Cases and Materials
on the English Legal System

Cross
g Centre
tr

Law in Context

Below is a listing of the more recent publications in the Law in Context Series

Editors: William Twining (University College, London) and Christopher McCrudden (Lincoln College, Oxford)

Cases and Materials on the English Legal System

Ninth Edition

Michael Zander QC

Emeritus Professor of Law, London School of Economics

LexisNexis™ UK

Members of the LexisNexis Group worldwide

United Kingdom	LexisNexis UK, a Division of Reed Elsevier (UK) Ltd, Halsbury House, 35 Chancery Lane, LONDON, WC2A 1EL, and 4 Hill Street, EDINBURGH EH2 3JZ
Argentina	LexisNexis Argentina, BUENOS AIRES
Australia	LexisNexis Butterworths, CHATSWOOD, New South Wales
Austria	LexisNexis Verlag ARD Orac GmbH & Co KG, VIENNA
Canada	LexisNexis Butterworths, MARKHAM, Ontario
Chile	LexisNexis Chile Ltda, SANTIAGO DE CHILE
Czech Republic	Nakladatelství Orac sro, PRAGUE
France	Editions du Juris-Classeur SA, PARIS
Germany	LexisNexis Deutschland GmbH, FRANKFURT, MUNSTER
Hong Kong	LexisNexis Butterworths, HONG KONG
Hungary	HVG-Orac, BUDAPEST
India	LexisNexis Butterworths, NEW DELHI
Ireland	Butterworths (Ireland) Ltd, DUBLIN
Italy	Giuffrè Editore, MILAN
Malaysia	Malayan Law Journal Sdn Bhd, KUALA LUMPUR
New Zealand	LexisNexis Butterworths, WELLINGTON
Poland	Wydawnictwo Prawnicze LexisNexis, WARSAW
Singapore	LexisNexis Butterworths, SINGAPORE
South Africa	LexisNexis Butterworths, DURBAN
Switzerland	Stämpfli Verlag AG, BERNE
USA	LexisNexis, DAYTON, Ohio

© Professor Michael Zander QC 2003

A CIP Catalogue record for this book is available from the British Library.

ISBN 0 406 96380 0

Printed in Great Britain by Clays Ltd, Bungay, Suffolk

Visit LexisNexis UK at www.lexisnexis.co.uk

Preface to the ninth edition

I have been surprised at how much has had to be changed since the last edition published as recently as 1999. There are some two hundred pages of new text, so that, despite a great deal of pruning, the book is about a hundred pages longer than the last edition.

Major developments since the eighth edition include Lord Justice Auld's almost 700-page *Review of the Criminal Courts*, the July 2002 White Paper *Justice for All*, the huge Criminal Justice Bill 2002/03 and the Courts Bill 2002/03. They required the rewriting of the text on many topics: the organisation of the criminal courts, a new system for charging suspects, reform of the rules regarding the admissibility of prior convictions and of hearsay evidence, eligibility for jury trial, trial on indictment without a jury and abolition of the double jeopardy rule. Four years of experience with the Woolf reforms of civil justice has resulted in significant new case law and some published research. There was the 2002 Joint Home Office-Cabinet Office Review of PACE and the massive revision of the PACE Codes which became operative as from April 2003. Costs in civil proceedings and conditional fees have been topics resulting in growing controversy and concern. In regard to the legal profession there was the fierce March 2001 report of the Office of Fair Trading, *Competition in Professions* and the Government's July 2002 Consultation Paper, *In the Public Interest?* (The very last addition made to the book notes the publication on 24 July 2003 of *Competition and regulation in the legal services market* announcing the setting up of the Clementi review.)

On 12 June 2003, as the book was almost completed, the Prime Minister made the sensational announcement that the office of Lord Chancellor was to be abolished, that the Lord Chancellor's Department was to become the Department for Constitutional Affairs, that the law lords were to be removed from the House of Lords and installed in a new supreme court, and that the appointment of the judges would be transferred to a judicial appointments commission. All references in the book to the Lord Chancellor's Department (LCD) must as from that date be read as referring to the Department for Constitutional Affairs (DCA). It was however too late to make that change for this edition. At the time of writing, the office of Lord Chancellor had not yet been abolished. Pending legislation to achieve that, Lord

Falconer of Thoroton QC held the two offices of Lord Chancellor and Secretary of State for Constitutional Affairs.

The book, other than being brought up to date, has basically the same format as before. From the reader's point of view the biggest change may be the reference throughout the book to publications available on the world wide web. Ready access to official reports without having to move from one's desk must be an enormous boon to the student.

When the book went for final printing, the Criminal Justice Bill introduced in November 2002 had completed its passage through the House of Commons and was less than half way through its Committee stage in the House of Lords; the Courts Bill, also introduced in November 2002, had completed its passage in the House of Lords and had had its Committee stage in the Commons. The latest available *Criminal Statistics* and *Judicial Statistics* were those for 2001.

My cordial thanks go once again to Julian Roskams, my highly efficient editor, and to those others at LexisNexis UK responsible for seeing the book through its various stages to publication which these days is achieved in an almost unbelievably short space of time.

MZ

London
August 2003

Preface to the first edition

This book is concerned with dispute settlement in courts and tribunals in England and Wales. The aim is to make available a selection of materials which reveal the actual workings of the system, its problems and difficulties, and which suggest ways in which it might be improved. The emphasis is contemporary and critical. The materials selected come from a wide variety of sources. Some, of course, are drawn from conventional legal sources – statutes and judicial decisions. But many more are taken from articles, official reports, books and surveys. Wherever possible they draw on empirical work, though there are still far too many areas of concern where no empirical investigation has yet been undertaken. The work is intended mainly as a source-book for those taking courses on the English legal system for a law degree or an equivalent course for a degree in some other subject. My intention is not merely to make a collection of scattered sources conveniently accessible, but also to stimulate constructively critical thought about the subject. I also hope that anyone who wishes to learn about the actual operation of the legal system or who is interested in its reform will find it useful.

The book does not attempt to cover all topics that are sometimes included in legal system courses, such as the sources of law, the legal profession, the machinery of law reform and sentencing. Excellent works on each of these topics are readily available, and it would not have been possible to do justice to these subjects within short compass. Nor does this book attempt to replace standard descriptive texts. Rather it attempts to supplement them by focusing through the basic texts on points where the legal system is under stress or is the subject of controversy. The aim is to give a better understanding of the reality of the law in action.

July 1972
London

Michael Zander

Contents

CHAPTER I

The organisation of trial courts   I

CHAPTER 4

The trial process   363

Chapter 5

The jury   463

CHAPTER 6

Costs and the funding of legal proceedings   537

CHAPTER 7

Appeals 619

Acknowledgments

All the materials in the book appear here with the permission of those who hold the copyright. I wish to express my sincere gratitude to all the individuals and institutions who have so kindly and generously allowed the material to be reprinted in this form. In particular I wish to thank the Controller of Her Majesty's Stationery Office for permission to include extracts from official publications; the Incorporated Council of Law Reporting for England and Wales for extracts from the *Law Reports* and the *Weekly Law Reports*; and LexisNexis UK for extracts from the *All England Law Reports*. I am indebted to the following publishers and journals for permission to use extracts: Sweet & Maxwell Ltd for extracts from *Civil Justice Quarterly*, the *Criminal Law Review* and the *Criminal Appeal Reports*; to the *Law Quarterly Review*, *Legal Action*, the *Magistrate*, the *Modern Law Review*, the *Solicitor's Journal*, the *Law Guardian*, the *New Law Journal*, the *Law Society's Gazette*, the *International and Comparative Law Quarterly*, *New Society*, *The Times* and *The Guardian*. The Social Administration Research Trust gave permission for use of an extract from Susanne Dell's book *Silent in Court*. The BBC and Sir Robert Mark gave permission for use of an extract from Sir Robert's Dimbleby lecture on BBC television. The *New Statesman* and CR Rolph allowed me to use the extract from Mr Rolph's 1969 article on police discretion.

Command papers, Hansard, House of Commons papers and other official publications excerpted

(in chronological order)

Books, pamphlets, memoranda and articles excerpted

Table of statutes

Table of cases

PAGE

PAGE

N

O

PAGE

P

PAGE

R

PAGE

PAGE

PAGE

PAGE

S

Chapter 1

The organisation of trial courts

Recent official reports – from Beeching to Auld

In the past quarter century there have been a number of official reports on the courts system leading to significant changes. The 1969 report of the Beeching Royal Commission on the Assizes and Quarter Sessions system looked at the conduct of both criminal and civil business outside London. The report led to the Courts Act 1971 which set up the Crown Court. The Civil Justice Review (1985-1989) led to the Courts and Legal Services Act 1990 which made major changes in the distribution of work between the High Court and the county court. More recently, a wholesale restructuring of civil justice flowed from the reports by Lord Woolf[1] on *Access to Justice*[2] which were implemented as from April 1999.[3]

In December 1999, Lord Irvine, the Lord Chancellor, asked Lord Justice Auld to report on the workings of the criminal courts. The Press Notice announcing the review said: 'This Review is a complement to the highly successful review that Lord

---

[1]   In 1994 when he was first asked to undertake the project Lord Woolf was a law lord. In 1996, when he completed his report, he was Master of the Rolls. He is now Lord Chief Justice.

[2]   *Access to Justice*, Interim Report, 1995; Final Report, 1996. For a book of essays commenting on the Interim Report see *The Reform of Civil Procedure–Essays on Access to Justice* (ed Zuckerman and Cranston, OUP, 1995). See also the lengthy note in 14 *Civil Justice Quarterly*, October 1995, pp 231-49. For the writer's critique of the Woolf project see in particular M Zander, 'The Woolf Report: Forwards or Backwards for the new Lord Chancellor?' 16 *Civil Justice Quarterly*, 1997, pp 208-27.

[3]   The Woolf reforms are enshrined in the new Civil Procedure Rules (CPR). They can be accessed on the Lord Chancellor's Department (LCD) website – www.lcd.gov.uk. The new system went live on 26 April 1999. For a general overview by the civil servant mainly responsible see D Gladwell 'Are you ready for Woolf?', 149 *New Law Journal*, 22 January, 1999, p 90.For a book of essays commenting on the Interim Report see *The Reform of Civil Procedure–Essays on Access to Justice* (ed Zuckerman and Cranston, OUP, 1995). See also the lengthy note in 14 *Civil Justice Quarterly*, October 1995, pp 231-49. For the writer's critique of the Woolf project see M Zander, 'The Woolf Report: Forwards or Backwards for the new Lord Chancellor?' 16 *Civil Justice Quarterly*, 1997, pp 208-27.

Woolf undertook of the civil courts'. The terms of reference were to inquire into 'the practices and procedures of, and the rules of evidence applied by the criminal courts at every level, with a view to ensuring that they deliver justice fairly, by streamlining all their processes, increasing their efficiency and strengthening the effectiveness of their relationship with others across the whole of the criminal justice system and having regard to the interests of all parties, including victims and witnesses, thereby promoting public confidence in the rule of law'.[4] The Auld *Review of the Criminal Courts*[5] was published in October 2001.[6]

The Government's response to the recommendations made in the Auld Report – inter alia, rejecting its main proposals in regard to re-organisation of the courts system – appeared in the White Paper *Justice for All* (Cm 5563, July 2002). An account of the Government's response to each of the recommendations in the Report was published at the same time in a separate appendix to the White Paper. Many of the proposals in the Auld Report were included in the Criminal Justice Bill introduced in the House of Commons in November 2002.[7]

The objectives of the system

The *General Issues Paper* of the Civil Justice Review (1987) suggested that the primary aim in all branches of civil justice was the pursuit of high-quality justice, which included fairness of procedures and methods of adjudication such as to ensure to each party an opportunity to present his case and to have it impartially considered, and quality, fairness and consistency of judicial decisions (para 55).

But the primary aim was not sovereign. It had to be balanced against a second aim, namely that of limiting to a level proportionate to the subject-matter, the incidence of delay, cost to the parties and cost to the court service. This aim (of efficiency) included the following elements: time targets for the handling of cases; effective deployment of judges, court staff and court facilities; the appropriate matching of judges to cases; the adoption of streamlined procedures for simple cases; and limiting costs to the parties and to the court service (para 56).

There was also the aim that the system should be effective–responsive to the variety of types of business; adaptable to changing economic and social circumstances; with

---

4   For a critique of the Review's working methods see M Zander, 'Reforming the criminal justice system: too difficult to be left to one individual?', 151 *New Law Journal*, 30 November 2001, p 1774.

5   Accessible on www.criminal-courts-review.org.uk and www.lcd.gov.uk.

6   For a summary of the recommendations see M Zander, 151 *New Law Journal*, 12 October 2001, pp 1462-63. See the special issue of the *Criminal Law* Review, April 2002. For the writer's 75-page critique of the Auld Review see www.criminal -courts-review.org.uk or www.lse.ac.uk/collections/law/news.

7   When the book was delivered to the publishers, the Criminal Justice Bill had been through all its stages in the Commons and had had its Second Reading in the House of Lords. It is referred to throughout the book as the Criminal Justice Bill 2002/03. The clause numbers are those in the 21 May 2003 print of the Bill for the start of the proceedings in the House of Lords.

court locations and court hours that were convenient; providing simple rules regarding jurisdiction, venue and procedure; and securing to litigants the assistance they needed with their cases.

One difference between civil and criminal business was that, while crime was relatively homogeneous, civil matters involved an enormous variety of matters. A whole variety of specialist jurisdictions had developed. This had both good and bad aspects. The advantages included the fact that specialist skills and familiarity with the business might speed up the despatch of business. But the danger was that specialist jurisdictions blocked mobility of transfer of judicial and court personnel, quasi-monopolies grew up amongst practitioners, traditions of separateness ossified and became difficult to reform and the different jurisdictions might not produce a rational allocation of resources.

Lord Woolf in his reports also proposed a list of prescriptions for a system of civil justice, many of which can be adapted for application equally to criminal justice. The system should be just in its results. It should be fair and be seen to be so by ensuring that litigants have equal opportunities, regardless of their resources, to assert or defend their legal rights, by providing litigants with the opportunity to state their case, and by treating cases alike. Procedures and cost should be proportionate to the nature of the issues involved. The system should deal with cases with reasonable speed. The system should be understandable by those who use it and responsive to their needs. It should provide as much certainty as possible and it should be effective – adequately resourced and organised. (*Interim Report*, 1985, pp 2-3)

See generally IR Scott, 'Problems in Court Structure and Processes', 44 *Current Legal Problems*, 1991, pp 15–38.

Before looking at these issues more closely, the next sections describe the existing structure as it has developed.

1. The work handled by the courts

(a) The civil courts

There are three different levels of trial courts for civil cases: the High Court, the county court and the magistrates' court.

(1) THE HIGH COURT

History[8]

The High Court is divided into three Divisions–the Queen's Bench Division, the Chancery Division and the Family Division. The High Court came into existence

---

[8]   For an outstanding historical account see B Abel-Smith and R Stevens, *Lawyers and the Courts* (Heinemann, 1967).

in the Judicature Acts of 1873–5, in replacement for the ancient Queen's Bench Court, Court of Common Pleas, Court of Exchequer, Chancery Court, and the Probate, Divorce and Admiralty Court. Under the 1873–5 legislation these five separate courts became the five Divisions of the High Court; but in 1888 the three common law courts (Queen's Bench, Common Pleas and Exchequer) were merged into a single Division, the Queen's Bench Division (QBD). The Probate, Divorce and Admiralty Division was broken up by the Administration of Justice Act 1970 which allocated its functions between the QBD, the Chancery Division and the new Family Division.

The High Court today

The jurisdiction of the High Court is now to be found in the provisions of the Supreme Court Act 1981.

The Queen's Bench Division (QBD) This consists of the Lord Chief Justice and some 70 High Court judges. It deals primarily with claims for contract and tort. The largest single category of work is for goods sold and delivered, work done, materials supplied or professional work done. The next largest categories typically are: claims for breach of contract, for personal injuries, for the recovery of land or property.

The number of cases dealt with by the QBD has been declining sharply in recent years, largely because of the transfer of cases from the QBD to the county court. In 1990 the number of proceedings started in the QBD was over 350,000. In 1997 it was down to some 121,000. By 2001 it had slumped to a mere 21,600![9]

The overwhelming majority of the claims are disposed of without a trial. During 2001, 2,479 cases were disposed of. Of these, just under a fifth were determined after a trial. The rest were settled or withdrawn before the hearing or in some instances struck out (eg because the case was considered to be frivolous).[10]

The QBD additionally has two special types of jurisdiction. One is the Admiralty Court, previously part of the Probate, Divorce and Admiralty Division until it was abolished by the Administration of Justice Act 1970. Admiralty cases typically concern collisions at sea, damage to cargo and personal injuries suffered at sea. (In 2001 there were 281 writs and summonses issued in admiralty cases but only seven cases were actually tried!) The second category is the Commercial Court, which has judges specially chosen for their experience to try heavy commercial cases. These consist of matters relating to ships, insurance, carriage of cargo and the construction and performance of mercantile contracts. Many of the cases have a strong international flavour.

What is called the Divisional Court of the Queen's Bench Division exercises a very important first instance jurisdiction by way of review of the acts of Ministers, civil servants and local councillors. Traditionally this was by way of the ancient prerogative

[9]   The figures are to be found in the annual Judicial Statistics.
[10]   *Judicial Statistics* Annual Report, 2001, Cm 5551, Table 3.5, p 31.

writs (certiorari, mandamus, prohibition and habeas corpus). More recently such cases were dealt with by an application for judicial review under what was Order 53 of the Rules of the Supreme Court (RSC). The part of the QBD that dealt with these applications was known as the Crown Office List. From October 2000 the Crown Office List was renamed the Administrative Court. (This was part of the response to the Report of the Bowman Report on the Crown Office List, 2000.)[11] The applicant now applies for mandatory, quashing and prohibiting orders. Unlike the position for ordinary actions, permission (formerly called 'leave') is required to start such proceedings. Applications for permission are heard normally by a single judge. In 2001 there were 4,700 applications to apply for judicial review in civil matters (no fewer than half of which concerned immigration issues).

The Chancery Division As has been seen, this is the successor to the ancient Chancery Court. It consists of the Vice Chancellor and some 17 High Court judges. They deal with corporate and personal insolvency disputes, business, trade and industry disputes, the enforcement of mortgages, professional negligence, intellectual property matters, copyright and patents, trusts, wills and probate matters. The Chancery Division also includes a specialist Companies Court and Patents Court. In 2001, the total number of proceedings was just over 37,000, of which some 20,000 were Companies Court matters and 9,300 were bankruptcy petitions.

The Family Division This was created in 1970 when the Probate, Divorce and Admiralty Division was split up. It consists of the President and some 17 High Court judges. It hears defended divorce cases and ancillary disputes over children and property. It also deals with wardship, guardianship of infants, adoption and legitimacy cases. The Family Division nominally also deals with non-contentious probate work but in practice this work is handled by administrative or bureaucratic rather than by judicial proceedings.

There are two other special jurisdictions to mention:

The Technology and Construction Court (formerly the Official Referees Court) The Official Referees Court was renamed the Technology and Construction Court in October 1998. Its jurisdiction remained the same, namely difficult or technical issues of fact on reference from the Queen's Bench Division or the Chancery Division after an application made by either party. Usually the cases involve complex building and construction disputes. The judges used to be circuit judges (lower in the judicial hierarchy than High Court judges), but on the renaming of the court in 1998, a High Court judge was put in charge for the first time and the Official Referees were renamed 'judges' to be addressed as 'My lord' instead of 'Your Honour'. In 2001 the court disposed of nearly 1,400 matters – most of which were 'struck out, settled or discontinued'. A total of 61 were tried.

---

[11]   *Practice Note* [2000] 1 WLR 1654, [2000] 4 All ER 1071. For commentary see (2001) 20 *Civil Justice Quarterly* pp 1-5; and (2001) *Public Law*, pp 4-20.

The Court of Protection This is responsible for the management and administration of the property and affairs of people suffering from mental disorder. Most of the work is done by masters and deputy masters (see below) rather than by judges. But judges of the Chancery Division do exercise some of the powers. There are normally some 30,000 estates under administration. In December 1997 the Government published a consultation paper, *Who Decides? Making Decisions on Behalf of Mentally Incapacitated Adults* based on the recommendations of the Law Commission in its report on *Mental Incapacity* (1995, Law Com 231). This proposed that the Court of Protection should cease to exist as an office of the Supreme Court and instead become a superior court of record. Its jurisdiction would be exercisable by any judge of the Chancery or Family Division or any circuit judge or district judge nominated by the Lord Chancellor. By mid-2003, no decision on this issue had been announced.

Interlocutory work in the High Court

Most actual trials are handled by judges. But the pre-trial ('interlocutory') work is conducted in London by masters in the Queen's Bench and Chancery Divisions and by district judges (formerly called registrars) in the Family Division. Outside London there are no masters. High Court interlocutory business outside London is handled in District Registries by district judges who are normally also the district judges for the county court. District Registries are physically located in county courts. There are over a hundred District Registries. All the District Registries deal with Queen's Bench, Chancery and Family Division work. Most, though not all, are authorised to take undefended divorce cases. County courts are now divided into Civil Trial Centres and Feeder Courts. Groups of feeder courts are supervised by Designated Circuit Judges who sit in the trial centres.

Judges in High Court cases

In 2001 the High Court case load was shared between High Court judges (51%); circuit judges (23%); Deputy High Court judges (sometimes practitioners and sometimes retired judges) (17%); district judges (8%); and Lords Justices of Appeal and recorders (practitioners sitting as part-time judges) (1%).

Sittings outside London

The Queen's Bench Division and the Family Division sit in London and over twenty locations throughout the country; the Chancery Division sits in London and eight other cities. The Divisional Court, the Court of Appeal and the House of Lords, traditionally sit only in London–but the Court of Appeal, both Civil and Criminal, occasionally sits outside London. The Divisional Court sits in Wales for cases arising under the devolution legislation, the Government of Wales Act 1998. The Judicial Committee of the Privy Council when hearing Welsh devolution cases can also sit in Wales.

Allocation of judges and separate High Court Divisions

The judges of the High Court are allocated on appointment to one or other division and usually then remain in that Division.

The 1987 Civil Justice Review General Issues Consultation Paper (para 68) said that there was no comprehensive planning or forecasting procedure available for the purpose of reviewing the total workload of the High Court and its Divisions. Each Division managed its affairs virtually independently of the others and this stood in the way of overall management of civil business. One of the country's leading experts on courts' management, Professor Ian Scott (who was also a member of the Civil Justice Review), has added: 'It may be argued that the present three-fold Division structure stands in the way of development of a range of procedures suited to the many varieties of business arising in the High Court and that what is required nowadays is not three divisions but multiple, "substance-sensitive" procedural and administrative arrangements reflecting the wide jurisdiction of the Court' (8 *Civil Justice Quarterly*, January 1989, p 5).

Lord Woolf's Interim Report in 1995 said that it could be argued that separate practices and a separate culture between the Chancery and the Queen's Bench Divisions might cause difficulties for outsiders. On the other hand, the Chancery Division provided a convenient umbrella for a number of specialist jurisdictions which were serviced by specialist judges and specialist members of the bar. These jurisdictions, which included companies, bankruptcy and the administration of estates and trusts, were of a quasi-administrative nature and required a different approach from other litigation. The sense of team spirit among the Chancery judges and their special relationship with the Chancery Bar resulted in a more effective and efficient disposal of work. Moreover, if the Chancery judges were amalgamated with the judges of the QBD they might just be absorbed to meet the needs of the QBD. Lord Woolf's conclusion (p 77, para 23) was that it was not desirable, at least at that stage, to merge the two Divisions. Implementing his other recommendations would involve other changes of a very substantial nature and it was preferable not to add to those changes the upheaval that a merger of the two Divisions would involve.

He would, however, follow the suggestion that judges should be nominated to lists according to their expertise, regardless of which Division to which the lists belonged. So a judge could be attached not only to lists in the Chancery Division but also to the Commercial Court in the QBD. If, however, the retention of the Chancery Division proved inimical to the uniform and flexible approach which he considered essential, the question of a merger could be reconsidered. In his Final Report, Lord Woolf confirmed that he accepted that, although the administration of the two divisions should be brought closer together, they should not be merged (p 261, para 6).

(2) THE COUNTY COURT

The county court was established in 1846 with a jurisdiction limited to £20 for actions in contract and tort. Over 150 or so years this rose from £20 to £5,000. Then in

1990 the ceiling was abolished.[12] As from 1 July 1991 county courts were able to deal with all contract and tort claims and recovery of land actions, regardless of value, plus equity matters where the value of the trust fund or estate does not exceed £30,000.

However most actions in the county court are for relatively small sums. In 2001, 40% of all claims were for sums under £1,000, 16% were for sums between £1,000 to £3,000, 13% between £3,000 and £5,000 and 16% were for amounts over £5,000, of which only 1% were for amounts over £25,000. The remaining 15% were for unquantified ('unliquidated') sums.[13]

Most of the business of the county courts is money claims. For reasons that are unclear the number of such claims issued has been steadily declining. In 1990 it was 3m; in 1996 that figure had reduced to 2.1m.; in 2001 it was down to 1.5m.

Actions of this kind are mainly for goods sold and delivered, work done, materials supplied and professional fees. The other largest categories of work done by the county court are undefended divorce[14] and ancillary relief in regard to children and matrimonial property and actions for the recovery of land and premises. The county court also has an admiralty and equity jurisdiction, can hear contested probate actions, and deals with bankruptcy and companies winding up.

Small claims

A 1970 study of the county court by the Consumer Council (*Justice out of Reach*) showing that individuals hardly ever used the county courts as plaintiffs led to changes in county court procedure designed to make them more 'user friendly' to ordinary citizens. The main reform was the introduction in 1973 of what was at first called 'arbitration' and is now called the small claims procedure. Its attractions included that hearings were in private,[15] the procedure is less formal than in ordinary trials and the costs rules were altered so that each side basically pays its own costs. (In regard to pre-trial procedure, see pp 111-12 below, in regard to less formal trial methods, see pp 381-87 below, and in regard to costs, see pp 554-55 below.)

The limit for small claims cases was originally £75. But, like the jurisdiction of the county court itself, it has increased hugely. It is now generally £5,000 – though £1,000 for personal injury and housing cases.[16]

---

12   During the first hundred years the jurisdiction was increased very slowly – to £50 in 1850, £100 in 1903 and £200 in 1938. In 1955 the jurisdiction of the county courts was raised to £400. In 1966 it went up to £500, in 1969 to £750 and in 1974 to £1,000. It next jumped to £2,000 in 1977 and in 1981 it was more than doubled to £5,000 – and in equity matters £30,000.

13   *Judicial Statistics*, 2001, p 37.

14   174 of the 220 county courts are authorised to deal with undefended divorce work.

15   This has been changed. To make the procedure compatible with the European Convention on Human Rights a trial now has to be conducted in public. See further p 403 below.

16   The £75 limit was raised to £200 in 1975. In 1979 it went up to £500 and in 1991 to £1,000. Lord Woolf's Interim Report in June 1995, proposed that it be increased to £3,000–save for

As the jurisdiction has expanded the small claims system has assumed increasing importance. In 1973, when it began, only 8% of defended actions in the county court were heard under the small claims procedure. A quarter of a century later the proportion had soared to over four-fifths. (In 2001, it was 81%.[17]) This is an astonishing development. As Professor Baldwin has written, 'It is no exaggeration to say that the development of the small claims procedure in England and Wales has for many years been slowly bringing about a revolution in civil procedures in the county courts'[18]

Who uses the small claims system? Although the main purpose of establishing the small claims system was to provide more user-friendly access to justice to individuals, in fact, like the county court itself, the small claims system is used to a significant extent by business concerns. In 2001, just under half of all claimants (46%) were businesses.[19]

It is also striking that, according to Baldwin, in the main, individual litigants using the small claims system are middle class. ('Most litigants contacted in this study, especially those who appeared as plaintiffs, were relatively well-heeled and articulate individuals. Over two-thirds of those in paid employment were in professional or managerial occupations . . . Very few litigants were from ethnic minority groups. The genuinely poor make few appearances at small claims hearings, and when they do, it is typically as defendants to face landlords or money-lenders.[20] ')

The advantages of 'repeat players'

The fact that most county court claimants are institutions of one sort or another is hardly surprising. Litigation is not something that the ordinary citizen is likely to want to undertake. He will be nervous about the likely costs, both in terms of time and money. He will worry whether he may have to appear in court–not knowing that most cases settle out of court. He will be unfamiliar with the procedures of the legal system and will not know how to 'use the system'. He will not be in regular contact with lawyers who can take up his case. He will not know how to calculate the pros and cons of taking up the cudgels in terms of the likely outcome as against the costs of the case.

None of these factors inhibit the large institution or, if at all, not nearly to the same extent. Professor Marc Galanter, a noted American scholar in the field of the sociology of law, in a famous study analysed the differences between parties who have only

---

personal injury cases. This was implemented in January 1996. When the Woolf reforms were implemented in April 1999, the jurisdiction was raised to £5,000.

17 In 1997, 1998 and 1999 the proportions were even higher – 83%, 87% and 87%.
18 J Baldwin, *Lay and Judicial Perspectives on the Expansion of the Small Claims Regime*, September 2002, LCD Research Series, No8/02, p 7.
19 *Judicial Statistics*, 2001, Table 4.9 – based on a three months' sample from selected county courts.
20 J Baldwin, *Small Claims in county courts in England and Wales* (Oxford, Clarendon, 1997), p 166.

occasional recourse to the law ('one-shotters') as against those who take part in litigation repeatedly ('repeat players').(M Galanter, 'Why the "Haves" Come out Ahead', 9 *Law and Society Review*, (1974), p 95 and 'Explaining Litigation', ibid, p 347.)

The repeat players' advantages included the following:
(1) Having done it before, they can structure the next transaction and thus gain over the one-shotter. It is the repeat player who writes the standard-form contract and who can adjust it if a particular clause has been interpreted unhelpfully in a previous case.
(2) Repeat players develop expertise, can employ specialists, enjoy economies of scale and have low start-up costs for any new case.
(3) Repeat players have developed informal relations with those who work the legal system, such as lawyers and court officials.
(4) Repeat players can play the odds. Because they have large numbers of cases they can afford to take risks with particular cases providing they come out ahead overall. The one-shotter by comparison cannot afford to lose his one case and therefore cannot take the risks involved in going for the maximum result.
(5) Repeat players can play to alter the rules through test-case litigation or even by lobbying for legislative or administrative changes. Repeat players can select from among their cases the most favourable ones to fight into the courts and up the appellate levels in order to achieve the best results. This gives them advantages in the area of law-making through litigation.

The computerised summons production centre In 1990, the computerised Summons Production Centre (SPC) was set up to process summons requests from major 'repeat players' – plaintiffs who issued more than 1,000 summonses a year. Issue and dispatch of summonses was guaranteed within 24-48 hours. Its main customers were banks, mail order companies, and utilities – gas, electricity and water companies. It issues roughly half of all summonses. (In 2001 the proportion was 52%.)

Note also the fact that, although both in the QBD and in the county court by far the majority of actions commenced are money claims, they are only a tiny fraction of those tried. This is because so high a proportion of debt cases are concluded by some means other than trial. Of the actions *tried* in the QBD, personal injury claims used to represent about three-quarters of the total case-load. (Today it would be less, due to the recent moves to transfer personal injury cases from the High Court to the county court.) In Galanter's sense, personal injury plaintiffs are one-shotters. The fact that they can bring actions against institutions (employers and insurance companies) was previously due to the levelling effect of legal aid and the support of trades unions and insurance companies. Now, as will be seen, conditional fee agreements (see pp 000-00 below) have taken the place of legal aid in most personal injury claims. But the repeat player still has many advantages including above all the fact that it is a matter of little overall consequence whether he wins or loses any particular case. This tells–especially in such matters as payment into court (p 81 below), credibility in bargaining (so that the threat to go the whole way by taking the case to court has to be seen as a real threat), and the fact that the repeat player can select the most advantageous cases to press.

(3) MAGISTRATES' COURTS

Magistrates' courts have always had a significant jurisdiction in the civil field. Most of it was in the field of domestic relations–especially maintenance for deserted wives and children, custody disputes, adoption, guardianship, and protection of battered wives. A different kind of civil jurisdiction is the collection of various statutory debts such as income tax, national insurance, social security, rates and legal aid contributions.

In the field of domestic relations there was a great deal of overlap between the jurisdiction of the magistrates and that of the county court. The issue of what to do about this jurisdiction culminated in the Children Act 1989 which led to a significant re-casting both of the relevant law and of the responsibilities of the different levels of civil courts. The magistrates' courts functions in this field have been renamed 'family proceedings courts'.

(4) THE DISTRIBUTION OF FAMILY COURT WORK

The Children's Act 1989, which was implemented in 1991, established for the first time a concurrent family jurisdiction across all tiers of civil courts:

County courts There are county courts with no family jurisdiction. There are divorce county courts which can issue all private law family law proceedings but contested matters are transferred to family hearing centres for trial. Family hearing centres can issue and hear all private law family law matters whether or not they are contested. There are care centres which have full jurisdiction in both private and public family law matters. There are also Specialised Adoption Centres.

(Public law cases are those usually brought by local authorities or the NSPCC and include care, supervision and emergency protection orders. Private law cases are brought by individuals generally in connection with divorce or separation.)

The High Court The High Court has jurisdiction to hear all cases relating to children and has an exclusive jurisdiction in wardship cases. It also hears appeals from family proceedings courts and cases transferred from the county court or the family proceedings courts.

Family Proceedings Courts Full private and public law jurisdiction except for divorce. Either lay magistrates alone or a district judge sitting with lay magistrates. They have been specially trained.

Public law cases must start in the family proceedings court but can be transferred to the county court to minimise delay or where the matter is grave, complex or important.

Private law cases can be started at any family proceedings court or county court.

For a wide-ranging consideration generally of the role of the civil courts, see Ross Cranston, 'What Do Courts Do?', 4 *Civil Justice Quarterly*, April 1986, p 123.

(b)   The criminal courts

There are two trial courts for criminal cases: the Crown Court and the magistrates' court.

(1)   THE CROWN COURT

The Crown Court dates from 1 January 1972, the day on which the Courts Act 1971 came into force. The Courts Act was the result of the *Report of the Royal Commission on Assizes and Quarter Sessions* (Beeching Report, 1969, Cmnd 4153). The Beeching Royal Commission was set up in 1966 in order to investigate and propose reforms to the system of assize and quarter sessions courts that had remained substantially unchanged for centuries.

The Royal Commission found that the then existing system was seriously defective. The ancient assize towns were no longer necessarily main centres of population; the fact that the same judge did both civil and criminal work meant that the civil cases always had to wait for the more urgent criminal cases to be finished first; the sittings of the assize courts were fixed long before anyone had any idea as to the likely case-load; when the allotted time was up the judge had to go to the next assize town, rather than finish the list; the judges spent too much of their time on the road travelling between assize towns and whilst he and the court staff were all travelling, the entire courts system was inaccessible.

The solutions recommended by the Beeching Commission to the ills it had diagnosed were clear cut:
(1) The abolition of Assizes and Quarter Sessions and their replacement by a new higher criminal court to be called the Crown Court. This court would sit as and where needed. The siting of Crown Courts would be based on the principle 'that virtually the whole population will be within reasonable daily travelling distance of at least one such site, and that no regard shall be paid to civic boundaries established for other purposes'.
(2) The division of the criminal from the civil business of the higher courts so that civil litigants would no longer have to wait for the completion of criminal cases.
(3) Instead of the judges processing from town to town, they should to a much greater extent sit in courts' centres in permanent or more or less permanent session. In addition, there should be mini-circuits to handle the criminal work that could not be dealt with in the main court centres.
(4) Cases should be divided into different categories and allocated to judges by reference to their gravity and the level of seniority of judge required.

(5) The judges should all be able to sit in any Crown Court anywhere in the country.

(6) County court judges should be restyled circuit judges, who should sit both in Crown Courts to conduct criminal cases and in county courts to conduct civil business.

(7) There should be a new title of recorder for part-time judges eligible to sit in any Crown Court, who could be solicitors as well as barristers.

(8) The country should be divided into six, as compared with the previous seven, circuits. Each circuit should be run by two Presiding judges and a Circuit administrator.

(9) There should be a unified court administrative service, appointed and paid by the Lord Chancellor.

(10) The Lord Chancellor should be the minister responsible for all the higher courts and the county court.

The Royal Commission was set up by a Labour Government but the report was implemented by the incoming Conservative Government. It accepted every one of the recommendations listed above. The Courts Act 1971 provided for the establishment of the Crown Court, whose business was to be handled by High Court judges, circuit judges and recorders. (The Crown Court for the City of London was, however, allowed to keep its hallowed name 'the Central Criminal Court', otherwise known as the Old Bailey.)

The Crown Court sits at some 90 locations throughout the country. The court centres are of three kinds. First-tier centres are those visited by High Court judges, circuit judges and recorders for the full range of Crown Court work–as well as by High Court judges of the Queen's Bench Division and Family Division for civil work. Second-tier centres are those at which Crown Court work (but not civil business) is dealt with by High Court judges, circuit judges and recorders. Third-tier centres are those visited only by circuit judges and recorders or deputy circuit judges and assistant recorders.

The distribution of business in the Crown Court is governed by directions given by the Lord Chief Justice with the concurrence of the Lord Chancellor. (For the latest see *Practice Direction* [2001] 4 All ER 635.) These divide offences, for the purposes of trial, into four classes.

The most serious (Class 1) are generally to be tried by a High Court judge. They include treason, murder and espionage. But murders can be released by or on the authority of the Presiding Judge for trial by a deputy High Court judge, a circuit judge or a deputy circuit judge who has been approved ('ticketed') for the purpose.

Offences in Class 2 must be tried by a High Court judge unless released by, or on the authority of, a Presiding Judge for trial by a circuit judge or recorder. The offences include manslaughter, rape and abortion. Rapes and other serious sex offences can only be released to judges who have been ticketed for such trials.

Offences in Class 3 may be listed for trial by a High Court judge or by a circuit judge, deputy circuit judge or recorder who has attended a continuation seminar at the Judicial Studies Board and has been ticketed by a Presiding Judge. The offences include all offences triable only in the Crown Court unless they are specifically assigned to classes 1, 2 or 4.

Cases in Class 4 can be heard by any judge eligible to sit in the Crown Court though they are normally heard by a circuit judge or recorder. They include grievous bodily harm with intent, robbery and conspiracy and all 'either way' offences.

Class 1 offences constitute some 1% of those dealt with by the Crown Court. Class 2 cases represent some 3% of the case-load. Class 3 cases are around 10% of the total. The balance (86% in 2001) are therefore, Class 4 offences.

'Ticketing' of judges

The system of 'ticketing' judges as suitable for particular types of cases was criticised by Lord Justice Auld in his *Review of the Criminal Courts*. There were, for instance, some 50 circuit judges approved to try murder cases and another 25 who were approved to try attempted murder. There were about 340 circuit judges approved to try rape or other serious sexual offences. This system of selection involved the Lord Chief Justice, the Senior Presiding Judge, the Presiding Judges, the Resident Judge of each court centre and his listing officer. The system, Lord Justice Auld said, was 'unduly bureaucratic and rigid' (para 22, p 236). It was a rough and ready means of marking suitability. It also made for invidious distinctions between judges. The system, he suggested, should be changed by giving Resident Judges responsibility for allocating cases at their court centres – subject to regular and systematic appraisal to determine the experience and interests of judges and a precondition of appropriate training by the Judicial Studies Board before taking particular types of cases

Committals for sentence only

Until now Crown Courts have also had a jurisdiction in sentencing defendants committed for sentence by magistrates once the case has been concluded in the magistrates' courts. (In 2001 there were close to 26,000 such committals.) This jurisdiction in the Crown Court has been exercised by a judge sitting with two lay magistrates. In his *Review of the Criminal Courts*, Lord Justice Auld recommended (p 200) that this jurisdiction be abolished – a recommendation that the Government broadly accepted and partly implemented in the Criminal Justice Bill 2002/03.[21]

Appeals heard by the Crown Court

The Crown Court also has a jurisdiction in hearing appeals in respect of conviction and/or sentence in criminal cases decided by magistrates. (In 2001, there were 12,700

---

[21]   The Bill retains the power only for cases where the defendant pleads guilty at what is called 'plea before venue' – see p 319 below.

such appeals.) These are heard by a judge sitting with two or sometimes one lay magistrate. The judge should be the resident judge or a specifically designated judge or an approved experienced recorder but failing that, another judge can be selected.

Discretion in listing

The dry recital of the basic principles on which allocation of cases is done conceals a fascinating and little-studied aspect of judicial administration, namely how cases are allocated to individual judges. That this is (or at least was) a subject worthy of inquiry emerged from a pilot study of sentencing in the 1980s which showed that court clerks who actually do the listing can be influenced by personal views as to what they think should be the outcome of the case. The study suggested that if they thought the defendant deserved a severe sentence they have the power, and sometimes exercised it, of making sure that he did not appear before someone they considered to be a lenient judge, or even of ensuring that he was dealt with by someone they thought would be suitably severe! (The finding was so embarrassing that the pilot study was stopped by the intervention of the then Lord Chief Justice.)[22]

Crown Court judicial manpower

The Beeching Royal Commission report in 1969 estimated that there would be a need for some 150 full-time circuit judges and 120 part-time recorders – totalling 270. To put it mildly, this proved to be a considerable underestimate. Only three years later, in 1972, there were 205 circuit judges and 287 recorders-a total of 561 or more than double the number. By 2003 that figure in turn had almost quadrupled to 605 circuit judges and 1,310 recorders – a total of 1,915. (Until 2000, part-time judges started as assistant recorders but this tier was merged with that of recorders as a result of the decision of the High Court of Justiciary in Scotland in *Starrs v Procurator Fiscal*.[23] The court held that temporary sheriffs were insufficiently independent of the executive for the purposes of Article 6 of the European Convention on Human Rights because they had insufficient security of tenure. (This was felt to apply equally to assistant recorders in England and Wales.[24])

In 2001, circuit judges handled three-quarters of Crown Court work (74%), recorders 21%, High Court judges 4%, deputy High Court and deputy Circuit judges 1%.

---

[22] See A Ashworth et al, *Sentencing in the Crown Court*, Centre for Criminological Research, Occasional Paper No 10, 1984, pp 60–64.) See also A Lovegrove, 'The Listing of Cases in the Crown Court as an Administrative Discretion' (1984) *Criminal Law Review*, p 738.

[23] [2000]1 LRC 718.

[24] In April 2000 the LCD announced that in future part-time judicial appointments would be for five years with a right of automatic renewal save in cases of misconduct or incapacity. For the various decisions taken by the Lord Chancellor after a review of the implications of the decision see *Judicial Appointments Annual Report 1999-2000*, paras 2.14-2.18.

(2) MAGISTRATES' COURTS

Magistrates' courts, which are manned mainly by lay justices, handle some 97% of all criminal cases. In 2001 there were 1.84 million cases tried in magistrates' courts. Of these, 0.77 million (43%) were minor motoring charges, 0.57 million (30%) were other cases that could only be tried in the magistrates' courts, and 0.5 million (27%) were cases that could have been tried in the Crown Court but the defendant chose instead to have the case dealt with summarily before the magistrates.[25] (On this last category, called 'either way' offences, see further below, pp 37-44.)

There are some 450 or so magistrates' courts, some of which sit every day, some of which sit only occasionally. They are manned by just under 30,000 lay and unpaid magistrates, men and women in more or less equal numbers, and by some 95 or so professional, full-time and paid magistrates formerly called 'stipendiaries' and from 1999 called District Judges (Magistrates' Courts).[26] The lay justices typically sit once a week. The jurisdiction of the District Judges (Magistrates' Courts) is the same as that of the lay justices except that the district judge normally sits on his or her own,[27] whereas the lay justices sit with one or, more usually, two others. Whatever its composition, the magistrates' court will have a court clerk who is supposed to be appropriately qualified to advise the bench on law and procedure. (On the issue of the qualification of court clerks see p 26 below.)

Considering the vast amount of attention given by commentators to trial by jury, trial in the magistrates' court gets rather short shrift. The point has been made forcibly by Dr Penny Darbyshire who for some years has been waging a battle to draw attention to the problems of the magistrates' courts . She pointed to the fact that by far the majority of criminal cases are heard in the magistrates' courts. Moreover, while it was true that well over 90% of defendants in the magistrates' courts plead guilty, there were far more contested trials in the magistrates' courts than in the Crown Court. ('The decisions which matter are those of the police and prosecutors as to charge, the defendant's decision as to plea and the magistrates' decisions as to verdict and sentence, aided by their clerks; yet the making, teaching and analysis of criminal law and evidence often proceeds as if things were as in Blackstone's day.')[28] Juries heard only 1% of all criminal cases that come before the courts; magistrates sentenced about 95% of all defendants who come before the criminal courts.

There had been an enormous growth in the jurisdiction of the magistrates during this century with indictable-only offences downgraded to either-way and either-way

---

25   *Criminal Statistics*, 2001, Cm 5696.

26   The change of title was made in the Access to Justice Act 1999, s 78. For the history of the office see P Seago, C.Walker and D Wall, 'The Development of the Professional Magistracy in England and Wales' [2000] Criminal Law Review 631.

27   But a district judge sits with lay justices in Family Proceedings Courts and in Youth Courts.

28   P Darbyshire, 'An Essay on the Importance and Neglect of the Magistracy' [1997] Criminal Law Review 627, 643.

offences to summary-only.[29] ('By 1997, the list of offences triable by magistrates includes: causing death by aggravated vehicle taking , wounding or inflicting grievous bodily harm, cruelty to and abduction of children, indecent assault and many other sex offences, most burglaries, thefts, frauds and forgeries, arson not endangering life, manufacturing, supplying and misusing all illegal drugs, some perjury, all betting and gaming offences and most firearms offences.'[30])

A combination of 'statutory downgrading, prosecutorial discretion and the exercise of choice and whim by victims, defendants and magistrates' resulted in very grave offences being dealt with summarily.[31] Magistrates also dealt with almost all young offenders. ('The importance of the youth court is impossible to exaggerate. . . [But] It is a jurisdiction almost entirely forgotten in traditional law books and by the public, probably because it goes on behind closed doors, unreported.'[32]) The Attorney-General had the power to appeal an unduly lenient sentence given by the Crown Court (p 632 below). There was no equivalent for unduly lenient sentences given by magistrates. The decisions of the Divisional Court on appeal from the magistrates' court got far less notice in the law reports than decisions of the Court of Appeal. ('When the Court of Appeal or House of Lords develop criminal law and evidence they speak in the language of trial on indictment and pay no regard to how their reasoning will apply to summary trial. Stipendiaries and justices' clerks are left to agonise on how to translate these *rationes* into their world, in articles sounding exasperated, in *The Justice of the Peace* and *Local Government Law*.'[33])

The same blindness affected many academics.[34] The Runciman Royal Commission on Criminal Justice had focussed almost exclusively on trials on indictment. The legislation that followed the Runciman Report had been flawed in its application to magistrates' courts.[35] Part of the problem lay in the weakness of justices' clerks, court clerks and magistrates as a lobbying force. Even the Law Commission was capable of producing reform proposals that completely ignored summary proceedings.

In a subsequent article,[36] Dr Darbyshire critically examined the rhetoric about magistrates and highlighted concerns for Lord Irvine, the then new Labour Lord Chancellor. The magistrates on the whole had a poor reputation. ('Praise of the

---

[29]   See pp 37-38 below for explanation of the distinction between these categories.
[30]   Darbyshire [1997] Criminal Law Review 630.
[31]   Darbyshire [1997] Criminal Law Review 630. Darbyshire referred to studies demonstrating the way charges are reduced in sexual offences and assault cases.
[32]   Darbyshire [1997] Criminal Law Review 633.
[33]   Darbyshire [1997] Criminal Law Review 635.
[34]   I was one of those criticised for the disparate treatment in this book of trial by jury and trial by magistrates (ibid, p 637.) I am indebted to her for prompting the addition of this section.
[35]   Dr Darbyshire instanced the botched attempt at abolition of committal proceedings, the new rules on disclosure and on preparatory hearings (ibid, p 638).
[36]   'For the New Lord Chancellor – Some Causes for Concern about Magistrates' [1997] Criminal Law Review 861-74.

magistracy is as rare as pro-jury rhetoric is common.')[37] Almost no one extolled the virtues of the magistracy who was not either a magistrate or the Lord Chancellor of the day addressing magistrates. Blackstone – 'for whom the jury was the most admirably constituted fact-finding body in the world' – had deplored the mischiefs that resulted from demoting cases from jury trial to trial before justices. In modern times Mr Michael Mansfield QC dismissed magistrates in his book *Presumed Guilty* (1993) with only a page of discussion. Lord Gifford QC in his book *Where's the Justice?* (1984) described lay justices as 'white, middle class, middle-aged people sitting in judgment over young, working class and often black defendants' (p 37). Mr Geoffrey Robertson QC condemned lay justices as 'ladies and gentlemen bountiful', politically imbalanced, unrepresentative of ethnic minority groups, and women, who 'slow down the system and cost a fortune'. We should replace them he told the House of Commons Home Affairs Committee with juries or 'sensible stipendiary magistrates'.[38] According to Bar lore the burden of proof was reversed in magistrates' courts where police evidence was too readily believed. The James Committee had cited defendants' negative view of 'magistrates, who inevitably become "case-hardened" and may be too ready to accept the prosecution case'.[39] Later surveys repeated this view.[40]

Given the continuing shift of criminal business from the jury to the magistrates, Dr Darbyshire suggested that it was 'fatuous' to suggest, as Michael Mansfield had done, that the right of trial by jury should be restored for all but the most trivial offences. 'It is not going to happen. It is high time we bore our responsibility as commentators to deal with what we have got.'[41]

The text that follows draws heavily on Dr Darbyshire's writings. It draws also on a report commissioned jointly by the Lord Chancellor's Department and the Home Office – Rod Morgan and Neil Russell, *The judiciary in the magistrates' courts*, 2000 ('Morgan and Russell') and on Lord Justice Auld's *Review of the Criminal Courts*, 2001 ('Auld'). See also Andrew Sanders, *Community Justice: Modernising the Magistracy in England and Wales*, 2001, IPPR.

Selection process [What follows describes the system as at mid-2003. Obviously it will be changed when the office of Lord Chancellor is abolished, if only to provide for the person or body to appoint magistrates. But at the time of writing it was unknown what other changes would be made regarding the selection process. The Magistrates'

[37]   *Criminal Law Review*, 1997, p 861.
[38]   House of Commons, 52-II, Home Affairs Committee, Third Report, *Judicial Appointments Procedures*, 1995-96, vol II, para 611. (The Report is referred to here as Home Affairs Report.)
[39]   *The Distribution of Criminal Business between the Crown Court and Magistrates' Courts*, Cmnd 6323, 1975, p 18, para 36.
[40]   Darbyshire cited A E Bottoms and J McLean, *Defendants in the Criminal Process*, 1976, p 89; D Riley and J Vennard, *Triable-either-way-cases:Crown Court or Magistrates' Court?*, 1988, Home Office Research Study No 98; C Hedderman and D Moxon, *Magistrates' Court or Crown Court? Mode of Trial Decisions and Sentencing*, 1992, Home Office Research Study No 125; J Vennard in *Contested Trials in Magistrates' Courts*, 1982, Home Office Research Study No 71, pp 2-3.
[41]   Darbyshire, *Criminal Law Review*, 1997, p 862.

Association hoped that basically the system would otherwise be left unchanged.] The Magistrates' Association, in evidence to the House of Commons Home Affairs Select Committee said: 'The present method of recruitment is shrouded in mystery but, as far as we can see from the outside, the system is a self-perpetuating oligarchy'.[42] That even the Magistrates' Association should describe the selection process in such terms speaks for itself. There are close to a hundred local Advisory Committees which nominate potential candidates to the Lord Chancellor. The names of the Secretary to the Advisory Committees are available – they are even given on the LCD's website. But the names of committee members are not easily available. (Two-thirds of the members are magistrates.)

Like all magistrates, the chairmen of Advisory Committees and of sub-committees are appointed by the Lord Chancellor – usually on the advice of the outgoing chairmen.[43] (The chairman of the local bench is not permitted to sit as a member of the local Advisory Committee.) Local Advisory Committees are left to determine their own ways of recruiting new magistrates. Both the Advisory Committee and the bench they are responsible for selecting are supposed broadly to reflect the local community in terms of gender, ethnic origin, geographical spread, occupation and political affiliation. But the Committee is left to obtain its own information in that regard. Auld comments[44] that without reliable information the Committees are not equipped to fulfill this responsibility.

Serving magistrates are recruited in different ways – nomination by local organisations, advertisements or being invited by existing committee members. The process of selection is now supposed to include interviews. Darbyshire noted: 'Many magistrates are councillors and many have multiple membership of other local organisations such as health authorities or trusts or school governing bodies.' [45] In some areas the Freemasons seemed to have disproportionate numbers. Darbyshire urged that advertising be undertaken by the LCD on a national basis and that it emphasise that anyone can apply. Auld said that many local Advisory Committees, 'largely rely on the network, and overlapping membership of local bodies, with the result that there is an undue draw towards the local "great and good".' [46] He contrasted the money devoted to attract members of the public to become magistrates (£35,000) to that devoted to attract them to serve in the Territorial Army (£4.7m). [47] He said he was concerned at the low level of financial assistance given to local Advisory Committees. He endorsed criticism of the Lord Chancellor's Department made by Morgan and Russell as to its failure to maintain a proper database as to the composition of the magistracy using the same classification as the national census[48].

---

[42]   Op cit, n 38 above at p 241.
[43]   Statement of Lord Mackay of Clashfern in evidence to the Home Affairs Committee, op cit n 38 above, para 504.
[44]   p 122, para 68.
[45]   Op cit, n 36, at 867.
[46]   p 121, para 66.
[47]   p 122, para 67.
[48]   p 122, para 69.

The LCD acted on this suggestion. [49] Also, as from 1999, an explanation of how to become a magistrate, the duties of magistrates and other relevant information, including the application form and notes for guidance, have been on the LCD's website.

The LCD issues a lengthy (150 or so pages) document advising Advisory Committees on the processes of selection. It covers functions, organisation and composition, appointments, sources of candidates, interviewing, ancillary matters and conduct.

Composition of the bench

On composition of the bench, Darbyshire wrote: 'Lay magistrates are too white, middle class, Conservative and, I would add, old'. [50]

Gender Lay magistrates are equally divided male and female. [51]

Age There are no figures as to the average age of magistrates. In 1995 the LCD told the House of Commons Home Affairs Committee that a 'recent' survey of 875 new appointments showed that 22% were under 40, 57% were between 41 and 50 and 21% were over 50. [52] A study of the composition of an anonymous North Midlands bench ('Whitechurch') of 116 magistrates published in 1997 showed over 80% were aged 50 or more and only 5% under 40. [53] Darbyshire reports that her observations suggest that sitting magistrates are skewed towards the retired. ('They have time to sit far more often than the required 26-day minimum. Clerks call on them to replace a sick justice or a late cancellation'. [54])

Ethnic minority representation Morgan and Russell wrote, 'the composition of the lay magistracy is now approaching ethnic representativeness, that is 2% black, 2% of Indian sub-continent or Asian origin and 1% other' – as against a national picture of 94% white, 2% black, 3% Indian sub-continent or Asian origin and 1% other. [55]

Social class mix It has been accepted for decades that there are insufficient numbers of 'working class' magistrates, despite strenuous efforts by successive Lord Chancellors to increase the proportion. One factor may be that magistrates are not paid, though

---

[49]   See Annual Report on Judicial Appointments for 1999-2000, para 5.21.

[50]   Darbyshire, *Criminal Law Review*, 1997, p 863.

[51]   *Judicial Statistics*, 2001, Table 9.4, p.96.

[52]   Home Affairs Committee Report, op cit n 38 above, p 150.

[53]   J Dignan and A Wynne, 'A microcosm of the Local Community?', 37 *British Journal of Criminology*, 1997, pp 170-93.

[54]   Op cit, n 36 above, at p 865. The Lord Chancellor recommended a maximum of 80 sessions a year but she had heard of magistrates who sat more than 100 times a year. Morgan and Russell reported that lay magistrates on average sit 41 times per year (Fig.2.3, p.19).

[55]   p 14. This assumed that the 11% of magistrates whose ethnic identity is recorded as unknown are all white.

they can claim travel expenses (including a per mile bicycle allowance!), a subsistence allowance and a modest financial loss allowance, on proof of actual loss. Another factor no doubt is the attitude of employers. Another is the fact that so few people seem to know that anyone can apply to be a magistrate. But the main factor may be the 'old boy network' of the selection process.

There have been a number of studies of the social class composition of the magistracy.[56] One by Dignan and Wynne (n 53 above, published in 1997 but based on 1989-90 data) is especially useful as they compared their data with those of previous surveys. The proportion of wage earners had risen from 15% of male magistrates in 1947 to 26% in 1989-90. Although an increase, this did 'nothing to dispel the overall picture of a magistracy that is still drawn from the middle classes' (p 188). The rateable value of their houses showed equally 'that magistrates in Whitechurch tend to be drawn from the more affluent sectors of the communities they reside in, irrespective of the overall prosperity of those communities' (p 189). A total of 17% were members of a Masonic lodge or Rotary organization – much lower than in the 1973 Rochdale study and unlike Rochdale, there was little overlap of membership between those two organisations. Morgan and Russell sent questionnaires to 1,916 lay magistrates in the 10 courts selected for their study. Just under three-fifths (58%) replied. Of these, 69% gave as their current or former occupation a professional or managerial position, 12% said they had a clerical or other non-manual jobs, 3% were skilled manual workers and 5% said they were unemployed. As many as two-fifths (40%) said they were retired (p 16). Possibly also relevant was the fact that 86% of those responding said they did not claim loss of earnings and almost a quarter (23%) said they seldom or never claimed expenses.

Political balance For many years it has been official policy that attention be given to the political balance on the bench. The policy developed from the report of two Royal Commissions (1909-10 and 1946-48) both of which suggested that the Conservative Party was over-represented on the bench and that it was important to have a broader mix. The directions to Advisory Committees state that the bench should reflect the political balance of the local electorate as judged from the result of the last two general elections. Nominees are asked to state their political affiliation, though not all do so. Nominating committees are asked to state the current balance of the parties on the bench and in the local electorate.

It is likely however that in many, if not most, cases the actual distribution of political allegiances is not 'balanced' as recommended in the directions. In the study by Dignan and Wynne (above), for instance, 'there was a marked contrast between the declared voting intentions of the Whitechurch bench and the pattern of voting in local council elections at the time. While the area returned a large majority of Labour councillors only just over a quarter of magistrates said they intended to vote Labour. Conversely, while almost half the magistrates identified with the Conservatives, the party had

---

[56] See for instance, J Baldwin, 'The Social Composition of the Magistracy', 16 *British Journal of Criminology*, 1976, p 171.

only 16% of local council seats at the time. (p 191) No fewer than 27 of the 70 wards in the division had no magistrates living in them, while five wards had 33 magistrates – almost a third of the total number (p 192).

In October 1998 the LCD issued a Consultation Paper ('Political Balance in the Lay Magistracy') raising the question whether the attempt to achieve a political balance on the bench should be scrapped in favour of a new system that would attempt to achieve a balanced bench on the basis of a broader range of socio-economic factors. The responses were inconclusive with about half in favour of the existing system and half in favour of a broader approach. Auld [57] said that the outcome of this consultation exercise was that the Lord Chancellor concluded 'though reluctantly, that for the time being the requirement for political balance should remain, but that work should continue on searching for a more appropriate measure of social balance, possibly using occupational groupings, either alone or with social groupings based on National Statistics classification'. In Auld's view that was the right approach. The only basis for the political balance to be used was that it was regarded 'as a crude proxy for occupational and/or social groupings' [58] Political views, he said, 'balanced or otherwise, are hardly relevant to the fairness or ability of a tribunal'. [59]

Auld [60] said there were various alternatives for making the magistracy more representative. One was to make the role and terms of service more manageable for a wider range of persons; another would be short term conscription like jury service; a third was co-option of citizens on a rotating basis – serving a specified number of times per year; a fourth was election. He thought that only the first was worthy of serious consideration. The only concrete suggestion he made in that regard was reviewing the sitting arrangements. ('There may be scope for magistrates to sit more or less often, for longer or shorter periods at a time and more flexibly, according to their individual circumstances. This might increase the pool of candidates for appointment. . .'[61]). One has to say that it is difficult to believe that changes in sitting arrangements of that kind would have much impact.

Training The LCD told the House of Commons Home Affairs Committee that until 1989 'training was negligible. It was really a matter of learning by experience.'[62] There was a brief induction course consisting of ten sessions, followed by some Basic Training in the first year and further Basic Training in the second and third year. The training consisted of courses following a syllabus. There was no evaluation or assessment process.

But as from 1998 a new system of training has been started based on competences – a combination of skills, knowledge and attributes. It considers not just knowledge of

---

57   P 128, para 85.
58   P 128, para 85.
59   P 128, para 85.
60   P 123, para 72.
61   P 124, para 73.
62   Op cit, n 38 above, p 151.

law and procedure but such topics as reaching impartial decisions (eg 'one's own conditioning and personal prejudices, labelling and stereotyping, language and cultural differences and body language'); and effective participation on the bench (eg ensuring equality of treatment to all court users, ensuring that witnesses are not bullied, note-taking, observing people/conduct, contributing to a structured decision-making process, challenging discriminatory views, helping to identify the issues etc). New magistrates are assigned experienced magistrates as mentors. Competences are assessed through appraisal. The appraisal system applies not only to new magistrates. Existing magistrates are also appraised, in principle, every three years – though benches are allowed up to five years for the first appraisal. There is now also training and appraisal for chairmen of benches. The required competences depend on the work that each magistrate is actually doing.

Reviewing the new training system, Auld [63] said that it had been much criticised for its complexity – 'for example there are 104 "competences" even for those who sit only as "a winger"'.[64] Two years after the introduction of the scheme no national standards had been set in regard to competences. The Judicial Studies Board had issued an evaluation of the new system[65] in which it concluded that although the basic concepts were sound there was too great a variation in the manner of its implementation. It recommended the introduction of national performance standards, the weighting of consequences and simplification of documents. Auld added that the lack of consistency as between areas applied to all the training of magistrates. This was a matter of legitimate concern 'particularly in its contribution to wide variations in the effectiveness of case management and in sentencing patterns'.[66] In his view there was 'an urgent need for clearer and simpler national standards in the training of magistrates and for more consistency in and monitoring of its provisions'.[67] The Judicial Studies Board, he said, should be made responsible for devising and securing the content and manner of training of magistrates.

The balance between lay and professional magistrates

In 1998, the LCD issued a Consultation Paper (*Unification of the Stipendiary Bench*) on whether there should be a single national judicial corps of stipendiary magistrates. The professional magistrates get through cases at a considerably greater rate than lay justices. The LCD's Consultation Paper (para 33) suggested that, according to research, a single stipendiary did the work of about 30 lay justices in the provinces and of 23 in London.

Morgan and Russell's report was a comparison between lay and stipendiary magistrates. It confirmed that stipendiaries dealt with their work more quickly. They

---

[63] Pp 131-2, para 92.
[64] The bench normally consists of the chairman and two 'wingers'.
[65] *Magistrates New Training Initiative: Evaluation of Implementation, Final Report* (December 2000).
[66] P 132, para 96.
[67] P 132, para 96.

knew the law and therefore did not need to consult their legal adviser. They sat alone and therefore did not need to consult colleagues. They therefore withdrew less often and for shorter periods. But they also asked more questions than lay magistrates. They granted fewer adjournments. They were less likely than lay justices to grant bail over police objections (19% compared to 37%), and more likely to give defendants immediate custodial sentences (25% compared to 12%)[68] The finding that stipendiaries are more severe in sentencing confirms earlier research.[69]

- If only direct costs were considered, Morgan and Russell said, lay justices were much cheaper as they were not paid and many did not claim loss of earnings or even travel expenses (£3.59 per appearance against £20.96). However, when the cost of buildings and court administration were included the gap obviously narrowed. (£52.10 against £61.78).

- The study found that in London where there are a large number of stipendiaries they did the full range of magistrates' courts work. Outside London their caseload was more slanted toward 'heavy business' (pp 26-27).

- A nationally representative sample of 1,753 members of the public were interviewed as to their views on and knowledge of the magistracy (ch 5). Most had heard of magistrates and magistrates' courts but only a minority had heard of lay as opposed to stipendiary magistrates. When the difference between them was explained, almost three-quarters (73%) said they were not aware of the difference. When comparing single magistrates with panels, a large majority thought that the more serious decisions of guilty/not guilty (74%) and imprisonment (76%) should be taken by panels.

The establishment in 1999 of Lord Justice Auld's Review of the Criminal Courts raised expectations in some quarters that he would recommend a change in the overall balance between lay and professional magistrates. But he did not do so. ('Nor can I see any basis for recommending any significant change in their respective numbers.'[70])

Auld also rejected the suggestion that lay and professional magistrates sit together in a hybrid magistrates' court. ('The overwhelming evidence in the Review is that they each do a good job in their separate ways. And neither magistrates nor District Judges would welcome such a general transformation and diminution of their respective roles.'[71]) However, somewhat inconsistently, he did recommend, that a new intermediate criminal court (District Division) be set up consisting of a professional judge and two lay magistrates (on which see below pp 45-46).

---

[68]   Op cit, sect 3.4.8.
[69]   See S S Diamond, 'Revising Images of Public Punitiveness: Sentencing by Lay and Professional English Magistrates', 15 *Law and Social Inquiry*, 1990, pp 191-221 and 'The Assessment of Sentencing Choice through Triangulation: A Reply to Walker', 17 *Law and Social Inquiry*, 1990, pp 115-22.
[70]   P 111, para 2.
[71]   P 109, para 40.

Extent of summary jurisdiction

Auld also rejected suggestions for either a general increase or decrease in summary jurisdiction. ('I can discern no wide or well-based support for a change in the general limit of six month's custody or £5,000 fine now applicable to District Judges and magistrates alike.' (p 101, para 20)) He acknowledged that their sentencing powers were greater than those given to lay tribunals in other countries but, in his view, 'they are increasingly well trained for their task and have their legal advisers to assist them, where necessary, on points of law or procedure'(ibid). There were remarkably few appeals from their decisions.

As will be seen(p 43 below), the Government disagreed. Hoping to reduce the proportion of cases committed for sentence to the Crown Court it included a provision in the Criminal Justice Bill 2002-2003 to extend magistrates' sentencing power from six months' to 12 months' imprisonment.

Justices' chief executives, justices' clerks and court clerks

The justices' clerk used to be the person responsible for the administration of the court – including keeping the accounts, handling the collection of fines and other enforcement procedures, for running the licensing sessions, for training the justices, for listing of cases and generally for advising the bench. In large court complexes the justices' clerk was so busy with administrative duties that he rarely sat in court. Some justices' clerks would have one or two benches; some had a large number. (Darbyshire stated that when in 1997 the Kent Magistrates' Courts Committee amalgamated the whole county under one clerkship the clerk would be serving 14 benches with 800 justices.[72])

In 1994 the Police and Magistrates' Courts Act established the post of justices' chief executive to act as the single head of service for each magistrates' courts committee. Each Magistrates' Court Committee was required to appoint a chief executive to manage the courts in its area. But justices' clerks continued to be responsible for many administrative matters. The Justices of the Peace Act 1997 separated the legal and administrative functions of the job. The Access to Justice Act 1999, s 87 took this process further in providing that the chief executive need not be someone qualified to be a justices' clerk. The policy was that justices' clerks should concentrate on their legal and judicial functions which were rapidly expanding.[73]

Lord Justice Auld said: 'The office of the justices' clerk has developed piecemeal over the centuries. Originating as the personal servant to the local justice of the peace in medieval times, its subsequent history is of steady accretion, diversification and

---

[72]   Op cit, n 36 above at p 873.
[73]   The LCD's Consultation Paper, 'The Future Role of the Justices' Clerk' said the Government intended to transfer responsibility for fines and fees accounts to the justices' chief executive and this was effected by the Access to Justice Act 1999, s 91.

professionalism as the business of the summary courts has increased and the law has become more complex ... As a result of recent legislation, Government policy and the current programme of amalgamation of Magistrates' Courts Committees (MCCs) and benches their numbers are depleting, their territorial responsibilities widening, their former broad administrative responsibilities diminishing and their legal role concentrating on the provision, mostly through other members of staff, of legal advice to magistrates, together with certain case management functions.' [74]

The court clerk – qualifications Each court is advised by a court clerk. Ideally the court clerk should be a qualified lawyer but many are not. A Consultation Paper issued by the LCD in 1998 (*The Professionalisation of Court Clerks*) said that some 40% of the 1,500 or so court clerks in magistrates' courts were not so qualified. Since 1980, all courts clerks are supposed to have at least a Diploma in Magisterial Law, though not all in fact satisfy that test. Darbyshire says: 'Diploma students and part-time distance learners may be authorised to clerk on completion of just one year of the course.'[75] The LCD's Consultation Paper invited views on a proposal that all court clerks should be professionally qualified as barristers or solicitors. The Consultation Paper presented two broad options. One was that from a given date only persons qualified as barristers or solicitors would be eligible to take courts. The second was that this would only apply to new entrants as from that date.

The Government initially decided that court clerks appointed after January 1999 would have to be fully qualified and that existing clerks would have to become so qualified within ten years. Subsequently, however, the Government retreated slightly in the face of criticism and announced that this new rule would not apply to serving clerks aged 40 or over.[76]

Auld said that in March 2001 there were some 1,800 legal advisers, two-thirds of whom were qualified. He warmly approved of the increasing professionalism of the court clerks but he recommended that District Judges, being themselves professionally qualified, should normally sit without a legal adviser[77]

The clerk and the bench The function of the court clerk vis-à-vis the bench has undergone important changes. Basically the function is to guide the justices on matters of law and procedure.

In the 1950s it was laid down that the clerk must be, and be seen to be, subservient to the bench and that although the clerk could, for instance, retire with the bench when

---

74   p 114, para 50.
75   Darbyshire, *Criminal Law Review*, 1997, p 872. Under the Justices Clerks, (Qualification of Assistants) Rules 1979 a person can serve as a court clerk if he has passed a preliminary professional examination and has served for two years or, in the case of clerks who had served for five years before 1980, if he has a 'certificate of competence' from the magistrates' court committee.
76   Press statement by Mr Geoff Hoon, MP, Minister of State, 12 November 1998.
77   P 117, para 53.

they went to consider their decision, he should do so only on invitation and should emerge before the justices.(See *Practice Direction* [1953] 2 All ER 1306.)

In recent years the crucial role played by the clerk has increasingly been recognised and the courts have now rather changed their emphasis when dealing with the delicate balance of power between the clerk and the bench.

The next *Practice Direction* was issued in July 1981 – [1981] 2 All ER 831. It said that '*if it appears to him to be necessary*' (emphasis supplied), or 'he is so requested by the justices', the clerk had the responsibility to 'refresh the justice's memory as to any matter of evidence and to draw attention to any issues involved in the matters before the court' as well as advising on the penalties available and giving guidance as to the choice of penalties. The clerk could advise the justices in their retiring room though if they wished to consult him about the evidence they should normally do so in open court.

For a strong argument that advice on law from the clerk should always be given in open court see A Heaton-Armstrong, 'The Verdict of the Court and its Clerk? Can Justice be Seen to be Done Behind Closed Doors?', (1995) *Justice of the Peace*, 31 May, p 340; (1995) *Justice of the Peace*, 7 June, p 357. This advice was taken and implemented in the *Practice Direction* issued on 2 October 2000, the day the Human Rights Act came into force:

Practice Direction [2000] 1 WLR 1886, [2000] 4 All ER 895

8. At any time, justices are entitled to receive advice to assist them in discharging their responsibilities. If they are in any doubt as to the evidence which has been given, they should seek the aid of their legal adviser, referring to his/her notes as appropriate. This should ordinarily be done in open court. Where the justices request their adviser to joint them in the retiring room, this request should be made in the presence of the parties in court. Any legal advice given to the justices other than in open court should be clearly stated to be provisional and the adviser should subsequently repeat the substance of the advice in open court and give the parties an opportunity to make any representations they wish on that provisional advice. The legal adviser should then state in open court whether the provisional advice is confirmed or if it is varied, the nature of the variation.

In recent years the trend has been to give more and more responsibility to the clerk and especially the clerk to the justices him (or her) self. The first step in that direction was taken in the Justices' Clerks Rules of 1970, which allowed clerks to hear applications for summonses and warrants, to grant adjournments, renew bail, to issue witness orders and take pleas, order a means inquiry and vary the payment of a fine.

It has been suggested that they should be allowed to rule formally on the admissibility of evidence and to sum up points for the justices. They would then be acting very much like the judge with a jury. One strong argument for such a development is that it would make the administration of justice more open. The parties would be able to see on what basis the case was being approached and what law was being applied. In February 1997, the Narey Report[78] proposed that justices' clerks should take over from magistrates many of the functions of court management such as handling pre-trial reviews or early administrative hearings, extending bail, varying conditions of bail, ordering defendants to produce his driving licence etc. The decision as to bail or custody would, however, remain one for the bench. In its response to the Narey Report the Government said it accepted in principle that there was a role for clerks to the justices in assisting in case management.

Under rules made by virtue of the Crime and Disorder Act 1998, ss 49 and 50 justices' clerks have the power to perform a variety of tasks recommended for transfer by Narey.[79] (As originally drafted the Crime and Disorder Bill would have given clerks even wider judicial powers – including varying of bail conditions without consent, remanding an accused in custody for a medical report, making an order for joint or separate trials, determining mode of trial on an additional charge and prohibiting press publicity. But after opposition from, inter alia, the Lord Chief Justice and the Magistrates' Association, s 49(3) was added expressly to prevent those functions being delegated to clerks.[80])

Auld said that the majority of justices' clerks were frustrated by the limitations of their newly-acquired jurisdiction and wanted enhanced powers. But Auld did not support this. ('I recommend that there should be no extension of justices' clerks case management jurisdiction.'[81]) The Government, so far at least, seems to have accepted that view.

See further on magistrates' courts: Sir Thomas Skyrme, *The Changing Image of the Magistracy*, Macmillan, (1979) and *History of the Justices of the Peace*, (1994); Pat Carlen, *Magistrates' Justice*, Martin Robertson, (1976); Elizabeth Burney, *Magistrate, Court and Community*, Hutchinson, (1979); P Darbyshire, *The Magistrates' Clerk*, Barry Rose (1984); S Brown, *Magistrates at Work*, 1991.

2. Managing the courts

In April 1979 the Court Service was launched as an executive agency of the Lord Chancellor's Department. The Service took over responsibility for administrative and operational functions of the Supreme Court of England and Wales (comprising the Court of Appeal, the High Court–including the probate service–and the Crown

---

78   *Review of Delay in the Criminal Justice System*, 1997. Mr Martin Narey was a senior Home Office official who shortly thereafter became Director-General of the Prison Service.

79   See The Justices' Clerks Rules, 1999 (SI 1999 No 2784).

80   See generally, P Darbyshire, 'A comment on the powers of Magistrates' Clerks', *Criminal Law Review*, 1999, pp 377-86.

81   P 119, para 58.

Court), county courts and seven tribunals.[82] It did not cover administrative support for the magistrates' courts.

The Court Service publishes an annual report. There is also an annual report entitled the *Judicial Statistics* published by the Lord Chancellor's Department. The Court Service periodically publishes a Charter for Court Users in which it sets out its current objectives: eg to answer telephone calls within thirty seconds, to give jurors not less than four weeks' notice of jury service, to provide separate waiting rooms for witnesses, to start Crown Court cases within 16 weeks of their transfer from magistrates' courts, to issue civil proceedings within five to ten days from receipt of all the documentation and the fee etc.

Magistrates' courts The magistracy is older even than the Justices of the Peace Act 1361, which in effect gave statutory recognition to the institution and made magistrates into a form of local government. They still have some essentially administrative tasks such as liquor licensing, but for at least the past century justices have been mainly concerned with judicial functions. The organisation of magistrates' courts was historically outside the national scheme under the Lord Chancellor which covered the civil courts and the Crown Courts. The magistrates' courts service was a local service locally administered. From 1949 the Home Office assumed the burden of financing 80% of the cost of the magistrates' courts. The actual level of funding was set by the local Magistrates' Courts Committee in consultation with the paying local authority. These committees consisted of magistrates elected by their fellow magistrates in the area. Subject to the approval of the Home Secretary, the Committee appointed the Justices' Clerk who, as has been seen, was both the chief administrator of the court and its chief clerk.

In 1979, a Home Office Scrutiny Report (the Le Vay Report) stated: 'There is no coherent management structure for the service. At the national level, the role of the Home Office is so uncertain, and its powers so limited, that it might be truer to say that there are 105 local services, each run by a committee of magistrates. But the local structure is just as confused, with 285 justices' clerks enjoying a semi-autonomous status, under committees which are fundamentally ill-suited to the task of management. It is impossible to locate clear management responsibility or accountability anywhere in the structure.' The Scrutiny proposed a radical solution, that the service be restructured as a single national service, operated as an executive agency.

In December 1991 it was announced that as from April 1992 ministerial responsibility for the magistrates' courts would be transferred from the Home Office to the Lord Chancellor's Department. The LCD took over responsibility for their

---

[82]   The Immigration Appellate Authorities, the Lands Tribunal, the Pensions Appeals Tribunal, the Social Security and Child Support Commissioners, the Value Added Tax and Duties Tribunals (including both the General and Special Commissioners of Income Tax) and the Transport Tribunal, the Banking Tribunal, and the Building Societies Tribunal.

finance, organisation and management. But the Government rejected the proposal of the Le Vay Scrutiny Report of a national executive agency to run the courts. Magistrates' courts continued to be a locally based service. There was however to be a new national inspectorate to improve efficiency. Also a local chief executive would take over the administrative responsibilities of the clerk to the justices. The Home Secretary would retain responsibility for criminal law and procedure.

The details of the Government's plans for the magistrates' courts were presented in February 1992 in a White Paper (*A New Framework for Local Justice*, Cm 1829, 1992). The White Paper stated, inter alia, that the number of magistrates' courts committees would be reduced from 105 to 50 or 60, that the committees would have a maximum of 12 members supported by a corporate management team of senior staff, that non-magistrates could be co-opted and that the pay of court clerks would be related to performance.[83]

The Magistrates' Courts Service Inspectorate was established on a non-statutory basis in autumn 1993. The chief function of the inspectorate is to carry out a rolling programme of efficiency and effectiveness inspections of the administration and management of all services provided by magistrates' courts committees.

In December 1993 the Government introduced in the House of Lords the Police and Magistrates' Courts Bill to implement the White Paper of February 1992. The Bill proved to be highly controversial with attention focussed in particular on the provisions that appointment of chairmen of magistrates' courts committees and renewal of contracts for justices' clerks would require the approval of the Lord Chancellor; on fixed term contracts and on performance related pay for clerks; the introduction of the new management tier of chief justices' clerks as line managers for justices' clerks; and the fear that concern about budgets would affect the advice given by clerks in regard to judicial decision making.

In the face of the formidable weight of criticism, the Government had to amend the Bill. The effect of the amendments was that chairmen of magistrates' courts committees would continue to be appointed by members of the committee without requiring the approval of the Lord Chancellor, the terms of contract between the chief justices' clerk or justices' clerks and their committee were left to local discretion and the Lord Chancellor therefore had no power to require that they be for fixed terms or that remuneration be related to performance, and the renewal of appointments of chief justices' clerks and justices' clerks did not require the approval of the Lord Chancellor. The title 'chief justices' clerk' was changed to 'justices' chief executive'. The chief executive had to be legally qualified but he only had power to act as a justices' clerk if so appointed by the magistrates' courts committee. He reported to, and was employed by, the committee.

The Act stated that when exercising legal functions a justices' clerk 'shall not be subject to the direction of the magistrates' courts committee, the justices' chief

---

[83]   The scheme was severely criticised by the Magistrates' Association, the Justices' Clerks Society, the Law Society and the Bar. (See, for instance, *Law Society's Gazette*, 23 October 1991, p 7.)

executive or any other person' and a member of the staff of a magistrates' courts committee shall likewise not be subject to direction by the committee or of the justices' chief executive (s 78).

In October 1997, the Lord Chancellor announced that the Government would take action to see that Magistrates' Courts Committees' boundaries were better aligned with those of the police service and Crown Prosecution Service regions. The first fruit of this initiative was the amalgamation of five MCCs in Merseyside which took effect in April 1999. At that date there were 84 MCCs. By 2003 the number of MCCs had been reduced to 42, consistent with the number of criminal justice areas.

Lord Justice Auld's Review

The criminal justice system currently operates on a budget of some £12 billion and consists of three government departments – the Department of Constitutional Affairs, replacing the Lord Chancellor's Department, the Home Office and the Attorney General – and a number of separate agencies. Describing the management for the system, Lord Justice Auld said,

> The whole edifice is structurally inefficient, ineffective and wasteful. . . .The basic problem lies in the shared, but also divided, responsibilities of the three Government departments for the system. Each, necessarily, must guard its constitutional independence and, in respect of some of its responsibilities, its functions from the others and have regard to its separate financial accountability to the Treasury and to Parliament. The Public Accounts Committee, in its 2000 Report, observed: 'The most common constraints to effective local inter-agency liaison include conflicting objectives and priorities, which can prevent agreement ... Current performance in progressing criminal cases is not satisfactory and needs to be improved through more concerted joint monitoring and management of performance across the criminal justice system.[84]

Auld continued,

> It does not have to be this way. It is axiomatic that over-all political accountability for investigation, prosecution and adjudication should remain separate. But beneath that level there needs to be a mechanism for securing some central direction and joint management of the achievement of shared objectives. [85]

He recommended that a Criminal Justice Board should replace all the existing national planning and operational bodies, including the Strategic Planning Group[86]

[84]   Chapter 8, para 14, pp 319-20.
[85]   Chapter 8, para 15, p 420.
[86]   It consisted of the Criminal Policy Directors and senior Finance Officers of the three departments, other senior officials including a representative of the Treasury and a member of the Prime Minister's Policy Unit. It met every six weeks. It made recommendations to the Ministerial Group chaired by the Home Secretary which included the Lord Chancellor and the Attorney General. According to a recent study by Professor Sue Richards cited by Auld,

and the Trial Issues Group (TIG)[87] It should be responsible for planning and setting criminal justice objectives, budgeting and the allocation of funds, securing the national and local achievement of its objectives, the development of an integrated IT system and research and development. The Board should be the means by which the government departments and agencies dealing with criminal justice provide over-all direction of the criminal justice system. It should have an independent chairman and should include senior civil servants from the three main departments and chief executives of the main criminal justice agencies plus a small number of non-executive members.[88]

The Government's White Paper *Justice for All* (para 9.5) stated that a new National Criminal Justice Board would be established to replace the Strategic Board It would be chaired by the Permanent Secretary at the Home Office and would include the Permanent Secretary at the Lord Chancellor's Department, the DPP, the chief executives of the criminal justice agencies, the president of the Association of Chief Police Officers and a senior judge. The Board would report to the Cabinet Committee, chaired by the Home Secretary and including the Lord Chancellor and the Attorney General whose function was to co-ordinate broad policy on criminal justice. The existing tripartite Criminal Justice Joint Planning Unit would be answerable to the Board and would establish co-ordinated business plans and priorities. The White Paper did not mention Auld's recommendation as to the Board's functions but it was clear that the Government did not accept that the Board would allocate budgets.

Auld recommended that local Criminal Justice Boards, replacing Area Strategy Committees and local Trial Issues Groups, should be responsible for giving effect at the local level to the national Board's directions and for management of the system at their level.[89]

The White Paper (para 9.11) said that the Government would set up 42 local Criminal Justice Boards to oversee the new joint working agreements between local agencies in each area. Local Chief Officers from the police, CPS and Probation Service as well as senior representatives of the courts would provide the core membership. Each local Board would be required to establish advisory and consultative machinery involving input from the judiciary, magistrates, voluntary groups and members of the community including victims. (para 9.12) The local Boards would agree annual local delivery contracts with the National Board and would

---

the Strategic Planning Group 'is not strategic and it does not plan'. (Auld, ch 8, paras 22, 25 pp 322, 323).

[87] Established in 1995. Consists of senior civil servants and officials drawn from all the main criminal justice agencies and organisations. Monthly meetings. A creature of the three departments. Operated as their planning and co-ordinating agent through sub-groups, pilot studies, instructions and guidance. Supported by six specialist sub-groups and local TIGs based on the 42 criminal justice areas.(Auld, Chap 8, paras 26-27, pp 324-25.)

[88] Chapter 8, paras 43-72, pp 330-43.

[89] Chapter 8, paras,73-77, pp 343-44.

be responsible and accountable for local delivery of criminal justice system objectives; improvements in the delivery of justice; the service provided to victims and witnesses; and in securing public confidence.

Auld said that the present Criminal Justice Consultative Committee was 'ill-equipped to undertake the wide-ranging and comprehensive consultative and advisory role that the government needs'.[90] It should be replaced by a strengthened Criminal Justice Council chaired by the Lord Chief Justice and with a proper secretariat and research staff to keep the whole system under review and to advise the Government.[91]

The White Paper (para 9.7) stated that the Criminal Justice Consultative Council would be replaced by a new Criminal Justice Council with membership from the Commission for Racial Equality, the Law Society, victim and witness organisations and academics, as well as the core membership of the judiciary, the Bar and the magistracy. There was no mention of the secretariat or research capacity.

Auld recommended that the Crown Court and the magistrates' courts should be replaced by a unified Criminal Court[92] .

The Government rejected this recommendation. The White Paper *Justice for All* (para 4.6) said that the benefits Auld saw flowing from unification could be realised through 'a closer alignment of the magistrates' courts and the Crown Court, without a complete re-ordering of the court system and without adversely affecting the civil and family jurisdictions' . The Government would legislate to bring the two courts closer together. They would be known as 'the criminal courts'. (See the Courts Bill below.)

Auld recommended that there should be a single centrally funded executive agency as part of the Lord Chancellor's Department responsible for the administration of all courts, civil, criminal and family (save for the appellate Committee of the House of Lords) replacing the Court Service and the Magistrates' Courts Committees[93]

In regard to the 42 MCCs and the Greater London Magistrates' Courts Authority, the White Paper (para 9.16) said that Lord Justice Auld had found their 'differences in practices, procedures, management and culture to be confusing, divisive and inefficient'. Organisational boundaries between the different court services in each area formed an institutional barrier to the effective management of the courts. There were wide variations in their performance.

The Government accepted Auld's recommendation of a new agency to replace the Courts Service. ('The aim of the new agency will be to enable management decisions to be taken locally by community focused local management boards, but within a strong national framework of standards and strategy direction … In an integrated

90   Chapter 8, para 79, p 347.
91   Chapter 8, paras 78-88, pp 346-51.
92   Chapter 7, paras 2-15, pp 270-73.
93   Chapter 7, paras 50-73, pp 287-95.

system, local managers will have much greater freedom to balance workloads across the civil, criminal and family jurisdictions ... Unification will also make it simpler to transfer cases from magistrates' courts to the Crown Court and easier for the courts to engage directly with other criminal justice agencies'.[94])

At the same time the White Paper said that management of the courts needed to reflect local considerations. ('The new structure will need to ensure sufficient local flexibility and devolved decision making about management issues of importance to the local area'.[95])

There also needed to be greater accountability to the local community. MCCs largely consisted of magistrates appointed by magistrates. ('There is no requirement for court users, the local community or local authorities to be consulted about key management decisions.'[96]) The Government said that it would expect managers of courts to be accountable to new local management boards which would include representatives drawn for example from the judiciary, the magistracy, local court user groups, victim support groups, local authorities and the local community.[97]

But local flexibility could not be used to excuse wide variations in performance. ('Local services will need to satisfy clear national standards in performance, financial reporting and meeting national policy aims.'[98]) The Chief Executive of the new agency would be accountable to Ministers and Parliament for national functions including setting and monitoring standards across the courts, stepping in to take action when an area was under-performing and managing major programmes and projects like IT.[99]

Auld recommended that a Joint Inspection Unit should be established under the collective control of the six Criminal Justice Chief Inspectors: – of the Crown Prosecution Service, of the Constabulary, of Prisons, of Probation, of the Magistrates' Court Service and of Social Services. The Magistrates' Courts Inspectorate should be superseded by an Inspectorate for the unified Criminal Court.[100]

The Government accepted both these recommendations. On joint inspections, it said, 'The more the CJS comes to be managed as one overall system, with consistent measures of performance, the more important it will be that future inspections are conducted and delivered in a cohesive and consistent manner.' (para 9.43) There was already a joint inspectorate secretariat. (para 9.45) (In March 2003 it was announced that the five inspectorates responsible for the police, Crown Prosecution Service, courts, prisons and probation, would undertake the first joint inspection –

94   White Paper, *Justice for All*, paras 9.17, 9.20.
95   White Paper, *Justice for All*, para 9.22.
96   White Paper, *Justice for All*, para 9.23.
97   White Paper, *Justice for All*, para 9.24.
98   White Paper, *Justice for All*, para 9.25.
99   White Paper, *Justice for All*, para 9.26.
100 White Paper, *Justice for All*, paras 351-52, pp 351-52.

of the criminal justice system in Gloucestershire.) On inspecting the courts, the White Paper said (para 9.46), 'We will set up a new independent inspectorate to look at improving administrative performance of the magistrates' courts, the Children and Family Court Advisory Service and, for the first time of the Crown Court and county courts'.

The Courts Bill 2002-2003

The Courts Bill introduced in the House of Lords on 28 November 2002 gave effect to some of these proposals.[101]

- Part I (Maintaining the Court System) – Clause 1 places a duty on the Lord Chancellor to provide an efficient and effective system to support the carrying on of the business of all the main courts in England and Wales, namely the Court of Appeal, the High Court, the Crown Court, the county courts and the magistrates' courts. The Bill does not set out a blueprint for the new agency. However the Explanatory Notes accompanying the Bill stated (para 6), 'This responsibility will be discharged, in practice, by a new executive agency, as part of the Lord Chancellor's Department, replacing the Courts Service and the 42 Magistrates' Courts Committees (MCCs).'[102] The agency will have local community links through Court Boards [103] Their members, appointed by the Lord Chancellor, must include a judge, two lay justices[104], two other persons with knowledge of the work of the courts in the area and two persons representative of the community in that area and may include others.[105] The office of justices' chief executive would be abolished.[106]

- Part 2 (Justices of the Peace) – largely re-enacts Part II of the Justices of the Peace Act 1997. The main change is to give lay magistrates a national jurisdiction, though they will be assigned to a local justice area (cl 10).

Justices' clerks will in future be appointed by the Lord Chancellor. They will have to have a five-year magistrates' courts qualification, or be a barrister or solicitor or have previously been a justice's clerk. (cl 22) The Lord Chancellor will be obliged to consult with the chairman of the lay justices before assigning a justices' clerk to a different area. Assistants to the justice's clerk will also be appointed by the Lord Chancellor. They will have to have a five-year magistrates' court qualification or

---

101   The Bill had its 2nd Reading in the House of Lords on 9 December 2002. It completed all its stages in the Lords on 19 May. By the time this work went for printing the Bill had completed the Committee Stage in the Commons.

102   Clause 6(1) abolishes the 42 MCCs and the London magistrates' courts authority.

103   The Bill as introduced called them Courts Administration Councils – with the unhappy acronym CACs - but the name was changed as a response to strong criticism in the Lords.

104   The Bill originally provided for only one.

105   Replacement cls 4 and 5 and a new schedule set out more detail about the Boards including their powers. These were to include approval of their area's estate strategy regarding the opening and closure of court houses, spending priorities and staffing structures.

106   Clause 6(2)(b).

such other qualification as is prescribed. (ibid) A clause headed 'Independence' states that when exercising their legal functions justice's clerks are not subject to the direction of the Lord Chancellor or any other person and that assistants are not subject to the direction of anyone other than the justice's clerk. (cl 24)

- Part 5 (Inspectors of Court Administration) – provides for the establishment of a new inspectorate to be known as Her Majesty's Inspectorate of Courts Administration to replace and build upon the work of the existing Courts Service Inspectorate. It would have the power to inspect all magistrates' courts, county courts and the Crown Court.
- Part 7 (Procedure Rules and Practice Directions) – provides for the amalgamation into a single new Criminal Procedure Rule Committee of the two existing separate Rule Committees for the Crown Court and the Crown Court.

The debates in the House of Lords focused particularly on the issue of centralisation of powers and the resulting loss of local input regarding the running of magistrates' courts. (For an article about the Bill by the Minister, published after the completion of the House of Lords stage, see Baroness Scotland, 'Courts Bill', 167 *Justice of the Peace*, 24 May 2003, p 384. The purpose of the article was plainly to persuade magistrates who had expressed considerable disquiet about the Bill that the Government's amendments sufficiently met their concerns.)

3. Problems of trial courts' organisation

(a)   The allocation of cases between higher and lower trial courts–criminal cases

Historically there were three criminal courts: assize courts, quarter sessions courts and magistrates' courts. The judges began to go out on assize to hear criminal cases from the early part of the 12th century. In 1361 a statute provided that justices of the peace were required to keep the peace and to arrest and punish offenders. The following year a further statute required them to meet four times a year–from which the origin of Quarter Sessions Courts is derived. In times of crisis such as the Wars of the Roses in the 15th century and the Civil War in the 17th century, when it was not possible to assemble the justices at Quarter Sessions, they started to sit to hear cases out of sessions without a jury. At first this was done without authority, but by the end of the 16th century powers of summary jurisdiction were conferred on these meetings, which came to be called Petty Sessions.

Until the middle of the 19th century there were only two categories of offence: those triable on indictment at either assizes or quarter sessions, and those triable only summarily by magistrates. From 1847 onwards, however, the legislature gradually gave magistrates power also to deal with various categories of indictable offence. In 1847 their powers of sentence were three months' imprisonment or a fine of £3. The modern maximum became six months' imprisonment or a fine of £5,000. The

Criminal Justice Act 1982, Part III, established a system of grading of offences which had five scale levels. Under the 1991 Criminal Justice Act the actual figures were altered: Level 5 up to £5,000; Level 4 to £2,500; Level 3 to £1,000; Level 2 to £500; Level 1 to £200.

THE RIGHT TO HAVE TRIAL BY JURY

It is widely believed that the defendant's right to claim trial by jury in more serious cases dates back to Magna Carta. This is a misconception. For centuries there was no question of choice. Until the middle of the nineteenth century the normal mode of trial in criminal cases was trial on indictment by judge and jury. Justices had a considerable jurisdiction when sitting at Quarter Sessions but there were only a small number of offences that the magistrates could deal with in the magistrates' court. The development of the magistrates' courts as the court where most criminal cases are handled only started in the mid-nineteenth century. In the Criminal Justice Act 1855 the magistrates' were given jurisdiction to try simple larceny cases involving sums of under five shillings but only with the defendant's consent. That was the first time the defendant was given a power to choose the mode of trial. In the Summary Jurisdiction Act 1879 the defendant was given the right to claim trial by jury for all offences carrying a maximum sentence of more than three months. Today, as will be seen, the right exists in relation to all 'either-way' offences which make up some 80% of all cases sent to trial in Crown Courts. If the defendant opts for summary trial (as most do), the magistrates' court retains the right to send the case for trial.

Where several defendants are charged with either-way offences, each defendant has an individual right of election. If one elects for trial at the Crown Court, this does not mean that the others can be forced to have a Crown Court trial. (*Nicholls v Brentwood Justices* [1991] 3 All ER 359, HL.)

The question of the allocation of cases between the higher and the lower criminal court has been on the political agenda for many years. From the perspective of government it has been fuelled mainly by a wish to reduce the cost of criminal proceedings. In 1993 the Runciman Royal Commission on Criminal Justice stated that the Home Office estimated that the average cost of a contested case in the Crown Court was some £13,500 as against £1,500 in the magistrates' court and the cost of a guilty plea case was £2,500 as against £500 in the magistrates' court–see Royal Commission Report, 1993, Cm 2263, p 5, para 18.

 In 1975 the issue was explored by the James Committee, whose report *(The Distribution of Criminal Business between the Crown Court and Magistrates' Courts*, 1975, Cmnd 6323) recommended the transfer of substantial categories of work to the lower court. It considered the criteria which should determine whether an offence ought to be tried at one or the other level. The primary, though not the only criterion, it thought, was its seriousness in the eyes of the community. It would be impracticable to categorize offences by reference to their gravity in the mind of the defendant since that would vary from person to person. The Committee said there should continue to be offences which were so serious that they should be triable only on indictment 'because the offences are so serious that trial on indictment is necessary in order to signify the gravity with which society regards them' (para 43). At the other end of the scale there were many offences for which the elaborate procedures and expense of trial on indictment would not be justified. But between these two categories it thought there should be an intermediate category of offences triable either way.

The Committee considered a variety of ways for determining the level of court for a trial of offences triable either way. It thought the defendant's right to elect for trial by jury should be retained. It was only used in about a tenth of the cases in which it could be exercised, but it was widely regarded as important both by defendants and by those who represented them.

If the defendant opted for trial summarily, the magistrates should, however, have the right to send the case for trial at the higher level– having first heard representations from the prosecution. That proposal was implemented in the Criminal Law Act 1977.

The Committee proposed, further, that some offences previously triable either summarily or on indictment should become summary-only offences. This should apply, for instance, to all drink-driving offences and theft of amounts under £20 or criminal damage where the value of the damage did not exceed £100. The Government accepted these recommendations and they were included in the Bill. But the proposals to make small theft and small criminal damage cases triable only summarily provoked great opposition, and the Government eventually dropped the proposal from the Bill. The Committee's other recommendations for making offences triable only summarily were implemented in the 1977 Act and in 1980 (in the Magistrates' Courts Act, s 22 and Sch 2) criminal damage cases involving amounts under £200 became triable only summarily.

The process of transferring cases to the summary-only category continued. In the Criminal Justice Act 1988, criminal damage cases became summary-only if they involved sums of under £2,000 and driving while disqualified, taking a motor vehicle without authority, and common assault and battery were all reduced to this category. The £2,000 limit for summary-only criminal damage cases was raised to £5,000 by the Criminal Justice and Public Order Act 1994.

A Consultation Paper produced by the Home Office in 1986 again raised for consideration the controversial question of whether small theft cases should be transferred to the summary-only category. A survey had shown that cases of theft and handling of goods worth less than £50 constituted 10% of the Crown Court's case load and 8.8% of court time (*The Distribution of Business between the Crown Court and Magistrates' Courts*, Home Office, 1986, para 21). The proposal floated in the Consultation Paper was that there should be a statutory presumption that indictable offences should be tried summarily but trial on indictment would be available 'where special circumstances made the offence one of exceptional gravity' (ibid, para 27). It would be for the magistrates to decide this question. There might also be a case for allowing a person with no prior conviction for dishonesty to elect for trial on indictment for an offence of that character.

The proposal again ran into considerable opposition and in the end the Government decided not to pursue it. (See House of Lords, *Hansard*, 19 November 1987, col 309.) But the Home Office returned to the issue in 1991 in its evidence to the Runciman Royal Commission on Criminal Justice in which it again proposed that small theft cases should become summary-only.

In 1990, Lord Taylor, the Lord Chief Justice issued *Practice Note (Offences triable either way: mode of trial)* [1990] 3 All ER 979 to assist magistrates in making the mode of trial decision. The court should never make its decision on grounds of convenience or expedition. The accused's prior record was irrelevant. 'In general, except where otherwise stated, either way offences should be tried summarily unless the court considers that the particular case has one of the features set out in the following pages [relating to named offences] *and* that its sentencing powers are insufficient.' This was intended to increase the proportion of cases dealt with summarily but it did not have a great impact.

In 1993, the Runciman Royal Commission on Criminal Justice (1993, Cm 2263, pp 85–89) recommended a radical change by proposing that the defendant should no longer have a right to demand trial by jury in either way offences. Instead, he should have a right only to *ask* for Crown Court trial. If the prosecution agreed that would be sufficient. If the prosecution disagreed, the matter would be decided by the magistrates after hearing representations from both sides. The magistrates' decision should be guided by statutory indications as to what factors should be taken into account. These should include the gravity of the offence, the defendant's prior record, if any, the complexity of the case, and the effect of conviction and the likely sentence on the defendant.

The reasons that led the Commission to this unanimous recommendation were various –

(1) The decision as to whether a case properly belongs in the higher or the lower court was one that should be made by the system not by the defendant. In regard to indictable-only and summary-only offences the decision was made by the legislature. In regard to either way offences it would be more rational that the decision be made by the court than by the defendant.

(2) Many defendants chose Crown Court trial because statistically juries acquitted more often than magistrates. But the defendant should no more have the right to choose the court that gave him a better chance of an acquittal than to choose a lenient judge.

(3) The great majority of those who asked for Crown Court trial in either way offences in fact eventually pleaded guilty. (The proportion was nearly 75% not 83% as wrongly stated in the Commission's Report, p 86, para 7.)

(4) These cases of last minute guilty pleas in the Crown Court (known in the jargon as 'cracked trials') clogged up the system, caused additional costs in preparation of cases that in the event were wasted, resulted in witnesses being brought needlessly to court, and added to the numbers in prison.

(5) According to Home Office research,[107] half of those who elected for trial by Crown Court did so in the mistaken belief that if convicted the sentence would be lighter. In fact when samples were matched judges were three times as likely to impose immediate custody and sentences were on average two and a half times as long. Overall, judges imposed seven times as much custody as on comparable cases in the magistrates' courts.

(6) The same research showed that one third of the defendants in the sample who elected Crown Court trial would, in retrospect, have preferred to have been dealt with at a magistrates' court.

(7) The research also showed that in over 60% of cases in which the magistrates declined jurisdiction, the Crown Court imposed a sentence that would have been within the power of the magistrates' to impose.

(8) The objection that justice in the magistrates' courts was inferior to that in the Crown Court was not a reason to preserve the defendant's right to insist on jury trial. Magistrates handled over 90% of all criminal cases and 'should be trusted to handle cases fairly' (ibid, p 88, para 18).

This proved to be the most controversial of all the 352 recommendations made by the Runciman Royal Commission. Defence of the accused's right to trial by jury aroused strong emotion. Critics of the Commission's proposal included the Bar, the Law Society and the greatly respected Lord Chief Justice, Lord Taylor. The Lord Chief Justice's objection was principally that the Commission's recommendation would lead to 'two-tier' justice: that is jury trial for those with no record and the most reputation to lose, but magistrates' trial for recidivists.

In July 1995 the Government published a Consultation Document *Mode of Trial* which canvassed three options. One was the recommendation made by the Runciman Royal Commission. The second was statutory reclassification of either way offences to summary-only. Thus reclassification to summary-only status of thefts of under £100 could divert an estimated 9,000 cases from the Crown Court each year. The third option was a new procedural device of requiring defendants to enter a plea *before* the mode of trial decision. A plea could not be entered when magistrates decided to commit for trial. If this rule were changed and the defendant pleaded guilty, the magistrates would deal with sentencing unless they considered their sentencing powers were insufficient, in which case they would transfer the case for sentence only. Home Office research had found that about two-thirds of defendants committed by

---

[107]   C Hedderman and D Moxon, *Magistrates' Court or Crown Court? Mode of Trial Decisions*, HMSO, 1992, Home Office Research Study, No 125.

magistrates reported that they were ready to plead guilty at the first opportunity available to them. This suggested that, if the defendant in such cases could enter a plea at the magistrates' court, some 25,000 defendants dealt with at the Crown Court might have been willing to plead guilty at the magistrates' courts and be sentenced there or have their case transferred to the Crown Court for sentence only.

Early guilty pleas in the magistrates' court would also be encouraged by sentence reduction for an early guilty plea first recognised in statute by the Criminal Justice and Public Order Act 1994, s 48 – see p 316 below. The Magistrates' Association Sentencing Guidelines issued in September 1993 advised magistrates that a timely plea of guilty might be regarded as a mitigating factor for which a sentencing discount of about one third might be given.

The Criminal Procedure and Investigations Act 1996, s 49(1) adopted a modified version of the plea before venue option. But rather than the defendant being required to enter a plea before the mode of trial decision, he was to be *invited* to indicate his plea. (On this see pp 319-23 below.)

The next development was in February 1997, with the publication of the Narey Report (*Review of Delay in the Criminal Justice System*). Narey basically agreed with the Runciman Commission's recommendation. He considered, however, that Runciman had been wrong to allow prosecution and defence to agree the mode of trial. In his view the question should always be decided by the court, on the basis of statutory criteria. This reform, he thought, would 'stop an improper manipulation of the justice system' by defendants (p 35). Narey (pp 35-36) also proposed that indictable-only cases should start in the Crown Court rather than having to begin in the magistrates' court before the defendant was committed for trial by the magistrates.

In July 1998 the Home Office issued a brief new Consultation Paper (*Determining Mode of Trial in Either-Way Cases*). The options, it suggested, were 1) to leave matters alone or 2) to reclassify some either-way offences as summary-only, or 3) to abolish the defendant's right to elect and to leave it to the court.

Mode of Trial Bill No1 In November 1999 the Government introduced the first of two unsuccessful legislative attempts to remove the defendant's right to elect trial in the Crown Court. Its first Criminal Justice (Mode of Trial) Bill provided that the magistrates should determine mode of trial (subject to a right of appeal to the Crown Court) after hearing representations from both sides and in light of a number of considerations. These were the nature and seriousness of the case, their powers of punishment, the effect of conviction and sentence on the defendant's livelihood and reputation and any other relevant circumstances. It added that whether the defendant had previous convictions could be mentioned so as to permit the court to consider the question of the effect of a conviction on reputation.

The Bill broadly reflected the recommendations of the Runciman Royal Commission, except that it preferred Narey's view that the mode of trial issue should always be determined by the court with no power for the parties to determine the matter by agreement. The Bill was much criticised. As Lord Justice Auld later said in his Report (p 190, para 143), the express mention of a defendant's livelihood and reputation as relevant was a particular target for criticism as creating 'two-tier justice' – the argument being that it would lead to magistrates' courts discriminating against the poor or unemployed and in favour of defendants with higher economic or social status. Auld suggested that two other factors contributed to criticism. One was the absence of any proposal to abolish committal for sentence (on which see pp 43-44 below). The other was reference to the fact that the Government's proposal would save £105m. The Bill reached the Committee stage in the Lords but, after a series of defeats, it was withdrawn.[108]

The Mode of Trial Bill No 2 The Government reintroduced the Criminal Justice (Mode of Trial) (No2) Bill – this time in the House of Commons. But when it reached the Lords it was again defeated and was again withdrawn.[109]

The crucial change between the (No 1) Bill and the (No 2) Bill was the removal of all but one of the factors the court was permitted to take into account when making the allocation decision. These were now reduced to 'the nature of the case' and 'the circumstances of the offence (but not of the accused)'. It no longer referred to appreciation of the relevant circumstances – such as previous convictions and reputation – mentioned in the previous Bill.[110]

The Auld Report Lord Justice Auld (p 200) agreed with Runciman and Narey that the decision as to mode of trial in either-way cases should be made by the court. ('I regard it as a matter of principle that the decision where a defendant should be tried is one for a court, not for the defendant. This is a decision in which the public as well as the accused have an interest, and the decision should be an objective one, bearing both in mind, not a subjective choice of the defendant based solely on his own self-interest.' (p 199, para 170)). He agreed with Narey that if the parties agreed on venue the matter should be determined by the magistrates after hearing representations from the parties. He differed from both Runciman and Narey in recommending that where the parties disagreed, the matter should be decided by a District Judge – with a right of appeal on paper only to a Circuit Judge at the Crown Court. As to the difference between the Mode of Trial Bill No 1 and No 2, it seemed that Auld preferred the approach of the No 1 Bill.[111]

However, no doubt wishing to avoid further political difficulties and defeats in the House of Lords, the Government announced in its July 2002 White Paper *Justice for*

---

[108]   The Committee stage on 20 January 2000 resulted in a defeat for the Government by 222 to 126 on the right of election.

[109]   It did not get beyond its Second Reading in the Lords on 28 September 2000.

[110]   For an explanation of the reasoning behind the Bill by the Home Secretary see Jack Straw's article in *New Law Journal*, 12 May 2000, p 670. For the writer's critique of the change made in the No2 Bill see M Zander, 'Why Jack Straw's jury reform has lost the plot', *New Law Journal*, 10 March 2000, p 366.

[111]   See p 195, para 158 and p 281, para 37.

All that it had decided to abandon the project altogether. The White Paper pointed out that nearly nine out of ten defendants (87%) in either way cases were dealt with by magistrates. 9% went to the Crown Court because the magistrates declined to take the case, 4% went because the defendant elected trial by jury.(p 73, para 4.20) The right to elect, it said, was open to abuse.

> All too often defendants will elect for trial, then after some time plead guilty in the Crown Court and receive a sentence which magistrates could have passed. Alternatively they will hope to avoid a trial altogether, or perceive a better chance of being acquitted although guilty. The motive will often be to prolong the process in the hope of reducing the chance of either the victim or necessary witnesses giving evidence. (p 73, para 4.21)

Despite this, the White Paper went on, 'We have decided that the right of defendants in these cases to elect trial by jury in the Crown Court ought to remain.' (p 73, para 4.22) But the right to elect,

> should not be abused by defendants who hope that a sufficient case against them will not be made if they protract the process, but when confronted by such a case then plead guilty. Such abuse and delay puts pressure on victims and witnesses, and threatens good justice. We also want to reduce the numbers of cases sent by magistrates to the Crown Court unnecessarily, because of uncertainties about the possible sentence. (ibid)

The White Paper announced two measures to address the issue.

One was to increase the sentencing power of magistrates. ('We will legislate to increase magistrates' sentencing powers to 12 months, and to allow us to increase them up to a maximum of 18 months, depending on the results of evaluations, and taking account of any necessary additional training requirements.' (p 72, para 4.19)) (As has been seen, the Auld Report had rejected the suggestion that magistrates' courts should be given greater sentencing powers (Auld, p 101, para 20). The Criminal Justice Bill 2002/03 had a clause implementing the Government's intention. Clause 146(1)[112] stated, 'A magistrates' court does not have power to impose imprisonment for more than 12 months in respect of any one offence.'[113]

The second was to stop defendants being sent to the Crown Court for sentence only. ('The practice of committing cases to the Crown Court for sentence after magistrates have agreed to take the case will be abolished. This means that defendants will always know the maximum sentence they could incur if they enter a not guilty plea but do not exercise the right to elect trial by jury.'(p 73, para 4.24)) Also, when deciding whether a case was suitable for them to deal with, magistrates would be made aware of the defendant's previous convictions.

---

[112]   In the original print of the Bill in the Commons this was cl 137.
[113]   Clause 148 gave the Home Secretary the power to increase 12 months to 18 months.

We expect these changes to lead to significant reductions both in the number of cases going to the Crown Court which can be dealt with more effectively and appropriately in the magistrates' courts, and in the abuse of the right to elect for jury trial. In deciding to retain the defendant's right to elect for jury trial we have recognised the issues of principle that arise over it, and that the number of defendants who elect for jury trial are a small and diminishing proportion of those who could do so. (p 73, para 4.25)

The Criminal Justice Bill gave effect to this proposal in Schedule 3. (The schedule is 26 pages long!) The Explanatory Notes (para 220) state that the power to commit for sentence only 'will no longer be available in cases where the magistrates' court has dealt with the case having accepted jurisdiction (whether as a contested case or a guilty plea) but will be limited to cases where a guilty plea has been indicated at plea before venue'. In other words, if the magistrates believe that they can deal with it, they will not be able to send the defendant for sentence to the Crown Court. But in cases they think are more serious, they will still have the power.

The likely effect of increasing magistrates' sentencing powers and of abolishing their power to commit for sentence only Professor Lee Bridges of Warwick Law Faculty has been in the forefront of those expressing concerns about the likely effect of increasing magistrates' power of sentencing. He points out that in recent years there has been a significant increase in the use by magistrates of short custodial sentence and in the number of cases they send to the Crown Court – both for trial and for sentence only. The reason for sending cases to the Crown Court is presumably that the magistrates consider that their sentencing powers are insufficient.

Figures in the Auld Report (p 678) showed that in 1999, of the 43,000 either way cases committed to the Crown Court for trial, 19,000 (44%) ended with a non-custodial sentence and a further 5,000 (12%) ended with a custodial sentence of under six months. Some of these would have been cases where the defendant elected trial by jury which would still go to the Crown Court. But the majority would have been cases where the magistrates decided the case was too serious for them to deal with. If they had the power to send the defendant to prison for up to 12 months, many would have had custodial sentences where the Crown Court gave a non-custodial sentence, or a longer custodial sentence than the Crown Court gave. It could also result in more defendants electing to be dealt with in the Crown Court to avoid the uncertainty and inconsistency of sentencing by magistrates.

Similarly, figures in Auld showed that in 1999, of the 20,000 committed by magistrates for sentence only, 7,000 (35%) received non-custodial sentence and another 5,000 (25%) received custodial sentences of under six months. If the magistrates had had the power to sentence these defendants to more than six months' imprisonment, presumably many would have received custodial sentences, or longer custodial sentences. The impact on prison overcrowding could be very significant.

(See also p 322 below for details of an empirical study showing that magistrates do not want to take more serious cases and that the increase in their sentencing powers may therefore not have the intended effect for that rather different reason.)

AULD'S PROPOSAL FOR A MIDDLE TIER OF JURISDICTION IS REJECTED

Lord Justice Auld proposed that there be a new court – to be called the District Division – between the magistrates' court and the Crown Court.

He accepted that indictable-only cases should continue to be heard by the Crown Court and that summary-only offences should continue to be heard by the magistrates' courts. The target category was that of either-way offences: 'Many, mostly "either-way" cases now dealt with in Crown Court are not sufficiently serious or difficult to warrant the use of what is a relatively slow, cumbersome and expensive process' (p 274, para 17). To make the point Auld cited statistics showing that over half (54%) of all adult custodial sentences were for six months or less and that the Crown Court accounted for about a quarter of these. It also imposed some 26,000 non-custodial sentences. (ibid) On the other hand, in regard to cases dealt with by magistrates, 'some may be essentially "jury" issues where a panel of magistrates might be thought by some to be more appropriate. Some may be legally or factually complex where a District Judge would often be the preferred tribunal. Some may fall into both categories where a mix of a judge and magistrates would be ideal.' (pp 274-275, para 18)

Auld said, 'There has been much support in the Review for a tier of jurisdiction between that of magistrates' courts and the Crown Court to be exercised by a tribunal consisting of a professional judge and two lay magistrates' (p 275, para 21). In the succeeding paragraphs of the Report, Auld argued why a mixed tribunal of a judge sitting with lay magistrates could be expected to do a satisfactory job. He did not, however, provide any clear answer to the question why the cases he had in mind should be allocated to the proposed new tribunal in preference to the court where they were now heard – in other words, as Sir Robin himself put it, the question whether a mixed tribunal would be 'a more appropriate and acceptable forum than consigning them to one or another of the present two very different forms of proceeding' (p 275, para 20).

The main rationale for mixed tribunals, Auld said, was 'that they combine the advantages of the legal knowledge and experience of the professional judge with community representation in the form of lay magistrates' (p 276, para 23). However, this 'main rationale' obviously applied only to the District Division as an alternative to trial by magistrates. It could not apply to the District Division as an alternative to trial by jury. Whatever the merits of the mixed tribunal, it obviously could not be suggested that it would be an improvement in terms of community representation over trial by jury.

It was clear that Lord Justice Auld thought that jury trial should be drastically reduced. The extent of this hoped-for reduction became clear later in his report. Dealing with preparation of cases, Sir Robin said, 'for trials of substance, *which under my proposals, would in future be the sole or main candidates for trial by judge and jury*'(p 522, para 24, emphasis supplied). This was a truly radical agenda for reform.

Under the Auld proposals some of the cases that would no longer be dealt with in the Crown Court would be heard by the magistrates' court, while some would go to the new intermediate tribunal. The reason for sending them to the new intermediate tribunal was explained by Auld thus:

> There should be a third tier for the middle-range of cases that do not warrant the cumbersome and expensive fact-finding exercise of trial by judge and jury, but which are sufficiently serious or difficult, or their outcome is of such consequence to the public or defendant to merit a combination of professional and lay judges, but working together in a simpler way.(p 277, para 26)

Such cases, Auld suggested, 'could be those where, in the opinion of the court, the defendant could face a sentence of imprisonment of up to, say, two years or a substantial financial or other punishment of an amount or severity to be determined' (p 277, para 26). The main criterion, it seemed, would be the severity of the likely penalty looking at the case 'at its worst, which would require consideration both as to the circumstances of the offence as well as of the defendant, including any previous convictions' (p 277, para 27).

Despite Auld's claim that there had been much pre-publication support for the proposal for the third tier or intermediate court, after publication of the Report it received a great deal of criticism and little support. It was argued, for instance, that quite apart from major issues of principle, magistrates might not be keen simply to sit with the judge as 'wingers', acting as fact-finders like jurors. If they had to sit on longer more complex cases which might go longer than one day, it would mean that mainly retired magistrates would have to be used, as working magistrates might not be able to spare the time. Also, there would be the expense of setting up a new court system with appropriate staffing. And the allocation decision would be more complex, often leading to allocation appeals.

The Government's July 2002 White Paper stated, 'We are not convinced that there is a strong enough case to justify introducing a new 'intermediate tier' court, as was recommended by Sir Robin Auld'. (p 72, para 4.19) The Government thought that the benefits this would provide could be achieved in other ways – such as increasing magistrates' sentencing powers.

(b) The allocation of cases between higher and lower trial courts – civil cases

Since 1846, when the county court was established, there has been the question of the proper relationship of the High Court and the county court. The two courts had concurrent jurisdiction up to the limit of the county court's jurisdiction. In 1846 the ceiling was £20. As has been seen, it was repeatedly raised [114] until in 1981 it became £5,000 and in 1991 the ceiling was abolished. There were costs incentives to

---

[114] Always over the strenuous opposition of the Bar. Such opposition was naturally fuelled by the fact that barristers enjoyed a monopoly over the right to appear in the High Court whereas in the county court barristers and solicitors had an equal right of audience. For the history see B Abel-Smith and R Stevens, *Lawyers and the Courts* (Heinemann, 1963).

encourage litigants to have the case dealt with in the cheaper county court. Thus when the county court ceiling was £5,000 and the plaintiff in the High Court recovered less than £3,000 he was penalised by getting his costs on the county court scale; if he recovered less than £600 he got no costs at all.[115] When the ceiling was abolished in 1991 the High Court was given the power to reduce the costs recoverable by the successful party by up to 25% if it thought the case should have been brought in the county court.[116] The courts had the power to transfer cases up or down either at the request of the parties or of its own motion.[117] Despite these incentives, a surprising number of cases within the jurisdiction of the county court were brought in the High Court.

In 1988, the Civil Justice Review (Cm 394) recommended that:(1) The High Court and the county court should remain separate (para 116). (2) There should be no upper limit for the jurisdiction of the county court (para 125). (3) There should be a lower limit of £25,000 for cases in the High Court. All cases below that should be heard in the county court unless they involved public law or specialist problems, or were cases of unusual complexity (para 124). (4) Cases involving amounts between £25,000 and £50,000 should be heard in either the High Court or the county court (para 124). (5) All personal injury cases should start in the county court (para 155). (6) Registrars should be given the title of district judge and have their jurisdiction increased to £5,000.

COURTS AND LEGAL SERVICES ACT 1990

The Lord Chancellor announced his broad acceptance of these proposals in April 1989 and they were implemented by the Courts and Legal Services Act 1990 and the High Court and county courts Jurisdiction Order 1991 (SI 1991/724).[118]

The effect of the changes was that cases were allocated for trial according to substance, importance and complexity. Generally, cases involving amounts below £25,000 were to be tried in the county court; those involving amounts above £50,000 in the High Court; and amounts in between, in either court depending on the criteria and judicial availability.

The 1991 Order abolished the financial limits on county court jurisdiction over many actions, including ordinary actions in contract and tort (art 2). Cases which included a claim for damages in respect of personal injuries had to be started in the county court unless the claim was worth more than £50,000 (art 5). If the High Court thought

---

[115] County courts Act 1959, ss 19, 20.

[116] Courts and Legal Services Act 1990, s 4 amending s 51 of the Supreme Court Act 1981.

[117] Supreme Court Act 1981, Sch 3, para 8 inserting new s 75A, Band C into County Courts Act 1959. See also *Practice Direction* [1991] 3 All ER 349.

[118] See also the county court (Amendment No 2) Rules 1991, SI 1991/1126 and (Amendment No 3) Rules 1991, SI 1991/1328 and the Rules of the Supreme Court (Amendment No 2) 1991, SI 1991/1329 which came into force on 1 July 1991.

that the person bringing the proceedings knew or ought to have known that the action should have been brought in the county court, the court could order that the proceedings be struck out.

The jurisdiction of registrars which was formerly limited to £1,000, was increased by the 1990 Act to £5,000 and their title was changed to district judge. But important or difficult cases were listed for hearing by a circuit judge rather than a district judge. (See *Practice Direction* [1991] 3 All ER 722.)

THE WOOLF REPORT

The origin of the Woolf Inquiry on civil justice (see p 0 above) was the Lord Chancellor's request to Lord Woolf to remove unnecessary differences between the procedural rules of the High Court and the county court. Lord Woolf got the Lord Chancellor's approval for expansion of this original remit to a much wider brief.

In his Interim Report in June 1995 Lord Woolf proposed that the rules of the High Court and the county court should basically be the same (and that he would produce a draft of a single code of rules for High Court and county court cases), that an action could be commenced at any court and that the court rather the parties should have the responsibility for allocating the case to the appropriate track. He suggested (p 73, para 4), that these recommendations, together with others he made as to case management, 'will mean that the question of whether a case is a High Court or a county court case will be of reduced significance'. (On the distinction between Lord Woolf's fast track and multi-track cases and on allocation see pp 56–57, 77–78 below.)

He had considered whether to recommend the unification or amalgamation of the two courts:

> **Interim Report of the Woolf** *Inquiry into Civil Justice, Access to Justice*, **1995, pp 73–75**
>
> 6. I have therefore considered whether to recommend the unification of the two courts. This would be an additional step in reducing the complexity of the system. It would be an advance since it would produce a single, vertically integrated court. However, very much the same result could be achieved if the movement towards aligning the jurisdiction of the county courts and the High Court was continued and the powers of Circuit judges were to be extended. This would make it generally unnecessary to identify the criteria which mark the boundary between the jurisdiction. . . .
>
> 8. I accept that for constitutional reasons it is essential that the separate status of the High Court judge is maintained and not undermined in any way. Although it is not impossible to preserve distinct judicial tiers in a single court (as, for example, in the Crown Court), this would become more difficult if the High Court itself were merged in a single court.

9. However, the further alignment of the jurisdictions of the High Court and the county courts should continue, both as to subject matter (the obvious example is defamation) and as to powers. For example, the restrictions on Circuit judges granting Mareva and Anton Piller injunctions should be removed.

10. I should make it clear that I am not proposing total alignment. There would be no point, for example, in extending the power to hear small claims to High Court judges or to confer on the High Court the various statutory jurisdictions of the county courts. Conversely, it would not be appropriate to give county courts general jurisdiction over judicial reviews (except for certain categories which I will consider further in my final report).

11. It is more appropriate and more effective for cases to be allocated to the correct level for trial as a result of a judicial examination of all the circumstances of the particular case, taking into account any general guidance which has been issued as part of the management of the case, than for the case to be allocated as a result of some technical rule as to jurisdiction. . .

13. The new unified rules will provide a common procedure for the conduct of civil business. A new, common approach to the handling of cases centred on the concept of judicial control and case management will introduce a strong unifying element into the way in which cases are handled by all the civil courts. This will be crucially reinforced by the appointment of the Head of Civil Justice, who will have overall responsibility for the management and organisation of civil business throughout England and Wales at every level in the system. The approach will be reinforced by a partnership between judges and administrators at key levels throughout the civil courts system.

14. The new multi-track will itself straddle the High Court and the county courts. Within it cases will be handled by High Court judges, Circuit judges, Masters and district judges. The courts, through the procedural judges, will have responsibility for ensuring that cases are dealt with at the appropriate level.

15. Out of London, the divide between the two courts has in any event become indistinct. The increasing use of the Chancery and Mercantile jurisdiction of the High Court in key centres means that heavy cases are often heard locally by Circuit judges. There will no longer be any reason to distinguish physically between the High Court and county courts outside London. Already outside London, the High Court and the county courts at the larger centres share the same buildings. There is at present, however, a separation of the administration which will become unnecessary when the new unified rules introduce a common procedure. I recommend that they should share the same administration, although there are many county courts where High Court business is most unlikely to be heard.

16. In London the situation is different. The Royal Courts of Justice are the permanent seat of the most complex and specialised litigation and of the two divisions of the Court of Appeal. They are administered separately from the Central London county court, where the heaviest county court litigation is dealt with. I see no reason for any change in these arrangements.

For a robust reply from a practising solicitor, rejecting Lord Woolf's negative approach to the question of amalgamation of the High and the county courts, see Richard Harrison, 'Why have two types of civil courts?', *New Law Journal*, January 15, 1999, p 65.

The question of the possible amalgamation of the High Court and the county seems to have disappeared as an issue.

The tribunal system

The work of the courts is supplemented by the large number of administrative tribunals. Tribunals sit for more days than the High Court and the county courts together and hear many more contested cases than the ordinary courts. The Leggatt inquiry into tribunals published in March 2001 (*Tribunals for Users: One System, One Service* (www.tribunals-review.org.uk)) stated that there were some 70 tribunals and that between them they dealt with nearly one million cases a year – though only 20 of the 70 tribunals dealt with more than 500 cases a year and many were defunct. Their quality varied from excellent to inadequate (p 5). The inquiry said that the so-called tribunal system was not a system at all:

> What we have found . . . is that the present collection of tribunals has grown up in an almost entirely haphazard way. Individual tribunals were set up, and usually administered by departments, as they developed new statutory schemes and procedures. The result is a collection of tribunals, mostly administered by departments, with wide variations of practice and approach, and almost no coherence. The current arrangements seem to us to have been developed to meet the needs and conveniences of the departments and other bodies which run tribunals, rather than the needs of the users. (p 15)

Leggatt said that the lack of coherence had brought with it many difficulties and weaknesses in the performance of tribunals. The Report outlined what would be a new 'single, overarching structure' (p 34). There would be nine subject divisions dealing with immigration; social security and pensions; land and valuation; financial including taxation; transport; health and social services; education; regulatory; and employment. Appeals would go to a single appellate division which would sit in panels related to the nine divisions. There would be a new Tribunals Service operating parallel to the Courts Service and under the Lord Chancellor – so that administration of tribunals would be taken away from their parent departments.

For responses to the Leggatt Review see www.lcd.gov.uk/tribunals.htm.

In March 2003, responding to Leggatt, the LCD announced that there would be a new unified Tribunals Service as the third part of the modernisation of the justice system. The Lord Chancellor said, 'We have substantially reformed the civil justice pillar and are embarking on major reform of the criminal pillar; the third is the administrative justice pillar, tribunals justice'. (LCD Press notice 106/03, 11 March 2003). The unified tribunal service would have as its core the top 10 non-devolved tribunals which currently existed: the Appeals Service; the Immigration Appellate Authority; the Employment Tribunals Service; the Criminal Injuries Compensation Appeals Panel; the Mental Health Review Tribunal; the Office for Social Security and Child Support Commissioners; Tax tribunals; Special Education Needs and Disability Tribunals; the Pensions Appeal Tribunal; and the Lands Tribunal.

More details, it was said, would follow in a White Paper to be published later in 2003 – though after the Lord Chancellor's Department was abolished in June, it was uncertain to what extent unification of the tribunals service would remain a priority for the new Secretary of State for Constitutional Affairs.

The previous great report on tribunals was that of the Franks Committee on *Administrative Tribunals and Enquiries*, 1957 which led to the Tribunals and Inquiries Act 1958 and the establishment of the Council on Tribunals. The Council, an advisory body, keeps under review and reports on the working of tribunals. It publishes an annual report - see www.council-on-tribunals.gov.uk.

Chapter 2

Pre-trial civil proceedings

I. Introduction

This chapter deals with the problems of the pre-trial stages of a civil action which set the stage for the trial- if there is one. There are two main reasons why the pre-trial stage of litigation is vital. One is that in the great majority of cases the proceedings never reach trial. Secondly, in the rare cases that go to trial, the outcome is usually determined by what has been achieved by way of collection and preparation of evidence in the pre-trial stage.

Pre-trial civil process has repeatedly been the subject of reports and inquiries – more than 60 over the past hundred years! (In other words these are issues and problems that seem not to go away.) Since 1968 there has been the report of the Winn Committee (*Committee on Personal Injuries Litigation*, 1968, Cmnd 369); the Report of the Cantley Committee (*Report of the Personal Injuries Litigation Procedure Working Party*, 1979, Cmnd 7476); the massive Civil Justice Review 1985-88;[1] the Heilbron-Hodge Working Party set up jointly by the Bar and the Law Society (*Civil Justice on Trial-the Case for Change, 1992*). The recommendations of these bodies were dealt with extensively in earlier editions of this work. For reasons of economy of space, they are treated here lightly, since the new system which took effect in April 1999 was based essentially on the recommendations made by Lord Woolf in his June 1995 Interim[2] and his July 1996 Final Report both entitled *Access to Justice*. Virtually every topic dealt with in this chapter is affected by the Woolf Report.

---

[1] For a full account of its recommendations, see the 30-page note in the *Civil Justice Quarterly*, 1988, pp 281–312. See also the reflections of a member of the Civil Justice Review formerly with the National Consumer Council: Richard Thomas, 'Civil Justice Review – Treating Litigants as Consumers', *Civil Justice Quarterly*, January 1990, p 51.

[2] For an extended account of its recommendations see the 30-page note in the *Civil Justice Quarterly*, October 1995, pp 231-49.

The gestation period from the Final Report of *Access to Justice* to implementation in April 1999 was just under three years. Given the radical nature of the changes made and their immense scope, this was a remarkable achievement.

The Woolf reforms, like those of previous attempts at reform of civil justice, were mainly aimed at the three problems of cost, delay and complexity. As will be seen, the main thrust of the project was to transfer the chief responsibility for progressing cases from the parties and their lawyers to the court.

The overriding objective At the heart of the new system is the 'overriding objective' which is set out in Part I, R1.1 of the new Civil Procedure Rules (CPR). The opening words of the new rules state 'These Rules are a new procedural code with the overriding objective of enabling the court to deal with cases justly'. Rule 1.1(2) then articulates what is meant by dealing with a case justly. 'Dealing with a case justly includes, so far as is practicable: (a) ensuring that the parties are on an equal footing[3] (b) saving expenses; (c) dealing with the case in ways which are proportionate (i) to the amount of money involved; (ii) to the importance of the case; (iii) to the complexity of the issues; (iv) to the financial position of each party; (d) ensuring that it is dealt with expeditiously and fairly; and (e) allotting to it an appropriate share of the court's resources, while taking into account the need to allot resources to other cases'.

These propositions are intended to have an impact at all times. CPR 1.2 states that these factors must be taken into account whenever the court exercises any power given to it by the rules or interprets any rule. Moreover, the duty to comply with the overriding objective applies not only to the courts but also to the parties. Rule 1.3 states 'The parties are required to help the court to further the overriding objective'. This applies to all stages of a dispute. So, for instance the Practice Direction on Pre-action Protocols (on which see p 61 below) states that the court will expect the parties, 'in accordance with the overriding objective' to act reasonably in exchanging information and documents and generally in trying to avoid the necessity for the start of proceedings (para 4).

Lord Woolf's Final Report said that the overriding objective 'provides a compass to guide courts and litigants and legal advisers as to their general course' and this has become a reality (p 275).

It will be noted that the listed considerations which make up the overriding objective are very broad and not necessarily consistent. In truth, they will justify any decision the court is minded to make. As the practitioner's bible *The White Book* says, 'It is probably true to say that, in almost any circumstances in which the court exercises a power given to it by the CPR, it would be possible to justify (at least in part) the particular manner in which the power is exercised in the light of one or other of the aspects of the overriding objective'. (*Civil Procedure*, 2003, vol 1, p 9)

---

3   It has been held that this concept of a 'level playing field' does not mean that it is wrong for one side to instruct a QC where the other has only a junior barrister (*Maltez v Lewis* [1999] 21 LS Gaz R 39 (1999) Times, 4 May.

In *Holmes v SGB Services plc* [2001] EWCA Civ 354 the judge granted an application to vacate the trial date, to amend particulars of claim and to re-instruct the expert. He said there was a tension between rules emphasising the maintaining of trial dates and the interests of justice in achieving a fair trial. Dismissing the other side's appeal, the Court of Appeal doubted whether any such tension existed. Buxton LJ said that in making the case management decision, the court has to balance all the criteria in CPR 1.1 without giving any of them undue weight. Striking a balance was a matter for the judge and it would be wrong for the Court of Appeal to give, or for judges to seek, any direction suggesting that one or other of the criteria was more or less important.

With due respect to the Court, it is unrealistic to say that the tension does not exist. Clearly it does. If, as in *Holmes*, two or more of the criteria point in different directions, the judge, having weighed them, must decide which he favours. So in each such case one or more of the criteria will be held to be 'more important' than others.

It is clear however that the Court of Appeal wants to leave the whole business of applying the criteria to the judges below. It will interfere only when it finds their decisions wholly unreasonable.

Despite its centrality and importance, the White Book editorially warns against excessive reliance by the courts on the overriding objective. ('Premature and unnecessary recourse to the overriding objective may lead to inadequate legal analysis of important procedural issues (thus hindering the proper development of the law), to radical provisions in the CPR not being consistently applied as intended and to an erratic "palm tree justice" approach to interlocutory work (leading to inconsistent treatment of like situations), and it is submitted, for these reasons should be avoided'[4]

The court's duty to manage cases

Traditionally civil litigation in the pre-trial stage was run by the parties, with the courts playing only a supporting or facilitating role, intervening basically only when requested. The new rules impose a positive duty on the courts to manage cases. CPR 1.4(1) states that the court must further the overriding objective by actively managing cases. It continues:

> 1.4 (2) Active case management includes:- (a) encouraging the parties to cooperate with each other in the conduct of the proceedings; (b) identifying the issues at an early stage; (c) deciding promptly which issues need full investigation and trial and accordingly disposing summarily of the others; (d) deciding the order in which issues are to be resolved; (e) encouraging the parties to use an alternative dispute resolution procedure if the court considers that appropriate and facilitating the use of such procedure; (f) helping the parties

[4]   *Civil Procedure*, 2003, vol 1, p 9. The General Editor of the *White Book* at that date was Lord Justice May, the then Deputy Head of Civil Justice.

to settle the whole or part of the case; (g) fixing timetables or otherwise controlling the progress of the case; (h) considering whether the likely benefits of taking a particular step justify the cost of taking it; (i) dealing with as many aspects of the case as it can on the same occasion; (j) dealing with the case without the parties needing to attend at court; (k) making use of technology; and (l) giving directions to ensure that the trial of a case proceeds quickly and efficiently.

The court is given power (unless a rule or other enactment prevents it) to exercise its powers on its own initiative. It may give a person likely to be affected an opportunity to make representations but it need not do so. A party affected by such an order has the right to seek to have it set aside, varied or stayed.

For a positive assessment of whether judicial detachment and impartiality is compatible with the new duty of active trial management see Mr Justice Lightman, 'The case for judicial intervention', 149 *New Law Journal*, 3 December 1999, p 1819 and www.lcd.gov.uk/judicial/speeches/ speechfr.htm.

THE THREE TRACKS

Under the CPR, cases must be assigned to one of three tracks: Small Claims, Fast-Track or Multi-Track. Each track has its separate regime.

Small claims

As has been seen, the limit for small claims cases is £5,000 except for personal injury and housing cases where it is £1,000. Under the Woolf reforms, small claims involve mainly very limited pre-trial court management, few, if any pre-trial hearings and a trial where the judge runs the proceedings in whatever way seems right to him.

Fast track

The fast track is for cases involving amounts between £5,000 and £15,000 unless they are unsuitable for this track. The original concept was a set timetable of no more than 30 weeks to trial, limited pre-trial procedure, a trial confined to no more than three hours, no oral evidence from experts and standard fixed costs recoverable from the other side. This, broadly, was the scheme that was implemented, though the proposed three-hour limit on the hearing was extended to five hours and fixed costs applied originally only to the costs of the actual hearing.

Multi track

The multi track is for cases involving amounts in excess of the fast track limit or for cases involving lesser amounts which are too complex or too important to be dealt with as small claims or fast track cases. They are given a more intensive form of court management probably including pre-trial hearings

The new Rules

One of the important parts of the Woolf reform project was the unification of the rules of the High Court in the White Book (formerly the *Annual Practice*, now *Civil Procedure*) with those for the county court in the Green Book (*County Court Rules*). Under the Civil Procedure Act 1997, a new Rule Committee was established, replacing the two committees previously responsible respectively for the Rules of the Supreme Court (RSC) and the County Court Rules (CCR). The new committee was charged with the task of preparing a new single procedural code, to be known as the Civil Procedure Rules (CPR).

Previously the rules were divided into Orders. In the CPR they are divided into Parts. Most Parts are accompanied by Practice Directions that amplify or clarify the rules. These have a major role. (Joseph Jacob has rightly said, 'The development of procedure is now by Practice Direction as much as by precedent or change of rule.'[5]) But whereas the Rules are made by the Rule Committee, the Practice Directions are made by Heads of the different divisions.[6]

The Civil Procedure Rules – as amended from time to time – are accessible on the LCD's website – www.lcd.gov.uk The fact that the website is up to date is of considerable value given the number of amendments and additions. From April 1999 to May 2003 there were no fewer than 31 supplements.

The significance of calling the CPR a 'new procedural code?' The White Book comments editorially that in many cases the judges have stressed the statement in r 1.1 that the CPR are 'a new procedural code'. It suggests that they do so to ensure that the innovative provisions in the CPR are given their full intended effect 'and are not limited by practices and attitudes that attached to the former rules of court' and also to make it clear that provisions that are plainly based on former rules will not necessarily be interpreted and applied in accordance with the old case law. But it warns that the assertion 'should not be relied upon as an excuse for dealing with important procedural issues as matters of first impression rather than as matters requiring rigorous legal analysis (in their historical context, if necessary)'[7]

---

[5]   *Civil Litigation practice and procedure in a changing culture*, 2001, pp 21-22.
[6]   For the QBD by the Lord Chief Justice, for the Chancery Division by the Vice Chancellor, for the Court of Appeal Civil Division by the Master of the Rolls and for the county courts by the Lord Chancellor. (See *Note on Practice Directions* first published in the HMSO version of the CPR, 23rd Supplement, May 2001 and see also JA Jolowicz, 'Practice Directions and Civil Procedure Rules', (2000) *Cambridge Law Journal*, pp 53-61.)
[7]   *Civil Procedure*, 2003, vol 1, 1.3.9.

Joseph Jacob has described the effect on precedent:

> The CPR are a step toward 'Teflon precedents'. Old decisions, even those after April 1999, will not stick. Of course, cases will continue to be reported, read by lawyers and to judges. What has changed is that a continued primacy is given to the Rules and even more importantly the spirit that underlies them (the Overriding Objective, CPR Part 1.2(b)). To this extent, the doctrine of precedent is being modified. Previous authority, even apparently binding authority, will become guidance. The judge, in managing cases, will have prime regard to the rules themselves not what some other judges have said about them.'[8]

THE HUMAN RIGHTS ACT AND THE CPR

There are many provisions in the CPR that arguably might provoke challenges under the Human Rights Act 1998 but the courts have made it clear that it is most unlikely that such challenges will be successful. The reason is that in the view of the senior judiciary the rules to be found in the CPR are consistent with the European Convention on Human Rights. Lord Woolf expressed this in *Walker v Daniels* [2000] 1 WLR 1382 in which he said the matter was more than adequately covered by the requirement in the CPR that the court deal with cases *justly*. There was therefore no need to pray in aid the ECHR.

> It would be unfortunate if case management decisions in this jurisdiction involved the need to refer to the learning of the European Court of Human Rights in order for them to be resolved. In my judgment, cases such as this do not require any consideration of human rights issues, certainly not issues under article 6. It would be highly undesirable if the consideration of case management issues was made more complex by the injection into them of Article 6 style arguments. I hope that judges will be robust in resisting any attempt to introduce those arguments. [at 1387]

USER-FRIENDLY LANGUAGE

One of the features of the new Woolf era was the scrapping of old-fashioned legal terms and, in particular, the banishment of time-honoured Latin phrases used by lawyers. Thus new terms for practitioners and judges to master included: 'claimant' instead of 'plaintiff'; 'disclosure' instead of 'discovery'; 'statement of case' instead of 'pleading'; 'application' instead of 'motion'; 'litigator's friend' instead of 'next friend and 'guardian ad litem'; 'without notice' instead of 'ex parte'; 'witness summons' instead of 'subpoena duces tecum' , 'with permission' instead of 'with leave'; 'service by an alternative method' instead of 'substituted service'; 'between parties' instead of

---

8   *Civil Litigation practice and procedure in a shifting culture*,2001, p 13.

'inter partes'; 'search order' instead of 'Anton Piller order'; 'freezing order' instead of 'Mareva injunction' etc. For lawyers such changes are minor irritants. Opinions differ as to whether it actually benefits lay people involved in litigation or whether it is not mainly a further manifestation of political correctness.

Further reading For basic pre-Woolf reading on the topic of this chapter, see especially the 1986 Hamlyn Lectures given by Sir Jack Jacob QC published under the title: *The Fabric of English Civil Justice* (Sweet & Maxwell, 1987). For an excellent assessment of the profound significance of the new system by Sir Jack's son see Joseph Jacob, *Civil Litigation practice and procedure in a shifting culture* (2001, Emis Professional Publishing, 152pp, £15).

For reference See the major commentaries issued annually – the White Book, *Civil Procedure* (Thompson-Sweet & Maxwell); *Civil Practice* (Blackstone); and *Civil Court Practice* (Lexis/Nexis). See also N Andrews, *English Civil Procedure*, 0UP, 2003.

For a valuable series of occasional articles commenting on the frequent amendments and other CPR related developments see Suzanne Burns, *Legal Action*, August 2000, p 27; December 2000, p 25; June 2001, p 18; October 2001, p 6; April 2002, p 20; May 2002, p 16; October 2002, p 20; February 2003, p 29; July 2003, p 12.[9]

2. Few cases are ever started and fewer reach court

If legal problems are seen in the form of an iceberg, the ones that reach a court are those at the very tip. The great majority never even get to a lawyer. Of those that get to a lawyer, the great majority get sorted out without any form of court hearing, sometimes before legal proceedings are started, sometimes between the initiation of legal proceedings and the hearing.

The first solid empirical evidence regarding the progress of claims came from a massive study of personal injury cases conducted in the 1980s by the Oxford Socio-Legal Centre (Don Harris et al, *Compensation and Support for Illness and Injury*, Clarendon Press, Oxford, 1984). The study was based on a huge national household survey which produced a random sample of 1,711 accident victims all of whom had suffered some impairment for at least two weeks. Of these, only 26% had even considered claiming damages, 14% had actually consulted a solicitor most of whom (12%) actually got damages (Fig 2.1, p 26). A writ was issued in just under 40% of the cases in which damages were obtained (p 112). There were only five cases which ended with a court hearing! This represented 2.7% of the 182 cases in which damages were obtained; but only 0.2% of the 1,711 accident cases in the sample.

In Professor Hazel Genn's study *Paths to Justice* (Oxford, 1999), 4,125 randomly selected adults were surveyed to find out how they had experienced and dealt with a

---

[9] See also her 'The Human Rights Act and civil procedure', *Legal Action*, September 2001, p 33 and 'The Woolf reforms in retrospect', *Legal Action*, July 2003, p 8.

variety of problems for which there might be a legal solution. About 40% of the sample had experienced one or more of 14 types of justiciable problems during the previous five years. Overall, about 5% had done nothing at all to try and solve the problem, about one third tried to resolve the problem without help and about 60% tried to resolve the problem with advice. The most common first adviser was a solicitor, followed by a Citizens' Advice Bureau. About one third of the problems were eventually resolved by agreement (in some 3% after the commencement of legal proceedings). Very limited use had been made of formal legal proceedings. In eight out of ten cases no legal proceedings were started, no ombudsman was contacted and no alternative dispute resolution (ADR) process was used. The matter ended with a court, tribunal or ombudsman's decision in 14% of all cases but the majority of these cases were ones in which the respondent to the survey was being pursued in court etc rather than him or herself initiating action. Among respondents having action taken against them, over half (56%) said their case had been decided by a court, tribunal or ombudsman, compared with only 9% of those who initiated action. (p 151)[10]

Most people are not even prepared to use the informal and 'user friendly' small claims system – see p 387 below.

Once a case begins there are immense pressures to settle, especially for what Galanter called the 'one-shotter' pp 9-10 above). This was always the case but it is even more so under the Woolf reforms which made achieving a settlement one of its main objectives.

On the process of negotiating a settlement, see further J Phillips and K Hawkins, 'Some Economic Aspects of the Settlement Process: A Study of Personal Injury Claims', *Modern Law Review*, 1976, p 497; and Hazel Genn, *Hard Bargaining: A Study of the Process of Out of Court Settlement In Personal Injury Actions 1987* (OUP, 1988). For a picture of the strategies of defence lawyers see R Dingwall, T Durkin, P Pleasence, WLF Felstiner and R Bowles, 'Firm handling; the litigation strategies of defence lawyers in personal injury cases', 20 *Legal Studies*, 2000, p 1.

For a powerful argument that settlement is not necessarily a good thing, see Owen Fiss, 'Against Settlement', *Yale LJ*, 1984, p 1073. For a valuable assessment of the role of settlement in light of the Woolf reforms see S Roberts, 'Settlement as Civil Justice', 63 *Modern Law Review*, 2000, p 739.

---

10   The Cantley Committee in their report in 1979 stated: 'In round figures, for every 9,000 personal injury writs issued in London there are no more than about 300 judgments. Outside the personal injuries field, for every 100,000 writs issued in London there are fewer than 300 judgments after trial. The figures for District Registries are not dissimilar.' (*Report of the Personal Injuries Litigation Procedure Working Party*, 1979, Cmnd 7476, para 9.)

LEGAL PRIVILEGES THAT PROMOTE SETTLEMENT

Negotiations designed to explore the possibility of settlement are assisted by legal privileges. One such is for negotiations conducted 'without prejudice'. This is the rule that if in the course of written exchanges headed with the magic words 'without prejudice' a party makes an offer or concession it cannot be used as evidence against him if in the event the negotiations break down and the case comes to court. For an illustration of the rule see *Rush & Tompkins Ltd v Greater London Council* [1988] 3 All ER 737, HL.[11] The trend is for the scope of the 'without prejudice rule' to be narrowed. See, for instance, *Prudential Assurance Co Ltd v Prudential Insurance Co of America* [2002] EWHC 2809 (Ch), (2003) Times, 2 January where the Vice Chancellor emphasised the importance of art 10 of the ECHR. The without prejudice rule, he said, should be applied with restraint and only in cases in which the public interest underlying the rule were plainly applicable. (See K Awadella, 'The privileged few', 147 *Solicitors' Journal*, 17 January 2003, p 43.)

Another example of rules to promote settlement is the privilege accorded to mediators or conciliators such as marriage guidance counsellers, clergymen, doctors or even family friends who are working with a couple in a matrimonial dispute. Unless they have the consent of both spouses, they may not reveal the content of any communication from either spouse. In effect such communications are treated as having been made 'without prejudice' – see *Mole v Mole* [1951] P 21, *Pool v Pool* [1951] P 470 and cf *Bostock v Bostock* [1950] P 154. The principle extends to cover direct negotiations between the spouses themselves where no third party intervenes: *Theodoropoulas v Theodoropoulas* [1964] P 311.

Conduct of the claim before action: the new pre-action protocols

One of the important innovations of the Woolf reforms is that the conduct of the parties in the pre-litigation stage will be taken into account by the court both during the case and at the end when it comes to allocation of costs. One of the chief means to this end are the pre-action protocols. This was an idea pioneered by Lord Woolf. They were developed by working parties of experts representing the different interest groups in litigation. By the time the new rules came into force in April 1999, pre-action protocols had been promulgated for personal injury litigation and the resolution of clinical disputes. By 2003 they existed also for construction and engineering, defamation, professional negligence and judicial review, all of which are supplemented by a Pre-Action Protocol Practice Direction.

This represents a major new development in civil litigation. The Practice Direction accompanying the protocols says their objective is to encourage the exchange of early

---

[11]   See C Mulcahy, 'Lifting the veil on without prejudice negotiations', 144 *Solicitors' Journal*, 12 May 2000, p 444; J Ross, 'The without prejudice rule', 152 *New Law Journal*, 4 October 2002, p 1488; and S Akhtar, 'Listen without prejudice', 153 *New Law Journal*, 11 April 2003, p 538.

and full information about the prospective claim, to enable parties to avoid litigation by settlement and, where litigation cannot be avoided, to support the efficient management of the litigation. The introduction to the personal injury protocol (PIP) says that its aims are more pre-action contact between the parties, better and earlier exchange of information, better pre-action investigation by both sides and to enable proceedings to run to the court's timetable and efficiently. ('The court will be able to treat the standards set in protocols as the normal reasonable approach to pre-action conduct' (para 1.4).)

The PIP says that it is designed especially for road traffic, tripping and slipping and accident at work cases in the fast track range. But the 'cards on the table' approach advocated in the PIP was 'equally appropriate to some higher value claims'. (PIP, para 2.4)

> The spirit, if not the letter of the protocol should still be followed for multi track type claims. In accordance with the sense of the civil justice reforms, the court will expect to see the spirit of reasonable pre-action behaviour applied in all cases, regardless of the existence of a specific protocol.' [para 2.4]

The PIP suggests that the claimant may wish at a very early stage to notify the defendant and his insurer that a claim is likely to be made. It includes a specimen letter of claim. This is completely different from the traditional uninformative letter before action. It should 'contain a clear summary of the facts on which the claim is based with an indication of the nature of any injuries received ... Sufficient information should be given in order to enable the defendant's insurer/solicitor to commence investigations and at least put a broad valuation on the risk' (paras 3.1, 3.5). It states that the defendant has a maximum of three months to investigate a claim and to respond stating whether liability is admitted, and if not, giving reasons (para 3.7). In the hope of getting agreement on a single expert, before either party instructs a medical expert, he should try to agree the name of an expert with the other side.

The pre-action protocol on medical negligence disputes is similar. It was based on extensive consultation with the major vested interests in the medico-legal system.

The Practice Direction accompanying all the pre-action protocols says (para 2.3) that if, in the opinion of the court, non-compliance with the protocols has led to the commencement of proceedings which might otherwise not have needed to be commenced, or has led to unnecessary costs being incurred, it can impose a financial penalty on the party at fault.

It also says (para 4.1) that in cases not covered by a specific protocol, 'the court will expect the parties, in accordance with the overriding objective and the matters referred to in CPR 1.1(2)(a), (b) and (c), to act reasonably in exchanging information and documents relevant to the claim and generally in trying to avoid the necessity for the start of proceedings'.

In October 2001, the LCD issued a consultation paper on whether there was a need for a general pre-action protocol. The responses were generally not favourable with many respondents stating that there would be difficulty in successfully producing a protocol capable of applying to all disputes, and that it would add to costs and lead to delays. But amendments to para 4 of the Practice Direction that came into force in April 2003 achieve much the same effect. (For details see D de Ferrars, 'Entry via the back door?', 153 *New Law Journal*, 4 April 2003, pp 519-20.)

ARE THE PROTOCOLS A SUCCESS?

Research commissioned by the Law Society and the Civil Justice Council[12] showed that those involved in personal injury and clinical negligence work felt positive about the protocols. ('By establishing clear ground rules on how claims should be formulated and responded to, protocols were thought to focus minds on the key issues at an early stage and encourage greater openness. This smoothed the way to settlement'.[13]) In fact housing practitioners reported similar changes even though there was no protocol covering their work.

On the other hand, it is generally agreed that one of the effects of the protocols has been 'front-loading' of costs not only for cases that are ultimately contested but equally for those that settle – including cases that would previously have settled at lower cost.

See also S Burns, 'Pre-action protocols under the CPR', *Legal Action*, October 2001, pp 6-9.

3.   Initiation of proceedings

Who can sue? Representative parties and group litigation

Traditionally, the system was based on the concept that legal proceedings were brought by individuals. But there was provision in the rules for persons to be represented in proceedings by other persons. They were known as ' representative proceedings'. (The old rules were in RSC Ord 15, r 12; the new rules are in CPR 19.6.[14])

The old rule required that those who were represented 'have the same interest' in the proceedings and this requirement is also in CPR 19.6. The requirement used to be

---

[12]   T Goriely, R Moorhead, P Abrams, *More Civil Justice? The impact of the Woolf reforms on pre-action behaviour*, Law Society 2002, Research Study No43, 420 pp. A 33-page summary is accessible on www.research.lawsociety.org.uk (Publications) The research was based on interviews with 54 lawyers, insurers and claims managers, of whom 30 specialised in personal injury (PI) work, 12 specialised in clinical negligence and 12 specialised in housing disrepair. In the case of PI work it also included comparison of 150 claimant solicitor files concluded before April 1999 ('pre-Woolf') and 150 opened and closed post-Woolf files.

[13]   Goriely et al, Summary of Research Study No 43, p v.

[14]   Inserted by the Civil Procedure (Amendment) Rules 2000, SI 2000/221.

interpreted very narrowly. The classic case was *Markt & Co Ltd v Knight Steamship Co Ltd* [1910] 2 KB 1021. But gradually the courts adopted a broader approach.[15] (See further J Seymour, 'Representative Procedures and the Future of Multi-party Actions', 62 *Modern Law Review*,1999, pp 564-84.)

In public law anyone with a 'sufficient interest' may apply for judicial review and the courts have given a generous interpretation to 'sufficient interest'. Organisations like Greenpeace and the Consumers' Association have been held to have a sufficient interest to bring proceedings. But in private law cases claimants must show that they themselves have a legal right which they are seeking to enforce. In February 2001 the LCD issued a Consultation Paper (*Representative claims: proposed new procedures*) which proposed that this distinction between public law and private law cases be removed and that it should be possible for a representative claim in private law to be brought by an appropriate body or person with a sufficient interest – such as consumer groups, environmental organisations and trade associations.[16] But in April 2002 the LCD issued a statement to the effect that a new general provision for claims of this nature would not meet the needs of the diverse situations where representative claims would be beneficial. Instead the Government would bring forward legislation dealing with specific topics.[17]

In recent years there has been considerable development of group or multi-party litigation. In the United States class actions are used on a significant scale. Rule 23 of the Federal Rules of Civil Procedures allow such actions where (1) the class is so numerous that joinder of all members is impracticable; (2) there are questions of law or fact common to the class; (3) the claims or defences of the representative are typical of the claims or defences of the class; and (4) the representative parties will fairly and adequately protect the interests of the class.

The first massive group action for damages along American lines in the English courts was the claim of some 1,500 plaintiffs against Eli Lilly, the manufacturers of the drug Opren. The actions were coordinated by a consortium of a small number of solicitors' firms. Instead of separate statements of claim, plaintiffs were using two-page schedules which referred to a master statement of the claim running to over a hundred pages. In July 1986 Hirst J ruled that a number of 'lead cases' should be chosen to be litigated on the different issues of liability. The remaining actions would then be stayed pending the result in these cases.

---

[15]   See, for instance, *John v Rees* [1970] Ch 345 permitting representation of members of the local Divisional Labour Party even though there was some division of opinion between the plaintiff and those he claimed to represent; and *Prudential Assurance Co Ltd v Newman Industries Ltd* [1981] Ch 229 permitting representation by minority shareholders of all other shareholders.

[16]   See on the Consultation Paper, P Bowden and M Bramley, 'Representative claims', 145 *Solicitors' Journal*, 6 July 2001, p 629; and a Note by Professor Ian Scott in 20 *Civil Justice Quarterly*, 2001, p 205.

[17]   LCD Press Notice 141/02, 26 April 2002.

Technically, the position is different from that in an American class action. Under the American procedure, the result binds all members of the class. In the English system this is not so. Any Opren litigant could in theory have continued to fight his own case after the conclusion of the 'test cases'. But this is pure theory. In reality, the members of the class in the English situation are just as much bound by the result. Those on legal aid would not be allowed to continue the case and those not on legal aid would not be able to afford to do so.

It had been thought that the procedural problems posed by the English rules for representative actions could be circumvented by the 'lead case' device where one strong case was selected as a test case. Typically, a plaintiff on legal aid poor enough to be on a nil contribution would be selected. The other plaintiffs would issue their proceedings but their claims would be stayed until the test case was determined. It was thought that the costs of the litigation could be thrown on to the state through this use of the legal aid fund. However in the Opren case the Court of Appeal held that if the action failed, the costs would have to be met by all the plaintiffs, other than those on legal aid. This in effect meant that, absent support from the legal aid fund, such actions were impossible to fund.

For the role of the legal aid fund in supporting multi-party litigation in a series of major disaster case – the Zeebrugge ferry disaster, the King's Cross fire, the Clapham and Purley rail crashes, the Lockerbie air crash, the Hillsborough football stadium tragedy and lawsuits against the makers of the Dalkon Shield contraceptive device and Benzodiazepene-based tranquillizers – see the article by the Director of Legal Practice at the Law Society, A Lockley, 'Regulating Group Actions', *New Law Journal*, 9 June 1989, p 798.[18] (For a discouraging assessment of the future for such cases see J Robins, 'Another one bites the dust', *The Lawyer*, 2 June 2003, p 18 – www.thelawyer.com/lawyernews.)

WOOLF AND MULTI-PARTY ACTIONS

Lord Woolf devoted 25 pages of his Final Report to multi-party actions and ended with 18 separate recommendations for procedural reform. (Final Report, pp 223-48). The new procedures should provide access to justice both where large numbers of individuals had a claim that was too small to make individual action uneconomic and when individual damages were large enough to make an action viable but the number of claimants made the case unmanageable.

---

[18] The Legal Aid Board played a major role in the development of this form of action. See its reports *Issues Arising for the Legal Aid Board and the Lord Chancellor's Department from Multi-Party Actions*, May 1994 and *When the Price is High*, 1997. This policy was continued by the Legal Services Commission (LSC). Its annual reports give information about multi-party actions funded by the LSC. Such cases are handled by the Special Cases Unit (SCU) as part of its remit with Very High Cost Cases. In 2000/01 six such cases were concluded. Only one ended successfully; the others were abandoned (p 23, para 2.77). In 2001/02, five were concluded of which two were settled and three were abandoned. (p 35, para 2.114)

There should be full-scale case management throughout. Where proceedings will or might require collective treatment, either the parties or the Legal Aid Board should make an application to the court for a declaration that the action meets the criteria for a multi-party situation (MPS). The court itself should equally have the power to initiate such an application. The criteria suggested by the Law Society were: 10 or more persons with claims in respect of the same or similar circumstances, a substantial number of which give rise to common questions of fact or law and the interests of justice would be served by treating the case as an MPS. Lord Woolf agreed subject to two modifications. The number 10 should be a guide not a rule. In some instances five might be sufficient. Secondly, the common issues need not necessarily predominate over issues affecting only individuals. The MPS format should be sufficiently flexible to handle all the different types of multi-party actions – local housing and environmental actions, consumer cases, financial actions such as the Lloyds litigation, single 'one-off' disasters and large-scale complex environmental actions and product liability cases, including pharmaceutical and medical cases.

The subsequent procedure would broadly follow the scheme proposed by the Law Society. The case should be certified as an MPS. A managing judge should be appointed to control all the cases. He would make decisions about notification of the action, lead lawyers, arrangements for representing the interests of the group, as to how to balance the generic issues and the individual cases, and as to how costs were to be dealt with. Individuals would participate by entering their names on a register. The judge would probably need the assistance of a master – who might be a deputy master or deputy district judge drawn from practitioners with experience of such cases.

Lord Woolf accepted that there was nothing wrong with lawyers 'taking the initiative in multi-party actions' (*Final Report*, p 242, para 70). The typical claimant in such cases was 'often poorly informed or ignorant of the particular facts, and it will only be the lawyer who recognises the potential for claiming' (ibid). But the interests of the lawyers and their clients could conflict. Both the Legal Aid Board and the court should supervise and control the way the case was handled by the lawyers. Clients might be represented by a 'trustee' appointed and paid for out of public funds who would maintain a watching brief on the public interest elements of the case. There was a strong case for requiring court approval of any settlement in such cases.

In 1997 the LCD issued a Consultation Paper, *Access to Justice – Multi-party Situations: Proposed New Procedures*.

The CPR deals with the matter in Part 19 rr 19.10-19.15 – headed Group Litigation. The rules provide a framework for the case management of 'claims which give rise to common or related issues of fact or law' (CPR 19.10). The court has power to make a group litigation order (GLO) enabling the court to manage the claims in a co-ordinated way. The GLO will contain directions about the establishment of a group register listing the claims and specifying the management court. Judgment orders and directions of the court will be binding on all claims within the GLO (CPR

19.12(1). The court will be able to select particular claims as test claims and to appoint individual solicitors to be the 'lead' solicitor for the claimant or defendants(CPR 19.13(b),(c) and 19.15). The Practice Direction allows costs to be apportioned in advance.

For the position regarding the vital matter of costs see pp 551-53 below.

Which court?

As has been seen, until 1990 the High Court and the county court had concurrent jurisdiction up to the limit of the county court's jurisdiction (which at that time was £5,000). So, in disputes within the jurisdiction of the county court, the plaintiff had a choice as to whether to start the action in the higher or the lower level court. Reforms in 1990-91 following the report of the Civil Justice Review aimed to shift a significant volume of High Court cases to the cheaper county court. Lord Mackay said that the reason was: 'Too many cases of relatively low importance, substance and complexity were being handled and tried at an inappropriately high level. This was wasteful of High Court resources, inflated the costs of smaller cases and clogged up the courts, exacerbating delay'. (Lord Mackay, 'Litigation in the 1990s' (1991) *Modern Law Review*, p 171.) It was provided that personal injury cases had to commence in the county court unless the amount in dispute was over £50,000. But for other cases there remained some degree of choice as between the two levels of court. As from April 1999, however, the rule is that no proceedings can be started in the High Court unless the amount claimed is over £15,000 or in personal injury cases, £50,000. (See Practice Direction to CPR, Part 7.) So the choice as to where to issue proceedings now applies only to cases involving sums of over £15,000 or in the case of personal injury claims, over £50,000.

There are various reasons why lawyers may prefer the High Court to the county court. They may feel they will get higher damages, the enforcement process is thought to be more efficient, the quality of the judges is likely to be better, the level of costs may be higher. But the court has the power to transfer a case from one level to the other. (CPR Part 30) The Practice Direction on Case Management in the High Court states that, if started in the High Court, cases involving sums of under £50,000 will generally be transferred to a county court. (CPR 29PD, 2.2)

What kind of proceedings should be started?

Until 1999, there were a variety of ways of starting legal proceedings: in the High Court, writ of summons, originating summons, originating motion and petition; in the county court, summons (also known as plaint). Lord Woolf's Interim Report stated that his new code of procedure would provide for a single method of starting all types of claim (p 209, para 11). Under the CPR, for most cases there is now only one claim form regardless of whether it is a case in the High Court or the county court. (See CPR, Part 7.) (However, if there is no substantial issue of fact, a claim in the form of what was previously an originating summons is retained – see CPR, Part 8. This is used extensively for instance in proceedings where the only issue is costs.

Contents of the claim form

Part 16 of the CPR and its supporting Practice Direction set out the matters that must be included in the particulars of claim (unless the originating summons procedure is used). A claim form must: contain a concise statement of the nature of the claim, specify the remedy claimed, including any claim for interest on the judgment and the grounds for claiming any aggravated or exemplary damages, and contain a statement of value of the claim. The particulars of the claim can either be stated on or with the claim form or they can be sent subsequently, in which case the claim form must state that they will follow.

Previously, the court could only grant a remedy that had been asked for and practitioners would end the request for remedies with general words to the effect of 'and such further or other relief as the court thinks appropriate'. The new rules give the court the power to award any remedy to which the claimant is entitled, even if this is not specified in the claim form.

The claim form asks for a statement of value in order to enable the court to allocate the case to the appropriate track. This is new. The claim form must state whether the claimant expects to recover more than £5,000, between £5,000 and £15,000 or more than £15,000, or that the claimant cannot say what the claim is worth. If the statement of value is omitted, the district judge will need more information in order to allocate the case to its proper track.

The law distinguishes between 'special damages' where the amount is based on specific amounts that can be precisely quantified – the cost of clothes damaged in the accident, taxi fares to and from the hospital, cost of rented car etc – and 'general damages' where there is no precise way of quantifying the amount claimed – such as damages for pain and suffering resulting from the injuries suffered in the accident. Claims for general damages have not in the past been quantified. Under the new rules, if a figure is given on a claim for general damages, this is treated by the court as the statement of value for the purposes of allocation to the right track. Moreover, if no defence is entered, the claimant is entitled to ask for judgment in the amount claimed, (though the defendant can apply to have the judgment set aside).

CONTENTS OF THE PARTICULARS OF CLAIM

The particulars of claim must include a concise statement of the facts on which the claimant relies. In a personal injuries case the particulars must include brief details of the claimant's injuries and a schedule of past and future losses. If medical evidence is relied on, a medical report must be served with the particulars.

It is optional whether the particulars include points of law relied on and the names of witnesses to be called.

THE STATEMENT OF TRUTH

In order to improve the quality of the documents exchanged between the parties, either the claim form or the separate particulars of claim must contain a statement by the claimant or the claimant's solicitor: 'I believe that the facts stated in these particulars are true'. Particulars that do not contain this statement are liable to be struck out. The same rule applies to defendants and to the statements of all witnesses. (See CPR, Part 22.) The purpose of the statement of truth is to eliminate claims in which a party has no honest belief and to discourage the pleading of cases unsupported by evidence which are put forward in the hope that something may turn up either pre-trial or at the trial – *Clarke v Marlborough Fine Art (London) Ltd (Amendments)* [2002] 1 WLR 1731, Ch D, per Patten J.

The drafting of documents – out with old-style pleadings?

The pleadings are the formal documents exchanged between the parties which define the issues in the case so as to enable each party to prepare its evidence for the trial. Strictly, parties are limited at the trial to matters which have been pleaded – though the court has a discretion to admit by amendment issues that were not pleaded. (For a case in which the pleadings determined the outcome of the case with disastrous results for the plaintiff, see *Esso Petroleum Co Ltd v Southport Corpn* [1956] AC 218.)

Under the old rules the pleadings were supposed to contain a statement of the facts on which the party relied in his claim or defence – not the evidence by which the facts were to be proved (RSC, Ord 18, r 7(1).) But although pleadings were intended to reveal to each side what the other's case would be, practitioners were adept at seeing that they did not have this effect. They drafted the pleadings in such a way as to conceal rather than reveal.

The Winn Committee made some acid comments on the state of modern pleadings (*Report of the* (Winn) *Committee on Personal Injuries Litigation*, 1968, Cmnd 369 p 237). 'A perusal of the RSC Ord 18 ... constitutes a fascinating experience, for a practitioner, in the nature of a trip through territory unknown to him and in a climate which he has not experienced in his daily life. No set of rules could have been more carefully devised, no judicial comment could be more cogently expressed; practice all too regrettably often reveals little relationship to the Rules; the judicial comments pass unregarded.'

> 252 ... .It is all-important to make clear in the pleading the causal connection between the facts alleged and the breach of duty which is alleged to flow from them. Thus it happens that a statement of claim pleads that the plaintiff sustained a fall at work (without saying how or why) and adds that this was

'caused' by the negligence and/or breach of statutory duty of the defendants. There follows an assortment of complaints, such as failing to fence a stock-bar, failing to maintain the floor, failing to provide protective clothing, etc. This may conceal a perfectly coherent case, eg that the plaintiff tripped in a cavity in the floor, caught his sleeve in an unfenced stock-bar, and was whirled across the room, falling and breaking his ankle, which would not have occurred had he been provided with boots instead of plimsolls. Yet the pleading discloses nothing.. . .

254. In road traffic cases, the statement of claim seldom requires any great intellectual effort and, perhaps for this reason, tends to be a shoddy product. Far too many such pleadings follow a stock form of which the dominant characteristic is that no cause of collision known to practitioners is omitted. In this type of litigation superfluity and irrelevance are rampant vices …

266. We have no hesitation in saying it is in defence that the current practice of pleading calls for the harshest criticism. One of the most experienced Queen's Bench Masters told us that at present 'The defence is a blot on our procedure' and he regrets that trial Judges seem to be unwilling to penalize unsuccessful formal denials by an order for costs (which is not easy to frame). 'The chief defect of our system,' he avers, 'is that a defendant is permitted to make wide denials.'

The position in the 1990s when Lord Woolf reported was much the same as that described in 1968 by the Winn Report.

Woolf on pleadings Lord Woolf's report referred to 'incomplete, obscure, evasive or long-winded pleadings' and to 'slapdash pleading and deliberate misuse'. He said that while he accepted that compliance with existing rules would improve the position, 'the fact that they are so often ignored only accentuates the need for a completely new approach and a change of culture' (Interim Report, p 154, para 6). The answer, he said, lay in a switch to a 'managed system of litigation' which must extend to the way in which parties set out their claims and defences. Mere exhortation would achieve little. It was time to return to the basic functions of pleadings–to state the facts of the case. He therefore proposed (Interim Report, p 155, para 9) that:
(1)   The claimant and defendant should each set out 'all the material matters on which they rely'.
(2)   The claim and defence would be considered by the procedural judge after the defence is filed.
(3)   The procedural judge gives directions which could include directions to clarify points in the claim or defence. If the factual allegations are so unclear that the matters in dispute cannot be identified, he would hold a case management conference. If the case was on the 'fast track', the conference would normally be on the telephone.

A major aim of the case management conference would be to produce an agreed statement of the issues in dispute. This would take over from the pleadings.

There were bound to be practical difficulties initially in obtaining a reliable record of any resulting changes in the pleadings but it was essential to make this approach work.

As a consequence, the need for further exchanges between the parties (requests for further and better particulars, notices to admit, interrogatories) should largely be eliminated.

The new rules of procedure for both High Court and county court, Lord Woolf said, should simplify the rules regarding pleadings. One aim would be to avoid technicality. There should be non-prescribed forms of claim for common types of proceedings– possibly in questionnaire format. Statement of claim and defence might face each other in the same document. Eventually this could be computerised. Parties should be required to identify the principal documents on which they relied and would be permitted though not required to attach them to the pleading.

In order to signal a change of culture the word 'pleading' which was synonymous with obfuscation should be replaced by 'statement of case' (p 162, para 33).

There is nothing in the new rules equivalent to RSC Order 18 dealing with the general principles of pleading. They have to be gathered by looking at what is required in particulars of claim and defences. Lord Woolf's hope, apparently, was that the judges would achieve the miracle of improving standards of drafting by a combination of exhortation based on scrutiny and criticism together with the application of sanctions.

In a decision given shortly after the new rules came into force Lord Woolf said that although pleadings could now be simpler than before, they were still necessary 'to mark out the parameters of the case that was being advanced by each party'. But contests over the precise terms of a pleading were to be discouraged and should take place, if at all, at a hearing where all relevant issues could be resolved. No more than a concise statement of the facts was required. (*McPhilemy v Times Newspapers Ltd* [1999] 3 All ER 775, 792-93.)

The cost of initiating proceedings

In recent years the cost of taking civil proceedings has risen very considerably. In 1988/1989 the then Conservative Government adopted a policy that the civil justice system should be self-financing. It did so without any public discussion or consultation with the judiciary. Initially the costs of the system that had to be financed by court fees excluded judicial salaries. But in 1991 the Government decided that judicial salaries should also be included. There were swingeing increases in court fees. This policy was fiercely criticised as unconstitutional by Sir Richard Scott (as he then was), the first holder of the office of Head of Civil Justice,

> The policy that the civil justice system should be self-financing is, I suggest, indefensible from a constitutional point of view. It treats civil justice as a market place commodity to be paid for by the customer who wants it ... The system of

civil justice is one of the three pillars on which the structure of justice in a civilised community must stand. The other two are the criminal justice system and the police. No-one could seriously suggest that the criminal justice or the police should be made self-financing. Why should the suggestion be made of the civil justice system? ... A policy which treats the civil justice system merely as a service to be offered at cost in the market place, and to be paid for by those who choose to use it, profoundly and dangerously mistakes the nature of the system and its constitutional function. [Transcript of speech to the County Court Advisers Group, 16 May 1997]

Sir Richard, now Lord Scott, hoped that the Government would 'consign the self-financing of the courts policy to the dustbin'. His call has been echoed repeatedly. In November 2002, the Civil Justice Council, in published advice to the Lord Chancellor urged that full cost recovery was impossible without inappropriate cross-subsidy, that it arbitrarily limited the nature and quality of the services provided by the civil justice system, limited access to the courts and was wrong in principle.[19] The following month, Lord Woolf, the Lord Chief Justice, added his voice to the chorus of condemnation in a powerful intervention on the Second Reading of the Courts Bill. [20] Indeed his leadership resulted in a defeat of the Government on the issue during the Committee stage. An amendment to the Courts Bill, carried by 90-87 on 27 March 2003 (col 917) required that when setting court fees, the Lord Chancellor must have regard to access to justice. But there was no sign that the Government would abandon its Treasury-driven policy.[21] It was reported in June 2003 that the Lord Chancellor had launched a review of court fees with a view to lift the £55m deficit faced by the Supreme Court and to make all civil courts profit making.[22]

Over the past several years the volume of civil litigation has been declining significantly which has a direct and serious impact on the revenues collected from court fees. It is not clear to what extent the rise in court fees itself has contributed to this phenomenon.

Court fees are not payable by those in receipt of certain benefits: income support, family credit, disability working allowance, income-based jobseeker's allowance. In 1996, Lord Mackay, the Lord Chancellor abolished this traditional waiver of fees for indigent litigants. But the action was successfully challenged by way of judicial review (*R v Lord Chancellor, ex p Witham* [1997] 2 All ER 779). The judges found that

---

[19]   *Full Costs Recovery* accessible on www.civiljusticecouncil.org.uk (Publications).

[20]   Lord Woolf, the Lord Chief Justice, added his voice to the chorus of condemnation in an intervention on the Second Reading of the Courts Bill – see House of Lords, *Hansard*, 9 December 2002, col 27. For the Legal Action Group's powerfully expressed view see N Ardill, 'Courting trouble', *Legal Action* , February 2003, p 6.

[21]   At the time of writing, the latest levels were fixed by the Supreme Court Fees (Amendment) Order 2003, SI 2003/ 646; the county court Fees (Amendment) Order 2003, SI 2003/648 and the Family Proceedings Fees (Amendment) Order 2003, SI 2003/645. For details see for instance 153 *New Law Journal*, 4 April 2003, p 507.

[22]   *The Lawyer*, 2 June 2003, p 2.

the Lord Chancellor had infringed a basic constitutional right of access to the courts which Mr Justice Laws described 'as near to an absolute right as any I can imagine'. The Lord Chancellor had the grace not to appeal the decision. (See R English, 'Wrongfooting the Lord Chancellor: Access to Justice in the High Court', 61 *Modern Law Review*, 1998, pp 245-54.) In 2003 it was estimated that some five million people were eligible for the automatic exemption from court fees (statement of the Minister during the House of Commons Committee Stage of the Courts Bill, Standing Committee 'D', 8 July 2003, col 169)

Another gesture in the same area was the decision announced in 2002 that the fee payable on allocation would no longer be required for claims of under £1,000.

Venue

Pre-Woolf, High Court cases could be started in the Royal Courts of Justice in the Strand or in any District Registry, as the plaintiff chose, subject to provision for transfer to another District Registry or the Royal Courts. Divorce proceedings could be started in any divorce county court. In the county court, by contrast, the rule was that the proceedings should be in the defendant's local court or the court with which the case was most closely connected.

Lord Woolf's Interim Report proposed that, irrespective of the nature of the proceedings, the plaintiff should be able to apply to *any* court and it would be for the court to allocate the case to the appropriate track and the appropriate court (p 36, para 14).

This recommendation was adopted in the CPR. The claim can be issued from any court – but if the defendant is an individual and the claim is for a specified amount of money the case will normally be transferred to the defendant's home court, if and when a defence is entered. (CPR 26.2)

Issue and service of proceedings

The claim must be 'issued' and it must be 'served' on the other side. Originally proceedings had to be served personally. In the High Court this was done until 1999 by the plaintiff or a professional process server on his behalf. In the county court it was formerly done by the bailiff on behalf of the court until it was stopped in 1983 as an economy measure, since when it was usually sent by the court through the post.

Under the 1999 reforms, service can still be personal but it can also be by first class post or by document exchange or by fax 'or other means of electronic communication in accordance with the relevant practice direction'. (CPR 6.2) Service will normally be by the court and the court can choose whichever method of service it prefers. (CPR 6.3(2)) (Exceptionally, the Administrative Court will not serve documents, leaving it to the parties to do so.) There are special rules as to how service should be effected on businesses and companies, on children and patients and members of the armed services. The 'deemed' date of service is the second day after it was posted rather than, as previously, seven days later.

There is a separate practice direction for the issue of proceedings by the computerised Summons Production Centre available to bulk issuers (p 10 above). A pilot scheme for issuing process online – Money Claim On Line (MCOL) – was launched in December 2001 for claims under £100,000. In the first year of its operation, over 16,000 claims were issued making it the fourth highest issuing source for money claims. [23]

If ordinary service is not possible because the defendant's whereabouts are not known, the court can be asked for permission to allow service by an alternative method (formerly 'substituted service'), for example by putting an advertisement in a local newspaper. Where a property owner is trying to get back possession of premises occupied by squatters, service on those on the premises (whose names would normally not be known) is allowed to be made by posting up a notice of the proceedings on the door or some other appropriate place.

There can be and often is a considerable delay between issue and service of a writ. The rules used to allow 12 months from issue of the writ for its service. Under the CPR 7.5 the general rule is that service of the claim form must take place within four months from the date of issue (or six months if service is outside the jurisdiction). If the particulars are not served with the claim, they must be served within 14 days thereafter and, in any event, within the overall four- or six-month, period (r 7.4).

The case law on this dry procedural topic is an object lesson in how the courts have been struggling to find the right approach to failures to comply with the new rules.

In *Vinos v Marks & Spencer plc*[24], V had suffered injuries at work. After lengthy negotiations failed to produce a settlement, his solicitor issued proceedings a week before the expiry of the limitation period but due to an oversight they did not serve the claim form until nine days after the expiry of the four-month period prescribed by the CPR. V applied for an extension of time. Under CPR 7.6 the court can extend the time 'only if (a) the court has been unable to serve the claim form; or (b) the claimant has taken all reasonable steps to serve the claim form but has been unable to do so; and (c) in either case, the claimant has acted promptly in making the application'. These provisions did not cover what happened. The court had not been asked to serve the claim form and V by his solicitor had not been unable to serve the form after taking all reasonable steps to do so.

Obviously a procedural slip had occurred, but the Court of Appeal refused to apply the 'slip rule' in CPR 3.10 which provides, 'Where there has been an error of procedure such as a failure to comply with a rule or practice direction (a) the error does not invalidate any step taken in the proceedings unless the court so orders; and

---

[23]   153 *New Law Journal*, 7 February 2003, p 163.
[24]   [2001] 3 All ER 784 CA.

(b) the court may make an order to remedy the error'. (The court said, 'The general words of CPR 3.10 cannot extend to enable the court to do what CPR 7.6(3) specifically forbids ... Interpretation to achieve the overriding objective does not enable the court to say that provisions which are quite plain mean what they do not mean, nor that the plain meaning should be ignored' (para 20).)

The harsh disciplinarian approach of *Vinos* was applied in *Godwin v Swindon Borough Council*[25]. In that case the claim form actually arrived in time but by virtue of the 'deeming' provision in CPR 6.7(1) it was deemed to have arrived three days late. In judgments that take 24 pages in the law reports, the Court of Appeal held that the deemed day of service was not rebuttable by evidence showing that service had actually been effected in time! Nor could the situation be rescued by application of CPR 6.1(b) (the rules apply except where the court orders otherwise) or CPR 6.9 (the court has the power to dispense with service altogether) – because that would be to condone failure to comply with the express terms of the rule about service.

The court's approach was slightly softened in *Anderton v Clwyd County Council*[26] involving five separate appeals basically on the same issue. The Court of Appeal agreed that the deemed day of service could not be rebutted by evidence of earlier receipt. The aim of CPR 6.7 was to achieve procedural certainty in the interests of all concerned. Justice and proportionality required that there were firm procedural rules which should be observed. General rules should not be construed to create exceptions and excuses whenever those who could easily have complied with the rules had slipped up. However, the power in CPR 6.9 to dispense with service altogether could be applied in exceptional circumstances at least where there had been an ineffective attempt to serve in time (as opposed to a case where the claimant had not even attempted to effect service).

In *Wilkey v BBC*[27], the Court of Appeal held that the decision in *Anderton* created a presumption that CPR 6.9 would be applied to cases prior to that decision unless the other party could show that he would suffer prejudice or some other good reason why it should not be applied. Avoidable delay would not be a good reason. But the dispensing power should ordinarily not be exercised where service had occurred after the decision in *Anderton*. In such cases a strict approach should generally be adopted. The deemed service rule and the highly desirable certainty which it provided would therefore continue to apply in all but the most exceptional circumstances after the *Anderton* decision.

The issue came back to the Court of Appeal for the fifth time in two years in *Cranfield v Bridgegrove Ltd*[28] a case involving five pre-*Anderton* cases. The Court said that in pre-*Anderton* cases, failure to serve in time could be excused, for instance, where the

25   [2001 EWCA Civ 1478, [2002] 1 WLR 997, [2001] 4 All ER 641.
26   [2002] EWCA Civ 933, [2002] 1 WLR 3174, [2002] 3 All ER 813.
27   [2002] EWCA] Civ 1561, [2003] 1 WLR 1, [2002] 4 All ER 1177.
28   [2003] EWCA Civ 656, [2003] 3 All ER 129.

failure had been caused by some error by the court itself, or, maybe, where the claim form though deemed to have arrived late had actually arrived in time. In post-*Anderton* cases, the court would ordinarily not exercise its discretionary power to disregard late service. But the court said that it could exercise its discretion where there had been some comparatively minor departure from the permitted method of service. However, the principle established in *Godwin* was important and was not to be subverted. It would be subverted unless the power to dispense with service retrospectively was confined to truly exceptional cases. So it seems as if the disciplinarian approach prevails.

Responding to a claim

A defendant served with a claim has a number of options. He can admit the claim by serving an admission under Part 14 of the Civil Procedure Rules. Or he can serve a defence under Part 19. Or he can admit part of the claim and serve a defence for the part he does not admit. Or he can file an acknowledgment of service under Part 10.

Acknowledgment of service

Acknowledgment of service was previously a procedure known only to the High Court. It is now available in all cases. It is appropriate when the defendant is unable to file a defence within 14 days of service of the particulars of claim. Filing the acknowledgment gives the defendant an extra 14 days. It is also used when the defendant wishes to dispute the court's jurisdiction. If the defendant can file the defence within 14 days, the stage of acknowledgment of service can be omitted. (Where a claim has been issued online, acknowledgement of service – as well as defence, part admission and counterclaim – can now also be made online.)

If the defendant fails to file an acknowledgment of service or a defence or an admission within 14 days, the claimant can move directly to ask for judgment. (See default judgments below.)

A defence

As has been seen (p 70 above), Lord Woolf severely criticised the drafting of defences especially for failing to reveal the nature of the defence case. Under the new rules, the defence has to be explicit. CPR 16.5 requires a defence to state, inter alia, which of the allegations are denied, which are admitted and which are neither admitted nor denied. Where the defendant denies an allegation he must state his reasons for doing so. If he intends to put forward a different version of the facts, the defendant must state his own version. A failure to deal with an allegation is taken as an admission in regard to that allegation. (CPR 16.5) Previously, the defendant could put in a simple, totally uninformative, denial and the plaintiff tried to get further information by requests for further and better particulars. The position under the new rules is wholly different. The defendant has no choice. In regard to each allegation he must admit it, or deny and explain why, or state that he cannot either admit or deny it.

CPR 3.4(2) gives the court the power to strike out a statement of claim, inter alia, if there has been a failure to comply with a rule or practice direction. The practice direction on striking out a statement of case states that a defence may fall within the rule where it consists of a bare denial or otherwise sets out no coherent statement of facts or if the facts it sets out would not, even if true, amount to a defence. The court can of its own motion strike out the defence or order the defendant to give additional information, and in default, order that the defence be then struck out.

Claimant's right of reply

In his Interim Report, Lord Woolf said that the plaintiff need not be given a right to reply. But his Final Report allowed that, at least in some circumstances, a reply should be permitted. CPR 16.7 states that a claimant who does not file a reply is taken to admit the matters stated in the defence and that a claimant who fails to deal with something raised in the defence is taken to require that matter to be proved.

Allocation to track

Allocation of the case to its proper track is based on answers given by both sides to a booklet called the allocation questionnaire (Form N150). The court sends the questionnaire to both sides after a defence is filed. It must be completed within the specified time, usually 14 days. The allocation decision is generally taken by a district judge or a master. (See CPR 26.6) The main consideration is the amount claimed but there are various additional relevant matters including the nature of the remedy sought, the complexity of the facts, law and evidence, the number of parties, the amount of oral evidence, the importance of the claim to persons who are not parties and the views of the parties. (CPR 26.8) If the amount in dispute is under £5,000, the normal track is small claims. But a personal injury claim where the claim for 'general'[29] (as opposed to 'special' damages) is over £1,000 is excluded. So is a residential tenant's claim for damages of more than £1,000 for repairs or if it is a claim for unlawful eviction or harassment. If the claim is for between £5,000 and £15,000 it will normally be allocated to the fast track but again there will be exceptions. To be fit for the fast track the procedural judge must consider that the trial can be completed within five hours[30] and that oral expert evidence will be limited to one expert per party in no more than two fields. All cases that are not allocated to the small claims or fast track are allocated to the multi-track.

---

[29]   Damages for pain, suffering and loss of amenity.
[30]   As has been seen, this was a retreat from Lord Woolf's original proposal of three hours.

The allocation questionnaire asks, inter alia, whether the parties wish there to be a one-month stay to attempt to settle the case. (A stay can be ordered without the parties' consent.) It asks whether they have complied with any pre-action protocol; what witnesses of fact it is intended to call and which facts they are witnesses to. There are several questions about expert witnesses, with the emphasis placed on the desirability of single experts jointly instructed. (The questions ask whether expert reports have been copied to the other side; the names of the proposed experts and their fields of expertise; whether the parties will be using the same expert(s) and, if not, why not; whether there is a wish that the expert(s) give oral evidence at the trial.) The parties require consent to use expert evidence at all. There are questions about trial location, legal representation and time estimates. The parties are asked to give an estimate of costs to date and likely overall costs. The final section invites agreed directions. (See CPR Practice Direction to Parts 26 to 29.)

By 14 days after the defence is entered, both parties are therefore required to know a great deal about the case in regard to the facts, the likely evidence and the costs. The Practice Direction makes it clear that the parties are expected to consult one another and to cooperate in completing the allocation questionnaire.

If the solicitors do not give sufficient replies, they are asked to attend an allocation hearing. The person attending the allocation hearing is required to be someone with personal knowledge of the case and with authority to deal with any issues likely to come up (CPR, PD, Part 26, 6.5).

There are costs sanctions for causing an allocation hearing by failure to return the allocation questionnaire. The party in default will be required to pay – forthwith – the other sides costs of the hearing on the indemnity basis (see p 541 below). If those costs are not paid within the stated time, the court can order that the statement of claim be struck out (CPR, Part 26, 6.6(2)).

Counterclaim

A counterclaim by the defendant is treated like a claim and the claimant can then file a defence to the counterclaim (see CPR, Part 20.3 and 20.4).

Seeking more information

CPR, Part 18 gives the court the power to order a party to clarify any matter that is in dispute or to give additional information in relation to any such matter 'whether or not the matter is contained or referred to in a statement of case'. A party replying to a request must include a statement of truth (p 69 above). The accompanying Practice Direction states that a request 'should be concise and strictly confined to matters which are reasonably necessary and proportionate to enable the first party [the requesting party] to prepare his own case or to understand the case he has to meet' (para 1.2).

If the person to whom the request is addressed (the second party) considers that complying with the request would involve disproportionate expense, he can say so in his reply, with his reasons (CPR, PD, Part 18, 4.1, 4.2). If the second party objects to a request or cannot reply within the stated time, he does not have to make an application to the court. He must simply write to the first party giving his reasons or saying when the reply will be ready.

If the second party fails to respond to the original application, the court will order that the request be replied to without a hearing. The court can make an order as to costs at the end of any such hearing. If it does not do so, the costs cannot be recovered later.

Making applications for pre-trial court orders

Applications (previously called 'motions') have to be in writing. They must be served on the other side as soon as practicable and, save in cases of urgency, at least three days before the application is to be heard. In some circumstances the application can be made by a telephone hearing or a video conference. Where the parties agree on the terms of the order, or agree that no hearing is needed, the court has power to deal with an application without a hearing. The court also has the power to make an order without a hearing if it does not consider that a hearing is appropriate.

Amendments

Once served, any amendment to an official document requires either the consent of the other party or of the court.

Judgment in default

If the defendant fails to file an acknowledgement of service or fails to file a defence – provided that in either case the time for doing so has expired – the claimant can normally ask the court to enter what is (and also was previously) called a default judgment. There are some types of case where default judgment cannot be obtained and others where a default judgment requires the consent of the court. (Consent is required, for instance, where the claim is against a child or a patient, or is against the Crown, or is a claim in tort by one spouse against another.) If the claim is for an unspecified sum of money, the default judgment is for an amount to be decided by the court plus costs.

But a default judgment can in some circumstances be set aside. It must be set aside if it was entered prematurely or in breach of any of the technical rules (CPR 13.2). If the default judgment is technically correct, the court may set aside or vary it if the defendant can show that he has a real prospect of successfully defending the claim or it appears to the court that there is some other good reason why it should be set aside or varied or the defendant should be allowed to defend the claim (CPR 13.3). In considering whether to exercise this discretion the court must have regard to whether the application to be set aside or vary was made promptly.

Summary judgment

Part 24 of the new rules gives the court extensive power to deal with hopeless cases by way of summary judgment. This power is an extension of the power that previously existed under RSC, Order 14. But whereas the power under Order 14 could only be exercised on application of a party, the power under Part 24 can be exercised by the court of its own motion.

The court can give summary judgment if it considers that the claimant or defendant has no real prospect of success and there is no other compelling reason why the case should be disposed of at trial. (CPR 24(2)) (On this new test see *Swain v Hillman* [2001] 1 All ER 91 CA.)

An application for summary judgment can be made in respect of the whole claim or a part of a claim. It can be based either on a point of law or on the evidence or both. At least 14 days' notice of the hearing must be given. If the application is based on a point of law, the notice must identify the point of law. If it is based on the evidence, the evidence supporting the application must be filed. If the respondent wishes to oppose the application, he must file his evidence at least seven days before the hearing. The applicant must file any reply at least three days before the hearing. Under the new rules an application can be made in a small claims case as well as in fast track or multi track cases.

The court's approach is treated in the Practice Direction (Part 24, PD, para 4.1). The old test under Order 14 was – no triable issue. The new test is – no reasonable prospect of success. Exceptionally, the court can permit the case to go forward on grounds of public interest even though the case appears hopeless.

For sharply critical comment on the new, more restrictive approach to summary judgment see D O'Brien, 'The New Summary Judgment: Raising the Threshhold of Admission', 18 *Civil Justice Quarterly*, April 1999, pp 132-48. He suggested that making the test at the summary hearing more demanding had a cost in terms both 'of the substantive accuracy of the adjudication and, more importantly, in terms of procedural fairness' (p 147). Moreover under the attenuated fast track procedures the parties were already 'being denied access to the full panoply of procedural weapons currently available' (ibid). Why then curtail even further their right to adjudication on the merits by insisting that their case have a realistic chance of success? (ibid) Also, to the extent that funding would increasingly be by way of conditional fee agreements (pp 599-607 below), there should be even less need to screen unmeritorious claims since that function would already have been performed by the claimant's solicitor in deciding whether to take the case. O'Brien said that the dramatic extension of the court's summary powers might turn out to be the most radical of Lord Woolf's reforms and one beset with difficulties. It would be a fertile field for satellite litigation 'with parties investing a great deal of their resources and energy to fighting and, if unsuccessful, then appealing applications for summary judgment' (p 148). The 'knock-on effects might be to undermine the very objectives the new rule was intended to achieve, namely speedy and cost effective resolution of disputes'.

There are other provisions in the CPR that could have a similar effect to summary judgment:

- CPR 1.4(1) states that the court must further the overriding objective by 'actively managing' cases. CPR 1.4(2) states that active case management includes, amongst other things: identifying the issues at an early stage (CPR 1.4(2)(b)), and deciding promptly which issues need full investigation and trial and accordingly 'disposing summarily' of the others (CPR 1.4(2)(c)).
- The court's 'general powers of management' include the power to exclude an issue from consideration' (CPR 3.1(2)(k)).(But the Court of Appeal has held that a claim arguable on the pleadings needs to be decided and should not be excluded by exercise of the court's powers under CPR 3.1(2)(k) – see *Royal Brompton Hospital NHS Trust v Hammond* [2001] EWCA Civ 550, (2001) Times, 11 May)
- CPR 3.4(2) states that the court may strike out a statement of case on the ground that (a) it discloses no reasonable grounds for bringing or defending the claim, (b) it is an abuse of the court's process or is otherwise likely to obstruct the just disposal of the proceedings or (c) that there has been a failure to comply with a rule, practice direction or court order.

Part 36 offers to settle and payment into court

'Payment into court' has for a long time been a device to promote settlement. The defendant paid a sum of money into a court account as an offer of settlement. If the claimant accepted the money, the case was ended and he got his costs as well. If the claimant refused the offer, the defendant could increase his payment-in. If the claimant still refused and the case went to trial, the matter was determined by the outcome. If the claimant recovered more than the amount paid-in, he got his damages plus the costs in the normal way. If, however, he did not recover more than the amount paid in, the court ordered that he pay the costs of both sides from the date of payment-in.

Pre-CPR the rule was applied inflexibly. The consequence of 'getting it wrong' was extremely serious as failing to beat the sum paid in could result in the plaintiff losing the greater part or even the whole of his damages.

The trial court would not be informed of the fact or the amount of any payment-in, lest its assessment of damages be influenced – though on appeal sometimes the Court of Appeal might become aware of it. Payment into court did not apply to small claims.

Technically the system applied only where the case concerned a damages claim. But the same principle was adapted for use in other cases. So, if the defendant made an offer of settlement 'without prejudice save as to costs', this was treated by the courts in virtually the same way as if it were a payment into court. (The technique was known as a Calderbank letter–after the case of *Calderbank v Calderbank* [1975] 3 All ER 333.) The Court of Appeal held in *Cutts v Head* [1984] Ch 290 that the court could look at a letter marked 'without prejudice' but expressly reserving the issue of costs. In a case where a payment into court was not practicable, this would suffice. Where payment-in was practicable, however, it would still be required to achieve the effect.

For an analysis of payment into court and other economic aspects of the settlement process, see Jenny Phillips and Keith Hawkins, 'Some Economic Aspects of the Settlement Process: A Study of Personal Injury Claims', 39 *Modern Law Review*, September 1976, p 497.

Woolf on payment into court Lord Woolf, in his Interim Report in June 1995, made a number of proposals regarding payment into court:

(1) That the actual payment-in of money should stop and that instead a Calderbank letter would suffice in all cases (p 194, para 5). [This was not adopted.]
(2) An offer should be capable of being made either in respect of the whole case or of specific issues (p 194, para 5). [This was adopted.]
(3) The plaintiff too should be able to make an offer to settle–as was already permitted in a number of Australian and Canadian jurisdictions. [This was adopted.]
(4) If the plaintiff's offer was refused and he then was awarded as much or more, he should be entitled to 'additional costs' in the form of costs on the indemnity basis (see p 541 below) plus interest at an enhanced rate. But the scope of this recommendation was qualified by the caveat that it should only apply to 'multi track cases' and therefore not to the much larger number of 'fast track cases' because 'it would detract from the pre-determined costs regime which is an integral feature of that track' (p 196, para 9). [Adopted as to payment of costs on the indemnity basis and as to interest at an enhanced rate, unless unjust to do so, – limited to 10% over base rate. (CPR 36.21). Not adopted as to the proposed limitation to multi track cases.]
(5) If the plaintiff beats the defendant's offer but not his own, Lord Woolf proposed that he should only be entitled to normal costs. [Adopted unless 'unjust to do so'.]
(6) An offer by either side should be capable of dealing either with the whole case or with one or more issues and should be capable of being made even before the start of proceedings (p 197, para 17). [Adopted.]
(7) Courts should have (and should exercise) a discretion to modify the normal cost rule in the light of the way in which offers are made–to take account, for instance, of sham offers, or last minute offers or withdrawals of offers (pp 197–8, paras 18–20).

The new rules on payment into court (CPR, Part 36) There are several significant differences in the new rules. First, the court can mitigate the harshness of the traditional rule under which the claimant would automatically be ordered to pay the costs of both sides if he failed to get a penny more than the amount paid- in by the defendant. When a claimant fails to get more than the amount paid-in, the claimant will normally still be ordered to pay the defendant's costs from the latest day for acceptance of the payment in. (As a rule, that is 21 days from the date the offer is made.) In *Neave v Neave (No 2)* [2003] EWCA Civ 325, the Court of Appeal said that the effectiveness of the Part 36 regime would be undermined if the ordinary consequences of the payment into court rule did not follow. The offeror was not to be deprived of his costs after having beaten the payment-in without good reason. But, if the court considers that that is 'unjust', it can decide otherwise. In considering this question, the factors the court can take into account include: the terms of any offer, the stage in the process reached, the information available at the time the offer was made and the conduct of the parties with regard to giving information (CPR 36.21(5)).

Secondly, the new rules provide for a claimant's offer – stating what he would accept by way of settlement. If in the event he obtains more, the court can assess costs on the higher indemnity basis (see p 541 below) and can allow interest at a rate that is no more than 10% above bank rate. The rules provide for Part 36 offers before commencement of proceedings. Such an offer would be taken into account by the court when deciding on costs at the end of the case. If the offer is by the defendant, it must be followed by a Part 36 payment of an equal or greater amount within 14 days of service of the claim form.

Payment-in applies to money claims. Where the claim is not for money the defendant can make a Part 36 offer (as opposed to a Part 36 payment) with the same basic rules. This is the equivalent of what was previously known as a 'Calderbank letter'.

Curiously, Part 36 only applies 'where at trial' the claimant fails to beat a Part 36 payment. It therefore does not apply to cases ending with summary judgment. However, in such cases, where appropriate , the court can order indemnity costs and enhanced interest (up to 10%).[31]

Part 36 is regarded as one of the successes of the Woolf reforms. The main caveat has been that the courts have been erratic in their approach to the award of costs:
* *Ford v GKR Construction Ltd*[32] – CA refused to interfere with judge's decision to award the claimant all her costs although she had failed to beat the sum paid in (£85,000 as against £95,000). She had been reasonable and the defendants had disclosed their damaging video regarding the claimant's mobility very late

---

[31]   *Petrotrade Inc v Texaco Ltd* [2001]4 All ER 853. Lord Woolf, giving judgment, speculated that Part 36 did not apply probably because the Rule Committee took the view that it should not apply to ordinary debt collecting. ('By making a Part 36 offer, a claimant could put himself in a position where indemnity costs and enhanced interest orders could be made when it was not appropriate.' (para 61))

[32]   [2000] 1 WLR 1397, [2000] 1 All ER 802.

- *Lloyds Bank plc v Parker Bullen*[33] – £100,000 paid in, judgment given for £400,000 but only 80% of costs awarded due to exaggeration of claim
- *Kinetics Technology International v Cross Seas Shipping Corpn (The Mosconici)*[34] – judgment beat payment- in but after conduct was considered the successful claimant was ordered to pay two-thirds of the defendant's costs from the date of payment-in
- *Budgen v Andrew Gardner Partnership*[35] – judgment for £330,000 beat payment-in by £44,000 but claimant only got 75% of his costs from date of payment-in because he lost on a point that took a substantial proportion of the seven day trial
- *Verrechia v Metropolitan Police Comr*[36] – claimant originally sought £141,500. Later made Part 36 offer of settlement of £98,600. Payment-in of £5,500. Judgment for £53,225. Without giving reasons the judge made no order of costs on the basis that the case had been 'an effective draw'. The Court of Appeal declined to interfere.
- *Huck v Robson*[37] – defendant offered 50-50 on liability; claimant made Part 36 offer of 95-5. Judge gave claimant 100% but did not give indemnity costs or interest because the 95-5 split was 'derisory'. Court of Appeal allowed the appeal.[38]

4. Getting the documentary evidence

Disclosure (formerly 'discovery') from one's opponent

Under the old rules (RSC Ord 24 and CCR Ord 14) the parties had to 'make discovery' after close of pleadings. Making discovery consisted basically of making available to each other all documents that the party had or had had in his possession, custody or power which related to any matter in issue.[39] The effect of the Woolf reforms was to retain the concept but to narrow its scope. Also, 'discovery' is now called 'disclosure'.

There were two stages – first, making a list of the documents, which had to be done within 14 days of the close of pleadings; secondly, physical production of the documents or giving an opportunity for their inspection or copying. The list of documents was in two categories – those that would be produced without objection and those discovery of which was opposed by virtue of a claim of legal professional

---

33   [2000] Lloyd's Rep PN 51.
34   (2001) 2 Lloyds Rep 313.
35   [2002] EWCA Civ 1125.
36   [2002] EWCA Civ 605, [2002] 3 All ER 385.
37   [2002] EWCA Civ 398, [2002] 3 All ER 263.
38   For comment see G.Exall, *Solicitors' Journal*, 29 March 2002, pp 288-89.
39   See *Compagnie Financière du Pacifique v Peruvian Guano Co* (1882) 11 QBD 55, 63.

privilege or public interest immunity (on which see pp 87, 90 below). Discovery took place automatically, but if the opponent defaulted on this obligation, an application could be made to the court for enforcement or appropriate penalty.

The duty to make disclosure as required by the rules lay on both parties and their lawyers. In *Rockwell Machine Tool Co Ltd v EP Barrus (Concessionaires) Ltd* [1968] 2 All ER 98, Megarry J pointed out that many litigants had little appreciation of the scope of discovery and the duty of making full disclosure: 'Accordingly it seems to me necessary for solicitors to take positive steps to ensure that the client appreciates at an early stage of the litigation, promptly after writ issued, not only the duty of discovery and its width but also the duty of not destroying documents which have to be disclosed.'

WOOLF ON DISCOVERY

In his Interim Report Lord Woolf stated that he had received many submissions that in a minority of complex cases discovery created a significant problem in terms of a burden of resources and cost. In his view discovery should be retained but curbed. He differentiated four categories of documents: (1) the documents relied on by the parties; (2) adverse documents, which could help the other side; (3) other relevant documents; (4) documents which could lead to a train of inquiry that might produce relevant documents. The category that generated most of the problem, he suggested, was the third.

Lord Woolf categorised (1) and (2) as suitable for 'standard discovery' and (3) and (4) as 'extra discovery'.

In regard to the fast track case, he proposed, only standard discovery should normally be permitted. But extra discovery could be ordered if a case could be made out. In fast track cases this would be very rare. The parties would have to certify that they had disclosed all documents required under standard discovery.

In multi-track cases Lord Woolf suggested that the approach would have to be adjusted to the needs of the case. The procedural judge would decide on the scope and extent of discovery at the case management conference – on which see p 00 below. Discovery might be ordered on the basis of a rolling programme.

The core of the problem was how to avoid lawyers having to trawl through all category (3) documents in order to eliminate the possibility of overlooking category (2) documents. The Bar suggested that initial disclosure should be confined to documents which are 'capable of being located without undue difficulty and expense'. Lord Woolf said that he supported this approach but he formulated the test slightly differently–'initial disclosure should apply to documents of which a party is aware at the time when the obligation to disclose arises' (p 171, para 34). It was for consideration whether this formula should be enlarged to include potentially adverse documents of which a party would have been aware if he had not deliberately closed his mind to their existence.

In making an order for extra discovery the procedural judge would have in mind the circumstances of the parties and of the case.

The new rules (CPR, Part 31)

Adopting the Woolf proposals, the new rules create a much more restrictive disclosure regime. Disclosure on the fast-track and the multi-track are subject to the principles of necessity and proportionality under the overriding objective of the rules (see p 54 above). There is no longer an automatic duty to disclose. Instead, disclosure is ordered by the court. Whether the court orders it and, if so, to what extent, depends on the court's view of what is appropriate having regard to the amount of money involved, the importance of the case, the complexity of the issues and the financial position of the parties. It is usually much more restrictive in fast-track cases than in multi track cases. The court can dispense with disclosure altogether. Also the parties can agree to dispense with disclosure – typically where disclosure has already occurred in pre-action exchanges.

As proposed in Lord Woolf's Interim Report, if a disclosure order is made, it will normally be for '*standard disclosure*'. This requires the party to disclose documents on which the party relies; or which adversely affect the party's case or another party's case; or which support another party's case; or which the party is required to disclose by a relevant practice direction. By way of example, the personal injury pre-action protocol suggests that in a tripping-on-the-highway case the highway authority should disclose (for the previous 12 months) the records of inspection, the maintenance records, minutes of meetings where the maintenance or repair policy had been discussed, records of complaints about the state of the highway and records of other accidents on that stretch of the road.

The definition of 'standard disclosure' represented something of a retreat from Lord Woolf's Interim Report which proposed that it should only cover documents that 'to a material extent' adversely affected a party's case or supported the case of another. The dropping of the words 'to a material extent' represented an enlargement of what must be disclosed. On the other hand, the new requirement of disclosure is obviously considerably narrower than the old rule.

As has been seen, the original suggestion was that disclosure was only required in regard to documents of which a party was 'aware'. But the new rules introduce a duty to search. A party has to conduct 'a reasonable search' for documents which are or have been in the party's control. In determining the extent of a reasonable search, account is to be taken of the number of documents involved, the nature and complexity of the proceedings, the ease and expense of retrieval of any document and the significance of any document likely to be located during the search. The Practice Direction accompanying Part 31 of the CPR says it may be reasonable to decide not to search for documents coming into existence before a certain date or to limit a search to particular categories of documents. (Part 31, PD, para 2)

The duty to disclose is a continuing one. If a party finds out about a new disclosable document there is a duty to inform the other party immediately (see on this *Vernon v Bosley (No 2)*[1999] QB 18, [1997] 1 All ER 614).

Disclosure has to be accompanied by a 'disclosure statement' signed not by the solicitor but by the party personally, saying: 'I state that I have carried out a reasonable and proportionate search to locate all the documents which I am required to disclose under the order made by the court on .... I did not search for documents: (1) predating ...; (2) located elsewhere than ...; (3) in categories other than ... I certify that I understand the duty of disclosure and to the best of my knowledge I have carried out that duty. I certify that the list ... is a complete list of all documents which are or have been in my control and which I am obliged under the order to disclose'. (Annex to PD 31)

If a party thinks that the other side's disclosure is inadequate, the court can be asked to order specific disclosure or specific inspection or even a specific search. (CPR 31.12) In deciding whether to make such an order the court will take into account all the circumstances, and in particular, the overriding objective, that the means should be proportionate. By the same token, refusal to permit inspection can be based not only as before on the grounds of legal professional privilege (see below) or public interest immunity (see p 90 below), but also on the ground that to permit inspection would be disproportionate. An unsuccessful application will result in an order to pay costs, summarily assessed and payable immediately.

As pre-Woolf, disclosure does not apply in small claims cases. The standard directions on that track merely require each party to supply the court and the other parties with copies of all documents, including experts' reports, to be relied on, not less than 14 days before the hearing and to bring the original documents to the hearing itself.

The main sanction for failing to comply with the disclosure rules is that the party will not be able to rely on the document without permission of the court (CPR 31.21).

NO DISCLOSURE IF LEGAL PROFESSIONAL PRIVILEGE APPLIES

It is important that clients should be able to communicate fully with their legal advisers without fear that these communications will become known to the other side. Legal professional privilege is therefore an exception to the principle of disclosure. It applies equally in criminal proceedings. Where it exists, legal professional privilege is absolute and is therefore not subject to the weighing of competing public interests – *R v Derby Magistrates' Court, ex p B* [1996] AC 487 overruling *Ataou* [1988] 2 All ER 321. In *Ataou* the Court of Appeal had held that the court must undertake a balancing exercise in deciding whether privilege applied where the issue was someone's innocence being established. The House of Lords unanimously held that even in that situation the privilege was absolute. The principle cannot be derogated from, for instance, by provisions in the CPR. (See *General*

Mediterranean Holdings v Patel [2000] 1 WLR 272 where the Divisional Court held that CPR 48.7(3) giving the court power to order the disclosure of a privileged document for the purposes of a wasted costs order was ultra vires.)

Privilege applies to documents prepared for the purposes of getting or giving legal advice whether or not in the context of litigation and to documents prepared with a view to litigation. It covers instructions and briefs to counsel and counsel's opinions.

In *Ventouris v Mountain* , *The Italia Express* [1991] 1 WLR 607, [1991] 3 All ER 472 the Court of Appeal held that privilege did not apply to documents obtained by solicitors for the purposes of preparing for litigation if the documents did not come into existence for the purposes of the litigation.

Normally, if an original document does not have privilege, a photocopy likewise does not have privilege even if the photocopy came into existence for the purpose of seeking legal advice.[40] But if a solicitor has exercised skill and judgment in selecting the document for consideration it may attract privilege.[41]

In *Alfred Crompton Amusement Machines Ltd v Customs and Excise Comrs (No 2)* [1974] AC 405, [1973] 2 All ER 1169, HL, the House of Lords held that privilege does not attach to a communication passing between a party and his non-professional agent or a third party, unless the communication was made after a decision which would lead to solicitors being instructed to start or defend legal proceedings.

Where a document is prepared for a dual purpose, the test of whether it is privileged is what was the dominant purpose. In *Waugh v British Railways Board* [1980] AC 521, [1979] 2 All ER 1169, HL, privilege was denied to a British Railways internal inquiry as to the circumstances of a fatal accident. The report had two purposes–the prevention of accidents for the future and assistance in dealing with the particular claim. The House of Lords held that its dominant purpose was the prevention of accidents and it therefore was not privileged. See similarly *Peach v Metropolitan Comr* [1986] 2 All ER 129.

The privilege is that of the client, and only the client can waive it. It is not lost because the client has died.[42] If, however, a copy of the document has somehow (even through improper means) come into the possession of the other side, evidence of its contents can be given unless the court can be persuaded to grant an injunction against such use on the ground that it would involve breach of confidence. (See *Calcraft v Guest* [1898] 1 QB 759, *Goddard v Nationwide Building Society* [1987] QB 670, [1986] 3 All ER 264; *Guinness Peat Properties Ltd v Fitzroy Robinson Partnership* [1987] 1 WLR 1027, [1987] 2 All ER 716; and *British Coal Corpn v Dennis Rye Ltd (No 2)* [1988] 1 WLR 1113, [1988] 3 All ER 816.) A document also loses its privilege and is therefore

---

[40]   *Sumitomo Corp v Credit Lyonnais Rouse Ltd* [2001] EWCA Civ 1152, [2002] 4 All ER 68 overruling *Dubai Bank Ltd v Galadari (No 7)* [1992] 1 All ER 658.
[41]   *Barclay's Bank plc v Eustice* [1995] 4 All ER 511, CA.
[42]   *Bullivant v AG of Victoria* [1901] AC 196.

disclosable where an expert in his report refers in passing to it after it has been supplied to him by the instructing solicitor as part of the background on which his report is based (*Clough v Tameside and Glossop Health Authority* [1998] 1 WLR 1478, [1998] 2 All ER 971).

In *Re L (a minor)* [1997] AC 16, [1996] 2 All ER 78 the House of Lords held by 3 to 2 that although legal professional privilege was absolute and could not be overridden even in wardship and care proceedings involving children, it did not cover a report by a pathologist prepared in the course of care proceedings at the request of the child's mother which the judge held could be disclosed to the police. There was a clear distinction between the privilege attaching to communications between solicitor and client and that attaching to reports by third parties prepared on the instructions of a client for the purposes of litigation. Litigation privilege had no place in care proceedings which were non-adversarial.

For criticism of the distinction drawn by the majority in *R L (a minor)* between litigation privilege and advice privilege see C Passmore, 'The future of legal professional privilege', *International Journal of Evidence and Proof*, 1999, vol 3, No 2, pp 71-86. Passmore argued that this is not an isolated exception to the general principle. He gave a series of other recent examples in case law and elsewhere, including money laundering legislation (see below) and the 1999 CPR, r 35(10) (an expert's report 'must state the substance of all material instructions, whether written or oral on the basis of which the report was written' and the instructions 'shall not be privileged'). He suggested that the time was ripe for debate as to the extent to which the rules on privilege need refinement to meet new policy objectives based on the principle of 'cards on the table'. See also D A Ipp, 'Lawyers Duties to the Court' (1998) *Law Quarterly Review* 63, 68-76.

In *Three Rivers District Council v Bank of England* [2003] EWCA Civ 474 the Court of Appeal handed down a decision which effectively narrowed the scope of advice privilege. Following the collapse of BCCI, the liquidators were suing the Bank of England for its part in the collapse. The Bank claimed legal professional immunity for documents prepared by bank employees in connection with a Government inquiry by Lord Bingham into the supervision of BCCI under the Banking Act. The Court of Appeal held that the documents only had advice immunity if they were sent to the client – the Bank's Bingham Inquiry Unit (BIU) – and by the client to the inquiry. It therefore did not attach to documents sent to the Bank's solicitors, nor to documents prepared with the dominant purpose of seeking legal advice which were in fact not sent to the solicitors. (The Court also held that the dominant purpose of preparing the documents was not seeking legal advice but presentation of the Bank's case in the most favourable light.)

For critical commentary see D Sandy, 'Privilege, precedent and principle: the perils of *Three Rivers*', 153 *New Law Journal*, 6 June 2003, p 885. The author compared the *Three Rivers* decision unfavourably with that given two months later by the Judicial Committee of the Privy Council in *B v Auckland District Law Society* [2003] UKPC

38. The Privy Council had emphasised that the privilege was a basic and absolute right on which the administration of justice depended and that it was in the public interest that clients should not be deterred from telling the whole truth to their lawyers. The documents for which privilege was claimed by the Bank of England had been brought into existence to give the lawyers a candid account of the story. If such documentation was not privileged it would discourage corporate clients from free and unfettered communication with their lawyers. The author suggested that the Privy Council would have reached a different decision in *Three Rivers* from that of the Court of Appeal and regretted that the House of Lords had refused leave for the Bank to appeal the decision.

It has been held that in the case of expert witnesses, legal professional privilege attaches to confidential communications between the solicitor and the expert, but it does not attach to the chattels or documents on which the expert based his opinion, or to the independent opinion of the expert himself: *Harmony Shipping Co SA v Davis* [1979] 3 All ER 177 at 181. This rule applies to criminal as well as to civil cases. Therefore in a criminal trial the Crown can subpoena as a witness a handwriting expert whom the defence has consulted but does not wish to call as a witness, and is entitled also to production of documents sent to the expert for examination and on which he based his opinion provided they are not covered by legal professional privilege: *R v King* [1983] 1 All ER 929. Lord Justice Dunn said: 'It would be strange if a forger could hide behind a claim of legal professional privilege by the simple device of sending all the incriminating documents in his possession to his solicitors to be examined by an expert' (at 931).

See generally IH Dennis, *The Law of Evidence* (2nd edn, 2002), ch 10.

NO DISCLOSURE IF PUBLIC INTEREST IMMUNITY APPLIES

The second main ground of immunity from disclosure is where it is contrary to the public interest. Such immunity may arise because of the contents of the document or because the document belongs to a class or category which has immunity regardless of its contents.

It is for the courts and not for the executive to determine whether a document has immunity (*Conway v Rimmer* [1968] AC 910).

Before deciding on a claim for public interest immunity the court can call for the actual documents in question and can look at them without showing them to the party applying for access to them. But in *Air Canada v Secretary of State for Trade (No 2)* [1983] 1 All ER 910, the House of Lords held that the court should only do this if the party applying for discovery had shown that the information in the documents was likely to assist his case, in the sense that there was a reasonable probability that it would and not just a mere speculative belief that it would do so. See also *Balfour v Foreign and Commonwealth Office* [1994] 1 WLR 681, [1994] 2 All ER 588 where the

Court of Appeal held that once there was an actual or potential risk to national security demonstrated by an appropriate certificate by a minister the court should not exercise its right to inspect the documents. The Court of Appeal applied the decision of the House of Lords in *Council of Civil Service Unions v Minister for the Civil Service* [1985] AC 374, [1984] 3 All ER 935, arising out of the banning of trades union at GCHQ. See generally N Zaltsman, 'Public Interest Immunity in Civil Proceedings: Protecting the Supply of Information to the Public Authority', *Public Law*, 1984, p 423.

There have been many examples over the years of public interest immunity. In *Alfred Crompton Amusement Machines v Customs and Excise Comrs (No 2)* [1974] AC 405, the House of Lords gave protection to information obtained confidentially by the Crown for the purposes of valuing goods for tax purposes; in *Gaming Board for Great Britain v Rogers* [1973] AC 388, the House of Lords protected confidential inquiries by the Gaming Board from the police as to applicants; in *D v National Society for the Prevention of Cruelty to Children* [1978] AC 171, the House of Lords upheld a claim to avoid disclosure by NSPCC of the name of an informant about child cruelty where the mother wanted to sue the informant or the NSPCC. See also: *Burmah Oil Co Ltd v Bank of England* [1980] AC 1090, [1979] 3 All ER 700, HL in which immunity was granted in relation to documents exchanged between government ministers and the Bank of England regarding the price to be paid by the Treasury for the purchase of Burmah Oil shares. In *Neilson v Laugharne* [1981] 1 All ER 829 and *Makanjuola v Metropolitan Police Comr* [1992] 3 All ER 617, immunity was allowed for statements given to the police in connection with an inquiry into a complaint against the police. But these decisions were overturned by the House of Lords in *R v Chief Constable of the West Midlands Police, ex p Wiley* [1995] 1 AC 274, [1994] 3 All ER 420. The House of Lords held there that a class claim to immunity in such cases was unjustified since it tended to defeat the object it was designed to achieve. By contrast, see *Taylor v Anderton* [1995] 1 WLR 447, [1995] 2 All ER 420, CA.

In *Williams v Home Office* [1981] 1 All ER 1151, immunity was refused to hundreds of pages of internal Home Office documents relating to the establishment of 'control units' in prisons. In *Evans v Chief Constable of Surrey* [1988] QB 588, [1989] 2 All ER 594 the Divisional Court said there could be no disclosure of reports from the police to the DPP about a murder in which the applicant was implicated. In *Re HIV Haemophiliacs, Litigation* [1990] NLJR 1349, the Department of Health was ordered by the Court of Appeal to hand over documents for which public interest immunity had been claimed regarding the plaintiffs' infection with AIDS. The 900 or so plaintiffs had shown a *prima facie* case against the department in negligence and the claim to immunity was overridden by the public interest in the full and fair trial of the plaintiffs' claim. (This decision led to an out-of-court aggregate settlement of £42m for the plaintiffs.)

The doctrine applies also to criminal cases. A spectacular illustration was the so-called Matrix Churchill case in which the trial judge, Judge Smedley, quashed public interest immunity certificates served by the prosecution, designed to suppress evidence about intelligence sources, about information held by the Security Service (MI5) and the Secret Intelligence Service (MI6), and high level inter-departmental and ministerial contact over a licence application to export material for a super-gun to Iraq. The judge's decision led to the collapse of the prosecution against the executives in the machine tool company who had been charged with deception in obtaining export licences. (See A Tomkins, 'Public Interest Immunity after Matrix Churchill', *Public Law*, Winter 1993, pp 650–68. For a detailed account of the case see D Leigh, *Betrayed: The Real Story of the Matrix Churchill Trial* (London, 1993).) It led also to the establishment of the 'arms for Iraq' inquiry by Lord Justice Scott.

Disclosure from someone who is not (or is not yet) a party

NON-PARTIES

Discovery was traditionally only available against the person who was the object of the proceedings. Information or documents in the possession of third parties could normally only be obtained by issuing a subpoena duces tecum requiring them to come to the trial with the documents.

The objection that discovery only applied if proceedings had actually started and only applied to parties was considered by the Winn Committee in 1968. It recommended that discovery by order of the court should be available where a claim in respect of personal injuries or in respect of someone's death was 'likely to be made'. The Administration of Justice Act 1970, s 31, implemented this recommendation, which only applied, however, to actions arising out of personal injuries or death. The power was to be found in s 33 of the Supreme Court Act 1981.

The Winn Committee proposed a second exception to the general rule in regard to claims for damages arising out of personal injuries or death. This was to allow a party to seek an order for discovery against a third party who was holding relevant documents. This recommendation was implemented in s 32 of the Administration of Justice Act 1970 and was to be found in s 34 of the Supreme Court Act 1981, and Ord 24, r 7A.

Lord Woolf proposed that pre-action disclosure both from likely parties and from non-parties should be extended to all cases and the Civil Procedure Act 1997, s 8[43] gave effect to this recommendation. (See CPR, rr 31.16 and 31.17.)

It is not necessary to establish on a balance of probabilities that the evidence will support the applicant's case or undermine the opponent's case – only that it may well do so.[44]

---

[43]   And Civil Procedure (Modification of Enactments) Order 1998, SI 1998/2940.
[44]   *Three Rivers District Council v Bank of England (No 4)* [2002] EWCA Civ 1182, [2002] 4 All ER 881.

Medical records

The Access to Health Records Act 1990 established a right for a patient, or someone authorised to apply on his behalf, to get medical records created after November 1990. Note also the Data Protection Act 1984 which gave a person a right of access to information about him which is held in computerised form. But the right to get data on computer is qualified by secondary legislation which states that there is no right to inspect a health record if access would be likely to cause serious harm to the physical or mental health of the applicant or would be likely to disclose another person's identity. (Data Protection (Subject Access Modification) (Health) Order 1987, SI 1987/1903.)

The pre-action protocols on personal injury claims and medical negligence claims (pp 61-63 above) had a wider provision for access to medical records. ('It is Department of Health policy that patients be permitted to see what has been written about them, and that healthcare providers should make arrangements to allow patients to see all their records, not only those covered by the Access to Health Records Act 1990.') Use of the forms was said to be entirely voluntary and did not prejudice any statutory rights. The aim was 'to save time and costs for all concerned for the benefit of the patient and the hospital and in the interests of justice. Use of the forms should make it unnecessary in most cases for there to be an exchange of letters or other enquiries.' (PD, Annex B.)

The Data Protection Act 1998, which came into force in 1999, replaced the Access to Health Records Act 1990. It broadly made similar access provisions – though s 8(2)(a) provides a new exemption where supply of the information would involve 'disproportionate effort'.

Disclosure from a third party to correct wrongdoing (the Norwich Pharmacal principle)

The courts developed a further exception to the general rule, under which discovery could be ordered against a third party who has information which is needed to deal with wrongdoing. Thus in *Norwich Pharmacal Co v Customs and Excise Comrs* [1974] AC 133, the House of Lords held that the Customs authorities had to disclose the names of persons importing materials allegedly in breach of the plaintiff's patent because dishonest traders did not deserve protection. Lord Reid said (at p 175) that 'if through no fault of his own a person gets mixed up in the tortious acts of others so as to facilitate their wrongdoing he may incur no personal liability but he comes under a duty to assist the person who has been wronged by giving him full information and disclosing the identity of the wrongdoer'. The same principle was applied by the House of Lords in *British Steel Corpn v Granada Television Ltd* [1981] AC 1096, to order Granada to hand over to British Steel the name of the 'mole' who had passed it confidential documents relating to the company's handling of the steel strike. Granada, like the Customs in Norwich Pharmacal, was an innocent third party, but the courts ordered discovery in order to permit the plaintiff to get a remedy in regard to wrongdoing.

The same doctrine was applied in *Bankers Trust Co v Shapira* [1980] 1 WLR 1274, [1980] 3 All ER 353, when the court ordered a bank to reveal the details of a customer's account in order to give effect to a defrauded plaintiff's equitable right to trace his money. (By contrast, see *Arab Monetary Fund v Hashim (No 5)* [1992] 2 All ER 911– disclosure by non-party not ordered because potential benefit was outweighed by detriment.)

Where the power to order such disclosure concerns the press it raises the issue of freedom of expression protected by s 10 of the Contempt of Court Act 1981 and Art 10 of the European Convention on Human Rights. In *Ashworth Hospital Authority v MGN Ltd* [2002] UKHL 29, [2002] 1 WLR 2033, [2002] 4 All ER 193 the House of Lords upheld the Court of Appeal's decision ordering the *Daily Mail* to reveal to the hospital the name of the person who supplied a journalist with information about the notorious 'Moors murderer' Ian Brady. The law lords concluded that it did not matter if the wrongdoing was tortious or in breach of contract. In the Court of Appeal Lord Woolf went further in suggesting, obiter (para 53) that it may extend to criminal wrongdoing – but this conflicts with the Court of Appeal's ruling in *Interbrew SA v Financial Times* [2002] EWCA Civ 274, [2002] 2 Lloyd's Rep 229 in which five media organisations were ordered to hand over to the company a leaked document about a contemplated take-over. In *Interbrew* the Court of Appeal said that if the purpose of the leak was to bring wrongdoing to public notice it would deserve a high degree of protection. But if the purpose was to wreck legitimate commercial activity it would be less deserving of protection. These two cases also establish that a *Norwich Pharmacal* order can be made even where the applicant does not intend to pursue court action against the wrongdoer. (See M Amos, 'A storm brewing' , *New Law Journal*, 9 August 2002, p 1230.)

In *X v Y* [1988] 2 All ER 648 the court refused to order a reporter to disclose the source of his story as a fine for contempt of court on the paper and a permanent injunction stopping the paper publishing the information was sufficient. In *Goodwin* both the Court of Appeal and the House of Lords held that a journalist had to pay a fine of £5,000 for contempt of court for refusing to disclose the source of an article. But the Strasbourg court held that this constituted a violation of Article 10 of the Convention. The interests of a democratic country in having a free press outweighed the company's interest in tracking down the source of the leak to the journalist.[45]

THE 'MERE WITNESS' RULE

The person against whom the order is made must somehow be involved. It would not be possible under the *Norwich Pharmacal* doctrine, for instance, to order a passer-by

---

[45] *Goodwin v United Kingdom* (1996) 22 EHRR 123.

who saw a road accident to reveal the name prior to the hearing of the action. He would be a 'mere witness'. This rule was prayed in aid in *Harrington v North London Polytechnic* [1984] 3 All ER 666, by lecturers at the polytechnic who had been ordered by the court to disclose the names of picketing students. The action was brought by Patrick Harrington, a member of the National Front, after he had been prevented from pursuing his studies by other students who objected to his presence. He obtained an injunction against the polytechnic, but when the injunction was ignored by picketing students, Harrington asked for a further order requiring certain teachers to identify persons in photographs taken of the picketing. The lecturers claimed they were not parties to the action and that they should be protected from the order by the 'mere witness' rule. They also said that an order against them would be contrary to public policy since it would damage the special relationship between staff and students. The Court of Appeal held that they were not 'mere witnesses'. In fact they were not witnesses at all since they had not been present at the time of the picketing. They could be made subject to such an order as employees of the polytechnic. But since they had not been given a chance to put their argument, the case was sent back to the High Court for proper argument on the public-policy aspects.

Subsequent use of disclosed document

The rule used to be that disclosure was made subject to an undertaking that the document disclosed would not be used for any 'improper, collateral or ulterior purpose'. (RSC Order 24, r 14A.) This has now been replaced by CPR 31.22 which states that a document that has been disclosed may only be used for the purpose of the proceedings in which it is disclosed except where '(a) the document has been read to or by the court, or referred to, at a hearing which has been held in public; (b) the court gives permission; or (c) the party who disclosed the document and the person to whom the document belongs agree'. Even where a document has been read by or to the court or referred to at a public hearing, the court can make an order restricting or prohibiting its use. (CPR 31.22(2)). Documents read by the judge out of court before the hearing on which he based his decision were held to be documents referred to at a hearing held in public – see *SmithKline Beecham Biologicals SA v Connaught Laboratories Inc* [1999] 4 All ER 498, CA, a decision under former RSC Ord 24, r 14A.

For considerations material to an order maintaining confidentiality after the trial has finished see *Lily Icos v Pfiza Ltd (No 2)* [2002] EWCA Civ 2, [2002] 1 WLR 2253.

See also SMC Gibbons, 'Protecting documents disclosed under pre-action protocols against subsequent use', 21 *Civil Justice Quarterly*, 2002, pp 254-70.

5. Getting evidence from witnesses

The first question addressed is whether there are any rules that inhibit a party to litigation or his lawyers from approaching a potential witness and whether there are any procedures for compelling such a person to give a statement.

There is no property in a witness

The formal position is that since 'there is no property in a witness' one can approach anyone and ask for a statement about the matter in issue. But the person approached is not under an obligation to cooperate. If he is from the opponent's camp, he will almost certainly decline – and, in the improbable event that he might be willing to give a statement, the opponent's lawyers would advise him not to do so. Even the neutral witness may decline, whether because he has already given a statement to the other side, or because he simply does not feel like it or for any other reason. There is no procedure that can compel the potential witness to give a statement. He can of course be compelled to give evidence at the trial by serving him with a *subpoena*. But no sensible lawyer would call a witness at the trial unless he had previously found out what the witness was going to say. So that is not a practical option. The rule that there is no property in a witness is set out in the Law Society's *Guide to the Professional Conduct of Solicitors* (online version May 2003 – www.lawsociety.org.uk):

21.10 Interviewing witnesses Principle

It is permissible for a solicitor acting for any party to interview and take statements from any witness or prospective witness at any stage in the proceedings, whether or not that witness has been interviewed or called as a witness by another party.

1. Principle 21.10 stems from the fact that there is no property in a witness and applies both before and after the witness has given evidence at the hearing.

2. A solicitor must not, of course, tamper with the evidence of a witness or attempt to suborn the witness into changing evidence. Once a witness has given evidence, the case must be very unusual in which a solicitor acting for the other side needs to interview that witness without seeking to persuade the witness to change evidence ... .

3. A solicitor should be aware that in seeking to exercise the right to interview a witness who has already been called by the other side or who to the solicitor's knowledge is likely to be called by them, the solicitor may well be exposed to the suggestion that he or she has improperly tampered with the evidence. This may be so particularly where the witness subsequently changes his or her evidence.

4. In order to avoid allegations of tampering with evidence it is wise in these circumstances for such solicitor to offer to interview the witness in the presence of a representative of the other side. If this is not possible, a solicitor may record the interview, ask the witness to bring a representative, and ask the witness to sign an additional statement to the effect that the witness has freely attended the interview and has not been coerced into giving the statement or changing his or her evidence.

In practice, in civil cases solicitors are very chary about even approaching a witness associated with the other side for fear of running foul of the prohibition on tampering with the evidence. By contrast in criminal cases, both the prosecution and the defence may find it necessary to interview the same witnesses. It was held to have been contempt of court for the police deliberately to impede inquiries by a private investigator working for the defence who was trying to find potential alibi witnesses in a murder case. The accused's alibi was that he stayed overnight at a hostel with three 'travellers' known to him only by their first names. The police had asked the hostel management to ensure that the hostel staff not talk to the investigator (*Connolly v Dale* [1996] QB 120).

The rule that there is no property in a witness applies also to expert witnesses. This was established by the Court of Appeal in *Harmony Shipping Co SA v Davis* [1979] 3 All ER 177. The plaintiffs in an action approached a handwriting expert to advise on the authenticity of a document the genuineness of which was crucial to their case. The expert advised that the document was not genuine. Subsequently he was approached for advice by the other side. Not realising that he had already advised the plaintiffs in the same case, he advised the defendants that the document was not genuine. Later he realised what had happened and told the defendants that he could not accept any further instructions in the matter from them. The defendants, who wanted him to testify as to the genuineness of the document, issued a subpoena requiring him to attend to give evidence. The plaintiffs tried to have the subpoena set aside on the ground that there was an express or implied contract that the expert would not advise both sides and that the defendants were therefore not able to call him.

The Court of Appeal unanimously rejected this contention. The court held that the rule that there was no property in a witness applied to experts as much as to witnesses of fact. The only difference was that an expert could not be required to give evidence about matters that were covered by legal professional privilege. Insofar as he had been told things in confidence by the solicitors, such information was privileged and could not be made the subject of testimony. But anything not covered by legal professional privilege was available to the defendants in the case as much as to the plaintiffs. (See also *Re L* [1996] 2 All ER 78, HL.)

In the United States, there is a procedure to permit a party to take a pre-trial statement from a potential witness and the rule that there is no property in a witness therefore has much more meaning there. Each party can require not only the other party but also anyone with knowledge of relevant facts to answer questions in an oral examination called 'taking a deposition' in regard to those facts and to produce all relevant documents. Any party may take the testimony of such a person either by way of oral examination or written interrogatories. Under the Federal Rules of Civil Procedure a witness, including a party, must give names, addresses and other details of all witnesses known to him. If the pre-trial examination of a witness is oral, his testimony can be used to impeach the witness (for example, to challenge the evidence that he gives at trial). For an evaluation of the pros and cons of this procedure see Geoffrey Bindman, 'Another Kind of Discovery', *Law Guardian*, May 1965. For a graphic illustration of the American system in action, see Richard Rashke, *The Killing of Karen Silkwood* (Sphere Books, 1983). The book, which was the basis of a film starring Meryl Streep, describes the case brought by Miss Silkwood's estate against her employers, alleging that her death was due to its negligence in regard to contamination by plutonium. Most of the inquiries made by the lawyers were pursued through the means of pre-trial depositions. In the end there were over 6,000 pages of such depositions. The case ended with a verdict awarding damages of $10 million. It is difficult to imagine that the case could have had a successful outcome in England, where there is no equivalent procedure permitting a party to require a potential witness of fact to answer questions pre-trial.

Interim remedies

The Civil Procedure Rules, like the old rules, provide for a variety of interim remedies that can be obtained before the hearing of the case. CPR 25(1) lists 19 different kinds of interim remedies, of which perhaps the best known is the interim injunction. They include interim declarations, orders for the inspection of, or the preservation of relevant property or for information to be provided. The procedure for obtaining an interim remedy is dealt with in CPR, Part 25. (It provides for application by telephone in urgent cases – though this facility is not available to litigants in person, only to lawyers! (PD 25, para 4.5(5)).)

Special rules apply to two particularly formidable interim remedies – for freezing assets and for searching premises. (They have been described as the 'two nuclear weapons of the law'). Because of their fearsome character they can only be granted by High Court judges or 'any other judge duly authorised'. (PD 25, para 1.1)

A *'freezing order' (formerly called Mareva injunction)* prevents the other party from transferring his assets abroad or disposing of them so as to defeat the plaintiff's hope of satisfying any judgment he may ultimately win. The power derives from a 1975 case, *Mareva Cia Naviera SA v International Bulkcarriers SA* [1980] 1 All ER 213n, [1975] 2 Lloyd's Rep 509, CA. The Court of Appeal held that an injunction to prevent assets from being removed could be granted in any case in which the court thought it to be just or convenient. (See especially, *Third Chandris Shipping Corpn v Unimarine SA* [1979] QB 645, 668–9; *The Siskina* [1979] AC 210, 261; *Barclay-Johnson v Yuill* [1980] 1 WLR 1259.) The new jurisdiction was recognised in the Supreme Court Act 1981, s 37, which made it clear that such orders can be made regardless of whether the subject of the order is domiciled, resident or even merely present within the jurisdiction.

Section 37(1) of the 1981 Act empowered the High Court to grant an injunction in all cases in which it appears to the court to be just and convenient to do so. Section 37(3) extended that power to restraining a party to any proceedings from 'dealing with' assets within the jurisdiction. 'Dealing with' includes disposing of, selling, pledging or charging an asset. The order in effect freezes the assets pending the outcome of the proceedings. It has been held that such an order can apply to assets worldwide: *Derby & Co Ltd v Weldon (No 2)* [1989] 1 All ER 1002, CA, but that such worldwide orders should be granted only in exceptional circumstances: *Republic of Haiti v Duvalier* [1990] 1 QB 202, CA.

Usually the order only relates to the amount of the claim–leaving the defendant free to use the rest of his assets. The defendant must be left enough to meet his reasonable living expenses and to meet certain debts (*PCW (Underwriting Agencies) Ltd v Dixon* [1983] 2 All ER 697). The defendant must also normally be allowed to make payments in the ordinary course of business conducted in good faith (*Iraqi Ministry of Defence v Arcepey Shipping Co SA* [1981] QB 65n).

Mareva injunctions became very popular. (In a case in 1986, Bingham J said that such applications had become 'commonplace, hundreds being made each year and relatively few refused'.[46])

The procedure is dealt with in the Practice Direction for CPR Part 25.

'Search order' (formerly called Anton Piller Order) *The other draconian order* originally *developed by the courts in* the 1970s was *the Anton Piller order*,[47] which permits the plaintiff to enter the defendant's premises to search for evidence. (The court's jurisdiction to make the order was put onto a statutory basis by the Civil Procedure Act 1997, s 7.)

The application is made without notice (previously *ex parte*) to the defendant and is generally heard *in camera* so as not to alert the other side to the application and thus risk that the material may be destroyed.

Search orders are governed by CPR 25.1(1)(h) and the Practice Direction accompanying Part 25. The plaintiff must satisfy the court that he has a very strong *prima facie* case on the merits, that he is likely to suffer very serious actual or potential damage from the defendant's actions, and that there is clear evidence that the defendant has incriminating material on his premises which he would be likely to destroy if no order were made. If the court is satisfied that the effect of such an order would not be excessive or out of proportion, it may order the defendant to permit the plaintiff to enter his premises, to search for goods or documents which are relevant to his claim and to remove, inspect, photograph or make copies of such material.

---

[46] *Siporex Trade SA v Comdel Commodities Ltd* [1986] 2 Lloyd's Rep 428 at 539.

[47] The name derived from the decision which initiated this development–*Anton Piller KG v Manufacturing Processes Ltd* [1976] 1 All ER 779, CA. The plaintiffs there wanted to restrain a breach of copyright by a rival firm. They feared that if the defendants knew, they would destroy the documents showing their guilt. They therefore applied for an *ex parte* order, which was granted. The Court of Appeal held that such an order should, however, only be made in an extreme case where there was grave danger of property being smuggled away or vital evidence destroyed.

The plaintiff has to give an undertaking that he will pay the defendant damages if a judge should later hold that damages ought to be paid because of the way the order was executed. The order must be precise. It should be enforced with circumspection and the claimant's solicitor being an officer of the court should be present. The defendant must be allowed to contact his solicitor and, unlike the police with a search warrant, if the defendant refuses entry, the claimant is not entitled to use force. But the defendant may find himself liable to proceedings, including committal to prison, for contempt of court.[48] The procedural requirements set out in *Universal Thermosensors* are now included in the Practice Direction to CPR, Part 25 of which deals at length with search orders. In particular, it requires that there always be a Supervising Solicitor to supervise the actual entry. (For a detailed appreciation of the importance of this institution by someone who had performed the role 20-30 times see Tony Willoughby, 'The role of the Supervising Solicitor', 18 *Civil Justice Quarterly*, April 1999, pp 103-12.)

A variety of other safeguards are covered in the Practice Direction: (1) execution should be on working days in office hours so that the defendant can get legal advice if he wishes to have it; (2) where the supervising solicitor is a man and the respondent is likely to be an unaccompanied woman, he must be accompanied by a woman; (3) unless it is impracticable, a detailed list of what is taken away must be prepared on the premises and the defendant must be given an opportunity to check the list before anything is removed.

The Supreme Court Act 1981, s 72 cancelled the privilege against self-incrimination in the context of proceedings for infringement of intellectual property (patents, trade marks, copyright etc) but provided that answers given or documents handed over cannot be used in subsequent criminal proceedings. A search order in such cases is therefore not covered by the privilege. A Consultation Paper issued by the LCD in 1992 (*The Privilege against Self-incrimination in Civil Proceedings*) recommended that the privilege should no longer apply in civil proceedings generally but this recommendation was not acted upon.

The 'search' (Anton Piller) order and the 'freezing order' (Mareva injunction) were developed primarily in intellectual property, passing off and other commercial matters. Anton Piller orders were often sought by employers against ex-employees to prevent them using confidential information such as customers' lists, price lists

---

48   For pre-CPR cases see especially *Rank Film Distributors Ltd v Video Information Centre* [1982] AC 380; *Vapormatic Co Ltd v Sparex Ltd* [1976] 1 WLR 939; *Yousif v Salama* [1980] 1 WLR 1540. In *Columbia Picture Industries Inc v Robinson* [1986] 3 All ER 338 it was held that the order had been carried out in an oppressive manner by the plaintiff's solicitors. The court ordered them to pay the defendant damages of £7,500, plus £2,500 for his company. For discussion and comment, see *Civil Justice Quarterly*, January 1987, p 10. See generally Anne Staines, 'The Protection of Intellectual Property Rights: Anton Piller Orders', 46 *Modern Law Review*, 1983, p 274 and M Dockray and H Laddie, 'Piller Problems' (1990) *Law Quarterly Review* 601. See also the strong decision of the Vice Chancellor in *Universal Thermosensors Ltd v Hibben* [1992] 3 All ER 257.

etc. They can be used equally in matrimonial proceedings. Thus in *Emanuel v Emanuel* (1982) 12 Fam Law 62 an Anton Piller order was granted to enable a wife to search at her former husband's home for documents which he had unreasonably refused to produce in regard to his income.

Stopping the defendant leaving the country In *Bayer AG v Winter* [1986] 1 All ER 733, the Court of Appeal held that in support of a Mareva injunction and Anton Piller order the court could also give further relief in the form of a requirement that the defendant hand in his passport and an order that he not leave the country.

Obtaining advance notice of one's opponent's witnesses and of their evidence

Traditionally there was no procedure to enable one party to obtain the names of his opponent's witnesses, let alone their statements, and there was equally no procedure for oral examination of the other side's witnesses in advance of the trial. But in this area there have been some dramatic changes which completely transformed English pre-trial procedure.

The Winn Committee in 1968 considered but rejected the proposal for compulsory exchange of witness statements (called 'proofs') and for pre-trial examination of the other side's witnesses. In regard to the suggestion that proofs of witnesses should be exchanged the Committee said simply: 'We do not think the time has yet come, if it ever will, when this fundamental change should be recommended'.[49] There was no further treatment of the subject nor any discussion of what made the suggestion inappropriate.

In regard to the suggestion that names of witnesses should be exchanged together with their addresses, the Committee said: 'we equally think that this should not take place. Foreign jurisdictions seem to be equally divided in relation to the exchanging of names of witnesses. Except in some American States the strong tendency of countries operating in a common law atmosphere is against exchange' (para 370). Again there was no further argument. In relation to the suggestion that the other side's witnesses should be examinable by some form of pre-trial examination, the Committee said this would so complicate, delay and increase the cost of litigation that it should be rejected (para 355).

But although the Winn Committee in 1968 was against a general principle of exchange of witness statements it did favour *some* exchange. It described the traditional approach to litigation as one of 'trial by ambush':

> Our present procedures ... adopt the adversary system as 'trial by ambush'. The courtroom resembles an arena. It is regarded as good tactics to keep the other side in the dark so far as it is possible, and if one party can spring a surprise

[49]　*Report of the Committee on Personal Injuries Litigation*, 1968, Cmnd 369, para 368.

upon the other, then an advantage has been obtained by which such party may profit [para 131].

Revolution in the rules for the exchange of evidence

The Winn Committee recommended that medical evidence be subject to a rule of exchange, and that where such exchange had been ordered, no medical evidence should be admitted at the trial unless its substance had been exchanged in advance. This recommendation became the basis of the rapid change in English procedure which resulted in new rules requiring each side in civil cases, save in exceptional circumstances, to give to the other pre-trial the statements of *any* witness they intend to call. Failure to comply normally results in not being permitted to call that witness at the trial. (For a detailed account of the successive stages of this reform process see a note in 12 *Civil Justice Quarterly*, 1993, pp 5–8 and the Note in 14 *Civil Justice Quarterly*, 1995, pp 228–30.)

By the time that Lord Woolf started his inquiry, pre-trial disclosure of statements of both expert witnesses (RSC Ord 38, rr 36, 37) and non-expert witnesses (RSC Ord 38, r 2A) had been mandatory in the High Court for several years. Indeed, the matter had gone further still in that the witness statement was normally used not merely pre-trial, but stood as the witness' evidence at the trial itself. That rule was promulgated in January 1995 by the Lord Chief Justice and the Vice Chancellor in a *Practice Note* ([1995] 1 All ER 385) stating: 'Unless otherwise ordered, every witness statement shall stand as the evidence-in-chief of the witness concerned'. This is equally stated to be the position in the new Civil Procedure Rules – see CPR, rr 32.4(2), 32.5(2).

In a matter of 10 years or so therefore the English system had gone from the position where witness statements were never available before trial to a position where they are virtually always available–and indeed normally constitute that party's evidence-in-chief at trial.

There are however exceptional situations where exchange will not be ordered. In *Richard Saunders & Partners v Eastglen Ltd* [1990] 3 All ER 946 it was held that an order would not be made under Ord 38, r 2A, where fraud was alleged and it might be necessary to preserve an element of surprise, or where exchange would be oppressive because there would be great difficulty or expense in obtaining a statement, or where the application is made too late and the preparation of witness statements at that stage would add to rather than save costs. In *McGuinness v Kellogg Co of Great Britain Ltd* [1988] 2 All ER 902 the Court of Appeal approved a decision to allow the defendants to show a video of the plaintiff made by the insurance company's inquiry agent in a personal injuries case–without first disclosing it pre-trial to the plaintiff or his advisers. But the Court of Appeal took the opposite view in a later similar case *Khan v Armaguard Ltd* [1994] 3 All ER 545 on the ground that it was precisely in cases where video evidence exposed the plaintiff's fraud that pre-trial disclosure was appropriate.

HAS THE EXCHANGE OF WITNESS STATEMENTS PROVED BENEFICIAL?

The exchange of witness statements was introduced as a way of improving the process of civil litigation but to some critics it has made matters worse. A county court judge, Judge Nicholas Brandt, published a letter to Lord Woolf in March 1995 in which he said: 'Exchange of witness statements was thought to promote settlements, and, in default, to speed up trials, thereby reducing expense. Experience has demonstrated the futility of these aspirations. The overwhelming majority of cases (about 97%) settle anyway and there is no evidence that this device has increased the percentage. There is overwhelming evidence that the preparation of these statements has turned into a cottage industry. I have talked to members of the Bar who cheerfully confess to spending hours drafting these documents. *Cui bono?*–not the litigant. Incidentally, some are badly drafted, containing much irrelevance and hearsay, leading to applications to strike out and more expense.' ('Some serious thoughts from Essex on civil justice', *New Law Journal*, 10 March 1995, p 350.) For a wide-ranging critique of the cost and delays inherent in the modern insistence on 'cards on the table'– discovery, witness statements, interrogatories, pleadings etc–see A Jack, 'Radical Surgery for Civil Procedure', *New Law Journal*, 18 June 1993, p 891. For similar views, expressed by a member of the Bar, see Anthony Speaight, 'A Bonfire of the Paper Mountain', *Counsel*, November/December 1994, p 4. Speaight suggested that witness statements gave a significant advantage to the wealthier litigant. If they stand as the witness' evidence-in-chief, the ascertainment of the truth becomes more difficult because the judge no longer has the opportunity of seeing the witness telling his story in his own words. The cost of trials had been considerably increased.

In the same issue of the Bar's journal *Counsel*, Fiona Bawdon said that witness statements had taken on a significance undreamed of hitherto–'witness statements are getting longer and longer, and lawyers are spending hours and hours working on them with their clients'. In many cases they became not so much witness statements as lawyers' statements. She quoted a leading commercial QC: 'The lawyer knows what has to be proved. It is lawyers' language which is used.' As a result of statements currently being so finely crafted, the potential for injustice increased. 'You are effectively manufacturing evidence.' On abuse of witness statements see also *ZYX Music GmbH v King* [1995] 3 All ER 1, per Lightman J and the note on the case in 14 *Civil Justice Quarterly*, October 1995, p 228.

Lord Woolf, in his Interim Report, said that his Inquiry had received 'a considerable volume of information indicating that the exchange of statements is not proving as beneficial as had been intended' (p 176, para 6). 'At a meeting of the Commercial Court Users' Committee on 1 February 1995, there was general agreement that it was having a devastating effect on costs. This was because statements were being treated by the parties as documents which had to be as precise as pleadings and which went through many drafts' (ibid). A Commercial judge said that 'an enormous amount of time is now spent by lawyers ironing and massaging witness statements; that is extremely expensive for clients, and the statements can bear very little relation to what a witness of fact would say' (op cit para 7). A leading QC said that in a case of his, £100,000 had been expended in preparing witness statements.

Lord Woolf concluded (p 176, para 9): 'There is justification for the concerns which are being expressed about the results of requiring witness statements to be exchanged. The problem is primarily in relation to the heavier litigation. Nonetheless, it does spread to more modest litigation and it needs to be addressed.' He nevertheless firmly endorsed the practice of requiring the exchange of witness statements as a way of ensuring that the parties are aware before the trial of the strengths and weaknesses of the case they have to meet. 'The sooner a party is aware of this, the more likely it is that the outcome of the dispute will be a just one, whether it is settled or tried' (p 177, para 10).

But the excesses should be eliminated. The new industry devoted to the creation of witness statements would be more likely to wither, Lord Woolf suggested, if the courts adopted a more relaxed attitude to the statements: 'If it is generally understood that a witness will be allowed to develop points already referred to in a witness statement, most of the benefits which are to be derived from the exchange of witness statements should still be achieved, but without the need for exhaustive drafting intended to achieve pedantic accuracy' (p 178, para 13). (To that end, the new rules state that a witness giving oral evidence may with the permission of the court 'amplify his witness statement' and also 'give evidence in relation to new matters that have arisen since the witness statement was served on the other parties' (CPR 32.5(3)).) Lord Woolf concluded this section with a hope repeated several times in his Interim Report: 'In the case of witness statements ... the solution to the present problem will depend on practitioners behaving in a sensible and co-operative way. If the court is prepared to adopt a more flexible attitude, the parties and their advisers will need to respond by adopting a more sensible approach to the preparation of witness statements. If they do not, the court must make it clear that they will bear the cost'(p 179, para 21).

A remarkable further proposal in Lord Woolf's Interim Report was that cross-examination on the contents of witness statements should only be allowed with the leave of the judge. 'Such leave should not be given for cross-examination in detail. Nor should it usually be necessary even when a more significant feature is relied upon. The advocate's comment will be all that the judge will usually require'! (p 179, para 18.) This proved too radical. In the new rules the proposal that cross-examination should require the permission of the court was adopted for hearings other than a trial but was not adopted for the trial itself (CPR 32.7).

WHO CAN INSPECT THE WITNESS STATEMENTS?

CPR 32.13(1) provides that a witness statement that stands as evidence-in-chief is open to inspection 'during the course of the trial' unless the court otherwise orders.

Anyone can ask for a direction that a witness statement is not open to inspection (CPR 32.13(2)). But the court will not give such a direction unless it thinks it should because of the interests of justice, the public interest, the nature of expert medical evidence, the nature of any confidential information in the statement, or the need to protect the interests of a child or patient. (CPR 32.13(3)).

Under the former rules[50] the presumption was that witness statements were not open to inspection but anyone, such as a media representative, could ask for a direction permitting inspection. If granted, such inspection could take place both during the trial and beyond the end of the trial. The presumption is now reversed but the time for inspection appears to be restricted to the trial. The White Book suggests that presumably an interested person could apply for a direction that inspection be permitted after the end of the trial.[51]

The expert witness in the pre-trial process

As has been seen, the pre-Woolf rules required the parties to exchange the reports and statements of the experts on whom they intend to rely at the trial. In his Interim Report Lord Woolf said that the subject of expert evidence had caused his Inquiry much concern. Concern had been expressed in particular that the need to engage experts was 'a source of excessive expense, delay and in some cases, increased complexity through the excessive or inappropriate use of experts' (p 181, para 1). Concern had also been expressed regarding a lack of independence of experts.

Most of the problems with expert evidence arose because the expert was initially recruited as part of the team and then had to change roles and seek to provide the independent expert evidence which the court was entitled to expect. The judges often exercised their power to ask the experts to meet to try to agree. But this did not seem to deal with the problem of the partisan approach of the respective experts. Before such meetings, the experts were quite often instructed by their respective parties not to agree to anything. Alternatively they were told that anything agreed between the experts had to be referred back to the lawyers for ratification.

Lord Woolf cited an editorial in the Bar's journal *Counsel* in November/December 1994 which said that expert witnesses today were 'hired guns'. There was, it suggested, a 'new breed of litigation hangers on, whose main expertise is to craft reports which will conceal anything that might be to the disadvantage of their clients'. The disclosure of expert reports 'which originally seemed eminently sensible, has degenerated into a costly second tier of written advocacy'. This 'deplorable development' had been unwittingly encouraged by a generation of judges who wanted to read experts' reports before coming into court, and by practice directions stipulating that the reports be lodged in court to enable them to do so.

Waiting for experts' reports, Lord Woolf said, was also a cause of much delay. It was not uncommon for six to nine months to elapse between a request for a report and its delivery (p 184, para 12).

---

[50] RSC Ord 38, r 2A(12) to (16) and CCR Ord 20, r 12A(12) to (16).
[51] *Civil Procedure*, 2003, p 754.

This unhappy situation had become institutionalised. Lawyers repeatedly instructed a limited class of consultants for reports. There was a serious shortage of suitable experts. The best doctors tended also to be the busiest.

Lord Woolf proposed various changes that would address these issues:

(1) In multi track cases the judge at the initial case management conference would distil the issues from the parties' statements of case and, if necessary, would decide what expert evidence was needed on each issue. The key issues should then be narrowed through exchange of experts' reports and through meetings of experts, so that only areas of disagreement would have to be decided by the court (p 185, para 18).

(2) In some cases the court should appoint an independent expert. There was already power to do so under RSC Ord 40 on application by either party–a power that was hardly ever used. Parties did not like it because the cost was in addition to their own experts and they did not trust the court expert. Lord Woolf said these were real concerns, but 'as long as they are borne in mind, there will be cases where it will be the best course to appoint an independent expert' (p 186, para 22). If the parties could not agree on the appropriate independent expert, the relevant professional body could be asked to make the appointment.

(3) Rules of court should permit the court to appoint an independent expert of its own motion and to limit the parties' power to call any expert save under the direction of the court (p 187, para 23). This would not however prevent the parties from having their own expert to guide them, especially in regard to cross-examination of any other expert who gave evidence. The additional cost of the neutral expert would usually be justified 'by helping to achieve a settlement, or in the assistance he will provide to the judge' (ibid).

In complex litigation the court could sometimes be assisted by the appointment of an assessor, as already happened in the Admiralty Court (p 187, para 24).

There should be a wide power for the court of its own motion to refer issues to experts either for determination or report.

(4) All experts should address their reports to the court. Any instructions they received from the party employing them should be disclosed in the report. The report should end by a declaration that it included everything the expert regarded as relevant (p 188, para 27).

(5) If experts met at the direction of the court it should be understood that they were under a duty if possible to reach any agreement that was appropriate. If they could not do so they should specify the reasons. It should be unprofessional conduct for an expert to accept instructions not to reach agreement at such a meeting. Once an expert had been instructed to prepare a report for use of the court, any communications between the expert and the client or his advisers should no longer be privileged (p 188, para 28).

(6) No subpoena for attendance of a medical expert should be issued without leave of the procedural judge (p 189, para 29).

(7) In fast track cases, because the timetable was very tight and trial would be limited to [three] hours, it would be necessary for the court to be able to resolve expert issues without oral evidence. In order to achieve that the court should choose from among the following options–(a) the joint appointment of an expert at the outset, chosen, if possible by the parties, if not by the court; failing that no more than one expert per side; (b) separate reports from the experts with the court deciding the issue on the basis of the reports plus argument by counsel; or (c) the reference of the issue to an expert to determine or report when the expert would communicate with experts appointed by the parties before coming to his conclusion (pp 189–90, para 32).

In his Final Report Lord Woolf devoted 15 pages to the problem of expert evidence. He said that there had been widespread agreement with his criticisms of the way in which expert evidence was used. But his specific proposals had 'provoked more opposition than any of [his] other recommendations' (p 137, para 5). Most respondents favoured the retention of the full-scale adversarial use of expert evidence and resisted proposals for wider use of single experts ('the idea is anathema to many members of the legal profession', p 140, para 16) and for disclosure of communications between experts and their instructing lawyers.

The basic premise of his approach, he said, was that the expert's function was to assist the court. He did not recommend a court-appointed expert or a single expert for every case. The court should have a range of options. The appointment of a single expert 'would not necessarily deprive the parties of the right to cross-examine, or even to call their own experts in addition to the neutral expert if that were justified by the scale of the case'. (p 141, para 17)[52]

Lord Woolf admitted that, given the strength of opposition to his proposals, 'it would not be realistic to expect a significant shift towards single experts in the short term' (p 141, para 20). But it was possible to initiate a shift in that direction. The rules should specify that as a general principle single experts should be used where the issue concerned an established area of knowledge and where it was not necessary to sample a range of opinions. Where two experts were appointed they should if possible write a joint report. Expert reports should contain the contents of all written and oral instructions.

The new rules In the rules, expert evidence is treated in Part 35. Rule 35.3 states that 'It is the duty of an expert to help the court' and 'this duty overrides any obligation' to those instructing him. (For cases illustrating the point see J Hughes, 'Expert evidence: three key lessons from recent case law', *New Law Journal* (Expert Witness Supplement) 28 February 2003, p 291.) No expert may be called and no expert evidence may be put in evidence without the court's permission. (CPR 35.4) The

---

52   In *Daniels v Walker* [2000] 1 WLR 1382 the Court of Appeal (including Lord Woolf) held that the fact that a joint expert had been instructed did not preclude a party who was dissatisfied with the joint expert's report being allowed to instruct and call his own expert.

court will consider whether an expert's report is necessary. (The White Book says, 'It can be very difficult for the parties and their lawyers to anticipate in advance when the court will decide that expert evidence is necessary.'[53]) The accompanying Practice Direction starts with the statement: 'Part 35 is intended to limit the use of oral expert evidence to that which is reasonably required. In addition, where possible, matters requiring expert evidence should be dealt with by a single expert.' In fast track cases an expert will only be directed to attend a hearing if it is necessary in the interests of justice. (CPR 35.5) That would not prevent either side from asking the expert to attend but that might have to be at their expense.

A procedural innovation was that each side can put written questions to the other side's expert. If the expert fails to answer such questions, the court can direct that the expert's evidence not be admitted or that his fees not be recoverable from the other side (CPR 35.6). The court can direct that the evidence on an issue be given by one expert only (CPR 35.7). If the parties cannot agree on selecting the single expert, the court can select him from a list prepared by the parties (CPR 35.7). The fact that the defendant does not object to the expert proposed and then used by the claimant does not mean that he should be regarded as an expert who has been jointly instructed whose report is available to both sides. The claimant retains his privilege regarding the expert's report.[54].

Both sides can instruct the single expert provided they send a copy of the instructions to the other party (CPR 35.8). However neither can meet with the expert in the absence of the other.[55] The court can limit the amount that can be paid to the expert[56] (CPR 35.8). The expert's report must state the substance of all material instructions, whether written or oral, on the basis of which the report was written. (CPR 35(10)) (For discussion of the problem of the loss of legal privilege in the context of this rule see 'C Phipps, ' Being frank with experts', 144 *Solicitors' Journal*, 4 February 2000, p 90.) Where there is more than one expert, the court can direct them to meet to try to reach agreement, failing which to report as to the nature of their disagreement (CPR 35.12).

In December 2001 the official Code of Guidance on Expert Evidence was published after a long gestation period.[57] The Code is not annexed to the CPR – though it is included in the *White Book*, at the end of Part 35. (It can be accessed on the website of the Expert Witness Institute – www.ewi.org.uk (the law and you).) The Guide

---

53   *Civil Procedure*, 2003, 35.4.1.
54   *Carlson v Townsend* [2001] EWCA Civ 511, [2001] 3 All ER 663.
55   *Peet v Mid-Kent Healthcare NHS Trust* [2000] EWCA Civ 1703, [2002] 1 WLR 210, [2002[3 All ER 688.
56   In February 1999 District Judge Frenkel wrote 'Under the present regime, the total cost of calling two orthopaedic experts can be £2,000' (*New Law Journal*, 19 February 1999, p 254).
57   On the draft code see District Judge M Walker, 'Guidance for experts' *New Law Journal*, Expert Witness Supplement, 26 November 1999, p 1767.

states that unlike lawyers, expert witnesses may not work on the basis of a contingency or conditional fee. The logic behind this has been queried.[58]

The new rules appear to be a revolution in the way that expert evidence is treated in the English courts. But are they?

There have been cases where the courts have exerted a new strong disciplinarian role vis-à-vis experts. In *Stevens v Gullis* [2000]1 All ER 527, for instance, the Court of Appeal dismissed an appeal after the trial judge had refused to allow an expert witness to be called after he had failed to comply with the requirements of PD35 (which only came into force a month later). Lord Woolf said of the expert that 'he demonstrated by his conduct that he had no conception of the requirements placed upon an expert under the CPR'.

The LCD's August 2002 report on the Woolf reforms[59] compared a sample of 1997 pre-CPR cases with a sample of 2000/01 post-CPR cases. In the 1997 sample, in 8% of the cases an expert had been appointed by one party only. In the post-CPR sample the proportion (9%) was about the same. In the 1997 sample, in 12% of cases both parties had appointed experts. In the post-CPR sample the proportion (9%) had gone down. In the 1997 sample there had been no cases of single joint experts. In the post-CPR sample there was a joint expert in 15% of cases.[60]

What is striking in these figures is that although single joint experts have clearly become an established feature of the system, especially in fast track cases, parties are still being allowed to employ their own experts where the case justifies it. As Sir Louis Blom-Cooper QC, Chairman of the Expert Witness Institute, put it,

> The underlying fear within the legal profession that the single joint expert would be the thin edge of the wedge, inexorably adopting the exclusivity of court-appointed experts in the European fashion, has distinctly not been realised. ... Expert witnesses are still called by the respective parties; as such the expert's overriding duty to the court, cannot of itself erase the image of partisanship so redolent of the English mode of civil trial. Thus the reforms in Part 35 do not substantially detract from, or even seriousdly impinge upon, the English way of conducting civil litigation.[61]

When there is a single joint expert it is usually someone agreed between the parties. Typically, the claimant's solicitor puts forward two or three names and the defendants agree to one. The process of having to get the other side's consent to a name obviously promotes the use of experts who have a reputation for being neutral and fair-minded as opposed to those known to be fiercely partisan. In the research by Goriely et al

---

[58]   'So, what then, is the difference between lawyers for whom conditional fees are ethical and expert witnesses for whom they are not?' (Joseph Jacob, *Civil Litigation practice and procedure in a shifting culture*, 2001, p 104.)

[59]   *Further Findings A continuing evaluation of the Civil Justice Reforms.*

[60]   Figure 9, p 15.

[61]   'Experts and Assessors: Past Present and Future', 21 *Civil Justice Quarterly*, 2002, 341, 350.

(*More Civil Justice? The impact of the Woolf reforms on pre-action behaviour*, 2002) respondents concerned with personal injury litigation were reported as welcoming the fact that experts were now less partisan and that they were instructed in a more neutral way.

But the single joint expert does not mean that the parties do not also have their own experts. Preparing effective instructions and written questions to a single joint expert requires skill in the relevant field, so the use of 'shadow' experts to advise rather than to write reports has increased.[62]

Sometimes the court, having first directed that there be a single joint expert, has agreed to allow a party dissatisfied with the joint expert's report to instruct a different expert.[63]

6. Pre-trial case management

Pre-trial case management can be achieved by directions given by the court without a hearing or by some form of pre-trial hearing. The purpose of pre-trial directions and pre-trial hearings is to prepare the case for trial in order to reduce cost and delay. A side effect may be to promote pre-trial settlement. In the past there have been various kinds of pre-trial hearings in the High Court and the county court. One was the so-called summons for directions. The Evershed Committee which reported in 1953 on how to simplify civil procedure, after deliberating for six years, said that the best hope for reducing delays and costs was a ' robust summons for directions' (*Final Report of the Committee on Supreme Court Practice and Procedure*, 1953, Cmd 8878). But this hope was not realised. The normal summons for directions continued to be a perfunctory affair lasting only a few minutes conducted by clerks in front of the master. (See Master Diamond, 'The Summons for Directions', 75 *Law Quarterly Review*, 1959, p 43.) In a paper prepared for a Workshop on Civil Procedure in London in 1970, Sir Jack Jacob wrote, 'in most personal injury actions the Summons for Directions is a very mild affair and cannot possibly be called robust, since the only order that is made is the limitation of medical and perhaps other experts, plans and photographs, and place and mode of trial, and setting down'.

Because the summons for directions had become a formality, the Winn Committee in 1968 recommended (para 352) that this should be recognised by making the process automatic. Provision, it said, should be made for automatic directions without a summons and without an order. This proposal was not, however, implemented then. The report of the Cantley Working Party in 1979 urged that it be implemented. The report said that 'in practice competent solicitors know what they want and agree

---

62   D Hall, 'Under Scrutiny', 145 *Solicitors' Journal*, 14 December 2001, Supplement, pp 18-19.
63   *Daniels v Walker* [2000] 1 WLR 1382 CA; *Cosgrove v Pattison*, [2001] CP Rep 68, (2001) Times, 13 February; cp *Popek v National Westminster Bank plc* [2002] EWCA Civ 42 where the Court of Appeal upheld the judge's decision not to allow a claimant's late application to be allowed to adduce additional expert evidence to that of the single joint expert.

it in advance or in chambers and a two minute hearing suffices in nearly all personal injury cases ... In fact the two minute hearing to obtain the Master's order on an agreed summons is in most cases quite unnecessary'. (*Report of the Personal Injuries Litigation Procedure Working Party* (1979, Cmnd 7476, para 33)

The proposal that there should be automatic directions unless the parties asked for something different was implemented for High Court cases in 1980 in Ord 25, r 8, in regard to personal injury actions. A similar change was made in Chancery cases in 1982.

The Civil Justice Review Body in its Final Report in 1988 recommended (para 254) that standard directions should be devised for all cases where such directions were appropriate. The parties should be free to apply to the court for additional or different directions or for a general stock-taking. The court should be entitled to initiate a general stock-taking on any hearing whether or not it was applied for by either of the parties.

In cases where there were no automatic directions it should continue to be possible to have a summons for directions or, in the county courts, a pre-trial hearing.

Lord Woolf's proposals

Lord Woolf's Interim Report and the January 1996 Consultation Paper for fast track cases envisaged a 'directions hearings'. The January 1996 Consultation Paper stated that there would be 'suitably tailored standard directions' linked to the timetable for the case. District judges would thus: see all defences when filed, decide venue, allocate cases to the appropriate track, give the necessary directions, set a timetable, and allocate a hearing week (p 14, para 59). Other options at the directions hearing would be an application for summary disposal, striking out of the claim if it had no realistic chance of success, or because no valid defence was shown (previously Order 13 and Order 14.)

The Woolf 'directions hearing' sounded remarkably like the 'robust summons for directions' envisaged in 1953 by the Evershed Committee!

Directions under the new rules

The 1999 rules provide for directions to be given by the court as part of its case management functions – in small claims and fast track cases usually without any actual hearing, on the basis of the allocation questionnaire.

SMALL CLAIMS

In small claims cases, after allocation, the court gives 'standard directions' or 'special directions' and fixes a date for the final hearing (CPR 27.4). 'Standard directions' are defined to mean a direction that each party shall at least 14 days before the date fixed for the hearing, file and serve on the other party copies of all documents (including any expert report) on which he intends to rely at the hearing (CPR 27.4). In road accident cases these may include witness statements, invoices and estimates for repairs, documents relating to loss of earnings, sketch plans and photographs. Before the hearing the parties should try to agree the cost of repairs and other losses. The accompanying Practice Direction gives similar indications in regard to building disputes, landlords claims for repairs, holiday and wedding claims. 'Special directions' are directions in addition to standard directions. (For examples see CPR, PD, Form F.)

FAST TRACK

Directions in fast track cases are given at two stages. One is at allocation. The other is on the filing of the listing questionnaire. A directions hearing is held 'if necessary and desirable' (PD, 28, 2.3). The directions fix a trial date not more than 30 weeks later or fix a period, not exceeding three weeks, within which the trial is to take place (CPR 28.2). An appendix to Part 28 sets out forms of directions regarding requests for further information, disclosure of documents, witness statements, expert evidence, filing of documents with the listing questionnaire, the date for the filing of the listing questionnaire and the documents that must be filed at that time. The Practice Direction states that a typical timetable from allocation might be: Disclosure (4 weeks); Exchange of witness statement (10 weeks); Exchange of experts reports (14 weeks); Sending of listing questionnaire by court (20 weeks); Filing of listing questionnaire (22 weeks); Hearing (30 weeks). On listing, the court confirms the trial date, specifies the place of trial and gives a time estimate. So far as possible, the court's further directions should be based on prior agreement between the parties.

The style of case management envisaged for the fast track was outlined by Lord Woolf in his Interim Report:

> The procedure I have outlined above envisages a pro-active role for the district judge in communicating with the parties or, more often, their legal advisers by telephone, letter or fax ... Where appropriate this should include tripartite discussions between the judge and the parties by means of a telephone conference facility. . .The fast track procedure is designed to dispense with any procedures which create uncertainty or unnecessary preparation or generate additional cost. Although there will be no case management conference or pre-trial review, the district judge will be able to ensure that the case is reasonably fit for the hearing by monitoring the checklist and the documentation. To enable district judges to fulfill this role effectively, it is essential that they are provided with appropriate information technology [pp 44, paras 14–15].

MULTI TRACK

Directions for multi track cases can be given at allocation, at a case management conference, at a pre-trial review or at listing. On the allocation of a claim to the multi track the court considers whether it is necessary or desirable to hold a case management conference straight away or whether it is appropriate instead to give directions on its own initiative. The directions should, so far as is appropriate, be based on agreement between the parties. To obtain the court's approval, agreed directions must set out a timetable by reference to calendar dates for the taking of steps for the preparation of the case. The court will not approve the timetable if it proposes a date for a case management conference that is later than is reasonably necessary. Agreed directions should also deal with such matters as filing of any reply or amended statement of case, dates for the requests for further information, the disclosure of evidence, the use of a single joint expert or the exchange of expert reports. If the court gives directions on its own initiative, its general approach will be based on standard disclosure, disclosure of witness statements by simultaneous exchange and a single joint expert ('unless there is good reason not to do so').If directions are not agreed and the court cannot give them on its own initiative, it will direct a case management conference to be listed (CPR, PD 29).

For approval of case management see Mr Justice Lightman, 'The case for judicial intervention', 149 *New Law Journal*, 3 December 1999, p 1819. For an appraisal of the significance of the reforms see N Andrews, 'A new Civil Procedural Code for England – Party Control "Going, Going, Gone"', 19 *Civil Justice Quarterly*, 2000, pp19-38. For a report on the range of judicial views regarding case management see Joyce Plotnikoff and Richard Woolfson, *Judges' Case Management Perspectives: the View of Opinion Formers and Case managers*, LCD 3/2002 – www.lcd.gov.uk/ researchintrofr

Case management conferences, pre-trial reviews, listing hearings

Lord Woolf's report envisaged an early case management conference sometimes for fast track cases and usually for multi track cases. Pre-trial reviews nearer the time of the hearing, he suggested, would be usual in multi track cases. These recommendations are reflected in the rules. Where one party has filed a listing questionnaire but the other has not, there will also be a listing hearing (PD 29, para 8.3(2)). The court will fix the trial date or the period in which the trial is to take place as soon as practicable (CPR 29.2(2)). Postponement of the trial will not occur unless it is unavoidable. ('Litigants and lawyers must be in no doubt that the court will regard the postponement of a trial as an order of the last resort' (PD 29, para 7.4(6).) The legal representative attending such a hearing must be personally familiar with the case and have authority to deal with issues that arise. Failure to comply will be punished by a wasted costs order (PD 29, para 5.2(3)). The lay party may also be required to attend (r 29.3).

The Practice Direction on the multi track covers a great variety of issues. The topics to be considered at a case management conference will include whether the case is clear, what disclosure of documents is necessary, what factual or expert evidence should be disclosed, what arrangements should be made for the putting of questions to experts, whether there should be a split trial or a trial of preliminary issues. The court will set a timetable for the steps to be taken. Case management is to be tailored flexibly to the needs of the case. It will generally be conducted by a master, a district judge or a circuit judge. In complex cases it should be conducted by the trial judge. (See *Morris v Bank of America National Trust* [2000] 1 All ER 954, CA.)

In small claims cases there will normally be no pre-trial hearings, but the court can hold a preliminary hearing where it considers that special directions are needed to ensure a fair hearing and it is necessary to get a party to court to ensure that he understands what he must do to comply with the special directions or to enable the court to dispose of the claim on the basis that one party has no real prospect of success. (PD, 27, para 27.6) If all parties agree, the preliminary hearing can be treated as the final hearing.

UTILITY OF PRE-TRIAL HEARING

It is common sense to suppose that a pre-trial hearing will reduce cost and delay – but the empirical evidence suggests that common sense may be wrong. The procedure for small claims cases introduced in 1973 originally included a pre-trial review. But this was dropped after it was found that it was more of a nuisance than a help. The preliminary-hearing concept also had a somewhat unsuccessful test in the Family Division. In 1979 it was announced that the 'pre-trial review' concept would in future be applied to contested matrimonial causes in the Family Division. The *Practice Direction* [1979] 1 All ER 112 stated that 'the prime objective behind the pre-trial review procedure is to enable the registrar to ascertain the true state of the case and to give such directions as are necessary for its just, expeditious and economic disposal'. In practice, where it had been tried experimentally it had been found that 'under the registrar's guidance the parties are often able to compose their differences, or to drop insubstantial charges and defences, and to concentrate on the main issues in dispute'. This scheme did not, however, prove successful. It ran as an experiment for fourteen months before being cancelled by a further Practice Direction in June 1981. (See *New Law Journal*, 1981, p 623). Research revealed that the reason for the failure of the scheme was that it did not sufficiently achieve the objectives of securing more settlements or even of clarifying issues for the trial.

A study of matched samples in 3,000 personal injury cases in New Jersey found that while pre-trial conferences improved preparation, they did not shorten trials. The researchers concluded that they therefore lowered rather than raised the efficiency of the system by absorbing a great deal of court time without any compensating savings.[64]

[64]   M Rosenberg, *The Pre-trial Conference and Effective Justice*, 1964, Columbia University Press, p 68.

What to do about delay?

The problem of what to do about delay in civil litigation is common to all legal systems.

The approach of the common law The traditional approach of the English courts was relatively relaxed. In *Allen v Sir Alfred McAlpine & Sons Ltd* [1968] 2 QB 229 the Court of Appeal held that the power to dismiss for lack of prosecution of the case should only be exercised where the court was satisfied either: (1) that the default had been intentional and contumacious, or conduct amounting to an abuse of the court; or (2) that there had been inordinate and inexcusable delay by the plaintiff or his lawyers and that such delay would give rise to a substantial risk that it was not possible to have a fair trial of the issues in the action or it had caused or was likely to cause serious prejudice to the defendant. These principles were approved by the House of Lords in *Birkett v James* [1978] AC 297. Moreover, the law lords said there that delay before issuing the writ within the limitation period was irrelevant. The delay under consideration must have occurred since the writ was issued, though it did accept that if he had delayed at first, it was incumbent on the plaintiff to move with all due speed after the writ was issued. But at that time the applicant had to be able to establish that the delay caused him serious prejudice. An adverse effect on the system as a whole was not sufficient.

Twenty years later in *Arbuthnot Latham Bank Ltd v Trafalgar Holdings Ltd* [1998] 2 All ER 181, decided in the count-down to implementation of the CPR, the attitude was very different. The Master of the Rolls, Lord Woolf, giving the Court of Appeal's decision, said that in *Birkett v James* the broader consequences of inordinate delay was not a consideration which was in issue, but in the new era of managed litigation it was going to be a consideration of increasing significance.

Litigants and their legal advisers must therefore recognise that any delay which occurs from now on will be assessed not only from the point of view of the prejudice caused to the particular litigants whose case it is, but also in relation to the effect it can have on other litigants who are wishing to have their cases heard and the prejudice which is caused to the due administration of civil justice. [at 191]

For discussion of the case see I R Scott, 'Disregard of procedural time-limits as abuse of process', 17 *Civil Justice Quarterly*, 1998, pp 83–7.

See also the study of serious fraud cases done by Professor Michael Levi for the Runciman Royal Commission on Criminal Justice. In regard to pre-trial reviews Levi said, 'None of the defence lawyers I interviewed argued that pre-trial reviews had any significant effect on the development of the case.' (*The Investigation, Prosecution and Trial of Serious Fraud*, Royal Commission on Criminal Justice, Research Study No 14, 1993, p 105.)

See to the same general effect the *Crown Court Study*. Judges in Crown Court cases were asked whether they thought the pre-trial review had saved much time and money at trial. Two-thirds (66%) said no; a quarter (24%) said a little, and 8% said a fair amount of time had been saved. Only 1% said a great deal of time had been saved. (M Zander and P Henderson, *Crown Court Study*, Royal Commission on Criminal Justice, Research Study No19, 1993, sect 2.8.9.)

THE SYSTEMS APPROACH OF OFFICIAL COMMITTEES

Since the Second World War the problem of delay was considered by no fewer than six committees: the Evershed Committee (1953), the Winn Committee (1968), the Cantley Committee (1979), the Civil Justice Review (1986-9), the Heilbron-Hodge Committee (1993) and Lord Woolf (1995/96).

The Evershed Committee[65] as has been seen, placed its faith in 'the robust summons for directions', but this totally failed. The summons for directions never became robust.

The Winn Committee[66] thought that delay was 'a very great reproach'. It proposed various remedies. One was interest on damages–to encourage insurance companies to pay up quicker. This was implemented in the Administration of Justice Act 1969, s 22. Another was the power to order interim payment of part of the damages in a case where it was reasonably clear that damages would ultimately be awarded. This was implemented in the Administration of Justice Act 1969, s 20. Thirdly, the Committee thought delays should be reduced by keeping the procedure on tighter reins so far as time-limits were concerned. The need, it thought, was to increase the penalties for delay.

The Cantley Committee[67] did not think that the problem of delay was so serious. Generally the system worked tolerably well.

> 8. The basic principle of litigation as at present conducted in our courts is that the litigation is the litigation of the parties: the court is there to assist the parties and finally to resolve the dispute between the parties if asked to do so, but the court does not intervene unless asked to do so by the parties. Some of the weaknesses of our system derive from this fact but so do many of its strengths and given a competent legal profession, which, with some exceptions, we have, one should not lightly interfere with this method of conducting litigation and encourage an undue degree of court intervention if to do so would lose the advantages of economy and flexibility which our system brings.

Most accidents which led to claims, it said, did not lead to writs and most writs did not lead to trial and judgment. These cases were settled 'and settlement is an essential ingredient in our system of disposing of actions' (para 9). Moreover, a delay which enabled and encouraged the parties to settle their dispute on reasonable terms was not an undue delay and 'any solution which brought cases to the point of trial more quickly but which brought more cases to trial than at present would have the double disadvantage of being more costly for those cases which might otherwise have settled: and, by bringing more cases to the point of trial, delay the trial itself' (para 9).

---

[65]   *Final Report on Supreme Court Practice*, 1953, Cmnd 8878.
[66]   *Committee on Personal Injuries Litigation*, 1968, Cmnd 369.
[67]   *Report of the Personal Injuries Litigation Procedure Working Part*, 1979, Cmnd 7476.

But Cantley agreed that there were some cases of egregious delay. Having canvassed various solutions to this issue, the one it most favoured was that if within 18 months after the issue of a writ in a personal injury case the action had not been set down for trial, the plaintiff's solicitor should be required to report to the court as to what stage the proceedings had reached. If appropriate, the court could then issue a summons for the purpose of giving directions. But this sensible proposal foundered because at that date – and for many years after – the court system had no way of identifying the *cases* in which a writ had not been set down 18 months after the issue of the writ.

The approach to the problem of delay of **the Civil Justice Review**[68] was very different from that of the Cantley Committee. Where Cantley emphasised that civil litigation was essentially a private matter between the parties, the Civil Justice Review thought of it rather as a matter of public concern.

(i)   It caused personal stress, anxiety and financial hardship to plaintiffs and their families.

(ii)   These pressures sapped the morale and determination of plaintiffs, resulting often in acceptance of low settlement offers.

(iii) It reduced the availability of evidence and eroded the reliability of the evidence which was available.

(iv)   It led to inefficient business dealing with files opened and reopened over months and years.

(v)   Compensation was delayed until long after it was most needed.

(vi)   It lowered public estimation for the legal system.[69]

The Civil Justice Review proposed a variety of remedies for delay. They included: 1) Reducing the time-limit for bringing a personal injuries action from 3 years to 1 year. [Not adopted.] 2) Requiring solicitors handling personal injury cases to have a specialist qualification. [Not adopted.] 3) Obliging a solicitor to start proceedings within a fixed period of his first meeting with his client. [Not adopted.] 4) A system of paper adjudication for cases involving amounts of under £5,000. [Not adopted.] 5) Laying down and enforcing a strict time-table for larger cases. [Adopted ten years later for Lord Woolf's fast track] 6) Requiring litigants personally to sign applications for adjournments. [Not adopted.] 7) Giving court administrators targets for trials. [Adopted in Lord Woolf's fast track.] 8) The court should control the time taken in litigation. [Adopted by Lord Woolf] 9.) Implementing the proposal made by Cantley that where a case had not been set down for trial within a stated time from the issue of the writ the lawyers should be asked to report the reasons. There should be different periods for different kinds of cases. 10) Better court management information. The net impact of the Civil Justice Reform project in terms of reducing delay was therefore negligible.

---

68   The Review produced five consultation papers on Personal Injuries (1986), Small Claims (1986), Commercial Court (1986), Enforcement of Debt (1987) and Housing Cases (1987). Its Final Report, *Report of the Review Body on Civil Justice*, Cm 394 was published in 1988.

69   Civil Justice Review, *The Personal Injuries Consultation Paper*, 1986, para 86.

In October 1990 a new rule was introduced in the county court without prior consultation or even warning – CCR Ord 17, r 11–providing for *automatic striking out* of an action if a request for a hearing had not been made within the time-limit. The time-limit was six months from the close of pleadings. The pleadings were deemed to be closed 14 days after delivery of a defence or 28 days after the delivery of a counterclaim.

Unless the court had already fixed a hearing, the action was automatically struck out if no request to fix a hearing was made within 15 months of the close of pleadings. The rule applied to any default or fixed date action ie one begun by plaint. This meant most actions.

The Civil Justice Review envisaged that the court would send out a warning notice but this did not happen–no doubt because the court lacked the technology to discover which cases were at risk of being struck out. Practitioners therefore had to watch the diary to make sure that they did not fall foul of the rule.

The court had a discretion to extend time-limits retrospectively but in *Rastin v British Steel plc* [1994] 2 All ER 641 the Court of Appeal held that the discretion should be exercised sparingly. The plaintiff had to be able to show that he had prosecuted the case with reasonable diligence.

The automatic strike-out rule resulted in thousands of cases being struck out.[70] It generated a flood of satellite litigation which in the end required drastic action by the Court of Appeal. In April and May 1997 three of its members (Saville, Brooke and Waller LJJ) in a seven-week period decided more than 100 appeals and applications arising out of Order 17, r 11.[71] This stopped the flood of cases to the Court of Appeal. A year later, in May 1998, Lord Justice Brooke said that there was only one case involving Order 17, r 11 awaiting decision.[72]

But the automatic strike out rule had been a catastrophic failure.

The Heilbron-Hodge Report[73] was produced by a committee established by the Bar and the Law Society. Surprisingly, given that it was a committee of practitioners, one of the main villains in regard to delay, it thought, were lawyers: 'Progress of actions lies with the parties and their lawyers rather than the courts. This is often a recipe for unacceptable and otherwise avoidable delay as well as unnecessary cost' (p 5, para 1.7(iv)). Heilbron-Hodge called for 'a radical reappraisal of the approach to civil litigation from all its participants' (p 6, para 1.8). It is time for many of the

---

70 According to Judge Greenslade there had been no fewer than 34,000 cases where the automatic striking out rule had been applied – *Reform of Civil Procedure–Essays on Access to Justice*, (ed AAS Zuckerman and R Cranston, Clarendon, 1995, p 122).

71 The decisions, which take 70 pages in the law reports, were reported in *Bannister v SGB plc* [1997] 4 All ER129 and *Greig Middleton & Co Ltd v Denderowitz, Olaleye-Oruene v London Guildhall University* [1997] 4 All ER 181.

72 *Cockerill v Tambrands Ltd* [1998] 3 All ER 97, 99.

73 *Civil Justice on Trial–the Case for Change*, 1992.

deeply ingrained traditions to be swept away and for their replacement by pragmatic and modern attitudes and ideas. In essence what is needed is a change in culture.

This allegedly much needed new ethos in the civil courts was embodied in ten basic principles of reform enunciated by Heilbron-Hodge. One was, 'Litigants and their lawyers need to have imposed upon them, within sensible procedural time-frames, an obligation to prosecute and defend their proceedings with efficiency and despatch. Therefore, once the process of the court is invoked, the court should have a more active and responsible role over the progress and conduct of cases' (p 6, para 1.8,(ii)). Judges should adopt a more interventionist role 'to ensure that issues are limited, delays are reduced and court time is not wasted' (p 6, para 1.8(iv)).

Under the heading of 'Court Control of Litigation' the Committee recommended that the issue of all originating process should be computerised. Each stage in an action should be computer monitored, triggering 'prompts' where the time prescribed by the procedural rules had expired without any extension of time being ordered or mutually agreed. The court should ensure that extensions of time agreed between the parties should only rarely be allowed beyond set limits (p 34, para 4.11).

The automatic striking out rule introduced by CCR Ord 17, r 11 should be applied to the High Court. (Heilbron-Hodge seemed unconcerned about the grave problems that the automatic strike out rule had caused.)

The proposed system of court control of litigation, the Committee said, should incorporate powers to dismiss claims which were not expeditiously prosecuted. The existing rules on dismissal for want of prosecution would then become redundant (p 39, para 4.30(i)).

Pending the introduction of such a system the decision in *Birkett v James* [1978] AC 297 should be reversed. (As has been seen, in that decision the House of Lords held that delay before issuing a writ did not count. Even if the claim had previously been dismissed for want of prosecution, if the plaintiff could issue a writ within the time-limit, the action should not be dismissed save in exceptional circumstances.)

Within a short period of setting down an action a 'pre-trial review' should be fixed. This should be heard by a High Court judge and in some long and complex cases by the trial judge. The matters to be dealt with would include identification of all witnesses and of the extent of documentation to be presented at the trial, estimates of length of trial, the agreement of non-contentious facts, and the fixing of an approximate trial date (pp 40–41, para 4.33(iii)).

It is clear that Heilbron-Hodge paved the way for the Woolf Report.

For a descriptive note about the Heilbron-Hodge report see 14 *Civil Justice Quarterly*, January 1994, pp 11–14.

In January 1994, the firm **KPMG Peat Marwick** published the results of a study into the causes of delay in the High Court and county courts. The study was commissioned by the Lord Chancellor's Department in July 1993. The research was based on court records of a small sample of personal injury cases and interviews with persons involved in the cases. The conclusion was that there were many causes of delay. They included: 1) The anatomy of the case itself. 2) Delay caused by the parties for some of which they could be blamed and some of which was not their fault. 3) Delay caused by the lawyers, especially solicitors, again, partly their fault, partly not. 4) External factors such as the difficulty of getting reports from medical and other experts. 5) The attitudes of the judiciary. 6) Court procedures. 7) Court administration and especially problems created by listing.

The report stated that the two factors that gave rise to the most significant delay were inexperience or inefficiency in the handling of cases by the parties' solicitors and time taken to obtain medical or other expert reports.

THE 1995 PRACTICE DIRECTIONS

In 1995, while Lord Woolf was preparing his Interim Report, the Lord Chief Justice, Lord Taylor unexpectedly entered the fray with a strongly worded Practice Direction – [1995] 1 All ER 385. It was headed 'Civil Litigation-Case Management' and it took effect in the Queen's Bench Division and the Chancery Division:

> **Practice Note (Civil Litigation–Case Management [1995] 1 All ER 385**
>
> The paramount importance of reducing the cost and delay of civil litigation makes it necessary for judges sitting at first instance to assert greater control over the preparation for and conduct of hearings than has hitherto been customary. Failure by practitioners to conduct cases economically will be visited by appropriate orders for costs, including wasted costs orders.

It then set out a series of new rules. The court would exercise its powers to limit: discovery, the length of oral submissions, the time allowed for the examination and cross-examination of witnesses, the issues to be addressed, and reading aloud from authorities. Unless otherwise ordered, witness statements would stand as the evidence-in-chief of the witness. The rules on pleadings would be strictly enforced. Parties should use their best endeavours to identify and limit the issues. Rules about court bundles would be strictly enforced. In cases lasting more than ten days a pre-trial review would be normal. Opening speeches should be succinct. The rule requiring skeleton arguments summarising submissions to be sent to the other side and to the court must be adhered to. The pre-trial check list required the lawyers to state whether alternative dispute resolution (ADR) had been considered.

Six days later a similar Practice Direction was issued by the President of the Family Division – see [1995] 1 All ER 586.

It is clear therefore that when Lord Woolf was working on his report in 1994/95 the conceptual basis for his eventual recommendations had already been laid in the reports of the Civil Justice Review, the Heilbron-Hodge Committee and the 1995

Practice Directions. But Lord Woolf's analysis of the problem was unique in that in his Interim Report he laid all the blame for the ills of the system on one cause–the uncontrolled nature of the litigation process[74]: 'In particular there is no clear judicial responsibility for managing individual cases or for the overall administration of the civil courts' (p 7, para 1).

The reason suggested was that without effective judicial control the adversarial process was 'likely to encourage an adversarial culture and to degenerate into an environment in which the litigation process is too often seen as a battlefield where no rules apply'. The consequence was that expense was often excessive, disproportionate and unpredictable and delay was unreasonable. This was because the conduct, pace and extent of litigation were left almost completely to the parties. There was no effective control of their worst excesses (p 7, para 5).

THE WOOLF REFORMS

As has been seen, the remedy prescribed by Lord Woolf was court control. Thus the first of the 124 recommendations in his Interim Report was: 'There should be a fundamental transfer in the responsibility for the management of civil litigation from litigants and their legal advisers to the courts' (p 223).

Apart from case management, the other chief remedy for delay in the Woolf reforms was the strict timetabling of fast-track cases with a trial date fixed at a relatively early stage. (In practice the court generally fixes a 'trial window' of one, two or three weeks rather than give an actual date.) The *White Book* states, 'Early fixing of the trial date or "trial window" – and insisting upon it – is of the essence of the fast track.'[75]

CPR 28.2 states that when the court allocates a case to the fast track, the court will give directions for the management of the case and set a timetable. 'The standard period between the giving of directions and the trial will be not more than 30 weeks'. (CPR 28.2.(4))

The LCD's August 2000 report on the Woolf reforms had several pages of figures and graphs showing the time from issue to hearing in the years 1994 to late 2001 based on data collected by the Court Service.[76] The figures provided some evidence that delay in multi-track and fast-track cases had decreased: 'Average time from issue to trial was lower post-CPR; 498 days in 2000/01 following a rise pre-CPR from 546 days in March 1994 to 639 days in September 1997 ... The decline in average time from issue to trial between 1997 and 2000/01 was spread across cases regardless of type or value.'[77]

---

[74] There was no reference in his report to the more nuanced view of delay in the report by KPMG Peat Marwick.

[75] *Civil Procedure*, 2003, para 28.2.3.

[76] *Emerging Findings*, pp 20-23.

[77] para 6.4. The figures for small claims showed fluctuations – see Fig 12, p 22.

The report by Goriely, Moorhead and Abrams for the Law Society and the Civil Justice Council[78] also had information on the length of time from issue to settlement. But since their figures were based on comparison of the solicitors' files for pre-CPR and post-CPR personal injury cases, the researchers were able also to take into account pre-issue work. This is critical for any proper evaluation of the effect of the Woolf reforms. The research was conducted between 20 and 28 months after the introduction of the Woolf reforms. It therefore only included small simple cases normally concluded within two years. The research measured the total time taken from the solicitor first receiving instructions to the conclusion of the matter.

This showed that the overall time had remained much the same. Both before and after the reforms, the average standard fast track case took 13 months to conclude. This is true whether one takes the mean or median figure. [p 171]

The early stages of a case had become slower. It now took longer to write the first letter of claim. (The median number of days pre-Woolf was 13 and post-Woolf was 36[79] Equally it took longer to instruct a medical expert- no doubt because the two sides had to try to agree on a name (The median number of days from first instruction to medical instruction had risen from 67 days pre-Woolf to 113 days post-Woolf[80]) There had been a slight increase in the delay before receipt of the medical report. (From a median of 64 days to 83 days.[81])

By contrast, the later stages, had become quicker. Once a medical report had been received, settlements were arrived at more quickly. (p 171).

But overall the delays were unchanged. The speeding up of one part was cancelled by the slowing down of the other.

American research on the effects of case management – the Rand Report

A few months after Lord Woolf published his Final Report, the Institute of Civil Justice at the Rand Corporation in California published a massive study of the effect of judicial case management in the United States. The study was based on a five-year survey of 10,000 cases in 20 Federal courts drawn from 16 states. The object was to investigate the impact of procedural reforms introduced under the Civil Justice Reform Act 1990. They included differential case management for different tracks, early judicial management, monitoring and control of complex cases. The results, to say the least, were discouraging. The package of reforms as implemented, it was found 'had little effect on time disposition, litigation costs, and attorney satisfaction

---

[78]   *More Civil Justice The impact of the Woolf reforms on pre-action behaviour*, 2002.
[79]   P 70.
[80]   P 131.
[81]   P 132.

and views of the fairness of case management' (p 1).[82] The reason was that whereas some of the changes introduced had a beneficial effect, these were cancelled by others that had an adverse effect. In particular, 'Early case management is associated with significantly increased costs to litigants, as measured by attorney work hours' (pp 1-2). The Rand Report explained that case management tends to increase rather than reduce costs because it generates more work by lawyers: 'Lawyer work may increase as a result of early management because lawyers need to respond to a court's management – for example, talking to the litigant and to the other lawyers in advance of a conference with the judge, travelling and spending time at the courthouse, meeting with the judge, and updating the file after conference. In addition, once judicial case management has begun, a discovery cut-off date has usually been established, and attorneys may feel an obligation to begin discovery' (p 14). Doing so, the Report said, 'could shorten time to disposition, but it may also increase lawyer work hours on cases that were about to settle when the judges began early management' (p 14). Experiments were conducted to see whether it made any difference if early case management was applied somewhat earlier or later. It did not. Reflecting on this, the Report said, 'This finding suggests that the *fact* (sic) of management adds to the lawyer work hours, not the "earliness" of the management'. (p 14) But of course the earlier the case management starts, the more cases are brought within its scope: ' starting earlier means that more cases would be managed because more cases are still open, so more cases would incur the predicted increase in lawyer work hours. Early management involves a trade-off between shortened time to disposition and increased lawyer work hours' (p 14). (There was no sign in Lord Woolf's two reports that this basic point had been absorbed.)

In regard to delay, the Rand study found that 'what judges do to manage cases matters'. 'Early judicial case management, setting the trial schedule early, shortened time to discovery cut-off, and having litigants at or available for settlement conferences are associated with a significantly reduced time to disposition' (p 1). Setting an early trial date was said to be 'the most important component of early management' (p 14). No other aspect of early judicial management had a consistently significant effect on time to disposition, costs or attorney's satisfaction or views of fairness.

On the US approach to case management and delay see Joyce Plotnikoff, 'Judges as Case Managers', *Civil Justice Quarterly*, April 1985, p 102–11, and 'Case Control as Social Policy: Civil Case Management Legislation in the United States', *Civil Justice Quarterly*, July 1991, pp 230–45. For an overall view by an American expert on the problem of delay, see Geoffrey Hazard, 'Court Delay: Toward New Premises', *Civil Justice Quarterly*, July 1986, p 236; see also Peter A Sallman, 'Observations on Judicial

---

[82] The quotations here are from the executive summary of the study, J S Kakalik et al, *Just, Speedy and Inexpensive? An Evaluation of Judicial Case Management under the Civil Justice Reform Act*, 1996. The results of the study were the subject of an article by the writer – *New Law Journal*, 7 March 1997, p 353. See also the writer's postscript – *New Law Journal*, 11 April 1997, p 539.

Participation in Caseflow Management', *Civil Justice Quarterly*, April 1989, pp 129–51.

For comments by American scholars on the 'managerial judging' proposals in Lord Woolf's Report see Richard Marcus, 'Déja Vu All Over Again', in *Reform of Civil Procedure–Essays on Access to Justice* (ed AAS Zuckerman and R Cranston, Clarendon, 1995) pp 219–43 and Samuel Issachoroff, 'Too Much Lawyering, Too Little Law', *Zuckerman and Cranston*, pp 245–51.

For description of the Australian approach to case management see Peter McManus, 'Case Management in the Family Court of Australia', 10 *Civil Justice Quarterly*, July 1990, pp 280–99 and BC Cairns, 'Managing Civil Litigation: An Australian Adaptation of American Experience', 14 *Civil Justice Quarterly*, January 1994, p 67.

Sanctions and the new rules

In his Final Report Lord Woolf devoted a whole chapter to sanctions. It started:

> When considering the problems facing civil justice today I argued in chapter 3 of my Interim Report that the existing rules of court were being flouted on a vast scale. Timetables are not adhered to and other orders are not complied with if it does not suit the parties to do so. Orders for costs which do not apply immediately have proved to be an ineffective sanction and do nothing to deter parties from ignoring the court's directions. There was overwhelming support from all sides for effective, appropriate and fair sanctions [p 72, paras 1, 2]

Lord Woolf said he would stress four important principles,

> The primary aim of sanctions is prevention, not punishment. (b) It should be for the rules themselves, in the first instance to provide an effective debarring order where there has been a breach, for example that a party may not use evidence which he has not disclosed. (c) All directions orders should in any event include an automatic sanction for non-compliance unless an extension of time has been obtained prospectively. (d) The onus should be on the defaulter to apply for relief, not on the other party to seek a penalty' [(p 72, para 4]

Striking out a claim or defence was a draconian sanction. 'Nonetheless, where parties do fail without reasonable excuse to comply with the court's directions, particularly where they do so more than once, the court must be willing to exercise appropriate discipline over them' (p 75, para11). Costs orders – to be paid immediately – also had 'an important part to play' (p 75, para 12). But parties might think a costs order 'a price worth paying for the delay and inconvenience which their action causes the other party' (p 72, para 13) .It was essential that 'case management itself, and other sanctions, should play their part in suppressing misbehaviour' (p 75, para 13).

Lord Woolf conceded that there should be a limited right to apply for relief from a sanction but the onus should be on the defaulter to apply, not on the other party to enforce the sanction (p 75 para 14). Relief should be given on the basis of the test in *Rastin v British Steel plc* [1994] 1 WLR 732 where the court was satisfied that the breach was not intentional, that there had been substantial compliance with other directions and that there was a good explanation.

Lord Woolf said that to a large extent the effectiveness of sanctions would revolve around judicial attitudes. ('There is no doubt that some judges at first instance, especially Masters and district judges, will need to develop a more robust approach to the task of managing cases and ensuring that their orders are not flouted' (p 76, para 15). They must, in particular, be resistant to applications to extend a set timetable, save in exceptional circumstances. And they would need to be supported by courts hearing appeals. ('Procedural decisions must not be overturned lightly...This is not simply a matter of limiting appeals. It goes to a change of culture in which judges can make orders confident that parties will not feel that they can ignore orders or that they can escape unscathed by appealing' (p 76, para 15).)

The new rules provide for seven different kinds of sanctions: striking out a statement of case; excluding argument or evidence;[83] orders for security for the sum in issue and for present and future costs; orders for payment (or non-payment) of costs, in some cases on the indemnity principle, and for the immediate assessment and payment of costs; orders for payment of interest at penal rates; proceedings for contempt; and wasted costs orders. The court can impose a sanction on its own initiative with or without holding a hearing and with or without an opportunity for the party affected to make representations (CPR 3.3). However a party whose case is struck out can apply to have it reinstated.

Thus, the court has the power to strike out a statement of claim if 'there has been a failure to comply with a rule, practice direction or court order' (CPR 3.4) or if the claimant does not pay the fee payable when an allocation questionnaire or listing questionnaire is served (CPR 3.7). Where a party has failed to comply with a rule, practice direction or court sanction, any sanction for such failure takes effect unless the party in default applies for and gets relief from the court (CPR 3.8). CPR 3.9 sets out nine considerations that the court should take into account. They include: the interests of the administration of justice; if the application for relief was made promptly; whether there is a good explanation for the failure; and the effect that granting relief would have on each party. As has been seen, there is also a general 'slip rule' giving the court power to cure any error in procedure such as a failure to comply with a rule or practice direction (CPR 3.10).

There is one new rule that somewhat eases the pressure created by time-limits. CPR 2.11 says that, unless the rules or a practice direction provide otherwise, the parties can give each other permission to extend time-limits by written agreement. The rule then cites the cases where this is not possible. One is where a rule, practice direction or court order requires something to be done within a specified time and also specifies

---

[83] For instance CPR 3.1(2)(k) where a claimant fails to provide further information or a schedule of damage, or R32.10 if a witness or summary is not provided within the time-limit.

the consequences of failure to comply (CPR 3.8(3)). Another is an extension of time that would cause alteration of the fast track case management timetable in respect of the return of the listing questionnaire or the date of the trial (or trial period) (CPR 28.4). A third is an extension of time that would cause alteration of the multi track timetable in respect of the case management conference, a pre-trial review, the return of the listing questionnaire, or the trial (or trial period) (CPR 29.5). In these instances, an extension of time requires the consent of the court.

There is no practice direction on how the courts should approach the application of sanctions and no specific reference, save in the overriding objective, to the doctrine of proportionality.

In his Report Lord Woolf made clear that adherence to the new rules had to be strictly enforced, especially in regard to time-limits. In regard, for instance, to the fast track,

> I regard adherence to the overall timetable, with strict observance of the set trial date, as an essential component of the fast track. For this reason, the directions order will be framed as a series of requirements which must be completed by specified dates and will include an automatic sanction for non-compliance, unless an extension order has been obtained prospectively. Parties will be in breach of the order unless they comply with the directions by the date specified.[Final Report, p 35, para 15.]

See to the same effect Mr Justice Lightman, lecturing at the Judicial Studies Board shortly before the Woolf reforms were due to take effect. At common law, he said, time was of the essence. Equity modified this rule. In equity, time was not of the essence. In 1873, with the merger of common law and equity, the rules of equity prevailed. That was the prevalent attitude in respect of rules in the pre-Woolf era. The traditional attitude of the courts had been that every default in respect of the rules was venal and so remediable. Save in exceptional circumstances every litigant should be allowed his day in court. That approach was no longer maintainable. It was out of accord with the new rules. In regard to time-limits, he said, ' time is now of the essence, but in cases where a sufficient cause exists, an application may be made for relief from the draconian sanctions for non-compliance and relief may be granted if to do so accords with the overriding objective'. There was therefore no scope for a presumption that apparently draconian provisions should be interpreted narrowly. 'The judges at the coal face must be robust.'[84]

For a very different philosophy see Sir Jack Jacob, doyen of civil proceduralists, in his dissent to the Report of the Winn Committee in 1968:

> The admonition by Lord Justice Bowen that 'courts do not exist for the sake of discipline' should be reflected in the principle that rules of court should not be framed on the basis of imposing penalties or producing automatic consequences for non-compliance with the rules or orders of the court. The function of rules

---

[84]   Lightman, J,'Sanctions under the new rules', *New Law Journal*, 5 March 1999, p 336.

of court is to provide guide-lines not trip wires and they fulfil their function most where they intrude least in the course of litigation.[85]

The first important post-CPR decision given by Lord Woolf in *Biguzzi v Rank Leisure plc*[86] sounded a distinctly more emollient note than his earlier rhetoric might have suggested. The claimant was injured in 1993. His action got bogged down through default on both sides. Shortly before the CPR came into force, the district judge struck out the action even though the delay had not caused serious prejudice to the defendants or to the chances of a fair trial – on the ground that there had been a wholesale disregard of the rules amounting to an abuse of process. After the CPR came into force an appeal was allowed mainly on the ground that there was nothing unfair in allowing the case to go forward largely because the defendant as well as the claimant had been guilty of serious default. The Court of Appeal upheld that decision. Lord Woolf said that the draconian step of striking-out, whilst available to a procedural judge in his wide-ranging discretion, was one which did not achieve justice in this particular case. Such an order simply led to hard fought appeals and satellite litigation with disproportionate costs. The advantage of the CPR over the previous rules, he said, was that the courts' powers were much broader than they had been. 'In many cases there will be alternatives which enable a case to be dealt with justly without taking the draconian step of striking the case out.' (at p 940) There were a range of alternative sanctions such as requiring the claimant to make a payment into court by way of security for costs or ordering the defendant to pay costs on the higher indemnity basis. The courts had to apply the overriding objective of dealing with cases justly which included a need to show that non-compliance with time-limits would not be tolerated.

This leaves the matter largely in the hands of judges at first instance. ('... judges have to be trusted to exercise the wide discretions which they have fairly and justly in all the circumstances, while recognising their responsibility to litigants in general not to allow the same defaults to occur in the future as have occurred in the past. When judges seek to do that, it is important that this court should not interfere unless judges can be shown to have exercised their powers in some way which contravenes the relevant principles. (at p 941.)

For a strongly expressed view that the tougher approach is best see A. Zuckerman, 'Dismissal for disobedience of peremptory orders – An imperative of fair trial', 20 *Civil Justice Quarterly* 2001, p 12.

When considering whether to grant relief from a failure to comply with a rule under r 3.9 the court will weigh the matters that are specifically listed and any others that seem relevant in the particular circumstances. The relevance of case law is debatable. Counsel try to persuade the court that they have precedents that are significant. The courts often indicate that each case must be judged in light of its particular facts and that precedents are therefore not useful.

---

[85]   *Report of the Committee on Personal Injury Litigation*, 1968, Cmnd 369, pp 151-52.
[86]   [1999] 4 All ER 934.

An assessment of the Woolf reforms four years on

The writer was consistently a critic of the Woolf reforms project.[87]

This was very much the minority view. For the most part, both branches of the legal profession, the judiciary, and both the lay and the legal press strongly supported the Woolf reforms.[88] The only serious problem about the Woolf proposals raised by those who supported them was whether the government would put in the necessary resources to make them work, notably in regard to IT.

Writing in 2003, some four years having elapsed since the reforms went live in April 1999, what do we know about their impact – and how do we know it? The latter is important as only solid research can produce solid results. (For an assessment of the research situation in March 1997 (ie pre-Woolf) plus recommendations see a report commissioned by the LCD – T Goriely, *Evaluating the Woolf reforms – obtaining baseline data on the cost and length of civil litigation*.[89])

Apart from the above-mentioned study by Goriely, Moorhead and Abrams commissioned by the Law Society and the Civil Justice Council, by May 2003 there had been no published studies that count as proper research. The LCD's publications on evaluation of the Woolf reforms – *Emerging Findings* (March 2001)[90] and *Further Findings* (August 2002[91] drew on a combination of sources: – reports of the Law Society's Woolf Network based on responses by some 130 solicitors knowledgeable in the field who agreed to answer periodic questionnaires on how in their view the reforms were working in practice[92]; surveys by the Expert Witness Institute, the Court Service User Satisfaction Surveys in March, November 2001 and June 2002. There have also been reports made by individual law firms. There are quite a number

---

[87]   See M Zander, 'Are There Any Clothes for the Emperor to Wear?', *New Law Journal*, 3 February 1995, p 154; 'Why Lord Woolf's Proposed Reforms of Civil Litigation Should be Rejected' in *Reform of Civil Procedure–Essays on Access to Justice* (ed AAS Zuckerman and R Cranston, Clarendon, 1995, pp 79–95); and the Chancery Bar Association lecture 'The Woolf Report: Forwards or Backwards for the new Lord Chancellor?', 16 *Civil Justice Quarterly*, July 1997, pp 208-27. Lord Woolf used the occasion of the Gee Lecture at the Royal College of Physicians to reply, 'Medics, Lawyers and the Courts', 16 *Civil Justice Quarterly*, October 1997, pp 302-17 and also on www.lcd.gov.uk/judicial/speeches/speechfr.htm. For the writer's riposte see 'Woolf on Zander', *New Law Journal*, 23 May, 1997, p 768. For a broader view of the issues see the writer's Lionel Cohen Lecture given at the Hebrew University in Jerusalem, 'What can be done about cost and delay in civil litigation?', 31 *Israel Law Review*, 1997, pp 703-23.

[88]   For a very positive early assessment of progress by the civil servant in charge of implementation see D Gladwell, 'Modern Litigation Culture: The First Six Months of the Civil Justice Reforms in England and Wales', 19 *Civil Justice Quarterly*, 2000, pp 9-18.

[89]   The 34-page report was published by Social Legal Research, 227a Richmond Road, Twickenham TW1 2NJ.

[90]   See www.lcd.gov.uk/civil/emerge/emerge.htm. For a summary of the main findings see 'Effects of the Civil Justice Reforms', 20 *Civil Justice Quarterly*, 2001, pp.301-02

[91]   www.lcd.gov.uk/civil/reform/ffreform.htm.

[92]   They have been published roughly twice yearly. No1 in September 1999; No 2 in March 2000; No 3 in February 2001; No 4 in February 2002; No 5 in September 2002. The 4th, 5th and subsequent reports are accessible on www.lawsociety.org (Civil Litigation).

of articles written by a variety of authors of the 'Woolf reforms one/two/three years on' variety based on a mixture of opinion and impression – and plenty of anecdotal evidence.

So far as the writer was able to ascertain, as at mid-2003, the only ongoing Woolf reform related research, properly so-called, were two studies on case management.[93]

APPARENT BENEFITS DERIVING FROM THE WOOLF REFORMS

The majority of those concerned with the civil litigation business seem to believe that the Woolf reforms are working quite well. Even those who have concerns are mainly, on balance, positive.

The indications from a variety of sources seem to justify the following propositions as to benefits flowing from the implementation of the Woolf reforms:

- A less adversarial culture is developing – confounding the views of pessimists such as the writer who considered such a development improbable.
- Pre-action protocols appear to be working to promote earlier settlement and probably more settlement.
- Since pre-action protocols result in more work being done earlier, cases that would have settled anyway are likely to settle on the basis of more relevant information.
- Part 36 – and especially the possibility of Part 36 offers by claimants – seems to be helping to achieve earlier and perhaps more settlements.
- The use of single joint experts is working better than critics feared. (However, unpublished research suggests that this may not save money and may even cost more. Also, in commercial cases, parties are hiring their own experts to shadow the joint experts. J Peysner, 'Controlling costs', *New Law Journal*, 25 July 2003, p 1147, 1148.)
- The fact that parties can be ordered to pay the costs of interlocutory applications right away has resulted in fewer interlocutory applications.

However there are important issues that give rise to concern and others still where there is uncertainty.

ISSUES OF CONCERN OR UNCERTAINTY

The fall in the number of cases issued

It was one of Lord Woolf's aims that more cases would settle without the need for legal proceedings.

---

[93] One, a mainly quantitative study, was being conducted in house by the LCD itself, the other, a qualitative study based on interviews, was being conducted by Professors John Peysner and Mary Seneviratne of Nottingham Trent. Both were scheduled to finish in 2004. Neither, however, was researching the issues surrounding costs generated by case management.

There has been a significant drop in the number of claims issued. The LCD report *Further Findings* (2002) stated 'Overall there has been a drop in the number of claims issued, in particular in the type of claim most affected by the new Civil Procedure Rules introduced in April 1999' (para 3.1). To test the matter it looked at the number of claims issued in the years 1997 to 2001. This showed that there was a peak early in 1999 and then a large drop in claims issued in the county court immediately after the introduction of the new rules. Although month by month the figures varied, the report said, 'this overall downward trend has now been stable for three years since April 1999 and would appear to be well established' (para 3.3).

However, a rather different picture emerges if one takes a longer time frame. In the years 1958-78 the figures for money claims issued in the county court were stable at a little over 1m. In 1988 they were double that at 2.1m. By 1998 they had jumped again to 3m and they rose to a peak of 3.5m in 1992. But since 1992, year by year there was a significant drop. In 1998, the year before implementation of Woolf the number at 2m was half that of 1990. By 2001 it had fallen to 1.5m. In other words, since there was a considerable fall year by year from 1992 onwards it plainly does not make sense to attribute the further fall since 1999 exclusively or even mainly to the Woolf reforms.

(As has been seen, one unfortunate side effect of the drop in the number of civil cases being litigated is a corresponding fall in the income derived from court fees. While the LCD, no doubt driven by the Treasury, continues to insist on the full recovery of the costs of the civil court system from litigants, this will have the inevitable result of forcing the level of court fees even higher, which could further reduce the number of cases ....)

Costs

It was an aim of the reforms that the cost of litigation would be more affordable, more predictable and more proportionate to the value and complexity of individual cases.

The research evidence, so far, derives from the above mentioned research by Goriely, Moorhead and Abrams and from the study conducted for the Civil Justice Council by P Fenn and N Rickman (*Cost of Low Value RTA claims 1997-2002*, January 2003.[94]

The study by Goriely, Moorhead and Abrams They looked at the effect of the Woolf reform on costs both through interviews with the players and by examining pre-Woolf and post-Woolf files of concluded cases.

---

[94]   www.civiljusticecouncil.org.uk. The study was of settled claims. It used various large data bases including 27,378 from one insurance company, 11,420 from a second, 150,000 cases handled by claims negotiators for 20 different insurance companies and 5,852 cases handled by a claimant solicitor's firm.

Claimant solicitors said that different changes had had different effects. The fact that fewer claims were issued was thought to lead to obvious cost reductions. It was also suggested that cases 'were now more focused with fewer unnecessary disputes over side issues' (p 172). The courts were also felt to put more emphasis on proportionality, with a consequent downward pressure on costs' (p 172). On the other hand, costs had been increased by 'front-loading' with more work needed at an earlier stage. More work was necessary before issue 'as the fast-track timetable left little time to obtain expert evidence or witness statements once litigation had begun' (p 172). 'By and large, claimant solicitors thought front-loading was right (in that it was work that should be done) but they suggested that inevitably, it had a cost impact. Claimant solicitors disagreed as to whether costs, overall, had gone up, down or had stayed about the same.

By contrast, insurers 'were united in their views. They all said that, since April 1999, the average cost of a personal injury claim had increased markedly. They felt this to be the reforms' "major weakness"'. (p 174)

After considering various sets of figures the researchers concluded: 'The evidence produced by the insurance industry is strong prima facie evidence that the cost of personal injury claims has increased.' (p 175) But the figures only related to claims settled in-house, before proceedings had been issued. 'One cannot be sure of the overall impact of the reforms, until one is able to take into account the costs of litigated claims. These may take another few years to work their way through the system' (p 175).

The authors also reported on the figures in the study of files of actual cases. These were all small cases that had settled quickly with little substantive dispute. The median amount paid by opponents in post-Woolf cases was £1,576, compared with £1,393 for pre-Woolf cases – a difference that was just statistically significant. (The mean rose from £1,580 to £1,761, a rise of 11% which was lower than in the figures produced by the insurance industry but higher than inflation (8%). (p 175)[95]

The study by Fenn and Rickman In their conclusions (p 17) they reported that for low value (<£15k) RTA cases at the end of July 2001, mean base costs (excluding disbursements) were approximately £2,000 and mean disbursements were approximately £500. This represented a rise of approximately 25% in base costs over the previous 18 months (ie from mid 2000 to end 2001) and of approximately 10% in disbursements.

The increases in base costs and disbursements were greatest in the cases in which legal proceedings had not been issued -50% and 25% respectively. ('To the extent that these agreed costs reflect legal inputs, it appears that much more work is being done at the pre-issue stage in cases settling from 2000 onwards. This is consistent with Woolf driven cost increases – though more work would be required to confirm this with statistical confidence.' (p 11)

[95]   The rise was not due to recoverable success fees (p 176).

The increases were not different as between conditional fee (CFA) cases and non-CFA cases.

Costs rose proportionately to damages and to the complexity of the case.

The authors ended their list of findings:

> The trends in costs we have reported *appear consistent* with the effect of Lord Woolf's reforms on the 'front loading' of casework. This is particularly the case given that the changes are concentrated on non-CFA, pre-issue cases, at a time when 'Woolf cases' were beginning to be settled in significant numbers.

But again the authors emphasised that more work was needed to establish with statistical confidence whether the apparent causal relation suggested by logic and timing between the Woolf reforms and the rise in costs, was real.

At the time of writing, there were no cost figures concerning the impact of case management – and the signs were that no such figures were likely to emerge. (As was seen above, regrettably, neither of the studies in hand were set up to produce such data.) But if the Rand study in the United States is relevant and if the indications of the effect on costs of front-loading in the study by Fenn and Rickman are confirmed, it would seem inevitable that Woolf-style case management too will have the effect of pushing up costs. The reality is that whenever the court gets lawyers to act, costs tend to go up. (Lord Woolf at a very late stage himself conceded this – in his Gee Lecture in May 1997: 'While I favour the greater case management which is now possible I recognise that case management does involve the parties in more expense'.[96]

As to predictability, the erratic decisions of the courts in regard to Part 36 offers and payment into court (above) and equally as regards the rule that costs follow the event (below) have introduced a major new degree of uncertainty into the litigation process.

Predictability in regard to costs will obviously be increased once the new system for fixed costs for RTA cases that settle without legal proceedings for under £10,000 is in place. (See p 000 below.)

Delay

The Goriely, Moorhead, Abrams study (p 63, n 12 above) suggests that the impact of the reforms on delay, at least in run-of-the-mill small cases that settle without proceedings, is neutral. The benefits from matters that went more quickly were cancelled by others that went more slowly.

The *Judicial Statistics* for 2001 reported that the average waiting time from issue of claim to trial in the county court decreased between 1998 and 1999 from 85 to 79 weeks and had since decreased further to 74 weeks (2000) and 73 weeks (2001).[97] In

---

[96]   16 *Civil Justice Quarterly*, 1997, 302, 314 and also www.lcd.gov.uk/judicial/speeches/speechfr.htm.)

[97]   Table 4.17.

the High Court, the average waiting time in 2001 was 173 weeks compared with 164 in 2000, 174 in 1999 and 178 in 1998.[98]

In the Woolf reports delay was presented as wholly bad. But this is not necessarily so. A study by the Rand Corporation found that litigants seem more concerned about the fairness of the process than about delays, or even whether they won or lost. (See M Zander, 'What Litigants Think of the Tort System', *New Law Journal*, 20 October 1989, p 1422.) See also R Dingwall, T Durkin and WLF Felstiner, 'Delay in Tort Cases: Critical Reflections on the Civil Justice Review', 9 *Civil Justice Quarterly*, October 1990, pp 353–65 which showed that for expert litigators delay was simply a resource to be managed in the best interests of the clients and Dingwall and Dinkin, 'Time Management and Procedural Reform: Some Questions for Lord Woolf' in *Reform of Civil Procedure–Essays on Access to Justice* (ed AAS Zuckerman and R Cranston, Clarendon, 1995, p 371–392).

Inconsistent decisions

One effect of the reforms is greatly to increase judicial discretion in the decision-making of pre-trial judges – district judges, masters, circuit judges, High Court judges. Appeals in interlocutory matters are not encouraged. The result is a great increase in inconsistent but unappealable decisions. (The Law Society's Woolf Network's responses to the periodic questions posed about the state of the reforms has highlighted this issue repeatedly. At the time of writing the most recent report from the Network was the 5th, dated December 2002. Respondents complained of inconsistency in regard to the assessment of costs, sanctions generally, time-table targets, the use and numbers of experts, case management decisions, pre-action disclosure, and security for costs.)

The Designated Civil Judge role was created to promote greater consistency and it no doubt has had some impact but in the writer's view the problem cannot be significantly improved whether by judicial training or supervision or guidance from appellate level courts or anywhere else. It is part of the price that has to be paid for the benefits of the reforms.

Unjust application of sanctions

When disproportionate sanctions are imposed – *pour encourager les autres* – the result is, by definition, unjust in the particular case. Lord Woolf insisted that the courts would need to enforce the rules and it is clear that to an extent they are doing so. The five Court of Appeal decisions described above (pp 74-76) on failures in regard to service of claims, illustrate the point. As those cases show, the Court of Appeal believes that enforcing procedural rules is even more important than achieving justice in the particular case.

98   Table 3.9.

Again, inconsistency aggravates the problem. Judges differ as to how rigorous they are prepared to be in applying the rules and sanctions for breach. Even individual judges who on one day are strict, may on the next day in similar circumstances be more lenient. The result is unpredictability.

Can the courts cope?

The extra burdens that fall on the courts as a result of the Woolf reforms pose a severe challenge. Complaints from all round the country suggest that the courts are – and are likely to remain – seriously under-resourced and the provision of IT, which Lord Woolf constantly said was vital to the success of the enterprise, remains woefully inadequate.

In May 2003, Lord Justice Brooke, the Judge in charge of Modernisation, reporting directly to the Lord Chief Justice, spoke about the current position:

> Far and away our greatest need is to introduce software systems which will enable court staff and judges to manage court business better in the civil and family courts. Today the courts are not networked … . we are miles behind most government departments and modern private sector businesses. In the autumn we also hope that testing will have begun for the new software systems we will use in future in all our courts. At present we rely on paper filing systems. It is not always easy to retain and motivate staff when files go missing, or get into a muddle quite so often. Nowadays court users have every reason to complain about some of the delays and inefficiencies that occur. Once modern software is in place, court staff and judges with case-management responsibilities will be able to handle cases far more efficiently before trial than is possible today. A modern electronic diary and listing system will enable trial dates to be fixed more quickly and judges' time to be more effectively used. Unfortunately, the Treasury decided not to back these plans, for the time being at least. On 15 July 2002 the Government published its spending plans up to April 2006 … . very large sums of money have been earmarked for IT in the criminal justice system, and within the next three years IT infrastructure should be installed in all our Crown Court centres. Attention has also been paid to the need for information to flow more easily between the different agencies in the criminal justice system. But so far as our civil and family courts are concerned, we are at present engaged in working out how we can best make progress over the next three years without Treasury backing on the scale for which we had hoped. We still do not know exactly what money will be available to us for the next three years.'[99]

The fact that the civil courts are supposed to be funded out of court fees and that the number of proceedings has been falling only adds to the problems of finding the money to establish appropriate IT technology for the courts.

[99]   Speech at a seminar in Leeds, 28 May 2003 – see www.lcd.gov.uk/judicial/speeches/ speechfr.htm.

CONCLUSION

On the basis of the evidence to date, the writer remains of the view that on balance the disadvantages of the reforms outweigh the advantages. He believes that if Lord Woolf had presented his package of reforms with an admission that, in addition to the great upheaval involved, they would end by costing most litigants more, that they would not greatly reduce delays (if at all) and that they would hugely increase uncontrollable judicial discretion, it is doubtful whether they would have been implemented. Certainly, benefits of various kinds are resulting from the reforms but in the writer's view they are not sufficient to compensate for the detriments. (For a generally downbeat overall assessment see also Suzanne Burns, 'The Woolf Reforms in retrospect', *Legal Action* July 2003, pp 8-11.)

Alternative dispute resolution – ADR

In the last few years there has been a dramatic upsurge in new schemes and systems of alternative dispute settlement (ADR) which now has a large literature of its own and much support. ADR has not yet become directly part of the court system– as has happened in the United States. But it has increasingly been brought into connection with the ordinary legal system – a development that was given great further emphasis through the CPR.

In December 1993, a Practice Direction in the Commercial Court introduced questions about ADR into the pre-trial check list to be answered by the parties. Legal advisers were urged to ensure that parties were fully informed of the most cost effective means of resolving disputes ([1994] 1 All ER 34). In January 1995, the Lord Chief Justice's Practice Direction (p 120 above) gave strong backing for the importance of ADR. The Practice Direction gave the text of the pre-trial check list to be lodged with the court. This specifically asked solicitors to state whether some form of ADR might 'assist to resolve or narrow the issues in this case' and whether there has been exploration with the client or the other side of the possibility of resolving the dispute (or particular issues) by ADR?

In 1996, the judges of the Commercial Court announced that in appropriate cases they would invite the parties to take positive steps to set in motion ADR procedures. The judge might adjourn the proceedings for a specified period of time to encourage and enable the parties to take such steps. If, after discussion with both sides, it appeared that an early neutral evaluation was likely to assist in the resolution of the matters in dispute, the judge might offer to provide that evaluation or to arrange for another judge to do so. The judge who provided the early neutral evaluation would, unless the parties agreed otherwise, take no further part in the case. (See on this development *Law Society's Gazette*, 19 June, 1996, pp 36, 39, *Solicitors' Journal*, 16 October, 1999, p 936; and more generally on ADR for heavy commercial cases, *Law Society's Gazette*, 5 November, 1997, p 22-27.)

Another field in which ADR, in the form of mediation, appeared to be making some progress was that of matrimonial disputes and divorce. Mediation is a method of resolving disputes by having a neutral third party guide the parties to their own solution. Lord Woolf's Report called it a form of 'facilitated negotiation'. In 1995, the Government announced that it intended that mediation should have a formal role in a new form of no-fault divorce. (White Paper, *Looking to the Future: Mediation and the Grounds for Divorce*, Cm 2799, 1995.) Mediation, it said, would reduce bitterness, would improve communication between couples and would help them reach agreement. Also, it should be more cost-effective. The White Paper said that the Government was satisfied that even when mediators were paid more than had been the case in the pilot studies, 'family mediation will still prove to be more cost effective than negotiating at arms length through two separate lawyers and even more so than litigating through the courts' (p 42, para 5.19).

Though mediation was not to be compulsory it was to be strongly promoted. Part II of the Family Law Act 1996 which provided for no-fault divorce, also included a requirement to attend an information meeting (s 8) at which the parties would get information about marriage counselling and on conflict resolution and mediation. Intending divorcees would be told that mediation might be a better alternative to litigation and confrontation in the courts. Part II also had a power for the court to direct that the parties attend a meeting to explain mediation (s 13). Part III provided that legal aid could be given for mediation in family matters (s 27). Before the Legal Aid Board could consider an application for legal aid, clients were supposed to attend an appointment with a mediation provider to see whether mediation would be suitable. Only if it was deemed to be unsuitable could the client get legal aid for representation for legal proceedings.

The Legal Aid Board initiated a number of pilot studies to test this system. But the pilot studies proved disappointing. Many tried to avoid the intake interview. Fewer were deemed suitable for mediation than had been hoped. The Advisory Board under the Act said in its Second Annual Report in May 1999, 'while the implementation of Section 29 has clearly already had some impact, the proportion of cases in the pilot franchises electing to use mediation remains as yet very small' (para 2.25). The result of low usage is that the average cost per case amongst mediation providers is high, as their fixed costs are spread over a small number of cases. Interim findings from research into the pilots conducted by Newcastle University suggested that only 7% of people who attended the s 8 information meetings went on to mediation. Four out of ten people reported that after attending these meetings they were more likely to go to a solicitor. (For the implications, see D Hodson, 'Family Law Act 1996; Where now?' *Solicitors' Journal* 2 July 1999, p 632 and *Law Society's Gazette* 21 July 1999, p 22, 31. For the background see S Roberts, 'Decision-Making for Life Apart', 58 *Modern Law Review*, 1995, pp 714-22. For discussion of the problem and possible solutions see G Bevan et al, 'Piloting a Quasi-Market for Family Mediation among Clients Eligible for Legal Aid', *Civil Justice Quarterly*, 1999, pp 239-48. See also A Baker and P Townsend, 'Is our Faith in Mediation Misplaced?', 163 *Justice of the Peace*, 20 March 1999, p 224.)

An announcement about implementation of Part II of the 1996 Act was expected in summer 1999 but in June 1999, in a Written Parliamentary Answer, Lord Irvine announced that implementation of Part II of the Act would be postponed until 2000 when the full results of the pilot studies would be available.[100] Experts predicted that in reality this spelled the end of the provisions – or at least that the Lord Chancellor had decided that they would not be implemented in the then current Parliament. They were proved to be right. By 2003 nothing further had moved on this front.

There was speculation as to the reasons. Had the Lord Chancellor been persuaded that mediation would not after all be cheaper? Was he worried about political rows over no-fault divorce? Did he see the compulsory information sessions to 'push' mediation instead of court proceedings as an infringement of civil liberties? Whatever the reason, the abandonment of the project was plainly a set-back for the mediation bandwagon.

Another technique of alternative dispute resolution is the *Ombudsmen* who deal with complaints in a variety of contexts in both the public and the private sector. The public sector ombudsmen include the Parliamentary Commissioner, the Local Government Commissioner, and the Legal Services Ombudsman.[101] Private sector ombudsmen existed in a number of industries such as insurance, building societies, pensions, banking and estate agencies.(The Financial Services and Markets Act 1999 amalgamated several of these schemes in the person of one 'overlord' Financial Services Ombudsman.) In his Interim Report Lord Woolf expressed the hope that the private ombudsmen system 'which has an impressive track record in relation to the service industries' should be extended to cover consumer complaints in the retail sector (p 139, para 16). They had many advantages including the fact that they are free and that complainants do not need the assistance of lawyers. Using the ombudsman did not prevent the complainant from taking legal proceedings if in the event the ombudsman was not able to provide a satisfactory outcome.

WOOLF AND ADR

Lord Woolf's Interim Report devoted a chapter to ADR. He did not propose that ADR should be imposed compulsorily on parties to civil litigation but he greatly welcomed the development and the strengthening of ADR. He suggested that in multi track cases at the case management conference and pre-trial review the parties should be required to state whether the question of ADR had been discussed and if not, why not. The Lord Chancellor and the Court Service should treat it as one of their responsibilities to make the public aware of the possibility offered by ADR. There should be a closer relationship between ombudsmen and the courts. Ombudsmen

---

[100] House of Lords, *Hansard*, 17 June 1999, vol 602, WA col 39.
[101] See on this subject, for instance, R Nobles, 'Access to Justice through Ombudsmen: the Courts' Response to the Pensions Ombudsman', 21 *Civil Justice Quarterly*, 2002, pp 94-117.

should have the right to apply to a court for a ruling on a point of law without requiring the complainant to commence legal proceedings. It would also be an advantage if the courts were able to refer issues to an ombudsman, subject to the parties' consent and that of the ombudsman in question. In any subsequent proceedings, the ombudsman's findings of fact would be accepted as being correct in the absence of evidence to the contrary. This would involve changes to the statutory position of public ombudsmen. The same concept should be applied to private sector ombudsmen if they thought it acceptable (p 140).

In his Final Report, Lord Woolf urged that people should be encouraged to use the growing number of grievance procedures, ombudsmen or other available ADR method before taking judicial review proceedings. (p 251, para 7) He repeated his Interim Report recommendations on ADR and added a new one – that when considering what order to make as to costs, the court should be able to take into account a party's unreasonable refusal to attempt ADR or lack of cooperation in ADR.

ADR features prominently in the new rules. CPR 1.4(1) states that 'the court must further the overriding objective by actively managing cases'. CPR 1.4(2) goes on by elaborating 12 different examples of what active case management means. The fifth of these is 'encouraging the parties to use an alternative dispute resolution procedure if the court considers that appropriate and facilitating the use of such procedure'. The duty is therefore that of the court but under CPR 1.3 the parties have the obligation of helping the court to further the overriding objective. When filing the allocation questionnaire a party may make a written request for the proceedings to be stayed 'while the parties try to settle the case by alternative dispute resolution or other means' (CPR 26.4). Also the court can order a stay of its own initiative. (CPR 26.4(2)(b)) As has been noted, legal aid is available for mediation. The courts should have details of local ADR facilities. Sabotaging the effort at ADR could be penalised in costs if the case comes back to the courts.

This happened in *Dunnett v Railtrack plc*[102] where the Court of Appeal refused to give the successful defendants their costs because they had refused to consider ADR which the trial judge had urged should be attempted when he granted leave to appeal from his decision.

In *Cable & Wireless plc v IBM United Kingdom Ltd*[103] the judge held that IBM could enforce a clause in the contract requiring that the parties should attempt in good faith to resolve the dispute through 'an Alternative Dispute Resolution (ADR) procedure as recommended to the parties by the Centre for Dispute Resolution' even though it also said, 'However, an ADR procedure which is being followed shall not prevent any party from issuing proceedings.' Colman J stayed the proceedings issued by Cable & Wireless on the grounds that there was a mutual intention that litigation

---

[102]   [2002] EWCA Civ 303, [2002] 1 WLR 2434, [2002] 2 All ER 850.
[103]   [2002] EWHC 2059 (Comm), [2002] 2 All ER (Comm) 1041.

should be a last resort, that the ADR clause was much more than an agreement to negotiate and, above all, that there were good public policy grounds for enforcing the clause. ('For the courts now to decline to enforce contractual references to ADR on the grounds of intrinsic uncertainty would be to fly in the face of public policy as expressed in the Civil Procedure Rules and as reflected in the judgment of the Court of Appeal in *Dunnett v Railtrack'*. For comment see C Newmark, 'In praise of ADR', 152 *New Law Journal*, December 13, 2002, p 1896.

Another landmark decision was *R (Cowl) v Plymouth City Council*[104] in which the Court of Appeal held that judicial review proceedings (regarding the closing of an old age home) should not be allowed to go ahead if a significant part of the issues could be resolved outside the litigation process. The lawyers on both sides were under a heavy obligation to resort to litigation only if it was really unavoidable.[105]

See also *Royal Bank of Canada Trust Corpn Ltd v Secretary of State for Defence*, LTL 14 May 2003, Ch D in which the judge refused to award any costs to the Department of Defence even though it had won on the substantive issue – because of its 'surprising' rejection of an offer of mediation by the claimants. The judge said he was influenced in particular by the Government's 2001 pledge that 'ADR will be considered and used in all suitable cases wherever the other party accepts it'.

But a litigant's refusal to engage in ADR will not always be treated as unreasonable. In *Watson Wyatt v Maxwell Batley*,[106] Colman J refused the claimant's application to block part of the defendant solicitors firm's costs because their refusal to mediate had not been unreasonable. The judge held that three separate invitations to mediate were not genuine but had been employed as an aggressive tactic. See similarly *Hurst v Leeming*[107] where Lightman J held that a barrister involved in professional negligence proceedings was entitled to his full costs even though he had refused to mediate. His refusal was not unreasonable because the personality of the opponent made it improbable that mediation would succeed.

Whilst, the 'mood music' of the courts is now increasingly in favour of ADR so far at least, ADR is making very slow headway on the ground as a means of resolving civil disputes.

The abandonment of mediation under the Family Law Act was an obvious example. Another was the rather modest success of the scheme to promote ADR set up in January 1996 at the Central London county court. All defendants facing non-family civil disputes of over £3,000 were offered mediation at the nominal rate of £25. Research on the project by Professor Hazel Genn of University College, London found that, despite the negligible cost, only 5% of litigants approached took up the

---

[104] [2001] EWCA Civ 1935, [2002] 1 WLR 803.
[105] For comment see K Ashton and J Halford, 'ADR and judicial review – a cultural revolution', *Legal Action*, June 2002, p 15.
[106] LTL, 15 November 2002, *Solicitors' Journal*, 29 November 2002, p 1072.
[107] [2001] EWHC 1051 (Ch), [2003] 1 Lloyd's Rep 379.

offer. Those who did use the service achieved a settlement in 62% of cases and generally were satisfied. The process promoted and speeded up settlement and reduced conflicts. But it was unclear to what extent the mediation saved costs – and, where the mediation was unsuccessful, the mediation had the effect of increasing costs. Also the level of damages was distinctly lower than that of the courts – a possible explanation why most practitioners seem less than enthusiastic.[108]

However the scheme has continued and indeed developed. By 2003 there were comparable schemes at four other county courts – Birmingham, Leeds, Exeter and Guildford.

In Spring 2002, the LCD published another study by Professor Genn – *Court based ADR Initiatives for non-family civil disputes: the Commercial Court and the Court of Appeal*[109] The Commercial Court had been identifying cases suitable for ADR since 1993 and the judge may make an order directing the parties to attempt ADR to resolve the dispute. The study covered the four-year period July 1996 to June 2000. The number of orders had grown considerably since the introduction of the CPR. Where pre-CPR, the average rate was about 30 annually; in the last six months there had been 68 such orders. During the whole period there were 233 cases in which an ADR order had been made. Information was available regarding 184. Of these, 103 (56%) tried mediation.

Summarising her research on ADR Orders in the Commercial Court, the Court of Appeal ADR scheme and the earlier Central London County Court mediation scheme, Professor Genn drew the following conclusions:[110]

- Voluntary take-up of invitations to enter ADR schemes remains at a modest level, even when the mediator's services are provided free or at a nominal cost
- Outside of commercial practice, the profession remains very cautious about the use of ADR. Positive experience of ADR does not appear to be producing armies of converts. Explanations may lie in the amount of work involved in preparing for mediation, the incentives and economics of mediation in low-value cases, and the impact of the Woolf reforms. More pre-issue settlements and swifter post-issue settlements may diminish the perceived need for ADR in run-of-the-mill cases.
- An individualised approach to the direction of cases toward ADR is likely to be more effective than general invitations at an early stage in the litigation process … .

---

[108] H Genn, *The Central London county court Pilot Mediation Scheme*, LCD Research Series 5/98. For a substantial report on the state of ADR in the UK construction industry see N Gould and M Cohen, 'ADR: Appropriate Dispute Resolution in the UK Construction Industry', *Civil Justice Quarterly*, April 1998, pp 103-27. The conclusion was that although formalised mediation was only rarely invoked it was a technique that was available for appropriate cases.

[109] LCD Research Series 1/2002.

[110] See the Executive summary at www.lcd.gov.uk (research).

- Subjective perceptions of the profession support the view that *successful* ADR saves the likely costs of proceedings to trial and may save expenditure by promoting earlier settlement than might otherwise have occurred. *Unsuccessful* ADR can increase the costs for parties.

ADR generally results in a high level of customer satisfaction.

It seems clear that, despite the hype and its success when used, ADR is only used in a tiny proportion of cases.

Reasons for the low take-up of ADR by litigants have been suggested by the Centre for Effective Dispute Resolution (CEDR):
- The process is unfamiliar to clients and practitioners. The latter in particular and not unnaturally prefer to stick to what they know and how they normally operate unless there are incentives to do otherwise.
- Classic positional negotiation behaviour in conflict makes it awkward for a party to suggest talks or even talks about talks.
- People resist going to third parties (including advisers and the courts) unless they either (1) are familiar with the process, (ii) see it as the only real option, (iii) accept it as a 'socially credible' (i.e. a known and acceptable) option.[111]

FURTHER READING

For some basic reading on ADR see: Karl Mackie (ed), *A Handbook of Alternative Dispute Resolution* (Routledge and Sweet & Maxwell, 1991); HJ Brown and AL Marriott, *ADR Principles and Practice* (Sweet & Maxwell, 2nd ed, 1999); National Consumer Council, *Settling Consumer Disputes: A Review of Alternative Dispute Resolution*, 1993; JS Auerbach, *Justice without Law* (Yale University Press, 1983); RL Abel, *The Politics of Informal Justice* (Academic Press, 1982); AH Bevan, *Alternative Dispute Resolution* (Sweet & Maxwell, 1992); and the special issue of the Modern Law Review, 'Dispute Resolution and its Alternatives', May 1993.

See also: R Williams, 'Should the State Provide Alternative Dispute Resolution Services?', *Civil Justice Quarterly*, April 1987, p 142; Richard Thomas, 'Alternative Dispute Resolution–Consumer Disputes', *Civil Justice Quarterly*, July 1988, p 206; R Young, 'Neighbour Dispute Mediation: Theory and Practice', *Civil Justice Quarterly*, October 1989, p 319; 'ADR in Commercial Disputes: CEDR', *Civil Justice Quarterly*, July 1991, p 210; 'Alternative Dispute Resolution, Courts and Legal Services Committee, The Law Society, 1991, 1992; Bar Council (Beldam) Committee on Alternative Dispute Resolution, Report, 1991; AF Acland, 'Simply Negotiation with Knobs On', *Legal Action*, November 1995, pp 8–9; P Brooker and A Lavers, ' Issues in the Development of ADR for Commercial and Construction Disputes', *Civil Justice Quarterly*, 2000, p 353; and P Brooker, 'Commercial and

[111]   CEDR *Response to LCD Discussion Paper on Alternative Dispute Resolution*, February 2000.

Construction ADR: Lawyers' Attitudes and Experience', *Civil Justice Quarterly*, 2002, p 327.

On some of the problems associated with the growth of ADR in the United States see J Resnick, 'Failing Faith: Adjudicatory Procedure in Decline', 53 *University of Chicago L Rev* , 1986, p 494; 'Many Doors? Closing Doors? Alternative Dispute Resolution and Adjudication', *10 Ohio State Jrnl on Dispute Resolution*, 1995, p 212.

Chapter 3

Pre-trial criminal proceedings

Introduction

This chapter deals with one of the most important aspects of any legal system – how suspects are dealt with pre-trial, and police powers. It offers a great deal of scope for discussion of matters of both principle and practice. It is also an area where a considerable volume of empirical work has been done.

The recent history of pre-trial criminal proceedings in England and Wales has been dominated by the enactment of the Police and Criminal Evidence Act 1984 ('PACE') a modern recasting of police powers. The Act was the product of the Philips Royal Commission on Criminal Procedure (1981, Cmnd 8092), which was established by a Labour Government in 1978[1] and reported to a Conservative Government in January 1981. Twenty years after its original enactment, although it had been developed by literally hundreds of amendments, PACE was still the central piece of legislation in the field.

The Act is accompanied by six Codes of Practice: Code A on Stop and Search; Code B on Search of Premises; Code C on Detention, Questioning and Treatment of Persons in Custody; Code D on Identification; Code E on Tape-recording of Interviews; and Code F on Visual Recording with Sound of Interviews. (The last was introduced in April 2002 in pilot areas only.) The Codes too have been revised from time to time. The latest major revision came into force on 1 April 2003.

The Codes are the result of extensive consultation with interested bodies and persons and have to be approved by Parliament.[2]

---

[1] For the background see M Zander, 'The criminal process – a subject ripe for a major inquiry' [1977] *Criminal Law Review* 249.

[2] The Criminal Justice Bill 2002/03 as originally published required only that new Codes be laid before Parliament but the Government retreated on this. The Lord Chancellor, Lord Falconer, confirmed on the 2nd Reading in the Lords on 16 June 2003, that an amendment would be moved to restore the requirement of an affirmative resolution.

Technically, the Codes are not law,[3] nor can a breach of the Codes be made the subject of an action for damages or a criminal prosecution against a police officer (PACE, s 67(10)). Originally PACE (s 67(8)) provided that a breach of the Codes was automatically an offence against the police disciplinary code, but this section was repealed by the Police and Magistrates' Courts Act 1994. (Hardly any disciplinary proceedings for breaches of PACE had in fact been brought.[4])

The main sanction behind the Codes is that a judge may exclude evidence obtained in breach of the rules and where the judge failed to do so, an appeal court may quash a conviction (s 67(11)). As will be seen below (p 000), this has happened often.

On PACE, see M Zander, *The Police and Criminal Evidence Act 1984* (Sweet & Maxwell, 4th edn, 2003). See also generally Andrew Ashworth, *The Criminal Process: an Evaluative Study* (Clarendon, Oxford 2nd ed 1998); A Sanders and R Young, *Criminal Justice* (Butterworths, 2nd ed, 2000); M McConville, A Sanders and R Leng, *The Case for the Prosecution* (Routledge, 1991); M McConville, J Hodgson, L Bridges and A Pavlovic, *Standing Accused* (Clarendon, Oxford, 1994).

At various points in this chapter reference is made to the Eleventh Report of the Criminal Law Revision Committee (CLRC) (*Evidence, General*), published in June 1972 (Cmnd 4991). This report made a number of fundamental and highly controversial recommendations for changes in the rules of evidence and procedure in criminal cases. The CLRC's Report was received with such a volume of criticism, notably on the problem of the right of silence, that its recommendations (including some that were not controversial) were not implemented at the time.[5] However many of its recommendations, including those on the right to silence, were implemented years later – notably in the Criminal Justice and Public Order Act 1994 (CJPOA 1994).

This chapter deals extensively with the Reports of the Philips Royal Commission on Criminal Procedure (above) and of the Runciman Royal Commission on Criminal Justice (Cm 2263, 1993).[6] (The writer was a member of the Royal Commission.)[7]

The latest significant report in this area was Lord Justice Auld's *Review of the Criminal Courts of England and Wales* published in October 2001.[8] For appraisal of the Auld

---

3   See, however, *McCay* [1991] 1 All ER 232 in which the Court of Appeal said that the Codes had the full authority of Parliament behind them and that therefore there was statutory authority (*sic*) for a breach of the normal hearsay rule!

4   See Report of the Runciman Royal Commission on Criminal Justice, 1993, p 48, para 102.

5   See M Zander, 'The CLRC Evidence Report – a Survey of Reactions', *Law Society's Gazette*, 7 October 1974.

6   The Philips Commission also produced 12 separate research reports. Runciman produced 22 such reports.

7   For a critical assessment of the Runciman Royal Commission's Report see for instance *Criminal Justice in Crisis* (ed M McConville and L Bridges, Edward Elgar, 1994).

8   The 686-page report is accessible on www.lcd.gov.uk (Major Reports).

report see, for instance, the April 2002 issue of the *Criminal Law Review*. See also the writer's 75-page Response.[9]

The Government gave its response to the Auld Review in the White Paper *Justice for All*, Cm 5563, July 2002. The Criminal Justice Bill 2002/03 contained a number of its proposals. (At the time when this book was handed to the publishers the Bill had completed its Commons stages and had just begun its passage in the House of Lords. Given the length of the Bill[10] this was likely to go on until October. It is referred to here as the Criminal Justice Bill 2002/03. The clause numbers used here are those in the version of the Bill printed on 21 May 2003 before the Second Reading in the House of Lords.)

Also relevant is the Joint Review of PACE and the Codes of Practice by the Home Office and the Cabinet Office published in November 2002. (For the text see www.policereform.co.uk. For highly critical commentary see M Zander, 'The Joint Review of PACE: a Deplorable Report', 153 *New Law Journal*, February 14, 2002, p 204.)

Evaluating criminal justice systems

The terms of reference of the Philips Royal Commission asked, 'having regard both to the interests of the community in bringing offenders to justice and to the rights and liberties of persons suspected or accused of crime and taking into account also the need for the efficient and economical use of resources', to consider whether changes were needed in the system. The Philips Commission referred frequently to the need to strike a fundamental balance between the interests of the suspect and of the prosecution.

The terms of reference of the Runciman Royal Commission required it to 'examine the effectiveness of the criminal justice system in England and Wales in securing the conviction of those guilty of criminal offences and the acquittal of those who are innocent, having regard to the efficient use of resources'.

The terms of reference of Lord Justice Auld's inquiry, somewhat narrower than those of Philips and Runciman, were to inquire into 'the practices and procedures of, and the rules of evidence applied by, the criminal courts at every level, with a view to ensuring that they deliver justice fairly, by streamlining all their processes, increasing their efficiency and strengthening the effectiveness of their relationships with others across the whole of the criminal justice system, and having regard to the interests of all parties including victims and witnesses, thereby promoting public confidence in the rule of law'.

---

[9] Accessible on www.lcd.gov.uk (Major Reports/Comments received) or on www.lse.ac.uk/collections/law/news.)

[10] 307 clauses, 32 schedules, 369 pages.

Superficially, the different terms of reference of the three inquiries might suggest that each had a different agenda. But the essence of each was the same. Sensible assessment of the criminal justice system unavoidably has to take account of the proper concerns of the relevant interests. The most obvious are those of the prosecution and of the defence and the need to achieve due economy and efficiency. Auld's terms of reference added the interests of the victim and witnesses. On some topics primary weight is given to the interests of the prosecution (sometimes called the 'crime control' perspective; on others to the interests of the suspect (sometimes called the 'due process' perspective); on others again to the need for economy and efficiency. The civil libertarian will strike the balance differently from the police officer. The task of an external inquiry such as that of a Royal Commission is to consider all the evidence and then reach a considered view as to the pros and cons of all the arguments. The 15-person Philips Royal Commission and the 11-person Runciman Royal Commission consisted of a mixture of people knowledgeable about the system (judges, lawyers, police officers etc) and lay people with no prior experience of the criminal justice system. Both were unanimous in the majority of their recommendations. Though he had an advisory body, Lord Justice Auld basically conducted his inquiry on his own.[11]

For the contrasting view that principle rather than a search for a proper balance should guide reform of criminal justice systems see *Ashworth* (p 144, above, especially chapter 10).

When a report from an official advisory body such as a Royal Commission or the Criminal Law Revision Committee is received by the Government of the day it must decide whether, and if so, to what extent and in what way, to implement the recommendations. On evaluating criminal justice see further *Sanders and Young* (above) pp 1–26.

The first substantive topic dealt with here is the questioning of suspects.

1.   Questioning of suspects by the police

(a)   The importance and quality of police questioning

The questioning of suspects nowadays plays a central part in the police handling of the functions of prosecution.[12] A Home Office study of 12,500 custody record forms and observation over a total of 4,000 hours in 25 police stations showed that six out of ten detainees were interviewed in custody.[13] The overwhelming majority (96%)

---

[11]   On that see M Zander, 'Reforming the criminal justice system: too difficult to be left to one individual?' 151 *New Law Journal*, 30 November 2001, p 1774.

[12]   See for instance M McConville and J Baldwin, *Courts, Prosecution and Conviction* (Clarendon Press, 1981), ch 7; B Mitchell, 'Confessions and Police Interrogation of Suspects', [1983] *Criminal Law Review*, p 596; McConville et al (1991) p 112 above, ch 4.

[13]   T Bucke and D Brown, *In police custody: police powers and suspects' rights under the revised PACE codes of practice*, 1997, Home Office Research Series No 174.

were interviewed only once. Even in serious cases only one in five was interviewed more than once. (p 31)

It was not always so. Thus the Royal Commission on Police Powers and Procedure in 1929 made it clear that at that time the law was that where an arrest was necessary the constable should make it clear that the person was under arrest on a specific charge and: 'thereafter he should not question the prisoner ... although he should make a note of anything he says and should bring him straight to the police station for formal charging' (para 137). Whether this is what actually happened is a different question but that was the formal position. It was only recently that the courts directly recognised that the police could hold a suspect for questioning: see p 198 below.

Various studies have found that over half of suspects in detention confess when questioned. In Bucke and Brown, 1997, (n 2 above) confessions were made by 58%. (p 34) White suspects confessed more often than Afro-Caribbean and Asian suspects – 60% compared with 48% and 51% respectively. (p 33) Having legal advice is associated with fewer confessions. Two-thirds (66%) of those who had not had legal advice confessed compared with 47 % of those who had had legal advice (p 34).

THE QUALITY OF POLICE INTERVIEWING

Until recently the police received little or no training in questioning. Research conducted for the Home Office by Professor John Baldwin of Birmingham University showed that the results were not unduly impressive. The research was to inquire into video-taping of interviews but a side product was the first independent assessment of the quality of police interviews.[14]

Overall, he found that 64% of interviews were conducted 'competently', 25% were 'not very well conducted' and 11% were conducted 'poorly' (Table 3, p 14).

The main weaknesses identified were: 'a lack of preparation, a general ineptitude, poor technique, an assumption of guilt, unduly repetitive, persistent or laboured questioning, a failure to establish relevant facts and the exertion of too much pressure' (ibid).

> The image of police interviewers as professional, skilled and forceful interrogators scarcely matched the reality. Officers sometimes emerged as nervous, ill at ease and lacking in confidence. Even in the simplest cases, they were unfamiliar with the available evidence, and the video cameras often showed them with their eyes glued to a written statement, clearly unacquainted with its contents ... Many officers enter the interview room with their minds made up. They treat the suspect's explanation, if they bother to listen to it at all, with

[14] The study was based on 400 video recordings and 200 audio recordings of interviews conducted by the police in the West Midlands, West Mercia and London – J Baldwin, *Video Taping Police Interviews with Suspects – an Evaluation* (Home Office, Police Research Series, Paper No 1, 1992).

extreme scepticism from the outset. They are not predisposed, either from training or temperament, to think that they might be wrong. The questions asked (often leading questions starting as they do, from an assumption of guilt) merely seek to persuade suspects to agree to a series of propositions. If this is unsuccessful, discussion tends to be unhelpfully polarised, with claims and counter-claims, allegations and denials following a familiar circular path, descending often into a highly repetitive series of questions ... Some officers adopted an unduly harrying or aggressive approach in interviewing, and though this arose in a relatively small number of cases, these were the ones in which the present writer felt greatest unease about the outcome, particularly where they involved juveniles and young persons.

Another part of the mythology is that the great majority of interviews are with suspects who are awkward or aggressive. There are of course some interviews which are of this nature, but the great majority are not. Most involve relatively simple and straightforward matters with reasonably compliant suspects. Because officers assume the opposite to be the case (as do most training manuals), training often fails to deal with the commonplace and the humdrum ... In only twenty seven cases (4.5% of the whole sample) did the officer's manner seem unduly harsh or aggressive. In almost two thirds of all cases, the style of interviewing could not even be described as confrontational, since no serious challenge was made to what a suspect was saying ... Fewer than one in eight suspects sought to exercise their right to remain silent in any significant way, and taking interviews as a whole, it emerged that four out of every five were with such cooperative or compliant individuals that they should have presented no serious difficulties to a moderately competent interviewer (pp 14 – 18).

Professor Baldwin suggested that 'The importance of this simple finding can scarcely be overstated' (p 18). For an account of research comparing the strikingly different tenor of police interviews as reflected in police summaries (pre-PACE) and tape-recording (post-PACE) see I Bryan, 'Shifting images: police-suspect encounters during custodial interrogations', 17 *Legal Studies*, 1997, no 2, pp 215-33.

For other writings by Professor Baldwin on this research see *New Law Journal*, 8 November 1991; 'Police Interview Techniques: Establishing Truth or Proof?', *British Journal of Criminology*, 1993, pp 325 – 52.

Partly in response to this research, partly because of concerns about police malpractice that led to the setting up of the Runciman Royal Commission, the police service commissioned outside experts to help it design a new interviewing training package. In its report in 1993 the Royal Commission referred with approval to this development. The new approach had been signalled in a Home Office circular[15] which stated, inter alia, 'The role of investigative interviewing is to obtain accurate and reliable information from suspects, witnesses or victims in order to discover the

---

[15]   22/1992, dated 20 February 1992.

truth about matters under police investigation... Investigative interviewing should be approached with an open mind ... . When questioning anyone a police officer must act fairly in the circumstances of each individual case.'[16]

A new training package based on these principles, involving a full week of training, was introduced in 1993. All police officers were supposed to be exposed to the course.[17] The essence of the interviewing method, one might say, was less talking and more listening!

(b)   The danger of false confessions

The phenomenon of false confessions is now widely recognised and accepted. One of the world's leading authorities on the subject has identified four different types of false confessions:

(1) false confessions borne of a desire to attract publicity or notoriety, or to relieve guilt about real or imagined misdeeds, or from an inability to distinguish between reality and fantasy;
(2) false confessions to protect others;
(3) false confessions to gain a short-term advantage such as respite from questioning, or bail;
(4) false confessions which the suspect is persuaded by the interrogator are true.

See further G H Gudjonsson, *The Psychology of Interrogations, Confessions and Testimony*, (Wiley, 1992); and 'The Psychology of False Confessions', *New Law Journal*, 18 September 1992, p 1277. See also *Justice of the Peace*, 24 July 1999, pp 586-91.

(c)   The Judges' Rules

For most of this century the process of questioning suspects was governed principally by the Judges' Rules. The Judges' Rules were rules formulated by the judges of the Queen's Bench Division in the form of a code. Technically they were not law, and breaches of the Judges' Rules did not necessarily give rise to any adverse consequence for the police. Evidence obtained in breach of the Judges' Rules could in theory be held to be inadmissible, but this hardly ever occurred unless the defendant's statements was held by the court to be 'involuntary' (see pp 448-51). There was also the theoretical possibility that a breach of the Rules (especially one revealed in court) could be made the occasion for police disciplinary proceedings against the officer concerned. That too, however, was very rare.

---

[16]   Royal Commission on Criminal Justice, Report, 1993, p 13, para 21.
[17]   For an article on investigative interviewing by one of those most responsible for its introduction see Chief Supt Tom Williamson, *Policing*, Winter 1992, pp 286 – 99. See also the series of articles by Det Sergt Gary Shaw in nine consecutive issues of *Police Review* starting 5 January 1996.

The Judges' Rules had three parts. There was, first, the preamble which set out five principles that were said to apply generally: (a) that citizens had a duty to help the police discover and apprehend offenders; (b) that no one could be compelled to come to the police station otherwise than by arrest; (c) that anyone in a police station could communicate with and consult privately with a solicitor at any stage provided that it did not cause unreasonable delay or hindrance to the processes of investigation or the administration of justice; (d) that when the officer had enough evidence to charge the suspect he had to cause that to be done without delay; and (e) that a precondition for the admissibility of any confession was that 'it shall have been voluntary in the sense that it has not been obtained from him by fear of prejudice or hope of advantage, exercised or held out by a person in authority, or by oppression'.

There then followed the actual Rules dealing with the stages of questioning. Rule I stated that the police could question anyone. Rule II required the police to caution the person being questioned as soon as the police officer had enough evidence to afford reasonable grounds for suspecting that he had committed an offence. The caution warned him that he was not obliged to say anything. Rule III required a second caution when he came to be charged and stated that thereafter questions should only be put in exceptional cases. ('Such questions may be put where they are necessary for the purpose of preventing or minimising harm or loss to some other person or to the public or for clearing up an ambiguity in a previous answer or statement'.) But a third caution had to be given before such further questions were asked. Rule IV regulated the taking of a statement and required the officer to allow the suspect to put it in his own words.

In addition to the Judges' Rules there were Administrative Directions accompanying the rules, drafted not by the judges but by the Home Office. These dealt with a variety of matters concerning the handling of suspects in the police station. (For the full text of the Rules and the Administrative Directions, see [1964] 1 WLR 152.)

The Judges' Rules and the Administrative Directions were criticised on various counts. One was that there were many aspects of the process of detention and questioning which they did not cover at all. Another was that they were badly drafted and that in many important respects they were vague. A third ground of objection was that they did not have the status of law. It seemed to be widely accepted that they were frequently flouted by the police and that breaches were usually ignored by the courts.

The Philips Royal Commission on Criminal Procedure concluded that it was desirable 'to replace the vagueness of the Judges' Rules with a set of instructions which provide strengthened safeguards to the suspect and clear and workable guidelines for the police' (para 4.109). The Code of Practice on Detention, Treatment and Questioning of Persons by Police Officers (Code C of PACE) laid down a mass of detailed rules regulating most aspects of the process of questioning. (In the 2003 HMSO version of the Codes, Code C ran to no fewer than 74 pages.)

(d) Whom can the police question?

The police can ask questions of anyone both before and after arrest. This right continues after arrest, though, as will be seen, according to the principles of the English system, questioning is normally supposed to cease after the suspect has been charged. From that moment he is notionally under the control of the court and the police should regard themselves as having completed their function.

(e) Is the citizen obliged to answer police questions?

The fact that the police are entitled to ask questions does not mean that the citizen must answer them. The rule of English law on this critical point is that there is normally no such duty. This is the citizen's so-called 'right of silence'. Thus a person who is silent in the face of questioning cannot be charged with obstructing the police in the exercise of their duties.

This fundamental rule was stated authoritatively by the Divisional Court in 1966 :

Rice v Connolly [1966] 2 QB 414 (Divisional Court)

[The appellant was seen by officers in the early hours of the morning behaving suspiciously in an area where on the same night breaking offences had taken place. On being questioned he refused to say where he was going or where he had come from. He refused to give his full name and address, though he did give a name and the name of a road, which were not untrue. He refused to accompany the police to a police box for identification purposes, saying, 'If you want me, you will have to arrest me.' He was arrested and charged with wilfully obstructing the policy contrary to the Police Act 1964, s 51(3).]

Lord Parker CJ: ... the sole question here is whether the defendant had a lawful excuse for refusing to answer the questions put to him. In my judgment he had. It seems to me quite clear that though every citizen has a moral duty or, if you like, a social duty to assist the police, there is no legal duty to that effect, and indeed the whole basis of the common law is the right of the individual to refuse to answer questions put to him by persons in authority, and to refuse to accompany those in authority to any particular place; short, of course, of arrest.

Mr Skinner has pointed out that it is undoubtedly an obstruction, and has been so held, for a person questioned by the police to tell a 'cock-and-bull' story to put the police off by giving them false information, and I think he would say: well, what is the real distinction? It is a very little way from giving false information to giving no information at all. If that does in fact make it more difficult for the police to carry out their duties, then there is a wilful obstruction.

In my judgment there is all the difference in the world between deliberately telling a false story – something which in no view a citizen has a right to do –

and preserving silence or refusing to answer – something which he has every right to do. Accordingly, in my judgment, looked upon in that perfectly general way, it was not shown that the refusal of the defendant to answer the questions or to accompany the police officer in the first instance to the police box was an obstruction without lawful excuse.

Marshall and James JJ concurred, though James J said he would not go so far as to say that silence combined with conduct could not amount to obstruction. Whether it did amount to obstruction would depend on the facts of the actual case.

But see *Ricketts v Cox* [1982] Crim LR 184 (Divisional Court). See also K Lidstone, 'Minding the Law's Own Business', *New Law Journal*, 14 October 1982, p 953. Silence together with awkward, abusive behaviour may constitute the offence of obstruction.

WHEN THE CITIZEN IS UNDER A DUTY TO ANSWER

The general principle of the common law is therefore that it is not a criminal offence not to answer questions – and especially questions the answer to which would be incriminating. But there are some exceptions to this fundamental rule.

Motorists In certain situations, for instance, the police have a right to arrest someone who refuses to give his name and address. The most common example is where the police officer has reasonable grounds for thinking that a vehicle has been involved in an accident or traffic offence. It is an offence not to give up one's driving licence and to state one's name and date of birth if one is driving a car and one is asked to do so by a police officer. The duty to provide information about the driver of a motorcar applies not only to the driver himself but also to 'any other person'. The Judicial Committee of the Privy Council held that it is not a breach of the Human Rights Act 1998 to require the motorist to give these details.[18]

Official Secrets There is a provision in the Official Secrets Act 1911, s 6 (as amended in 1939), that if a chief constable is satisfied that there is reasonable ground for suspecting that an offence under the Official Secrets Act has been committed and for believing that someone is able to furnish information about the offence, he can ask the Home Secretary for consent to use powers of coercive questioning. If such permission is granted, an officer not below the rank of inspector can require the person concerned to attend at a stated time and place and to answer questions. Failure to comply is a criminal offence.

Companies Act, bankruptcy, insolvency, liquidations, banking There are extensive powers in the Companies Act 1985 (which repeat powers previously in the Companies Act 1948), to require officers and agents of companies to assist inspectors appointed to

---

18   *Brown v Stott (Procurator Fiscal Dunfermline)* [2001] 2 All ER 97, PC – a simple question or two was not a disproportionate response to the problem of road accidents. See also *DPP v Wilson* [2001] EWHC Admin 198, [2002] RTR 37.

investigate the affairs of the company under ss 431, 432 and 447. In essence they are powers to require production of books and documents and explanations. But refusal to answer questions can be dealt with under ss 431 and 432 as contempt of court and under s 447 as a criminal offence. Similar powers exist in a variety of other regulatory contexts – eg under the Financial Services Act 1986, for administrators, receivers and liquidators of insolvent companies under the Insolvency Act 1986, ss 236 and 237, under the Insurance Act 1982, s 43A, under the Banking Act 1987, ss 41 and 42. The Serious Fraud Office (SFO) has the same power under the Criminal Justice Act 1987, s 2 – though in that case the statements taken can only be used in evidence in criminal proceedings to challenge an inconsistent statement (s 2(8)).

In the case of Ernest Saunders the European Court of Human Rights (ECHR) ruled that statements taken compulsorily (in that case by the Serious Fraud Office) cannot be used in evidence in subsequent criminal proceedings as they infringe the right not to incriminate oneself guaranteed by art 6 of the Convention. (*Saunders v United Kingdom* (1996) 23 EHRR 313.) This decision affected a whole range of statutory provisions and in February 1997 the Attorney-General advised prosecutors that statements taken compulsorily under statutory powers should not be used in future in evidence either as part of the prosecution case or in cross-examination.[19]

In order to comply with the ruling in the *Saunders* case, the Youth Justice and Criminal Evidence Act 1999, s 9 and Sch 3 prohibited the use of evidence obtained by the prosecution under a number of statutory powers, mostly concerning financial investigations, eg. Insurance Companies Act 1982, Companies Act 1985, Insolvency Act 1986, Financial Services Act 1986.

Terrorism and drugs trafficking A power to require answers on pains and penalties for refusal exists also under the special legislation concerning terrorism and drug trafficking. Thus, the Prevention of Terrorism (Temporary Provisions) Acts 1974 and 1976, s 11 made it an offence for a person who had information which he knew or believed might be of material assistance in preventing an act of terrorism or to secure the arrest, prosecution or conviction of anyone involved in terrorism offences, to 'fail without reasonable excuse to disclose that information as soon as reasonably practicable'.

In his 1978 report on the operation of the Act, Lord Shackleton recommended that this provision be allowed to lapse on the ground that 'it has an unpleasant ring about it in terms of civil liberties.'[20] However, the second inquiry into the operation of the Act reached the opposite conclusion. Up to the end of 1982 a total of 14 people had been charged under s 11, of whom nine were convicted. (Seven of these received

---

[19] *New Law Journal*, 13 February, 1998, p 208. See Paul Davies, 'Self-Incrimination, Fair Trials, and the Pursuit of Corporate and Financial Wrongdoing', in B Markesinis (ed) *The Impact of the Human Rights Bill* (OUP, 1998), pp 31-61. See also N Hood, 'Compulsory questions', *New Law Journal*, 25 July 2003, p 1140.

[20] *Review of the Operation of the Prevention of Terrorism Acts*, 1978, Cmnd 7324, para 133.

sentences that were non-custodial and one of those imprisoned got a sentence of under a year.) Nevertheless Lord Jellicoe thought retention of the section was warranted[21] and it was retained as s 18 of the 1989 Prevention of Terrorism (Temporary Provisions) Act. But Lord Lloyd of Berwick's *Inquiry into legislation against terrorism* (Cm 3420, 1996) also recommended that it be dropped and the Government followed the recommendation in the Terrorism Act 2000.

The Criminal Justice Act 1993 made it a criminal offence to fail to disclose to the police as soon as practicable knowledge or suspicion acquired in the course of one's trade, profession, business or employment that someone is providing financial assistance for terrorism. This is now Terrorism Act 2000, s 19.

ARREST FOR FAILURE TO GIVE NAME AND ADDRESS

The Police and Criminal Evidence Act did not alter the law regarding the duty to answer questions. However, as will be seen, it did give the police a new power to arrest someone for a non-arrestable offence where the officer cannot find out the name of the suspect or his address for the purpose of serving a summons on him (s 25(3)(a), (b) and (c)). This is close to creating for suspects a duty to reveal one's name and address.

A similar but even stronger power exists in Scotland originally under the Criminal Justice (Scotland) Act 1980 and now under the Criminal Procedure (Scotland) Act 1995, s 13:

> where a constable has reasonable grounds for suspecting that a person has committed or is committing an offence at any place, he may require (a) that person ... to give his name and address and may ask him for an explanation of the circumstances which have given rise to the constable's suspicion; (b) any other person whom the constable finds at that place ... who the constable believes has information relating to the offence, to give his name and address.

The officer can require such a person to remain with him for such time as may be necessary to note the name, address and explanation given and to verify the name and address. But he may only require the person to remain with him for this purpose briefly. The requirement ceases if there is unreasonable delay in obtaining verification of the name and address. Reasonable force may be used to ensure that the person does remain with the officer, and failing to give a name and address or failing to remain with the officer are both offences. But failing to proffer an explanation is not made an offence and to that extent the right of silence is preserved in Scotland (ibid).

---

21   *Review of the Operation of the Prevention of Terrorism (Temporary Provisions) Act 1976*, Cmnd 8803, 1983, ch 9.

OBSTRUCTING THE POLICE

The right of silence must be distinguished from the question of actively misleading or hindering the police. This can constitute an offence. In *Ingleton v Dibble* [1972] 1 All ER 275, for instance, it was held to be obstruction of the police in the execution of their duty for a motorist to take a swig of whisky to defeat a breathalyser test. In *Willmott v Atack* [1977] QB 498, it was held not to be obstruction for a person to intervene between a police officer and a motorist who was resisting arrest when the purpose of the intervention was to help the police officer by persuading the motorist to desist. The motorist did in fact obstruct the officer, but the Divisional Court held that it had to be shown that he had intended to impede the officer. In *Moore v Green* [1983] 1 All ER 663, by contrast, it was held to be obstruction for a probationer police officer to warn the landlord of a public house that his premises were under police surveillance and that a raid to enforce the licensing laws was to be made that evening.

The Criminal Law Act 1967, s 4, made it an offence to do anything intended to impede the apprehension or prosecution of someone who is known or believed to have committed an arrestable offence.[22] Section 5 of the same Act also made it an offence to accept money or other consideration for not disclosing information that would lead to the prosecution of an arrestable offence. See also *Albert v Lavin* [1981] 3 All ER 878, in which the House of Lords held that it was not merely the right but also the duty of a citizen in whose presence a breach of the peace is being, or appears about to be, committed, to attempt to stop it, if necessary by detaining the person responsible.

(f) The legal consequences of silence in the face of police questioning

The citizen's right of silence in the face of police questioning was supported by two main rules of law. One was that already shown in *Rice v Connolly* – namely that silence cannot be made the subject of a charge of obstructing the police in the execution of their duties or, with a few exceptional instances, any other criminal offence. The second was the rule that the prosecution could not comment on the fact of silence and the judge could not suggest to the jury that silence was evidence of guilt. The second, as will be seen below, has however now been abolished by the Criminal Justice and Public Order Act 1994.

THE CRIMINAL LAW REVISION COMMITTEE (CLRC)

In its Eleventh Report (*Evidence (General)*), the CLRC recommended that failure during police questioning to mention any fact on which the defendant sought subsequently to rely at his trial could be made the subject of adverse comment by the

---

[22] See Glanville Williams, 'Evading Justice' (1975) *Criminal Law Review*, pp 430, 477, 608.

prosecution and the court, and adverse inferences could be drawn against the accused from such silence or failure. The accused would still have the right to silence, but he would exercise it at the risk that adverse inferences might be drawn against him if the jury or magistrates thought that it would have been reasonable to expect him to have mentioned the facts in question while being questioned. This would apply not only to facts raised in his own evidence but equally to facts referred to in the evidence of any of his witnesses:

> To forbid it seems to us to be contrary to common sense and, without helping the innocent, to give an unnecessary advantage to the guilty. Hardened criminals often take advantage of the present rule to refuse to answer any questions at all, and this may greatly hamper the police and even bring their investigations to a halt. Therefore the abolition of the restriction would help justice .... [para 30]

The Committee said that if this proposal regarding silence under interrogation were accepted, it would mean a change in the caution required by the Judges' Rules. The Committee said that the caution was of no help to an innocent person, 'indeed it might deter him from saying something which might serve to exculpate him'. On the other hand the caution 'often assists the guilty by providing an excuse for keeping back a false story until it becomes difficult to expose its falsity'. The caution, it said, stemmed from the ancient fallacy that fairness in criminal trials required that a guilty person should not be allowed to convict himself too easily. It was illogical for the police to have to start an interrogation by saying that the suspect need not say anything (para 43).

The Committee's proposals on the right of silence and the caution provoked furious controversy. Most of the comment was hostile (see note 5, p 144, above) and it was this above all that led at the time to the rejection of the CLRC's entire report. It was argued by the critics that to allow adverse comment on silence would amount almost to a reversal of the burden of proof. It would put a premium on a suspect's articulateness when most suspects were notoriously inarticulate as well as confused and frightened. The critics also denied that silence necessarily indicated guilt. There were many possible innocent reasons for silence, including a desire to protect someone else, fear, contempt for the accusation or failure to understand the accusation.

The matter was next considered by the Philips Royal Commission on Criminal Procedure.

THE PHILIPS ROYAL COMMISSION'S PROPOSALS

The Philips Royal Commission felt that basically the law should not be changed. In relation to the situation before an arrest, it regarded the decision in *Rice v Connolly* (p 151 above) as correct. ('We adhere to the decision in *Rice v Connolly* that the duty to assist the police is a social one and not legally enforceable.' (para 4.47)) Once a suspect was arrested the situation was different since he then had to submit to being questioned. But if adverse inferences could be drawn from the fact of silence it might 'put strong (and additional) psychological pressure upon some suspects to answer questions without knowing precisely what was the substance of and evidence for the accusations against them'. (para 4.50) This, in the Commission's view, 'might well increase the risk of innocent people, particularly those under suspicion for the first time, making damaging statements'. (ibid) On the other hand a guilty person who at present remained silent would still tend to remain silent since it would be more prudent to hope that the case against him would not be proved in spite of any adverse inferences.

Moreover, 'to use a suspect's silence as evidence against him seems to run counter to a central element in the accusatorial system at trial'. (para 4.51) There was an inconsistency of principle 'in requiring the onus of proof at trial to be upon the prosecution and to be discharged without any assistance from the accused, and yet in enabling the prosecution to use the accused's silence in the face of police questioning under caution as any part of the case against him at trial'.

A minority of the Commission agreed with the police view that the right of silence should be abolished, but the majority concluded 'that the right of silence in the face of police questioning after caution should not be altered'. (para 4.53) The Conservative Government accepted this recommendation.

The caution The Commission proposed that the first caution should be administered not when the police had enough admissible evidence to justify suspicion but when they had enough evidence to justify an arrest. (para 4.56) This was accepted by the Government. Code of Practice C (para 10.1) states that 'a person whom there are grounds to suspect' must be cautioned 'before any questions about it ... are put to him'.

Under the Code of Practice the suspect had to be cautioned again before he was interviewed at a police station. The text of the caution was formerly: 'You do not have to say anything unless you wish to do so, but what you say may be given in evidence'.

The text of the caution has now changed to take account of the 'abolition of the right to silence' (see pp 160-61 below) but the suspect still has to be cautioned and the rules as to when cautions are required have not changed. As will also be seen, whether the suspect is given the 'old' caution' or the 'new' caution now depends on whether he has or has not been given an opportunity to get legal advice (see pp 160-61 below).

If questioning is interrupted, the suspect must be made aware that he is still under caution when it is resumed (Code C, para 10.8). After he is charged he must again be cautioned (Code C, para 16.2).

The Code of Practice continues the rule under the Judges' Rules that from that point he should be questioned only where questions are necessary 'to prevent or minimise harm or loss to some other person or the public to clear up an ambiguity in a previous answer or statement or in the interests of justice for the detainee to have put to them, information concerning the offence which has come to light since they were charged'. Before such questions are put he should be cautioned again (Code C, para 16.5).

The debate reopened

In July 1987, the then Home Secretary, Mr Douglas Hurd, reopened the debate by a speech in which asked whether it was really in the public interest for experienced criminals to be able to refuse to answer questions ' secure in the knowledge that a jury will never hear of it'. In 1988 he announced the setting up of a Working Party to consider not so much whether the CLRC's 1972 proposal should be adopted, but 'the precise form of the change in law which would best achieve our purposes'.

In October 1988 the Secretary of State for Northern Ireland laid before Parliament the draft Police and Criminal Evidence (Northern Ireland) Order 1988 which was first approved and then made on 14 November and came into force one month later (SI 1989 No 1341).

The Northern Ireland Order permitted the court to draw adverse inferences from the accused's failure before being charged or on being charged to mention any fact relied on in his defence at trial. As recommended by the CLRC in 1972, the Order stated that such silence could also be corroboration of other evidence.

The Northern Ireland Order also provided that adverse inferences could be drawn where someone who had been arrested and cautioned about the matter failed to explain 'any object, substance or mark' that the officer reasonably believed suspicious (art 5). Similarly, adverse inferences can be drawn from failure to explain one's presence at the scene of the crime. In Northern Ireland it can also be corroboration of other evidence (art 6).

Report of the Home Office Working Group

The *Report of the Home Office Working Group on the Right of Silence* was published in July 1989. It recommended changes that were similar but not identical to those already introduced for Northern Ireland. The Government, however, did not implement the recommendations of the Working Group, possibly out of a sense that it would be inappropriate in a climate dominated by the concern about miscarriages of justice generated in particular by the trio of IRA cases, the Guildford Four, the Maguires and the Birmingham Six.

THE RUNCIMAN ROYAL COMMISSION

The Runciman Royal Commission, like the Philips Royal Commission, recommended by a majority that the traditional protection for the right to silence be retained. The majority of nine considered that to allow the prosecution and the judge to suggest that silence was evidence of guilt could produce false confessions and therefore more miscarriages of justice.

> The majority of us, however believe that the possibility of an increase in the convictions of the guilty is outweighed by the risk that the extra pressure on suspects to talk in the police station and the adverse inferences invited if they do not may result in more convictions of the innocent. They recommend retaining the present caution and trial direction unamended. In taking this view, the majority acknowledge the frustration which many police officers feel when confronted with suspects who refuse to offer any explanation whatever of strong *prima facie* evidence that they have committed an offence. But they doubt whether the possibility of adverse comment at trial would make the difference which the police suppose. The experienced professional criminals who wish to remain silent are likely to continue to do so and will justify their silence by stating at trial that their solicitors have advised them to say nothing at least until the allegations against them have been fully disclosed. It may be that some more defendants would be convicted whose refusal to answer police questions had been the subject of adverse comment; but the majority believe that their number would not be as great as is popularly imagined.

> It is the less experienced and more vulnerable suspects against whom the threat of adverse comment would be likely to be more damaging. There are too many cases of improper pressures being brought to bear on suspects in police custody, even when the safeguards of PACE and the codes of practice have been supposedly in force, for the majority to regard this with equanimity. [Report, pp 54 – 55, para s 22, 23]

The Report then cited with approval the view of the Philips majority (cited above) to the effect that if adverse inferences could be drawn from silence it might put strong additional pressure on some suspects and might result in more false confessions.

> The minority of two of the Runciman Commission however favoured the view that both the prosecution and the judge should be permitted to invite the jury to draw adverse inferences from silence. In the view of many police officers 'a significant number of suspects, by refusing to answer questions, seriously impede the efforts of investigators to fulfil their function of establishing the facts of the case.'

The minority recommended that silence in response to questions 'asked in a room with audio or visual recording, preferably with a legal representative present, but at least after the suspect has been offered the opportunity of taking legal advice, would qualify for later comment at trial'. (p 51, para 10)

THE CRIMINAL JUSTICE AND PUBLIC ORDER ACT 1994

The Home Secretary, Mr Michael Howard, made his position clear shortly after the Royal Commission reported. Speaking at the Conservative Party Conference that October he said:

As I talk to people up and down the country, there is one part of our law in particular that makes their blood boil ... It's the so-called right of silence. This is of course a complete misnomer, what is at stake is not the right to refuse to answer questions. But if a suspect does remain silent should the prosecution and the judge or magistrates be allowed to comment on it? Should they have the right to take it into account in deciding guilt or innocence? The so-called right to silence is ruthlessly exploited by terrorists. What fools they must think we are. It's time to call a halt to this charade. The so-called right to silence will be abolished.

Mr Howard made good his promise in the provisions of the Criminal Justice and Public Order Act 1994 (CJPOA 1994). There are five sections that are especially relevant.

CJPOA 1994, s 34 gave the court the power to invite the jury (or in the case of the magistrates, themselves) to draw an adverse inference from silence. The right arises only if the suspect has been cautioned and if he is being questioned by a constable 'trying to discover whether or by whom the offence had been committed'.[23] The inference can be drawn if he 'failed to mention any fact relied on in his defence' or failed to mention any such fact on being charged, being a fact 'which in the circumstances existing at the time the accused could reasonably have been expected to mention when so questioned' or charged (s 34(1)). The inferences to be drawn can be 'such inferences from the failure as appear proper' (s 34(2)).

The new caution to take account of the change in the law in CJPOA 1994, s 34 is more complex than the old caution: 'You do not have to say anything. But it may harm your defence if you do not mention when questioned something which you later rely on in court. Anything you do say may be given in evidence' (Code C, para 10.5). (The old much simpler caution was misunderstood by many suspects. The new more complex caution poses even more difficulties.[24] A team of psychologists read the new caution to 109 ordinary people. On average about half thought it made sense but only one in four actually understood the first part which tells the individual of his right to remain silent; one in eight understood the second element which warns that exercise of the right may harm one's defence later; and one in three understood the third part which says that anything said may be used in evidence. They concluded that the length and complexity of the new formula 'ensures that it is beyond the ability of most people in the street to absorb, let alone comprehend'.[25])

A further complication has now been added by legislation preventing a court from drawing adverse inferences until the suspect being interviewed at the police station

---

[23]   So if the police know that they are going to charge before the interview starts no inference can be drawn – *Pointer* [1997] Crim LR 676 CA. But if they still have an open mind pending the results of the interview, inferences can be drawn – *McGuiness* [1999] Crim LR 318, CA.

[24]   See I Clare and G Gudjunsson, *Devising and Piloting an Experimental Version of the 'Notice to Detained Persons'* (Royal Commission on Criminal Justice, Research Study No 7, 1992).

[25]   *Counsel*, September – October 1995, p 4.

has had the opportunity to get legal advice.[26] This applies even to terrorism suspects. So someone who is interviewed before he has 'been allowed an opportunity to consult a solicitor' must be cautioned in terms of the old formula. If he is then interviewed after he has had an opportunity to get legal advice he must be cautioned again in terms of the new formula! (See PACE Code C, para s10.4-10.10.)

CJPOA 1994, s 35 provides that adverse inferences may be drawn from the accused's failure to give evidence at his trial: see pp 443-44 below.

CJPOA 1994, s 36, like the Northern Ireland rule, permits the court to invite adverse inferences from the accused's failure or refusal to account for suspicious objects, substances or marks. Section 37, again like the Northern Ireland rule, permits adverse inferences from the accused's failure or refusal to account for his presence at the scene of the crime at the time it was committed. In both cases the suspect must first have been cautioned by the constable. Under ss 36 and 37 adverse inferences can be drawn from the mere failure to respond to the question. It is not necessary, as under s 34, to show that the defendant relied on a fact in his defence that he failed to disclose when being questioned. But he must have been cautioned by the appropriate 'special warning'. Under s 36 he must have been advised that the objects, marks or substances found on his person, or his clothing or footwear seem suspicious and must be asked for an explanation. Where the suspect is arrested at the scene of the crime at the time it is committed, the s 37 caution must inform him what offence is being investigated, what fact he is being asked to account for, that the officer believes that fact may be due to his having taken part in the offence and that failure to account for the fact could lead to adverse inferences being drawn at the trial. (Home Office research has shown that when such special warnings are given they rarely result in any satisfactory account being given.)[27]

CJPOA 1994, s 38(3) states that silence on its own can never be enough. There must always be a prima facie case before any adverse inference can be drawn.

The new provisions can result in the defence solicitor being called as a witness in regard to the advice he gave his client in the police station. (See on this see D Wright, 'The solicitor in the witness box' [1998] *Criminal Law Review*, p 44.)

For an evaluation of the practical effect of the reform see T Bucke, R Street, D Brown, *The right of silence: the impact of the Criminal Justice and Public Order Act 1994*, Home Office Research Study (2000). For an assessment of the Northern Ireland experience see J Jackson, M Wolfe, K Quinn, *Legislating Against Silence: The Northern Ireland Experience* (Northern Ireland Office, 2000).

---

[26] Youth Justice and Criminal Evidence Act 1999, s.58; Criminal Evidence (Northern Ireland) Order 1999, SI 1999, No 2789, art 36. These statutory provisions resulted from decisions of the Strasbourg Court – *Murray (John) v United Kingdom* (1996) 22 EHRR 29, para 66, *Averill v United Kingdom* (2001) 31 EHRR 839.

[27] T Bucke and D Brown, *In police custody: police powers and suspects' rights under the revised PACE codes of practice*, 1997, Home Office Research Series No 174, p 38.

For separate, caustic, overall assessments of the new law by two leading scholars see D Birch, 'Suffering in Silence: A Cost-Benefit Analysis of Section 34 of the Criminal Justice and Public Order Act 1994' [1999] *Criminal Law Review*, 769–88 and I Dennis, 'Silence in the Police Station: the Marginalisation of Section 34' [2002] *Criminal Law Review*, 25–38.

See also R Pattenden, 'Silence: Lord Taylor's Legacy' (1998) 5 *International Journal of Evidence and Proof* 141; and D Wolchover, *Silence and Guilt* (2001).

There is a bibliography on the right to silence in M Zander, *The Police and Criminal Evidence Act 1984* (4th edn, 2003), pp 440-41.

JUDICIAL INTERPRETATION OF THE RIGHT TO SILENCE PROVISIONS

In 1994, the House of Lords deciding *Murray (Kevin Sean)* [1994] 1 WLR 1 on the Northern Ireland provisions held that adverse inferences may be drawn if they are suggested by the application of common sense.[28] The case law has become incredibly voluminous but the theme of common sense has continued to be dominant.[29]

Among the propositions that seem to have been established by the cases, the more important include the following:

Strict interpretation Because the provisions restrict important rights they must be construed strictly.[30]

Reliance on facts need not be in defendant's evidence It can occur through evidence of others, or cross-examination.[31] But mere hypothesising is not reliance.[32] Nor is a bare admission of facts in the prosecution's case.[33]

The failure to mention a fact could be at any stage up to time of being charged[34] It could consist of lying in the interview and asserting 'the truth' at trial[35]

'The accused' means the actual accused with such qualities, apprehensions, knowledge and advice as he was shown to have had. 'When reference is made to the "accused" attention is drawn not to some hypothetical, reasonable accused of ordinary phlegm and fortitude but to the actual accused with such qualities, apprehensions, knowledge and advice as he is shown to have had.'[36]

---

[28]   Referred to in *Report of the Working Group on the Right of Silence*, Home Office, 1989, App C.
[29]   On the case law see, for instance, M Zander, *The Police and Criminal Evidence Act 1984* (4th edn, 2003), pp 425-34.
[30]   *Bowden* [1999] 2 Cr App Rep 176 at 181.
[31]   *Bowers* [1998] Crim LR 817 CA.
[32]   *Nickolson* [1999] Crim LR 61 CA.
[33]   *Betts and Hall* [2001] EWCA Crim 224, [2001] 2 Cr App Rep 257.
[34]   *Dervish and Anori* [2001] EWCA Crim 2789 , [2002] 2 Cr App Rep 105.
[35]   *Ashton* [2002] EWCA Crim 2782.
[36]   *Argent* [1997] 2 Cr App Rep 27, at 33.

The fact that the defendant was advised to be silent by his lawyer must be given appropriate weight[37] ('If it is a plausible explanation that the reason for not mentioning facts is that the particular appellant acted on the advice of his solicitor and not because he had no or no satisfactory answer to give then no inferences can be drawn'[38]) But see *Howell*[39]: whether legal advice to be silent will prevent adverse inferences being drawn will depend on whether the jury consider it to be plausible that that was the reason he was silent, rather than that he had no or no satisfactory answer to give. ('There is a public interest in reasonable disclosure by an accused when confronted with incriminating facts. This would be thwarted if silence based on legal advice allowed the systematic evasion of the drawing of adverse inferences. For comment see C Jowett, 'Inferences from silence', *New Law Journal*, 7 March 2003, p 344 and AL-T Choo and AF Jennings, ' Silence on legal advice revisited: *R v Howell*' [2003] 7 Int'l Jrnl of Ev and Proof, pp185-190.)

Valid reasons for advising silence include: little or no disclosure by the police so the solicitor cannot advise the suspect (*Roble*[40]); the suspect's condition – ill-health, confusion, intoxication, shock), or genuine inability to recollect events without reference to documents or other persons (*Howell*).

Explaining the reasons for legal advice to be silent will probably amount to a waiver of privilege – Bowden[41].

The jury may draw whatever inferences they think proper – Cowan[42], *Beckles and Montagu*[43] The test is common sense – *Murray (Kevin)*[44], *Argent*[45].

EMPIRICAL EVIDENCE ON THE RIGHT TO SILENCE CHANGES

Pre-CJPOA 1994 empirical evidence showed that relatively few suspects actually relied on their right of silence. David Brown of the Home Office conducted an analysis of studies on the right of silence for the Runciman Royal Commission on Criminal Justice. His conclusion was that 'outside the Metropolitan Police District, between 6% and 10% of suspects exercise their right to silence to some extent, while within the Metropolitan police district the equivalent percentage is between 14% and 16%. The number of those who refuse to answer any questions at all is estimated at 5% at most in provincial police force areas and 9% at most in the Metropolitan police district' (Runciman Report, p 53, para 15). A different Home Office study based on

---

37   *Condron v United Kingdom (No 2)* (2001) 31 EHRR 1, [2000] Crim LR 679.
38   *Betts and Hall* [2001] EWCA Crim 224, [2001] 2 Cr App Rep 257.
39   [2003] EWCA Crim 1, [2003] Crim LR 405.
40   [1997] Crim LR 449.
41   [1999] 2 Cr App Rep 176.
42   [1996] QB 373, 381-2, CA.
43   [1999] Crim LR 148, CA.
44   [1994] 1 WLR 1, 12, HL.
45   [1997] 2 Cr App Rep 27, at 33.

a sample of 4,250 suspects detained between September 1993 and March 1994 found 10% refused to answer all questions and another 13% refused to answer some questions.[46]

The first Home Office research on the impact of the changes made by the CJPOA 1994 (Bucke and Brown, n 13, p 146 above) was conducted at the same police stations as has had been in the pre-CJPOA 1994 Home Office study (Phillips and Brown, n 46). It showed a reduction in suspects using the right of silence. Where in the pre-CJPOA 1994 study, 10% gave 'no comment' interviews by refusing all questions from officers, in the post-CJPOA 1994 study this had fallen to 6%. Where 13% had answered some questions in the 'pre' study, in the 'post' study this had fallen to 10%. The downward trend was observed across all police stations. Even more significant was that reductions in the use of silence were greatest among those receiving legal advice, presumably because lawyers advised of the dangers of remaining silent under the new provisions.

The same data were used again in Bucke, Street and Brown, *The Right of Silence: the impact of the Criminal Justice and Public Order Act 1994*, Home Office Research Study 199, 2000. In 2000 the Northern Ireland Office published a similar study.[47]

The results of the two studies and of the position generally were assessed by Professor John Jackson.[48] The Home Office study established that the silence provisions had had a marked effect on both pre-trial and trial practices but that it was much less clear that they had increased the likelihood of defendants being charged and convicted. It was more common for investigating officers to disclose the main features of the evidence against the accused, thus enabling legal advisers to give suspects better advice as to whether and, if so, how to respond to police questions. This in turn meant that stories could be checked out earlier, weak cases could be stopped and in cases that went to court, the prosecution's hand could be strengthened. More defendants were testifying but, on the other hand, the silence provisions made trials more complex. Judges had to exercise extreme care in directing juries on the right to silence issue. Jackson suggested (p 173) that the overall effect had been to make the police interview a formal part of the proceedings against the accused without certain basic procedural safeguards. The suspect had no right to disclosure of the police case at that stage and legal advice as to whether or not to say anything was problematic since

[46]   C Phillips and D Brown, *Entry into the Criminal Justice System: a survey of police arrests and their outcomes*, Home Office Research Study No 185, 1998, p 75 .

[47]   J Jackson, M Wolfe and K Quinn, *Legislating against Silence: the Northern Ireland Experience*, 2000. For a summary see M Zander, 'Silence in Northern Ireland', *New Law Journal*, 2 February 2001, p 138. The study was based on examination of all trials in Belfast Crown Court for 1990-95; more detailed examination of 30 terrorism trials in 1995; comparison with all trials in the same court in 1987 and 1991; statistics on legal advice in 1997; and interviews with judges, lawyers and police officers.

[48]   'Silence and proof: extending the boundaries of criminal proceedings in the United Kingdom', 5 *International Journal of Evidence and Proof*, 2001, pp 145-73.

the courts had left to the jury the question whether it was reasonable for the suspect to accept this advice.

2.   Safeguards for the suspect

The suspect in the police station is in a very vulnerable position. The question arises as to how he can be protected from police abuse of power. A variety of approaches have been developed in recent years, of which the most important are treated below: access to a lawyer; informing the outside world of the fact of arrest; tape-recording of the interview; and rules to regulate the regime in the police station and to prevent oppressive questioning.

(a)   Access to a lawyer

The presence of a lawyer during questioning provides the accused with much-needed advice and at the same time helps to minimise the risk of oppressive interrogation.[49]

Until 1986 when the Police and Criminal Evidence Act came into operation, access to a solicitor in the police station was governed by the Judges' Rules and some judicial dicta. The Preamble to the Judges' Rules (c) stated that the Rules did not affect the principle: 'That every person at any stage of an investigation should be able to communicate and to consult privately with a solicitor. This is so even if he is in custody, provided that in such a case no unreasonable delay or hindrance is caused to the processes of investigation or the administration of justice by his doing so.' This appeared to give a qualified right of access to a solicitor in the police station. The Administrative Directions drafted by the Home Office supplemented the Rules by stating in para 7(a) that provided no hindrance was reasonably likely to be caused to the processes of investigation or the administration of justice, 'he should be allowed to speak on the telephone to his solicitor or to his friends'. Para 7(b) stated that not only should persons in custody be informed of their right orally, but notices describing this right should be displayed at convenient and conspicuous places and the attention of persons in custody should be drawn to them.

In practice, however, the police were reluctant to allow a suspect to summon a solicitor. All the studies that were done before PACE agreed that the proportion of suspects who actually saw a solicitor was very small.[50]

---

[49]   However in two of the most celebrated cases in which oppressive questioning led to confessions in murder cases being held to be inadmissible the suspect had had a legal adviser present throughout: see p 453 below.

[50]   P Softley, *Police Interrogation: An Observational Study in Four Police Stations*, 1980, p 68; J Baldwin and M McConville, 'Police Interrogation and the Right to See a Solicitor' (1979) *Criminal Law Review*, pp 145 – 52; M Zander, 'Access to a Solicitor in the Police Station' (1972) *Criminal Law Review*, p 342 and 'The Investigation of Crime' (1979) *Criminal Law Review*, p 215; B Mitchell, 'Confessions and Police Interrogation' (1983) *Criminal Law Review*, pp 597, 599 – 600.

THE PHILIPS ROYAL COMMISSION

The Philips Royal Commission on Criminal Procedure in 1981 thought the availability of legal advice for suspects was a matter of considerable importance. In the Commission's view a suspect should be informed of his right to have a lawyer though it rejected the view that there should be an absolute right to have a solicitor. There were situations in which the police should be entitled to refuse access to a lawyer – for instance, where a solicitor could alert associates of the arrested person. On the other hand, 'conferring the discretion to withhold access must not bring with it the risk that it will be used improperly' (para 4.90). In particular the Commission did not think it sufficient justification for withholding access that a solicitor might advise his client not to speak – that was the suspect's right. Nor should the police refuse access 'where secrecy is desirable but not imperative' (ibid).

The Commission summarised its view as follows:

> 4.91. Accordingly our general view is that the power to refuse access should be exercised only in exceptional cases. In the first place it should be limited to cases where the person in custody is suspected of a grave offence. Further, even in the case of such offences, the right should be withheld only where there are reasonable grounds to believe that the time taken to arrange for legal advice to be available will involve a risk of harm to persons or serious damage to property; or that giving access to a legal adviser may lead to one or more of the following: (a) evidence of the offence or offences under investigation will be interfered with; (b) witnesses to those offences will be harmed or threatened; (c) other persons suspected of committing those offences will be alerted; or (d) the recovery of the proceeds of those offences will be impeded.

The Commission estimated that if all the 720,000 suspects interviewed at police stations in connection with indictable offences were to take up their right to see a solicitor the cost would be some £30m but likely take-up, it thought, would be of the order of one-fifth which would mean an annual cost of some £6m. (In 2002-03 the cost of legal advice in police stations in some 750,000 cases was £168m!)

PACE

PACE s 58(1) provides that 'a person arrested and held in custody in a police station or other premises shall be entitled, if he so requests, to consult a solicitor privately at any time'. The right is both to have legal advice before being interviewed and to have the lawyer present during the interview. Even a suspect arrested under the Terrorism Act has those rights – though in some circumstances a senior officer can instruct that an interview with a terrorism suspect can be conducted in the sight and hearing of an inspector.

The provision of the lawyer is free regardless of the suspect's means. A suspect who comes to the police station under arrest or is arrested there must be informed of the right to have free legal advice both orally and in writing. (Code C, para s 3.1, 3.2, 6.1)

If a person makes such a request it must be recorded in the custody record and, subject to the exceptions that are mentioned, he must be allowed to have access to a solicitor 'as soon as is practicable' (PACE s 58(2) and (4)). Delay in compliance with such a request is only permitted where (1) the detainee is being held in connection with a serious arrestable offence (as defined in the Act: see p 172 below); and (2) an officer of the rank of at least superintendent authorises delay.

Delay The circumstances in which such authorisation may be given are defined in s 58(8):

. ... an officer may only authorise delay where he has reasonable grounds for believing that the exercise of the right [of asking for a solicitor]

(a) will lead to interference with or harm to evidence connected with a serious arrestable offence or interference with or physical injury to other persons; or

(b) will lead to the alerting of other persons suspected of having committed such an offence but not yet arrested for it; or

(c) will hinder the recovery of any property obtained as a result of such an offence.

If such a delay is authorised, the detainee must be told the reason for it, the reasons must be recorded on the custody record (see below) and, once the reasons cease to exist, he must be allowed to see a solicitor. (The House of Lords has held that breach of the statutory duty to give reasons for authorising delay of an arrested person's right of access to a solicitor did not give the arrested person a private law remedy in damages – *Cullen v Chief Constable of the Royal Ulster Constabulary* [2003] UKHL 39, [2003] 1 WLR 1763.) The maximum period of delay is 36 hours, or in the case of terrorism suspects held under the Terrorism Act 2000, 48 hours. (Code C, Annex B, para s 8-11)

There has been a considerable amount of case law on the interpretation of PACE s 58(8). Most of the cases have involved defence assertions that the police wrongly delayed access to a solicitor and that subsequent confessions or admissions should not be (or should not have been) admitted. The leading case is *Samuel* [1988] QB 615. The suspect was being questioned in connection with robbery and burglary offences. He asked for a solicitor but the request was refused on the ground that the offences were serious and that there was a risk of accomplices being inadvertently alerted. Subsequently he confessed. The trial judge admitted the interview in which he confessed. The Court of Appeal quashed the conviction. The right of access to a solicitor, it held, was a 'fundamental right of a citizen' and if a police officer sought to justify refusal of the right he had to do so by reference to the specific circumstances of the case. It was not enough to believe that giving access to a solicitor *might* lead to the alerting of accomplices. He had to believe that it probably would. This would be very rare, especially where the lawyer called was the Duty Solicitor. (See to like effect *Parris* [1989] Crim LR 214.)

A Note for Guidance in Code C says that an officer's decision to delay access to a specific solicitor 'is likely to be a rare occurrence' and is permissible only if he has reasonable grounds to believe that the suspect is 'capable of misleading that particular solicitor and there is more than a substantial risk that the suspect will succeed in causing information to be conveyed which will lead to one or more of the specified consequences' – alerting accomplices etc (Code C, Annex B, Note B3).

Research shows that the police hardly ever claim to be entitled to delay access to a solicitor. In a massive study carried out by David Brown of the Home Office Research Unit involving two samples each of 5,000 taken in 1991, there was only one case (!) of legal advice delayed.[51] In the post-CJPOA Home Office study of 12,500 cases by Bucke and Brown there was not a single one in which the power to delay legal advice had been used (n 27, p 161 above below, at p 23.) Not surprisingly, in terrorism cases, delay is more frequent. A special study of this problem by David Brown showed that delay of access to a solicitor was authorised in 26% of cases.[52]

The fact that there has been a breach of s 58(8) does not mean that the court will automatically exclude the resulting statement. It will depend on the court's evaluation of all the circumstances. Thus in *Dunford* [1991] Crim LR 370 the Court of Appeal took into account the fact that the suspect had a record and was therefore familiar with the police station. He answered several questions with 'No comment' and before reaching the police station he declined to answer any questions. The court held that the judge had been entitled to allow in the confession. In *Walsh* (1989) 91 Cr App Rep 161 the Court of Appeal said that to admit evidence obtained following a 'significant and substantial' breach of s 58 would inevitably have an adverse effect on the fairness of the proceedings within the meaning of s 78 (see pp 457-59 below). But that did not mean it had necessarily to be excluded. The task of the court was not only to consider whether there would have been an adverse effect on the fairness of the proceedings but *such an adverse effect* that justice required the evidence to be excluded. Where the suspect knows his way around in the police station situation it is less likely that a breach of s 58 will result in exclusion of the evidence. (See also *Alladice* (1988) 87 Cr App Rep 380.)

GETTING A LAWYER

PACE originally required the Law Society to establish Duty Solicitor schemes for police stations. They are now run by the Legal Services Commission established by the Access to Justice Act 1999.

[51]   Brown et al, *Changing the Code: Police Detention under the revised PACE Codes of Practice* (Home Office Research Study, 1992), p 68.

[52]   D Brown, *Detention under the Prevention of Terrorism Provisions Act 1989: Legal Advice and Outside Contact* (Home Office Research and Planning Unit Paper No 75, 1993, p16).

If the detainee does not know of a solicitor, he must be told of the availability of a Duty Solicitor and be shown a list of solicitors who have indicated they are available for this purpose. In about two-thirds of all cases the suspect asks to speak to his own solicitor, rather than the Duty Solicitor. But the state pays the cost regardless of means in any event.

STATISTICAL DATA

In Brown's first 1991 sample of 5,000 taken before April 1991, 24% asked for legal advice. The 1991 revision of the Code required that the suspect be specifically told legal advice was free and that posters advertising the fact be put up in police stations. The 1997 study by Bucke and Brown showed that the take-up had risen to 40%.[53]

Afro-Caribbean and Asians were much more likely to request legal advice (46% and 44%) than white suspects (36%) (ibid, p 20). Afro-Caribbeans were more likely to have been arrested for violence against the person, robbery and fraud and forgery than whites, all of which are offences for which there is a relatively high request rate.

A factor in take-up could be the way the police communicate the right to consult a solicitor. Sanders and Bridges identified a long list of 'ploys' used by the police to discourage suspects from asking for solicitors. These included speaking too quickly or saying that the charge was not very serious, that getting a solicitor would involve considerable delays, that the solicitor probably would not come anyway, or that one was unnecessary.[54] The Code (Code C, para 6.5) requires the custody officer to ask the suspect who declines legal advice for his reasons. But Bucke and Brown found that this rule is often honoured in the breach. Less than half of those refusing legal advice were asked for their reasons[55].

Since 1991, the Code has specifically stated that no attempt may be made to dissuade a suspect from obtaining legal advice (Code C, para 6.4). Brown's research conducted before and after the 1991 change did not find much evidence of 'ploys' if that word is taken to connote conscious attempts to dissuade or discourage the suspect from seeking legal advice. (In the great majority of cases 'details of rights were given in exemplary fashion, both slowly and clearly' – though in some cases it was given too quickly or incompletely or the language used was not readily comprehensible.)

The fact than one asks for legal advice and that the police allow one to have it does not always mean that such advice is actually obtained. Earlier research showed a non-contact rate as high as a quarter. But this seems to have gone down. Bucke and Brown found no contact was made with an adviser in only 11% of cases (p 23).

---

53 n 27, p 161 above, at p 19.
54 A Sanders and L Bridges, *Advice and Assistance at Police Stations and the 24 hour duty solicitor scheme* (LCD, 1989).
55 n 27, p 161 above, at p 21.

Sometimes the reason for 'non-contact' is that the suspect changes his mind, or he is released from custody before the adviser arrives or he decides to see the lawyer at court instead. Overall, a third of suspects (34%) actually had legal advice (p 24).

Often the solicitor does not actually go to the police station, he advises over the telephone. Code C, para 6.1, says the communication with the solicitor may be 'in person, in writing or by the telephone'. The Duty Solicitor rules were changed in light of research findings so as to require the solicitor normally to attend in person where (1) the police intend to interview the suspect for an arrestable offence under s 24 (see p 192 below), or (2) the police intend to hold an identification para de or (3) the suspect complains of serious maltreatment by the police. In Bucke and Brown, 1997, 56% of suspects who had advice, received it at the police station, 18% had it over the phone and another 26% it by phone and at the station. (pp 24-25)

But even if the solicitor advises in person it does not mean that he will necessarily stay while the suspect is interviewed. In Bucke and Brown, 1997, of 2,181 suspects interviewed in custody, just over half (52%) had no legal advice, just over a third (37%) had their legal adviser present at all interviews, just under 10% (9%) received advice only pre-interview and the remaining 2% had the adviser present at some but not all interviews (p 32). This showed a considerable rise from previous studies in the proportion of cases of the adviser being present during interviews.

THE ADVISER IN THE POLICE STATION

The police are not allowed to refuse someone access to a solicitor because he might advise the suspect to be silent or because he has been asked to act by someone else – providing the suspect does actually want to see the solicitor. (Code C, Annex B, A, 4)

Note 6J to Code C, as revised in 2003, states that a person consulting a solicitor in the police station 'must be allowed to do so in private' and that 'This right to consult or communicate in private is fundamental'. It specifies that the right will be compromised if the advice is listened to, overheard or read.

If a person has asked for legal advice he may not be interviewed or continue to be interviewed until he has received such advice unless an officer of the rank of superintendent reasonably thinks that one of the specified grounds for allowing legal advice to be delayed applies. (Code C, para 6.6).

If a person who wanted legal advice changes his mind, an interview may take place if that person agrees in writing or on tape and an officer of the rank of inspector or above, having asked the suspect for his reasons, agrees. (para 6.6 (d))

The right to get legal advice under s 58 contemplates that the adviser will be a solicitor but in practice this often is not the case. Lee Bridges and Jacqueline Hodgson (1995) said: 'it appears from the available research evidence that a significant proportion, probably between two-fifths and one-half, of all attendances at police stations by legal advisers are carried out by persons other than fully qualified solicitors'.[56] Often the adviser is a former police officer! The use of non-solicitors as police station advisers is particularly common when the firm used is the client's own solicitor (as opposed to the duty solicitor). (As has been seen, suspects in the police station call for their own solicitor in about two-thirds of all cases.)

The most recent research shows that the proportion of advisers who are solicitors is rising. In Bucke and Brown, 1997, when the advice at the police station was given through the duty solicitor scheme, the adviser was a qualified solicitor in 92% of instances. When the advice was given by the suspect's own firm, the adviser was a solicitor in 75% of cases. (p 27).

The quality of legal advice in police stations has been criticised in several research studies.[57] Thus McConville and Hodgson in a study done for the Runciman Royal Commission found that in 86% of cases, the adviser made no inquiries about the case of the custody officer. In half the cases the adviser spent under 10 minutes in private conversation with the client and many such consultations appeared cursory in nature.[58] Dixon et al reported that 'legal advisers are largely passive and non-interventionist in police interrogations'. The role of many was 'to act purely as witness to the proceedings.'[59] Baldwin, in a study of 182 audio or video tapes of police interrogations where a legal adviser was present, found that in two-thirds of these cases the adviser said nothing at all in the interview.[60]

Concern about the quality of the work done in police stations led the Law Society to produce an elaborate new training scheme for police station advisers. It led also to the Legal Aid Board insisting that it would only pay for advice done by persons who have qualified themselves under the new 'accreditation scheme'. As from February 1995, Legal Aid only paid for police station work done by 'own solicitor' representatives if they were on the accreditation list. In January 1995 it was announced that duty solicitor representatives and trainee solicitors were also being brought into the accreditation scheme.[61]

For discussion of the effect of poor legal advice on cases especially in regard to exclusion of evidence see E Cape and J Hickman, 'Bad lawyer, good defence', *New Law Journal*, 2 August 2002, p.1194.

---

[56]   Lee Bridges and J Hodgson, 'Improving Custodial Legal Advice' *Criminal Law Review* (1995), p 104.

[57]   For a review of this evidence see Bridges and Hodgson, 1995, n 56 above.

[58]   M McConville and J Hodgson, *Custodial Legal Advice and the Right to Silence*, Royal Commission on Criminal Justice, Research Study No 16, 1993).

[59]   D Dixon et al, 'Safeguarding the Rights of Suspects in Police Custody' (1990) 1 *Policing and Society*, 124.

[60]   J Baldwin, *The Role of the Legal Representatives at Police Stations* (Royal Commission on Criminal Justice, Research Study No 3, 1992), p 49.

[61]   See *Law Society's Gazette*, 11 January 1995, p 29. For a detailed assessment see L Bridges and J Hodgson, 'Improving Custodial Legal Advice' *Criminal Law Review* (1995), pp 106 –13.

Bucke and Brown noted the length of consultations. Nearly half took less than 15 minutes. Only 2% lasted over an hour. The more serious the offence, the longer the consultations (p 27).

For more details of the rules and the research data on the many aspects of legal advice to suspects in the police station see M Zander, *The Police and Criminal Evidence Act 1994* (4th edn, 2003) pp 180-201 and Bridges and Hodgson (1995).

NOTE – 'SERIOUS ARRESTABLE OFFENCES' (PACE, S 116 AND SCH 5)

'Serious arrestable offences' are defined in Sch 5 of the Act to mean any of certain specified offences such as murder, manslaughter, rape, using explosives to endanger life or property, and possession of firearms with intent to injure or with criminal intent. Apart from the named offences, under s 116 an offence is a serious arrestable one if it is arrestable (see pp 191-93 below) and it either has led or is likely to lead to serious harm to the security of the state, serious interference with the administration of justice or the investigation of offences, or death or serious injury or substantial financial gain or loss to anyone. Loss is serious if, having regard to the circumstances, it is serious for the person who suffers it (s 116(7)). This might cover £50 stolen from a pensioner – see *McIvor* [1987] Crim LR 409.

Research has shown that, according to the police, only about 2% of suspects are identified as being involved in serious arrestable offences (D Brown, *Detention at the Police Station under the PACE Act 1984* (Home Office, 1989), pp 48 – 9). In Brown et al's later study (1992) serious arrestable offences again constituted between 1 and 2% of the samples (see n 51, p 168 above, at p 68).

(b)   Informing someone that one has been arrested

Since the Criminal Law Act 1977, a suspect has been entitled to have the fact of his arrest and his whereabouts communicated, to someone reasonably named by him – without delay or, where some delay is necessary in the interests of the investigation or prevention of crime or the apprehension of offenders, with no more delay than is so necessary (s 62).

CLA 1977, s 62 was recreated with minor modification in s 56 of the Police and Criminal Evidence Act. The person to be informed is now 'one friend or relative or other person who is known to him or who is likely to take an interest in his welfare' (s 56 (1)).

Delay is only permitted where the offence in question is a serious arrestable one and is authorised by an officer of at least the rank of inspector. [62] The only permitted ground is that informing someone of the fact of the suspect's arrest 'will lead to

---

[62]   It was altered from superintendent by the Criminal Justice and Police Act 2001, s 74.

interference with or harm to evidence connected with a serious arrestable offence or interference with or physical injury to other persons, or will lead to alerting of other persons suspected of having committed such an offence but not yet arrested for it; or will hinder the recovery of any property obtained as a result of such an offence' (s 56(5)). If delay is authorised, the person must be told the grounds and they must be recorded on his custody sheet (s 56(6)). The right to have someone informed of his whereabouts applies anew every time that the suspect is brought to a new police station (s 56(8)).

The Code of Practice (Code C, section 5) adds further details. Thus the suspect has the right to have someone informed of his whereabouts at public expense. If one person cannot be reached he has the right to nominate someone else. The police right to delay informing someone does not apply in the case of a juvenile or someone who is mentally disordered or vulnerable.[63] Efforts must be made to notify his parent or guardian, or, where he is subject to a supervision order, his supervisor and the appropriate adult (see pp 180-81 below).

The Code of Practice also provides for a foreign national or Commonwealth citizen to be allowed to communicate with his embassy, high commission or consulate at any time, and this right may not be suspended or delayed (para 7.1 and note 7A).

It seems that under one-fifth of suspects seek to avail themselves of this right: D Brown, 'Detention at the Police Station under PACE', Home Office Research Study No 104, 1989, p 34. Delays are hardly ever imposed by the police. Brown et al (1992, p 68) found that delays were imposed in only 0.1% of cases.

(c) Tape-recording of interviews

It would be a very unusual suspect who could take a note (let alone a coherent note) of the questioning he undergoes in the police station. The police on the other hand are well placed to make an official record of the process. For many years there was a serious issue as to the accuracy of this record. It happened not infrequently that the suspect claimed that he had (in the jargon) been 'verballed', meaning that an alleged admission or confession had been invented by the police.

The best way to safeguard the accused from police malpractice of this kind is obviously to have the entire transaction on tape. The tape also protects the police from false accusations of improper questioning or fabrication of evidence. Tape recording has been compulsory since January 1992 for all interviews in connection with all offences other than summary only offences. But it took a considerable period to reach this position.

In 1972, a majority of the CLRC thought the time was not yet ripe to make tape-recordings compulsory. It suggested, however, that the Home Office mount an

---

63   Code C, Annex B, note B3.

experiment. The Philips Royal Commission in its 1981 report considered various options. It recommended the most modest – that only the final stage of police questioning be tape-recorded, namely the formal 'statement stage'. This is the stage when the police assist the suspect to put his previous more rambling account of the matter into a coherent statement. Taping of the whole interview, the Royal Commission thought, would prove too costly.

To its credit, the Conservative Government nevertheless went ahead with an experiment into taping the whole interview. The police were initially extremely hostile. The results soon convinced the police, however, and they became as enthusiastic about tape-recording as any civil libertarians. The reason was that the presence of tape-recording seems to increase the proportion of guilty pleas and to reduce challenges to prosecution evidence. Moreover, police fears that tape-recording would diminish the flow of confessions or information about offences committed by suspects were not realised. Rather surprisingly, suspects seemed just as ready to 'help the police with their inquiries' on tape as before. For an account of the sea-change in the attitude of the police see J Baldwin, 'The Police and Tape Recorders' (1985) *Criminal Law Review*, p 659.

Tape-recording is done under the procedure laid down in PACE Code E which deals with all the details. It provides that tape-recording must be done openly. The master tape is sealed in the presence of the suspect. The second tape is the working copy. There should be a time coding to ensure that the tape is not changed by the police. The fact of breaks, with timings, is supposed to be recorded.

If the suspect objects to the interview being tape-recorded, the officer can, but need not, turn the recorder off.

The police also have to make a record of the interview. A 1991 Home Office Circular to the police on tape-recorded interviews (39/1991) said that the summary was supposed to be a 'balanced, accurate and reliable summary of what has been said which contains sufficient information to enable the Crown Prosecution Service to decide whether or not a criminal prosecution is appropriate and whether the charges are appropriate'. The summary was supposed to include a verbatim written record of all questions and answers containing admissions by the suspect. (See, however, J Baldwin and J Bedward, 'Summarising Tape Recordings of Police Interviews' (1991) *Criminal Law Review*, p 671 and J Baldwin, 'Getting the Record Straight', *Law Society's Gazette*, 3 February 1993, p 28 to the effect that summaries are often inaccurate.)

Research by Price Waterhouse funded by the Home Office showed that summaries prepared by civilian employees were generally of higher quality than those prepared by police officers. They were more consistently free from bias either toward prosecution or defence and they were better in terms of coverage, accuracy, relevance and literacy. Also they were cheaper. (See A Hooke and J Knox, 'Preparing Records of Taped Interviews', Home Office Research and Statistics Department, Research Findings No 22, November 1995.) Based on this research, all forces were advised by an efficiency scrutiny in July 1995 to implement a programme to employ civilians to prepare records of taped interviews.

The efficiency scrutiny led in 1995 to further major changes, the main purpose of which was to cut down significantly on police paperwork. In straightforward cases where the defendant is likely to plead guilty in the magistrates' court the police are now supposed to send to the CPS an Abbreviated File with Short Descriptive Notes (SDNs) of taped interviews instead of a Record of Taped Interview (ROTI). The SDN should be brief, should refer to relevant tape counter times, and should use reported speech. The Abbreviated File would have a statement of the victim and of key witnesses. The full file has typed copies of all witnesses. (For an account of this story and an assessment of the then latest changes see A Mackie, J Burrows, R Tarling, 'Preparing the prosecution case' [1999] *Criminal Law Review*, pp 460-69. For subsequent developments see a report in May 2003 by the Cabinet Office Regulatory Impact Unit entitled *Making a Difference: Reducing Bureaucracy and Red Tape in the Criminal Justice System* – www.cabinet-office.gov.uk/regulation/PublicSector/reports.htm section 2.2.)

The defence have full access to the tape-recording unless there is a valid claim of public interest immunity.[64]

But in fact it is relatively rare for either the prosecution or the defence lawyers to listen to the actual tapes. They tend instead to work from the summary of the tape. In 1994 the Law Society laid down guidelines as to when solicitors should listen to the tape. (See *Law Society's Gazette*, 20 April 1994, p 29.)

Until recently, tape-recording did not apply to interviews with terrorism suspects. There was a fear that giving the defence access to the tapes might result in the identification of the officers involved in questioning such suspects, with possible risk to their lives. But in March 1990 the Home Secretary announced a two-year experiment in London and Merseyside in which the police would tape-record summaries of interviews with terrorism suspects. The experiment lasted until 1995 and taping continued after that on a voluntary basis. No report was ever published on the experiment. In 2001 a new system came into force for the mandatory audio recording of terrorism interviews under the Terrorism Act 2000 in England, Wales, Scotland and Northern Ireland. In Northern Ireland in addition there has been video-taping of terrorism interviews as from February 2001.

For an account of a major early study of tape-recording see Carole Willis, J Macleod and P Nash *The Tape Recording of Police Interviews with Suspects*, 2nd Interim Report, Home Office Research Study No 97, 1988. For an account of an equivalent study in Scotland see Scottish Home and Health Department, 'Tape Recording of Police

---

64   In *R v X Justices, ex p J* [2000] 1 All ER 183, Div Ct, the prosecution successfully argued that the tapes should not be released to the defence as to do so would put an undercover agent with a distinctive voice at risk. But copies of the transcripts were released.

Interviews: An Interim Report – the First 24 Months', 1982. On guidance to the courts on the handling of tape recordings see *Rampling* [1987] Crim LR 823, and *Practice Direction* (Crime: Tape Recording of Police Interviews) [1989] 1 WLR 631. For a comparison of pre-PACE with post-PACE cases in regard, inter alia, to the effect of tape-recording see I Bryan, ' Shifting images: police-suspect encounters during custodial interrogations', 17 *Legal Studies*, 1997, p 215.

Video-taping pilot study A Home Office sponsored pilot experiment with the video-taping of interviews with ordinary suspects began in April 2002 . It is taking place in six police force areas under the provisions of new PACE Code F. The rules for the handling of video recording are very similar to those for audio recording. Like audio tapes, the master tape has to be sealed in the presence of the suspect. In terrorism cases and other cases where an officer believes that recording or disclosing his identity would put him in danger he is permitted to use his identification number instead of his name and he can have his back to the camera. Receipt of the video tape by the defence is subject to an undertaking by the lawyer that it will not be given to the defendant for fear that it will be used improperly to identify the police officers involved.

Another possible (and most desirable) development would be the tape-recording of interviews with significant witnesses. For a two-part article by two barristers see D Wolchover and A.Heaton-Armstrong, 'Tape-recording witness statements', *New Law Journal*, 6 June, 1997, p 855, 13 June, p 894.

EXCHANGES THAT ARE NOT RECORDED

It is clear that exchanges take place between suspects and police officers that are not recorded – in the street, in private homes or other premises, in the police car and at the police station. Research done for the Runciman Commission showed that the arresting officers reported having interviewed suspects before arrival at the police station in 8% of cases.[65] The Royal Commission called for more research on the pros and cons of attempting to tape-record such exchanges outside the police station (Report, pp 27 – 28), but nothing further seems to have occurred in that regard.

It is to be noted in this context that Code C, para 11.1 states that save for exceptional circumstances 'Following a decision to arrest a suspect he must not be interviewed about the relevant offence except at a police station'. No doubt this is because it is only when he gets to the police station that the suspect is advised of his full rights and, in particular, it is only then that he is told about and enabled to get legal advice. Now that silence after caution can 'count' for the prosecution it is at least possible

---

[65]   S Moston and G Stephenson, *The Questioning and Interviewing of Suspects outside the Police Station* (Royal Commission on Criminal Justice, Research Study No 22, 1993).

that the courts will be faced with more situations where the police question (and therefore 'interview' – see below) suspects outside the police station.[66]

The Runciman Royal Commission recommended that the public parts of police stations should be under constant 24-hour a day surveillance through both audio and video recording. That would include the area around the custody officer's desk (the 'custody suite') and the corridors leading to the cells. It would not include the cells themselves. The purpose would be to reduce the danger of unauthorised and improper exchanges, as well as to monitor the nature of any physical interaction between suspects and police officers (Report, pp 33 – 34). The Government's Interim Response to the Royal Commission's Report in February 1994 indicated that this recommendation was accepted in principle.

(d) The regime in the police station – the Codes of Practice and the custody officer

The Administrative Directions accompanying the Judges' Rules made some provision for the way the suspect was to be looked after in the police station. These dealt with such matters as the way the statement was to be taken and recorded, the record of the questioning, reasonable comfort and refreshment of suspects, special rules for questioning children, young persons and mentally handicapped persons, rules regarding the questioning of foreigners and access to writing materials.

The PACE Codes of Practice very significantly added to these rules and laid on the police a large number of detailed new requirements in regard to the way that suspects must be handled. The difference between the old Administrative Directions and the Codes may be seen from their respective length – the Directions ran to some two pages; the 2003 version of Code C for the Detention, Treatment and Questioning of persons by the police, runs to over 70.

Code C starts with the statement that 'all persons shall be dealt with expeditiously and released as soon as the need for detention has ceased to apply' (para 1.1).

Most of the Code deals with the situation in the police station. It deals with the duties in particular of the custody officer – the person in each police station designated to be responsible for the well-being of suspects. The Police and Criminal Evidence Act states there has to be a custody officer on duty in each police station and that normally he should be of the rank of sergeant or above. It is the custody officer's duty to ensure 'that all persons in police detention at that station are treated in accordance with this Act and any code of practice issued under it ... and that all matters relating

---

66 In *Williams* (1992) Times, 6 February W claimed that he had been persuaded to confess during an hour-long post-charge 'social visit' in his cell by investigating officers. The Court of Appeal rejected his appeal that the confession given at a later formal interview should have been excluded by the trial judge.

to such persons which are required by this Act or by such codes of practice to be recorded are recorded in the custody records relating to such persons' (s 39(1)). The custody officer must, if possible, be someone other than the arresting or investigating officers. Where the arresting officer is higher in rank than the custody officer and there is some disagreement between them regarding the handling of the suspect, the custody officer has to refer the matter to an officer of the rank of superintendent or above responsible for that police station (s 39(6)).

The Code requires the custody officer in each police station to maintain the custody record containing the details of all the relevant events of the detention. A person is entitled to a copy of any part of the custody record and he must be told of his right to have a copy.

INFORMATION TO THE PERSON IN CUSTODY

One of the most important provisions in the Code relates to the information that must be given to the suspect. The custody officer, before any questioning of the suspect, must tell him the ground of his detention and tell him both orally and in writing of his right to have someone informed about his arrest, to have free legal advice and of his rights under para 5 to send messages to the outside world.

PACE s 5 (the right not to be held incommunicado) permits the suspect at his own expense to send letters, or telegrams or make telephone calls, providing Annex B does not apply. (Annex B states that the implementation of certain rights may be delayed if an officer of the rank of inspector (formerly it was superintendent) or above has reasonable grounds to believe that it would lead to 'interference with or harm to evidence connected with a serious arrestable offence', or to the alerting of other persons suspected of having committed such an offence, or will hinder the recovery of property obtained in the course of such an offence.) If letters are sent from the police station, the police are permitted to monitor their contents – other than in the case of letters to a solicitor (para 5.7).

As has been seen, the custody record must show that the suspect has been told about his rights, either by his signed acknowledgement or a note that he refused to sign. If he wishes to waive the right to legal advice, this too must be signed (para 3.2).

The police must warn the suspect that anything he says in a letter, phone call or telegram may be used in evidence (para 5.7).

RECORDS OF INTERVIEWS

The provisions in Code C regarding the process of keeping proper records of any interview with the suspect require records to be kept of the place of interviews, the time they begin and end, and the time of any breaks. The person interviewed must be given the chance to read the record and to sign it as correct or to indicate what he thinks is not accurate. Persons making statements must be allowed to make them in their own words. If the officer writes the statement he should use the words actually spoken by the suspect. (Paras 2.6, 11.7 – 11.14 and Annex D.)

One important addition to the old rules is that records of interviews should so far as practicable be made contemporaneously, or failing this as soon as possible after the interview (para 11.7(c)). This has caused the police much concern. Also a full written record of the interview must be made and the suspect must be given a chance to read it and to sign it as correct. Where a third person is present at an interview, he has to be given the opportunity to read the written record of the interview and to sign it as correct or to indicate the aspects in which he thinks it is inaccurate. If he refuses to do so, this fact should be recorded (para s 11.12, 11.14). For definition of an interview see Code C, 11.1A. But the definition is less important since a record must now be made of relevant comments even if they are made outside the context of an interview (para 11.13).

For an evaluation of the value of the recording rules see H Fenwick, 'Confessions, Recording Rules and Miscarriages of Justice: a Mistaken Emphasis' [1993] *Criminal Law Review* , p 174.

CONDITIONS OF DETENTION (SS 8 AND 9)

The Judges' Rules and Administrative Directions made some, but only rather general, reference to the conditions of detention. The Code puts detailed flesh and blood on the existing skeleton.

So far as practicable there should be no more than one person per cell. Cells and bedding should be aired and cleaned daily. There should be reasonable access to toilet and washing facilities. Replacement clothing should be of reasonable standard and no questioning must take place unless the suspect has been offered clothing. There should be at least two light and one main meal per 24 hours and any dietary requirements should be met so far as possible. Brief outdoor exercise should be permitted daily, if possible.

A child or young person should not be placed in police cells unless he is so unruly as to be a danger to person or property or there is no other secure accommodation available. Only an inspector or above can authorise such detention.

No more than reasonable force may be used by a police officer to secure compliance with reasonable instructions, to prevent the suspect's escape, or to restrain him from causing injury to persons or damage to property or evidence.

If any ill-treatment or unlawful force has been used, any officer who has notice of it should draw it to the attention of the custody officer who in turn must inform an officer of at least the rank of inspector not connected with the investigation. He in turn must summon a police surgeon or other health care professional to examine the suspect. A complaint from the suspect to this effect must be reported to an inspector or above.

MEDICAL TREATMENT (s 9(b))

The Code requires that appropriate action be taken by the custody officer to deal with any medical condition – whether or not the person in custody asks for it. This applies not only to obvious medical conditions but where the person is unable to appreciate the nature of the proceedings, or he is incoherent or somnolent and the custody officer is in any doubt as to the circumstances of his condition. The Code specifically warns that a person who appears to be drunk may in fact be suffering from the effects of drugs or some injury. If in doubt the police should call the appropriate health care professional. (Note 9C).

The advice of an appropriate health professional should equally be obtained if the suspect says he needs medication for a serious condition such as heart disease, diabetes or epilepsy (Code C, para 9.9).

CONDUCT OF INTERVIEWS (s 12)

In any period of 24 hours the suspect is supposed to be given eight continuous hours for rest, free from questioning, travel or other interruption and, if possible, at night. If he goes to the police station voluntarily, the period is calculated from arrest.

Before a detainee is interviewed, the custody officer, in consultation with the officer in charge of the case and appropriate health care professionals as necessary, must assess whether the detainee is fit to be interviewed. (para 12.3 and Annex G)

Interview rooms are supposed to be adequately heated, lit and ventilated. The suspect should not be required to stand. The interviewing officer should identify his name and rank (or in terrorism cases or if in other cases, revealing his identity would put him at risk, his number). In addition to meal breaks there should also be short breaks for refreshment approximately every two hours unless this would prejudice the investigation.

THE QUESTIONING OF JUVENILES, AND MENTALLY DISORDERED AND OTHERWISE MENTALLY VULNERABLE PERSONS (s 3(b) AND ANNEX E)

There are detailed provisions in the Code regulating the questioning of persons who are mentally disordered, mentally vulnerable or youthful. Broadly, they require that normally questioning should only take place in the presence of an 'appropriate adult' who is either a parent or guardian or a person in whose care he is. If the adult thinks that legal advice should be taken, the interview should not commence until such advice has been taken. However, an interview may take place in the absence of the responsible adult or lawyer if an officer of the rank of superintendent or above reasonably believes that the delay in waiting would involve the risk of immediate harm to persons or serious loss of or damage to property. (para 11.18)

The Runciman Royal Commission (p 44, para 86) recommended that an expert working party be appointed to consider the role of the appropriate adult. The Home Office set up a Review Group which reported in June 1995. It recommended, inter alia, that local panels of appropriate adults should be set up and that guidance as to the role should be available in the form of leaflets. Panels of lay people who volunteer to be on call as appropriate adults now exist in some parts of the country.

Juveniles make up around one-fifth of suspects in police stations. Home Office research showed that 91% of juvenile suspects had an appropriate adult present for all or some of their time in custody. In three-fifths of cases (59%) it was a parent; in another 8% it was another relative and in almost a quarter of cases (23%) it was a social worker.[67]

Mentally disordered or mentally vulnerable detainees are a smaller group. In the same Home Office study, 2% of detainees were treated as being in those categories (p 7) – though other research has suggested that the actual proportion is considerably higher. Appropriate adults, usually a social worker, attended police stations in two-thirds of such cases (66%) (p 8).

For discussion of the various problems raised by the appropriate adult see J Hodgson, 'Vulnerable Suspects and the Appropriate Adult' [1997] *Criminal Law Review*, pp 785-95.

INTERPRETERS (s 13)

The Administrative Directions accompanying the Judges' Rules referred to statements made by those who could not speak English being translated by an interpreter. But they did not positively require the interpreter to be called. The Code remedies this deficiency and states categorically that a person who has difficulty in understanding English shall not be interviewed save in the presence of someone who can act as interpreter. (para 13.2)

QUESTIONING OF DEAF PERSONS (s 13)

The Code also provides that where there is a doubt as to a person's hearing, arrangements should be made to have a competent interpreter. If he wishes, no interview should take place without the interpreter. On the other hand, if he does not insist on having an interpreter, the person should sign a waiver to that effect.

---

67   T Bucke and D Brown, *In police custody: police powers and suspects' rights under the revised PACE codes of practice*, 1997, Home Office Research Series No 174, p 6.

(e)   Rules preventing improper pressure on suspects

It goes without saying that police officers may not use physical violence or the threat of violence against suspects. Any such action would of course constitute the criminal offence of assault (or worse). It would also be actionable in civil proceedings for damages. But civil and criminal proceedings are usually difficult to launch because of the problem of proving the allegations. The use or the threat of physical violence could also be the basis of a formal complaint against the officers concerned.

Apart from the inhibiting effect of these possibilities there is also the long-established principle that statements to be admissible in evidence must be voluntary. The requirement that all confessions or admissions be voluntary is considered in chapter 4. It will be seen there that the Philips Royal Commission proposed that the common law rules be modified and that the Police and Criminal Evidence Act partly adopted the Commission's proposals. Under the scheme of the Act, confessions obtained as a result of oppression, violence, the threat of violence, or inhuman or degrading treatment are wholly inadmissible. Likewise inadmissible are statements obtained in circumstances that make it likely that any confession obtained in those circumstances would be unreliable. Moreover it is for the prosecution to prove beyond reasonable doubt that the statement was not obtained as a result of such conduct. But if these conditions are met, the confession can be admissible even though it was obtained as a result of inducements. (See further pp 454-55.)

3. Detention and arrest

(a)   Can a person be held in the police station if he is not under arrest?

It is common to read in the newspapers that a man is 'helping the police with their inquiries'. When asked, the police normally assert that he is not under arrest.

The legal position of such a person is stated in s 29 of PACE which provides that where a person attends a police station voluntarily 'for the purpose of assisting with an investigation', he is entitled to leave at will unless placed under arrest (s 29(a)). Secondly, he must be informed 'at once that he is under arrest if a decision is taken by a constable to prevent him from leaving at will' (s 29(b)). The only gap in the system is that there is no duty on the police to advise the person in question that he need not accompany the officer to the police station unless he wishes to do so. This would be the equivalent of the duty to caution him about his right of silence. But it does not exist and neither the Philips Royal Commission on Criminal Procedure nor PACE made any reference to the issue.

However, if someone who is voluntarily helping the police with their inquiries, whether at a police station or elsewhere, is cautioned he must be informed that he is not under arrest, if that is the case (Code C, para s 3.21 and 10.2).

(b) In what circumstances can someone be stopped in the street?

The police can ask anyone any questions – but can they lawfully stop a citizen who does not wish to be stopped, without arresting him? This question has arisen in a variety of contexts. In 1967 the Divisional Court gave a clear response to this question:

Kenlin v Gardiner [1967] 2 QB 510 (Divisional Court)

[Two schoolboys were going from house to house to remind members of their rugby team about a game. Two plainclothes police officers became suspicious and, producing a warrant card, asked what they were doing. The boys did not believe they were police officers. One boy made as if to run away. The police officer took hold of his arm. The boy struggled violently, punching and kicking the officer. The other boy got involved and struck the other officer. Both were charged with assaulting a police constable in the execution of his duty.

Appeal by case stated.

Winn LJ gave the judgment of the court:]

The boys undoubtedly assaulted the police officers: there cannot be any doubt about that, they struck them and kicked them, but the question is whether that was a justifiable or unjustified assault; and that again, as Mr Rogers agreed, depends entirely on whether the answer of self-defence was available to these two boys in the particular circumstances. ... So one comes back to the question in the end, in the ultimate analysis: was this officer entitled in law to take hold of the first boy by the arm – of course the same situation arises with the other officer in regard to the second boy a little later – justified in committing that technical assault by the exercise of any power which he as a police constable in the precise circumstances prevailing at that exact moment possessed?

I regret, really, that I feel myself compelled to say that the answer to that question must be in the negative. This officer might or might not in the particular circumstances have possessed a power to arrest these boys. I leave that question open, saying no more than that I feel some doubt whether he would have had a power of arrest: but on the assumption that he had a power to arrest, it is to my mind perfectly plain that neither of these officers purported to arrest either of these boys. What was done was not as an integral step in the process of arresting, but was done in order to secure an opportunity, by detaining the boys from escape, to put to them or to either of them the question which was regarded as the test question to satisfy the officers whether or not it would be right in the circumstances, and having regard to the answer obtained from that question, if any, to arrest them.

I regret to say that I think there was a technical assault by the police officer. From which it follows that the justification of self-defence exerted or exercised by these two boys is not negatived by any justifiable character of the initial assault. ...

For these reasons I think that this appeal should be allowed and this conviction quashed.

To the same effect see *Ludlow v Burgess* [1971] Crim LR 238, and *Pedro v Diss* [1981] 2 All ER 59. A case that seems at first sight to be at variance with *Kenlin v Gardiner* is *Donnelly v Jackman*.

Donnelly v Jackman [1970] 1 All ER 987 (Divisional Court)

[Talbot J gave the judgment of the court:]

The facts found by the justices were these: at about 11.15 am on Saturday, 5 April, the appellant was lawfully walking along a pavement when PC Roy Grimmett in uniform came up to him for the purposes of making inquiries about an offence which the officer had cause to believe the appellant had committed or might have committed. The officer spoke to the appellant asking him if he could have a word with him. The appellant ignored that request, and continued to walk along the pavement away from the officer. The officer followed close behind him and apparently repeatedly asked him to stop and speak to him. At one stage the officer tapped the appellant on the shoulder, and apparently shortly after that the appellant turned round and in turn tapped the officer on the chest saying 'Now we are even, copper'.

It became apparent to the officer, so the finding proceeds, that the appellant had no intention of stopping to speak to him. The officer then again touched the appellant on the shoulder with the intention of stopping him, whereupon the appellant then turned round and struck the officer with some force. The finding is that the officer did not touch the appellant for the purpose of making any formal arrest or charge, but solely for the purpose of speaking to him. Following the striking of the officer, the appellant was arrested for assaulting the officer in the execution of his duty and taken to the police station. The justices convicted the appellant, finding the summons proved.

[The Divisional Court then distinguished *Kenlin v Gardiner* on the ground that there each officer had taken hold of one of the boys and had in fact detained him. They continued:]

Turning to the facts of this matter, it is not very clear what precisely the justices meant or found when they said that the officer touched the appellant on the shoulder, but whatever it was that they really did mean, it seems clear to me that they must have felt that it was a minimal matter by the way in which they treated this matter and the result of the case. When one considers the problem: was the officer acting in the course of his duty, in my view one ought to bear in mind that it is not every trivial interference with a citizen's liberty that amounts to a course of conduct sufficient to take the officer out of the course of his duties.

In my judgment the facts that the justices found in this case do not justify the view that the officer was not acting in the execution of his duty when he went to the appellant and wanted to speak to him. Therefore the assault was rightly found to be an assault on the officer while acting in the execution of his duties, and I would dismiss this appeal.

In a later case the Divisional Court, on facts virtually identical with those of *Donnelly v Jackman*, went the other way (*Bentley v Brudzinski* [1982] Crim LR 825). The respondent and his brother were stopped and questioned by a police officer at 3.30 am. They answered his questions truthfully and identified themselves. After waiting some 10 minutes while the officer unsuccessfully tried to verify their identities by radio, they walked away. Another officer who came up at that point stopped the respondent by putting his hand on his shoulder and was punched in the face. The Divisional Court held that this was more than a trivial interference with the respondent's liberty and amounted to an unlawful attempt to stop and detain him. Accordingly the respondent was not guilty of assaulting an officer in the execution of his duty. Lord Justice Donaldson added, however, that the respondent would have had no defence to a charge of common assault if one had been laid. (For comment, see (1982) *Criminal Law Review* pp 481 and 826.) See also the contrasting cases of *Collins v Wilcock* [1984] 1 WLR 1172; *Weight v Long* [1986] Crim LR 746; *Smith v DPP* [2001] EWHC Admin 55, [2001] Crim LR 735; and *R (on the application of Bucher) v DPP* [2003] EWHC Admin 580. For discussion of the last case see N Parpworth and K Thompson, ' Physical Contact and a Police Officer's Execution of Duty', 167 *Justice of the Peace*, 7 June 2000, p 426.)

One exception to the general rule is under the Road Traffic Acts. RTA 1988, s 163 (formerly RTA 1972, s 159) gives the police the power to stop a vehicle on any ground whatever. It is an offence to fail to stop. This power of stopping the vehicle does not, however, give the police any right to search it unless the driver agrees. As has been seen, the officer can, however, demand to have the name and address of the driver or the owner. The Divisional Court held in 1972 that the power to demand that a motorist give his name and address includes the power to block his passage for the purpose: *Squires v Botwright* [1972] RTR 462.

The courts have held that the police have the right to detain motorists for a short period while they administer the breathalyser – see, for instance, *Coleman* [1974] RTR 359 or *Squires v Botwright* above. See also *Lodwick v Sanders* [1985] 1 All ER 577. The police stopped a lorry driver who had no excise licence, index plate or brake lights. In the course of the subsequent exchange, the police officer became suspicious as to whether the lorry was stolen. The officer took the ignition keys when the driver tried to leave. There was a minor fracas. The driver was charged with assault on the police, but was acquitted on the ground that the officer had not been acting within his duty. Held, on appeal, that this was incorrect. He was entitled to stop it in the first place and, being suspicious, to detain it for a reasonable period while checking out whether it was stolen. He had therefore been acting in the execution of his duty.

As has been seen, in Scotland since 1980, (now under the Criminal Procedure (Scotland) Act 1995) where a constable has reasonable grounds for suspecting that a person has committed an offence he can ask him for his name and address and 'an explanation of the circumstances which have given rise to the constable's suspicion' (s 13(1)). He can also ask anyone whom he thinks has information relating to that offence to give his name and address. Secondly, the officer can require anyone whose name and address he has asked for to remain with him while he verifies the name and address – provided it can be done quickly. It is an arrestable offence not to comply (s 13(7)).

The Philips Royal Commission did not recommend that the police should have any power short of arrest to detain persons as suspects. It also specifically rejected the idea that witnesses should be liable to arrest if they refused to give their name and address (para 3.90). They preferred the approach that citizens should be left to make up their own minds as to whether to co-operate with the police. Only in one situation should the rule be otherwise. This was where there had been some grave incident (such as a murder on a train of football supporters). The police should then have the right to detain potential witnesses 'while names and addresses are obtained or a suspect identified or the matter is otherwise resolved' (para 3.93).

But PACE contained no provision which gave the police any power to detain suspects other than through arrest. (See also the next section below.)

Note however that under the Terrorism Act 2000, s 89 an officer may stop a person 'for so long as is necessary to question him to ascertain (a) his identity and movements, (b) what he knows about a recent explosion or another recent incident endangering life; (c) what he knows about a person killed or injured in a recent explosion or incident'.

The Terrorism Act 2000, ss 32-36 also gives the police the right to cordon off an area for the purposes of a terrorist investigation. Note that in *DPP v Morrison* [2003] EWHC Admin 683, (2003) Times, 21 April, the Divisional Court held that the police had a common law power to set up a cordon in a shopping mall as a crime scene because they were entitled to assume that the owner of private land over which there was a public right of way would have consented to the cordon. Hooper J went further in adding obiter that he doubted whether consent in such a situation could lawfully be withheld.[68]

However the power to stop and search persons arises solely under statute. There are a number of statutes which give the police this power. Pre-PACE the best known of these was the power under s 66 of the Metropolitan Police Act 1839 to stop and search anyone in the metropolitan area reasonably suspected of carrying stolen goods. This power also existed by virtue of bye-laws in a few other cities. A similar power exists nationally in relation to drugs under the Misuse of Drugs Act 1971 and firearms

[68]   See further on the case N Parpworth and K Thompson, 'The Lawfulness of a Police Cordon', 167 *Justice of the Peace*, 5 July 2003.

under the Firearms Act 1968. There are also a variety of archaic powers to stop and search persons suspected eg under the Badgers Act, the Pedlars Act, the Poaching Prevention Act and the Protection of Birds Act. [69]

In *Daniel v Morrison* [1980] Crim LR 181, the Divisional Court held that the power under s 66 of the Metropolitan Police Act 1839 to stop, search and detain anyone suspected of having stolen goods included the power to question them as well, if only briefly. Similarly, in *Geen* [1982] Crim LR 604, the court held that the power to search someone suspected of carrying prohibited drugs under the Misuse of Drugs Act 1971 included a power to question him briefly.

THE PHILIPS ROYAL COMMISSION'S PROPOSALS

The Philips Royal Commission proposed that the Metropolitan police power to stop and search for stolen goods should apply throughout the country. It also proposed a new power to stop and search for something possession of which was prohibited in a public place – such as offensive weapons (para 3.20).

The majority of the Royal Commission thought that the danger of abuse of power could be avoided by the incorporation of proper safeguards, together with the fact that search would only be possible where there were reasonable grounds for suspicion. ('If parliament has made it an offence to be in possession of a particular article in a public place, the police should be able to stop and search persons suspected on reasonable grounds of committing that offence' (para 3.21).) The safeguards proposed were: the officer should have to record every search and the reason for it; supervising officers should have a duty to collect and scrutinise figures of searches and their results for evidence that they were being carried out randomly, arbitrarily or in a discriminatory way; the person stopped should have a right to get a copy of the record; and numbers of stops and searches should be given to chief constables' annual reports (para 3.26). The Commission also thought that searches on the street should be limited to fairly superficial examination of a person's clothing and baggage.

For pre-PACE research on stop and search see David Smith, *Police and People in London: I.A. Survey of Londoners*, 1983; David Smith and Jeremy Gray, *Police and People in London: IV. The Police in Action*, 1983.; Carole Willis, *The Use, Effectiveness and Impact of Police Stop and Search Powers* (Home Office Research and Planning Unit, Paper 15, 1983).

PACE

The Government did not wholly accept the Royal Commission's proposals on stop and search powers. It rejected the argument that there should be a general new power

---

[69] For a full list see *Report of the Royal Commission on Criminal Procedure: Law and Procedure*, 1981, Cmnd 8092 – 1, pp 75 – 9.

to stop and search anyone reasonably suspected of carrying something possession of which in a public place was forbidden. The police therefore have to continue to manage under the various specific statutes which give them stop and search powers.

But the Government did include in PACE a new power to search someone reasonably suspected of carrying housebreaking implements or an offensive weapon. [70] The Act also provided for the extension nationally of the power under the Metropolitan Police Act 1839, s 66 to search persons suspected of carrying stolen goods.

RECORDS OF STOPS AND SEARCHES

Under PACE s 2 the police officer who proposes to carry out a stop and search must state his name and police station, and the purpose of the search. A plain clothes officer must in addition produce documentary evidence that he is a policeman. The officer must give the grounds for the search. (This seems in fact to have been the common law already: see *McBean v Parker* [1983] Crim LR 399.) A search in the street must be limited to the outer clothing. The police officer is required to make a record of the search immediately, or if this is not practicable, as soon as possible (s 3). The record is supposed to state the name of the officer, the name of the person stopped, if known, the object of the search, the ground of the search and its result (s 3).

Recording of stops that do not result in a search The Macpherson Report on the murder of Stephen Lawrence recommended that the police should be required to make records of *all stops* including voluntary stops (Recommendation 61). Despite criticism that this would hugely increase the burden on the police to little advantage to anyone, the Government initially accepted the recommendation subject to feasibility trials. The draft of Code A issued in April 2002 laid down rules for the recording of any stop where the police require the person to account for himself. But when the revised version of Code A was laid before Parliament in December 2002 these provisions had been dropped. The Government announced that it still adhered to the policy subject to pilot studies but it seemed that the idea might eventually be quietly dropped.

One of the chief objections is that quite apart from causing aggravation for both the police officer and the citizen, it would produce no worthwhile new information. Since a stop does not have to be justified by reasonable suspicion, there would be no way of assessing whether any particular stop or any series of stops was reasonable.

THE CODE OF PRACTICE FOR THE EXERCISE OF POWERS OF STOP AND SEARCH

Code A on stop and search has been amended several times, most recently as of 1 April 2003. Many of the changes in the 2003 version of the Code had their origins in debates

---

[70]   Defined in the same way as under the Prevention of Crime Act 1953, s 1, as 'any article made or adapted for use for causing injury to the person, or intended by the person having it with him for such use by him or by some other person' (s 1(9)).

and research prompted by the Macpherson inquiry into the death of Stephen Lawrence. Six reports were published in September 2000 in the Home Office Police Research Series.[71]

Section 1 of Code A starts with the words, 'Powers to stop and search must be used fairly, responsibly, with respect for people being searched and without unlawful discrimination'. (para 1.1) The person stopped can be questioned prior to a search and, if such preliminary exchanges indicate that the suspicion is ill-founded, no search need take place. But a person cannot be stopped in order for grounds for a search to be found. Normally, there has to be prior reasonable suspicion that the person was carrying something possession of which justifies exercise of the power. Reasonable suspicion requires an objective basis 'based on facts, information, and/or intelligence' (para 2.2) 'A person's race, age, appearance, or the fact that the person is known to have a previous conviction cannot be used alone or in combination with eachother as the reason for searching that person' (ibid) Nor can a search be based on 'generalisations or stereotypical images' (ibid).

There is a striking contrast between the terms of the Code of Practice on the need for reasonable cause to legitimate a stop, and the decision of the Divisional Court in *Chief Constable of Gwent v Dash* [1985] Crim LR 674, in which it was held that random stopping of motorists to see whether they were driving with excess alcohol was not unlawful – though randomly requiring motorists to give a specimen of breath would be unlawful. The court said that, provided there was 'no malpractice, caprice, or opprobrious behaviour', there was no legal restriction on the stopping of motorists by a police officer in the execution of his duty.

For a long and helpful evaluation of the problem of police discretion and its control in arrest and stop and search, see CL Ryan and KS Williams, 'Police Discretion', *Public Law*, Summer 1986, p 285; see also D Dixon et al, 'Reality and Rules in the Construction and Regulation of Police Suspicion', 17 *International Journal of the Sociology of Law*, 1989, p 185.

---

[71] *The Impact of Stops and Searches on Crime and the Community* by J Miller, N Bland and P Quinton (Paper 127); *Upping the PACE? An evaluation of the recommendations of the Stephen Lawrence Inquiry on stops and searches* by N Bland, J Miller, P Quinton (Paper 128); *The Views of the Public on Stops and Searches* by V Stone and N Pettigrew (Paper 129); *Police Stops, Decision-making and Practice* by P Quinton, N Bland and J Miller (paper 130); *Profiling Populations Available for Stops and Searches* by MVA and J Miller (Paper 131); *Managing the Use and Impact of Searches: A review of force interventions* by N Bland, J Miller and P Quinton (Paper 132). See also Marian Fitzgerald, *Searches in London*, Final Report, December 1999, London, Metropolitan Police (www.met.police.uk.); P Jordan, *Stop/Search: Impact on crime and impact on public opinion*, Police Foundation, 2000 (www.police-foundation.org.uk); and M Fitzgerald, M Hough, I Joseph, T Qureshi, *Policing for London* (Willan, 2002).

POWER TO STOP AND SEARCH RANDOMLY

There are now a number of statutes that permit stop and search even though there is no reasonable ground to suspect the particular person. The Criminal Justice and Public Order Act 1994 provided for this in s 60 (powers to stop and search in anticipation of serious violence) and in s 81 (to prevent acts of terrorism). Both sections require that a senior officer (under s 60, an inspector,[72] under s 81 an assistant chief constable or equivalent) to designate the area in which such powers can be exercised for a limited period (24 hours under s 60, 28 days under s 81). Section 81 only applied to vehicles and their drivers and passengers. The Prevention of Terrorism (Additional Powers) Act 1996 filled a gap by permitting stop and search also of pedestrians. (See now Terrorism Act 2000, s 44.) The Crime and Disorder Act 1998, s 25 permitted an officer acting under CJPOA 1994, s 60 to require the person to remove any item such as a face mask that is being worn wholly or mainly to conceal his identity. (The revised Code A, Note 4 advises that 'where there may be religious sensitivities about ordering the removal of such an item, the officer should permit the item to be removed out of public view'.)

ABOLITION OF 'VOLUNTARY' SEARCHES

Originally the rules on stop and search did not apply where the search was voluntary. Obviously, if this concept is given a wide interpretation there is a danger that a 'coach and four' will be driven through the procedural safeguards of PACE. The Home Office Circular on PACE issued to police said, 'Voluntary search must not be used as a way of avoiding the main thrust of the safeguards.' However not all forces and all personnel concerned took this message to heart. In too many situations the concept of the consensual or voluntary search was used as a way of avoiding the main thrust of the safeguards. [73]

An attempt to address the problem was made in 1991 by a requirement that 'in these circumstances, an officer should always make it clear that he is seeking the consent of the person concerned'[74]. In 1995 an amendment went considerably further by requiring the officer to say not only that the person need not consent but that *that without his consent he will not be searched*"[75]. The 1995 version also added 'Juveniles, people suffering from a mental handicap or mental disorder and others who appear not to be capable of giving an informed consent should not be subject to a voluntary search'.[76]

---

[72] Under s 81 of the CJPOA it had to be a superintendent but the Knives Act 1997, s 8 replaced this by an inspector.

[73] See D Dixon, C Coleman and K Bottomley, 'Consent and Legal Regulation of Policing', 17 *Journal of Law and Society*, 1990, p.345.

[74] Code A, Note 1D(b).

[75] Emphasis supplied.

[76] Note 1E.

The 2003 version of the Code drops both the requirement that the person be told that without his consent he cannot be searched and the specific ban on voluntary searches of juveniles and others deemed incapable of giving consent. Instead, the new preliminary 'Principles governing stop and search' state unambiguously:

> An officer must not search a person, even with his or her consent, where no power to search is applicable. Even where a person is prepared to submit to a search voluntarily, the person must not be searched unless the necessary legal power exists, and the search must be in accordance with the relevant power and the provisions of this Code. [para1.5]

The only exception where an officer does not require a specific power to search applies to searches of persons entering sports grounds or other premises 'carried out with their consent given as condition of entry' (ibid). This means that the concept of voluntary search is now effectively banned for adults as much as for juveniles. A search can only be done if there is the legal power, including reasonable suspicion, and if the Code of Practice is complied with.

STATISTICS

The annual Home Office statistics on stop and search[77] show that the two most common categories are stolen property and drugs. (In 2001-02 they accounted respectively for 39% and 36% of all recorded stops and searches.) Offensive weapons accounts for a very small proportion. (In 2001-02 only 7%.)

The 'hit rate' in the sense of arrests following a stop and search, which was 17% in both 1986 and 1987, has been between 10 and 13% in the years since 1993. (Table PA)The proportion of all arrests that result from stop and search is currently around 8% but in the Metropolitan Police District the proportion is considerably higher. In 2001-02 it was 17%. (Table AC)

(c)   The power to arrest

There are two forms of arrest, lawful and unlawful. In *Spicer v Holt* [1977] AC 987, HL, Lord Dilhorne said (at p 1000): 'Whether or not a person has been arrested depends not on the legality of the arrest, but on whether he has been deprived of his liberty to go where he pleases.' (See to same effect, *R v Inwood* [1973] 2 All ER 645; *R v Bass* [1953] 1 QB 680.) So, if a person is being detained by the police against his will, he is under arrest, but whether the arrest is lawful will depend on whether the conditions for a lawful arrest have been fulfilled. (*Dawes v DPP* [1995] 1 Cr App Rep 65.) If the arrest is not lawful there is a right to use reasonable force to avoid it, but

---

[77]   *Arrests for Notifiable Offences and the Operation of Certain Police Powers under PACE.* The latest available was that for 2001-02.

this is clearly not a right to be lightly exercised since the legality of the arrest is best tested after the event when the dust has settled.

A lawful arrest is one authorised by law. There are three basic types of lawful arrest.

(1)   ARREST UNDER WARRANT

The normal procedure is laid down in the Magistrates' Courts Act 1980, s 1(1) which gives a magistrate power to issue a warrant upon written information being laid before him on oath 'that any person has, or is suspected of having, committed an offence'. Under the Criminal Justice Act 1967, s 24(1) it is provided that a warrant for the arrest of someone should not be issued unless the offence in question is indictable or is punishable with imprisonment. This reflects the policy that minor offences should be dealt with by summons rather than arrest.

(2)   ARREST WITHOUT WARRANT AT COMMON LAW

Until 1967 the law of arrest at common law revolved around the distinction between felonies and misdemeanours. Felonies and misdemeanours were abolished by the Criminal Law Act 1967 which substituted the concepts of arrestable and non-arrestable offences.

There is now only one remaining common law power to arrest – where a breach of the peace has been committed and there are reasonable grounds for believing that it will be continued or renewed, or where a breach of the peace is reasonably apprehended. (See *Wershof v Metropolitan Police Comr* [1978] 3 All ER 540; *Hickman v O'Dwyer* [1979] Crim LR 309; *Howell* [1981] Crim LR 697.)

(3)   ARREST WITHOUT A WARRANT UNDER STATUTE

The general power of arrest which formerly was set out in the Criminal Law Act 1967, s 2, is now to be found in PACE s 24 and Sch 1A. Section 24 provides that the police may arrest without a warrant for arrestable and certain other offences. An arrestable offence is one for which the sentence is fixed by law (ie murder and treason); any offence which carries a liability to five years' imprisonment or more; any offence specifically listed in Schedule 1A[78]; and any attempt to commit any of the above.

The Act gave constables and ordinary citizens slightly different powers of arrest in relation to these various offences:

---

[78]   Previously the ever-growing list was in s 24(2) but it was transferred to a new Sch 1A of PACE by PRA 2002, Sch 6. At the time of the passage of the 2002 Act there were 25 offences on the list.

Police and Criminal Evidence Act 1984, s 24

(4) Any person may arrest without a warrant –
(*a*) anyone who is in the act of committing an arrestable offence;
(*b*) anyone whom he has reasonable grounds for suspecting to be committing such an offence.

(5) Where an arrestable offence has been committed, any person may arrest without a warrant –
(*a*) anyone who is guilty of the offence;
(*b*) anyone whom he has reasonable grounds for suspecting to be guilty of it.

(6) Where a constable has reasonable grounds for suspecting that an arrestable offence has been committed, he may arrest without a warrant anyone whom he has reasonable grounds for suspecting to be guilty of the offence.

(7) A constable may arrest without a warrant –
(*a*) anyone who is about to commit an arrestable offence;
(*b*) anyone whom he has reasonable grounds for suspecting to be about to commit an arrestable offence.

Under sub-s (5) the arrest was only lawful if an arrestable offence had actually been committed. So in *Self*[79] the jury acquitted S of theft and he therefore could not be guilty of assault with intent to resist arrest by a member of the public. A Government amendment to the Criminal Justice Bill 2002/03 dealt with this by inserting a new sub-s (5A): 'Any person may arrest without warrant, any person who is accused by an apparently credible witness of having committed an arrestable offence shortly before the accusation is made'.

Arrest for non-arrestable offences In addition to the powers of arrest under s 24, the Act also gave the police new powers of arrest in regard to non-arrestable offences. Section 25 provides that 'where a constable has reasonable grounds for suspecting that an offence has been committed or attempted, or is being committed or attempted, he may arrest any person whom he has reasonable grounds to suspect of having committed the offence or of being in the course of committing or attempting to commit it if it appears to him that service of a summons is impracticable or inappropriate because any of the general arrest conditions is satisfied'. The 'general arrest conditions' are that the officer does not know and cannot find out the suspect's name or address (or he has reasonable grounds to think that he has been given a false name or address), or he has reasonable grounds for believing that an arrest is necessary to prevent someone causing: physical harm to himself or someone else; or loss of or damage to property; or an offence against public decency; or an obstruction of the highway (s 25(3)(d)).

[79]   (1992) 95 Cr App Rep 42, CA.

Reasonable ground to suspect Most statutes that grant a power of arrest require that the arresting person has reasonable grounds to suspect. The House of Lords considered this well-worn phrase in deciding *O'Hara v Chief Constable of the Royal Ulster Constabulary* [1997] AC 286, [1997] 1 All ER 129. O had been arrested for murder committed in the course of a terrorist act in Northern Ireland. The arresting officer had attended a briefing given by a superior officer at which he was told to arrest O because he had been involved in the murder. The officer's suspicion was based solely on that briefing. The trial judge and the Court of Appeal of Northern Ireland held that enough information had been given to the officer to enable him to form the required state of mind. On appeal to the House of Lords it was argued that reasonable grounds had to exist in fact, that the test was objective and therefore required proof of more than what was in the officer's mind. Dismissing the appeal, the House of Lords unanimously rejected this argument. The court need look no further than what was in the officer's mind. The officer's suspicion could be based on what he had been told – even by an anonymous informant. It did not have to be established that the facts were true. But in each case it had to be considered whether the officer had enough information to form reasonable grounds for suspicion. Being ordered to make an arrest by a superior officer was not in itself enough. Here, although the information disclosed to the arresting officer at the briefing had been scanty, it was sufficient.

(4)   DETENTION FOR 30 MINUTES BY A CIVILIAN

The Police Reform Act 2002 (PRA 2002) gives unprecedented powers to civilians acting in support of the police. The Act creates various categories of support with different powers – 'community support officers', 'detention officers', 'escort officers', 'investigating officers' and 'accredited persons' under community safety accreditation schemes.[80] When the Bill was first introduced in the House of Lords it included a power for community support officers to detain people in the street for up to 30 minutes pending the arrival of a police officer. The Government was defeated over these powers. When the Bill went to the Commons the Government successfully moved an amendment to restore the power for community support officers. It did not attempt to restore the power for 'accredited persons'. However, anticipating further defeat in the Lords, it announced on the Third Reading [81] that the power to detain would not be implemented nationally until, first, it had been piloted in up to six force areas over a two-year period and, secondly, there had been a report on the pilot by the Chief Inspector of Constabulary.

The powers of the community support officer (CSO) relate to minor misconduct such as issuing fixed penalty notices for being drunk in a public place, cycling on a

---

[80]   The powers are set out in Pt.4 and Schs 4 and 5 of the 2002 Act on which see, for instance, M Zander, *The Police and Criminal Evidence Act 1984* (4th edn, 2003), ch 12; L Jason-Lloyd, *Quasi-Policing* (Cavendish, 2003).

[81]   House of Commons, *Hansard*, 10 July 2002, cols.980-981.

pavement, littering etc. A CSO can detain someone reasonably believed to have committed such an offence if he refuses to give his name and address or gives what appears to be a false one. Government ministers repeatedly insisted that detention for up to 30 minutes backed by use of reasonable force did not amount to arrest – merely 'a power of enforcement'[82], whatever that may be.

(d) Procedure on arrest

The law does not lay down any particular procedure to effect a lawful arrest. In *Alderson v Booth* [1969] 2 QB 216, Lord Parker CJ said:

> ... whereas there was a time when it was held that there could be no lawful arrest unless there was an actual seizing or touching, it is quite clear that that is no longer the law. There may be an arrest by mere words, by saying 'I arrest you' without any touching. ... Equally it is clear ... that an arrest is constituted when any form of words is used which in the circumstances of the case were calculated to bring to the defendant's notice and did bring to the defendant's notice that he was under compulsion.

See *R v Inwood* [1973] 2 All ER 645 and *Dawes v DPP* [1995] 1 Cr App Rep 65. See also Glanville Williams, 'When is an arrest not an arrest', 54 *Modern Law Review*, 1991, p 408.

The other requisite of a valid arrest is that the officer must ensure that the suspect knows immediately, failing which, as soon as practicable (1) that he is under arrest – *R v Inwood* [1973] 1 WLR 647 and *Pedro v Diss* [1981] 2 All ER 59 – and (2) the ground of arrest – *Christie v Leachinsky* [1947] AC 573, HL; *Grant v Gorman* [1980] RTR 119; *Waters v Bigmore* [1981] Crim LR 408; *Pedro v Diss*, above. In the famous case of *Christie v Leachinsky* Viscount Simon in a classic statement said (at p 589):

> ... (1) If a policeman arrests without warrant upon reasonable suspicion of felony, or of other crime of a sort which does not require a warrant, he must in ordinary circumstances inform the person arrested of the true ground of arrest. He is not entitled to keep the reason to himself or to give a reason which is not the true reason. In other words a citizen is entitled to know on what charge or on suspicion of what crime he is seized. (2) If the citizen is not so informed but is nevertheless seized, the policeman, apart from certain exceptions, is liable for false imprisonment. ... If a policeman who entertained a reasonable suspicion that X has committed a felony were at liberty to arrest him and march him off to a police station without giving any explanation of why he was doing this, the prima facie right of personal liberty would be gravely infringed. No one, I think, would approve a situation in which when the person arrested asked for the

---

82   House of Commons, Official Report, Standing Committee B (Police Reform Bill), 20 June 2002, col 266.

reason, the policeman replied 'that has nothing to do with you: come along with me. ...'

The common law is reflected in PACE s 28 which states that an arrest is not lawful unless, at the time of or as soon as practicable after the arrest, the person arrested is informed (a) that he is under arrest, and (b) of the ground of the arrest. Moreover it is specifically stated that this applies even where the fact of the arrest or its ground is obvious.

The legal consequences of failing to give grounds of arrest were considered by the Divisional Court in *DPP v Hawkins* [1988] 3 All ER 673 and by the Court of Appeal in *Lewis v Chief Constable of South Wales Constabulary* [1991] 1 All ER 206. In *Hawkins*, the court held that failure to state the reasons for an arrest at the moment when it became practicable to do so had the effect of rendering the initially lawful arrest unlawful as from that moment and not as from the outset. The court therefore refused to allow the lawful arrest to be invalidated retrospectively. In *Lewis* the officers had told the plaintiffs of the fact of arrest but delayed telling them the grounds for 10 minutes in one case and 23 minutes in the other. The Court of Appeal (without referring to the *Hawkins* case) said that arrest was not a legal concept but was a matter of fact arising out of the deprivation of a person's liberty. It was also a continuing act and therefore what had been an unlawful arrest could become a lawful arrest. The remedy for the plaintiffs was merely the damages they had been awarded by the jury for the 10 minutes and 23 minutes of illegality – £200 each. (For critical comment see J Marston, 'The Reasons for an Arrest', *Justice of the Peace*, 2 March 1991, p 131. See also *Kulynycz* [1970] 3 All ER 881.)

Under s 30 of PACE, a person who has been arrested must be taken to a police station 'as soon as practicable', unless his presence elsewhere is reasonably necessary for the investigation. (But see p 260 below for the new concept of 'street bail' given by a police officer included in the Criminal Justice Bill 2002/03.)

SUMMONS OR ARREST

Accused persons will either have been charged after an arrest or they will have been summonsed by post, after an information has been laid before a magistrate or a justice's clerk.

The proportion arrested for categories of offences varies dramatically. In 2001, of those dealt with for indictable offences, no fewer than 91% were arrested, compared with 42% of those dealt with for summary offences other than motoring charges, and 18% of those dealt with for motoring offences (*Criminal Statistics*, 2001, Cm 5696, Table 8.1, p 132).

But there are great variations in the policies of different police forces. A study done for the Philips Royal Commission showed, that in Cambridgeshire, Cleveland and the Metropolitan Police District only 1% of adults accused of indictable offences were summonsed, compared with over 40% in places such as Thames Valley, West Yorkshire, Wiltshire and North Wales, (See R Gemmill and RF Morgan-Giles, 'Arrest, Charge and Summons', *Philips Royal Commission, Research Study No 9*, 1981, Appendix A, p 42.)

The Philips Royal Commission (para 3.77) urged that the less intrusive procedure of summons be used wherever possible. But, for whatever reason, the trend is moving instead in the opposite direction. In 1984 and 1986 the proportion of suspects summonsed for indictable offences was 22%. But since then it declined and has been below 10% in each year since 1996. (In 2001 it was 8%.) (*Criminal Statistics*, 2001, above, Table 8.l)

Lord Justice Auld recommended that the procedure for issuing a summons on an information laid before magistrates should be abolished and provisions to implement the recommendation were included in the Criminal Justice Bill 2002/03, Part 4. The new procedure would simply entail the issue of a written charge together with a requirement ('a requisition') for him or her to appear before a magistrates' court to answer to the charge.

NOTE — REMEDIES FOR UNLAWFUL ARREST

A victim of an unlawful arrest has three possible remedies. First, he can attempt to initiate proceedings for habeas corpus. This is by no means simple. The writ can be applied for by the person unlawfully detained or by someone else on his behalf. There is always supposed to be a duty judge available at or through the Royal Courts of Justice to hear applications. In emergencies the initial application to the judge can even be by telephone. But many lawyers are not familiar with this procedure and legal aid may not be available. Moreover, the Divisional Court to whom application must be made is not easily persuaded to grant the writ.

On the rare occasions when habeas corpus proceedings are brought on behalf of someone who is allegedly detained by the police without charges, the normal response from the police is to charge him before the case comes to be heard.

The second remedy is to use the illegality as the basis of an argument that the subsequent proceedings should be declared null and void. This is unlikely to succeed because of the rule of English law (see p 457 below) that evidence illegally obtained can nevertheless be admissible. Similarly, *R v Kulynycz* (p 196 above) shows that the courts may be ready to cure an initial illegality if it was subsequently corrected.

The third remedy is to bring an action for damages for false imprisonment. In cases like *Christie v Leachinsky* or *R v Kulynycz* this is of little use since the amount of damages awarded would be purely nominal. But sometimes this can be a significant remedy. In *Wershof v Metropolitan Police Comr* [1978] 3 All ER 540, the plaintiff, a young solicitor, got £1,000 for being arrested and detained for about an hour before being released on bail. In *Reynolds v Metropolitan Police Comr* [1982] Crim LR 600, the Court of Appeal rejected an appeal against a jury's award of £12,000 damages for false imprisonment. The plaintiff was arrested in the early hours of the morning in connection with charges of arson for gain. The journey to the police station took two and a half hours. She was detained until 8pm the same day, when she was told there was no evidence against her. She got home by around 11pm. The trial judge in her action for damages against the police ruled that they had had reasonable grounds for suspecting her of involvement in the crimes. See also *Allen v Metropolitan Police Comr* [1980] Crim LR 441 – damages of £1,115 for unnecessary force used in an arrest.

But in *Hsu v Metropolitan Police Comr* [1997] 2 All ER 762, CA the plaintiff was physically assaulted and racially abused when he refused to allow three police officers to enter his house. He was arrested and detained for about 75 minutes during which time his house was entered. He suffered post-traumatic stress disorder. The jury awarded compensatory damages of £20,000 and exemplary damages of £200,000 but the Court of Appeal reduced the total to £35,000. It held that £50,000 was the maximum that should be awarded for exemplary damages. Similarly, in *Goswell v Metropolitan Police Comr*, unreported, *Legal Action*, September 1998, p 21, the Court of Appeal reduced exemplary damages of £170,000 awarded by a jury for false imprisonment and assault to £15,000.

(e)   The legality of detention for questioning

An arrest has to be based on reasonable suspicion that the person arrested has committed, is committing or is about to commit the offence in question. This is, however, not the same as the degree of suspicion necessary to base a charge. Could the police lawfully hold an arrested person for questioning in order to decide whether there was enough evidence to charge him? The question was only properly settled at common law at around the time that PACE was being enacted.

The House of Lords held in *Holgate-Mohammed v Duke*[83], that the police were entitled to hold a suspect for questioning without charges. The plaintiff had been arrested after the theft of jewellery from premises where she was a lodger. She was detained for six hours but was not charged. She brought an action for damages against the police and at first instance won damages of £1,000. The judge held that detention had not been too long and she had been allowed to see a solicitor. Also there had been no improper pressure. But the purpose of detention had been to put her under greater pressure through having her in custody under arrest than would have existed if she had been interviewed without being arrested. The House of Lords confirmed the Court of Appeal's decision allowing the appeal, and said that it was legitimate for the police to question someone in order to dispel or confirm the officer's reasonable suspicion which led to the arrest.

The first reference to the concept of detention for questioning in any English statute was in PACE. Section 37(2) states that before an arrested person is charged the only

---

[83]   [1984] 1 All ER 1054.

ground for detaining him is that there are 'reasonable grounds for believing that his detention without being charged is necessary to secure or preserve evidence relating to an offence for which he is under arrest *or to obtain such evidence by questioning him*' (emphasis supplied).

(f) The time-limits on detention for questioning

Before PACE the law on time-limits for detention without charges was in a state of muddle. There was a common belief that the police were required to bring a suspect before the courts within 24 hours of arrest. But this was based on a misunderstanding. The only relevant provision that mentioned a time-limit was the Magistrates' Courts Act 1980, s 43(1) (formerly Magistrates' Courts Act 1952, s 38(1)), which stated, in effect, that a person charged with an offence that was not serious who could not be brought before a magistrates' court within 24 hours had to be bailed from the police station to appear before the court. But there was no requirement in the section that he be brought before the court within 24 hours – only that if he was not, he should be bailed unless the offence was a serious one. (There was no definition of the concept of 'serious offence', which was therefore left to the police to define.)

The only statutory time reference regarding police detention prior to 1984 was the provision in s 43(4) of the Magistrates' Court Act 1980 (formerly MCA 1952, s 38(4)) that 'Where a person is taken into custody for an offence without a warrant and is retained in custody he shall be brought before a magistrates' court as soon as practicable'. There was no indication as to what was intended by the words 'as soon as practicable'. But it was clear from police practice that this was interpreted by them to mean as soon as practicable after he had been charged and not as soon as practicable after being taken into custody. In his evidence to the Philips Royal Commission, the Commissioner of the Metropolitan Police suggested that the words 'as soon as practicable' were intended to recognise the need to keep some people in custody while inquiries were pursued in order to see whether there was enough evidence for a charge. A person aggrieved by the delay could apply to the Divisional Court for habeas corpus.

For common law decisions on time-limits for detention, see *Houghton and Franciosy* (1978) 68 Cr App Rep 197; *Hudson* (1980) 72 Cr App Rep 163; *Re Sherman and Apps* (1981) 72 Cr App Rep 266, (sub nom *Holmes, ex p Sherman*) [1981] 2 All ER 612 ; *Nycander* (1982) Times, 9 December.

NB The legislation giving effect to the report of the Scottish Thompson Committee – the Criminal Justice (Scotland) Act 1980, s 2 – authorised detention only for up to six hours as proposed in the Committee's report.

THE PHILIPS ROYAL COMMISSION

Research conducted for the Philips Royal Commission established that most suspects spend a relatively short time in police custody. About three-quarters of all suspects were dealt with in six hours or less, and about 95% within 24 hours. Virtually none were held for more than 48 hours. A study based on nearly 50,000 detainees in the Metropolitan Police District showed that the proportion held for more than 72 hours was 0.4%. (*Report of the Royal Commission*, para 3.96, p 52)

In the Royal Commission's view the proper length of police detention before a suspect had to be brought before a court was a maximum of 24 hours. It proposed a scheme under which after six hours the custody officer in the police station would review the need for further detention. Within 24 hours the suspect would either have to be charged or released or an application would have to be made to a magistrates' court for permission to hold him for another 24 hours. The suspect would have a right to be present at any such hearing and he would equally be permitted legal representation on legal aid. Thereafter the police would be entitled to go back to the magistrates for further extensions of 24 hours at a time. After 48 hours' detention, there would be a right of appeal to a judge against continued detention. The Royal Commission did not propose any upper limit of time for such extensions. In theory the magistrates would be free to grant any number of 24-hour extensions.

PACE

The Government did not wholly accept the Royal Commission's scheme. When an arrested person is being held under s 37(2) for questioning (p 000 above) he can be held in the first instance, for up to 24 hours. At that point the necessity of further detention must be considered by a superintendent. He may give authority for further detention until the 36 hour point. (s 42)

The superintendent's authority to extend detention beyond 24 hours related only to 'serious arrestable offences' (as to which see p 172 above). But the Criminal Justice Bill 2000/03 included a provision to apply it to all arrestable offences. [84]

The 24-hour period is measured from arrival at the police station. If the suspect is arrested by another force, it starts from the moment he arrives in the police station in the area where he is wanted. If he comes from outside England and Wales, the 24-hour period has in any event to start within 24 hours of his first arrest (s 41).

After 36 hours, there has to be a hearing in the magistrates' court with the suspect present and, if he wishes, legally represented (s 43). The magistrates can grant a warrant of further detention for up to a further 60 hours – making a total of 96 hours, as under the original version of these proposals (ss 43 and 44). But the maximum period of time allowable by magistrates is 36 hours at a time. It follows that if the police want to ask for the full 96 hours they have to return to the magistrates for a second hearing (ss 43(12) and 44).

---

[84]   The provision was based on a recommendation by the Home Office/Cabinet Office Joint Review of PACE, 2002.

The magistrates can only authorise further detention if the offence in question is a serious arrestable offence (see p 172 above), is being investigated diligently and expeditiously, and if further detention is necessary to secure or preserve evidence relating to an offence for which the suspect is under arrest or to obtain such evidence by questioning him (s 43(4)).

The Act specifically preserves habeas corpus (s 51(*d*)). But such applications will presumably fail if detention has been properly authorised by the magistrates and the conditions for further detention still apply. If they no longer apply, further detention will be unlawful and habeas corpus is available.

The time for which a suspect can be held under PACE is affected by the following provisions:

(1) The custody officer is under a duty to order the immediate release of an arrested person if the grounds for holding him cease to apply and there are no other valid grounds for holding him (s 34).

(2) When the suspect first comes to the police station, the custody officer has to decide whether there is at that stage enough evidence to charge him and, if so, he should be charged forthwith (s 37(1) and (7)). Research has shown that this duty is not performed. Custody officers rubber-stamp the arresting officer's decision to bring the suspect in for questioning. (See I McKenzie, R Morgan and R Reiner, 'Helping the Police with their Inquiries: The Necessity Principle and Voluntary Attendance at the Police Station' (1990) *Criminal Law Review*, pp 23 – 4, and M McConville, A Sanders and R Leng, *The Case for the Prosecution* (Routledge, 1991), pp 42 – 4, 119. See also E Cape, 'Detention without charge: What does "sufficient evidence to charge" mean?' [1999] *Criminal Law Review*, pp 875-85.)

(3) The necessity of further detention must be reviewed regularly throughout the period of detention by an officer of the rank of inspector – initially after the first six hours and thereafter every nine hours. The suspect and/or his legal adviser must be given an opportunity to make representations (s 39).

(4) After being charged the arrested person must be released, with or without bail, unless:
(i)   it is necessary to hold him so that his name or address can be ascertained; or
(ii) the custody officer reasonably thinks that it is necessary to hold him for his own protection or to prevent him from causing physical injury to anyone or from causing loss of or damage to property; or
(iii) the custody officer reasonably thinks that he needs to be held because he would otherwise fail to answer to bail or to prevent him from interfering with witnesses or otherwise obstructing the course of justice; or
(iv) if he is a juvenile, he needs to be held 'in his own interests' (s 38(1)).

(5) Once he has been charged, if he is not released, he must be brought before a magistrates' court, as soon as practicable, and not later than the first sitting after

being charged (s 46(2)). If no court is sitting on the same day as he is charged or the next day (other than Sunday), the custody officer is under a duty to inform the clerk to the justices so that a court sitting can be arranged (s 46(3)).

Note – 'holding charges'

The police commonly lay charges in regard to less serious offences while pursuing inquiries over more serious matters. Under Code C (para 16.1,as amended) they may delay charging the suspect until they are ready to charge him on the other matters. However, if the other charges are more serious the suspect must be made aware of the fact at an early stage, so that he can consider whether he wants legal advice and how to respond to questions. (See *Kirk* [1999] 4 All ER 698 – convictions for manslaughter and robbery quashed.) Subject to that, the rules require that once they have enough evidence to justify a charge, the police must charge the suspect and must not question him about an offence, save 'to minimise harm or loss', to clarify ambiguities or to deal with *new* matters (paras 16.1, 16.5).

TERRORISM CASES

The time-limits for detention without charges in terrorism cases are longer. Under successive Prevention of Terrorism (Temporary Provisions) Acts a terrorism suspect could be detained for 48 hours in the first instance and then, with the written permission of the Home Secretary for a further five days.

The Strasbourg Court held that detention for four days and six hours under this legislation was a breach of art 5(3) of the ECHR,[85] but the Government then entered a derogation from the Convention on the ground of the national situation in Northern Ireland.

During the passage of the Criminal Justice Bill 2002/03 the Commons approved a Government amendment to extend the maximum length of detention that could be authorised under the Terrorism Act from a total of 7 days to a total of 14 days (cl 284).

Another change made by the Bill is that authority for detention of terrorism suspects beyond 48 hours is no longer obtained from the Home Secretary. The Terrorism Act 2000 substituted for the Home Secretary a 'judicial authority' – defined in the Act to mean either the Senior District Judge (Chief Magistrate) or another District Judge (Magistrates' Court) designated for the purpose by the Lord Chancellor.[86]

---

[85]   *Brogan v United Kingdom* (1989) 11 EHRR 117.
[86]   Schedule 8, para 29.

INDEFINITE DETENTION WITHOUT CHARGES

In the aftermath of the infamous September 11 attack on the Twin Towers in New York the Government rushed through the Anti-terrorism, Crime and Security Act 2001 which gave the Home Secretary exceptional powers to detain some terrorism suspects indefinitely without charge. If the Home Secretary reasonably believes a person to be a suspected international terrorist whose presence in the UK is a risk to national security he may issue a certificate under ACSA 2001, s 21. The definition of terrorist under the Act includes being a member of, belonging to, or having links with an international terrorist group.[87] (Having links with includes supporting or assisting.[88]) An international terrorist group is defined as one that is subject to the control or influence of persons outside the UK which the Home Secretary suspects of being concerned in the commission, preparation or instigation of acts of international terrorism.[89] Ministers explained that this draconian power was aimed at a small number of persons who cannot be prosecuted for insufficiency of admissible evidence nor deported because they would face death or torture. (If they find a country prepared to take them, they have a right to go.)

During the passage of the Bill most of the controversy centred on the detained suspect's means of challenging certification by the Home Secretary. The Bill provided that appeal would lie to the Special Immigration Appeal Commission (SIAC) established by the 1997 Act of that name, which sits with a High Court judge, an immigration judge and a security expert. The hearings are in camera and the Commission can hear evidence that is not shown to the detainee or his lawyer, though a security vetted lawyer appointed to represent him would be shown such evidence. An appeal from the Commission lies to the Court of Appeal and House of Lords on a point of law.

The Bill provided that no court or tribunal other than the SIAC could entertain proceedings for questioning the Home Secretary's certificate. During the debates the Government amended the Bill by raising the status of the SIAC to that of a superior court of record, one of the results of which is that it is not subject to judicial review. But the Attorney-General pointed out that the SIAC was in some respects more powerful than a court in that it could review the Home Secretary's certificate on the merits.

It was reported in March 2003 that a special self-contained unit would be set up at Woodhill jail in Milton Keynes to house persons held under the ACSA 2001. Thirteen suspects were being held at different prisons. They would have a choice as to whether to move to the unit or stay where they were. The self-contained unit had been recommended by Lord Carlile of Berriew QC in his review of the operation of the Act. He reported that detainees under the Act complained of being held together

---

[87]   ACSA 2001, s 21(2).
[88]   ACSA 2001, s 21(4).
[89]   ACSA 2001, s 21(3)(b).

with convicted criminals. [90] The authorities had issued no names, no charges had been brought and no explanations for detention had been given. [91]

For commentary on the Act see H Fenwick, 'The Anti-Terrorism, Crime and Security Act 2001: A Proportionate Response to 11 September?', *Modern Law Review*, 2002, pp 724-62. On the power of indefinite detention see J Sawyer, 'Detention appeals', 152 *New Law Journal*, p 1357; M Darwyne, 'The crumbling pillars of justice', *Counsel*, April 2003, p 27.

STATISTICS ON LENGTH OF DETENTION AND CHARGES

The annual Home Office statistics on length of detention give no figures as to average periods of time. They do however show the total number of cases in which the police apply to the magistrates for a warrant of further detention authorising detention beyond 36 hours. In the decade from 1991 to 2001/02 the annual number of applications to magistrates for warrants of further detention beyond 36 hours has remained remarkably stable – from a low of 220 to a high of 343. [92]

Evidence of average periods of detention prior to charge was given in the two Home Office studies by David Brown, *Detention at the Police Station under the Police and Criminal Evidence Act 1984* (HMSO, 1989) and Brown et al, *Changing the Code: Police Detention under the revised PACE Codes of Practice* (HMSO, 1992). The 1989 report showed (p 62) that only 1% of all suspects in the sample of some 5,500 were held for more than 24 hours. As many as 32% were out of the police station within two hours, 59% in four hours and 76% in six hours. 11% were held more than twelve hours. The mean length of detention was 5 hours 10 minutes with a median of 3 hours 19 minutes. The later study showed that the position had basically not changed. The mean period in 1990 was five hours one minute, and in 1991, five hours 18 minutes. The median in 1990 was three hours 13 minutes and in 1991 was three hours 20 minutes (pp 104 – 105). In the study of just over 4,000 people detained at 10 police stations in 1993-94 by Phillips and Brown, the mean time that suspects were held without charge was six hours and 40 minutes. In very serious cases (murder, rape) it was just under 22 hours. For moderately serious offences it was just over seven hours. For less serious offences the average was just under four hours. [93]

Not surprisingly, in terrorism cases the period is distinctly longer. A study of 253 persons detained under the Prevention of Terrorism Act, again by David Brown, found an average period of detention of nearly 29 hours with a median of 16 hours 24 minutes. But just under 40% of the detainees had been released within 12 hours

90   'Jail within jail to hold terrorist suspects', *The Times*, 7 March 2003.
91   R Ford and D McGrory, '15 Foreign suspects held without trial in top-security jail', *The Times*, 17 January 2003.
92   Home Office Statistical Bulletin, *Arrests for Notifiable Offences and the Operation of Certain Police Powers under PACE*, November 2002, p 16.
93   p 164, n 46 above, at p 109.

and nearly two-thirds within 24 hours. (D Brown, *Detention under the Prevention of Terrorism Act 1989: Legal Advice and Outside Contact* (HMSO, 1993, p 50.)

4. Police powers of search and seizure

(a) On arrest

SEARCHING THE ARRESTED PERSON

Pre-PACE the common law position was by no means fully supportive of the police wish to search arrested persons. In *Lindley v Rutter* [1981] QB 128 the Divisional Court held that the police had not been justified in forcibly removing a female suspect's bra. The officers had been acting in accordance with their chief officer's standing order as to searching of prisoners but the court said the order could not be justified since it was not adapted to the circumstances of particular cases. In *Eet* [1983] Crim LR 806 the court held that officers had not been entitled to use force to search a driver suspected of having stolen the car to establish his identity. In *Brazil v Chief Constable of Surrey* [1983] 3 All ER 537 the court held that the police were not acting in execution of their duty when they searched a female suspect without informing her of the reason for the search. In *King* [1969] 1 AC 304, PC it was held that where police are searching premises under a search warrant, they are not permitted to search persons there unless the warrant specifically so states.

SEARCHING PREMISES AFTER AN ARREST

It was for a long time common police practice after arresting someone to go to his home and to search there. The Royal Commission on the Police in 1929 said it was unlawful and should either be permitted by statute or stopped. But no statute was passed to deal with the matter and the practice continued.

In *McLorie v Oxford* [1982] QB 1290 the Divisional Court took a very restrictive view of the powers of the police to search premises after an arrest. The police went to M's home looking for a car which they thought had been used by M's brother in an attempt to murder someone. The brother was arrested later that evening at the house where he lived with his father and brother. Subsequently the police saw the car in the backyard of the house and asked M's father for permission to remove it for forensic examination. After the father refused to give permission, the police returned in strength and removed the car forcibly. M, who had resisted the seizure, was charged with assaulting the police and convicted. Quashing the conviction, the Divisional Court held that the police had not been acting lawfully. They would have been entitled to follow a motorist onto his own property in 'hot pursuit' and that would have entitled them to remove the car for forensic examination. But this was not a case of hot pursuit.

Such is the importance attached by the common law to the relative inviolability of a dwelling house that we cannot believe that there is a common law right without warrant to enter one either in order to search for instruments of crime, even of serious crime, or in order to seize such an instrument which is known to be there. Certainly if there were, we would expect it to be reflected in the books and it is not. [per Donaldson LJ]

The Philips Royal Commission

The Philips Royal Commission thought that the police should not routinely make full searches of all suspects and that the question of how far a search should go should be considered by the station officer. A superficial search should always be permissible. Strip searches, on the other hand, should be rare. If they required search of intimate parts of the body they should be permitted only in grave offences and only on the authority of a senior officer, and should always be conducted by a doctor.

Search of the arrested person's premises and vehicle should be allowed subject to safeguards. The chief safeguard should be that there must be reasonable suspicion that evidence material to the offence may be found on those premises. Search of any other premises should have to require a warrant. The reasons for any search should be recorded by the station officer before the search, in order to minimise the risk of 'fishing expeditions' (para 3.121). Evidence of other offences found in the course of such a search should be admissible if a warrant could have been obtained to look for it, even though no such warrant had been obtained. Searches should be conducted in a manner appropriate to what was being searched for (para 3.122).

PACE

PACE broadly enacted these recommendations. Section 18 empowers a constable to enter premises occupied or controlled by a person arrested for an arrestable offence to search for evidence relating to that or connected offences. He must have reasonable grounds for believing that there is evidence on the premises that relates to the offence in question or to some offence 'which is connected with or similar to that offence' (s 18(1)). Authorisation must normally be given in advance by an officer who is at least an inspector.[94] The officer who authorises such a search in advance (or approves one after the event) must make a written record of the grounds for the search and of the nature of the evidence sought.

PACE s 32 authorises search of an arrested person and any premises (including a vehicle) on which the arrest took place in which he was when arrested or immediately before. It cannot be used to justify a search several hours after the arrest.[95] A search under s 32 can be for anything that can be used to assist an escape or for evidence relating to *any* offence (s 32(2)).

---

[94]   See *Badham* [1987] Crim LR 202.
[95]   Ibid. See also *Churchill* [1989] Crim LR 226.

PACE s 19 authorises an officer who is lawfully searching any premises (whether after an arrest or not) to seize any article (other than one covered by legal professional privilege) if he reasonably believes that it is evidence relating to the offence which he is investigating 'or any other offence', and that 'it is necessary to seize it in order to prevent its being concealed, lost, damaged, altered or destroyed'.

INTIMATE SEARCHES (S 55)

Section 55 of PACE permits a search of bodily orifices (called an 'intimate search'). An intimate search can only be for a weapon or other article that might be used to cause injury or for Class 'A' drugs (ie not for 'evidence'), and it has to be conducted by a doctor or nurse or, in the case of a weapons search only, a police officer of the same sex provided that a superintendent or above reasonably considers that it is not practicable for the search to be conducted by a doctor. In practice virtually all such searches are carried out by doctors.

A full record has to be kept of such searches. In David Brown's 1989 Home Office study (see p 204 above) intimate searches were found in only seven cases of 5,519 (0.1%) (p 53). The Home Office annual statistics (*Arrests for Notifiable Offences and the Operation of Certain Police Powers under PACE*) show that the number of such searches annually ranges from a few dozen to a couple of hundred or so. Most are for Class A drugs. (In 2001-02 there were 102, of which 88 (86%) were for Class A drugs. Such drugs were found in 18 cases (20%).)

The Joint Parliamentary Committee on Human Rights has suggested that intimate searches under PACE may contravene Article 3 of the European Convention on Human Rights which prohibits 'inhuman or degrading treatment'.[96] Article 3 is absolute and permits no justification. The Government told the Committee that it did not agree that the rules contravened the Convention.

For provisions designed to ensure that intimate searches are only undertaken in exceptional circumstances see Code C, Annex A.

INTIMATE (S 62) AND NON-INTIMATE (S 63) SAMPLES

PACE also made provision for the taking of bodily samples from the suspect as part of the process of criminal investigation. With the development of DNA analysis this power is assuming major importance.

The Act distinguishes between two kinds of sample – 'intimate' samples (s 62) and 'non-intimate' samples (s 63). The main practical difference is that intimate samples,

---

[96]   First Report, Criminal Justice and Police Bill, Session 2000-2001, HL Paper 69, (2001, HL) para 75. The Committee's reports are available on www.parliament.uk/parliamentary_committees/joint_committtee_on_rights.cfm

other than urine, may only be taken with the suspect's written consent, and only by a doctor. Provided an inspector's authority is given, non-intimate samples may be taken, without consent and by a police officer.

PACE defined intimate samples as samples of blood, semen, other tissue fluid, urine, saliva, pubic hair or a swab taken from a body orifice. The Runciman Royal Commission (Report, pp 14 – 15, para 29) recommended that the definition be changed so as to permit the taking of saliva by mouth swab without consent. This was done in the Criminal Justice and Public Order Act 1994 (CJPOA 1994) by making saliva a non-intimate sample. Previously intimate samples could only be taken if the investigation concerned a serious arrestable offence. Now under the CJPOA 1994 it need only be a recordable offence which means an offence carrying a penalty of imprisonment. It requires the consent of an inspector[97] and the written consent of the suspect

Non-intimate samples are defined (s 65) as a sample of hair, other than pubic hair, a sample taken from a nail or under a nail, a swab taken from any part of the body including the mouth, other than a body orifice, saliva and a footprint or similar impression of part of a body. A non-intimate sample can be taken without the written consent of the person concerned if an officer of the rank of inspector[98] or above has authorised compulsory taking of the sample.

Section 63 permits the taking of a non-intimate sample without consent in three situations: 1) following charge with a recordable offence; 2) where the person is in police detention (or is being held in custody by the police on the authority of a court), on the authority of an inspector which can only be given if he reasonably believes that the sample will tend to confirm or disprove his involvement in the offence; 3) following conviction for a recordable offence.

The Criminal Justice Bill 2002/03, cl 8 would extend the power to take a non-intimate sample without consent to anyone who has merely been arrested for a recordable offence regardless of whether it might confirm his involvement in the offence. (Clause 7 makes a similar extension in regard to the taking of fingerprints without consent.) In other words, cll 7 and 8 are mainly to help build up the national DNA database.[99]

A pilot study in several force areas of additional powers to take non-intimate samples for drug testing began in 2001 under new ss 63B and 63C.[100] It arises if an adult has been charged with any on a list of 'trigger offences' or if drug misuse is reasonably suspected. It permits the taking of a urine sample or a saliva swab.

---

[97] The requirement that it be a superintendent was altered by the Criminal Justice and Police Act 2001, s 80(1) despite concerns expressed by the Parliamentary Joint Committee on Human Rights – First Report, Session 2000-2001, HL, Paper 69 (2001) HC 427, para 81.

[98] The requirement that it be a superintendent was altered by the Criminal Justice and Police Act 2001, s 80(1).

[99] See C McCartney, ' The future of the National DNA database', 167 *Justice of the Peace*, 24 May 2003, p 386.

[100] Inserted into PACE by the Criminal Justice and Court Services Act 2000, s 57.

DESTRUCTION OF SAMPLES NO LONGER REQUIRED

PACE s 64 required samples (and fingerprints) to be destroyed if, in the event, the person from whom they were taken was acquitted. But after two decisions[101] holding that s 64 meant what it said provoked public criticism and legislation was swiftly passed to change the rule.[102] The amending provision was made retrospective and therefore covers the large number of samples improperly held on the DNA database.

The police expect the database for DNA samples eventually to hold some 5 million records. (The Metropolitan Police decided in 1999 to take a DNA sample from all those arrested save in very minor cases.) The CJPOA 1994 added a new requirement for both intimate and non-intimate samples that the person from whom the sample is taken must be informed that it can be made the subject of a search (called 'a speculative search') against other records.

In Bucke and Brown's 1997 study just over half of the suspects in custody gave their consent to the taking of a non-intimate sample. Usually the sample was taken by a mouth swab. Custody officers said that mouth swabs were the preferred method 'despite hair when plucked by the root apparently being much better for DNA analysis' (n 27, p 161 above, at p 44).

The taking of intimate samples was very rare. Only 40 out of 10,496 suspects (0.38%) provided such samples. (p 46)

(b) Powers to enter premises other than after an arrest

AT COMMON LAW

There is no general common law power to enter private premises in order to investigate criminal acts . In *Davis v Lisle* [103] a police officer, believing that D's employees had created an obstruction in the highway with a lorry, followed to D's garage. The officer neither had permission to be on the private property nor a warrant. He was first asked, and then told to leave but did not do so. D then struck the officer. He was convicted of assaulting a police officer in the execution of his duty. On appeal the Divisional Court that the officer was not acting in the execution of his employment. In remaining despite having been asked to leave he was a trespasser. See, to like effect, *Lambert v Roberts* [104], in which the Divisional Court held that a police officer was not entitled to administer a breathalyser test on a motorist he had

---

[101] Both decisions were given by the same court on the same day. One was a murder case, the other a rape case. The rape case went to the House of Lords. *Re A-G's Reference (No 3 of 1999)* [2000] 4 All ER 360.
[102] Criminal Justice and Police Act 2001, s 82.
[103] [1936] 2 KB 434.
[104] [1981] 2 All ER 15.

followed home when the motorist asked him to leave. But in *Snook v Mannion* [1982] RTR 321, on virtually identical facts the decision went the other way. The officers followed the motorist home after observing his erratic driving. They asked him to take a breathalyser test which he refused, and he told them to 'fuck off'. The magistrates held that this was mere abuse, not a revocation of their implied licence to be on his drive. He was therefore convicted of driving with an excess of alcohol in his blood and the Divisional Court upheld the decision. See also *Morris v Beardmore* [1981] AC 446, HL; *Clowser v Chaplin, Finnigan v Sandiford* [1981] Crim LR 643, HL; *Hart v Chief Constable of Kent* [1983] Crim LR 117.

The particular problem in relation to motoring law was altered by the provisions of the Transport Act 1981. TA 1981, s 25 stated: 'for the purposes of arresting a person under the power conferred by s 5 [driving, or being in charge of a motorcar while unfit] a constable may enter (if need be by force) any place where that person is or where the constable, with reasonable cause, suspects him to be. This power may not, however, cover the situation where the officer wishes to administer a breathalyser test. TA 1981 also gave the police a power of entry where an accident has taken place: see Sch 8. But these statutory provisions confirm that at common law there is no such power.

On the force that can be used by the police in effecting entry, see *Swales v Cox* [1981] 1 All ER 1115.

Lawful entry A police officer who enters premises without lawful excuse commits a trespass. Prior to PACE, there were various kinds of lawful excuse.

(1) *Under the authority of a search warrant* There are many statutory provisions that permit the police to ask magistrates for a search warrant. In dealing with an application for a search warrant, the magistrate is supposed to satisfy himself that in all the circumstances of the case it is reasonable to grant it. But in the nature of the situation it is difficult for the magistrate to differ from the police officer's view. The search warrant must, however, specify the correct premises. If it says Flat 45, the police cannot lawfully search Flat 30 even though that was what they actually intended when they asked for a search of Flat 45: *R v Atkinson* [105]

(2) *To execute an arrest without warrant* This power which arose formerly under the Criminal Law Act 1967, s 2(6), now arises under PACE, s 17(1).

(3) *To deal with emergency situations* There was a common law power to enter premises to deal with, or prevent, a breach of the peace: see *Thomas v Sawkins* [106]. The power also extended to saving life or limb. In *McLeod v Metropolitan Police Comr* [107] the Court of Appeal held that on the facts the police believed that there was a real and imminent risk of a breach of the peace sufficient to justify an entry while items were removed from the house by the divorced husband in the absence of the wife. (The European Court of Human Rights subsequently took a different view: [1999] Crim LR 155.)

[105]   [1976] Crim LR 307.
[106]   [1935] 2 KB 249.
[107]   [1994] 4 All ER 553.

It was held by the Divisional Court in 1985, that once the police were on premises lawfully for one purpose, they were there lawfully for any purpose. They could therefore search persons for drugs (which was their real object in being there) even though they had not got a warrant under the Misuse of Drugs Act, because they were lawfully on the premises to check out the premises under the Greater London Council (General Powers) Act 1968: *Foster v Attard*. [108]

According to survey evidence given by the police to the Philips Royal Commission, most searches of premises were under warrant. The survey showed that 61% of such searches in London (compared with only 24% in the provinces) were backed by a warrant. [109].

By far the fullest study of the operation of the search-warrant power pre-PACE was published in August 1984 (KW Lidstone, 'Magistrates, Police and Search Warrants' (1984) *Criminal Law Review*, p 449). The survey by Mr KW Lidstone of Sheffield University showed that search warrants for stolen or prohibited goods represented a mere 8% of all the search warrants issued in that period. (As many as 86% were issued to the Gas and Electricity Boards.)

The researchers observed 32 warrant applications. The magistrate asked questions of the police officer in only four and in only two were the questions directed to the grounds for the application. It does not appear, therefore, that the power is exercised with much care. (Surprisingly, stipendiary magistrates were no more likely to ask questions than lay magistrates.)

The information supplied to magistrates was usually minimal – limited to the name of the police officer, the name of the occupier, the address and the nature of the case. The grounds for the application were rarely stated. (Usually it was 'As a result of information received, there is reason to believe' or something similar.) Only occasionally was there any indication that the police had verified the information or had supporting evidence. (The Lord Chancellor's guidance to magistrates is that police officers should not be required to identify an informant but that it is legitimate to ask whether he is known to the officer and whether it has been possible to make other inquiries.)

The comment from Ken Lidstone was that:

> The reality is then that the judicial hurdle of the warrant application is no more than a stepping stone. Magistrates see the 'information from a reliable source' formula as an impenetrable barrier beyond which they cannot or will not go. This, together with an almost unquestioning trust in the police, the clerk, or both, allied to a lack of knowledge of how the police actually operate and an over-glamorised view of specialist squads, combine to impair the proper exercise of the independent judicial function [pp 452 – 3].

---

[108]   [1986] Crim LR 627.
[109]   *The Investigation and Prosecution of Criminal Offences in England and Wales: The Law and Procedure*, Cmnd 8092 – 1, 1981, pp 126 – 9.

THE PHILIPS ROYAL COMMISSION

The Royal Commission on Criminal Procedure recommended that existing powers to get a search warrant to look for prohibited goods such as stolen goods, drugs, firearms, explosives, etc should be confirmed (para 3.39). In addition, however, there should be a new power to search for evidence whether from guilty persons or from persons totally unconnected with the offence. But this power, it thought, should be used very sparingly and subject to strict controls It should be granted only in exceptional circumstances and in respect only of grave offences. The seriousness of the intrusion could also be marked by making the issuing authority a circuit judge. The procedure for obtaining access to evidence might have two stages. The court would first order the person holding the material to make it available to the applicant. Non-compliance could result in a search warrant being issued. If there was a danger that the evidence would disappear, there would be power for the court to issue a search warrant at the first stage.

PACE

When the first Police and Criminal Evidence Bill was published it provided for two different procedures. The normal method for getting permission to search for evidence on private premises was to be by getting an ordinary warrant from the magistrates. The Government said it took the view that the magistrates already granted search warrants in so many different situations that there was normally no need to require a judge's permission to search in this class of case. But where the material sought was held in confidence and related to a serious arrestable offence (p 172 above) an order from a circuit judge would be required. Application to the judge would normally be made in the absence of the other side by the police.

These proposals provoked an outcry of protest from a variety of quarters – notably from doctors, priests, journalists and Citizens' Advice Bureaux – claiming that the police would be given the right to search through confidential files and records. As a result the Government made a number of major changes in the proposals. First, it was provided that any hearing before a judge (called a 'special procedure' application) would be inter partes unless the police had reason to suspect that the person from whom the material was sought was implicated in the crimes in question. Secondly, categories of 'excluded material' were defined which would be exempt from any kind of search by the police. (Though if the material could pre-PACE have been the subject of a search warrant it could be made the subject of a special procedure application[110] (see below).) Excluded material covers:

---

[110]   Also under the terrorism legislation even excluded material can be the subject of an access order by a court. Only material covered by legal professional privilege is protected from such an order. See now Terrorism Act 2000, s 37 and Sch 5, para 6 (ed).

(1) Personal records held in confidence and acquired in the course of any 'trade, business, profession or other occupation'. 'Personal records' for this purpose means documents or records concerning individuals relating to their physical or mental health, spiritual counselling, social work or similar work involving counselling or assistance and other activities relating to a client's personal welfare or counselling and assistance given by voluntary organizations (ss 11, 12). Thus the files and records of doctors, priests, social workers and Citizens' Advice Bureaux are normally exempt from any kind of police search under PACE (but see p 214 below). Excluded material also covers human tissue or tissue fluid taken for the purpose of treatment or diagnosis. But if a doctor has the gun used in the crime or the patient's bloodstained clothing, the police would be able to ask a judge for an order requiring it to be produced. They would not be excluded material because they are not 'records' (s 12).

(2) Journalistic material in the form of documents or records held in confidence. 'Journalistic material' for this purpose means material acquired or created for the purposes of journalism. It is not required that the material be for publication in a national newspaper or that the person holding it be a member of one of the journalists' unions. The material is only 'journalistic material', however, if it is held in confidence and is in the possession of someone who acquired or created it for the purposes of journalism (ss 11 and 13).

PACE also provided that items held subject to legal professional privilege could not be made the subject of a search warrant application to magistrates (s 8(1)(d)). Nor can such material be made the subject of a special procedure application or even seizure under s 19 if actually found during a lawful search.

(3) Items covered by legal professional privilege consist of material exchanged between the client and his lawyer or anyone else acting for the client regarding legal advice; material exchanged between the client and the lawyer or anyone else acting for the client or between the client and such other person in connection with legal proceedings; and items enclosed with or referred to in such communications.

However, items held with the intention of furthering a criminal purpose are not subject to legal privilege (s 10). On this issue see the House of Lords' decision in *R v Central Criminal Court, ex p Francis & Francis*[111], which established that the criminal intent need not be that of the client or the solicitor. It can be that of a third party. Note also *R v Crown Court at Inner London Sessions, ex p Baines & Baines*[112], in which it was held that material consisting simply of records of the financing and purchase of a house was not covered by privilege because they were not concerned with the giving of legal advice.[113] See also *R v Customs and Excise Comrs, ex p Popely*[114] where it was held that a search warrant cannot authorise seizure of items covered by legal

[111] [1989] AC 346.
[112] [1987] 3 All ER 1025.
[113] See L Alt, 'Raids: Against the Law', *Solicitors' Journal*, 15 November 1991, p 1248.
[114] [1999] STC 1016 ,Div Ct.

professional privilege but if in the course of a lawful search of a solicitors' office, especially if the solicitor is himself suspected of involvement, the officer inadvertently seizes material which includes items subject to legal privilege, the execution of the warrant is not thereby rendered unlawful.

SPECIAL PROCEDURE MATERIAL

If the police seek evidence that is held in confidence but which is not excluded material, they must go to a circuit judge for permission to seek 'special procedure material'. The procedure is set out in Sch 1 of PACE. This requires that the judge be satisfied: (1) that there are reasonable grounds for thinking that a serious arrestable offence has been committed; (2) that there is 'special procedure material' on premises specified in the police application; (3) that it is likely to be of substantial value to the investigation and that it is likely to be relevant evidence; (4) that other methods of obtaining the material either have been tried or have not been tried because they would be bound to fail; and (5) that it is in the public interest that the material should be produced having regard, on the one hand, to the benefit likely to accrue to the investigation and, on the other, to the circumstances in which it is held. Those are called 'the first set of access conditions'. Alternatively, the application can sometimes be made under the 'second set of access conditions'. But these only apply if pre-PACE the police could have obtained a search warrant to search for the material in question. The applicant must satisfy the court that the issue of a search warrant would have been appropriate. Most applications are made under the first set of access conditions.

If so satisfied, the judge orders the person who appears to be in possession of the material to produce it to the police or to give them access to it, within seven days from the date of the order. The person against whom the order is sought must normally be given due notice of the application so that he can appear to contest the application. Once a person is served with an order to produce the material, he must not conceal or destroy it. If he disobeys the order he can be dealt with by proceedings for contempt but not normally by the issue of a search warrant.

Special procedure applications have been made very frequently by the police, especially against banks and other financial institutions. Usually they are uncontested hearings. Ken Lidstone reported over 2,000 such applications between 1986 and 1989: see 'Entry, Search and Seizure', 40 *Northern Ireland Legal Quarterly*, Winter 1989, p 333 at 342.

In certain circumstances the police can ask the judge for a search warrant instead of an order to produce and in that case the hearing is ex parte not inter partes.

One is where service of notice of the proceedings would seriously prejudice the investigation. PACE also provides that the special procedure applies to any search for excluded material or special procedure material under previous statutes. In other words, in so far as the previous law already allowed any search for confidential material on a magistrates' warrant or otherwise (for instance, under the Official

Secrets Act), the police now have to get a judge's order authorising such a search. But the judge will be required to issue a warrant if he is satisfied that it is appropriate to do so. He cannot apply all the other tests that he has to apply before authorising access to other special procedure material. (See Sch 1, para s 3, 4, 11 and 12.)

See further Ken Lidstone, 'Entry, Search and Seizure', 40 *Northern Ireland Legal Quarterly*, 1989, pp 333 – 62. For criticism of the way the courts deal with the seizure of journalistic material see R Costigan, 'Fleet Street Blues: Police Seizure of Journalists' Material' [1996] *Criminal Law Review*, pp 231–39.

Terrorism cases The terrorism legislation (now the Terrorism Act 2000, Sch 5, para s 4-17) gives the police far wider powers to acquire protected information. The judge must be satisfied that a terrorist investigation is underway, that the material would be of substantial value to the investigation and that disclosure would be in the public interest. The person thought to be in possession of the material can be required to state where to the best of his knowledge and belief it is. A production order under the legislation takes effect notwithstanding any restriction on disclosure or obligation of secrecy – an obvious threat to journalists who might have to disclose material and thereby endanger an informant. But material covered by legal professional privilege is protected.

(c)   Getting a search warrant

The Philips Royal Commission on Criminal Procedure proposed (para s 3.46 – 7) that new rules should be laid down to regulate the procedure for getting a search warrant, and these recommendations were adopted in PACE. This provides (s 15) that an application for a warrant must state the grounds for making the application, the statutory authority covering the claim and, in as much detail as possible,[115] the object of the warrant and the premises concerned. The application must be supported by an information in writing.[116] The constable must answer any questions put by the justice of the peace on oath. Each warrant can authorise only one entry. The warrant must specify the name of the person applying for it, the date of issue, the statutory power under which it is issued, and, so far as possible, the articles sought and when the search is to take place. The Act also requires a report to be made by the police to the issuing judicial authority (s 16(9)). If it is executed, it must be endorsed with a statement showing whether the articles specified or any other articles were seized.

---

[115] In *IRC v Rossminster Ltd* [1980] 1 All ER 80, the Inland Revenue obtained a search warrant to look for evidence of suspected tax fraud from the homes of two directors of Rossminster Ltd and its offices. Piles of documents were taken away for inspection. The House of Lords, reversing the Court of Appeal, held that the warrant was sufficiently detailed since it stated that the search was for evidence of tax fraud. It was not necessary, and might be impossible, to be more specific before the documents had been examined. See also *Reynolds v Metropolitan Police Comr* [1984] 3 All ER 649.

[116] This will continue after laying an information to get a summons is abolished under the provisions of the Criminal Justice Bill 2002/03.

This must be made forthwith after the search. If the warrant is not executed within one month, it must be returned at that point (s 16(10)).

The utility of these requirements must, however, be somewhat undermined by the evidence of the study by Ken Lidstone (p 211 above) showing how magistrates actually grant search warrants. He argued that the police were much more likely to use their powers under PACE s 32 (search after an arrest) or s 19 (general power of seizure of evidence found incidental to a lawful search), than the power to get a search warrant. Since the police could normally get access to and the right to search premises without having to get a search warrant they would presumably prefer that. (See also S Sharpe, 'Search warrants: due process protection or process validation?', *International Journal of Evidence and Proof*, 1999, vol 3, no 2, pp 101-34.)

(d)   Executing a search warrant and search by consent

Where the occupier of the premises to be searched is there, PACE requires that the constable identify himself, produce a copy of the warrant and give him a copy (s 16(5)). If he is not in uniform, the officer must produce documentary evidence that he is a constable (s 16(5)(*a*)). Code B on the searching of premises requires that, where it is proposed to search by consent without a warrant or arrest, the police must, if it is practicable, get the occupier's consent in writing before the search (para 5.1) and they must tell him that he is not obliged to give such consent (a new caution) and that anything taken may be produced in evidence (para 5.2). Under the April 1991 revised Code B the police must, unless it is impracticable to do so, give the occupier a Notice of Powers and Rights stating whether the search is under warrant or with consent, explaining the rights of the occupier and the powers of the police (para 6.7). If the person is not suspected of an offence he should be told so (para 5.2).

A warrant for the search of premises does not legitimise a search of persons on the premises. (See *Chief Constable of Thames Valley Police v Hepburn* [2002] EWCA Civ 1841, (2002) 147 Sol Jo LB 59. The Court of Appeal increased damages of £600 awarded to H to £4,000 for arrest and detention in a drugs bust of a pub in High Wycombe. Drugs were found in the room in which he was held but there had been no reasonable grounds to suspect him at the time of his arrest. He had not been charged with any offence arising from the event.)

An officer executing a warrant may use such force as is reasonable but no more than the minimum degree of force is to be used (Code B, para 6.6). Searches must be conducted 'with due consideration for the property and privacy of the occupier and with no more disturbance than necessary' (para 6.10). To have the media in attendance during the execution of a search warrant, even if they do not enter the premises, could be a breach of this provision. In *R v Marylebone Magistrates' Court, ex p Amdrell Ltd, trading as 'Get Stuffed', and Robert and Pauline Sclare* [117] the applicants sought judicial

[117]   (1998)162 JP 719, [1998] NLJR 1230.

review of the magistrates' decision to issue search warrants, inter alia, on the ground that the police had invited unauthorised persons, namely the press, to attend. The application failed but Lord Justice Rose for the Divisional Court said that save in exceptional circumstances 'it does not seem to me to be in the public interest that legitimate investigative procedures by the police, such as the execution of search warrants, or, for that matter, the interviewing of suspects, which may involve the innocent and may not lead to prosecution and trial should be accompanied by representatives of the media encouraged immediately to publish what they have seen'. Such publication might lead to new witnesses coming forward but it was far more likely 'to impede proper investigation and cause unjustifiable distress or harassment to those being investigated'.

The occupier must be allowed to have a friend, neighbour or other person to witness the search, unless the officer reasonably believes that the presence of the person asked for would seriously hinder the investigation or endanger officers or others. (para 6.11)

If the search is for special procedure material under Sch 1 of the Act or the Terrorism Act 2000, Sch 5, the officer should ask the occupier to produce the material. He may also ask to see any index to files and to inspect files which according to the index appear to contain any of the material sought. But a more extensive search of the premises can only be made if access to the material is refused, or it appears that the index is inaccurate or incomplete, or if 'for any other reason the officer in charge of the search has reasonable grounds for believing that such a search is necessary in order to find the material sought' (para 6.15).

CONDUCT OF SEARCHES

It has been a fundamental rule for centuries that the police may not ransack a person's home looking generally for evidence against him. The common law rule against 'general warrants' was laid down in the great case of *Entick v Carrington* (1765) 2 Wils 275.

Any lawful entry upon premises for the purposes of a search must always be for a specified reason and the search must be consistent with that reason.

PACE provides that 'a search under warrant may only be a search to the extent required for the purpose for which the warrant was issued' (s 16(8)). This would obviously make unlawful a search for stolen refrigerators under the floor-boards. But if the search was for drugs, such a search would presumably be permitted. The same section also states that entry and search must be at a reasonable time of day 'unless it appears to the constable executing it that there are grounds for suspecting that the purpose of a search may be frustrated on an entry at a reasonable hour' (s 16(4)). Code B adds that a search under warrant may not continue once the things specified in the warrant have been found or the officer in charge is satisfied that they are not there (para 6.9A and B).

(e)   'Bug and burgle' and other intrusive surveillance by the security agencies and police

Covert surveillance by the security service and the police is not new. But in recent years it has come more to public attention as a result of two quite different developments. One is the extraordinary growth of technical means available for such surveillance. The other is the pressure exerted by application of the European Convention on Human Rights to regularise such activities through legislation. The traditional ways of handling the problem – informal systems, unpublished non-statutory guidelines, official nods and winks condoning plain illegality[118] – no longer pass muster. Nowadays, such activities have to be 'in accordance with the law' if they are not to run foul of art 8 of the ECHR which guarantees everyone the right to respect for 'his private life and family life, his home and correspondence'.

There have been three major recent pieces of legislation in this area: the Security Service Act 1989 as amended in 1996, the Police Act 1997 and the Regulation of Investigatory Powers Act 2000.

The Security Service Act 1996 MI5's traditional role as defined in the Security Service Act 1989 was to protect national security, especially against threats from espionage, terrorism and sabotage from the activities of agents of foreign powers 'and from actions intended to overthrow or undermine parliamentary democracy' (s 1(2)) and also 'to safeguard the economic well-being of the United Kingdom against threats posed by the actions or intentions of persons outside the British Islands' (s 1(3)). The SSA 1989 gave the Home Secretary the power to issue warrants for 'the taking of such action as is specified in the warrant in respect of any property so specified' – namely entry of premises for the purpose of bugging.

As a result of the end of the Cold War, MI5 was looking for a new role – and employment for its staff of about 2,000. In 1996, to this end, the Government introduced the Security Service Bill to amend the Security Service Act 1989 by extending MI5's functions to 'act in support of the prevention and detection of serious crime'. In response to fears expressed by civil libertarians that this would give MI5 a roving brief to act on its own, the Government amended the Bill by clarifying that such actions could not be free-standing but had to be 'in support of the activities of police forces and other law enforcement agencies'.

The SSA 1996 also defined the offences in relation to which the Home Secretary could issue such warrants. The definition was broad – conduct that 'involves the use of violence, results in substantial financial gain or is conduct by a large number of persons in pursuit of a common purpose' or alternatively, the offence is one for which someone over 21 with no previous convictions could expect to get a term of three or more years' imprisonment. (This definition was taken from the Interception of Communications Act 1985.) The Minister assured the House of Commons that the

---

[118]   As described for instance in *Spycatcher* (1987), the celebrated international bestseller by former MI5 officer Peter Wright.

Security Service Act would only be used against what the ordinary citizen would understand to be organised and serious crime. [119]

The Minister also stated that the Government intended to introduce legislation to regulate the position regarding police surveillance and bugging operations. He acknowledged that it was not satisfactory that the Security Service should be subject to the requirement of getting a warrant for a bugging operation from the Home Secretary while the police could authorise it themselves.[120]

The Police Act 1997 The Police Bill was introduced in 1996 and received Royal Assent in March 1997. Part III regulating intrusive surveillance devices came into force in February 1999. The Act provides that 'no entry on or interference with property or with wireless telegraphy shall be unlawful if it is authorised by an authorisation' under the Act (s 92). Authorisation can only be given if the authorising officer believes that 'it is likely to be of substantial value in the prevention or detection of serious crime' and that the objective cannot reasonably be achieved by other means (s 93(2)). The definition of serious crime is the same as that quoted above from the Security Service Act (which was taken from the Interception of Communications Act 1985).

Until the PA 1997, entry on premises by the ordinary police for the purpose of bugging had been governed by unpublished Guidelines issued by the Home Secretary in 1984. Under the Guidelines a chief constable or assistant chief constable could authorise 'encroachment on privacy' through the use of surveillance devices. Though not formally published, the Guidelines were extensively quoted by the Lord Chief Justice, Lord Taylor, giving the judgment of the Court of Appeal in *R v Khan*[121], a case that arose from the placing of a bug on the exterior wall of a house which enabled the police to tape-record a conversation inside the house about drug smuggling. [122]

In the debates on the Bill a great deal of attention was focussed on the question of who would be entitled to authorise a bugging operation by the police and in particular, whether and, if so, when the police would have to get approval from someone external to the police service. The Act provides that authorisation must normally be obtained from the chief constable or, in an urgent case, where this is not reasonably practicable, from an officer of assistant chief constable rank. (ss 93, 94) It must be in writing though in a case of urgency it can be given orally but it will then lapse after 72 hours unless renewed in writing (s 95). Any authorisation must be notified as soon as practicable to the Chief Commissioner appointed under the Act (s 96). The authorisation requires renewal after three months.

However, in certain circumstances, the chief constable's authorisation does not take effect until it also has the written approval of one of the Commissioners appointed under the Act (s 97(1)). The circumstances are where the property to be bugged is

---

[119]   House of Commons, Standing Committee A, 1 February 1996, col 44.
[120]   House of Commons, Standing Committee A, 1 February 1996, col 78.
[121]   [1994] 4 All ER 426 at pp 430 – 31.
[122]   See also *R v Chalkley* [1998] 2 All ER 155, 161.

used wholly or mainly as a private dwelling or as a bedroom in a hotel or consists of office premises or the bugging is likely to involve (1) matters subject to legal professional privilege[123] (ie bugging of lawyers' offices); or (2) confidential personal information;[124] or (3) confidential journalistic material[125] (s 97(2)). But this requirement of prior approval from a Commissioner does not apply when the chief constable believes the case is one of urgency. The Commissioner must then be notified with reasons for the urgency as soon as practicable and has the power to quash or cancel it (ss 97(3) and 103(2)).

Commissioners under the Act must be persons who hold or have held high judicial office (s 91(2)).

The Act is accompanied by a Code of Practice on Intrusive Surveillance setting out the detailed procedures to be followed. The Code requires the authorising officer to 'satisfy him/herself that the degree of intrusion into the privacy of those affected by the surveillance is commensurate with the seriousness of the offence'. (para 2.3) It says that this is ' the case where the subjects of the surveillance might reasonably assume a high degree of privacy, for instance in their homes, or where there are special sensitivities, such as where the intrusion might affect communications between a minister of any religion or faith and an individual relating to that individual's spiritual welfare or where medical or journalistic confidentiality or legal privilege could be affected' or where confidential social security records are involved.

The Home Office press release issued when the Code of Practice was laid before Parliament stated that it was estimated that in 1996 there were some 2,550 chief officer authorisations by the police and customs throughout the United Kingdom. The majority related to the use of tracking devices on vehicles.

Part III of the Act only covers equipment whose placement may cause an act of trespass, criminal damage or interference with wireless telegraphy – for example, bugging devices in a home, a covert video camera in a hotel room and an electronic tracking device attached to a vehicle. It does not cover long-distance microphones or equipment based on laser-beam or microwave technology whose use does not involve interference with property. It also does not apply where the police are acting with the consent 'of a person able to give permission in respect of relevant property' (Code, para 2.1). This could raise difficult questions, for instance, in a landlord-tenant case as to who can give such consent. But presumably an employer could agree to an employee being bugged. The bugging of police cells would always have the approval of the police and would not require the approval of a Commissioner.

The 1984 Home Office Guidelines continue to apply to any surveillance operations not covered by the PA 1997.

123   See s 98.
124   See s 99.
125   See s 100.

See further Madeleine Colvin, 'Part III Police Act 1997', *New Law Journal*, 26 February 1999, p 311; and Steve Uglow, 'Covert Surveillance and the European Convention on Human Rights', [1999] *Criminal Law Review* pp 287, 296.

The Regulation of Investigatory Powers Act 2000 Prior to the 2000 Act (RIPA 2000), the UK had no system of statutory or judicial controls on undercover investigations. In so far as there was any regulation it was in the form, again, of semi-published Guidelines (first issued in 1969 [126] and reissued by the Association of Chief Police Officers (ACPO) in 1999.[127])

RIPA 2000 puts onto a statutory basis, inter alia,: 'directed surveillance'[128]; 'covert human intelligence' ie the use of informers; and 'intrusive surveillance' in residential premises or private vehicles including '(a) monitoring, observing or listening to persons, their movement, their conversations or their other activities or communications; (b) recording anything monitored, observed or listened to in the course of surveillance; and (c) surveillance by or with the assistance of a surveillance device'.

However, the 'bug and burgle' provisions of the Police Act 1997 (above) remain in being. The provisions of RIPA 2000, ss 32-40 apply in regard to the surveillance of private property that does not require the physical placing of a device in or on the property. If the activity involves physical trespass on the property, the PA 1997 governs.

The authorising officer, designated in the legislation, has to be satisfied the authorised surveillance is proportionate and necessary. Authorisation of 'directed surveillance' and of 'covert human intelligence sources' requires only internal oversight which could be from the organisations carrying out the surveillance (ss 28, 29). For the police it is normally at superintendent level.

Authorisation of 'intrusive surveillance' is more narrowly restricted, requiring the decision of the Home Secretary or of one 'of the senior authorising officers'. Senior authorising officers for the police are chief constables (s 32) (In cases that are urgent authorisation can be obtained from an Assistant Chief Constable.) But even when such authority has been obtained, the further step is required of notifying the Surveillance Commissioner [129] who must decide whether to approve the authorisation based on a consideration of the relevant grounds and the issue of proportionality

---

[126]   Home Office Circular 97/1969 set out in *New Law Journal*, 1969, p 513.

[127]   They were on the NCIS website – www.ncis.co.uk but are now subsumed in the Code under the RIPA 2000.

[128]   Defined as surveillance 'undertaken (a) for the purpose of a specific investigation; and (b) in order to obtain information about or to determine who is involved in the matter under investigation'(s 26(2)).

[129]   The Chief Surveillance Commissioner is the same Commissioner appointed under s 91 of the Police Act 1997. RIPA 2000, s 62 states that his duties cover intrusive surveillance under both Acts.

(s 35). The authorisation only takes effect when approved in writing by the Surveillance Commissioner (s 36).

It should be noted that RIPA 2000 does not impose a duty to obtain authorisation nor does it make unauthorised activity unlawful. If the activity was lawful before passage of the Act it remains lawful even if it is not authorised under RIPA 2000 (s 80). What it does do is to make lawful activities that have been authorised which would otherwise be unlawful.

It should also be noted that the fact that evidence has been obtained by means that are unlawful does not mean that it will necessarily be held to be inadmissible (as to which see pp 457-59 below).

See further, Y Akdeniz, N Taylor, C Walker, 'Regulation of Investigatory Powers Act 2000 (1): Bigbrother.gov.uk: State surveillance in the age of information and rights' [2001] *Criminal Law Review*, pp 73-90; E Cape, 'The right to privacy – RIP', *Legal Action*, January 2001, pp 21-23.

(f) Seizure of evidence

The law of seizure is closely related to, but is nevertheless separate from, the law of search. Traditionally, the common law required that search be by warrant and that the warrant be particular and faithfully followed. Thus, as already seen, in *Entick v Carrington* (1765) 2 Wils 275 it was held that the police could not ransack a man's house on a general warrant looking for evidence of a crime. In *Price v Messenger* (1800) 2 Bos & P 158, it was said that a constable who finds goods while searching under a warrant, which are not covered by the warrant, commits a trespass by seizing them.

However, in the late 1960s and the 1970s the common law on this crucial topic considerably modified the strict rule. [130] The topic is no longer of practical importance and is therefore no longer covered in this work.

THE PHILIPS ROYAL COMMISSION

The Philips Royal Commission dealt with the problem posed by seizure of evidence not covered by the search warrant:

Restrictions upon seizure for evidential and other purposes

3.48. Restriction on seizure of goods provides another method of controlling the execution of warrants. We do not think it desirable to limit seizure only to

---

[130]   See *Elias v Pasmore* [1934] 2 KB 164; *Chic Fashions (West Wales) Ltd v Jones* [1968] 2 QB 299; *Ghani v Jones* [1969] 3 All ER 1700; *Garfinkel v Metropolitan Police Comr* [1972] Crim LR 44; *Frank Truman Export Ltd v Metropolitan Police Comr* [1977] 3 All ER 431. See also *R v Waterfield*, *R v Lynn* [1964] 1 QB 164; *Jeffrey v Black* [1978] 1 All ER 555; and *McLorie v Oxford* [1982] QB 1290.

prohibited goods or to the evidence specified in the warrant. It defies common sense to expect the police not to seize such items incidentally found during the course of a search. At the same time the risk that premises may be ransacked as soon as a warrant is granted in respect of any offence must be minimised. The present law seems to us to be uncertain and of little help in this respect.

3.49 We wish to preclude a specific warrant being used to legitimise general searches. Accordingly when the police have lawful authority to enter premises upon one of the warrants proposed in para graphs 3.39 and 3.42, they should be entitled to seize the items specified in that warrant and any other prohibited goods or evidence of a grave offence (that is items for which they could have obtained a warrant) which they find incidentally in the course of a lawful search, that is one conducted in accordance with the terms of the warrant and in the manner appropriate to the items being searched for. The procedure for giving a receipt should apply to such additional material that is seized and the receipt should specify the suspected offence in respect of which the material has been seized. Items seized otherwise than in this way may not be used in evidence. We appreciate that the obligatory exclusion of evidence at trial may appear an inflexible restriction, but the right of members of the public to be free from general searches must be respected.

PACE

The Government did not wholly accept the Commission's recommendations. Section 19 of PACE gives the police power to seize articles where a search is carried out lawfully either with the consent of the occupier or under any statutory power. The article may be seized if the officer reasonably believes that it is evidence in relation to an offence which he is investigating *or any other offence* or that it has been obtained in consequence of the commission of an offence and that it is necessary to seize it in order to prevent its concealment, loss or destruction. The only articles exempted are those covered by legal professional privilege (s 19(6)) – and even they may be seized under the new power to 'seize and shift' (below). It is immaterial whether an arrest has or has not taken place and equally whether the occupier is suspected of any involvement in criminal activity.

An article may be held for use as evidence at the trial, for forensic examination or, where it appears to be stolen, for restoration to its lawful owner (s 22(2)). If requested by the occupier or the person having possession of the article, the police must give that person a record of what was seized (s 21(1)) or a photocopy or photographs of items seized (s 21(3)). Alternatively, the officer should be prepared to grant access, under supervision, to the items in question (s 21(3)). But neither photographs, nor photocopies nor access need be granted if 'the officer in charge of the investigation has reasonable grounds for believing that to do so would prejudice the investigation' (s 21(8)).

Power to 'seize and sift' In *R v Chesterfield Justices, ex p Bramley* [2000] 1 All ER 411 the Divisional Court confirmed that the police could not lawfully take away material that included items covered by legal professional privilege in order to sift and sort them at leisure at police premises. If such material was taken it had to be returned immediately and damages might have to be paid. The Government moved swiftly to change this. The Criminal Justice and Police Act 2001[131], gives the police a power to remove material for the purpose of sifting it elsewhere where it is not practicable to examine it on the spot. The power applies not only to seizure under PACE but to other legislation covering law enforcement agencies. The Police Reform Act 2002 extended the power to civilian investigating officers.

Having sifted the material, they can retain only what they are permitted to seize under the previous seizure powers – though they can hold on to 'inextricably linked material' that cannot be separated. Anyone with a sufficient interest in the material being held can apply to a High Court judge for its return.

(g) The power to freeze the suspect's assets

A new development in the law in recent years has been the power to freeze assets of a defendant prior to a trial. It is similar to developments in civil procedure, especially of 'freezing orders' (formerly Mareva injunctions) (p 98 above).

The first step was taken in *West Mercia Constabulary v Wagener* [1981] 3 All ER 378, where the police used civil process to seize and preserve property of a suspect. The High Court judge granted the police an injunction to restrain the alleged proceeds of fraud from being withdrawn from a bank account. The court said that since magistrates could not issue a search warrant to deal with proceeds of an alleged crime held in a bank account, the High Court would fill the gap. The new power was applied by the Court of Appeal in *Chief Constable of Kent v V* [1982] 3 All ER 36, even though the alleged proceeds of crime had been mingled with the defendant's own moneys. But in *Chief Constable of Hampshire v A Ltd* [1984] 2 All ER 385, the mingling of the alleged proceeds of crime with other moneys proved fatal to the police request for the same injunction. The Court of Appeal distinguished the earlier decision. In that case there was one victim of fraud and the fraud was easily identifiable. In the Hampshire case there were large numbers of transactions and much of the money in the relevant accounts would not be the result of fraud. The Court of Appeal in the Hampshire case seemed concerned to restrict the ambit of the new doctrine to cases where it could be shown that they were the proceeds of crime and could be identified. See similarly *Chief Constable of Leicestershire v M* [1988] 3 All ER 1015, per Hoffmann J holding that the *proceeds* of crime could not be the subject of an interlocutory injunction. In *A-G v Blake* [1998] 1 All ER 833 the Court of Appeal granted the Crown an injunction to stop the notorious spy, George Blake, from receiving royalties from his autobiography. It was held to be part of the court's support for the criminal law

---

[131]   CJPA 2001, ss 50-66 and Schs 1 and 2. See also Code B, para s.7.7-7.12.

to enforce public policy by restraining receipt by the criminal of further benefit from his crime.

But the common law power to freeze the defendant's assets was supplemented by the Drug Trafficking Offences Act 1986. The basic scheme of the DTOA 1986 was to give the court powers to freeze property or assets, whether in the hands of a defendant or a third party, which might subsequently be needed to satisfy the confiscation order for which the Act made provision. (Under the DTOA 1986 the court was required to make a confiscation order on every person convicted of a drug-trafficking offence who had received any payment or reward in connection with drug trafficking at any time. The requirement was mandatory. The confiscation order was in addition to any sentence including a fine. The amount was the amount assessed by the court to be the full value of the offender's drug-trafficking activities. (For this purpose the court could assume that, unless the contrary was shown, all the offender's assets plus any assets he had had in the previous six years, represented the proceeds of drug trafficking.) The similar powers under Part VI of the Criminal Justice Act 1988, by contrast, applied only to offences where the court was satisfied that the proceeds of the crime were more than £10,000.

The power to confiscate the proceeds of crime was hugely expanded by the Proceeds of Crime Act 1995 which is not restricted to offences involving more than £10,000. The Act provides extraordinary ancillary civil powers which permit the High Court to make a restraint order preventing any dealing with the defendant's assets. Such an order is similar to a 'freezing order' (Mareva injunction), and the prosecutor is given priority over unsecured creditors. The High Court can make disclosure orders requiring disclosure by affidavit of the nature and extent of assets. (See *Re O* [1991] 1 All ER 330.) It can also make receivership orders to manage assets or to realise them to enforce payment of a confiscation order made by the Crown Court. (See K Talbot, 'The Proceeds of Crime Act 1995', *New Law Journal*, 15 December 1995, p 1857; and K Rees, 'Confiscating the proceeds of crime', *New Law Journal*, 6 September, 1996, p 1270.)

5. The prosecution process

(a) The police have a wide discretion

The police have a major field of discretion in deciding whether and how to respond to criminal conduct. A former police officer turned journalist described once how he had walked from Waterloo Station to Holborn in order to see how many criminal offences he could identify:

CR Rolph, 'Police Discretion', *New Statesman,* **2 February 1969**

I got the following bag:
- A girl feeding the pigeons inside Waterloo Station.

- Two cars with expired Excise Licences.
- Three cars with none at all.
- Twenty-three cars parked wholly or partly on the footway.
- One lorry with its lowered tailboard hiding the rear number plate while in motion.
- A furniture van with its rear number chalked on the back.
- One flag-day girl shaking a collecting box in people's faces.
- One boy throwing a half-eaten egg sandwich into the roadway.
- Three shop awnings that you had to duck under.
- A cycling window cleaner carrying a ladder on his shoulders.
- And a painter on a window - sill wearing no means of preventing a fall.

I would say it was a typical lot. And among the things too numerous to count were cars bearing advertising 'stickers', vehicles waiting on double yellow lines, and disembarking bus passengers throwing their tickets away.

I've known policemen who would have hated to let any of these escape. They would all have been seen as personal affronts. But even a policeman like that couldn't have coped with more than one of them. If he chose the cycling man with the ladder, who was actually the most dangerous, all the rest would have got away. So perhaps he would have chosen the three shop blinds, on the ground that they might have knocked his helmet off (they ought to be 8ft 6in from the ground).

But it has to be faced that the great majority of policemen would have chosen none of them. Which in itself would have been a choice. And the chief constable's 'discretion' is merely the same choice writ large, with the difference that chief constables, who have no time to go around looking for car licences, number plates, flag-day offences, litter bugs, men on window-sills, don't exercise their choice until an offence is actually reported and the papers come before them.

A more systematic exploration of the discretionary element in policing was part of a study of policing conducted in the late 1960s by John Lambert. What he wrote then is as relevant today:

John Lambert, 'The Police Can Choose', *New Society*, 18 September 1969

The policeman is not, and never has been, simply a 'law-enforcement officer'. He has *discretion*, in almost all circumstances except catching a murderer actually on the job, about whom he will arrest, investigate or harass, and whom he won't. In this sense, the problem is that of 'normal' policing, because in this exercise of discretion, which is central to all his work, the policeman's own private view of the world comes into play: his opinion, as a citizen, of other citizens; his reaction, as a member of one class or race, towards other classes or races.

The part that discretion plays, necessarily, in British police work is seldom acknowledged publicly. The legal philosophy of a democratic society sees police activities as potentially threatening to individual liberty. So the police, in enforcing the law, are themselves bound by numerous regulations. The theory is that laws apply to all men and the police must enforce the law always, everywhere equally.

Yet *full* enforcement is not possible. Law-breaking is so common that to investigate every infringement, to prosecute every known offender, would require police forces of a size, and involve expenditures on a scale, that would be impracticable and intolerable. So small police forces with small budgets have to enforce laws selectively. Both as an organization and as individuals, the police have considerable choice about how to organize, which crimes and criminals to prosecute, how to allocate what number of men to different law enforcement tasks, and so on. It's almost a question of artistry, and certainly it's craftsmanship ...

Crime occurs unevenly in different neighbourhoods of towns and cities. This puts more policemen in some areas than others, with different opportunities to discover offences and to find offenders to process as clients. Opportunities abound for legalistic policemen to cram police cells with the drunk and disorderly and police offices with papers relating to motoring offences. In practice, many are seen but few are processed. How the drunk or the motorist reacts to the policeman's intervention determines the outcome.

What matters is whether the client shows deference or respect to the policeman. And which of these is shown depends very much on a two-way perception of status, rank, position and power between policeman and client. Thus law enforcement depends quite precisely on relations between police and public. The legal role of the police is defined by the perceptions of policemen and their ability to manage relationships.

CLASS BIAS IN PROSECUTIONS

Research conducted by Andrew Sanders, then of Birmingham University, explored the question of how far prosecution policy was influenced by class bias. He took 1,200 (non-motoring) cases from six police divisions (two from a large metropolitan county force, two from a small rural force and two from a force that policed both rural areas and a city). He compared police decisions with those of non-police agencies and especially the Factory Inspectorate (HMFI). (See A Sanders, 'Class Bias in Prosecutions', *The Hansard Journal*, vol 24, 1985, p 176.)

He found:
(1)   That the police cautioned very little – in about 4% of cases; whereas the HMFI used cautions as the norm – in the period 1978 to 1982 cautions were used in 65 – 73% of cases.

(2) The overwhelming majority of HMFI prosecutions are directed at the middle class, that is companies and managers, whereas most police prosecutions are of working-class or unemployed (previously working-class) persons. Despite considerable demographic differences, the police divisions produced very similar class patterns with around only 5% from the middle or upper class. (Also a statistically significant difference emerged in the ability of middle-class persons suspected of crime to avoid prosecution by the police.)

(3) In the police, the decision to prosecute is taken at a relatively junior level (inspector), while the decision not to prosecute is made at a relatively high level (superintendent or above). In the HMFI it is the other way round. The junior (inspector) can caution but it requires a more senior officer to institute a prosecution. Prosecutions are only started by the HMFI for what are regarded as the most serious of the serious cases, whereas the police often prosecute trivial cases.

(4) The police do not take poverty into account when deciding whether to prosecute. By contrast, if a factory owner or trader says he broke the law because he could not afford to comply, it would be taken into account and would be regarded as a valid reason for not prosecuting.

(5) Whereas in the police there was an institutional bias in favour of prosecution (reflected in the phrase 'let the court decide'), the HMFI regarded prosecutions as a last resort. The role of HMFI officials was one more of advice and persuasion, getting firms to comply with the law. The police saw their role in prosecutions as such.

In Sanders' view the different decisions of the agencies were the result not of the people concerned but rather of the perspective of the agencies. The police in some circumstances behaved in a similar way – eg in fraud cases where it was widely agreed that prosecution was thought of as a last resort for the real rogues. In tax evasion, too, very few are prosecuted. In 1980 there were 22,000 serious cases of tax evasion. One in 122 was prosecuted. By contrast there were 107,000 social security frauds, of which one in four were prosecuted. The total value of social security fraud was estimated at some £108m in 1979 compared to £3 – 3.5bn in tax evasion in the same year. Tax evasion therefore resulted in 30 times more loss to the public purse and yet there were far more prosecutions of social security fraud. On when the CPS can prosecute although the Inland Revenue has accepted a pecuniary settlement see Sylvia Elwes and R Clutterbuck, 'Tax and Criminal Prosecutions', (1999) *Criminal Law Review*, 139-43.

On class bias see also the research sample reported by McConville, Sanders and Leng in *The Case for the Prosecution* (Routledge, 1991), p 123.

For evidence of remarkable regional differences in prosecution policies see research by Dr Gary Slapper referred to at p 253 below.

(b)   Proposals for an independent prosecution process

In most countries the police start criminal proceedings but they are then continued (or not) by some form of public prosecution service such as the district attorney in the United States, the procurator fiscal in Scotland, or the procureur in France. Until 1986, England was one of the few countries in the world which left a major prosecution function to the police. In the magistrates' courts the police themselves generally prosecuted, though they would often use lawyers. In cases dealt with in the Crown Court, the police, like solicitors, did not have a right of audience and therefore had to instruct both solicitors and barristers.

As from 1986 onwards, under the Prosecution of Offences Act 1985, the police no longer had any role in continuing prosecutions beyond the stage of charge. Once a suspect had been charged the papers went to the Crown Prosecution Service (CPS), which decided whether to proceed, and, if so, on what charges. It was then the CPS which carried the prosecution forward. The change represented a revolution in the actual practice of prosecutions, especially in magistrates' courts. (As will be seen, under the provisions of the Criminal Justice Bill 2002/03 a new system was due to come into force under which, save in routine or serious cases, the CPS rather than the police would formulate the initial charge.)

The 1970 JUSTICE Report The origin of the Crown Prosecution Service was a report by JUSTICE, the prestigious British Section of the International Commission of Jurists, which argued that the police role in prosecutions should be restricted to very minor cases or should be eliminated altogether (*The Prosecution Process in England and Wales*, 1970). The main thrust of the JUSTICE report was that even the honest, conscientious police officer may become psychologically committed to successful prosecution. 'He wants to prosecute and he wants to win.' He is therefore more likely to continue with a prosecution where the evidence may be weak. Also, the police were not well suited to evaluate the public policy aspects of the discretion not to prosecute. The police should not both collect the evidence and conduct the proceedings.

The JUSTICE Committee concluded:

> 9. ... we think that two basic points can legitimately be made against the existing procedure:
> (a) It confuses two quite distinct and disparate functions and responsibilities, namely the vigorous investigation of crime; and the cool, careful objective assessment of the whole of the evidence and probabilities needed for a correct decision as to whether a prosecution should be started or, if started, continued.
> (b) It offends against the principle that the prosecution should be – and should be plainly seen to be – independent, impartial and fair: concerned only with the pursuit of truth and not with winning or losing. This is of cardinal importance in an accusatorial system. ...

The Committee recommended the introduction of the Scottish system where the decision to prosecute in all but very minor cases is taken by prosecutors, the procurators fiscal, under the Lord Advocate, who are wholly independent of the police. The police report all cases to the procurators fiscal, who decide whether a prosecution is warranted.

THE PHILIPS ROYAL COMMISSION'S REPORT

The terms of reference of the Philips Royal Commission included the question whether changes were need 'in the process of and responsibility for the prosecution of criminal offences'.

Its Report said that for a variety of reasons a new system was needed. There were three key objectives: to secure fairness, to secure efficiency and to secure accountability in the prosecution system. A fair system meant one that brought to trial only those against whom there was an adequate and properly prepared case and whose prosecution was justified in the public interest. It also required a high standard of competence, impartiality and integrity in those who operate the system. The service also had to be efficient and accountable. Efficient in the sense that it achieved the objectives set for it with minimum use of resources and the minimum delay. Accountable in the sense that those who made the decision to prosecute or not could be called publicly to explain and justify their policies and actions so far as that was consistent with protecting the interests of suspects and accused.

What it proposed was based on the following features: The initial decision to charge a suspect should continue to be taken by the police. Thereafter all decisions would be taken by a prosecution agency, including any decision to alter or drop the charges. Each area would have a prosecuting solicitors' department presided over by a Crown Prosecutor of equal status to the chief constable and answerable to the same authority. Each police authority area should have a new committee to be known as the Police and Prosecution Authority, to which the crown prosecutor and the chief constable would both be accountable. The Minister responsible for the prosecution system should be either the Home Secretary or the Attorney-General.

THE GOVERNMENT'S REACTION

The Government rejected the Royal Commission's view that the new prosecution system would be based on local committees. [132] The Government proposed that there should be a single prosecution service, controlled and directed by the DPP. The investigation of criminal offences would remain with the police and they would continue to lay the initial charges but thereafter the responsibility for all prosecution decisions (including the dropping or alteration of charges) would be that of the

[132]   For the history of the proposals see the 6th edition of this work, p 220.

prosecution service. The Government said it believed 'that the establishment of an independent prosecution service on this basis would promote consistency and fairness; would reduce the proportion of cases pursued despite lack of sufficient evidence; would improve the preparation and presentation of cases in court; would provide an attractive career structure; and would lead to greater efficiency and better accountability for the use of resources' (White Paper, *An Independent Prosecution Service for England and Wales*, Cmnd 9074, 1983 para 6).

(c)   The Crown Prosecution Service (CPS) 1986-2003

The Crown Prosecution Act 1985 established the Crown Prosecution Service (CPS) as a national prosecution service for the whole of England and Wales under the general direction of the Director of Public Prosecutions (DPP).

The country was originally divided into areas – 29 in England and 2 in Wales – with each area headed by a chief crown prosecutor, responsible to the DPP for the operation of his area. In 1993 this structure was altered. The 31 areas were amalgamated into 13 larger areas, including one for the whole of London.

The function of the CPS is to conduct all criminal cases against both adults and juveniles (apart from minor motoring offences which have been excluded from the system) that are instituted by or on behalf of the police.

It was also given a power in CPA 1985, s 23 to discontinue proceedings which is used very often (see further below). This is in addition to the power not to start proceedings where charges have been laid. In summary cases before the court has heard any evidence, and in proceedings in the Crown Court before it or the magistrates' court has heard any evidence, the proceedings can be stopped by notice to the court with reasons. They can also be stopped where someone has been arrested without a warrant before the court has been informed of the charge by notice to the suspect.

The CPS does not, however, have its own investigation machinery or facilities. It relies for that role on the police. Nor, unlike the procurator fiscal in Scotland, can the CPS direct the police to carry out an investigation or further investigations. It can only request. The Runciman Royal Commission considered whether the CPS should be given such a power but by a majority of 10 to 1 decided against it. Any dispute between the CPS and the police as to such a question should, it thought, be resolvable between the two agencies, if necessary with the help of the Chief Inspector of Constabulary (Report, p 74, para 26).

A rocky start The CPS started operation in 1986. Over the years since then the CPS has mainly had a poor press. In the early years of the service there were many media stories of muddle and confusion, of lost files, delays and cases bungled. There is general agreement that the operational efficiency of the service has greatly improved. Such stories are now much rarer. But the CPS continues to be the butt of criticism, often coming from the police because of decisions to discontinue cases, on which see further (pp 243-44 below).

There was also a continuing problem of staff morale – due partly to issues of management. A survey in November 1993 by the First Division Association (FDA) the union which represents three-quarters of CPS lawyers, found that their morale was at an all-time low and that the majority had no confidence in the senior management. A poll of the entire membership of the union in November 1995 found the lowest morale and highest dissatisfaction was in the CPS section. Members complained that management was poor and that government-imposed efficiency and economy drives had put intolerable pressures on them. Disaffection was especially pronounced among senior staff. (See D Bindman, 'Crown Jewels', *Law Society's Gazette*, 7 February 1996, p 22).

The restructuring which had reduced 31 areas to 13 was also a source of criticism. In April 1997, just before the general election, the Labour Party published a document in which it promised that the CPS would be re-organised yet again – this time into 42 areas each with the same boundaries as the 42 police areas. It also announced that there would be a review of the working of the CPS by a three-man team headed by Sir Iain Glidewell, a former Lord Justice of Appeal. A month before the report was published, Dame Barbara Mills QC, who had been DPP for nine years, announced that she would be resigning. In November 1998 it was announced that the Chairman of the Criminal Bar Association, Mr David Calvert-Smith QC, would replace her. He served until 2003.

THE GLIDEWELL REPORT

The Glidewell Report (*Review of the Crown Prosecution Service*, 1998, Cm 3960, £21) was published in June 1998.[133] It proved to be a hard-hitting, wide-ranging document highly critical of the CPS. The 216-page report made 75 recommendations for changes. The basic themes were:
* a need for improved staff morale
* greater devolution of decision making from the centre – approval for the Government's decision to move from 13 areas to 42
* senior lawyers to spend less time on administration and more on casework and prosecuting
* headquarters should be 'slimmer, tougher and more directly in control of matters with which it is properly concerned' (p 165)
* the chief executive should be a lay person
* better working arrangements for the interface with the police
* the police to retain responsibility for investigation and charging
* better support for prosecuting barristers in the Crown Court.

---

[133]   For a summary and editorial comment see [1998] *Criminal Law* Review, pp 517-20.

THE GOVERNMENT'S RESPONSE TO GLIDEWELL

The Government's reaction to the Report was basically positive. [134] But the Government did not accept the Glidewell recommendations that would have resulted in a transfer of power or responsibilities from the police to the CPS. It saw the future rather in collaboration and partnership between the two organisations. The Attorney-General told the House of Commons, 'co-location, common administration and integrated working' would 'streamline casework and file handling processes, remove duplication and unnecessary burdens and reduce delay'. But the police would retain their responsibility for file preparation and witness warning. The Government had decided 'that it would not be practical or a proper reflection of the respective constitutional priorities of the CPS and the police, to require a transfer of responsibilities. Collaboration was being promoted by a new Criminal Justice Units Project Group chaired jointly by the CPS and the Association of Chief Police Officers (ACPO). (Attorney-General, House of Commons, *Hansard*, 19 April, 1999, WA col 398.)

THE AULD REVIEW (2001)

Lord Justice Auld in his Review said that most of the Glidewell recommendations had been adopted after local pilots. CPS staff were increasingly located in or close to police stations working in liaison with the police in criminal justice units and were receiving papers for review shortly after charge. Early signs were that the new system was producing some improvements in efficiency and some savings though not, in the main, in the accuracy of charging. [135]

(d)   The CPS to take on the task of charging

The Auld Report, disagreeing with both Runciman and Glidewell, recommended that charging of suspects should to a large extent be taken over by the CPS. ('I recommend that the Crown Prosecution Service should be given greater legal powers, in particular the power to determine the initial charge and sufficient resources to enable it to take full and effective control of cases from the charge or pre-charge stage, as appropriate'[136]) The chief reason given for this proposition was overcharging by the police. ('A significant contributor to delays in the entering of pleas of guilty and in identifying issues for trial and, in consequence, the prolonged and disjointed nature of many criminal proceedings, is "over-charging" by the police and failure by the Crown Prosecution Service to remedy it at an early stage.'[137]) Overcharging,

---

[134]   See statement of the Attorney-General on publication, House of Commons, *Hansard*, 1 June, 1998, vol 313, col 42 and Written Answers, 30 November, 1998, col 67.

[135]   *An early Assessment of Co-located Criminal Justice Units* – available on the CPS website www.cps.gov.uk.

[136]   Chapter 10, p 399, para 12.

[137]   Chapter 10, p 408, para 35.

Auld said, led the defence to maintain tactical pleas of not guilty until the last minute. It could also give rise to 'hasty, ill-considered and inappropriate' acceptances by the prosecution of guilty pleas which bewildered and distressed victims.[138]

Auld thought that 'consideration should be given to a move towards earlier and more influential involvement of the Crown Prosecution Service in the process to the point where, in all but minor, routine cases, or where there is a need for a holding charge, it should determine the charge and initiate the prosecution.

In response to the Auld proposal, the Home Secretary and the Attorney-General decided to start a pilot scheme within the then current legal framework. This took place on nine sites in five areas from February to August 2002. Reports on the pilot were commissioned from independent researchers, PA Consulting Group. [139]

The pilot involved 3,324 cases in which the CPS gave the police oral advice as to charge and 2,875 cases in which the advice was written. The reported results were very positive:

- Conviction rates improved in six of the nine pilot areas.
- Discontinuance rates were lower than the pre-pilot sample in all areas.
- The proportion of defendants who pleaded guilty increased and the pleas came at an earlier stage.
- There was a consistent fall in all areas in the number of cases where charges were changed or dropped. The early intervention of the CPS, it seemed, made it more likely that the charge was right from the start.
- The proportion of last-minute changes of plea ('cracked trials') decreased.
- The time from arrest to charge increased by an average of 24 days but the time from charge to completion reduced by 10 days.
- There was some evidence that the quality of files had improved – and not just the files in the pilot.

The Executive Summary of the Report said that all areas were 'fully supportive of early charging advice' and were continuing with the scheme even though the formal pilot had ended. It added, 'We must also highlight the qualitative benefits which have been seen in all areas including enhanced joint working, better quality, skills transfer, and improved confidence, trust and mutual respect'. (p vii)[140]

In the meanwhile the Government's White Paper *Justice for All* (Cm 5563, July 2002, para 3.31) had indicated that Auld's recommendation would be adopted and provisions to give it effect were included in Part 4 and Schedule 2 of the Criminal Justice Bill 2002/03.

---

[138]   Chapter 10, p 408, para 35.

[139]   See *Crown Prosecution Service Charging Suspects: early involvement by CPS. A pilot Final Evaluation*, April 2003.

[140]   An earlier assessment of the proposed placement of police officers in police stations to offer pre-charge advice to police investigators had been sceptical about its likely benefits – see J Baldwin and A Hunt, 'Prosecutors Advising in Police Stations'(1998) *Criminal Law Review*, 521-36.

Under these provisions, s 37 of PACE is amended to require that the custody officer have regard to guidance from the DPP when determining whether the suspect should be released without charge but on bail, or without charge and without bail or charged. Where the case is referred to the CPS to determine whether proceedings should be instituted and, if so, on what charges, the defendant would be released on police bail with or without conditions.

A new six-months pilot scheme to test the concept in five areas was started in March 2003. [141]

(e)   The decision whether to prosecute

The CPS decision as to whether to prosecute is based on the Code for Crown Prosecutors. The current version is on the CPS website (www.cps.gov.uk) and is also published at the back of the annual report. The following text gives key passages as regards the evidential test and the public interest test:

Code for Prosecutors, 2003

2.2 Crown Prosecutors must be fair, independent and objective. They must not let any personal views about the ethnic or national origin, sex, religious beliefs, political views or sexual orientation of the suspect, victim or witness influence their decisions. They must also not be affected by improper or undue pressure from any source ...

4. The Code Tests

4.1 There are two stages in the decision to prosecute. The first stage is the evidential test. If the case does not pass the evidential test, it must not go ahead, no matter how important or serious it may be. If the case does pass the evidential test, Crown Prosecutors must decide if a prosecution is needed in the public interest.

4.2 This second stage is the public interest test. The Crown Prosecution Service will only start or continue a prosecution when the case has passed both tests...

5. The Evidential Test

5.1 Crown Prosecutors must be satisfied that there is enough evidence to provide a 'realistic prospect of conviction' against each defendant on each charge. They must consider what the defence case may be, and how that is likely to affect the prosecution case.

---

[141]   See *Solicitors' Journal*, 8 March 2002, p 200.

5.2 A realistic prospect of conviction is an objective test. It means that a jury or bench of magistrates, properly directed in accordance with the law, is more likely than not to convict the defendant of the charge alleged.

5.3 When deciding whether there is enough evidence to prosecute, Crown Prosecutors must consider whether the evidence can be used and is reliable. There will be many cases in which the evidence does not give cause for concern. But there will also be cases in which the evidence may not be as strong as it first appears ...

6. The Public Interest Test

6.1 In 1951, Lord Shawcross, who was Attorney-General, made the classic statement on public interest, which has been supported by Attorneys-General ever since: 'It has never been the rule in this country, I hope it never will be, that suspected criminal offences must automatically be the subject of prosecution'. (House of Commons Debates, vol 483, col 681, 29 January 1951.)

6.2 The public interest must be considered in each case where there is enough evidence to provide a realistic prospect of conviction. A prosecution will usually take place unless there are public interest factors tending against prosecution which clearly outweigh those tending in favour. Although there may be public interest factors against prosecution in a particular case, often the prosecution should go ahead and those factors should be put to the court for consideration when sentence is being passed.

Factors stated to militate *in favour* of prosecution (para 6.4) are: (1) the likelihood of a significant sentence; (2) a weapon was used or violence was threatened; (3) the offence was committed against someone who serves the public such as a police or prison officer or a nurse; (4) the accused was in a position of authority or trust; (5) the accused was the ringleader or an organiser; (6) the offence was premeditated; (7) that it was carried out by a group; (8) the victim was vulnerable, or was put in fear or suffered personal attack, damage or disturbance; (9) the offence involved discrimination on grounds of ethnic or national origin, sex, religion, political belief or sexual orientation; (10) a marked difference between the actual or mental ages of the accused and the victim, or if there is an element of corruption; (11) the relevance of the accused's record; (12) whether the accused was subject to a court order; (13) the likelihood of repetition; (14) the offence, though not serious in itself, is widespread in that area.

Factors stated to militate *against* prosecution (para 6.5) are: (1) the likely penalty would be very small or nominal; (2) the offence was committed as a result of a mistake or misunderstanding; (3) the loss or harm is minor; (4) long delay between the offence and the trial, unless the offence is serious or it has only just come to light; (5) prosecution will have a very bad effect on the accused's physical or mental health, always bearing in mind the seriousness of the offence; (6) the accused is old, suffering from significant mental or physical ill health, unless the offence is serious or there is a real possibility of it being repeated; (7) the accused has already made reparation or paid compensation ('but defendants must not avoid prosecution simply because they pay compensation'); (8) details may emerge at the trial which could harm sources, international relations or national security.

The CPS prosecutes on behalf of the public at large and not in the interests of any individual. 'However, when considering the public interest test Crown Prosecutors should always take into account the consequences for the victim of the decisions whether or not to prosecute, and any views expressed by the victim or the victim's family' (para 6.7). It was important that a victim is told about a decision which 'makes a significant difference to the case' (para 6.8).

In regard to young offenders the Code has recently rather changed its approach. It formerly stated that the CPS should have in mind that the stigma of a conviction could cause very serious harm to the prospects of a young offender and that they could sometimes be dealt with without going to court. The Code no longer contains this sentence. Instead it states that unless the charge is very serious, cases are usually only referred to the CPS when the juvenile has already had a reprimand and final warning. In other words attempts to divert the youth from the court system have not been effective. 'So the public interest will usually require a prosecution in such cases, unless there are clear public interest factors against prosecution' (para 6.10).

For analysis of the 'public interest element' see Andrew Ashworth, 'The "Public Interest" Element in Prosecutions' (1987) *Criminal Law Review* p 595. See also A Ashworth and J Fionda, 'Prosecution, Accountability and the Public Interest' (1994) *Criminal Law Review*, p 894; and Roger Daw, 'A Response', ibid, p 904. A Hoyano et al, 'A Study of the Impact of the Revised Code for Crown Prosecutors'(1997)] *Criminal Law Review* pp 556-64.

For a strongly argued view that the evidential requirement in the Code is misconceived, see Glanville Williams, 'Letting off the Guilty and Prosecuting the Innocent' (1985) *Criminal Law Review*, p 115. Professor Williams' contention was that if the test for proceeding is whether a conviction was likely to succeed (the '51% or realistic prospect of conviction) rule' many prosecutions that ought to be brought would not be. The test rather should be whether the prosecutor is satisfied on the evidence that the suspect is guilty, subject to the public interest questions as to whether a prosecution is desirable. Certainly there had to be at the least a reasonable possibility of a conviction. But the effect of the rule that there must be a reasonable probability of a conviction meant, for instance, that corrupt police officers might not be prosecuted because it was notoriously difficult to get a jury to convict a police officer. Where the prosecutor did not believe that the accused was guilty, he should drop the case. An exception to this principle might be where failure to charge someone may bring about a loss of public confidence in the integrity of the prosecution service.

It is not only the Code for Crown Prosecutors that influences the decision whether or not to start and continue a prosecution. Another consideration is the CPS staff member's concern to maintain his employer's approval by not having too many cases that go wrong – ie end in acquittal. In an era when performance targets dominate thinking, that will tend to militate in the direction of dropping cases when there is a doubt as to the prospects of a conviction. In former times the prosecution might have left the issue to be resolved by the jury. The same tendency is promoted by the current concern to reduce costs which powerfully affects the members of all public agencies.

(In addition to the published Code CPS staff also work under the influence of the unpublished *Policy Manual* which is for internal use only.)

GUIDE TO CASE DISPOSAL

A step in the direction of reducing both discretion and prosecutions came in 1995 with the issue to the police of a new Case Disposal Manual. This ranked every offence, motoring, criminal and alcohol-related, on a scale of points from one to five. *Five-point offences*, such as murder, would always be prosecuted. *Four-point offences* have what the manual terms 'a high probability of prosecution'. This category includes GBH, forgery, arson, perjury, burglary and perverting the course of justice. *Three-point offences* include indecent assault, theft, handling stolen goods, buggery, prostitution offences, resisting arrest, criminal damage and ABH. In three-point offences the decision whether to charge is to be made by listing the 'aggravating' and the 'mitigating' factors. The manual lists general factors, for instance, the impact on the victim, the accused's prior criminal record, the likelihood of penalty and whether the crime is a prevalent offence causing local concern. The manual also indicates factors specific to particular offences. So possession of drugs (even Class A substances such as cocaine, crack and heroin) will usually be cautioned if only 'small amounts, for personal use' are involved! The possessor of an offensive weapon will not be prosecuted under the manual's guidelines if there was 'no risk, weapon not on display, mistaken belief that there would be no offence if carried for protection only'. Deception offences will not be prosecuted if they were 'committed over a short period, low value' or 'driven by poverty/personal need'. ABH would not be prosecuted if it is a single blow causing only superficial injury. *Two-point offences* are those where there is a high probability of a caution and the decision maker needs to be able to justify the decision not to caution. This category includes begging, kerb-crawling and being drunk and incapable in a public place. A charge for this offence will only be laid if the offender is arrested four times for the same offence within a four-week period. *One-point offences* are minor offences for which a Formal Warning is appropriate or where there is a decision not to proceed with a prosecution. They include such things as throwing litter in the street or sending someone to buy liquor for a person who is under age.

David Rose, Home Affairs Correspondent of *The Observer*, described and commented on this remarkable development in his book *In the Name of the Law: The Collapse of Criminal Justice* (Jonathan Cape, 1996, pp 163 – 64):

The *Case Disposal Manual*, introduced at first in London and several counties, with others rapidly following suit, enlarges police discretion on an unprecedented scale. It requires that officers of junior rank take fundamental decisions with massive implications for the lives of those they arrest, without reference to any court or outside authority. The judgments it demands are even more subjective than some of those required by the Code for Crown Prosecutors. How, for example, do you measure whether a sexual assault is 'trivial'? It is inescapable that many of those judgments will be shaped by factors which have nothing to do with the true merits of the case: the officer's workload; his opinion of the suspect; and the possibility that he may, in return for non-prosecution, become a useful informant in future .... The Manual, drawn up after consultation between the Metropolitan Police, the Association of Chief Police Officers and the CPS, alters institutionalised police practice significantly, but its introduction took place without any trace of public or parliamentary debate.

REDUCING DISCRETION BY NEW 'CHARGING STANDARDS'

In August 1994 the police and the CPS introduced a new piece of machinery, 'charging standards', designed to standardise the decision to charge throughout the country. The first such standards were for assault. (*Justice of the Peace*, 20 August 1994, pp 554 – 55.)

The standards defined the degree of injury that would justify charges respectively of common assault (Criminal Justice Act 1988 s 37), assault occasioning actual bodily harm (CJA 1988, s 47, 'ABH'), unlawful wounding/inflicting grievous bodily harm (Offences Against the Person Act 1861, s 20, 'GBH') and wounding/causing grievous bodily harm with intent (OAPA 1861, s 18).

But although the motive for this innovation was stated to be to increase consistency of decision making it seemed likely that there were other more questionable reasons behind the decision. One was to minimise the occasions when the CPS incurred the anger of the police by reducing charges. If they were reduced initially by the police this problem did not arise. Another, probably much more important, was to reduce costs especially by increasing the number of cases charged as common assault which can only be tried summarily. The concern expressed in some quarters was that the overall effect would be to downgrade offences. (See for instance FG Davies, 'CPS Charging Standards: A Cynic's View', *Justice of the Peace*, 1 April 1995, p 203.) Another concern expressed was that in many cases police officers might arrest someone for ABH knowing full well that he would be charged only with common assault which is not an arrestable offence. This would be an abuse of power. 'The charge should relate to the evidence available, not to a set of instructions. Parliament intended the custody officer to charge according to the evidence. If there is to be a change in this, it is to be made by Parliament not by an agreement between the police and the prosecutor.' (J Woods, 'The Metropolitan Police Assault – Charging Offences – Are they Based on Law?', *Justice of the Peace*, 21 January 1995, p 43.)

The Glidewell Report (1998, p 203 above) said, 'We are very much in favour of Charging Standards as a useful guide to both members of the police and the CPS', though it did have some reservations about the wording of the standards (p 83). On the question of downgrading of offences, Glidewell said that although it suspected that charges were sometimes downgraded when they should not be, it had no evidence on the question. It noted that charges were only rarely upgraded. Downgrading was usually where the defendant was pleading guilty (pp 84-85).

At the time of writing it was not clear what would be the future for Case Disposal and Charging Standards in the new regime where the CPS would take over the main role in the laying of charges.

CAUTIONING AS AN ALTERNATIVE TO PROSECUTION

An important form of prosecution discretion is whether to caution or to prosecute offenders. A police caution is a formal warning, given orally by a senior police officer in uniform, to a person who admits his guilt. This is distinct from an informal warning. The caution becomes part of that person's record and can be referred to in subsequent court proceedings.(Technically a caution is not a conviction, but if it is cited in subsequent proceedings its effect may be like that of a previous conviction.[142])

An informal caution does not become part of the offender's record and cannot be mentioned in later proceedings. A caution cannot be made dependent on the offender complying with some requirement or performance of some task. It is technically not a sentence. (In some force areas there are 'caution plus' schemes under which the suspect agrees voluntarily to make reparation or pay compensation or to undertake counselling or other help but these schemes are only slowly becoming official.)

Cautioning of juveniles has been a part of the system for many years. It has only fairly recently started to be important for adults as well. In the mid-1980s the Home Office officially encouraged cautioning. (See Home Office, 'Cautioning by the Police', Consultative Document, 1984.) A Home Office circular in 1985 said: 'There is no rule of law that suspected offenders must be prosecuted. It has long been recognized in the case of juveniles that there may be positive advantages for society as well as for the individual in using prosecution as a last resort. Cautioning provides an important alternative to prosecution in the case of juvenile offending; it also represents a possible course of action in the case of adults.' (Home Office Circular, 14/1985, *The Cautioning of Offenders.*)

---

142   See Judge Richard May, 'The Legal Effect of a Police Caution' (1997) *Criminal Law Review*, pp 491-3; and R Evans, 'Challenging a Police Caution using Judicial Review' [1996] pp 104-08. For a warning about the unreliability of cautions and therefore the danger of treating them like previous convictions by citing them in subsequent proceedings see *Criminal Law Review* [1996] 453.

But practice varied considerably from force to force.[143] The Runciman Royal Commission on Criminal Justice recommended that cautioning practice should be 'subject to national guidelines and applied more consistently across police force areas than appears to be the case' (Report, p 82, para 57). Police cautioning, it thought, should be governed by statute, under which national guidelines, drawn up in consultation with the CPS and police service among others, should be laid down in regulations (ibid).

The Home Office guidelines on cautioning were changed in 1990, largely because of the research showing wide variations in cautioning rates between forces. They were also partly the result of a drop in cautions of persons over 17. Under the new guidelines cautioning was supposed to be considered where there was evidence of guilt sufficient to give a realistic prospect of conviction and an admission of guilt and consent to the caution by the offender or in the case of a juvenile by his parent. The criteria for cautioning were the same as before: the nature of the offence, the likely penalty, the offender's age and health, and his or her criminal record and attitude towards the offence. The presumption in favour of not prosecuting juveniles and the elderly was now to be extended also 'to other groups – young adults and adults alike – where the criteria for caution are met'.

However, Mr Michael Howard, who became Home Secretary in 1993, took a less positive view of cautioning at least for more serious offences. His tougher approach was reflected in a new circular (18/1994) issued in March 1994 which replaced and cancelled the 1990 circular. Its purpose was to provide guidance on cautioning and in particular 'to discourage the use of cautions in inappropriate cases, for example for offences which are triable on indictment only; to seek greater consistency between police forces; and to promote the better recording of cautions' (para 1).

The circular said that, despite earlier discouragement of cautions for the most serious offences, cautions had been administered for offences as serious as attempted murder and rape. This 'undermines the credibility of the disposal' (para 5).

See further C Wilkinson and R Evans, 'Police Cautioning of Juveniles' (1990) *Criminal Law Review*, p 165; D Westwood, 'The Effects of Home Office Guidelines on the Cautioning of Offenders' (1991) *Criminal Law Review*, p 591; R Evans, 'Police Cautioning and the Young Adult Offender' (1991) *Criminal Law Review*, p 598; M McConville and A Sanders, 'Fairness and the CPS', 31 January 1992, p 120; S Uglow, A Dart, A Bottomley and C Hale, 'Cautioning Juveniles-Multi-Agency Impotence' (1992) *Criminal Law Review*, p 632 and K Soothill, B Francis, B Sanderson,' A Cautionary tale: the Sex Offenders Act 1997, the Police and Cautions', (1997) *Criminal Law Review*, pp 482-90.

---

[143] This was shown by research done for the Philips Royal Commission (1981, Cmnd 8092 – I, App 23, p 203.) See also annual *Criminal Statistics* and H Giller and Norman Tutt, 'The Police Cautioning of Juveniles: The Practice of Diversity' (1983) *Criminal Law Review*, pp 587 – 95; (1987) *Criminal Law Review* pp 367–74.

For a mainly positive assessment of a new form of cautioning where the victim and others affected by an offence are invited to participate in a cautioning session see R Young and B Goold, 'Restorative Police Cautioning in Aylesbury – From Degrading to Reintegrative Shaming Ceremonies?' [1999] *Criminal Law Review*, pp 126-38.

Conditional cautions The Criminal Justice Bill 2002/03 introduced a new concept of conditional cautions for adults – namely a caution with conditions attached. The conditions must be ones which have either or both of the objectives of reparation for the offence or rehabilitation of the offender (cl 22). The requirements are: (1) that the CPS consider that there is sufficient evidence to charge the individual; and (2) the individual signs a document admitting that he committed the offence, his consent to the cautions and the conditions imposed (cl 23). Failure without reasonable excuse to comply with the conditions makes the person liable to prosecution for the offence (cl 24). The Home Secretary must produce a Code of Practice with the criteria for conditional cautions, how they are to be given, by whom, the conditions that may be imposed, for what period and the arrangements for monitoring (cl 25).

Replacing cautions for juveniles with 'reprimands' and 'warnings' – Crime and Disorder Act 1998

The Crime and Disorder Act 1998 (CDA 1998), ss 65 and 66 provided for the replacement of cautions of juveniles by 'reprimands and warnings'. As has been pointed out, this was partly an exercise in semantics since the 'reprimand' is the equivalent of the old-style first caution – a term that is retained for over 18-year-olds.[144] But s 65(3) provides that if the offender has previously been reprimanded he cannot be reprimanded a second time unless the offence was committed two years after the last warning – and no one can be warned more than twice. The 'warning' ('final warning') is similar to what has come to be called 'caution plus' schemes which provide some kind of counselling, mentoring or other community support for the young person. The offender is referred to a Youth Offending Team (YOT)[145] which will determine whether a rehabilitation programme is appropriate. This may involve some form of mediation. The Home Office has indicated support for the restorative-cautioning initiative pioneered in the Thames Valley area. A first offence by a young offender can therefore be met with a reprimand, a final warning or criminal charges depending on its seriousness. After a reprimand, a further offence leads either to a warning or charge. Following a warning, any further offences will normally result in a charge being brought.

For an early and highly critical assessment see R Evans and K Puech, ' Reprimands and Warnings: Populist Punitiveness or Restorative Justice?' [2001] *Criminal Law Review*, pp 794-805. Their conclusion was that rather than providing an opportunity

[144]   J Dignan, 'The Crime and Disorder Act and the Prospects for Restorative Justice', (1999) *Criminal Law Review*, pp 48,51.
[145]   Under CDA 1998, s 39.

for new style restorative justice, 'the legislation is punitive and controlling in principle and in practice' (p 804). Many of the young people and YOT workers saw the warning scheme as 'arbitrary, unfair, and disproportionate especially as it may involve compulsory participation in a rehabilitation (change) programme' (ibid). It suggested that that there was a considerable gap between the rhetoric of the Home Office and the Youth Justice Board and what was actually happening on the ground.

(f)   Discontinuance by the CPS

One of the stated objectives for setting up the CPS was better and earlier identification of cases that for any reason should not go forward to prosecution. The 1983 White Paper *An Independent Prosecution Service for England and Wales* said the objectives of the CPS included the promotion of greater consistency of policy and uniformly high standards of case preparation and decision-making across the country. The effect, it was said: 'should be that cases which are unlikely to succeed should be weeded out at an early stage' (Cmnd 9074, p 14). But the CPS' power to drop a prosecution has given rise to much controversy.

The Code for Prosecutors states:

> Prosecutors may decide to continue with the original charges, to change the charges or sometimes to stop the case.

> Review is a continuing process so that Crown Prosecutors can take into account any change in circumstances. Wherever possible, they talk to the police first if they are thinking about changing the charges or stopping the proceedings. This gives the police the chance to provide more information that may affect the decision. The Crown Prosecution Service and the police work closely together to reach the right decision, but the final responsibility for the decision rests with the Crown Prosecution Service. [paras 3.1–2]

The CPS drops around 12%-13% of the cases. Is this too high, too low or about right? It is difficult to make a sensible judgment. The police often complain that the CPS drops too many cases, but there is also some evidence that it drops too few. (The *Crown Court Study* done for the Runciman Royal Commission showed that in the view of both prosecuting and defence barristers and of judges, the prosecution was weak in about one-fifth of contested cases and that over 80% of these cases ended in acquittal.[146])

Another possible indication comes from acquittal statistics. There are three kinds of acquittals – ordered acquittals , directed acquittals and jury acquittals. 'Ordered acquittals' are where the prosecution offers no evidence at all. The case is dropped at court because the prosecution decide at the last moment not to pursue it, perhaps

---

146   M Zander and P Henderson, *The Crown Court Study* (Royal Commission on Criminal Justice, Research Study No 19, 1993, pp 184 – 5, Table 6.20, 6.21).

because a crucial witness fails to turn up or refuses to give evidence. (The rules do not permit the CPS to discontinue a case between committal for trial by the magistrates and trial at the Crown Court. They must therefore go through the process of formally offering no evidence even in cases which their process of review has identified as too weak to continue.) 'Directed acquittals' are where the judge stops the case – usually half way, after a submission by the defence that the prosecution's case is not strong enough even to require a response. Jury acquittals are where the jury has deliberated and found the defendant not guilty. At first blush, ordered and directed acquittals seem to be in the category of weak cases that arguably could and should have been aborted earlier.

In the six years leading to the establishment of the CPS the proportion of acquittals that were either ordered or directed acquittals ranged from a low of 43% in 1982 to a high of 48% in 1985. It might have been expected that with the establishment of the CPS and its presumably better screening methods, the proportion of ordered and directed acquittals would go down. In fact, however, it went up It is now some two-thirds of all acquittals (In 1996 it was 62%. In 2001 it was 66% (See annual *Judicial Statistics*, Table 6.10).)

There have been a number of studies as to the reasons why cases are terminated by the CPS or by the court[147] and various initiatives have been tried – but it is not clear that much impact has yet been made on the issue.

(g)   Judicial control of police discretion in prosecution policy

The problem of controlling police discretion in regard to prosecuting has only rarely come before the courts. The first modern examples of importance were the cases brought by a private citizen, former Member of Parliament Mr Raymond Blackburn, to compel the police to enforce the gambling and then the obscenity laws.

R v Metropolitan Police Comr, ex p Blackburn [1968] 2 WLR 893 (Court of Appeal)

[In April 1966, a confidential instruction was issued to senior officers of the Metropolitan Police. Underlying this instruction was a policy decision not to take proceedings against clubs for breach of the gaming laws unless there were complaints of cheating or they had become the haunts of criminals. The applicant, being concerned at gaming in London clubs, brought proceedings for mandamus to get the Commissioner to withdraw the confidential instruction.]

---

[147]   See D Crisp and D Moxon, *Case Screening by the Crown Prosecution Service: How and Why Cases are Terminated*, Home Office Research Study 137, 1994; B Block, C Corbett and J Peay, *Ordered and Directed Acquittals in the Crown Court*, Royal Commission on Criminal Justice Research Study No 15, 1993; the study reported in CPS Annual Report, 1994 – 95, pp 7 – 8; and figures cited in the Glidewell Report, 1999 at p 90.

Lord Denning MR: the result of the police decision of 22 April 1966, was that thenceforward, in this great metropolis, the big gaming clubs were allowed to carry on without any interference by the police ...

The duty of the Commissioner of Police of the Metropolis

I hold it to be the duty of the Commissioner of Police in the Metropolis, as it is of every chief constable, to enforce the law of the land. He must take steps so to post his men that crimes may be detected; and that honest citizens may go about their affairs in peace. He must decide whether or not suspected persons are to be prosecuted; and, if need be, bring the prosecution or see that it is brought. But in all these things he is not the servant of anyone, save the law itself. No Minister of the Crown can tell him that he must, or must not, prosecute this man or that one. Nor can any police authority tell him so. The responsibility for law enforcement lies on him. He is answerable to the law and to the law alone. That appears sufficiently from *Fisher v Oldham Corpn*,[148] and *A-G for New South Wales v Perpetual Trustee Co Ltd*[149].

Although the chief officers of police are answerable to the law, there are many fields in which they have a discretion with which the law will not interfere. For instance, it is for the Commissioner of Police of the Metropolis, or the chief constable, as the case may be, to decide in any particular case whether inquiries should be pursued, or whether an arrest should be made or a prosecution brought. It must be for him to decide on the disposition of his force and the concentration of his resources on any particular crime or area. No court can or should give him directions on such a matter. He can also make policy decisions and give effect to them, as, for instance, was often done when prosecutions were not brought for attempted suicide. But there are some policy decisions with which, I think, the courts in a case can, if necessary, interfere. Suppose a chief constable were to issue a directive to his men that no person should be prosecuted for stealing any goods less than £100 in value. I should have thought that the court could countermand it. He would be failing in his duty to enforce the law.

... On 30 December 1967, the Commissioner issued a statement in which he said: 'It is the intention of the Metropolitan Police to enforce the law as it has been interpreted.' That implicitly revoked the policy decision of 22 April 1966; and the Commissioner by his counsel gave an undertaking to the court that the policy decision would be officially revoked. We were also told that immediate steps are being taken to consider the 'goings-on' in the big London clubs with a view to prosecution if there is anything unlawful. That is all that Mr Blackburn or anyone else can reasonably expect.

[148] [1930] 2 KB 364, 46 TLR 390.
[149] [1955] AC 457.

See also *R v Metropolitan Police Comr, ex p Blackburn (No 3)* [1973] 1 All ER 324 and *R v Chief Constable of Devon and Cornwall, ex p Central Electricity Generating Board* [1981] 3 All ER 826. In the second *Blackburn* case the applicant was again asking for mandamus to require the police to enforce the law – this time in respect of pornography. The application was refused on a showing by the Commissioner that he was doing his best to stem the tide of obscene publications. (A subsequent series of trials of senior members of the Obscene Publications Squad on corruption charges later suggested that the Court of Appeal had not been put wholly in the picture regarding the zeal with which the police discharged their duties in this area. But at the time nothing was known of this.)

In the second case, mandamus was sought by the Electricity Board to require the police to help clear squatters off ground that the Board wanted to survey as a site for a nuclear power station. The Chief Constable refused to help the Board to remove them on the ground that he had no statutory power of arrest in the circumstances nor any common law power of arrest since there had been no breach of the peace and none was anticipated, nor was there any unlawful assembly to disperse. The Court of Appeal held that since it was for the police on the spot and not the Court to decide when and how to exercise their power, mandamus would not be issued. In the event the police did move in a few days later with the Board, and the protesters were removed peaceably. [150]

REMEDIES FOR THE PROSECUTION'S FAILURE TO PROSECUTE

In *R v DPP, ex p C* [1995] 1 Cr App Rep 136 the Divisional Court, most unusually, allowed an application for judicial review of the decision of the CPS not to prosecute for buggery of a wife by a husband on the ground that the prosecutor had not had in mind certain relevant considerations. Several of the cases have involved ethnic minority complaints about the failure of the CPS to prosecute police officers involved in deaths in police custody of family members. [151]

For the argument that courts should be prepared to review prosecutorial decisions see generally, Y Dotan, 'Should Prosecutorial Discretion Enjoy Special Treatment in Judicial Review? A Comparative Analysis of the Law in England and Israel.' (1997) *Public Law*, pp 513-31.

In 1988, the House of Lords ruled that the police could not be held liable in negligence for failing to prevent crimes. There was no duty of care to individual members of the public to identify and apprehend an unknown criminal, even though

---

[150]   See also *Coxhead* [1986] Crim LR 251, CA; *R v General Council of the Bar, ex p Percival* [1990] 3 All ER 137, 149 – 52 , Div Ct: In *R v Chief Constable of Kent County Constabulary, ex p L* and *R v DPP, ex p B (a minor)* [1993] 1 All ER 756 Div Ct; *R v IRC, ex p Mead* [1993] 1 All ER 772; *R v Chief Constable of Sussex, ex p International Trader's Ferry* [1999] 1 All ER 129, HL.

[151]   See *R v DPP, ex p Manning* [2001] QB 330 in which the Divisional Court quashed the decision not to prosecute after a death in custody and M.Burton, '*Reviewing Crown Prosecution Service decisions not to prosecute*' [2001] Crim LR 374-84.

it was reasonably foreseeable that harm was likely to be caused to a member of the public if the criminal was not detected and apprehended. Even if such a duty did exist, it would be against the public interest to hold the police liable (*Hill v Chief Constable of West Yorkshire* [1988] 2 All ER 238, a case brought by relatives of one of the victims of Peter Sutcliffe, the 'Yorkshire Ripper').

But the principle on which this decision was based has been thrown into doubt by the ruling of the European Court of Human Rights in *Osman v United Kingdom* [1999] Crim LR 82, (1998) Times, 5 November. A teacher had formed an attachment to a 15-year-old pupil. He changed his name to that of the boy, broke windows at the family home and slashed car tyres. The school met with the police to discuss the matter. Eventually the teacher shot and killed the boy's father and seriously injured the boy. The Court of Appeal rejected an action for negligence against the police in light of the decision in *Hill*. The ECHR held unanimously that there had been a violation of art 6 of the Convention which guarantees a right to have one's civil rights and obligations determined by a court or tribunal. The ECHR accepted that in *Hill* there were sufficient public policy reasons for excluding liability. But in *Osman* the proximity test seemed to be satisfied, as the police appeared to have assumed some responsibility for the Osmans' safety. A blanket immunity for the police established by the House of Lords decision in *Hill* was therefore a disproportionate restriction on the applicant's right of access to a court. (For critical reaction see Lord Hoffmann, 'Human Rights and the House of Lords' (1999), 62 *Modern Law Review*, pp 159-67. See also Laura CH Hoyano, 'Policing Flawed Police Investigations: Unravelling the Blanket', (1999) *,Modern Law Review*, pp 912-36.) See now also *Menson v UK* (ECHR, Application No 47916/99) and discussion in P O'Connor QC and H Hill, 'Scrutinising the bill', *New Law Journal*, 1 August 2003, p 1194.

(h) Is the CPS 'independent of the police?

A central part of the case for the establishment of the CPS was that it should be more independent of the police. In one sense the CPS certainly is independent of the police in that it is the CPS that takes the decision whether to proceed with the case. Indeed, under the arrangements being established by the Criminal Justice Bill 2002/03 the CPS will in the future now commonly determine the charge from the very outset. But the police still play a crucial role which to a great extent constrains the CPS.

The entire investigation of the offence is in the hands of the police. The CPS gets the file prepared by the police and nothing much else. [152]

---

[152] In *R (on the application of Joseph) v DPP* [2001] Crim LR 489 the Divisional Court held that the CPS had been entitled to rely on summaries of video evidence given by the police which led it to discontinue the case despite the fact that in interview one of the alleged culprits admitted carrying a weapon which undermined the self-defence argument on which the CPS decision was based. The commentator in the *Criminal Law Review* wrote : 'This is simply another example of the dependence of the CPS on the accuracy and bona fides of the police in preparing and disclosing material' (p 490).

The Philips Royal Commission envisaged that the CPS would supervise and check the work of the police but in practice this does not happen and the Runciman Royal Commission did not recommend any change in that regard. One reason is simply the lack of manpower resources. Another is that it would generate tensions between the two agencies. Thirdly, since the CPS has no investigatory powers under the Act, it lacks the standing to do so. The role of the CPS is simply to vet the work done by the police which is inconsistent with performing an active supervisory role.

A study of over 1,000 cases by M McConville, A Sanders and R Leng, *The Case for the Prosecution* (Routledge, 1991) supports this view:

> Police influence over a case is said to be confined to the investigation and case preparation stages with ultimate decision making by the prosecutor applying rigorous tests of public interest and evidential sufficiency. The reality is a system of routinised decision-making embodying an overwhelming propensity to prosecute, bolstered by the presumption that earlier decisions were properly made and should not be overturned. The system is dominated throughout its stages by the interests and values of the police, with the CPS playing an essentially subordinate and reactive role [p 126].

> The image of the proposed prosecution service conjured by both sides of the debate was of a body which would *displace* the police from their central role in prosecution decision making and relegate the police to a new subservient role in investigating crime and preparing cases for the new prosecution service. The reality is of a Crown Prosecution Service which is in many respects subordinate to the police. The police retain total control over many key decisions, such as decisions to take no further action, informally warn and caution. [p 141].[153]

Even in Scotland where the prosecutors *do* have investigatory powers they tend to 'rubber stamp' most police decisions. Research as to how the Scottish system actually works showed that the fiscals prosecuted in about 92% of cases referred to them. They acted almost invariably on the basis of information supplied by the police. They had the power to ask for further information but rarely did so - in the study, in only 6% of cases. In other words the police largely determined the exercise of the fiscal's discretion as to whether to prosecute. In most cases the papers made it clear and the decision-making was largely routine. (In 63% of cases the decision was taken on the same day that the fiscal received the papers.) The real discretion of the fiscal came in the 'trial avoidance arrangements' – bargaining over a guilty plea to lesser charges in return for other more serious charges being dropped. (See S Moody and J Tombs, *Prosecution in the Public Interest*, Scottish Academic Press, 1982.)

---

[153]   Advice was sought in only 51 of the 711 prosecution decisions taken after the establishment of the CPS – and in 48 cases the advice was sought by one force which was simply continuing its pre-CPS practice of consulting lawyers (p 142) (ed).

At the time when the CPS was established it was regarded as vital that the new organisation be moved physically into its own buildings away from the police. But, as has been seen, the trend is now in the opposite direction toward co-location. Glidewell welcomed closer cooperation and did not think it threatened the independence of the prosecutor.('When they are working in close proximity to a police station and in association with one or more police officers, they will, we are confident, continue to maintain that professional independence' (p 132).)

THE THREE STAGES OF THE CPS' HISTORY

In January 2003, Lord Goldsmith QC, the Attorney-General, summed up what he described as the first two stages of the CPS' history.[154]

1986-1999 In this first stage the professional culture of the Crown Prosecution Service was established. It is marked, rightly, by a great emphasis on establishing the independence of the CPS from the police. It was essential to move from what had essentially been a solicitor/client relationship with the police to establish instead a culture of independence, and to bring home that a new organisation had come into being.

These were difficult times. The idea was good in concept, but the execution was poor. The CPS was undoubtedly under-resourced. The organisation itself struggled to find the right balance between local autonomy and central direction. It probably became over-bureaucratic. There was a long period of inadequate work, loss of public confidence, and a lack of self-worth. But despite all these pressures, a strong professional culture did develop. For much of this time, the training provision within the CPS was excellent. Guidance was produced on policy which helped to create a consistent approach to prosecutions throughout the country. The Code for Crown Prosecutors, though occasionally amended, has stood the test of time. The process and development of the CPS in this phase was entirely true to the recommendations and the reasoning of the Phillips Commission.

1999-2003 The second phase began in early-1999 after the present Government in its first term set about reform. It commissioned the Glidewell Report, and put its recommendations into effect. The CPS was restructured into 42 areas which matched police force boundaries... .

The process was started of creating Glidewell co-located units where much police and CPS work could be done under one roof, increasing efficiency and reducing bureaucracy.

In this phase too, this Government addressed the historic under-funding of the CPS. This chronic under-funding, which meant far too few Crown

---

[154]   Speech to the Crown Prosecution Service Senior Management Conference.

Prosecution staff having to do far too much work, has now been remedied by this Government. In 2001, the CPS received a net increase in funds of 23%. This year it received a further 6% increase in real terms and the figure for the forthcoming financial year is 9% in real terms. These are substantial figures. A nearly 40% increase in resources is a substantial uplift. It takes time for extra resources to translate into additional staff recruited, trained and in post, especially in organisations where a very high degree of professional expertise is required. So we are only now starting to see the benefits of these extra resources in terms of additional, qualified staff on the ground, delivering results.

The next period heralded the third stage for the CPS.

I see the third stage of the CPS especially as one in which the CPS is more outward facing and outcome focused. It is one in which the CPS has an enhanced role at every stage of the criminal process working in cooperation with our criminal justice partners while retaining that independence of prosecution decision-making which is the hallmark of the CPS. But it also means increasing the efficiency and the accountability which were also part of its reason for being.

Some of it would involve a change of culture. Lord Goldsmith listed the features of the new era:

Getting the cases right from the start: This is the most important part of what happens later. The CPS will have an increased role through a new relationship of cooperation between the police and the CPS. The Criminal Justice Bill will give the CPS the responsibility for determining the charge in all but routine cases.

Building on the Glidewell co-location and so improving the administration of cases; reducing bureaucracy; getting operational officers in touch with operational lawyers.

Improving the review of cases: the focus of review will be not only to keep careful track of changes which are taking place to see whether cases should be continued but seeing what should be done to strengthen weak cases. This is a very important element and part of the culture change needed.

Taking charge of witnesses: far too many cases fail because witnesses do not turn up to give evidence. Changing this is a key part of improving performance. The West Midlands pilot will show the potentials for one agency to be in the lead in handling witnesses and that this agency should be the CPS.

Seeing that the victim's voice is heard in sentencing: I believe that prosecutors need to play a larger role in the sentencing of offenders: we need to be clear all the aggravating features of a case are drawn to the attention of the judge; prosecutors need to be ready and willing to draw to the attention of the Court the relevant sentencing authorities; they will ensure that the confiscation provisions of the law are properly and robustly enforced. Ensuring victims' personal statements are taken into account and challenging unfair and inaccurate mitigation. [The traditional role of the prosecution in sentencing in England has been either to remain totally silent or to confine any participation to simply drawing the court's attention to its powers. (ed)]

And the new powers will give a role to the prosecutors even at the outset: the new power for prosecutors' cautions in the Criminal Justice Bill [see below (ed)] and greater emphasis on getting cases in the right court as changes to magistrates' sentencing powers take place means prosecutors will have from the start to be concerned with what the eventual disposal ought to be.

The past concentration on establishing a professional standard of fairness and independence might have meant that it had 'fallen into the trap of suggesting that the CPS is concerned only with process and not with outcome'.

But now, given the legislative changes that are planned, and the resources that are being provided, you have the room and the ability to come into your own. Why should not prosecutors and the public see you as fighters for justice, your role being to ensure that the guilty are brought to justice – as part of the key safeguards in fighting crime and keeping the streets safe? Of course that does not mean using the means that are not fair. Being fair is a key part of what the CPS does and of maintaining public confidence in it. But you can be firm as well as fair; effective in seeing the guilty brought to account as well as just.

Ensuring that the guilty are brought to justice will involve, of course, preventing the innocent getting into the system. The CPS has a significant role in preventing such miscarriages of justice, through the proper application of the Code tests and through the proper application of disclosure. This reflects the CPS contribution to protecting the rights of defendants as part of our target on raising public confidence.

Between that type of case and those cases which are very strong there is of course a middle ground where a prosecution is properly brought but an acquittal may properly be obtained, because of course it is not right that every case should result in a conviction. To achieve that result, prosecutors would have to be very cautious about the cases that they brought. They would only prosecute certainties, and that would result in injustice as well, because it would mean that many cases that should have been brought before the court would not be brought.

Lord Goldsmith concluded his speech:

... for too long the CPS has been seen as the ones at the back of the criminal justice system: the bit between the people who do the real work: the investigators and those who try cases. That is unfair and untrue. You are the ones who take the brunt if things go wrong in court, but miss out on praise if things go well.

The prosecutor will now come centre stage: the decision-makers, the people who decide which cases should be brought to court, and bring them home.

I see the image of the prosecutor, not as someone at the back of the court, but as the visible, committed fighter for justice, receiving a stream of police officers to give sound and well-received advice; respected in court as they give advice to magistrates on which cases they should keep and which they should send to the Crown Court; efficiently and relentlessly bringing cases to court in good order and bringing the defence up to the mark; and increasingly in the Crown Court as they help judges manage cases and raise the quality of rulings.

(j)   Other prosecutors

THE LAW OFFICERS

The Attorney-General (assisted by the Solicitor-General) has two main functions in respect of prosecutions. First, he possesses the power to enter a *nolle prosequi* in cases tried on indictment, which has the effect of stopping the proceedings. Secondly, he can give or refuse his permission (known as *fiat*) in the considerable number of cases where by statute his consent is required for a prosecution. (The Director of Public Prosecutions likewise is required by many statutes to give permission before a prosecution can be brought.) The Law Commission has reported on the requirement of consent of the Attorney-General or of the Director of Public Prosecutions. It found that it was difficult to discover a rational basis for some of them and recommended that such requirements be removed save in those categories of case where it was still required in the public interest. [155] Lord Justice Auld in his Review agreed. [156] But so far the Government has not acted on the recommendation. (On whether the DPP should publicise the criteria for prosecution in cases of assisted suicide see the view of the DPP himself – Sir David Calvert-Smith and S O'Doherty, ' Legislative Technique and Human Rights: A response' [2003] *Criminal Law Review*, p 384.

PROSECUTION BY PUBLIC BODIES

Many prosecutions are conducted by government departments, nationalised industries, local authorities and other statutory bodies. A study done for the Philips Royal Commission on Criminal Procedure showed that they amounted to something like one-quarter of all prosecutions. Prosecutions were conducted, in order of frequency, by: the Post Office (mainly for television-licence offences); the British Transport Police (eg for non-payment of fares); the Department of the Environment (in relation to vehicle excise licences); the Department of Social Security (for social security frauds); HM Customs and Excise; and Regional Traffic Commissioners (for offences connected with the use of heavy lorries). Other public bodies with some

[155]   *Consents to Prosecution*, Law Comm No 255, 1998.
[156]   Chapter 10, para s 51-52.

prosecution functions included the Health and Safety at Work Inspectorate, Water Authorities, the Inland Revenue, Department of Trade, and Ministry of Agriculture. (See KW Lidstone, R Hogg and F Sutcliffe, 'Prosecutions by Private Individuals and Non-Police Agencies', *Royal Commission on Criminal Procedure, Research Study No 10*, 1980, Table 2.3, p 15.) Following a devastating review of Customs and Excise prosecutions it was announced in July 2003 that their power to prosecute was to be given to a new independent body - see *New Law Journal*, 25 July 2003, p 1135.

Recent research has shown that there are extraordinary regional variations in such prosecutions. Analysis of all 9,689 prosecutions brought by organisations other than the CPS at three magistrates' courts in London, Milton Keynes and Newcastle showed that the 2,320 cases prosecuted by the Department of Transport and DVLA, 80% were in Milton Keynes and only 1% was in the London court. Of the 97 cases brought by the Environment Agency, 89% were in the Newcastle court. (G Slapper, *Organisational Prosecutions*, Ashgate, 2001.)

PRIVATE PROSECUTIONS

A private person can bring a prosecution even though he has no direct interest in the matter. (So private bodies such as the NSPCC or NSPCA can bring prosecutions.) The private prosecutor must persuade a magistrate to issue a summons which will be refused if it appears to be a vexatious or improper proceeding. He would also normally have to bear his own costs and if the prosecution fails he might in addition have to pay something in respect of the costs of the defence. The DPP has the right to take over a private prosecution and the Attorney-General has the power to stop one by entering a *nolle prosequi*.

A study done for the Philips Royal Commission showed that private prosecutions were 2.4% of all prosecutions. [157] The great majority were for common assault. In some areas the police had a policy of not prosecuting in shoplifting cases and all prosecutions for this offence were brought by retail stores.

When the CPS refuses to prosecute, or refuses to bring appropriate charges, sometimes the victim (or in cases of death, a relative) wants to bring a private prosecution. In *R v Tower Bridge Metropolitan Stipendiary Magistrate, ex p Chaudhry* [1994] 1 All ER 44 the mother of the deceased victim of a driving accident tried to get a summons for causing death by reckless driving. The driver had been charged with summary only traffic offences. The Divisional Court held that the decision whether to allow a private prosecution to go forward should be based on consideration of various matters. One was whether the case had already been investigated by a responsible prosecuting authority which was pursuing what it considered to be appropriate charges. Regard should be had to para 7 of the Code for Crown Prosecutors – whether the charges reflect the seriousness of the offence, give the

---

[157]   Lidstone, Hogg and Sutcliffe, *Prosecutions by Private Individuals and Non-Police Agencies*, Royal Commission on Criminal Procedure, Research Study No 10, 1981 Table 2.13, p 23.

court sufficient sentencing powers and whether the charges can be presented in a clear and simple manner. A second consideration would be whether the issue of a summons for a more serious offence would override the discretion of the CPS in a way that would be oppressive to the defendant. Thirdly, the court should bear in mind that the DPP could always intervene to discontinue the proceedings under s 6(2) of the Prosecution of Offences Act 1985 or to reduce the charges under s 23. Lord Justice Kennedy suggested that there would have to be special circumstances 'such as apparent bad faith on the part of the public prosecutor' (at p 51). The court refused the application for judicial review. See also *R v Bow Street Stipendiary Magistrate, ex p South Coast Shipping Co Ltd* [1993] 1 All ER 219.

In 1995 the family of 18-year-old Stephen Lawrence succeeded in launching a private prosecution for murder after the CPS dropped charges against two teenagers who had been charged with the killing. It was believed to be the first time that a private prosecution had been brought in this country in a murder case. Stephen Lawrence, who was black, was stabbed by a white gang while waiting for a bus in South East London in April 1993. The murder aroused much public attention and a fund was established to pay for the private prosecution. However, in the event, the trial of the three defendants collapsed after the judge ruled that crucial eye-witness evidence for the prosecution was too unreliable to be put before the jury. (See national press 26 April 1996.) (For discussion of the legal issues see Edward Saunders, 'Private prosecutions by the victims of violent crime', *New Law Journal*, 29 September 1994, p 1423. For sharp criticism of the Lawrence family's lawyers for having launched a private prosecution that was bound to fail see M Mears, 'Mansfield, Kamlish and Khan - the three wise men', *New Law Journal*, 26 March, 1999, p 463.) See further on this subject, J Kodwo Bentil, 'The Unenviable Task of Seeking to Institute a Private Prosecution' 154 *Justice of the Peace*, 26 May 1990, p 324.

See also *Elguzouli-Daf v Metropolitan Police Comr* [1995] 1 All ER 833, CA, holding that the CPS owes no duty of care toward defendants such that they could sue for failure to dismiss charges earlier where the forensic evidence had been discredited.

Lord Justice Auld in his Review said that although a strong case had been advanced for abolition of the right of private prosecution he was not inclined to recommend it. It was not much used but 'its strength might lie in its availability when needed rather than in the extent of its use'. [158] But in his view there was need for an effective system for alerting the DPP to the initiation of such prosecutions, so that he could consider his power to intervene. He recommended that any court which authorised the initiation of a private prosecution should be required to notify the DPP of it in writing.[159]

[158]   Chapter 10, para 48, p 414.
[159]   Chapter 10, para 48, p 415.

(k)   Duties of prosecuting lawyers

The classic statement on the role and approach of prosecuting counsel was expressed by a judge as long ago as 1865 – they 'are to regard themselves as ministers of justice, and not to struggle for a conviction' [160].

At the time of the establishment of the Crown Prosecution Service, the Bar set up a committee on the duties and obligations of counsel when conducting a prosecution. The chairman was Mr Justice Farquharson, as he then was. The Committee produced what have come to be called the Farquharson Guidelines. [161] The introductory passage of the 1986 Guidelines referred to the special position of prosecution counsel:

> There is no doubt that the obligations of prosecution counsel are different from those of counsel instructed for the defence in a criminal case or of counsel instructed in civil matters. His duties are wider both to the court and to the public at large. Furthermore, having regard to his duty to present the case for the prosecution fairly to the jury he has a greater independence of those instructing him than that enjoyed by other counsel. It is well known to every practitioner that counsel for the prosecution must conduct his case moderately, albeit firmly. He must not strive unfairly to obtain a conviction; he must not press his case beyond the limits which the evidence permits; he must not invite the jury to convict on evidence which in his own judgment no longer sustains the charge laid in the indictment. If the evidence of a witness is undermined or severely blemished in the course of cross-examination, prosecution counsel must not present him to the jury as worthy of a credibility he no longer enjoys. Many of the important decisions counsel for the prosecution has to make arise during the trial itself, and then because he has the conduct of the prosecution case, he is the person best fitted to make them. Information will be available to him and not, for example, to the judge of the reliability and background of the witnesses he is proposing to call. It is for these reasons that great responsibility is placed upon prosecution counsel and although his description as a 'minister of justice' may sound pompous to modern ears it accurately describes the way in which he should discharge his function.

The Farquharson Guidelines were reissued in a revised version in 2002.[162] Strangely, the new version did not include anything about the fundamental issues regarding prosecuting counsel's role explained in the original text. But there can be no doubt that the fundamental principle remains unchanged.

At the core of the principle is that prosecution counsel is independent. This is a vital part of the role of the barrister in private practice and most of all for prosecution

---

[160]   *Puddick* (1865) 4 F & F 497, per Crompton J.
[161]   The original Guidelines were published in the *Law Society's Gazette*, 26 November 1986, p 3599.
[162]   Published on the CPS website at www.cps.gov.uk and the Criminal Bar's website at www.criminalbar.com.

counsel. In his introduction to the revised version of the Guidelines the Lord Chief Justice said that the prosecution advocate 'plays an important public role and as such may be considered a cornerstone of an open and fair criminal justice system'. He cannot be that cornerstone unless he is independent. But what does independence of prosecution counsel mean in practice?

THE PROSECUTOR AND THOSE INSTRUCTING HIM

One critical aspect of the issue is prosecuting counsel's relationship with those instructing him – the CPS and, through the CPS, the police. To what extent is counsel free to take what he considers to be the right decisions in regard to the case he is prosecuting?

The 1986 Guidelines said on this issue that in case of disagreement between counsel and those instructing him, counsel's view should prevail subject to the right of the CPS to take a second opinion or to withdraw the instructions and brief another barrister. From a certain point of time, however, it would no longer be practicable to withdraw instructions.

The 2002 revised Guidelines laid down detailed guidance [163]:

The Role and Responsibilities of the Prosecution Advocate

1. (a)*Pre-trial preparation* It is the duty of Prosecution Counsel to read the Instructions delivered to him expeditiously and to advise or to confer with those instructing him on all aspects of the case well before its commencement. . .

2. (b) *Withdrawal of Instructions* A solicitor who has briefed Counsel to prosecute may withdraw his instructions before the commencement of the trial up to the point when it becomes impracticable to do so, if he disagrees with the advice given by Counsel or for any other proper professional reason. . . .

3. (c) *Presentation and conduct* While he remains instructed it is for Counsel to take all necessary decisions in the presentation and general conduct of the prosecution. . . .

4. (d) *Policy decisions* Where matters of policy fall to be decided after the point indicated in (b) above (including offering no evidence on the indictment or on a particular count, or on the acceptance of pleas to lesser counts), it is the duty of Counsel to consult his Instructing Solicitor/ Crown Prosecutor whose views at this stage are of crucial importance. . . .

---

[163] For reasons of economy of space, the extract that follows only states each main proposition without the explanatory paragraphs.

(e) In the rare case where Counsel and his Instructing Solicitor are unable to agree on a matter of policy, it is subject to (g) below, for Prosecution Counsel to make the necessary decisions. . . .

(f) *Attorney-General* Where Counsel has taken a decision on a matter of policy with which his Instructing Solicitor has not agreed, then it would be appropriate for the Attorney-General to require Counsel to submit to him a written report of all the circumstances, including his reasons for disagreeing with those who instruct him. . . .

5. (g) *Change of advice* When Counsel has had the opportunity to prepare his brief and to confer with those instructing him, but at the last moment before trial unexpectedly advises that the case should not proceed or that pleas to lesser offences should be accepted, and his Instructing Solicitor does not accept such advice, Counsel should apply for an adjournment if instructed to do so [to permit other counsel to be instructed].. . .

6. (h) *Prosecution's advocate's role in decision making at trial* Subject to the above, it is for Prosecution Counsel to decide whether to offer no evidence on a particular count or on the indictment as a whole and whether to accept pleas to a lesser count or counts. . . .

THE BARRISTER AND THE JUDGE

The Farquharson Guidelines also deal with the relationship between prosecuting counsel and the judge especially as to whether counsel is right to accept a plea to a lesser charge. The revised Guidelines in 2003 restated the position set out in the original version in 1986:

7.(i) If Prosecution Counsel invites the Judge to approve the course he is proposing to take, then he must abide by the judge's decision. . . .

(j) If Prosecution Counsel does not invite the Judge's approval of his decision, it is open to the Judge to express his dissent with the course proposed and invite Counsel to reconsider the matter with those instructing him, but having done so, the final decision remains with Counsel. . . .

(k) In an extreme case where the Judge is of the opinion that the course proposed by Counsel would lead to serious injustice, he may decline to proceed with the case until Counsel has consulted with either the Director [of Public Prosecutions[164]] . . .

Barrister David Jeremy, while welcoming the new Guidelines, expressed anxiety as to whether they would operate as intended. Writing in the *Criminal Bar Association*

---

[164] Commonly referred to simple as 'the Director'.

Newsletter [165] he claimed that the independence of the prosecuting barrister had been ignored by both the Bar Council and the Crown Prosecution Service:

> When it comes to the important policy questions such as acceptance of plea, or continuing with a prosecution, a whole generation of barristers has grown up with the idea that they are no more than a conduit between the CPS and the defendant. The pantomime of experienced counsel explaining a serious case over the telephone to a CPS lawyer, who may be totally unfettered by knowledge of the case, and then awaiting the latter's 'instructions', sometimes without even being asked to give his own opinion, has brought the prosecution process into disrepute. It fails to make use of the expertise of the Bar. And it renders the CPS vulnerable to defensive decision-making, That is decision making that is motivated by a desire to conceal errors or omissions, that gives too much weight to the views of others such as the police, or that simply seeks the easiest option
> ...
>
> The reason why we have been reduced to this situation is presumably because the Crown Prosecution Service perceives a need to appear to be in sole control of decision-making, and the Bar in turn has paid excessive regard to the fact that the CPS is a provider of work. By being too fearful of where the next brief is coming from, we have contributed to the abandonment of any valid claim to be independent prosecutors.

For a valuable review of many of the relevant problems see M Blake and A Ashworth 'Some Ethical Issues in Prosecuting and Defending Criminal Cases' [1998] *Criminal Law Review*, pp 16-34. The authors consider a variety of issues: defending a person believed to be guilty; believing that perjury has been committed; the lawyer knows that an error of law or fact has been made which favours the other side; the defence lawyer thinks the client would be better advised to plead guilty but the client wishes to plead not guilty; the client and his lawyer disagree as to how to conduct the defence; the prosecutor realises that evidence has been obtained unfairly; the prosecutor negotiates for a guilty plea even though he suspects that the prosecution case would fail.

6. Bail or remand in custody

There are many reasons for concern as to whether accused persons should be held in custody while their cases are still pending. Remand in custody for someone who has not yet been convicted is despite the fact that he is formally presumed to be innocent. To be remanded in custody is a serious matter for the person concerned.

Remand prisoners are disadvantaged in preparing their cases for trial. The remand prisoner will be hindered in getting access to lawyers to prepare his defence, in

---

[165]   June 2002, 3,4.

looking for witnesses and collecting evidence or preparing evidence in mitigation of sentence. If the prison where he is held is remote, he may find that lawyers are not willing to come there at all. Even when it is relatively close to main centres of population he will find it difficult to have the kind of access to advisers that would be possible if he were at liberty. If someone is sent to the prison it is often a clerk rather than a qualified solicitor just because of the amount of time involved in making the visit.

There is evidence that, *other things being equal*, those who are held in custody are more likely to plead guilty, to be found guilty and to be given a custodial sentence than those who are on bail. In other words, the mere fact of being imprisoned seems to have an effect on one's prospects in the criminal justice system. (See AK Bottomley, *Decisions in the Penal Process*, Martin Robertson, 1973, pp 88 – 93.)

Also, the defendant in custody is unable to continue with his normal life, may lose his job, may fall behind in paying rent and both he and his family may suffer other financial and other practical difficulties, as well as obvious emotional upset or even trauma. The National Association for the Care and Resettlement of Offenders (NACRO) carried out a study based on interviews in 1991 and 1992 with 3,449 prisoners in eight male and two female prisons. Nearly one third of the sample (31%) were on remand. Two-fifths of the remand prisoners had lost their homes as a result of being in prison. Over one third (35%) of the remand prisoners had lost jobs through being imprisoned. ('Bail-Some Current Issues', Penal Affairs Consortium, October 1995, p 2 –referred to here as the 'Penal Affairs Consortium Paper, 1995'). A Home Office study of 415 unconvicted prisoners at Brixton, Holloway and Feltham stated that the prisoners reported problems with depression (59%), loneliness (49%), relationships with partners (45% of those who had partners). ('The Welfare Needs of Unconvicted Prisoners' 1994, Home Office Research and Planning Unit Paper No 81 – cited in the Penal Affairs Consortium Paper, 1995, pp 2–3.)

The suicide rate of remand prisoners is significantly higher than the rate for prisoners who are not on remand. Between 1990 and 1994, remand prisoners were between a fifth and a quarter of the prison population but they accounted for over half the suicides (122 out of 240) – Penal Affairs Consortium paper, 1995, p 3. It is generally assumed that the reason is the anxiety and uncertainty of the situation of awaiting trial or sentence, the higher proportion of mental disturbance among remand prisoners and the depressing effect of the poor conditions and restricted regimes in which remand prisoners are held.

Remand prisoners are a serious issue also from the point of view of prison overcrowding. Remand prisoners who have not yet been convicted or are awaiting sentence make up around one-fifth of the prison population. (Of these, roughly, two-thirds are unconvicted, the remaining third are awaiting sentence.) Because of the rapid turn-over of remand prisoners, they are, of course, an even higher proportion of all *receptions* into prison. Remand prisoners may even be held in police station cells for lack of space in the prisons.

Conditions in prisons for remand prisoners are theoretically better than for convicted prisoners. They are allowed more visits; they can send more letters; they can wear their own clothes and be attended by a doctor of their own choice (provided they meet the cost); they can work if they wish like convicted prisoners but cannot be required to do so; they cannot be required to have their hair cut; they can have more cigarettes and may use private cash for purchases from the prison shop. But in practice the regime for remand prisoners is in most ways worse than for those who have been convicted. A paper presented in 1992 to the Criminal Justice Consultative Committee prepared by the Director General of the Prison Service (referred to here as 'The Director General's paper') stated, 'Taken as a whole, however, the regime for unconvicted prisoners is in practice far from satisfactory, and is often worse than for the convicted. A variety of factors contribute to this, including antiquated accommodation, a transient and sometimes volatile population, and the pressures placed on establishments by the demands of courts and other work' (para 4.3). In many prisons they are locked in their cells as much as 23-hours a day.

The Director General's paper included a Statement on Unconvicted Prisoners which he said reflected a model regime that had been agreed by the Prisons Board and Ministers (para 7.9). It said that unconvicted prisoners 'are presumed to be innocent'. It continued:

> Subject to the duty to hold them and deliver them to court securely and to the need to maintain order in establishments, they will be treated accordingly and, in particular, will be allowed all reasonable facilities to: seek release on bail; preserve their accommodation and employment; prepare for trial; maintain contact with relatives and friends; pursue legitimate business and social interests; obtain help with personal problems. They will receive health care appropriate to their needs. They will have opportunities for education, religious observance, exercise and recreation and, where possible, for training and work.

But the Director General candidly admitted that this represented hope not reality:

> The model regime has been agreed by the Prisons Board and Ministers. But it is important to be clear about its status. It represents the sort of regime we believe that we ought to offer prisoners, not what we feel fully equipped to offer them at the moment.

It is unfortunately the case that the model regime bears little, if any, relation to the situation in the prisons today.

The question of bail arises in two situations, the police station and the court – and in future will also arise in the street:

(a) Bail on the street

The Criminal Justice Bill 2002/03 introduced the radically new concept of bail granted by a police officer in the street. The Explanatory Notes accompanying the

Bill[166] (para 99) said this 'provides the police with additional flexibility following arrest and the scope to remain on patrol where there is no immediate need to deal with the person concerned at the [police] station'. It was intended to allow the police 'to plan their work more effectively by giving them new discretion to decide exactly when and where an arrested person should attend at a police station for interview' (para 92).

Clause 3 of the Bill amends s 30 of the Police and Criminal Evidence Act 1984 which requires the police to take an arrested person to a police station. The arrested person must be given a written notice stating the offence for which he was arrested and the ground[167]. If he is not told at that time where and when he must attend at a police station he must be so informed later. No condition other than attendance at a police station may be imposed. Failure to attend at the specified time makes the person liable to arrest.

(b)   Bail from the police station

If a person is arrested on a warrant, the warrant will state whether he is to be held by the police in custody or released on bail. But if, as is much more common, he is arrested without a warrant the police will have to decide whether or not to release the suspect after they have charged him. PACE lays on the custody officer the duty to consider whether further detention is appropriate. Before a suspect has been charged, he can only be detained in the police station if the custody officer reasonably thinks that such detention is 'necessary to secure or preserve evidence relating to an offence for which he is under arrest or to obtain such evidence by questioning him' (s 37(2)). There is no distinction drawn between serious and other offences.

After a person has been charged, he has to be released from the police station unless his name and address are not known or the custody officer reasonably thinks his detention is necessary for his own protection or to prevent him causing injury to a person or damage to property or because he might 'skip' or interfere with the course of justice (s 38(1)(a)). A juvenile can be held in custody, in addition, 'in his own interests' (s 38(1) (b)).

The Criminal Justice and Public Order Act 1994 gave the police the power to grant bail subject to conditions very similar to the power to grant bail subject to conditions traditionally enjoyed by the court. (On the courts' power to set conditions for bail see p 265 below.) The power, established by CJPOA 1994, s 27, followed a recommendation of the Runciman Royal Commission (Report, p 73, para 22) based on the belief that it would result in release of far more persons from police custody.

The Runciman Commission envisaged that conditional bail would apply to arrested persons regardless of whether they had been charged, but the power to impose

---

166   As reprinted for the Lords.
167   New s 30B of PACE inserted by cl 3(7) of the Criminal Justice Bill.

conditions under CJPOA 1994, s 27 only applied to persons who had been charged. This will change, however, when the provisions of the Criminal Justice Bill 2002-03 come into force since it recognises release on bail subject to conditions for persons who have not been charged. [168]

Conditions should only be imposed if it appears to the custody officer that they are necessary to secure that the defendant (a) surrenders to custody, (b) does not commit further offences while on bail, (c) does not interfere with witnesses or otherwise obstruct the course of justice (CJPOA 1994, s 27(3)). The police, unlike the court, cannot order reports to be prepared nor can the police order the defendant to live in a bail hostel.

The conditions of bail can be made more onerous or less onerous by the original or another custody officer (ibid).

The CJPOA 1994, s 29 gave the police for the first time a power to arrest someone who did not answer to police bail.

The great majority of those arrested are bailed by the police. This applies even to arrests for indictable offences. In 2001, of the 539,000 who were arrested for indictable offences, 82% were bailed from the police station. (*Criminal Statistics*, 2001, Cm 5696, Table 8.1, p 132.)

(c)   Bail decisions by courts

When a court adjourns a case – whether overnight or for a week or a month – it has to decide whether the defendant should be remanded on bail or in custody. Until the Bail Act 1976 the system of bail was to permit the release of the defendant, usually on his own recognisance (his promise to pay a stated sum of money if he absconded and was caught) and often also the promise by sureties that they too would pay a stated sum of money in the same event. (No money had to be provided by the surety unless the defendant did 'skip'.) Bail could be granted either with or without conditions. Police objections to bail could be based on a variety of grounds – for example, the likelihood that the defendant would abscond, would interfere with witnesses, or would commit further offences.

Historically the chief reason for refusing bail was that the accused might abscond. In fact in the nineteenth century it seems to have been the sole reason (*Re Robinson* (1854) 23 LJQB 286) and this remained the case well into this century. But gradually the courts began to accept other grounds as well. In 1955 Lord Goddard changed the position by recognising the notion that persons with a bad record and especially those who were housebreakers should not normally be granted bail. (*Pegg* [1955] Crim LR 308; *Wharton* [1955] Crim LR 565; *Gentry* [1956] Crim LR 120.) One of

---

[168]   See new s 37D(3) inserted by Sch 2, para 3.

the main justifications for this new approach was that it would help to prevent the defendant from committing further offences while on bail.

THE BAIL ACT 1976

Statutory presumption of bail The Bail Act 1976 created a statutory presumption of bail for remand cases (including remands after conviction for reports to be made). This means that the court *must* grant bail unless one of the statutory exceptions applies – even if the defendant does not apply for bail (s 4). (The importance of the presumption was shown by the results of a study carried out over six months in Cardiff. There were almost 500 cases (496). In 395 the police did not object to bail, nothing was said about bail on behalf of the defendant and bail was simply granted. (MJ Doherty and R East, 'Bail Decisions in Magistrates' Courts', 25 *British Journal of Criminology*, 1985, Table 2, p 256.))

The main exceptions are set out in the Bail Act itself, Sch 1. They provide that a court need not grant bail to a person charged with an offence punishable with imprisonment if the court is satisfied that there are substantial grounds for believing that, if released on bail, the defendant would (a) fail to appear, (b) commit an offence while on bail, or (c) obstruct the course of justice. Bail also need not be granted if the court thinks he ought to stay in custody for his own protection (or, in the case of a juvenile, for his own welfare), or if there has been insufficient time to obtain enough information about the defendant for the court to reach a decision, or he has previously failed to answer to bail (Sch 1, Pt I, paras 2 – 6).

In determining whether it is likely that the defendant would skip or commit an offence or obstruct justice, the court should have regard to (a) the nature and seriousness of the offence (and the probable way the court will deal with the defendant), (b) the character, antecedents, associations and community ties of the defendant, (c) his record in regard to any previous grant of bail and, (d) except where the remand is for reports, the strength of the evidence against him (Sch 1, Pt I, para 9). (For criticism of the structure of the Bail Act provisions see *Criminal Law Review* (1987) p 438 – 9, and (1993) p 1.)

Exceptions to the statutory presumption the case of someone charged with an offence punishable with imprisonment who is remanded for reports, bail need not be granted if it appears to the court impracticable to complete the inquiries or make the report without keeping the defendant in custody (Pt I, para 7).

Where the defendant is charged with an offence not punishable with imprisonment, the permissible grounds for refusing bail are narrower. He can be refused bail if he has previously failed to answer to bail and if the court believes, in view of that failure, that he will again fail to surrender to custody if released on bail (Sch 1, Pt II, para 2).

Further exceptions to the statutory presumption for bail were introduced by Mr Michael Howard as Home Secretary. The most severe was for anyone on a charge of murder, attempted murder, manslaughter, rape or attempted rape who had previously been convicted for one of those offences. The Criminal Justice and Public Order Act 1994, s 25 provided that in such cases bail was not permitted at all. But this absolute prohibition only lasted four years before it was removed by Mr Jack Straw's Crime and Disorder Act 1998, s 56. This allows bail in such cases if the court finds it is justified by 'exceptional circumstances'. Michael Howard's s 25 was contrary to the European Convention on Human Rights – see *CC v United Kingdom* [1999] Crim LR 228. Despite doubts raised in some quarters[169], the Law Commission concluded that the revised s 25 could be interpreted compatibly with the Convention on the basis that where the defendant would not pose a real risk of committing a serious offence on bail that would constitute 'an exceptional circumstance'. [170] This view was upheld by the Divisional Court in *R (on the application of O) v Harrow Crown Court* [2003] EWHC 868 Admin, (2003) Times, 29 May.

Of greater practical significance was s 26 of Mr Howard's CJPOA 1994 which removed the statutory presumption of bail in regard to anyone charged with an offence which is not a purely summary offence where the alleged offence occurred while the defendant was on bail. This was to deal with the alleged scandal of so called 'bail bandits' – on which see p 272, n 187 below. The court was not bound to refuse bail in such cases; it simply was not subject to the statutory presumption in favour of bail. The Law Commission recommended that this provision might conflict with the ECHR and that it should be amended to make it clear that offending on bail was only one of the considerations to be taken into account rather than in itself an independent ground for refusing bail.[171] This recommendation was accepted by the Government and the necessary amendment was introduced in the Criminal Justice Bill 2002/03, cl 14 which provides that the court should give that matter 'particular weight'.

The same Bill however created a new restriction on the grant of bail to drug users. The Explanatory Notes accompanying the Bill said (para 148) there was a concern that such offenders if granted bail would merely reoffend in order to fund their drug use. Accordingly the Bill [in cl 19] states that an alleged offender aged 18 or over who has been charged with an imprisonable offence will not be granted bail where three conditions exist unless he demonstrates that there is no significant risk of his committing an offence while on bail. The three conditions are that there is drug test evidence that he has a Class A drug in his body, the court is satisfied that there are substantial grounds for believing that misuse of a Class A drug caused or contributed to the alleged offence and he refuses to undergo an assessment as to his drug dependency.

---

169   See, for instance, P Leach, 'Automatic denial of bail and the European Convention' [1999] *Criminal Law Review*, pp 300-05.

170   *Bail and the Human Rights Act 1998* (Law.Com No.269, 2001), para 8.45. See on this subject also J.Burrow, 'Bail and the Human Rights Act 1998', *New Law Journal*, 2000, pp 677 and 736.

171   1998 Bail Report, para 4.12.

Bail on condition If bail is granted, it can be conditional or unconditional. Unconditional bail means that the defendant must simply surrender to the court on the appointed date. Failure to do so without reasonable cause is an offence (s 6(1)), punishable in the magistrates' court with three months' imprisonment and/or a fine, or in the Crown Court with 12 months' imprisonment or a fine.

Conditions can be attached where the court thinks it is necessary to ensure the defendant's presence at court, or so that he does not commit further offences or interfere with witnesses or obstruct the course of justice, or to ensure that he makes himself available for reports or for an interview with lawyers.[172].

The most common conditions relate to such matters as reporting to the police daily or weekly, handing in one's passport, living in particular premises or with particular persons, or *not* associating with particular persons or not going to particular places. In 2001, electronic tagging was added as a possible condition for juvenile defendants.[173] The Criminal Justice Bill 2002/03 added a further ground – the protection of the defendant. [174] In *R (on the application of Crown Prosecution Service) v Chorley Justices* the Divisional Court upheld the lawfulness of a 'door stepping' condition, under which the defendant is subject to a curfew backed by a condition that he must show himself at the door if asked to do so by the police. [175]

See generally BP Block, 'Bail Conditions: Neither Logical nor Lawful', 154 *Justice of the Peace*, p 83; JN Spencer, 'Bail Conditions: Logical or Illogical?' *Justice of the Peace*, 24 March 1990, p 180; JW Raine and MJ Willson, 'The Imposition and Effectiveness of Conditions in Bail Decisions', *Justice of the Peace*, 3 June 1995, pp 364 – 67.

It seems that conditions are imposed on about two-thirds of grants of bail.[176]

There was previously no right of appeal as such against conditions imposed on the grant of bail. Lord Justice Auld in his Review said this was sensible – 'Otherwise the appellate process could be corrupted by endless wrangling over conditions'.[177] But he recommended that the defendant should be given a right of appeal against conditional grants of bail in respect of conditions to live away from home and to provide sureties or to give security (on which see below).[178] This recommendation was accepted by the Government and a provision to give it effect was included in the

---

[172] Section 3(6). The last category was added by the Crime and Disorder Act 1998, s 54(2).

[173] Criminal Justice and Police Act 2001, s 131 adding new s 6ZAA to the Bail Act 1976.

[174] Cl 13, following the recommendation of the Law Commission Report, n 172 above, para 9A.27.

[175] [2002] EWHC 2162 (Admin), (2002) 166 JP 764. For discussion suggesting that the condition is useless see P Tain, 'Shut that door' *Solicitors' Journal*, 20 December 2002, p 1155.

[176] R Morgan and N Russell, *The Judiciary in the magistrates' court* (Home Office, RDS Occasional Paper No 66, 2000) p 49.

[177] Chapter 10, para 88.

[178] Chapter 10, para 88.

Criminal Justice Bill 2002/03 (cl 16) which extended the right of appeal also to conditions of curfew and electronic tagging.

The Bail Act 1976 did not create an offence of breaking conditions imposed by the court. But s 7(3) gives the police a power to arrest a defendant on conditional bail where they reasonably suspect that he is likely to break the conditions or that he has already done so. Anyone arrested under this subsection must be brought before a justice of the peace within 24 hours. The justice of the peace may then reconsider the question of bail. If he is not brought before the magistrates within 24 hours, they cannot remand him in custody since they have no jurisdiction over him (*R v Governor of Glen Parva Young Offender Institution, ex p G* [1998] 2 All ER 295). It has been held that a hearing to deal with alleged breach of bail conditions is not a hearing of a criminal offence so as to give the accused rights under Article 6 (Right to a Fair Trial) of the ECHR and that, although Article 5 (Right to liberty and security) is applicable, it does not impose any new procedural requirements. But the court must take proper account of the quality of the material available to it. [179]

Sureties The Bail Act 1976 abolished personal recognisances whereby the defendant agreed to pay a sum of money if he failed to appear on the appointed day. The only exception was where the court thought there was a danger the defendant might go abroad, in which case he could be asked to give monetary security. But the Crime and Disorder Act, 1998, s 54(1) restored the general power to order the defendant to give a personal recognisance. Giving a personal recognisance does not require the production of the actual money – only providing sufficient evidence to satisfy the court that one has it.

The Bail Act preserved the ancient right of the court to ask for sureties as a condition of bail. The sureties promise to pay in the event that the defendant does not turn up. The court then has a discretion as to whether to order that the amount put up by the sureties be forfeited (technically called 'estreated'). The Crime and Disorder Act 1998, s 55 changed the position by making the surety's recognisance forfeit automatically if the defendant fails to appear – but the court then fixes a hearing to enable the surety to show cause why he should not be ordered to pay the sum in which he was bound. (For the principles applied by the courts see *R v Uxbridge Justices, ex p Heward-Mills* [1983] 1 WLR 56; *R v Southampton Justices, ex p Green* [1976] QB 11; and A Eccles, 'New Developments in the Law of Forfeiture of Recognisance' (1982) *Justices of the Peace*, p 146.)

Standing surety for someone can have catastrophic consequences. In a case in December 1982, for instance, Bow Street magistrates' court demanded payment of £120,000 from a travel agent who promised that amount as surety for two men he hardly knew charged with VAT frauds of over £20 million. See also *R v Bow Street Magistrates' Court, ex p Hall and Otobo* [1986] NLJ Rep 1111. For a more lenient attitude see *R v Crown Court at Reading, ex p Bello* [1992] 3 All ER 353. The Divisional

---

[179]   *R (on the application of the DPP) v Havering Magistrates' Court* [2001] 1 WLR 805, [2001] Crim LR 902, Div Ct.

Court had upheld the judge's order that the surety lose £5,000, which was half the sum he had agreed to stand for, even though he was entirely blameless. In the view of the Divisional Court it was not necessary to show that the surety was at fault. But the Court of Appeal disagreed. The court should always consider the question of fault. ('If it was satisfied the surety was blameless throughout it would then be proper to remit the whole of the amount of the recognisance'.) However, in *R v Crown Court at Maidstone, ex p Lever* [1995] 2 All ER 35 the Court of Appeal held that the absence of culpability on the part of the surety was not by itself a reason to reduce or remit entirely the forfeiture of a recognisance if the defendant absconded. It upheld forfeiture of £35,000 out of £40,000 and of £16,000 from £19,000 even though the surety had been in no way at fault.

In *ex p Bello* (above) the Court of Appeal held that the surety had to be informed of the date when the defendant was required to attend at court. Since he had not been so informed that was in itself sufficient ground to allow the appeal. See also *R v Crown Court at Wood Green, ex p Howe* [1992] 3 All ER 366 holding that courts should consider the surety's ability to pay when deciding how much of the sum promised should be forfeited.

The surety's responsibilities cease when the trial starts. In 1990 the financier Asil Nadir fled Britain for Cyprus after he had been arraigned at the start of his trial for fraud offences. The judge Mr Justice Tucker required a Mr Guney who had stood as surety in the amount of £1 million to forfeit £650,000. The Court of Appeal (the Master of the Rolls dissenting) held that since from the moment that the defendant was arraigned at the start of the trial the surety was no longer at risk, the decision to forfeit the surety's money had been wrong (*R v Central Criminal Court, ex p Guney* [1996] 2 All ER 705).

The Bail Act 1976, s 9, specifically made it a criminal offence to agree to indemnify a surety – for example, where the defendant or his associates agree to reimburse the surety if he is asked by the court to pay the money he has promised to pay. This is treated as a conspiracy to pervert the course of justice.

The Act provides that a surety can be relieved of his obligations if he notifies the police that the bailed person is unlikely to surrender. The police can then make an arrest without a warrant. But *R v Crown Court at Ipswich, ex p Reddington* [1981] Crim LR 618, established that the surety was not automatically relieved simply by going to the police. Mrs R had stood surety in the amount of £2,000 on condition that the accused reside with her and report daily to the police station. She feared that the accused was not reliable and went to the police to say that she thought he might not surrender to his bail. When in fact the accused did not appear, the court ordered that half of her surety be estreated. On appeal, it was held that the Crown Court judge had not sufficiently taken into account the efforts she had made and he had erred in law in saying that she had done the wrong thing to have gone to the police station. Also there should have been an inquiry as to her means. The case was sent back for rehearing.

There is some authority that the surety can himself make an arrest but in practice this is hardly likely to be done: see (1981) *Criminal Law Review*, p 619. See generally, K Parsons, 'Duties of a surety: a summary of the current law', *Solicitors' Journal*, 20 February, 1998, p 154.

Procedural formalities The Act requires that the bail decision be recorded and that reasons must be given to the defendant if it is refused or conditions are attached to the grant of bail. Reasons must also be given if bail is granted over the objections of the prosecution. [180] If the defendant is unrepresented and is refused bail, he must be told of his right to apply to a higher court for bail (s 5).

What determines the decision on bail? Both the theory and law of bail is that the decision as to whether the defendant is remanded in custody or on bail is made by the court. But in practice the decision is often actually determined by other actors in the criminal justice system. In a study by the Home Office Research Unit it was found that the factor which was most highly correlated with the bail rate in courts was whether the police had given the defendant bail from the police station (F Simon and M Weatheritt, *The Use of Bail and Custody by London Magistrates' Courts Before and After the Criminal Justice Act* (HMSO, 1984), p 15). See further A Hucklesby, 'Remand Decision Makers' (1997) *Criminal Law Review* pp 269-81. The author conducted a study in three London courts over a three-year period, observing 1,524 remand hearings and analysing court records for 2,069 cases. She also interviewed magistrates, court clerks, CPS staff, defence solicitors, police officers and probation officers. She found that only 9% of all remand hearings were contested. In 85% of cases the CPS did not oppose a remand on bail. When the CPS did oppose bail, the defence did not contest the matter in 42% of those cases (p 271). In her view, in most cases the police, the CPS and the defence lawyers were the effective decision makers. Usually the remand decision was made informally before the defendant appeared in court. Even when there was a contested bail application, the magistrates generally agreed with the CPS assessment of bail risk.

(d)   How many bail applications?

An unconvicted person could not be remanded in custody for more than eight days. This ensured that his case would be reconsidered every week and repeated applications could be made to have him released by the magistrates.

However, in 1980 in *R v Nottingham Justices, ex p Davies* [1980] 2 All ER 775, the Divisional Court held that no fresh application for bail could be made to magistrates unless the circumstances had in some way changed since the last application.

One effect of the decision in the *Nottingham Justices'* case was that even competent defence counsel delayed making an application for bail lest the client was prejudiced by the rule. As a result, a client might be remanded in custody much longer than

---

[180]   Criminal Justice and Police Act 2001, s 129.

would otherwise have been the case. See B Brink and C Stone, 'Defendants Who Do Not Ask For Bail' (1987) *Criminal Law Review*, p 152. This article led to Criminal Justice Act 1988, s 154, which requires courts to consider bail at *each* hearing. [181]

Moreover, under s 154, at the first hearing after the defendant has been remanded in custody his lawyers can deploy any arguments they please, whether or not they have been advanced previously. But at any subsequent hearing the court need not hear arguments heard previously. This helped to defuse part of the problem created by the *Nottingham Justices* case. But there is a doubt as to whether if the defence do not advance any argument regarding bail at the first hearing they are restricted to two hearings or whether the first 'unargued' hearing should be disregarded and not count. It seems that many courts adopt a strict approach and in effect hold that the defendant who does not utilise his first opportunity of arguing for bail has wasted it. (See M Hinchcliffe, *Law Society's Gazette*, 1 July 1992, p 19)

LENGTH OF PERIODS OF REMAND

Remands traditionally were for a maximum of one week. The Criminal Justice Act 1982, s 59 and Sch 9, provided for the longer remand in custody of defendants over 17 who are legally represented even though they are not physically before the court. The defendant could be remanded in custody for three one-week periods providing this was explained to him when he was first remanded in custody and he gave his consent. This meant that he had to be produced at least every four weeks. But if he wished to change his mind during that period, he could. His lawyer would not normally appear for him in his absence either.

At first this was introduced as an experiment (Criminal Justice Act 1988, s 155) but in 1991 all courts were given the power to remand a defendant for up to 28 days at a time providing he has been remanded in custody for the offence at least once before. In other words, this power cannot be used on the first occasion. The purpose was to reduce court hearings, to reduce time taking prisoners to and from courts and prisons, and to save legal aid money. (Magistrates' Courts (Remand in Custody) Order 1991, SI 1991/2667). In 1997, the power to remand the accused in custody for 28 days on the second remand was extended to defendants under 17 (Criminal Procedure and Investigations Act 1996, s 52(2)).

(e)   Appeals against a refusal of bail

There were three alternative methods of appealing against a refusal of bail – other than applying again to another bench of magistrates, which was considerably restricted by the *Nottingham Justices* decision.

---

[181]   The section added a new Part IIA to Sch 1 of the Bail Act 1976.

The first was to apply to the judge in chambers through a barrister or a solicitor. The basic procedure for such applications is set out in CPR SC79.

The alternative was to apply for assistance to the Official Solicitor. The prisoner filled out a form in prison which requested the Official Solicitor to forward an application to the judge in chambers. There was no oral argument. The papers were simply presented to the judge by an official. There was no charge for the service.

Unsurprisingly, the chances of success were much greater through an oral argument presented by lawyers than in appeals by the Official Solicitor. According to a Parliamentary Answer, the success rate for Official Solicitor applications in 1980 was 9% compared with 69% for those privately represented (House of Commons, *Hansard*, 23 November 1981, Written Answers, cols 274–5). (See to like effect Nan Bases and Michael Smith, 'A Study of Bail Applications Through the Official Solicitor to the Judge in Chambers' (1976) *Criminal Law Review*, p 541.)

The third method of seeking to obtain bail after it has been refused by magistrates was through the Crown Court. The magistrates issued a certificate saying that they heard full argument on the application for bail before they refused bail. Such appeals could be made in summary cases as well as in cases that were indictable. If the applicant was legally aided, the legal aid order covered an application under this procedure. If not, neither the Crown Court nor the magistrates' court had the power to issue a legal aid order for the purposes of a bail application alone.

Auld recommended that the appeal system be reformed by removal of the right of application to a High Court judge after determination of the matter by either magistrates or the Crown Court. Reopening of the bail issue should be restricted to an appeal on a point of law only. [182] This recommendation was accepted. and provisions to give it effect were included in the Criminal Justice Bill 2002/03 (cl 17). But cl 16 of the Bill would create a right of appeal to the Crown Court against the imposition by magistrates of certain listed conditions of bail – such as requirements relating to residency, provision of a surety or giving a security, curfew or electronic monitoring. This complements the removal by cl 17 of the High Court's power to hear such appeals.

(f)   Appeals against a grant of bail

The Bail (Amendment) Act 1993 gave the prosecution a right of appeal where a magistrates' court granted bail to a person who was charged with or convicted of an offence carrying a sentence of five years' imprisonment, or an offence of taking a conveyance without the owner's consent (contrary to the Theft Act 1968, s 12), or aggravated vehicle taking (contrary to the Theft Act 1968, s 12A). (The Criminal Justice Bill 2002/03, cl 18 would apply the right to any imprisonable offence.) The

---

[182]   Chapter 10, para s 84-87.

right of appeal is against the grant of bail only, and therefore cannot be used to challenge conditions imposed.

Lord Justice Auld's Review recommended that these criteria were too strict and that the prosecution should have a right of appeal in respect of all offences that would on conviction be punishable by a custodial or partly custodial sentence.[183] The recommendation was accepted by the Government and a provision to give it effect was included in the Criminal Justice Bill 2002/03 (cl 18).

In order to exercise the right the prosecution must strictly follow the set procedure. First, the prosecution must have objected to bail during the bail hearing (s 1(3)). At the conclusion of the bail hearing the prosecution must immediately[184] state in open court that it proposes to exercise its right of appeal (s 1(4)). The clerk of the court announces the time at which this oral notice was given and issues a warrant of detention authorising the detention of the defendant for the time being. This is also recorded in the court register.

If the defendant is unrepresented, the clerk has to tell him that he has the right to ask the Official Solicitor to represent him at the appeal.

The prosecution must serve written notice on the court and the defendant (not his legal representative). If this is not done within two hours, the appeal is deemed to have been dropped (s 1(7)).

The appeal hearing must start within 48 hours of the day on which oral notice of intention to appeal was given, not counting weekends and public holidays (s 1(8)). The hearing is before a single judge in chambers in the Crown Court (s 1(9)). The defendant has no right to be present.

For a review of this system five years on by an experienced prosecutor see D Tucker, 'The Prosecutor on the Starting Block: the Mechanics of the Bail (Amendment) Act 1993' (1998) *Criminal Law Review*, pp 728-31. He suggests that the way for the CPS to avoid an unseemly rush after an adverse decision is to decide beforehand whether an appeal would be taken.

Note

1. Time spent in custody pre-trial or pre-sentence can generally be deducted from the ultimate sentence. This is by virtue of s 67(1) of the Criminal Justice Act 1967. But this is not always the case: see N Yell, 'Credit for Time Spent Remanded in Custody', *Justice of the Peace*, 1982, p 275; *Criminal Law Review* (1986) pp 270-1; *New Law Journal*, 3 October 1980, p 937.

---

[183]   Chapter 10, para 90.
[184]   But five minutes delay is acceptable – *R v Isleworth Crown Court, ex p Clarke* [1998] 1 Cr App Rep 257 (DC).

2. No compensation is paid to persons who have been remanded in custody and then are found not guilty. By contrast in West Germany, France, Holland and Sweden, persons who are detained and then acquitted can sometimes be compensated.

(g)   Causes for concern

Bail/remand in custody is a subject that perennially attracts critical comment from all quarters.

The civil libertarians are concerned especially that:
* Around a half of those remanded in custody pre-trial are either acquitted or receive non-custodial penalties. (In 2001, 21% were acquitted and another 21% were given a non-custodial sentence. [185])
* There are considerable variations in the policy of different courts in remanding defendants on bail or in custody.
* Bail decisions are too hasty. Research showed 62% of bail hearings lasted less than two minutes, and 96% less than 10 minutes. Even when bail was refused, 38% were heard in under two minutes and 87% in less than 10 minutes. (MJ Doherty and R East, 25 *British Journal of Criminology*, 1985, Table 2, p 256.)
* Remand prisoners tend to be held in highly unsatisfactory conditions in prisons or in police cells
* Some remand prisoners spend very long periods of time in custody. (In 2000, 1,970 prisoners had spent over 6 months on remand, of whom 270 had spent over 12 months in prison.)
* Many of those held on remand have a variety of problems – drug misuse, poor educational attainment, mental illness and unstable accommodation are particularly prevalent among remand prisoners.[186]

At the same time, other discontents and anxieties are expressed by the police and the media. One such is that too many commit offences while on bail – the problem of what the media call 'bail bandits'. [187]

The legislature has taken a number of steps directed at the problem of offences committed while on bail:

---

[185]   *Criminal Statistics*, 2001, Cm 5696, Table 8.8, p 139.
[186]   *Reducing   re-offending   amongst   ex-prisoners*,   Social   Exclusion   Unit   2002. www.socialexclusionunit.gov.uk
[187]   For the facts see for instance 'Offending While on Bail: a Survey of Recent Studies', Home Office Research and Planning Unit, 1992, Paper No 65. This concluded that the percentage of offenders who were convicted of offences committed while on bail had varied little over the previous decade. The studies consistently showed that 10- 12% of persons granted bail were convicted of offences committed while on bail. Six years later another Home Office study found that the proportion was 12% for those bailed by the police and 15% for those bailed by the court. (D Brown, 'Offending on bail and police use of conditional bail', Home Office, *Research Findings No 72*, 1998.)

- A provision in the Criminal Justice Act 1991 required magistrates to give reasons for rejecting police objections to bail in murder, manslaughter or rape cases (s 29(2)).
- The Criminal Justice Act 1993, s 66 provides that an offence committed by a person on bail should be treated by the court sentencing for that offence as an aggravating factor .
- The Criminal Justice and Public Order Act 1994, s 25 as has already been seen (p 264 above), removed the power to grant bail in certain cases – though that had to be modified because of the ECHR. It also removed the presumption in favour of bail where the defendant is accused of offences committed while on bail (s 26).

The Criminal Justice Bill 2002/03, cl 14 (1) provided that a person charged with an offence committed while on bail may not be granted bail 'unless the court is satisfied that there is no significant risk of his committing an offence while on bail'[188]

Another concern is that 'Too many people skip'. (In 2001, of the 543,00 persons bailed by magistrates' courts, 13% failed to appear at court. The proportion for indictable offences was 15%. (*Criminal Statistics*, 2001, Cm 5696, Table 8.9, p 140.)) The Criminal Justice Bill 2002/03 included a provision (cl 15) that someone who previously did not without reasonable excuse surrender to custody while on bail may not be granted bail unless the court is satisfied that there is no significant risk of his jumping bail again.

The prison authorities are concerned about the cost of remand prisoners, the burdens they create for the prison system including the burden of escorts for prisoners going to court, the rapid turnover in receptions and discharges, and in terms of the problem of prison overcrowding and providing a tolerable regime while they are in custody.

(h)   New developments

One helpful relatively recent development is the Bail Information Scheme now operating in over a hundred magistrates' courts. (They began in the mid-1980s as a result of the initiative of the Vera Institute of Justice of New York.[189]) Under these schemes probation officers provide the CPS and the court with verified information about the defendant – his employment status, where he lives, his family situation and other community roots and the like. Research has shown that the provision of bail information has a significant effect. A Home Office study of three schemes at magistrates' courts showed, for instance, that at Hull the CPS made no objection to bail in 39% of cases where bail information was provided, compared with 13% where

---

[188]   Inserting a new para 2A of Part I of Sch 1 to the Bail Act 1976.
[189]   The concept, based on pioneering work by the Vera Institute in New York, was first proposed in this country by the writer in the late 1960s – see M Zander, 'Bail: A Reappraisal', *Criminal Law Review*, March 1967.

it was not provided. The equivalent figures at Blackpool were 19%, compared with 15% and at Manchester (where the scheme concentrated on the most serious cases), 58% and 40%. The figures for court decisions were even more striking. At Hull, when information was provided, 69% of decisions favoured bail, compared with 38% where no information was provided. In Blackpool the figures were 58%, compared with 38% and in Manchester 80%, compared with 50%. 72% of homeless defendants who had information presented were bailed (mostly to bail hostels), compared with 15% where no information was provided. ('Bail Information Schemes: Practice and Effect', Home Office Research and Planning Unit, Paper No 69, 1992.)

But despite their value, it is clear that courts often lack the information they need. The Auld Review said[190], 'As to information, despite the introduction in 1998 of bail information schemes, it is often incomplete and for that and other reasons inaccurate'. A 1998 study commented on the lack of ready availability to the police, prosecutors and courts of the defendant's criminal record and other relevant information. [191]

Since September 1999 all remand prisons have been required and funded to provide bail information schemes.[192] But the Prison Inspectorate's thematic report in 2000 on the treatment and conditions of remand prisoners recorded wide variation in performance by establishments throughout the country and pretty poor overall performance.[193]

Another helpful development has been the establishment of bail hostels and other facilities where defendants can be sent by courts. There are also a growing number of bail support schemes usually run by probation involving arrangements to help defendants on bail – through contact with bail support workers, residence requirements, volunteer befriending schemes, debt counselling and the like.

But these more hopeful developments must be seen against a background of a continuing huge remand population in prison, held for the most part in their cells for 23 out of 24 hours a day.

Auld recommended that courts take more time over bail, that better information be provided to them and that they should always record their bail decisions. [194]

---

190   Chapter 10, para 78.
191   R Morgan and P Henderson, *Remand Decisions and Offending on Bail: Evaluation of the Bail Process Project*, 1998 (Home Office Research Study 184).
192   Auld Review, Ch 10, para 71.
193   *Unjust Deserts*, 2000, para s.4.09-4.17 – www.homeoffice.gov.uk/justice/prisons/inspprisons.
194   *Unjust Deserts*, 2000, para s.4.09-4.17 – www.homeoffice.gov.uk/justice/prisons/inspprisons.

THE LAW COMMISSION ON BAIL AND THE ECHR

In June 2001 the Law Commission published a report entitled *Bail and the Human Rights Act 1998* [195] on whether the law on bail complied with the European Convention on Human Rights. It concluded that there were no provisions in the existing law which when interpreted as required by the 1998 Act could not be applied in a manner which complied with the Convention, nor which, given appropriate training, decision-takers would be likely to apply in a way which would violate Convention rights. However the report identified certain areas of the law that would benefit from legislative reform which were adopted in the Criminal Justice Bill 2002/03.

7. Information supplied to the opponent

(a) Evidence the prosecution intend to call or use

Lord Justice Auld said in his Review, 'The law is somewhat muddled in its provision for advance notification of the prosecution case and/or evidence, but reasonably satisfactory in its operation'.[196]

Technically the position is different for the two levels of court and for different categories of case.

Cases tried in the magistrates' court The statutory rule is that for either-way cases there is no duty on the prosecution to supply its evidence to the defence in advance of the trial unless the defence requests it. In that event the prosecution has a choice whether to supply copies of witness statements or a summary of their statements. [197] Because of the ease of photocopying, normally the statements themselves are supplied.

For summary-only offences there is no equivalent rule. The defence was expected to manage somehow on the day without any advance notice.

However the position for both types of cases has now changed as a result of Guidelines on Disclosure issued by the Attorney-General in November 2000 – see www.lslo.gov.uk. They included the following bald statement (para 43):

> The prosecutor should ... provide to the defence all evidence upon which the Crown proposes to rely in a summary trial. Such provision should allow the accused or their legal advisers sufficient time properly to consider the evidence before it is called. Exceptionally, statements may be withheld for the protection of witnesses or to avoid interference with the course of justice.

---

[195] Law Com No 269.
[196] Chapter 10, para 117.
[197] Magistrates' Courts (Advance Information) Rules 1985, SI 1985 601, r4.

This statement covers both summary-only and either-way cases tried in the magistrates' courts. Technically, the Guidelines do not have the force of law but it is clear that the Attorney-General expects them to be followed. In a covering Foreword he highlighted this development as one of the new Guidelines' 'highly significant changes addressing areas not covered by legislation'.

Cases going to the Crown Court The rule for cases committed for trial in the Crown Court was that the prosecution had to provide the defence prior to the committal with copies of enough of the prosecution evidence to constitute a prima facie case (*R v Epping and Harlow Justices, ex p Massaro* [1973] QB 433; *R v Grays Justices, ex p Tetley* (1979) 70 Cr App Rep 11). Before the trial took place or at least before the end of the prosecution's case, any other evidence the prosecution intends to call must also be handed over.

As will be seen below, several categories of case have in recent years been sent or transferred directly to the Crown Court without committal proceedings in the magistrates' court and the Criminal Justice Bill 2002/03 contained provisions finally to abolish committal proceedings. In cases sent directly to the Crown Court the rule has been that copies of the prosecution's evidence must be provided to the defence 42 days after the first preliminary hearing there. [198]

Also, the Divisional Court has recognised a residual common law duty on prosecutors to serve proposed evidence earlier, where it is in the interests of justice to do so – for instance, to assist a bail application or an application to stay the proceedings as an abuse of process. [199]

The need for the defence to have speedy advance disclosure of the prosecution's case is now the greater because of changes that have recently been made in order to process cases, and especially guilty plea cases, more quickly. These include asking the defendant to indicate his plea before the magistrates decide whether he should be tried at the higher or lower level ('plea before venue' under the Criminal Procedure and Investigations Act 1996, s 49, pp 319-323 below); and the rule that when someone is granted bail by the police the return date when he is required to appear at court should, if possible, be the next sitting of the court (Crime and Disorder Act 1998, s 46.) The case for this is made by D Sunman, 'Advancing Disclosure: Can the Rules for Advance Information in the Magistrates' Courts be Improved?'[1998] *Criminal Law Review*, pp 799-801.

Lord Justice Auld said time between charge and service of the prosecution's evidence was 'dead time' in the life of the case. The Philips Royal Commission had recommended the introduction of a formal and comprehensive framework of rules for advance prosecution disclosure of proposed evidence in all courts, but no rules

---

[198]   Magistrates' Court Act 1980,s 5B(2)(c); Crime and Disorder Act 1998 (Service of Prosecution Evidence) Regulations 2000, SI 2000/3305, reg 2.

[199]   *R v DPP ex p Lee* [1999] 2 All ER 737.

were made'[200] Auld said he supported that recommendation. The precise time-scale should be prescribed by rules.[201]

(b)   Evidence the prosecution do not intend to use ('unused material')

The rules regarding disclosure to the defence of material the prosecution do not intend to use (known as 'unused material') were formerly a mixture of common law and guidelines laid down by the Attorney-General. They are now however statutory.

[The 8th edition of this work treated this subject historically over 50 years, at some length (pp 252-62) from a common law decision in 1946 to the Criminal Procedure and Investigations Act 1996. For reasons of economy of space this historical account has been drastically reduced here.]

Common law 1946-1981 The first judicial pronouncement on the subject merely required the prosecution to supply the defence with the name and address of any witness who they knew could give material evidence but whom they did not intend to call as a witness. [202] There was judicial disagreement as to whether this duty extended to the witness statements themselves.[203]

Attorney-General's 1981 Guidelines In December 1981 the Attorney-General issued Guidelines for trials on indictment. These stated that all 'unused material' should normally be made available to the defence solicitor 'if it has some bearing on the offence(s) charged and the surrounding circumstances of the case'. 'Unused material' for this purpose was defined to mean (1) all witness statements and documents not included in the committal bundles served on the defence; and (2) where edited statements are included in the committal bundle, the unedited version of such statements or documents.

There were stated exceptions: when disclosure might lead to improper pressure on the witness, where it was untrue and where it was against the public interest on account of being 'sensitive', for instance, because it dealt with national security, the identity of an informer or the source of surveillance.

In the case of any doubt, the material ought to be submitted to counsel for advice. A balance should then be struck between the competing values. If, for instance, the material established the accused's innocence or even if it only tended to show him to be innocent, it should either be disclosed in full or at least with the sensitive passages excised. Any doubt should be resolved in favour of disclosure. If the material was too sensitive to show to counsel, it must be sent to the DPP. (The Guidelines were set out in full in *Practice Note* [1982] 1 All ER 734 and in 74 Cr App Rep 302.)

---

[200] Chapter 10, para s 119-20.
[201] Chapter 10, para 120.
[202] *R v Bryant and Dickson* (1946) 31 Cr App Rep 146; *R v Leyland Justices, ex p Hawthorn* [1979] 1 All ER 209.
[203] *Dallison v Caffery* [1964] 2 All ER 610, 618, 622. See also *R v Hennessey* (1978) 68 Cr App R 419 at 426.

Technically, the Guidelines were not law but the courts treated failure to comply with them as the basis for quashing convictions: see for instance *R v Lawson* (1989) 90 Cr App Rep 107.

Strictly, the Guidelines only applied to trials on indictment, but in 1987 the Attorney-General told the House of Commons that in summary trials the prosecution were under a general duty of being fair, which required them, inter alia, to supply to the defence any materially inconsistent statement, written or oral, of any prosecution witness of which the prosecutor became aware at any stage (House of Commons, *Hansard*, 5 November 1987, col 713). The Divisional Court held that this view was correct in *R v Bromley Magistrates' Court, ex p Smith and Wilkins, R v Wells Street Magistrates' Court, ex p King* [1995] 4 All ER 146. The court asserted the principle that, 'An accused is as much entitled to the safeguards designed to ensure a fair trial in the magistrates' court as in the Crown Court' (p 149). The court was told that, except in non-imprisonable, summary only traffic offences, after a not guilty plea the routine practice was for the CPS to provide disclosure either by way of the material itself or by way of a schedule inviting access to the disclosable material.

The duties laid down by the Guidelines also applied even when the prosecution was private, provided the case had been committed for trial. Cf *R v Gregory Pawsey* [1989] Crim LR 152 with *R v DPP, ex p Hallas* [1988] Crim LR 316.

Whether the Attorney-General's Guidelines were being followed was another question. A JUSTICE Committee in December 1987 said that it was the experience of the Committee that the spirit of the Attorney-General's Guidelines on disclosure to the defence was frequently ignored and that the practice of disclosure varied considerably from area to area (JUSTICE, *A Public Defender*, 1987, para 25).

Common law 1989 – 1995 The law relating to prosecution disclosure of unused material developed rapidly in the years after 1989 so that in effect the Attorney-General's Guidelines were to a significant extent displaced. This process began with the decision of Mr Justice Henry, as he then was, in the first of the so-called Guinness prosecutions in August 1989 (*Saunders*) when he ruled that unused material included all preparatory notes and memoranda which led to the making of witness statements. The breadth of this ruling caused consternation among prosecution agencies.

In June 1992 the Court of Appeal developed the rule further in quashing the conviction of Judith Ward (*R v Ward* [1993] 2 All ER 577). The Court held that the accused should have the same opportunity of reviewing all the available material as the crown has. It followed that copies of all police officers' notebooks should be provided to the defence *without request*, as should observation logs, crime reports, photofits, artists impressions from all witnesses, notes of oral descriptions and car registration numbers.

In *R v Preston* [1993] 4 All ER 638 at 664 the House of Lords held that the test for the disclosure of unused material was materiality not admissibility. The Attorney-General had advised that prosecuting counsel should not receive the product of the tapping of the defendants' phones because it was inadmissible in evidence. The House of Lords held that the Attorney-General had been wrong so to advise. Prosecution counsel's role as arbiter between the adversarial interests of the prosecution and the broader dictates of justice could not be performed effectively unless he knew everything material. In *Ward* (above) the Court of Appeal said that although the Attorney-General's Guidelines created an exception for material that was 'sensitive' or subject to public interest immunity, neither ground for withholding could be used without informing the defence of its nature or getting a ruling of the court.

Attorney-General's 2000 Guidelines In November 2000 in response to growing concern about the unsatisfactory working of the disclosure system the Attorney-General issued a new set of Guidelines on Disclosure. (Accessible on www.lslo.gov.uk.) Their main focus was to tighten up existing procedures and to clarify the responsibilities of police investigators and disclosure officers, prosecutors and defence practitioners. For the most part they restated and emphasised what was already the position. New provisions included the statement (as seen above) that prosecutors must disclose all their evidence in summary cases, that open access must be given to the defence in respect of material seized but not examined by the prosecution and a list (in para 40) of items that would normally be disclosed as a matter of course if relevant to the defence.

RECOMMENDATIONS OF THE RUNCIMAN ROYAL COMMISSION

The Runciman Royal Commission was persuaded by evidence given mainly by the police that the disclosure regime introduced by Mr Justice Henry's decision in Guinness I and by the Court of Appeal's judgment in *Ward* resulted in some cases in excessive burdens on the prosecution.

> 41. ... Even in some straightforward cases the amount of material collected during the course of the investigation can be voluminous. In major inquiries, even with computerised logs of all the information collected during the investigation, it is scarcely possible to be sure that all the material that has been generated has been listed.

> 42. Against this background, the defence can require the police and prosecution to comb through large masses of material in the hope either of causing delay or of chancing upon something that will induce the prosecution to drop the case rather than to have to disclose the material concerned. The defence may do this by successive requests for more material, far beyond the stage at which it could reasonably be claimed that the information was likely to cast doubt upon the prosecution case. Although it may be time consuming and wasteful of resources for the police to check all the material requested, they may have to do so if they are to be sure that they can properly be released. For example, the information may have been given to the police in response to a broadcast appeal promising confidentiality to those providing the information. Or some

witnesses may have given statements to the police naming third parties... The police may well feel that the information should not be divulged and may in some cases decline to divulge it even if it means dropping the case. This does not seem to us to be in the interests of justice.

43. These problems are particularly acute where informants or undercover police officers are concerned. Their lives may be at stake if their existence, let alone their identities, are suspected' (Report, p 93, para 43).

The Attorney-General's Guidelines had left it to the prosecution, in consultation with prosecution counsel when necessary, to decide whether material should be withheld on public interest or sensitivity grounds. In *Ward* the court said it was not for the prosecution to be judge in its own cause. But where sensitivity was not the issue the present position was not satisfactory. The Commission said

49. ... We strongly support the aim of the recent decisions to compel the prosecution to disclose everything that may be relevant to the defence's case. But we accept the evidence that we have received that the decisions have created burdens for the prosecution that go beyond what is reasonable. At present the prosecution can be required to disclose the existence of matters whose potential relevance is speculative in the extreme. Moreover, the sheer bulk of the material involved in many cases makes it wholly impracticable for every one of what may be hundreds of thousands of individual transactions to be disclosed.

50. In our unanimous view a reasonable balance between the duties of the prosecution and the rights of the defence requires that a new regime be created with two stages of disclosure. The first stage of primary disclosure, would, subject to appropriate exceptions, be automatic. The second stage, of secondary or further disclosure would be made if the defence could establish its relevance to the case. Where the prosecution and defence disagreed on this aspect, the court would rule on the matter after weighing the potential importance of the material to the defence.

51. We envisage, therefore, that the prosecution's initial duty should be to supply to the defence copies of all material relevant to the offence or to the offender or to the surrounding circumstances of the case whether or not the prosecution intend to rely upon that material. Material relevant to the offender includes evidence which might not appear on the face of it to be relevant to the offence but which might be important to the defence because for example it raises questions about the defendant's mental state, including his suggestibility or propensity to make false confessions (as happened in the case of Judith Ward). In addition, the prosecution should inform the defence at this stage of the existence of any other material obtained during the course of the inquiry into the offence. This part of its duty should be discharged by the CPS or other prosecuting authority disclosing to the defence the lists [which could in many cases be by reference to categories, such as 'house-to-house inquiries on a housing estate'] or schedules which it had obtained from the police and other

key participants in the investigation such as expert scientific witnesses. This would enable the defence to go through the lists and see whether there was any material which might be relevant to the defence but which the prosecution had not thought to be relevant in its initial selection of items for full disclosure.

Thereafter, if the defence wanted more disclosure it should be under an obligation to justify such a request by reference to the case it intended or hoped to present. As will be seen below, the Commission by a majority of 10 – 1 recommended that the defence should be required to give outline details of the defence in all cases. The dissenter was the writer. But the writer agreed with the other 10 members of the Royal Commission that where the defence wanted further disclosure, that should be on the basis of disclosure of enough of the defence case as to persuade a judge that such an order should be made.

Disclosure of scientific evidence

In *R v Ward* (above) the Court of Appeal dealt specifically with the duty of disclosure in regard to scientific evidence (at p 628):

> We believe that the surest way of preventing the misuse of scientific evidence is by ensuring that there is a proper understanding of the nature and scope of the prosecution's duty of disclosure ... [The court then dealt with the Advance Notice of Expert Evidence Rules, 1987 which enabled the defence to ask the prosecution to provide a copy or an opportunity to inspect 'the record of any observation, test, calculation, or other procedure on which [any] finding or opinion is based'.] The new rules are helpful. But it is a misconception to regard them as exhaustive; they do not in any way supplant or detract from the prosecution's general duty of disclosure in respect of scientific evidence. That duty exists irrespective of any request by the defence. It is also not limited to documentation on which the opinion or findings of an expert is based. It extends to anything that may arguably help the defence ... Moreover, it is a positive duty, which in the context of scientific evidence obliges the prosecution to make full and proper inquiries from forensic scientists in order to discover whether there is discoverable material. Given the undoubted inequality as between prosecution and defence in access to forensic scientists, we regard it as of paramount importance that the common law duty of disclosure, as we have explained it, should be understood by those who prosecute and defend.

The Runciman Royal Commission also emphasised the crucial importance of prosecution disclosure to the defence where exhibits are sent to a lab for analysis. Sir John May's inquiry into the case of the Maguires[204] and the Court of Appeal's judgment in the Judith Ward case (above) had demonstrated the serious risk of a miscarriage of justice if there were not full disclosure of scientific evidence to the defence. 'Forensic

---

204   *Interim Report on the Guildford and Woolwich pub bombing* 1990, (HC 556) and *Second Report on the Maguire Case*, 1992 (HC 296).

scientists are therefore under a categorical obligation to disclose to the police, and the police to pass on to the CPS, all the scientific evidence that may be relevant to the case' (Report, p 154, para 45). This duty of disclosure, it said, extended to anything that might help the defence.

> Following disclosure, the defence are entitled to access to notebooks and test results and to information about similar evidence discovered in other or related cases, especially where this tends to undermine the identification of the defendant as the offender. We interpret the Court of Appeal judgment in *Ward* as meaning that, if expert witnesses are aware of experiments or tests, even if they have not carried them out personally, which tend to disprove or cast doubt upon the opinions that they are expressing, they are under an obligation to bring the records of them to the attention of the police and prosecution.

The Royal Commission said that it had 'no hesitation in endorsing the main thrust of the Court of Appeal's judgment in *Ward* as regards the disclosure of scientific evidence and it was pleased to be able to say 'that this is also accepted by the public sector laboratories concerned' (p 154, para 47). If the defence thought there might be material at the laboratory which threw doubt on the prosecution's test results, 'they should in our view be entitled to have access to the original notes of the experiment in order to test that belief'. It continued:

> We believe that this is in fact the position, since we have been told by defence experts that they now have full access to everyone and everything relevant to the case in question.

The Royal Commission recommended that when exhibits were taken for analysis by the prosecution, regard should be had to the potential desire of the defence in due course to carry out their own tests on the material. Where practicable, sufficient material should be collected for the purpose and, so far as practicable, the scene of the crime should remain undisturbed. After a suspect had been charged the defence should have an enforceable right to observe any further scientific tests carried out or the right to remove some of the material for their own analysis (Report, p 155, para 52).

Defence access to scientific or forensic material and testing

A JUSTICE Committee said in December 1987 that although the police theoretically made their forensic science laboratory facilities available to the defence, 'in practice little or no use can be made of them'. The police would not permit re-examination of an exhibit already examined by one of their own scientists. They would allow their own scientists to conduct tests for the defence or a defence scientist to use their laboratories. But they insisted that their own scientists had to be present, which meant that the prosecution were fully apprised of the experiments and the results. This was 'wholly unacceptable' and 'an erosion of the principle that it is for the prosecution to establish their case' (JUSTICE, *A Public Defender*, 1987, para 30).

Generally the defence did not take advantage of the possibility of using police facilities. Indeed if they did, and if evidence favourable to the prosecution emerged, it would be a gross breach of duty by the defence solicitor to the client.

In 1989 the House of Commons Home Affairs Committee reported on the Forensic Science Service (*The Forensic Science Service*, 1988 – 9, HC 26 – 1). On the issue of access for the defence it thought that it was valuable that defence lawyers had a choice of using independent scientists or the Forensic Service.

In April 1991 the Forensic Science Service (FSS) became an Executive Agency of the Home Office as part of the Thatcher Government's policy for making public bodies somewhat independent and financially accountable. It started to charge the police and others using its services. (Previously even the defence experts had the use of the facilities free of charge.) The Framework Document provided that the Agency was free to take on work for the defence. But it seems that was developing slowly. (See Russell Stockdale. 'Running with the Hounds', *New Law Journal*, 7 June 1991, p 772, raising the question of how to provide adequate forensic scientific services to the defence.)

The problem of provision of adequate scientific facilities for the defence was in the terms of reference of the Runciman Royal Commission. The Royal Commission said that the public sector forensic science laboratories were prepared to work for the defence for its normal charges – provided the same lab was not already working on the case for the prosecution. The exception was the Metropolitan Police Forensic Science Laboratory, and it intended to change this policy. But it was rare that the defence were dissatisfied with tests carried out for the prosecution. It was more likely to be a matter of interpretation of the results. Defence scientists were allowed to use the public sector facilities (Report, p 146, para 11).

The Commission proposed that 'all the public sector laboratories should look upon themselves as equally available to the defence and the prosecution and we would expect to see considerable development of the provision of services to the defence as time goes by' (Report, p 149, para 24).

The Royal Commission thought that the defence should have complete freedom to choose between public sector and private sector forensic scientists (Report, p 156, para 55). It did not think that public funds should be devoted to establishing separate facilities for the defence.

THE CRIMINAL PROCEDURE AND INVESTIGATIONS ACT 1996 AND THE CODE OF PRACTICE

The recommendations of the Runciman Royal Commission regarding disclosure were basically implemented in the Criminal Procedure and Investigations Act 1996. Having first issued a Consultation Paper in May 1995 (Cm 2684), the Conservative Government published the Bill that November. The Bill received the Royal Assent in July 1996 and came into force together with regulations[205] and the Code of Practice in April 1997.

There is general agreement that it has not worked well.

The provisions of prosecution and defence disclosure are closely linked though they cover different types of material. The duty of prosecution material to be disclosed under the rules relates to unused material, ie the material the prosecution does not intend to use. The prosecution's duty to disclose its own evidence is unchanged by the new legislation. The duty of the defence to disclose material under the Act relates to its case. (For the treatment of the defence disclosure provisions see below at p 000.)

The police are placed under a duty to record and retain information and material generated in the course of an investigation. The Code of Practice deals with the length of time for which material has to be retained.

The Code (para 6.2) states that 'material which may be relevant to an investigation, which has been retained in accordance with this code, and which the disclosure officer believes will not form part of the prosecution case, must be listed on a schedule'. If any of the material is 'sensitive' (which the officer believes it is not in the public interest to disclose) it must be listed on a separate schedule. Both schedules must be given by the police to the prosecution lawyers. The lawyers must also be given records of the first description of any suspect given by potential witnesses; information given by an accused person which indicates his explanation; any material casting doubt on the reliability of a confession or the reliability of a witness; and any material which the investigator believes may fall within the test for primary prosecution disclosure (para 7.3).

Primary prosecution disclosure Section 3(1) required the prosecutor to disclose to the accused any prosecution material 'which in the prosecutor's opinion *might undermine* the case for the prosecution against the accused' (emphasis supplied), or alternatively to give the accused a written statement that there is no material of that description. (As will be seen, the Criminal Justice Bill 2002/03 will change this.)

Under the Act, the duty to give primary disclosure arises with a period to be prescribed measured from 'the relevant day'. For cases dealt with in the magistrates' court the relevant day is the day the defendant pleads not guilty and for cases dealt with at the Crown Court, it is the day the proceedings are committed to the Crown Court.[206] Although a time-limit was envisaged by the Act, none has actually been fixed for prosecution disclosure other than 'as soon as practicable'. But in *R v DPP, ex p Lee* [1999] 2 All ER 737 the Divisional Court laid down the very important principle

---

205 Crown Court (Criminal Procedure and Investigations Act 1996) (Disclosure) Rules 1997; Magistrates Court (Criminal Procedure and Investigations Act 1996) (Disclosure) Rules 1997; Criminal Procedure and Investigations Act 1996 (Defence Disclosure Time-limits) Regulations 1997.

206 Sections 3(8), 12 and 13(1).

that the prosecutor must always be alive to the need to make advance disclosure of material of which he is aware (either from his knowledge or because his attention has been drawn to it by the defence) and which he as a responsible prosecutor recognises should be disclosed at an early stage. The prosecutor had a continuing duty between arrest and committal to ascertain whether immediate disclosure was required in the interests of justice and fairness.

Under the disclosure rules the defence do not have the advantage of primary prosecution disclosure before deciding whether to plead guilty in the magistrates' court.

Also, in cases where the police anticipate a guilty plea in the magistrates' court, under the Act they do not have to pass information to the prosecution lawyers as to the weaknesses of the prosecution's case. The duty on the police to prepare a disclosure schedule for consideration by the prosecution lawyers only arises if the accused is likely to be tried in the Crown Court or is likely to plead not guilty in the magistrates' court. (If the defendant changes his mind and pleads not guilty at the last moment, the disclosure schedule has to be prepared as soon as is reasonably practicable.)

The Act requires the prosecutor when making primary disclosure, at the same time to give to the accused (a) a document indicating the nature of any prosecution material which relates to the offence, which has not been disclosed to the accused, and which the prosecutor believes is not sensitive, or (b) a written statement that there is no material of that kind.

Secondary prosecution disclosure After defence disclosure has been made under s 5 or 6 (p 295 below), the prosecutor must make secondary disclosure of any prosecution material not already disclosed which 'might be reasonably expected to assist the accused's defence as disclosed by the defence statement given to the prosecutor under s 5 or 6' or give the accused a written statement that there is no such material (s 7(2)).

If the accused thinks the prosecution have not complied with their obligation to disclose, he can apply to the court for an order requiring such disclosure (s 8(2)). The court need not make such an order if it does not think such disclosure to be in the public interest (s 8(5)). This decision must however be kept under continuing review by the court (s 15(3)).

The prosecutor too must keep the question of what should be disclosed under continuing review (s 9(2)).

DISCLOSURE OF SENSITIVE MATERIAL — PUBLIC INTEREST IMMUNITY (PII)

The doctrine of public interest immunity enables the prosecution to withhold disclosure of material where in the courts' view, the public's interest in non-disclosure outweighs the defendant's interest in having access to the material. In a series of decisions it was held that the court, not the prosecution, is the arbiter of what could be withheld from disclosure.[207] The court must carry out a balancing exercise, though where non-disclosure may lead to a miscarriage of justice the court should always order disclosure[208] – so that if the prosecution decides that disclosure is not an option the case against the defendant has to be dropped.

The Runciman Royal Commision (Report, Ch 6, para 47) said it believed 'that the procedure laid down in *Johnson, Davis and Rowe* for the disclosure of material that may attract public interest immunity strikes a satisfactory balance between the public interest in protecting such material and the legitimate need of the defence in some cases to see it or to be aware of its existence.

The Criminal Procedure and Investigations Act 1996 in effect codified the common law. [209] There are three possible situations. Wherever possible the prosecutor should inform the defence that he intends to apply for a ruling with both parties present. The second is where the prosecutor considers that he cannot reveal the category of material in issue. He informs the defence that an application will be made in the absence of the defence. Or, where even notifying the defence that an application is to be made reveals too much, an application can be made in the absence of, and without notice to the defence. The court is required to keep its decision under review as the case progresses.

In February 2000 the Strasbourg Court in *Rowe and Davis v United Kingdom*[210] agreed that in exceptional circumstances evidence could be withheld from the defence but found that there had on the facts of the case been a breach of the ECHR. The general rule was that a fair trial included a duty on the prosecution to reveal all its evidence to the defence. (para 60) But this might in some circumstances have to give way to other competing considerations such as national security, protection of witnesses and preserving secrecy of police investigations. (para 61) However, art 6(1) of the Convention only permitted exceptions that were strictly necessary. The procedure followed at the applicants' trial whereby the prosecuting authorities decided to withhold material evidence without informing the trial judge did not meet this standard and the Court of Appeal, which had itself considered the material, was not able to remedy the position as it had not seen the witnesses give their evidence and had to rely on transcripts.

By contrast, in *Jasper v United Kingdom* and *Fitt v United Kingdom*[211] the public interest immunity (PII) application had been made in proper form to the trial judge and the Strasbourg Court held there was no breach of the ECHR. The court rejected the argument that the defence had to be represented by 'special counsel'.

---

[207]   *Ward* (1993) 96 Cr App Rep 1, CA; *Davis, Johnson and Rowe* (1993) 97 Cr App Rep 110, CA; *Keane* (1994) 99 Cr App Rep 1, CA.

[208]   *Keane* (1994) 99 Cr App Rep 1, CA.

[209]   See Crown Court (Criminal Procedure and Investigations Act 1996) (Disclosure) Rules 1997, SI 1997 No 698, reproducing the procedure laid down in *Davis, Rowe and Johnson*.

[210]   (2000) 30 EHRR 1, [2000] Crim LR 584 and commentary at 585.

[211]   (2000) 30 EHRR 1, and 441, [2000] Crim LR 586. But see now also the potentially important decision in *Edwards and Lewis v UK* (2003) Times, 29 July, ECHR.

Lord Justice Auld's Report said that there was 'widespread concern in the legal professions about lack of representation of the defendant's interest [in such hearings] and anecdotal and reported instances of resultant unfairness to the defence'.(Ch10, para 193) He proposed the introduction of a scheme for instruction in such cases by the court of special independent counsel to represent the interests of the defendant both at trial and on appeal.

In July 2003, Sir David Calvert-Smith QC, the Director of Public Prosecutions, announced the new Joint Operational instructions on prosecution disclosure including new rules on public interest immunity applications. A PII application should only be made if disclosure would cause real harm to a genuine public interest.[212]

LORD JUSTICE AULD'S REPORT ON DISCLOSURE GENERALLY

Lord Justice Auld said that the report in 2000 of the CPS Inspectorate in its Thematic Review of the Disclosure of Unused Material, found 'that the 1996 Act was not working as Parliament intended and that its operation did not command the confidence of criminal practitioners' (Ch 10, para 163).

It highlighted the failure of police disclosure officers to prepare full and reliable schedules of unused material; undue reliance by the prosecutors on disclosure officers' schedules and assessment of what should be disclosed; and the 'awkward split of responsibilities between the police and the CPS in the task of determining what should be disclosed.' (para 163)

Auld said that Joyce Plotnikoff and Richard Woolfson in their research study[213] had reached the same conclusions. ('Our findings confirmed the conclusion of the CPS Inspectorate's Thematic Review that poor practice in relation to disclosure was widespread.' (Auld, Ch 6, para 164).) They had found that government objectives for improvement in efficiency had not been achieved; that in the Crown Court the average length of trial had not fallen as hoped and that the scheme was expensive. ('It had been expected that it would be "cost-neutral" for the criminal justice system, but in fact it was so resource intensive that it cost the CPS as much or more than it saved the police and produced no identifiable, significant savings for the courts.' (para 164))

Auld concluded,

> To summarise: the main concerns about the disclosure provisions of the 1996 Act are: a lack of common understanding within the CPS and among police forces of the extent of disclosure required, particularly at the primary stage; the conflict between the need for a disclosure officer sufficiently familiar with

---

[212] 'Getting it right – prosecution disclosure of unused material', *New Law Journal*, 4 July 2003, p 1020.

[213] *A Fair Balance? Evaluation of the Operation of Disclosure Law*, Home Office, 2002.

the case to make a proper evaluation of what is or may be disclosable and one sufficiently independent of the investigation to make objective judgment about it; the consignment of the responsibility to relatively junior officers who are poorly trained for the task; general lack of staffing and training for the task in the police or the CPS for what is an increasingly onerous and sophisticated exercise; in consequence, frequent inadequate and late provision by the prosecution of primary disclosure; failure by defendants and their legal representatives to comply with the Act's requirements for giving the court and the prosecutor adequate and/or timely defence statements and lack of effective means of enforcement of those requirements; seemingly and confusingly different tests for primary and secondary prosecution disclosure; and the whole scheme, whether operated efficiently or otherwise is time-consuming and otherwise expensive for all involved. The outcome for the criminal justice process is frequent failure to exchange adequate disclosure at an early stage to enable both parties to prepare for trial efficiently and in a timely way. (Ch 6, para 167)

Auld said that reform was needed but that there was no consensus as to what form it should take. One suggestion was for a reversion to the common law position obtaining immediately before the introduction of the 1996 Act. Another, and more widely supported, suggestion was for automatic disclosure by prosecutors of all non-sensitive unused material held by the prosecution. [214] This was supported by the Criminal Bar Association, by many judges, the Law Society and by JUSTICE. There had already been a move toward automatic exchange of certain categories of documents and the Attorney-General's Guidelines in 2000 had recommended blanket disclosure of large quantities of material (see p 279 above).

Automatic disclosure of the whole police file apart from sensitive material, could involve 'enormous and unnecessary cost for the police and prosecutors, particularly in large cases'. (Ch 10, para 169.). Such savings as might accrue in identifying disclosability of documents would in many instances be eclipsed by the costs of compilation by the prosecution and of examination by the defence of vast volumes of irrelevant material. (para 169)

In Auld's view the best way forward was first to require automatic disclosure at the primary stage of some forms of documents (crime reports, incident report books, police officers' notebooks, custody records, draft versions of witness statements where the draft differs from the and experts' reports). It could also include certain types of material by reference to their subject matter as distinct from the category of document.

Beyond that he favoured building on and improving the present system of two-stage prosecution disclosure coupled with greater defence disclosure.

---

[214] The writer would favour one or other of these two suggestions – see his Response to the Auld Report, www.lcd.gov.uk(Major Reports, Comments) at pp 47-54.

- The test for primary and secondary prosecution disclosure should be made the same.
- The duty of recording unused material should remain with the police but with improved training, rigorous 'spot audits' by HM Inspectors, and non-compliance being treated as a police disciplinary offence.
- Prosecutors should carefully check police schedules against witness statements and unused material.
- Transferring from the police prosecutors responsibility for identifying disclosable material.[215]

THE GOVERNMENT'S RESPONSE TO AULD ON PROSECUTION DISCLOSURE

The White Paper *Justice for all* (Cm 5563, July 2002) devoted one-and- half pages to disclosure mostly on defence disclosure [216]. In regard to prosecution disclosure it said:

- The two-stage process for prosecution disclosure would remain (para 3.48).
- There should be a single test of disclosability at both stages (ibid). (The Criminal Justice Bill 2002/03 made a significant change in this respect by changing the test from subjective to objective – for material that ' in the prosecutor's opinion might undermine' the prosecution's case it substituted 'might reasonably be considered capable of undermining' the prosecution case, and added 'or of assisting the accused'. [217] The prosecutor's duty to apply this test continues throughout the case. [218])
- Work already in progress would continue to ensure 'consistent and efficient delivery of prosecution disclosure duties' which would 'in turn ensure that the defence has the necessary information to play its part in the disclosure procedure more effectively' (para 3.51).
- The Government wanted 'to see greater protection for sensitive information in organised crime cases'. Options were being developed in consultation with the police (para 3.53).

For commentary on disclosure see especially R Ede and E Shepherd, *Active Defence: A Lawyer's Guide to Police Investigation and Prosecution and Defence Disclosure*, The Law Society, revised ed, 1998. See also J Sprack, 'The Duty of Disclosure', (1997) *Criminal Law Review*, pp 308-20; R Leng, 'Defence strategies for information deficit: negotiating the CPIA', *International Journal of Evidence and Proof*, 1997, (1), no 4, pp 215-31. For consideration of the impact of the Human Rights Act 1998 see for instance S D Sharpe, 'Article 6 and the Disclosure of Evidence in Criminal Trials'

---

[215] Plotnikoff and Woolfson, n 213 above at p 134, recommended to the contrary that primary responsibility remain with the police – a view shared by the writer.

[216] For the White Paper's proposals on defence disclosure see p.000 below.

[217] Clause 31 amending CPIA 1996, s 3(1)(a).

[218] Clause 32 inserting a new CPIA 1996, s 7A.

[1999] *Criminal Law Review*, pp 273-86. See also JA Epp, 'Achieving the aims of the disclosure scheme in England and Wales' (2001) 5 *International Journal of Evidence and Proof*, 2001(5), pp 188-98; and P Plowden and K Kerrigan, 'Cards on the Table?' *New Law Journal*, 18 May 2001, p 735, 1 June 2001, p 820.

The subject was treated at length in the writer's Response to the Auld Report – www.lcd.gov.uk (Major Reports, Comments at pp 47-54 – including extensive reference to the discouraging findings of the Plotnikoff-Woolfson research.)

(c)   Other issues of prosecution disclosure

Where a prosecution witness is of known bad character, the prosecution is under a duty to inform the defence of the fact (*R v Collister and Warhurst* (1955) 39 Cr App Rep 100). In *Paraskeva* [1983] Crim LR 186, the Court of Appeal quashed a conviction because the prosecution had failed to comply with this duty. The complainant in a charge of robbery and assault had had a conviction for theft. The Appeal Court said that the defence should have been told, since either the prosecution or the defence were lying and the jury should have had this information in making up their minds which it was. It has been laid down in a Practice Statement that details of the previous convictions of the accused himself must be supplied by the prosecution to the defence – *Practice Direction* [1966] 1 WLR 1184.

See also *Edwards* (1991) 93 Cr App Rep 48, where the Court of Appeal quashed convictions because disciplinary findings against police witnesses had not been made known to the defence or the court. The court held that the defence were entitled to cross-examine police officers not only about disciplinary findings but also about any earlier trial in which their evidence had been rejected by the jury in circumstances suggesting that they were not believed. The Runciman Royal Commission thought this went too far. It recommended that the prosecution should only be required to disclose disciplinary findings against police witnesses in so far as those records were relevant to an allegation by the defence about the conduct of the witness in the present case. The Royal Commission thought that the prosecution should also not be required to disclose cases in which there has been an acquittal following evidence given by an officer where it would seem that his evidence must have been disbelieved by the jury. Since research in the jury room was not permitted there was no way of knowing why the jury had rejected particular evidence (Report, p 97, para 56).

The prosecution must disclose to the defence copies of any statement or report made by any prison doctor as to the mental capacity of the defendant. Also the results of any examination carried out by the Home Office Forensic Science Laboratory should be handed over to the defence. But generally the prosecution are not under an obligation to disclose material that goes solely to the credibility of defence witnesses – *R v Brown (Winston)* [1997] 3 All ER 769, HL. For a report of the case, comparison with *R v Rasheed* (1994) 158 JP 941 and comment see also *New Law Journal*, 8 July 1994, p 939.

(d)   Disclosure by the defence

It has been a fundamental principle that the defendant's right of silence in the police station extended also to the preparatory stages before the trial and to the trial itself. Subject to a few exceptions, the defence was not under any obligation to give advance notice of its case. But this has now changed.

The first exception was the Criminal Justice Act 1967, which in s 11 laid down that an alibi defence must be notified to the police in advance of the trial, so that it could be checked.

In 1975, the James Committee (p 37 above), in spite of its strong recommendations for more disclosure by the prosecution, did not think that the defence should be asked to disclose more – or at least not without more detailed consideration. It observed that: 'there is considerable strength in the argument that it is wrong in principle, in a system which presumes innocence until guilt is proved, to require disclosure of the defence before the details of the evidence for the prosecution are disclosed' (para 229).

The Philips Royal Commission on Criminal Procedure also considered whether the principle of disclosure accepted in alibi defences should be extended to other forms of evidence. It did not think that the defence should generally be required to disclose its case. It thought there was an 'objection of principle' to any formal requirement of general disclosure by the defence because the burden of proof was upon the prosecution (para 8.20). It considered that it would be impossible to devise effective sanctions against a defendant who failed to comply with the requirement, since it seemed unlikely that in practice courts would be prepared to prevent a defendant from introducing evidence that demonstrated his innocence. (The experience with the alibi defence rule is that courts are normally lax about insisting on compliance by the defence and in reality the sanction is the comment permitted to prosecution and judge on failure to comply.) The Commission cited research evidence that even police officers thought that new facts introduced at the trial resulted in unjustified acquittals only in about 1% of cases (para 8.21). But it agreed with the Scottish Thomson Committee in its report in 1975 (Cmnd 6218, para 37.11) that special defences should be notified to the prosecution in advance. The obvious examples, it thought, were defences depending on medical or forensic evidence on which the prosecution would wish to consider calling expert testimony.

Section 81 of PACE granted power to make Crown Court rules to require any party to proceedings before the Crown Court to disclose to the other party any expert evidence which he proposes to adduce in the case.

The new rules (Crown Court (Advance Notice of Expert Evidence) Rules, SI 1987/716) provided for the disclosure, as soon as practicable after committal, of a statement in writing of any finding or opinion of an expert upon which a party intended to rely. Failure can be penalised by the court refusing permission to adduce the expert evidence, but, like alibi notices, it is not strictly enforced by the courts.

ROSKILL REPORT

The problem of disclosure by the defence was also considered by the Roskill Committee in its report on Fraud Trials (HMSO, January 1986).

It concluded, subject to one dissent, that the defence should be required to outline its case in writing at the preparatory stage. Failure to do so should be capable of attracting adverse comment from the prosecution and the judge, and the jury could be invited to draw adverse inferences (para 6.82).

It considered, but ultimately rejected, the case for advance disclosure by the defence of the names of its witnesses and for advance notification to the prosecution as to whether the defendant himself intends to give evidence (para s 6.83 – 4).

In his Note of Dissent, Mr Merricks said that he would restrict the use that could be made of the defence outline of its case at the trial. No reference to it should be permitted during the trial save with the leave of the judge. This would be to avoid the danger that prosecution counsel would use the defence advance disclosure statement in examining his own witnesses, so as to discredit the defence. By the same token, there would be a danger that the defence might be hampered in cross-examining the prosecution witnesses. It was a normal aspect of cross-examination that counsel would probe and test the veracity and credibility of the other side's witnesses. But if the defence were revealed in advance the judge might rule irrelevant any line of questioning which was not germane to the defence as outlined.

CRIMINAL JUSTICE ACT 1987

The Government, however, accepted the majority's recommendation. The Criminal Justice Act 1987 provided that in serious fraud case investigations notices can be given under s 2 requiring persons to give information and to produce documents. This power has been used extensively. But in addition under s 7 a Crown Court judge can order a special preparatory hearing in cases of 'fraud of such seriousness and complexity that substantial benefits are likely to accrue from' such a hearing, for the purpose of identifying the issues, assisting the comprehension of such issues, expediting the proceedings or assisting the judge's management of the trial. An order for a preparatory hearing may be asked for by either the prosecution or the defence.

The judge can order the prosecution to 'prepare and serve any documents that appear to him to be relevant' and having made such an order and the prosecution having complied with it, the judge can then make an equivalent order for the defence to provide relevant documents (s 7(3)).

Under this provision the defence can be required to give the court and the prosecution: (1) a statement in writing setting out in general terms the nature of his defence and indicating the principal matters on which he takes issue with the prosecution; (2) notice of any objections he has to the prosecution's case statement; (3) notice of any points of law he intends to take, including any on the admissibility of evidence; and

(4) notice of the extent to which he agrees with the prosecution as regards documents and other matters and the reason for any disagreements (s 9(5)).

Section 10 provides that, in the event of any departure from the case disclosed at the preparatory hearing or any failure to comply with the obligation to make advance disclosure, the judge and, with the judge's leave, the other party, may make such comment as he thinks appropriate. (In deciding whether to give such leave the judge is required to have regard to the extent of any departure and whether there was any justification for it.) When making an order to the defence to make advance disclosure, the judge must warn the defence of the possibility of such comment (s 9(7)).

For a report on how the powers under the CJA 1987 have been utilised see M Levi, *The Investigation, Prosecution and Trial of Serious Fraud*, Royal Commission on Criminal Justice, Research Report No 14, 1993.

A Working Group chaired by the Lord Chancellor's Department recommended in 1991 that legislation should be introduced requiring the defendant to state the nature of his defence at a plea and directions hearing in the Crown Court (*Working Group on Pre-Trial Issues*, November 1991, para 244[219]). The report said that it was not suggested that a defendant should specify the substance or detail of his case or the evidence he will call to establish his defence, but he should be asked to reveal the essential issues in dispute and the principal facts (ibid). This could achieve substantial savings in court time.

RUNCIMAN ROYAL COMMISSION ON CRIMINAL JUSTICE

The Runciman Royal Commission too, by a majority of 10 – 1, recommended that after the prosecution had produced its case, the defendant should be asked to indicate in outline the nature of his defence:

> 59. With one dissentient, we believe that there are powerful reasons for extending the obligations on the defence to provide advance disclosure. If all the parties had in advance an indication of what the defence would be, this would not only encourage earlier and better preparation of cases but might well result in the prosecution being dropped in the light of the defence disclosure, an earlier resolution through a plea of guilty, or the fixing of an earlier trial date. The length of the trial could also be more readily estimated, leading to a better use of the time both of the court and of those involved in the trial; and there would be kept to a minimum those cases where the defendant withholds his or her defence until the last possible moment in the hope of confusing the jury or evading investigation of a fabricated defence [p 97].

The majority thought this would not infringe the right of defendants not to incriminate themselves – anymore than this right was infringed by the duty to advance one's

---

[219] The Report, which made 165 recommendations, was not published in the normal sense. The work of this committee was taken over in January 1996 by a new Trial Issues Group.

defence at trial. Moreover defendants would still be entitled to remain silent throughout (pp 97 – 8, para 60). It was true that 'ambush defences' were relatively rare but the present system encouraged late preparation of cases which was undesirable.

68. In most cases disclosure of the defence should be a matter capable of being handled by the defendant's solicitor (in the same way that alibi notices are usually dealt with at present). Standard forms could be drawn up to cover the most common offences, with the solicitor having only to tick one or more of a list of possibilities, such as 'accident', 'self-defence', 'consent', 'no dishonest intent', 'no appropriation', 'abandoned goods', 'claim of right', 'mistaken identification' and so on. There will be complex cases which may require the assistance of counsel in formulating the defence. Where counsel are involved, they should if practicable stay with the case until the end of the trial: where this is impracticable, the barrister who has been involved with the pre-trial work should pass on his or her preparation to the barrister who is to present the case at trial [p 98].

The writer dissented:

1. The most important objection to defence disclosure is that it is contrary to principle for the defendant to be made to respond to the prosecution's case until it has been presented at the trial. The defendant should be required to respond to the case the prosecution makes, not to the case it says it is going to make. They are often significantly different.

2. The fundamental issue at stake is that the burden of proof lies throughout on the prosecution. Defence disclosure is designed to be helpful to the prosecution and, more generally, to the system. But it is not the job of the defendant to be helpful either to the prosecution or to the system. His task, if he chooses to put the prosecution to the proof, is simply to defend himself. Rules requiring advance disclosure of alibis and expert evidence are reasonable exceptions to this general principle. But, in my view, it is wrong to require the defendant to be helpful by giving advance notice of his defence and to penalise him by adverse comment if he fails to do so... .

8. In serious fraud cases under the Criminal Justice Act 1987 the defence can be required by the judge to produce a case statement setting out the defence 'in general terms'. But a study done for the Royal Commission by Professor Michael Levi shows that this has proved largely ineffectual because it is not sufficiently specific.[220] If it does not work in the serious fraud area, it probably will not work in other areas.

---

[220]   Michael Levi, *The Investigation, Prosecution and Trial of Serious Fraud*, Royal Commission on Criminal Justice Research Study No 14, 1993, pp 104, 182.

9. Moreover, a general requirement of defence disclosure would involve significant extra delays, costs and inefficiencies. The lay client would have to be seen to take his instructions. Getting the lay client to come into the solicitor's office or going to see him in prison is often troublesome. Counsel would quite frequently be involved both to advise and often actually to settle the defence disclosure. It could hardly be expected that defence lawyers would go out of their way to be helpful to the prosecution. The prosecution would therefore often find it right to ask for 'further and better particulars', with resulting further delays and costs. These extra costs would apply not only to cases that ended as trials but also to those that ended as last-minute guilty pleas ('cracked trials').

10. The present much criticised lack of continuity in counsel's involvement in the case would pose even greater problems than in relation to ordinary pre-trial matters. From the defendant's point of view, the last minute appearance of a barrister he has never seen before would be even more upsetting in a regime where pre-trial defence disclosure was a requirement. It is bad enough that the client should so often be faced on the day of the trial with a new barrister. It would be worse if he knew that the new barrister's ability to represent him was restricted by decisions regarding defence disclosure made by another barrister at an earlier stage whether on paper or at a pre-trial hearing.

11. Moreover it is extremely unlikely that defence disclosure rules would be enforced. The rule requiring advance notice of an alibi defence is honoured more in the breach than in the observance. Where there has been a breach of the rule the judge can refuse to allow the alibi defence to be put. But breaches are generally not penalised by the judges – because they are understandably reluctant to prevent a defendant from putting forward his defence. The judges would I believe be equally slow to penalise failure to make this new form of defence disclosure, whether by adverse comment or by sanctions imposed on the lawyers.

12. In summary, I am against defence disclosure because it is wrong in principle, and because it would cause extra delay, cost and general inefficiency in the system, to little, if any, purpose [pp 221–23].

THE CRIMINAL PROCEDURE AND INVESTIGATIONS ACT 1996

The Criminal Procedure and Investigations Act provided for a new regime of compulsory disclosure by the accused in response to primary disclosure by the prosecution (on which see p 284 above). Section 5 said that the accused must give a defence statement to the prosecutor –

(6) For the purposes of this section a defence statement is a written statement–
(a) setting out in general terms the nature of the accused's defence,

(b) indicating the matters on which he takes issue with the prosecution, and

(c) setting out, in the case of each such matter, the reason why he takes issue with the prosecution.

In the case of an alibi the particulars to be provided included the name and address of any such witness, failing which, information as to how to find him (s 5(7)).

The Consultation Paper issued in 1995 (Cm 2684) had made the proposal that the defence would as a matter of rule have to give the police advance notice of the names and addresses of their witnesses. This was criticised and it was not included in the Act.

The regulations impose a tight time-limit for defence disclosure. The defence statement must be served within 14 days of the prosecution's service of prosecution material or statement that there is none. The defence can apply for an extension of time.

On the question what use, if any, the prosecution can make of the defence statement see J Sprack, 'Will defence disclosure snap the golden thread?', *International Journal of Evidence and Proof*, 1998, vol 2, no 4, pp 224-31; S Thompson, 'Defence Statements – Weighting the Scales or Tipping the Balance on a Submission of No Case?' (1998) *Criminal Law Review*, pp 802-07; C Parry and M I Tregilgas-Davey, 'Prosecution use of defence statements', *Solicitors' Journal*, 28 May, 1999, p 520.

If the defendant fails to comply with the obligation to give a defence statement or does so late, or sets out inconsistent defences, or at his trial puts forward a defence inconsistent with what appeared in the defence statement, or advances an alibi of which he has not given advance notice, the judge and, with leave of the court, the prosecution 'may make such comment as appears appropriate' (s 11(3)(a)). Also 'the court or jury may draw such inferences as appear proper in deciding whether the accused is guilty' (s 11(3)(b)).

The Runciman Royal Commission and expert evidence

The Royal Commission unanimously recommended that if the defence propose to contest the prosecution's scientific or other expert evidence they should give advance notice of the grounds on which they dispute that evidence – *whether or not they intend to call expert testimony of their own* (Report, p 157, para 60). The *Crown Court Study* done by the writer for the Royal Commission showed that the defence called an expert in only one-third of the cases in which they contested the prosecution's scientific evidence. In two-thirds of cases, the challenge was purely in the form of cross-examination. But it is very common in that situation for the defence to be advised by an expert even though he is not called at the trial. The present rules only require advance disclosure of evidence one intends to adduce at the trial. The defendant does not have to give notice of tests done which support the prosecution theory of the case.

The Royal Commission recommended that where the defence were calling an expert at the trial, the experts for both sides should be required to meet 'in order to draw up a report of the scientific facts and their interpretation by both sides' (Report, p 158, para 63). That document would then be available at the trial as a statement of what was agreed and what remained in dispute. If substantial disagreement on scientific issues was recorded, a preparatory hearing should be held in front of the trial judge to see whether disagreement could be narrowed before the trial unless both sides certify that this is unnecessary (Report, p 159, para 68). (The Commission did not refer to the problem identified in Lord Woolf's Interim Report (p 183, para 9) of experts being instructed by the lawyers not to agree anything.)

Where the defence intended to dispute the prosecution's scientific evidence without calling their own expert they should be required to indicate what was in dispute. Five members of the eleven-member Commission would have gone further to require the defence experts to participate in pre-trial discussion with the prosecution expert. But the majority did not support that recommendation.

The Commission considered, but rejected a proposal that the judge should be given the power to order that further scientific tests be done or that a third independent expert be asked for his opinion. It concluded that that 'might well add greater complexity to the pre-trial and trial phases, because it would be necessary for the third expert to be subjected to examination and cross-examination by both sides, without necessarily bringing about any decisive answer to the questions in issue' (p 158, para 67). But the judge should have a power to direct the experts on both sides to meet to discuss and to try to resolve their differences (ibid). (As has been seen, (p 75 above) Lord Woolf's Interim Report was more radical in recommending that, at least in some cases, the court should appoint an independent expert even though the parties would also have their own experts (p 187, para 23). See CPR 35.7.)

LORD JUSTICE AULD'S REPORT

In his report Lord Justice Auld said,

> [M]any defence statements do not comply with the requirements of the 1996 Act. They do not set out in general terms the nature of the defence or the matters on which issue is taken with the prosecution case and why. Often defence statements amount to little more than a denial, accompanying a list of material that the defence wish to see and without explanation for its potential relevance to any issues in the trial. Most judges, Crown Prosecution Service representatives or practitioners who have commented on the matter in the Review and to the Plotnikoff and Woolfson Study [221] have said that the statements, in the form in which they are generally furnished, do little to narrow the issues at, or otherwise assist preparation for, trial. (Ch 10, para 158)

[221] *A Fair Balance*, Home Office, 2002, p.13.

The 14-day time-limit for filing the defence statement was tight and sometimes insufficient. Prosecution primary disclosure might be defective or late, defendants for all sorts of reasons might not give their solicitors instructions or do so in time, the solicitors might misunderstand the instructions, or neither might focus sufficiently on the issues. Judges were likely to be very cautious in permitting the jury to draw adverse inferences from a failure to comply with the requirements. (para 159)

Auld said that he had considered whether to recommend that the defence be under an obligation to identify defence witnesses and the content of their expected evidence but had concluded against it. Many would find it objectionable as going beyond definition of the issues and requiring the defendant to set out an affirmative case. (para 180, p 470) There were too many instances when the prosecution amended the charges late in the day or failed to provide adequate or timely primary disclosure. There could be no question of punishing a defendant by barring an unannounced defence and only rarely of allowing adverse inferences. Often it would be difficult to establish whether the fault for non-compliance lay with the lawyer or the defendant. Financial penalties, whether on the lawyer or the defendant, were equally unworkable. (para s 180-83)

Although Auld did not recommend changes in the requirements for defence statements he did propose a variety of ways for making them more effective (Ch 10, para 183):

- to have full and timely prosecution disclosure
- to pay defence lawyers a proper and discrete fee for preparatory work
- to make defendants in custody more accessible to their lawyers (including provision of video-conferencing facilities)
- for prosecution lawyers to request particulars of inadequate defence statements, seeking court directions if necessary
- through professional conduct rules, training, guidance and in the rare cases where it was appropriate, discipline, '[T]o inculcate in criminal defence practitioners and through them their clients, the principle that a defendant's right of silence is not a right to conceal in advance of trial the issues he is going to take. Its purpose is to protect the innocent from wrongly incriminating themselves, not to enable the guilty, by fouling up the criminal process, to make it as procedurally difficult as possible for the prosecution to prove their guilt regardless of cost and disruption to others involved'. (para 183)

THE GOVERNMENT'S EXTENSION OF THE DUTY OF DEFENCE DISCLOSURE

The White Paper *Justice for All* (Cm 5563, July 2002) indicated the Government's intention to make important changes in regard to defence disclosure:

- Widening the matters on which an adverse inference could be drawn to include significant omissions that the defendant could reasonably have been expected to have mentioned in the defence statement. [222] This was included in the Criminal Justice Bill 2002/03. [223]

- Removing the requirement for permission from the judge before commenting on discrepancies between the defence statement and the defence at trial. This was included in the Criminal Justice Bill 2002/03. [224]

- Incentives and strengthened sanctions aimed at getting prosecution counsel to play a more active role in advising on and challenging the adequacy of defence statements. (para 3.54)

- Giving the prosecution a right to apply for an early judicial hearing to enable the prosecution to challenge unreasonable defence requests for prosecution documents. (para 3.54)

- Enhancing the requirements of the defence statement (para 3.54). This was included in the Criminal Justice Bill 2002/03. (See below.)

- Requiring the judge to alert the defence to inadequacies in the defence statement from which adverse inferences may be drawn. (para 3.54) This was included in the Criminal Justice Bill 2002/03 and extended to other failings of defence disclosure. [225]

- Requiring the defence to provide, in advance, details of any unused expert witness reports. (para 3.57) In August 2002 the Home Office issued a consultation paper on this issue. (For the details and a critical response see M Zander, 'Advance Disclosure', *Solicitors' Journal*, 20 September 2002, 824. The writer's full 17-page Response to the Consultation Paper is accessible on www.lse.ac.uk/collections/law/news.) Reacting to criticism, the Government dropped the proposal that defence expert reports should be disclosed, but the Bill contained a provision requiring the defence to disclose the name and address of any expert consulted by the defence. [226] In the debate on the measure in the Commons the Home Office Minister said that the purpose was to 'enable the prosecution to approach and consult expert witnesses with a view to obtaining evidence to support the prosecution case' [227] Could the prosecution call a defence expert as a prosecution witness? The Minister said, 'It would be open to them to do so ... Of course the legal professional privilege rule would prevent the expert from

---

[222] Paragraph 3.52.

[223] New s 11(2)(e) and (f) of the CPIA 1996 inserted by cl 38 of the Criminal Justice Bill 2002/03.

[224] Under the CPIA 1996, s 11(3) adverse comment on 'faults in disclosure by the accused' could be made only with the leave of the court. By contrast, the equivalent provision in the clause replacing s 11 had no requirement of leave of the court save where the 'fault' was giving a witness notice late or calling a witness who was not named in the witness notice (s 11(4), (5), (6) inserted by cl 38 of the Bill).

[225] New CPIA 1996, s 6E(2) inserted by cl 35 of the Bill.

[226] New CPIA 1996, s 6D inserted by cl 34 of the Bill.

[227] HC Official Report Standing Committee B (Criminal Justice Bill) 9 January 2003, cols 254–55.

being questioned about any work done for the defence.' [228] The House of Commons Home Affairs Committee in its report on the Bill said that while it accepted the need for the provision it was not convinced that it would work. The Home Secretary giving evidence to the Committee had admitted, 'There would be little or no sanction in practice... In terms of the actual trial, if [defence solicitors] had deliberately or negligently failed to identify the names of all experts and the trial has taken place then there is not much that can be done about that'.[229]

- Requiring details of defence witnesses. (para 3.57) Implemented by a provision in the Bill that the defence serve on the court and the prosecutor a notice giving the name, address and date of birth of any proposed defence witness together with any information known to the accused which 'might be of material assistance in identifying or finding' the witness. Any changes or further information must be notified by an amended notice. [230] The House of Commons Home Affairs Committee recommended that the Bill be amended so that when the prosecution wish to interview a defence witness, they should be required to notify the defence and offer to interview the witness in the presence of the defence. Also that the interview should be tape-recorded. [231] The Government broadly accepted the Committee's suggestions but said they would be dealt with in a Code of Practice rather than by amending the Bill. An amendment to require such a Code of Practice was introduced during the Lords Committee stage debate on 14 July, see col 744.[232] The section states that the code must include, in particular, guidance as to: the information that must be provided to both the interviewee and the accused regarding such an interview; the attendance of the interviewee's solicitor and the accused's solicitor at the interview; and the attendance of any other appropriate person having regard to the age and any disability of the interviewee.

The Criminal Justice Bill 2002/03 made other changes regarding defence disclosure by inserting new provisions in the 1996 Act:

- The accused required to provide a more detailed defence statement. [233] Thus where previously the Act required disclosure 'in general terms' of the nature of the defence, there would now be an obligation to set out 'the nature of the accused's defence, including any particular defences on which he intends to rely' (s 6A(1)(a)) and details of any point of law he wishes to take (s 6A(1)(d)). (The Home Office Minister agreed in the Committee stage of the Bill that the defendant could not be penalised if his lawyers failed in their duty to notify points of law to be raised)

---

[228]   HC Official Report Standing Committee B (Criminal Justice Bill) 9 January 2003, col 255.
[229]   HC 83, 2nd Report 2002-03, para s 77-78.
[230]   New s 6C of the 1996 Act inserted by cl 33 of the Bill.
[231]   HC 83, 2002-03, para 71.
[232]   New s 21A of the CPIA.
[233]   New CPIA 1996, s 6A inserted by cl 32(2) of the Bill.

- The Home Secretary given the power to prescribe in regulations further details that have to be contained in defence statements. [234] In the Committee stage in the Commons, the Government accepted an amendment to require that any such change would require the approval of an affirmative resolution passed by both Houses of Parliament.
- The defence must update the defence statement, as required by regulations. [235]
- Either on his own motion or on the application of any party, the judge may direct that the jury be given a copy of the defence statement (edited to remove any inadmissible evidence) if that would help the jury 'to understand the case or to resolve any issue in the case'. [236]
- Failure to comply with any of the rules regarding defence disclosure can lead to comment by the court or 'any other party' and adverse inferences being drawn.[237]

The defence disclosure provisions in the Bill were debated in the House of Lords during the Committee stage on 14 July 2003. [238] They were severely criticised by speaker after speaker from all sides of the House. Although no vote was taken on these clauses it was clear that the issue would come up again on Report in the autumn with the possibility that the Government might be defeated – as it was on 15 July regarding trial on indictment without a jury, on which see p 522 below.

8. The guilty plea

The guilty plea plays a critical role in the criminal process since the great majority of defendants do plead guilty. In the Crown Court the proportion is currently around 60%. (According to the *Judicial Statistics*, Table 6.8, in 2001, 61% pleaded guilty to all charges and 3% pleaded guilty to some charges.) In the magistrates' courts there are unfortunately no official figures. Obviously, in the great mass of minor motoring cases the accused pleads guilty in virtually all cases. But even in categories of more serious offences, most plead guilty. (In a sample of 3,000 cases in five offence categories – shoplifting, assaulting a police officer, possession of cannabis, criminal damage and social security fraud – as many as 83% of the defendants pleaded guilty (*Report of a Survey of the Grant of Legal Aid in Magistrates' Courts*, Lord Chancellor's Department, 1983, p 5).)

One very curious aspect of the statistics on guilty pleas is how they consistently show very different patterns in different parts of the country. (Thus the guilty-plea rate

---

234 Subsection (4) of the new CPIA 1996, s 6A.
235 New CPIA 1996, s 6B inserted by cl 32(3) of the Bill.
236 New CPIA 1996, s 6E(4),(5) inserted by cl 35.
237 New CPIA 1996, s 11(5) inserted by cl 38 of the Bill.
238 On cl 32 (Defence disclosure) see cols 691-99; on cl 33 (Notification of intention to call defence witnesses) see cols 715-25; on cl 34 (Notification of names of experts instructed by defendant) see cols 726-37.

nationally in 2001 was 61% but it varied from a high of 71% on the North Eastern circuit to a low of 47% in London.[239])

It seems likely that the main reason why accused persons plead guilty is that they *are* guilty, they know they are guilty, they believe that the police know it and can prove it, and they cannot see any advantage in pleading not guilty. Frequently they have made a tape-recorded or signed statement admitting the facts alleged against them in the police station, and this in turn has followed from admissions made in the course of the earlier period of questioning by the police. (A study of a large sample of cases tried in the Crown Court in Birmingham and London showed that 88% of those who made statements confessing to the charges pleaded guilty in Birmingham and two-thirds in London: see J Baldwin and M McConville, 'Confessions in Crown Court Trials', *Royal Commission on Criminal Procedure, Research Study No 5*, 1980, p 14.)

Sometimes, however, innocent persons plead guilty.

(a)   The innocent who plead guilty

There have been three formal studies which have produced substantial evidence that this is a real issue. The first was that of Mr Clive Davies, a barrister, who conducted interviews with 418 men charged with burglary in the course of a study of the bail system. Of these, eight men volunteered the information that although they were not guilty they intended to plead guilty to the charges. A further 21 either said that they were not guilty or said they intended to plead not guilty, but subsequently pleaded guilty. Davies concentrated his focus on the eight who said they would plead guilty from the outset:

Clive Davies, 'The Innocent who Plead Guilty', *Law Guardian*, March 1970, pp 9, 11

AB, a man with no previous convictions of crime, was walking home from a dance late at night with a friend. In the High Street they were stopped by three policemen, who pointed out a broken shop door and accused AB and his friend of having broken it with intent to steal. AB (who declares that until that moment he had no knowledge whatsoever of the broken door) and his friend were cautioned, taken to the police station and charged with the offence of burglary. After four hours at the police station (11 pm to 3 am) they both agreed to 'do a deal' by pleading guilty to causing malicious damage in return for the charge of burglary being withdrawn. AB insisted to me that he had nothing whatever to do with the broken door, and agreed to admit the charge because: (1) No one would believe his word and that of his friend against the word of the three police officers, who, he said, were going to testify that they caught the two men

---

[239]   *Judicial Statistics*, 2001, Table 6.9.

in the act of pushing against the shop door; (2) His wife, who resented his being out late, would be staying up awaiting his arrival home, and would be 'doing her nut' at the lateness of the hour; (3) The case, with a plea of guilty, would entail the loss of only two days' work through appearance in court, while a plea of not guilty, especially if taken to Quarter Sessions, would involve the loss of many day's work, spread over several weeks or months, and possibly of AB's job, a matter of some importance to him, because he had a wife and family to support and numerous hire-purchase payments to keep up; and (4) As a first offender, he could expect to escape with a fairly small fine. He did plead guilty, and fines and compensation amounted to some £30, rather less than the probable total cost of even a successful defended case.

CD, also a man without previous convictions, left a public house at about eleven o'clock with EF, a friend with a long criminal record. Both were fairly drunk and both wanted to urinate. They went into an alley, where they saw an open outhouse door and (with the logic of the drunken) thought it would be a good idea to relieve their aching bladders in the darkness and privacy of the outhouse. They came out to find two plain-clothes policemen waiting for them in the alley, and they were subsequently charged with being found on enclosed premises with intent to steal a motor-cycle, even though neither of them knew how to ride one. CD's solicitor strongly advised him to plead guilty, as did a fellow employee at CD's place of work 'who used to be the clerk of the Court': no one, said these well-informed persons, would believe him, especially in view of EF's previous convictions. When I saw him, CD had firmly made up his mind to plead guilty – 'to get it over with' as he said, and to bring an end to the intolerable state of anxiety that was depriving him of his appetite and sleep. It is a cardinal rule of social research that the investigator must not intervene so as to alter the situation he is studying, but most rules have their exceptions, and in this case it seemed essential to try to intervene. ... So I spent upwards of an hour trying to make him see the folly of pleading guilty if he was not: in this I was supported by his mother, who shared my views, but had succumbed in their two-week period of misery to CD's own mood of hopelessness. Whether or not as a result of this persuasion, CD pleaded not guilty, and both he and EF were acquitted. They were bound over to keep the peace, presumably on account of their undoubtedly illegal and somewhat offensive trespass. According to CD there were unsavoury undertones in his case which never came to the attention of the court. He has the appearance and manner of a 'female' homosexual, and was found to be carrying a perfume bottle when given a routine search after arrest. ... He said that he was told at the police station that unless he pleaded guilty to the garage-breaking charge he would be charged with something very much more serious, from which he inferred (as well he might) that allegations of a homosexual offence would be made.

On the basis of this study Davies calculated that some thousands of persons each year pleaded guilty to charges of which they were innocent.

In a study based on interviews with women in Holloway prison it was found that a significant number pleaded guilty to offences they claimed not to have committed. Of 527 women who had been tried at magistrates' courts, there were 56 such cases. The reasons they gave were similar to those mentioned by Davies – police advice or pressure, to save time and avoid remands, fear that pleading not guilty would lead to harsher penalties or the feeling that there was no point, when the police evidence would inevitably be preferred (Susanne Dell, *Silent in Court*, Occasional Papers in Social Administration, Number 42 (Bell, 1971), p 30).

In a later study by John Baldwin and Michael McConville of last-minute change of plea cases tried at the Birmingham Crown Court, 'over half of the sample made some claim to be innocent, and often very vehemently, either of the whole of the indictment to which they pleaded guilty or of individual counts within it' (*Negotiated Justice*, Martin Robertson, 1977, p 61). No fewer than 70 of the 121 defendants interviewed (58%) claimed to be innocent. Some of these claims according to the researchers were somewhat limp, others were scarcely believable and seemed far-fetched to the interviewer. Others were based on a misunderstanding of the law. But there were some whose stories could not be so lightly dismissed. The reasons given for pleading guilty were variations on a few themes – 'the feeling of hopelessness at attempting to rebut the evidence of police officers and the severity of sentence they anticipated if they failed to do so; the weariness caused by the case dragging on for months on end and the consequent anxiety and social disruption caused by frequent remands (especially if in custody); the attractiveness of the bargain held out to them or perhaps merely the negative pressure exerted by counsel' (p 65).

No fewer than a third of the defendants who claimed innocence alleged that the police had falsely attributed verbal admissions to them. Some of these allegations the researchers found credible, others less so. Another factor in the decision to plead guilty was the advice of counsel. Some defendants said that their barristers had made it clear that they had no real prospect of an acquittal (p 70). The independent assessors who examined the cases concluded that in 79% of these cases the likelihood was that the defendant would be convicted; but in 21% they thought there was some chance of an acquittal and in some instances that the chances of an acquittal were good (p 74).[240]

One of the main contentions of the Baldwin and McConville study was that some guilty pleas are induced by *improper pressure* by the barrister. This suggestion produced a strong and angry response from the Bar. But a later piece of analysis of

---

[240]   The *Crown Court Study* conducted by the writer for the Runciman Royal Commission on Criminal Justice appeared at first to be a fourth such study. In a pre-publication lecture about the early results of the study, the writer suggested that the study included 53 such cases. (M Zander, 'The Royal Commission's Crown Court Study' *New Law Journal*, 11 December 1992.) However further analysis of these cases showed that very few, if any, were in reality cases of innocent persons pleading guilty. (For further details see M Zander, 'The "Innocent" who Plead Guilty'. *New Law Journal*, 22 January 1993, p 85. See also the Royal Commission's Report, p 11, para 43.)

the same data by the same two authors revealed the very significant fact that the proportion of guilty pleas varied dramatically from one barrister to another (*New Law Journal*, 27 October 1977, p 1040). Some apparently like a fight more than others and some may be more inclined to exert pressure on the client to plead guilty. No doubt the barrister honestly believes this to be in the best interests of his client but, because of his psychological 'set', he may take insufficient notice of the client's protestations of innocence. (There has been no follow-up study to investigate this sensitive issue further.)

It has already been seen that guilty-plea rates vary also as between different circuits. Ole Hansen (in the *New Law Journal*, 27 June 1986, p 601) reported on an informal inquiry into the reasons behind these marked and remarkable variations. Michael Huebner, then Circuit Administrator in Leeds, said that the abnormally high guilty-plea rate in his (North Eastern) circuit reflected the robustness of the bench and the legal profession 'and a good dollop of northern common sense'.

But, Hansen suggested, what seemed like robustness to a circuit administrator might look rather different from the defendant's perspective. A Leeds solicitor had told him that 'the local bar was not prepared to fight enough cases'. One of the reasons that he used London counsel a lot was that they were more ready to fight – and they usually won their cases.

Moreover the problem was not confined to the Bar. 'Many solicitors had a similar attitude. They did not believe their client's defences were valid and therefore did not investigate cases fully – preferring instead to maximise their fee income from magistrates' court advocacy. The end result was a client under pressure to plead guilty in the Crown Court'.

In Newcastle a further reason was that the local lay magistrates were so punitive that many solicitors would advise clients to go to the Crown Court for a more lenient sentence.

Another explanation for the high guilty-plea rate was that the judge, the defending and the prosecuting barristers all frequently came from the same chambers, which made defence counsel 'anxious not to appear to "waste" the courts' time'. Also, in the provinces, if a barrister had a number of guilty-plea cases in a session he could get a higher level of remuneration than if he only had the one not-guilty-plea case. He might therefore have a financial incentive to get his client to plead guilty.

There is no doubt that many guilty pleas result from skilful handling of the suspect by the police. See B Smythe, 'Police Investigation and the Rules of Evidence' 117 *Solicitors' Journal*, 5 October 1973, p 718 written by a former police officer. See further McConville, Sanders and Leng, *The Case for the Prosecution* (Routledge, 1991), pp 60 – 65.

Sometimes a guilty plea occurs despite the fact that the prosecution do not have enough evidence to prove the case. (See J Baldwin and M McConville, *Negotiated Justice* (Martin Robertson, 1977), p 74; S Moody and J Tombs, *Prosecution in the*

Public Interest (Scottish Academic Press, 1982), p 307; and McConville, Sanders and Leng, *The Case for the Prosecution* (Routledge, 1991), p 159.)

In the *Crown Court Study* prosecution barristers in guilty plea cases were asked: 'If the defendant had pleaded not guilty but the prosecution had gone forward, do you think he/she would have stood a fair chance of an acquittal?' There were 767 responses. In 9% it was 'Yes, the defendant would have had a fair chance of an acquittal' sect 6.5.5).

In the United States discussions regarding plea are assisted by the fact that the prosecutor is permitted to make recommendations to the court as to the appropriate sentence. He can therefore state in the 'plea bargaining stage' that if the suspect agrees to plead guilty he will ask for a lesser sentence, and actual figures can be mentioned. In the English system this is not possible since the prosecutor does not recommend any particular sentence. (There is no suggestion (at least as yet) that the Attorney-General's vision for an enhanced role for prosecutors (see pp 250–52 above) will change this tradition.) However, the prosecutor can promise to 'put in a good word' for the defendant. He can also change the charges, by dropping the most serious.

NOTE – TICS

There is a very different form of 'confession' – the admission by someone who either pleads guilty or is found guilty that he committed *other* offences. If this happens before the court case, they are mentioned in court and 'taken into consideration' for the purpose of sentencing. (Hence they are called TICs.) The advantage for the accused is that they cannot later be brought up against him. The advantage for the police is that they can 'clear the books' – the success rate of cleared-up crime in that force area improves.

In recent years the police on some forces have taken this one step further by visiting defendants in prison after they have been sentenced to see whether they can get them to admit to other offences.

It is of course quite possible that not all of these admissions are in fact true. In August 1986 detectives from Scotland Yard investigating allegations that police officers in Kent had been falsifying crime statistics with bogus confessions, made an unprecedented series of surprise raids on 13 police stations in Kent. It was the sort of police operation usually directed against leading criminals, complete with a 6am briefing at the Yard and a simultaneous swoop on target stations at 10am. Teams of officers from the Serious Crime Branch were investigating allegations made by a serving Kent officer, PC Ron Walker, that detectives in the area had been 'cooking the books'. He had alleged that the fake confessions were boosting the clear-up rate in some areas by as much as 50%. He also claimed that in return for making false confessions, some criminals were given a licence to commit further crimes on release from prison.

(b)   The sentence discount

A powerful incentive to pleading guilty (whether one *is* guilty or not) is the prospect of a lighter sentence if one pleads guilty than if one contests one's guilt and is then convicted. The judges have made it abundantly clear that a person who pleads guilty is entitled to expect some 'sentence discount'.

There are many cases that make the point that a guilty plea can legitimately result in a lower sentence. In *Turner* (p 310 below), Lord Parker CJ said that counsel for the defence was entitled to advise his client ('if need be in strong terms') that a guilty plea 'showing an element of remorse is a mitigating factor which may well enable the court to give a lesser sentence than would otherwise be the case'. In *Cain* the Court of Appeal stressed that defendants should appreciate that, in general, a plea of guilty attracts a lesser sentence and that this was 'a glimpse of the obvious'. Lord Widgery said: 'Everybody knows that it is so and there is no doubt about it. Any accused person who does not know about it should know about it. The sooner he knows the better' ([1976] Crim LR 464). In *Davis* in 1978 the Court of Appeal said: 'It is common knowledge, that it is an almost universal practice for some such discount to be made on a plea of guilty' ([1979] Crim LR 327). For more recent cases confirming the policy see, for instance, *Costen* (1989) 11 Cr App Rep (S) 182; *Hussain* [2002] EWCA Crim 67, [2002] Crim LR 327.

The usual range of discount from the notional appropriate sentence is in the region of 25 to 30%. For decisions on the question of the extent of the discount for a guilty plea, see *Williams* [1983] Crim LR 693 and commentary at p 694. See also *Pyne* [1984] Crim LR 118, and *Barnes* [1984] Crim LR 119.

One would assume that this must act as an incentive to plead guilty in a proportion of cases. For a practitioner's view, see James Morton, 'Plea Bargaining', *New Law Journal*, 10 May 1985, p 457; 24 May 1985, p 515; 7 June 1985, p 564.

Although almost all the literature and case law on the sentence discount relates to the Crown Court, the concept also applies in the magistrates' court. The first mention of it in the Magistrates' Association's Sentencing Guidelines appeared in 1989. A study published in 1990 found that magistrates did not regard a guilty plea as a significant matter in mitigation of sentence.[241] But the 1993 official Guidelines stated unequivocally:

> The guideline sentences represent a broad consensus of view and are based on a first-time offender pleading *not guilty*. A *timely* guilty plea may be regarded as a mitigating factor for which a sentence discount of approximately one-third might be given. (Emphasis in the original.)

---

[241]   RJ Henham, *Sentencing Principles and Magistrates' Sentencing Behaviour*, Avebury, Aldershot, 1990.

Moreover, since 1994 the magistrates' courts have been under the same obligation as Crown Courts to state in open court what discount it gave in respect of a guilty plea.[242] For an empirical study of the operation of the sentence discount see R Henham, "Reconciling Process and Policy: Sentence Discounts in the Magistrates' Courts' [2000] *Criminal Law Review*, pp 436-51. The study confirmed that the discount was in regular (if erratic) use.

NOTE — SUPERGRASSES AND OTHER INFORMERS

A rare but important situation is where an accused is given total immunity from prosecution in return for evidence for the Crown. A celebrated instance of this was the case in 1974 of Bertie Smalls, who was charged with taking part in a number of robberies. In return for a guarantee of immunity he promised to tell the police about a whole series of robberies. As a result, 26 defendants were arrested, charged and ultimately convicted on Smalls' evidence of robberies involving £1.2m in stolen money. Smalls was arraigned at the Old Bailey but the prosecution offered no evidence against him and a verdict of not guilty was entered.

The Court of Appeal said that undertakings of immunity to criminals might have to be given in the public interest. They should, however, never be given by the police. They should be given only by the Director of Public Prosecutions, and then only most sparingly. In serious cases it would be prudent of him to consult the Law Officers (*The Times*, 25 March 1975, p 18).

After the Smalls case the practice in England seemed to be to prosecute in such cases and hope that a combination of a recommendation from the prosecutor, a lenient judge and an even more lenient Home Office would secure a sufficiently short sentence for supergrasses to make the advantages of adopting this course outweigh the pressures the other way.

In Northern Ireland, however, total immunity was still being given at least so long as the supergrass was not himself directly linked to murder. In 1982 and 1983 the security forces and police were having more and more success largely due to the assistance of supergrasses. In autumn 1983 this led to considerable press publicity for various groups and individuals who expressed unease about this development. The campaign was triggered largely by the case of Joe Bennett, whose evidence led to 14 people being given sentences of some 200 years. *The Sunday Times* wrote on 11 September 1983 that Bennett had in reality been involved in at least one murder. According to the *Sunday Times* story, there were at that date some 300 people awaiting trial on 700 charges arising out of the activities of 26 supergrasses.

The main concern about supergrasses was that they were being allowed to get away with it, that the courts were relying on their uncorroborated evidence and that, in

---

[242]   The obligation was created by the Criminal Justice and Public Order Act 1994, s 48 – on which see p 316 below.

Northern Ireland, charges in terrorism cases are dealt with in the special 'Diplock courts' without juries. (On Diplock courts, see pp 523-24 below.) Even the Rev Ian Paisley, a hard-line opponent of the IRA, was quoted as saying that the use of supergrasses was 'undermining the rule of law'. The concern was heightened when it became known in October 1983 that supergrasses were being offered significant financial inducements in the form of cash and resettlement grants. In October 1983, the then Attorney-General Sir Michael Havers in a Written Parliamentary Answer said that the DPP had given instructions that the chief constable would in every case 'furnish him with a statement of all financial arrangements for the support of the witness and his family and any arrangements for future financial payment to the witness or for his benefit, and that these particulars will be disclosed to the defence and will be available to the court of trial' (House of Commons, *Hansard*, 24 October 1983, vol 47, cols 3 – 5). So far as was known, no such disclosure had until then ever been made either to the defence or to the judge.

On the very day when the Attorney-General made his statement, the case against eight alleged terrorists based entirely on the evidence of supergrass Patrick McGurk collapsed when McGurk announced that he would not after all be giving evidence. Crown counsel read a statement to the court in which McGurk said he had lost his nerve after waiting for 20 months for the trial to come on. Only a few days earlier another major supergrass, Robert Lean, had withdrawn his evidence against no fewer than 28 people. He had previously been given immunity against prosecution in regard to any crimes he admitted and therefore could not be prosecuted for the many serious terrorist acts he had himself committed.

The case of Robert Lean marked a turning point. After that everything seemed to go wrong for the authorities in these cases. In 1985 the DPP decided not to proceed with a case against Terry Davis, a supergrass who had implicated 40 to 50 other people in serious burglaries. Many had been picked up but in the end they were released without charges being brought. In 1986 the convictions of 18 defendants on the evidence of supergrass Christopher Black were quashed by the Criminal Appeal Court. Black had been given immunity for a murder charge in exchange for evidence against 38 people charged with 184 terrorist offences. The case against 20 defendants accused on the evidence of William Allen collapsed when the trial judge described his evidence as 'unworthy of belief'. The 14 men convicted on the evidence of Joseph Bennett all had their convictions quashed on appeal. In October 1986 the DPP decided not to offer any evidence against 19 defendants accused of terrorist offences on information given by Northern Ireland's first woman supergrass Angela Whoriskey. It seemed that the whole policy of using supergrasses in Northern Ireland had fallen apart.

See generally A Jennings, 'Supergrasses and the Northern Ireland Legal System', *New Law Journal*, 1983, p 1043; Tony Gifford, *Supergrasses*, Cobden Trust, 1984; E Grant, 'The Use of "Supergrass" Evidence in Northern Ireland 1982 – 1985', *New Law Journal*, 8 November 1985, p 1125; Steven C Greer, 'The Rise and Fall of the Northern Ireland Supergrass System' (1987) *Criminal Law Review*, p 663; D Bonner,

Modern Law Review 1988, p 23; Steve Greer, 'Supergrasses and the Legal System in Britain and Northern Ireland', 102 *Law Quarterly Review*, 1986, p 198.

(c)   The judge's involvement in plea discussions

The courts have tried over the years to arrive at an acceptable approach to the problem of communication regarding the plea between the defendant and his lawyers, on the one hand, and the prosecution lawyers and the judge, on the other. The defendant speaks to his lawyer who in turn may have had discussions with counsel for the prosecution, with the judge or with both as to plea. Such discussions are normally designed to see whether there is a basis for advising the defendant to plead guilty on the understanding that he will get a certain kind of sentence. Thus if the judge indicates that he will not send the defendant to prison, his counsel may be able to get him to change his plea to guilty and thus bring the proceedings to an early halt. These discussions are generally referred to as plea (or charge) bargaining.

Whatever is agreed between the lawyers, the judge has the final word. He can reject the 'deal' struck between the lawyers. This was illustrated in the 'Yorkshire Ripper' case in 1981. The prosecution and defence agreed that Peter Sutcliffe would plead guilty to manslaughter on the grounds of diminished responsibility. But the judge refused to accept the plea and there was then a long trial, at the end of which the jury found the accused guilty of murder and rejected the diminished responsibility defence.

In a minority of cases the judge himself becomes directly involved in the bargaining process. This has certain dangers, and the courts in recent years have had many occasions to express views on the subject. The *locus classicus* of advice to counsel on the practice of discussing these issues with the judge is *R v Turner*.

R v Turner [1970] 2 QB 321 (Court of Appeal, Criminal Division)

[The defendant pleaded not guilty at his trial on a charge of theft. He had previous convictions, and during an adjournment he was advised by his counsel in strong terms to change his plea; after having spoken to the trial judge, as the defendant knew, counsel advised that in his opinion a non-custodial sentence would be imposed if the defendant changed his plea, whereas, if he persisted with the plea of not guilty, with an attack being made on police witnesses, and the jury convicted him there was a real possibility of a sentence of imprisonment being passed. Repeated statements were made to him that the ultimate choice of plea was his. He thought that counsel's views were those of the trial judge; nothing happened to show that they were not and the defendant changed his plea. He did not receive a custodial sentence but still appealed against his own plea.

Lord Parker CJ gave the judgment of the court:]

... The court would like to say, with emphasis, that they can find no evidence here that Mr Grey exceeded his duty in the way he presented advice to the appellant. He did it in strong terms. It is perfectly right that counsel should be able to do it in strong terms, provided always that it is made clear that the ultimate choice and a free choice is in the accused person.

The matter, however, does not end there, because albeit it may be sufficient in the majority of cases if it is made clear to a prisoner that the final decision is his, however forcibly counsel may put it, the position is different if the advice is conveyed as the advice of someone who has seen the judge, and has given the impression that he is repeating the judge's views in the matter. As I have said, the court is quite satisfied Mr Grey was giving his own views and not the judge's at all. But it had been conveyed to the appellant that Mr Grey had just returned from seeing the deputy chairman. What was said gave Mr Laity the impression that those were the judge's views, and Mr Grey very frankly said that in the circumstances the appellant might well have got the impression that they were the judge's views. ...

Accordingly, though not without some doubt, the court feels that this appeal must succeed. ...

Before leaving this case, which has brought out into the open the vexed question of so-called 'plea-bargaining', the court would like to make some observations which may be of help to judges and to counsel, and, indeed, solicitors. They are these:

1. Counsel must be completely free to do what is his duty, namely to give the accused the best advice he can and, if need be, advice in strong terms. This will often include advice that a plea of guilty, showing an element of remorse, is a mitigating factor which may well enable the court, to give a lesser sentence than would otherwise be the case. Counsel of course will emphasise that the accused must not plead guilty unless he has committed the acts constituting the offence charged.

2. The accused, having considered counsel's advice, must have a complete freedom of choice whether to plead guilty or not guilty.

3. There must be freedom of access between counsel and judge. Any discussion, however, which takes place must be between the judge and both counsel for the defence and counsel for the prosecution. If a solicitor representing the accused is in the court, he should be allowed to attend the discussion if he so desires. This freedom of access is important because there may be matters calling for communication or discussion, which are of such a nature that counsel cannot in the interests of his client mention them in open court. Purely by way of example, counsel for the defence may by way of mitigation wish to tell the judge that the accused has not long to live, is suffering maybe from cancer, of

which he is and should remain ignorant. Again, counsel on both sides may wish to discuss with the judge whether it would be proper, in a particular case, for the prosecution to accept a plea to a lesser offence. It is of course imperative that so far as possible justice must be administered in open court. Counsel should, therefore, only ask to see the judge when it is felt to be really necessary, and the judge must be careful only to treat such communications as private where, in fairness to the accused person, this is necessary.

4. The judge should, subject to the one exception referred to hereafter, never indicate the sentence which he is minded to impose. A statement that on a plea of guilty he would impose one sentence but that on a conviction following a plea of not guilty he would impose a severer sentence is one which should never be made. This could be taken to be undue pressure on the accused, thus depriving him of that complete freedom of choice which is essential. Such cases, however, are in the experience of the court happily rare. What on occasion does appear to happen however is that a judge will tell counsel that, having read the depositions and the antecedents, he can safely say that on a plea of guilty he will, for instance, make a probation order, something which may be helpful to counsel in advising the accused. The judge in such a case is no doubt careful not to mention what he would do if the accused were convicted following a plea of not guilty. Even so, the accused may well get the impression that the judge is intimating that in that event a severer sentence, maybe a custodial sentence, would result, so that again he may feel under pressure. This accordingly must also not be done.

The only exception to this rule is that it should be permissible for a judge to say, if it be the case, that whatever happens, whether the accused pleads guilty or not guilty, the sentence will or will not take a particular form, eg a probation order or a fine, or a custodial sentence.

Finally, where such discussion on sentence has taken place between judge and counsel, counsel for the defence should disclose this to the accused and inform him of what took place.

QUESTIONS

1. In Rule 1 the court indicated that counsel could inform his client that a guilty plea could be a mitigating factor. In Rule 4 it said that the judge must not give any indication that the plea could make any difference to his judgment. Are these two propositions consistent?

2. In Rule 2 the court said that the accused must have complete freedom of choice as to whether to plead guilty or not. Is this realistic? Is his freedom of choice not seriously qualified by the pressure of the advice to plead guilty?

3. The court is prepared to countenance solicitors at discussions about plea and sentence with the judge, but there is clearly no thought that the defendant himself might be there. Is this justifiable?

The final words of the extract from *Turner* emphasised the duty of counsel to relay to his client what had happened in the judge's room. This critical issue came up for more detailed scrutiny in *Cain* [1976] Crim LR 464. At the trial Mr Justice Melford Stevenson had sent for counsel for both sides and had said that he thought the defendant had no defence at all. If he persisted in his not guilty plea he said that he would get a very severe sentence indeed but that a change of plea would make a considerable difference. Counsel reported this to the accused who eventually agreed to plead guilty to three counts, the prosecution having agreed to accept those pleas. The judge gave him four years' imprisonment. Cain then appealed on the ground that he had been pressured into pleading guilty. The Court of Appeal quashed the conviction and ordered a new trial. Lord Widgery referred to Lord Parker's remark in *Turner* about counsel passing on to his client what the judge had said. That statement admitted exceptions, for example where counsel who did not know the judge and was not familiar with the tariff, wished to obtain guidance as to the sentence the judge had in mind so he could properly advise the defendant. If he had to disclose what the judge had said, the confidentiality between judge and counsel would be broken.

This decision gave rise to considerable confusion as to what counsel was and was not permitted to say to his client, and in July 1976 the Court of Appeal issued a Practice Direction which stated that in so far as *Cain* and *Turner* were inconsistent, *Turner* should prevail: [1976] Crim LR 561. This did little to clarify matters.

Since then there have been many further decisions.[243] The principles that can be distilled from these cases are, first that the judge should not engage in over-precise indications, let alone bargaining as to what he intends, and, secondly, private discussions between counsel and the judge should not take place unless it was absolutely necessary. The Court of Appeal has said many times that the discussion should take place in open court in the absence of the jury.

In *R v Harper-Taylor and Bakker* [1988] NLJR 80, the Court of Appeal warned that one of the dangers of going into chambers was that the more relaxed atmosphere of the private room could blur the formal outlines of the trial. The fact that the accused was not present meant that he had to be informed of what had happened at second hand. The lawyers for either side might hear things that they would rather not hear that would put them into conflict between their duty to the client and their duty to preserve the confidentiality of the private room.[244]

---

[243] *Llewellyn* (1978) 67 Cr App Rep 149; *Bird* [1978] Crim LR 237; *Atkinson* [1978] Crim LR 238; *Davis* [1979] Crim LR 167; *Smith* [1990] Crim LR 354.
[244] But see *Agar* (1990) 90 Cr App Rep 318.

This passage was cited by the Court of Appeal in *R v Pitman* [1991] 1 All ER 468 in which Lord Lane LCJ said that there continued to be a steady flow of appeals to the Court of Appeal arising out of visits by counsel to the judge. ('No amount of criticism and no amount of warnings and no amount of exhortation seems to be able to prevent this happening' p 470.) The court quashed a conviction because of undue pressure by the trial judge on the accused by saying to counsel in chambers that there seemed to be no defence to the charge (although counsel had advised the client to plead not guilty), and that he would get substantial credit for a guilty plea. The plea was a matter for the defendant and if he was accepting blame for the incident (death of a motorist in a collision) and was contrite, his plea was the best evidence of that. The defendant changed his plea and was given a nine months' prison sentence.

A learned commentary on *Pitman* sums up the effect of the case law in this vexed area as follows:

Patrick Curran, 'Discussions in the Judge's Private Room' (1991) *Criminal Law Review*, pp 79, 85–6[245]

It is submitted that the following principles may be identified in the case law which has developed from the original guide-lines in *Turner*:

1. An accused person must have a completely free choice of plea.

2. Defending counsel must be quite free to do his duty, which is to give the accused the best advice he can, if need be in strong terms. He is entitled to tell the accused that a plea of guilty is a mitigating factor which may result in a lighter sentence than would otherwise be imposed. Counsel must however emphasise that the accused must not plead guilty if he has not committed the offence.

3. There must be freedom of access between counsel and the judge. However, a judge should not initiate discussions in private. Both prosecuting and defence counsel must be present at any private discussion.

4. Such discussions should not take place unless they are really necessary. Pre-trial reviews should take place in open court.

5. A judge should only give an indication of sentence (a) when he is in possession of all the material facts; and (b) when he is of the view that a particular form of sentence is appropriate irrespective of plea. Any suggestion of different kinds of sentence following a guilty plea on the one hand and a conviction by the jury on the other is fundamentally wrong. This applies even where the judge is silent as to the alternative sentence after conviction by the jury

6. No discussion should take place in the judge's private room without the presence of a shorthand writer or tape-recorder to record exactly what is said.

---

[245] The footnotes with case references have been eliminated.

The fundamental problem is that the Court of Appeal wants to have it both ways. On the one hand, it wants defendants to appreciate that if they plead guilty they will get a lesser sentence. On the other hand, it does not want judges to provide defendants with concrete information as to how great the discount will be.

The courts have given two reasons for refusing to provide a defendant with this information. One is that it will create undue pressure on him to plead guilty. But the pressure is already created by the fact of the sentence discount. To quantify the discount can hardly increase the pressure – on the contrary, it may reduce it by making it clear that the defendant's fears about the penalty for pleading not guilty are exaggerated. The second reason is that it is thought unseemly for the court to be in any sense bargaining or haggling with the defendant. As was said in *Cain*, 'What was being condemned was a more precise offer because the judge was then inviting the defendant to bargain with him.'

(d) Should plea bargaining be more explicit?

Should the process of 'bargaining' be explicit or implicit, detailed or vague? Is it better for the judge to give a general indication of the kind of sentence he has in mind which is conveyed to the accused without too detailed an account, or should the accused be told more precisely what his options are?

The judges and barristers who took part in the *Crown Court Study* were asked 'Do you think that *Turner* should be reformed to permit full and realistic discussion between counsel and the judge about plea and especially sentence?' 86% of prosecution barristers, 88% of defence barristers and 67% of judges answered this question 'Yes' (Report, p 145, sect 4.13.1).

In 1992 a committee of the Bar Council chaired by Mr Robert Seabrook QC recommended that unofficial plea bargaining should be replaced with a formal system with graduated sentence discounts depending on the stage at which the guilty plea was entered. The report included a table which proposed that a guilty plea at the committal stage should receive a minimum of 30% discount, while those who waited longer would get less – a minimum of 10% was suggested for a plea made between the first Crown Court listing and arraignment (*The Efficient Disposal of Business in the Crown Court*, June 1992. For a fierce critique of the Seabrook proposals see M McConville and C Mirsky, 'To Plea or not to Plea', *Legal Action*, February 1993, p 6.)

THE RUNCIMAN ROYAL COMMISSION REPORT

The Runciman Royal Commission said of the sentence discount:

> Provided that the defendant is in fact guilty and has received competent legal advice about his or her position, there can be no serious objection to a system of inducements designed to encourage him or her so to plead (p 110, para 42).

It thought that the system of sentence discounts should remain but that it should be made more effective, in particular by promotion of earlier guilty pleas so as to reduce the very high proportion of last minute guilty pleas (known as 'cracked trials'). In the *Crown Court Study*, of the total of cases listed, 39% were listed as guilty pleas, 26% were listed as not guilty pleas but 'cracked' (ie became guilty pleas), 31% were contested and 3% ended without a plea when the defendant was bound over or the case was allowed to lie on the file (Royal Commission Report, p 111, note 15).

> Cracked trials create serious problems, principally for all the thousands of witnesses, police officers, experts and ordinary citizens, who come to court expecting a trial only to find that there is no trial because the defendant pleads guilty at the last minute. This causes unnecessary anxiety in particular for victims whose evidence has up to that point been disputed (Report, p 111, para 45).

The Court of Appeal had stated that other things being equal, an earlier plea ought to attract a higher discount:

> This court has long said that discounts on sentence are appropriate, but everything depends on the circumstances of the case. If a man is arrested and at once tells the police that he is guilty and cooperates with them ..., he can expect to get a substantial discount. But if a man is arrested in circumstances in which he cannot hope to put forward a defence of not guilty, he cannot expect much by way of a discount. In between come this kind of case, where the court has been put to considerable trouble as a result of a tactical [late] plea. The sooner it is appreciated that defendants are not going to get a full discount for pleas of guilty in those circumstances, the better it will be for the administration of justice' (*R v Hollington and Emmens* (1985) 82 Cr App Rep 281).

The Royal Commission said it agreed with the view expressed by the Court of Appeal that, other things being equal, the earlier the plea the higher the discount (p 111, para 47).

This was given statutory effect in the Criminal Justice and Public Order Act 1994, s 48(1) which provided that when determining what sentence to pass on an offender who has pleaded guilty the court shall take into account (a) the stage in the proceedings for the offence at which the offender indicated his intention to plead guilty and (b) the circumstances in which this indication was given. Section 48(2) states that if the court, in consequence of taking into account the matters referred to in subs (1), 'imposes a punishment on the offender which is less severe than the punishment it would otherwise have imposed, it shall state in open court that it has done so'. (Section 48 subsequently became s.152 of the Powers of Criminal Courts (Sentencing) Act 2000 and was cl 137 of the Criminal Justice Bill 2002/03.)

A study of the impact of s 48 based on 310 guilty plea cases in six Crown Court centres showed that it was working very imperfectly. In almost half the cases in the sample the judge did not comply with the requirement of saying that he had given a discount for the guilty plea. Of those who did say it, only a third went on to give any explanation of the basis on which they had reached their decision. Under 10% of the whole sample gave a full explanation. Surprisingly, a third of the sentencers told the researchers they regarded a guilty plea 'not particularly important' or 'not important at all' and half attached no importance (35%) or no particular importance (15%) to the stage when the guilty plea was entered. (See also on this n 254, p 320 below.) There were considerable differences in the way the section was treated in different courts as well as differences in the discounts given for offences. [246]

'SENTENCE CANVASS'

The Runciman Royal Commission recommended a new system of formalised plea bargaining. Under this system, which the Commission called 'sentence canvass', the defendant's lawyer would be permitted to ask a judge at a hearing in chambers what sentence he would impose on a guilty plea. Prosecution and defence would present the case to the judge who would, if he felt able and willing, give an indication as to sentence. If the defendant accepted that sentence, the case would be adjourned into open court and the parties would go through it all again in public. If the defendant did not accept it he would be free to contest the case in the normal way. (See Runciman Report, pp 113 – 14, para s 50 – 55.) The proposal was based on a recommendation in the report of a Bar Council Working Party. But it was not well received. In particular, the Lord Chief Justice, Lord Taylor, indicated that he opposed the proposal. At the time it seemed most unlikely that any version of this recommendation of the Runciman Royal Commission would be implemented.

However, in 2000 the Fraud Advisory Panel made proposals to the Lord Chancellor which included a sentence canvass for fraud cases very similar to that proposed by the Runciman Commission and, as will be seen, also by Lord Justice Auld.[247]

For a powerful argument urging that the sentence discount is wrong in principle and should be abolished see Professor Andrew Ashworth, *The Criminal Process An Evaluation Study* (OUP, 2nd ed,1998), pp 286-97). Ashworth argues that the sentence discount is against the spirit of four fundamental rights and freedoms recognised by the ECHR – the presumption of innocence, the privilege against self-incrimination, the right to be treated fairly and without discrimination, and the right to a fair and public hearing.

See also P Darbyshire, 'The Mischief of Plea Bargaining and Sentencing Rewards' [2000] Crim LR 895-910 (Darbyshire, as well as arguing the case, cites the recent literature.)

---

[246] R Henham, 'Bargain Justice or Justice Denied? Sentence Discounts and the Criminal Process' (1999) 62 *Modern Law Review*, pp 515-38. The article also covers the case law and recent literature on the subject.

[247] *New Law Journal*, 17 March, 2000, pp 398,399.

THE AULD REPORT

Lord Justice Auld's Report rehearsed and gave his response to the objections raised powerfully by Professor Andrew Ashworth, Dr Penny Darbyshire and others. [248]

- *The sentence discount for a guilty plea gives the defendant a benefit he does not deserve since the plea does not reduce either his culpability or the need for his punishment and/ or containment* In Auld's view it flies in the face of reason to exclude the defendant's admission of guilt when sentencing him. It is as right to take it into account as other factors that do not bear on culpability such as prior convictions, age, state of health etc
- *It is contrary to the presumption of innocence to give the convicted defendant a heavier sentence for putting the prosecution to its proof* The presumption of innocence is not the same as the right to put the prosecution to its proof, it is only one of the incidents of that presumption. It does not require that once found guilty the sentence should be the same.
- *The sentence discount creates improper pressure to plead guilty* If the sentence discount led to significant numbers of innocent defendants to plead guilty there might be cause for concern. The sentencing system should not be tailored to encourage the guilty defendant to try his luck.
- *In Scotland no discount is given for a guilty plea* Auld did not comment on this point.
- *Victims may be unhappy that the defendant gets a lower sentence secured by the plea and untested mitigation* Auld agreed that it is vital that victims should be fully informed of the course of the case and be able to indicate to the court the effect on them of the crime but the sentence discount did not affect those imperatives.
- *The system discriminates against defendants from ethnic minorities who tend to plead not guilty more often* If there is indirect discrimination it is self-inflicted. That is not a reason to skew the system to meet one element of society's perceptions of it. (But Auld said there was a case for research as to why ethnic minority defendants plead not guilty more often than white defendants. [249])

Auld did not agree with the Runciman Royal Commission that informing the defendant of the maximum sentence on a plea of guilty and the possible sentence on conviction after trial would amount to unacceptable pressure – 'that comparison is precisely what a defendant considering admitting his guilt wants to know.' (para 112, p 442))

THE WHITE PAPER

The White Paper *Justice for All* (Cm 5563, July 2002) stated that the Government broadly accepted Auld's proposal. ('We therefore intend to introduce a clearer tariff of sentence discount, backed up by arrangements whereby defendants could seek

[248]   Chapter 10, paras 101-08.
[249]   The literature on this issue is referred to in R Henham, 'Reconciling Process and Policy: Sentence Discounts in the Magistrates' courts' [2000] *Criminal Law Review* p 440, n 24.

advance indication of the sentence they would get if they pleaded guilty.' (para 4.42))
The procedure would have to be initiated by the defendant formally in court sitting
in private in the presence of the prosecution. The proceedings would be recorded.
But, agreeing with Runciman rather than Auld, the court's indication of sentence
would not include what it might be after a trial (para 4.43). The system would not
apply to summary-only proceedings but it would apply to either-way cases. The law
would be changed to provide that when making their decision magistrates would be
informed about the defendants prior convictions. A trial conducted by magistrates
after an advance indication would be handled by a different bench. (para 4.44)

The Criminal Justice Bill 2002/03 dealt with this issue in Sch 3. It implements the
proposal that the magistrates should be informed of the defendant's prior convictions
when deciding whether an either-way case is suitable for summary trial.[250] If they
reach that view, the defendant 'may then request an indication ('an indication of
sentence') of whether a custodial sentence or non-custodial sentence would be more
likely to be imposed if he were to be tried summarily for the offence and to plead
guilty'[251] So the indication of sentence would only go to the question of custody or
not. The court may, but it need not, give such an indication.[252] If the defendant opts
for trial in the Crown Court, the judge there would not have his hands tied by the
indication of sentence given by the magistrates.[253] There was nothing in the Bill
regarding a 'clearer tariff of sentence discount'.

The Bill confined 'sentence indication' to magistrates' courts but the Government
took the view that the new system could be applied in the Crown Court without
legislation.

(e) Taking a plea before mode of trial decision

As a way of reducing the numbers of cases going to the Crown Court the Government's
Consultation Document on Mode of Trial issued in July 1995 (Cm 2908) put forward
a new idea that was not considered by the Runciman Royal Commission. This was
to oblige the defendant to enter a plea before the mode of trial decision was taken.
The Consultation Document stated that this procedural innovation had long-term
potential for retaining significantly more work at magistrates' courts.

Under the then existing procedure the law did not permit the defendant to enter a
plea when magistrates decided to commit a case for trial. Under the system proposed
by the Government this would change. The defendant would be required to enter a
plea before the magistrates decided whether to commit/transfer the case to the Crown
Court. In respect of defendants who pleaded guilty, the magistrates would then hear

---

[250]   New MCA 1980, s 19(2)(a) inserted by Sch 3, para 5 of the Bill.
[251]   New MCA 1980, s 20(3) inserted by Sch 3, para 6 of the Bill.
[252]   New MCA 1980, s 20(4).
[253]   New MCA 1980, s 20A(3).

a recital of the facts of the case by the prosecution. If the magistrates thought their sentencing powers were insufficient, the defence would be given an opportunity to try to persuade the court to retain the case. If the magistrates decided to retain the case, they would then move to sentence.

Home Office research had shown that nearly three-quarters (73%) of defendants who had been dealt with at the Crown Court because magistrates declined jurisdiction, would, had they had the choice, have chosen to be dealt with at a magistrates' court and another 4% had no preference (D Moxon and C Hedderman, *Magistrates Court or Crown Court? Mode of Trial Decisions*, Home Office Research Study, Paper No 125, 1992, p 21).

It did not take the Government long to conclude that this idea should be pursued and a modified version was included in the Criminal Procedure and Investigations Bill introduced in the House of Lords in November 1995.

The main modification was that, instead of the new procedure being compulsory, it is merely optional. If the defendant declines to indicate how he would plead, the bench decides whether the case should be tried summarily or at the Crown Court in the ordinary way. But he will then be entitled to a lower sentence discount if he later decides to plead guilty. (*Rafferty* [1998] Crim LR 433[254]) The second modification was that asking the defendant to indicate how he would plead would not technically constitute taking a plea.

Section 49 of the CPIA 1996[255] provides that the magistrates' court must explain to the accused charged with an either way offence that 'he may indicate whether (if the offence were to proceed to trial) he would plead guilty or not guilty'. If he indicates that he would plead guilty the court then proceeds as if it had been a summary trial – either to sentence him or to commit him to the Crown Court for sentence only. The guilty plea is taken into account by magistrates together with the matters that they would previously have taken into account (set out in s 19 of the Magistrates' Courts Act 1980) in considering whether their powers of sentencing were sufficient.

If the case is sent to the Crown Court, the defendant remains free to change his plea to one of not guilty, at the risk of that raising his sentence if he is convicted. For the problems created by CPIA 1996, s 49 see *R v Warley Magistrates' Court, ex p DPP* [1998] Crim LR 684 and commentary pp 687-90.

---

[254] This proposition has to be treated with some reserve since research suggests that sentencers pay little or no attention to the decision in *Rafferty* – '... defence solicitors in all three sample courts indicated that full credit was almost always given for a guilty plea at the Plea and Directions hearings in the Crown Court despite the guidance given by the Court of Appeal in *Rafferty* that the maximum sentence discount is reserved for those who indicate a guilty plea at the plea before venue hearing in the magistrates' court.' (A Herbert, 'Mode of Trial and Magistrates' Sentencing Powers: will increased powers inevitably lead to a reduction in the committal rate?' [2003] *Criminal Law* Review, pp 314, 319, n 28.)

[255] By inserting new ss 17A, 17B and 17C into the Magistrates' Courts Act 1980.

An assessment in 1999 of the effect of s 49 by Professor Lee Bridges showed that although the number of cases in which the magistrates sent cases for trial in the Crown Court had declined, it had not had the desired effect of reducing the number of cases going to the Crown Court. The reason was that the number of cases being committed for sentence had risen by even more.

> Between 1996/97 and 1998/1999 , the number of either way cases ordered by magistrates to the Crown Court for trial decreased by 4,700 while the number of committals for sentence increased by 15,600, over three times as much. Plea before venue has therefore not led to a reduction in cases being sent to the Crown Court but rather to a change in the status of those cases. Whereas before magistrates would have declined jurisdiction and sent either way defendants to the Crown Court for trial, where many of them would then have entered guilty pleas, now such defendants will indicate their guilty pleas in the magistrates' court and be sent, as convicted defendants to the Crown Court for sentence. This change does bring some administrative savings, but the vastly increased use by magistrates of their power to commit defendants to the Crown Court for sentence still involves a considerable waste of resources. And any promise that plea before venue held out for defendants of having their cases retained for sentencing in magistrates' courts, because of their early guilty pleas, has proved to be illusory.[256]

Professor Bridges made the same point in giving evidence to the House of Commons Home Affairs Committee in its inquiry on the Criminal Justice Bill 2002/03.[257]

In his memorandum Professor Bridges suggested that 'plea before venue' introduced in 1997 was doomed in light of the provisions in the Bill for advance 'indication of sentence'. Under the existing procedure the defendant was asked to indicate a plea before magistrates decided whether the case was suited for summary trial. Under the provisions of the Bill magistrates would decide on venue before the defendant was asked to indicate his plea. If they decided that it was suitable for summary trial, they would then be able to give an 'indication of sentence' to help the defendant make up his mind as to how to plead.

The effect of taking the decision as to venue before knowing the defendant's plea, Bridges suggested, could be to increase the number of cases going to the Crown Court, thereby reversing the effect of 'plea before venue'. Further, the result of 'indication of sentence' was that much greater information on the circumstances of offences and defendants would need to be routinely available to magistrates at an early stage of the proceedings, with likely resulting delays and costs. The Government, he thought, had failed to think through the implications of its plans for sentence indications.

---

[256] L Bridges, 'False starts and unrealistic expectations, *Legal Action*, October 1999, pp 6-7.
[257] His memorandum is accessible on the Committee's website on www.parliament.uk.

The Home Affairs Committee made no mention of these concerns in its report on the Bill.

A further spanner in the works emerged from new research into plea before venue and the reasons for magistrates' decisions declining jurisdiction and sending cases to the Crown Court.[258] The research was conducted in three magistrates' courts in the Midlands and Home Counties during 1999 and 2000.[259] The researcher reached the important conclusion that the idea that magistrates are the chief decision makers regarding mode of trial is mistaken.

> There was ... considerable evidence in this study to suggest that most mode of trial decisions were effectively not taken by magistrates, but were the result of prior negotiation between lawyers. Defence solicitors only challenged the recommendation of the Crown in 11% of cases and in many of these [about half] adopted various recognised techniques to ensure that the magistrates realised that a contested application was only being made in order to comply with their client's instructions. Lay magistrates reached a decision contrary to the agreed or unchallenged recommendation of the Crown Prosecution Service (CPS) in only one case out of an observation sample of 123'. (p 318).)

Herbert said that the plea before venue provisions had had two prime motivations:

> The first was the crime control objective of encouraging defendants to admit guilt by providing them with the opportunity, at least theoretically, to obtain the maximum sentence discount. The second was to facilitate the completion of more cases by magistrates by giving them the opportunity to consider all offence and offender information and apply the discount before determining whether or not their sentencing powers were sufficient. [p 319]

The responses of defendants and magistrates provided two major explanations for the limited effect of plea before venue.

In regard to the first objective, fewer defendants were prepared to plead guilty at that stage than had been anticipated. Only about half the defendants (51%) indicated a plea at the plea before venue hearing . One reason was what was felt to be inadequate pre-trial prosecution disclosure. Another was the understandable reluctance to plead guilty at the plea before venue in light of the charges as they stood at that stage.

> There was a consensus of opinion among all interviewed court participants, that the majority of mode of trial decisions, possibly as many as 75%, were obvious. They were, however, only obvious on the basis of the charge or charges faced at the mode of trial hearing. As an example, magistrates in the largest

---

[258]   A Herbert, 'Mode of Trial and Magistrates' Sentencing Powers: will increased powers inevitably lead to a reduction in the committal rate?' [2003] *Criminal Law* Review 314.

[259]   The data collection consisted of observation of court cases, analysis of court registers regarding more than a thousand cases over a three-month period and interviews with 38 court participants – lay and stipendiary magistrates, legal advisers and defence solicitors.

sample court unsurprisingly declined jurisdiction in 11 cases of violent disorder. Yet not one of these defendants was ultimately convicted of that offence, and all those who admitted lesser offences of violence in the Crown Court received community orders. Increased sentencing powers will not influence this predicament. ... There would appear to be little incentive for solicitors to address this perceived problem given their apparent belief that cases which initially present as being serious are better suited to be resolved in the Crown Court. [p 321]

Whether that will change when the CPS rather than the police initiate the charge remains to be seen.

As regards the second main reason behind plea before venue, Herbert's research showed that magistrates were very reluctant to consider taking cases that they felt might be outside their sentencing powers. This was demonstrated by their attitude to ordering pre-sentence reports. According to the philosophy behind plea before venue, the appropriate course of action in a case that appears on the facts to warrant a sentence of nine months was to order a pre-sentence report and postpone any decision until all the information is available. But the research suggested that magistrates have not adopted – and do not agree with – this approach. They appeared to view the decision to order reports as equivalent to a decision to accept jurisdiction. The result was that they were unwilling, or at least reluctant, to order reports in cases that might be outside their sentencing powers, preferring instead to commit the defendant to the Crown Court at the plea before venue. Only 5% of 315 defendants for whom reports were ordered were committed for sentence after consideration of the report. The magistrates interpreted this statistic with approval as an indication that their colleagues had made the right decision at plea before venue. The theory behind plea before venue is that magistrates would make their decision as to venue after considering all the relevant facts. But in fact almost half (45%) of those committed had received a sentence that could have been given by the magistrates and four-fifths of them had been committed without a pre-sentence report. (p 320)

9. Committal or transfer proceedings

If the charge is one on which there is a choice between the magistrates' court and the Crown Court, the defendant must be told of his right to ask for trial at the higher level. As has been seen, most then opt for summary trial. If the defendant asks for trial at the higher level, his preference always prevails. If, however, he asks for summary trial and the prosecutor prefers to have the case tried at the Crown Court, the court will decide. The court can also override the defendant's choice of summary trial if it thinks the case too serious for trial in a magistrates' court.

Hitherto, if the case was to be tried in the Crown Court, the defendant had to be committed for trial by the magistrates' court. In other words, even cases that are dealt with in the Crown Court had to start in the magistrates' court.

The history of committal proceedings was set out by the Royal Commission on Criminal Procedure in *The Investigation and Prosecution of Criminal Offences in England and Wales: The Law and Procedure* (1981, Cmnd 8092 – 1, pp 67 – 8):

a. Historical background

184. Before the establishment of regular police forces it was the duty of magistrates to pursue and arrest offenders and it was the magistrates who could be referred to as 'detectives and prosecutors'. They had responsibility for the taking of depositions as long ago as the 16th century. These were equivalent to the statements taken from witnesses by the police today. The examination of the witnesses took place in private and the accused had no right to be present. In the early part of the 19th century the responsibility for enquiring into offences began to pass to the police. In 1848 changes were made in the procedure. The Administration of Justice (No 1) Act of that year set out to consolidate the law relating to the duties of magistrates in relation to the functions of investigating and inquiring into offences, with such changes as were deemed necessary. The most important change was a provision whereby the accused was entitled, for the first time, to be present at the examination of the witnesses against him. But the inquiry was not required to be in open court, that is in public. The nature of the inquiry by the magistrates was changing before 1848 and continued to do so after that year. During this transitional period, the position of the police as investigators and prosecutors was becoming more clearly established. During the same period, the magistrates' inquiry became a judicial instead of an investigative function. Indeed, by 1848, or soon after, the magistrates' examination (that is committal proceedings) usually took place in open court. As a result of these changes there became grafted onto the system a preliminary judicial hearing.

b. Committal proceedings in the modern era

185. This preliminary judicial hearing continues today, with modifications, as committal proceedings. The link with the magistrates' former investigative functions is evidenced by the statutory reference to committal proceedings as an inquiry into an offence by examining justices, and by the procedure which envisages that the charge will not be formulated until after the 'examining justices' have heard the evidence of the prosecution and that it is the magistrates who will decide upon what charge the accused will be committed for trial. These terminological and procedural relics have no practical effect today. As the police became the principal investigators of crime, so the magistrates' inquiry became a judicial function with the object of ensuring that there was sufficient evidence for the accused to stand trial. In 1848 when this practice was codified (in the Administration of Justice (No 1) Act 1848) all crimes proper were triable only at assizes or quarter sessions so it may be said that the normal criminal procedure envisaged a preliminary judicial hearing before a person could be put on trial.

186. From 1848 until the present time there has been a continuous tendency to confer jurisdiction on magistrates' courts to try criminal offences. Today, those courts try as many as 80% of all indictable offences. Consequently, a preliminary judicial hearing is held in only the 20% of such cases which are committed for trial at the Crown Court.

c. Purpose of committal proceedings

187. The purpose of committal proceedings now is to ensure that no person shall stand trial at the Crown Court unless there is a *prima facie* case against him. It is not a purpose of committal proceedings that the defence may hear all the prosecution witnesses, or any particular witness or witnesses, give their evidence in chief or that such witnesses shall be made available for cross examination. The prosecution are not required to call all their witnesses at committal proceedings; if they can make out a *prima facie* case without calling any particular witness or witnesses, even an important witness, they are entitled to do so and neither the defence nor the court can require any witness to be called.[260] It follows that committal proceedings are not necessarily a means whereby the defence may obtain full disclosure of the prosecution case before trial. In most cases, however, the prosecution do present all their evidence at the committal proceedings, and if they do not, they should give notice before the trial of any additional evidence they propose to call.

(a)   The introduction of 'paper committals' in 1967

Before the Criminal Justice Act 1967, committal proceedings were lengthy affairs in which all the evidence had to be taken laboriously, translated into depositions and then signed. In the overwhelming proportion of cases the defendant was committed for trial. The Criminal Justice Act 1967 introduced changes designed to abbreviate this procedure and thus save the time of courts, lawyers, police and witnesses. Instead of the witnesses having to come to the magistrates' courts to have their statements taken down, the statements were now sent to the defence. If the defendant was legally represented, he could agree to be committed for trial on the basis of the prosecution statements. The procedure in that event lasted only a few minutes. If, however, he wanted all or some of the prosecution witnesses to be called for examination and cross-examination, this was open to him. (The procedure was to be found in Magistrates' Courts Act 1980, s 6(1) – paper committals and s 6(2) – old style full committals.)

In a large Home Office study in 1985 it was found that there was no evidence that full committals resulted in the weeding out of a higher proportion of weak cases than paper committals. The rate of acquittals directed by the judge was considerably

---

[260]   *R v Epping and Harlow Justices, ex p Massaro* [1973] QB 433; *R v Grays Justices, ex p Tetley* (1979) 70 Cr App Rep 11. See also *R v Governor of Pentonville Prison, ex p Osman* [1989] 3 All ER 701; and *Galbraith* [1981] 2 All ER 1060, CA (ed).

higher in the full committal cases – 15% as against 5% (P Jones et al, 'The Effectiveness of Committal Proceedings as a Filter in the Criminal Justice System' (1985) *Criminal Law Review*, pp 355, 360). Also, full committals resulted in considerably greater delays.

(b)   Reform or abolition?

The Philips Royal Commission on Criminal Procedure thought that committal proceedings were an inadequate filter against weak cases. It proposed the abolition of full committal proceedings and the institution of a new procedure ('application for discharge') whereby the defence could ask for a hearing before the magistrates at which to make a submission of no case to answer. The Royal Commission also proposed the abolition of paper committals, on the ground that sifting of weak cases would be done by the proposed new independent prosecution service. The defence should, however, be able to apply to the magistrates for rulings on bail, witness orders, mode of trial, etc (para s 8.24 – 8.31).

The Roskill Committee on Fraud Trials in its report in January 1986 also recommended that something drastic should be done about committal proceedings. With regard to full committals, they were time-consuming. Sometimes in complicated cases they lasted for weeks and occasionally even months. The defence desire to use the committal stage as a dress-rehearsal for the trial could be an abuse. Sometimes, for instance, the defence would cross-examine prosecution witnesses simply in the hope of turning up something that would assist the defence.

The Committee recommended a new procedure whereby fraud cases could be sent for trial direct to the Crown Court by the new prosecution authorities recommended by the report. They would issue a 'transfer certificate' subject to the right of the accused to apply to a judge for a discharge on the ground that the prosecution's evidence failed to disclose a *prima facie* case. (See para s 4.31 – 4.40.)

This recommendation was implemented in the Criminal Justice Act 1987, ss 4–6. A transfer certificate can be issued under s 4 by the DPP (and therefore anyone in the Crown Prosecution Service), the Director of the Serious Fraud Office, the Commissioners of Customs and Excise or the Home Secretary. The basis of a transfer certificate is (1) that in the opinion of one of the above the evidence of the offence would be sufficient for the person charged to be committed for trial and (2) that it reveals a case of fraud 'of such seriousness and complexity that it is appropriate that the management of the case should without delay be taken over by the Crown Court' (s 4(1)(b)).

Further erosion of the value of committal proceedings occurred in the Criminal Justice Act 1991, s 55(7), which removed the right of the accused personally to cross-examine a child victim in sex and assault cases at the committal stage. The debate as to what to do about committals continued. (For the history between 1986 and 1992 see the 6th edn of this work, pp 304 – 06.)

In 1992 a study of some 3,000 either-way cases in five Crown Court areas and interviews with magistrates and justices' clerks showed that they thought that full committals rarely achieved any useful purpose. (Carol Hedderman and David Moxon, *Magistrates' Court or Crown Court? Mode of Trial Decisions and Sentencing*, Home Office Research and Planning Unit, Paper No 125, 1992.) Occasionally they were useful but the resources they absorbed were quite out of proportion to any benefits. Equally there was a strong view that 'paper committals' served no judicial purpose and that there was no point in retaining them in their existing form.

(c)   The Runciman Royal Commission

The Runciman Royal Commission, like the Philips Commission and the Roskill Committee, recommended that committal proceedings be abolished on the grounds that paper committals were a waste of time and that there were better ways of achieving the objective of weeding out weak cases than by old style full committals. It commented on the cumbersome procedure of full committals. The Commission said that it did think however that there ought to be a way for the defendant to argue that the case against him was so weak that it should not be allowed to proceed. The defendant ought therefore to have the right to submit that there was no case to answer. Such a submission should be considered on the papers, without calling any evidence. The parties should, however, be permitted to present oral argument. In indictable only cases the submission of no case to answer should be made to the Crown Court; in either way cases it should be made to the magistrates' court but they should be heard by stipendiary magistrates rather than lay justices. (Report, pp 90–91, para s 25–32.)

(d)   Apparent abolition – Criminal Justice and Public Order Act 1994, s 44

The Government accepted the recommendation. Committal proceedings were seemingly abolished by s 44 of the Criminal Justice and Public Order Act 1994. Instead cases were to be transferred under provisions set out in Sch 4 of the 1994 Act. It had originally been intended that the transfer provisions would come into force in May 1995 but major snags in the drafting of Sch 4 were discovered by the Law Society – which caused successive postponements, first to July 1995, then to September 1995, then to a date in 1996 and then to a later date in 1996. Finally, to the Government's embarrassment, the difficulties raised by the Law Society and others proved insurmountable. On 25 April 1996 the Home Office wrote to the relevant interested parties that it had decided to move amendments to the Criminal Procedure and Investigations Bill totally abandoning the whole idea of transfer proceedings.

Instead, uncontested 'paper committals' under s 6(2) of the Magistrates' Courts Act 1980 were retained without change. Contested 'old style committals' under s 6(1) were reformed by the removal of the right to call witnesses to give oral evidence.

Contested committal proceedings therefore proceeded simply on the basis of witness statements and other documentary material presented by the prosecution and oral argument by both prosecution and defence as to whether there was a case for committal. (See Criminal Procedure and Investigations Act, ss 44, 45 and Sch 1.) For further explanation see A Edwards, (1997) *Criminal Law Review* 322-25.

NB Sch 2 of the Act made dramatic changes in the rules for the giving of evidence at the Crown Court. Any statement which formed part of a committal bundle was to be read at trial as evidence of its truth unless the defence asked for the attendance of the witness for cross-examination. Even if the defence did require the attendance of the witness for cross-examination, the judge at the Crown Court had the power to overrule the request and to rule that the evidence should be read.

(e)   Abolition of committal proceedings for indictable only offences

The Labour Government made a further intervention in this area in the Crime and Disorder Act 1998, in the provision for indictable-only cases to be sent direct to the Crown Court without any committal proceedings. Section 51 was headed 'No committal proceedings for indictable-only offences'. Subject to the power to adjourn, the court was required at the first hearing to send the accused direct to the Crown Court for trial. The transfer applied also to any related either way offences and any connected summary only offences carrying imprisonment or disqualification. The defendant was able to have an early hearing to ask the Crown Court judge to dismiss the charge on the ground that there was not sufficient evidence for a properly directed jury to convict. An experienced defence solicitor suggested that this test could be more demanding than the test in the magistrates' courts. (See A Edwards, [1999] 'Improving Criminal Procedure?', *Criminal Law Review*, p 33.) If a charge was dismissed, no further charges could be brought on the dismissed charge except by way of a voluntary bill of indictment. (See below.)The defence would be able to raise issues of admissibility, unlike the new procedure on committal. The judge can hear live evidence if it is in the interests of justice to do so (Sch 3, para 2(4)).

(f)   Transfer proceedings to replace committal

The new procedure for indictable-only cases was piloted in six areas from January 1999. The pilots were evaluated by Ernst & Young. Their study found that the average time taken from charge to completion in bail cases was reduced from 228 days to 194 days and in custody cases from 172 days to 141. The average number of magistrates' court hearings was reduced from 4.6 hearings per case to 1.4 hearings. That was accompanied by only one additional Crown Court hearing. On a national basis this represented savings of an estimated £16m. On that basis the Government decided to roll out the change nationally. Implementation began in January 2001.

The magistrates are supposed to send the case to the Crown Court on the first hearing, though they have the power to adjourn. The reasons for an adjournment might be to enable the prosecution to decide whether it is indeed an indictable-only case, for the defendant to get a surety for a bail application or because co-defendants are involved. The first hearing in the Crown Court has to take place within eight days of the magistrates' court hearing in custody cases and within 28 days in bail cases. [261] In the pilots most magistrates' courts made 'through legal aid orders' to cover proceedings for the whole case to trial. In the Crown Court, most first hearings were presented by a CPS lawyer, not by counsel but the defendant was usually represented by counsel. At the first hearing the court would ask the defendant to indicate his plea and in contested cases would set the timetable for the case.

An application by the defendant to have the case dismissed can be made not later than 14 days after service of the papers by the prosecution.[262] (See generally S O'Doherty, 'Indictable only offences – the new approach', *New Law Journal*, 22 December 2000, p 1891.)

The Auld Report recommended that committal proceedings be abolished and that all either-way cases going to the Crown Court should be 'sent' in the same way as indictable-only cases under s 51 of the Crime and Disorder Act 1998.[263] The Government accepted the recommendation which was implemented in Sch 3 of the Criminal Justice Bill 2002/03 by applying the s 51 procedure to either-way cases allocated for trial on indictment. [264] The same clause of the Bill also includes sending to the Crown Court of cases where the defendant is under 18[265] and of serious fraud cases previously dealt with under the Criminal Justice Act 1987[266]

10. The voluntary bill of indictment

There was one procedural device to avoid committal proceedings – the voluntary bill of indictment. This was an application to commit a defendant direct to the Crown Court without going via the magistrates' court. The application was made to a High Court judge.[267] Normally it was made when the committal proceedings were already completed and subsequently a further defendant emerged. Instead of starting the committal proceedings again, the defendant was belatedly sent for trial on the basis of the evidence already available. The applicant supplied the judge with the committal papers, including proofs of all witnesses, depositions and witness statements. Under the procedure which obtained until August 1999, prosecutors can and often did refuse to give the defence copies of the documents presented to the judge in support of the

---

[261] The time-limit runs from receipt of the notice in the Crown Court with the magistrates having four days to send the notice.

[262] Crime and Disorder Act 1998 (Dismissal of Charges Sent) Rules 1998.

[263] Auld Report, ch 10, para 172.

[264] New CDA 1998, s 51 inserted by cl 18 of Sch 3 of the Bill.

[265] New CDA 1998, s 51A.

[266] New CDA 1998, s 51B.

[267] The procedure goes back to 1859. It is now regulated by the Administration of Justice (Miscellaneous Provisions) Act 1933, s 2 Indictment (Procedure) Rules 1971, SI 1971/2084 and the Practice Direction (Crime: Voluntary Bills) [1990] 1 WLR 1633.

voluntary bill. The defendant was normally not even given leave to oppose the application which was usually dealt with by a High Court judge without a hearing simply on the papers.

Once the High Court judge had authorised a voluntary bill, the Court of Appeal would not inquire into the exercise of the judge's discretion[268] Nor was judicial review available.[269] But a Crown Court judge had an inherent jurisdiction to prevent injustice or abuse of process.[270]

The previous *Practice Direction* stated that the judge could invite representations from the proposed defendant but this was not normally done. The procedure was therefore outside the normal rules of fairness and natural justice and, arguably, was contrary to art 6 of the European Convention on Human Rights - see S Farrell and D Friedman, 'Voluntary Bills of Indictment: the Administration of Justice or a Rubber Stamp?' (1998) *Criminal Law Review*, pp 617-26. It seems that this point was taken because on 29 July 1999 a new *Practice Direction (Crimes: Voluntary Bills)* was issued. Prosecutors were required to give the prospective defendant notice of the application and to serve on him a copy of all the documents delivered to the judge. He had to be informed that he could make written submissions to the judge within nine working days. If this procedure was not followed, the judge had to be so informed. The judge was entitled to hold an oral hearing before deciding. [271]

There are no statistics as to the extent of the use of the procedure. The Roskill Committee on Fraud Trials said that it had been told that it was used at the Central Criminal Court in about 6 to 12 cases each year (1986 p 53, n 24).

Lord Justice Auld in his report [272] suggested that once committal proceedings were abolished there would be little point in preserving the voluntary bill procedure. However neither the White Paper nor the Criminal Justice Bill 2002/03 mentioned voluntary bills.

II. Pre-trial preparation

(a)   Pre-trial hearings

'In recent years, and given added momentum by the Civil Justice Reforms, the role of the court in case management has come to the fore.' These were Lord Justice Auld's introductory words to the section in his Report on Pre-trial hearings (Chap 10, para 204, p 481). Echoing the approach of the Woolf reforms (Chap 2 above) he said that 'For many, the sooner the court takes hold of the case at an early preliminary stage,

---

[268]   *Rothfield* (1937) 26 Cr App Rep 103.
[269]   *R v Manchester Crown Court, ex p Williams and Simpson* [1990] Crim LR 654.
[270]   *Wells* [1995] 2 Cr App Rep 417.
[271]   [1999] 4 All ER 63.
[272]   Chapter 10, para .58, pp 418-19.

the better' (ibid). The rationale was that the parties did not prepare the case for trial as speedily or efficiently as they should and they needed the goad of the court to make them do their job properly. 'The vehicle for the application of the goad is a pre-trial hearing of some sort.'(ibid) These take various forms.

Plea and Directions Hearings (PDH) Every Crown Court case (other than serious fraud and other complex or long cases for which statutory preparatory hearings are appropriate) has a PDH. This system was put in place by a Practice Direction in 1995. [273]

The main purpose of the plea and directions hearing (PDH) is to try to identify the cases that can be dealt with either immediately or very quickly, especially those in which the defendant intends to plead guilty. Where a not guilty plea is confirmed, the judge questions counsel for both sides with a standard questionnaire[274] with a view to identifying the issues and giving directions that would assist preparation for trial.

Preparatory hearings under the Criminal Justice Act 1987, ss 7-10 for serious or complex fraud cases The 1987 Act provides that a preparatory hearing can be ordered by the judge for the purpose of identifying the issues likely to be material to the verdict of the jury, assisting their comprehension, expediting the proceedings or assisting the judge's management of the trial (s 7(1)). He can order the prosecution to prepare and serve any documents that appear to him to be relevant (s 7(3)) .In particular, he can order the prosecution to produce a case statement setting out the principal facts, the witnesses who will speak to those facts, any relevant exhibits and any proposition of law on which the prosecution intends to rely (s 9). Providing the prosecution have complied with such an order, the judge can order the defendant to prepare and serve any documents that appear to him to be relevant. In particular, he can require the defendant to give a statement in writing 'setting out in general terms the nature of his defence' and indicating the principal matters on which he takes issue with the prosecution, giving notice of any objections to the prosecution's case statement, informing the court of any point of law he wishes to take and as to the extent to which he agrees with the prosecution documents.

Pre-trial rulings under the Criminal Procedure and Investigations Act 1996 The Government's Consultation Document *Improving the Effectiveness of Pre-Trial Hearings in the Crown Court*, issued in July 1995 (Cm 2924) proposed that judges should have a power to make binding rulings at any point after the transfer of a case

---

[273] See now Crown Court: Plea and Directions Hearings) [2002] 3 All ER 904 Practice Direction – consolidation – Part 41 at p 930. It had been recommended by the Government's Working Group on Pre-Trial Issues in a report issued but not published in November 1990. The Runciman Royal Commission by 10-1 recommended a much more elaborate pre-trial regime – see Report Ch 7, para s 1-36, described in the 8th edn. of this work at p 291. The writer, dissenting, urged that the Commission's proposed pre-trial regime would make the system less rather than more efficient and urged the introduction of PDHs – Report, pp 223-33.

[274] For the text see [2002] 3 All ER pp 957-60.

to the Crown Court. This proposal was implemented by s 40 of the Criminal Procedure and Investigations Act 1996. The section enables the court to make a ruling as to the admissibility of evidence or any other question of law before the trial, whether on application or on its own motion. The start of a trial is defined to mean when the jury is sworn (s 39(3)). This therefore avoids having to swear-in a jury and then send them away for hours or days while lawyers argue legal points.

CPIA 1996, s 40 enables a judge who makes a ruling under the section to order that the ruling is binding, but then goes on to say that such a ruling can be varied by the trial judge 'if it appears to him that it is in the interests of justice to do so' (sub-s (4)). Neither party can seek to obtain a variation in a binding pre-trial ruling unless there has been some material change in circumstances (s 40(5)).

Preparatory hearings under the Criminal Procedure and Investigations Act 1996 The same Consultation Document proposed that, subject to a satisfactory pilot, a scheme of preparatory hearings similar to those that operate in serious fraud cases under the Criminal Justice Act 1987 should be introduced for other complex and potentially lengthy cases tried in the Crown Court. CPIA 1996, s 29 enables a judge, on application or otherwise, to order a preparatory hearing in a case of such complexity or such length that he thinks substantial benefits will accrue from such a hearing. The purpose of such a hearing is to identify material issues, to assist the jury's comprehension of the issues, to expedite the trial or to assist the management of the trial (s 29(2)). The judge at such a hearing can make binding rulings .

Magistrates' courts – Early administrative hearing (EAH) The EAH is intended for defendants who intend to contest their guilt. The court typically takes a plea before venue (p 319 above), determines mode of trial and sets pre-trial review and trial dates as necessary. The Crime and Disorder Act 1998, s 50 gave single magistrates and court clerks the power to run EAHs. [275]

Magistrates' courts – Pre-trial review (PTR) Many magistrates' courts developed their own local forms of pre-trial reviews (PTR) as a way of dealing with pre-trial matters such as which witnesses need to attend, refinement of charges, assessment of the time needed for the hearing and similar aspects of case management.

In his influential 1997 report for the Home Office, *Review of Delay in the Criminal Justice System*, Mr Martin Narey commended such PTRs.('It is clear that properly conducted, PTRs can make a significant contribution to case progress' (p 26)). The functions exercised by clerks at PTRs, he said, varied from area to area: 'The most effective PTRs seem to be those where through local consent the clerk is given a great deal of latitude in managing the case' (p 26). But some aspects of such case management were beyond the powers of clerks and therefore depended on consent

---

[275] For an assessment of the pilot studies of EAHs see P. Tain, 'Reducing delay: case management', *Solicitors' Journal*, 15 October, 1999, p 959.

of the parties. Narey (pp 26-27) suggested that legislation should be passed to give the clerks a long list of case management powers. The recommendation was implemented by the Crime and Disorder Act 1998, s 49.

EMPIRICAL EVIDENCE ABOUT THE VALUE OF PRE-TRIAL HEARINGS

The existing empirical evidence about pre-trial hearings of whatever kind suggests that, contrary to what common sense would suggest, instead of simplifying trials or saving costs, such hearings tend to do the opposite. They increase costs and lengthen trials. The evidence for this proposition is now rather extensive:

– In the *Crown Court Study*, judges were asked whether they thought the pre-trial review had saved much time and money. As many as two-thirds (66%) said No. A quarter (24%) said that a little time and money had been saved. In 8% a fair amount of time and money had been saved. A 'great deal' had been saved in only 1%.[276]

– Professor Michael Levi's study for the Runciman Royal Commission of serious fraud cases stated in regard to ordinary pre-trial reviews,[277] 'none of the defence lawyers I interviewed argued that pre-trial reviews had any significant effect on the development of the case ... The problem is that the judge in the pre-trial reviews is seldom the trial judge, has seldom read the papers, and therefore understandably does not wish to become embroiled in complex matters.'[278]

– The fate of the more formal preparatory hearings under the Serious Fraud regime is equally discouraging. The Roskill Committee said that a full day should be set aside for preparatory hearings.[279] In fact, however, in many of the cases brought by the Serious Fraud Office, preparatory hearings have taken weeks or even months. (In Guinness I, the preparatory hearing took three months.)

– As already noted, the only proper study of the impact of pre-trial conferences, using *matched* samples, conducted in 3,000 personal injury (ie civil) cases in New Jersey,[280] concluded that although they improved preparation, they did not shorten trials. The researchers concluded that they therefore lowered rather than raised the efficiency of the system by absorbing a great deal of court and judge time without any compensating saving in the time required for trials.[281]

---

[276] Section 2.8.9.
[277] Pre-trial reviews are not the special preparatory hearings envisaged for serious fraud cases by the Roskill Committee which were established by the Criminal Justice Act 1987.
[278] Royal Commission Research Study No 14, 1993, p 105.
[279] *Fraud Trials Committee Report*, 1986, HMSO, para 6.52.
[280] M Rosenberg, *The Pre-Trial Conference and Effective Justice*, 1964, Columbia University Press, p 68.
[281] Civil cases are of course not the same as criminal. But if pre-trial conferences do not achieve their intended results in civil cases, it is arguable that they are even less likely to work in criminal cases where the adversarial nature of the proceedings is greater and the defendant is understandably therefore even less inclined to be co-operative or helpful.

(b)　Auld on pre-trial hearings

Lord Justice Auld was considerably less convinced of the value of pre-trial hearings in criminal cases than Lord Woolf was for civil cases. PDHs in the Crown Court he suggested were mainly perfunctory – 'taking the form of a report on progress, good or bad, and the fixing of a trial date or the judge chivvying the parties into getting on with basic matters of preparation and to resolving the issues that they may or may not have discussed before then' (Chap 10, para 209, p 483). The lawyers were not paid adequately for pre-trial work which as a result tended to be done by more junior lawyers than those who would appear at the trial. The courts had no effective sanctions to make the parties prepare cases properly. There were also problems in tailoring the time-tabling of pre-trial hearings to the parties progress or lack of it in preparing for trial. The time-limits for holding PDHs were no doubt 'a reassuring target for the Court Service with its own targets and key performance indicators in mind and for the Government with its commendable aim of speeding the criminal justice process' (Chap 10, para 212, p 484) But for cases not needing such a hearing it was 'an unnecessary and expensive intrusion in getting the case to trial' while for cases needing a PDH 'the timing is often too tight' (ibid). Often disclosure had not been completed so that by the time of the PDH the parties were 'nowhere near identification of the issues or assessment of the evidential and other requirements for trial, far less a realistic joint estimate of the likely length of the case to enable the court to fix a firm date for listing' (ibid). So further costly PDHs might be needed. Or the parties might commit themselves to a trial date for which they were not ready.

In magistrates' courts, Auld suggested, the PTR 'should perform the same function as plea and directions hearings in the Crown Court, but usually fails to do so... because of lack of targets, lack of enforceable sanctions for failure to achieve them, lack of clarity about the aims of the hearing and local variations in practice'(Chap 10, para 206, p 482).

Auld said that in the view of some judges and practitioners pre-trial hearings were a useful means of getting the parties together to focus on the matter of the plea, and in the event of a contest, the issues and the likely evidence required. There was also the convenience to defence practitioners of having defendants in custody brought from prison to court for a conference.

> Frequently the last factor is the most important in the exercise. [For various reasons] defence lawyers are often unable – and sometimes unwilling – to visit and take instructions from clients in custody. In my view this is a major blot on our system of criminal justice. It should be a fundamental entitlement of every defendant, whether in custody or on bail, to meet at least one of his defence lawyers in order to give him instructions and to receive advice at an early stage pf the preparation of his case for trial, and certainly before a pre-trial hearing. (Chap 10, para 214, p 485)

The problem to which Auld alluded is serious. According to defence barristers in the *Crown Court Study* (sect 2.6.1) there was no pre-trial conference with counsel in

58% of cases. According to defence solicitors there was none in 59%. Not surprisingly, it was considerably more common to have had no conference when the defendant ended by pleading guilty. But, according to the barristers, there was no pre-trial conference in 37% of contested cases, and according to defence solicitors in 46%. Whichever figure was correct, the proportion is considerable.

Auld suggested the problem could be addressed by promoting video links both to enable remand prisoners to confer with their lawyers and for the holding of court pre-trial remand hearings. [282] The Government's policy paper *Criminal Justice: The Way Ahead* announced that every prison handling remand prisoners would have a video link to a magistrates' court by March 2002, (Cm 5074, 2001, p 107). However, this commitment extends only to magistrates' courts and Auld was clearly right in saying (p 503, para 260) that 'there is an equally compelling case for extending this facility to all pre-trial hearings in the Crown Court'. Auld urged that they should be not only available for court hearings. 'They should also be available to enable representatives to speak to their clients and take instructions during the course of the preparation of the case.'

Auld's overall view was that

> [O]ral pre-trial hearings should become the exception rather than the rule. They should take place only in cases which, because of their complexity or particular difficulty, require them. In the majority of cases they are unnecessary, expensive, time-consuming and often, because of their timing and the failure of trial advocates to attend, ineffective. Paradoxically ... they also often serve to delay rather than speed disposal of cases. (Chap 10, para 218, p.487)

Save for an initial preliminary hearing, pre-trial resort to the court, in Auld's view, should be 'a last recourse' used only when the case requires it. (Chap 10, para 219, p.487) (For the contrary view that, on balance, the PDH is worth preserving for all Crown Court cases see the writer's Response to the Auld Report accessible on www.lcd.gov.uk (Major Reports, Comments) at pp 55-63.)

Auld's thesis was that,

> In courts at all levels the main players – the police, prosecutors and defence lawyers – should take the primary responsibility for moving the case on. They should concentrate on improving the quality of the preparation for trial rather than trying to compensate for its poor quality by indulging in a cumbrous and expensive system of, often unnecessary and counterproductive court hearings. (p 487, para 220)

The way to do that, he said, was 'by adequate organising and resourcing of the police, prosecutors, defence practitioners and the courts, including the provision of a common

---

[282] See, in particular, p 502, para 259 where Auld describes experiments that have been conducted and the encouraging results of evaluation .J Plotnikoff and R Woolfson, *Video Link Pilot Evaluation*, Home Office 1999 and *Evaluation of Information Video Link Pilot Project at Manchester Crown Court* (Court Service and HM Prison Service, 2000).

information system of information technology for all of them and the Prison and Probation Services'. (ibid)

Whether these hopes are realistic hopes is a different question. Provision of a common IT system for all the different criminal justice agencies would take many years and the expenditure of vast sums of money. It would also require a solution to a problem that has so far proved intractable – that each major part of the system has its own IT system.

Adequate organising and resourcing of the various parts of the criminal justice system must also be regarded as highly problematic. But even in the unlikely event that the Treasury released sufficient funds, it is not certain that it would make much impact on the problem under consideration here, namely the better preparation of cases for trial.

(c) Auld on 'pre-trial assessment'

Auld suggested that in all Crown Court cases and as appropriate in the magistrates' courts, 'the court and the parties should set a provisional time-table by reference to a suitably adapted standard checklist or case management questionnaire, including a date before which trial should start' and that thereafter 'the parties should liaise with each other, informally communicating progress or lack of it, on key tasks to the court and any others involved'. (Chap 10, para 221, p 488) Courts now had 'case progression officers' whose function it was to remind the parties of imminent deadlines. Such officers could assume a wider role, not only chasing progress but also involving themselves in arrangements for listing and where appropriate obtaining and transmitting written directions of the judge. (Chap 10, para 210, p 484, para 221, p 488) In the event of a failure of such liaison the case could be listed for a pre-trial hearing.

The Bar Council had suggested a more formal model in the form of a 'paper' PDH coupled with front-loading of fees to cover preparatory work.[283] Such 'paper' PDHs were being tested in a pilot study in three court centres. (Indications were that the pilot showed paper PDHs to be ineffective.)

The process, Auld said, should culminate in a 'pre-trial assessment' by the parties and the court, the parties 'signifying in writing to eachother and the court their readiness or otherwise for trial and the court responding in writing as appropriate'(Chap10, para 224, p 489) Where outstanding matters could not be resolved by written directions, there would be an oral pre-trial hearing. Wherever

---

[283] Building on the PDH Judge's Questionnaire and requirement of a defence statement, the defence advocate would be required to advise on evidence and as to a trial plan. There would be a fixed date for the 'paper' hearing based on the parties' answers to an extended questionnaire served on the court and eachother.

possible the defendant in custody should be asked to consent to participating by video-link. The judge at such hearings should be able to make binding rulings on law, evidence or procedure subject to variation at trial as justice might require. It was vital that trial advocates should attend any pre-trial hearing. All court orders should be recorded (which was not the case at present) and immediately or rapidly issued to the parties in writing. Ideally, it should be done electronically – though, Auld admitted, 'unfortunately the CREST computer system used in the Crown Court does not have this basic facility'(Chap 10, paras 225-27, pp 489-90).

Auld's 'pre-trial assessment' sounds much like what existed before which did not work. The Runciman Commission (p 103, para 10) said that in 1982 a Working Party under the chairmanship of Lord Justice Watkins recommended a system of pre-trial discussion between the parties based on the exchange of forms giving information about the likely length of the case, the witnesses to be called, pleas and so on. But an experiment set up to try out the scheme had produced disappointing results. The use of the forms was patchy. Similarly, in the *Crown Court Study*, court clerks said that just under half (47%) of the listing information forms that were supposed to be sent in by the lawyers had not been received and of those that were sent in, many were returned late. (sect 2.2.8)

(d)   Auld on sanctions as a management tool in criminal justice

Lord Justice Auld in his Review accepted that sanctions are mainly useless or inappropriate in promoting good standards in pre-trial work in criminal cases.

> Throughout the Review I have anxiously searched here and abroad for just and efficient sanctions and incentives to encourage better preparation for trial. A study of a number of recent and current reviews in other Commonwealth countries and in the USA shows that we are not alone in this search and that, as to sanctions at any rate it is largely in vain. In a recent report, the Standing Committee of Attorneys General in Australia commented: '... the primary aim is to encourage co-operation with pre-trial procedures. There are inherent practical and philosophical difficulties associated with sanctions for non-co-operation' (Ch 10, para 231)

This conclusion stands in marked contrast to the views expressed in the Court Service's Consultation Paper *Transforming the Crown Court* issued under the imprimatur of the Lord Chancellor in September 1999 and in the Report of the National Audit Office, *Criminal Justice: Working Together* published in December 1999. The Court Service's Consultation Paper repeatedly stated that compliance with protocols and other case management performance standards must be enforced by sanctions. These it suggested should include on-the-spot fines or fixed financial penalties imposed by judges or by court staff under judicial direction. Financial penalties would apply to the police and other agencies. Consistent failure to comply could lead to agencies' budgets being capped. The National Audit Office Report equally urged that sanctions should play a central part in court management. It recommended (at p 110) that, 'In taking forward its proposals to change Crown Court procedures, the Court Service should ensure that appropriate forms of sanctions are introduced to help manage robustly'. It identified the sanctions available to the courts as costs orders against the lawyers, reprimand in open court, reprimand in the judge's chambers, a report to the head of chambers or, as the case may be, to the senior partner of the firm of solicitors, and reference to the practitioner's professional body. The same view was taken by the other Commissioners on the Runciman Royal Commission. Sanctions, they thought should include docking fees, wasted costs orders, or a report to the head of chambers or to the leader of the circuit.

There is, in other words, a powerful contemporary disposition to imagine that sanctions are an answer to the fact that pre-trial process does not function according to the rules. (The same philosophy informed Lord Woolf's Report on *Access to Justice*.) Not that that they are frequently used. The National Audit Office, which was so enthusiastic about their use, said:

> For sanctions to be effective they need to be workable and appropriate. Magistrates and court staff we spoke to criticised costs orders, which they considered to be overly cumbersome since a lawyer's right to make representations against an order can prove time consuming and expensive. They are also felt to be inappropriately severe, since a single costs order can damage the reputation of an advocate, leading to hostility rather than co-operation between local defence solicitors and Crown Prosecution Service staff. Additional hearings may entail expenditure greater than the award itself. (p 90, para 4.67)

In the paper entitled 'What on Earth is Lord Justice Auld Supposed to Do?', the writer urged Sir Robin to reject this fashionable current philosophy. ('[I]t is time that the belief in the value of sanctions in securing compliance with performance targets in the context of the justice system is challenged. People on the whole do their work as best they can according to their abilities, so far as circumstances permit. If in the mass of cases the system is not working as it is supposed to do it is probably not the fault of those doing the work. Sometimes the fault lies in the design of the system, but often there is no fault.' [284]) I expressed the hope that, if Sir Robin was persuaded of this 'it would be very helpful if he said so in plain terms'. He did precisely that and he set out the reasons (p 491, para 230). These may be summarised as follows:

- An order for costs against the defendant is usually not an option because of his lack of means and because he cannot be blamed for the faults of his lawyers.
- The fairness of the trial is threatened if the defendant is under threat of sanctions if he or his lawyers misjudge the extent of their obligations to co-operate with pre-trial procedures.

[284] [2000] *Criminal Law Review* p 419 at 429.

- Judges are reluctant to make costs orders against the prosecution involving a transfer of funds from one public body to another.
- In attempting to make wasted costs orders it is difficult to identify who was at fault – on the prosecution side, counsel, those instructing him, or the police, on the defence side, counsel, his solicitor or the defendant. [There are of course many other possible culprits – quite apart from the possibility that no one was at fault. (ed)] Wasted costs proceedings are an impracticable and expensive way of achieving efficient preparation for trial.
- There are considerations of public interest, including the fairness of the trial, in extending the court's power to draw adverse inferences against a defaulting party or in seeking to import from civil process the notion of 'strike out', for example by depriving the defendant from advancing part of his case or by too ready a use of the court's power to stay a prosecution for abuse of process.

Despite his conclusion that 'there is little scope for improving on existing sanctions against the parties or their representatives for failure to prepare efficiently for trial' (p 492, para 232), Sir Robin suggested two exceptions. In regard to his proposal that the parties shoulder primary responsibility for the task, having recourse to a pre-trial hearing only when there are matters they cannot reasonably resolve between them, he suggested that they should be penalised if they unnecessarily asked for a pre-trial hearing. The penalty would be loss of the fee for the unnecessary hearing. That would be open to all the same objections that Sir Robin levelled against wasted costs orders. The penalty would be used very rarely – and when used, would result in lengthy and costly debate and successful appeals. It would also be likely to have the effect of discouraging lawyers from asking for a pre-trial hearing in cases where one was actually needed.

Secondly, he suggested, the Bar Council and the Law Society should 'incorporate more stringent and detailed rules in their codes of conduct about preparation for trial' and should issue clear guidance 'as to the seriousness with which the court will view professional failures in this respect' (p 492, para 234). The danger is that, if implemented, this could be not only useless but counter-productive. The more stringent and detailed the rules, the more they will not be complied with. And to say that the courts will regard failure to comply with the stringent and detailed rules with 'seriousness' – having just acknowledged that there are no workable sanctions – is to invite cynicism.

(e) Case Preparation Project

On 30 June 2003, Lord Falconer, newly installed as Secretary of State for Constitutional Affairs and Lord Chancellor, spoke at the national launch of the Case Preparation Project (CCP). The theme was 'Delivering justice – effective trial management'. CCP involves all the key players in the criminal justice system – the police, CPS, the judges and magistrates, court staff and the defence. There were six core proposals that would be tested by pilot studies in seven areas.

- *Clearer definition of roles and responsibilities* The responsibilities of the defence, the prosecution and the police in preparing cases at each stage of the case management process from the point of charge to disposal in the courts to be laid down in national protocols with accompanying quality standards. Responsibilities for the courts and the judiciary in supervising the process to be clearly defined.

- *A new Case Progression function* In each Criminal Justice area, each agency – the CPS, defence, police, the magistrates and Crown Courts – to nominate a person or persons (Case Progression Officers) for progressing cases through the system to the specified protocols and standards. This role to be adequately resourced. The Case Progression Officers (including whoever has been nominated by the defence) to work together as a 'virtual team' to ensure that cases are managed effectively. Primary responsibility to be on the parties to ensure timely and adequate case preparation. The Case Progression function in the defence, CPS and police to ensure witness availability information is accurate and up-to-date and fed to the courts for listing. The court based CPO to support the judiciary, identifying cases that require intervention and working closely with the Listing office to ensure that cases are listed appropriately for trial based on accurate information. Judges and magistrates to have an explicit responsibility for supervising case progression. They will question the parties as to their conduct of the case, and will intervene where issues in dispute need to be resolved, where cases are not making appropriate progress and/or where the parties are not meeting the required standards and responsibilities for case preparation. In the magistrates' courts, specially trained legal advisers will have an enhanced role in supporting the lay magistracy in managing cases consistently – for instance by conducting case progression hearings.

- *Process changes in the courts*
  - *Magistrates' courts* Make the first hearing more effective. Magistrates, with the legal adviser, to conduct a robust review of the case, deal with allocation decisions, take pleas, identify case needs, make directions and fix a realistic timetable. Legal advisers to carry out pre-trial readiness checks/assessments outside the courtroom. CPOs to oversee progress and compliance with directions and orders given by the court.
  - *Crown Courts* The new more robust first hearing in the magistrates' court will mean that fewer cases 'sent' to the Crown Court will require a preliminary 'Narey' hearing in the Crown Court. There will be a flexible approach to PDHs – the judiciary, assisted by the court CPO and the parties, will decide whether an oral PDH is needed or whether an electronic or paper PDH is more efficient. The judiciary actively to inquire whether the parties have identified the issues, are preparing adequately for trial and are complying with directions and the agreed timetable. Where appropriate sanctions may be used to penalise poor performance. For certain cases the parties to be required to prepare a Case and Issues Summary to clarify the issues to be decided by the jury. (Not part of the pilots as it probably requires

legislation.) The parties responsible to certify the court that they are ready for trial in advance of the trial date.

The new Criminal Procedure Rules Committee to be asked to make rules giving the judges the necessary authority to manage cases.

o *Listing* To provide greater certainty, reduce the number of ineffective trials, increase confidence and value for money. More fixed dates. Revised listing practices to be built into a national framework.

- *Interventions to support better case management* The agencies will be given consistent targets and performance measures – for instance in regard to ineffective trials and witness measures. Examples of interventions being considered include, for the agencies, warnings at the local level, warnings at the national level, external inspections or audits; and for the defence, audit by the Legal Services Commission or formal inspection.

  Local Criminal Justice Boards to monitor and manage performance against the new targets and to consider what interventions are needed to keep everyone up to the mark. The Criminal Justice Joint Planning Unit to work on CCP as part of its drive to improve delivery nationwide.

- *Actions to 'incentivise' defendant behaviour* The judiciary to apply appropriate sanctions for hindering and obstructing the process – for instance by deliberately failing to attend hearings or keep appointments with lawyers. Requirements of the defendant to be linked to conditions of bail. Sanctions that could be applied could include financial penalties, a period in custody or community service. Defence representatives to be responsible for informing the court if the defendant persistently fails to attend meetings to take instructions or if there is a likelihood that the trial might be jeopardised.

- *Actions to 'incentivise' lawyers to case progression* The solicitor's and barrister's responsibilities for case preparation, case progression and their duty to the court to be articulated in protocols and standards. Fee structures to be adjusted to ensure that these responsibilities are appropriately and explicitly remunerated. This might include front-loading of fees and efficiency payments where cases are brought and concluded expeditiously.

Persistent failures by an individual practitioner or professional practice (prosecution or defence) to fulfil the case preparation protocols and to meet the agreed standard subject to a range of possible interventions. For the prosecution this could include individual warnings, warnings at national level, inspections or audits. For the defence this could include warnings from the Legal Services Commission (LSC) mandatory audits by the LSC, withholding of fees, peer review and ultimately withdrawal of LSC contracts.

Plainly this is an extremely ambitious and far-reaching project to which the Government is committing serious resources. The headquarters unit alone had some 50 persons. The pilots in seven areas were scheduled to take from summer 2003 to summer 2004 with an evaluation over 9-12 months. (The contract for the evaluation had been awarded to Accenture.)

Commenting on the launch, the writer expressed reservations about the project:

Michael Zander, 'Can the Criminal Justice System be licked into shape?' *New Law Journal*, 11 July 2003, p 1049

Lord Falconer made clear that this programme of criminal justice reform was 'an absolute priority of the government'.

The overall plans involve all the relevant agencies and, remarkably, at least at this stage, they seem to be on board. (Ken Macdonald QC, the new chair of the Criminal Bar Association, for instance, pledged the full support of the CBA for the reforms.) The project will be well resourced. There will be pilot studies and external evaluation. The plans at this stage are fluid and will be adjusted in light of experience.

Given all this constructive effort aimed at laudable objectives it seems churlish to raise serious doubts about the project. The doubts fall into four distinct categories.

Even though the concerted reform effort is greater than ever before, many of the problems addressed may be too deep-seated to be solved. Experience with one attempt at reform after another suggests that any system that requires the parties to take responsibility for the proper and timely preparation of criminal cases, for monitoring eachother, for notifying the court of problems as necessary, for completing forms, will fail in too a large proportion of cases to make successful enforcement action a practical proposition. Frustration at failure will tend to generate either resignation or more and more punitive sanctions – with little practical effect.

Although significant resources are being put into the project, they will be insufficient to test whether the new ideas are practicable. To take only the most obvious example, it will be years before the court IT system is adequate to the task . In the meanwhile the cost of providing sufficient human resources to give the system a chance of working as proposed will be prohibitive.

Worse, some of the proposed solutions to the problems will be counter-productive. Wasted cost orders, for instance, as Lord Justice Auld recognised, tend to generate cumbrous satellite proceedings. Paying lawyers more for pre-trial work will put more money in their pockets, thus pushing up costs to the taxpayer, but will probably not generate either savings or other benefits elsewhere.

More fundamentally, to the extent that the reforms do work, the effort and expense required could be out of proportion to the attainable gains. Ironically, in the very week of the CCP conference, both the Prime Minister and the Trade and Industry Secretary, Patricia Hewitt, acknowledged that maybe the Government had been wrong to devote so much energy to 'delivery' and performance targets. As the Audit Commission recently said, targets and indicators may ' encourage counter-productive activity (for example allocating disproportionate resources to certain activities because they are being measured)'[285].

Lord Falconer said at the conference that his priority was to produce a criminal justice system 'which people trust and above all respect'. The extent of people's trust and respect for the system is based on a complex and shifting bundle of factors. It seems improbable that it could be affected much, if at all, by the outcome of this initiative. The project will be worthwhile if evaluation shows that it has achieved useful results proportionate to the costs and effort expended – regardless of whether the general public knows or cares.

12. Preparation of cases by the defence

A depressing picture of the way cases are (or at least were) prepared by defence lawyers emerged from research conducted by Professor Michael McConville and colleagues Jacqueline Hodgson, Lee Bridges and Anita Pavlovic, published as *Standing Accused* (Clarendon Press, Oxford, 1994). The study was the first to try to explain what defence lawyers actually do. It was based on examination of files, attending police stations, sitting in on legal advice sessions in police stations, attending questioning of suspects by police officers; interviews with clients; attending interviews with clients in the solicitors' office and at court and conferences with counsel. Interviews were also conducted with the lawyers and their staffs.

The main research was conducted over a three-year period starting in October 1988. In that period the researchers observed the practices of 22 firms of solicitors in cities and towns in the South West, East Anglia, the South, Central and North Midlands, the North West and the North East of England. 'The firms were chosen for the most part because of their status as mass deliverers of legal services in criminal cases in their localities' (p 15). In some cases the researcher spent several months with the firm. For most the observation period lasted between four and eight researcher weeks. Shorter periods were spent with firms with smaller practices. The average time spent with each firm was six and a half researcher weeks. In addition to this main sample, another twenty six firms and three independent agencies were targeted by police station advice and interrogation observation. The average period spent observing this sample of firms was about two weeks. In total therefore there were 48 firms in the study and the research covered 198 researcher weeks of observation.

The research came to the following conclusions:

Almost all those interviewed in the firms 'came to see criminal defence practices as geared, in cooperation with the other elements of the system, toward the routine production of guilty pleas' (p 71). ('In the process, any notions they have carried with them into practice of criminal defence work being based in an adversarial process and involving careful investigation and construction of the individual's case are disabused' (ibid).)

Many suspects in the police station do not appreciate the significance of the right to free legal advice, some are dissuaded by the police, and some are confronted by solicitors who do not want to attend the police station. Many of those who do police station work are former police officers. Non-solicitor clerks generally cannot offer legal advice. 'Advisers of all grades fall in with police routines and are responsive to police expectations that the private interview with the client will be over in a matter of minutes. Consultations are hurried and produce only an outline of the client's account sufficient to enable the adviser to slot the case into one of the "typical case" categories with which advisers are familiar' (p 100).

Defence advisers present during interviews conducted by the police make few if any objections to the way the interview is conducted.

> Looked at as a whole, advisers who attend police stations accept uncritically the propriety and legitimacy of police action, even where what they witness themselves, what they hear from clients, and what they suspect goes on, leaves them convinced that the police break the rules and in other ways are beyond the law. The reason for this is that many advisers, like the police, instinctively believe, without requiring substantiation through evidence, that there is a case to answer, and that it is the client who must give the answer. This in turn springs from a working assumption that the client is probably factually guilty' [pp 126–7].

'Defence-advisers, most of whom are non-qualified staff, are less concerned with establishing the circumstances relating to the alleged offence than with securing from the client a promise to plead guilty.' ('Their dealings with the clients, based in personal relationships, operate on the principle that the client has done something and should plead' (p 159).) Clerks do not assiduously test for the existence of defences or satisfy themselves that all legal requirements of guilt are met, nor do they have the skills to undertake such an inquiry ... many solicitors are court-based, keep a distance from clients and delegate all tasks short of advocacy to non-qualified staff on an ungraded and unsupervised basis' (ibid).

Legally aided clients are not generally encouraged to tell their stories. In so far as their version emerges they are taught that it is not worth recording, that it will not persuade any court, and should be abandoned in the face of police evidence. Statements of clients are routinely disregarded. The adviser persuades the client that his case is not worth pursuing. Those that survive to trial do so despite not because of the process. 'Conviction is achieved in the office of their own adviser through a process whose methodologies most nearly resemble those of the police themselves' (p 160).

Plea settlement and pleas in mitigation are dealt with in a routine manner. Magistrates' courts are seen by solicitors as places where clients can be processed through guilty pleas. Defence solicitors fail to see their own central role in the production of guilty pleas.

> In magistrates' courts, the principal strength of prosecution cases lies in their heavy reliance upon evidence from the police. Such evidence assumes legitimacy because it is practised, assertive and depersonalised. Supported by notebook entries and the testimony of fellow officers, the self-legitimating and mutually supporting character of police evidence commends itself to magistrates ... Against this there is often no separate, competing case for the defence. 'The general lack of investigation and preparation by solicitors and their staff, throws the burden of the defence onto the defendant' [p 237] So far as conviction or acquittal is concerned, any success defence solicitors have at trials themselves tends to be a product of what they can achieve "on their feet" in court and whatever "turns up" on the day. [p 238].

For Crown Court cases a few firms were exceptional in employing competent and experienced staff:

> Here the case was prepared well in advance and a real effort made to engage in proactive defence work. Witnesses were sought and pursued until contacted; enquiry agents were sent to draw up plans of the scene of the crime; and forensic experts were employed in response to the client's assertion of inaccurate or fabricated evidence. However, these individuals were quite exceptional, even within the firms in which they were employed. In the majority of practices much preparatory work is undertaken by non-qualified staff, and solicitors themselves have little contact with routine Crown Court cases ... In an unacceptably high number of cases, evidence is still being gathered long after the time when it was first available, sometimes during the trial itself ... The role definition applied to staff, leads solicitors to employ junior, casual or part-time individuals who are not otherwise involved in the case at all. The fact that the rates of remuneration are so low shows that it is not just solicitors who undervalue these tasks but the state itself ... With occasional outstanding exceptions, the average solicitor has little involvement in preparing these cases, and what work is done is often too little and too late [pp 267 – 8].

A few barristers were strongly committed to cases and were careful to test the underlying basis of a guilty plea, but most barristers were not:

> Strikingly on the hearing day at court, but also in conferences in chambers, barristers evince little interest in scrutinising the evidence or in attempting to convince the defendant of its weight and probative value. Rather, conferences are treated as "disclosure interviews", the purpose of which is to extract a plea of guilty from the client. In this process, what the prosecution alleges, what witnesses may say, and what the client wishes to say, are not discussed ... In place of evidence, a whole gamut of persuasive tactics is deployed against clients enabling barristers to take control of cases and to prevent most clients from becoming, in any real sense, defendants. [pp 268 – 9].

For a very different picture given by participants in the process see M Zander and P Henderson, *Crown Court Study* (Royal Commission on Criminal Justice, 1993). This confirmed that a high proportion of briefs are received by the barrister in the case at the last minute – 40% of prosecution barristers and 25% of defence barristers got the brief in contested cases after 4pm of the day before the trial (p 30). 59% of prosecution barristers and 44% of defence barristers said it was a returned brief (p 32). A quarter of all barristers said the brief was not adequate (p 33). But despite this almost all the barristers thought they had enough time to prepare the case (pp 30 – 31) and 71% of prosecution barristers and 83% of defence barristers said they had been able to rectify inadequacies in the brief (p 33).

The judges were asked whether counsel was well-prepared. Nearly half the judges (47%) thought the prosecution counsel was 'Very well prepared' and the same proportion thought counsel was 'Adequately prepared'. The remaining 6% thought counsel was 'Not well prepared' (p 47). The judicial assessment of defence counsel was precisely the same (pp 59 – 60).

13. Publicity and contempt of court

It is a principle of fundamental importance both at common law and under the European Convention on Human Rights that the trial of an accused person should not be prejudiced by inappropriate pre-trial publicity or by publication of prejudicial material during the trial itself. Traditionally, English law controlling the media in regard to publication of pre-trial material has been strict; in practice in recent years it has become far less so. There are two main different kinds of approach to the problem – to prohibit certain kinds of publication and to penalise breaches by proceedings for contempt of court or, alternatively, to grant a stay or to quash proceedings in the case which is the subject of the publicity. Until very recently almost all English law has been of the former kind. But in recent years there has emerged also the question whether proceedings should be stayed in advance or be annulled retrospectively because of excessive media publicity. (For a general review of developments up to the mid-1990s see D Corker and M Levi, 'Pre-trial Publicity and its Treatment in the English Courts', (1996) *Criminal Law Review*, pp 622-32. For research evidence that, unsurprisingly, pre-trial publicity has little or no impact on jurors see pp 351–52 below.)

Under the Contempt of Court Act 1981 it is unlawful to publish anything which 'creates a substantial risk that the course of justice in the proceedings will be seriously impeded or prejudiced' (s 2(2)). The rule takes effect from the moment when proceedings are 'active', which in criminal cases is from the moment of arrest without a warrant, or from the issue of a warrant or from the charging of a suspect (Sch 1, para s 3–5).

Publicity before criminal proceedings are active Publication of prejudicial material at a point in time where there is as yet no suspect would therefore not fall foul of the statutory rule though it could still be common law contempt of intending to prejudice potential criminal proceedings. This was held to apply to The Sun newspaper in 1988 when it delayed laying an information before magistrates for a private prosecution it was funding until after it had published its story about a doctor allegedly raping an eight-year old girl. The sub judice period did not begin until the information was laid so that the 1981 Act had not been breached. But after the doctor had been acquitted, the paper was held to have committed a common law contempt by proclaiming the doctor's guilt. A fine of £75,000 was imposed. (*A-G v News Group Newspapers plc* [1988] 2 All ER 906.) By contrast in *A-G v Sport Newspapers Ltd* [1992] 1 All ER 503, *The Daily Sport* published the previous convictions of a man the police suspected of kidnapping a girl, after the police asked the media not to publish the information. No warrant had yet been issued for the arrest of the man. The editor said that he got the message about the police request not to publish the information too late. The court held that there would not be liability for common law contempt unless there were overwhelming evidence of intent to prejudice the proceedings. The court criticised the paper but did not find such intent. The decision was somewhat surprising as the paper knew that the man was likely to be arrested and obviously appreciated that publication of his previous convictions would be highly prejudicial.

Publicity when criminal proceedings are active Once criminal proceedings are 'active' the media publish prejudicial material at their peril. They are liable for contempt even though it cannot be proved that they intended to prejudice a fair trial. There is an exception, however, if they can show that they did not know and had no reason to know that criminal proceedings were active (s 3(1)). It is also a defence if it can be established that publication was part of a discussion of public affairs or matters of public interest, if the risk of prejudice to the proceedings is incidental to the discussion (s 5).

Proceedings to enforce the law are brought by the Attorney-General In recent years the standard of compliance with the spirit of the law of contempt in criminal cases has slipped considerably. The media now frequently publish material in the early stages of a case which in former times would have resulted in severe penalties on editors. In the sensational case of the 'Yorkshire Ripper' most of the press published quotes from the police on the day of the arrest of the suspect, Peter Sutcliffe, indicating that the police were jubilant at having caught the man they were hunting. The search for the Ripper was over. One or two papers even published photographs of him in spite of the fact that there might well have been issues of identification evidence. The Attorney-General happened to be out of the country at the time. The Solicitor-General merely issued a letter to editors reminding them of the law of contempt, but no proceedings followed.

Another huge wave of media publicity followed the arrest of Michael Fagan in 1982 after he had been found in the Queen's bedroom at Buckingham Palace. This time proceedings *were* brought against several newspapers for publishing material about Fagan that showed him to be feckless, that he had been a 'junkie' and had marriage problems and that other criminal proceedings were pending against him. As *The*

Times said (12 February 1983): 'It was fortissimo and it was as lurid as the pettiness of the material permitted. Any idea that while a man has a criminal charge outstanding against him his character is in baulk[286] was thrown to the wind.' But, to general surprise, the Divisional Court, with the Lord Chief Justice presiding, rejected all but one of the charges against the papers. It therefore set a lower standard of conduct for the press than would have been thought right before (*A-G v Times Newspapers* (1983) Times, 12 February).

In 1994 the Court of Appeal quashed the conviction for murder of two sisters Michelle and Lisa Taylor because of prejudicial pre-trial publicity and material irregularities at the trial. (*R v Taylor and Taylor* (1993) 98 Cr App Rep 361.) The Court of Appeal referred the case to the Attorney-General and asked him to consider bringing proceedings for contempt against the newspapers concerned but the Solicitor-General declined to do so. In December 1994 the two sisters were given leave to bring proceedings for judicial review against the Attorney-General's failure to take proceedings against the newspapers. But in August 1995 the Divisional Court dismissed the proceedings on the ground that, even though some of the newspaper reports crossed the acceptable limits of fair and accurate reporting, the Attorney-General's discretion not to act could not be reviewed by the courts. (For comment see B Naylor, 'Fair Trial and Free Press: Legal Responses to Media Reports of Criminal Trials', 53 *Cambridge Law Journal*, 1994, pp 492-501.)

In 1995, the trial judge refused to stay the proceedings against the Maxwell brothers, Kevin and Ian (sons of Robert Maxwell), who had been the subject of a great deal of adverse pre-trial publicity before their trial for fraud. In the event, the jury acquitted the defendants. Mr Justice Phillips (now Lord Phillips MR), spoke of the way in which, especially in a long case, all the participants in the case are dominated by the experience:

> It is something that it is impossible to exaggerate. As the weeks go by the trial becomes not merely part of life, but the dominant feature of it so that the stage is reached when one can hardly see behind or beyond it, and I am quite sure that this is true of all who are involved in the trial. The responsibility of reaching verdicts is a heavy one in any case, but in a case such as this it is one of which the jury will be particularly aware. I do not believe that their verdicts will be influenced by anything they may have read about individual defendants before the trial begins.

In October 1995 a trial judge stopped a trial of Geoff Knights, partner of *EastEnders* star Gillian Taylforth, because of what the judge called 'unlawful reporting and scandalous reporting'. (Knights was charged on 17 April 1995. On the following day the *Daily Mail* and *Today* published interviews with witnesses, the *Daily Star* said he 'had gone berserk with an iron bar after catching Miss Taylforth with another man' and a few days later the *Daily Mail* published a lengthy interview with a potential witness along with an account of Knights' previous convictions.) The case was believed

---

[286]   A billiards term meaning 'out of play' (ed).

to be the first where the trial was abandoned before it started simply because of pre-trial publicity. (See national newspapers 5 October 1995 and E Crowther, 'Publish and Then be Damned', *Justice of the Peace*, 13 January 1996, p 26.)

The Attorney-General in a Parliamentary Answer in October 1995 said that at least five trials, including that of Knights, had been halted in the previous three years because the trial judge decided that media coverage would make a fair trial impossible. (House of Commons, *Hansard*, 26 October 1995, vol 264, cols 797-807.)

In July 1996 the Attorney-General brought proceedings against various newspapers for contempt of court arising out of the case of Geoff Knights. But he failed. The Divisional Court held that the saturation media coverage given over previous years to the relationship between Geoff Knights and Gillian Taylforth, including his violent behaviour on previous occasions and his previous convictions, had continued until a month before the incident in 1995 which led to the abortive proceedings. It could not be said that any of the publications in April/May 1995 had created a greater risk of prejudice than that which had already been created (*A-G v MGN Ltd* [1997] 1 All ER 456).

In 1996 the Court of Appeal upheld the conviction of Rosemary West who with her husband Fred West had been charged with multiple horrific murders. After his suicide, she was eventually convicted of 10 murders. There had been massive pre-trial press coverage. The question, the Court of Appeal said, was whether it was possible to have a fair trial after such intensive and unfavourable publicity. Lord Taylor, Lord Chief Justice, said, 'to hold otherwise would mean that if allegations are sufficiently horrendous so as inevitably to shock the nation, the accused cannot be tried. That would be absurd'. The jury had been adequately directed that they must act only on the evidence given in court (*West* [1996] 2 Cr App Rep 374).

In *A-G v Birmingham Post and Mail Ltd* [1998] 4 All ER 49 the Attorney-General did succeed in contempt of court proceedings in respect of an article suggesting that a murder which was then the subject of a trial had been carried out by members of a notorious gang. The article had not identified any of the defendants but the judge had stopped the trial and it started again with a different jury in a different town and ended with convictions. A fine of £20,000 was imposed on the newspaper. See also *Andrews (Tracey)* [1999] Crim LR 156.

In April 2001 the trial judge stopped the trial on charges of affray of two famous Leeds United footballers, Lee Bowyer and Jonathan Woodgate, after he found that an article in the *Sunday Mirror* had been 'seriously prejudicial'. The article, which framed the case as racially motivated, was published shortly before the end of a long trial. The wasted costs were estimated to be in the region of £8m. A 10-week retrial ended that December with the acquittal of Bowyer and the conviction of Woodgate on a minor charge. [287] The newspaper was fined £75,000 for contempt. It was this

---

[287]   The publicity over the case was the subject of research published in TM Honess, S Barker, E A Charman and M Levi, 'Empirical and Legal Perspectives on the Impact of Pre-trial Publicity', (2002) *Criminal Law Review*, pp 719-27.

case that prompted the Government to include in the Courts Bill 2002/03 a provision permitting a court to make 'a third party costs order' where 'there has been serious misconduct (whether or not constituting a contempt of court), and the court considers it appropriate, having regard to that misconduct' to make such an order.[288]

Committal and transfer proceedings Until 1967, committal proceedings provided much lurid material for the press which was lawful since it amounted to reporting of court proceedings. But it was often said that such reporting prejudiced the prospects of a fair trial since the jury might remember what they had read and be affected by it. This was the more so since the normal practice was for the prosecution to present its case at the committal stage but for the defendant to refrain from revealing his defence. The press accounts of the case would therefore inevitably be very one-sided.

The matter came to a head after the trial of Dr Bodkin Adams in 1957 for the murder of one of his elderly patients. The prosecution at the committal proceedings led evidence of the circumstances in which two other patients had died but this was not introduced at the trial. The massive newspaper coverage of the case from the arrest of the doctor to his ultimate acquittal gave the impression that he had been guilty of several murders. As a result of the case, in June 1957 a Departmental Committee under the chairmanship of Lord Tucker was appointed to consider whether there should be restrictions on reports of committal proceedings.

The report of the Committee (*Proceedings Before Examining Magistrates*, 1958, Cmnd 479) recommended that restrictions should be imposed, and these recommendations were eventually enacted in the Criminal Justice Act 1967, s 3 (see now s 8 of the Magistrates' Court Act 1980), which made press reporting of the evidence at committal proceedings unlawful save where asked for by the defence. The press could only publish the formal basic facts and not the evidence (8(4)): the identity of the court; the names, addresses and occupations of the parties and witnesses and the ages of the accused and witnesses; the offence or offences, or a summary of them, with which the accused was charged; any decision of the court to commit the accused for trial and the charges.

The restrictions regarding reporting of committal proceedings have been applied to proceedings in the magistrates' court for transferring or sending cases to the Crown Court first, under the Criminal Justice Act 1987 for the transfer of fraud cases, then under s 51 of the Crime and Disorder Act 1998 in respect of the sending of indictable-only cases, and most recently under the Criminal Justice Bill 2002-03 for sending of either-way cases. (See Sch 3, para 19 inserting a new s 52A into the 1998 Act.)

Publicity at the time of the trial prejudicing a retrial In October 1998, Michael Stone was convicted of the savage killing of Lin Russell and her daughter Megan and of the attempted murder of her other daughter Josie. The case received a great amount of media coverage. In February 2001 his conviction was quashed by the Court of

---

[288]   Cl 88 inserting a new s 19B into the Prosecution of Offences Act 1985.

Appeal on the ground of the unreliability of fellow-prisoner prosecution witnesses. The court ordered a retrial. The defence had argued that because of the publicity it would be impossible to have a fair retrial. The Court of Appeal rejected the argument. The court was not satisfied on the balance of probabilities that the publicity, three years on, was such as to make a retrial oppressive or unfair or make a verdict in a retrial unsafe.[289] (At the retrial, Stone was reconvicted.)

Power to order postponement of reports The 1981 Contempt of Court Act, s 4(1) states that a person is not guilty of contempt of court under the strict liability rule in respect of a 'fair and accurate report of legal proceedings held in public, published contemporaneously and in good faith'. Section 4(2) gives the court the power to order that publication of a report of the proceedings of any court be postponed for such period as the court thinks 'where it appears to be necessary for avoiding a substantial risk of prejudice'. In the past the power was very rarely used by magistrates but was used quite often by Crown Courts: see C Walker et al, 'The Reporting of Crown Court Proceedings and the Contempt of Court Act 1981', *Modern Law Review*, September 1992, p 647. More recently it has been used increasingly by magistrates' courts – see M Dodd, 'Lifting the Veil of Secrecy: reporting Restriction Orders', 165 *Justice of the Peace*, 2001, pp 498, 522.

The Court of Appeal held in 1982 that this power applied to committal proceedings. It held, however, that the only risk the court could take into account was a risk of prejudice to the committal proceedings – not any possibility of risk of prejudice to the later trial. (See *R v Horsham Justices, ex p Farquharson* [1982] 2 All ER 269.)

Publishing material not heard by the jury The media are not permitted to publish evidence held to be inadmissible. This would normally preclude publication of what takes place in the absence of the jury even though it is fair and accurate and contemporaneous and relates to what occurred in open court. It would not be published 'in good faith' – since it would normally be obvious that it was not intended to be seen by jurors and if published might prejudice a fair trial. The contrast with the comparable rule in the USA emerged clearly in the televised trial of OJ Simpson during which viewers around the world frequently heard evidence not heard by the jury. In the United States the jury in a criminal case is quite often kept together (sequestered) throughout the trial. That means they are kept overnight in a hotel or other suitable facility. In England this only happens after the jury starts to deliberate and under the Criminal Justice and Public Order Act 1994, s 43 the judge has a discretion to allow them to go home overnight even then.

Research evidence as to the (minimal) effect of pre-trial publicity

A study conducted for the Law Commission of New Zealand explored the effect of pre-trial publicity on jurors. The researchers took a sample of 48 high profile jury

---

[289]   [2001] *Criminal Law Review* p 465 and lengthy commentary.

trials conducted in different parts of the country in 1998. Questionnaires were given to all potential jurors on their arrival at court at the start of the week in which a sample case was starting. These asked whether they knew anything about two or three of the cases starting that week and, if so, from what source. Jurors in the sample cases who agreed were interviewed after the trial. From a potential sample of 575 jurors, 312 were interviewed – an average of 6.5 per jury. [290]

Given that all the sample cases were high profile, a surprising finding was that so few of the jurors were even aware of the pre-trial publicity. In over half the cases (25 out of 48) no juror recalled seeing any pre-trial publicity. In all, only 58 of the 312 jurors (19%) recollected seeing any and only 16 jurors admitted to knowledge of any details of the alleged offence or the accused's involvement (para s 7.48, 7.52) When jurors who had seen the pre-trial publicity were asked whether it had any impact on their thinking about the case, only two acknowledged that it had.

> In summary, therefore, jurors were only rarely aware of sufficient details of pretrial publicity to enable them to form any bias or prejudgment. When they were, for the most part they reported that they consciously made an effort to put that aside and focus upon the evidence alone; and when they did not, other jurors in the process of collective deliberations generally overrode any individual bias or predetermination. [para 7.57]

As to publicity during the trial:

> While some other jurors were more affected by media coverage during the trial, there is similarly no evidence that any of the collective deliberations of the juries in the sample were ultimately driven or even influenced by this. [ibid]

Anonymity for victims (and defendants) in sexual offence cases

Since 1976 the victim of rape has been given a measure of anonymity. The Sexual Offences (Amendment) Act 1976 provided anonymity for the victim after someone had been accused of rape, but not earlier. Also the judge could lift the protection pre-trial if he thought that would cause witnesses to come forward or if the accused's defence would otherwise be prejudiced. At the trial he could lift the protection if satisfied that it was an unreasonable restriction on reporting and that it was in the public interest. The 1976 Act also gave the defendant the same protection.

The Criminal Justice Act, 1988, s 158 extended the protection of anonymity to the victim from the moment of the allegation but withdrew the protection of anonymity from the defendant.

The 1976 and 1988 Acts dealt with rape, attempted rape, incitement to rape and accomplices to such offences. They did not deal with conspiracy to rape or burglary

---

[290]   W Young, N Cameron and Y Tinsley, *Juries in Criminal Trials Part Two: A summary of the research findings*, New Zealand Law Commission, November 1999 – www.lawcom.govt.nz

with intent to rape. The Sexual Offences (Amendment) Act 1992 extended the statutory anonymity of rape victims to other sexual offences.

Under the SO(A)A 1992 the accused can ask for the prohibition to be lifted if he can satisfy the judge that it is necessary to induce witnesses to come forward because the conduct of the defence would otherwise be substantially prejudiced. At the trial, the prohibition can be lifted if the judge considers that the effect of the prohibition is to impose a substantial and unreasonable restriction on reporting and that it is in the public interest to remove it.

Anonymity for defendants In December 2002, the House of Commons Home Affairs Committee in its report on the Criminal Justice Bill 2002-03 said there was a case for extending the anonymity for victims of sex crimes to those accused of such crimes. There was a basis for distinguishing this category of offence in that, first, there was a risk of mistaken prosecutions and, secondly, the stain on a person's reputation was serious and permanent. It urged the Home Secretary to consider amending the Bill to provide for this. [291]

The Home Secretary declined the invitation. However, at the Report stage of the Sexual Offences Bill Lord Ackner successfully moved an amendment to restore the defendant's right to anonymity in rape cases that he had between 1976 and 1988. The Government was defeated on the issue by 109-105. [292] At the time of writing it was not known whether the Government would seek to reverse the defeat when the Bill reached the House of Commons and, if so, whether the House of Lords would stand its ground or concede the point.

No reporting of names of young victims, witnesses or offenders or of frightened witnesses – the government climbs down

The Youth Justice and Criminal Evidence Bill 1998-99, as originally drafted would have made it a criminal offence to identify a person under 18 who might be a victim, a witness or a perpetrator of crimes under investigation unless one of the exceptions applied. Not surprisingly, this extraordinarily far-reaching proposal met with intense opposition, especially from the press and eventually the Government dropped – or at least suspended – the proposal in so far as it affected victims and witnesses. The Bill was amended to require that the provision affecting witnesses and victims be activated by a specific Order in Council and the indications were that this was not likely to happen. The YJCEA 1999, s 44 maintained the previous rule that a child cannot be identified as the alleged perpetrator of the offence unless the court gives permission on grounds of public interest. It also provided for a new right of appeal against court decisions to lift or not to lift reporting restrictions in the interests of

---

[291]   HC 83, December 2002, para 145.
[292]   House of Lords, *Hansard*, 2 June 2003, cols 1084-95.

justice and for a right of appeal to the Crown Court against such decisions made in the magistrates' courts.

The YJCEA 1999, s 46 also gave the court the power to prohibit the reporting of information that would lead to an adult witness being identified in any criminal case if the court considers that coverage will lead to him being intimidated or that his cooperation or his evidence would be adversely affected by fear or distress. The Explanatory Notes to the Bill stated, 'Neither "fear" nor "distress" was intended to cover a disinclination to give evidence on account of simple embarrassment.' Nevertheless this provision is obviously very far-reaching. The court can lift the restrictions on grounds of the interests of justice. Also the person himself may waive the protection given.

14. Delays in criminal cases

The extent of delays in the criminal justice system is a perennial concern. There are various indications of the extent of delays. One is the proportion of cases in which the defendant was dealt with in under eight weeks from committal to trial. The annual *Judicial Statistics* show the fluctuations. In the mid 1970s it was over half. In the 1980s it declined to a third. By 1990 it was up to nearly a half but in 1994 it had slipped down to a third. Three years later it was again over half. In 2001 it was 41%. The average wait from committal to trial in 2001 was 14.6 weeks.

In the magistrates' courts the delays are of course less. In March 2002 the average time for all cases from first listing to completion was some five weeks (34 days). In either way cases it was eight weeks (56 days). In the youth court it was seven weeks (48 days). Just over half of all cases were completed on the first hearing. [293]

Not surprisingly, guilty pleas are dealt with much more quickly. In 2001, 54% of guilty pleas were dealt with inside eight weeks from committal – compared with 16% of not guilty pleas. On average, defendants who pleaded guilty waited 11.2 weeks, while those who pleaded not guilty waited 19.8 weeks. Defendants on bail wait longer than those in custody – in 2001, 16.0 weeks compared with 9.1 weeks.

The Narey Report In February 1997 the Home Office published a 50-page report by Mr Martin Narey, who had been asked 'to identify ways of expediting the progress of cases through the criminal justice system from initiation to resolution, consistently with the interests of justice and securing value for money'.

The Government accepted and implemented most of Narey's 33 recommendations. Implementation was mainly by way of pilots. (See 'The Narey Recommendations', *Justice of the Peace*, vol 163, 24 April, 1999, p 329.)

---

[293]　*Time Interval for Criminal Proceedings in Magistrates' Courts: March 2002*, Lord Chancellor's Department, June 2002.

In August 1999 the Government announced that pilot studies to test the Narey proposals had proved highly effective in reducing delays and that the schemes would be introduced nationwide as from November 1999. They included location of CPS staff in police stations, use of CPS non-lawyer case workers to review files and to present certain cases, 'early first hearings' for straightforward guilty pleas, 'early administrative hearings' for all other cases, and changes to the powers of single justices and justices' clerks, (See Ernst and Young: *Reducing Delay in the Criminal Justice System: Evaluation of the Pilot Schemes*, Home Office, 1999.)

Government Ministers said of the apparent success of the pilots that they were 'a major breakthrough' (the Lord Chancellor), that they would have 'a dramatic impact on delivering swifter punishment to offenders and speedier justice for victims' (Home Office Minister), and that they demonstrated a 'potential to make significant inroads into delay without diminishing the quality of justice' (Solicitor-General). Professor Lee Bridges was more sceptical. [294]

The Labour Party's manifesto for the 1997 General Election pledged that it would halve the time from arrest to sentence in cases involving persistent young offenders which in 1996 was 20 weeks (142 days). By 2002 this had been achieved. In the second and the third quarter of 2002 the average was just under 10 weeks (68 days).[295] But the *Justice of the Peace*[296] sounded an editorial warning: 'Of course, we fully support the general aim of reducing delay'. But there was a risk 'that speeding up the process will reduce opportunities for thorough and effective review'. The new immediate-transfer-to-the-Crown Court provisions (under s 51 of the Crime and Disorder Act 1998, p 289 above) and 'early first hearings' (under s 46 of the CDA 1998, p 295 above) were both examples of new procedures that might work injustice for lack of crucial information. It concluded: 'We hope that meeting targets will not become an obsession, as so often happens when statistical goals are set. ... Accelerating the progress of cases is desirable only if the quality of decisions does not suffer.'

For a perceptive analysis of the reasons for delays in the criminal justice system see I Kelcey, 'Delays, the truth, the whole truth and nothing but the truth', *New Law Journal*, 15 November 2002, p 1726.

(a)   Time-limits

OVERALL TIME-LIMITS

In Scotland there is a rule that a jury trial must commence within 110 days of committal if the accused is in custody (subject to the court's power to grant an extension) and

---

[294]   L Bridges, 'False starts and unrealistic expectations', *Legal Action*, October 1999, pp 6-8.

[295]   Lord Chancellor's Department Press Notice 432/02 based on the statistical bulletin *Average time from arrest to sentence for persistent young offenders* – available on www.lcd.gov.uk/statistics/statpub.

[296]   Volume 163, 24 April 1999, p 321.

within one year if he is on bail. If either deadline is passed the prosecution is stayed. The only equivalent in the English system is the rule that summary offences in the magistrates' courts must be started within six months of the alleged offence.[297]

Lord Justice Auld in his Report addressed himself to the question whether the English system should adopt the Scottish approach. He was clear that it should not. The Scottish experience was not encouraging:

> [T]he availability of these time-limits does not, in general, contribute to the aim of efficient and speedy preparation for trial. To comply with them procurators fiscal [298] frequently have to list cases for trial even when they are not, or may not be, ready and then seek repeated adjournments while the parties continue to prepare for trial. Not only does such necessity defeat the purpose of the time-limits, but it also causes much waste of time and other inconvenience to defendants, witnesses, victims and all others involved in the process. In Canada a decision of the Supreme Court[299] interpreting the constitutional right of defendants charged with serious offences to trial within a reasonable time, led to so many motions to stay, that the prosecution dropped thousands of cases awaiting trial. The resultant public outcry contributed eventually to the legislature reclassifying a broad range of offences so as to take them outside that relatively loose time bar.

> Similar experiences in other jurisdictions suggest that the Secretary of State has been well advised in not introducing overall time-limits here. Compliance with arbitrary and rigid time-limits is likely to give only an illusion of speedy preparation for trial, hiding the reality of injustice in substantive and procedural compromises that they may impose on the criminal justice process. At their worst, they may prevent conviction of the guilty while doing little to speed the trial of both guilty and innocent. Neither is conducive to public confidence in the system. [300]

CUSTODY TIME-LIMITS

Custody time-limits have been part of the English system since the middle 1980s.[301] When a time-limit is exceeded the result is not, as in Scotland, that the case is stayed but rather that the defendant has to be released on bail.

---

[297]   Magistrates' Courts Act 1980, s 127.
[298]   The Scottish equivalent of the CPS.
[299]   *R v Askov* (1990) 79 CR (3rd) 273, 56 CCC (3rd) 449 (SCC).
[300]   Chapter 10, paras 263-64, p 504.
[301]   The Prosecution of Offenders Act 1985, s 2 empowered the Secretary of State to set time-limits for the preliminary stages of criminal proceedings by regulations. The time-limits are specified in the Prosecution of Offences (Custody Time Limits) Regulations 1987 and the (Amendment) Regulations 1999.

In summary-only or either-way cases, the maximum custody period from first appearance to summary trial is 56 days. For either-way cases, the limit to trial or committal is 70 days unless the court takes the decision . For indictable only offences, the limit is 70 days before committal and 112 days from committal. If the case is 'sent' under s 51 of the Crime and Disorder Act 1998 the limit is 112 days including time spent in custody at the instance of the magistrates' court or 112 days whichever is the longer.

Each charge has its own time-limit. In *R (Wardle) v Leeds Crown Court*[302] W was charged with murder. On the day the time-limit expired the prosecution offered no evidence on that charge but laid a new charge of manslaughter. The House of Lords held that a new 70-day time-limit began on that day. But the prosecution had to show that the new charge had not been brought solely (Lord Hope and Lord Clyde) or primarily (Lord Slynn) to obtain a fresh custody time-limit.[303]

Auld recommended that the present maximum custody periods should continue, save that in the event of the Government accepting his recommendation for the abolition of committal proceedings, the periods should be 56 days for all cases tried summarily and 182 days for those tried at the Crown Court. As has been seen, the recommendation for the abolition of committal proceedings was followed in the Criminal Justice Bill 2002/03. Presumably, the Custody Time Limit Regulations 1987 were to be amended before the provisions in the Bill became operative.

See generally, K Parson, 'Custody time-limits', 143 *Solicitors' Journal*, 26 November 1999, p 1110.

EXTENSION OF CUSTODY TIME-LIMITS

A court may extend the custody time-limit if it is satisfied that the need for it is due to 'some...good and sufficient cause'[304] and 'that the prosecution has acted with all due diligence and expedition'[305] These two concepts have generated a great deal of case law which now takes in consideration of the Human Rights Act 1998.

In *R v Governor of Winchester Prison, ex p Roddie* [1991] 2 All ER 931, the accused was charged with robbery. The prosecution asked for an extension of time because of delays in getting the papers ready due to the police being drastically understaffed. The Divisional Court held that neither the seriousness of the offence, nor the fact that the extension was for a short period, nor that the police were understaffed constituted good and sufficient grounds for an extension of time. Once the time-

---

[302] [2001] UKHL 12, [2001] Crim LR 468 and commentary at 469.

[303] Note the powerful dissents by Lords Scott and Nicholls - who said respectively that the majority view was 'absurd' and 'simply nonsense'.

[304] The two words are separate and have separate meanings: *R v Central Criminal Court, ex p Abu-Wardeh* [1997] 1 All ER 159.

[305] Prosecution of Offences Act 1985, s 22(3).Prior to the amendments introduced by the Crime and Disorder Act 1998 the requirement was only 'all due expedition'.

limit had expired there was no discretion to extend it. The accused was held unlawfully for six weeks until the date of his committal. (A person being held unlawfully because of a breach of the custody time-limits rules can apply for release on bail or by way of habeas corpus. But he cannot obtain damages as the time-limit rules do not create a right of action (*Olotu* [1997] 1 All ER 385).)

In November 1998, the Lord Chief Justice, giving an important judgment in five appeals in the Divisional Court, said that the exercise of the discretion to grant an extension was for the judge, taking into account all the relevant factors. It was neither possible nor desirable to try to define what may or may not amount to good and sufficient cause for granting an extension. The Divisional Court would be most reluctant to interfere with the judge's decision (*R v Crown Court at Manchester*, *ex p McDonald* [1999] 1 All ER 805.) But the case also stands for the proposition that custody periods should be as short as possible and that the prosecution must prepare cases with all due diligence and expedition. The parties were not permitted to enter consent orders. Great caution should be exercised over a request for an extension by the prosecution based on a shortage of judges or courtrooms. If a case was not remarkable it could be tried by any judge of the appropriate status. Difficulties in listing cases would normally not be a ground for granting an extension of time.

An application for an extension has to be made *before the time-limit expires* after two days' notice had been given.[306] This has given rise to considerable difficulties. In *R v Sheffield Justices, ex p Turner* [1991] 1 All ER 858 the accused was charged with murder. Both the CPS and the defendant's solicitor miscalculated the time-limit and thought it ended on 23 August when in fact it ended the previous day. The application for an extension of the time-limit which was granted on 23 August was therefore technically too late. The Divisional Court ruled that the accused was held unlawfully from 23 August until his committal on 20 September, but that from 20 September he was again held lawfully because on that date he had been committed for trial. The fact that the time-limit had expired on 22 August did not invalidate the committal on 20 September.

Auld recommended amendment of s 22 of the 1985 Prosecution of Offenders Act to enable a court to consider and grant an extension of the custody time-limit after it has expired – providing that it is narrowly drawn, including a provision that the court must be satisfied that there is a compelling public interest. Also there should be a right of appeal against a refusal of an extension.[307]

See generally, A Samuels, 'Custody Time-limits', (1997) *Criminal Law Review*, pp 260-68; and J Burrow, 'Pre-committal custody time-limits', *New Law Journal*, 5 March 1999, p 330 and 'A Ashworth, 'Trial within a reasonable time: applying

---

[306]   In *R v Governor of Canterbury Prison, ex p Craig* [1990] 2 All ER 654, the Divisional Court held that the notice requirements are directory not mandatory and the court can give an extension if satisfied that there is a good and sufficient reason to do so.

[307]   Chapter 10, paras 267-70, pp 505-07.

article 6', 10 *Archbold News*, 18 December 2002, p 3 both of which consider case law and the potential impact of the Human Rights Act. See also K.Parsons, 'Custody time-limits – an overview', *Solicitors' Journal*, 26 November 1999, 110-12.

STAY OF PROSECUTION BECAUSE OF DELAY

If delay in bringing the prosecution is excessive it may be stopped ('stayed') as an abuse of the process of the court. But the courts are very reluctant indeed to entertain such an application. See *A-G's Reference (No 1 of 1990)* [1992] 3 All ER 169 and *A-G's Reference (No 2 of 2001)* [2001] EWCA Crim 1568, [2002] Crim LR 207 and commentary at 208. On the doctrine of abuse of process see F Davies, 'Abuse of Process: An Expanding, Exponential Doctrine', *Justice of the Peace:* vol 162, 1998, pp 4, 19, 39, 61, 81 and vol 163, 1999, pp 187, 247, 309.

15. Computerisation in the criminal justice system

The story of computerisation of the criminal system is not a happy one.

The Glidewell Report on the CPS in June 1998 described the position as at that date:

> Since the late 1980s when the technology became available, the vision of a fully integrated case preparation, case management and case recording system for the whole criminal justice system has been widely discussed and is now accepted as something which could, with determination and co-operation, be realised. So why has so little progress been made? One problem is that each of the institutions in the criminal justice system (including 42 separate police forces) has approached the computerisation of their processes and management of their information systems in separate ways, and on different time-scales. For each the priority has been to meet its own requirements rather than those of the criminal justice system as a whole. The result has been some successes, some major failures and overall a range of systems which are significantly less effective than they should have been. The position today is that each criminal justice agency has made commitments and stakes out its position. While there may be agreement on the ultimate goal, there seems to be reluctance to subsume sectional interests to the greater benefits of all (p 184).

As long ago as 1986 the Goldman Report had identified the common data and information which criminal justice agencies needed for the conduct of their business and made the case for 'a single point of data capture and for multiple usage' (p 185). The Committee for the Co-Ordination of Computerisation in the Criminal Justice System (CCCJS) had been set up in 1988, nearly a decade earlier. It saw itself 'as a strategic, even visionary, organisation'. In 1993/94 it produced a 'high level strategy for IT in the criminal justice system' (ibid). But in 1995 a Government study (the

Masefield Report) while commending what had been achieved said progress had been 'very slow' and 'a step change is now needed'. ('There is a pressing need for agencies to share goals, to work more proactively together to improve systems and to be far more outward-facing in their strategies. The systemic nature of the criminal justice must be more effectively recognised and managed if major inefficiencies and seriously under-optimal investment is to be avoided' (ibid).) Having quoted these words from the Masefield report, Glidewell continued: 'What is sad is that this statement of the obvious can be repeated with equal relevance three years later' (ibid). Only now there was even greater urgency because of the major commitments that already existed or were about to be made by the various agencies. Contracts with providers would be for 7-12 years and would be difficult and/or costly to alter.

> The fact that within the criminal justice system a number of largely unco-ordinated projects are about to be contracted seems to us, at best, to be a sure recipe for sub-optimisation and at worst, to signal the possibility of near disaster (p 186).

Urgent decisions were needed.

The problem was that the Ministerial Direction recommended by Masefield had not been implemented and the management structure for IT did not have the effective power to deliver results across agencies. Glidewell recommended the setting up of a Criminal Justice Information Technology Organisation (CJITO) on which all the agencies would be represented. CJITO would be responsible for the development of all cross-agency systems.

In 1999 the same problem was described in the National Audit Office's Report, *Criminal Justice: Working Together* [308]

> Each organisation in the criminal justice system is independently responsible for developing its own business processes and information flows, and for identifying, developing and procuring information technology to support them. As a result, information systems have historically been developed in isolation. Moves toward the automated exchange of information have been slow and constrained by the different systems in use and the fact that they were not designed to communicate with each other.

In October 2001, Lord Justice Auld in his Report (p 353, para 92) again repeated this analysis:

> Each of the main criminal justice agencies has introduced, or is about to introduce, a system designed for its own needs, and with varying or no ability

---

[308]   HC 29, Session 1999-00, at 117, para .6.6.

to communicate direct its electronically stored information to other agencies that need it.[309]

Auld (para 94, p 354) described as 'a public disgrace' the fact that manual systems still played an important part in the operation of the criminal justice system. But the inefficiency of the development of IT for the criminal justice system was even more of a public disgrace. ('At best the system is inefficient and wasteful', Report, para 99, p 355.) He made a series of recommendations (pp 308 and 365-366), the most important of which was that the project of linking the six main IT systems in the criminal justice system be scrapped in favour of a single integrated system for all the agencies.

Given the history and the many problems of achieving a satisfactory IT system, including its immense cost, one has to be pessimistic as to the likelihood of this being achieved.

---

[309]   Chapter 8, para 92, n 73. said that that there were, or were about to be, no fewer than six separate systems: Police: 'NSPIS', Custody and Case Preparation (in progress); 'Connect 42', provision of personal computers and an email facility to lawyers and caseworkers (in progress); 'Compass', a case management system (contract yet to be awarded); Magistrates' Courts: 'LIBRA',(still partly in pilot and yet to be installed nationwide); Crown Court: 'CREDO' (yet to be introduced); National Probation Service: 'CRAMS' (yet to be introduced) and 'Copernicus' (yet to be introduced); Prison Service: 'Quantum' (about to be installed).

Chapter 4

The trial process

This chapter deals with the trial itself. The first section considers the particular characteristics of the English, adversary method of trial as compared with the inquisitorial method followed on the Continent, and examines the role of the judge. The second and third sections concern the advantages of representation and the difficulties faced by the unrepresented person in an English trial. The following sections look at the orality of procedure and the evidence of social psychologists that evidence on questions of fact is more apt to be unreliable than the participants appear to realize. The sixth section deals with the most important problems of the rules of evidence.

I. The adversary system compared with the inquisitorial

The common law method of trial has often been described as 'adversary' or 'accusatorial'–as distinct from the continental 'inquisitorial' method. The essence of the distinction is that, whereas in the inquisitorial system the dominant role is played by the court, in the adversary system it is played by the parties. In the adversary system the judge is supposed to remain a mainly passive and silent umpire, listening to the evidence produced by the two parties. The parties decide what witnesses to call and in what order, the parties examine and cross-examine the witnesses and, if both sides decide not to call a witness who has potentially relevant evidence, there is nothing the court will do about it. The burden of preparing the case and of presenting it falls on the parties themselves, which means that a party without a lawyer is at a distinct disadvantage. By contrast, in the inquisitorial system the judge calls the witnesses and examines them, while the parties or their lawyers play a supporting or subsidiary role.

To be sure, as already seen and as will be noted further, the 'pure' adversary system as it has been conducted in England in modern times has been considerably affected as regards civil trials by the implementation of the Woolf reforms with their emphasis on the active judge. But the pure model applies still in criminal trials and to a considerable extent in civil cases.

(a)   The adversary system

JUDICIAL INTERVENTION

A classic statement of the pure adversary system was given by Lord Denning deciding that the trial judge (Mr Justice Hallett) had intervened too often:

Jones v National Coal Board [1957] 2 QB 55, CA

We are quite clear that the interventions, taken together, were far more than they should have been. In the system of trial which we have evolved in this country, the judge sits to hear and determine the issues raised by the parties, not to conduct an investigation or examination on behalf of society at large, as happens, we believe, in some foreign countries. Even in England, however, a judge is not a mere umpire to answer the question 'How's that?' His object, above all, is to find out the truth, and to do justice according to law; and in the daily pursuit of it the advocate plays an honourable and necessary role. Was it not Lord Eldon LC who said in a notable passage that 'truth is best discovered by powerful statements on both sides of the question'? See *ex p Lloyd*.[1] And Lord Greene MR who explained that justice is best done by a judge who holds the balance between the contending parties without himself taking part in their disputations? If a Judge, said Lord Greene, should himself conduct the examination of witnesses, 'he, so to speak, descends into the arena and is liable to have his vision clouded by the dust of conflict': see *Yuill v Yuill*.[2]

Let the advocates one after the other put the weights into the scales–the 'nicely calculated less or more'–but the judge at the end decides which way the balance tilts, be it ever so slightly ... The judge's part in all this is to hearken to the evidence, only himself asking questions of witnesses when it is necessary to clear up any point that has been overlooked or left obscure; to see that the advocates behave themselves seemly and keep to the rules laid down by law; to exclude irrelevancies and discourage repetition; to make sure by wise intervention that he follows the points that the advocates are making and can assess their worth; and at the end to make up his mind where the truth lies. If he goes beyond this, he drops the mantle of a judge and assumes the robe of an advocate: and the change does not become him well. Lord Chancellor Bacon spoke right when he said that:[3] 'Patience and gravity of hearing is an essential part of justice; and an overspeaking judge is no well-tuned cymbal.'

---

[1]   (1822) Mont 70, 72 n.
[2]   [1945] P 15, 20, [1945] 1 All ER 183, 61 TLR 176.
[3]   'Of Judicature', *Essays or Counsels Civil and Moral*.

For a criminal case see *R v Perks* [1973] Crim LR 388. In *Gunning* [1980] Crim LR 592, the conviction was quashed where the judge asked 165 questions compared with 172 from counsel. In *Matthews* (1983) 78 Cr App Rep 23, the Court of Appeal declined to quash a conviction where the judge put 524 questions to counsel's 538. On any view, the court said, the number of judicial interventions and questions was excessive but they did not quite go so far as to divert counsel from his own line of questioning. The court said that a large number of interruptions put the appeal court on notice of the possibility of a denial of justice but the critical issue was not the number but the quality of the interventions. 'The critical aspect of the investigation is the quality of the interventions as they relate to the attitude of the judge as might be observed by the jury and the effect that the interventions have either upon the orderly, proper and lucid deployment of the case for the defendant by his advocate or upon the efficacy of the attack to be made on the defendant's behalf upon vital prosecution witnesses by cross-examination' (at pp 32–33). Nor will the court interfere merely on the ground that the judge has been guilty of discourtesy, even gross discourtesy, to counsel: *R v Ptohopoulos* [1968] Crim LR 52.

In *Hamilton* [1969] Crim LR 486 (quoted more fully in (1973) 58 Cr App Rep 378 at 382), Lord Parker LCJ said the Court of Appeal would overturn a conviction on account of excessive intervention (a) where the interventions invited the jury to disbelieve the defence evidence in such strong terms that they could not be cured by the usual formula that the facts are for the jury; (b) where they prevented defence counsel from carrying out his duty to present the case for the defence; and (c) where the defendant himself was prevented from telling his own story. (See, for instance, *Rabbitt* (1931) 23 Cr App Rep 112; *Clewer* (1953) 37 Cr App Rep 37; *Renshaw* [1989] Crim LR 811; *Sharp* [1993] 3 All ER 225; and generally Sean Doran, 'Descent to Avernus', *New Law Journal*, 1 September 1989, p 1147.)

For the role of the judge in influencing or directing the jury to convict or acquit, see pp 505-09 below.

But in recent years the traditional concept of the judge as a passive umpire, as in a tennis match, simply 'hearkening to the evidence' has in regard to civil cases become greatly altered. One reason is that whereas in former times it was normal for the judge to come into court with little knowledge of the case, today far more material is supplied to the court and pre-reading is normal which means that the judge will form provisional views on the basis of which he can ask questions on matters of evidence as well as questions of law. As has been seen, the Woolf reforms are largely built on the concept of a more active, interventionist judge. The primary focus of the Woolf reforms was, no doubt, on making the court more active in the pre-trial stage but the reforms have their impact on the trial stage too. Pre-Woolf the idea of the active judge was well established in small claims cases. Now it is normal, even required, for all courts.

It is important also to appreciate that the nature of the role of the judge described in Lord Denning's judgment in *Jones v National Coal Board* only applied to the evidence. It had no application to legal argument. Legal argument in a common law case involves the judge very actively. Counsel makes his points and submissions but the judge will feel free to engage him in discussion by asking questions, raising objections, putting contrary points. The process may sometimes almost resemble a seminar. The same is true on appeal. As Dr Kate Malleson wrote of the Court of Appeal Criminal Appeal, 'The role of the judges in the Court of Appeal is not that of neutral referees but active participators in the proceedings. They ask questions of counsel, make comments, discuss problems, suggest answers, express their opinions and raise new matters in a way which more closely resemble an inquisitorial hearing'.[4]

The higher in the system, the more extensive the exchanges between counsel and the court. (In his book *The Law Lords* (Macmillan, 1982) Professor Alan Paterson reports that in the argument in *Cassell v Broome* there were 99 judicial interventions on the first day alone, 61 of which came from the presiding judge (at p 70).)

Even on points of law, however, the adversary system works on the basis that the court is not supposed to undertake its own research and is not supposed to go beyond the arguments presented by the parties. For consideration of the weaknesses of this rule see NH Andrews, 'The Passive Court and Legal Argument', *Civil Justice Quarterly*, 1988, p 125.

CALLING WITNESSES

The basic common law rule was and remains that it is for the parties, not the court, to call and to examine the witnesses. The parties decide what witnesses to call, in what order, and what questions to ask them. In civil cases the court cannot call a witness unless the parties agree–see for instance *Briscoe v Briscoe* [1966] 1 All ER 465 (Div Ct). In criminal cases the judge technically has the right to call a witness but virtually never does so. For a rare example that was upheld by the Court of Appeal see *Bowles* [1992] Crim LR 726. By contrast, in *Grafton* [1992] Crim LR 826 the judge's decision led to the conviction being quashed. After evidence by the defendant and a friend of his the prosecution said it would offer no further evidence. The judge decided to go ahead and call the remaining witness for the Crown. Prosecution counsel took no further part. The jury convicted. The Court of Appeal said that the judge's role was to hold the ring impartially and to direct the jury on the law. By acting as he had done, he had taken over the prosecution. But see *R v Haringey Justices, ex p DPP* [1996] 1 All ER 828 where the Divisional Court held that if magistrates considered that it would be unfair to the defence if a witness were not called they should call the witness rather than dismiss a case as an abuse of process. See also *Oliva* [1965] 1 WLR 1028.

The position in regard to expert testimony is different. Before Lord Woolf's reforms, under RSC Ord 40, r 1(1) the court could, on the application of either party, appoint

---

4   'Decision-making in the Court of Appeal: The Burden of Proof in an Inquisitorial Process', *The International Journal of Evidence and Proof*, vol 1, 1997, pp 175, 178.

an expert 'to inquire and report upon any question of fact or opinion not involving questions of law or construction'. But the power required the request of at least one of the parties – and in any event it was virtually never used. (See A Jack, 'Lord Woolf and Expert Evidence', *New Law Journal*, 5 August 1994, p 1099; and J Basten, 'The Court Expert in Civil Trials–A Comparative Appraisal', 40 *Modern Law Review*, 1977, p 174.)

In 'The Expert Witness in the Criminal Trial' (1987) *Criminal Law Review*, p 307, the author DJ Gee, Professor of Forensic Medicine at Leeds University, argued that the position of the expert witness in the adversary system was most unsatisfactory. The adversary system, he suggested, was inimical to the presentation of expert evidence in a way that was scientific. ('Indeed a real danger lies in the possibility that the scientist could become more concerned to be an effective witness than a conscientious scientist', p 308.) The scientist prepared his report without knowing what the other side would say. He gave his report to the lawyers for his side. He will have had a brief consultation with his own counsel, usually just before he gave evidence. He would have only a slight idea of the facts of the case and would rarely attend for longer than his evidence. It was rare for him to see the depositions of the other witnesses. He often would not know what precisely counsel wanted to elicit from him. Inadequate knowledge of the facts could affect the way in which he presented his evidence.[5]

A major step in redefining the role of the expert in a less adversary role was taken in *The Ikarian Reefer* [1993] 2 Lloyd's Report 68. Mr Justice Cresswell listed the requirements for expert witnesses. These included being independent, objective and non-partisan. His evidence should indicate the limits of his expertise and make it clear when his report was provisional.

The Civil Procedure Rules (Part 35 and the Practice Direction) and the Code for Guidance for Experts build on those principles. The duty of the expert to help the court overrides any duty to the client (Part 35.3)[6] The expert must act in an independent way at all stages. No party can call expert evidence or even put an expert's report in evidence without the permission of the court (Part 35.4).It can direct that the evidence be given by a single expert (Part 35.7) The court can direct the experts to try to reach agreed opinions (Part 35.12).

For a case illustrating the limits of the adversary system see *Crozier* [1991] Crim LR 138, where the Court of Appeal held that a psychiatrist instructed by the defence in a criminal trial might in exceptional circumstances be justified in showing his report to the prosecution–even though that would be contrary to the wishes of the defence. The circumstances must be such that the public interest in the disclosure of his views

---

[5]   On the problem of the expert witness in the adversary system as it was pre-Woolf see further MN Howard QC, 'The Neutral Expert: A Plausible Threat to Justice' (1991) *Crim Law Review*, p 98, and JR Spencer, 'The Neutral Expert: An Implausible Bogey' (1991) *Crim Law Review*, p 106.

[6]   *Anglo Group plc v Winther Browne & Co Ltd* (2000) 144 Sol Jo LB 197.

to the prosecution was stronger than his duty of confidentiality to his patient. The defendant had pleaded guilty to attempted murder of his sister. The psychiatrist thought that the defendant was a serious danger to his family and should be detained in Broadmoor. When he came into the courtroom, he found to his consternation that the judge was in the process of imposing sentence–a nine-year term. He told prosecution counsel of his report and as a result the prosecution applied for the sentence to be altered. The judge quashed his own sentence of imprisonment and substituted a hospital order with an unlimited restriction of time on release. The Court of Appeal held that the public interest in having the information divulged was greater than in the confidential relationship between doctor and patient. (See to like effect *W v Egdell* [1990] 1 All ER 835.)

The rule is that each party is bound by the evidence of his own witness. One cannot impeach the evidence of a witness one has called by cross-examination to show that he is in error, save where the court is persuaded to allow cross-examination on the ground that the witness is 'hostile'. (See M Newark, 'The Hostile Witness and the Adversary System' (1986) *Criminal Law Review*, p 441.) This means that each side may suppress a witness for fear of what he may say.

The possibility that the parties may suppress evidence that they do not intend to call was illustrated in *Causton v Mann Egerton* [1974] 1 All ER 453. The plaintiff was considering suing his employers for injuries to his eye suffered through their alleged negligence. He agreed to be examined by the insurers' doctors. They were pessimistic about the prospects of his regaining his sight. He was also examined by doctors on his own behalf. On request from the defendants' solicitors, the reports of his doctors were disclosed to them. But when the plaintiff's solicitors asked for reciprocal disclosure of the reports prepared by the insurers' doctors, this was refused.

The Court of Appeal (Lord Denning dissenting) held that the refusal was legitimate in law. Disclosure could be compelled if a party was intending to rely on the evidence. But neither the opposite party nor the court could require a party to produce privileged testimony which it did not intend to call. Lord Denning said that the defendants' doctors apparently took a more serious view of the plaintiff's injuries than did his own doctors. The defendants accordingly wished to keep their own reports away from the court and the plaintiff. This would be unfair. 'Counsel for the defendants sought to excuse their conduct by saying that litigation in this country is based on the adversary procedure. By that he means, I suppose, that it is permissible for an insurance company to refuse to cooperate in the doing of justice. It can play with a poker face with the cards hidden from view. I cannot subscribe to that view. Although litigation is based on the adversary procedure, we require the adversaries to play it fairly and openly. The defendants have made the plaintiff put his cards on the table. They should put theirs too' (at p 458).

But Lord Denning was overruled by his two fellow judges. Lord Justice Roskill said that to decide otherwise would be to ride roughshod over the clear rule that in the absence of the parties' consent, the court could not order the production of privileged documents. ('So long as we have an adversary system a party is entitled not to produce documents which are properly protected by privilege if it is not to his advantage to produce them and even though their production might assist his adversary or his solicitor were aware of their contents or might lead the court to a different conclusion from that to which the court would come in ignorance of their existence' (at p 460).) See also *Air Canada v Secretary of State for Trade (No 2)* [1983] 1 All ER 910; and *General Mediterranean Holdings SA v Patel* [1999] 3 All ER 673.

In research conducted in Crown Courts for the Royal Commission on Criminal Justice judges were asked 'Were you aware of any important witness(es) who were not called by either side?' In nearly a fifth (19%) of 743 cases the judge answered Yes.[7] The Royal Commission (Ch 8, para 18) recommended that judges be prepared in suitable cases, where they become aware of a witness who may have something to contribute, to ask counsel in the absence of the jury why the witness has not been called and, if they think appropriate, urge them to rectify the situation. In the last resort judges should be prepared to exercise their power to call the witness themselves. There is no reason to believe that judges adopted either recommendation.

Lord Justice Auld in his Report said that in his view judges were right to use the power only in exceptional cases. (Ch.11, para 36) The parties might have good reasons, which they cannot divulge, consistent with justice and the interests of a fair trial, for not calling a witness. Also, if the witness helped the prosecution, the judge might be thought to be playing the role of auxiliary prosecutor.

(b)   Modifications or exceptions to the adversary system

There are some situations where the normal principles of the adversary system – that the court is basically passive and it is for the parties to make the best case they can – do not apply.

COURT ACTING OF ITS OWN MOTION

The pre-1999 rules had some provisions permitting the court to act of its own motion.[8] But there were few of these. Since one of the chief purposes of the reforms in civil litigation initiated by Lord Woolf was to put the court in charge of managing cases, it is hardly surprising that the new rules have many such powers.[9]

---

[7]   M Zander and P Henderson, *The Crown Court Study*, Royal Commission on Criminal Justice, Research Study No 19, sect 4.3.12.

[8]   For example the power to transfer a case from High Court to county court or vice versa.

[9]   Thus, in addition to any other power, the court may extend or shorten the time for compliance with any rule, practice direction or court order; adjourn or bring forward a hearing; require a party or a party's legal representative to attend the court; and stay the whole or any part of a case (CPR 3.1(2)).

SMALL CLAIMS HEARINGS

In small claims cases in the county court the judge is given complete control of what rules of evidence and procedure to adopt. For the first years many of the judges followed the traditional approach of leaving it to the parties to make their case. But gradually and increasingly they took a more active role in getting the parties to make their case. By 2002, Professor John Baldwin reported that 'almost all' the district judges who were interviewed in his study were 'thoroughly enthusiastic about playing a pro-active, interventionist role at hearings'.[10]

WHERE THE INTERESTS OF CHILDREN ARE CONCERNED

The courts have held that the ordinary principles of the adversary system do not necessarily apply in wardship or care proceedings where the primary concern is the welfare of children. The policy was reflected in a dictum of Lord Scarman in *Re E (SA)* [1984] 1 WLR 156, 158-59 in which he pointed out that in wardship proceedings the court was not exercising an adversarial jurisdiction:

Its duty is not limited to the dispute between the parties: on the contrary, its duty is to act in the way best suited in its judgment to serve the true interest and welfare of the ward. In exercising wardship jurisdiction, the court is a true family court. Its paramount concern is the welfare of its ward. It will, therefore, sometimes be the duty of the court to look beyond the submissions of the parties in its endeavour to do what it judges to be necessary.

See to the same effect *Oxfordshire County Council v M* [1994] Fam 151, [1994] 2 All ER 269, per Sir Stephen Brown; and *Re L (a minor)* [1996] 2 All ER 78. Both cases raised the question whether legal professional privilege applied to reports of experts prepared for the purpose of litigation. The court in both cases ordered the disclosure of the reports. For other cases see *Livesey v Jenkins* [1985] AC 424 at 437, HL; and *Official Solicitor to the Supreme Court v K* [1965] AC 201 at 240, HL.

PROSECUTION DISCLOSURE

As has been seen, there are rules requiring the prosecution to reveal to the defence material that tends to undermine the prosecution's case (see pp 277-81 above).

PROFESSIONAL RULES OF CONDUCT

Lawyers arguing a point of law in court are subject to the rule that they must put before the court all relevant authorities whether they help or hinder the case being made.

---

[10]   *Lay and Judicial Perspectiveson the Expansion of the Small Claims Regime*, (September 2002, LCD Research Series, No.8/02) p 89.

Another exception to the rule that it is for the parties to make their case is the rule of professional conduct which places limits on the extent to which a lawyer can knowingly lend himself to deception of the court. In 1962 sentence of suspension from practice was confirmed on a prominent Queen's Counsel, Mr Victor Durand, for misleading the court in an action for damages against the police. Mr Durand had put his witness, a police officer, on the stand and examined him as Mr G without alluding to the fact that he had been demoted for misconduct. The original sentence of three-year suspension from practice was later reduced to one year. (See *The Times*, 24 November 1961 and 12 January 1962.)

If his client confesses his guilt to his own barrister, the barrister is not required to report the fact to the authorities nor need he give up the case. But he may not 'assert as true that which he knows to be false.'. He may take points by way of objection to the jurisdiction of the court, to the admissibility of evidence, or to the form of the proceedings. But he may not call evidence which he knows to be false. He is entitled to test the prosecution's case by cross-examination and he may argue that the prosecution have failed to produce enough evidence to establish their case. Further than that he should not go.[11]

In *Vernon v Bosley (No 2)* [1999] QB 18, [1997] 1 All ER 614, just before the judge gave judgment, defendant's counsel received anonymously information that showed that his opponents had knowingly presented a false picture as to their client's medical/psychiatric state, a material matter in the litigation. The Court of Appeal allowed an appeal based on the new material. Stuart LJ said that it was the duty of counsel to advise his client to make the appropriate disclosure, failing which he should withdraw from the case. Thorpe LJ went further and said that in such circumstances, counsel should himself disclose the material to his opponent. (For analysis and comments see A Speaight QC, 'A change of expert opinion', *New Law Journal*, 7 February, 1997, pp 163-66. See also J Goodliffe, 'Fair play between lawyers', *New Law Journal*, 5 September, 1997, p 1268.)

A more robust approach still was adopted by Jacob J in a patent case *Honeywell Ltd v Alliance Components Ltd* (22 February 1996, unreported). Jacob J said that where parties relied on experiments they should notify the opponent of any experiments they had conducted which did not support their argument or which undermined it. But in *Electrolux Northern Ltd v Black and Decker* ([1996] FSR 595) his colleague in the Patent Court Laddie J disagreed. If *Honeywell* was right other potentially fruitful avenues would have to be disclosed and costs and delay would be increased. (See 'B McConnell, 'Opposing views', *New Law Journal*, 28 November, 1997, p 1754.)

Another example of the duty to disclose is where an application is made in the absence of the other side ('without notice' – formerly '*ex parte*'). In that situation, by definition, the adversary system is not operating and it is therefore the lawyer's duty to make

---

11   *Code of Conduct of the Bar of England and Wales*, 7th ed 2000, Miscellaneous Guidance N, paras.13.3-13.5.

full disclosure to the court so that the decision is made on a fully informed basis.[12] The same is true where an application is made for a 'freezing' (formerly *Anton Piller)* order (p 99 above). The lawyer making such an application is under an especially high duty to take care to see that his lay client realises the need for candour and full disclosure.[13]

However the duty of confidentiality to the client (legal professional privilege) overrides the duty of disclosure.

See further a valuable and instructive article by DA Ipp, 'Lawyers Duties to the Court' [1998] 114 *Law Quarterly Review*, pp 63-107, especially pp 67-76.

LORD WOOLF AND THE RUNCIMAN ROYAL COMMISSION ON THE ADVERSARY SYSTEM

As has been seen, Lord Woolf's Interim Report *Access to Justice* published in June 1995 blamed the excesses of the adversary system for much of the cost, delay and complexity of the civil justice system (p 7):

> 3. By tradition the conduct of civil litigation in England and Wales, as in other common law jurisdictions, is adversarial. Within a framework of substantive and procedural law established by the state for the resolution of civil disputes, the main responsibility for the initiation and conduct of proceedings rests with the parties to each individual case, and it is normally the plaintiff who sets the pace. The role of the judge is to adjudicate on issues selected by the parties when they choose to present them to the court.

> 4. Without effective judicial control, however, the adversarial process is likely to encourage an adversarial culture and to degenerate into an environment in which the litigation process is too often seen as a battlefield where no rules apply. In this environment, questions of expense, delay, compromise and fairness may have only low priority. The consequence is that expense is often excessive, disproportionate and unpredictable; and delay is frequently unreasonable.

> 5. This situation arises precisely because the conduct, pace and extent of litigation are left almost completely to the parties. There is no effective control of their worst excesses. Indeed, the complexity of the present rules facilitates the use of adversarial tactics and is considered by many to require it. As Lord Williams, a former Chairman of the Bar Council, said in responding to the announcement of this Inquiry, the process of law has moved from being 'servant to master, due to cost, length and uncertainty'.

At various points in the Report, Lord Woolf called for the parties to behave in a more co-operative and less combative or adversarial manner. He stated that one of

---

[12]   *Brinks-Mat Ltd v Elcombe* [1988] 1 WLR 1350.
[13]   *Chappell v United Kingdom* [1989] FSR 617.

the objectives of judicial case management would be 'the encouragement of a spirit of co-operation between the parties and the avoidance of unnecessary combativeness which is productive of unnecessary additional expense and delay' (p 30, para 17(c)).

Sir Jack Jacob wrote, 'the passive role of the English court greatly enhances the standing, the influence and the authority of the judiciary at all levels and may well account for the high respect and esteem in which they are held' (*The Fabric of English Civil Justice*, 1987, p 12).

Lord Woolf, by contrast, proposed that the judge should exercise control both before and during trial not only to marshall the case but to control the quantity and quality of evidence received by the court. (p 178, paras 14,15) This policy was enshrined in the CPR. Part 32.1 starts: '(1) The court may control the evidence by giving directions as to – (a) the issues on which it requires evidence; (b) the nature of the evidence which it requires to decide those issues; and (c) the way in which the evidence is to be placed before the court. Part 32 continues: '(2)The court may use its power under this rule to exclude evidence that would otherwise be admissible. (3) The court may limit cross-examination.' Thus, the judge, if he chooses to exercise it, has enormous power to decide which witnesses of fact are called and how they are to give their evidence. Similarly he has some power over the evidence of the expert witnesses. In particular, no expert can be called without the court's permission.

In the view of some this imperils both the search for truth and the court's appearance of impartiality–see for instance the severe criticisms of Conrad Dehn QC 'The Woolf Report: Against the Public Interest?' in Zuckerman and *Reform of Civil Procedure– Essays on Access to Justice* (Clarendon, OUP, 1995), p 162; and of Neil Andrews, 'The Adversarial Principle: Fairness and Efficiency Reflections on the Recommendations of the Woolf Report', ibid, pp 171–183. See also J A Jolowicz, 'The Woolf Report and the Adversary System', 15 *Civil Justice Quarterly*, 1996, pp 198-210. Professor Jolowicz showed how the French civil justice system, which, contrary to popular belief, traditionally was mainly adversary, had in recent years become more and more inquisitorial. He suggested that the Woolf reforms would push the English system in the same direction.

For a powerful piece supporting Professor Jolowicz's view see Mr Justice Lightman, 'The case for judicial intervention',[14] published a few months after the Woolf reforms had gone live. In the 'old days', he said, the parties did not have to give advance disclosure of their case. The only information the other side had was what little was revealed by the pleadings, the judge did no pre-reading because, apart from the pleadings, there was nothing to pre-read. In those circumstances it was natural and right for the trial judge to be basically silent and passive. Now there was full advance disclosure of the evidence and a requirement of skeleton arguments in which each side set out their submissions and authorities. The judge usually found time to read these before the trial. In Lightman's view it was not merely acceptable but positively

14   *New Law Journal*, 3 December 1999, p 1819.

desirable that the judge should ask questions based on his reading of the skeleton arguments. This showed the advocate the issues on which the court needed to hear argument. Having read the witness statements in advance the judge was also in a position to ask questions of the witnesses. ('He does not need to wait to see if the question is asked and then what answer is given, and he need not accept the sufficiency of an answer just because the advocate does.' (p 1835)). However the judge needed to tread very carefully. ('His questioning out of turn may frustrate a planned cross-examination, and if he asks (as he is entitled to) leading questions, (questions suggesting their own answer), the witness may psychologically find it difficult to resist the perceived judicial pressure to give that answer' (p.1835)).

But it is noteworthy that the CPR do not include a new power for the judge to *call* witnesses nor did Mr Justice Lightman urge such a power.

The position in regard to criminal cases remains much more in the traditional mould. By contrast with the view of Lord Woolf, the Runciman Royal Commission on Criminal Justice did not call for any move towards a less adversary procedure–though it did make some relatively minor proposals for alterations in the way that expert evidence is prepared–see pp 296-97 above. It rejected the idea of the court calling its own expert. (Report, p 160, para 74.) It equally rejected the concept of judicial supervision of the pre-trial stage of a criminal investigation. Partly its reason was cultural, but partly it was substantive:

> Every system is the product of a distinctive history and culture, and the more different the history and culture from our own the greater must be the danger that an attempted transfer will fail. Hardly any of those who gave evidence to the Commission suggested that the system in another jurisdiction should be adopted in England and Wales; and of those who did, none argued for it in any depth or with any supporting detail [Report, p 4, para 13].

> Our reason for not recommending a change to an inquisitorial system as such is not simply fear of the consequences of an unsuccessful cultural transplant. It is also that we doubt whether the fusion of the functions of investigation and prosecution, and the direct involvement of judges in both are more likely to serve the interests of justice than a system in which the roles of police, prosecutors, and judges are as far as possible kept separate and the judge who is responsible for the conduct of the trial is the arbiter of law but not of fact. We believe that a system in which the critical roles are kept separate offers a better protection against the risk of unnecessarily prolonged detention prior to trial [ibid, para 14].

For the research evidence on the inquisitorial system done for the Royal Commission, see p 377 below.

As has been seen, Lord Justice Auld equally accepted that a judge should call a witness in a criminal case only in exceptional circumstances.

(c) The inquisitorial system compared

In the continental inquisitorial system the main burden of presenting the case at court falls on the court itself. The court calls the witnesses and there is, therefore, not the same danger as exists in the common law systems of the evidence of a particular witness being suppressed because neither side wishes to call him. The witnesses are questioned ('examined') by the presiding judge. The role of the lawyers is supplementary. They can suggest the names of further witnesses that the court should call. They can ask questions of witnesses after the court has finished asking its questions. But the lawyers play a subsidiary role.

The essential differences between the two systems in regard to the taking of evidence was captured 50 years ago by the Evershed Committee in its *Final Report on Supreme Court Practice*, 1953, Cmnd 8878:

> 250. (a) There is no doubt that the difference between the English and the continental systems in regard to evidence, ie in regard to the rules of evidence and the way in which evidence is taken, is very marked; and equally there is no doubt that the difference is one of the main reasons for the fact that litigation in England is substantially more costly than (for example) in France or Germany.
>
> (b) In both France and Germany all (oral) witnesses are the court's witnesses, though generally speaking they are tendered by the parties. In both countries the system is (as has been said), unlike the English system, 'inquisitorial'. There is substantially no cross-examination and for practical purposes none at all by the parties or their legal representatives. The witness in effect makes a deposition before the examining judge who decides what witnesses shall be summoned. The process of taking evidence is almost invariably at an early stage of the proceedings, long before the 'trial' proper.
>
> (c) The witness makes his statement in his own words—there being no 'hearsay' rule. It is for the court to decide the value of what has been said. It is, however, to be noted that the parties themselves are, generally, not competent witnesses in Germany; and in France parents, relatives and servants of the parties and certain other categories of persons are not competent.
>
> (d) In both France and Germany, oral testimony is regarded as of far less significance than in England.

One of the points frequently made in comparisons between the English and the civil law systems of trial is their different approach to the 'search for the truth'. This was the theme of a leading practitioner who is also a scholar, in a book about a famous murder case:

Louis Blom-Cooper, *The A6 Murder*, 1963, pp 72, 80–2

In the Continental trial system the starting point of the trial is the accused man. The first thing the court learns about is his medical and criminal antecedents;

the court then feels more able to adjudge the man's conduct in relation to the crime, both for testing his culpability in arriving at a verdict and his responsibility for the crime in assessing the treatment he should receive.

The English form of trial is more professional, more aseptic, than the Continental system, a kind of surgical operation, a great deal less painful to the public who are immune from the range of a Continental system of inquiry. The English trial is precise and coldly analytical within the narrow confines marked out by the accusatorial system. Every piece of the puzzle is fitted into a framework which is delineated by the nature of the trial, an accusation on a specific charge against a specific person with all else ruthlessly excluded. The rapier of the prosecution is thrust out; the defence's task is merely to parry it, with no concern other than that the rapier thrust should not strike home. A successful parry means an acquittal and that is that. This precision is claimed to be the English virtue, and certainly the construction of the English trial system does mean that the rules of the game are well defined, and that an accused can prepare himself for it. A more roving inquiry means that the accused may find himself outflanked and may mean also that other suspects may find, in the course of the judicial process, that the pointer of guilt as it swings away from the major suspect shifts towards them.

The Continental system of law, called by contrast the inquisitorial system, believes that a human being is on trial and that the acts of a human being, judged to be criminal, are highly complex. To affix criminal responsibility on an accused, it is not enough to inquire: did this man do the specific act alleged against him? The Continental lawyer wishes to probe deeper in order to determine the full criminal responsibility and the certainty, so far as certainty can be achieved, that the crime is laid at the door of the right perpetrator. It is in essence a search for the truth about the crime.

If your system searches for the truth of the crime, what better start can be made than that the chief suspect 'the accused' should be examined by the court? He must, if any one does, know most about the crime. And so immediately at the outset the scope of the trial is altogether wider. The stage of the trial is taken a step further by the defence and prosecution being allowed to show the real, extended context of the act with which the accused is charged. This intense search for the truth is wholly commendable, since the public, through the agency of the judicial system, is entitled to know not only the criminal but the nature of the crime. For to find out the crime is to make absolute at one fell swoop the nature of responsibility without qualification, and to hamstring the power of the court when determining the sentence. In English law the two functions are kept quite distinct. The mitigating features of the accused's acts are kept away from the eyes and ears of the court—except when. . . the defence chooses to put in a record of the accused's character ...

The Continental system is therefore fairer to the public, in whose name the trial is being conducted, than it is to those who are the personalities engaged in the trial.

The Runciman Royal Commission on Criminal Justice looked at the question whether it should recommend a move toward the inquisitorial system as proposed by some of those who submitted evidence. It invited Professor Leonard Leigh and Dr Lucia Zedner to advise it upon the suitability of the French or German models of procedure for adoption or adaptation in England and Wales'. In their report[15] Leigh and Zedner rejected the notion that the inquisitorial model was 'better' or that it should be adopted: 'We do not believe that adoption, certainly in the crude form which is sometimes suggested in respect of the examining magistrates, is either feasible or desirable' (p 67). In some respect the protections afforded to the suspect in England and Wales were already more extensive than those in France and Germany.[16] 'To reproduce the best features of a foreign system in this country would require much more than the introduction of an office found in the foreign jurisdiction. It would be expensive and time-consuming and would not in our submission, produce better results than could be achieved by an intelligent adaptation of the existing English system' (ibid).

The Royal Commission's own verdict on this issue was categorical:

Our reason for not recommending a change to an inquisitorial system as such is not simply fear of the consequences of an unsuccessful cultural transplant. It is also that we doubt whether the fusion of the functions of investigation and prosecution, and the direct involvement of judges in both, are more likely to serve the interests of justice than a system in which the roles of police, prosecutors, and judges are as far as possible kept separate and the judge who is responsible for the conduct of the trial is the arbiter of law but not of fact. We believe that a system in which the critical roles are kept separate offers a better protection for the innocent defendant, including protection against the risk of unnecessarily prolonged detention prior to trial. [Report, p 4, para 14.]

Most writing in English contrasting the adversary/inquisitorial features of the common law and continental systems focuses on criminal cases. Professor JA Jolowicz has traced the way in which the French civil justice system has moved from a basically adversary position to one where the judge has more and more responsibility for establishing the facts. ('The Woolf Report and the Adversary System', 15 *Civil Justice Quarterly*, 1996, pp 198-210.) According to a decree of 1971, substantially re-enacted in 1975, cases can be allocated for trial ('*audience*') on the short route if the exchanges between the parties shows that the case is ready for hearing. Otherwise the case must

---

[15]   *A Report on the Administration of Criminal Justice in the Pre-trial phase in France and Germany*, Royal Commission Research Study No 1, 1992.

[16]   For details of the French system after the reforms of 1993 and 2000 see the very valuable articles by Dr Jacqueline Hodgson in the bibliography below.

follow the long route which means that the preparation of the evidence (the *'instruction'*) takes place under the control of the *juge de la mise en état*. He must not only see that delay is minimised but ensure that the case is prepared so that the *audience* can focus on the real question raised by the litigation. It is still for the parties to identify the subject matter of the litigation by their claims and defences and it is for them to prove the facts on which they rely. But a new art 10 of the civil code passed in 1972 stated that 'Everyone is bound to cooperate with the administration of justice with a view to revelation of the truth'. The judge can, of his own motion, order any legally admissible *mesures d'instruction* and he can proceed to personal verification of the facts in issue by a variety of means, such as visiting the scene. He can invite the lawyers to deal with matters on which they have made no submissions and to provide explanations on matters of fact or of law as he considers necessary to resolve the litigation. He can call them before him and can draw inferences from their replies to his questions. Also, since he will be a member of the court that takes the *audience* his impressions will play a part there as well. The *mesures d'instruction* include the taking of oral evidence and obtaining expert reports. When oral evidence is taken it is the judge who decides what are the facts requiring proof and the judge examines the witnesses. He can on application of a party or of his own motion take evidence from anyone else whose evidence would be useful 'to manifestation of the truth'. The expert is appointed by the court and it is the judge who defines the questions to be addressed in the report. Professor Jolowicz summarised: 'Put another way, whereas in the past it was the role of the judge only to evaluate the proofs adduced by the parties, now, as a result of the new rules, he has come to play an active part in searching for the truth' (at p 208).

The extract that follows describes the operation of the civil justice system in Germany from which it appears that some of the basic inquisitorial features already observed above seem to operate in civil cases there as well. The procedure has been described by an English lawyer writing about the German system:

John Ratliff, 'Civil Procedure in Germany', 2 *Civil Justice Quarterly*, July 1983, p 257

The absence of a 'day in court'

There is no single, continuous, oral hearing in German law. Instead proceedings take the form of a series of meetings interwoven with the taking of evidence. German law adheres to the principle that officials should direct the case. This means that the court itself, or an office thereof, is responsible for the initial service of the writ and subsequent exchange of pleadings. Pleadings are sent to the court, which keeps one copy for the official file and sends on two copies to the opposing side, one for the party and one for his lawyer. There is an initial meeting at which the court, after discussion with the parties and on the basis of the written pleadings, decides on what points it will take evidence. The court is not bound to take evidence in any particular order and often hears what it considers to be the decisive evidence first. The actual examination of witnesses takes place in a separate hearing. After the taking of evidence there will be a discussion on what the evidence proves and further appointments for the taking of evidence may be made. This process of taking evidence in instalments succeeded by discussion continues until the court considers the case adequately clarified. One judge is delegated the task of 'reporting' the case, compiling a factual summary of the evidence. At the final hearing the court asks the parties' lawyers if they wish to make any concluding remarks, however, usually a lawyer makes only a 'ritualized reference' to his pleadings. A short discussion on one or two points may follow. The court then retires to come to judgment. The principle of collegiality renders judgment 'off the cuff' impossible. Judgment is later given in court and sent to the parties or their lawyers by registered post or placed in the 'postboxes' which many lawyers' firms have at the courts for receipt of official communications.

In recent years it has increasingly been appreciated in Germany that there may be value at least in some cases in having a trial more in the English sense instead of a series of meetings and written communications between the parties, their lawyers and the court. A new method of handling civil cases (called 'the Stuttgart procedure') was therefore developed. Its essence is to prepare the case so thoroughly beforehand that it can be determined conclusively in one hearing– possibly with the support of a single preliminary meeting. Under the Code of Civil Procedure the judge can if he wishes adopt this mode of proceeding.

See also CN Ngwasiri, 'The Role of the Judge in French Court Proceedings', *Civil Justice Quarterly*, 1990, p 167.

FURTHER READING

For further reading about the English system of trial, see: Glanville Williams' classic work, *The Proof of Guilt* (3rd edn, Stevens, 1963); Sybille Bedford, *The Faces of Justice* (Collins, 1961) and *The Best We Can Do* (Collins, 1963; Penguin, 1961); see also Richard du Cann, *The Art of the Advocate* (revised edn, Penguin, 1993); Patrick Devlin, *The Judge* (Oxford University Press, 1979), pp 54–85; Stephen Landsman, 'The Decline of the Adversary System', 29 *Buffalo Law Review*, 1980, p 487; S Landsman, 'A Brief Survey of the Development of the Adversary System', 44 *Ohio St LJ*, 1983, p 713; and Sir Jack Jacob, *The Fabric of English Civil Justice* (Sweet and Maxwell, 1987), pp 5–19.

On the inquisitorial system, see Sybille Bedford, *The Faces of Justice*, op cit; B Kaplan et al, 'Phases of German Civil Procedure', 71 *Harvard law Review*, 1957–8, pp 1193, 1443; B Kaplan, 'Civil Procedure–Reflections on the Comparison of Systems', 9 *Buffalo Law Review*, 1959–60, p 409; M Damaska, 'Evidential Barriers to Conviction and Two Models of Criminal Procedure: A Comparative Study', 121 *University of Pennsylvania Law Review*, 1973, p 506; 'Structures of Authority and Comparative Criminal Procedure', 84 *Yale Law Journal*, 1975, p 480; and John Langbein, 'The German Advantage in Criminal Procedure, 52 *University of Chicago Law Review*,

1985, p 230. Langbein's article provoked SR Gross 'The American Advantage: The Value of Inefficient Litigation' (1987) 85 *Michigan Law Rev* 734; and RJ Allan et al, 'The German Advantage in Civil Procedure: A Plea for More Details and Fewer Generalities in Comparative Scholarship' (1988) 82 *Northwestern Law Rev* 705 and his reply 'Trashing the German Advantage' (1988) 82 *Northwestern Law Rev* 763.

For an American view that the two systems are not in fact as different as is often thought, because the *juge d'instruction* is only rarely involved and, even when he is, there is still much scope for independent police action, see A Goldstein and M Marcus, 'The Myth of Judicial Supervision in Three Inquisitorial Systems: France, Italy, and Germany', 1977 *Yale Law Journal*, pp 240–83. For a comment on this article and a reply to the comment, see *Yale Law Journal*, 1978, pp 1549, 1570. See also Abraham Goldstein, 'Reflections on Two Models: Inquisitorial Themes in American Criminal Procedure', 26 *Stanford Law Review*, 1974, pp 1009, 1016–25, and Patrick Devlin, 'The Judge in the Adversary System', in *The Judge* (OUP, 1979), p 54.

For further basic information about the two systems see Alain Cornec, 'You Can Say Accident in French', *Law Society's Gazette*, 28 November 1984, p 3328; P Dugdale, 'The West German Court System', *Law Society's Gazette*, 10 September 1986, p 2665. See also H Kötz, 'The Role of the Judge in the Court Room: The Common Law and Civil Law Compared' (1987–91) *Journal of South African Law*, p 35.

On the French system see J R Spencer,' French and English Criminal Procedure: A Brief Comparison' in *The Gradual Convergence*, (ed B.S.Markesinis, Oxford, Clarendon, 1994), pp 33-45 and M Delmas-Marty, 'The *Juge d'instruction: Do the English Really Need Him?*, ibid, pp 46- 58.

On the French system since the reforms of 2000[17] see a series of very helpful articles by Jacqueline Hodgson: 'The Police, the Prosecutor and the *Juge d'Instruction*', 41 *British Journal of Criminology*, 2001, pp 342-61; ' Reforming French criminal justice', *Legal Action*, November 2001, pp 6-8; 'Suspects, Defendants and Victims in the French Criminal Process: The context of recent reforms', 51 *International and Comparative Law Quarterly*, 2002, pp 781-816; 'Heirarchy, Bureaucracy, and Ideology in French Criminal Justice: Some Empirical Observations', 29 *Journal of Law and Society*, 2002, pp 227-57; 'Constructing the pre-trial role of the defence in French criminal procedure: an adversarial outsider in an inquisitorial process?, 6 *International Journal of Evidence and Proof*, 2002, pp 1-16.[18]

For a comprehensive review and comparison of the criminal procedure of England, France and of Germany originally prepared in the context of the Runciman Royal

---

[17]　Loi no 2000-516 du 15 juin 2000 *renfor?ant la protection de la présomption d'innocence et les droits des victimes.*

[18]　According to Hodgson: 1) Interviews with juveniles must be video-recorded but apart from that there is no requirement of tape or video recording; 2) the defence lawyer has the right to 30 minutes with the suspect at the start of detention and again after 20 hours and 36 hours – previously it was 30 minutes after hours; 3) the police must inform the suspect, at the start, of the date and nature of the offence being inquired into; 4) in cases being supervised by the *juge d'instruction* the suspect and his lawyer have the right of full access to the *dossier* – however

Commission's inquiries see *Comparative Criminal Procedure* (eds John Hatchard, Barbara Huber and Richard Vogler, British Institute of International and Comparative Law, London, 1996, 255 pp).

For a comparison of the English and Dutch systems under the title 'Are Inquisitorial and Adversarial Systems Converging?' see N Jorg, S Field and C Brants, in *Criminal Justice in Europe: A comparative Study* (eds P Fennel, C Harding, N Jong and B Swart, Clarendon, Oxford, 1995) pp 41-56.

For description (by two of its chief authors) of radical reform of the Italian system in 1988 see Ennio Amodio and Eugenio Selvaggi, 'An Accusatorial System in a Civil Law Country: The 1988 Italian Code of Criminal Procedure', 62 *Temple Law Review*, 1989, p 1211. The article was the subject of M Zander, 'From Inquisitorial to Adversarial – The Italian Experiment', *New Law Journal*, 17 May 1991, p 678.

For a lengthy consideration of the adversary/inquisitorial spectrum and where on the spectrum Diplock- non-jury trials in Northern Ireland (p 523 below) should be placed see J Jackson and S Doran, *'Judge Without Jury: Diplock Trials in the Adversary System* (Clarendon, Oxford, 1995) especially chaps.3 and 10. The conclusion of the study was that judges in Diplock courts did not act in a more inquisitorial manner than when sitting with a jury. They varied somewhat in the extent to which they were interventionist but the differences arose from individual characteristics and not from the method of trial.

(d) Small claims – a special procedure

The jurisdiction As has been seen, the small claims jurisdiction was established in 1973 as a way of creating a more user-friendly system that would encourage ordinary people to bring their cases to court. (Originally, and for no obvious reason, the scheme was called 'arbitration' but this was dropped as from 1999.) The jurisdiction, which began with a maximum jurisdiction of £75, now covers claims up to £5,000.[19]

---

this affects only some 7% of all cases; 5) in all other cases supervision of the police inquiry is by the prosecutor (*procureur*) – normally conducted over the telephone and by fax; 6) the Ministry of Justice circular says that the suspect should not be told his right to silence at the start of the questioning (neither desirable nor legally required and to do so would encourage the suspect to be silent which would be against his own interest); 7) there is no requirement of an appropriate adult; 8) duty solicitors (*avocat commis d'office*) are mainly young and inexperienced doing it as part of their training; 9) the maximum period of pre-trial detention (*détention provisoire*) is 2 years or 4 years depending on the gravity of the offence.

19   See J Baldwin, 'Increasing the small claims limit', *New Law Journal*, 27 February 1998, p 27; *Monitoring the Rise in the Small Claims Limit*, LCD Research Series 1/97, Lord Chancellor's Department, 1997 and *Lay and Judicial Perspectives on the Expansion of the Small Claims Regime*, LCD, Research Series 8/02, September 2002. See also more generally J Baldwin, *Small Claims in the County Court in England and Wales: The Bargain Basement of Civil Justice* (Oxford, Clarendon, 1997) and 'Litigants Experiences of Adjudication in the County Courts', *Civil Justice Quarterly*, January 1999, pp 12-40.

The small claims court now handles roughly four out of five contested cases in the county court. (In 2001, 58,333 cases (or 81%) were disposed of as small claims, compared with 13,430 (19%) as ordinary contested hearings.[20])

The allocation decision Before April 1999, a case within the jurisdiction would go to 'arbitration' unless it raised a difficult question of law or fact or was of exceptional complexity or the parties agreed that the case should be tried in court or that it would be unreasonable. (CCR Ord 19, r 1(5)). Under the Woolf regime, the court allocates the case to its appropriate track. The Practice Direction on small claims says, 'The small claims track is intended to provide a proportionate procedure by which most straightforward claims with a financial value of not more than £5,000 can be decided, without the need for substantial pre-hearing preparation and the formalities of a traditional trial, and without incurring large legal costs' (26PD8.1(1)(a)) 'Cases generally suitable for the small claims track will include consumer disputes, accident claims, disputes about the ownership of goods and most disputes between a landlord and a tenant other than those for possession (26 PD 8.1(1)(c)).

Nature of hearing From the outset, one of the most important features of the small claims system has been its informality: The Civil Procedure Rules (CPR 27.8(1)) continue this approach:

> The court may adopt any method of proceeding at a hearing that it considers to be fair.
> ...
> (2) Hearings will be informal.
> (3) The strict rules of evidence do not apply.
> (4) The court need not take evidence on oath.
> (5) The court may limit cross-examination.
> (6) The court must give reasons for its decisions.

The judge therefore has complete discretion as to the conduct of the case.

It is true that in *Chilton v Saga Holidays plc* [1986] 1 All ER 841 the Court of Appeal held that the special rules for small claims did not mean that the basic principles of the adversary system could be set aside. The registrar who heard the case had refused to allow solicitors for the defendants to cross-examine the plaintiff and his wife. ('In cases where one side is unrepresented, I do not allow cross-examination. All questions to the other side will be put through me.') The county court judge upheld the registrar's decision. But the Court of Appeal held that their view was wrong. The Master of the Rolls said that, although the procedure was designed to be informal, it was fundamental to the adversary system 'that each party shall be entitled to ask questions designed to probe the accuracy or otherwise, or the completeness or otherwise, of the evidence which has been given'.

The Courts and Legal Services Act 1990, s 6, provided that county court rules may prescribe the procedure and rules for small claims cases and that such rules 'may, in

[20]   *Judicial Statistics*, 2001, Table 4.7.

particular, make provision with respect to the manner of taking and questioning evidence'. The Explanatory Notes specifically related this provision to the problem created by the Court of Appeal's decision in *Chilton v Saga Holidays plc*. The right to cross-examine lay on the border between procedural rules and the law of substantive evidence, and an enabling power was therefore needed to permit a rule to be made which gave the court the right to dispense with the right. But although the CPR rule (32.1(3)) states that the court may 'limit' cross-examination it does not say that it may prevent it altogether.

In his most recent research on the way the system is functioning Professor John Baldwin was full of praise for the way in which the district judges handled these cases:

> . . .district judges have made enormous strides in the past twenty years in providing a pleasant and relaxed setting in which litigants can present their cases at small claims hearings, with or without legal representation. . . It would not be much of an exaggeration to say that what district judges in England and Wales have achieved in providing a congenial arena in which litigants in person can function effectively at hearings has not been equalled at other levels of the judiciary. Moreover, the writer's knowledge of what happens at small claims hearings in other jurisdictions leads him to believe that the judiciary of no other country has achieved a comparable measure of success in this regard.[21]

The judge is expected to be interventionist Despite the decision in *Chilton*, judges are encouraged to take an active role. The rules not only permit informality. The 1999 Practice Direction states, for instance, that the judge may 'ask questions of any witness himself before allowing any other person to do so'.[22] This would be regarded as completely unacceptable in ordinary cases.

Not surprisingly, the judges vary in their willingness to take on this kind of activist role. Professor John Baldwin, writing about this, said:

> The interventionist role is not, however, always easy to play, particularly for judges who (as in this country) have been used to practising within an adversarial setting. It is in fact a role that bears remarkable similarities to the inquisitorial judge. Yet unless adjudicators play this role – and what is more, play it competently and enthusiastically – small claims procedures simply will not work.[23]

Any observer, he said, 'is likely to be struck by the enormous variations between district judges in their interpretation of what it means to be interventionist'.[24] It was

---

[21]   *Lay and Judicial Perspectives on the Expansion of the Small Claims Regime*, LCD Research Series No8/02, September 2002, pp 88, 89 – www.lcd.gov.uk

[22]   PD 27, 4.3(1).

[23]   J Baldwin, 'Small Claims Hearings: The "Interventionist" Role Played by District Judges', 17 *Civil Justice Quarterly*, January 1998, pp 20, 21.

[24]   Baldwin, 17 *Civil Justice Quarterly*, January 1998, p 22.The same had been the finding in an earlier study of the small claims system in 30 courts - George Appleby, *Small Claims in England and Wales*, Birmingham Institute of Judicial Administration, 1978, pp 30-33.

rare for the judge to read the papers beforehand. Most did not explain the purpose of the hearing or the nature of the procedure they intended to adopt, whereas some took great pains over the introduction.[25] But most of the judges showed evident relish in playing an interventionist role.

It can, indeed, be said that the judicial shift from the traditional adversarial approach to active interventionism has been achieved in small claims and, however reluctant they may have been in the past, few district judges now show much hesitation about intervening at hearings or express misgivings about doing so.[26]

Baldwin identified four main approaches to being interventionist. One was 'going for the jugular' – identifying the central issues and insisting that the parties stick to them. A second was to allow the parties to say what they want to say. A third was to sit passively and then just ask a few questions. A fourth was to try to achieve a compromise solution like a mediator. The different styles could affect the outcome of cases. Thus, for instance, judges vary in their approach to the frequent failure of litigants in person to bring all the evidence they need. Preliminary hearings are rare and are discouraged by the rules. It is rare for parties to come with witnesses.(In one of his many studies, in 91 out of 109 hearings observed by Baldwin, there were no witnesses.)[27] To avoid an adjournment, a robust judicial approach tended to be adopted. But judges differed widely in their ability and their inclination to ask the pertinent question and to fill in the gaps in the evidence. They varied also in whether they felt bound to apply the law. A minority thought they should; 'a majority said they were entitled to disregard the law in making decisions if in their view strictly applying it would produce injustice'.[28] In his Interim Report Lord Woolf said (p 109) 'it is questionable whether such differences are acceptable even in a jurisdiction limited to £1,000' and that any inclination to follow common sense rather than the principle of law should be resisted in the interests of consistency. Baldwin agreed with Lord Woolf:

> While there is little doubt that the district judges who compromise the application of law in the broader interests of "doing justice" act out of laudable motives, it can be dangerous to apply common sense notions even in small claims. Decision making can easily become inconsistent, capricious, uncertain, even biased, and in the process, the substantive legal rights of individuals may be undermined. Moreover, while flexibility is doubtless desirable in dealing with small claims, it can create great uncertainty for lay litigants and their advisers.[29]

---

25   Baldwin, 17 *Civil Justice Quarterly*, January 1998, p 23.
26   Baldwin, 17 *Civil Justice Quarterly*, January 1998, p 24.
27   Baldwin, 17 *Civil Justice Quarterly*, January 1998, p 28.
28   Baldwin, 17 *Civil Justice Quarterly*, January 1998, p 29.
29   Baldwin, 17 *Civil Justice Quarterly*, January 1998, p 31.

For Baldwin, the variable approaches adopted by district judges 'inevitably weakens one's enthusiasm for the small claims procedure'.[30] Lord Woolf had argued for more guidance and training for district judges in playing the interventionist role to achieve greater consistency.[31] Baldwin suggested that,

> With the trebling[32] in the small claims limit, it is surely no longer acceptable simply to allow the parties to prepare their cases in whatever way they think appropriate and then ask the district judges to make the best of it at hearings. If endless adjournments are to be avoided, then careful attention needs to be paid at an early stage in proceedings to ensure that cases are adequately prepared and, where they are not, that proper directions are given to rectify deficiencies. This tends at present to be done in only a superficial way in many courts, yet it can have a critical bearing upon the fairness of the court procedure.[33]

However, in a further study carried out only a few years later, Baldwin was much reassured at the way the courts had adapted to the increase in jurisdiction and he no longer considered that the way the court handled the case was much, if at all, influenced by the amount involved.[34]

Research on small claims hearings in Canada found, just as Professor Baldwin found, that judges varied greatly in their approach, from the strict legalists to those who seek rather to do justice.[35]

Litigants' perspective Research has confirmed that the small claims system is popular amongst those who use the civil courts. Professor Baldwin interviewed 352 county court litigants who had used either ordinary or the small claims procedure. The interviews took place in 1996 and 1997. The respondents were a cross-section of plaintiffs and defendants, business and lay, regulars and first timers, winners and losers. The main purpose of the study was to examine the two kinds of county court procedures through the eyes of the litigants.

Most of the litigants in both samples (whether they were private individuals, the representatives of businesses or court 'regulars') said they very much favoured informality of procedures in resolving their disputes. The great majority of small claims litigants accepted without much question the relatively simple and crude methods adopted by district judges and welcomed the opportunity to participate directly in the resolution of their disputes. There were few complaints from the small

---

30   Baldwin, 17 *Civil Justice Quarterly*, January 1998, p 33.
31   *Access to Justice*, Interim Report, pp 108-10, Final Report, p 98.
32   As has been seen, the limit has since been further increased to five times what it was in 1995.
33   Baldwin, 17 *Civil Justice Quarterly*, January 1998, p 34.
34   Baldwin, *Lay and Judicial Perspectives on the Expansion of the Small Claims Regime*, LCD Research Series No8/02, September 2002, p 64
35   R A Macdonald, 'Judicial Scripts in the Dramaturgy of the Small Claims Court', 11 *Canadian Journal of Law and Society*, 1996, p 63. The study was described and discussed by the writer: M Zander, 'Consistency in the exercise of discretionary powers', *New Law Journal*, 1 November, 1996, p 1590.

claims litigants. But these high levels of satisfaction, Baldwin said, 'were certainly not paralleled in the interviews with litigants who had experienced "open court" trial. Almost every interview with litigants in the latter category produced complaints of varying degrees of seriousness. Some produced a veritable catalogue.'[36] Individual litigants complained about the formality and the wigs and gowns. Many were greatly affected by the costs and especially the threat of having to pay the other side's costs if they lost. ('Even though the sums in dispute were in all cases in the sample under £3,000, the costs incurred by some individuals ran into thousands of pounds.'[37]) They were more likely than the small claims litigants to complain about their lawyers and the legal advice they had received. (Whereas 87% of small claims litigants were satisfied with their lawyers, only 45% of 'open court' litigants were.[38]) In short, 'No matter what criterion of litigant satisfaction was adopted, the small claims regime came out ahead – and by a wide margin.'[39]

Baldwin's positive view was confirmed by his further study published in 2002 which ended: 'Although there may be continuing problems and dilemmas in small claims that are yet to be satisfactorily tackled, the small claims procedure is widely acknowledged to be the great success story of civil justice in England and Wales'.[40] He thought it would be worth considering transferring at least a proportion of personal injury claims from the fast track – 'even if such moves would require modification of existing arrangements and would in any event be resisted by sections of the legal profession'.[41]

Had the increase in jurisdiction made any difference? Baldwin suggests that although the threefold increase in the small claims jurisdiction from £1,000 to £3,000 had produced some changes – in the kind of litigant using the system, increases in the level of claim and changes in legal representation – 'one is nevertheless struck ... by how little things are changing, not by how much'.[42] It was especially disappointing that there had been no real increase in the overall number of litigants using the county court. The main consequence of increasing the jurisdiction seemed to be to shift a certain proportion of ordinary county court cases to the small claims system.

He reached much the same conclusion in the study published in 2002 which focussed on the increase in jurisdiction from £3,000 to £5,000:

> What has been striking about recent developments is, therefore, how little difference they have made, not how much. The effects of the dramatic increases

---

36　J Baldwin, 'Litigants' Experience of Adjudication in the County Courts', 18 *Civil Justice Quarterly*, January 199, pp 12-40 at 20.

37　Baldwin, 18 *Civil Justice Quarterly*, January 1999, p 28.

38　Baldwin, 18 *Civil Justice Quarterly*, January 1999, p 24.

39　Baldwin, 18 *Civil Justice Quarterly*, January 1999, p 39.

40　N 31 above at p 91.

41　N 31 above at p 86.

42　J Baldwin, *Monitoring the Rise in the Small Claims Limit*, LCD Research Series 1/97, 1997, p 116.

in the small claims limit, insofar as they have been noticed at all, have been absorbed without serious disruption.[43]

Most people wont use the courts – even the small claims court Professor Baldwin asked why all the changes in court procedure to make the small claims system more 'user friendly' had had such little success in attracting would-be litigants. The answer, in his view, lay in the nature and the image of the courts themselves:

Although there is a hard-core of regular court users – for the most part business people for whom an occasional county court appearance is an inevitable, if somewhat disagreeable, part of commercial life – for most of the rest of the population, the courts are regarded as institutions that are to be avoided at all costs. It is, it seems, only idealists ... who see the county courts as providing a mechanism through which legal wrongs can be remedied. For most people, it is more accurate to say that a situation has to become desperate before legal action in the county courts would ever be contemplated.[44]

(e) Tribunals and the adversary system

For an evaluation of the tribunal system as to its 'adversary' and 'inquisitorial' features see Gabrielle Ganz, *Administrative Procedures* (Sweet & Maxwell, 1974), pp 29–35. For a very critical view of the decision-making process in industrial tribunals, see Alice Leonard, *Judging Inequality* (Cobden Trust, 1987). Leonard studied 300 industrial tribunal cases relating to sex discrimination and equal pay over a three-year period. Her conclusions were disturbing. She found considerable ignorance and misunderstanding about the relevant legislation in the decisions. Many tribunals applied the wrong legal standard. Tribunals were found to be superficial in their analysis of the evidence, too ready to accept vague and generalized statements even when these were inconsistent with other evidence or based on irrelevant considerations. There was a great lack of uniformity in the quality of decision-making as between different tribunals. Some were much more expert than others. The lack of uniformity applied also to the expertise of those assisting applicants. Most claims failed because of the failure by the complainant and his representative to present relevant evidence. The usual pattern was for the parties to present only oral evidence with no more than one or two pre-existing documents. They failed to call supporting witnesses, failed to cross-examine witnesses effectively and made little or no use of statistical or comparative evidence. Complainants who had representatives who were more experienced and knowledgeable about the legislation had much better success rates.

---

[43] N 31 above at pp 85-86.
[44] N 31 above at p 88.

Leonard adopted the view of a previous study[45] that the tribunal should perform an inquisitorial rather than an adversarial function. But in addition to an expert tribunal there would be a need for some form of expert to help the tribunal by organizing the presentation of the cases, 'an individual expert in the legislation who in each case reviews the available information, determines what evidence and witnesses would be appropriate and ensures that they are produced by the parties' (p 147).

2.   The advantages of being represented

It would appear obvious that in an adversary system the party who is unrepresented is likely to be at a distinct disadvantage. But there is remarkably little statistical evidence one way or the other on this important question.

The problem is mainly one that affects the lower courts and proceedings in tribunals since in the higher trial courts it is rare for the parties to be unrepresented.

(a)   Representation in magistrates' courts

In a study by the Lord Chancellor's Department in some 60 magistrates' courts there were 566 criminal cases in which the defendant pleaded not guilty. The proportion acquitted for those who were granted legal aid was 42%, for those who refused legal aid but were represented privately was 52%, and for those who were not represented was virtually the same, 51%. This suggested that representation was not necessarily so significant. (See Lord Chancellor's Department, *Report of a Survey of the Grant of Legal Aid in Magistrates' Courts*, 1983, Table 17.)

(b)   Representation in small claims cases

In its original 1973 pamphlet which first proposed a small claims court, the Consumer Council recommended that legal representation not be permitted in the small claims court. But this recommendation was not adopted. Representation by a lawyer was permitted from the start in 1973 and representation by a non-lawyer has been permitted since 1992.[46] Representation by non-lawyers seems to be very rare. Professor John Baldwin reported that in 109 hearings he observed there were only five that featured a lay representative.[47]

---

[45]   J Corcoran and E Donnelly, 'Report of a comparative analysis of the provisions for legal redress in member states of the EEC in respect of Article 119 of the Treaty of Rome and the Equal Pay, Equal Treatment and Social Security Directive', 1984.

[46]   The Lay Representation (Rights of Audience) Order 1992 giving effect to s 11 of the Courts and Legal Services Act 1990.

[47]   *Civil Justice Quarterly*, January 1998, p 20, 31, n 31.

Baldwin compared legal representation in the 1996 sample of over 2,500 cases with his 1993 sample of just under 2,000 cases. There were some striking differences. In 1993, in 82% of the cases neither side was legally represented, in 1996 the figure had dropped to 55%. In both 1993 and 1996 only the plaintiff was legally represented in 12% of cases. In 1993 only the defendant was legally represented in 4% of cases. The 1996 figure of 5% was virtually the same. But whereas in 1993 both sides had been legally represented in only 2% of cases, in 1996 that figure had risen to 27%.[48] This was an astonishing change over so short a period.

In a previous study for the LCD, Baldwin had established that increases in legal representation were not occurring across the board but were confined to road accident cases. 80% of litigants involved in such cases were legally represented compared with only 14% in other categories of cases.[49] The increase in legal representation seemed therefore to be the result of the fact that many more road accident cases were being handled in the small claims system.

According to the 1996 sample, plaintiffs were significantly more likely to be legally represented than defendants. When the plaintiff was a company or a firm they were legally represented in, respectively, 51% and 41% of cases. Individuals as plaintiff were legally represented in a third of cases. This difference was less marked in the case of defendants. (27% of companies, 30% of firms and 33% of individual defendants were legally represented.)[50] It is worth noting that even firms and companies are not legally represented in the majority of cases in which they are involved – though they may, of course, be represented by a staff member who is familiar with court procedures.

Baldwin's 1996 figures suggest that legal representation improved a litigant's chances of success by about 10%. He had reached the same conclusion in his earlier study.[51] A more important question is whether legal representation makes a difference when the other side is unrepresented. The 1996 figures showed that it made little difference.[52] Baldwin reflected that this confirmed his earlier research which had indicated how problematic the legal representative's role is likely to be in the small claims context where the court is encouraged to be interventionist. (He had found that the lawyers in small claims cases tended to take a back seat and were side-lined by district judges who preferred to talk directly to the parties.[53])

[48] J Baldwin, 'Increasing the small claims limit', *New Law Journal*, 27 February 1998, p 275.
[49] J Baldwin, *Monitoring the Rise in the Small Claims Limit*, LCD Research Series 1/97, Lord Chancellor's Department, 1997.
[50] Baldwin, *New Law Journal*, 27 February 1998, p 275.
[51] Baldwin, *New Law Journal*, 27 February 1998, p 276.
[52] In 87% of the 2,563 cases the plaintiff got an award. When both sides were legally represented the figure was 90%. When neither side was legally represented it was 86%. When the plaintiff alone was legally represented it was 87%. When the defendant alone was legally represented it was 86% (ibid).
[53] J Baldwin, *Small Claims in the County Court in England and Wales: The Bargain Basement of Civil Justice* (Oxford, Clarendon, 1997) at pp 116-20.

(c)   Representation in tribunals

Another set of statistics regarding the benefit of representation relates to proceedings before national insurance tribunals and supplementary benefit appeals tribunals. In a study by Professor Kathleen Bell and colleagues, conducted in Scotland and the northern region of England in the 1970s, it was found that out of 4,456 cases in national insurance tribunals, the appellant was represented in just over 20%. Representation in three-quarters of the cases was by a trade-union representative, in 19% by a relative or friend and in only 3% by lawyers. Overall, the success rate of appeals was 21%, but the success rate was distinctly higher for those who had been represented, regardless of who was the representative. (Kathleen Bell, 'National Insurance Local Tribunals', 4 Journal of Social Policy, 1975, p 16. See to like effect vol 885 House of Commons, Hansard, 1 May 1973, cols 264–5.)

The Benson Royal Commission on Legal Services in 1979 cited new evidence to similar effect in regard to the success rate in over 50,000 supplementary benefit appeal tribunal cases in 1976. (Cmnd 7648, 1979, para 15.9, p 169).

The most sophisticated inquiry into the issue is, however, the study by Hazel and Yvette Genn, *The Effectiveness of Representation at Tribunals*, July 1989, published by the Lord Chancellor's Department. The data showed that the presence of a representative 'significantly increases' the probability that cases will be won. In social security appeals the presence of a representative increased the probability of success from 30% to 48%. In hearings before Immigration Adjudicators it went up from 20% to 38%. In Mental Health Review Tribunals it increased the success rate from 20% to 35%. In Industrial Tribunals the impact depended on whether the respondent was represented. When he was not, the presence of a representative for the applicant pushed the success rate up from 30% to 48%. Where the respondent was represented and the applicant was not, the success rate went down to 10%. What was as striking as the statistical difference in success rate between those who were represented and those who were not, was that, again, the nature of the representation made little difference. Thus in immigration appeals, solicitors, barristers and the United Kingdom Immigrants' Advisory Service (UKIAS), which used mainly non-legally qualified advocates, succeeded with virtually identical rates. (ibid, p 84). E Heslop, 'Trends and threats in employment tribunals', *Legal Action*, February 2003, p 7 expressed concern about applicants' lack of access to representation in Employment Tribunals.

See also G Bull and J Seargeant, *Approaches to Tribunal Representation: A study of the tribunal work of advice agencies*, Policy Studies Institute,1996 – a study aimed at providing advice as to the criteria for giving legal aid for tribunal representation should legal aid become available;

3.   Handicaps of the unrepresented

The formality of English proceedings is often referred to by commentators. Where both parties are legally represented, as they normally are in the High Court or the higher criminal courts, this may not be quite so important. But where they are not legally represented it may be of great significance. There are no figures as to the proportion of defendants in the magistrates' courts who are unrepresented but it is certainly several hundred thousand each year. The essence of the situation was captured by Mrs Susanne Dell's study based on interviews with a random sample of 565 prisoners at Holloway prison. The study was conducted many years ago but it would be surprising if the situation of an unrepresented defendant today is very different.

(a)   In the lower courts

Susanne Dell, Silent in Court, 1971, pp 17–19

Many of the women who were unrepresented were seriously handicapped by the lack of legal help. An inexperienced defendant is at a disadvantage in court even if well educated and articulate,[54] but for those who have little education, who are scared, nervous and unable to express themselves in the kind of language they believe is expected in court, the handicap can be crippling, particularly if they wish to deny the offence or to plead mitigating circumstances.

. . . when the unrepresented defendant first appears in court, she is in several ways at a disadvantage. The proceedings may be bewildering and unintelligible to her to an extent the court can hardly appreciate. One remanded girl, when asked by the interviewer whether she had asked for bail in court, replied 'What is bail? Is it the same as legal aid?' Many others, even by the time they were interviewed, were confused about the correct meaning of terms like 'remand' and 'bail'. This kind of ignorance was not restricted to first offenders, although for them the position is particularly difficult; they do not know what to expect, how to behave, when to speak, and when to be silent. As one girl put it, 'I kept being told to get up and sit down.' It is not easy in such circumstances to do justice to one's own defence.

Frequently, the women said that they had not been able to catch what was being said: a typical comment was 'The Judge mumbles away, and you don't know whether or not he's supposed to be speaking to you'. Many remanded women said they had left the court room without realising what the magistrate had decided: and it was then the police who had had to explain to them that they could not go home, as they had been remanded to Holloway. One first offender who caught the words 'two weeks' thought she was being put on probation for

---

[54]   Not many women in the sample fell into that category, but an example was a professional woman, who was arrested with others at a political demonstration. She appeared in court with the others, unrepresented, and was remanded in custody untried. When asked by the interviewer why bail had not been allowed, she said she did not know. She knew the police had opposed it, but said that all she heard was a policeman saying that the reason was 'the same as before'. It had not occurred to her to ask in court what bail meant.

that period, until the police disabused her in the cells. This ignorance and lack of understanding can be a practical handicap to the unrepresented person: if a woman who has been remanded in custody is not aware of the fact before she leaves the court room, she cannot ask for bail, nor can she ask for it if she does not understand the meaning of the term. If she is remanded in custody for medical reports while unaware 'as virtually all such women were' that bail could be granted for such a purpose, she is also precluded by her ignorance from asking for it. When a person is represented, her ignorance on such matters is immaterial: her solicitor will ask for bail, and present what arguments there may be against the use of custody. But it is unrealistic to assume that most unrepresented persons can properly look after their own interests in these matters. ... The impossibility of expressing themselves in court weighed heavily on many women: not infrequently those who had given the interviewer full accounts of the background to their offences, said that the court had not known of the mitigating circumstances, as they had found themselves tongue-tied and silent at the appropriate moment. ... A few women complained that they never had a chance to explain themselves in court: this, no doubt, reflected their failure to understand the procedure, since they had probably been interrupted when trying to speak at the wrong moment. But the most common situation among the unrepresented was that when invited to do so, they failed to give the court any explanation of their behaviour. When asked 'What have you to say?' they seemed to think that the response expected was a short stereotype like 'I'm sorry' and they felt it impossible and inappropriate in the formality of the atmosphere to talk about the background to their offence. One woman described her feelings when she was invited to speak in court and failed to respond, much as she wished to: 'I was too over-awed and frightened–I didn't want to make a fool of myself–I would only have cried.'

A similar impression of the situation of the defendant in the magistrates' court was given in a book based on observation in magistrates' courts–Pat Carlen, *Magistrates' Justice*, 1976, see especially pp 83–5.

(b)   In the tribunals

The 1957 Franks Committee on Administrative Tribunals said (p 9) that tribunals had certain characteristics which distinguished them from courts – cheapness, accessibility, freedom from technicality and expert knowledge of the tribunal members. It identified three main objectives for the system: namely, openness, fairness and impartiality. But as H Genn and Y Genn (*The Effectiveness of Representation at Tribunals*', Lord Chancellor's Department, 1989, p 111) pointed out, the Franks Committee did not acknowledge that, to an extent, there is a conflict between the two sets of objectives. Cheapness and informality may be in conflict with fairness and impartiality.

They found that tribunals were decidedly 'more informal and procedurally more flexible than courts' (p 112). But the price was paid in quality of decision making, since much of the law dealt with in tribunals is difficult and to present a coherent case on fact and law is not easy. The notion that tribunal cases were straightforward and that therefore there was no great need for a representative was unrealistic (ibid, ch 4).

> The experience of unrepresented appellants and applicants is overwhelmingly of feeling ill-equipped to present their case effectively at their hearing. They are intimidated, confused by the language and often surprised at the formality of the proceedings. Those who are subjected to cross-examination find the experience stressful, and feel unable to conduct cross-examination themselves. It is difficult to convey the degree of incomprehension common among appellants and applicants who appear unrepresented at tribunals, or the extent of the difficulties experienced by ordinary people trying to present their case in a legal forum.

> Representatives perform a number of functions. They prepare the case, act as a mouthpiece, and protect and support appellants and applicants. They act as a physical buffer between the appellant and the tribunal, and between the appellant and the opposing side. Most importantly, representation reduces the sense of being at a disadvantage experienced by unrepresented appellants. It increases the likelihood that those who appear before tribunals will perceive the process as fair. (p 241)

(c)   Litigants in person

A litigant always has the right to represent himself in any court. But if he is not legally represented, can he come with some other kind of person to assist him? In *McKenzie v McKenzie* [1971] P 33, CA, the Court of Appeal held that the judge in a defended divorce case had been wrong to exclude an Australian barrister who attended to assist the husband petitioner appearing in person. He had been sitting beside the petitioner prompting and advising him. The court cited the words of Chief Justice Tenterden in *Collier v Hicks* (1831) 2 B & Ad 663 at p 669:

> Any person, whether he be a professional man or not, may attend as a friend of either party, may take notes, may quietly make suggestions, and give advice; but no one can demand to take part in the proceedings as an advocate, contrary to the regulations of the court as settled by the discretion of the justices.

> ... Mr Payne submitted, in my opinion rightly, that the judge ought not to have excluded Mr Hanger from the court, or, rather, ought not to have prevented Mr Hanger from assisting the husband in the way that he proposed to do. And, goes the submission, justice was not seen to be done in those circumstances ...

This decision led to the start of a new form of assistance in courts known as the 'McKenzie man'.

The 'McKenzie man' concept has gone through different phases and has been the subject of conflicting judicial decisions. (For a valuable review and critique of the decisions see R Moorhead, 'Access or Aggravation? Litigants in Person, McKenzie Friends and Lay Representation', 22 *Civil Justice Quarterly*, 2003, pp 133-55.)

In the 1990s it came up in the context of hearings for non-payment of community charge (poll tax). In *R v Leicester City Justices, ex p Barrow* [1991] 2 All ER 437 the Divisional Court held that no party to court proceedings had a 'right' to the assistance of a 'McKenzie friend'. It was a matter for the judge or justices to decide whether or not such assistance should be permitted as an exercise of discretion. On appeal the Court of Appeal [1991] 3 All ER 935 disagreed. It held that in civil proceedings to which the public had a right of access, the court, as part of its duty to administer justice fairly and openly, was under a duty to permit a litigant in person to have all reasonable facilities for exercising his right to be heard in his own defence. This included quiet and unobtrusive advice from another member of the public accompanying him as an assistant or adviser. A litigant did not need leave from the court for this. But in the exercise of its inherent jurisdiction the court could restrict the assistance of an adviser or even require him to leave the court if it became apparent that his assistance was unreasonable or not *bona fide* and was harmful to the proper and efficient administration of justice. There was no evidence that either the applicants or the person who was helping them had any intention of disrupting the court proceedings and the court should have allowed such assistance. (For an account of this litigation see PA Thomas, 'From McKenzie Friend to Leicester Assistant: the Impact of the Poll Tax', *Public Law*, 1992, pp 208–20.)

The leading case now is *R v Bow County Court, ex p Pelling* [1999] 4 All ER 751. Dr Pelling was an experienced McKenzie friend who charged for his services. He had been refused permission to attend to assist G, a father, in an application before the senior civil judge. No explanation was given. Dr Pelling brought judicial review proceedings challenging his exclusion. He failed, first, because he had no standing to bring such proceedings. The right to have a McKenzie friend was that of the litigant not of the McKenzie friend. But Lord Woolf, giving the Court of Appeal's judgment, went on to distinguish *Pelling* from *McKenzie*. G's application was straightforward and G would not have been prejudiced by presenting it on his own. (As Moorhead observed, how can the court know ahead of the hearing whether the litigant in person will be able to manage without help?) Ultimately, Lord Woolf said, the decision was a matter of discretion for the court, with stronger or weaker presumptions one way or the other depending on whether the hearing was in private. (A hearing in chambers is sometimes in private and sometimes in public.)

Moorhead summarised the effect of the decision in *Pelling*:

> 1) If the proceedings are in public whether in court or in chambers, a litigant in person should be allowed to have the assistance of a McKenzie friend unless the judge is satisfied that the interests of justice do not require it.

2) If the hearing is in private, the nature of the proceedings may make it undesirable in the interests of justice for the litigant to have a McKenzie friend.[55]

3) The judge should always give reasons for excluding the McKenzie friend.

Moorhead argues persuasively that the more open approach of the Court of Appeal in *Barrow* is to be preferred to that of Lord Woolf in *Pelling*. ('There should be a strong presumption in all cases (whether taking place in chambers and whether private or public) that a court should permit a litigant in person to have the assistance of a McKenzie friend.' (at 153)) That applied especially to lay assistance short of advocacy. Advocacy, especially when it was provided for payment, was more problematic. Competition for the legal profession from lay representatives who charged fees but did not have formal qualifications, or insurance, or rules of conduct did pose issues. But Moorhead suggests that the question for the courts should be providing help for needy litigants rather than protecting the interests of the legal profession.

In *Izzo v Phillip Ross & Co, New Law Journal*, 5 October 2001, p 216, it was held by a Chancery Division judge that allowing a McKenzie friend to address the court (as opposed to simply advise and assist the litigant in person) was an indulgence 'which the court would not lightly accord' – but it was allowed in that instance. (See also *Paragon Finance Ltd v Noueiri* [2001] EWCA Civ 1402, [2001] 1 WLR 2357.)

THE OTTON WORKING PARTY ON LITIGANTS IN PERSON IN THE ROYAL COURTS

In June 1995 a committee under the chairmanship of Lord Justice Otton established by the Judges' Council, reported on the problem of litigants in person in the Royal Courts of Justice ((RCJ).[56] It said there had been a significant increase in the number of such litigants in the RCJ. The largest number and proportion were in the civil division of the Court of Appeal. In 1993–94, litigants in person were one in three of applicants for leave to appeal but only 10% of actual appellants. The litigant in person was ultimately successful in only 4% of cases–a much lower rate than litigants who had representation (p 10). One reason was that some simply had no case at law. Others were prejudiced by the complexity of the proceedings, their lack of knowledge of procedure, and the non-availability of low cost or free legal advice and assistance. Court staff gave as much assistance as they could but they could not become legal advisers without prejudicing the independence of the court.

The Working Party endorsed the call by Lord Woolf in his Interim Report for additional support for the Citizens' Advice Bureau (CAB) in the Royal Courts of Justice in the Strand which handles some 18,000 inquiries a year. Lawyers from

---

[55]   In *G (Chambers Proceedings: McKenzie Friend),Re* [1999] 1 WLR 1828, the McKenzie friend, a solicitor, was refused permission to attend a chambers wardship hearing in private unless he was the solicitor on the record. The Court of Appeal declined to intervene.

[56]   The report was obtainable at the time from the Courts Business Section, Supreme Court Group, Room W08, Royal Courts of Justice, Strand London WC2A 2LL.

leading firms of solicitors gave free advice at the CAB. Also, it suggested, the Bar and the Law Society should each have a scheme for the provision of free advisory services for such litigants. (See B McConnell, 'Watch these LIPs', *New Law Journal*, 20 October 1995, p 1549–52).

In 2003 it was reported that the CAB in the Royal Courts was threatened with closure after the Association of London Government planned to withdraw its grant of £58,000 a year.[57]

4. Establishing the facts in court: the unreliability of human testimony

Law teachers often make it appear that most of the courts' time is taken up with legal problems. This is far from the case. The majority of trials on both the civil and the criminal side involve issues of fact, not problems of law. One of the difficulties faced by the courts is the danger of perjury by those giving evidence.

(a)   Perjury

This is an area where little is known–though everyone connected with the justice business would agree that perjury is quite common. The number of prosecutions is tiny – usually 200-300 cases a year.[58] These obviously represent only the tip of the iceberg. An attempt to get some kind of line on the problem was reported by a practising barrister in 1986 (*New Law Journal*, 28 February 1986, p 181). David Wolchover had been at the Bar since 1971. His aim was to discover how much perjury was committed by police officers. His method was to inquire of his fellow barristers. He accepted that it was far from ideal as a basis for an assessment, but said he thought that there was none better and that it might not be wildly wrong.

He considered that having practised for many years he 'had sufficient experience and acumen to be capable of making a reasonably confident judgment from the details of facts and circumstances in a given case whether police officers were committing perjury'. It had become apparent to him that 'police perjury occurs with great frequency in London' where he practised. His belief that this was so 'was reinforced by hearing, in chambers, in the robing room and Bar mess, the casual and matter of fact way in which the Bar tends to refer to police perjury. It was regarded as commonplace' (p 183). Over a two-year period he conducted an informal and statistically haphazard poll of fellow barristers to ask how many shared that view. In

---

[57] *The Lawyer*, 5 May 2003, p 5.

[58] A spectacular example of a perjury prosecution was the case brought against former Cabinet Minister Jonathan Aitken arising out of his failed libel proceedings against *The Guardian* and Granada's *World in Action* programme. Aitken pleaded guilty and was sentenced in June 1999 to 18 months' imprisonment. (For an absorbing account of the story see L Harding, D Leigh and D Palliser, *The Liar: The Fall of Jonathan Aitken* (Penguin, 1997).)

the large majority it was shared. Most were between five and twenty years since call to the Bar and took part in prosecution and defence work in about equal proportions.

In Mr Wolchover's estimation, perjury took place in as many as three out of every 10 criminal trials both summary and on indictment. Forty-one of the 55 barristers (75%) he asked thought that this was 'a reasonable estimate with which they could readily concur'. Eight thought it occurred in only one or two out of ten. Four thought its frequency was less than one in ten. Two thought it happened in as many as 50% of their cases (one of these did more prosecution than defence work). Averaged out roughly, this would mean that police perjury was observed to occur in a little over a quarter of all trials.

Mr Wolchover observes that this figure relates only to perceptible lying under oath. There would be many other cases (possibly more) where the police officers lied in ways that were not perceptible to the barristers in the case or where the issue of police perjury never became relevant because the defendant pleaded guilty. There would almost certainly be cases where innocent defendants pleaded guilty to trumped-up charges (see p 302 above) or where some of the prospective evidence was invented– the gilding of the lily.

(b) Human fallibility

But the problem of perjury in the courts is minor by comparison with the problems created by the fallibility of honest witnesses. There is now a mass of evidence based on the experiments conducted by psychologists and others showing how deplorably inaccurate human beings are in their powers of observation, recall and reporting. (See in particular DS Greer, 'Anything But the Truth?–The Reliability of Testimony in Criminal Trials', 11 *British Journal of Criminology*, 1971, p 13; Dr Eliot Slater, 'The Judicial Process and the Ascertainment of Truth', 24 *Modern Law Review*, 1961, p 721; Dr LRC Haward, 'Some Psychological Aspects of Oral Evidence', 3 *British Journal of Criminology*, 1962–3, p 342; LRC Haward, 'A Psychologist's Contribution to Legal Procedure', 27 *Modern Law Review*, 1964, p 656; D Farrington, K Hawkins and S Lloyd-Bostock, *Psychology, Law and Legal Processes* (Macmillan, 1979), especially Part IV; D Yamey, *The Psychology of Eye-Witness Testimony* (Free Press, 1979).

Professor Greer, for instance, said (11 *British Journal of Criminology*, 1971, p 13):

On the whole, it seems, psychological theory in the field of perception is fairly well advanced. It is now generally recognized that there is an important distinction between 'actual' and 'perceived' characteristics of the environment. In other words, 'We all live in a world of our own psychological reality, a world of personal experience separated from the real world (whatever we choose to mean by that) and from the psychological world of others by a complex neuro-physiological process. ... This process selects, organises and transforms objective information according to conditions existing in the observer at the time' (Haward, 1964, op cit, p 663). In short, what a witness recognises perceptually is not necessarily an exact reproduction of the data presented and for legal purposes at any rate the most important finding in this area is that there can be a very considerable discrepancy between the two.

Many of the causes of this discrepancy are already well known, eg the adverse effect on accuracy of testimony of poor lighting, long distance, short duration of exposure, etc. Less well-known factors influencing perception include emotion, interest, bias, prejudice, or expectancy, on the part of the perceiver. Take, for instance, the effect of 'expectancy' or 'set'. It is a well-documented fact that we frequently perceive what we expect to perceive. If we expect to see an individual performing a particular action we are more likely than not to interpret a stimulus which is in fact ambiguous as evidence that the person is performing the expected action.

One example of this is provided by a Canadian case where a hunter was mistaken for a deer and shot by his companions. The hunters, who were eagerly scanning the landscape for deer, perceived the moving object (the victim) as a deer. Before the trial, the police recreated the scene under the same conditions, using another man in the place of the deceased. They reported at the trial that the object was clearly visible as a man. But the important psychological difference between the first and second 'shooting' was that the hunters, expecting to see a deer, 'saw' a deer; the police expected to see a man and therefore 'saw' a man.

More recently, a psychologist was called in by the defence in an English case where two men were charged with having committed an act of gross indecency in a public convenience. Complaints had been made to the police that the convenience was being used for indecent purposes and the accused were apprehended by two policemen who were keeping the convenience under secret observation. The defendants denied that any criminal acts had taken place. The psychologist reproduced the defence version of the facts (ie no criminal act) in a series of photographs and he showed these to twelve adults under different conditions of light, for varying lengths of time, and with reference to three different question: In A they were merely asked to say what they saw in the pictures; in B they were asked if they could see any crime being committed in any of the pictures; in C they were told that some of the pictures actually portrayed criminal acts being committed and they were asked to identify the pictures concerned.

The result was that the number of errors increased considerably from A to B to C. In other words, the witnesses most frequently erred in asserting that a crime was being committed when they were led to expect to see this criminal behaviour. The police, therefore, expecting to see an indecent act being committed might well have put an erroneous interpretation on innocent facts. In the event, the accused were acquitted.

A revealing account of a personal experience of being a witness was written in 1973 by *New Society's* legal correspondent (now a distinguished Queen's Counsel):

'Diogenes', New Society, *31 August 1973*

Just over two years ago, I witnessed a minor accident. It happened in this way. I was riding in a bus which had new automatic doors at its exit. On reaching the bus stop where I wanted to get off, I found myself behind an old lady who was stepping onto the pavement with some caution. The bus driver evidently had his view of the exit in the mirror blocked because, before she had completed her manoeuvre, he started the bus up. Her arm was caught in the closing doors. Fortunately, my shouts caused the bus driver to stop and the old lady was saved from nothing worse than slight shock, bruises to her arm, and a cut on her shin.

At the time, with a barrister's instinct for a possible civil claim by the old lady against the city bus company, I gave her my name (as a witness, not an advocate), and on my return to my parents' house, some ten minutes later, I wrote out a statement of what I had seen. I was, in other words, the perfect witness. I was on the spot. I had appreciated at once the need for an accurate account of what had happened. I was trained to understand what was and what was not relevant to a claim for negligent driving. And I made a statement within minutes.

Yet, even within that short space of time I found myself forgetting certain details. Had I been directly behind the old lady, or were there other passengers between us? Where had her arm been when it was trapped? How fast was the bus going before it stopped? I argued several points with my wife, who had been with me; and, later that evening, when I furnished another statement to the police, I found myself making minor modifications to my account.

A magistrates' court hearing followed a few months later. I gave my evidence as well as I could; but, by that time, I could not honestly say that I remembered more than the bare outlines of the event, and would have been lost without an ability to refer to my contemporary record–something admissible in evidence like the policeman's notebook. The driver was, however, convicted, in my view quite properly. I felt sorry for the defence solicitor.

I have not been summoned to give evidence in civil proceedings. Nowadays, once a driver has a conviction in respect of an accident, the fact of which can be adduced in evidence, his chances of defending a civil claim are slim indeed. And, I assume, the claim has been settled by the city bus company's insurers.

But, in the ordinary run of things, a trial of a personal injury claim two years after the event would be nothing unusual; slow for a county court, but average for the high court. And, if I am called on as a witness at this length of time, what do I really retain except a memory of the kind of accident that it was and a feeling that it was the driver's fault?

The point of this reminiscence? Only that every day witnesses purport to give truthful accounts, in the box, of accidents that occurred in split-second circumstances, and in which they were often themselves involved; and that thousands of pounds, indeed an individual's future, may depend on the outcome of the case.

Research has been done on both sides of the Atlantic to discover whether different groups of people are aware of the factors that influence the accuracy of eye witness evidence. To an alarming extent they do not. Even police officers have little appreciation of the relevant factors–and length of service, rank or nature of employment (in uniform or CID) seem not to affect the matter one way or the other (Peter Bennett and Felicity Gibling, 'Can We Trust Our Eyes?' 5 *Policing*, Winter 1989, p 313 and p 320).

For the entertaining and instructive reflections of an experienced judge on the problems of finding the facts in civil cases, see T Bingham (later to become in turn, Master of the Rolls, Lord Chief Justice and senior law lord), 'The Judge as Juror', *Current Legal Problems*, 1985, p 1.

5.   The principle of orality

One of the fundamental features of an English trial is the oral examination of witnesses. The principle of orality has always been at the heart of the English trial, partly because of the dominant role played for centuries by the jury, though, as will be seen, its importance is gradually being somewhat eroded, especially in civil cases. The exceptions to the general rule are quite numerous and they are increasing.

One minor and very understandable exception is the evidence of someone who cannot come to the trial–because of age, infirmity or physical distance. The court can order that his evidence be taken by an examiner on behalf of the court with both sides present. (Or his evidence may be allowed in as an exception to the rule against hearsay evidence – see p 427 below. (The Youth Justice and Criminal Evidence Act 1999, s 24 provided for evidence to be given by live link and this may increasingly be used for witnesses unable to come to court for any of these reasons.)

Another more important exception is evidence given on affidavit, a procedure that is common, for instance, in the Chancery Division. The evidence in interlocutory injunction cases is normally taken on affidavit, eg in trade union disputes. So, too, is the evidence on the basis of which the Administrative Court decides applications for judicial review of administrative action, formerly under RSC Order 53 ,now under CPR Part 54. In theory, the person whose evidence is being read to the court (the deponent) can be asked to come to court to be cross-examined. But this is very rare. This means that the procedure is not well adapted to dealing with disputes as to the facts.

The concept of written evidence was developed in a different way by the Practice Directions issued in 1995 for the Queen's Bench Division, the Chancery Division and the Family Division each of which (as has been seen, p 120 above) stated that 'unless otherwise ordered, every witness statement or affidavit shall stand as the evidence-in-chief of the witness concerned': [1995] 1 All ER 385, para 3; [1995] 1 All ER 586, para 3. The 1999 rules restated this principle: 'Where a witness is called to give oral evidence under paragraph (1), his witness statement shall stand as his evidence in chief unless the court otherwise orders'. (CPR, r 32.5(2))

Another inroad into orality is the rule for fast track cases that expert evidence must normally be given in writing. ('The court will not make a direction giving permission for an expert to give oral evidence unless it believes it is necessary in the interests of justice to do so' (CPR, PD 28, 7.2(4)(b)).

Another exception is when hearsay evidence is given in the form of a witness statement when the witness is not called at all. Under the Civil Evidence Act 1995 the evidence can be given in this form provided notice has been given to the other side and no request has been made for the witness to be brought to court (see CPR, r 33.2).

Nearly all divorces are obtained through the 'special procedure', which is virtually divorce by post. The court simply looks at the petition and the supporting affidavits and, if they are in order, pronounces the divorce. Normally there is no one present from either side.

Another exception to the general principle that evidence must be given orally in open courts is in relation to criminal cases. The Magistrates' Courts Act 1980, ss 6 and 102, provided for the committal stage to be drastically shortened by the acceptance as evidence of written statements of witnesses, providing that they were signed, that they had been sent in advance to the other side and that the other side did not object. Even if the other side did not object, the court retained an overriding discretion to call a witness whose statement had been produced as evidence, but in practice this was rarely exercised. As has been seen, the Criminal Procedure and Investigations Act 1996, ss 4, 45 and Sch 1 took this development further by eliminating oral evidence in committal proceedings altogether – before committal proceedings themselves were abolished.

Section 9 of the Criminal Justice Act 1967 had an even wider provision since it related to any criminal case, whether tried summarily or on indictment. It permitted the admission as evidence of a written statement subject to the same conditions as applied to committal proceedings under the Magistrates' Courts Act 1980.

See generally C Glasser, 'Civil Procedure and the Lawyers–the Adversary System and the Decline of the Orality Principle', 56 *Modern Law Review*, 1993, pp 307–24.

For the argument that commitment to the orality principle seriously weakens the special measures available to protect vulnerable witnesses under the Youth Justice and Criminal Evidence Act 1999 (pp 410, 411 below) see L Ellison, *The Adversarial*

Process and the Vulnerable Witness (OUP, 2001). The book is a critique of the traditional model of oral, adversary trial and its partial reform by the 1999 Act.[59]

6. Justice should be conducted in public

It is an old adage that justice must not only be done but must be manifestly seen to be done – a phrase attributed to Lord Hewart C J in *Sussex Justices, ex p McCarthy* [1924] 1 KB 256 at 259.('Publicity is the very soul of justice. It is the keenest spur to exertion and the surest of all guards against improbity. It keeps the judge himself while trying under trial.'[60]) It is therefore axiomatic that judicial business should be transacted in public. There are various distinct issues involved in this phrase. One is physical access to the hearing for the public, including the press. A second concern is access for non-parties to the judgment. A third is the special position of the press and the right to publish an accurate account of the proceedings and of the judgment.

(a) Physical access to the proceedings

Although the principle is clear there are situations where the basic maxim gives way to other even more important considerations. An obvious example is where a case is heard *in camera* because of the national security implications of the evidence. And there are other situations where for one reason or another the public and the press have no access to the proceedings. The list is long and seems to be growing.

In *Scott v Scott* [1913] AC 417, the House of Lords held that although normally a court must sit in public, it can sit *in camera* if this is necessary to achieve justice. The rule has been applied, for instance, to protect a secret trade process, or national security, or the affairs of the mentally ill or to prevent tumult or disorder. Convenience, however, is not sufficient reason to sit *in camera*. In 1982 the Divisional Court ruled that magistrates in Reigate had erred in going into camera for a hearing of charges against a 'supergrass' who had committed his offences *after* he had been given a light sentence for informing. Both defence and prosecution asked for the matter to be dealt with *in camera* but the Divisional Court said the decision to comply was wrong (*R v Reigate Justices, ex p Argus Newspapers* (1983) 5 Cr App Rep (S) 181).

The protection of public decency is normally not a sufficient basis for proceeding in private–see *Scott v Scott* above at p 439. But in *R v Malvern Justices, ex p Evans* [1988] 1 All ER 371 (Div Ct) the court held the magistrates in a criminal case had been entitled to sit *in camera* to spare the defendant from giving embarrassing evidence about her husband that could affect her pending divorce case. See also *A-G v Leveller*

---

59   For a lengthy review of the book see 7 *International Journal of Evidence and Proof*, 2003, pp 71-74.

60   Bentham – cited by Butler-Sloss P in *Clibbery v Allan* [2002] 1 All ER 865 at 872.

Magazines [1979] AC 440, HL and see generally James Michael, 'Open Justice: Publicity and the Judicial Process', 46 *Current Legal Problems*, 1993, pp 190–203.

The Civil Procedure Rules state that the general rule is that a hearing is to be in public. (CPR 39.2 (1)) The court is not, however, required to 'make special arrangements to accommodate members of the public' (CPR 39.2(2)).(See below for the position regarding small claims.)

The rules state that a hearing may be in private if (a) publicity would defeat the object of the hearing; (b) it involves national security; (c) publicity would damage confidential information; (d) a private hearing is necessary to protect the interests of a child or patient; (e) the hearing is one in the absence of the other side ('without notice' – formerly called *ex parte*) and it would be unjust to the absent respondent to have it in public; (f) it concerns uncontentious matters relating to the administration of trusts or of a deceased person's estate; (g) the court considers it to be in the interests of justice (CPR 39.2(3)).

ARE SMALL CLAIMS HEARINGS IN PUBLIC?

Small claims hearings in England have generally been held in private in the judge's own chambers. The parties are typically seated across the table from each other, with the district judge at its head. The fact that the hearing was in private was said to be one of its most attractive features for people unfamilar with court procedure. It was therefore surprising that the Practice Direction accompanying the 1999 rules for small claims stated: 'The general rule is that a small claims hearing will be in public'. (PD 27, 4.1(1)) It seems that this change was prompted by fear that a hearing in private might run foul of art 6 of the European Convention on Human Rights, that in the determination of his civil rights and obligations everyone is entitled 'to a fair and public hearing'.(See *Scarth v United Kingdom* (1999) 27 EHHR CD 37.)

The rules state that, although the hearing will generally be held in public, the judge can order a small claims case to be heard in private 'if the parties agree or there is some special reason for holding it in private' (PD 27,4.1(2)). No doubt, the parties commonly agree and things go on much as before.

Moreover, 'in public' does not necessarily mean in the courtroom. It can be 'in public' even if it is in the judge's private room. The small claims Practice Direction says (PD27, 4.2): 'A hearing ... will generally be in the judge's room but it may take place in a courtroom.' Presumably, if the parties agree and the members of the public wishing to attend (if there be such) can be fitted into the judge's room, it will continue to be held there. A different Practice Direction not restricted to small claims (PD 39, 1.10) says that unless there is a notice on the door stating that the proceedings are private 'members of the public will be admitted where practicable.' If the hearing is in the judge's room, the concept of it being 'in public' is obviously more notional than real.

SPECIAL MEASURES DIRECTIONS

The Youth Justice and Criminal Evidence Act 1999 (Pt II, Ch I) added a further dimension to the closed court issue in the form of a 'special measures directions' under which (as will be seen below, see p 408), a court can seek to protect a vulnerable witness, inter alia, by clearing the court of the public, including the press, though one member of the press must be allowed to stay to represent the press (s 25(3)). Vulnerable witnesses for this purpose include anyone under 17, anyone suffering from a mental or physical disorder or disability or significant impairment of intelligence and social functioning and complainants in sexual offence cases.

In *Richards* [1999] Crim LR 764 the Court of Appeal dismissed an application for leave to appeal based on Art 6 of the European Convention on Human Rights against the trial judge's decision to clear the court when a witness to a murder refused to give evidence unless this was done. There was no suggestion that the 18 year old witness qualified as 'vulnerable' but the court held that that there was a common law power to do what was required in the interests of justice.

ACCESS TO COURT DOCUMENTS AND THE JUDGMENT

So far as concerns the judgment, in *Forbes v Smith* [1998] 1 All ER 973, 974, Mr Justice Jacob said: 'The concept of a secret judgment is one which I believe to be inherently abhorrent'. Only in cases where there was cause for secrecy such as in a trade secrets case should the judgment be regarded as a secret document. A judgment given in chambers was normally to be regarded as a public document unless it was given *in camera* – as in that particular case.

However it is increasingly the case that courts make decisions on the basis of material that has not been read out in open court.

Under RSC Ord 63, r 4 a member of the public could inspect for a fee a copy of any writ or other originating process and any judgment or court order. Curiously, the same did not apply in the county courts. CCR, Ord 50, r 10(2) stated that someone who was not a party to the proceedings could only obtain copies of documents from the court records with the leave of the court.

The 1999 rules give a non-party the right to inspect and to take a copy of the claim form that has been served and of a judgment given in public[61] – unless a practice direction made any other provision.[62] If a non-party wishes to inspect and copy any other document, he must seek the leave of the court.[63] (This does not yet apply however in the county courts where the facilities for computer searching are not yet in place.)

---

[61] CPR 5.4(2).
[62] CPR 5.4(4).
[63] CPR 5.4(2)(c).

Practice Direction 39 1.11 states that when a hearing takes place in public, members of the public may obtain a transcript of any judgment . PD 39 1.12 states that when a judgment is given or an order is made in private, a member of the public must get the leave of the judge to obtain a transcript.

Witness statements which stand as evidence (ie where the written statement is taken as evidence) are open to inspection during the trial unless the court otherwise orders. (CPR 32.13)

See also *Practice Statement* [1998] 2 All ER 667 on access to judgments for the press and law reporters.

Discovering what happened in chambers Open access to decisions given in chambers was the subject of *Hodgson v Imperial Tobacco Ltd* [1998] 2 All ER 673 an action by cancer sufferers against tobacco companies. The Court of Appeal held that what happened during proceedings in chambers was private but not confidential or secret. Information about such proceedings and the judgment or order could and should be made available to the public when requested. Moreover, save in the exceptional circumstances identified in the Administration of Justice Act 1960, s 12(1) or where a court with power to do so ordered otherwise, it was not contempt of court to reveal what occurred in chambers provided any comment made did not substantially prejudice the administration of justice. The judge had therefore been wrong to make a 'gagging order'.

Wardship, guardianship and adoption cases are usually heard in chambers. In undefended divorce cases no evidence is heard in open court. Ancillary proceedings concerning maintenance and custody of children are normally heard in chambers. Domestic proceedings in magistrates' courts are in private. In the Family Division a commentator has observed that, since 'chambers' hearings are the rule and open court hearings the exception, 'a situation has been created which is causing concern even among some judges'. So little in the way of reported decisions were emerging from this quarter that 'lawyers specialising in divorce related cases are faced with a virtual famine of modern day case law': Roger P Pearson, 'Open Justice', *Solicitors' Journal*, 19/26 December 1986, p 969.

But in *Clibbery v Allan* [2002] 1 All ER 865 the Court of Appeal held that although family proceedings involving children or ancillary relief were protected from publication without the court's permission, that did not apply to all family proceedings heard in private. Whether they were protected would depend on the nature of the proceedings and whether the administration of justice would be impeded by publication.

PHYSICAL ACCESS TO PROCEEDINGS IN CHAMBERS

A chambers hearing can be in the judge's private room or it can be in the normal courtroom with a notice stating that the court is sitting in chambers. But, even when held in chambers, the proceedings are normally to be regarded as being in public. This was recognised by Mr Justice Jacob in *Forbes v Smith* [1998] 1 All ER 973. ('A chambers hearing is in private, in the sense that members of the public are not given admission as of right to the courtroom.' (p 974).) Courts, the judge said, sat in chambers or in open court generally only as a matter of administrative convenience. Thus in the Chancery Division the normal practice was for urgent applications for interlocutory injunctions to be made in open court, whereas in the Queen's Bench Division they were made in chambers. There was no logic or reason for the difference. It was abolished by the Civil Procedure Rules. The Commercial Court sat in chambers but with its doors open. So normally did the Patent Court. If there was an appeal from a chambers hearing to the Court of Appeal it was heard in open court.[64]

(b) Press reports of judicial proceedings

The question of reporting of court proceedings is a separate issue. Normally proceedings can be reported. Thus the Contempt of Court Act 1981, s 4 states: 'subject to this section, a person is not guilty of contempt of court under the strict liability rule in respect of a fair and accurate report of legal proceedings held in public, published contemporaneously and in good faith'.

Section 4 of the Act gives the courts the power to direct that publication be postponed 'where it appears to be necessary for avoiding a substantial risk of prejudice to the administration of justice'. Such orders must be formulated with precision–see *Practice Direction (Contempt: Reporting Restrictions)* [1982] 1 WLR 1475. On s 4 orders see especially *R v Horsham Justices, ex p Farquharson* [1982] QB 762; *R v Leveller Magazines Ltd* [1979] AC 440, HL.

Under s 11 of the Contempt of Court Act 1981, a court, having power to do so, may direct that a name or other material not be published if it appears to the court to be necessary. Use of this power by the courts has proved very controversial. Until 1988 there was no right of appeal against the exercise of the power by the Crown Court or higher courts, but this was changed by s 159 of the Criminal Justice Act 1988. There have, however, been a number of decisions, mainly by the Divisional Court, on challenges to s 11 orders made by magistrates. From these it seems clear that the courts should not, for instance, prevent publication of the name of a witness or party simply to protect them from embarrassment. Thus, in 1987 the Divisional Court held that justices in Malvern and Evesham had been wrong to prohibit publication of a former Conservative MP's name and address when he appeared on a motoring charge. He had claimed that publication of the details would expose him to harassment

---

64   In *Storer v British Gas plc* [2000] 1 WLR 1237 the Court of Appeal quashed a decision of an industrial tribunal because the room in which the hearing took place was in an area marked 'Private. No admittance to the public beyond this point' the door to which was fitted with a push-button lock.

by his wife. Lord Justice Watkins said that s 11 of the 1981 Act was not enacted 'for the benefit of the comfort and feelings of defendants' (*R v Evesham Justices, ex p McDonagh* [1988] 1 All ER 371). See to similar effect *Trustor AB v Smallbone* [2000] 1 All ER 811. See also *Scarth v United Kingdom* (1999) 27 EHRLR CD 37. But it would be legitimate to ban reporting of a witness's name in a blackmail case.

Even chambers' hearings to which the public are not admitted are generally capable of being reported. The Administration of Justice Act 1960, s 12(1), states: 'The publication of any information before the court sitting in private shall not of itself be contempt of court'. So if reporters can find out what happened in chambers they can publish it. The exceptions are for matters affecting juveniles, national security, secret processes and where the court, having power to do so, has specifically prohibited publicity.

Reporters who attend the youth court in the magistrates' courts (which again is not open to the public) cannot report anything which would lead to the child being identified unless the court permits it. (Children and Young Persons Act 1933, s 49 (as amended)) By contrast, by virtue of s 39 of the same Act, in the Crown Court and the magistrates' court the press can identify a juvenile unless the court prohibits such publication.

See further Geoffrey Robertson and Andrew Nicol, *Media Law* (Penguin, 4th edn, 2002).

TELEVISING TRIALS

Cameras are not permitted in court. So television of legal proceedings, now commonplace in the USA[65], is not permitted. It was reported in March 2003, however, that the Lord Chancellor had given permission for an experiment with televising of appellate level cases. The pilot would allow broadcasters to produce news bulletins, features and documentary material but only for demonstration purposes. They could not be broadcast. If the material was deemed unobjectionable there might be legislation to lift the ban.[66]

(c)   Protecting the witness

In child abuse cases child witnesses have been allowed to give their evidence from behind a screen, but the identity of the witness is known. It is simply a device to spare the child the trauma of giving evidence in the face of the court and, more especially, of the accused.

---

65 But not in the US Supreme Court.
66 Frances Gibb, 'Irvine ready to allow TV cameras in Appeal Court', *The Times*, 10 March 2003.

Courts have also had to decide whether in exceptional circumstances the identity of witnesses such as members of the security service can be concealed even from the other side. In a trial in Belfast in June 1989 Hutton LCJ held that in the particular circumstances of the case such an order could be made, but in that instance the defence raised no objection. The defendants Murphy and Maguire were accused of taking part in the gruesome murder of two British army corporals who became entangled in an IRA funeral in March 1988. The prosecution asked the court to rule that some 27 media witnesses could give their evidence without being identified and that they should not be seen by the accused, the public or the press, but only by the court and the lawyers for each side. Their evidence mainly concerned television footage. The judge held that the witnesses could give their evidence behind a large curtain.[67] (See Gilbert Marcus, 'Secret Witnesses', *Public Law*, Summer 1990, p 207.)

SPECIAL MEASURES DIRECTIONS' FOR VULNERABLE WITNESSES

The 1999 Youth Justice and Criminal Evidence Act, Part II, Chapter 1, has no fewer than 18 sections giving courts the power to give a 'special measures direction' to assist witnesses (not including the defendant) who might have difficulty giving evidence or who might be reluctant to do so. They include those under the age of 17; persons who suffer from a mental disorder, mental impairment or significant learning disability, or physical disorder or disability which the court considers likely to affect the quality of their evidence; persons whom the court is satisfied would give less than their best evidence because of fear and distress caused by giving evidence. A witness alleged to be the victim of a sexual offence will be presumed to need assistance with giving evidence, unless the complainant specifically tells the court that she does not wish to be considered eligible (s 17(4)). This makes it possible to tell rape victims that they will definitely be given protection in the court room unless they specifically say they do not want it, where previously it was in the discretion of the judge. Either the prosecution or the defence can apply for such a direction but the court has the power to make a direction of its own motion.

The special measures that can be authorised are: screens to ensure that the witness cannot see the accused; allowing the witness to give evidence from outside the court by live television link; clearing the press and public from the court so that evidence can be given in private; not wearing the court dress of wigs and gowns; allowing an interview with the witness video-recorded before the trial to be shown at the trial as the witness's evidence-in-chief (as recommended for the evidence of children by the Pigot Committee); allowing a witness to be cross-examined before trial about their evidence and a video recording of that cross-examination to be shown at trial in place

---

[67]   In June 1999 the Divisional Court held that the inquiry into the shootings in Londonderry on 'Bloody Sunday' had acted unreasonably in denying a claim for anonymity of 17 members of the paratroop regiment. Knowing their names was not vital for the inquiry to perform its task, while disclosing them put their lives at risk. (*R v Lord Saville of Newdigate, ex p A* [1999] NLJR 965. The Court of Appeal upheld the ruling [1999] NLJR 1201.)

of calling the witness; allowing an approved intermediary to help the witness communicate with the legal representatives and the court. Whether a direction is made and its terms will be in the discretion of the court. But in the case of young witnesses there will be a presumption that their evidence will be given by pre-recorded video, failing which by live television link from outside the court.

In general, a witness whose evidence-in-chief is given in the form of a video recording has to be called at the trial unless the special measures direction provides for the witness's evidence on cross-examination to be given otherwise than by testimony in court (s 27(5)). If such direction provides for cross-examination to be conducted by video recording it will be made in the absence of the accused but in the presence of such persons as the direction or rules of court specify. The accused must be able to 'see and hear any such examination and to communicate with any legal representative acting for him' and both the judge and the lawyers must not only be able to see and hear the examination but to communicate with the persons in whose presence the examination is being conducted (s 28).

Chapter I of Part II of the 1999 Act finally came into force in June 2002. The Home Office published guidance on the new procedures: *Achieving best evidence in Criminal Proceedings: Guidance for Vulnerable or Intimidated Witnesses, including children* (Available on www.cps.gov.uk and www.homeoffice.gov.uk.)[68] See also L Ellison, *The Adversarial Process and the Vulnerable Witness*, (OUP 2001); Di Birch, 'A Better Deal for Vulnerable Witnesses?' [2000] *Criminal Law* Review, pp 223-49; and LCH Hoyano, 'Striking a Balance between the Rights of Defendants and Vulnerable Witnesses: Will Special Measures Directions Contravene Guarantees of a Fair Trial? [2001] *Criminal Law Review*, pp 948-69.

7. The taking of evidence

In a civil case the case starts with an opening speech for the claimant (formerly 'plaintiff'). In a criminal case tried in the Crown Court the case opens with a speech from the prosecution. (In the magistrates' court the prosecution will not necessarily make an opening speech beyond a statement as to the nature of their case.) The purpose of the opening speech is to set out that side's case and what the witnesses will establish. In Scotland, by contrast, the case starts right away with the first witness– no opening speech is permitted. The danger of the English system is that when there is a jury, it will be prejudiced against the accused by counsel's address, and the more so because the prosecution may not actually succeed in proving what counsel's opening speech foreshadowed.

The Runciman Royal Commission on Criminal Justice proposed that unless the judge gave leave, the prosecutor's opening speech should not be longer than 15

---

[68]   See D Heraghty, 'Gearing up for greater use of video evidence', *New Law Journal*, 28 March 2003, p 460.

minutes and that opening speeches should be limited to an explanation of the issues at trial. They should refer to the evidence to be called only if that was essential to the jury's understanding of the case. The prosecution should not seek to suggest that particular matters would be proved by the prosecution (p 120, paras 8, 9).

The Royal Commission also proposed (p 121, para 10), that the defence should have the option of making their opening speech immediately after the prosecution's opening. This is in fact occasionally done.

The next stage is 'examination-in-chief' when the claimant (formerly 'plaintiff') or prosecutor calls and examines his witnesses. But, in civil cases, as has already been seen, this stage is nowadays normally skipped as the witness' statement is treated as his evidence-in-chief unless the court otherwise orders. The new Civil Procedure Rules state that a party may amplify his witness statement or testify in relation to anything new that has happened since the witness statement was served (CPR, r 32.5(3)).

In a criminal case, however, the oral witnesses are still normally examined in-chief by each side. The prosecution goes first. Examination-in-chief consists of taking the witness through his story stage by stage. The advocate will base his examination of the witness on the information supplied by his instructing solicitors based on their meetings with the witness, which they have reduced to his statement (or 'proof').

In order to minimise the danger of 'coaching of the witness', the rule in England has been that prosecutors are not permitted to speak about the evidence to their own witnesses prior to the trial. The only general exceptions were the client and an expert witness.[69]

Since the Youth Justice and Criminal Evidence Act 1999 another exception has been made for interviews with vulnerable witnesses. In civil cases there is no longer a rule that prohibits a barrister from seeing witnesses but the Code of Conduct states that a barrister should not appear as advocate in a case if he has 'taken' a witness statement – as distinguished from 'settling' a witness statement taken by someone else.[70]

However, the Damilola Taylor case in 2002 led to a reconsideration of this important rule for criminal cases.(In April 2002 the trial of four boys for the murder of 10-year-old Damilola ended in a blaze of publicity with all four being acquitted after the 14-year-old chief prosecution witness had been shown to be a completely unreliable witness.) On 1 May 2003, the CPS launched a Consultation Paper inviting views as to whether the prosecutor should in future be permitted to interview key witnesses in order to assess their credibility.[71]

---

[69]   See Bar Council's Code of Conduct, Written Standards for the Conduct of Professional Work, paras 6.1.3, 6.1.4 and 6.3.1; www.barcouncil.org.uk. There is no equivalent for solicitors – see Law Society's Guide to Professional Conduct, para 21.10.

[70]   Code of Conduct, Written Standards for the Conduct of Professional Work, para 6.2.6; www.barcouncil.org.uk.

[71]   See *Pre-trial Interviews by Prosecutors*, www.cps.gov.uk. The Consultation Paper included an appendix showing the position in other countries.

Examination-in-chief should not generally include 'leading questions'. A leading question is one that suggests the answer ('Did you see the accused at that point raise his arm in a threatening way?' as opposed to 'What did you see then?'). Leading questions are, however, permitted for matter that is wholly uncontroversial ('Is your name John Smith and do you live at ?'). They are also allowed when the purpose is to elicit a denial from the witness ('Did you kill the deceased?').

At the end of the examination-in-chief, the witness is offered to the other side for cross-examination. Cross-examination is the attempt to show that the witness was lying or mistaken, or that he is not a person who can be relied on to tell the truth. It may also be used to establish evidence favourable to the cross-examiner's side. Leading questions are permitted. The witness can be cross-examined about his previous convictions, his bias and his reputation for untruthfulness. But the Bar's *Code of Conduct* says that a barrister must not suggest that a witness or other person is guilty of crime, fraud or misconduct or attribute the crime to someone else unless such allegations go to a matter in issue (including the credibility of the witness) which is material to the lay client's case 'and which appear to him to be supported by reasonable grounds'[72]. Also a barrister must not make statements or ask questions which 'are merely scandalous or intended or calculated only to vilify insult or annoy either a witness or some other person' (ibid, para 5.10 (e)).

As will be seen (see p 447 below), in rape cases the defendant's representative is restricted as to the questions that can properly be put to the complainant regarding her sexual experience with other persons.

New rules introduced in the Youth Justice and Criminal Evidence Act 1999, ss 34, 35, also state that someone charged with a sexual offence if acting in person (ie without legal representation), may not cross-examine either the victim ('the complainant') or a child witness or any other witness if the court so orders. In such a case the court must invite the defendant to arrange for a legal representative to act for him for the purpose of cross-examination, failing which it may appoint a representative for the purpose (s 38). The rules were introduced because of public outrage at a small number of cases in which a defendant accused of rape subjected the victim to the ordeal of lengthy and humiliating direct cross-examination.[73]

In May 1998 the Lord Chief Justice issued new guidelines to judges to take a more interventionist approach in such cases and either halt questioning, if it sought to humiliate, or order the installation of a screen so that at least the victim did not have to see and be seen by the defendant (*The Times*, 7 May, 1998). The Lord Chief Justice thought that the judges were capable of dealing with the problem without legislation. But the Government decided that legislation would be better.

---

[72] Code of Conduct, Written Standards for the Conduct of Professional Work, para 5.10(h)).
[73] In 1997, Ralston Edwards, wearing the same clothes as he wore during his 16-hour attack on her at her home, spent *six days* cross-examining his victim in his rape trial at the Old Bailey. In another case, in November 1997, the defendant Brown sacked his defence team and subjected his victim to merciless cross-examination. (Both men were convicted by the jury.)

The general rule is that evidence is not admissible to contradict answers given in answering questions put in cross-examination. The reason is to confine the scope of the case within reasonable limits. But if the witness has made a prior statement which is inconsistent with his evidence he can be cross-examined about it.

Occasionally, effective cross-examination can be based simply on what the witness has said, by pointing up inconsistencies or improbabilities; usually, however, it requires other material based on work done by those responsible for preparation of the case. Cross-examination is a difficult art and it is not very often that it significantly dents the witness's evidence.

One of the duties of the cross-examiner is to 'put his client's case'. This is because of the technical rule that one cannot call evidence to contradict the opponent's case unless one has challenged the disputed evidence in cross-examination. That is why one so frequently hears counsel say to the witness 'I put it to you that... ' – to which the usual reply is some variation on 'No, that is not so.' Nothing much is achieved by such exchanges other than fulfilment of the requirement that the case be 'put' to the witness.

For an assessment of the rules on cross-examination of police witnesses by the defence so as to bring out past discreditable incidents, see David Wolchover, 'Attacking Confessions with Past Police Embarrassments' (1988) *Criminal Law Review*, p 573.

At the close of cross-examination, the witness is offered back to the opponent for re-examination. The purpose of re-examination is not to go over the same ground again, but to clarify or to explain evidence that has emerged during cross-examination. Thus, if in cross-examination reference has been made to part of a conversation favourable to the cross-examiner, questions could be put to draw out other parts of the conversation which put a different and less attractive gloss on the matter.

This process of examination-in-chief, cross-examination and re-examination is repeated for each witness in turn. When that process is complete, each party makes a closing speech. In a criminal case the defence has the last word (Criminal Procedure (Right of Reply) Act 1964). In a civil case it is the claimant/plaintiff who goes last.

Historically the courts have allowed counsel to take as long as they need to present their case. But increasingly this relaxed attitude is giving way to a new concern to see that litigation does not take more time than is necessary. Thus, the Practice Directions issued in 1995 for proceedings in the Queen's Bench Division and the Chancery Division and for the Family Division stated that the court would increasingly exercise its discretion to limit the length of opening and closing oral submissions, the time allowed for the examination and cross-examination of witnesses, the issues on which it wished to be addressed and reading aloud from documents and authorities. ([1995] 1 All ER 385, para 2.) Courts have increasingly used counsel's time estimates as a way of trying to control the length of the case. In *A-G v Scriven* (4 February 2000, unreported, CA) Simon Brown LJ said: 'The courts are not required to listen to litigants, whether represented or not, for as long as they like. It is for the court to control its own process, and it is well entitled to bring arguments to a close when it concludes that its process is being abused and that nothing of value will be lost by ending it.'

The final stage is the process of actual decision. In a case with a jury, the judge sums up on the facts and the law (see pp 502-05 below) and the jury then decides. In a criminal trial with a jury the question of sentence is solely for the judge. Juries, as will be seen, are rare in civil cases. Usually, therefore, it is simply a matter of the court reaching and announcing its decision.

In the High Court, but not always in the county or magistrates' court, it will normally also give a reasoned judgment. There is growing pressure generated by the Human Rights Act for judicial decisions to be properly reasoned but the requirements in the lowest courts are as yet not very demanding.[74] In the Crown Court, the jury does not give reasons (as to which see pp 511-12 below). Nor does the judge since it is the jury rather than the judge that gives the decision. The exception is sentencing which is done by the court. The Criminal Justice Bill 2002/03, cl 167 imposes on the court a general statutory duty to give reasons for, and to explain the effect of, the sentence passed. The Explanatory Notes state that in doing so, 'it seeks to bring together in a single provision many of the obligations on a court to give reasons when passing sentence which are currently scattered across sentencing legislation' (para 454).

On the conduct of trials generally see Richard du Cann's excellent book, *The Art of the Advocate* (Penguin, revised edn, 1993).

8. The exclusionary rules of evidence

One of the chief differences between the English and the continental systems is that the English excludes various categories of evidence in spite of the fact that they are relevant to the matters in dispute. The exclusionary rules of evidence fall into three main categories: (a) evidence excluded because it might be unduly prejudicial; (b) evidence excluded because it is inherently unreliable; and (c) evidence excluded because it is against the public interest that it be admitted. In all three areas, and especially in the first two, there have been important recent developments notably in regard to the admissibility of hearsay evidence and of prior convictions Both topics were the subject of proposals in the Government's White Paper *Justice for All* (July 2002) and both were included in the Criminal Justice Bill 2002/03. In regard to the third topic there is a constant flow of judicial decisions.

See generally IH Dennis, *The Law of Evidence* (2nd ed, Sweet & Maxwell, 2002); J McEwan, *Evidence and the Adversarial Process* (2nd ed, OUP, 1998).

(a)   Evidence excluded because it might be unduly prejudicial

BAD CHARACTER AND PRIOR CONVICTIONS

An exception to the basic rule that relevant evidence is admissible is that evidence of previous misconduct by the defendant or the defendant's disposition or propensity to act in a particular way is inadmissible. There are said to be two reasons. First, the fact that the defendant behaved in a particular way before does not in itself provide evidence that he did the act of which he is now accused. Secondly, insofar as it does provide such evidence there is a danger that a jury would give it undue weight. So, as a general rule, the defendant's previous convictions have not been admissible in evidence until after a trial has ended in conviction – at which point they are of course considered as part of the question of the appropriate sentence. (By contrast, as has been seen, in systems based on the continental civil law the defendant's character and background are fully admissible in evidence. In the United States, his prior convictions *are* admissible if the defendant gives evidence.)

In the Crown Court Study conducted for the Runciman Royal Commission, the defendant in contested cases had previous convictions in no less than 77% of cases.[75] In other words, this is an issue that affects a very high proportion of defendants.

EXCEPTIONS TO THE GENERAL RULE

The English system has recognised several exceptions to the general rule:
(1) One is where the defendant himself wishes to introduce his own prior record.
(2) Another is that if he asserts that he is a person of good character, the prosecution are permitted to demolish the claim by producing evidence to the contrary. (The courts have held for instance that the defendant put his character in issue when he claimed to have earned an honest living for a considerable time[76] or to be a regular churchgoer.[77])
(3) *The 'tit for tat' rule* Where the defence makes imputations attacking the character of prosecution witnesses, the prosecution in cross-examination may be permitted to introduce the defendant's previous convictions – in order to show the jury the kind of person 'throwing mud'.[78] What is considered to be an imputation for these purposes is not straightforward.[79] The court has a discretion to disallow such cross-examination if it considers that the prejudicial value of the information exceeds its probative value.[80] It has been said that the discretion should be exercised if there was nothing more than a denial 'however emphatic or

---

[74] In regard to the duty to give reasons of magistrates see *R (on the application of McGowan) v Brent Justices* [2001] EWHC Admin 814, [2002] Crim LR 412 and commentary at 413; and *R v Civil Service Appeal Board, ex p Cunningham* [1992] ICR 816.

[75] M Zander and P Henderson, *The Crown Court Study*, Royal Commission on Criminal Justice, Research Study No.19, 1993, sect 4.6.1.

[76] *Powell* [1985] 1 WLR 1364.

[77] *Ferguson* (1909) 2 Cr App Rep 250. See also *Stronach* [1988] Crim LR 48.

[78] Criminal Evidence Act 1898, s 1(f)(ii).

[79] See *Britzman and Hall* [1983] 1 WLR 350 for guidance. In that case the defendants denied having made admissions to a police officer and denied having had a shouted conversation from one cell to another involving further admissions. The suggestion that the police had lied allowed the prosecution to introduce the previous convictions.

[80] *Selvey v DPP* [1970] AC 304; *Davison-Jenkins* [1997] Crim LR 816.

offensively made', of an act or even a short series of acts amounting to one incident or in what was said to have been a short interview. The purpose of the cross-examination is supposed to be discrediting the defendant as a witness not to show disposition to commit the offence in question.[81] Where the defence necessarily involves such imputations (as in 'the drugs were planted on me'), the court may exercise its discretion. But there is no rule to that effect.

(4) *'Cut throat defences'* The 'tit-for-tat rule' also applies where a defendant gives evidence assisting the prosecution against a co-defendant.[82] Where this would lead to injustice the court can order separate trials.

(5) *Similar fact evidence* This is the main exception to the exclusionary rule. The term 'similar fact evidence' covers evidence of misconduct by the defendant which is said to be evidence of his propensity or disposition to misconduct either in general or in specific ways. It extends to evidence of bad character or conduct that is not criminal.[83] For a classic example of 'striking similarity' see *Straffen* [1952] 2 QB 911. At S's trial for murder of a child the prosecution was allowed to introduce evidence that he had been charged with two previous murders of children to which he was found unfit to plead by reason of insanity. In each case the killing had been by strangulation and in each case the bodies had been arranged in a particular way. See also *DPP v Boardman*[84] But in *DPP v P* the 'striking similarity' test was stated to be only one of the ways in which the relevance of similar fact evidence may be found.[85] P was charged with rape of, and incest with, his two daughters. The trial judge allowed the evidence of both sisters in the same case. The Court of Appeal quashed the conviction on the ground that there had not been such striking similarities in the girls' accounts of their father's behaviour as to justify the evidence of one to be used in the trial of the counts relating to the other. The House of Lords allowed an appeal by the prosecution. The Lord Chancellor, Lord Mackay, said in that case, 'the essential feature of evidence which is to be admitted is that its probative force. . . is sufficiently great to make it just to admit the evidence, notwithstanding that it is prejudicial to the accused in tending to show that he was guilty of another crime' (at 460).

(6) *Theft Act 1968, s 27(3)* On a charge of handling stolen goods the prosecution may establish that the defendant knew that the goods were stolen by introducing evidence of previous convictions for possession of stolen goods.

Overriding discretion

Even when the evidence of previous misconduct was technically admissible the prosecution might decide not to use it. The court always retained the power to refuse

---

81   *McLeod* [1994] 1 WLR 1500, 1511.
82   Criminal Evidence Act 1898, s 1(f)(iii). See for instance *Murdoch v Taylor* [1965] AC 574.
83   *Ball* [1911] AC 47. At one time it was thought that the rule required 'striking similarity'.
84   [1975] AC 421.
85   [1991] 2 AC 447, 460.

to allow the prosecution to use the evidence where it considered that its prejudicial effect outweighed its probative value.

PROPOSALS FOR REFORM OF THE RULES

In 1972 the Criminal Law Revision Committee (CLRC) in its report 'Evidence (General)' proposed that the 'tit-for-tat' rule should not apply where the 'imputations' were necessary in order to put the defence case. So a person charged with assault should be allowed to put forward the defence that the alleged victim was the actual aggressor without fear that his previous convictions for violence would be admitted in evidence.[86] The CLRC also proposed a new exception to the exclusionary rule when the accused admitted the facts (the *actus reus)* and denied only that he had the necessary knowledge or intent (*mens rea*) – as in 'I did take the little girl into the wood but we were only looking for butterflies'.[87] The jury could then be told that he had previous convictions for indecent assaults on children. This proposal was supported by the Runciman Royal Commission on Criminal Justice.[88]

The Runciman Royal Commission recommended that the whole question of the admissibility of prior convictions should be referred to the Law Commission. This was done in 1994. In July 1996 the Law Commission published a Consultation Paper.[89] It took another five years, until October 2001, for the Commission to produce its final Report.[90]

The scheme proposed by the Law Commission was that evidence of bad character should only be admissible with the leave of the court. It defined evidence of bad character as evidence showing or tending to show the commission of an offence, or that the person has behaved, or is disposed to behave, in a way that might be viewed with disapproval by a reasonable person. Its proposals covered both witnesses and defendants. Witnesses, it said, should be much better protected from attacks on their character than under the existing law. Leave could only be given in respect of the bad character of a *witness* if the evidence had substantial explanatory value, or substantial probative value in relation to a matter in issue which was of substantial importance in the context of the case as a whole. Such leave could be given in respect of the bad character of a *defendant* in four situations:

---

[86]   Cmnd 4991, paras.123-30.

[87]   Paras 92-94.

[88]   Report, p 126, para.31.

[89]   *Evidence in Criminal Proceedings: Previous Misconduct of a Defendant*, Consultation Paper No 141. For commentary and discussion see special issue of the Criminal Law Review, February 1997. The recommendations in the Consultation Paper were described in the 8th edn of this work at pp 363-64.

[90]   *Evidence of Bad Character in Criminal Proceeding*, Cm 5257, Law Com, No 273. For commentary and discussion see J.McEwan, 'Previous Misconduct at the Crossroads: Which "Way Ahead"?' [2002] *Criminal Law Review*, pp 180-91; P.Mirfield, 'Bad character and the Law Commission', (2002) 6 *International Journal of Evidence and Proof*, pp 141-62.

- if the evidence has the same degree of explanatory value as would be required in the case of a non-defendant, and in addition if the interests of justice require it to be admissible despite its prejudicial effect;
- if the evidence has substantial probative value in relation to a propensity to be untruthful, leave may not be given unless also;
- the defendant has suggested that someone else has a propensity to be untruthful and adduces evidence in support of that suggestion of that person's bad character; and
- without the evidence of the defendant's bad character the fact-finders would get a misleading impression of the defendant's propensity to be untruthful in comparison with that other person.

Leave could be given to the prosecution if:
(a) the defendant is responsible for an assertion which creates a false or misleading impression about the defendant;
(b) the evidence has substantial probative value in correcting that impression; and
(c) the interests of justice require it to be admissible.

Leave could be given to a co-defendant if the evidence has substantial probative value in a matter in issue between co-defendants, which is of substantial importance in the context of the case as a whole. If it has probative value only in showing that D1 has a propensity to be untruthful, leave may not be given unless in addition, D1's case is such as to undermine that of D2.

The Law Commission's draft Bill set out the factors to be taken into account when assessing the probative value or the interests of justice. In assessing the probative value of the evidence the court would have to assume its truth unless no court or jury could reasonably find it to be true.

Empirical evidence The Law Commission's 1996 Consultation Paper referred to empirical evidence of how jurors treat evidence of previous misconduct based on a study conducted for the Commission.[91] The research showed that recent convictions for similar offences increased the perceived probative effect of the offence charged. Knowledge of a previous conviction for an offence of dishonesty did not decrease the defendant's credibility as a witness but a previous conviction for indecent assault on a child has a distinct negative impact on the jurors' perception of the defendant's credibility whatever the charge. For critical assessment both of the empirical data and of the Law Commission's reliance on it see M Redmayne, 'The Law Commission's character convictions' (2002) 6 *International Journal of Evidence and Proof*, pp 71-93.

---

[91] Published as an appendix to the Commission's Paper and separately as S Lloyd-Bostock, 'The effects on Juries of Hearing about the Defendant's Previous Criminal Record: A Simulation Study' [2000] *Criminal Law Review*, p 734 and *The Effects on Magistrates of Learning that the Defendant has a Previous Conviction*, LCD Research Series No 3/00 (2000).

In the same month that the Law Commission published its Final Report, Lord Justice Auld's *Review of the Criminal Courts of England and Wales* was published. He said that the present law on the admissibility of bad character evidence was unduly complex and difficult to apply, that it often failed to distinguish between relevant and irrelevant evidence and arguably left too much discretion to judges. In his view there was much to be said 'for a more radical view than has so far found favour with the Law Commission, for placing more trust in the fact finders and for introducing some reality into this complex corner of the law'.[92] But, given that the Law Commission was about to produce its final report, he did not make any specific recommendations.

The Government's White Paper Justice for All In its White Paper in July 2002 the Government said that it opposed the routine introduction of all previous convictions as evidence in a case as that might prejudice the fact finders unfairly against the accused. ('Juries and judges need to make their decisions on the basis of the evidence of whether or not the defendant committed the crime with which he is charged rather than his previous reputation.' (para 4.55)) But it continued,

> We favour an approach that entrusts relevant information to those determining the case as far as possible. It should be for the judge to decide whether previous convictions are sufficiently relevant to the case, bearing in mind the prejudicial effect, to be heard by the jury and for the jury to decide what weight should be given to that information in all the circumstances of the case'. (para 4.56)

That, it added, should be so for witnesses as well as defendants. So, where a doctor was charged with indecent assault against a patient, which the doctor denied, the judge should be able to rule that the prosecution could introduce evidence that the doctor had previously been acquitted in two previous separate trials on the similar charges involving other patients. Or, where the defendant was charged with assaulting his wife, the judge should be able to rule that previous convictions for assault occasioning bodily harm and evidence by witnesses of past occasions when he was seen striking his wife be admitted in evidence. Unless the court thought the information would have a disproportionately prejudicial effect, the fact finders should be allowed to know about previous convictions and other misconduct relevant to the offence. (para 4.57)

The Criminal Justice Bill 2002-2003

In November 2002, the Government introduced the Criminal Justice Bill, Part 11 Chapter 1 of which had 16 clauses[93] on evidence of bad character to replace the common law rules governing the admissibility of such evidence.

Clause 90 defines bad character evidence as evidence of a person's bad character which shows or tends to show '(a) that he has committed an offence, or (b) he has

---

[92] Ch 11, p 567, para 120.
[93] When first published, they were cll 81-97. When the bill was reprinted for the House of Lords on 21 May 2003 they were cll 90-106.

behaved, or is disposed to behave, in a way that, in the opinion of the court, might be viewed with disapproval by a reasonable person' (cl 81(1)). This adopted the definition proposed in the Law Commission's draft Bill attached to its October 2001 report. The Explanatory Notes on the Bill (para 320[94]) said that the words 'tend to show' would cover evidence suggesting that a person has been involved in an offence even though he has been acquitted. This preserves the effect of the controversial decision in Z [2000] AC 483 where in a rape case the House of Lords held that the trial judge and the Court of Appeal had been wrong to hold that the three separate complaints which resulted in the defendant's three prior acquittals for rape were inadmissible. An example of behaviour that might be viewed with disapproval by reasonable people would be 'evidence that a person has a sexual interest in children, even if they have not acted on it in a criminal way' (Explanatory Notes, para 321). This too would be within the present rules of admissibility.

Clause 92 set out the circumstances in which evidence can be given of the previous misconduct of someone other than the defendant. It might be a witness or some other person who was alleged by the accused to be the real perpetrator. Evidence of their bad character could only be given with leave of the court and only if it met one of three conditions: that it is important explanatory evidence, that it is of substantial probative value to a matter in issue and that issue is one of substantial importance in the case, or that the parties agree that the evidence should be given. For evidence to be admissible as 'important explanatory evidence' 'it must be such that, without it, the court or jury would find it impossible or difficult properly to understand other evidence in the case' and 'its value for understanding the case as a whole is substantial' (cl 92 (2)). The court would be required to take into account factors such as the nature and number of previous events and when they occurred. If the evidence was tendered to show that someone else was responsible for the crime, the court would have to consider the extent to which it showed or tended to show that to be the case. These rules would give witnesses considerably more protection than under the current law.

Clauses 93 to 101 set out the circumstances in which evidence of the defendant's bad character would be admissible. Instead of the previous exclusionary rule with exceptions – which the Law Commission thought should be continued – the approach is inclusionary subject to limited judicial discretion to exclude such evidence where to admit it would be unfair.

Clause 93(1) provides that evidence of a defendant's bad character is admissible where any of the following apply:
(a) the parties agree to it being given
(b) the defendant introduces the evidence himself
(c) it is 'important explanatory evidence'
(d) it is evidence of the defendant's previous conviction for an offence 'of the same description or of the same category' (cl 95 gives the Home Secretary the power to prescribe by order what offences are 'of the same category')

---

[94] The numbering here too is for the version reprinted for the Lords as at 21 May 2003.

(e)   it is relevant to an important issue between the defendant and the prosecution – which includes, if relevant, whether he has a propensity to commit that kind of offence or to be untruthful (cl 96)

(f)   it has significant probative value in relation to an important issue between the defendant and a co-defendant – available only to defendants between themselves (cl 97)

(g)   it corrects a false impression given by the defendant about himself (for instance that he is a person of good character)

(h)   the defendant has attacked the character of another person – mainly aimed at informing the jury as to the defendant's creditworthiness but the Explanatory Notes (para 347) state that it is not intended that the jury should be expected to put the information out of their minds when considering other issues.

Of these, (a), (b), (f), (g) and (h) are based on the existing law; (c), (d) and (e) are new. It is specifically stated that under (d), (e) and (h) the defendant can apply for the evidence not to be admitted on the ground that admitting it would have such an adverse effect on the fairness of the proceedings that the court ought not to permit it (cl 93 (3)). It follows that under (a), (b), (c), (f) and (g) the court does not have that discretion to exclude the evidence.

If bad character evidence emerges but later in the trial it transpires that the evidence is contaminated, for instance by collusion between witnesses or because it is false or misleading, and the court considers that it would make a conviction unsafe, the court must either direct the jury to acquit or order a retrial (cl 100 (1)).

The Government's proposals were strongly criticised by the all-party House of Commons Home Affairs Committee in its report on the Bill. It did not agree that prior similar convictions should be admitted automatically unless the defendant succeeded in persuading the trial judge to rule against admissibility. ('We believe that these provisions could lead to miscarriages of justice in some cases. In particular we are concerned at the prospect of using a defendant's previous record to prop up what might otherwise be a weak case. We are also concerned that this will increase the temptation for the police to pursue "the usual suspects"'.[95]) It agreed with the Criminal Bar Association that 'propensity for misconduct should not justify automatic admission of the defendant's bad character'[96] It was concerned that the test for admitting the defendant's bad character was lower than that for admitting the bad character of witnesses. ('In our view, there should be a standard test requiring the bad character to have "substantial probative value" in relation to a matter in issue, which is itself of substantial importance in the context of the case as a whole.'[97]) Its overall conclusion was blunt: 'We recommend that Clauses 84 to 92 [93 to 101 in the version reprinted in May 2003], which relate to the admissibility of a defendant's bad character, be deleted from the Bill'.[98]

[95]   2002-203, 2nd Report, December 2002, HC 83, para 116.
[96]   Para.119.
[97]   Para 122.
[98]   Para 123.

Lord Woolf, Lord Chief Justice, too was highly critical of these provisions:[99]

13. The provisions as a whole are extremely confusing and will prove very difficult to interpret. They will result in lengthy arguments in court, more appeals and more scope for technical errors on the part of the trial judge that could give rise to convictions being overturned. Evidence that would previously have been considered neither admissible nor relevant will apparently be treated as both admissible *and* relevant.

14. The definition has two limbs. First, evidence that the person 'has committed an offence'. There is no difficulty here. However, it is then provided that evidence 'which shows or intends to show that . . . he has behaved or is disposed to behave in a way that, in the opinion of the court, might be viewed with disapproval by a reasonable person' is also evidence of bad character. This latter test of bad character is far more uncertain than it should be and is likely to give rise to a prolonged argument during a trial as to whether particular conduct falls within it. Furthermore it is likely to lead to appeals ...

15. An example of the sort of complications that are likely to arise as a consequence of chapter 1 is provided by clause 96. That clause is designed to introduce into a trial an issue as to whether a defendant has a propensity to commit an offence or a propensity to be untruthful and then allow evidence of bad character to be given. This evidence of propensity is particularly dangerous. A trial should relate to whether an accused has committed an offence or is untruthful and not questions as to whether the defendant has a *propensity*. Again the judiciary consider this provision is likely to complicate proceedings and prolong trials without any benefit ...

16. Another curiosity relates to the provisions as to the defendant's bad character. The judge is allowed to exclude evidence of bad character if it would have 'such an adverse effect on the fairness of the proceedings that the court ought not to admit it', but this discretion does not apply to all the situations where evidence of bad character can be admitted. In addition, the clause addresses when the judge is to exclude the evidence. It would be preferable if this clause and many similar clauses gave the judge a discretion to admit such controversial evidence and not to exclude it. (clause 93(3))

17. The situations not included are set out in subclauses (c), (f) and (g). Sub-clause (c) refers to 'important explanatory evidence'. Sub-clause (f) relates to evidence that has substantial probative value in relation to an important matter in issue between the defendant and a co-defendant. Sub-clause (g) is evidence

---

[99]   In 'Background Notes' to his speech on the 2nd Reading of the Bill on 16 June 2003. In his speech (at col 574) he told the Lords that, since he did not have time to deal with all the matters in issue, he was delivering to the Lords Library a lengthy document setting out 'what the judiciary, whom I represent, regard as being the problem areas'. The writer (with permission) published the gist of the 12-page document in the *New Law Journal*, 8 August 2003, pp 1228, 1242 and 15 August, pp 1264-66.

to correct a false impression given by the defendant. What is not clear is whether the general discretion of a judge to exclude evidence because its prejudicial value exceeds its probative value is excluded. If it is intended to be excluded, then it certainly should not be.

For a thoughtful, general response to the proposal to broaden admissibility of previous convictions see Professor Nigel Walker, 'What does fairness mean in a criminal trial?', 151 *New Law Journal*, 17 August 2001, p 1240.

Use of prior convictions in civil proceedings

Previous convictions could not be admitted in evidence in civil proceedings arising out of the same facts. A conviction for dangerous driving was therefore not admissible in subsequent proceedings for damages resulting from the same incident. This rule, known as the rule in *Hollington v F Hewthorn & Co Ltd* [1943] KB 587, was abolished by the Civil Evidence Act 1968, s 11. The conviction is now rebuttable evidence of the facts involved in the offence, save in libel proceedings where the conviction is deemed to be irrebuttable evidence of the facts.

(b) Evidence excluded because it is inherently unreliable

(1) EVIDENCE OF CHILDREN

The law affecting the evidence of children has always caused problems.

Children's evidence on oath The basic rule at common law was that evidence had to be given on oath. In order to take the oath the witness had to understand its significance. Until 1991 there was no statutory rule as to the age at which a child was allowed to take the oath. It was regarded a matter for the judge in the case to determine whether the child had an appreciation of the solemnity of the occasion and of the special responsibility to tell the truth conveyed by the oath. In *Hayes* [1977] 1 WLR 234 the court said that the dividing line was probably between eight and ten. In 1972 the Criminal Law Revision Committee recommended that in criminal cases children under 14 should always give evidence unsworn. This was implemented 20 years later in the Criminal Justice Act 1991.[100]

Children's unsworn evidence Although the basic rule was that evidence had to be given on oath, in fact the courts would accept unsworn evidence. In criminal cases this was already known in the seventeenth century in cases of 'rape, buggery, witchcraft, and such crimes which are practised upon children' (Hale, *History of the Pleas of the Crown*, 1736, p 284). But in 1779 it was held that a child could only give evidence on oath (*Brasier* (1779) East PC 443). It took another century until the Criminal Law

---

[100] Section 52 inserted a new s 33A into the Criminal Justice Act 1988: 'A child's evidence in criminal proceedings shall be given unsworn.'

Amendment Act 1885 before children were allowed to give unsworn evidence. The 1885 Act applied only in cases involving unlawful sexual intercourse with girls under 13. It was extended to all criminal cases by the Children and Young Persons Act 1933, s 38 though the 1933 Act provided that the unsworn evidence of a child required corroboration. Curiously however, unsworn evidence from children was not permitted in civil cases until the Children's Act 1989.

As to the age at which unsworn evidence could be admitted, in 1958 a court ruled that it had been wrong to accept the unsworn evidence of the five-year old daughter who was the victim of her father's alleged incest. (*Wallwork* (1958) 42 Cr App Rep 153) In *Wright* (1987) 90 Cr App Rep 91, this was extended to a six-year-year old. But in *B* (1990) Times, 1 March the Court of Appeal refused to grant leave to appeal against a conviction for incest based on the unsworn evidence of a child of six. Similarly, in *Z* [1990] 2 QB 355 the Court of Appeal upheld the trial judge's decision to hear unsworn evidence from a six year-old child.

Recent reforms

The rules in regard to the evidence of children have recently been altered partly in response to a more positive attitude to the evidence of children[101] and partly in response to a concern about the difficulty of getting convictions in sex abuse cases involving young children.

Competence The Youth Justice and Criminal Evidence Act 1999 makes it clear that the question of competence to give evidence in criminal cases is not to be treated as a matter of age. Section 53(1) states that a person of any age is competent to give evidence in a criminal case. A person is not competent, however, if he cannot understand questions put to him or give understandable answers (s 53(2)).[102] In order to assess whether a child can give intelligible testimony the judge should either watch any video taped interview or should ask the child questions (or both) so as to

---

[101] For a review of empirical research evidence, see JR Spencer and Rhona Flin, 'Child Witnesses–Are They Liars?', *New Law Journal*, 24 November 1989, p 1603. Their conclusion was that the evidence did not support the traditional view that children are more likely to tell lies than adults, and it contradicted the view that the younger the child, the more likely it is that he or she will lie. On the empirical evidence' evidence see also Ray Bull, 'Children as Witnesses', 4 *Policing*, 1988, p 130; and D Birch, `Children's Evidence [1992] CLR 262, 263-64. One piece of research was reported by G Davies, A Tarrant and R Flin, 'Close Encounters of the witness kind: children's memory/a simulated health inspection', *British Journal of Psychology*, 1989. The study tested 128 boys and girls split into age groups of 6 to 7 and 10 to 11. The test involved direct confrontation between the child and an adult stranger in which the child was touched and an article of clothing (shoes) removed. The two age groups did not differ in their ability to help produce a photofit of the man. The report says 'Even the youngest subjects tested could have provided evidence on a number of points relevant to the main theme of events which would have been accurate in essentials and of interest to the court.'

[102] For an application of s 53 in a case where the videoed interview of an 81-year-old rape victim who had long-term delusional problems and had been diagnosed with early Alzheimer's disease was allowed see *R v D* [2002] EWCA Crim 990, [2003] QB 90.

determine if he or she can understand questions and answer them in a coherent and comprehensible manner. (cp *DPP v M* [1997] 2 All ER 749.)The question is one on which expert evidence can be received[103] (s 54(5)).

The oath As has been seen, in 1991 the rule was adopted that children aged 14 should give evidence on oath while the evidence of children under 14 would always be unsworn. The Youth Justice and Criminal Evidence Act 1999, s 55 confirms this in a provision which states that a witness in a criminal case may not be sworn unless he has reached the age of 14 – 'and he has a sufficient appreciation of the solemnity of the occasion and of the particular responsibility to tell the truth which is involved in taking the oath' (s 55(2)). The test has however now been significantly watered down. If the witness is able to give intelligible testimony, the Act provides that it is to be presumed that the witness is fit to take the oath unless evidence to the contrary is given. Giving intelligible testimony means understanding questions put to him and giving answers that can be understood (s 55(8)). Expert evidence can be given on the matter (s 55(6)).

Corroboration The second reform was in regard to the requirement that the unsworn evidence of children in criminal cases had to be corroborated (Children and Young Persons Act 1933, s 38). This was joined with a further rule that the unsworn evidence of one child could not corroborate the unsworn evidence of another child, however cogent the evidence (*Hester* [1973] AC 296). The effect of these rules was to make it impossible in some cases to get convictions of offenders in extremely serious sexual abuse cases.

The requirement of corroboration for the unsworn evidence of children was abolished by the Criminal Justice Act 1988, s 34(1). Section 34(3) also provided that unsworn evidence could corroborate the evidence, whether sworn or unsworn, of anyone.

Prior to 1988 the sworn evidence of a child did not technically require corroboration but the judge had to warn the jury of the danger of relying on such uncorroborated evidence. The requirement of that warning has now also been abolished by s 34(2) of the 1988 Act–unless such a warning is required in relation the evidence of an adult witness.

Evidence by video-link and pre-recorded interview The third area of reform was in regard to the way that children give evidence in criminal cases. The issue is whether children should be able to give evidence by live video link or even by pre-recorded interview instead of in the actual courtroom. The first step taken in that direction was s 32(1) of the Criminal Justice Act 1988 which allowed children under 14 in Crown Court cases of violence, sexual assault or cruelty to give evidence by live closed circuit

---

[103] This cancelled the 1997 decision that it was not appropriate to permit expert evidence to be given on the issue on the ground that the question was one well within the competence of a judge or magistrate (*G v DPP* [1997] 2 All ER 755).

television with the permission of the court. The aim was to protect the child from having to face the allegedly abusing adult.[104] The reform did not permit pre-recorded video interviews to be admissible as recommended the following year by the Pigot Committee (*Report of the Advisory Group on Video Recorded Evidence*, Home Office, December 1989[105]). At the time that was considered too controversial.[106]

The second step was the Criminal Justice Act 1991 which represented a compromise approach to this vexed issue. Section 54 inserting a new s 32A into the 1988 Act permitted the Crown Court or a youth court at the trial of a case to which s 32 of the 1988 Act (above) applied to admit as evidence-in-chief a video- recording of an interview with a child unless: (a) the child was not available for cross-examination; or (b) there had been a failure to comply with rules about disclosing the circumstances in which the recording was made; or (c) it would not be in the interests of justice to admit the recording. The child had to be called and could be cross-examined, but not by the accused himself (s 55(7)).

The Home Office and the Department of Health jointly produced a *Memorandum of Good Practice on Video Recorded Interviews with Child Witnesses for Criminal Proceedings* (HMSO, 1992). For description see Brian Ward, 'Children's Evidence', *Solicitors' Journal*, 3 July 1992, p 644 and by the same author, 'Interviewing Child Witnesses, *New Law Journal*, 6 November 1992, p 1547.

The Youth Justice and Criminal Evidence Act 1999, Part II, Chapter 1 scrapped the 'half Pigot' regime created by the 1988 and 1991 Acts and substituted an 'almost Pigot' regime. The Act provides for the availability of 'special measures' in all criminal cases for various categories of witnesses. One is witnesses under 17. They are automatically eligible for special measures. There are three groups: children giving evidence in a sexual offence case; children giving evidence in a case involving an offence of violence, abduction or neglect; and those giving evidence in any other case. In all three categories there is a statutory presumption that the witness' evidence in chief will be given by a pre-recorded video, unless this would not improve the

---

[104]   For a description of how this procedure operates and of some of its problems, see C Champness, 'Children's Evidence in Criminal Proceedings', *Law Society's Gazette*, 8 March 1989, p 14.

[105]   There is also an important Scottish report by the Scottish Law Commission ('The Evidence of Children and Other Potentially Vulnerable Witnesses', Discussion Paper No 75, June 1988). For an evaluation of this report in the light of English law and practice, see Jenny McEwan, 'Child Evidence: More Proposals for Reform' (1988) Criminal Law Review, p 813.

[106]   The pros and cons of this have been fiercely contested. See, for instance, Glanville Williams, 'Video-taping Children's Evidence' *New Law Journal*, January 30 1987, p 108; April 10, 1987, p 351; April 17, 1987, p 369; JR Spencer, 'Child Witnesses, Video-technology and the Law of Evidence' (1987) *Criminal Law Review*, p 76. See also David PH Jones, 'The Evidence of a Three-year-old child' (1987) *Criminal Law Review*, p 677. For the contrary view, see for instance James Morton, 'Videotaping Children's Evidence – A Reply', *New Law Journal*, 6 March 1987, p 2126. See on this issue Champness, 'Children's Evidence', *Law Society's Gazette*, 8 March 1989, p 14, which gives some information about the approach to the problem in the USA.

quality of the evidence. In the case of the first two groups, which are described as being in need of 'special protection', there are further measures. In sexual offence cases, the witness will be cross-examined at a recorded pre-trial hearing unless the court is persuaded that the witness does not want this protection. In violent offence categories evidence of child witnesses will be given through a live link at the trial.

For discussion of the implications and complexities of the 1999 Act in regard to child witnesses see Laura C H Hoyano, 'Variations on a Theme by Pigot: Special Measures Directions for Child Witnesses' [2000] *Criminal Law Review* 250-73.

See also a report published by the Home Office in 1992 which showed that child witnesses using video links gave more consistent evidence, more audibly and were less unhappy than those giving evidence in open court (Graham Davies and Elizabeth Noon, *An Evaluation of the Live Link for Child Witnesses*, Home Office, 1992).

(2) PERSONS OF DEFECTIVE INTELLECT

Where it is alleged that a witness lacks the mental capacity to testify, it is for the judge to decide whether he understands the nature of the oath.

(3) PARTIES

Until modern times, both in civil and criminal cases, the parties themselves were not permitted to give evidence, because it was thought that their evidence would be unreliable. This was changed for civil cases in 1851 by the Evidence Act of that year. In criminal cases defendants were not permitted to give evidence on oath until 1898, though before that date the judges allowed accused persons to make an unsworn statement from the dock. The present rules regarding occasions when parties need not give evidence fall under the different heading of evidence excluded for reasons of public policy–see below.

(4) SPOUSES OF PARTIES

The spouse of a party was incompetent as a witness on the same basis as the party himself on the grounds of the likely unreliability of the evidence. It was not until the Evidence Amendment Act 1853 that a spouse became a competent witness in a civil case and in the 1898 Criminal Evidence Act that a spouse became a competent witness for the defence in a criminal case. (As will be seen (pp 440-41 below), the spouse is not normally competent for the prosecution.) It seems, however, that a spouse is not a compellable witness for the defence. See TMS Tosswill, 'The Accused's Spouse as a Defence Witness' (1979) *Criminal Law Review*, p 702, and Michael Cohen, 'Are Wives Really so Incompetent?' (1980) *Criminal Law Review*, p 222.

(5) HEARSAY EVIDENCE

Hearsay evidence is excluded mainly on the ground that it is inherently unreliable. Hearsay evidence very simply defined is that of someone who is not present in court as a witness. If A is the witness, what B said to A is first-hand hearsay; whilst what B said to C, who told A, is second-hand hearsay. A document is hearsay evidence unless its author is there to introduce it in evidence. See also the definition in *Cross and Tapper on Evidence*:[107] 'an assertion other than one made by a person while giving oral evidence in the proceedings is inadmissible as evidence of any fact or opinion asserted'. This definition was adopted by the Law Commission in its report on the subject (see below)[108].

The rule has been regarded as one of the essential features of the basic common law principle that a trial, especially in a criminal case, should be based on evidence given by live witnesses in open court subject to cross-examination.

At the Nuremberg trial of the Nazi war criminals there was a clash between the continental systems which permit hearsay evidence, for what it is worth, and the common law systems which basically reject it. In that situation the common law countries agreed to accept hearsay evidence.

A dramatic example of the impact of the exclusion of hearsay evidence is *Sparks v Reginam*:

Sparks v R [1964] 1 All ER 727 (Judicial Committee of the Privy Council)

[A girl of three was sexually assaulted. The mother asked what the person who did it looked like. She said, 'It was a coloured boy.' The defendant, a staff sergeant in the US Air Force, was a white man. The trial court ruled that the mother could not give her daughter's statement in evidence. On appeal, inter alia, against this ruling, Lord Morris, giving the judgment of the Board, said (at p 733):]

It becomes necessary therefore to examine the contentions which have been advanced in support of the admissibility of the evidence. It was said that 'it was manifestly unjust for the jury to be left throughout the whole trial with the impression that the child could not give any clue to the identity of her assailant'. The cause of justice is, however, best served by adherence to rules which have long been recognised and settled. If the girl had made a remark to her mother (not in the presence of the appellant) to the effect that it was the appellant who had assaulted her and if the girl was not to be a witness at the trial, evidence as to what she had said would be the merest hearsay. In such circumstances it would be the defence who would wish to challenge a contention, if advanced,

---

[107]   C Tapper (ed) (7th edn 1990), p 509.
[108]   In the 9th edn, 2002, 'statement' replaced 'assertion' and 'stated' replaced 'or opinion asserted' (p 530).

that it would be 'manifestly unjust' for the jury not to know that the girl had given a clue to the identity of her assailant. If it is said that hearsay evidence should freely be admitted and that there should be concentration in any particular case on deciding as to its value or weight, it is sufficient to say that our law has not been evolved on such lines, but is firmly based on the view that it is wiser and better that hearsay should be excluded save in certain well-defined and rather exceptional circumstances. [Fortunately, the appeal was allowed on other grounds.]

In an even more remarkable case, *Myers v DPP* [1965] AC 1001, the prosecution foundered because of the hearsay rule. The accused took part in a conspiracy involving the purchase of wrecked cars with their log books, then disguising stolen cars so as to make them conform to the log books of the wrecked cars and selling them as renovated wrecks. In order to prove that the cars were the stolen rather than the wrecked ones, the prosecution called an officer in charge of the records of the manufacturers of the stolen cars to produce microfilms of the cards filled in by workmen showing the numbers of the cylinder blocks which coincided with the cylinder block numbers of the cars sold by the defendants. The majority of the House of Lords held that the admission of the records would be a breach of the rule against hearsay evidence because, as Lord Reid said, 'The entries on the cards were assertions by the unidentifiable men who made them that they had entered numbers which they had seen on the cars'. The problem was dealt with almost immediately by statute in the Criminal Evidence Act 1965, which made business or trade records admissible. For a striking, more recent case, see also *R v Kearley* [1992] 2 AC 228, [1992] 2 All ER 345, HL. K was accused of possession of drugs with intent to supply. Drugs had been found in his flat. While the police were there, 10 phone calls were received in which the caller asked to speak to him about getting drugs. The prosecution wanted to introduce evidence of these calls through evidence of the police officers who intercepted the calls. After five days of argument the House of Lords ruled (3-2) that the calls were inadmissible as hearsay evidence!

There have always been a variety of exceptions to the hearsay rule, some statutory, some common law, and in recent years there have been a succession of statutory exceptions and amendments of the rule. As will be seen, p 433 below, in 1995, on the recommendation of the Law Commission, the hearsay rule was effectively abolished in civil cases. In the same year the Law Commission published a report recommending drastic reform of the rule for criminal cases (see p 435 below). The Government accepted the recommendations in full but, in the event, they were not implemented. Instead, the Government introduced an even more radical reform in the Criminal Justice Bill 2002-2003.

The rule only applies if the statement in question is to be introduced in order to establish the truth of its contents. If it is to be introduced for some other purpose, it does not count as hearsay evidence. This is confusing not only for the student. It causes confusion even for the courts. The distinction drawn is between 'hearsay' and 'direct evidence'. Thus, for instance, the printout from an intoximeter measuring blood alcohol level has been treated not as hearsay but as direct ('real') evidence of the mechanical process. (*Castle v Cross* [1985] 1 All ER 87) In *Taylor v Chief Constable of Cheshire* [1987] 1 All ER 225, the prosecution case depended in part on what three police officers had seen in a video-recording allegedly showing the appellant committing theft from a shop. But the video had mistakenly been erased before the trial. The evidence of what was on the video was held by the Divisional Court not to be hearsay at all but rather direct evidence of what was seen happening at a particular time and place. Similarly, the courts have held that a sketch made by a police officer from a description given by a witness was not hearsay (*Smith, Percy* [1976] Crim LR 511), that a photofit picture compiled by a police officer was not hearsay (*Cook* [1987] Crim LR 402), and that in some circumstances computer printout is not hearsay–*Wood* [1982] Crim LR 667.

However, in *Townsend* [1987] Crim LR 411, the court refused to extend this to a piece of paper on which a victim of a mugging had written the assailant's car number with a defective ball-point pen which only made indentations. The police had been able to blow up the indentations which matched the defendant's car number, but they had lost the original piece of paper. (The commentator in the *Criminal Law Review* on *Cook* and *Townsend* points to the unsatisfactory nature of these cases.)

Another form of evidence which looks as if it should be treated as hearsay evidence is where it is introduced simply to permit a witness to refresh his memory (for instance in the very common situation where a police officer is permitted to 'refresh' his memory from his notebook), or to show a previous inconsistent statement or a prior consistent statement. Another example of non-hearsay is where the statement is introduced not to show the truth of the statement but rather to show a person's mental state. Thus in *Subramaniam v Public Prosecutor* [1956] 1 WLR 965, the court allowed evidence of threats allegedly made by terrorists to the appellant to be admissible not to show that they intended to carry out those threats but to demonstrate his state of mind where his defence to the charge was duress. (Cf *Blastland* [1986] AC 41 where the House of Lords ruled that the out-of-court statement could only be introduced to show a state of mind where the state of mind was in issue. The charge was murder and buggery. The defence was that the offences had been committed by someone else. The defence wished to introduce statements made by that person to others revealing knowledge of the murder at a time when it was not generally known. The House of Lords held that the purpose of introducing the statement was not to show the other person's state of mind but to show that he had committed the murder. It was therefore not admissible.)

A cynical comment on these examples of 'non-hearsay' is to see them all as ways simply of avoiding the rule–a view expressed by Adrian Zuckerman in his *Principles of Criminal Evidence* (Clarendon, 1989) at p 197:

> The methodology just described illustrates a fairly common tendency in this area. A certain type of statement is taken to be reliable. To avoid exclusion the

court searches for a convenient tag which may be given to this type of evidence so that it may pass for something other than hearsay. To fulfil its function the tag or label must be associated with admissible evidence ... Once the label is attached to a piece of evidence, the inhibiting effect of the hearsay rule disappears as if by magic.

There are in addition a long list of exceptions to the rule.

EXCEPTIONS TO THE HEARSAY RULE

Aet common law, an early exception recognised was that a deposition taken before a coroner or justice of the peace might be read at a subsequent trial if the witness was dead, *or too* ill to travel. The exception did not, however, extend to cases where the witness was simply untraceable, even if it could be shown that diligent efforts had been made to find him. (These exceptions are now in the Criminal Justice Act 1925 s 13 (4) (*a*), which provides also for the situation where the witness whose deposition is to be read is proved to be insane or kept out of the way by means of the procurement of the accused or on his behalf.)

Another common law exception was for the *dying declaration*. This allowed the prosecution in a murder or manslaughter case to introduce in evidence a statement made by the deceased purporting to identify his assailant, providing he had a 'settled and hopeless expectation of death'. If he believed he had a chance of recovery the exception did not apply. For a modern example of the rule, see *Nembhard v R* [1982] 1 All ER 183, where the Judicial Committee of the Privy Council upheld a conviction for murder where the only evidence against the accused was the deceased's alleged statement to his wife that he was going to die and that the defendant had shot him. See also *Lawson (Raymond)* [1998] Crim LR 883.

A more important common law exception in criminal cases is for *admissions or confessions*. If it were not for this exception, a police officer would not be able to tell the court about the accused's alleged self-incriminatory statement. The rationale for the exception was that people do not make false statements to the police to their own detriment; therefore there would be an inherent probability that the statement was true, which would avoid the vice of hearsay statements that they are inherently unreliable and not subject to cross-examination. The rationale is patently unconvincing. First, as is nowadays well known, people do make untrue confessions and admissions–whether to protect others or out of some form of pressure or psychological weakness. Secondly, the issue in regard to confessions in a contested case is often not whether the confession was true or false but whether it was made at all. The real reason for the exception is the need for it if criminals are to be brought to book.

Another common law exception was for a statement made so close to the event as in effect itself to be part of the event (the *'res gestae'* rule). It used to be thought that the statement had to be actually contemporaneous with the event. Thus in *Bedingfield* (1879) 14 Cox CC 341 the court refused to admit under the *res gestae* doctrine a statement by the victim who came out of her house with her throat slit ('See what Harry's done') because it was not made at the moment of the murderous attack. But this requirement has now been abandoned. See the House of Lords decision in *Andrews* [1987] 1 All ER 513. A was charged with murder by stabbing. The victim was found bleeding heavily a few minutes after the stabbing. A police officer arrived a few minutes later. The victim told the police that the defendant had carried out the stabbing. This statement was admitted as part of the *res gestae* and the ruling was upheld by the House of Lords. Lord Ackner's judgment said that a *res gestae* statement was admissible if it was made in circumstances which were sufficiently spontaneous and contemporaneous with the event to preclude the possibility of concoction or distortion. It had to be so closely associated with the event that the victim's mind was still dominated by it. The decision in *Bedingfield* was overruled. (See to like effect *Turnbull* (1984) 80 Cr App Rep 104, where the court admitted a statement made in a pub some 200 yards away from the scene of the attack and some 45 minutes after it had occurred.)

The common law also allowed statements in *public documents* such as a birth or marriage certificate to be admitted without requiring that the author of the document has to come to court to give evidence. At common law, however, the rule required that the document be available for public inspection. So in *Lilley v Pettit* [1946] KB 401 the court held inadmissible the regimental records of the army unit of the defendant's husband where she had been charged with falsely entering her husband's name as father of her child. The prosecution wanted to prove that the husband had been abroad at all material times. The evidence was not admissible because the records were not public.

There is another, somewhat odd, category of common law exception to the hearsay rule–for family law matters especially where they affect children. The attitude of the courts has been somewhat erratic. In several cases the courts decided that in family law cases the strict hearsay rule can be relaxed. (See for instance *Official Solicitor v K* [1965] AC 201; *Hurwitt v Hurwitt* (1979) 3 FLR 194; *Edwards v Edwards* [1986] 1 FLR 187; *Thompson v Thompson* [1986] 1 FLR 212n; *Webb v Webb* [1986] 1 FLR 541.) But in other cases the courts have insisted on strict compliance with the rules. (See especially *H v H; K v K* [1990] Fam 86; *Bradford City Metropolitan Council v K and K* [1990] Fam 140 ('the *Bradford* case' and 9 *Civil Justice Quarterly* 1990, p 228).

Concern over the last two of these decisions prompted a late amendment to the Children Act 1989 enabling the Lord Chancellor to provide by order for the admissibility of hearsay evidence in children's proceedings. This was done by the Children (Admissibility of Hearsay Evidence) Order 1990, which was then repeated in the 1991 Order of the same name (SI 1990/1115). The 1990 Order provided that the hearsay rule did not apply in civil proceedings before the High Court or a county court concerning the upbringing, maintenance or welfare of a child. The Order also provided that the hearsay rule did not apply in relation to such proceedings in juvenile courts. This refers in particular to care and related proceedings. The 1991 Order extended the new rule to magistrates' courts.

CIVIL CASES — RECENT DEVELOPMENTS

In civil cases the main statutes until 1995 were the Civil Evidence Acts of 1938, 1968 and 1972. Under the 1938 Act, statements in original documents could be admitted to establish a fact of which direct oral evidence would be admissible if the maker of the statement had personal knowledge of the matter or it was part of a continuous record in the performance of a duty and the witness could not attend because he was dead, ill or abroad, or if all reasonable efforts to find him had been made without success. It also allowed the statement to be admitted if the witness was present to avoid delay or cost. The maker of the statement had to have personal knowledge of the facts stated and there were specific requirements that he authenticate the document. Also the statement had to be one made in writing.

The Civil Evidence Act 1968 broadened admissible hearsay to oral statements and also to mechanically recorded statements made by someone under a duty to record such information supplied to him by someone with personal knowledge of the facts. Procedural safeguards required notice to be given in advance to the other side, with full particulars of the hearsay statement in question. If the other party objected, the person whose statement was to be given had to be called in person, unless he was dead, ill or abroad or could not reasonably be expected to remember the matter. The Civil Evidence Act 1972 made the evidence of expert witnesses admissible in the form of their reports without having to call them.

In January 1991 the Law Commission proposed that the hearsay rule should be completely abolished for civil proceedings. The proposal was made in a Consultation Paper (*The Hearsay Rule in Civil Proceedings*, Consultation Paper No 117). The proposal was a provisional one, subject to the consultation exercise. The alternative would be to reform the Civil Evidence Act 1968 and procedural rules of court so as to simplify the rule. The Law Commission suggested that, despite reform of the hearsay rule, it was not only difficult to understand but increasingly difficult to reconcile with recent procedural developments such as pre-trial exchange of witness statements. The Commission also drew attention to the fact that the hearsay rule in civil proceedings had already been abolished in Scotland by the Civil Evidence (Scotland) Act 1988. There was still a case for keeping the hearsay rule in criminal proceedings, especially in jury trials. But jury trials in civil cases were now exceedingly rare. (In 1989 there were only 104 in county courts out of 22,259 trials (para 3.19, p 52).)

The Law Commission said that the chief advantage of abolition of the rule was to simplify the rules of evidence and the elimination of technical objections to the admissibility of relevant evidence. It should be for the parties to decide what evidence would assist their case. In practice they would resort to hearsay evidence only where it was the best they could find.

The Law Commission's views were broadly confirmed in its final report published in 1993 (*The Hearsay Rule in Civil Proceedings*, (Law Com No 216)). The Government implemented the recommendations of the report in the Civil Evidence Act 1995 which came into force in January 1997. The same rules were extended to civil proceedings in magistrates' courts as from April 1999.[109]

The guiding principle in the 1995 Act is that evidence is not to be excluded on the ground that it is hearsay but the court will decide what weight to give to the evidence. The concept of hearsay evidence remains and it will often be regarded as less persuasive than direct evidence. But it is no longer to be excluded on that ground.

Parties are under a duty to give each other notice of their intention to adduce hearsay evidence. (See now CPR, r 33; D Barnett, 'Civil Evidence Act, when do the new rules apply?', *New Law Journal*, 9 May 1997, p 701.)

Failure to give notice does not mean that the evidence cannot be introduced but the court can take that failure into account in considering what weight to place on the evidence and when making costs orders (s 2). The Law Commission Report (Pt III, para 3.7) said that it appeared that the notice requirement under the previous English legislation had 'fallen into disuse' and that 'the prescribed time-limits were not complied with'. Under the Civil Evidence (Scotland) Act 1988 hearsay evidence is admissible without any requirement of advance notice. (One commentator suggested that we would have done better to follow the Scotland Act – see J Peysner, 'Hearsay is dead! Long live hearsay', *International Journal of Evidence and Proof*, 1998, vol 2, No 4, pp 232-46.)

A party can call for cross-examination of a person whose statement has been tendered as hearsay evidence and who has not been called to give oral evidence (s 3). Section 4 guides the court as to what factors to weigh in such evidence. These include factors such as whether it would have been reasonable and practicable to have called the maker of the statement, and when the statement was made eg was it made contemporaneously, or whether there was any motive to conceal or misrepresent matters.

See D O'Brien, 'The Rule Against Hearsay RIP', *New Law Journal*, 2 February 1996, p 153; I Grainger, 'Hearsay Evidence Admissible', *New Law Journal*, 31 May 1996, p 536; and A Hogan, 'The Civil Evidence Act 1995', *New Law Journal*, 14 February 1997, p 226.

CRIMINAL CASES – RECENT DEVELOPMENTS

In criminal cases, too, the hearsay rule was gradually weakened by statute, though not as much as in the civil field.

---

[109] Magistrates' Courts (Hearsay Evidence in Civil Proceedings) Rules 1999, SI 1999/681.

The Criminal Justice Act 1967, s 9, made admissible written witness statements where they are signed, a copy has been served in advance on the other party and no counter-notice has been served objecting to the statement being tendered in evidence. This was very frequently used. Section 2 of the 1967 Act (then s 102 of the Magistrates Courts Act 1980) made written statements admissible in committal proceedings on a similar basis–namely, that they are written, signed and tendered in advance. Again, this was used all the time. The Criminal Procedure and Investigations Act 1996 carried this much further by making *any* written statement and deposition admitted in evidence in committal proceedings admissible at trial providing the statement was signed by a magistrate. The accused can object to the statement or deposition being read as evidence at his trial but the trial court can overrule the objection if it considers it 'to be in the interests of justice'.[110] For a savage critique of this new provision see R Munday, 'The drafting smokescreen', *New Law Journal*, 30 May 1997, p 792, 6 June 1997, p 860. Dr Munday suggested that the provision would eventually be declared to be contrary to Art 6 of the European Convention on Human Rights.

As has been seen, the Criminal Evidence Act 1965 was passed to reverse the House of Lords decision in *Myers v DPP* (p 428 above), by making business and trade records made under a duty to record the information admissible. But this legislation was superseded by the much wider provisions of the Police and Criminal Evidence Act 1984, which in turn was superseded by the even wider provisions of the Criminal Justice Act 1988.

The Police and Criminal Evidence Act, s 68, made admissible statements in any document that form part of a record compiled by a person under a duty or on the basis of information supplied by someone acting under a duty, where the maker of the document is unavailable to give evidence. The supplier of the information must be dead, ill or physically unable to give evidence, abroad or not known, or it must be a situation where it would not be reasonable to expect him to remember the matters recorded.

Section 68 of PACE, however, was replaced by Part II and Schedule 2 of the Criminal Justice Act 1988. The purpose of Part II was to establish a new basis for the admissibility of documentary hearsay in criminal proceedings. It classified documents into three categories: first-hand hearsay, business documents and documents which may fall into either category which are prepared specifically for the purpose of criminal proceedings. The 1988 Act, s 23 made any first-hand hearsay admissible provided the maker is unavailable to give evidence because he is dead or unfit or abroad and it is not reasonably practicable to secure his attendance; or that he cannot be found in spite of all reasonable steps taken. These provisions are similar to those in s 68 of the 1984 Act, but it is no longer possible to tender someone's hearsay statement on the basis that he cannot reasonably be expected to remember the matter. Nor can the maker's statement be admitted when he could not be identified

---

[110] Section 68 and Sch 2, paras 1, 2.

after reasonable efforts made. So documents prepared by unidentified workmen seem now not to be admissible under s 23.

Section 24 considerably widened the previous exception for business records by no longer requiring that the business document have been made by someone acting under a duty. It is only necessary to prove that the information contained in the document was supplied by someone who had or might reasonably be supposed to have had personal knowledge of the matter.

Where a statement was prepared for the purposes of a criminal investigation or prosecution it can be introduced in evidence on proof regarding the absence of the maker that he is dead, unfit, abroad, etc, or that he does not give evidence 'through fear or because he is kept out of the way'. See further DJ Birch, 'The Criminal Justice Act–The Evidence Provisions' (1989) *Criminal Law Review*, pp 15–31.

The Runciman Royal Commission on Criminal Justice (Cm 2263, 1993) expressed the view that 'in general, the fact that a statement is hearsay should mean that the court places rather less weight on it, but not that it should be inadmissible in the first place' (p 125, para 26). The probative weight of the evidence should, it thought, 'in principle be decided by the jury for themselves' (ibid). It recommended that 'hearsay evidence should be admitted to a greater extent than at present' (ibid). But because of the complexity of the hearsay rule it thought that the issues needed thorough exploration by the Law Commission.

The Government referred the question of the hearsay rule to the Law Commission in April 1994 and in July 1995 the Commission produced Consultation Paper No 138, *Evidence in Criminal Proceedings: Hearsay and Related Topics*. The Consultation Paper, which was 266 pages long, suggested that it was right to retain the rule in criminal cases as a protection to the accused. In civil cases the finders of fact were judges; in criminal cases they were jurors and magistrates. But the rules needed reform– 'The rule is excessively complex; this complexity leads to confusion, anomalies and wasted time, both for the court and for the parties. The rule results in the exclusion of cogent evidence even when it is the defence that seeks to adduce it' (para 9.2).

The Commission proposed that as a general rule hearsay should remain inadmissible subject to listed statutory exceptions. These would be first hand oral or documentary hearsay of identified witnesses. The categories of exception would be: (1) where the witness was dead or too ill to attend court; (2) where such steps had been taken as were reasonably practicable to secure his attendance but without success and he was abroad or could not be found; or (3) where the witness refused to give evidence although physically available. They would not extend to evidence of any fact of which the witness' oral evidence would not be admissible.

The Commission proposed that there should be a residual discretion to admit hearsay falling outside the stated categories and other preserved exceptions which would extend to multiple as well as first hand-hand hearsay. This should be available only if it appeared to the court that (1) the evidence was so positively and obviously trustworthy that the opportunity to test it by cross-examination could safely be dispensed with, and (2) the interests of justice required that it be admitted.

The Commission also recommended that s 69 of PACE regarding computers should be repealed. In the absence of evidence to the contrary it should be assumed that a computer or other mechanical instrument was functioning properly. This was effected by s 60 of the Youth Justice and Criminal Evidence Act 1999.

The Law Commission's Final Report (Law Com 245, Cm 3670, 1997) reaffirmed the main recommendations in the Consultation Paper. For commentary on the Law Commission's Consultation Paper see especially A A S Zuckerman, 'The Futility of Hearsay', (1996) *Criminal Law Review*, pp 4-15; DC Ormerod, 'The Hearsay Exceptions', ibid, pp 16-28; J R Spencer, 'Hearsay Reform: A Bridge Not Far Enough', ibid, pp 29-33; P Murphy, 'Hearsay: the road to reform', *International Journal of Evidence and Proof*, 1997, vol 1, no 2, pp 107-27 and 'Practising safe hearsay: surrender may be inevitable, but shouldn't we take precautions?' ibid, 1997, vol 1, no 3, pp 105-21. For commentary on the Final Report see J D Jackson, 'Hearsay: the sacred cow that won't be slaughtered?' *International Journal of Evidence and Proof*, 1998, pp 166-90).

In December 1998 the Government announced that it accepted all the recommendations of the Law Commission's Report – lock, stock and barrel (House of Lords, *Hansard*, 17 December, 1998, vol 599, WA, col 184). However, the legislation to give effect to this commitment was delayed for years and in the end it was not implemented.

In October 2001 Lord Justice Auld's *Review of the Criminal Courts* said of the hearsay rule:

> It is common ground that the present law is unsatisfactory and needs reform. It is complicated, unprincipled and arbitrary in the application of the many exceptions. It can exclude cogent and let in weak evidence. It wastes court time in requiring it to receive oral evidence when written evidence would do. And it confuses witnesses and prevents them from giving their accounts in their own way. (p 557, para 96)

The Law Commission's proposals, Auld said, looked at individually, represented useful improvements on the present law. They relaxed some of the rigidity of the present rule through a widening of the exceptions and the introduction of a limited inclusionary discretion. But, 'their implementation would not significantly change the present landscape nor, I believe, remove much of the scope for dispute that disfigures and interrupts our present trial process.' (p 559, para 102) He suggested that a further review be undertaken with a view to making hearsay evidence 'generally admissible subject to the principle of the best evidence, rather than generally inadmissible subject to specified exceptions as proposed by the Law Commission' (p 560). Fact finders should be trusted to assess the weight of the evidence.

The Government's July 2002 White Paper *Justice for All* said:

> We believe the right approach is that, if there is good reason for the original
> maker not to be able to give the evidence personally (for example, through
> illness or death) or where records have been properly compiled by businesses,
> then the evidence should automatically go in, rather than its admissibility being
> judged. Judges should also have a discretion to decide that other evidence of
> this sort can be given. This is close to the approach developed in civil
> proceedings. (para 4.61)

The Government did not adopt Lord Justice Auld's recommendation that the topic
should be further studied by another committee. Instead the Criminal Justice Bill
2002/03 contained a complete restatement of the law on the subject consisting of 22
clauses taking some 25 pages of print. (As originally printed they were cll 98 to 125;
when reprinted for the Lords in May 2003 they were cll 107 to 129.)

Clause 107(1) established that hearsay evidence, whether oral or written, would be
admissible under four headings: (a) under the statute itself; (b) under any common
law rule specifically preserved by the statute; (c) if the parties agreed; and (d) if the
court was satisfied that it would not be contrary to the interests of justice for it to be
admitted. The last category gives the judge the possibility of admitting hearsay that
does not fit into any other category. It could extend to any form of hearsay evidence
including multiple hearsay ('A said that B said that C shot the deceased'). In regard
to (d), cl 107 (2) set out the kind of factors that the court must take into account when
deciding whether the evidence was reliable enough to admit – the probative value of
the evidence and how important it was, the circumstances in which it was made, the
reliability of the maker of the statement, how reliable it was that the statement had
been made, why oral evidence was not available, the difficulty of challenging the
statement and what other evidence there was.

Clause 109(2) set out a series of categories under which first-hand hearsay evidence,
oral or documentary, was admissible, provided that the witness was unavailable to
testify because he is (a) dead, (b) ill, (c) absent abroad, (d) has disappeared or (e) is in
fear (which para (3) says must be widely construed and includes fear of the death or
injury of another person or of financial loss but leave under this head can only be
given if it is in the interests of justice). Business and other documents permitted under
s 24 of the Criminal Justice Act 1988 are permitted under cl 110. Clause 111 preserved
eight categories of hearsay evidence permitted at common law, including 'public
information' (such as dictionaries, maps, birth certificates or court records), *res gestae*
(see pp 430–31 above) and confessions – but not including dying declarations. Clause
112, reversing the traditional rule, provides that previous inconsistent statements
become evidence of their truth.

The court has a discretion to exclude hearsay evidence on the ground that it would
result in undue waste of time having regard to its likely value (cl 119 (1)).

Lord Woolf, Lord Chief Justice, said of these provisions:[111]

22. [W]e question whether the complexity of the provisions is necessary. What has happened is that the complex common law rules are being replaced by complex statutory rules, some of which are a repetition of the common law rules.

23. What happens now in civil proceedings is that a judge has a general discretion to determine how matters are to be proved. The judge has to exercise the discretion in the interests of justice. . . .If it is not first-hand evidence, then it has the disadvantage that it has not been tested by cross-examination. Whether this matters depends on the circumstances. If we have got to the stage where it is considered that it is safe to allow juries to hear hearsay evidence, then we must be accepting that they can be trusted to use that evidence in accordance with the directions of the judge. Instead of the detailed and complex provisions which are contained in Chapter 2, what is needed is a simple rule putting the judge in charge of what evidence is admissible and giving him the responsibility of ensuring that the jury use the evidence in an appropriate manner.

(6)   EVIDENCE OF IDENTIFICATION

Possibly the most notorious source of miscarriages of justice is identification evidence. It has therefore been suggested by some that such evidence ought to be wholly excluded in criminal cases unless corroborated. The question was examined by the Devlin Committee on *Evidence of Identification in Criminal Cases*. In its report (House of Commons paper 338, 1976) it rejected this view but recommended (pp 94–5) that the judge should be required to warn the jury that it was unsafe to convict on the basis of eyewitness evidence unless the circumstances of the identification were exceptional or there was substantial evidence of some other sort. A judge who gave such warning should indicate the kind of case where exceptionally it might be reasonable to rely on eyewitness evidence. Failure to give the warning would be grounds to quash the conviction. So too would a finding by the Court of Appeal that the case was not such as to justify reliance on eyewitness evidence or that there was insufficient supporting evidence.

Only a few weeks after the report was published, the Court of Appeal in *R v Turnbull* [1977] QB 224 acted on the report but it did not give full effect to the Committee's recommendation. The Court, sitting with five judges, laid down new guidelines for trial judges in cases involving disputed identification evidence. Lord Widgery for the court said that the trial judge should warn the jury of the special need for caution before relying on identification evidence. He should instruct them as to the reason for such warning and should refer to the possibility that a mistaken witness was a convincing one and that even a number of such witnesses could be mistaken. Secondly,

---

[111]   In his 'Background Notes' to his 2nd Reading speech – see n 99, p 421 above.

he should direct the jury to examine very closely the circumstances in which the identification came to be made: 'How long did the witness have the accused under observation? At what distance? In what light? Was the observation impeded in any way, as for example by passing traffic or a press of people? Had the witness ever seen the accused before? How often? If only occasionally, had he any reason for remembering the accused? How long elapsed between the original observation and the subsequent identification to the police? Was there any material discrepancy between the description of the accused given to the police by the witness when first seen by them and his actual appearance?' (at p 228). If there were such discrepancies, the prosecution should inform the defence.

The court said that in setting out its guidelines it had tried to follow the recommendations of the Devlin Committee. A failure to follow the guidelines was likely to result in a conviction being quashed. For cases in which convictions were subsequently quashed as a result of a failure to follow the guidelines, see, for instance, *R v Hunjan* (1978) 68 Cr App Rep 99; *Bentley* [1991] Crim LR 620; *Fergus* (1993) 98 Cr App Rep 313. But the courts have resisted the suggestion that *Turnbull* requires them to follow a formula – see, for instance, *Mills* [1995] Crim LR 884 and *Mussell; Dalton*, ibid, p 887. See also E Grayson, 'Identifying Turnbull' (1977) *Criminal Law Review*, p 509; and JD Jackson, 'The Insufficiency of Identification Evidence Based on Personal Impression' (1986) *Criminal Law Review*, p 203.

The rules for identification procedures are now to be found in PACE Code of Practice on Identification Evidence (Code D) as revised as from 1 April 2003. (See M Zander, *Police and Criminal Evidence Act 1984* (4th edn, Sweet & Maxwell, 2003, pp 274-89. For cases on the admissibility of evidence obtained in breach of the identification rules see ibid, paras 8-116 and 8-121.

Judicial warnings regarding uncorroborated evidence

Until very recently the judges were required to give the jury a warning about the danger of relying on the uncorroborated evidence of children (see p 424 above), accomplices giving evidence for the prosecution, and complainants in a sexual offence. The Law Commission recommended in 1991 that the rules *requiring* such warnings should be abolished–*Corroboration of Evidence in Criminal Trials*, Cm 1620, 1991. This was effected in the Criminal Justice and Public Order Act 1994, s 32(1). In *Makanjuola; Easton* [1995] 3 All ER 730, [1995] 2 Cr App Rep 469, the Court of Appeal held that although there was no longer a rule requiring a warning about uncorroborated evidence, one could be given on a discretionary basis where the judge thought it necessary. It gave guidelines as to how the matter should be approached. The guidelines provoked a good deal of debate. See commentary in (1996) *Criminal Law Review* 44 at 45 and 815 at 816; and D J Birch, 'Corroboration: Goodbye to All That?' (1995) *Criminal Law Review* pp 524-39; P Mirfield, 'Corroboration after the 1994 Act', (1995) ibid, pp 448-60; J Hartshorne, 'Corroboration and care warnings after *Makanjuola*', *International Journal of Evidence and Proof*, 1998, vol 2, no 1, pp 1-12. See also *Warwick Muncaster* [1999] Crim LR 409.

Section 33 of the 1994 Act also abolished the requirement of actual corroboration for a number of offences under the Sexual Offences Act 1956.

(c)   Evidence excluded because its admissibility would be against the public interest

There are various categories of excluded evidence that can conveniently be collected under this head:

(1)   THE EVIDENCE OF SPOUSES IN CRIMINAL CASES

A spouse was generally not able to give evidence for the prosecution in a criminal case even if willing to give evidence (see *R v Mount* (1934) 24 Cr App Rep 135). She was not competent as a witness. There were some exceptions where the wife was permitted to give evidence but was not compellable, mainly involving offences against the wife herself, her property or against their children. In *Hoskyn v Metropolitan Police Comr* [1978] 2 All ER 136, the House of Lords held that a woman who married the defendant two days before the trial could not be *compelled* to give evidence against her new husband in a case arising out of a serious assault on her! See also *R v Pitt* [1982] Crim LR 513, in which the Court of Appeal said a wife who was competent but not compellable to give evidence for the prosecution against her husband remained free to decide whether to give evidence until the moment that she entered the witness box, and was unaffected by whether she had previously given a statement to the police or had given evidence at the committal proceedings. But once she decided to give evidence she became like any other witness and had to answer all questions save those that might incriminate her. Moreover, she could be treated as a hostile witness if that would be legitimate with an ordinary witness. But this ought to be explained to her before she started to give evidence. The general exclusionary rule applied even after judicial separation and possibly after divorce in regard to matters that occurred during the marriage.

In its 1972 11th Report, the Criminal Law Revision Committee said the question of the continuation of this exclusionary rule involved a balancing of the need to get the right verdict, on the one hand, and, on the other hand, the objection that such evidence would disturb marital harmony and be harsh on the spouse compelled to testify. It thought that the rule should at least be modified to make the wife *competent* to give evidence for the prosecution if willing to do so. She should also be compellable (as opposed to being merely competent) in cases involving violence against her or against children of the household under 16 (paras 149–50). If the parties were divorced, the Committee thought that they should be treated for all purposes as if they had never been married–even in regard to matters occurring during the marriage. (But see M Cohen, 'Are Wives Really So Incompetent?' (1980) *Criminal Law Review*, p 222.)

The Police and Criminal Evidence Act, 1984, s 80, broadly carried into effect the proposals of the Criminal Law Revision Committee. It provides, first, that a spouse is always competent for the prosecution save where he or she is charged jointly with the same offence. (The exception does not apply, however, where he or she is no longer liable to be convicted for that offence by virtue of having pleaded guilty or otherwise.) The Act, secondly, made the spouse always compellable for the defence–save for the same exception where she is charged jointly with him.[112] The Act extended the CLRC's proposals by making a spouse *compellable* for the prosecution not only in cases of violence to children of the family under 16, but also in cases of violence or a sexual offence against anyone under 16 whether or not they were family members. Fourthly, the Act adopted the CLRC's proposal that a spouse should be competent for a co-accused regardless of whether his or her spouse consented. Fifthly, the Act laid down that after the marriage has been terminated, both spouses become competent and compellable as if they had never been married– even regarding events that occurred during the marriage.

(2) EVIDENCE OF A WITNESS THAT MIGHT INCRIMINATE HIM

Any witness in any case, other than the defendant himself, is entitled to refuse to answer a question that might expose him to a criminal charge. If the privilege is invoked, it is for the judge to decide whether the questions have to be answered. It seems that the privilege may extend to cover answers that could incriminate a spouse, but it does not go beyond that to protect other family members.

In *Re O (disclosure order)* [1991] 1 All ER 330 the Court of Appeal held that convicted persons could be required to make full disclosure of their assets for the purposes of potential confiscation proceedings under the Criminal Justice Act 1988, but because of the principle of not requiring a person to incriminate himself the order would be subject to a condition that no disclosure made in compliance with the order should be used as evidence in the prosecution of an offence alleged to have been committed by the person required to make the disclosure.

(3) THE ACCUSED IS NOT A COMPELLABLE WITNESS

An accused person in a criminal case has a right to remain silent in the dock. That was and remains the case. In fact the great majority of defendants who plead not guilty do give evidence. (In the Crown Court Study done for the Royal Commission on Criminal Justice over 70% of defendants gave evidence.)[113]

---

112 In *R (on the application of CPS) v Registrar General of Births, Deaths and Marriages* [2002] EWCA Civ 1661, [2003] 1 All ER 540 the Court of Appeal held that it was not contrary to public policy for the defendant to marry in order to take advantage of s 80. The prosecution were therefore not entitled to ask the prison authorities and/or the Registrar of Births, Deaths and Marriages to refuse to allow the wedding until after the defendant's trial.

113 M Zander and P Henderson, *The Crown Court Study* (Royal Commission on Criminal Justice, Research Study No 19, 1993, p 114).

The basic common law rule was that the prosecution were not permitted to comment on the fact that the defendant chose not to go into the witness box. (Criminal Evidence Act 1898, s 1(*b*).) (But see *R v Brown and Routh* [1983] Crim LR 38 where it was held the rule had not been infringed even though the prosecution counsel did comment on the defendants' failure to give evidence in the sense that he said the prosecution's case was uncontradicted.)

The judge was allowed in his discretion to draw the jury's attention to the fact but he could not suggest that silence constituted evidence against the defendant. The position was explained by the Lord Chief Justice, Lord Taylor, in *R v Martinez-Tobon* [1994] 2 All ER 90 concerning the importation of cocaine. The trial judge had told the jury in his summing up that that they were not to conclude from the fact that the defendant had not given evidence that he was guilty but that they might think that if he had thought that D was bringing in emeralds rather than cocaine that the defendant would have been very anxious to say so. The Court of Appeal upheld the conviction. Provided the judge told the jury that they should not assume guilt from a refusal to give evidence at least in some circumstances comment was permitted. Where the defence case involved facts which were at variance with the prosecution's case and which were within the defendant's knowledge, such comment might be legitimate. The nature and strength of such comment was a matter for the judge.

Until 1982, if the defendant chose to give evidence he could either go into the witness box and thereby subject himself to cross-examination or he could make a statement from the dock on which he could not be cross-examined.

The CLRC in its 1972 11th Report recommended drastic reform of the rules:
(1) That if the prosecution had established a *prima facie* case, the accused should formally be asked to go into the witness box and told that, if he failed to do so, adverse inferences could be drawn. Failure to do so could also amount to corroboration where corroboration was required. In the view of the Committee the existing rule was much too favourable to the defence. Normally it should be incumbent on the accused to give evidence, but it would not become contempt of court to refuse.
(2) The prosecution and judge should be entitled to comment on the accused's failure to give evidence. The prohibition on comment was wrong in principle and entirely illogical.
(3) The right to make an unsworn statement from the dock should be abolished. It was rarely exercised in trials on indictment save in cases where the accused wanted to attack prosecution witnesses without making himself liable to the revelations of his own prior convictions. (See on this point, p 414 above.) It was wrong to give the accused this choice (Criminal Law Revision Committee, 'Evidence (General)', *Eleventh Report*, 1972, Cmnd 4991, paras 102–13).

These proposals were received with much less criticism than those made by the CLRC in regard to the right of silence in the police station.

The Philips Royal Commission on Criminal Procedure disagreed with the CLRC on the first two points. It did not favour putting pressure on the accused to give evidence or allowing comment on his refusal to testify. But it did agree that the right of the defendant to make an unsworn statement from the dock should be abolished. It was anomalous that a defendant should be able to give evidence without being subject to the possibility of perjury proceedings. He should be required to submit himself to the oath and cross-examination. (Report, paras 4.63–7.)

The Government followed the same line. The Criminal Justice Act 1982, s 72, abolished the right of the defendant to make an unsworn statement from the dock. However, it preserved the right of an unrepresented accused to address the court in the same way that counsel could, by way of submissions or in mitigation of sentence.

The Runciman Royal Commission on Criminal Justice said that the balance was held correctly in the standard direction given to juries:

> The defendant does not have to give evidence. He is entitled to sit in the dock and require the prosecution to prove its case. You must not assume that he is guilty because he has not given evidence. The fact that he has not given evidence proves nothing one way or the other. It does nothing to establish his guilt. On the other hand, it means that there is no evidence from the defendant to undermine, contradict, or explain the evidence put before you by the prosecution.

Where the defendant did not give evidence, the prosecution could question and the judge could comment on the explanation given by counsel but, the Commission said, 'neither the prosecution nor the judge should invite the jury to draw from the defendant's failure to give evidence the inference that his or her explanation is less deserving of being believed' (Report, p 56, para 27).

The Government, however, rejected the view of the two Royal Commissions and instead implemented the recommendation of the CLRC made in 1972. The Criminal Justice and Public Order Act 1994 (CJPOA), s 35 states that at the trial of someone [who has attained the age of fourteen years],[114] at the conclusion of the prosecution's case, the court must 'satisfy itself ... that the accused is aware that the stage has been reached at which evidence can be given for the defence ... and that, if he chooses not to give evidence, or having been sworn, without good cause refuses to answer any question, it will be permissible for the court or jury to draw such inferences as appear proper from his failure to give evidence or his refusal without good cause to answer any question' (s 35(2)). The court or jury may draw such inferences as appear proper from the failure to give evidence or refusal to answer questions (s 35(3)).

The new rule does not apply if it appears to the court that 'the physical or mental condition of the accused makes it undesirable for him to give evidence' (s 35(1)(b)).

A Practice Direction issued by the Lord Chief Justice dealt with the procedure to be

---

[114]   The words in square brackets were removed by the Crime and Disorder Act 1998, s 35.

followed (*Practice Direction* (Crown Court: evidence: advice to defendant) [1995] 1 WLR 657). If the defendant is legally represented and the court is informed that he does not intend to give evidence the judge should, in the presence of the jury inquire of the lawyer: 'Have you advised your client that the stage has now been reached at which he may give evidence and if he chooses not to do so, or, having been sworn, without good cause refuses to answer any questions, the jury may draw such inferences as appear proper?' If this assurance is given the case proceeds. If not, the case should briefly be adjourned for that to be done.

If the accused is not legally represented the judge should say to the defendant:

> You have heard the evidence against you. Now is the time for you to make your defence. You may give evidence on oath, and be cross-examined like any other witness. If you do not give evidence, or having been sworn, without good cause refuse to answer any question, the jury may draw such inferences as appear proper. That means they may hold it against you. You may also call any witness or witnesses whom you have arranged to attend court. Afterwards you may also, if you wish, address the jury by arguing your case from the dock. But you cannot at that stage give evidence. Do you now intend to give evidence?

In *Cowan* [1996] QB 373 the Lord Chief Justice, Lord Taylor, for the Court of Appeal said there were certain essential matters on which the judge must direct the jury under s 35, namely:

- The burden of proof remains on the prosecution at all times.
- The defendant is entitled to remain silent.
- An inference from failure to give evidence cannot on its own prove guilt.
- The jury must be satisfied that the prosecution have established a case to answer before drawing an inference from silence.
- The jury may draw an adverse inference if, despite any evidence relied on by the accused to explain his silence or in the absence of such evidence, the jury conclude the silence can only sensibly be attributed to the accused having no answer or none that would stand up to cross-examination.

There needs to be some evidential basis or some exceptional factors in the case to justify the judge NOT permitting the jury to draw an adverse inference from the failure to give evidence. For other cases see pp 162-63 above.

For the recommended text of the Judicial Studies Board's latest specimen direction for the judge to give to the jury see the JSB's website – www.jsboard.co.uk (Publications – Bench Books – Specimen Directions, No39).

(4)   LEGAL PROFESSIONAL PRIVILEGE

As has been seen (pp 87-90) communications between a client and his legal adviser generally cannot be given in evidence by the lawyer without the permission of the client if they were made either (1) with reference to proceedings in being or then contemplated, or (2) to enable the client to receive, or the lawyer to give, legal advice.

The privilege is that of the client not the lawyer and can only be waived by the client. (There is no equivalent privilege for communications between doctor and patient, priest and penitent, or journalist and his source, though, as has been seen (pp 212–215 above), these categories do now have a comparable immunity under the Police and Criminal Evidence Act in regard to certain pre-trial police searches.) The privilege is intended to promote candour between a client and his lawyers.

In the Police and Criminal Evidence Act 1984 legal professional privilege is defined to include not only communications but also documents and other articles mentioned in or enclosed with privileged communications if the communication was in connection with the giving of legal advice or in connection with or contemplation of legal proceedings and for the purpose of such proceedings (s 10). It also includes not only communications for these purposes between the client and the lawyer, but also with third persons such as accountants or others involved in legal advice or legal proceedings. (See TRS Allen, 'Legal Privilege and the Principle of Fairness in the Criminal Trial' (1987) *Criminal Law Review*, p 449.)

Legal professional privilege and money laundering rules The Proceeds of Crime Act 2002 creates serious problems for lawyers. It makes it an offence if, knowing or suspecting, or having reasonable grounds for knowing or suspecting, that someone is engaged in money laundering, by reason of information which came to him in his professional capacity, he fails to report the situation as soon as practicable. The information can relate to any party, not just to the lawyer's client. There is a limited exception for privilege. A professional legal adviser has a valid defence under s 330(7) if he receives the information in privileged circumstances as defined in ss 10 and 11. They state that information is received in privileged circumstances if it is not communicated or given for the purpose of furthering a criminal purpose and it is from a client in connection with the giving of legal advice or from someone seeking legal advice or from someone in connection with actual or contemplated legal proceedings.

(5)   EVIDENCE OBTAINED AT A 'TRIAL WITHIN A TRIAL'

It is a common feature of Crown Court cases that the admissibility of evidence is considered by the judge, usually in the absence of the jury. This is known technically as a *voir dire*, or, less formally, as a 'trial within a trial'.

If the accused makes admissions during the *voir dire*, can the prosecution give evidence of them once the trial resumes? The point came up in *R v Brophy* [1981] 2 All ER 705, an appeal to the House of Lords from Northern Ireland. B was accused of 49 counts of terrorism offences including 12 murders by explosions. There was no evidence against him other than admissions made during interrogations. He challenged the admissibility of these statements. During the trial within a trial on this issue, he admitted he had for years been a member of the IRA. The trial judge ruled that the statements made in the interrogations were inadmissible as having been obtained improperly. This meant that there was no evidence against B on any of the first 48 counts. But the 49th count was being a member of the IRA. This was allowed to be proved by reference to the admissions made by the defendant during the *voir dire*. On appeal, the House of Lords held that this was not proper, even though it had been a voluntary admission in answer to questions from his own counsel. Anything which emerged only at the *voir dire* and was relevant to the *voir dire* could not be admissible at the trial: 'if such evidence, being relevant, were admissible at the substantive trial, an accused person would not enjoy the complete freedom that he ought to have to contest the admissibility of his previous statements' (at p 709, per Lord Fraser). He would not feel free if what he said at the *voir dire* could be used against him at the trial. See also *Wong Kam-Ming*[1980] AC 247, PC. For discussion of whether there are any exceptions to the rule either at common law or as a result of the new rules on inferences from silence see P Mirfield, 'Two Side-effects of Sections 34 to 37 of the Criminal Justice and Public Order Act 1994', (1995) *Criminal Law Review*, 612, 617-24.

If, however, he used the *voir dire* to boast of having committed the offences in question or used the occasion to make a political speech, that would be irrelevant to the issue of admissibility and different considerations would apply.

When the trial is in the magistrates' courts, a challenge to the admissibility of a confession cannot easily be conducted in the same way. There is no jury to withdraw while the court makes up its mind on the question of admissibility. On the other hand, it is not satisfactory for the magistrates to consider admissibility at the same time as considering the question of weight and truth. In *F (an infant) v Chief Constable of Kent* [1982] Crim LR 682, Lord Lane CJ said: 'where matters are being conducted before magistrates, there is no question of a "trial within a trial" because magistrates are judges of both fact and law and determine questions of guilt and innocence'. But this does mean that, where a confession is to be challenged, the chances of a fair trial are inevitably greater in the Crown Court than in the magistrates' court. (See, for discussion of this issue, WMS Tildesley and WF Bullock, 'Challenging Confessions in the Magistrates' Courts', *Justice of the Peace*, 16 April 1983, p 243.)

In *R v Liverpool Juvenile Court, ex p R* [1987] 2 All ER 668, it was argued on behalf of the juvenile accused that the *Chief Constable of Kent* case had in effect been displaced by the provisions of s 76 of the Police and Criminal Evidence Act 1984 which dealt with the admissibility of confessions (see below). The Divisional Court upheld the contention. It ruled that, where the question of the admissibility of a confession is raised by the accused, the magistrates must hold a trial within a trial at which the defendant would be entitled to give and call evidence relating purely to the question of admissibility. (For comment see B Gibson, 'Justices and Trials Within Trials– Yet Again', *Justice of the Peace*, 2 May 1987, p 275.)

(6) TO PROTECT POLICE INFORMERS, ETC

The courts have for decades recognised the principle that the identity of police informers should, if possible, be kept secret and that surveillance methods should not necessarily become known to the defence. As long ago as 1890 Lord Esher MR referred to the rule protecting the disclosure of the name of an informant as a rule in public prosecutions. (*Marks v Beyfus* (1890) 25 QBD 494.) In *Rankine* [1986] QB 861 the appellant argued on appeal that his conviction was unsafe and unsatisfactory because he had not been allowed by the trial judge to cross-examine the police witnesses as to the location of the observation point from which they had allegedly seen him repeatedly selling drugs. The Court of Appeal refused to quash the conviction. See to the same effect *Johnson* [1988] 1 WLR 1377.

However, this principle of public interest exclusion of evidence may have to give way to the even higher principle that the defendant should not be unfairly impeded from establishing his innocence. Thus in *Brown* (1987) 87 Cr App Rep 52 the Court of Appeal quashed convictions because the trial judge had refused to allow police officers to be questioned about the details of their surveillance operation.

Note that no equivalent tenderness toward the defendant is shown when his case on appeal is that the jury considered material that should not have been known to them. The principle in such cases is that the Court of Appeal will not permit such a contention to be put (see *Thompson*, pp 515–16 below).

See generally JA Andrews, 'Public Interest and Criminal Proceedings', 104 *Law Quarterly Review*, 1988, pp 410–21.

(7)   CROSS-EXAMINATION OF RAPE VICTIMS

At common law a rape victim giving evidence against her alleged attacker could be cross-examined about her sexual past. The purpose of the Sexual Offences (Amendment)Act 1976, s 2 was to restrict such questions. No such questions could be asked without the leave of the judge and no such questions could be asked about the sexual experience of the complainant with anyone other than the defendant. Moreover the Act provided that the judge should only give such consent if satisfied that it would be unfair to the defendant to refuse to allow the evidence to be adduced. But it was felt that the 1976 Act did not do the job[115] and the Youth Justice and Criminal Evidence Act 1999 returned to the issue.

Section 41 of the Act provided that evidence or questioning about a complainant's sexual conduct was not admissible as evidence of whether he or she consented to the offence except where the evidence or questions related to acts at or about the time of the incident that was the subject of the charge. Evidence or questioning about sexual behaviour was admissible, however, in relation to whether sex took place or whether the defendant believed his alleged victim consented, provided it related to specific instances of sexual behaviour at or about the time in question and that its main purpose was not to impugn the witness's character.[116]

---

[115] See Louise Ellison, 'Cross-Examination in Rape Trials', (1998) *Criminal Law Review*, pp 605–15.

[116] See N Kibble, 'The sexual history provisions: Charting a course between inflexible legislative rules and wholly untrammelled judicial discretion' [2000] *Criminal Law Review*, p 274.

In *R v A (No 2)* [2001] 3 All ER 1 the House of Lords held that, despite the wording of section 41, the complainant could be asked questions about her sexual conduct that if excluded would endanger the defendant's right to a fair trial under Article 6 of the ECHR. The defendant had been barred by the trial judge from asking questions about their sexual relationship in the three weeks before the alleged rape. The House of Lords upheld the Court of Appeal's decision thereby overturning the trial judge's ruling – and Parliament's intention in passing s 41.[117]

(8)   EVIDENCE OBTAINED BY IMPROPER MEANS

The common law made a distinction between *confessions* that were improperly obtained and other kinds of evidence obtained in regular ways. Broadly, confessions were liable to be excluded, whilst other evidence was normally admitted in evidence.

(i)   Confessions

THE COMMON LAW

There was a well-established common law rule going back some two hundred years that a confession could not be admitted in evidence if it was 'involuntary', which was defined to mean obtained as the result of a threat or promise held out by a person in authority.[118]

The rule was expressed in the Judges' Rules, principle (e) of the preamble of which stated: 'it is a fundamental condition of the admissibility in evidence against any person ... that it shall have been voluntary in the sense that it has not been obtained from him by fear of prejudice or hope of advantage, exercised or held out by a person in authority or by oppression.' An example of the principle being applied was *R v Smith*, decided in 1959:

R v Smith [1959] 2 QB 35 (Courts Martial Appeal Court)

[The appellant, a soldier, was charged with the murder by stabbing of a soldier of another regiment during a barrack-room fight. Immediately after the fight the appellant's regimental sergeant-major put his company on parade and

---

[117]   For discussion see J Temkin, 'Sexual History Evidence: Beware the Backlash' [2003] *Criminal Law Review*, p 217; and Di Birch, 'Untangling Sexual History Evidence: A rejoinder to Professor Temkin', [2003] *Criminal Law Review*, p 370.

[118]   This was held to include a father–see *R v Moore* (1972) 56 Cr App Rep 373; and *R v Cleary* (1963) 48 Cr App Rep 116. In *R v Thompson* (1978) Times, 18 January, it was held to include also a social worker who said: 'Do not admit something you have not done but it is always the best policy to be honest. If you were concerned tell him about it and get the matter cleared up for your own sake.' The judge excluded the accused's confession. On the concept of the person in authority, see P Mirfield, 'Confessions–the "Person in Authority" Requirement' (1981) *Criminal Law Review*, p 92.

indicated that the men would be kept there until he learnt who had been involved in the fighting. At the trial the judge-advocate admitted in evidence a statement made by the appellant to the sergeant-major at that parade, confessing to the stabbing. Evidence was also given of a subsequent confession made the following day to a sergeant of the Special Investigation Branch after a caution had been administered.

Lord Parker CJ, giving the judgment of the court, stated the facts and continued:]

The court is quite clear that while there was nothing improper in the action taken by the regimental sergeant-major, the evidence of what took place was clearly inadmissible at the prisoner's trial. What the sergeant-major did might well have been a very useful course of action in order to enable further inquiries to be made, but the court is satisfied that if the only evidence against the prisoner was a confession obtained in those circumstances, it would be quite inadmissible at his trial. It has always been a fundamental principle of the courts, and something quite apart from the Judges' Rules of Practice, that a prisoner's confession outside the court is only admissible if it is voluntary. In deciding whether an admission is voluntary the court has been at pains to hold that even the most gentle, if I may put it in that way, threats or slight inducements will taint a confession. To say to all those on parade, 'You are staying here and are not going to bed until one of you owns up' is in the view of this court clearly a threat. It might also, I suppose, be looked upon as an inducement in that the converse is true, 'If one of you will come forward and own up, the rest of you can go to bed'; but whichever way one looks at it, the court is of opinion that while the action was perfectly proper and a useful start no doubt to inquiries, evidence in regard thereto was clearly inadmissible.

The court then considered the second confession made by the accused the next morning. It ruled that this was admissible because the effect of the threat or inducement was then spent.

The *Smith* case did not end in the defendant's conviction being quashed. An even more striking case was that of *R v Zaveckas* [1970] 1 All ER 413 because the court there did quash the conviction when it found that the confession had followed upon an improper promise. The case was even more remarkable in that the promise came as the result of a request from the accused. He was told by the police that an identification parade had been arranged and if he was not picked out he would be allowed to go. He asked whether he would be given bail at once if he made a statement. The officer said 'yes' and he then made a statement admitting guilt. The Court of Appeal Criminal Division ruled that the statement should have been held inadmissible because it was an inducement held out by a person in authority. With regret, the court said, it had to quash the conviction. Similarly, in *Northam* (1967) 52 Cr App Rep 97, the Court of Appeal quashed a conviction based on a confession after the accused had asked a police officer whether it would be possible for a second offence to be taken into consideration at his forthcoming trial rather than being the basis of a later separate trial. The police officer said the police would have no objection. The Court of Appeal said this amounted to a fatal inducement.

The common law objection to the admissibility of confessions obtained through *oppression* appears to be more recent than for confessions obtained by threats or promises. The preamble to the Judges' Rules mentioned 'oppression' as one reason for a confession being found 'involuntary'. For judicial statements on the subject see for instance *Prager* [1972] 1 WLR 260; *Westlake* [1979] Crim LR 652; *Hudson* [1981] Crim LR 107; *Gowan* [1982] Crim LR 821.

Confessions obtained as a result of threats, promises or oppression were inadmissible in law. Once they were classified in this way the judge had no discretion. Confessions obtained in breach of the Judges' Rules, by contrast, were only inadmissible in the judge's discretion, though it was not easy to get the judges to exercise this discretion. In *Prager* [1972] 1 WLR 260, Lord Justice Edmund Davies dealt with the submission by counsel that a statement was inadmissible because the police had not cautioned the defendant before questioning him, even though they plainly had plenty of evidence justifying reasonable suspicion, and that the questioning was therefore in breach of Rule 2 which required a suspect to be cautioned when the police had sufficient admissible evidence reasonably to suspect him. (The defendant was taken from his house in the early hours of the morning and on arrival at the police station was questioned at length about complicity in espionage activities.) The Court of Appeal refused to hold that the confession should have been excluded.

See, to same effect, *Conway v Hotten* [1976] 2 All ER 213 and *Greaves v D* [1980] Crim LR 435. A breach of the Judges' Rules alone was not therefore likely to commend itself as a reason for excluding evidence. For a more recent application of the doctrine in dramatic circumstances see, however, the Privy Council's quashing of a murder conviction in Hong Kong (*Lam Chi-ming* [1991] 3 All ER 172) because of misbehaviour by the police.

Later changes in the admissibility rules regarding confessions In its 1972 11th Report, the Criminal Law Revision Committee recommended by a majority that confessions should only be excluded where it was likely that the threat or inducement would produce an unreliable confession. It would be for the judge to imagine that he was present at the questioning and to consider in the light of all the evidence 'whether at the point when the threat was uttered or the inducement offered, any confession which the accused might make as a result of it would be likely to be unreliable'. The proposed test applied not to the confession actually made but 'to any confession which he might have made in consequence of the threat or inducement' (para 65). The Committee did not make it clear whether the test should relate to the reasonable defendant in that situation or to the accused himself–ie whether it should be objective or subjective.

This proposal was not at first implemented by legislation but in the period between the CLRC's Report and the Police and Criminal Evidence Act 1984 the common law changed and came somewhat into line with the approach adopted by the CLRC.

This was mainly achieved by two cases. In the first, *DPP v Ping Lin* [1975] 3 All ER 175, the defendant confessed after the officer in the case had assured him 'If you show the judge that you have helped the police to trace bigger drug people, I am sure that he will bear it in mind when he sentences you.' The House of Lords upheld the trial judge's decision to allow the confession to be given in evidence. The question of voluntariness, the law lords held, was one of fact and causation.

The second case, *Rennie* [1982] 1 All ER 385, went even further. The officer admitted that the defendant confessed in return for a promise from the officer that he would in that event not bring the suspect's sister and mother into the affair. The Court of Appeal upheld the trial judge's decision to admit the confession. Giving judgment Lord Lane LCJ said it was for the court simply to take a commonsense view of whether the confession had been of the defendant's own free will. The fact that his confession was induced wholly or in part because he hoped the police would then not charge his mother or his sister did not make it involuntary.

Plainly, the test of whether a confession was voluntary had undergone a sea-change since decisions like *Smith* in 1959 and *Zaveckas* in 1970.

THE PHILIPS ROYAL COMMISSION

The Royal Commission on Criminal Procedure (1981) criticised the common law rule in regard to confessions (as it then stood), on the ground that it was unrealistic. It assumed, first, that suspects in the police station could be free from fear of prejudice or hope of advantage and, secondly, that it was possible to tell to what extent any particular suspect was affected by such fear or hope. Both assumptions, the Commission said, were false. Research conducted for the Commission by Dr Barrie Irving showed that even a trained psychologist present at the questioning of suspects could not tell what pressures were responsible for suspects making statements. But fear of prejudice and hope of advantage were in the very nature of the situation–regardless of what precisely was said or done by the police. (Report of the Royal Commission, 1981, para 4.73; based on B Irving, *Police Interrogation: A Case Study of Current Practice*, Royal Commission Research Study No 2, 1980.)

The Commission thought it would be better to abandon the vain attempt to distinguish between voluntary and involuntary confessions and to concentrate instead on the behaviour of the police officer. If the suspect was subjected to torture, violence, the threat of violence or inhuman or degrading treatment, any subsequent confession should be inadmissible. This would mark society's 'abhorrence of such conduct' (*Report*, para 4.132). But any lesser breach of the rules of questioning should only be liable to the consequence that the trial judge would warn the jury of the danger of relying on the resulting confession if there was no independent evidence (*Report*, para 4.133).

PACE

The proposal that the voluntariness test should be abolished met with considerable opposition, and the Conservative Government did not accept it. The Police and Criminal Evidence Act instead based its approach on the inadmissibility of any confession obtained as a result of oppression (as defined) or which was obtained in consequence of something 'likely in the circumstances to render unreliable any confession which might be made by the accused in consequence thereof':

Police and Criminal Evidence Act 1984, s 76

(1) In any proceedings a confession made by an accused person may be given in evidence against him in so far as it is relevant to any matter in issue in the proceedings and is not excluded by the court in pursuance of this section.

(2) If, in any proceedings where the prosecution proposes to give in evidence a confession made by an accused person, it is represented to the court that the confession was or may have been obtained–

(a) by oppression of the person who made it; or

(b) in consequence of anything said or done which was likely, in the circumstances existing at the time, to render unreliable any confession which might be made by him in consequence thereof,

the court shall not allow the confession to be given in evidence against him except in so far as the prosecution proves to the court beyond reasonable doubt that the confession (notwithstanding that it may be true) was not obtained as aforesaid.

'**Oppression**' as defined in s 76(8) 'includes torture, inhuman or degrading treatment, and the use or threat of violence'.

Various points arise:

(1) The burden of proof on questions of the admissibility of confessions lies on the prosecution–s 76(2).

(2) When any question of the admissibility of a confession arises it is for the judge to rule as to whether the evidence is admissible and for the jury to decide on whether it is to be believed (see *McCarthy* (1980) 70 Cr App Rep 270; *Ragho Prasad s/o Ram Autar Rao v R* [1981] 1 All ER 319).

(3) There is supposed to be a trial within a trial to determine the admissibility of a confession–even in the magistrates' court (see *R v Liverpool Juvenile Court, ex p R* [1988] QB 1). Moreover, the Court of Appeal has said obiter that the question of its admissibility cannot be considered by the court after the confession has been given in evidence (*Sat-Bhambra* (1988) 88 Cr App Rep 55, [1988] Crim LR 453). But this seems questionable.[119]

---

[119] See Professor JC Smith – a comment on the case after the report in the *Criminal Law Review*.

(4)   There have only been a few cases in which the courts have held that there was oppressive conduct by the police (s 76(2)(*a*)). In *Fulling* [1987] QB 426 the Court of Appeal made it clear that oppression would exist only very rarely. It gave the word its meaning in the *Oxford English Dictionary* as 'The exercise of authority or power in a burdensome, harsh or wrongful manner; unjust or cruel treatment of subjects, inferiors etc; the imposition of unreasonable or unjust burdens'.

In *Beales* [1991] Crim LR 118 the trial judge in the Norwich Crown Court found that questioning of the suspect for 35 minutes (!) 'stepped into the realm' of oppression because the police officer deliberately misled the suspect as to the existence of evidence of the offence. But the judge said that even if the police conduct was not oppressive under s 76(2)(*a*) the confession was certainly unreliable under s 76(2)(*b*). On the facts of the case it seems unlikely that the Court of Appeal would have upheld the trial judge's finding that there was evidence of oppression.

In *Davison* [1988] Crim LR 442, where there had been a whole series of breaches of the Act and the Codes of Practice, the judge held that the prosecution had failed to discharge the burden of proof on it to show that the confessions in a series of interviews had not been obtained as a result of oppression. He seemed to regard the unlawful detention of the suspect as of prime significance.

In the case of Timothy West in 1988 the trial judge held that police had been oppressive in constantly interrupting the defendant, shouting at him, using foul language to indicate that he was lying, and making it clear that they would continue questioning him until he confessed.

In *Paris, Abdullahi and Miller* (1992) 97 Cr App Rep 99 (the case of the 'Cardiff Three'), the Lord Chief Justice in the Court of Appeal said the court had been horrified by the hectoring and bullying manner of the police questioning of Miller who denied the murder charge over 300 times before making admissions. ('Short of physical violence, it is hard to conceive a more hostile and intimidating approach to a suspect. It is impossible to convey on the printed page the pace, force and menace of the officer's delivery.') The Court of Appeal quashed all three convictions.

In the George Heron case in November 1993, Mr Justice Mitchell ruled that confessions and admissions to the murder of a seven year old girl were inadmissible because they had been obtained by oppression. The questioning had been conducted without any hectoring or shouting. But the judge held that oppression existed in falsely telling the accused that he had been identified, in pounding him with being a killer and with sexual motives for the killing and in telling him that it was in his interest to tell the truth when it had been made clear that the police regarded the truth to be that he had done the killing. The police had been engaged in breaking the defendant's resolve to make no admissions.

It is worthy of note that in both the Cardiff Three case and the George Heron case the suspect had had his legal adviser present throughout the interviews.

UNRELIABILITY (S 76(2)(b))

The formula adopted in s 76(2)(b) (p 452 above) was effectively that recommended by the Criminal Law Revision Committee in its 1972 Report. The fact that the new test abandoned the previous law as reflected in decisions like *Zaveckas* (p 449 above) is confirmed by the provision in Code C that if a suspect asks an officer 'what action will be taken in the event of his answering questions, making a statement or refusing to do either, the officer may inform him what action he proposes to take in that event provided that the action is itself proper and warranted (Code C, para 11.5). But officers are still admonished not to indicate 'except in answer to a direct question' what action will be taken if the person being interviewed answers questions, makes a statement or refuses to do either (ibid).

The issue of reliability of confessions has given rise to a number of different points:
(1) The words 'in consequence of anything said or done' mean said or done by someone other than the suspect–*Goldenberg* [1988] Crim LR 678.
(2) The test of 'likely in the circumstances existing at the time' is objective and hypothetical. It is not what the officer thought was the suspect's mental state but what it actually was.[120] The circumstances existing at the time can include the fact that the suspect had a very low IQ or was very suggestible. (See *Silcott, Braithwaite and Raghip* (1991) Times, 9 December; *McKenzie* (1992) 96 Cr App Rep 98, CA.) Also the truth or otherwise of the confession does not come into the question.
(3) But although the words of the subsection seem to require a causal link between what was said and done in fact, in some of the cases the courts have found a confession to be unreliable where there was no such link. The courts have treated breaches of the Code as sufficient to establish unreliability even without any evidence that the breaches led directly to the admissions or confession. (See for instance *DPP v Blake* [1989] 1 WLR 432; and *Doolan* [1988] Crim LR 747.[121])

Examples of things said or done which have been held to constitute grounds for holding a confession to be unreliable include: an offer of bail;[122] minimising the significance of a serious (sex) offence and suggesting that psychiatric help might be appropriate;[123] saying to a defendant who has previously denied the offence, 'Do I gather that you are now admitting the offence?';[124] falsely telling the suspect that his voice has been recognised on tape;[125] falsely telling the suspect that he has been identified by a witness;[126] indicating that the suspect will have to stay in the police station until the matter is cleared up.[127]

---

[120] *Everett* [1988] Crim LR 826.
[121] This was an especially striking case since some of the breaches considered relevant by the court occurred *after* the confession.
[122] *Barry* (1991) 95 Cr App Rep 384, CA.
[123] *Delaney* (1988) 88 Cr App Rep 338, CA.
[124] *Waters* [1989] Crim LR 62, CA.
[125] *Blake* [1989] 1 WLR 432.
[126] *Heron*, text, p ? above.
[127] *Jasper* (24 April 1994, unreported), CA.

Examples of things *not* said or done which have been held to be grounds for holding a confession to be unreliable include: failure to obtain a solicitor;[128] breaches in the provisions of Code C;[129] or failure to see that the suspect has an appropriate adult.[130] But such grounds will not *necessarily* result in a confession being held to be inadmissible.[131]

Runciman Royal Commission The Runciman Commission, by a majority of eight to three, rejected the suggestion that a confession should only be admissible if corroborated. But it recommended that the judge should be required to give the jury a warning, adapted to the circumstances of the case similar to that in identification cases, about the dangers of relying on an uncorroborated confession (Report, p 68, para 87).

For further reading on confession evidence see especially: DJ Birch, 'The PACE Hots Up: Confessions and Confusions under the 1984 Act' [1989] *Criminal Law Review*, p 95; Birch, 'The Evidence Provisions', *Northern Ireland Legal Quarterly*, 1989, p 411; Ian Dennis, 'Miscarriages of Justice and the Law of Confessions: Evidentiary Issues and Solutions', [1993] *Public Law*, pp 291–313; M Zander, *The Police and Criminal Evidence Act 1984* (4th edn, Sweet and Maxwell, 2003), pp 313-27; I H Dennis, *The Law of Evidence* (2nd edn, Sweet and Maxwell, 2002) ch 6.

(ii) Evidence, including confessions, illegally or improperly obtained

Whereas, as has been seen above, the common law historically took a strict view of the admissibility of confession evidence, its approach to other evidence was different. Until 1979 the rule was that the courts had a discretion as to whether such evidence should be admitted. There were many cases in which this proposition had been stated. The origin of the doctrine was a dictum of Lord Chief Justice Goddard, giving the judgement of the Privy Council in *Kuruma, Son of Kaniu v R* [1955] AC 197 at 204: 'No doubt in a criminal case the judge always has a discretion to disallow evidence if the strict rules of admissibility would operate unfairly against the accused. ... If, for instance, some admission of some piece of evidence, eg a document, had been obtained from a defendant by a trick, no doubt the judge might properly rule it out'.

See also *Jeffrey v Black* [1978] 1 All ER 555 in which Widgery LCJ said that the discretion, though not often exercised, certainly existed: 'But if the case is exceptional, if the case is such that not only have the police officers entered without authority, but they have been guilty of trickery or they have misled someone, or they have been oppressive or they have been unfair, or in other respects they have behaved in a manner which is morally reprehensible, then it is open to the justices to apply their discretion and decline to allow the particular evidence to be let in as part of the trial.'

---

128   *McGovern* (1990) 92 Cr App Rep 228, CA; *Chung* (1990) 92 Cr App Rep 314, CA.
129   *Delaney* (1988) 88 Cr App Rep 338, CA.; *Doolan* (1991) 12 Cr App Rep (S) 634, CA.
130   *Everett* [1988] Crim LR 826. *Moss* (1990) 91 Cr App Rep 371, CA.
131   *Waters* [1989] Crim LR 62; *Maguire* (1989) 90 Cr App Rep 115, CA.

In spite of the existence of the discretion, there were few cases in which it was exercised (see Gerald Coplan, 'The Judicial Discretion to Disallow Admissible Evidence', *Solicitors' Journal*, 18 December 1970, p 945). But the House of Lords in *Sang* [1980] AC 402 either abolished the discretion or at least drastically curtailed it. The case concerned a defence of entrapment–the defendant claimed that he had been induced to commit the offence by an informer acting on the instructions of the police. All the judges in the House of Lords ruled that there was no such defence as entrapment in English law. But they went on to consider the more general question whether a judge had a discretion to exclude relevant evidence. They ruled, again unanimously, that (save for confessions or evidence tantamount to a confession) no discretion existed to exclude evidence simply on the ground that it had been illegally or improperly obtained! Such illegality might be a factor to be taken into account in sentencing, or might be the basis for civil proceedings or disciplinary action against the police. The only basis for excluding relevant evidence was where its effect would be unduly prejudicial–for example, evidence of previous similar acts as in *Noor Mohamed v R* [1949] AC 182 or *Harris v DPP* [1952] AC 694–or where it would be unfair to admit it. But unfairness could not be shown merely by the fact that the evidence had been illegally obtained. In fact the nature of 'unfairness' that would entitle the judge to exclude evidence in his discretion is obscure. Lord Scarman, for instance, said that each case must depend on its circumstances: 'All I would say is that the principle of fairness, though concerned exclusively with the use of evidence at trial, is not susceptible to categorisation or classification, and is wide enough in some circumstances to embrace the way in which, after the crime, evidence has been obtained from the accused' (at p 290).

For comment on the *Sang* case, see JD Jackson, 'Unfairness and the Judicial Discretion to Exclude Evidence', *New Law Journal*, 1980, p 585. See, generally, JD Heydon, 'Illegally Obtained Evidence' (1973) *Criminal Law Review*, p 690, and AJ Ashworth, 'Excluding Evidence as Protecting Rights' (1977) *Criminal Law Review*, p 723.

THE PHILIPS ROYAL COMMISSION

The Royal Commission on Criminal Procedure recommended that the admissibility of improperly obtained evidence other than confessions be substantially confirmed. It did not accept the view that illegally or improperly obtained evidence should basically be excluded, as it is in the United States by the doctrine that the fruit of the poisoned tree should not be eaten.

The Commission said it was not appropriate to use the rules as to the admissibility of evidence to discipline the police or to discourage police malpractice. First, it could only affect the small minority of cases where the defendant pleaded not guilty and would therefore not discourage improper behaviour by the police in the majority of cases. Secondly, the challenge on admissibility would be so distant in time from the moment of the improper conduct as not to be an effective deterrent. Experience in the United States suggested that it was not effective as a deterrent to misconduct by the police. The proper way to deter or to deal with misconduct by the police was through police disciplinary and supervisory procedures, civil actions for damages and the machinery of complaints against the police (Report, paras 4.123–8).

The Commission equally did not favour the 'reverse onus' exclusionary rule recommended by the Australian Law Reform Commission, under which improperly obtained evidence is inadmissible unless the prosecution can satisfy the judge that there was some special reason why the impropriety should be condoned. Such a rule, the Commission said, would be difficult to administer in a uniform way. It would not reduce trials within trials. The fact that the judge had a discretion would weaken the deterrent effect on the police.

The Royal Commission's Report attracted severe criticism from some quarters for its failure to recommend an exclusionary rule–see, for instance, Jim Driscoll, 'Excluding Illegally Obtained Evidence–Can We Learn from the United States?', *Legal Action Group Bulletin*, June 1981, p 131. See also by same author, 'Excluding Illegally Obtained Evidence in the United States' (1987) *Criminal Law Review*, p 553.

PACE

The Government disagreed with the Royal Commission. At a very late stage it included a provision to introduce an expanded version of the common law discretion. The final version of s 78 provided:

> 78. (1) In any proceedings the court may refuse to allow evidence on which the prosecution proposes to rely to be given if it appears to the court that, having regard to all the circumstances, including the circumstances in which the evidence was obtained, the admission of the evidence would have such an adverse effect on the fairness of the proceedings that the court ought not to admit it.
>
> (2) Nothing in this section shall prejudice any rule of law requiring a court to exclude evidence.

The impact of s 78 has been remarkable. Contrary to what most commentators expected, the judges have forged the somewhat ambiguous words of s 78 into a powerful weapon to hold the police accountable for breaches of the law and of the Codes of Practice.

There are now a very large number of cases interpreting and applying s 78 which is by far the most frequently used section of the Act. A high proportion of the decided cases are Court of Appeal decisions. Reviewing this mass of case law for the 2003 edition of his book on PACE the writer expressed his impression:

> Not that the courts have articulated a consistent and all-embracing theory for the application of s 78. Various principles explaining the exercise of the discretion to exclude evidence have been suggested by academic commentators. These include the Reliability principle (to promote the reliability of evidence),

the Disciplinary principle (to penalise the police for breaches of the rules as a way of promoting adherence to the rules), and the Protective principle (to protect the accused).[132] Many cases could be said to fall within those broad approaches–though there is little or no sign that the judges themselves deal with the problems in that way. The evidence from the cases is to the contrary.[133]

The writer believes rather that s 78 has become both established and accepted as a means for the courts to determine what breaches of the rules or improper conduct are unacceptable on a case by case basis without any clearly articulated theory. Usually, even when there has been some breach or impropriety, the court allows the evidence in and even when it finds there to have been impropriety, the Court of Appeal usually ends by dismissing the appeal. But there have also been many cases, including non-confession cases, in which the appeal court has quashed a conviction because of such improprieties. In the great majority of such cases the court's chief concern seems to be that the verdict should be based on reliable evidence. But sometimes, the court is expressing a more fundamental concern directed not so much to the result in the particular case as to a view that the system demands a minimum of procedural correctness and moral integrity.[134]

To some extent the decisions of the courts applying s 78 can be systematised. Certain basic distinctions have emerged. But there remains (and will always remain) a significant and irreducible degree of discretion left to the court.... Professor Diane Birch, writing about the entrapment cases, has suggested that 'The more principled the discretion can be said to be, and the more its underlying aims can be articulated, the more consistent will be the decisions made under it'.[135] She cites another academic view of the need to avoid the 'mushiness and unpredictability of a general doctrine of exclusion for "unfairness"'.[136] Consistency in the application of a discretion to exclude evidence on the grounds of unfairness may be desirable but in the end it is

---

[132]   See especially AJ Ashworth, 'Excluding Evidence as Protecting Rights' [1977] Crim LR 723, and *The Criminal Process*, 2nd edn, Clarendon, Oxford, 1998; and AAS Zuckerman, *The Principles of Criminal Evidence* (1989).

[133]   See M Hunter, 'Judicial Discretion: Section 78 in Practice' [1994] Crim LR 558 reporting on an empirical study in Leeds Crown Court. The judges she interviewed were unanimous in rejecting the idea that they considered any of these theoretical principles when deciding whether to exclude disputed evidence. The writer cannot say that he is surprised at this finding which would probably be equally true of the Court of Appeal.

[134]   See further Ian Dennis, 'Reconstructing the Law of Criminal Evidence' [1989] 42 *Current Legal Problems* 21; and AAS Zuckerman, 'Illegally Obtained Evidence: Discretion as a Guardian of Legitimacy', [1987] 40 *Current Legal Problems*, 55.

[135]   'Excluding Evidence from Entrapment: What is a "fair cop"?' [1994] *Current Legal Problems*, 73 at p 89.

[136]   JD Heydon, 'Entrapment and Unfairly Obtained Evidence in the House of Lords' [1980] Crim LR 129 at p 134.

unattainable. [*M Zander, The Police and Criminal Evidence Act 1984* (4th edn 2003, Sweet & Maxwell), pp 334-335.]

See also IH Dennis, *The Law of Evidence* (2nd ed, Sweet and Maxwell), Ch 8.

By far the most common basis for the Court of Appeal to apply s 78 has been 'significant and substantial' breaches of the PACE rules. The cases concern (1) breaches of the Act and or the Codes such as failure to tell the suspect (D) his rights, not giving D access to a solicitor, not cautioning D, not providing an appropriate adult, not complying with the formalities regarding interviews, not complying with identification procedures; and (2) obtaining evidence by tricks, undercover police work and the like. (For references to the actual cases see the writer's book on PACE, *The Police and Criminal Evidence Act 1984*, pp 336-48.)

The Court of Appeal has repeatedly said that each case must be decided on its own facts. It has refused to lay down guidelines as to how the discretion under s 78 should be exercised. The decision to exclude evidence is not taken to penalise the police. (See for instance *R v Delaney* (1988) 88 Cr App Rep 338, CA.) In order to succeed under s 78 the defence have to establish that a significant and substantial breach of the rules or other impropriety has occurred, that it affects the fairness of the proceedings which is sufficiently serious as to require that the court exclude the evidence. In *R v Walsh* (1989) 91 Cr App Rep 161, the Court of Appeal said: 'The task of the court is not merely to consider whether there would be an adverse effect on the fairness of the proceedings, but such an adverse effect that justice requires the evidence to be excluded.'

For the view that the courts tend to exercise the discretion in s 78 against professional criminals see M Doherty, 'Judicial discretion: victimising the villains?', *International Journal of Evidence and Proof*, 1999, vol 3, no 1, pp 44-56.

THE ECHR AND THE FAIRNESS OF TRIALS

In *Khan (Sultan) v United Kingdom* [137] the European Court of Human Rights held that although there had been violations of Arts 8 and 13 of the Convention, the defendant had not been deprived of his right to a fair trial under Art 6(1) of the Convention. The case concerned reception of evidence from a listening device installed on his home by the police.[138] The European Court reached the same decision in *P G and J H v United Kingdom*[139] which concerned covert listening devices both at the suspects' home and at the police station. The House of Lords adopted the same

---

[137]   (2000) 31 EHRR 1016, [2000] Crim LR 684.
[138]   For critical comment see Professor Ashworth's commentary in the *Criminal Law Review* at 684-86.
[139]   [2002] Crim LR 308.

approach in *Sultan Khan*[140] and in *P*[141] In both it held that the question whether the trial was fair should be judged by application of section 78.

Further reading A Ashworth, 'Article 6 and the Fairness of Trials', (1999) *Criminal Law Review*, 261-72; Sir Robert Walker, 'The Impact of European Standards on the Right to a Fair Trial in Civil Proceedings in United Kingdom Domestic Law', (1999) *European Human Rights Law Review*, 4-14; Francis G Jacobs, 'The Right to a Fair Trial in European Law', (1999) *European Human Rights Law Review* 141-56. For fuller treatment see, for instance, B Emmerson and A Ashworth, *Human Rights and Criminal Proceedings*, (1999, Sweet and Maxwell); B Emmerson and A Ashworth, *Human Rights and Criminal Justice* (2001, Sweet and Maxwell); Lord Lester and D Pannick (eds) *Human Rights Law and Practice*, (1999, Butterworths), pp 133-60.

ABUSE OF PROCESS

There is a separate common law doctrine known as 'abuse of process' that the court can stop a case if it regards it contrary to the public interest to permit it to continue. Thus in *R v Horseferry Road Magistrates' Court, ex p Bennett* [1994] AC 42, [1993] 3 All ER 138 the House of Lords ruled that a stay was appropriate where B had been forcibly abducted and brought to this country to face trial in disregard of extradition laws. Lord Griffiths said that the judiciary should not 'countenance behaviour that threatens either human rights or the rule of law' and that if a serious abuse of power has occurred the court 'should express its disapproval by refusing to act upon it.'[142] Cp *Latif and Shahzad* [1996] 1 All ER 353 where the House of Lords refused to apply the doctrine in a case where S was lured by a customs officer to come to this country to collect a shipment of heroin S had sent here. ('The conduct of the customs officer was not so unworthy or shameful that it was an affront to the public conscience to allow the prosecution to proceed.' (per Lord Steyn, p 361)). In a speech, with which the other four Law Lords agreed, Lord Steyn said:

> The speeches in *Bennett* conclusively establish that proceedings may be stayed in the exercise of the judge's discretion not only where a fair trial is impossible, but also where it would be contrary to the public interest in the integrity of the criminal justice system that a trial should take place. An infinite variety of cases could arise. General guidance as to how the discretion should be exercised in particular circumstances will not be useful. But it is possible to say that in a case such as the present the judge must weigh in the balance the public interest in ensuring that those who are charged with grave crimes should be tried and the competing public interest in not conveying the impression that the court will adopt the approach that the end justifies any means'. (p 361)

---

[140]   [1997] AC 558.
[141]   [2001] 1 AC 146, HL.
[142]   P 62.

See further M Mackarel and C Gane, 'Admitting Irregularly or Illegally Obtained Evidence from Abroad into Criminal Proceedings – a Common Law Approach' (1997) *Criminal Law Review* 721-29. The authors criticise the laxity of common law courts in the United States, Canada, Australia and this country for their failure to apply the standard set in *Bennett*. Lord Steyn in *Latif and Shahzad* said that the court had to undertake a balancing exercise. Mackarel and Gane suggest that 'the balance has been tipping heavily in favour of the requirements of effective crime control, to the extent that the irregular and illegal activities of law enforcement agencies are considered to have little bearing on the fairness or the propriety of any subsequent trial' (p 728).

There are also other applications of the doctrine of abuse of process – for instance to stop cases where there has been egregious delay.[143]

---

[143]   See *R v Derby Crown Court, ex p Brooks* (1985) 80 Cr App Rep 164; *A-G's Reference (No 1 of 1990)*(1992) 95 Cr App Rep 296. See generally the series of five articles by F G Davies in *Justice of the Peace*, vol 162, 1998, 3, 10, 17, 24 and 31 January and the three 1999 follow-up articles, vol 163, 6, 27 March and 17 April.

Chapter 5

The jury

1. The origins of the jury system

The original concept of the jury was precisely the opposite of what it later became. The members of the jury were chosen as persons who were likely to know what had happened or, if not, they were supposed to find out before the trial. In the thirteenth century it was 'the duty of the jurors, so soon as they have been summoned, to make inquiries about the facts of which they will have to speak when they come before the court. They must collect testimony; they must weigh it and state the net result in a verdict' (F Pollock and FW Maitland, *The History of English Law*, 2nd edn 1898, pp 624–5). Medieval juries came more to speak than to listen.

The transformation of the medieval active jury into the passive courtroom triers of fact is not well understood either in its timing or its causes. Probably in the later fifteenth century, but certainly by the sixteenth, it had become expected that the jury would be ignorant of the facts of the case.

2. Eligibility for jury service

Until 1974 eligibility for jury service was governed largely by wholly out-of-date property qualifications. This was the subject of inquiry by the Morris Committee, which reported in 1965 and whose report was implemented by the Juries Act 1974.

(a) Composition of the jury list

Report of the (Morris) Departmental Committee on Jury Service, 1965, Cmnd 2627, paras 38–42

38. Under the present qualifications eligibility is in practice confined to 'householders'. In general, this is taken to mean the person who is liable to pay

the rates in respect of separately rated accommodation. In most families this is the husband (which is why, as will be seen later, only a relatively small proportion of jurors are women).

29. Another restriction on the householder's eligibility is that his premises must be rated at not less than £30 in the counties of London and Middlesex and not less than £20 elsewhere. At the time the Juries Act 1825 was passed, there must have been relatively few houses with the necessary rateable value. Successive revaluations have enormously increased the number of houses rated at the qualifying value, and we were informed by the Government Social Survey that 81% of domestic hereditaments in England and Wales are at present rated at £30 or more; no figure is readily available for those rated at £20 or more, but we have been told that for the country as a whole the proportion excluded by the rateable value limitation is now unlikely to exceed 10%. ...

42. It is estimated that there are 7.15 million names marked as eligible for jury service on the 1964 electoral registers for England and Wales, which is 22.5% of the 31.77 million names on the registers. This estimate was supplied to us by the Social Survey Division of the Central Office of Information, and was based on counts made of a sample of pages of the registers for 48 parliamentary constituencies.

The Morris Committee recommended that, subject to certain exempted categories, juries ought to be selected from all those on the electoral register. This was eventually implemented. See the Juries Act 1974. Under this Act a person is eligible for jury service who is between 18 and 70, on the register of electors[1] and has been resident in the UK for at least five years since the age of thirteen. (Until 1988 the age limit was 65 but the Criminal Justice Act 1988, s 119 provided that a person who is between 65 and 70 is eligible though he cannot be required to serve.)

(b)   Those ineligible, disqualified or excused

Certain persons, however, have been 'ineligible', 'disqualified' or 'excused'. Those *ineligible* were basically persons who it was thought would exercise undue influence in the jury room by virtue of their professional knowledge about the justice business – judges, lawyers, other fee earners in solicitors' offices, court staff, police officers, prison officers, probation officers and the like. In *R v Salt* [1996] Crim LR 517, the Court of Appeal quashed the conviction when the supervising usher in the court contacted his son when there were insufficient numbers to serve on a jury. This had

---

1   Lord Justice Auld's Report (ch 5, para 23, p 144), recommended that this should be broadened to include persons on other specified publicly maintained lists or directories, for instance, by the Driver and Vehicle Licensing Authority, the Department for Work and Pensions, the Inland Revenue and telephone directories. The proposal was intended to address the finding of Home Office research that close to 10% of those eligible to register on the electoral roll are not registered. This proposal was not adopted by the Government.

happened on other previous occasions. The court held that the selection of the son of an usher who regularly attended as a juror fell within the spirit of the disqualification in Sch 1 of the Juries Act 1974 which made the officers and court staff of any court ineligible for jury service. The selection of this juror was outside what was permissible in terms of random selection so far as practicable.

The list of those ineligible also includes clergymen of any religious denomination on the ground that they might exert undue influence in the jury room by virtue of their office. The Runciman Royal Commission on Criminal Justice recommended that this last category of exclusion from jury service be abolished. ('We do not see why clergymen and members of religious orders should not be eligible for jury service' (Report, p 132, para 57).)

In many states in the United States, ineligibility on grounds of occupation has recently been eliminated. Even judges and lawyers are now thought to be eligible to serve on juries!

Lord Justice Auld in his Report urged that we follow the American example. ('In my view, no one should be automatically ineligible or excusable from jury service simply because he or she is a member of a certain profession or holds a particular office or job.'[2]) The recommendation was adopted in the Criminal Justice Bill 002/03. Schedule 27 of the Bill removes the status of 'ineligibility' for jury service except for persons who are 'mentally disordered'[3] or disqualified[4] Anyone who previously was ineligible who does not wish to serve must apply for excusal or delay (on which see below).

Disqualified The Juries Act 1974 (Sch 1, Part 2) has a list of categories of persons disqualified from jury service by reason of their criminal convictions. Lord Justice Auld did not propose any change in this category of exclusion from jury service but the Criminal Justice Bill 2002/03 brings the list up to date.[5]

The Runciman Royal Commission said that research might show that 'contrary to general belief, the role played by jurors with prior criminal convictions is indistinguishable from the role played by any other category of juror' and

---

[2]   Chapter 5, para 14, p 140.

[3]   Defined in new Sch 1, Pt.1 of the 1974 Act inserted by Sch 27, para 15 of the Bill.

[4]   New JA 1974, s 1 inserted by Sch 27, para 2 of the Bill and repeal of JA 1974, s 9(1) by Sch 27, para 3 of the Bill.

[5]   It provided that those disqualified include: (1) persons who have ever been sentenced to life imprisonment or to a term of youth custody or detention of more than five years or to be detained during Her Majesty's pleasure; (2) anyone who in the previous ten years has served any part of a prison sentence, youth custody or detention or has been detained in a young offender institution or has had a suspended sentence of imprisonment or has been the subject of a community service order, community punishment order or community order as defined in the Criminal Justice Act 2003; and (3) anyone who in the previous five years has been subject to a probation order or a community rehabilitation order. (New Sch 1, Part 2 of the JA 1974 inserted by Sch 27, para 15 of the Bill.)

recommended that s 8 of the Contempt of Court Act (see p 518 below) be amended to permit research on juries to be done. This has not been implemented.

Concern has been expressed about persons who are disqualified from serving on juries. In *R v Mason* [1980] 3 All ER 777 the Court of Appeal held that it was lawful for the police to scrutinise jury panels. If names showed up with disqualifying criminal convictions the information could be passed to prosecuting counsel who could eliminate such people from a case by using the procedure known as 'stand by for the Crown' – see p 476 below. (See also the *Annex to the Attorney-General Guidelines on Jury Checks: Recommendations of the Association of Chief Police Officers* [1988] 3 All ER 1086 authorising checks in cases where the police thought it particularly important that disqualified persons should not serve on the jury.)

In 1987 the Home Secretary announced that in future the police would make random checks of would-be jurors to see whether any were disqualified. An unpublished Home Office study had shown that one in every 24 juries had on it a disqualified person. The checks would be made between the time that the jury was summoned and the date of jury service. (*The Times, The Guardian*, 26 September, 1987). The system was instituted in 1988. Each Crown Court Centre outside London was supposed to provide the police quarterly with a batch of names for checking. But the Runciman Royal Commission (p 133, para 60) said that the Association of Chief Police Officers (ACPO) had told it that often courts did not fulfil this requirement and frequently the information given was insufficient to enable a search of the records to be made. No doubt sometimes too the police fail to make the checks. It has been held that it is not correct for the judge to institute inquiries as to whether a particular juror is disqualified. (In *Obellin, Williams and Martin* [1997] 1 Cr App Rep 355 the Court of Appeal quashed convictions for robbery because the judge asked the prosecution to carry out a Criminal Records Office check on one juror after they had begun their deliberations.)

It may be that the new Central Summoning Bureau (see p 469 below) will sort out this problem. Lord Justice Auld's Report said that one of the first things the new Bureau should do was to establish an electronic link with the police criminal records system 'to enable automatic checks on any previous convictions of potential jurors'[6]

Excusals Some persons were excused as of right, if they wished, being persons deemed to have more important business elsewhere, such as MPs, members of the House of Lords, full-time members of the forces, and doctors, dentists and others in the medical profession.

Lord Justice Auld recommended that excusal as of right be abolished[7] The Government accepted the recommendation[8] and it was included in the Criminal

---

[6]   Chapter 5, para 16, p 141.
[7]   Chapter 5, para 37, p 150.
[8]   White Paper *Justice for All*, CM 5563, July 2001, para 7.27.

Justice Bill 2002/03. [9] As has been seen, the new principle is that no one is excusable from jury service unless they can show good reason, in which case jury service should normally be deferred to another date. The Solicitor General told the House of Commons that it was estimated that removing the categories of 'ineligible' and 'excused as of right' would add some four million names to the pool from which jurors are drawn. [10]

It has always been possible to request excusal on an individual ad hoc basis and this is very common. Something like a quarter of a million persons are summoned for jury service per year. A 1999 Home Office research study, based on a sample of 50,000 people summoned for jury service, found that only about a third (34%) were actually available for service. Those who were ineligible, excused as of right or disqualified accounted for 13% of the sample. Some 8% had moved from their address and another 7% simply failed to attend. One of Auld's recommendations was that there should be 'rigorous and well-publicised enforcement of the obligation to undertake jury service' with fixed penalties subject to a right of appeal . [11]

No fewer than 38% of the Home Office sample were excused ad hoc on an individual basis. [12] Lord Justice Auld's Report said of this category that '[i]t is taken up in the main by those who are self-employed or in full-time employment who can make out a case for economic or other hardship for themselves or others if they have to give up their work for even a short period and also by parents who are unable to make alternative arrangements for the care of their children' [13] In fact however the Home Office research study on which this statement was based shows a somewhat different picture. The most common reason for excusal (not mentioned by Auld) was medical – accounting for no less than 40% of the total. Care of children and the elderly accounted for another 20%. The juror being an essential worker or financial reasons accounted for another 20%. The great variety of miscellaneous other reasons included not being a resident (9%), being a student (6%) and transport problems (overall only 1% but in some rural areas as much as 30%).

The Home Office study found that of the 34% of the sample who were available for jury service nearly half had had their jury service deferred, in quite a few cases more than once. Reasons for deferral were similar to those for excusal but prior holiday arrangements accounted for a third (34%).

Applications for excusal which formerly went to the court's Summoning Officer now have to be made to the new national Central Summoning Bureau (see p 469 below) but there is a right of appeal against refusal to the court.

---

9   Sch 27, para 3 repealing JA 1974, s 9(1) which gave persons listed in Sch 1, Part 3 of the Act excusal as of right.
10   House of Commons, Standing Committee B, February 13, 2003, col.1057-58.
11   Chapter 5, para 26, p 145.
12   J Airs and A Shaw, *Jury Excusal and Deferral*, Home Office Research and Statistics, Research Findings No 102, 1999.
13   Chapter 5, para 39, p 151.

The court has power to discharge a jury summons if it considers that the person will not be able to act effectively as a juror on account of disability [14] or 'insufficient understanding of English' [15]

There is no formal literacy test for jury service. The Runciman Royal Commission said in regard to the question whether there should be, that the Crown Court Study carried out for the Commission[16] showed that jurors and jury foremen broadly claimed to understand the issues they were trying. Inevitably this was a subjective judgment and moreover there were some jurors and even some whole juries who were confused. The subject, it said, should be the subject of research (Report, p 135, para 72).

Lord Justice Auld said that it was becoming increasingly necessary for jurors to have a reasonable command of written English. Even in simple cases there were usually documents that they must be capable of understanding. But there was no obvious solution to the problem. The present system of leaving the judge as the final filter during the process of jury selection was 'probably the best that can be achieved' [17] The judge should give the panel 'an ample and tactfully expressed warning of what they are in for, and offer them a formula that would enable them to seek excusal without embarrassment'. [18] If all else failed, the prosecution had its right to 'stand by' (see p 476 below).

The judge also has a discretion to excuse jurors on special grounds–for instance in relation to long, complicated or sensitive cases. It is common in these immensely long cases for the judge to ask jurors whether they can manage such a case and to excuse any who say they cannot. The jury is in a sense therefore 'self-selected'. (On this see further p 470 below.)

3. The process of jury selection

The random nature of jury selection has been described as the essence of the jury system: see *R v Sheffield Crown Court, ex p Brownlow* [1980] QB 530. In *Tarrant* [1998] Crim LR 342 the trial judge discharged the first jury selected and ordered a jury to be drawn from a different area because it was thought there was a danger of intimidation. The Court of Appeal quashed the conviction on the ground that the judge had improperly interfered with the jury selection process which was basically an administrative rather than a judicial function. The judge had the power to discharge individual potential jurors on the ground that they might not be able to perform their

---

[14] Juries Act 1974, s 9B.
[15] Juries Act 1974, s 10.
[16] M Zander and P Henderson, *Crown Court Study*, Royal Commission on Criminal Justice, Research Study No 19, 1993.
[17] Chapter 5, para 50, p 155.
[18] Chapter 5, para 50, p 155.

duties but he could not interfere with the composition of the jury panel or of an individual jury.

Until recently the actual process of selecting the names for the panel was somewhat haphazard. Each summoning officer had his own method and many were hardly 'random' in any sense recognisable by a statistician. In 1981 a new system, developed by the Lord Chancellor's Department in consultation with the Royal Statistical Society, was introduced nationally.

However, even then the system as it was actually operated was less than completely random. An article in *The Law Magazine*, 30 October 1987, p 20, pointed out that the randomness of jury selection was qualified by the following facts:

(1) The electoral register was not wholly representative of the population. Nearly 7% were on the register wrongly because they had moved or died; about one-fifth of those from the new Commonwealth were not registered, and nearly one-fifth of those between the ages of 21 and 24 were not registered because of their mobility.

(2) It was up to the summoning officer to decide which of his electoral registers to use. Each court had a collection of registers from which to choose.

(3) It was also up to the summoning officer to select his mini-panel of 18 or so names for a particular case and then to decide in which order to draw the names. ('Some even seem to look through the pack as they pick out names'.) Also, of course, courts would vary in what excuses they would accept as grounds for not serving for personal reasons.

A report on Jury Selection issued by the Criminal Bar Association in November 1988 described the system as 'remarkably primitive' (para 2.5). It recommended that the system be computerised in order to produce the best statistically verifiable results. (It suggested that the present system threw up bizarre juries of an unrepresentative kind. It was remarkable for instance how when there were rail strikes or other transport problems jurors drawn from a huge catchment area often lived close enough to each other to share taxis!)

The jury summoning officer calculates how many jurors will be required and, having made a random selection from the electoral lists, sends out his summonses so as to give at least four weeks' warning. The summons comes with an explanatory leaflet about jury service, a leaflet on jurors' expenses including a form regarding claims for loss of earnings, and a reply envelope to return a form stating that the person concerned is either qualified to serve or is not qualified, with the reason. Failure to give this information or giving false information is an offence.

In 2001 a single Central Summoning Bureau was established for the whole country. The Auld Report said, 'It is designed to overcome the deficiencies of the former system, principally in securing a better match in numbers of jurors summoned to the workload of each court, in providing better communication with potential jurors and accommodation of their needs, and in bringing greater consistency to the treatment of their applications for excusal or deferral'.[19] There is also now a website which has a 15-minute presentation for persons summoned for jury duty – www.juror.cjsonline.org.

The method of determining the composition of the jury for the particular case varies somewhat from court to court. Ballotting is supposed to be done by putting the appropriate number of cards into the ballot box and drawing them in such a way that the jury bailiff cannot see the names on the cards. The cards are then transferred to the courtroom ballot box for the final ballot.

Usually about twenty or so names are drawn and these individuals are brought into the back of the court. (They are often called 'the jury in waiting'.) The clerk of the court is given cards, each of which has the name and address of a juror in waiting. He reads out twelve names and those persons go into the jury box.

The same Criminal Bar Association report referred to above said that in former times 'there were many courts where rigging juries was an open secret ... convicting juries were kept together by order of judges and connivance of the court staff' (para 5.1). Rigging also occurred for benevolent reasons such as wishing to steer female jurors from nasty sex cases. The Association said 'We have no evidence that this is a reality any more.' Nevertheless practice varied. 'Whether the actions of some court clerks can strictly be interpreted as a proper ballot in accordance with the Act is doubtful –the shuffling and selection of jury cases certainly has little appearance of it' (ibid). The process of ballotting, it said, should be made more mechanical, independent of the whim of court staff and uniform throughout the country.

(a) Jury selection for long cases–the Maxwell fraud case

The trial of Kevin and Ian Maxwell, sons of the business magnate Robert Maxwell, which started in June 1995 was scheduled to last some six months. The trial judge, Mr Justice Phillips (now Lord Phillips MR) adopted a highly unusual method of selecting the jury. First, two groups of 400 potential jurors were summoned to the Old Bailey on two separate days. Of these, 650 were immediately excused for reasons of personal non-availability including holiday plans, child-minding responsibilities, work commitments and the like. The remaining 150 were invited to complete a 20-page questionnaire with some 40 questions specifically relating to the Maxwell trial. This was designed to test their availability for an unusually long case and was directed also to their knowledge of the case and possible resulting prejudice. The judge and counsel in open court then went through the list of these 150 questionnaires classifying them as A (no reason to exclude), C (should be excluded for any reason, including illiteracy) and B (uncertain). There were 52 Cs. The jury was then selected by ballot drawn from the remaining 100 or so jurors. As each name was drawn, if counsel or the judge had any queries on the basis of the questionnaire or the

[19] Chapter 5, para 16, p 141.

classification, the juror was asked to come into the court room and they were asked questions by the judge to clarify the issue. The individual then left the court room and the judge and counsel together decided whether that person should or should not serve as a juror.

In *R v Tracey Andrews* [1999] Crim LR 156 and commentary at 157; *New Law Journal*, 4 December 1998, p 1812 the Court of Appeal said that the use of a questionnaire to establish whether potential jurors were biased should be avoided save in most exceptional circumstances.

(b)   Compensation for jurors

Jurors receive a financial loss allowance graduated depending on the length of the case. In 2003, for the first ten days they were paid a flat rate of £52.63 a day even for the retired and unemployed. After that the loss-of earnings allowance was subject to a maximum of £105.28 a day. They are also paid a subsistence allowance –in 2003 from £4.51 per day plus travel expenses.

4. Challenging of jurors

At common law, either party can challenge the whole panel on the ground that the person conducting the summoning acted improperly or was biased. This form of challenge ('challenge to the array') is nowadays virtually unheard of. But the parties also have the right to challenge individual jurors ('challenge to the polls').

The position of the parties in regard to selection of the jury was historically somewhat different. The prosecution could only challenge jurors if they had some reason ('challenge for cause', see below). But they could also exercise a right known as 'stand by for the Crown' or simply 'stand by', which means that the prospective juror stands to one side. If a jury can be empanelled without him (as would almost always be the case), he is not required. If not, he must be accepted unless the prosecution can show cause why he should not be a juror in that case. (See JF McEldowney, 'Stand by the Crown: An Historical Analysis' (1979) *Criminal Law Review*, p 272.) In practice, the prosecution only rarely exercise their right either of stand by or of challenge for cause.

(a)   Peremptory challenge

The defence in a criminal case have traditionally had the right to challenge numbers of prospective jurors without giving any reason–the so-called right of 'peremptory challenge'. Originally the number of such challenges permitted was 35. In 1509 this was reduced to twenty; in 1948 it was reduced to seven and in 1977 to three. After all peremptory challenges had been exhausted, the defence had only a right of challenge for cause–with no limit to the numbers that could be challenged in that way. But from the mid-1980s the right of peremptory challenge became highly controversial.

It was suggested that the right was being 'abused' by defence lawyers who would use it, especially in London, to eliminate from the jury persons who were educated or looked intelligent or middle class. There was no hard evidence to support the allegation but it gained some currency.

In January 1986 great impetus was given to the campaign to abolish the right of peremptory challenge in the Report of the Roskill Committee on Fraud Trials. The Committee was divided on the issue but by a majority of seven to one it recommended that the right should be abolished. It thought that the interests of the accused could be adequately safeguarded by the right of challenge for cause.

The majority said that the right conflicted with the principle that the jury should be selected randomly. Since co-accused could each exercise three such challenges, the panel might be reduced by a considerable number. It concluded:

> We have considerable sympathy with the exercise of the right of peremptory challenge in pursuit of an aim of securing a better racial or sexual balance on a jury. But we have no sympathy with its exercise where that exercise is, as the evidence suggests is too often the case, largely tactical. The aim of the jury is to secure a verdict which is just to prosecution and defence alike after a proper appraisal of the evidence. That aim ought not to be hampered by the use of the right of peremptory challenge in the hope of replacing a juror whose appearance and address may suggest a capacity to understand the real issues or a bias in favour of the prosecution by one whom it is hoped may be less able to understand or may be more likely to be biased in favour of the defence [para 7.29]. ... Our evidence shows that the public, the press and many legal practitioners now believe that this ancient right is abused cynically and systematically to manipulate cases toward a desired result. The current situation bids fair to bring the whole system into disrepute. We conclude that in respect of fraud trials such manipulation is wholly unacceptable and must be stopped [para 7.37].

In a White Paper published in March 1986 the Home Office said that peremptory challenge was sometimes used for entirely proper reasons–such as to save time or possibly embarrassment to someone who would otherwise be challenged for cause, or to adjust the age, sex or race balance on the jury, or to remove someone suspected of being biased against the accused. But it was contrary to the interests of justice that persons should be removed because they were thought to have insight or respect for the law which was inimical to the defence. The problem was most acute in cases involving several defendants if they pooled their challenges. The Government had no wish to interfere unnecessarily with a long-standing right that could be used in ways that were consistent with justice. But as far as practicable, and providing it did not seriously prejudice a defendant's right to a fair trial, juries should be composed of a random selection of those who were neither ineligible nor disqualified. The question was whether that could be achieved without either leaving defendants with an understandable sense of grievance or opening up challenge for cause to an unseemly and disturbing degree. (*Criminal Justice: Plans for Legislation*, March 1986, Cmnd 9658, para 35).

The empirical evidence did not support the view that the use of peremptory challenge affected the outcome of trials.[20]

The 1986 White Paper was followed by legislation in the Criminal Justice Act 1988, section 118 of which provided simply 'The right to challenge without cause in proceedings for the trial of a person on indictment is abolished'.

The Crown Court Study[21] reported on the views of both barristers and judges as to whether the right to peremptory challenge should be restored. A slight majority of prosecution barristers (56%) thought the right should not be restored. Exactly the same proportion of defence barristers thought that it should be restored. The judges sided strongly with the view expressed by a majority of prosecution barristers–82% thought it should not be restored (sect 6.2.5, p 174). The Runciman Royal Commission made no recommendation on the subject.

(b)   Challenge for cause

In the United States prospective jurors can be asked questions to establish whether they are biased.[22] Sometimes this process can take hours and even days or weeks. Selection of the jury in the trial of Jack Ruby for killing Lee Harvey Oswald, the alleged assassin of President Kennedy, took 15 days. Selection of the jury in the celebrated trial of OJ Simpson took 40 days, from 26 September to 4 November, 1994.

In England, by contrast, questions may not be put unless a foundation of fact has first been laid,[23] which means that in practice challenges for cause are extremely rare. Since normally nothing is known about the prospective jurors other than their names and addresses, there is usually no basis on which a challenge for cause can be launched. Formerly, the lists available to the parties also showed the jurors' occupations, but in August 1973 the Lord Chancellor issued a directive (under the provisions of s 32(1) of the Courts Act 1971) that in future jury lists should no longer include the occupations of those on the jury panel. The intention, again, was to make it more difficult for counsel to 'select' the jury. The Bar Council issued a statement

---

20   See Julie Vennard and David Riley, 'The Use of Peremptory Challenge and Stand By of Jurors and Their Relationship to Final Outcome' [1988] *Criminal Law Review*, p 731.

21   M Zander and P Henderson, *The Crown Court Study*, Royal Commission on Criminal Justice, Research Study No 19, 1993.

22   For description see Mark George, 'Jury Selection, Texas Style', *New Law Journal*, 24 June 1988, p 438 and R May, 'Jury Selection in the United States: Are there Lessons to be Learned?' [1998] *Criminal Law Review*, p 270-73.

23   *Chandler (No 2)* [1964] 1 All ER 761.

on 7 May 1974 regretting the directive: 'It is felt that the new directive will hamper both the prosecution and the defence, and it is not in the interests of the administration of justice.'

Those entitled to inspect the list of names on the panel include the defendant, solicitor and counsel for any party, and police officers involved in the case. Instructions to Crown Court staff state that requests from anyone else, or if the official is in any doubt, should be referred to a superior officer. A record of any request to inspect the panel list must be kept. Concern about 'jury nobbling' has increased in recent years[24] but it has not reached the point where it has been thought that the right to look at the panel should be withheld.

Some consideration has been given to the problem of challenge for cause. The basic English rule was set out in a Practice Note issued in 1973 as a result of what happened in the so-called Angry Brigade case in 1972. The case concerned the trial of alleged anarchists for attempts to bomb the homes of various prominent Conservative politicians. The trial judge, in order to avoid any possibility that the trial might be thought to be unfair, acceded to a defence request that he put questions to prospective jurors. He asked them to exclude themselves for a variety of reasons, for instance if they were subscribing members of the Conservative Party, if they had relatives in the police force or serving in the armed forces in Northern Ireland, or if they were constituents of any of several prominent persons whose homes were alleged to have been the subject of actual or projected bombings. As a result, 39 people were challenged on behalf of the 8 defendants, and another 19 admitted they fell into one or other of the judge's categories (see *The Guardian*, 31 May 1972).

Shortly after the case was concluded, however, the Lord Chief Justice issued a Practice Note obviously designed to stop such questions.[25] This *Practice Note* was reissued in a revised form in 1988 ([1988] 3 All ER 177). The new text was:

> Jury service is an important public duty which individual members of the public are chosen at random to undertake. The normal presumption is that, unless a person is excusable as of right from jury service under Pt III of Sch 1 to the Juries Act 1974, he or she will be required to serve when summoned to do so. There will however be circumstances where a juror should be excused, for instance where he or she is personally concerned in the facts of the particular case or is closely connected with a party or prospective witness.

---

[24] The Runciman Royal Commission recommended that an acquittal should be cancelled and a retrial be instituted where it was subsequently established that jurors had been bribed or intimidated (p 177, para 74). This was implemented in the Criminal Procedure and Investigations Act 1996, s 54. As will be seen, p 529 below, the Criminal Justice Bill 2002/03 includes provision for trial without jury if jury tampering has occurred or there is 'a real and present danger' that it will occur.

[25] See [1973] 1 All ER 240.

He or she may also be excused on grounds of personal hardship or conscientious objection to jury service. Each such application should be dealt with sensitively and sympathetically.

Any person who appeals to the court against a refusal by the appropriate officer to excuse him or her from jury service must be given an opportunity to make representations in support of his or her appeal.

THE JUDGE'S DISCRETION

In *R v Ford* (1989) 89 Cr App Rep 278 at p 280 Lord Lane CJ said that the trial judge has a residual discretion to discharge a juror who ought not to be serving even in the absence of any objection by any party. 'The basic position is that a juror may be discharged on grounds that would found a challenge for cause. In addition jurors who are not likely to be willing or able properly to perform their duties may also be discharged.' This was the discretion exercised by Mr Justice Phillips in the selection of the jury in the trial of the Maxwell brothers (p 470 above).

The question of conscientious objection to jury service was considered in *R v Crown Court at Guildford, ex p Siderfin* [1989] 3 All ER 7, in which the Divisional Court held that a member of the Plymouth Brethren could be entitled to excusal not because of her beliefs as such but because they prevented her from taking part in the jury's deliberations. Since 'she would not participate at all in the usual discussion between jurors which is an integral part of the jury system', she would be unable to perform her duties as a juror. (The court also held that a judge hearing an appeal from a chief clerk's refusal of such an application to be excused jury service should consider sympathetically any request for the person to be legally represented.)

JURY SELECTION AND PRE-TRIAL PUBLICITY

As was seen above, it is not a valid ground of objection that the juror has previous knowledge of the case from the media. In *R v Maxwell* Phillips J said that because the minds of potential jurors might have become 'clogged with prejudice' by pre-trial publicity about the case he would permit questions to be put in the jury questionnaire and further questions to be posed when he questioned potential jurors in open court (see above). But in a ruling on jury selection given on 27 April 1995 he said 'The fact that a juror may have read or heard prejudicial matter about a defendant, *and even formed an adverse opinion of him on the basis of it, does not of itself disqualify the juror on the ground of bias*' (emphasis supplied). He cited a dictum of the Ontario Court of Appeal in *R v Hubbert* (1975) 29 CCC (2d) 279 at p 291:

In this era of rapid dissemination of news by the various media, it would be naive to think that in the case of a crime involving considerable notoriety, it would be possible to select 12 jurors who had not heard anything about the case. Prior information about a case and even the holding of a tentative opinion about it, does not make partial a juror sworn to render a true verdict according to the evidence.

Mr Justice Phillips cited with approval the observation of the High Court of Australia in *R v Glennon* (1992) 173 CLR 592 'in the past too little weight may have been given to the capacity of jurors to assess critically what they see and hear and their ability to reach their decisions by reference to the evidence before them'.[26]

Defence counsel had argued that the extent of the pre-trial publicity about the Maxwell case had established a prima facie case justifying a challenge for cause of any juror selected by ballot. He cited *R v Kray* (1969) 53 Cr App Rep 412, per Lawton J as authority for the proposition. Prosecution counsel argued that challenge for cause would only arise where having regard to the answers to the questionnaire a prima facie case of bias was made out. The judge said that in practice there was little difference between these positions. It was always necessary to show prima facie grounds for a challenge and the answers to the questionnaire could be used for that purpose.

PROCEDURE FOR CHALLENGE FOR CAUSE

In 1989 the Judicial Studies Board published a recommended procedure for challenge for cause based on recommendations of the Law Commission. If counsel can state the ground of challenge without prejudicing his client in the eyes of the jury, or embarrassing the juror, the matter can be dealt with in open court. If not, the sworn jurors should be sent to the jury room and the rest of the panel, *including the challenged juror*, should leave the court. The judge should then decide whether to exclude the press and the public. Challenges should never be heard in the judge's room.

(c)   Stand by for the Crown

When the defence right of peremptory challenge was abolished, the Attorney-General issued guidelines (*Practice Note* [1988] 3 All ER 1086) as to how the prosecution's right to 'stand by for the Crown' was to be used:

Attorney-General's guidelines on the exercise by the Crown of its right of stand by

1. Although the law has long recognised the right of the Crown to exclude a member of a jury panel from sitting as a juror by the exercise in open court of the right to request a stand by or, if necessary, by challenge for cause, it has been customary for those instructed to prosecute on behalf of the Crown to

---

[26]   The study carried out for the New Zealand Law Commission (pp 351–52 above) confirms the view that pre-trial publicity is not the threat to the jury's decision-making that has been feared.

assert that right only sparingly and in exceptional circumstances. It is generally accepted that the prosecution should not use its right in order to influence the overall composition of a jury or with a view to tactical advantage.

2. The approach outlined above is founded on the principles that (a) the members of a jury should be selected at random from the panel subject to any rule of law as to right of challenge by the defence, and (b) the Juries Act 1974 together with the Juries (Disqualification) Act 1984 identified those classes of persons who alone are disqualified from or ineligible for service on a jury. No other class of person may be treated as disqualified or ineligible.

3. The enactment by Parliament of s 118 of the Criminal Justice Act 1988 abolishing the right of defendants to remove jurors by means of peremptory challenge makes it appropriate that the Crown should assert its right to stand by only on the basis of clearly defined and restrictive criteria. Derogation from the principle that members of a jury should be selected at random should be permitted only where it is essential.

4. Primary responsibility for ensuring that an individual does not serve on a jury if he is not competent to discharge properly the duties of a juror rests with the appropriate court officer and, ultimately, the trial judge. Current legislation provides, in ss 9 and 10 of the Juries Act 1974, fairly wide discretions to excuse or discharge jurors either at the person's own request, where he offers 'good reason why he should be excused', or where the judge determines that 'on account of physical disability or insufficient understanding of English there is doubt as to his capacity to act effectively as a juror'.

5. The circumstances in which it would be proper for the Crown to exercise its right to stand by a member of a jury panel are: (a) where a jury check authorised in accordance with the Attorney-General's Guidelines on Jury Checks[6] reveals information justifying exercise of the right to stand by in accordance with para 9 of the guidelines and the Attorney-General personally authorises the exercise of the right to stand by; or (b) where a person is about to be sworn as a juror who is manifestly unsuitable and the defence agree that, accordingly, the exercise by the prosecution of the right to stand by would be appropriate. An example of the sort of exceptional circumstances which might justify stand by is where it becomes apparent that, despite the provisions mentioned in para 4 above, a juror selected for service to try a complex case is in fact illiterate.

(d)   Juries and the problem of race

The question whether the courts have any way of achieving a racial mix in a case where that seems to be desirable has been the subject of a number of conflicting court decisions–see *Binns* [1982] Crim LR 522 and 823; *Danvers* [1982] Crim LR 680; *Newton Rose* (1981) Times, 11 November; *Bansall, Bir, Mahio, and Singh* [1985] Crim

LR 151; *McCalla* [1986] Crim LR 335; *Frazer* [1987] Crim LR 418. (See further A Dashwood, 'Juries in a Multi-racial Society' (1972) *Criminal Law Review*, p 85.)

The issue of racially mixed juries was considered by the Court of Appeal in the case of *Ford* [1989] 3 All ER 445. The trial judge refused an application for a multi-racial jury in a case where the defendant was accused of reckless driving and driving a vehicle without authority. Lord Lane, the Lord Chief Justice, giving the judgment of the Court of Appeal, said that the judge had a discretion to discharge a particular juror who was unfit to serve, for instance because he was deaf or blind or otherwise incompetent to serve. In *Mason* [1980] 3 All ER 777 another example given was someone for whom taking part in a long trial would be unusually burdensome. But this discretion did not extend to discharging a competent juror in order to secure a jury drawn from a particular section of the community nor otherwise to influence the overall composition of the jury. 'For this latter purpose the law provides that "fairness" is achieved by the principle of random selection' (p 449).

The Court disapproved suggestions to the contrary in earlier cases such as *Binns*, *Bansall* and *Thomas* (1989) 88 Cr App Rep 370. Lord Lane said that there was no principle that juries should be racially balanced–for that would depend on an underlying premise that jurors of a particular racial origin were incapable of giving an impartial verdict in accordance with the evidence. Given that the right of peremptory challenge has now been abolished, it therefore seems that there is no way in which the court can achieve a racially mixed jury by design.

In its evidence to the Runciman Royal Commission on Criminal Justice, the Commission for Racial Equality (CRE) argued that something had to be done to ensure that a jury be racially mixed where this seemed relevant. Restoration of the right of peremptory challenge would help. But on its own it would not be sufficient. One way would be to give the trial judge a statutory right to stand by jurors in order to achieve a racially mixed jury. If the judge refused to exercise this power, the CRE proposed that the defence counsel should have the right to stand by unlimited numbers of jurors until an acceptable racial mix was achieved–ie the equivalent right to the prosecution's right of 'stand by for the Crown'.

See further S Enright, 'Race, Justice and Trial by Jury', *Solicitors' Journal*, 15 November 1991, p 1238.

The Runciman Royal Commission was persuaded by the CRE that in a small number of racially sensitive cases something needed to be done to secure that the jury should be racially balanced. ('The Court of Appeal in *Ford* held that race should not be taken into account in selecting juries. Although we agree with the court's position in regard to most cases, we believe that there are some exceptional cases where race should be taken into account' (p 133, para 62).)

The Royal Commission proposed that in such a case either the defence or the prosecution should be permitted to ask the judge to authorise a special procedure so as to achieve that the jury contain up to three members of ethnic minority communities. If the judge agreed, the jury bailiff would continue drawing names randomly until three such people were drawn. But this procedure should not apply, as the CRE had proposed, merely because the defendant thinks that he cannot get a fair trial from an all-white jury. The judge would have to be persuaded that it was reasonable because of the special and unusual features of the case. Thus, a black defendant charged with burglary would not normally succeed with such an application. But black people accused of violence against a member of an extremist organisation who had been making racial taunts against them and their friends might succeed (p 133, para 63).

The CRE thought it would be impracticable to provide that the ethnic minority members of the jury should be drawn from the same ethnic minority group as the defendant but the Royal Commission thought that this should be an issue that the judge could be asked to consider.

The Royal Commission's proposal proved controversial. The Lord Chief Justice, Lord Taylor, for instance, indicated that he was against it. Speaking to the Leeds Race Issues Advisory Council he said: 'Though put forward for the best of motives, this proposal seems to me the thin edge of a particularly insidious wedge. The jury is the foundation of our system. It is drawn at random from the law-abiding inhabitants of the locality in which a case is tried. We must on no account introduce measures which allow the State to start nibbling away at the principle of random selection of jurors'. Jurors must not be seen as 'representing the views of the community, or of discrete parts of it, nor indeed of representing either the complainant or the victim'. (*The Times*, 1 July 1995.)

Lord Justice Auld in his Report made the same recommendation as the Runciman Royal Commission. Juries, he admitted, were clearly at risk of one or more of their number bringing prejudice of one sort or another to their task. But such prejudice was usually invisible and 'we are content to assume that it will be overcome or cancelled by differing views of other members' [27] Membership of a race is usually visible and, he argued, 'it is this quality of visible difference and the prejudice that it may engender that singles out race for different treatment from other special interest groups in the courtroom'.[28]

The Government rejected the proposal. In its White Paper *Justice for All* it gave six reasons. Implementing the proposal, it said, [29] would potentially:

- undermine the fundamental principle of random selection and would not achieve a truly representative jury of peers;
- assume bias on the part of the excluded jurors when no prejudice had been proved;
- place the selected minority ethnic jurors in a difficult position – as if they were expected to represent the interests of the defendant or the victim;

[27] Chapter 5, para 59, p 158.
[28] Chapter 5, para 59, p 158.
[29] White Paper, *Justice for All*, July 2001, para 7.29.

- generate tensions and divisions in the jury room;
- place undue weight on the views of the specially selected jurors;
- place a new burden on the court to determine which cases should attract an ethnic minority quota and provide a ground for unmeritorious appeals.

The writer, as a member of Runciman Royal Commission, was party to its unanimous recommendation on ethnic minority representation. This is the only one of its recommendations on which he later changed his mind – see Response to the Auld Review, www.lcd.gov.uk (Major Reports/Comments), p 13.

5. Jury vetting

In 1978 during the so-called 'ABC' trial of a soldier and two journalists under the Official Secrets Act, it was revealed that in some cases the prosecution vet the jury panel. On the first day of the trial, counsel for one of the defendants learned from the clerk of the court that prosecution counsel had had a list of the potential jurors. 'Anyone who is known to be disloyal would obviously be disqualified', said Mr John Leonard QC for the prosecution. But in fact the Crown had not taken objection to anyone on the list.

It later emerged that the foreman of the jury had been a member of the elite SAS (Special Air Service Regiment). The jury was discharged when this fact was made known on television. As a direct result, in October 1978 the Attorney-General, Mr Sam Silkin QC published the guidelines for vetting of jury panels which he had actually established three years earlier. (See *The Times*, 11 October 1978.)

These guidelines have subsequently been redrafted several times. The latest version is [1988] 3 All ER 1086:

3. There are, however, certain exceptional types of case of public importance for which the provisions as to majority verdicts and the disqualification of jurors may not be sufficient to ensure the proper administration of justice. In such cases it is in the interests of both justice and the public that there should be further safeguards against the possibility of bias and in such cases checks which go beyond the investigation of criminal records may be necessary.

4. These classes of case may be defined broadly as (a) cases in which national security is involved and part of the evidence is likely to be heard in camera, and (b) terrorist cases.

5. The particular aspects of these cases which may make it desirable to seek extra precautions are (a) in security cases a danger that a juror, either voluntarily or under pressure, may make an improper use of evidence which, because of its sensitivity, has been given in camera, (b) in both security and terrorist cases the danger that a juror's political beliefs are so biased as to go beyond normally reflecting the broad spectrum of views and interests in the community to reflect the extreme views of sectarian interest or pressure groups to a degree which

might interfere with his fair assessment of the facts of the case or lead him to exert improper pressure on his fellow jurors.

6. In order to ascertain whether in exceptional circumstances of the above nature either of these factors might seriously influence a potential juror's impartial performance of his duties or his respecting the secrecy of evidence given in camera, it may be necessary to conduct a limited investigation of the panel. In general, such further investigation beyond one of criminal records made for disqualifications may only be made with the records of police Special Branches. However, in cases falling under para 4(a) above (security cases), the investigation may, additionally, involve the security services. No checks other than on these sources and no general inquiries are to be made save to the limited extent that they may be needed to confirm the identity of a juror about whom the initial check has raised serious doubts.

Such checks require the personal approval of the Attorney-General. If the check shows that any juror should be excluded from the trial it is done by telling prosecution counsel who would ask that juror to 'stand by for the crown'.

Use made of jury vetting

There is little information about the use of jury vetting. In his original statement in 1978 the Attorney-General said that in the three years since he had laid down his guidelines jury vetting had only occurred in 25 cases. Since then the categories of case in which it is permitted have been narrowed (by the elimination of big gang trials) and the requirement of consent of the Attorney-General has been added. Also the authorities know that each such case that comes to light usually provokes a row (as in a case involving charges against six anarchists when *The Guardian* (20 September 1979) printed details of information obtained from the police computer through jury vetting). The number of such cases is therefore presumably even fewer today than in the late 1970s.

For strong criticism of the practice of vetting, see Harriet Harman and John Griffith, *Justice Deserted* (National Council for Civil Liberties, 1979); Peter Duff and Mark Findlay, 'Jury Vetting–the Jury Under Attack', *Legal Studies*, 1983, p 159. See also Robert J East, 'Jury Packing: A Thing of the Past?', 48 *Modern Law Review*, 1985, p 518. East took an even more serious view of jury vetting, seeing it as part of a general erosion of civil liberties.

6. The size of the jury

As Lord Justice Auld's Report said, the fact that the English jury consists of 12 persons is 'a matter of tradition rather than logic'.[30] (In Scotland the number is 15.) Auld

---

30   Chapter 5, para 17, p 142.

made no recommendation for a change in this regard. But he did suggest that in long cases, where they consider it appropriate, judges should have a right to swear alternate or reserve jurors, to meet the contingency of the jury being reduced in number by illness or any other reason of necessity. [31] This recommendation was not adopted by the Government.

7. **Who serves on juries?**

There are two substantial studies of jury composition in England. The first was an investigation of 326 juries empanelled in 1975 and 1976 in the Birmingham Crown Court. During the study the court authorities kept records of each juror's sex, age, occupation and race and the number of times he had previously sat on a jury. The study showed that the recommendations of the Morris Committee had had a considerable effect. According to Lord Devlin, in 1956 juries were 'predominantly male, middle-aged, middle-minded and middle class'. This was no longer so. The researchers found that 'the juries in question had acquired a distinctly working class character: indeed a majority of jurors were manual workers, or the wives of manual workers' (J Baldwin and M McConville, *Jury Trials* (Clarendon, 1979), p 95). Nevertheless, when compared with census data for the area, manual workers and especially unskilled manual workers were still somewhat under-represented. (The census figures showed 8.8% of the local population in the category of unskilled Social Class V, as compared with 3.4% in the sample of jurymen (ibid).) In regard to age, there was 'a remarkable congruence' between those who sat on juries and residents of Birmingham (ibid, p 97). In regard to sex, women were distinctly under-represented–72% of jurors were male. The authors explained this by two facts– more women than men asked for excusal and, as a result, an unofficial policy (since discontinued) was followed of calling twice as many men as women for jury service.

The other great discrepancy between the jury and the local population was in regard to an under-representation of racial minorities. Only 28 out of 3,912 jurors (0.7%) were of West Indian or Asian origin, when the census figures suggested that one could expect 10 to 15 times that number (p 98).

The researchers investigated whether jury decisions could be correlated with any of these factors, but found that 'however one regarded the material, no consistent patterns were apparent' (p 100). The presence of women, younger or working-class jurors appeared to make no difference to jury results. They concluded: 'We can confidently state that no single social factor (nor, so far as we could detect, any group of factors operating in combination) produced any significant variation in the verdicts returned , . .'The truth of the matter is that most juries in Birmingham were extremely mixed, and it is to be expected that the amalgam of personal and social attributes that make up a jury will produce verdicts that reflect that unique social mix rather than the broad social characteristic of the individuals concerned' (pp 104–5). This finding

---

[31]   Chapter 5, para 20, p 143.

appears to be confirmed by an unpublished Home Office study which compared the overall acquittal rate on a national basis for three months before the changes made by the Juries Act 1974 with three months after the Act came into force. No significant differences emerged (cited by Baldwin and McConville, op cit p 96, n 24).

The Crown Court Study carried out by the writer for the Runciman Royal Commission[32] included responses from over 800 juries sitting in every completed contested case in every Crown Court in the country for a two week period in February 1992. Returns were received from some 8,300 jurors. The profile of jurors that emerged from this national sample showed:

Sex Males were slightly over-represented – 53% as against 48% in the whole population; foremen were much more disproportionately male – 78% (sect 8.13.1).

Age Young jurors were almost exactly proportionate to their numbers in the population (18–24, 15%, compared with 14% in the general population, 21–34, 21%, compared with 20% in the general population). There was no jury in the sample where any age group dominated disproportionately. The average age of the 8,338 jurors was in the middle band (35–44) (p 236). In 65% of juries the number of young jurors (18–24) ranged from one to three (ibid). In one fifth of juries there were no such young jurors. The acquittal rate of juries with an average age of 25–34 was 42% – a little lower than the 44% for juries with an average age of 35–44 or 45–54 (Table 8.39, p 237).

Work status The great majority of the jurors were working (69% full-time, 13% part-time). Only 2% had been unemployed for over 2 years. 6% were retired persons (sect 8.13.3).

Social class The social class measures were somewhat crude but it appeared (Table 8.41, p 238) that 19% were skilled manual (compared with 23% in the general population), 7% were unskilled manual (exactly the same as the general population), 29% were professional/managerial (compared with 31% in the general population).

Ethnic mix Jurors were asked to identify their own race or ethnic background on a list of seven categories. The results showed a very close approximation between the sample and the general population. Whites were 95% of the jurors–almost exactly the same as the general population. Non-white jurors were 5% of the sample, compared with 5.9% of the total population according to the 1991 census. In fact Black-Caribbean and Indian were over-represented, each being 2% of the sample, compared with 1% of the national population. In 65% of juries there were no non-white jurors, in 16% of juries there was one non-white person, in 9% there were two, in 5% there were three, in 5% there were more than three (pp 241–42).[33]

---

32   N 21 p 473 above.

33   Official permission for the jury study was conditional on it being a national sample with no regional breakdown and no linkage with the other parts of the study. It was therefore not possible to test the jury composition against the population mix in different regions.

Language problems 96% of the sample said that English was their first language. Of the 273 who said English was not their first language, 32 said they had a little difficulty in following the case. None said they had a lot of difficulty (sect 8.13.7, p 242).

Concerns about the jury's composition Defence counsel in the Crown Court Study said they had no concerns about the composition of the jury in 83% of cases. Of those who expressed concerns, the most frequently mentioned issue was the racial mix (Table 6.14, p 176). When the defendant was black, defence counsel expressed concern about the racial mix on the jury in 18% of cases, and therefore had no concern in just over 80% of these cases (p 176).

Concerns of defence counsel did not correlate with the result of cases. Defence counsel had no concerns about jury composition in 80% of cases ending in acquittal, and in 81% of cases ending in conviction (ibid).

8. The extent to which juries are used

(a) Civil cases

There is a *right* to have trial by jury only in the following civil cases: libel, slander, malicious prosecution, false imprisonment and allegations of fraud. Since the Supreme Court Act 1981, the right to trial by jury in the categories listed above has been subject to the proviso in section 69(1) that the court can refuse jury trial if it is of the opinion that 'the trial requires prolonged examination of documents or accounts or any scientific or local investigation which cannot conveniently be made with a jury'.[34] In 1994 the Court of Appeal denied an application from two unemployed environmental campaigners that the libel action brought against them in respect of a leaflet by McDonald's fast food chain should be heard by a jury. The Court of Appeal said that the scientific issues would make it impossible for the case to be tried satisfactorily by a jury. The two campaigners conducted their own case which went on for over a year and became the longest libel action in recorded history.[35]

---

[34] See *Goldsmith v Pressdram Ltd* [1987] 3 All ER 485; *Viscount De L'Isle v Times Newspapers Ltd* [1987] 3 All ER 499; and *Beta Construction Ltd v Channel Four Television Co Ltd* [1990] 2 All ER 1012. Both parties in the 'Holocaust denial' libel action brought by David Irving against Penguin Books and Professor Deborah Lipstadt agreed that the case was too complex for a jury. The trial, which lasted from January to April 2000, ended with a devastating 150-page judgment by Gray J demolishing Irving's arguments. (For an account of the case see R Evans, *Telling Lies About Hitler* (Verso, 2002).)

[35] See national newspapers 26 March 1994, and a year later Dan Mills, '"McLibel 2" bite back against Big Mac', *Legal Action*, April 1995, p 9.) See also *Taylor v Anderton* [1995] 2 All ER 420, CA. In *Racz v Home Office* [1994] 1 All ER 97 the House of Lords upheld the Court of Appeal's denial of jury trial even though the action could have raised the issue of an award of exemplary damages.

In other cases trial is without a jury unless the court 'in its discretion orders it to be tried with a jury' (Supreme Court Act, 1981, s 69(3)). (For a brief review of the cases see *Civil Justice Quarterly*, April 1995, p 152.)

Prior to the 1981 Act the judges had what appeared to be a complete statutory discretion as to whether to order trial by jury. The Administration of Justice Act 1933 provided that 'any action to be tried in the Queen's Bench Division could, in the discretion of the court or judge, be ordered to be tried either with or without a jury'.

In 1933, the Court of Appeal sitting with five judges, said that the question of trial by jury was really one for the discretion of the court–*Hope v Great Western Rly Co* [1937] 2 KB 130. Lord Wright (at p 138) said the discretion of the judge was 'completely untrammelled'. The *Annual Practice*, the practitioners' bible, in interpreting the decision said 'the discretion of the judge is absolute'. When the Rules of the Supreme Court were revised in 1958, Ord 36, r 1(3) was amended to read: 'The discretion of a court or judge in making or varying any order under this rule is an absolute one.'

In 1966 the issue came again before the Court of Appeal sitting again with five judges in a case where jury trial had been allowed for a claim for damages in a road accident which left the plaintiff a permanent quadriplegic. Lord Denning gave the judgment of the court:

Ward v James [1966] 1 QB 273 (Court of Appeal, Civil Division)

Lord Denning MR:

Relevant considerations today

Let it not be supposed that this court is in any way opposed to trial by jury. It has been the bulwark for our liberties too long for any of us to seek to alter it. Whenever a man is on trial for serious crime, or when in a civil case a man's honour or integrity is at stake, or when one or other party must be deliberately lying, then trial by jury has no equal. But in personal injury cases trial by jury has given place of late to trial by judge alone, the reason being simply this, that in these cases trial by judge alone is more acceptable to the great majority of people. Rarely does a party ask in these cases for a jury. When a solicitor gives advice, it runs in this way: 'If I were you, I should not ask for a jury. I should have a judge alone. You do know where you stand with a judge, and if he goes wrong, you can always go to the Court of Appeal. But as for a jury, you never know what they will do, and if they do go wrong, there is no putting them right. The Court of Appeal hardly ever interferes with the verdict of a jury.' So the client decides on judge alone. That is why jury trials have declined. It is because they are not asked for. Lord Devlin shows this in his book [The Hamlyn Lectures, eighth series, *Trial by Jury*, ch 6, p 133].

This important consequence follows: the judges alone, and not juries, in the great majority of cases, decide whether there is negligence or not. They set the standard of care to be expected of the reasonable man. They also assess the damages. They see, so far as they can, that like sums are given for like injuries. They set the standards for awards. Hence there is a uniformity of decision. This has its impact on decisions as to the mode of trial. If a party asks for a jury in an ordinary personal injury case, the court naturally asks: 'Why do you want a jury when nearly everyone else is content with judge alone?' I am afraid it is often because he has a weak case, or desires to appeal to sympathy. If no good reason is given, then the court orders trial by judge alone. Hence we find that nowadays the discretion in the ordinary run of personal injury cases is in favour of judge alone. It is no sufficient reason for departing from it simply to provide a 'guinea-pig' case: see *Hennell v Ranaboldo*.

Lessons of recent cases

... recent cases show the desirability of three things: First, *assessability*: In cases of grave injury, where the body is wrecked or the brain destroyed, it is very difficult to assess a fair compensation in money, so difficult that the award must basically be a conventional figure, derived from experience or from awards in comparable cases. Secondly, *uniformity*: There should be some measure of uniformity in awards so that similar decisions are given in similar cases; otherwise there will be great dissatisfaction in the community, and much criticism of the administration of justice. Thirdly, *predictability*: Parties should be able to predict with some measure of accuracy the sum which is likely to be awarded in a particular case, for by this means cases can be settled peaceably and not brought to court, a thing very much to the public good. None of these three is achieved when the damages are left at large to the jury. Under the present practice the judge does not give them any help at all to assess the figure. The result is that awards may vary greatly, from being much too high to much too low. There is no uniformity and no predictability. ...

The case caused a great hullabaloo. The Court of Appeal, it was said, had struck down one of the sacred rights of an Englishman–the right to trial by jury. This was in fact not the case, the civil jury had already virtually ceased to exist even before the decision. In 1963, three years before *Ward v James*, the number of jury trials in London in the Queen's Bench Division was 27 out of a total of 962 (2.8%). (For the history of the decline of the civil jury, see Lord Devlin, *Trial by Jury*, chapter 6.) Nevertheless, the Court of Appeal was obviously concerned to allay public disquiet and almost immediately found a case in which it disclaimed any intention to abolish civil juries:

Hodges v Harland and Wolff Ltd [1965] 1 All ER 1086 (Court of Appeal, Civil Division)

[The plaintiff, while employed by the defendant, was operating a diesel driven air compressor. The spindle on that machine was not properly guarded as required by the relevant Regulations, 1960. The spindle caught and tore the plaintiff's trousers and avulsed his penis and scrotal skin. One effect of the injury was that the plaintiff still had the sexual urge without the ability to perform the sexual act. On the summons for directions, trial by jury was ordered by the judge after considering the reported cases and the principle of uniformity of awards and after taking other relevant considerations into account. On appeal:}

Lord Denning MR: ... Naturally enough, we have been referred to the recent decision of this court in *Ward v James*. It is a mistake to suppose that this court in that case took away the right to trial by jury. It was not this court but Parliament itself which years ago took away any absolute right to trial by jury and left it to the discretion of the judges. This court in *Ward v James* affirmed that discretion and said that, as the statute has given a discretion to the judge, this court would not fetter it by rigid rules from which the judge was never at liberty to depart. What *Ward v James* did was this. It laid down the considerations which should be borne in mind by a judge when exercising his discretion: and it is apparent that, on those considerations, the result will ordinarily be trial by judge alone. It will not result in trial by jury save in exceptional circumstances. That is no great change. It has been the position for many years. As it happened, in *Ward v James* itself, the result was trial by jury.

In this present case the judge, it seems to me, has borne all the relevant considerations in mind. He said, 'this is a unique case.' So it is. Counsel for the defendants urged that there were one or two cases in the books where a man had retained the sexual urge without the ability to perform the sexual act. That may be so, but they were very different from this. I think that the judge was well entitled to take the view that this was an exceptional case, and in the circumstances to exercise his discretion in favour of trial by jury. Indeed, when a judge exercises his discretion and takes all the relevant considerations into account, it is well settled that the burden is on anyone coming to this court to show that he was wrong. I see nothing wrong in the way that Lyell J dealt with this case in ordering trial by jury. ...

I think that this case was properly decided by the judge. The appeal fails and must be dismissed.

Davies and Salmon LJJ agreed.

The same issue of the unsuitability of juries in personal injury cases was addressed by the Court of Appeal 26 years later, in *H v Ministry of Defence* [1991] 2 All ER 834. By a strange coincidence the case again concerned injury to the penis. The plaintiff, a soldier, was suing for the catastrophic effects of an operation which was intended as a skin graft but which resulted in amputation of the major part of his sex organ. Liability was admitted; the only issue was as to damages. Lord Donaldson MR, giving judgment for himself and Lords Justices Woolf and Mann, said that since *Ward v James* in 1966 the only reported case in which trial by jury had been ordered in a personal injury case was that of *Hodges v Harland and Wolff*. 'Whereas under the 1933

Act there was no legislative bias for or against trial by jury, other than in cases specified in s 6, s 69(3) of the 1981 Supreme Court Act disclosed a change involving a bias against such a trial'.

Where the case called for an award of compensatory damages for personal injuries, a jury trial would normally be inappropriate 'because the assessment of such damages must be based upon or have regard to conventional scales of damages'. But jury trial might be appropriate if the question were one of exemplary damages (for instance where the injury resulted from deliberate abuse of authority), which would be somewhat similar to a claim for malicious prosecution or false imprisonment 'in respect of which there was a legislative intention that there should be a jury trial, unless there were contra indications'.

In 1995 the Law Commission in a Consultation Paper (*Damages for Personal Injury: Non-Pecuniary Loss*, Paper No 140, 1995, at p 125) said that not only did it agree with the Court of Appeal's decisions in *Ward v James* and *H v Ministry of Defence* (above), it went further and thought that juries should *never* be used for personal injury cases:

> We agree with these two decisions. Indeed we go further. Given the difficulty of assessing damages for non-pecuniary loss in personal injury cases and the judicial tariff that has been developed to ensure a measure of consistency and uniformity, we consider it unsatisfactory that juries might ever be called upon to assess compensatory damages for personal injury. Juries do not have the benefit of knowledge of the scale of values that has been developed and the inevitable consequence is unacceptable inconsistency with awards in other cases [para 4.83].

Like the Court of Appeal in *Ward v James*, the Law Commission rejected the idea that the jury should be provided with a scale of values, or upper and lower sums, leaving it for them to fix the actual amount.

JURIES FOR LIBEL AND SLANDER CASES — THE FAULKS COMMITTEE

The role of the jury in libel and slander actions was considered by the Faulks Committee set up in 1971. In its report (*The Law of Defamation*, 1974, Cmnd 5709) the Committee concluded that juries should no longer be available as of right in defamation actions but that instead there should be the same discretion to permit a jury as in all other cases. They had several reasons:

(1) Although juries were perfectly able to determine some questions that arose in defamation actions, there were other matters (such as whether a plea of justification succeeded, or technical legal concepts such as fair comment and qualified privilege) where a judge was normally more competent.

(2) Libel actions often turned on barbed subtleties, specialist jargon or group attitudes of warring factions where the jury was not likely to have any relevant insight or knowledge.

(3) Contrary to the popular view that judges were remote from the life of the community, they were in fact well in touch with the emotions, conventions, language and way of life of the rest of the community. ('The idea that judges live in an ivory tower is wholly out-dated. They go by train and bus, they look at television and they hear, in matrimonial, criminal, accident and other cases, every kind of expression which the ordinary man uses, and they have learnt how he lives' (para 484)).

(4) Judges gave their reasons, whereas juries did not. It was more satisfactory for both sides to know the reasons.

(5) Juries had difficulties with complex cases.

(6) Juries were unpredictable.

(7) Trial by jury was more expensive.

(8) The existing rule gave the right of decision as to mode of trial to whichever side wanted jury trial. No matter how strong the case against jury trial, the party who wanted it would prevail. This was unjust to the other party and wrong in principle.

The Committee concluded by saying that it believed that 'much of the support for jury trials is emotional and derives from the undoubted value of juries in serious criminal cases where they stand between the prosecuting authority and the citizen' (para 496).

It did not recommend that the possibility of jury trial should be removed altogether because there were some cases in which a jury would be better than a judge:

> We recognise it to be undesirable, that a judge sitting alone should be embroiled in a matter of political, religious or moral controversy. The same might be true where any party has been outspokenly critical of the Bench. Broadly, where the issue is whether the words were true or false and the subject is one that raises strong feelings among the general public so that a judge alone might be suspected, however mistakenly, of prejudice conscious or unconscious, we should expect that trial by jury might be awarded–but that in cases which did not involve such controversial questions a judge alone would be more likely to be selected [para 503].

However, the Committee did have a recommendation on the subject of whether juries should continue to deal with damages.

JURIES AND DAMAGES IN DEFAMATION CASES

The Faulks Committee came to the conclusion that it was not right that juries should continue to award damages. The jury simply lacked the necessary knowledge and experience. There were two possible alternatives. One was that the judge should fix the amount of damages without any help from the jury. The other was that the judge would fix the actual amount having had guidance from the jury as to the appropriate scale. The Committee favoured the second. The jury should determine whether the damages were to be 'substantial/moderate/nominal or contemptuous' and the judge should fix the actual amount (para 513). Also the Committee said that the Court of Appeal should be empowered to review the amount of damages and should have the power to substitute its own figure for that of the jury (para 514).

At first nothing was done to implement these recommendations. In its 1995 Consultation Paper on *Damages for Personal Injury: Non-Pecuniary Loss* (above), the Law Commission said that it had reluctantly come to the conclusion that the Faulks' Committee's recommendation to split the determination of liability and damages between judge and jury was unworkable in libel actions.

In the late 1980s the question of the jury's competence in the assessment of damages came into issue again as a result of some astronomic libel awards:

- £450,000 to Martin Packard against a Greek newspaper (with circulation of 50 copies in England), 1987
- £300,000 to Koo Stark against the *Daily Mirror* regarding an alleged relationship with Prince Andrew, 1988
- £500,000 to Jeffrey Archer against the *Daily Star* regarding an allegation that he had visited a prostitute, 1988. (The money later had to be paid back with costs and interest after Archer was imprisoned for perjury in the case.)
- £650,000 against *Private Eye* for Sonia Sutcliffe, wife of the 'Yorkshire Ripper', regarding an allegation that she had cashed in on his notoriety,1989. (The award was set aside by the Court of Appeal which ordered a retrial. She eventually accepted £60,000 in settlement.)

These cases led to a change in the rules so as to permit the Court of Appeal to substitute its own award for that of the jury–as had been recommended in 1974 by the Faulks Committee. But the problem continued.

- £250,00 against Mirror Group Newspapers for broadcaster Esther Rantzen regarding her reputation and integrity as someone concerned about sexual abuse of children. Reduced on appeal to £110,000–*Rantzen v Mirror Group Newspapers* [1993] 4 All ER 975. The Court of Appeal said the award was excessive by any objective standard of reasonable compensation. It invoked art 10 of the European Convention as one of the reasons for its decision. The courts' previous reluctance to intervene should be re-examined. The courts, it said, should subject large awards of damages to more searching scrutiny than had been the case in the past. The question to be asked was whether a reasonable jury could have thought the award was necessary to compensate the plaintiff and re-establish his reputation.

The Law Commission, in its Consultation Paper on *Damages for Personal Injury: Non-Pecuniary Loss* issued in December 1995, proposed that the judge in directing the jury in defamation or other cases should inform the jury of the range of awards for non-pecuniary loss in personal injury cases (para 4.103). The Law Commission's view had hardly been expressed when it became the law of the land through a ruling by the Court of Appeal in a case brought by rock star Elton John against the *Sunday Mirror*. (*John v Mirror Group Newspapers Ltd* [1996] 2 All ER 35.) The court reduced what it called the jury's 'manifestly excessive' award of £350,000 to £75,000. In doing so it held that in future lawyers and judges could and should give juries clear guidance in regard to damages. It described juries in libel actions as 'sheep loosed on an unfenced common with no shepherd'. Sir Thomas Bingham MR said:

> It is in our view offensive to public opinion, and rightly so, that a defamation plaintiff should recover damages for injury to reputation greater, perhaps by a significant factor, than if that same plaintiff had been rendered a helpless cripple or an insensate vegetable. The time has in our view come when judges, and counsel, should be free to draw the attention of juries to these comparisons.

Mentioning figures would not, it thought, develop into an auction. Figures mentioned by counsel would tend to be the upper and lower bounds of a realistic bracket. The jury would remain free to choose a figure within or outside the bracket.

The Court of Appeal took the same approach in *Thompson v Metropolitan Police Comr* [1997] 2 All ER 762. The Court held that in cases involving actions for unlawful acts by police officers, juries should be told about damages awarded in personal injury cases even if the case did not involve personal injuries and about the figure the judge considered appropriate to award in the circumstances. Exemplary damages should be from £5,000 to £25,000 with £50,000 an absolute maximum. (The court reduced damages of £220,000 awarded by the jury to £35,000.)

But in *The Gleaner Co Ltd v Abrahams* (2003) Times, 22 July, the Privy Council said that because damages in personal injury cases could be mentioned in defamation cases in one jurisdiction did not mean that it was necessarily right in another jurisdiction. There was an element of deterrence in libel cases which did not exist in personal injury cases. It dismissed the defendant's appeal against an award of 35 million Jamaican dollars (equivalent to £533,000).

(b)   Criminal cases

Cases tried at the Crown Court (called 'trial on indictment') where the accused pleads not guilty to one or more charges have hitherto always been heard by juries. (As will be seen, pp 522-29 below, Part 7 of the Criminal Justice Bill 2002/03 provides for trial by judge alone in certain circumstances.)

Cases tried on indictment are of two kinds: the very serious offences that can only be tried at the higher level and offences triable either way. [36] The great majority of either way cases are tried summarily.

---

[36]   For the problem of allocation of such cases see pp 37-44 above.

The basic concept regarding the disposition of either way cases has been that if either the magistrates or the defendant thought the case should be heard in the Crown Court that view prevailed. So, the magistrates could not insist on summary trial if the defendant wanted trial by Crown Court; equally, the defendant could not insist on summary trial if the magistrates thought it should be dealt with by the Crown Court. As has been seen, the Criminal Justice Bill 2002/03 retains this fundamental principle.

Where a number of defendants are jointly charged with an either-way offence and one elects to be tried on indictment, all must be sent for trial on indictment–*R v Brentwood Justices, ex p Nicholls* [1990] 3 All ER 516.

9. Aids to the jury

The question of whether, and if so how, to assist the jury has exercised a succession of official committees. The Morris Committee in 1965 recommended that jurors be sent a leaflet with information about their duties and about local arrangements. It did not think that they should be encouraged to take notes, though if they wished to do so, facilities to do so should be provided. ('The process of note-taking is one that requires a good deal of experience and skill. Because of their training, judges are able to make accurate and reasonably complete notes, and at the same time to observe all that is happening and to keep control over the proceedings. Not all jurors can be expected to have the same skill and training. Experience shows that as a general rule it may well be better for jurors to concentrate on listening, observing and reflecting.'[37]) The Crown Court Study done for the Runciman Royal Commission found that in the great majority of cases one or more members of the jury did take notes and most jurors said that they found their notes to be useful (p 173, sect 6.2.3).

The Morris Committee was equally doubtful whether jurors should be informed that they could ask questions. ('If positive encouragement were given to jurors to ask questions there would be a risk in a criminal case of some question prejudicial to the accused being asked inadvertently, and there would also be some risk of the proceedings getting out of hand.'[38]) In the Crown Court Study, the great majority of jurors (70%) said that they had been told they could ask questions, but of those who had wanted to do so, only 17% had had the courage to do so (p 174, sect 6.2.4).

The Lord Chancellor's Department produces a leaflet which is sent out with jury summonses to inform jurors about the process. It has a few lines on each of a variety of topics. Thus it describes the process of selection for cases, including the right of challenge and of asking jurors to stand by for the Crown. It tells the jurors to inform

[37]   Report of the (Morris) Departmental Committee on Jury Service, 1965, Cmnd 2627, para 282.

[38]   Report of the Morris Committee, para 283.

the clerk of the court if they have personal knowledge of the case or of anyone involved in it.

Jurors are told that during the trial they may be asked to retire whilst the judge hears submissions on matters of law. They are warned that they should not make up their mind about the case until they have heard all the evidence. They are also warned that they must not discuss the case with anyone except with other jurors and then only in the jury room. Even after the case is concluded they should not disclose what happened in the jury room.

They are also told about the duty to elect a foreman to act as chairman, but no guidance is given as to how this should be done. It is stated that they may take notes if they wish during the trial. It is also mentioned that in certain circumstances the judge may be able to take a majority verdict but that they must reach a unanimous verdict if possible.

In 1992 the Lord Chancellor's Department produced a video that is now routinely shown to all jurors at the start of their period of jury service.

The Roskill Committee gave attention to ways of making the jury's task easier, especially in complex cases. The prosecution, it said, should prepare schedules and summaries of the relevant contents of documentary evidence. Glossaries of technical terms should be made for the jury. Modern techniques of presentation of information should be utilized, including any appropriate forms of visual aid.

This exhortation has been very much taken to heart. Cases run by the Serious Fraud Office rejoice in a full battery of hi-tech methods. The two specially designed court rooms in Chichester Rents in Chancery Lane, for instance, have a proliferation of TV monitors and computer systems for presentation of evidence to the jury. The jury itself have four TV monitors on which they can see the head and shoulders of the witness. But the TV monitors are constantly in use also to project documents and graphics. In these huge cases with thousands of documents, the IT expert is now a vital member of the lawyers' support team. (See also Criminal Justice Act 1988, s 31, which permits the court to approve special means for conveying complex information.) But the Court of Appeal has discouraged attempts to persuade the jury by giving mathematical values to non-scientific evidence – see *R v Adams* [1996] Crim LR 898 and the valuable editorial note on the case which dealt with the utility of Bayes Theorem to guide the jury. The Court of Appeal said it had grave doubts whether the theorem could be used at all since it trespassed on a question that was peculiarly one for the jury, namely how to evaluate one piece of evidence against another.

The Runciman Royal Commission addressed the same issues and also made recommendations designed to ease the jury's task. It thought that writing materials should always be provided, that technological aids should be provided where appropriate and that the judge should explain to the jury that they have a right to ask questions and to take notes (pp 134–35).

Lord Justice Auld devoted considerable attention to the problem of providing more assistance to the jury. His recommendations included the following:

- Jurors should be provided with a copy of the indictment or charge.
- The judge should give jurors a fuller introduction to their task including the structure and practical features of the trial, a word about their manner of working, for example as regards note-taking and the time and manner of their deliberations.
- He should give them a summary of the case and the questions they are to decide supported with a written aide-memoire (a Cases and Issues Summary) agreed in draft by the lawyers and approved by the judge. The judge's summary should identify the nature of the charges, the evidence agreed, the matters of fact in issue and a list of the likely questions for their decision. If the issues narrow or widen in the course of the trial, the Case and Issues Summary should be amended and re-issued. (ch 11, paras 21-23, pp 520-21.)

Auld acknowledged that 'many criminal practitioners may not initially welcome the proposal for an agreed Case and Issues Summary' (ibid, para 24, p 522). They might believe 'that it would be impracticable in the hurly burly of their life, preparing cases for trial – often in the cracks of the day while engaged in the trial of other cases' (ibid.)

There are a considerable number of reasons why Auld's proposal of an agreed Case and Issues Summary poses problems:

- It is common in Crown Court cases for both prosecution and defence barristers to receive the brief for the trial at the very last minute – the day before the trial or the morning of the trial. [39] In that situation how could there be an agreed case statement?
- Counsel at trial is frequently different from counsel who dealt with the matter before. Again, this is true for both the prosecution and the defence. [40]
- There is no system that reliably enables counsel to know the name of opposing counsel in advance of the trial. In more substantial cases they might have that knowledge but in ordinary run-of-the-mill cases, usually they would not. [41] How could they agree a document if they do not know each other's identity?
- Even if counsel does know the name of the then opposing counsel, since it is normal for counsel to change during the pre-trial stage, there would be no way

---

[39]   In the Crown Court Study, half (51%) of all prosecution barristers and one third (31%) of defence barristers in contested cases received the brief in the case on the day before the hearing or on the day itself. (sect.2.1.3)

[40]   The Crown Court Study showed that close to half of all briefs were returned. Prosecution barristers in contested cases said their brief had previously been returned in 59% of cases. For defence barristers the proportion was 44%. (sect.2.1.6) It could not be assumed that a statement drafted by the (usually more junior) counsel who acted earlier would be thought adequate by the trial advocate.

[41]   The Court Service's *Review of the Effectiveness of Plea and Directions Hearings in the Crown Court*, January 1998 asked counsel when they were informed of opposing counsel's identity. 92% of defence counsel and 96% of prosecution counsel answered on the day of the PDH. (para 5.31)

of knowing whether that counsel will still be acting when the matter comes to trial.

- If, as would often happen, the appreciation of the facts changes as the case preparation moves along, the Case and Issues Summary would have to be up-dated – with further resulting problems of getting agreement

- Presumably the Case and Issues Summary would have to be settled by counsel. But what would be the role of the defence solicitors and the CPS? The Auld Report said nothing about this. Many solicitors would find it very unsatisfactory to be excluded from the process, but having them involved would add significantly to the complication and delay involved.

- Would the lawyers in practice get instructions from the defendant? There are, notoriously, serious difficulties in criminal cases in getting instructions from the defendant. If he is on bail, he frequently does not manage to get himself to his solicitors' office; if he is in custody, his solicitors and barristers commonly do not manage to get to the prison.

- Since there would be no advantage to the defendant in agreeing a statement such as Auld had in mind, defendants and their lawyers would drag their feet and would not be co-operative. Why should they be? This is well known to be the case with defence disclosure despite the fact that failure to produce a defence disclosure statement may result in adverse comment by the judge (CPIA 1996, s11(3)). Plotnikoff's and Woolfson's research[42] establishes that this is virtually a dead letter. The defence statement is generally either framed in a way that reveals little, or it is not entered at all. Yet prosecutors generally do not ask the court to direct that further particulars be given nor do they generally ask the judge to comment adversely on the absence or inadequacy of the defence statement.[43] One reason is that judges seem to be as unenthusiastic about enforcing the statutory obligation as prosecutors. If that is true of defence statements which are supposed to be helpful to the prosecution, how much more would it be true of Auld's proposed case statements which would mainly be intended to be helpful only to the jury?

10. The quality of jury decision-making

There is as yet no systematic study of the jury based on observation or recording of their deliberations. The Contempt of Court Act 1981 makes this impossible. According to s 8 of the Act it is contempt of court 'to obtain, disclose, or solicit any particulars of statements made, opinions expressed, arguments advanced or votes cast by members of a jury in the course of their deliberations in any legal proceedings'. (The lengthy questionnaire addressed to jurors in the Crown Court Study done for the Runciman Royal Commission was not exempt from the provisions of the 1981

---

[42]   J Plotnikoff and R Woolfson, *A Fair Balance? Evaluation of the operation of disclosure law*, Home Office, RDS Occasional Paper No 76, 2001 – available on www.homeoffice.gov.uk/rds/index.html

[43]   Plotnikoff and Woolfson research study.

Act. The questions asked were all carefully drafted and officially approved on the basis that they did not infringe the provisions of s 8.) The Runciman Commission recommended that section 8 of the Contempt of Court Act should be amended to permit authorised research in the jury room. [44]. Lord Justice Auld disagreed. [45]

Studies of jury decision-making have mainly been based on the impressions of judges, lawyers, or police officers, or on simulations with 'shadow' or 'mock' juries.

One major such study was the Chicago project based on the impressions of judges conducted by Professors Harry Kalven, Jr and Hans Zeisel of Chicago University and published as *The American Jury* (Little Brown & Co, 1966). The work was based on 3,576 actual criminal trials and the replies to a questionnaire from the 555 trial judges involved. (Jurymen could not be approached.) The results showed that judges and juries agreed to acquit in 13% of cases and agreed to convict in 62% of cases, yielding a total agreement rate of 75%.

In cases where judge and jury disagreed, it was found that the jury was more lenient than the judge in 19% and less lenient in 3%. Just over half of the disagreements which seemed explicable were caused by different approaches to the evidence. Nearly one-third were due to jury reaction to the law and about one-tenth were due to jury sentiments about the defendant himself. Summarising their conclusions in *New Society*, the authors said:

Harry Kalven, Jr and Hans Zeisel, 'The American Jury', *New Society*, 25 August 1966, p 290

It may be useful to put quite general and interrelated questions: why do judge and jury ever disagree, and why do they not disagree more often?

The answer must turn on the intrinsic differences between the two institutions. The judge very often perceives the stimulus that moves the jury, but does not yield to it. Indeed it is interesting how often the judge describes with sensitivity a factor which he then excludes from his own considerations.

The better question is the second. Since the jury does at times recognize and use its *de facto* freedom, why does it not deviate from the judge more often? Why is it not more of a wildcat operation? In many ways our single most basic finding is that the jury, despite its autonomy, spins so close to the legal baseline.

The study does not answer directly, but it does lay the ground for three plausible suggestions. As just noted, the official law has done pretty well in adjusting to the equities, and there is therefore no great gap between the official values and the popular. Again, the group nature of the jury decision will moderate and brake eccentric views. Lastly, the jury is not simply a corner gang picked from the street; it has been invested with a public task, brought under the influence of a judge, and put to work in solemn surroundings. Perhaps one reason why

[44]   Recommendation 1, p 188
[45]   Chapter 5, paras 82-87, pp 166-68.

the jury exercises its very real power so sparingly is because it is officially told it has none.

The jury thus represents a uniquely subtle distribution of official power; an unusual arrangement of checks and balances. It represents also an impressive way of building discretion, equity, and flexibility into a legal system. Not the least of the advantages is that the jury, relieved of the burdens of creating precedent, can bend the law without breaking it.

Whether or not one comes to admire the jury system as much as we have, it must rank as a daring effort in human arrangement to work out a solution to the tensions between law and equity and anarchy.[46]

The first English study, by the Oxford Penal Research Unit, was based primarily on the views of barristers and the police. Its principal finding was that most acquittals were 'attributable to a single cause—the failure of the prosecution (normally the police) to provide enough information, or to present it in court in a way that would convince both judge and jury of the defendant's guilt'. (See Sarah McCabe and Robert Purves, *The Jury at Work* (Blackwell, 1972), p 11.) Very few verdicts were found to be perverse.

The present writer's study of acquittals at the Old Bailey and the Inner London Crown Court was based on questionnaire interviews with the barristers for the prosecution and the defence. It was striking that there was no great difference of view between prosecution and defence lawyers as to the likely reasons for the acquittals. Again, there was little evidence of perverse verdicts. (See M Zander, 'Are Too Many Professional Criminals Avoiding Conviction?' 37 *Modern Law Review*, 1974, p 28.)

For the report of a series of experiments with 'mock' juries who listened to tape-recorded trials, see AP Sealy and WR Cornish, 'Juries and their Verdicts', 36 *Modern Law Review*, 1973, p 496, and LSE Jury Project, 'Juries and the Rules of Evidence' (1973) *Criminal Law Review*, p 208.

A study based on 30 cases heard by 'shadow' juries conducted by the Oxford Penal Research Unit showed the jury approaching its task very soberly. The shadow juries listened to real cases and when the real jury withdrew to consider their verdicts, so did the shadow jury. The authors summarized their results:

Sarah McCabe and Robert Purves, *The Shadow Jury at Work*, 1974, pp 60–3

Of course the 'shadow' jury discussions and verdicts were not comparable with those of the real jury since the future of the defendant was not at risk, but the

---

[46]   For an extended discussion of the book, see (1967) *Criminal Law Review*, pp 555–86. But for doubts about the statistical methodology of the study, see AE Bottoms and Monica Walker, 'The American Jury: A Critique', 67 *Journal of the American Statistical Association*, 1972, p 773. For the authors' rejoinder, see ibid, p 779. For an assessment in 1991 see Valerie Hans and Neil Vidman, 'The American Jury at Twenty-Five years', *Law and Social Inquiry*, 1991, p 323.

fact that many of our volunteers felt like jurors encourages us to make certain comparisons where real and 'shadow' jury verdicts agree.. .

Summary of results

3. The 'shadow' juries showed considerable determination in looking for evidence upon which convictions could be based; when it seemed inadequate, they were not prepared to allow their own 'hunch' that the defendant was involved in some way in the offence that was charged to stand in the way of an acquittal ...

5. There was little evidence of perversity in the final decisions of these thirty groups. One acquittal only showed that sympathy and impatience with the triviality of the case so influenced the 'shadow' jurors' view of the evidence that they refused to convict. One other unexpected acquittal seemed to be wholly due to dissatisfaction with the evidence.

A less favourable view of jury decisions emerged from a later piece of research– *Jury Trials* by John Baldwin and Michael McConville (Clarendon, 1979). They selected a random sample of 500 defendants in the Birmingham Crown Court who pleaded not guilty. In the event, 116 of these were acquitted by the judge before the case had run its full course and another 14 changed their plea to guilty during the case. This left 370, of which 114 ended in acquittal. The researchers asked the trial judge, the defence solicitor, the prosecuting solicitor, the police and the defendant himself about these cases–the first three groups by questionnaire and the last two by interview. The response rate was very high (over 95% for the judges, the prosecuting solicitors and the police). The table below shows the opinions of the different groups regarding the 114 acquittal cases.

	Judge	Defence solicitor	Prosecuting solicitor	Police
	%	%	%	%
No strong view expressed that the acquittal not justified	62	83	64	48
Some doubts about acquittal	6	7	9	8
Serious doubts about acquittal	32	10	26	44
Total	100 (114)	100 (114)	100 (114)	100 (114)

(Source: Jury Trials, Table 5, p 46.)

The acquittal was seen as doubtful or highly questionable by one respondent in 30 instances (27% of the 114), by two respondents in 16 (14%) and by three or more respondents in 28 (25%)–ibid, Table 6, p 47. There were 41 cases in which both judge and one other respondent found the acquittal doubtful (p 54).

Convictions were less often found doubtful or highly questionable, but 8% were so regarded by one or more respondents (2% by one respondent, 3% by two and 3% by three or more respondents–Table 9, p 51).

The researchers concluded that in respect of a few acquittals it might be said 'that the jury's verdict was primarily conditioned by its sympathy for the defendant or antipathy towards the victim' and 'some questionable convictions can possibly be explained on the basis of sympathy with the victim or prejudice against the defendant'. But in general 'the performance of the jury did not always appear to accord with the principle underlying the trial system in England that it is better to acquit those who are probably guilty than to convict any who are possibly innocent. On the contrary, the jury appeared on occasion to be over ready to acquit those who were probably guilty and insufficiently prepared to protect the possibly innocent' (p 128). There was nothing in the composition of the jury (age, sex or social class)that correlated with the decisions.

The study is significantly different from previous studies in suggesting a considerable measure of disagreement between jury verdicts and those of the other key actors.

The Crown Court Study (p 243, n 146 above), was based on the responses of jurors, prosecution and defence barristers, judges and police officers concerned in some 800 contested cases in every Crown Court in England and Wales in a two week period in February 1992.

The results were broadly very positive:

Did the jury understand the evidence? Jurors were asked, 'How difficult was it for you to understand the evidence in this case?' Over 90% thought it 'Not at all difficult' (50%), or 'Not very difficult' (41%) (p 206, sect 8.2.1). The same question was asked in cases where there was scientific evidence. Surprisingly, the results were very similar – 56% 'Not at all difficult', 34% 'Not very difficult' (p 206, sect 8.2.2).

Jurors were then asked 'Do you think the jury as a whole was able to understand the evidence?' The response broadly was Yes. Over 90% thought that all the jury understood the evidence (56%) or that most understood (41%). The response from jury foremen was virtually identical (p 207, sect 8.2.3). There were 143 juries (17% of the 821 in the study) in which one or more jurors said 'Only a few understood' or 'None of them understood'. 116 juries had one such member, 20 had two such members, 6 had three and one had four (ibid).

The prosecution and defence barristers were asked whether they thought the jury had trouble understanding the evidence. 94% of prosecution barristers, and 90% of defence barristers thought they had no trouble (p 177, Table 6.15). As a result of an oversight this question was not put to the judges, but they were asked whether the jury could understand the scientific evidence in cases where there had been some. In no fewer than 93% of these cases the judges thought all the scientific evidence was understandable by the jury (ibid).

The answers for the question could the jurors remember the *evidence* were much the same. [47]

Was the jury's verdict surprising? Different participants in the trial were asked 'In your view, was the jury's decision surprising in the light of the evidence?' In the great majority of cases the answer was No. The verdict was surprising in the view of 27% of the CPS, 25% of the police, 18% of the defence solicitors, 15% of the prosecution barristers and 14% of the judges and the defence barristers (p 163, Table 6.5).

The great majority of respondents in all the categories thought the verdict was understandable in the light of the evidence. Those who thought it was against the weight of the evidence but explicable gave a long list of explanations: sympathy for the defendant, antipathy toward the complainant, case too trivial or stale, misconduct by the police, concern over sentence, quality or lack of quality of the respective counsel. Hardly any respondents thought the decision was against the judge's direction on law.

The prosecution and defence lawyers and the judges all agreed that 2–4% of jury decisions were inexplicable. The police thought that 8% were inexplicable.

When the judges, the prosecution barristers and the police thought that the verdict was against the weight of the evidence it was an acquittal in about 90% of instances. When defence barristers and defence solicitors thought the verdict was against the weight of the evidence just under half were acquittals (Table 6.9).

On the basis of these figures it appears that 'problematic jury acquittals' constituted 31% of all jury acquittals for prosecution barristers, 29% for the judges and 16% for defence barristers (p 170).

Jury acquittals are about one-third of all acquittals in the Crown Court (see p 520 below). On that basis, problematic acquittals would be around one-tenth of all acquittals.

The Crown Court Study also showed that there were some (though far fewer) problematic convictions. Judges and prosecution barristers thought that 2% of convictions were problematic, whereas defence barristers thought that 17% were problematic (pp 170–71).

Length of jury deliberations In most cases the jury was out for a very short period– in over half (52%) for under two hours, and in three-quarters (77%) for under four hours (Table 8.23, p 225.) There were eight cases (1%) in which the jury stayed together overnight. (At the time of the survey it was a rule that once the jury had begun their deliberations, they were not allowed to separate until they reached their verdict, known as 'sequestration of the jury'. Now, under the Criminal Justice and Public

---

[47]   P 209, Table 8.9; p 178, Table 6.16.

Order Act 1994, s 43 it is in the judge's discretion whether he permits the jury to go home while they are deliberating.)

Not surprisingly, the length of jury deliberations was closely associated with the length of the case. Thus where the case lasted under half a day, the jurors reported being out for under two hours in 96% of cases. When the case lasted 3 to 4 days the jurors were back within two hours in only 15% of cases. When it lasted over two weeks, the jurors took more than four hours in three-quarters of the cases (p 225). (The English record is probably the Maxwell trial in 1996 where the jury were out for seven days of deliberations spread over 10 days and 11 nights.)

For an unscientific and distinctly jaundiced account of the experience of serving on a jury, see the lecture of the late Professor Ely Devons of the London School of Economics – 'Serving as a Juryman in Britain', 28 *Modern Law Review*, 1965, p 561. See also various articles in *New Law Journal* 14 September 1990, pp 1264–76; 'Jury Service: A Personal Observation', 1979 *LAG Bulletin*, p 278.

Research by Julie Vennard, then of the Home Office Research and Planning Unit, tends rather to support the view that juries decide rationally and on the basis of the evidence. (See J Vennard, 'The Outcome of Contested Trials', in *Managing Criminal Justice*, ed D Moxon, 1985, pp 126–51; and 'Evidence and Outcome: a Comparison of Contested Trials in Magistrates' Courts and the Crown Court', Home Office Research and Planning Unit, *Research Bulletin*, No 20, 1986, p 48.)

11. Respective roles of judge and jury

During the trial the jury is normally passive, simply listening to the case as it develops. Sometimes the jury will ask a question by passing a note to the judge. The judge will then decide whether, and if so how the question should be answered. Sometimes he will invite the views of the lawyers for both sides. At each break they are usually warned by the judge not to discuss the case among themselves or with anyone else until they reach their deliberations at the end.

The judge's role in the adversary system, as has been seen, is also largely passive if the comparison is with that of the judge in the continental system. But by comparison with the jury, the judge is quite actively involved. In particular, he will have to rule on points of law as they arise, especially in regard to the admissibility or otherwise of evidence. If this involves lengthy debate, the jury will be asked to withdraw. The judge knows more about the case than the jury in that he has access to the pre-trial papers and he also knows whether the defendant does or does not have previous convictions. At the close of the prosecution's case he may have to deal with a submission that there is no case to answer (see p 506 below). (For the view that there should be greater interaction between judge and jury in regard to fact finding see J Jackson and S Doran, 'Judge and Jury: Towards a New Division of Labour in Criminal Trials', 60 *Modern Law Review*, 1997, pp 759-78.)

The judge is supposed to sum up for the jury on both the law and the facts.

(a)   Summing up the law

In McVey[48] *the Court of Appeal spelled out the minimum content of every summing up:*

> It is trite to say that every summing up must contain at least a direction to the jury as to the burden and standard of proof, and as to the ingredients of the offence or offences which the jury are called upon to consider.

The problem of what is meant by this dictum was considered in a lecture entitled 'Summing Up the Law' at Nottingham University in 1989 by the late Professor Edward Griew:[49]

> Directing the jury as to the burden of proof means telling them who has to prove the case; it means telling them that the prosecution must prove the defendant's guilt, not the defendant his innocence. Directing them as to the standard of proof means telling them that the case has to be proved beyond reasonable doubt–commonly expressed by saying that they may convict the defendant only if they are sure of his guilt.

(For a study of what magistrates, ordinary citizens and professionals in the criminal justice system understand by the admonition 'only convict if you are sure of the defendant's guilt' see M Zander, 'The criminal standard of proof – how sure is sure?', *Criminal Law Review*, 20 October 2000 p 1517.)

In recent years the Court of Appeal has laid down 'model' or 'specimen' directions or standard forms of words in which directions on particular matters can or ought to be given. Quite a number are now embodied in a document issued to all judges who sit in the Crown Court by the Judicial Studies Board with the approval of the Lord Chief Justice. They are published on the Board's website.[50]. The Foreword warns, 'They are an invaluable tool – but must be a servant not a master. . .They must be adapted to the needs of the individual case.'

In his lecture, Professor Griew criticised the tendency of judges to give the jury more law than it needed for the purpose of its decision[51] and to use overly technical and complex language. American research showed that a good many judicial directions on law to juries were 'totally incomprehensible to an alarming percentage of jurors'.[52] No doubt similar research in this country would yield similar results. 'Our juries continue to be addressed in language relatively rich in abstract and latinate words and in sentences that are often very long.'

---

[48] [1988] Crim LR 127.

[49] [1989] Crim LR 768.

[50] www.jsboard.co.uk(Publications – Bench books – Specimen Directions).

[51] Professor Griew suggested (at pp 770–1) that in *McVey*, above, the Court of Appeal quashed a conviction of a plainly guilty person because the judge's direction on the ingredients of the offence was insufficient even though the missing words were unnecessary to the jury's decision.

[52] Notably Robert P Charrow and Veda R Charrow, 'Making Legal Language Understandable: A Psycholinguistic Study of Jury Instructions' (1979) 79 *Col L Rev*, 1306; William W Schwarzer, 'Communicating with Juries: Problems and Remedies' (1981) 69 *Calif L Rev* p 731.

In the *Crown Court Study* done for the Runciman Royal Commission, 61% of jurors said they found the judge's summing up 'not at all difficult' to understand and another 33% found it 'not very difficult' to understand. When asked if other members of the jury found it difficult, a quarter were not sure but 65% thought they did not.[53] But saying that they understood does not mean that they did understand. Even less does it show whether the jury followed the judge's direction on the law.[54]

(b) Summing up on the facts

The job of the judge in summing up the facts according to the Court of Appeal in a recent case is to 'state matters impartially, clearly and logically'.[55] His task therefore is to remind them of the evidence and to marshal it in a convenient way which is fair to both sides.[56]

But to what extent can he go beyond this to comment on the evidence and thereby seek to influence the jury's decision? There is no doubt that English judges do this.(It is famously said that Sergeant Sullivan at the end of an Old Bailey trial invited the judge to ask the jury whether they found for the defendant or his Lordship.) In the notorious case of the 'Birmingham Six' who were charged with IRA pub bombings resulting in numerous deaths and injuries, Mr Justice Bridge (as he then was), during a three-day summing up gave innumerable indications that in his view the prosecution's evidence was to be preferred to that of the defence. Nor did he see anything wrong with leading the jury to its conclusion. 'I am of the opinion', he told the jury, '–that if a judge has formed a clear view, it is much better to let the jury see that and say so and not pretend to be a kind of Olympian detached observer.'

For an unusually strong summing up on the facts in a civil case see that of Mr Justice Caulfield in the impudent libel action unwisely brought in 1987 by Mr Jeffrey Archer against *The Star*, arising out of the allegation that he had visited a prostitute [57] There was, the judge said, no accounting for the tastes of happily married men and the fact that the jury would not expect Mr Archer, deputy chairman of the Conservative Party, to visit a prostitute, did not mean that it was not possible. But he asked the jury to

53   Royal Commission on Criminal Justice. Research Study No 19, paras 8.6.2-3.

54   For references to other literature on whether jurors understand judges' directions on the law see Law Commission, *Evidence in Criminal Proceedings: Previous Misconduct of a Defendant*, Consultation Paper No 141, 1996, pp 127-28.

55   *Berrada* (1989) 91 Cr App Rep 131n. The trial judge had said that the defendant's allegation that police officers had fabricated an interview was 'really monstrous and wicked' and 'utterly monstrous'. The court quashed the conviction.

56   It seems that in a short case in which the issues are simple it is not necessarily a fatal defect in a summing up that the evidence has not been discussed: see *Attfield* (1961) 45 Cr App Rep 309.

57   Four years later Lord Archer was imprisoned for perjury and perverting the course of justice in the libel proceedings.

consider whether it was probable. He invited the jury to remember the evidence of Mrs Mary Archer. 'Your vision of her will probably never disappear. Has she elegance? Has she fragrance? Would she have, apart from the strain of his trial, a radiance?' Mr Archer, the judge said, was a sportsman. 'You may think he's fit looking ... Is he in need of cold, unloving, rubber-insulated sex in a seedy hotel?' (*The Times*, 24 July 1987.)

The danger that the judge will try to influence the jury is the greater in cases where the accused has previous convictions, because the judge knows of their existence from the outset. They are in his file, allegedly so that he can steer counsel away from questions which might otherwise lead to their becoming admissible. It seems that judges in Scotland manage without this.

In the United States, by contrast, the rule in most states is that the judge in a criminal trial must express no opinion on the weight or credibility of the evidence of witnesses or on the merits of either side.

Even if judges were to be prevented from commenting, they could probably still convey to the jury their basic view through a mixture of inflexion of the voice, 'body language', timing and other signs which would not register in the official transcript. (The Court of Appeal has, however, indicated that in extreme cases it would allow evidence from those present in court as to 'non-verbal communication' by the trial judge trying to persuade the jury–*Hircock* [1969] 1 All ER 47.) The only way to prevent such influence would be to prohibit the judge from summing up at all on the facts – which is the usual rule in the USA.

There is little doubt that when the judge sums up for a conviction the impression of impartial justice being done is diminished. See generally David Wolchover, 'Should Judges Sum Up on the Facts?' [1989] *Criminal Law Review*, p 781.

In the Crown Court Study, the barristers, the CPS, the defence solicitor and the judge were asked, 'Did the summing up favour either side?' In each category of respondents the majority said No. But of those who said Yes, more in each category thought it favoured the prosecution than the defence. (Table 4.21, p 130.) Defendants were asked about the fairness or otherwise of the judge during the trial and in the summing up. The defendant thought the judge had been fair in the summing up in 73% of cases and unfair in 27%. (p 132).

The Runciman Royal Commission thought it would be wrong to lay down a rule as to how far the judge should sum up on the facts. Cases and circumstances varied. Sometimes there would be no need for a summing up at all. The need to be fair to both sides, the Commission said, required 'that judges should be wholly neutral in any comment that they make on the credibility of the evidence' (p 124, para 23). It was 'inappropriate for judges to intrude their own views of whether or not a witness is to be believed' (ibid). Implementation of that recommendation would presumably require some kind of ruling or Practice Statement by the Lord Chief Justice. There is no sign that this will happen. (For support for the Royal Commission's view that it should happen, see D Osborne, `Breaking New Ground', *Counsel*, February 1998, pp 16-17.)

Lord Justice Auld took a radical approach to the judge's summing up: 'The judge should no longer direct the jury on the law or sum-up evidence in the detail that he now does.' (ch 11, para 44, p 533) His basic recommendations were:

- so far as possible, the judge should not direct the jury on the law, save by implication in the questions of fact that he puts to them for decision;
- the judge should continue to remind the jury of the issues and, save in the most simple cases, the evidence relevant to them, and should always give the jury an adequate account of the defence; but he should do it in more summary form than is now common;
- the judge should devise and put to the jury a series of written factual questions, the answers to which could logically lead only to a verdict of guilty or not guilty; the questions should correspond with those in the updated Case and Issues Summary, supplemented as necessary in a separate written list prepared for the purpose; and each question should be tailored to the law as the judge knows it to be and to the issues and evidence in the case; and
- the judge, where he considers it appropriate, should be permitted to require a jury to answer publicly each of his questions and to declare a verdict in accordance with those answers. (ch 11, para 55, pp 537-38)

In Auld's view 'simplification of the way in which judges direct and sum up to juries is essential for the future well-being of our system of trial by judge and jury' (ibid, para 49, p 535. (The Auld Report did not mention the findings of the Crown Court Study (p 499 above) suggesting that the jury may not in fact have as great difficulties with the summing up as some believe.) He did recognise however 'that the task of extricating us from our present tradition would be formidable' (ibid). The Court of Appeal bore ultimate responsibility for the elaborate and complex structure now enshrined in the Judicial Studies Board's specimen directions. What was needed, he suggested, was 'a fundamental and practical review of the structure and necessary content of a summing up with a view to shedding rather than incorporating the law and to framing simple factual questions that take it into account'. (ibid.) Perhaps, he thought, 'a body drawn from the judiciary and the Judicial Studies Board could be given a blank sheet of paper and charged with the task'. (ibid.)

The Auld Report was published in October 2001. At the time of writing, a year and a half later, there was no sign that such a body would be established. In the writer's view there was little likelihood that Auld's radical approach to the judge's summing up would be adopted.

(c)   Directing an acquittal

Acquittals directed by the judge comprise a high proportion of all acquittals. As has been seen, there are two forms of such acquittal: (1) where the prosecution enter no evidence at all (called an 'ordered acquittal') and (2) after a submission by the defence at some stage after the case has begun and usually at the end of the prosecution's case that there is no case to answer (a 'directed acquittal').

The withdrawal of a case from the jury poses a delicate problem. Can the judge decline to put the case to the jury if he thinks that the prosecution's case is merely weak? The Court of Appeal considered this question in *R v Galbraith* [1981] 1 WLR 1039. Lord Lane, the Chief Justice, said there were two schools of thought. One was that the judge should stop the case if in his view it would be unsafe or unsatisfactory to convict. (See for instance *Mansfield* (1977) 65 Cr App Rep 276.) The other was that the judge should only stop the case if there was no evidence on which a jury properly directed could properly convict. Before the Criminal Appeal Act 1966 the second test had been applied. But under the 1966 Act the Court of Appeal was required to quash a conviction where it found that under the circumstances it was unsafe or unsatisfactory (see p 660 below). Since then a practice had grown up of asking the trial judge to take a view as to whether conviction would be safe by submitting that there was no case. This involved the judge invading the province of the jury. It invited the trial judge to consider the weight and the reliability of the prosecution's evidence–precisely the issues that had to be considered by the jury. Lord Lane answered the question in this way (at 1042):

> How then should the judge approach a submission of 'no case'? (1) If there is no evidence that the crime alleged has been committed by the defendant, there is no difficulty. The judge will of course stop the case. (2) The difficulty arises where there is some evidence but it is of a tenuous character, for example because of inherent weakness or vagueness or because it is inconsistent with other evidence. (a) Where the judge comes to the conclusion that the prosecution evidence, taken at the highest, is such that a jury properly directed could not properly convict upon it, it is his duty, upon a submission being made, to stop the case. (b) Where however the prosecution evidence is such that its strength or weakness depends on the view to be taken of a witness's reliability, or other matters which are generally speaking within the province of the jury and where on one possible view of the facts there *is* evidence upon which a jury could properly come to the conclusion that the defendant is guilty, then the judge should allow the matter to be tried by the jury. It follows that we think the second of the two schools of thought is to be preferred.

For comment and discussion see Rosemary Pattenden, 'The Submission of No Case–Some Recent Developments' (1982) *Criminal Law Review*, p 558; D Wolchover, 'Stopping the Trial in Suspect Cases', *New Law Journal*, 1982, p 527. For the effect of this ruling in magistrates' courts, see N Yell, 'Submissions of "No Case to Answer"', *Justice of the Peace*, 1981, p 406 and Pattenden, op cit, at p 564.

Even where the judge has rejected a submission of no case he may still direct the jury to acquit if in light of the developing defence case he subsequently comes to the conclusion that no reasonable jury properly directed could convict. (*Brown (Davina)* [2001] Crim LR 675, CA.) But such a power must be exercised very sparingly.

The Runciman Royal Commission (p 59, para 41) recommended that *Galbraith* should be reversed so that a judge could stop a case if he or she took the view that the prosecution's evidence was demonstrably unsafe or unsatisfactory or too weak to be allowed to go to the jury. This recommendation has not been acted upon.

Sometimes the judge, whilst not going so far as to direct the jury to acquit, makes it very clear in his summing up that he thinks an acquittal is the right result. He sums up strongly for an acquittal. There is nothing to prevent this even if the judge goes beyond the proper limits. The matter is unlikely to become the subject of comment from the Court of Appeal since the prosecution has no right of appeal against an acquittal (other than on a point of law taken by the Attorney-General, the outcome of which does not affect the defendant–see p 631 below). (For a classic instance of the judge 'summing up for an acquittal' see the summing up of Mr Justice Cantley in the Jeremy Thorpe case (*Daily Telegraph*, 19, 20 June 1979.)

(d)   Directing a conviction

Views differ as to whether it is ever legitimate for the judge to direct the jury to convict. Lord Devlin thought it to be unconstitutional. (See *Trial by Jury*, 1966, p 84 and App II.) There is no doubt that the judge must leave to the jury any issue that has to be decided by them. In *Leer* [1982] Crim LR 310, the Court of Appeal considered a direction to convict where the accused had been charged with possessing an offensive weapon after being found with a fishing knife. The judge ruled that his answers to police questioning as to why he had the knife did not amount to a reasonable excuse and that he therefore had no defence to put forward, and he directed them to convict. The Court of Appeal quashed the conviction because the judge should have left the issue to the jury. It would have been surprising if the jury had decided to acquit but such a decision on the evidence would not have been perverse. See also *R v Clemo* [1973] RTR 176n.

But what if an acquittal would be perverse? Can the judge direct a conviction then? In *DPP v Stonehouse* [1978] AC 55, the House of Lords by three to two held that he could not. Lord Salmon said there was a difference between directing the jury to acquit or to convict. If there was no evidence on which they could reasonably convict, he should direct an acquittal. This rule had been established a long time ago to protect the accused against being wrongly convicted. 'But there is no converse rule. ... If the judge is satisfied that on the evidence, the jury would not be justified in acquitting the accused and indeed that it would be perverse of them to do so, he has no power to pre-empt the jury's verdict by directing them to convict. The jury alone has the right to decide that the accused is guilty' (at p 80). But Lord Salmon did accept that it would be perfectly in order for the judge to sum up to the jury 'in such a way as to make it plain that he considers the accused is guilty and should be convicted' (ibid). Lord Edmund-Davies said there was an unfortunate tendency in the courts these days to withdraw issues from the jury which were properly theirs. Whether this sprang from distrust of the jury's capacity, 'or from excessive zeal in seeking to simplify their task, it needs careful watching' (at p 88). The judge could give a strong lead to the jury but he should not direct them to convict. Lord Keith said that if judges had a right to decide in their discretion whether to direct a conviction it would widen the field for appeals. 'The wiser and sounder course, in my opinion, is to adhere to the principle that, in every case where a jury may be entitled to convict, the application of the law to the facts is a matter for the jury and not for the judge' (at p 9). See also *R v Lawn* [1984] Crim LR 114.

The view expressed in *Stonehouse* was confirmed in *Gent* [1990] 1 All ER 364, in which the Court of Appeal said the judge ought not to direct a conviction save possibly in a wholly exceptional case such as where there has been a formal admission of guilt. Accordingly the defendant is entitled to have the verdict of the jury even though, on the evidence, only one verdict is possible and an acquittal would in the judge's view be perverse. (See to like effect *Gordon* (1987) Times, 11 May.)

The only situation in which a direction to convict may be lawful is where the defence is based on a pure point of law and the judge rules against the defence on the matter of law–see *Hill and Hall* (1988) 89 Cr App Rep 74, [1989] Crim LR 136. But even that exceptional principle is dubious, especially in cases where it is conceivable that the jury might wish to acquit simply because it disapproves of the law or the way it has been applied.

An example was the famous case in 1985 of Clive Ponting, the civil servant prosecuted under the Official Secrets Act for leaking to an MP information about the sinking of the Argentinian ship *The General Belgrano* during the Falklands War. On the view of the law taken by the judge, McCowan J, Mr Ponting had no defence. He therefore intended to direct the jury to convict but was dissuaded from doing so by counsel for the prosecution who drew the judge's attention to what he termed 'recent authorities'. The judge said that, although all the elements of the offence had been made out and there was no defence, he told the jury that they were at liberty to bring in whatever verdict they considered right. The jury proceeded to acquit–presumably because they felt that Mr Ponting had acted honourably and perhaps correctly.

For a similar principled acquittal see the case of Pat Pottle and Michael Randall who were tried at the Old Bailey in July 1991 for helping the spy George Blake to escape from prison 25 years earlier. They were prosecuted after they wrote a book about their exploit. The trial judge ruled that they had no defence to the charge. In his closing speech to the jury Pat Pottle said, 'We do not deny the things we are accused of doing. Not only do we not deny it, we say it was the right thing to do.' The jury acquitted both men (*The Times*, 5 July, 1991).

See also TA Green, *Verdict According to Conscience: Perspectives on the English Criminal Trial, 1200–1800* (Chicago University Press, 1985), which suggests that part of the historic role of the jury was to mitigate the rigour and harshness of the criminal law and its penalties by acquitting guilty defendants, not just in the occasional case but on a massive scale.

(e)   Should the jury be prohibited from returning a perverse verdict?

In one of the most controversial passages in his report, Lord Justice Auld recommended 'that the law should be declared, by statute if need be, that juries have no right to acquit defendants in defiance of the law or in disregard of the evidence, and that judges and advocates should conduct criminal cases accordingly' [58] In his view, the ability of juries to acquit in defiance of the law and in disregard of their oaths was 'a blatant affront to the legal process and the main purpose of the criminal justice system – the control of crime – of which they are so important a part'.[59] The jury's role was 'to find the facts and, applying the law to those facts, to determine guilt or no'. [60] They were not there 'to substitute their view of the propriety of the law for that of Parliament or its enforcement for that of the appointed Executive, still less on what may be irrational, secret and unchallengeable grounds'. [61]

The writer was sharply critical of this proposal in his Response to the Auld Report[62]:

> I regard this proposal as wholly unacceptable – a serious misreading of the function of the jury. The right to return a perverse verdict in defiance of the law or the evidence is an important safeguard against unjust laws, oppressive prosecutions or harsh sentences. In former centuries juries notoriously defied the law to save defendants from the gallows. In modern times the power is used, sometimes to general acclaim, sometimes to general annoyance, usually one imagines to some of each.

> Auld quotes EP Thompson's eloquent passage in describing the function of the jury:

>> The English common law rests upon a bargain between the Law and the People. The jury box is where people come into the court; the judge watches them and the jury watches back. A jury is the place where the bargain is struck. The jury attends in judgment, not only upon the accused, but also upon the justice and humanity of the law.... [*Writing by Candlelight*, 1980]

> This exactly captures the position, which I would say is part of the unwritten constitution of this country. Auld says that he regards the ability of juries to acquit and to convict in defiance of the law and in disregard of their oaths, as a 'blatant affront to the legal process and the main purpose of the criminal justice system – the control of crime – of which they are so important a part' (p 175, para 105). I believe that this statement, perhaps the least attractive sentence in the whole report, reflects deep distrust of the jury. It is based I believe on an authoritarian attitude that disregards history and reveals a grievously misjudged sense of the proper balance of the criminal justice system.

[58]   Chapter 5, para 107, p 176.
[59]   Chapter 5, para 105, p 175.
[60]   Chapter 5, para 105, p 175.
[61]   Chapter 5, para 105, p 175.
[62]   Accessible on www.lse.ac.uk/collection/law/news and www.lcd.gov.uk(Major Reports – Comments).

In the Introduction to his Report (p 10, para 8) Sir Robin quotes, with apparent approval, from the concluding sentence in my Dissent to the Report of the Runciman Royal Commission, 'the integrity of the criminal justice system is a higher objective than the conviction of any individual'. But the concern for justice and for the integrity of the system is too important to be entrusted solely to the judges. The jury have a role in that regard too.

The Runciman Royal Commission dealt with this issue in a short paragraph – which was not mentioned by Auld:

> Although juries are under a solemn duty to return a verdict in accordance with the evidence, they do from time to time perversely return a verdict contrary to the evidence. Until there is research on jury deliberations it is impossible to say confidently why this happens. But it is plausible to suppose that it is because the jury has taken an unfavourable view of the prosecution or of the law under which it is brought or the likely penalty. We do not, however, think that these cases justify the introduction of a right of appeal against acquittal. (p 177, para 75)

I cannot imagine that on a constitutional matter of this importance any government would prefer the view of an individual judge, however distinguished, to the unanimous contrary view of a recent Royal Commission. I believe that the present system provides the right balance in telling the jury that they must decide the case in light of the law and the evidence but allowing them to ignore either or both if they believe that to be the right course. We have lived with that system for hundreds of years. I believe that there is no acceptable reason to consider changing it.

The Government did not accept Lord Justice Auld's recommendation. ('Nor do we intend to legislate to prevent juries from returning verdicts regarded as perverse where the verdict flies in the face of the evidence, as has happened very occasionally.'[63])

(f)   Asking the jury questions

The jury does not give reasons for its decisions. In a criminal case it simply says 'Guilty' or 'Not Guilty'. In a civil case it finds for the plaintiff or defendant and, if for the plaintiff, it may have to determine the damages. But in a decision in February 1999 the Court of Appeal (Rose LJ, Ognall and Burton JJ) created an exception to the general rule. It held that where there was more than one possible basis for a verdict of guilty of manslaughter 'it might be convenient and desirable' for the judge to invite the jury to indicate the basis on which they returned that verdict. The purpose of such an inquiry would be to assist the judge in regard to sentence. Lord Justice Rose said that in summing up, the judge might hand to the jury written questions identifying the different possible verdicts, as between murder and manslaughter and also as to the reasons for manslaughter. Alternatively, after a manslaughter verdict was returned

---

[63]   White Paper, *Justice for All*, CM 5563, July 2001, para 4.50.

a judge might ask the jury what was the basis of that verdict – provided that he had warned the jury in his summing up of his intention to ask that question. But there was no obligation on the jury to answer. Nor was there any requirement of unanimity as to the reasons for the verdict (*R v Jones (Douglas)* (1999) Times, 17 February.)

The decision seems completely novel and highly problematic.

(g) Is the jury's unreasoned verdict compatible with the European Convention on Human Rights?

Article 6 of the ECHR states that one of the incidents of a fair trial is a public pronouncement of a reasoned decision .If this applies to jury trial, the Strasbourg Court could hold jury trial with its inscrutable verdict to be contrary to the Convention. Addressing this question in his Report, Lord Justice Auld said: 'For a number of reasons, I incline to the view of a number of eminent British commentators[64] that the Strasbourg Court, in taking account of the way in which our system of jury trial works as a whole, would not consider our juries' unreasoned verdicts to breach Article 6.'[65]

He instanced the following reasons:
* The Strasbourg case law was not precise about the content of reasons required to satisfy the fair trial test.
* The test was not exacting. As well as allowing for different national traditions, the Court had stressed that the general duty to give reasons did not require detailed answers.
* Courts were not required by the Strasbourg case law to indicate the evidence they accept and why.
* The Strasbourg Court had ruled that the publicly unreasoned decision of a Danish jury was not contrary to the Convention.[66]
* In *Condron v UK*[67] the Court had said (at para 57) , 'the fact that the issue of the applicant's silence was left to a jury cannot of itself be incompatible with the requirement of a fair trial'. This, Auld suggested, showed that the Court was prepared to accept the jury's verdict as the final word in a judgment of which the summing up furnished the overt reasoning process.
* In considering the fairness of the trial the Strasbourg Court looked at the trial and the appeal process together. The Court of Appeal did have a limited capacity to quash a conviction if it considers that it was contrary to the evidence. [68]

---

64   He cited Professor John Spencer in his advice to the Review and Harris, O'Boyle and Warbrick, *The Law of the European Convention on Human Rights* (1995) p 215.
65   Chapter 5, para 92, p 170.
66   *Saric v Denmark*, application no.31913/96, decision of 2 February 1999.
67   (2000) 31 EHRR 1.
68   However Auld cited the Court's statement in *Condron v UK* (above, at para 46) that jury verdicts in England 'are not accompanied by reasons which are amenable to review on appeal'.

- There was no general continental consensus as to what is meant by the reasoning ('motivation'), of a judicial decision. In France, for instance, it could mean no more than an indication of the legal principles applied by the court.

But Lord Justice Auld did consider that 'the time has come' for the trial judge to give the jury a series of written factual questions leading logically only to a verdict of guilty or not guilty. [69]

12. Majority jury verdicts

In Scotland, since time immemorial, there has been a majority verdict based on a bare majority of eight or more out of the fifteen who sit on a Scottish jury. Historically in England, however, the jury's decision had to be unanimous. The reality of unanimity must sometimes have been questionable. It seems probable that in some cases dissenters would 'give in' rather than have a hung jury–or even just to bring the proceedings to a speedy conclusion. (For the particular danger of this happening on a Friday afternoon see Penny Darbyshire, 'Notes of a Lawyer Juror', *New Law Journal*, 14 September 1990, p 1264, 1266–7.)

In 1967, the then Home Secretary, Mr Roy Jenkins, introduced proposals in the Criminal Justice Bill to permit a majority verdict of not less than ten out of twelve. The reason he gave was the spate of recent 'jury nobbling' cases. But the evidence for this was thin. The total proportion of jury disagreements resulting in a retrial appeared to be about 4% and few of these, presumably, would have been due to any form of tampering with the jury.

The proposal provoked great controversy at the time, but in the interim it seems to have become accepted. (See, however, G Maher, 'Jury Verdicts and the Presumption of Innocence', *Legal Studies*, 1983, p 146, for a powerful argument that majority verdicts are inconsistent with the requirement that proof of guilt be beyond a reasonable doubt.) Lord Justice Auld dealt with this topic in nine lines. His Review had 'produced little support for change either in the levels of the required majorities or for reversion to unanimity in all cases or for any form of intermediate verdict, such as that of "not proven" in use in Scotland'. [70]

The current annual proportion of guilty verdicts by majority is just over a fifth. (It was 21% in both 1999 and 2000, and 23% in 2001– *Judicial Statistics*, Table 6.11.) There are no equivalent official figures for the proportion of acquittals by a majority, since the jury are not permitted to reveal that an acquittal was by a majority, for fear that it would be treated as a second-class acquittal.[71] (In the Crown Court Study conducted for the Runciman Royal Commission it was possible to establish

---

[69]   Chapter 5, para 97, p 172.
[70]   Chapter 5, para 75, p 164.
[71]   Criminal Justice Act 1967, s 13(2).

from the jury questionnaires that the proportion of acquittals by a majority was exactly the same as convictions by a majority (p 162).)

The court is not supposed to consider the possibility of a majority verdict until at least two hours and ten minutes have elapsed (*Practice Direction* [1970] 1 WLR 916). In a complex case the judge will wait much longer than that.

In *R v Reynolds* [1981] 3 All ER 849, the Court of Appeal Criminal Division quashed a conviction for theft because the foreman of the jury stated that there was a majority of ten in favour of conviction but he did not also state that there were two members of the jury who disagreed. The court held that the provisions of s 17(3) of the 1967 Act were mandatory in stating that the court 'shall not accept [a majority verdict] unless the foreman of the jury has stated in open court the number of jurors who respectively agreed to and dissented from the verdict'. In *R v Pigg* [1983] 1 All ER 56, the Court of Appeal Criminal Division applied the ruling in *Reynolds* and quashed a conviction for attempted rape on the same grounds. The Crown appealed, and the House of Lords overruled *Reynolds*. The law lords held unanimously that, although it was a mandatory requirement that the number who agreed on conviction and the number who dissented must be made known, the precise form of words used was not an essential part of that requirement. It was enough if the words used by the foreman of the jury and the clerk of the court made it clear to an ordinary person how the jury was divided. If the foreman said that ten agreed to convict it could be inferred that two dissented!

But what if the jury is completely deadlocked? For many years the judge was permitted in that situation to give what was known as the *Walhein* direction, approved in the case of that name (1952) 36 Cr App Rep 167. In that case, the jury told the judge that they were having difficulty in reaching a unanimous verdict. (At that date there was no such thing as a majority verdict.) The judge then directed them:

> You are a body of twelve men. Each of you has taken an oath to return a true verdict according to the evidence; but, of course, you have a duty not as individuals, but collectively. No one must be false to that oath; but in order to return a collective verdict, the verdict of you all, there must necessarily be argument and a certain amount of give and take and adjustment of views within the scope of the oath you have taken; and it makes for great public inconvenience and expense if jurors cannot agree owing to the unwillingness of one of their number to listen to the arguments of the rest. Having said that, I can say no more.

This direction, seemed, however, to condone pressure on the dissenting minority to fall into line. Since the introduction of majority verdicts in 1967 it has seemed inappropriate. In *Watson* [1988] QB 690 the Court of Appeal approved a new direction to replace that in *Walhein*:

> Each of you has taken an oath to return a true verdict according to the evidence. No one must be false to that oath, but you have a duty not only as individuals

but collectively. That is the strength of the jury system. Each of you takes into the jury box with you your individual experience and wisdom. You do that by giving your views and listening to the views of the others. There must necessarily be discussion, argument and give and take within the scope of your oath. That is the way in which agreement is reached. If, unhappily, [ten of] you cannot reach agreement you must say so. It is a matter for the discretion of the Judge as to whether he gives that direction at all and if so, at what stage of the trial. There will usually be no need to do so.

(See further MJ Reville, 'Directing the Hung Lamp of Freedom', *Law Society's Gazette*, 26 October 1988, p 19 and P Robertshaw, 'Exhorting Hung Juries' (1997) *Criminal Law Review* 805.)

13. Retrials on jury disagreement

When the jury disagrees and cannot reach a verdict, the prosecution are entitled to start afresh. It is a matter of discretion over which the court has no control – though occasionally the judge remonstrates with the prosecutor about the desirability of pursuing a particular case. (It has been argued that the prosecution should have to ask leave and that the court should take into account the same factors regarded as relevant when the Court of Appeal considers whether to order a retrial on quashing a conviction.[72])

There are no regular statistics about the extent to which retrials occur as a result of jury disagreements. But in 1981, according to a Home Office Research Unit paper, there were some 370 retrials due to this cause–about 1.5% of the 25,000 or so contested cases in the Crown Court that year. (See Sid Butler, 'Acquittal Rates', Home Office Research and Planning Unit Paper 16, 1983, p 7.) On the juror's duty to reach a decision see *R v Schot and Barclay* [1997] Crim LR 827. In P Robertshaw's article referred to above it is stated (p 805) that in 1991 there were 90 hung trials in the whole country – of which 79 (88%) occurred in one court, the Inner London Crown Court!

14. Will the Court of Appeal consider what happened in the jury room?

Occasionally an appeal is based on some alleged irregularity in what happened in the jury room or in some other aspect of the jury's handling of the case. What attitude do the courts take to such an appeal?

---

[72]   J Hall, 'Hung Juries and Retrials' *Archbold News*, 27 June 2001, p 6.

Boston v WS Bagshaw & Sons [1966] 1 WLR 1135n (Court of Appeal, Civil Division)

Lord Denning MR: This is a motion for a new trial. We are told that there are affidavits from all the twelve jury men, in which they wish to go back on some of the answers given by them in open court. They were given several questions to answer. They deliberated for five hours and came back into court with answers which were as clear as could be. It is not possible that there could be any misunderstanding as to the questions or the answers. In respect of each of two publications the jury were asked: 'Were the defendants actuated by malice?' To each they answered: 'No' The associate asked them, in accordance with the time-honoured practice: 'Are they the answers of you all?' The foreman answered 'They are.' The answers were duly recorded and they were discharged. On the next day the judge, after argument, held that on those answers the plaintiff failed and the defendants were entitled to judgment.

It appears that the jurors did not anticipate the result. They read it in the newspapers and some of them communicated with the plaintiff and his solicitors. Further inquiries were made. Then all the twelve jurors made affidavits indicating that they gave those two answers under a misapprehension; that they meant to find malice; and that they would, if they could, change those answers so as to say that the defendants were actuated by malice. Mr Hirst asks us to receive those affidavits and to order a new trial.

To my mind it is settled as well as anything can be that it is not open to the court to receive any such evidence as this. Once a jury has given their verdict, it is accepted by the judge, and they have been discharged, are not at liberty to say they meant something different. ...

The reasons are twofold: first, to secure the finality of decisions arrived at by the jury; secondly, to protect the jury themselves and to prevent them being exposed to pressure or inducement to explain or alter their views. If this were to be permitted, where is it to stop? After a jury have solemnly found a man 'Guilty' and he has been sentenced, are they to be at liberty next day to return and say they meant to find him 'Not Guilty'? It cannot be. ...

Harman LJ: I agree. It would be destructive of all trials by jury if we were to accede to this application. There would be no end to it. You would always find one juryman who said: 'That is not what I meant' and you would have to start the whole thing anew. Interest *reipublicae ut sit finis litium*.

Diplock LJ: I agree.

In criminal cases the rule is the same:

R v Thompson [1962] 1 All ER 65 (Court of Criminal Appeal)

[The appellant was convicted of certain offences by a jury, and sentence was postponed until the next day. In the intervening period, a juryman was alleged to have told a member of the public that, whilst in the jury room, a majority of the jurors had been in favour of acquitting the appellant until the foreman produced a list of the appellant's previous convictions, and that thereupon the jury agreed to convict. Leave to appeal against conviction was given, limited so that the Court of Criminal Appeal might rule whether there was jurisdiction to inquire into the subject of the alleged statement.

Lord Parker CJ gave the judgment of the court:]

... There is absolutely no doubt that information as to the prisoner's previous convictions must be kept from a jury, and if what was said to have happened did happen it would have been highly improper. This court is now asked to inquire into the matter, and to adjourn the case in order to see whether the alleged statement by the juryman can be supported by some statement or affidavit made by him. The court has come to the conclusion that it is perfectly idle to adjourn the case for that purpose because the court is quite satisfied that they would have no right at all to inquire what did occur in the jury room. It has for long been a rule of practice, based on public policy, that the court should not inquire, by taking evidence from jurymen, what did occur in either the jury box or the jury room. The court finds it unnecessary to go through all the cases.
. . .

Atkin LJ put the matter in his own words as follows:

The reason why that evidence is not admitted is both in order to secure the finality of decisions of fact arrived at by a jury, and, also, which is a matter of great importance for the protection of jurymen themselves, to prevent their being exposed to pressure that might otherwise be put on them with a view to explaining the reasons which actuated them individually in arriving at their verdict. To my mind, it is a principle which is of the very highest importance in the interests of justice to maintain, and an infringement of the rule appears to me to be a very serious interference with the administration of justice.... The court would also like to refer in passing to what Lord Hewart CJ said on the question of jurymen divulging what occurred in *R v Armstrong*:

If one juryman might communicate with the public upon the evidence and the verdict, so might his colleagues also, and if they all took this dangerous course, differences of individual opinion might be made manifest which, at the least, could not fail to diminish the confidence that the public rightly has in the general propriety of criminal verdicts.[73]

This appeal is dismissed.

---

[73]   [1922] 2 KB 555 at 568, [1922] All ER Rep 153 at 197.

See, to like effect, *R v Chionye* (1988) 89 Cr App Rep 285 and *Millward* [1999] Crim LR 164. In *Millward* the foreman incorrectly reported that the guilty verdict had been unanimous. She later wrote to the court to explain. The Court of Appeal dismissed the appeal on the ground that it was not a matter into which the court could inquire. See similarly *Miah and Akhbar* [1997] 2 Cr App R 12; *Qureshi* [2001] EWCA Crim 1807, [2002] 1 WLR 518, [2002] Crim LR 62; and *Mirza* [2002] EWCA Crim 1235, [2002] Crim LR 921. (Cp *Igwemma v Chief Constable of Greater Manchester* [2001] EWCA Civ 953, [2001] 4 All ER 751 in which the Court of Appeal held that the trial judge had been entitled to allow the jury to reconsider and then change the verdict it had already delivered in open court because it realised from what was said after that verdict that they had misunderstood the instruction they had been given.)

In *Sander v UK* (2001) 31 EHRR 1003 the Strasbourg Court held that the defendant had not had a fair trial because the trial judge had not taken sufficiently robust action to deal with an allegation by one juror of racial prejudice by other jurors. (See also *Remli v France* (1996) 22 EHRR 253 but cp. the Strasbourg Court's decision in *Gregory v UK* (1998) 25 EHRR 577 in which the Court held that the trial judge had dealt appropriately with such an allegation.) [74]

Lord Justice Auld in his *Review of the Criminal Courts* said that the effective bar that s 8 of the Contempt of Court Act put on an appellate court inquiring into and remedying possible bias or other impropriety in the course of a jury's deliberations was 'indefensible and capable of causing serious injustice'[75] The Act, he recommended, should be amended to permit such inquiry. However, there was nothing in the Criminal Justice Bill 2002/03 to give effect to this recommendation.

Where the alleged impropriety amongst jurors occurs outside the jury room the appeal courts have on occasion inquired into the matter. In *Spencer* [1986] 2 All ER 928 the House of Lords quashed convictions of nurses who had been found guilty of violence against patients at Rampton Hospital, when someone who had been removed from the jury because of possible bias against the defendants had given lifts to and from the trial to three of the jurors. See also *Prime* (1973) 57 Cr App Rep 632; *Blackwell* (1995) 2 Cr App Rep 625 and *Young* [1995] QB 324. (In the last of these the Court of Appeal ordered a retrial after it emerged that during an overnight adjournment in a hotel some members of the jury had used a Ouija board to consult the deceased in a séance!)

15. Publication of the secrets of the jury room

Jurors are told in the leaflet they receive on being summoned for jury service that they must not reveal anything that occurs in the jury room either during the trial or

---

[74]   For critical comment on the decision in *Sander* see M Zander, 'The complaining juror' *New Law Journal*, 19 May 2000, p 723.

[75]   Chapter 5, p 173, para 98.

after it has finished. But what is the position if the press publish details of jury deliberations? The question came up for decision after the sensational Jeremy Thorpe case[76] when the *New Statesman* on 27 July 1979 published an interview with a member of the jury in which he gave details of the jury discussions. Proceedings for contempt were instituted by the Attorney-General but, surprisingly, the Attorney-General lost (*A-G v New Statesman and Nation Publishing Co Ltd* [1980] 1 All ER 644). The Divisional Court held that disclosure of the secrets of the jury room could be contempt but it depended on the circumstances. It would be contempt if disclosure tended to imperil the finality of jury verdicts or to affect adversely the attitude of future jurors or the quality of their deliberations. In this particular case there were no special features which made publication a contempt. There had been no payment of money to the juror. The article did not suggest that anything improper had occurred. In fact it showed that the jury had approached their task in a sensible and responsible manner. There was no suggestion that the article could have interfered with the administration of justice in the case in question.

The media's victory was shortlived. The Contempt of Court Act 1981, s 8, made it contempt 'to obtain, disclose or solicit any particulars of statements made, opinions expressed, arguments advanced or votes cast by members of a jury in the course of their deliberation in any legal proceedings'. It makes no difference whether the case is identified or whether any payment is made for such disclosure. The clause was introduced against the advice of the Government by Lords Hutchinson and Wigoder and was supported by the Criminal Bar Association, the Senate of the Four Inns of Court and the Lord Chief Justice. The Lord Chancellor, Lord Hailsham, declared it to be 'far too draconian'. However, he was defeated in the House of Lords and the Government did not seek to have the clause overturned when the Bill returned to the House of Commons. It would seem to rule out even properly controlled academic research. The Runciman Royal Commission (p 2, para 8) recommended that the Contempt of Court Act should be amended to permit properly controlled research. But this recommendation has not been implemented.[77]

It is noteworthy that when the issue had been put to the Criminal Law Revision Committee for consideration in 1967 it did not think there was any need for legislation. It said juries were reminded of their duty to maintain secrecy by a notice on the walls of the jury room and that there seemed to be few breaches of this understanding: 'We are of opinion that secrecy has been well maintained and that such breaches or attempts to break it as have become known so far have not established a mischief so extensive or serious that it calls for legislation and punishment' (Criminal Law Revision Committee, Tenth Report, *Secrecy of Jury Room*, 1968). It accepted that it was not then a criminal offence to disclose what had happened in the jury room though in certain circumstances it might amount to contempt of court.

---

76   The leader of the Liberal Party was charged with conspiracy to murder his alleged homosexual lover. He was acquitted after a trial lasting 31 days.

77   For a discussion of the issue see M Zander, 'The case for jury research', 38 *Medicine, Science and Law*, 1998, pp 106-11.

But it did not think the problem was sufficiently serious to warrant legislation. For one thing it did not think it right to make punishable the inevitable minor disclosures as people spoke to their families and friends after the case about the experience of being jurymen. Such disclosures, the Committee said, though they should not be encouraged, few would regard as deserving of punishment. Under the Contempt of Court Act 1981 such disclosures could theoretically be the subject of proceedings for contempt–though in practice it is unlikely to be used for cases other than publication in the press.

See further Jacob Jaconelli, 'Some Thoughts on Jury Secrecy', *Legal Studies*, March 1990, p 91.

In *A–G v Associated Newspapers Ltd* [1994] 1 All ER 556 the House of Lords rejected an appeal by the owners of the *Mail on Sunday* which had been fined £60,000 for contempt in publishing views of jurors in the Blue Arrow fraud case. The information had been obtained not from the jurors directly but from transcripts of paid interviews purportedly carried out by way of 'research' by an American. The House of Lords held that it made no difference whether the publication of what had transpired in the jury room came directly from jurors or indirectly from others.

16. Does the jury acquit too many defendants?

The suggestion that too many guilty defendants are acquitted was powerfully urged on a number of occasions by Sir Robert Mark, when he was Commissioner of the Metropolitan Police. The best-publicised occasion for the expression of these views was his 1973 Dimbleby Lecture on BBC 1:

Sir Robert Mark, 'Minority Verdict', BBC, 1973, pp 8–14

What we do know about trials in higher courts doesn't justify any complacency. Indeed, there is one fact I can mention which should be enough in itself to demand some kind of enquiry. This is the rate of acquittals. Of all the people in England and Wales who plead not guilty and are tried by jury, about half are acquitted.. . .

Every acquittal is a case in which either a guilty man has been allowed to go free or an innocent citizen has been put to the trouble and expense of defending himself. There must be some rate of failure. We can't always expect to convict the guilty or never to prosecute the innocent. But in my opinion a failure rate of one in two is far too high. I doubt whether it would be tolerated in many other kinds of activity, so I think it's something that certainly needs looking into. In the absence of any reliable research no one can say with any certainty why the acquittal rate is so high. A fairly high number of acquittals are undoubtedly by direction of the judges, as soon as they've heard the prosecution case. Since 1967 cases are no longer sifted effectively by a Magistrate, and the higher courts are cluttered up by cases which in my opinion should never have got there at all. This probably accounts for what seems to be an increase since 1966 from 39% to about 50% in acquittals and tends to obscure the problem I'm discussing.

My own view is, nevertheless, that the proportion of those acquittals relating to those whom experienced police officers believe to be guilty is too high to be acceptable. ...

I wouldn't deny that sometimes common sense and humanity produce an acquittal which could not be justified in law, but this kind of case is much rarer than you might suppose. Much more frequent are the cases in which the defects and uncertainties in the system are ruthlessly exploited by the knowledgeable criminal and by his advisers.

Sir Robert Mark's strictures on the high 'failure rate' in English trials need some further explication and comment:

The percentage of acquittals when Sir Robert Mark spoke was around half. It is now even higher. In 1993, it was 58%; in 1997, 60%; in 2001, 66%. This seems, and perhaps is, very high. But the facts are more complex than Sir Robert Mark suggested.

The acquittal rate is based on contested cases, whereas the majority of defendants in the Crown Court plead guilty. The proportion pleading guilty in Crown Courts currently is around three-fifths. (In 2001, of the 74,318 defendants tried in the Crown Court, 61% pleaded guilty to all charges and another 4% pleaded guilty to some charges.[78]) (The proportion is lower than it was. For many years it was around 70%.)

The proportion of defendants pleading not guilty who are acquitted on all counts is currently just over a fifth. (In 2001 it was 23%. (ibid))

But only a minority of acquittals are by the jury. In 2001, no fewer than 54% of all acquittals were ordered by the judge when the prosecution offered no evidence at the start of the case and another 12% were directed by the judge at the close of the prosecution's case on the ground that there was insufficient evidence to put to the jury. In other words, the jury were only responsible for 33% of all acquittals–which represented 7% of all cases.[79]

The fact that some 7% of those tried in the Crown Court are acquitted by the jury might be largely attributable to the fact that the burden of proof is a high one. Even assuming that all those acquitted were guilty (obviously a wholly impermissible and unrealistic assumption), a significant number would rightly be acquitted simply because the prosecution failed to prove its case beyond a reasonable doubt. If proof must be beyond a reasonable doubt (and no one has suggested otherwise), it is inevitable that a considerable number of guilty defendants will be acquitted because the evidence of their guilt cannot be produced.

[78]   *Judicial Statistics*, 2001, Table 6.9.
[79]   *Judicial Statistics*, Tables 6.10 and 6.9.

There is no evidence to suggest that professional criminals do better in the criminal justice system than others, and there is a considerable amount of evidence to the contrary. Taking defendants with a prior record, the evidence is that they have a statistically *lower* chance of an acquittal than defendants with no prior record[80] Moreover, the worse the record, the worse the chances of an acquittal.[81] In Baldwin and McConville's 1979 study they got from the police details not only of prior convictions but also of prior acquittals and of suspected involvement in criminal activity. From this they built up a profile of each defendant on a scale of criminal professionalism. For this exercise there were close to 5,000 defendants in the sample– 2,406 in Birmingham and 2,292 in London, a total of 4,698. Of these, 2,265 (48%) were defined by the police information as 'low' on the criminal professionalism score, 1,448 (31%) as 'medium', 647 (14%) as 'high' and 227 (5%) as 'very high'. When these scores were compared with acquittals and especially the 'questionable acquittals', it was found that 'only a minuscule proportion of all cases end in the questionable acquittal of any defendant who, on the measures used here, could be regarded as a professional criminal. Indeed, of those scoring highly on the professionalism scale in each city, no more than one in eighty was said to have been questionably acquitted'.[82]

The only evidence that provides *any* support for Sir Robert Mark's thesis is that of John Mack, who contrasted the careers of the top criminals in his area of research (from names supplied by the police), with that of two other categories of lesser criminals. He called his three groups the Main Group, the Lesser Group and the Small Fry. On average the Small Fry were convicted on 85% of charges brought against them, the Lesser Group on 80% and the Main Group on 75%.[83] This does show that the Main Group were somewhat more successful in avoiding charges than the others, but the difference can hardly be said to be great and the police success rate in getting convictions in three-quarters of the charges brought against the top villains seems, if anything, remarkably high. Moreover, as Mack showed, when the serious criminals are convicted they tend to get longer sentences. Mack compared the time not spent in prison from the age of 17 for his three groups. The Small Fry spent on average 83% of their time not in prison compared with 70% for the Lesser Group and 74% for the Main Group.[84]

Nor was Sir Robert's attack on crooked lawyers supported by the small amount of evidence on this issue. Thus in Baldwin and McConville's study of 370 contested jury trials in Birmingham they interviewed the police officers in the cases about the

80   This is shown by a number of studies including even one conducted by the Metropolitan Police – see M Zander, *Modern Law Review*, 1974, p 39, Table 3; McCabe and Purves, *The Jury at Work* (Blackwell, 1972) p 39, Table 4; Metropolitan Police, *Law Society's Gazette*, 1 March 1973, Table 1.

81   M Zander, *Modern Law Review*, 1974, p 41.

82   *Jury Trials* (1979), pp 110–12.

83   J Mack, *Modern Law Review*, 1976, p 255.

84   J Mack, *Modern Law Review*, 1976, p 252.

reasons for the acquittals. They reported, 'There was not a single serious allegation of any practice which could possibly be described as corrupt' (*Jury Trials*, 1979, p 118). In another study the same two authors looked at 2,000 cases heard in seven London Crown Courts in the light of the 'solicitors blacklist' maintained by Scotland Yard. (They had been sent a copy anonymously.) The firms on the list appeared on behalf of 223 defendants in the sample. Of these, 50% pleaded guilty–a proportion that was slightly *higher* than for the rest of the sample. Of those who pleaded not guilty, the acquittal rate was 53%, which was not very different from that of 47% of the rest of the sample. Of the defendants identified to the researchers by the police as serious professional criminals, only 10 out of 72 had employed firms on the blacklist (Baldwin and McConville, 'Allegations Against Lawyers' (1978) *Criminal Law Review*, pp 744–5).

Finally, the minority of cases that are contested are likely, by definition, to be the doubtful ones in which one might expect a fairly high acquittal rate. This common-sense view is supported by the evidence, which shows that many not-guilty pleas are based on a defence that the accused lacked the necessary knowledge or intent (mens rea) to be guilty of the offence. It is perhaps not surprising that, in such cases particularly, the jury (or magistrates) will interpret conflicting testimony by giving the defendant the benefit of the doubt.

17. Trial on indictment without a jury

Hitherto in England and Wales trial on indictment has meant trial by jury. The Criminal Justice Bill 2002/03 Part 7 ('Trials on indictment without a jury') provided for trial on indictment by a judge without a jury in three situations: 1) on application by the defendant (cl 41); 2) on application by the prosecution on the ground of the complexity or length of the case (cl 42); and 3) on application by the prosecution where there is a danger of jury tampering (cl 43).

The House of Lords Committee stage debate on these provisions took place on 15 July 2003. Twenty peers spoke. Apart from the Minister, Baroness Scotland QC, only two of the twenty supported the Government. There were 17 speeches denouncing the provisions as an unacceptable incursion on the sanctity of trial by jury. After a debate of three and a half hours, the Lords rejected all three clauses by the overwhelming majority of 210 to 136.[85] (The vote was taken on clause 41 but the debate grouped all the Part 7 provisions together so that defeat for clause 41 meant defeat for them all.)

The Government immediately announced that it would restore the Part 7 provisions when the Bill returned to the Commons in the autumn but since there seemed little prospect that the House of Lords would concede on the issue, the fate of the provisions – and indeed of the whole Bill – was uncertain. (If the Government insisted on

[85]   House of Lords, Hansard, vol 651, 15 July 2003, cols 768-814.

restoring Part 7 and was unable to get the Lords to agree, the Bill would fail. It could be reintroduced not less than 12 months later and, under the Parliament Acts 1911 and 1949, can secure Royal Assent without the agreement of the House of Lords. But the Parliament Acts procedure requires that the second Bill be precisely the same as that first introduced in the Commons – so it could not contain the many Government amendments made during the passage of the first Bill.)

This section on trial on indictment without a jury begins with consideration of the Diplock courts in Northern Ireland.

(a)   'Diplock courts' in Northern Ireland

A survey of all cases tried in the first six months of 1973 in Belfast (a time of 'The Troubles') showed an acquittal rate of 16% for Protestant defendants as against 6% for Catholics. A Committee headed by Lord Diplock was sent to inquire into the problem of jury verdicts in terrorism cases. The Committee's Report identified various problems including intimidation of witnesses by terrorists and the danger of perverse acquittals of Loyalist terrorists by predominantly Protestant juries. The Committee recommended the suspension of jury trial for certain offences (*Report of the Commission to Consider Legal Procedures to Deal with Terrorist Activities in Northern Ireland*, 1972, Cmnd 5185). This was implemented in the Northern Ireland (Emergency Provisions) Act 1973 in relation to 'scheduled offences', broadly those regularly committed by terrorists–murder, other serious offences against the person, firearms and explosives charges, arson, robbery, aggravated burglary and intimidation.

The system of trial in 'Diplock courts' was basically left intact subject to certain significant innovations: a decision to convict requires a reasoned judgment (and reasoned judgments are normally also given for acquittals); there is an automatic right of appeal against conviction, sentence or both; and if the judge rules that a confession is inadmissible, he can withdraw and direct that the trial be conducted by a different judge. There were also changes made in the rules governing the admissibility of confessions.

A major study of the system published in 1995 stated that from 1973 to then, well over 10,000 defendants had passed through Diplock courts, 'the average annual figure having decreased from over 1,000 in the early years to a level of over 400 in each year from 1991 to 1993' (J Jackson and S Doran, *Judge without Jury: Diplock Trials in the Adversary System* (1995 Clarendon, Oxford), p 19.)

The study by Jackson and Doran showed (Table 2.2, p 35) that although the acquittal rate in Diplock courts for each of the ten years from 1984 to 1993 ran below that in ordinary jury trials, in seven of those ten years it was over 40% and in four of the ten years it was over 50%. The guilty plea rate in Diplock court cases was not significantly different from the rate in ordinary trials. In both Diplock courts and ordinary Northern Ireland trials the guilty plea rate was considerably higher than in jury cases in England and Wales. In Northern Ireland between 1984 and 1993 it was over 80%

in seven out of ten years in Diplock courts and in six out of ten years in ordinary trials. (ibid, Table 2.3, p 41).

The authors of the study found that although in Diplock courts the judges had more possibility for involving themselves in the fact-finding process than in jury trials, they generally did not do so. ('There was, however, no clear evidence from our survey that judges necessarily acted in a more inquisitorial manner when sitting in the absence of the jury. The general, though not universal view expressed by the judges who spoke to us was that it was inappropriate to deviate from the umpireal role required in adversarial proceedings' (ibid, p 288)).

(On the Diplock courts see also, K Boyle, T Hadden and P Hillyard, *Law and State* (Martin Robertson 1975) and by the same authors, *Ten Years on, Northern Ireland* (Cobden Trust, 1980); and J Jackson, 'Diplock and the Presumption against Jury Trial: a Critique' [1992] *Criminal Law Review*, p 755.)

In 1987 the Government decided to abolish the right of trial by jury in civil actions in Northern Ireland where previously jury trials were used in the overwhelming majority of such cases. In a strongly worded protest, the Northern Ireland Bar said the move had been engineered by employers' organisations such as the CBI and the insurance industry which argued that jury trials resulted in higher awards and therefore in higher insurance premiums which was bad for employment in the province. It called for the move to be stopped. But it went ahead notwithstanding. (Jury Amendment (Northern Ireland) Order, SI 1987/1283.)

(b)   Defendant allowed to opt for trial by judge alone

The Runciman Royal Commission did not mention 'jury waiver', namely permitting defendants to opt for trial by judge alone. This is widely used in the United States[86] and to some extent in Canada[87], New Zealand[88] and Australia. Lord Justice Auld proposed that, subject to the consent of the court, the defendant be given the choice in all trials on indictment. The judge should decide after hearing representations from both sides. He did not favour making the defendant's option subject to the consent of the prosecution as was the case in most jurisdictions in the United States.

In his view, trial by judge alone had a potential for providing 'a simpler, more efficient, fairer and more open form of procedure than is now available in many jury trials, with the added advantage of a fully reasoned judgment'.[89]

---

[86]   According to the Auld Report (ch 5, para 111, p 178.), in 1993 some 14% of all serious Federal cases were tried by judge alone.

[87]   It has applied to all indictable offences since 1985 – Canadian Criminal Code, RSC C-46, ss.473,476.

[88]   Offences carrying a maximum of 14 years' imprisonment or a mandatory life term are excluded – Crimes Act 1961, ss.361 A-C and 361B(5).

[89]   Chapter 5, para 117, p 180.

To avoid 'judge shopping', the defendant should be required to opt for trial at an early stage. Where the defendant had co-defendants who did not want trial by judge alone the best solution was that adopted in New Zealand where the judge would order that either all or none be tried by judge alone. [90]

The Government accepted the recommendation that the defendant be permitted to opt for trial by judge alone [91] and included it in the Criminal Justice Bill 2002/03. Clause 41 provides that if the defendant makes such an application it *must* be granted unless any of the circumstances described in sub-ss (5) to (8) apply. Subsection (5) applies where the defendant has co-defendants who do not want trial by judge alone. In that case, the application must be refused. Subsection (6) applies where (a) the defendant is or was in employment connected with the administration of civil or criminal justice (as explained in sub-s (9)), for example a judge, prosecutor or police officer, and (b) the judge is satisfied that if the defendant were convicted questions would arise as to his fitness for that office, and (c) the judge is satisfied that the matters referred to in (a) and (b) give rise to exceptional circumstances which make it desirable in the interests of justice for the trial to be conducted with a jury. There is no requirement that the charges arise out of the defendant's official functions.

Subsection (7) applies, regardless of the identity or functions of the defendant, where the charges raise issues whether the administration of justice has been prejudiced or brought into disrepute and this gives rise to exceptional circumstances making trial by jury desirable in the interests of justice.

Subsection (8) applies to any other case where exceptional circumstances make it necessary in the interests of justice to have trial by jury.

(c)   Non-jury courts for fraud trials

There have for many years been a variety of voices raised to urge that long, complex fraud cases should be tried by some form of special tribunal. In 1983, for instance, such a call was made separately by the Chairman of the Law Commission, Mr Justice Gibson, by the Lord Chief Justice, Lord Lane, by a law lord, Lord Roskill, and by Lord Hailsham, the Lord Chancellor, in the Hamlyn Lectures. The campaign for some such reform had been going on since the late 1960s when it was promoted in particular by the then Lord Chief Justice, Lord Parker. It seemed that little progress was being made, but in November 1983 the Government set up the Roskill Committee 'to consider in what ways the conduct of criminal proceedings arising from fraud can be improved, and to consider what changes in existing law and procedure would be desirable to secure the just, expeditious and economical disposal of such proceedings'.

---

[90]   Chapter 5, para 118, pp 180-81.
[91]   White Paper, *Justice for All*, Cm 5563, July 2001, para 4.27.

The Roskill Committee concluded that long fraud cases were so complex that it was not reasonable to expect jurors to be able to cope. There were often multiple defendants and many charges. 'The background against which frauds are alleged to have been committed – the sophisticated world of high finance and international trading – is probably a mystery to most or all of the jurors, its customs and practices a closed book' (para 8.27). The language of accountancy would be unfamiliar. The evidence often ran into hundreds or even thousands of documents. Research conducted for the Committee by the Medical Research Council's Applied Psychology Unit at Cambridge on understanding by jurors of a one-hour summing up in a fraud case confirmed the 'view of experienced observers and the promptings of commonsense, that the most complex of fraud cases will exceed the limits of comprehension of members of a jury' (para 8.34). Many jurors were simply out of their depth in such cases.

There was one dissentient, Mr Walter Merricks. In a powerful statement he effectively demolished the Committee's reasoning. First, he pointed to the weight of expert evidence received by the Committee which was 'overwhelmingly in favour of retaining the jury' (p 192, para C5). The vast majority of the solicitors' profession (from both prosecution and defence), the magistrates, the Bar and even the police had opposed the removal of jury trial. The judges had been divided but many judges had grave reservations about removing the right to trial by jury. Both the Society of Conservative Lawyers and the Society of Labour Lawyers had been 'emphatic in insisting on the retention of jury trial' (p 192). The submissions from the Bar were almost unanimous. Those who were against the jury came mainly from the financial and accountancy world and, when pressed in oral evidence, 'it became clear that most of them based their views on generalised impressions' (para C8). The Committee thought there were cases that were not prosecuted because of the difficulty of presenting very complex cases to the jury. But analysis by the DPP of all his fraud cases in 1983 showed that there was only one out of 71 not prosecuted in which the decision not to prosecute was caused by the complexity of the evidence.

Mr Merricks suggested that it had become a convention of the unwritten constitution that citizens should not be subjected to more than a short period of imprisonment otherwise than on a jury's verdict. Parliament should not be invited to abrogate this constitutional right without evidence that jury trial had broken down in serious fraud cases *and* that all possible procedural improvements had been considered and found inadequate. 'A mere hunch, unsupported by tested evidence, that the system might at some time in the future prove inadequate should not be enough' (para C7). The burden was on those who proposed to change the system. There was no hard evidence as to the extent of jury incomprehension. But the anecdotal evidence received by the Committee had not clearly supported the view that juries were unable to follow the evidence in these cases. 'Most judges and lawyers who made submissions to us thought that juries mostly reached the right result, or at least an understandable result' (para C17). There was a danger that if a special expert tribunal were set up, the trial would become simply an exchange between lawyers and the tribunal in impenetrable jargon.

The function of a trial as a publicly comprehensible exposition of the case would be threatened. Moreover, the fundamental issue in most fraud trials was one of dishonesty. It would be dangerous to entrust this judgment to experts. The legal standard of dishonesty was the standard of the ordinary man and experts were not ordinary men. It would also be difficult to define the cases in which the special tribunal would be appropriate.

Mr Merricks' dissent attracted much notice and support in comments on the Roskill Committee Report. Clearly he had had the better of the argument. The Government gave the report generally a warm welcome but its proposal on this particular issue was clearly too controversial and, after hesitating for a period, the Government announced that it would not be implemented.

But the debate rumbled on. In 1993 the Runciman Royal Commission (p 136, para 76) said that in the absence of research into juries it had no basis for making any recommendations for dispensing with juries in long fraud cases.

In February 1998, a year into the life of the Blair Government, the Home Office published a Consultation Document (*Juries in Serious Fraud Trials*) which invited views on whether the system should be altered and, if so, how. It referred to the Court of Appeal's decision in the *Blue Arrow* trial quashing the conviction on the ground that the case had become unmanageable and said that there was a significant risk of a miscarriage of justice resulting from the volume and complexity of the issues presented to the jury. In *R v Jones* the trial judge had discharged the jury from returning verdicts after the prosecution had presented its case, on the ground that by the time the jury came to consider its verdict it would not be able to recall the vital features of the case. The Consultation Paper canvassed a number of possible options: special juries, a judge sitting on his own, a special tribunal, and a judge sitting with a jury.

Views were asked for by June 1998 but in fact nothing further happened in regard to this issue before Lord Justice Auld was appointed in December 1999 to undertake his review of the criminal courts.

LORD JUSTICE AULD'S REPORT

Auld recommended that in serious and complex fraud cases, the trial judge should be empowered to order trial by himself sitting with lay members (or, where the defendant has opted for trial by judge alone, by himself alone). Either party should have a right of appeal against the judge's decision to the Court of Appeal.

Of the various arguments, Auld said that the two that weighed most heavily with him were 'the burdensome length and increasing speciality and complexity of these cases, with which jurors, largely or wholly strangers to the subject matter, are expected to cope' [92] The average length of cases prosecuted by the Serious Fraud Office was six

---

[92]   Chapter 5, para 183, p 204.

months. ('The fact is that many fraud and other cases ... now demand much more of the traditional English jury than it is equipped to provide.'[93])

Auld rejected having special juries made up of persons with special qualifications. It would be too difficult to compose lists of persons with the requisite qualifications and it would be unreasonable to expect them to serve for such long cases. He said that there had been little support for the idea of trial in such cases by a panel of judges. He agreed with those who argued that this would unduly strain valuable and limited judicial resources. He said that he had wavered as to whether trial in such cases should be by judge alone or by judge sitting with lay members. In the end he considered that the defendant should be entitled to express a preference, with the decision left to the judge. If he decided that trial should be with lay members, he should, after hearing representations, determine which (if any) speciality(ies) they should be drawn from. The Lord Chancellor, after consulting professional bodies, could establish and maintain a panel of suitable persons.[94] In the first instance the new system might be restricted to cases prosecuted by the Serious Fraud Office.

THE WHITE PAPER (JUSTICE FOR ALL)

In its White Paper *Justice for All* (Cm 5563, July 2001), the Government said that that there were a small number of serious and complex fraud trials that placed a huge strain on all concerned and where the time commitment was a burden on jurors' personal and working lives. As a result it was not always possible to find a representative panel of jurors. (para 4.28) The Government had concluded there should be a more effective form of trial in such cases. It rejected Auld's view that trial in such cases might be by judge with lay members. It recognised that the expertise of such persons could help the trial proceed. 'However, identifying and recruiting suitable people raises considerable difficulties, not least because this would represent a substantial commitment over a long period.' It therefore proposed that such cases should be tried by judge alone. It did not expect there to be more than 15-20 such trials a year. (para 4.30) It asked for views as to whether trial by judge alone should be extended to other long and complex cases.

THE CRIMINAL JUSTICE BILL 2002-2003

In the event the Government decided to extend trial by judge alone to a much wider category of cases. The Criminal Justice Bill 2002/03 dealt with the matter in Part 7. Clause 42 provided for the prosecution to apply for a trial on indictment in the Crown Court to be conducted by judge alone on grounds of length or complexity. Such an application would have to satisfy two tests.

---

93   Chapter 5, para 183, p 204.
94   Chapter 5, paras 185-85, 206, pp 205-09, 213.

The first concerns the likely impact of the trial on the jurors. The length or complexity of the trial must be such that it was likely to be so burdensome on the jury as to make it necessary in the interests of justice to conduct the trial without a jury (sub-s (4)(a)); or that the trial would be likely to place an excessive burden on the life of a typical juror (sub-s (4)(b)). The Explanatory Notes accompanying the Bill said that in deciding whether the burden on a typical juror would be excessive, the judge would need to take account of factors such as the impact of the trial on his or her working and private life, and the physical and mental demands it would make (para 231).

The second condition that must be satisfied relates to the sort of issues and evidence that the jury would have to consider – that the complexity or length (or both) would be attributable to the need to address arrangements, transactions or records of a financial or commercial nature or that relate to property (sub-s (5)(a)) and to the likely nature or volume of the evidence (sub-s (5)(b)).

The Explanatory Notes accompanying the Bill (para 228) said that in making his decision the judge might be expected to have regard to such things as the seriousness of the offence charged and the seniority of the defendant's position – though all relevant factors would have to be taken into account.

(d)   Trial by judge alone because of jury tampering

The White Paper *Justice for All* (July 2001) said that where an attempt had been made to intimidate or influence the jury the judge had a common law power to stop the trial but no power to continue the trial without a jury. The Government intended to legislate to give the judge power to continue the trial without the jury. (para 4.32) It asked for views on the further question whether this power should also exist where it was anticipated that there was a serious risk that the jury would be subject to bribery or intimidation. In such cases the courts currently ordered police protection for the jury. Quite apart from being extremely costly and burdensome for the police, such protection might have to continue over a period of months, and could be extremely disruptive and an unreasonable intrusion in the lives of jurors (para 4.33).

Clauses 43 and 45 of the Criminal Justice Bill 2002/03 gave effect to this intention. Under cl 43 the prosecution can apply to the judge for the trial to be conducted without a jury on the basis that 'there is a real and present danger that jury tampering would take place' (sub-s (4)) and that either of both of the following conditions apply: (1) that police protection for the jurors would be required, the level and duration of which would place an excessive burden on the life of a typical juror (sub-s (5)); (2) that even if police protection were provided, jury tampering was sufficiently likely to occur to make it necessary in the interests of justice to have trial by judge alone (sub-s (6)). Such an application would be made at a preparatory hearing where the parties would have an opportunity to make representations.

Under cl 45 the judge (exercising his common law powers) may discharge the jury during the trial because jury tampering appears to have taken place. If he is minded to discharge the jury on such grounds, he must allow the parties to make representations. If he then discharges the jury he must order that the trial continue without a jury unless in the interests of justice he decides that he must terminate it. If he decides instead to stop the trial he may order that a new trial will be conducted without a jury – providing he is satisfied that the condition set out in cl 43(4) and either or both of the conditions in cl 43(5) and (6) are likely to be met.

Applications under cll 41, 42 or 43 have to be made at a preparatory hearing (cl 44(2)). Decisions under any of those clauses or under cl 45 are subject to appeal to the Court of Appeal (cll 44 and 46).

(e) Young defendants

Defendants under 18 charged with an indictable offence other than murder must be tried summarily unless the offence is one of certain grave offences for which they may be sentenced to a long term of imprisonment or where they are charged with an adult and the magistrates consider it to be in the interests of justice that all should be tried together. Lord Justice Auld stated that in 1999 close to 5,000 young defendants were committed for trial in the Crown Court and nearly 1,000 were committed to the Crown Court for sentence.

Auld recommended that all cases involving young defendants at present committed to the Crown Court for trial or sentence should instead be put before a special sitting of the youth court constituted by a judge sitting with at least two experienced youth panel magistrates and exercising the full powers of the Crown Court. (ch 5, para 211, p 216) The court should have the power to sit in private. ('Notwithstanding the public notoriety that such cases now attract through intense media coverage, I consider that the court proceedings should normally be entitled to the same privacy as those in the present youth court.'[95]) The only exception should be where the young defendant is tried jointly with an adult. Such cases should continue to be subject to the Practice Direction issued in February 2000[96] as a result of the cases of Thompson and Venables both 11 years old when they were convicted at the Crown Court of the murder of two-year-old James Bulger. The European Court of Human Rights held in December 1999 that they had not had a fair trial.

The Practice Direction stated that the trial of young defendants should, if practicable, be in a courtroom in which all the participants are on the same level (para 9); the defendant should be allowed to sit with family members and where he has easy, informal communication with his legal representatives (para 10); the trial should be conducted in language that he can follow (para 11) and on a timetable that takes

[95]   Chapter 5, paras 185-85, 206, pp 205-09, 213.
[96]   [2000] 1 Cr App Rep 483; [2000] 2 All ER 285.

account of his concentration span (para 12); robes and wigs should not be worn unless the defendant asks that they should or the court orders that they should (para 12); the court should be prepared to order that attendance be restricted to a small number of persons. Facilities for reporting the trial must be provided but they can be restricted in the courtroom itself. If so, they must be relayed to another room to which the media have free access (para 13).

The Government's White Paper *Justice for All* (July 2001) said that many welcomed the proposal in Auld to take young defendants out of the Crown Court. Certainly, the younger the defendant, the stronger that case. 'There was however some concern over those in the older age group.' One option would be to give the Crown Court a discretion to retain cases involving 16 and 17 year olds. (para 4.38) As regards young defendants charged with adults, the Government invited further views. The option it preferred was to give the court a discretion to decide the venue in light of all the circumstances. (para 4.39) The Criminal Justice Bill 2002/03 did not include any provisions on this issue.

18. The operation of the jury (and trials) in former times

An American scholar, Professor John Langbein of the University of Chicago, writing in 1978, demonstrated from the Old Bailey Sessions Papers for the period 1670 to 1730 that at that time the criminal trial proceeded in a way that would now be regarded as most improper. The Old Bailey Sessions Papers were so-called 'chap books'– pamphlets written by non-lawyers for sale to the general public, each pamphlet recounting the details of the latest cases. They ran from 1674 for nearly two and a half centuries. During that time they underwent major changes of format and function, from chap books to newspapers to true law reports. The newspaper phase had been reached by the mid-1680s. At that time they were published regularly and they recounted a considerable number of cases. The Old Bailey sat eight times a year and a Sessions paper was produced for each session. In the early years they ran to four pages and everything was highly compressed. In the 1720s they were eight pages long and in the 1730s they burgeoned to twenty-page pamphlets. In the late 1730s the reports of a single session required two twenty-page pamphlets. They were seemingly written mainly for laymen and are therefore not an ideal source for understanding of the system of trial. But Langbein says that they 'are probably the best accounts we shall ever have of what transpired in ordinary English criminal courts before the late eighteenth century'. (JH Langbein, 'The Criminal Trial Before Lawyers', 45 *University of Chicago Law Review*, 1978, pp 263, 271.)

The features of the trial at that time included the following:

(1) A single jury was empanelled to hear a large number of cases. Typically, there were only two twelve-man juries for the whole sessions–a London jury and a Middlesex jury. A session lasted several days and processed 50–100 felony cases. In

December 1678, for instance, there was a two-day session. On the Wednesday morning the London jury tried two cases, the Middlesex jury tried seven. In the afternoon the London jury tried three cases. The next morning the Middlesex jury had eight cases and the London jury six. On Thursday the London jury was discharged whilst the Middlesex jury had six cases. Between them the two juries returned verdicts in 32 cases involving 36 accused in two days!

(2) The cases were commonly tried and decided in batches. The jury would hear a number of trials and would then go off to deliberate on all the cases together. In the cases in December 1678, for instance, the Middlesex jury which heard twenty-one cases deliberated only three times. The first batch consisted of seven cases, the second of eight cases and the last of six cases.

(3) Many of the jurors were veterans of earlier sessions. Jurors it seemed were drawn from a tiny cohort.

(4) As is obvious from the facts already related, trials took place at amazing speed. Most cases were not-guilty pleas but they were disposed of in short order. Typically a jury heard twelve to twenty cases in a day. Many of the not-guilty pleas, it is true, were somewhat half-hearted. The accused made no reply or offered no evidence or brought only character witnesses. One reason for the striking speed of events was that trials tended to take place within a few weeks of the event and the recollection of witnesses was therefore fresh. Most of the trials at the December sessions concerned crimes that had occurred in October or November. Also the cases were normally based on committal papers prepared and even presented by the justice of the peace or his clerk. The committal procedure often resulted in the accused making a statement or confession and the not-guilty plea that then followed was more pro forma than real. There were no lawyers either for prosecution or defence. The prosecution was at least allowed to have a barrister whereas the defence was not. In important cases, reported as State Trials, the prosecution was always represented, but in ordinary cases normally it was not. In the December 1678 session, for instance, there was no mention of any prosecution counsel in any of the 32 cases. In the absence of a lawyer there was no opening and closing speech, no examination or cross-examination of witnesses and no motions on points of evidence. Questioning of witnesses was done by the judge himself, or by the accused. The accused could not give sworn evidence but he could question both prosecution witnesses and call and question defence witnesses. He would be asked by the judge what reply he made to prosecution evidence and it was normal for him to respond rather than to rely on any right of silence or right not to incriminate himself. (Langbein says that in the entire 60-year period from the 1670s he did not come across a single case in which an accused person refused to speak in reliance on the right of silence.) Also the judge gave few instructions to the jury about each case. Jury deliberations were often perfunctory. Sometimes the jury did not even retire to reach a verdict.

(5) The judge played a far more directing role than would be permissible today. In *Bushell*'s case in 1670 the principle was established that jurors could not be fined for

returning a verdict contrary to the trial judge's instructions. But *Bushell*'s case was untypical. The Old Bailey Sessions papers show the judge normally exercising so much influence over the jury that Langbein suggests 'it is difficult to characterise the jury functioning autonomously' (at p 285). The judge often served in effect as examiner-in-chief of both the witnesses and the accused. In this capacity, as well as in summing up to the jury, he exercised what seems to have been a wholly unrestricted power to comment on the merits of the case. Sometimes the judge did not bother to use the power. But when he felt like it he would tell the jury what verdict to find, and normally the jury followed the judge's indications.

(6) Sometimes if the judge did not think the evidence for one side or the other was sufficient, he would stop the trial and tell the party in question to get evidence on the point in question and start again. Today the double-jeopardy rule prevents the prosecution from stopping a case that is going badly and starting afresh. But in the seventeenth and eighteenth centuries this occurred not infrequently. The power seems to have been used mainly in order to assist the prosecution rather than the defence.

(7) There is evidence in the reports of some instances of exchanges between the judge and the jury as the case was proceeding. The jury would comment as the case was developing, or would ask questions or would ask for certain witnesses to be called. Moreover it often gave reasons for its decisions and sometimes would be questioned about the verdict by the judge.

(8) In some instances the judge rejected a verdict, probed the jury's reasoning, argued with the jury, gave further instructions, and told it to go away to deliberate afresh. If the judge did not agree with a jury's conviction of the defendant, it was common for him to recommend a pardon or commutation of sentence and such recommendations were often influential.

(9) The Old Bailey Sessions Papers also threw light on the rules of evidence that were then applied. Hearsay evidence seemed to be admitted quite commonly. If the judge ruled that hearsay evidence should be excluded, no warning was normally given to the jury to disregard the excluded evidence. Nor was the jury sent out of the court room while the argument went on as to the admissibility of the evidence. Since there was normally no lawyer for either side, this was not appropriate.

The Sessions papers also show that, contrary to the modern rules, evidence of previous convictions was frequently considered by the jury as part of the evidence.

Langbein suggests that the modern concept of fairness to the accused requiring exclusion of evidence that would taint the jury had not developed by that time. At a time when the judge dominated the jury there was little thought of keeping prejudicial evidence away from them. The law of evidence, with its modern exclusionary rules, developed not in order to control the judges but as part of the rise of the lawyer as a participant in the criminal process. The rise of lawyers cost the judges their commanding role and thereby made the jury more dangerous, since the judge could not control it so well.

The rule that the accused could not have a lawyer started to break down in about the 1730s. Until then, according to Langbein, the absence of defence counsel was justified by three main arguments. First, the trial judge was supposed to serve as defence counsel. Secondly, the requirement of a high degree of proof was regarded as a safeguard. If proof of that level could be mustered against the prisoner it would be useless for him to have a lawyer since he would plainly be guilty. Third, the accused knew more about the case than anyone else and could not therefore be properly served by an intermediary. On the other hand, curiously, lawyers *were* allowed for misdemeanour cases though not normally for felonies. Lawyers were also permitted if there was some point of law to argue. If the court did not see the point, however, it was left for the accused himself to raise it and to persuade the judge to allow him to have a lawyer. Defence lawyers began to play a role in examining and cross-examining witnesses in the 1730s, though the accused himself continued to play the same role as before as well. There was no real differentiation of function between counsel and the accused. But gradually the role of the lawyer developed and, as Langbein puts it, the lawyers eventually broke up the ancient working relationship between judge and jury 'and cost the judge his mastery of the proceedings' (at p 314).

In the period covered by the Sessions Papers studied by Langbein, the accused in effect therefore lacked the safeguards both of the inquisitorial and of the adversarial systems. There was neither proper investigation of claims of non-guilt nor rules of evidence, the assistance of counsel nor appropriate rules for the selection, instruction and control of the jury.

Another American scholar, Professor Malcolm Feeley of the University of California, conducted a study of 3,500 cases at the Old Bailey from 1687 to 1912. He found that in the 1830s, trials accounted for no less than 95% of all adjudications. But trials were completely different from what we now think of when we use that word:

Typically defendants were not represented by lawyers; they rarely confronted witnesses in any meaningful way; they rarely challenged evidence or offered defences of any kind. And when the accused or someone in his or her behalf did occasionally take the stand, more often than not, they did not offer a spirited defence, but offered perfunctory excuses or defences, pleas for mercy, or in the case of witnesses, offered testimony as to good character or mitigating factors. Indeed the eighteenth and early nineteenth century trial (and earlier) more closely resembled the modern sentence hearing or plea bargaining process than it does a full-fledged modern jury trial.' (Malcolm M Feeley, 'Legal Complexity and the Transformation of the Criminal Process: The Origins of Plea Bargaining', 31 *Israel Law Review*, 1997, 183, 188.)

On the origins of defence lawyers see J Langbein, 'The Prosecutorial Origins of Defence Counsel in the Eighteenth Century: the Appearance of Solicitors', 58 *Cambridge Law Journal*, 1999, pp 314-65.

See also an illuminating, long article by Stephen Landsman, 'The Rise of the Contentious Spirit: Adversary Procedure in Eighteenth Century England', 75 *Cornell Law Review*, 1990, pp 498-609.

Further reading on the jury system

J Baldwin and M McConville, *Jury Trials* (Clarendon, 1979)

Z Bankowski and G Mungham, 'The Jury as Process' in P Carlen (ed), *The Sociology of Law* (University of Keele, 1976)

WR Cornish, *The Jury* (Penguin, 1971)

Penny Darbyshire, 'The Lamp that Shows that Freedom Lives–Is it Worth the Candle?' (1991) *Criminal Law Review*, p 740

Penny Darbyshire, 'What can we learn from Published Jury Research? Findings for the Criminal Courts Review 2001' (2001) *Criminal Law Review*, pp 970-79. [97]

Lord Devlin, *Trial by Jury* (Stevens, 1966); and 'The Conscience of the Jury', 107 *Law Quarterly Review, 1991*, p 398

P Duff and M Findlay, *The Jury Under Attack* (Butterworths, 1988)

S Enright and J Morton, *Taking Liberties: The Criminal Jury in the 1990s* (Weidenfeld and Nicolson, 1990)

MDA Freeman, 'The Jury on Trial' (1981) *Current Legal Problems*, p 65

Harry Kalven Jr and Hans Zeisel, *The American Jury* (Little Brown, 1966) and the review of their book by E Griew, 'The Behaviour of the Jury–A Review of the American Evidence' (1967) *Criminal Law Review*, p 569.

For an overview of the jury in continental countries see Roderick Munday, 'Jury Trial, Continental Style', *Legal Studies*, July 1993, pp 204–24. For developments in Spain and Russia see articles by the American scholar Professor Stephen Thaman: `Spain Returns to Trial by Jury', 21 *Hastings International and Comparative Law Review*, 1998, pp 291-537; and `The Resurrection of Trial by Jury in Russia', 31 *Stanford Journal of International Law*, 1995, pp 61-274.

For information and assessment of juries in England, Scotland, Ireland, Canada, America, New Zealand, Spain and Russia see 'Juries of the World', a special issue of *Law and Contemporary Problems*, vol 62, 1999, Neil J Vidmar (ed).

For an even broader survey of countries around the world under the title 'The Lay Participation in the Criminal Trial in the XXIst century' see *Revue Internationale de Droit Penal*, 2001 (1) and (2) – some 600 pages (almost all in English).

---

[97]   The full study is on the LCD website together with the Auld Review – www.lcd.gov.uk (Major Reports)) It is available in hard copy as Occasional Paper Series 49 from Kingston Law School, Kingston University.

Costs and the funding of legal proceedings

The problem of costs bedevils all legal systems – how to assess them, who should pay them, how to keep them under control, what can be done to assist those unable to afford them – these are the main topics addressed in this chapter.

(For treatment of the rules on costs in civil matters the best source is the practitioner's bible *Cook on Costs* published annually by LexisNexis UK.)

The rules distinguish between costs for 'contentious' and for 'non-contentious' matters. Cases which result in legal proceedings being initiated are contentious, even if they settle before any court hearing. In contentious matters, there were different rules for the High Court and the county court. In April 1999, as part of the implementation of the Woolf reforms, the difference between costs in the High Court and the county court was abolished.

The rules now are to be found in Civil Procedure Rules (CPR) Parts 43-48 – replacing Rules of the Supreme Court (RSC) Order 62 and County Court Rules (CCR) Order 38.

1. The new rules

The court's power to award costs in contentious matters flows from the Supreme Court Act 1981, s 51 which provides that, subject to statute and rules of court, 'the costs of and incidental to all proceedings ... shall be in the discretion of the court'. CPR 44.3(1) says that the court has a discretion as to 1) whether costs are payable by one party to another, (b) the amount of those costs, and (c) when they are to be paid.

(a) Who pays?

Under the old rules the position was clear and almost mechanical. Theoretically the court had a complete discretion. In fact, save in exceptional circumstances, the loser paid. At the end of the case, counsel for the winner asked for the 'usual order as to costs' which was made more or less automatically. The application was dealt with in seconds. Where a case settled, the settlement was normally on the basis that the loser paid the winner's costs.

CPR 44.3(2) states that the general rule still is 'that the unsuccessful party will be ordered to pay the costs of the successful party'. But the new rules made several major changes from the previous system. The most important was that the court has a much wider duty to exercise its discretion as to who pays costs at the end of a case. CPR 44.3(4) states that in deciding what order to make, the court must take into account all the circumstances including (a) the conduct of all the parties and (b) whether a party has succeeded on part of his case even though he has not succeeded overall. So a party that has lost may still get his costs in respect of matters on which he won. For the contrast between the old 'winner takes all' approach and the new more nuanced approach see *Re Elgindata Ltd (No 2)* [1993] 1 All ER 232 as compared with, say, *Johnsey Estates (1990) Ltd v Secretary of State for the Environment* [2001] EWCA Civ 535, [2001] All ER (D) 135 (Apr); or *Jones v University of Warwick* [2003] EWCA Civ 151, [2003] 1 WLR 954 (defendants got no costs even though they won the issue at the hearing as to the admissibility of a video of the claimant filmed secretly in her home, because of the way in which the film had been obtained). For a dozen or so examples of the application of the new approach see J Ross, 'Apportionment of costs – winner does not take all', 152 *New Law Journal*, 15 March 2002, p 401; M Goodwin, 'Costs losers', 146 *Solicitors' Journal*, 15 November 2002, p 104; M Ditchburn, 'Winner takes all?', 147 *Solicitors' Journal*, 28 February 2003, p 216.

Assessing who has won on particular issues can be a time-consuming exercise. In *Verrechia v Metropolitan Police Comr*[1] the Court of Appeal said that an order allowing or disallowing costs by reference to success on particular issues should only be made if there was no other order that could appropriately reflect the justice of the case. The costs of making the determination might be disproportionate to the benefit gained. A 'percentage' order would often produce a fairer result than an 'issues based' order. Wherever practicable, the judge should endeavour to form a view as to the percentage of costs to which the winning party should be entitled, or alternatively, whether justice would be done by awarding costs from or until a particular date.

(b)   Factors to take into account

CPR 44.5 states that when determining the amount of costs, the court must take into account not only matters that had previously to be taken into account (the amount involved, the importance and complexity of the matter, the skill required, the time spent) but also '(a) the conduct of all the parties including in particular (i) conduct before, as well as during, the proceedings; and (ii) the efforts made, if any, before and during the proceedings in order to try to resolve the dispute.' Thus the court can

---

[1]   [2002] EWCA Civ 605, [2002] 3 All ER 385.

take into account whether it was reasonable to raise or to pursue particular allegations, whether a party exaggerated his claim, and the way in which the case was pursued or defended.

The overall effect of the new rules is summarised in *Cook on Costs 2003:*

> The new Rules are not a mere codification of what was already there. They introduced a new philosophy and approach to costs. In the past the court had been concerned only to decide whether or not to award costs to one party or the other at the end of a hearing, with any costs awarded being quantified at the end of the proceedings if the parties could not agree them. Now costs permeate every aspect of civil litigation: the courts are charged with the responsibility of managing cases to ensure that the work undertaken by the parties (and therefore the costs they incur) are proportionate to the issues, while costs orders may be made as sanctions to ensure that the conduct of the parties (both before and during the proceedings) is in compliance with the new procedural code. As well as seeking to achieve proportionality and using costs orders as sanctions, the new regime also aims to make the amount of costs more predictable by requiring the parties to provide estimates of their costs at various stages of the litigation, and for costs on the fast-track to be fixed, initially for the trial only, but eventually for the whole action ... The concepts of proportionality and of the winner of litigation no longer virtually automatically receiving all, or indeed any, of his costs, have also brought about fundamental changes in the conduct of litigation.' (p 78)

(c)   Assessment of costs

If the loser is ordered to pay the winner's costs it does not mean *all* those costs but only such costs as are assessed to be due, which will depend on the basis on which the court has ordered them to be paid. The assessment is carried out by court officials and judges. This assessment was previously known as taxation and those who conducted the process were Taxing Masters. From April 1999 taxation was renamed 'detailed assessment' and 'summary assessment'. Taxing Masters became 'Costs Judges'. Taxing Officers became 'Authorised Court Officers'. The Supreme Court Taxing Office (SCTO) became the 'Supreme Court Costs Office (SCCO). Any party aggrieved at a decision in a detailed assessment hearing can appeal to a judge of the next tier. The appeal from the Authorised Court Officer is as of right. In most other cases the aggrieved person will need permission (formerly, leave) to appeal.

Summary assessment is where the court that has heard the case assesses the costs right away – (CPR 43.3) so that the actual amount to be paid by the loser can be determined there and then. The Practice Direction states that 'the general rule is that the court will make a summary assessment of the costs' in a fast-track case and at the end of any other hearing lasting less than a day (CPR, PD 44.7). That means that in county court cases summary assessment is the norm. It also generally applies in interlocutory (pre-trial) hearings where the court decides that one party should pay the costs 'in any event' regardless of the ultimate outcome of the case. But summary assessment does not apply where there is substantial dispute about the costs. Failure to produce a summary statement can be treated as a waiver of a claim for costs.

Judge Michael Cook (author of *Cook on Costs*) has written[2] 'It is a truth universally acknowledged that the costs provisions are the least successful part of the Civil Procedure Rules (CPR) and that the least successful part of the costs provisions is summary assessment'. The reason, he said, was that the judges were performing a function that was not within their competence,

> at the end of an exhausting fast-track hearing, there is often the pantomime of two barristers addressing a former barrister (the trial judge) who has had a one-hour Judicial Studies Board crash course on costs, on matters of which none of them have any practical experience. There is a one-page statement of costs prepared by someone who is not present in court, which contains references to a file of papers which is also conspicuous by its absence. The judge has to choose between two sets of figures apparently plucked from the air, or arrive at his own by the same route.

Detailed assessment is when the bill is assessed at some point, weeks or months after the case is finished. (See M Bacon, *Solicitors' Journal*, 1999, pp 680, 740.) It is common for the bills to be prepared by specialist costs draftsmen – itself a costly business.

Costs estimates Under the new rules, in fast-track and multi-track cases the parties are supposed to file cost estimates at various stages – with the allocation questionnaire, with the pre-trial checklist, and at other stages as ordered by the court. The estimates should show costs under ten different headings and to differentiate between costs already incurred and those to be incurred (Costs Practice Direction 6.1 to 6.6). Copies must be served not only on the court and the other side but also on the lay client. The purpose is to permit the court to use the estimates in deciding what case management decisions to make. In *Griffith v Solutia (UK) Ltd* [2001] EWCA Civ 736, [2001] All ER (D) 196 (Apr), the Court of Appeal encouraged courts to use the estimates to set budgets for the case. Some judges do this. In *AB v Leeds Teaching Hospitals NHS Trust* [2003] EWHC 1034, QB Gage J set a cap on costs in a case for damages for unlawful retention by hospitals of organs of deceased patients. Over 2,000 claims had been notified. The potential damages were between £10m and £15m. The lawyers' estimate was that they would need 3,410 hours in preparing the case. Despite the fact that the lead solicitors had agreed cost plans with the Legal Services Commission, the judge reduced this to 1,750 hours and put a cap on the claimants' costs in respect of the generic issues of £506,500.[3] The cap limits what the claimants can recover if they succeed, unless the court orders otherwise.

---

2   'Costs rules are a plodder's charter', 17 *Litigation Funding*, February 2002, p 8.
3   153 *New Law Journal*, 23 May 2003, p 792; 12 *Independent Lawyer*, July/August 2003, p 11.

The different bases of costs The level of costs depends on the basis of the assessment ordered by the court. Before 1986 there were five different costs orders that could be made at the end of the case as to the basis of 'taxation'. They were: 'party and party costs', 'common fund costs', 'trustee basis', 'solicitor and own client basis', 'indemnity basis'. (These five categories of costs were described by Sir Robert Megarry, Vice Chancellor, in *EMI Records Ltd v Wallace Ltd* [1982] 2 All ER 980.) In 1986 the system was changed. 'Party and party' costs was replaced by the 'standard basis' of taxation which became the norm for both privately funded and legal aid cases. On the standard basis all costs were allowed that were reasonably incurred, with any doubts being resolved in favour of the paying party. The other bases of costs (trustee, common fund, and solicitor and own client) were abolished and replaced by the 'indemnity' basis under which all costs were to be allowed except insofar as they are of an unreasonable amount or have been unreasonably incurred, with doubts being resolved in favour of the party being paid.

These definitions were slightly modified in the April 1999 rules. Thus standard fees still do not allow costs that have been unreasonably incurred or that are unreasonable in amount – but they must also be 'proportionate to the matters in issue' – a new concept. As before, any doubts are resolved in favour of the paying party (CPR 44.4). Costs assessed on the indemnity basis are to presumed to have been reasonably incurred and to be of a reasonable amount if they were incurred with the express or implied approval of the client. They are presumed to have been unreasonably incurred if they are of an unusual nature or amount and the solicitor did not warn the client that as a result he might not recover all of them from the other party (CPR 48.8).

It was held in *McPhilemy v Times Newspapers Ltd (No 2)*[4] that an order for indemnity costs is not penal and carries no stigma or implied disapproval of the defendant's conduct and that the claimant could get interest on indemnity costs.

The difference between contentious and non-contentious costs If there are no proceedings or they are in a tribunal,[5] costs are non-contentious. Non-contentious matters are governed by the Solicitors' (Non-Contentious Business) Remuneration Order 1994, art 3 which prescribes that a solicitor's remuneration shall be such sum as may be fair and reasonable having regard to all the circumstances and in particular to, the complexity of the matter, or the difficulty or novelty of the issues raised, the skill and responsibility involved, the time it takes, the number of documents, where the work is done, the amount of money involved and the importance of the matter to the client.

Costs-only proceedings The 1999 reforms introduced the new concept of proceedings solely for assessment of costs when there is complete agreement on all other matters. (CPR 44.12A) The application is made under CPR Part 8. This innovation has been used in an enormous number of such cases.

---

[4]   [2001] EWCA Civ 933, [2001] 4 All ER 861, [2002] 1 WLR 934.
[5]   Other than the Lands Tribunal.

Orders for payment of costs must now be paid within 14 days Pre-CPR, an assessment of interim costs was not made until the end of the case. The significance of CPR 44.8 requiring payment within 14 days is that it powerfully concentrates the minds of those considering whether to make interim applications. They have to be ready to back their judgment that an interim application is worthwhile with real money. Apparently it has had the intended effect of significantly reducing the number of such applications.

Proportionality CPR 1.1(2) states that 'proportionate' refers to the amount of money involved, the importance of the case, the complexity of the issues and *the financial position of each party*! The Practice Direction supplementing CPR 44.5 expressly states that 'proportionate' does not necessarily mean a fixed percentage as there will be costs that have to be incurred even in small cases and that solicitors 'are not required to conduct litigation at rates which are uneconomic' (para 11.2).

In *Lownds v Home Office*[6] the Court of Appeal addressed the question of the relationship between 'reasonable' and 'proportionate'. Pre-CPR the test had been reasonableness. The trouble with that test, Lord Denning said, was that 'it institutionalised, as reasonable, the level of costs which were generally charged by the profession at the time when the professional services were rendered.'[7] If a rate of charge was commonly adopted it was taken to be reasonable. Now the court also had to consider whether the costs were proportionate. CPR 44.3 in fact does not use the word proportionate but, Lord Denning said, 'the considerations which should be taken into account when making an order for costs are redolent of proportionality' (para 3). But where there is a clash between proportionality and reasonableness, which takes precedence? The claimed costs in that case were £17,000 plus VAT in a medical negligence case that settled for £3,000. The District Judge allowed costs of just under £15,000 plus VAT. Most of the costs had been incurred before the CPR came into force and on that ground the Court of Appeal said it would not interfere with the decision. But it considered what its approach would be in respect of costs post-CPR. The crucial point to emerge from the decision is that costs that are necessarily incurred should be allowed even if the result is disproportionate. There should be a two-stage process. First look to see if the costs as a whole are disproportionate. If they are not, check to make sure that each item was reasonably incurred and that the cost for each item was reasonable. If the global costs are disproportionately high, check to see whether any costs have been incurred unnecessarily. Costs that have been incurred unnecessarily may be recoverable from one's own client but they are not recoverable from the losing party.

In *Giambrone v JMC Holidays Ltd* [2002] EWHC 2932 (QB), [2003] 1 All ER 982 action was brought by 652 claimants against a company that ran holidays. After a costs hearing lasting two and a half days the costs judge held that the claimed costs

---

6   [2002] EWCA Civ 365, [2002] 1 WLR 2450.
7   At para 2.

were disproportionate. The claimants appealed unsuccessfully. Morland J who heard the appeal said that a costs judge should be able to deal with overall proportionality in a matter of an hour or less. He also said that appeals against a preliminary decision on proportionality were to be discouraged. (para 56)

2. Controls on fees

There are a variety of methods for seeking to protect the payer of costs from excessive charges.

(a) Assessment of costs by the court

As has been seen, assessment of contentious costs (previously called taxation) is assessment by the court. By far the most common is where the loser asks for the winner's bill to be assessed – now called 'between party' (formerly known as 'party and party') assessment. But such assessment does not reduce the total bill. It only determines what each party is to pay – the distribution of the burden of costs as between winner and loser. The procedure to reduce the bill absolutely is for the client to challenge his own lawyer's bill by what is called a solicitor and own client taxation, or assessment, under the Solicitors' Act 1974, Part III. The client does not have to pay the amount by which the bill is reduced. Such assessments are extremely rare – probably because clients feel embarrassment at challenging their solicitors' bills, partly through ignorance of the availability of the facility and partly because unless the client succeeds in getting the bill reduced by more than one-fifth he has to bear the costs of the taxation. The solicitor is required to inform the client of this right – but only at the stage of issuing legal proceedings to sue for unpaid fees – and now, before entering a conditional fee contract (see pp 599-607 below.) So, many clients probably pay the bill without ever realising that they have a statutory right to challenge it. The right of challenge exists even if there is a written agreement between lawyer and client as to the level of fees and even if the bill has already been paid.

(b) Remuneration certificates in non-contentious matters

The Law Society has traditionally provided a free service in reviewing bills in non-contentious matters. The client asks for a remuneration certificate. If the certificate suggests a lower fee, that is then the fee that the solicitor may charge. Remuneration certificates cannot result in the bill being increased. This procedure too is very little used. As from 1994 the system was modified so that it applies only if the bill is for an amount under £50,000 and only if the client has paid half the solicitors' costs plus disbursements and VAT. The solicitor must pay back to the client any amount paid him which the remuneration certificate states is excessive. In exceptional circumstances the requirement to pay half the bill can be waived by the Law Society.

(c)   Fixed costs and scale fees

For certain standard items in civil litigation there are fixed costs. This is true, for instance, for photocopies, attendance to issue or serve summonses, attendance to deliver documents, issuing proceedings, entering a judgment, enforcing a judgment etc. They apply where the claim is for a specified sum of money and summary judgment is obtained or the claim is one where the court gives a fixed date for the hearing when it issues the claim and judgment is given for delivery of goods.

In small claims cases the only costs normally recoverable are fixed costs attributable to issuing the claim, court fees, experts' fees not exceeding £200 each and loss of earnings by a party or witness up to £50 a day. If the case involves seeking an injunction the cost of obtaining legal advice up to £260 can be recovered. Costs on a summary assessment in relation to an appeal may also be allowed.[8] A party who acts unreasonably can be ordered to pay such costs as are assessed.

In other cases in the county court the level of fees was formerly controlled by scales depending on the amount in issue. (Until 1991 there were four scales; from 1991 there were three.[9]) In the High Court, the old approach of scales for the different items of work was replaced in 1986 by discretion which meant the solicitor had to justify each item in his detailed bill of costs.

Lord Woolf in his reports had expressed the hope that *all* fast-track costs would be fixed, but in the event, the only part of the case for which fixed costs could be agreed by April 1999 when the CPR were implemented was in respect of the day in court. The fixed amounts, which include the fee for preparation for advocacy, are the same regardless of the length of the trial. [10] (Fast-track cases are supposed to be finished within one day but that does not guarantee that one day will always suffice.) But the court has a discretion to increase or decrease the amounts because of the conduct of the parties or of the lawyers (CPR 46.3).

The question of fixed *pre-trial* costs in fast-track cases was subsequently taken forward by the Civil Justice Council through its Predictable Costs sub-committee chaired by Professor John Peysner of Nottingham Trent University. This bore important first fruit in December 2002 when there was agreement between all the interest groups on fixed costs for road accident claims of under £10,000 that settle without recourse to legal proceedings. The costs would be on a sliding scale of £800 plus 20% of the agreed damages up to £6,000 and 15% from £6,000 to £10,000. (For a brief description see John O'Hare, 'Fixing costs', *New Law* Journal, 20 December

---

8   For a horror story illustrating this exception see *Gregory v Turner* [2003] EWCA Civ 183, [2003] 2 All ER 1114.

9   Lower Scale – under £100, Scale 1 – £100-£3,000, Scale 2 – over £3,000.

10   The hearing fees are on a scale depending on the value of the claim. Where the award does not exceed £3,000 the fixed fee is £350; where it is between £3,000 and £10,000 it is £500; where it is over £10,000 the fixed fee is £750. Where a solicitor attends with counsel, a fixed sum of £250 is added. (CPR 46.2)

2002, p 1931. For further details see the Civil Justice Council's website www.civiljusticecouncil.gov.uk; and two valuable articles by Professor Peysner: 'Searching for Predictable Costs', *Journal of Personal Injury Litigation*, 2002, 162; and 'Finding Predictable Costs', *Civil Justice Quarterly*, Autumn 2003, forthcoming.) This scheme was due to become effective as from October 2003.

Lord Woolf intended that his proposed fixed-costs regime for fast-track cases under which between parties costs would be subject to a ceiling would also affect the level of costs charged by solicitors to their own clients.[11] But so far at least there is no such rule. CPR 48.8 provides that a solicitor can charge his own client more than the amount he can recover from the other side providing there is a written agreement with the client expressly permitting it. The proposed fixed costs scheme devised by the Civil Justice Council for road accident cases only applies to between parties costs, so CPR 48.8 would apply there too.

Scale fees for non-contentious work Conveyancing, which was formerly the single largest source of solicitors' work, used to be subject to scale fees that were treated as both maxima and minima–the fee was set by reference to the value involved and the Law Society allowed no competition between solicitors through undercutting. In 1973 this system was replaced by a requirement that the charge be 'fair and reasonable', and from 1984 solicitors were permitted to advertise their fees. These reforms introduced competition and caused fees to come down.[12] But the Law Society has continued to the present day to issue 'guidance' on how to calculate the value element in non-contentious work, based on a percentage of the value of the property. There are fee scales in the form of 'guidance' covering domestic conveyancing, probate and charges when acting for a mortgage lender.

The Office of Fair Trading (OFT) in its 2002 report *Competition in professions* (www.oft.gov.uk) said that although charges had dropped over the past decade, the fact that conveyancing and probate charges varied widely suggested that the market was not highly competitive. ('A greater degree of price convergence would be expected in the presence of strong competition or price transparency.' (para 217, pp 64-65 and similarly para 219.) (It also noted that bank charges for probate work were even higher than those of solicitors.) The OFT said that especially in the field of probate work the fee guidance might inhibit or distort competition.

Conveyancing of residential property, which in the mid 1960s represented half of solicitors' gross income, had reduced by the end of the 1990s to some 10%[13].

[11] Such a system operated in Germany. Woolf Report, Annex V, p 263. For fuller treatment see Dieter Leipold, 'Limiting Costs for Better Access to Justice' in Zuckerman and Cranston (eds) *Reform of Civil Procedure-Essays on 'Access to Justice'* (Clarendon, Oxford, 1995 pp 265, 266–75.)

[12] A Law Society Working Party stated in 1994 that solicitors' conveyancing charges fell in real terms between 1986 and 1993 by no less than 45%: 'Adapting for the Future', *Report of the Law Society's Special Working Party on Conveyancing Services*, 1994, p 9.

[13] See J Jenkins, *The Changing Legal Market Place in England and Wales*, Law Society, 1999, para 7.1.

(d) Legal aid work

Legal aid work is subject to fee rates and systems laid down by statutory rules and regulations. Payments for legal aid work are subject to a variety of controls. Much legal aid work is paid under hourly rates set by the LCD. So the basic hourly rate for civil legal aid court work in non-family law matters in 2003 was a paltry £74. This rate was the same for the whole country irrespective of the level of fee earner. (This basic rate had not been increased since 1994!) Payments for prescribed family law work are paid on somewhat higher rates.

The prescribed rate can be increased if the work is done with exceptional competence, skill or expertise, with exceptional dispatch or if it involves exceptional circumstances or complexity. In the county court the remuneration allowed can be doubled; in the High Court it can be trebled. Curiously, it seems however that solicitors generally do not claim such enhancement. ('It appears that many practitioners prefer to whinge about their unhappy lot rather that use their minds and energies in taking advantage of remedies that available to them.' *Cook on Costs* (2003), p 387.)

Standard and graduated fees From the mid-1980s the Government has increasingly paid legal aid fees by way of either standard or graduated fees. The standard fee is either wholly, or more or less, fixed for the category of case. So in the Crown Court, for instance, standard fees were introduced for solicitors in respect of contested cases lasting under two days, guilty pleas, committals for sentence and appeals The solicitor claimed either 'the lower standard fee' or 'the principal standard fee' or he delivered a bill in the traditional way. The determining officer decided the appropriate fee. In the case of barristers, the standard fee lays down one fee.[14]

The graduated fee is more flexible because it takes more variables into account. Graduated fees were introduced in 1996. They initially applied to all Crown Court cases other than those lasting more than 10 days or where there were more than 80 witnesses or over 1,000 pages of material. The system provided a base fee determined by the most serious offence charged. The base fee could then be increased by five factors: the size of the brief; the length of the trial; the number of defendants represented; other hearings pre-and post trial and certain other work by counsel.[15] In January 1998, the Bar proposed the extension of graduated fees to cases lasting up to 20 days. The Government suggested that cases up to 25 days in length should be

---

14   For information as to how it works see 'Standard fees in the Crown Court', *Law Society's Gazette*, 23 September 1987, p 2672; A Edwards, 'Standard fees: a survival guide', *New Law Journal*, 7 October 1988, p 722.

15   For description of the history and of the system see *Counsel*, May/June 1996, pp 12-15; *Criminal Bar Association Newsletter*, September 1995, pp 12-14; *Archbold Criminal Pleadings, Evidence and Practice* carries full information on costs, fees and legal aid. For a brief explanation of some the vagaries of the system see G Cooke, 'On graduated fees', 10 *Archbold News*, 18 December 2002, p 4. The author makes the point for instance that the fee for an adjournment is a mere £55 whereas the fee for a guilty plea could be over £1,000. The temptation to persuade the client to plead guilty rather than have the case adjourn is obvious.

brought into the scheme. The Bar accepted that. The Bar also accepted that for the very long cases the right method of payment was by individual fixed-cost contracts.

In May 2001 graduated fees were introduced for payment of barristers in family work in magistrates' courts, county courts and the High Court.[16] There were four categories of work each with its own fee scale: injunctions, public law children; private law children; ancillary relief and other family proceedings. The four categories were broken down into five functions each attracting a function fee: pre-issue; injunctive, declaratory or enforcement; interim or review hearings; conferences; main hearing. (Thus for instance the rate for pre-issue work done by junior counsel in public law children was £70; a conference was £60; the main hearing was £430 for the first day and £220-£230 for any subsequent day.) QCs were paid at 2.5 the rate for junior counsel. Slightly higher fees (Special Issue Payments or SIPs) can be paid if the case has special features such as complexity.

There are special provisions for Very High Cost Cases. Thus in civil cases the first £25,000 costs are paid at the normal rate. Thereafter the rate depends on the circumstances. If it is expected that the other side will pay costs if the case is successful, the rate is £70 per hour for solicitors, £50 per hour for junior barristers and £90 for senior counsel. If the prospects of success are not good, the rate is higher to reflect the solicitor's greater risk of not getting paid.

See generally *Cook on Costs*; *Butterworths Costs Service*.

(e)   Wasted costs orders

The Courts and Legal Services 1990 Act, s 4 provided for 'wasted costs orders' against legal representatives. Under the section (and under ss 111 and 112) the court may disallow, or as the case may be, order the legal representative concerned to meet, the whole or any part of the wasted costs (s 4(6)). Wasted costs are defined as costs incurred by any party (a) as a result of any 'improper, unreasonable or negligent act or omission on the part of any representative or any employee of a representative' or (b) which, in the light of any such act or omission, the court considers it is unreasonable to expect that party to pay.

However, the wasted costs order jurisdiction has been fraught with difficulties. A series of test cases on 'wasted costs orders' were decided by the Court of Appeal in January 1994 in *Ridehalgh v Horsefield* [1994] Ch 205, [1994] 3 All ER 848. The Court of Appeal held that before such an order is made the court must be satisfied that the conduct in question directly caused the wasted costs complained of. 'Improper' conduct covered any significant breach of a substantial duty in a code of professional conduct or according to the consensus of professional opinion, whether it violated the letter of a professional code or not. 'Unreasonable' meant vexatious,

---

[16]   See Community Legal Service (Funding) Counsel in Family Proceedings) Order 2001, SI 2001 No 1071.

designed to harass the other side. There was no need to show improper motive. It could arise from excessive zeal. 'Negligent' was to be understood in an untechnical way to denote failure to act within the competence reasonably to be expected of ordinary members of the profession. On the facts, the court allowed all six appeals and declared in each case that the order should not have been made. The conduct complained of in the appeals, variously, was: both parties' solicitors misconstrued a complex statute; solicitors, like their own expert and counsel, failed to realise that the client had fundamentally (and fatally for the claim) misdescribed the location of a piece of machinery; solicitors failed to serve the other side with notice of legal aid even though it is supposed to be done by the county court; solicitors pursued a misconceived application in reliance on specialist counsel and failed to progress negotiations even though counsel advised the parties were too far apart to achieve a sensible compromise; honest solicitors relied on client's untruthful instructions; counsel instructed at eleventh hour was inadequately prepared at hearing.

The Lord Chief Justice's 1995 Practice Statement (p 620 above) had emphasised the importance of wasted costs orders: 'The paramount importance of reducing the cost and delay of civil litigation makes it necessary for judges sitting at first instance to assert greater control over the preparation for and the conduct of hearings than has hitherto been customary. Failure by practitioners to conduct cases economically will be visited by appropriate orders for costs, including wasted costs orders' ([1995] 1 All ER 385, para 1). But the Court of Appeal's decision in *Ridehalgh v Horsefield* suggested that an appeal by the lawyers from a wasted costs order would often, if not usually, succeed. For a case in which a wasted costs order was made, where the judge delivered severe criticism of the barristers, including QCs, see *Re G (care proceedings)*[1999] 4 All ER 371.

In *Persaud v Persaud*[17] the Court of Appeal, citing *Ridehalgh* and *Medcalf v Weatherill* [2002] UKHL 27, [2003] 1 AC 120, said that there had to be something akin to abuse of process for a wasted costs order to be made. Mere negligence was not sufficient.

> Wasted costs are dealt with in CPR 48.7 and the accompanying Practice Direction. The Practice Direction states that the court will generally take the question in two stages. First it should be satisfied that there is evidence which 'if unanswered would be likely to lead to a wasted costs order being made' and that the wasted costs order proceedings are justified 'notwithstanding the likely costs involved'. The second stage is for the court, having heard the lawyer, to consider whether it is appropriate to make a wasted costs order (PD 48, 2.6).

Lord Justice Auld, in his report on the criminal courts, was distinctly unenthusiastic about wasted costs orders: ' The third possible financial sanction is to make a wasted costs order against the legal representatives on one side or another. But again there are often practical limitations on the court of identifying who is at fault on the

---

17   (6 March 2003, unreported) Case No.AC9500972, CA, 147 *Solicitors' Journal*, 14 March 2003, p 301.

prosecution side, counsel, those instructing him or the police – and on the defence side, counsel, his solicitor or the defendant. And wide use of such cumbrous satellite proceedings would be both an impractical and expensive way of achieving efficient preparation for trial' (p 491, para 230).

A study of the case law and of insurance statistics confirmed Auld's concerns: Hugh Evans, 'Wasted Costs' (2001) *Modern Law Review*, 51-62. ('The wasted costs jurisdiction was flawed for six reasons ... .First, it is very costly proportionate to the amount recovered.[18] Secondly, judges can initiate a wasted costs enquiry, which is unfair and even more disproportionately costly. Thirdly, it is procedurally complex. Fourthly, it is unpredictable whether the client would waive privilege; and what the consequences will be ... Fifthly, it is not possible for solicitors and barristers to make contribution claims against each other. Sixthly, it is mostly used against lawyers representing legally aided litigants from whom costs cannot be recovered' (p 51)). [19]

NB *Advocates' former immunity from suit is ended* Until 2000 both barristers and solicitors had immunity from actions for negligence in regard to the work they did in court and in preparation of court work: *Rondel v Worsley* [1969] 1 AC 191, HL and *Saif Ali v Mitchell & Co* [1980] AC 198, HL. See also *Kelley v Corston* [1997] 4 All ER 466. However in *Arthur JS Hall & Co v Simons* [2002] 1 AC 615, [2000] 3 All ER 673 the House of Lords, sitting with seven judges, changed that rule. They held that advocates no longer had immunity from suit, unanimously in respect of their conduct of civil proceedings and by a majority of 4-3 in respect of criminal proceedings.(The judgments take some 80 pages in the law reports.)[20]

3. Should costs follow the event?

(a) Civil cases

The rule that costs generally follow the event is one of the chief characteristics of the English system. In the United States the rule is the opposite – namely each side generally pays his or its own costs. There is a great deal of debate in the United States as to the merits and demerits of the 'cost shifting rule' (as it is known there). By

---

[18] In *C v C Wasted Costs Order* [1994] 2 FLR 34 the wasted costs hearing lasted 14 days and cost some £150,000, more than the original costs and far more than the costs which the court thought had been wasted. In the five years after *Ridehalgh* insurers had paid out £569,000 on successful claims at a cost of £849,000 and three-quarters of the claims (76%) were unsuccessful (Evans, p 55).

[19] For earlier articles see P Lewis, 'Wasted Costs: Has the Balance been Restored?', *Solicitors' Journal*, 18 February 1994, p 144; J Lambert, 'Cutting Costs', *Law Society Gazette*, 21 June 1995, p 20 and 'Bad Conduct', ibid, 5 July 1995, p 23; P Jones and N Armstrong, 'Living in Fear of Wasted Costs', *Civil Justice Quarterly*, July 1994, pp 208–32; A Murdie, 'Costs against non-parties and wasted cost orders against representatives', *Legal Action*, January 1998, p 20.

[20] See M Seneviratne, 'The rise and fall of advocate's immunity', 21 *Legal Studies*, 2001, pp 644-62.

contrast, in England there is remarkably little discussion of the pros and cons of the costs rule.

As was seen above, the rule that the loser pays the allowable costs of the winner is no longer so hard-edged and clear-cut as pre-CPR but the CPR recognises that that remains the general rule (CPR 44.3(2))

The alleged advantages of the rule include the following:
(1)   It 'makes the winner whole' – restores him financially somewhat to the position that he was in before the wrong done to him.
(2)   It recognises that the winner has won. By contrast, if he had to pay his own costs, the fruits of the litigation would be diminished by his costs, which to that extent would diminish his victory. In smaller cases the costs would eat up a huge proportion or even all of the damages.
(3)   If the client is advised that he has good prospects of success, the costs-follow-the-event rule encourages meritorious litigation. (The overwhelming majority of plaintiffs win – whether on a settlement or after a trial.)
(4)   The rule also helps to discourage unmeritorious or nuisance actions. A person with no reasonable prospects of success will think twice before bringing an action if he is told that he will have to pay his opponent's as well as his own costs.

The alleged disadvantages of the rule include the following:
(1)   The rule operates harshly where both sides have been responsibly and competently advised that they have good prospects of success. If both sides have acted reasonably why should the loser pay most of the winner's costs? (That remains the case under the post-Woolf reforms.)
(2)   The rule operates harshly where the outcome of the litigation turns on uncertainties and complexities of the law. It is unfair that the losing litigant should bear such a heavy burden of costs because the law is obscure (Again, that unfairness is not reduced by the post-Woolf rules.)
(3)   The rule operates harshly where one party loses on most of the issues raised at the trial but wins overall on a point that absorbs very little of the time in the case. Why should the opponent pay such a heavy price when he succeeded in regard to a high proportion of time taken by the trial? (The post-Woolf rules impact on that problem to the extent that the court allocates the burden of costs in accordance with the costs of the issues won and lost.)
(4)   The rule may deter meritorious as well as unmeritorious litigation. Some would-be litigants will not be willing to take the risk of losing even if they are advised that they have good chances of success.
(5)   The pressure to abandon sound causes of action for fear of the cost of losing will bear most heavily on the economically weaker party.
(6)   The rule has an inflationary effect on the cost of litigation as each side tends to spend more and more in order to ensure success and thereby avoid the risk of paying costs. Often the litigation is actually more about who pays the costs than about the apparent subject of the litigation. (That could be affected by the post-

Woolf emphasis on keeping costs in proportion to the amount at stake but it would be surprising if it made a big dent on the problem.)

(7) Moreover, the rule certainly does not prevent nuisance actions – they are a well-known phenomenon.

(8) The rule increases the unpredictability of the costs factor in litigation. It is bad enough that one cannot know what one's own lawyers are going to charge, it is worse that one may also have to pay an unknown amount in respect of one's opponent's costs. (That will be affected if and when a system of fixed costs for fast-track cases is instituted and also if there is progress in restricting costs chargeable to one's own client to the costs that one is permitted to recover from the other side.)

Lord Woolf said in his Interim Report in June 1995 that, on balance, the indemnity rule should be retained subject to a requirement that the court take account of the conduct of the parties in its allocation of costs (p 204, paras 23-24).

For an assessment of the effect of the new rule permitting costs orders in Employment Tribunals introduced in 2001 see S Hynes, 'Impact of costs rules changes reviewed', *Legal Action*, November 2002, p 8.

For an economist's assessment of the effect of fee shifting and other systems in light of the experience of several countries see A Cannon, 'Designing Cost Policies to Provide Sufficient Access to Lower Courts', 21 *Civil Justice Quarterly*, 2002, 198-253.

THE COSTS-FOLLOWS-THE-EVENT RULE AND GROUP ACTIONS

Special problems arise when there are many plaintiffs suing collectively as a group. The question became a matter of acute public concern in 1987, in the course of the litigation brought by over 1,000 plaintiffs for the effects suffered as a result of use of the anti-arthritis drug Opren. The court held that if the action was to go ahead, all the plaintiffs, other than those on legal aid, had to be regarded as being liable for their share of the ultimate costs of the action if they failed.[21]

One of the plaintiffs in the case then challenged the power of the court to make an order regarding costs before the end of the case. RSC Ord 62, r 3, said that costs should follow the event except when the court saw fit to make some other order. To follow the event, the plaintiff argued, must mean that the case was finished. The Court of Appeal rejected the argument. Normally the order would be made at the end of

---

21 Most of the plaintiffs were elderly pensioners. Obviously they could not afford this risk and it seemed as if the cases brought by non-legally aided plaintiffs would have to be withdrawn. At the last moment, however, a 'fairy godparent' in the form of a wealthy philanthropist Mr Godfrey Bradman came forward and guaranteed the costs of the non-legally aided plaintiffs, which it was thought would be well in excess of a million pounds. (See *The Times* and *The Guardian*, 23 July 1987.)

the case but it could be made earlier if the interests of justice required it. In any event, the judge's order in this case had not been for payment but for apportionment between plaintiffs: *Davies v Eli Lilly & Co* [1987] 3 All ER 94. See also *Nash v Eli Lilly & Co* [1993] 4 All ER 383, CA.

In *Aiden Shipping Co Ltd v Interbulk Ltd, The Vimeira* [1986] 2 All ER 409, the House of Lords held that the court had the widest possible discretion to order anyone to pay costs – even if they were not parties to the proceedings. The only proviso was that the order must be fair in the circumstances. Such an order was highly appropriate where some 'lead actions' were selected, raising common issues which could be litigated in order to settle those issues. In *Ward v Guinness Mahon & Co* [1996] 4 All ER 112 it was held that each of the 99 claimants should only be liable for one-ninety-ninth's part of the overall costs, in other words several not several and joint liability.

Group actions, as has been seen (pp 65-67 above), are now governed by CPR Part 19 which provides for the making of a Group Litigation Order (GLO). CPR 48.6A was made in July 2000 to codify the guidance in the case law on costs issues in such cases. It provides that unless the court orders otherwise, any order for common costs[22] against group litigants imposes on each such litigant several, rather than several and joint, liability for an equal share of those costs. However, in respect of liability toward his own solicitors, a group litigant is responsible for his own solicitor and client costs as well an equal share of the common costs.

The court may make provision for the costs contribution of a party who joins the group late, or leaves it early. In December 2001 the Court of Appeal gave a single decision in three GLO actions respectively concerning the MMR vaccine, oral contraceptives and exposure to asbestos in each of which there was an almost identical cost-sharing order made by the trial judge.[23] The chief question was whether the share of generic costs of discontinuers and those who settled were to be determined when they discontinued or settled or rather at the end of the case. If the former, funders of the litigation, notably the Legal Services Commission, would not be able to recover their costs even if they had funded a successful claim. The Court of Appeal held that the proper time for that decision was at the end of the case. So defendants cannot get pre-emptive orders exempting them from paying the common costs of discontinuers even though they might end up losing in respect of those common issues. Writing about the case the co-ordinating solicitors for the solicitors said: 'The judgment means practitioners involved in representing claimants in group claims can breath a sigh of relief and the Legal Services Commission is able to look positively again on funding these claims ... The only people unhappy with the judgment will be the

---

[22] 'Common costs' are defined as (1) costs incurred in relation to the GLO issues, (ii) individual costs incurred while it is a test case or (iii) costs incurred by the lead solicitor in administering the group litigation – see CPR 48.6A(2)(b).

[23] *Afrika v Cape plc; X v Schering Health Care Ltd; Sayers v Merck, SmithKline Beecham plc* [2001] EWCA Civ 2017, [2002] 1 WLR 2274.

defendants'[24] (See also on this important decision M Mildred, 'Cost-sharing in Group Litigation: Preserving Access to Justice', 65 *Modern Law Review*, 2002, pp 597-602; and M Goldberg, 'Counting the cost of group actions', 152 *New Law Journal*, March 22, 2002, p 437.)

For an account of the development of this area of litigation and discussion of the issues raised see CJS Hodges, *Multi-Party Actions* (Oxford University Press, 2000) and M Mildred, 'Group Actions' in GG Howells (ed) *The Law of Product Liability* (Butterworths, 2000).

THE COSTS-FOLLOW-THE EVENT RULE AND CONDITIONAL FEE AGREEMENTS – CAN THE LAWYERS BE MADE TO PAY?

Conditional fee agreements ('CFAs', dealt with more fully at pp 599-607 below) – often known as 'no win, no fee agreements' – have been permitted only since 1995. Lawyer and client agree that if the case is successful the lawyer will get a success fee on top of his normal fee, whereas if the case is lost the client pays him nothing (or sometimes just his disbursements). The success fee is an agreed percentage of the solicitors' normal costs and can be up to 100% of the solicitors' normal costs. A question raised was whether where the claimant had a CFA, a successful defendant could get his costs from the claimant's lawyers on the ground that they had financed (in the ancient legal jargon, 'maintained') the litigation. This argument was rejected by the Court of Appeal in *Hodgson v Imperial Tobacco Ltd* [1998] 2 All ER 673 a case brought by cancer sufferers against three tobacco companies. The court held that in regard to liability for costs, the position of the lawyers under CFAs was the same as that of lawyers normally. (The action collapsed a year later when 47 of the 53 claimants abandoned their action after a pre-trial ruling by the judge suggested they were unlikely to succeed. The plaintiff's solicitors, Leigh Day & Co and Irwin Mitchell, who had been funding the litigation under the CFA, were said to have lost £2.5m (*The Times*, 27 February 1999).)

(b)   Criminal cases

The principle that costs follow the event in criminal cases affects both the defence costs and those of the prosecution. Where the defendant is convicted, in addition to any contribution he may have had to make in respect of his own defence, he can be ordered to pay something toward the costs of the prosecution. The courts vary in their policy as to whether to order such payments. The power to order costs arises under s 18 of the Prosecution of Offences Act 1985[25], which says that where the

---

[24]   M Day and G Matthews, 'Fairer multi-party actions', 146 *Solicitors' Journal*, February 15, 2002, p 142. They began their article, 'It is no exaggeration to say that the future of multi-party actions hung by a thread while the judgment of the Court of Appeal was awaited'.

[25]   Supplemented by the Costs in Criminal Cases (General) Regulations 1986, SI 1986 No 1335.

defendant is convicted at the Crown Court or a magistrates' court he can be ordered to pay the whole or any part of the prosecution costs. For further details see *Practice Note* [1991] 2 All ER 924, [1991] 1 WLR 491. The court may make any order it considers just and reasonable. For a helpful statement of the principles to be applied see *R v Northallerton Magistrates' Court, ex p* Dove [1999] Crim LR 760: the sum ordered to be paid should be within the defendant's means and should not be grossly disproportionate to the fine; it should not be greater than the costs actually incurred; the purpose of the order is to compensate the prosecution not to punish the defendant.

The Attorney General told the House of Commons in November 1987 that it was the policy of the Crown Prosecution Service always to make an application for costs against all convicted defendants unless in the particular circumstances it was apparent that such an application would 'lack merit or that an order for costs would be impractical' (House of Commons, *Hansard*, 6 November 1987, col 819).

A defendant who is acquitted and who has paid some or all of his defence costs, may be entitled to ask for the whole or part of his costs to be paid out of public funds.

Under s 16 of the Prosecution of Offences Act 1985, when a defendant is acquitted the court may make an order ('a defendant's costs order') of such amount as the court 'considers reasonably sufficient to compensate him for any expenses properly incurred by him in the proceedings' (sub-s (6)).

> Where the defendant is acquitted, he ought normally to be awarded his costs. This is the rule, laid down repeatedly by a series of Practice Notes. The latest, issued in 1999, provides that such an order should normally be made 'unless there are positive reasons for not doing so, as where, for example the defendant's own conduct has brought suspicion on himself and has misled the prosecution into thinking that the case against him is stronger than it is'. ([1999] 4 All ER 436, para 2.2)

But in fact costs are only rarely given to the acquitted defendant by magistrates, probably because they tend to feel that such an order reflects badly on the prosecution. A refusal of an order is supposed to be exceptional, but in fact it is the order itself that is exceptional.

4. Exceptions to the rule that costs follow the event

There are a variety of situations where the costs-follow-the-event rule does not apply.

(a)   No costs in small claims in county courts

As was seen, in cases allocated to the small claims track, unless he has behaved unreasonably, the loser pays only 'restricted costs' (CPR 27.14): the fixed costs payable on issue of the proceedings; the fee payable on allocation (which is not payable if the claim is for under £1,000); the travelling expenses of a witness; up to £50 a day loss of earnings for each party or witness; a sum not exceeding £200 for an expert's fees plus travelling expenses; and costs of enforcement. But restricted costs only apply after the case has been allocated to the small claims system by the district judge. There is therefore a possibility of having to pay costs in respect of things done before the case was allocated.

The costs rule in small claims litigation is designed to facilitate and encourage use of the courts by ordinary citizens. The theory is that if they conduct the case themselves and then lose they have little in the way of costs to pay and they will therefore not be frightened to bring the case. The trouble with the theory is that the inability to recover costs may penalise rather than benefit the litigant by in practice denying him the use of a lawyer. He either has to be prepared to pay for it or do without. It is for that reason that so far at least, personal injury and housing cases involving sums of between £1,000 and £5,000 are excluded from the small claims system. The exception officially recognises that the services of a lawyer in such cases may often be crucial and the winning claimant should be able to recover the cost from the other side.

(b)   Legal aid cases

Under the former legal aid scheme, an assisted litigant was protected against the normal operation of the costs-follows-the-event rule by a special rule which limited what he could be asked to pay in respect of his opponent's costs to the same amount, if any, as he had been required to contribute toward his own costs. (Something between 80% and 90% of those who got civil legal aid were not subject to a contribution in regard to their own costs and were therefore not at risk of having to pay anything if they lost.) This rule applies equally under the new arrangements which came into force in April 2000 when the legal aid scheme became the Community Legal Service and the Legal Aid Board was replaced by the Legal Service Commission.[26]

Where a non-assisted person succeeds in an action against a legally aided person the effect of the rule meant that usually such a person got little, if anything, by way of costs from his defeated opponent. The Legal Aid Act 1988, s 18 provided that a person in that situation could make a claim on the Legal Aid Fund in respect of first instance proceedings by showing that he would otherwise suffer 'severe financial hardship'[27] and in all cases that it was 'just and equitable in all the circumstances' for such an order. This system too was continued under the new arrangements in 2000.[28]

---

[26]   Access to Justice Act 1999, s 11 and the Community Legal Service (Costs) Regulations 2000, SI 2000/441.

[27]   Lord Mackay, in his 1996 White Paper, said that the test would be eased to permit recovery by the unassisted successful litigant if he could show that he would otherwise suffer financial hardship. The requirement that it be 'severe' would be dropped (p 34, para 4.30). Lord Irvine's 1998 White Paper *Modernising Justice* confirmed that Labour would make the same change (p 36, para 3.29). But this promise was not kept.

[28]   See Community Legal Service (Cost Protection) Regulations 2000, SI 2000/824, Reg.5 and 30 *Focus*, pp 32-33.

In regard to proceedings at the appellate level it has been held to be 'just and equitable' to make an order in favour, inter alia, of building societies, insurance companies, a police authority and local authorities. In *R v Secretary of State for the Home Department, ex p Gunn* [2001] EWCA Civ 891, [2001] 3 All ER 481 the Court of Appeal held that an order could be made in favour even of a government department despite the fact that under the new rules the court had to have regard to the resources of the non-funded party in deciding what was just and equitable.

(c)　Some costs of litigants in person

The traditional rule was that a successful litigant in person, unless he was a practising solicitor, could not recover anything in respect of his own time and labour in preparing his own case.[29] The reason for the rule, given in 1884, was 'private expenditure of labour and trouble by a layman cannot be measured. It depends on the zeal, the assiduity, or the nervousness of the individual.'[30] Such considerations did not apply where the litigant was a solicitor. A practising solicitor could recover costs in respect not only of his own skill and labour, but also that of his clerk or that of his firm.[31]

In 1973 the House of Lords held that a successful litigant in person was entitled to claim for payments made to a solicitor who assisted him with the preparation of his case. Lord Reid said he should have 'such sums as were reasonably necessary for him to spend in order to prepare his written case and equip himself to appear and argue his case in person'.[32]

In 1975 the Litigants in Person (Costs and Expenses) Act took the matter further. It provided that litigants in person are entitled to recover costs, including compensation for their own time and effort. But the level of remuneration was and remains pitifully low. It was originally set at a nominal £9.25 per hour and that figure has not been increased. (In *Mainwaring v Goldtech Investments Ltd* [1997] 1 All ER 467 a litigant in person put in a bill for £87,250 charging her time at a basic rate of £75 per hour, uplifted to £125 in respect of research and £200 an hour in respect of preparation and advocacy. The court held that she was only entitled to charge at the going rate for litigants in person who suffered no pecuniary loss, namely £9.25 per hour!)

However, the 1975 Act provided that if the litigant in person in a civil case has suffered actual financial loss by reason of the work done on the c such loss can be recovered – subject to a maximum of two-thirds of the rate that would have been allowed if a solicitor had done the work[33]. This two-thirds restriction now also applies if the litigant in person is himself a practising solicitor, though not if he employs another

---

[29]　*Buckland v Watts* [1970] 1 QB 27 CA.
[30]　*London Scottish Benefit Society v Chorley* (1884) 13 QBD 872 at 877.
[31]　*Malkinson v Trim* [2002] EWCA Civ 1273, [2003] 2 All ER 356.
[32]　*Malloch v Aberdeen Corpn (No 2)* [1973] 1 All ER 304.
[33]　Previously, RSC Order 62 r 18(2), now CPR 48.6 (2).

firm.[34] A barrister who conducts his own defence in a criminal case can recover remuneration in respect of his professional time and skill – see *Khan v Lord Chancellor*[35]

In *R (on the application of Wulfsohn) v Legal Services Commission*[36] the Court of Appeal awarded the litigant in person, who had spent over 1,200 hours on the case, total costs of £10,460. (The trial judge had awarded him £120.) In *Hart v Aga Khan Foundation (UK)*[37], the Court of Appeal held that an actress who spent some 250 hours in studying technical matters in connection with her action could only recover for 40 hours' worth because that is what it would have taken a solicitor. An amendment to the rules in October 2002 stated, that where the litigant can prove financial loss, recoverable costs include 'the amount that he can prove he has lost for time reasonably spent on doing the work' (CPR 48.6(4)(a)). But if he cannot prove financial loss, he can only claim £9.25 per hour for 'the time reasonably spent on doing the work' (CPR 48.6(4)(b)).

One useful change made in the CPR in 1999 is the rule that the litigant in person can recover 'payments reasonably made by him for legal services relating to the conduct of the proceedings' (CPR 48.6(3)(b)). This would seem to permit 'unbundled' legal services where the litigant in person does much of the work on his case but uses professional lawyers as and when needed and, if he wins, can then recover their proper costs. A further amendment to the rules in October 2002 added to recoverable costs ' the costs of obtaining expert assistance in assessing the costs claim' (CPR 48.6(3)(c)).

Note that the litigant in person costs rules do not apply to cases brought in the small claims system, the limit for which, as has been seen, was increased in 1996 to £3,000 and in 1999 to £5,000. In small claims cases, as has been seen, the litigant normally cannot recover costs whether he employs lawyers or acts in person.

(d)   Where the winner is not liable to pay – the problem of the indemnity principle partly resolved

The costs-follow-the-event rule provided, as has been seen, that when the winner is indemnified against his costs, the indemnity covers his actual costs and no more. It follows that if he won the case and had no costs because his solicitor had agreed to work for nothing, nothing could be recovered from the other side. This was the principle –and the problem - of the indemnity principle. Why, however, should the lawyer not be permitted to promise his own client that he will charge him nothing and still recover his proper costs from the other side if the case succeeds? As will be

---

[34]   This is the effect of CPR 48.6(6) which now includes a practising solicitor in the definition of a litigant in person. Pre-1999 the rule (RSC Order 62, r 18(6)) specifically excluded from the definition of litigant in person anyone who was a practicing solicitor.

[35]   [2003] EWHC 12 (QB), [2003] 2 All ER 367.

[36]   [2002] EWCA Civ 250, [2002] All ER (D) 120 (Feb).

[37]   [1984] 1 WLR 994.

seen below, if the arrangement qualifies as a Conditional Fee Agreement, the matter is now regularised by statute. But if not, the indemnity rule has applied – until it was modified as from June 2003.[38]

In its May 1999 Consultation Paper *Controlling Costs*, the LCD asked whether in light of recent developments the indemnity principle should be abolished. The indemnity principle having become 'increasingly marginalised by the changes which have taken place in recent years' (p 16, para 11) the question arose whether there was any point in keeping the rule. The Lord Chancellor was considering abolishing the indemnity rule but was 'concerned that its removal should not lead to an increase in legal costs being awarded by the courts' (p 16, para 12). The indemnity principle provided a cap on the costs which could be recovered from the loser. Without it solicitors would technically be free to claim costs without bounds, subject only to assessment by the court.

The Access to Justice Act 1999, s 31 paved the way for abolition of the indemnity principle. It provided that Rules of Court might make provision, inter alia, for securing that the amount awarded to a party in respect of costs to be paid by him to his representatives 'is not limited to what would have been payable by him to them if he had not been awarded costs'. The Explanatory Notes to the Act stated that the purpose was 'to limit or abolish the common law principle known as the indemnity principle'. However, it was not until 2 June 2003 that this actually happened.[39] As from the same date a new rule provides that recoverable costs in CPR Parts 44 to 48 include costs incurred by the provision of advocacy or litigation services under a Conditional Fee Agreement (CFA) where the client is only liable to pay his lawyers fees and expenses to the extent that they are recovered 'whether by way of costs or otherwise'.[40] 'By way of costs' means from the loser; 'or otherwise' would cover from the damages.[41] The Explanatory Note to the statutory instrument says:

> This in effect abrogates in relation to this type of conditional fee agreement the so-called indemnity principle – the principle that the amount which can be awarded to a party in respect of costs to be paid by him to his legal representatives is limited to what would have been payable by him to them if he had not been awarded costs. Solicitors will to this extent be able to agree lawfully with their clients not to seek to recover by way of costs anything in

---

[38]   *Gundry v Sainsbury* [1910] 1 KB 645; *General of Berne Insurance Co v Jardine Reinsurance Management Ltd* [1998] 2 All ER 301; Solicitors Act 1974, s 60(3).The authorities were described and the issues discussed in the writer's 'Will the revolution in the funding of civil litigation in England eventually lead to contingency fees? 52 *DePaul Law Review*, 2002, 259, at 271-78. (The text is also available on the LSE website in a draft of the article – www. lse.ac.uk/collections/law/news.)

[39]   Access to Justice Act 1999 (Commencement No 10) Order, SI 2003/1241.

[40]   Civil Procedure (Amendment No 2) Rules 2003, SI 2003/No1242.

[41]   See D Marshall, 'The new CFA Regulations', 153 *New Law Journal*, 30 May 2003, p 833. For the background see J Peysner, 'A Revolution by degrees: From Costs to Financing and the end of the Indemnity Principle', www.webjcli.ncl.ac.uk

excess of what the court awards, or what it is agreed will be paid, and will no longer be prevented from openly contracting with their clients on such terms.

(e) Contemptuous damages

If the claimant wins only contemptuous damages he will normally be ordered to pay the costs despite having technically won the action. The order that he pay the 'loser's' costs reflects the true meaning of the result. Contemptuous damages are traditionally expressed in the form of the smallest coin then in circulation. In *Dering v Uris* [1964] 2 QB 669 Dering, a Polish prisoner doctor at Auschwitz, sued for libel over a passage in Leon Uris' well-known novel *Exodus* in which he was said to have participated in more than a hundred atrocious experimental operations at the concentration camp. The author, defending, brought witnesses who had survived the operations whose evidence showed Dering's conduct at Auschwitz in extremely poor light. The libel action in effect turned into a war crimes trial of Dering. In the event, the jury awarded him a halfpenny damages and the judge ordered that he pay the costs, which were enormous.

(f) No order as to costs in public interest cases

The court sometimes exercises its discretion by making no order as to costs where it takes the view that the losing party does not deserve to be penalised in costs. For an expression of this policy by Lord Woolf giving judgment for the Privy Council see *New Zealand Maori Council v A-G of New Zealand* [1994] 1 AC 466 at 484. The case concerned threats to the survival of the Maori language (taonga):

> Although the appeal is to be dismissed, the applicants were not bringing the proceedings out of any motive of personal gain. They were pursuing proceedings in the interests of taonga which is an important part of the heritage of New Zealand. Because of the different views expressed by the members of the Court of Appeal on the issues raised on this appeal, an undesirable lack of clarity inevitably existed in an important area of the law which it was important that their Lordships examine and in the circumstances their Lordships regard it as just there should be no order as to the costs on this appeal.

In *R v Lord Chancellor, ex p Child Poverty Action Group* [1998] 2 All ER 755 counsel for CPAG argued that where the case raises public as opposed to private law issues the court should be more prepared to make no order as to costs. He cited the Privy Council's decision in the Maori language case. He also cited the view of the Ontario Law Reform Commission in 1989 that the court should not order costs to be paid by the applicant if the case concerned issues whose importance extended beyond those of the parties, if the applicant had no self-interest in the outcome and if the respondent had clearly superior capacity to bear the costs of the case. Counsel suggested that the court should have in mind for instance: (1) whether the point of law was one of importance that ought to be litigated; (2) was it one that would otherwise probably not be litigated; (3) would legal aid probably have been granted if it was for a significant sum of money; (4) was the applicant a suitable person or body to bring the matter to court; (5) was the respondent in a position to meet its costs. Dyson J refused to grant the pre-emptive costs order requested. He also ruled that the indemnity rule should normally apply even in public law cases. But he did accept that there was a category of exceptional case where the court would make no order as to costs – and an even more exceptional category where it would make an early pre-emptive order in public interest challenge cases providing that the public body should in effect subsidise proceedings brought against it.

The first ever such order was made in December 2002 in *R (on the application of Campaign for Nuclear Disarmament) v Prime Minister* [2002] EWCA 2712 (Admin) (Case No AC9500930). The relevant rule is now CPR 44.3. The order in that case – which concerned an attempt to have the then impending war in Iraq declared illegal – was the more remarkable in that it was made before permission had been given to make the judicial review application.

A variant of this is the quite common practice of granting leave to appeal to the Inland Revenue in a tax case on terms that the Revenue will pay the taxpayer's costs in any event. The courts take the view that if the Revenue want a point of tax law cleared up, it should be done at the expense of the general body of taxpayers.

On the role of the Legal Services Commission in promoting litigation 'in the public interest' see below.

5. The legal aid system

Introduction

It has been recognised in most civilised countries that there is a significant denial of justice if the state does not assist poor persons to meet the costs of lawyers. In England this recognition goes back decades. The first major legislation establishing the legal aid system on a modern footing was the Legal Aid Act 1949 passed by the Attlee Government in the post-Second World era.

The scheme, one might say, has so far had three main stages. The first was from 1949 to 1989 when the scheme, though funded by the state, was run by the Law Society under the authority of the 1949 Legal Aid Act. The second, from 1989 to 1999, was when it was run by the statutory Legal Aid Board established by the Legal Aid Act 1988. The third era which began in April 2000 is the current system run by the Legal Services Commission under the authority of the Access to Justice Act 1999. The second stage could be seen as a seamless progression from the first. But the third marks a radical break.

The scheme as it developed from 1949 had certain main characteristics:
- it covered both civil and criminal proceedings in all the courts
- it also covered legal advice and assistance short of legal proceedings
- though funded by the Treasury the service was at first wholly and later mainly provided by private practitioners
- to get legal aid for representation in court there was a means test and a merits test
- the legally aided person could be asked to pay a contribution toward the cost
- although there was an annual budget, there was no ceiling on total expenditure.

These characteristics were in the second as much as in the first stage and with the exception of the last they are still in the scheme as it now operates. The fundamental difference between the third stage which began in April 2000 and the preceding 50 years is that there is now supposedly a ceiling on expenditure. From this many consequences flow. In particular, there now have to be ways of managing and controlling resources that are different in kind and extent from those that previously existed.

Although the new scheme was introduced by the Blair Labour Government it was foreshadowed by the previous Conservative administration. The new era was heralded in July 1995, when Lord Mackay, then the Conservative Lord Chancellor, announced major proposals for changing the scheme in a Green Paper, *Legal Aid – Targeting Need* (Cm 2854).) The most significant aspect of the proposal was that legal aid expenditure, which had previously been demand-led and therefore open-ended as to total expenditure, should be subject to a ceiling. The Green Paper provoked a fierce critical reaction from both lawyer and non-lawyer organisations concerned with the provision of legal services.[42]

At the time, Lord Irvine was Shadow Lord Chancellor. He attacked the policy of the Green Paper and especially the policy of capping expenditure. ' Capping', he said, 'is crude.' It would 'lead at worst to substantial exclusion from justice and at best to long waiting lists'. The availability of legal aid should not depend, he wrote, on where the individual lives or when application is made. It should depend on means and merits.[43]

In July 1996, Lord Mackay fleshed out his thoughts in a White Paper, *Striking the Balance* (Cm 3305), which broadly confirmed the plans outlined in the 1995 Green

[42] See for instance, *Legal Action*, June 1995, p 9, August 1995, p 8, October 1995, p 6. The Law Society published a 77-page response *A Better Way Forward*, September 1995. The Bar published a 76-page response in October 1995. For an overall analysis see T Goriely, 'The Government's Legal Aid Reforms' in Zuckerman and Cranston (ed,) *Reforming Civil Procedure-Essays on 'Access to Justice'* (Clarendon, Oxford, 1995) pp 347-69. See also M Zander, 'Twelve Reasons for Rejecting the Legal Aid Green Paper', *New Law Journal*, 21 July 1995, p 1098.

[43] Lord Irvine, 'The Legal System and Law Reform under Labour' in D Bean (ed) *Law Reform for All* (Blackstone, 1996). He cited with approval the writer's critique of the Green Paper proposals referred to in n 41 above.

Paper. His introduction to the White Paper stated, 'Implementing the changes will take some years. I am determined to make progress with care, learning as we go and ensuring, through pilots and detailed consultation, that new machinery and ways of delivering services work properly before they become a permanent part of the reformed legal aid scheme'. Again the reaction was mainly critical.

But, by the time of the General Election in May 1997 none of the proposed radical changes had actually been implemented. Lord Irvine, who became Lord Chancellor when Labour took office, commissioned a swift report from a former Treasury mandarin, Sir Peter Middleton, as to whether he should adopt the Conservative Government's strategy for legal aid (as well as the proposed Woolf reforms for civil litigation). Sir Peter's report,[44] published at the end of September 1997 urged the Lord Chancellor basically to proceed full steam ahead and, within days, on 18 October, Lord Irvine startled the audience at the Law Society's Annual Conference with announcements that were more radical even than anything proposed by Lord Mackay. In particular, he said that conditional fee agreements (pp 599-607 below) would be extended to all money and damages actions and that legal aid for such claims would be abolished. This caused consternation. The plans were strongly condemned by the Bar Council, the Law Society, the National Consumer Council, the Consumers' Association, Shelter, the Child Poverty Action Group, JUSTICE, the Legal Action Group, the Law Centres Federation, the National Association of Citizens' Advice Bureaux and the Advice Services Alliance. A joint letter from 11 of these organisations said they believed 'that the withdrawal of legal aid for money and damages claims could lead to the exclusion from the justice system of millions of the poorest and most vulnerable in society'.[45]

In March 1998 Lord Irvine published a Consultation Paper (*Access to Justice with Conditional Fees*) which outlined those of its proposals that could be implemented without primary legislation. It confirmed that conditional fees would be extended to all money and damages claims and that legal aid would be abolished for all personal injury claims other than medical negligence cases. But legal aid would continue to be available, at least for the time being, for housing cases, judicial review work and where a person claimed he was the victim of action by public authorities.

The White Paper (*Modernising Justice* (Cm 4155) setting out the Government's detailed proposals for legal aid, was published in December 1998[46]

---

[44]   Sir Peter Middleton, *Review of Civil Justice and Legal Aid*.

[45]   For a study commissioned by the Law Society of the impact on solicitors of the proposed replacement of legal aid by conditional fee agreements see J Shapland et al, *Affording Civil Justice*, Law Society, Research and Policy Planning Unit, Study No 29, 1998.

[46]   For analysis and comment see M Zander, 'The Government's Plans on Legal Aid and Conditional Fees', 61 *Modern Law Review*, 1998, pp 538-50.

The 1998 White Paper

In its December 1998 White Paper *Modernising Justice*, the Labour Government stated that legal services would in future be run by a new body, the Legal Services Commission. The chief responsibility of the Commission would be to take the lead in establishing a Community Legal Service (CLS). The CLS would tackle the current lack of planning and coordination in the advice sector. The longer term aim was 'to ensure that every community has access to a comprehensive network of legal service providers of consistently good quality, so that people with actual or potential legal problems are able to find information and help they need' (p 14, para 2.6). There was a multiplicity of sources of advice on legal matters. In addition to some 80,000 lawyers in private practice, there were some 30,000 volunteers together with nearly 6,000 professional staff working in the almost 2,000 agencies which provided advice services. In addition to the 700 main Citizens' Advice Bureaux with a further 1,760 outlets, there were over 800 independent advice centres, many specialising in particular fields and over 50 law centres (salaried lawyers in poverty areas, funded by a mixture of grants from local authorities and in some cases from the Legal Aid Board and legal aid moneys). Altogether these agencies received some £150m a year from a variety of different sources, including local authorities, charities, central government and the Legal Aid Board. They performed a vital role and the taxpayer would continue to fund them but the advice sector had grown up randomly. Most provision was not based 'on a rational assessment of need' and 'different types of service are spread unevenly across the country' (*Modernising Justice*, p 14).

The White Paper said that the Government believed that the solution lay in two key developments. There should be common systems, developed centrally and agreed by all funders, for defining and assessing needs and priorities and for setting and monitoring appropriate standards of service; and there should be a system for coordinating the plans of the various funders, 'so that the resources available to them are put to the best effect overall'. It was also important to coordinate the provision of information and basic advice with that of more specialised services such as detailed advice on mediation and representation in litigation by a lawyer. In addition to the £150m a year spent on the advice sector, some £800m a year was spent on advice, assistance and representation by lawyers through civil legal aid. 'In future, these two sorts of spending will be considered as a whole' (*Modernising Justice*, p 15, para 2.10).

The Legal Services Commission (LSC) would be funded by central Government but would be managed independently by a board of directors. Its functions would be to 'develop, in cooperation with local funders and other interested bodies, local, regional and national plans to match the provision of legal services to identified needs and priorities' (*Modernising Justice*, p 15, para 2.11). It would report annually to the Lord Chancellor. The LSC, it was said, would also manage the Community Legal Service fund which would replace legal aid in civil and family cases. It would find ways to work in partnership with local communities, local government and other funders.

'These partnerships will build on the links and structures already established by the Legal Aid Board through its Regional Legal Services Committees'.[47]

The Government would prepare for the start of the Community Legal Service by:

(1) Pioneering different systems for assessing need and planning provision of legal services. There would be pioneer partnerships bringing together the local authority, the Legal Aid Board, other local and national funders and local providers.

(2) Developing core quality criteria to form the basis of a common 'kitemark' recognised by all funders. Providers would have to obtain the kitemark as a condition of obtaining a contract with the LSC. The kitemark would be integrated with the Legal Aid Board's existing franchising scheme.

(3) Setting up a website on the Internet to provide a new source of information and advice about legal problems. (*Modernising Justice*, p 15, para 2.13)[48]

WEAKNESSES OF THE OLD LEGAL AID SCHEME

The White Paper (*Modernising Justice*, pp 28-9, para 3.8) said that the existing legal aid scheme was too heavily biased toward expensive court-based solutions. Because the scheme was open-ended it was impossible to target resources on priority areas, or on the most efficient and effective ways of dealing with a particular problem. Legal aid was spent almost entirely on lawyers' services and in practice lawyers decided where and how the money was spent. Legal aid was sometimes criticised for backing cases of insufficient merit and for allowing people to pursue cases unreasonably. There was little control over quality and no scope for competition to keep prices down. Lawyers' fees were calculated after the event, based on the amount of work done, so there was little incentive to work more efficiently.

THE OBJECTIVES OF THE NEW SYSTEM

The White Paper stated that the objectives of the new system for civil cases would be: to direct resources to where they were most needed; to ensure that disputes were resolved in a manner fair to both sides; to provide high quality services that achieved the best possible value for money; and to have a budget that was affordable to the tax payer and that was under control (*Modernising Justice*, p 28, para 3.6).

The areas that should have the greatest priority, it said, were social welfare cases – for example about people's basic entitlements like a roof over their heads and the correct social security benefits; 'other cases of fundamental importance to the people affected ... cases involving major issues in children's lives (like care and adoption

---

[47]   The first of these was established in 1977 in the north west. See annual reports of the Legal Aid Board.

[48]   See p 592 below.

proceedings) and cases concerned with protecting people from violence; and cases involving a wider public interest such as test cases or challenging the actions or failure to act of public bodies including cases under the Human Rights Act or alleging that public servants have abused their position or power' (*Modernising Justice*, p 28, para 3.7).

The CLS would operate under a controlled budget – 'with finite resources, there should be no expectation of an entitlement to public funding' (*Modernising Justice*, p 29, para 3.9). But the new scheme would be more flexible and adaptable than legal aid. ('It will be possible to re-deploy resources to meet unexpected demand and adopt different approaches to reflect changing priorities and new opportunities in the future'.)

The three basic elements of the new system would be 1) a planning system to allocate resources in the light of national and regional priorities; 2) contracting with providers which would set quality standards and increase value for money by introducing fixed prices and an element of competition ; and 3) a new funding assessment to decide which cases should receive help which would be better focused than the present 'merits' test, which would take account of priorities and would be adaptable when priorities changed.

The planning system would be based on an overall budget with sub-budgets for civil and for family cases. (On the crucial question whether the budget for civil legal services was to be 'ring-fenced' against being diminished by expenditure on criminal defence services see pp 577-85 below.) There would be a policy framework setting out priorities and objectives. The priorities would include one or more 'top priority' categories, for example child care proceedings, where the LSC would be required 'to ensure that funding is available in every case' (*Modernising Justice*, p 31, para 3.14). The LSC would allocate budgets to its regional offices. Each office would draw up a detailed regional plan for letting contracts for the different types of service and categories of case. The plan would be based on the advice of the Regional Legal Services Committees. The LSC would retain a budget at the centre for very expensive cases which would be funded on a case-by-case basis through individually negotiated contracts.[49]

Contracting would be with providers of legal services. The LSC would decide what services to buy and who to buy them from.

This was a fundamental change from the legal aid scheme, under which any lawyer could take a case and submit a bill to the Legal Aid Board for payment. In future lawyers and other providers would only be able to work under the scheme if they had a contract with, or a grant from, the LSC (*Modernising Justice*, p 31, para 3.17).

The Government had already announced that all advice and assistance and all representation in family litigation would be provided under such contracts as from

[49]   See further pp 574, 583, 597 below.

the end of 1999. In the first instance contracts would provide for payment for each case individually. Block contracts would come later. The Government's intention was that block contracts (bulk contracts for specified services at fixed prices) should eventually operate for most legal aid.

The White Paper said that contracting was the key to meeting the Government's objectives. Contracts would enable the LSC to meet its priorities for work to be done, to control its budgets (by determining expenditure in advance), and to ensure the quality of the work to be done by only contracting with providers who meet the required standard. It would promote better value for money through price competition. Prices would be fixed to promote greater efficiency. By fixing prices contracts could provide greater certainty about cost and cash flow which was good for providers. It would also be good for the parties as it should be possible to tell them at the outset how much they might have to pay in contribution or cost.

Contracts would run for up to three years and new contracts would be let in several tranches throughout the year so that at any given time a provider would have a number of contracts in place at different stages of the life cycle.

Quality would be a major concern. The work done under contract would be monitored. ('Under a contracted scheme, it will be particularly important to tailor monitoring systems to balance the incentives created by different price structures. For example, where a fixed price is being paid, monitoring must be designed to identify providers who under-prepare cases.' (*Modernising Justice*, p 33, para 3.20).) Quality standards would be based on the new CLS kitemark (above) and the Legal Aid Board's franchising scheme. Only firms with franchises would be permitted to provide legal aid.

To get a contract, a firm needed to be accepted onto a bid panel, put in a franchise application (if not already franchised), and then bid for the contract – unless it was in family, immigration or mental health field in which case the contract was assured once the firm had passed a preliminary audit. The Law Society predicted that there would be about 6,000 offices doing legal aid work.[50] It was predicted that although there was not yet a minimum volume turn-over requirement, one would eventually be introduced as it would not be cost effective for the Board to administer a large number of small contracts.[51]

The Funding Code The White Paper said there would be a published Funding Code setting out how decisions would be made as to which cases would qualify. It would be laid before Parliament. Under the legal aid scheme applicants had to satisfy a

---

[50]   The Minister of State, Mr Geoff Hoon, said in April 1999 that 96% of all the legal aid money spent on family work went to about 6,000 firms and that it was anticipated that some 5,000-6,000 firms would apply for franchises. (House of Commons, Standing Committee 'E', April 27, 1999, cols 31-2.)

[51]   See generally *Law Society's Gazette*, 14 April 1999, pp 22-26.

merits test and a means test. The Funding Code would replace the merits test. The test would vary depending on the priority of the category of case concerned.

The funding assessment would consider three key questions: (1) Would another type of service be a better way of dealing with the case? (For example, in some family cases it would be necessary to show that the case was unsuitable for mediation to qualify for representation by a lawyer.) (2) Could the matter be funded in some other way? (Could the client get a conditional fee arrangement? – see below). (3) Do the merits of the case 'in the context of the Government's priorities and available resources, justify public funding? The general test would still be whether a reasonable person able to fund the case with his or her own money would be prepared to pursue it. But the criteria applied would not only be the strength of the case and the prospects of success. They would also include 'the importance and potential benefit to the assisted person and the likely cost', 'the wider public interest' and 'the availability of resources and the likely demands on those resources' (*Modernising Justice*, p 34, para 3.26). The Funding Code would set out how the criteria would apply in different categories of case. In many cases the prospects of success and the ratio of potential benefit to likely cost would be quantified. This would make the funding assessment 'tougher and more transparent than the current merits test' (*Modernising Justice*, p 35, para 3.27). But where the case had highest priority not all the criteria would have to be considered. (Legal representation would for instance be automatic when the question was whether a child should be taken into care.)

The Access to Justice Act 1999

These proposals were incorporated in the Access to Justice Act 1999. Section 8(1) requires the LSC to prepare a code setting out the criteria for funding. Section 8(2) requires the LSC to consider the extent to which the criteria ought to reflect the following factors:

(a) the likely cost of funding the services and the benefit which may be obtained by their being provided;

(b) the availability of sums in the Community Legal Service Fund for funding the services and (having regard to present and likely future demands on that Fund) the appropriateness of applying them to fund the services;

(c) the importance of the matters in relation to which the services would be provided to the individual;

(d) the availability to the individual of services not funded by the Commission as part of the Community Legal Service and the likelihood of his being able to avail himself of them;

(e) if the services are sought by the individual in relation to a dispute, the prospects of his success in the dispute,

(f) the conduct of the individual;

(g) the public interest; and

(h) such other factors as the Lord Chancellor may require the Commission to consider.

In January 1999 the Legal Aid Board published a 98-page Consultation Paper (*The Funding Code*) describing its approach to the Government's proposals.[52] In October 1999 the Board published a draft code for consultation. Some amendments were made and in January 2000 the revised code was sent to the Lord Chancellor. He approved it on 14 January 2000. It became operative as from 1 April 2000 when the Legal Services Commission and the Community Legal Service were formally established.[53]

GLOSSARY OF TERMS

The legal aid scheme had several parts. The new scheme changed the names and to some extent the nature of the categories and added a number of new features[54]:

- The 1999 Act established the Legal Services Commission (LSC) with functions relating to the Community Legal Service (CLS) and the Criminal Defence Service (CDS)
- 'Legal aid for civil proceedings' – became 'Legal representation', sub-divided into 'Investigative Help' limited to making inquiries to permit assessment in cases likely to be expensive and 'Full representation'
- 'Legal aid for criminal proceedings' – became funded services provided by the CDS
- 'Legal advice and assistance' for matters that had not reached court proceedings (widely known as the Green Form scheme) – became Legal Help
- 'Assistance by way of representation' (ABWOR) – permitting representation in certain cases without a full legal aid certificate.[55] – became 'Help at Court'
- 'Duty solicitor scheme' in the police station – no change
- 'Duty solicitor scheme' in the magistrates' court – no change
- 'Support funding' (new) – a funding mix of the state plus a conditional fee agreement (CFA) divided into 'Investigative Support' (new) and 'Litigation Support' (new)
- 'Approved Family Help' (new) – help in family cases short of Full Representation
- 'General Family Help' (new) covering negotiations in a family dispute where no mediation is in progress
- 'Family Mediation' (new) for disputes relating to children, money or property

---

[52] The Law Society produced a 77-page response in April 1999.

[53] For the text of the Funding Code see www.legalservices.gov.uk .For an overview see Legal Services Commission, 30 *Focus*, April 2000, pp 19-30. For the relevant regulations see 29 *Focus*, March 2000, pp 28-57.

[54] For a fuller glossary of new terms see 30 *Focus*, April 2000, pp 42-43.

[55] It applied, for instance, to domestic proceedings in magistrates' courts and mental health review tribunals and to police applications for warrants of further detention under the Police and Criminal Evidence Act 1984.

THE LEGAL SERVICES COMMISSION

The Legal Services Commission, like the Legal Aid Board, has a mixed board of lawyers and non-lawyers.[56] The first chairman, Mr Peter Birch, was a non-lawyer, the second, Mr Philip Ely, appointed in 2003, was a solicitor and a past President of the Law Society.

The Commission is responsible for publicly funded civil and criminal legal services. (It took over responsibility for Crown Court expenditure as from April 2003.)

Like its predecessor the Legal Aid Board, the Commission publishes a detailed annual report – though less detailed as to statistics than the Board's reports. The annual report, and other publications issued by the Commission can be accessed on its website – www.legalservices.gov.uk. Note especially *Focus* published several times a year by the Commission with the latest information on both the civil and the criminal schemes and *Focus on CDS* which concentrates just on the CDS. Both are accessible on the website.

The annual *Judicial Statistics* give the global net expenditure on legal aid (including criminal legal aid in the Crown Court). (In 2001 total net expenditure was £1.75bn.[57])

THE NATURE OF PROVISION

The Legal Services Commission funds civil legal services under the headings of Controlled and Licensed Work.

'Controlled Work' covers all Legal Help and Help at Court and Legal Representation before Mental Health Review Tribunals, the Immigration Appeal Tribunal and Immigration Adjudicators. These services are provided under the terms of the provider's General Civil Contract where the decision as to whether to provide services is made by the provider under a contract that limits the number of cases that may be taken (known as 'matter starts'). The firm gets a global sum calculated by the LSC on the basis of the number and kind of its 'matter starts'. The contract specifies the number of matter starts under different headings – family, actions against the police, clinical negligence, debt, education, public law, welfare benefits etc. By far the largest number of contracts are issued in regard to family matters.[58]

The number of matter starts can be adjusted on application. The annual report for 2001/02 stated, 'There has been no need to ration matter starts' (para 2.15, p 10).

---

[56]   Details of the members and their business, financial and other interests appear in the annual report.

[57]   *Judicial Statistics, 2002*, p 104.

[58]   In 2002/03 family contracts were 42% of all contracts issued. Personal injury and clinical negligence accounted for 19%, housing for 8%, immigration and welfare benefits each for 7%. (LSC *Annual Report*, 2002-03, Table CLS 1, p 9.)

In regard to Controlled Work there are limits to the amount that may be spent on the case without further authority from the LSC. (The current limit for Legal Help is £500 for most cases, but £2,000 for immigration/asylum cases handled by fully franchised firms. In cases where Controlled Legal Representation is provided before a tribunal the limit is £1,500 for fully franchised firms.)

A firm with a contract for Controlled Work also has the right to apply to the LSC for a certificate to provide representation in civil proceedings. Certificates are issued on a case-by-case basis. (Emergency work can be conducted without prior authority.)

The number of solicitors' offices with Controlled Work contracts in the year to 31 March 2003 was 4,383 (down from 4,543 in the year to 31 March 2002). In addition there were 420 Not for Profit agencies with such contracts (up from 389 in the previous year).

'Licensed Work' covers other Legal Representation (not including very expensive cases which are managed under individual contracts). Licensed Work contracts do not limit the number of cases that can be started. Instead, an application for funding has to be made in each case and a decision is made on the basis of financial eligibility of the client and the merits of the case. Licensed Work is typically for firms that handle specialised litigation. In the year to 31 March 2003 there were 258 firms (down from 389 in the previous year) with contracts just for Licensed Work.

The total number of contractors as at March 2002 was therefore 5,061 (compared with 5,321 in the previous year). It will be recalled that the Law Society had optimistically predicted that the number of firms providing publicly funded services would be 6,000. If the not for profit non-solicitor firms are excluded the number of solicitor firms involved in this work is now well under 5,000 and declining.

THE FUNDING PRIORITIES

A direction given by the Lord Chancellor under AJA 1999, s 6(1) together with guidance issued under s 23 set the funding priorities as envisaged in the White Paper.[59] In drawing up its plans the LSC is required to give top priority to certain Children Act proceedings (as defined in the Funding Code[60]) and to civil proceedings where the client is at real and immediate risk of loss of life or liberty. Any such case should be funded provided it meets the merits test criteria. After that the LSC 'should generally give the following categories higher priority than others' namely:

- help with social welfare issues that will enable people to avoid or climb out of social exclusion, including help with housing proceedings and advice relating to debt, employment rights, and entitlement to social security benefits;

[59] See 29 *Focus*, March 2000, pp 17-18.
[60] Public law child protection cases for which legal aid was previously available without a means or merits test.

- domestic violence proceedings;
- proceedings concerning the welfare of children (including those under Part IV or V of the Children Act, adoption proceedings, and proceedings concerning residence);
- proceedings against public authorities alleging serious wrong-doing, abuse of position or power or significant breach of human rights

(a) The former legal aid scheme and what has changed

The legal aid schemes for civil and criminal proceedings operated on the basis of eligibility under both a means test and a merits test, with the possibility of a contribution from the assisted person. Legal advice and assistance had only a means test. The duty solicitor schemes had neither.

In its 1998 White Paper, the Labour Government said that these features would remain save that there would no longer be a preliminary means test for criminal legal aid and that contributions, which had been abolished to reduce the numbers eligible, would be re-introduced for legal advice and assistance. In the debates on the Access to Justice Bill it also emerged that the Government had decided that there would be no means test for an initial diagnostic interview.

(b) Legal aid in civil proceedings

The first question has always been whether the category of work is within the legal aid scheme. Prior to the Access to Justice Act 1999 the scope of the civil legal aid scheme was determined very simply. Proceedings in all the courts (and a few tribunals) were within the scheme unless they were included in the list of excepted proceedings. This list was very short: defamation, relator actions, election petitions and judgment summonses.

EXCLUSIONS FROM THE SCHEME

The Access to Justice Act 1999 (AJA) has a longer list of excluded categories. The Act excludes, in particular, services relating to allegations of negligently caused injury, death or damage to property, other than allegations of clinical negligence. (AJA 1999, Sch 22, para 1(a)) These matters are excluded on the ground that they are suitable for funding under conditional fee agreements (CFAs – see below). Personal injury due to something other than negligence is not excluded. Other areas of work excluded are conveyancing, boundary disputes, the making of wills, matters of trust law, defamation and malicious falsehood, company or partnership law and other matters arising out of business. (AJA 1999, Sch 2, para 1(a)) It is not thought that such matters have sufficient priority to justify public funding.

EXCEPTIONS TO THE EXCLUSIONS

The Lord Chancellor may give directions under AJA 1999, s 6(8)(a) permitting the Legal Services Commission (LSC) to fund in specified circumstances services that are generally excluded. The categories include cases that have a significant wider public interest; and cases against public authorities alleging serious wrong-doing, abuse of position or power, or a significant breach of human rights. Another category is personal injury cases with very high investigative costs before it can be determined whether the case could be funded under a CFA. Under s 6(8)(b) the Lord Chancellor may authorise funding in individual cases following a request from the Commission.

The Lord Chancellor's Guidance states that funding of a case in an otherwise excluded category may be considered where '(i) there is significant wider public interest; or (ii) the case is of overwhelming importance to the client; or (iii) there is convincing evidence that there are other exceptional circumstances such that without public funding for representation it would be practically impossible for the client to bring or defend the proceedings, or the lack of funding would lead to obvious unfairness in the proceedings'.[61]

The Commission has established a Public Interest Advisory Panel. A summary of its reports on individual cases is published in *Focus* and also on the website – www.legalservices.gov.uk (Guidance – Public Interest Reports).

See also K Ashton, 'Public interest litigation – realising the potential', *Legal Action*, July 2001.

In addition to establishing that the matter in question is within the scope of the scheme, the applicant has to satisfy a merits test and a means test.

THE MERITS TEST

Under the previous scheme an applicant could not get civil legal aid unless he satisfied the Legal Aid Board that he had reasonable grounds for taking, defending or being a party to the proceedings' (Legal Aid Act 1988, s 15(2)). He could be refused legal aid if in the circumstances it appeared to the Board 'unreasonable that he should be granted representation' (LAA 1988, s 15(3)).

The first part of the test was whether there were sufficient prospects of the client being successful. The second part, the 'reasonableness test', was more elastic. The usual interpretation was whether a reasonable solicitor would advise a reasonable client, who had the means, to spend his own money on the case. This excluded most small claims, as solicitors would not normally advise their clients to proceed.

---

61   The third category was added in light of *R (on the application of Jarrett) v Legal Services Commission* [2001] EWHC Admin 389 [2001] All ER (D) 111 (Jun), LT which concerned the exclusion of director disqualification cases.

But although financial benefit as compared with the cost was the normal criterion, it did not always apply. There were cases affecting the applicant's status, reputation or dignity where legal aid could be appropriate even though the financial benefit was small.

The Access to Justice Act 1999 and the Funding Code issued under it radically transformed the merits test. It now requires consideration of wider criteria and different measures of likely success depending on the type of case.[62] The essence of the matter is not merely prospects of success but cost-benefit. The tests are set out in the General Funding Code (the Code), s 5:

THE STANDARD CRITERIA

- For Legal Help (5.2) – Is there sufficient benefit to the client having regard to the circumstances, including the personal circumstances of the client to justify the work and is it reasonable for the work to be funded out of the Community Legal Service Fund (CLS Fund) having regard to any other potential sources of funding?
- For Help at Court (5.3)– The same and also, is advocacy appropriate? Will it be of real benefit to the client? Would Legal Representation be more appropriate?
- For Legal Representation and Support Funding (5.4) – Is alternative funding available? Are there alternative ways of solving the matter? Is litigation premature? Is it reasonable for the CLS to fund the litigation?
- For Emergency Representation (5.5) – Is it in the interests of justice?
- For Investigative Help (5.6)– Should the work be done under a CFA or should only Investigative Support be provided? Is it a case where the prospects of success are uncertain and substantial investigative work is required before the prospects can be determined? Would the damages be likely to exceed £5,000? Are there reasonable grounds for believing that the claim will be strong enough, in terms of prospects of success and cost benefit, to satisfy the criteria for Full Representation?
- For Full Representation (5.7):
  o Will be refused if the prospects of success are unclear or poor; or are borderline and the case does not appear to have a significant wider public interest or to be of overwhelming importance to the client
  o If the claim is for damages and it does not have significant wider public interest, will be refused unless:-
    ▪ If prospects of success are very good (80% or better), likely damages will exceed likely costs

---

62 For research by the Legal Aid Board into the capacity of solicitors to judge prospects of success see P Pleasence, 'Can solicitors pick winners?', *New Law Journal*, 29 January 1999, p 138.

- ▪ If prospects of success are good (60%-80%), likely damages exceed likely costs by 2:1
- ▪ If prospects of success are moderate (50%-60%), likely damages exceed likely costs by 4:1
- o If the claim is not primarily for damages (including one which has overwhelming importance to the client) but does not have a wider public significance, Full Representation will be refused unless the likely benefits justify the likely costs, such that a reasonable private paying client would be prepared to litigate. If the claim does have a significant wider public interest, it may be refused unless the likely benefit to the applicant and others justify the likely costs, having regard to the prospects of success and all other circumstances.
- For Litigation Support (5.9):
  - o Will be refused unless there is a satisfactory CFA supported by satisfactory insurance cover
  - o Will be refused unless the disbursements are likely to exceed £5,000 or the costs, excluding disbursements, are likely to exceed £15,000. (These threshold figures may be varied if the case has a significant wider public interest.)
  - o Will be refused if the prospects of success are unclear, borderline or poor
  - o Unless the case has a significant wider public interest, will be refused unless the ratios of likely costs to likely damages are the same as for Full Representation (above)
  - o If the case does have significant wider public interest it may be refused unless the likely benefit to the applicant and others justify the likely costs, having regard to the prospects of success and all other circumstances
- For Very High Cost Cases[63] (section 6):
  - o Will be refused unless it appears reasonable for funding to be granted in the light of the resources available and likely future demands on those resources. But this Affordability criterion does not apply to Special Children Act Proceedings; judicial review proceedings in which funding is to continue by virtue of 7.5.2 (see below); or other proceedings in which the life or liberty of the client is at risk. These cases are handled by the Special Cases Unit (SCU). Each case has an individual contract based on an agreed Case Plan with prices costed for each stage, though the plan may change as the case develops. (See 32 *Focus* pp 12-13.)
- For Judicial Review (section 7):
  - o If the court has not yet given permission or permission is not required, Full Representation will be refused if the prospects are unclear or poor, or borderline and the case does not appear to have significant wider public

---

[63]   In respect of Investigative Help or Full Representation cases where costs are likely to exceed £25,000; in respect of Litigation Support cases where a conditional fee agreement is in place and funding is sought for costs above £15,000 or disbursements above £5,000.

interest, to be of overwhelming importance to the client or to raise significant human rights issues (7.4.5). It may be refused unless the likely benefits justify the likely costs, having regard to the prospects of success and all other circumstances (7.4.6).

o   If permission has been granted and the case has significant wider public interest, or is of overwhelming importance to the client or raises significant human rights issues, then provided the Standard criteria in Section 4 are met, funding 'shall be granted' unless in light of further information 'it appears unreasonable' (7.5.2).

o   If permission has been granted but the case does not appear to have significant wider public interest or to be overwhelming importance to the client or to raise significant human rights issues, Legal Representation will be refused if prospects of success are borderline or poor or the likely benefits do not appear to justify the likely costs having regard to the prospects of success and all the circumstances (7.5.3).

Further similar criteria are stated in regard to claims against public authorities (s 8), clinical negligence (s 9), housing (s 10), family (s 11), mental health (s 12), and immigration (s 13).

THE MEANS TEST AND CONTRIBUTIONS

Under the legal aid scheme there were three categories of applicant: (a) those who qualified for free legal aid; (b) those who qualified for legal aid subject to a contribution; and (c) those who did not qualify for legal aid because of excessive income or capital or both.

The great majority (around 85%) of those who got civil legal aid paid no contribution. (In 1999-2000, 84% were on a nil contribution, 6% had a maximum contribution of up to £500, and 10% of over £500.[64])

The Community Legal Service has the same basic structure of eligibility tests regarding income and capital and for calculating eligibility.[65] The rates for the year have hitherto been announced to come into force each April. Thus, for the year from April 2003:

•   For Legal Help, Help at Court and Legal Representation before Immigration Adjudicators and the Immigration Appeal Tribunal the gross income limit was £2,228 per month (more with five or more dependent children), the limit for 'disposable income' was £621 per month and the capital limit was £3,000. There is no contribution.

•   For all other levels of service, the gross income level was the same as above but the disposable income limit was £707 per month and the capital limit was £8,000.

64   *Legal Aid Board Annual Report 1999-2000*, p 93.
65   The details were set out in 36 *Focus*, November 2001, pp 16-23.

A contribution in respect of income was payable for those whose monthly disposable income was above £267 and below £707. The contribution was assessed in three income bands:

o   For a monthly disposable income between £268 and £393 – 1/4 of income in excess of £263

o   For a disposable income between £394 to £522 – £32.50 + 1/3 of income in excess of £522

o   For a disposable income between £523 to £707 – £75.50 + 1/2 of income in excess of £522.

For someone whose disposable capital is between £3,000 and £8,000 the contribution is either the excess capital over £3,000 or the likely costs whichever is the lesser. If capital is under £3,000 there is no contribution in respect of capital.

To arrive at the figure for disposable income or disposable capital a considerable number of deductions are allowed from the gross figures. Thus for income, allowable deductions include national insurance, tax, child care expenses incurred because of employment, rent or mortgage payments up to £545 per month and a fixed amount for each dependent relative. In calculating capital one may exclude the value of one's home up to £100,000 after allowing for any mortgage again up to £100,000.

THE STATUTORY CHARGE

When a legally aided person won his case, the legal aid fund recouped itself for his costs first from costs paid by the loser, secondly from his contribution and thirdly from any damages awarded to him or from property recovered or preserved by the litigation. This so-called 'statutory charge' on the damages could in some cases have the effect of wiping out the net benefit of the litigation. Some forms of property were exempt – notably maintenance, or money or property not over £2,500 transferred in divorce proceedings. The Board had the power to delay activating the statutory charge (*Hanlon v Law Society* [1980] 2 All ER 199). This power to delay was commonly used to avoid a sale of the matrimonial home by the wife when it had been awarded to her in the matrimonial proceedings for her and the children to live in. But the claim remained effective and was met when the wife later sold. Pre-CLS the statutory charge was the cost of the funded services or the value of the house whichever was the lesser.

Under the CLS, the statutory charge is in most respects essentially the same. It does not apply to sums expended by the LSC in funding Legal Help, Help at Court, Family Mediation or Help with Mediation[66] The first £3,000 (increased from £2,500) recovered in family proceedings is exempt. However one difference is that when the operation of the charge is postponed the charge now applies to the whole cost of the

---

[66]   Unless in the case of Legal Help, Help at Court or Help with Mediation the work was in connection with family, clinical negligence or personal injury proceedings or a dispute which might give rise to such proceedings.

funded services so that if the value of the property increases in value above the amount due, the Commission can take its full pound of flesh. (See further 29 *Focus*, March 2000, pp 11-13.)

(c)   Criminal legal aid

The 1998 White Paper (*Modernising Justice*) also set out the Government's plans for criminal legal aid. The section of the White Paper was headed 'Criminal Defence Service'. The Government would set up a new Criminal Defence Service to replace the current criminal legal aid system.[67] Something new was needed because of the problems of the existing scheme. First, the cost of criminal legal aid had been rising alarmingly. In 1992-93, the taxpayer spent £507m on criminal legal aid. By 1997-98 the figure was £733m, an increase of 44% as against a rise in general inflation over that period of 13%. In the same period the number of legal aid orders for representation in criminal cases had gone up by 10%. In the Crown Court, the most expensive part of the system, the cost had risen by 58% while the number of cases had remained constant (p 60, para 6.6).

The framework for determining lawyers' rates of remuneration was 'inflexible and outdated' (p 60, para 6.7). Standard fees had increased control but larger and more complex cases were still dealt with by the traditional system of calculating the bill after the event. As a result, lawyers were under 'inappropriate financial incentives' – to seek unnecessary adjournments, to delay guilty pleas of clients until the last moment and to take cases to the Crown Court unnecessarily. Also a few, very expensive cases were taking an increasingly disproportionate share of the budget. Thus in 1996-97, 42% of legal aid spending in the Crown Court was on just 1% of the cases. In civil cases it was (and is) the same story. A sample of 1,269 legal aid files closed in 1998/99 showed that only 5% of cases in the sample had gross costs of over £25,000 but they consumed 44% of total net costs. Also the system for assessing defendant's means was flawed.

About 94% of defendants in the Crown Court obtained legal aid without making a contribution. So in most of these cases, the means assessment was a waste of time and money. On the other hand, free legal aid was sometimes granted to a defendant with an apparently wealthy lifestyle. This was usually because the defendant's assets had been frozen for the duration of the case, which was the only period when contributions were payable. This had undermined public confidence in legal aid (p 61, para 6.8).

Finally the scheme was highly fragmented with five different parts to the scheme which could lead to duplication and delay.

---

[67]   See generally on the previous scheme an excellent collection of essays in *Access to Criminal Justice: Legal Aid Lawyers & the Defence of Liberty*, ed R Young and D Wall, Blackstone, 1996 – referred to here as '*Access to Criminal Justice, 1996*'

The next section of the White Paper was headed 'Fundamental reform'. The new Criminal Defence Service (CDS) would be separate from the Community Legal Service (CLS) which would run the civil scheme.

The two schemes would have separate budgets. The Lord Chancellor caused consternation when he said in the debates on the Access to Justice Bill, 'what is available for civil legal aid is what is left over from the budget after the prior claims of criminal legal aid have been met.'[68] Explaining these words later, the Solicitor-General said there would be separate sub-heads on the departmental vote, 'which means that there will be separate accounting in the annual appropriation accounts for the two services'.[69] The accounts would explain any transfer during the year between the sub-heads. The Solicitor-General added: 'The Government have also undertaken to announce immediately to Parliament any transfer beyond a small sum' – though the transfer would not require Parliamentary approval.[70] But budgets had to be set and spending on legal services had to be planned just like that for health and education. The Government was determined that the CLS should be properly funded but the budget had to be, and be seen to be, under control.

Both budgets would be run by the Legal Services Commission. The CDS scheme would cover the whole of the existing scheme. 'Change will focus on securing better quality and value for money, by developing more efficient ways of procuring services – contracting and directly employed lawyers – and by streamlining the arrangements for granting representation' (p 61, para 6.11). In future most publicly-funded criminal defence services would be provided by lawyers in private practice, under contracts, working wherever possible on prices fixed in advance. Fixed prices created an incentive to keep delay to a minimum; they rewarded efficiency and allowed quick and certain payment. So far as possible, contracts would cover the full range of criminal defence services from advice in the police station to Crown Court representation. This would 'eliminate the fragmentation that bedevils the current scheme' (p 62, para 6 14). If a case required the services of a specialist advocate this would be provided under a separate contract. Very expensive cases – defined as those expected to last more than 25 days – would be handled by individually negotiated contracts. If the CDS and the firm chosen by the defendant could not agree on terms, the client might be required to choose a different firm from the panel (p 62, para 6.15). This would enable the CDS to keep a tight rein on expenditure instead of handing over a blank cheque as the existing system effectively did.

---

68   House of Lords, *Hansard*, 21 January 1999, col 738.

69   In a report to the Lord Chancellor in October 1998, the Board said that in regard to Green Form work it envisaged that family law work should initially continue at the same level of expenditure but that in other civil categories of work there should be a 25% shift toward an allocation based on the distribution of income support claimants: Law Society, *Reforming the civil advice and assistance scheme: exclusive contracting*, October 1998, p 1.

70   House of Commons, Standing Committee 'E', 29 April 1999, col 83. See also Standing Committee 'E', 4 May 1999, col 122.

All contracts would include quality requirements starting with the existing franchising scheme. But firms would have to give assurances that both solicitors and their unqualified representatives had the appropriate knowledge and skills. The Law Society's accreditation scheme first introduced for police station advice (p 171 above) could be developed for this purpose or, if that did not happen, the CDS would be expected to start its own.

Clients would still have choice of firm provided it had a contract. Change of firm would require the consent of the CDS and would not normally be possible. (The Government later stated that if a client asked for the duty solicitor in the police station he would normally be required to stay with the duty solicitor's firm for the rest of the case. If however, he asked for his own solicitor in the police station but ended up with the Duty Solicitor he would have the right to change to the solicitor of his choice.) Most firms that undertook a significant amount of criminal work would remain part of the scheme. But they should have to compete for work. One way to meet both these objectives would be to make firms bid for a larger or smaller share of the work available. Firms would be awarded more or fewer duty solicitor 'slots', on the basis of the prices they offered both for that work and for subsequent representation (para 6.14, p 62).

WHAT HAS CHANGED

The CDS became operational as from 2 April 2001. From that date funding of private practice solicitors to provide advice and assistance on criminal matters, including in the police station and representation in the magistrates' court, had to be through the General Criminal Contract. Crown Court work was excluded. It remained under the authority of the LCD.

Under the new system, applications for funding for legal representation are made, as before, to the court, but the means test only operates at the end of the case and then only in a small minority of cases.

THE MERITS TEST

The merits test previously was simply whether it was 'in the interests of justice' (Legal Aid Act 1988, s 21(2)). Prior to the Legal Aid Act 1988 the statutory formula of 'the interests of justice' was not further defined. Instead there was a non-statutory list of criteria that were supposed to be applied to the interpretation of the test for cases to be heard in the magistrates' courts. These non-statutory so-called 'Widgery criteria'[71] were replaced with a statutory gloss on the 'interests of justice' in s 22 of the Legal Aid Act 1988. This is now to be found in virtually identical language in Sch 3 of the

---

71   So called because they were formulated by the (Widgery) Report of the Departmental Committee on *Legal Aid in Criminal Proceedings*, 1966, Cmnd 2934, para 180.

Access to Justice Act 1999, para 5(2) ('Criteria for grant of right')'. The criteria for the grant of what is now called a 'right to representation' are whether the defendant is likely to face a sentence depriving him of his liberty or loss of livelihood or serious damage to reputation; whether the case involves a substantial question of law; or the defendant may be unable to understand the proceedings or to state his own case; whether the defence involves the tracing and interviewing of witnesses or expert cross-examination; or that it is in the interests of someone else that the defendant is represented. Schedule 3, para 5 (3) adds (perhaps ominously) that the mentioned factors may be varied or that new ones may be added by order.

Where the case was being tried in the Crown Courts, it was and still is normally regarded as being in the interests of justice for legal aid to be granted, as can be seen from the remarkable fact that year on year some 95% of those tried in the Crown Court , regardless of whether they plead guilty or not guilty, are represented out of public funds. (In 2001, it was 94% of those tried and 82% of those who appeared for sentence only.[72]) Unlike the position in most countries, members of the Criminal Bar, including its most eminent members, spend most of their working lives representing publicly funded defendants.

But whether a particular applicant for legal aid in the magistrates' court got it has depended as much as anything on the accident of which court he applied to. Notoriously, and probably unavoidably, courts varied considerably in their policy as regards the granting of legal aid.[73]

Research found considerable differences in interpretation of the criteria. It also found that many (perhaps most) grants of legal aid were made in situations where the criteria did not apply, or where, if they did apply, they were given little weight by court clerks. Instead, the system that seemed to operate in most courts was that for some offences legal aid was automatically granted, for others almost automatically refused, while in the middle was a grey area where the arguments presented by or, more likely, on behalf of the applicant could make a difference. Some court clerks were too generous some were too severe.[74] The problem has not been the subject of recent inquiry but probably that is still the case.

The Legal Aid Act 1988, s 21(7) provided that where a doubt arose as to whether legal aid should be granted to a person, 'the doubt shall be resolved in that person's favour'. There is no equivalent in the Access to Justice Act 1999.

---

[72] *Judicial Statistics*, 2001, p 103.
[73] R Young, 'The Merits of Legal Aid in the Magistrates' Courts' (1993) *Criminal Law Review* 336–44 and 'Court clerks, legal aid and the interests of justice', *New Law Journal*, 18 September 1992, p 1264 both reporting on research conducted for and published by the Legal Aid Board under the title *In the Interests of Justice? The Determination of Criminal Legal Aid Applications by Magistrates' Courts in England and Wales* by R Young, T Moloney, and A Sanders.
[74] (1993) *Criminal Law Review*, 336, 343.

The number of cases in which defendants got legal aid orders for trials in the magistrates' courts in the years 1993 to 1998 fluctuated between 432,000 and 494,000. In 1998/99 it rose to 503,000. In the following two years it was down to 475,000 and 467,000. But in 2001/02, it rose extraordinarily to 598,000.[75] There was speculation that reasons for the jump might have been the impact of the Human Rights Act and also the abolition of the means test. Understandably, it caused alarm at the LCD – see the Consultation Paper issued in June 2003, pp 596-98 below. In 2002/03, the figure was given as 576,000.[76]

THE MEANS TEST AND CONTRIBUTIONS

Means testing in criminal legal aid was normally done by court clerks who generally lack both expertise and interest in the subject. The process of means testing created serious problems.

The basis of the means test was somewhat imprecise. Courts were supposed to follow broadly the same financial tests as applied civil cases. The general test was whether it appeared to the court that the applicant's means were such that he required assistance in meeting the costs. Unlike the civil scheme, however, the criminal scheme had no upper limit – so even a relatively rich person could qualify if the case was likely to be a long and costly one. The test was what a person could reasonably be expected to afford without altering their life style.

As has been seen, there is no longer a means test for legal representation in either the magistrates' court or the Crown Court.

However, there is a means test for preliminary Advice and Assistance (old Green Form) in regard to criminal matters. As at April 2003, in regard to Advice and Assistance on criminal matters, the limit for disposable income was £91 a week and for disposable capital was £1,000 for those with no dependants, £1,335 for those with one dependent, £1,535 for those with two dependants with £100 increase for each additional dependant.

There is also a means test in regard to what is called Advocacy Assistance – namely preparation of the case and representation in certain types of non-criminal cases in the magistrates' courts such as civil fine matters or failure to obey an order of the court where there is a risk of imprisonment. The limit for disposable income in April 2003 was £192 per week and on the capital side was £3,000 (or £3,335 for those with one dependent, £3,535 for those with two dependants with £100 increase for each additional dependant).

75   The figures for 1993 to 2001 appeared in the Legal Services Commission's *Annual Report* 2000/01, p 51. In the annual report for 2001/02 there was no equivalent table. The figure for that year is a composite from Tables CDS 2 and CDS 4, pp 44-45.
76   *Annual* Report 2002/03, Table CD3, p 50.

Both of these forms of service are non-contributory. Defendants are ineligible if either their income or their capital exceeds the limits.

Contributions The criminal legal aid scheme had a contribution aspect but this was on a very different basis from that in the civil scheme. Until 1982, the court had a complete discretion as to whether to ask for a down-payment or to demand a contribution after the completion of the case. Both the contribution order and its amount were entirely in the discretion of the court and, inevitably, courts varied considerably in their approach. This was changed by the Legal Aid Act 1982, the chief purpose of which was to raise more revenue from contributions. The Act proceeded on the basis that defendants facing the might of the state and threatened with criminal penalties should nevertheless have to pay for their legal defence whatever they could afford according to rigid criteria as in civil cases. This policy was carried on by the Legal Aid Act 1988.

However, as already noted, contributions in criminal cases were of doubtful value. A study done for the Legal Aid Efficiency Scrutiny as long ago as 1986 showed that in 1984–85 only 3% of criminal legal aid orders were contributory and that the total sum collected through contributions was only £1.8m as against gross expenditure of £134m. (The costs of assessing means were estimated at £800,000.) The main reason why so few contribution orders were made, the Scrutiny Report stated, was that some two-thirds of applicants were unemployed (*Scrutiny Report*, 1986, vol 2, II.2, para 8).

The unimpressive rate of recovery of contributions has been a constant. In 2000, the total bill for criminal legal aid was £623.9m. The total amount recovered by way of contributions was £5.9m (0.94%).[77] In May 1999, during the committee stage of the Access to Justice Bill, Mr Geoff Hoon, Minister of State, said that fewer than 1% of applicants were refused legal aid on the grounds of means. Another 5% were asked to pay contributions which had to be repaid after they were acquitted. 'The total value of contributions collected is barely enough to pay for the direct costs of running the system'.[78] All this had been known for many years but the Government was finally grasping the nettle by abolishing means testing at the stage of application.

It was not only because the system was unproductive but also because it was erratic and inefficient. The system of vetting legal aid applications was severely censured by the National Audit Office and by the annual reports of the Comptroller and Auditor General.

The Government's solution, Mr Hoon told the Standing Committee on the Access to Justice Bill, was to scrap means testing for applicants and instead 'all courts other than magistrates' courts should have a duty to consider at the end of a case, whether a defendant should pay his defence costs. That would be done by a Recovery of Defence Costs Order' (House of Commons Standing Committee 'E', 11 May 1999, col 239).

[77]   *Judicial Statistics*, 2000, p 102, Table 10.7.
[78]   House of Commons, Standing Committee 'E', 29 April 1999, col 83.

The new system abolishing up-front contributions became effective as from 2 October 2000.[79] From that date anyone who successfully applies for a Right to Representation Order gets legal representation without charge. Those tried in the magistrates' courts, or who are sent to the Crown Court for sentence only, or who appeal to the Crown Court are never asked to make a contribution. Save in exceptional circumstances, the same is true for someone who is acquitted in the Crown Court. But anyone committed for trial who is convicted or who pleads guilty can be liable for defence costs.

Such a person has to fill in a Form B. If no Form B is filled in, save in exceptional circumstances, the judge *must* order the defendant to pay the full amount of the defence costs to the Legal Services Commission.[80] If Form B is filled out and discloses sufficient income or other assets, the court can make a Recovery of Defence Costs Order (RDCO). The regulations exempt the first £3,000 of the defendant's capital, the first £100,000 of the equity in his principal home and income of up to £25,000 per annum. The judge has a duty to consider making an order at the end of the case. The judge must decide whether the information before him is sufficient. His powers include the power to investigate the defendant's partner and any other third party where it appears that the defendant has deliberately removed assets.

If in doubt, the judge can refer the matter to the Legal Services Commission for a report.[81] The Commission then sends a report to the judge setting out the available amounts and he can make any necessary further inquiry.[82] In its 2001/02 annual report the Commission said it had had 809 referrals from Crown Courts. In 177 it had decided there was little merit in opening a full investigation. The remaining 632 cases required full investigation. It had reported back to the courts in 292 cases. The court had informed the Commission of 223 RDCOs made during 2001/02 valued at £315,000. It had collected £117,000 and had written off £9,000. This was against a cost of representation in the Crown Court in 2001 of £465m.[83] The amount and nature of any order to pay is completely in the discretion of the judge. Inevitably therefore there will be inconsistency in their approach to the matter. But defendants given prison sentences, especially if they are long sentences, are unlikely to be the subject of a RDCO. So all defendants in the magistrates' courts and most defendants in the Crown Court now get their legal representation wholly at the state's expense. (But see the proposals in the June 2003 Consultation Paper, pp 596-98 below.)

HIGH COST CASES

Special rules apply in high cost criminal cases – defined as any case predicted to last for 25 days or more at trial or where defence costs will exceed £150,000. As previously

---

79   Legal Aid Act 1988 (Modification) Regulations 2000.
80   Criminal Defence Service (Recovery of Defence Costs Orders) Regulations 2001, SI 2001, No 856, reg 13.
81   SI 2001, No 856, reg 7.
82   SI 2001, No 856, reg 12(b).
83   Legal Services *Commission, Annual* Report 2001-02, at p 51.

noted, such cases absorb a grotesquely large proportion of the total criminal defence budget – 1% of Crown Court cases accounting for 49% of all expenditure. Regulations provide that such cases require an individual case contract. Remuneration for both barristers and solicitors links payment to the weight and complexity of the case. The Commission's annual report for 2002-2003 (para 3.33, p 53) said it entered in 86 contracts in the year. Serious fraud cases are now restricted to a panel of specialist solicitors.

DUTY SOLICITOR SCHEMES IN MAGISTRATES' COURTS

A national scheme for the establishment of duty solicitor schemes in magistrates' courts was provided for by the Legal Aid Act 1982. The basic idea was that the defendant who comes to court without having seen a lawyer should have someone to provide preliminary advice – as to his plea, whether to ask for an adjournment, and whether to apply for legal aid or bail – and representation. Originally the scheme was run by the Law Society through regional committees. The running of the schemes became part of the responsibility of the Legal Aid Board when it took over the management of the scheme in 1988.

In its last annual report, for 1999-2000, the Board stated that all magistrates' courts were covered by the scheme. The number of persons assisted in that year was 259,000, at a total cost of £25m.

The scheme continued in the main unaffected by the transfer of responsibility to the Legal Services Commission. In 2000-2001, the numbers assisted under the scheme was 465,000 at a total cost of £48m. The large increase in numbers, the Commission said, was due to national implementation of the Narey proposals for Early First and Early Administrative Hearings, part of the package of measures designed to speed up the administration of criminal justice. (*Annual Report*, 2000/01, p 37. This figure is unfortunately not stated in subsequent annual reports.)

DUTY SOLICITOR SCHEMES IN POLICE STATIONS

As was seen above (p 168), duty solicitor schemes were set up under PACE to assist detainees in the police station. Like the schemes for courts, they were originally run by the Law Society and subsequently by the Legal Aid Board. They work on either a rota or a panel basis[84] with local practitioners. There are now such schemes covering all the nearly 2,000 police stations. There are elaborate rules as to the qualifications required and the selection process involved for those participating in these schemes. The Legal Aid Board and then the Law Society, and now the Legal Services

[84]   In rota schemes the solicitors are nominated in advance for a set period during which they must make themselves fully available–night or day. In panel schemes the phone service running the scheme calls one solicitor after another until it finds one available. Rota schemes tend to be used in urban areas, panel schemes in less busy rural areas.

Commission, have made serious attempts to improve the quality of the advice given under the scheme, especially by non-solicitors, through the scheme for accreditation of non-solicitor representatives and trainee solicitors. In 1999-2000 the number of suspects assisted under the scheme was 749,600 at an overall cost of £109m. In 67% of cases the solicitor called out was the suspect's own solicitor; in 31% it was the duty solicitor; in the remaining 2% it was both. These proportions are very consistent year on year. The state scheme pays in either case.

According to the Commission's statistics, in 2002-03 the number of cases of persons not yet charged who were assisted under the scheme was 717,000 at a total cost of £158m.[85]

There is (as yet) no means test and no contribution in respect of assistance under either of the duty solicitor schemes. (But see the proposals in the June 2003 Consultation Paper, pp 596-98 below.)

(d)   Legal advice and assistance ('the Green Form scheme') – now 'Legal Help'

Since 1973 a client with a legal problem who qualified under the means test was entitled to go to any solicitor participating in the Green Form scheme (most did), to ask for oral or written advice or assistance. Advice and assistance covered a great variety of types of help, short of representation at a hearing. It was within the discretion of the solicitor what work he undertook within the scheme. He could write letters, negotiate, vet or draft a document and even prepare an argument for the client to present in a court or tribunal. The only limitation was that the lawyer could not go beyond roughly two hours' worth of work without getting authority to continue.

There was no merits test other than the decision of the solicitor to provide the help. There was, however, a fairly stringent means test administered on a somewhat rough and ready basis by the solicitor himself. Until 1993 a contribution was payable by those just above the free limit but as from April 1993 Green Form help was only available to those eligible to obtain it free. That remains the position under the new scheme.

As noted above, what was previously the Green Form Scheme is now called Legal Help. As before it extends to all assistance short of actual representation. In 2002/03, Legal Help accounted for 811,000 acts of assistance.[86]

The lawyer can do up to two hours work (or three hours in divorce work). If the matter requires more work, the lawyer must apply for an extension.

---

85   *Annual Report*, 2002-03, Table CDS 2, p 49. The above figures exclude the immigration cases and standby claims which appear in the table.

86   *Annual Report*, 2002-03, Table CLS 4, p 21.

(e)   Assistance by Way of Representation (ABWOR) – now 'Help at Court'

Assistance by Way of Representation, known as ABWOR, was a scheme to enable representation in certain matters to be handled without the full requirement of a legal aid certificate. It applied to domestic proceedings in magistrates' courts, proceedings before mental health review tribunals, representation in police applications under PACE for a warrant of further detention, and representation in certain child care proceedings. In 1999-2000 it cost some £14.7m.

From April 2000, under the new scheme, ABWOR has only been available for criminal proceedings. In civil proceedings, whether in the magistrates' court or the county court, the equivalent is called Help at Court which can only be provided by solicitors with a contract in the relevant field of law. It is for the solicitor to determine whether the client is financially eligible and whether the case is within the scope of the Act.[87] Again there is no contribution from the client.

(f)   Public defenders

The most controversial proposal in the 1998 White Paper (*Modernising Justice*) was that, in addition to contracting with lawyers in private practice, the CDS would also be able to use salaried lawyers. Evidence from other countries, it said, suggested that properly funded salaried defenders could even be more cost-effective and could provide a better service than lawyers in private practice. (The White Paper cited Tamara Goriely, *Legal Aid Delivery Systems: which offer the best value for money in mass casework?*[88]) But before taking the first steps in this direction, the CDS would take account of the pilot scheme involving public defence solicitors which was currently running in Scotland (p 63, para 6.18).

The Scottish pilot scheme with a Public Defence Solicitors' Office (PDSO) started in October 1998, as a five-year experiment under the Crime and Punishment (Scotland) Act 1997. The main motive seems to have been the prospect of providing the service at a lower cost. The crucial question was whether cost savings could be achieved without lowering the quality of the work done or the satisfaction of clients. The pilot was based in Edinburgh. It had six full-time lawyers. It was expected to handle about 15% of the summary business in Edinburgh. Clients come from two sources. Anyone whose date of birth fell in January or February was required to consult PDSO if they wanted criminal legal aid. The second source was self-referral by people in the area. (See A Watson, 'The Public Defence Solicitors' Office: The Background to its Introduction in Scotland', *Scottish Law Gazette*, September 1998, p 117.)

The Government believed that in the longer term the best approach would prove to be a mixed system combining both private and 'staff' lawyers. The main reason was

---

87   29 *Focus*, March 2000, p 14.
88   LCD Research Series 10/97, December 1997.

'value for money for the taxpayer'. ('The cost of the salaried service will provide a benchmark, which the CDS can use to assess whether the prices charged by private lawyers are reasonable. Staff lawyers will also give the CDS flexibility.') The client would have the choice.

But the plan ran into heavy opposition from the profession and in the House of Lords principally on the ground that state salaried lawyers could not be expected to perform with the independence demanded from defence lawyers. The Government was defeated twice on the issue – first on the Report stage of the Bill by 189-134and then on Lords consideration of Commons amendments by 145-85.[89] But when the Government brought the clause back again, the Lords observed the usual constitutional convention and did not press the matter to a vote.[90]

In June 2000 the LCD published a Consultation Paper, *Criminal Defence Service: establishing a Salaried Defence Service and Draft Code of Conduct for Salaried Defenders Employed by the Legal Services Commission*. In March 2001 the LCD published the Government's conclusions following consultation on the code of conduct which resulted in several changes in the Code. In April 2001 it published the Government's conclusions on the plans for the PDS. None of the plans had been changed as a result of the consultation. (All of these documents can be accessed on the PDS' website: www.legalservices.gov.uk/pds/intro.htm.)

The Legal Services Commission's first annual report for 2000/01 stated that during the year it had opened the first three Public Defender offices in Liverpool, Swansea and Middlesborough. By July 2003 eight offices had opened (Annual Report, 2002/03, para 1.28.)

Clients had a free choice and it had been decided not to give the PDS offices a disproportionate share of duty solicitor work. So the offices had to build up their client basis from a cold start. Professors Lee Bridges of Warwick University and Avrom Sherr of the Institute of Advanced Legal Studies were conducting a four-year research study into the PDS. The Commission had appointed Anthony Edwards, a Commission member and a very experienced private practice defence lawyer as Professional Head of Service for the PDS. It was his responsibility to ensure that the staff complied with the Code of Conduct, for issuing guidance under the Code and for monitoring and if necessary addressing complaints about the services provided by the PDS.[91]

The PDS issued its own review of its first year of operation (2001-02) and declared it to have been 'a considerable success'.

Private practitioners understandably felt aggrieved about the level of funding provided by the PDS for staff, premises, and other facilities but Anthony Edwards

---

[89]   House of Lords, *Hansard*, 16 February 1999, cols 551–69 and 14 July 1999, cols 412-22.
[90]   House of Lords, *Hansard*, 26 July 1999, cols 1295-1308.
[91]   On his role see 1 *Independent Lawyer*, May 2002, pp 8-10.

told the Criminal Law Solicitors' Association (CLSA) annual conference in 2001 that although the PDS plainly was unfair competition this was to miss the point. Setting up a pilot PDS was a part of the Labour Party's manifesto at the last election. 'Like it or not, fair or not, an elected government is entitled to carry out its manifesto commitments.' But although some firms were raging, others were forging links with the new service.

Also, since the Government was likely to take the cost of the PDS as a benchmark for the proper cost of private practice, the profession should be cheering on the PDS 'to more and more palatial offices'.

In its Consultation Paper 'The Future of Publicly Funded Legal Services' issued in February 2003 the Law Society canvassed the idea that a salaried public defender (and civil legal) service might be a solution to the crisis in legal aid funding. The legal aid practitioner's journal *The Independent Lawyer* described this as a 'spectacular volte face' by the society which had previously been, at best, deeply skeptical about salaried provision for legal services.[92] Ironically though, the Law Society was warming to the PDS just as government seemed to be losing enthusiasm for the project. Patricia Scotland QC, the Government Minister, in a letter to the Legal Aid Practitioner Group, had confirmed that expansion of the pilot project from its existing eight offices had been halted. ('No new PDS offices will be opened in 2003 ... unless external factors, such as the collapse of coverage in a particular area, necessitates the [Legal Services Commission] starting a new office.') The Minister's statement followed confirmation by the Commission[93] that the PDS was more expensive than private practice – 'which would seem to rule out a nationwide service being a solution to the funding crisis'[94]

See generally: D O'Brien and JA Epp, 'Salaried Defenders and the Access to Justice Act 1999', 63 *Modern Law Review*, 2000, 394-412. Their conclusion was that the primary reason for the reforms was the desire to control legal aid costs. But if lessons were learnt from other jurisdictions, a well managed state salaried service could provide a service that would match the quality of the service provided by private practitioners. Equally, if managed poorly, it would be an inferior service. In other words, no delivery model was inherently inferior or superior. But the PDS should offer a complementary service not one that simply competed with private practice.

JUSTICE in its report *Public Defenders: Learning from the US experience*, 2001 said that 'what was clear without exception was that, within each US jurisdiction, the public defender system was acknowledged to be superior, in terms of quality, support and resources, to the publicly funded private bar operating alongside it' (p 7). Criticisms of US public defender systems it said were 'not based on arguments about the inadequacy of salaried as against private providers, but rather on the inadequate

---

[92]   Issue 8, March 2003, p 3.
[93]   See 5 *Independent Lawyer*, October 2002, p 10.
[94]   8 *Independent Lawyer*, March 2003, p 3.

resourcing and running of the indigent defence system as a whole in many states; but where nevertheless the salaried defender is likely to produce the best service on offer' (p 7).

See also the evaluation of the Scottish public defender system (PDSO) by the Institute of Advanced Legal Studies, *The Public Defence Solicitors' Office in Edinburgh: an independent evaluation*, Scottish Executive, 2001. It found that the quality of the PDSO's advocacy was similar to that of private practice though there were differences in the ways they processed cases. PDSO cases were more likely to end with a conviction (88% compared with 83% of private practice clients). The difference appeared to be a tendency on the part of the PDSO clients to plead guilty earlier, whereas if the case was dragged out there was a possibility the prosecution would drop the case. Client satisfaction with salaried defenders was lower than that of private practice clients. Only 39% strongly agreed that the PDSO had stood up for their rights compared with 71% of private clients. PDSO clients were also less likely to say they would use the office again.

Overall the research found the costs of the two systems broadly similar though public defenders had the potential to be cheaper if they had sufficient volume.

First indications as to the relative cost of the PDS in England and private practice suggests that the PDS costs *more* – but this may be due to the fact that the offices were staffed from the outset so as to provide a 24-hour, seven days a week service even though initially there was not the client base to justify such a level of staffing. (See 2001-2002, 1st annual report, para 5.18.)

Law centres

Most legal aid expenditure has been for services provided by lawyers in private practice (known in the US as 'Judicare'). A minuscule proportion of the resources disposed of by the Legal Aid Board went to law centres – lawyers, mainly in poverty areas, who are not in private practice. The first law centre was set up in 1970. Since then some 50 or so have been established. Their funding came variously from ordinary legal aid, grants from local authorities, from foundations and charities and in a few cases grants from the Legal Aid Board. The Legal Services Commission took over these grants. But by 2003 it had been decided that it would only support law centres through contracts like other providers. At that time the Commission was putting some £7.4m into 53 law centres.

Legal aid for tribunals?

With a few exceptions tribunals have always been outside the legal aid scheme. (The exceptions currently are the Employment Appeal Tribunal, the Mental Health Review Tribunal, the Immigration Adjudicators, the Immigration Appeals Tribunal, the Protection of Children Act Tribunal, the Proscribed Organisations Appeal

Tribunal and certain proceedings before the Special and General Commissioners of Income Tax.)

Not that legal representation in tribunals is regarded as irrelevant. It is widely recognised that legal representation does make a difference in tribunal cases as much as in court cases. (The Legal Aid Board in November 1995 in its response to the Lord Chancellor's Consultation Paper *Legal Aid – Targetting Need* stated that research it had commissioned concluded that 'the literature shows clearly that representation [in tribunals] has a significant impact on the outcome of cases' (p 6).[95]) The explanation simply has always been insufficiency of funds.

The not-for-profit sector in legal services

There is state funding, mainly from other sources, for advice given by non-lawyer agencies (known as 'the advice sector' or the 'not-for-profit sector'). By far the biggest are Citizens' Advice Bureaux (CABx). The 700 or so CABx, with over 2,000 outlets, dealt in 2001-02 with 5.7m problems. Many have a legal component. The advice given by bureaux is free of charge and non- means tested. The advisers are some 19,700 lay volunteers plus some full-time staff. The budget in 2001-02 was £103m. The funding for local bureaux comes mainly from local authorities and the Legal Services Commission (in 2001-02, 54% and 19% respectively). The central organisation, National Association of Citizens' Advice Bureaux (NACAB) is mainly funded by a grant from the Department of Trade and Industry. (In 2001/02 the DTI grant was worth £17.8m out of total budget of £25.9m – or some two-thirds.) The service provided now includes an online advice service – www.adviceguide.org.uk.

For the annual report see www.nacab.org.uk.

(g) The Legal Services Commission (LSC) at work

The LSC's annual reports give a great deal of information about it, its activities and achievements:

- *Staffing* The LSC was created as an executive non-departmental body which came into being in April 2000. It has staff of over 1,500 working in 12 offices around the country. The head office is in London. The website is www.legalservices.gov.uk.
- *Responsible for* The Community Legal Service (CLS) and the Criminal Defence Service(CDS).
- *Contracts with providers of services* The number of solicitors' offices with contracts from the CLS as at March 2003 was 4,641. There were also contracts with 420

95   For the report of the research see G Bull and J Seargeant, *Approaches to Tribunal Representation*, Policy Studies Institute, 1996.

Not for Profit (NfP) agencies. (The NfP sector represented 17% of expenditure on Legal Help). (2002-03, p 3).

- *Regional Legal Services Committees(RLSCs)* The LSC took over from the Legal Aid Board the 12 RLSCs covering the whole of England and Wales whose function is to provide an independent element in the strategic planning process and to assess the need for legal services in their regions. They also work to establish links with local and regional initiatives and with the regional Government offices.

- *Community Legal Service Partnerships (CLSPs)* CLSPs bring together organisations offering legal and advice services – solicitors, law centres, Citizens' Advice Bureaux, local authority advice services and the like. By March 2003 over 99% of the population of England and Wales was covered by a CLSP. (2002-03, para 2.159) By 2003 there were over 200 CLSPs. The CLS employed some 100 staff engaged in planning and partnership work.[96]

- *Research into need* The LSC's research centre published *Local Legal Need* (January 2001) providing guidelines for the conduct of local need surveys. The LSC together with the LCD also started the Measurement and Evaluation of Legal Needs Research Project to monitor the levels of need across the country using a national survey, a set of statistical legal needs models and an analysis of administrative data. (2000/01, para 2.47) For the first results of the research see *Summary of the findings of the first LSRC periodic survey of legal need (1) and(2)*, 2002-03, www.lsrc.org.uk.

- *CLS Quality Mark* The Quality Mark (QM) or Specialist Quality Mark (SQM) is a quality assurance standard for legal information, advice and specialist services launched together with the CLS in April 2000. Providers of services apply for the Quality Mark at the appropriate level depending on the services they offer. The CLS publishes annually a Directory split into regional volumes of organisations that have applied for or obtained a Quality Mark. By May 2003 there were some 10,340 organisations quality marked at one or more of the five levels: Self Help Information, Assisted Information, General Help, General Help with Casework and Specialist. (2002-03, para 2.132, p 37)

- A CLS Quality Mark for barristers' chambers (QMB) was launched in autumn 2002.[97] When the QMB was introduced, the LSC said that ultimately it would be compulsory for chambers doing publicly funded work but this threat was withdrawn after complaints by the Bar Council that such restriction of client choice would breach the Human Rights Act. By May 2003, the LSC had had 46 applications, about half of which came from chambers that already had BarMark, the Bar Council's own quality standard. At that date 33 chambers had been

---

[96] For a critical assessment of CLS partnerships see a paper prepared by the Advice Services Alliance entitled 'Partnerships and the Community Legal Service' accessible at www.asauk.org.uk and A Griffith, 'Time to rethink CLS partnerships?' *Legal Action*, February 2003, p 9. See also R Moorhead, 'Third Way Regulation? Community Legal Service Partnerships', 64 *Modern Law Review*, 2001, pp 543-62.

[97] 6 *Independent Lawyer*, November/December 2002, p 10.

awarded QMB.[98] The requirements for the solicitors' Quality Mark (SQM) are more rigorous than those for barristers' chambers.

- *CLS Directory Line* Callers are provided with details of providers in their area – if possible at least one solicitor and one NfP provider (In 2002-03 there were 93,300 callers – up from 55,300 in the previous year.)
- *Methods of Delivery Pilot* The LSC continued and extended pilots originally started by the Legal Aid Board to test out new ways of delivering services (2000/01, para 2.101).
- *The Just Ask website* (www.justask.org.uk) The website of the Community Legal Service – has, inter alia, the CLS leaflets and Advice Search with access to 300 other sites providing information and advice.
- *CLS legal information leaflets* The CLS had a contract with the Consumers' Association to produce leaflets on legal problems, vetted by the Plain English Campaign. There are now 24 leaflets with six more in the development stage. Over two million copies had been distributed to a wide variety of agencies including councils, public libraries, prisons etc. Ten were available in braille. They are available free of charge through a dedicated Leafletline (Tel.0845 3000 343) and can be downloaded from the LSC's website, the JustAsk website and the Consumers' Association website.
- *CLS Information Points* The CLS works to get other bodies to become CLS Information Points. In 2001/02 the number had risen to 2,088 including all libraries in the Eastern region. Applications to become approved Information Points had been received on behalf of county courts, prisons and police stations. Negotiations were in progress with the NHS and with the Post Office (2001/02, para 2.67).

See also R Naylor, *Post-implementation review of the Community Legal Service*, February 2002 a 45-page report commissioned by the LCD, accessible on www.legalservices.gov.uk/partners/pir-cls-review-Feb02. It was summarised in K Mackay, 'The CLS reviewed', *Legal Action*, April 2002, pp 9-10. The report dealt in particular with CLS partnerships, the Quality Mark, the JustAsk website and publicity.

For an assessment by the National Audit Office see its report *Community Legal Service: the introduction of contracting*[99] and for gloomy comments arising from the NAO's report J Robins, 'The price is right', *The Lawyer*, 10 February 2003, p 22.

A SIGNIFICANT PROPORTION OF THE POPULATION IS NOT ELIGIBLE FOR LEGAL AID

The proportion of the population eligible for legal aid depends on the relationship between the means test and the resources of the members of the population.

---

[98]   10 *Independent Lawyer*, May 2003, p 8.

[99]   House of Commons 89, Session 2002-03, 28 November 2002 (www.nao.gov.uk - Publications).

In 1991, a Government Consultation Paper (*Eligibility for Civil Legal Aid*) commented critically on the view that a particular proportion of the population 'should' be eligible for legal aid. This view presupposed that the distribution and level of means in the population remained constant relative to the cost of litigation. Also it did not relate means to costs. The figures did show a decline in eligibility – whether one looked at proportion of households (from 77% eligible in 1979 to 61% in 1990) or population (from 74% eligible in 1979 to 66% in 1990) (Table 3, p 85). The 75% of adults eligible in 1979 were made up of 29% eligible for free legal aid and 46% eligible for legal aid subject to a contribution. In 1990, the report said, the proportion of adults eligible had fallen to 56%, made up of 22% eligible for free legal aid and 34% subject to a contribution (Table 4, p 85).

At the end of the 1980s it was thought that around half of the population were eligible for legal aid.[100]

A report by the LSC's Legal Services Research Centre found that in 2001/2002, 28.4% of 'benefit units'[101] were fully eligible for Legal Representation and another 18.5% were eligible for Legal Representation on a contribution basis. The comparable percentages in 1998/1999 were 26% and 22%.[102]

(h)   Legal aid's uncertain future

To say that there is an air of crisis about legal aid is to say nothing new. But the present sense of crisis is greater than it has been at any time in the writer's experience over some 40 years. The main issue, as it has always been, is funding. Legal aid lawyers accept that their level of remuneration will be significantly less than that for private sector work. But if the work is actually unremunerative it is no longer viable.

In 2001 the Government announced a range of increases to legal aid remuneration. After 10 years during which there had only been two increases – and small ones at that – legal aid lawyers hoped that the period of year-on-year cuts in real terms might be over. But in 2002 the Lord Chancellor said yet again that there was no money for any increase in the rates. Richard Miller, of the Legal Aid Practitioners Group, said, 'Rightly or wrongly, many firms will now draw the conclusion that the Government's commitment to legal aid is illusory'.[103]

In its 2nd annual report published in July 2002 , the Legal Services Commission said:

---

[100]   See further Cyril Glasser, *Law Society's Gazette*, 9 March 1988, p 11; 20 April 1988, p 11; and 5 April 1989, p 9; and Michael Murphy, *Legal Action*, October 1989, p 7.

[101]   A 'benefit unit' refers to a single adult or couple living as married and any dependent children. Benefit unit is a standard government term.

[102]   Alexy Buck and Graham Stark, *Means Assessment: Options for Change*, Legal Services Research Centre, Research Paper 8, February 2001, p 9 – accessible at www.lsrc.org.uk (Publications).

[103]   R Miller, 'Legal aid: back to business as usual?' 152 *New Law Journal*, 12 April 2002, p 545.

We are picking up intelligence through our regional offices that up to 50% of firms are seriously considering stopping or significantly reducing publicly funded work. The likelihood of a substantial number of firms leaving is confirmed by other studies by the Legal Aid Practitioners' Group (LAPG) and the Law Society. We believe this to be overwhelmingly because of remuneration and profitability. Our studies show that at current legal aid rates many firms are at best marginally profitable. The LAPG study claimed that 54% of firms said that legal aid work was unprofitable. With increasing costs it is likely that more firms will choose to leave publicly funded work.[104]

One problem identified in the LSC's report was an upward trend in the cost of advice which was 'much higher than anticipated'. ('For example, in family the average cost has increased by 15% over 12 months, while that for social welfare law has increased by 21% and the average across all categories (excluding immigration) is a rise of 20%. This trend, or more importantly its impact on future contracts and the number of clients who may be helped, is not sustainable if the CLS continues to be funded at its existing levels' (para 2.17).)

In February 2003 the Law Society issued a Consultation Paper entitled 'The Future of Publicly Funded Legal Services' (accessible on www.lawsociety.org.uk), canvassing some possible ways forward.[105] The Foreword pointed out that in the previous 10 years the costs of running a solicitors' practice rose by 67.5%, while legal aid rates increased by only 26.3%. In the past the Law Society had argued that more money was needed. But that appeal had largely fallen on deaf ears.

There were four core principles – quality of service, geographical access, choice of solicitor, and proper funding. If a way had to be found to reduce eligibility, one would be to lower the means test thresholds that gave entitlement. Solicitors might be allowed to charge 'top up' fees. Conditional fee arrangements might be extended. The number of providers could be reduced. There was the possibility of creating a state salaried Public Defender service. The Not for Profit sector might take on work currently done by the private profession. Legal expenses insurance could be expanded. Responses were requested by the end of April 2003.

The editorial in the April 2003 issue of *Legal Action* ('Back to a cuts agenda?') began, 'Things, it seems, can only get worse for legal aid.' Over the previous year audible consternation about the number of organisations abandoning legal aid had included not only the Legal Services Commission, but the National Audit Office and even the Public Accounts Committee. A number of different causes, it said, lay behind the situation.'[A] £100m overspend and a negligible Spending Review settlement from the Treasury have plunged the legal aid scheme into further crisis. Increases in the number of orders made in the magistrates' courts, a jump in expenses relating to

---

104   2001/02, para 2.7.
105   For a summary of the paper see N Cobb, 'Resolving the funding black hole', 153 *New Law Journal*, 21 March 2003, p 427.

high cost criminal cases, a huge growth in expenditure on immigration cases and an overall increase of 15% in the average cost of cases have all contributed to the overspend.'

The LSC's long-serving chief executive Steve Orchard had been making it clear privately that there could be no guarantees that legal aid eligibility and scope would not be cut in the near future. It went without saying that an increase in remuneration was highly unlikely. 'So, despite all the changes and upheaval of the Access to Justice Act 1999 and the introduction of contracts, we may be about to see the government return to using cuts in essential entitlements as a method of controlling the legal aid budget.' It was a depressing reflection of the government's attitude 'that legal aid was little more than outdoor relief for lawyers, rather than an essential public service that contributes to helping individuals and communities out of poverty and disadvantage, and protects some of the most vulnerable people in our society'. Legal aid had been constantly ignored by the social exclusion and regeneration agendas and had been 'left to fight its own corner'. None of the factors leading to the rising legal aid budget had come out of the blue. Contracts had not delivered the anticipated costs controls – which was predictable 'given that contracting did not tackle the problem of rising costs'. The LCD had known for many years that the average cost of cases rose at a rate above that of inflation but no research had been done to identify the cause.

To add to the growing sense of gloom, in April 2003 the Legal Services Commission gave 12 months' notice that the General Criminal Contract would be terminated. This affected all solicitors doing criminal legal aid work. What did it mean? Comment in the *New Law Journal* said that civil servants at the LSC maintained that neither they nor the LCD had any idea what was in store. 'It would seem that the reason for the termination is that the Government is considering reforms to the criminal justice system and that the Contract is being terminated just in case its current terms do not cover what is decided on.' [106] But what reforms?' Some thought that it portended the wholesale introduction of a salaried defence service. But the LSC had given categorical assurances that there were no plans for this. What *was* on the cards was to bring in payment by results. 'Despite the evidence that defence lawyers are no more guilty of causing delay than prosecution lawyers, policemen or witnesses, the political line about financial penalties for "manipulative" lawyers has now been repeated so often that it can't be withdrawn' – though 'there is no prospect of saving money this way'.

Another misguided idea would be to take the task of granting legal aid from the magistrates' court where it was done on the spot and align it with the system for granting civil legal aid. Again it was 'difficult to see that more paperwork, more delay, more opportunities for discussion, will, in the end, save money'. Or the Government

[106] G Morgan, 'Notice of termination of the General Criminal Contract', *New Law Journal*, 2 May 2003, p.653.

might go so far as to reduce the scope of the legal aid service. But Article 6 of the European Convention on Human Rights which guaranteed the right to a fair trial might limit the possibilities. If the funded work was cut, many legal aid firms 'hanging on by their fingernails' would be put out of business. The Human Rights Act required representation in court. 'If they destroy private practice and can't afford a Public Defender System, to whom will the Government turn to fulfil these functions?' All of this was having a serious effect on the profession. 'How is any partnership to take a trainee on a two-year training contract or even agree to rent office space when it cannot prepare a business plan beyond April 2004?'

Steve Orchard, told a meeting of 300 criminal lawyers in Birmingham that expenditure on criminal defence services had increased by an 'unsustainable' 25% over the past four years. Decisions would have to be made by Ministers.[107] Mr Orchard who, ran the Legal Services Commission from the start, left it at the end of May 2003 an angry man. At one of his last public appearances he said, 'We are approaching crisis point ... If government is not very careful, it will find itself in the same position as with the health service, where it has had to bung in buckets of money to try to put right years of neglect'. It was 'immensely disappointing' that despite all the reforms of recent years, pay rates seemed unlikely to go up. The LSC and the profession had delivered 'everything that could have been expected' but LSC plans for inflation-linked pay rises had been blown out of the water by changes elsewhere in the justice system.[108]

Pending Government announcements, Geoffrey Bindman, a leading legal aid lawyer, suggested that the solution to the funding problem lay in the hands of the legal profession. The bulk of the profession had turned its back not only on legal aid but even on the recognition that it had any responsibility toward those who cannot pay for justice. ('Dr Johnson's aphorism that "every man is a debtor to his profession" is largely forgotten.') It was time to revisit the idea of a fund or foundation to support access to justice, to be financed by a levy on the profits of the most affluent firms and by the undistributed interest on client accounts. 'Without a bold initiative of this kind, legal aid as we have known will not survive.'[109]

(i)   The Government's Consultation Papers of June 2003

In June 2003 the LCD published two Consultation Papers outlining its ideas for retrenchment of expenditure on legal aid.[110]

---

[107]   153 *New Law Journal*, 4 April 2003, p 499.

[108]   10 *Independent Lawyer*, May 2003, p 4.

[109]   *The Times*, 29 April 2003, www.timesonline.co.uk/law.

[110]   *Delivering Value for Money in the Criminal Defence Service*, CP 05/03 and *Public Consultation on Proposed Changes to Publicly Funded Immigration and Asylum Work*, CP 07/03. Both were available on www.lcd.gov.uk.

CRIMINAL DEFENCE SERVICE

The Consultation Paper (Annex B) showed that for the Community Legal Service the annual net cost rose from £775m in 1995/96 to £844m in 1998/99 but then dropped to £734m in 2001/02. Over that period acts of assistance under the scheme fell each year from 1.5m in 1995/96 to 906,000 in 2001/02.

In the same years the net cost of the Criminal Defence Service rose from £1.4b in 1995/96 to £1.7b in 2001/02. The acts of assistance under that scheme fluctuated up and down between 1995/96 and 2000/01 but then dropped significantly from 2.1m in that year to 1.8m in 2001/02.[111]

Responses were requested by August 2003 for proposals including:

- *Reducing the cost of Very High Cost Cases* by £193m over three years – by reducing the fees paid to the lawyers
- *Reducing entitlement to free advice in the police station* Abolition of the right to free legal advice for less serious matters 'where solicitors can provide no worthwhile advice' – eg where a drink driving suspect is there for a blood or urine test or arrest for failure to attend court. Alternatively, advice in such cases to be available only over the telephone
- *Abolition of post charge advice and assistance for non serious cases* Post charge advice and assistance only to be available in the more serious cases that pass the interests of justice test. (This would leave solicitors either unable to work until a representation order was made or not knowing whether such work would be paid for.)
- *Savings on court duty solicitor schemes* Exclude clients on bail on non-imprisonable offences, or apply an interests of justice test, or pay the duty solicitor for shorter periods of time
- *Restrict representation orders to cases where imprisonment is a likely sentence* – as a response to the dramatic increase in the numbers getting legal aid since the abolition of the means test
- *Require the court to make a Recovery of Defence Costs Order* – RDCOs for all persons convicted subject to ability to pay

The potential estimated savings over three years – in addition to the estimated £191m for Very High Cost cases – would be some £91m.

For sharply critical comment see A Keogh, 'Value for money – but at what cost?' 153 *New Law Journal*, 13 June 2003, p 897 ('these measures may prove to be the final straw for many already troubled firms'). An editorial in *Justice of the Peace* criticised the LCD for not knowing what is actually going on:

---

[111] The global figures concealed great differences in the patterns. Thus legal aid in the Crown Court rose in cost in the last two years from £422m to £474m while the acts of assistance fell slightly from 114,300 to 113,300. The cost of legal aid in the magistrates' courts rose in those two years from £247m to £508m while the acts of assistance rose hugely from 467,600 to 598,200.

Why, for example, has higher court criminal legal aid expenditure increased so greatly when the graduated fee rates have fallen in real terms and plea before venue has reduced the numbers committed for trial? Why are the top 1% of Crown Court cases so expensive? If it is right that magistrates' courts have been granting more representation orders since the abolition of means testing and, if so, is this mere coincidence or is there a connection? The business community would be aghast at the thought of an organisation with an annual spend of £2bn knowing where its money was going, but not why. It is time for the LCD to do a bit of investing in research and analysis (which the paper to some extent, but not adequately, recognises). [vol 167, 14 June 2003, p 44]

IMMIGRATION AND ASYLUM WORK

Legal aid work in this area was carried out by 617 contracted suppliers. Costs had risen from £81m in 2000-01 to £174m in 2002-03. The rise was due to various factors including increases in the numbers of asylum seekers, faster processing by the Home Office resulting in more appeals (19,395 in 2000, 64,125 in 2002). The quality of some advice work was poor. Proposals for consultation to reduce expenditure and improve the quality of advice included:

- Clients to be identified by a unique file number to eliminate potential for fraudulent claims
- Time limits for number of hours of advice paid for different types of matter (five hours for initial advice in an asylum case, three hours for non-asylum cases) and maximum amounts allowed for disbursements. The maxima to attach to the client and to apply therefore if the client changes advisers
- Maximum fees for preparing appeals or for applying for leave to appeal (but not for substantive hearings)
- Payments only to accredited advisers
- Accreditation scheme to be applied also to interpreters
- Exclude from the scheme useless attendances – for instance at interviews with the Home Office

The proposed five-hour cap on initial advice is in contrast to the 14-20 hours allowed in the LSC's April 2003 Manual. Chris Randall, a member of the Immigration Law Practitioners Association and one of the LSC's peer reviewers, described the five-hour cap as 'disastrous'. 'You cannot prepare cases properly within these new time frames. The firms who care about the work, will find themselves having to do pro bono work as a matter of basic routine – and of course their budgets can't cope with that.'[112]

---

[112]   12 *Independent Lawyer*, July/August 2003, p3.

6. Conditional fees and contingency fees

The English system traditionally rejected contingent fees as a method of financing litigation. Under the contingency fee system, a client either pays nothing or less than the full fee if he loses, whereas if he wins, the lawyer takes his fee out of the damages. The fee charged by the lawyer in the event of a win is normally assessed on a percentage basis. In the United States contingency fees are the normal method of financing personal injury litigation. What is less well known is that they are also permitted in every Canadian province.[113]

From the client's point of view the great attraction of a contingency fee is that he normally pays nothing unless and until the case is won – and that the amount paid to the lawyers is then directly related to the amount obtained by way of damages. Typically it is one third of the recovery. The cost of losing is wholly, or at worst, mainly, borne by the lawyer. Normally the client is not even required to put up any money to cover disbursements.

The original objection to contingency fees in England was that they are maintenance (the financial support of someone else's litigation) and champerty (the taking of a financial interest in the outcome of someone else's litigation)[114]. Maintenance and champerty were illegal until the Criminal Law Act 1967, but in abolishing the criminal offences of maintenance and champerty the 1967 Act expressly preserved the rules making such arrangements improper for solicitors. (See *Wallersteiner v Moir (No 2)* [1975] 1 All ER 849, Denning MR dissenting.) The concern was that a lawyer who has a financial stake in the outcome of the litigation may be tempted into unethical conduct.[115]

Despite the objection to contingency fees, the English system, somewhat illogically, does now permit 'conditional fees' which is another form of payment by results.

Conditional fee agreements (CFAs) came out of Lord Mackay's 1989 Green Papers on reform of the legal profession. One Green Paper (Cm 571, 1989) was entitled 'Contingency Fees'. It asked for views as to whether it was right to abolish the English system's prohibition of contingent fees. It suggested that possible reform might take three different forms. One option was to allow unrestricted contingency fees. (The Green Paper said (para 4.9): 'It is considered that this would not be in the public interest.') A second option was to have contingency fees but to control the percentage of the damages that could be taken by the lawyers ('restricted contingency fees'). A third option was to adopt the Scottish system of 'speculative fees' under which the

---

[113] See M Zander, 'Contingency fees – the Canadian experience' (*Litigation Funding*, June 2002, p.12 ; and 'Green light for contingency fees', December 2002, p 16. See also *McIntyre Estate v Ontario*,[2002] OJ 3417, CA.)

[114] For a recent review of the history and rationale of maintenance and champerty see *Giles v Thompson* [1993] 3 All ER 321, 328-26 per Steyn LJ.

[115] For a more recent application of the unenforceability of a champertous agreement see *Aratra Potato Co Ltd v Taylor Joynson Garrett* [1995] 4 All ER 695 (Div Ct).

solicitor agreed that he would only be paid if he won the case. A possible variant would be to agree that if the case was won the lawyer would get an agreed success fee based on a percentage of his costs.

The White Paper issued in July 1989 stated that there had been a clear consensus in favour of the third option (*Legal Services: A Framework for the Future*, 1989, Cm 740, p 41). The Courts and Legal Services Act 1990, s 58 gave effect to this by legitimising 'conditional fee agreements' (an improvement on the more racy sounding 'speculative' fees). The permissible level of success fee (then called 'uplift') was to be set by statutory instrument.

The Lord Chancellor Department's subsequent Consultation Paper suggested that, at least in the first instance, the maximum uplift might be set at 10% and that this would not be part of any costs order payable by the opponent. It also suggested that conditional fees be restricted for the time being to personal injury cases.

Responding to the Consultation Paper both the Law Society and the Consumers' Association argued that an uplift of 10% was too low to lure lawyers into taking on potentially difficult and complex cases. The Law Society said it hoped the maximum would be raised to 20%, though there could be an argument for 100% – on the basis that this would enable the lawyer to break even if half the cases taken on a conditional fee basis were successful. (See *Law Society's Gazette*, 1 May 1991, p 10.)

In the event, the Lord Chancellor agreed on a maximum uplift of 100%. In other words, what had been previously discussed as a modest charge to the client of 10-15% of the fees was at the last moment changed to the very different proposition, that in the event of winning the case, the lawyer might receive double his fee. Moreover whereas the basic fee is made up of overheads and profit, the success fee would be pure profit, though profit that would have to fund the cost of cases that were lost where no fee was earned.

It took five years before CFAs became operational. The rules for the new system were in the Conditional Fees Agreements Regulations 1995 which came into force in July 1995 (SI 1995/1674). There had to be a legally binding contract between the client and the solicitor setting out the details of the arrangement. The technical requirements of the contract were extensive – which later proved to be a serious matter. The Law Society published a non-mandatory model agreement to be entered into between the solicitor and the client. It recommended that solicitors' success fee should never take more than 25% of the client's damages. For a full guide to the topic see Michael Napier and Fiona Bawden, *Conditional Fees – a Survival Guide*, Law Society, 2nd edn 1999.

The Law Society's model agreement (*Law Society's Gazette*, 28 June 1995, p 30) provided that if the case was won, the client was liable to pay disbursements, basic costs and a 'success fee', plus VAT, though it also explained that normally disbursements and basic costs would be recovered from the other side. If the case was lost, the client was liable to pay the solicitor's disbursements (which might or might not include barristers' fees–see below), and the other side's costs and disbursements.

The model agreement recited that the solicitor had explained to the client whether he was eligible for legal aid, the situation as regards liability for costs and disbursements, and the right to have the solicitor's bill vetted by a solicitor and own client taxation (now called assessment, for which see p 543 above).

Where the barrister in the case has a conditional fee agreement with the solicitors, his fee is a disbursement recoverable from the other side. But if he wins, the client has to pay the barrister's success fee in addition to the solicitors' success fee. If he loses, the client pays nothing in respect of the barrister's fee.

However, under a CFA the client who lost was still at risk of having to pay the other side's costs. The insurance market quickly saw that this was a risk that could be covered by insurance and a great variety of insurance products have been developed. Legal expenses insurance (LEI) was already quite well established. (See pp 613-15 below). But that was insurance taken out before the event. The product now developed was insurance taken out after the event (ATE). There are said to be some 60 providers of ATE insurance.

In October 1997, as was seen (p 562 above), Lord Irvine, then the new Lord Chancellor, provoked uproar when he announced that conditional fee agreements would replace legal aid for all damages and money claims. This threat was subsequently somewhat modified, but essentially the Lord Chancellor stuck to his basic policy. In March 1998 he published a Consultation Paper (*Access to Justice with Conditional Fees*). This stated that the Government wished to extend CFAs to any proceedings other than family and criminal cases. More significantly, the Consultation Paper also asked for views as to whether the losing defendant should have to pay the ATE insurance premium payable by the plaintiff to cover against the risk of losing and/or the success fee payable by the plaintiff. The Government said that it was minded to make these changes but was 'keen to learn whether they would be welcomed in making conditional fees more useful and attractive'.

As was to be expected, there were a variety of reactions. The Legal Aid Board[116] said it could see no objection to the general availability of CFAs for money claims. Making insurance premiums recoverable had the disadvantage that defendants with the strongest case would end up paying the highest amount as the success fee would be highest in such cases. If the success fee were recoverable, solicitors would have an incentive to charge an excessive uplift even on claims with a low risk. 'There would be a danger of lawyer-driven litigation as lawyers would have an incentive to pursue claims regardless of whether the damages claimed were small or trivial.' It might be so attractive to lawyers that litigation might be encouraged even between wealthy or corporate litigants who might otherwise settle without going to court.

---

[116] *The Legal Aid Board's response to the Lord Chancellor's Consultation Paper*, May 1998.

The Bar argued that abolishing legal aid in personal injury cases would be premature, unfair, illogical, unnecessary and contrary to the public interest. It should be retained in any event for a variety of types of cases. Children and patients were such a case. They could not look after themselves. Multi-party actions was another. ('It is inconceivable that those who are victims of mass disaster, or the terrible consequences of a defective drug, should be expected to hawk their claims on the CFA open market.') Industrial disease was another. Costs in such cases were very high. Funding them could only be done by legal aid. The Bar said that it agreed with the Government that in CFAs the success fee and the premium should be recoverable. The Law Society's response[117] was similar. The Legal Action Group agreed that the success fee and the insurance premium should be recoverable but the 25% cap on damages should be made statutory to prevent solicitors and their clients agreeing an unreasonably high success fee.

The Government moved swiftly. The first step was to extend the scope of conditional fees. Under s 58 of the Courts and Legal Services Act 1990 CFAs were originally limited to three categories of litigation – personal injury, insolvency and cases brought in Strasbourg under the European Convention on Human Rights. In July 1998, under the Conditional Fee Agreements Order 1998, they were extended to cover all civil cases other than family work.

This policy of expanding the role of CFAs was further elaborated in the provisions of the Access to Justice Act 1999. There were several developments. One was to extend CFAs to family work solely relating to financial matters and property.[118] (But all cases involving issues about the welfare of children as well as criminal proceedings remain outside the scope of conditional fees.) A second development was to extend CFAs to proceedings other than court proceedings, such as arbitrations.[119] The third development was to make a premium payable for an ATE insurance policy against the risk of having to pay costs recoverable from the losing defendant. The policy need not be one associated with a CFA.[120] The fourth, and perhaps the most important, development was that a success fee payable by the client was also recoverable from the losing defendant.[121]

---

[117]   *Ensuring Justice?*, April 1998.
[118]   Access to Justice Act 1999, s 27, inserting a new s 58A into the 1990 Act: see sub-s (1).
[119]   Section 58 of the CLSA 1990 did not cover arbitrations. It was held in *Bevan Ashford v Geoff Yeandle (Contractors) Ltd* [1998] 3 All ER 238 that CFAs in arbitration cases were nevertheless lawful because of the policy implicit in s 58. As has been seen, this decision was confirmed by s 27 of the Access to Justice Act 1999 inserting a new s 58A into the Courts and Legal Services Act 1990. Section 58A(4) applies CFAs to 'any sort of proceedings for resolving disputes (and not just proceedings in a court)'.
[120]   Access to Justice Act 1999, s 29.
[121]   New s 58A(6) in the CLSA 1990 inserted by s 31 of the Access to Justice Act 1999 states that a costs order against someone who has a CFA can include any 'success fees' payable under the CFA.

The recoverability of the ATE insurance premium and of the success fee had dramatic and far-reaching effects. It obviously made CFAs much more attractive to claimants. Now a client with a 'no win, no fee' CFA and an ATE policy could litigate free from financial risk. He was in an even better position than a legally aided litigant on a nil contribution since there was no 'statutory charge' to deprive him of part of his damages. Claimants' lawyers were also well satisfied. Instead of looking to their own clients for payment of the success fee out of the damages, they could now collect it from the loser's insurers. The Law Society's recommendation that the success fee should not result in taking more than 25% of the damages was no longer necessary and was dropped. Claimants' insurers had a booming business. There was a new phenomenon of 'claims management companies', run by non-lawyers offering various forms of 'no win, no fee' deals through mass marketing on television and in the press.[122]

From the point of view of the defence insurance industry these developments were most unwelcome. Instead of having to pay just the winner's damages and costs, it now also had to finance the ATE premium and the success fee. And moreover the marketing success of the claims management companies was resulting in significant growth in the number of claims.

This led to two developments. One was the proliferation of a new breed of 'costs negotiators', employed by insurance companies to negotiate settlements with claimants' lawyers, paid on a commission basis by reference to their success in reducing the bill.[123]

The second was a wave of satellite litigation, with insurers taking every conceivable point (and some inconceivable ones) to try to avoid, or at least delay, having to shoulder these new and unexpected liabilities for which they had not budgeted. As each point was litigated there were thousands, tens of thousand and even hundreds of thousands of other cases that were held up awaiting the outcome. Commonly there was no dispute between the parties as to liability or damages. The dispute was purely as to

---

[122] For a time these firms prospered. Claims Direct, which spent up to £1.5m per month on advertising, announced a pre-tax profit in 2000 of £10.1m on a turnover of £39.6m. The Accident Group (TAG) with some 700 solicitor firms on its panel had a turnover in 2002 of £243m. But for a variety of reasons both went bust, respectively in 2002 and 2003. Partly it was the result of press criticism based on the experience of disgruntled clients. Also, the courts held that the premiums charged to clients and the fees charged to panel solicitors were wholly or in part irrecoverable. (See 153 *New Law Journal*, 10 January 2003, p 6; *Solicitors' Journal*, 10 January 2003, p 2; J Robins, 'Accidental Success' *The Lawyer*, 24 February 2003, p 15; and 'Happy Ending' *The Lawyer*, 16 June 2003, p 20.)

[123] However, in *Ahmed v Powell* (19 February 2003, Case No BU 01 1986, accessible on www.courtservice.gov.uk/judgments) Chief Costs Judge Master Hurst held that employees of costs negotiators did not have rights of audience and that the fees they charged insurers were irrecoverable as champertous. See M Bacon, 'No right of audience', 147 *Solicitors' Journal*, 28 February 2003, p 215. Permission was given to appeal. It was unclear what effect the decision, if upheld on appeal, would have for the future of cost-negotiators and the industry as a whole. In the judgment it was stated that in a period of two years one such firm, acting on behalf of an insurer in some 27,700 claims, had achieved reductions in costs of £20.8m.

the costs – fought out under the new procedure introduced in 1999 by the Civil Procedure Rules for Part 8, costs-only proceedings. (Some felt that the introduction of costs-only proceedings had proved to be one of the less helpful features of the Woolf reforms of civil procedure.)

Insurers said, for instance, that they would not reimburse the success fee and ATE insurance premium where the case settled without legal proceedings being issued on the ground that until proceedings were issued there was no insurable risk. The point was well taken in logic but it was rejected unanimously by the Court of Appeal in *Callery v Gray*[124] The chief reason was the practical consideration that that was the result required if CFAs were to survive as a viable marketable proposition. ('There is overwhelming evidence from those engaged in the provision of ATE insurance that unless the policy is taken out before it is known whether a defendant is going to contest liability, the premium is going to rise substantially. Indeed the evidence suggests that cover may not be available in such circumstances.'[125]) The court held that the claimant could recover a reasonable success fee and a reasonable ATE insurance premium for cover against the risk of losing arranged when the solicitor was first instructed. In *Callery v Gray (No 2)*[126] the Court of Appeal held that the premium of £350 that had been charged was reasonable and therefore recoverable in full. It also held that in modest and straightforward claims for compensation arising from road traffic accidents, it was reasonable for a success fee of a maximum of 20% to be agreed at the outset. It posited, obiter, that it might be appropriate for there to be a two-stage success fee –initially of 100%, but reducing to as little as 5% if the claim settled before the end of the protocol period. That would encourage defendants and their insurers to settle early.

On appeal, the House of Lords unanimously dismissed the appeal on the recoverability of the success fee and by 4 to 1 dismissed the appeal on the recoverability of the ATE insurance premium. (The Law Lords were told there were 150,000 cases awaiting the outcome of the case.) It in effect washed its hands of the whole business saying that regulation of CFAs was a matter for the Court of Appeal. (None of the five judgments mentioned the two-stage success fee.)[127]

In September 2002 the Court of Appeal deciding *Halloran v Delaney*[128] dropped a bombshell by holding that in simple cases that are settled without the need to start proceedings the recoverable success fee should normally be 5% unless the court was

---

124 [2001] EWCA Civ 117, [2001] 3 All ER 833, [2001] 1 WLR 2112.
125 [2001] EWCA Civ 117, [2001] 3 All ER 833, [2001] 1 WLR 2112 at para 99.
126 [2001] EWCA Civ 1246, [2001] 4 All ER 1, [2001] 1 WLR 2142.
127 [2002] UKHL 28, [2002] 3 All ER 417, [2002] 1 WLR 2000. For a critical review of these judicial decisions see M Zander, 'Where are we now on conditional fees? – or why this emperor is wearing few, if any, clothes', 65 *Modern Law Review*, 2002, 919-30. This Case Note said that Lord Hoffman's speech had ripped to pieces the theoretical basis of the Court of Appeal's approach to the issue.
128 [2002] EWCA Civ 1258, [2003] 1 All ER 775, [2003] 1 WLR 28.

persuaded that a higher uplift was appropriate. (To add insult to injury, it added for good measure that the 5% normal success fee should apply retrospectively to any case decided since August 2001 when both *Callery* decisions were available, even though the success fee approved there was 20%.[129]) The Court referred again to the two-stage success fee. As has been seen (pp 544-45 above), a 5% success rate was also agreed as the appropriate success fee in fixed fees for road traffic cases where a settlement was achieved for under £10,000 without proceedings being issued. By implication, there would be a significantly higher success fee if the case does not settle at that stage or at all.

The costs war between insurers and claimants has also involved many cases that raised only pure technicalities. The CFA regulations which had been drafted to protect clients proved to be a minefield to be exploited by lawyers for the insurers whose objective was to discover some failure by the claimant's lawyers to comply with the regulations which would make the CFA unenforceable so that they could avoid having to pay up. The absurdity of these cases is that since both the success fee and the ATE insurance premium became recoverable, protection of the client is pointless since the client is no longer at risk.[130]

However, also in May 2003, the Court of Appeal gave a judgment that was clearly intended to put an end to the extraordinary wave of satellite litigation in which insurers challenged CFAs on minor technicalities. Six consolidated appeals were heard together in *Hollins v Russell and other appeals* [2003] EWCA Civ 718, [2003] All ER (D) 311 (May). Lord Justice Brooke giving the judgment of the court said that a CFA would only be unenforceable if in the circumstances of the particular case the conditions applicable to it by virtue of s 58 of the Courts and Legal Services

---

129   For further critical comment see M Zander, 'Where are we heading with the funding of civil litigation?', 22 *Civil Justice Quarterly*, 2003, 23, 29-32.

130   For a recent example see *Woods v Chaleff*, Decision of Master Rogers 30 April 2002 – see 152 *New Law Journal*, 16 August 2002, p 1276. For articles examining a slew of such cases see G Wignall, 152 *New Law Journal*, 16 August 2002, p 1268; 6 December 2002, p 1836; 2 May 2003, p 676; G Exall, 'Civil litigation brief', 146 *Solicitors' Journal*, 28 June 2002, p 582 and 20 December 2002, p 1160; SJ Brown, 'CFAs – privilege, disclosure and non-compliance', 152 *New Law Journal*, p 1812; A Dennison, 'Muddy waters' , 153 *New Law Journal*, 17 January 2003, p 49.

   The last of these concerned the 'TAG Test Case, Tranche 1' which was said to affect almost 250,000 cases and 700 firms of solicitors. The senior costs judge held that it was not a breach of the CFA regulations for the firms to delegate the function of explaining and agreeing the funding arrangements to non-solicitor agents. Victory for the claimants in those cases. But in May 2003 the same costs judge, deciding the 2nd Tranche of the TAG Test case, held that a large part of the moneys (which totalled close to £1,000 per case) paid in respect of the funding arrangements were not genuine ATE insurance premiums and were therefore not recoverable under the 1999 Act – see *The Accident Group Test Cases, Tranche 2 issues Sharratt and London Bus Central Bus Co,* Case No PTH0204771, 15 May 2003, accessible on www.courtservice.gov.uk/judgments/judge_home.htm. If upheld on appeal, this decision had extremely serious financial implications for the hundreds of solicitors' firms using that particular method of funding 'no win, no fee' arrangements.

Act 1990 had not been complied with in light of their statutory purposes. Costs judges should consider whether the particular departure from a regulation or statutory requirement, either on its own or together with any other such departure, had had a materially adverse effect on the protection afforded to the client or upon the proper administration of justice. If the answer was 'no', then the departure was immaterial and the statutory conditions were satisfied. The parliamentary purpose was to enhance access to justice, not to impede it, and to create better ways of delivering litigation services, not worse ones. These purposes would be thwarted if those who rendered good service to their clients under CFAs were at risk of going unremunerated at the culmination of the bitter trench warfare which had been such an unhappy feature of the recent litigation scene. Satellite litigation about costs had become a growth industry that was a blot on the civil justice system. CFAs should only be declared unenforceable if the breach mattered and if the client could have relied on it successfully against his own solicitor.

New rules introduced as from 2 June 2003 create what has been called a 'CFA Lite' or 'CFA Simple' under which many of the troublesome consumer protection rules introduced to safeguard the CFA client have been swept away.[131] In June 2003 the Department for Constitutional Affairs (successor to the LCD) issued a Consultation Paper entitled *Simplifying CFAs*[132].

So both the courts and the Government were finally moving to sort out the mess and to put CFAs onto a better footing. But the courts refused to recognise any other form of contingency arrangements. The clearest example was *Awwad v Geraghty & Co* [2000] 1 All ER 608. The defendant solicitors agreed to act for the claimant in libel proceedings on the basis of normal full rate fees if he won but a lower rate if he lost. The agreement was made in 1993 – so, after the Courts and Legal Services had authorised CFAs but before 1995 when they first became operational. The case settled and the solicitor sent a bill to the client at the lower rate. The client refused to pay and initiated the taxation of costs procedure whereby the court vets the lawyer's bill. The judge at first instance held that the agreement was unlawful and unenforceable so that the firm was not entitled to recover any costs.

On appeal the firm argued that the common law did not make the fees irrecoverable or, if it did, they were entitled to recover reasonable remuneration on a *quantum meruit* basis. The Court of Appeal held that it was against public policy for a solicitor to act under a contingency arrangement – even one specifying a normal fee – save if the agreement was sanctioned by statute. The courts would not enforce such an agreement and where public policy refused enforcement, there could be no *quantum meruit*. The court conceded that there were many considerations that favoured such

---

[131] See Conditional Fee Agreements (Miscellaneous Amendments) Regulations 2003, SI 2003 No 1240 and D Marshall, 'The new CFA Regulations', 153 *New Law Journal*, 30 May 2003, p 833, 837.

[132] Accessible on www.lcd.gov.uk (Legal aid and conditional fees) to test views as to a variety of ways in which the regulations for conditional fees could be made simpler still.

arrangements. Such an agreement was of advantage to the client. It did not increase the costs liability of the losing party. It did not involve any division of the spoils as a contingency fee agreement did. There was therefore no extra incentive for the lawyer to stir up litigation. The temptation for the lawyer to act improperly was less than where there was a contingent fee arrangement or one where the lawyer got a success fee on winning. There was nothing improper in a lawyer agreeing to act for his normal fees but having in mind – for reasons of friendship or in order to foster future work – not to exact the fee if the client lost. But Parliament had recently addressed itself to the problem, first in the 1990 Act and more recently in the 1999 Access to Justice Act. Lord Justice Schieman said, 'I see no reason to suppose that Parliament foresaw significant parallel judicial developments of the law'[133]

The position at the time of writing (summer 2003) was therefore fraught. The costs issues arising from the introduction of conditional fees was so bedevilling the litigation system as to cause massive and unprecedented disruption. Solicitors' firms that went in for CFA agreements on a large scale were going unpaid while one test case after another wound its way its way through the courts. Some were facing bankruptcy – though the decision in *Hollins v Russell* will have brought them some cheer.

Conditional fees, introduced in 1995 by the Lord Chancellor as his solution to the financing of civil litigation, had thrown up a plethora of unexpected teething problems and recoverability of success fees and ATE insurance premiums, introduced in 1999, had thrown the system into chaos. The question increasingly being asked was whether banned contingency fees might be a better option.

SHOULD CONTINGENCY FEES BE PERMITTED?

The principal reason given for banning contingency fees has always been a concern over ethical standards – the fear that the claimant's lawyer might stoop to 'dirty tricks' in order to make sure of winning and earning his fee. No win, no fee. And, on the other hand, the greater the damages, the fatter the fee. The lawyer's direct financial interest in the outcome of the litigation might act not simply as a spur to greater activity but a temptation from the path of righteous conduct.

However, this pass was sold with the introduction of conditional fees. In a conditional fee arrangement, the lawyer also has a direct financial interest in the outcome. If the case is won, the lawyer can charge a substantial success fee up to 100% of the basic costs which in many ordinary cases can be as much or more than the damages.[134] (It

---

[133]   At 628. See however, *R (on the application of Factortame Ltd) v Secretary of State for Transport, Local Government and the Regions (No 8)* [2002] EWCA Civ 932, [2003] QB 381, [2002] 4 All ER 97 where the Court of Appeal upheld a contingency fee for a firm of accountants who assisted the lawyers in litigation, to be paid out of the damages.

[134]   The Interim Report of Lord Woolf's Report showed that in a sample of cases in the Supreme Court Taxing Office, the average costs allowed in cases worth £12,500 or less were £12,044.

is also worth noting in this context that the new fixed fee for road traffic offences that settle without proceedings for under £10,000 (pp 544-45 above) has a sliding scale for the fee, dependent on the level of damages.)

In his 1977 Report to the Lord Chancellor (p 562 above), Sir Peter Middleton said,

> There is no essential difference in principle between conditional and contingency fees. Indeed, in some ways the latter may be preferable. Contingency fees create an incentive to achieve the best possible result for the client, not just a simple win. And they reward a cost-effective approach in a way that conditional fees, where the lawyers' remuneration is still based on an hourly bill, do not. Opponents of contingency fees usually cite the experience of them in the United States of America. However, considering the differences between the two jurisdictions – notably the cost-shifting rule and the fact that juries here do not generally set damages – we should re-assess whether those concerns may be misplaced.[135]

Contingency fees create a problem of potential conflict of interest between the lawyer and the client as the lawyer's financial interests may or may not be the same as those of the client. But the same is the true of CFAs.

While CFA success fees remain recoverable from the losing litigant, claimants are unlikely to prefer a contingency fee arrangement under which the lawyer would take his fee out of the damages. Under the existing arrangements, the claimant with a CFA can both have his cake and eat it. He gets his full damages and his lawyer receives his costs and his success fee from the other side.

But it is by no means obvious that this is the ideal solution. The recoverability of success fees has not only spawned a monstrous wave of satellite litigation. It has also thrown a considerable burden of extra costs on defendants' insurance companies – costs that naturally will be passed on to the general body of premium payers. If success fees are a proper inducement to get lawyers to engage in cases where there is a risk of getting no fee if one loses, it may be fairer that the cost should be borne by the client as a deduction from his damages rather than by the general public.

But it would now be a considerable step to put the genie of 'recoverability' back into the bottle. That step would be the more difficult politically if it was associated with permission for lawyers to enter into contingency fee arrangements. But the question whether contingency fees should be permitted is now on the legal-political agenda.

The advantages of contingency fees over conditional fees include the following:
* They are much simpler to explain to the client
* Since contingency fees are calculated as a percentage of the recovery they are, by definition, proportionate to the damages. (Concern that the lawyer's contingency fees may in big cases nevertheless be unreasonably high can to some extent be controlled by regulation requiring a sliding scale of percentages.)

---

[135] *Report to the Lord Chancellor, Review of Civil Justice and Legal Aid* 1997, para.5.49.

- The client may benefit from the incentive for the lawyers to maximise the damages
- Unlike CFAs, contingency fees do not have a built-in incentive for lawyers to pad their costs in order to earn higher success fees.
- Contingency fees would probably not generate the incredible volume of satellite litigation that has been stirred up by conditional fees.

Contingency fees are compatible with the English 'fee-shifting' rule as is clear from Canada where the loser pays the winner's costs, as in England, and contingency fees are permitted, as in the US. Ontario was the last Canadian province to accept contingency fees which it did in the recent case of *McIntyre Estate v Ontario*[136] . The Ontario Court of Appeal in that case had to decide whether the 1897 Ontario Champerty Act meant what it said – 'All champertous agreements are forbidden'. The court held that it did not. The reason that contingency fees had been thought to be against public policy was that they were thought to be open to abuse but, the court said, there was no evidence that lawyers who acted on a contingency basis performed to a lower ethical standard than those who were paid regardless of outcome. From a public policy point of view, the attitude towards permitting the use of contingency fees had undergone enormous change over the previous century. All the other Canadian provinces had enacted legislation to permit such arrangements and , 'Overwhelmingly, those studying these issues have recommended that for reasons of promoting access to justice, contingency fee agreements should be permitted'. (para 62) Whether a particular contingency fee was unlawful, the Court said, turned on whether the lawyer had an improper motive, which in turn depended, inter alia, on whether the agreed fee structure was fair and reasonable. (In the particular case the Court said that could not be decided until the end of the case.)

A few days later in *Raphael Partners v Lam*[137] the Ontario Court of Appeal upheld as reasonable and enforceable a contingency fee of 15% of the first $1m recovered and 10% of each additional $1m *plus* any costs recovered. (The total recovery was $2.5m plus the costs of $461,000.)

In Ontario therefore the move to legitimate contingency fees was initiated by the courts re-interpreting public policy on maintenance and champerty.

If contingency fees were to be legitimated in England either by the courts or by the legislature, the question would be whether the claimant's lawyers should have the contingency fee from damages *and* costs from the other side, as in *Raphael v Lam*, or simply the contingency fee from the damages, as in the United States, or whether there should be some combination of contingency fee and ordinary costs. If the successful litigant's lawyers were entitled to recover both full costs in the ordinary way and the full contingency fee, the contingency fee would be somewhat like the

---

[136]   [2002] OJ No.3417, September 10, 2002 (Docket No.C36074).
[137]   [2002] OJ No.3605, September 24, 2002 (Docket No.C36894).

CFA success fee but paid by the client out of the damages rather than by the losing litigant. It would build up the lawyers' 'war chest' to meet the costs in cases that are litigated and lost or where after investigation the case does not go forward – and it would increase profits, making this form of practice the more economically attractive to lawyers. But to allow the lawyers to take both costs from the loser and the contingency fee out of the damages could result in them getting remuneration that was unreasonably high.

These issues came under active consideration in Ontario in the aftermath of the decision in September 2002 in *McIntyre Estate*. In October 2002, only weeks after that decision, the Law Society of Upper Canada acted by amending the Rules of Professional Conduct to allow contingency fee agreements, save in family and criminal matters. (Revised Rule 2.08(3)) The Commentary to the Rule stated that in determining the appropriate percentage or other basis of a contingent fee 'the lawyer and the client should consider a number of factors, including the likelihood of success, the nature and complexity of the claim, the expense and risk of pursuing it, the amount of the expected recovery and who is to receive an award of costs.' It continued, 'If the lawyer and client agree that the costs award is to be paid to the lawyer, a smaller percentage of the award than would otherwise be agreed upon for the contingent fee after considering all relevant factors, will generally be appropriate.' It concluded, 'The test is whether the fee in all of the circumstances is fair and reasonable'.

A few weeks later, the Ontario legislature passed the Justice Statute Law Amendment Act 2002.[138] It amended the Solicitors Act by making it clear that contingency fee arrangements, providing they are in writing, are permissible, save in a criminal or family law matter. (new s 28.1) The new provisions state that a court should not reduce an order of costs solely because there is a contingency fee agreement in existence. (new s 20.1) This was to deal with cases where the fee payable under the contingency arrangement would not adequately compensate the lawyer for the work he had done. But the approval of the court is required for payment of both the contingency fee and the whole or part of ordinary costs and under the legislation such approval can only be given if there are exceptional circumstances. (new s 28(8)). At the time of writing the regulations required to bring these provisions into force had not yet been made.

Dissatisfaction in England among the higher judiciary with the results of the recoverability regime introduced by Lord Irvine's Access to Justice Act 1999 make it conceivable that the Ontario legislation could become a model for changes in the English system. It is even conceivable, if the right case came before it, that the House of Lords would adopt the robust attitude of the Ontario Court of Appeal that the time has come to declare contingency fees lawful at common law.

---

[138]   The Act received Royal Assent on 9 December 2002.

WHAT DOES RESEARCH ON CFAs SHOW?

The first published research on CFAs, conducted before many of the cases had been completed,[139] showed:

- The average level of uplift agreed between lawyer and client was 43%.
- The voluntary cap on the success fee as a percentage (25%) of the damages had become standard (but this cap was removed by the Law Society after the success fee and insurance premium become recoverable from the loser).
- There was serious cause for concern as to the accuracy of risk assessment by solicitors' firms. (The uplift appeared to be 'too low or (more often) too high, in almost half the cases than would be justified to compensate the solicitor for losing the case.'[140])

Subsequent research conducted after CFA cases had been completed[141] showed:

- The vast majority of completed CFA cases (93%) were successful in the sense either of achieving a settlement or a judgment wholly or partly in favour of the client. This was in contrast to the pessimism about the likely success rate shown by solicitors in the earlier study. Thus, 'a 41% average success fee would be appropriate to a case with a 70% chance of success, whereas in fact 93% of cases succeeded. The success fee appropriate to a case with a 93% chance of success would be only 8%.'[142]
- The success fees written into the CFA 'were higher than would have reflected the actual, very low, risk of losing'.[143]
- The mean success fee actually taken by solicitors (29% of costs) was lower than the mean success fee agreed in the CFA (43% of costs). In some cases the reason may have been that the amount taken was affected by the then still existing voluntary 25% cap on the percentage of the damages that should be taken. In a few cases the reason may have been that the solicitor shared the success fee with the barrister. In some cases the reason was that the solicitors did not take the full success fee to which they were entitled.
- Nevertheless, 'Despite this reduction, the mean success fee taken was still higher than the very high success rates would suggest were appropriate.'[144]

---

139   S Yarrow, *The Price of Success – Lawyers, Clients and Conditional Fees* (1997). The study was based on a sample of 200 CFA personal injury cases undertaken by 121 firms all of which were personal injury specialists. For comment at the time see M Zander, 'Two cheers for conditional fees – maybe' ,147 *New Law Journal*, 3 October 1997, p 1438.

140   S Yarrow, *The Price of Success – Lawyers, Clients and Conditional Fees* (1997), at p xviii.

141   S Yarrow, *Just Rewards?* (University of Westminster, 2000). The study was based on a sample of 197 cases supplied by a representative sample of 58 solicitors' firms specialising in personal injury work. The research consisted of interviews with lawyers in 16 of the 58 firms and details of just over half of the 197 cases (56%) that were completed. Fieldwork ended in March 2000.

142   S Yarrow, *Just Rewards?* at p 31.

143   S Yarrow, *Just Rewards?* at p 7.

144   S Yarrow, *Just Rewards?* at p 8.

Further reading

For discussion of ethical problems in England raised by conditional fees and/or contingency fees *see* D Luban, 'Speculating on Justice: The Ethics and Jurisprudence of Contingency Fees' in *Legal Ethics and Legal Practice* (eds S Parker and C Stamford, 1995); S Simkins, 'An ethical choice? A practical reaction to the death of legal aid in personal injury and medical negligence claims', *Journal of Personal Injury Litigation*, 1998, p 128; C Graffy, 'Conditional Fees: Key to the Courthouse or the Casino', 1(1) *Legal Ethics*, p 70 (1998); S Yarrow and P Abrams, 'Conditional Fees: The Challenge to Ethics', 2(2) *Legal Ethics*, 1999, p 192; R O'Dair, 'Legal Ethics and Legal Aid: The Great Divorce?', 52 *Current Legal Problems*, 1999, p 419; *The Ethics of Conditional Fee Arrangements*, Society for Advanced Legal Studies (2001).

For writing about contingency fees in England see especially RCA White, 'Contingent Fees: A Supplement to Legal Aid?', 41 *Modern Law Review*, 1978, p 286; T Swanson, 'The Importance of Contingency Fee Agreements', 11 *Oxford Journal of Legal Studies*, 1991, p 193; N Rickman, 'The Economics of Contingency Fees in Personal Injury Litigation', 10(1) *Oxford Review of Economic Policy*, 1994, p 34; J Peysner, 'What's Wrong with Contingency Fees?', 10(1) *Nottingham Law Journal*, 2001, p 22; M Zander, 'If conditional fees, why not contingency fees?', 152 *New Law Journal*, May 24, 2002, p 797.

For consideration of contingency fees in the USA see, for instance, Herbert M Kritzer, 'Seven dogged myths concerning contingency fees', 80 *Washington University Law Quarterly*, 2002, pp 730-94. (Professor Kritzer has published a series of articles on the subject accessible on his website:www.polisci.wisc.edu/~kritzer/research/research.htm.) See also Symposium on Contingency Fee Financing of Litigation in America, 47 *DePaul Law Review*, 1998, pp 227-477.

Contingency Legal Aid Fund (CLAF)

A Contingency Legal Aid Fund (CLAF) is created from contributions paid by successful litigants who agree that if they win they will pay a stated percentage of their damages into the Fund which is used to pay the costs of unsuccessful claimants. The concept avoids the main alleged danger of contingency fees of lawyers being tempted into unethical conduct because of the financial importance of winning.

The CLAF concept, though supported by JUSTICE, the Law Society and the Bar, has never been implemented. One obvious problem (known as the problem of 'adverse selection') is how sufficient numbers of clients with promising actions could be persuaded to agree to give up a percentage of their damages to make the system economically viable. This difficulty was compounded when under CFAs the success fee and the ATE insurance premium became recoverable from the losing litigant. The cases where the litigant was most likely to want the CLAF are the less promising ones where a CFA is not available. But such cases would not generate sufficient moneys in the Fund to make it viable.

In the debates on the Access to Justice Bill the CLAF concept was discussed – with Lord Goodhart taking the lead.[145] Though unpersuaded of the merits of a CLAF alongside CFAs, the Lord Chancellor eventually agreed to introduce a clause to permit the establishment of a CLAF and this was in fact done during the House of Commons Committee stage.[146] (See Access to Justice Act 1999, s 28.) But, whatever its theoretical merits, the CLAF concept seems likely to continue to be a talking point that is not actually put to the test.[147] The problem of 'adverse selection' cannot be magicked away.

A question of greater practical significance may be whether before-the-event legal expenses insurance is likely to make much progress.

7. Legal expenses insurance (LEI)

The concept of before-the-event (BTE) insurance against legal costs has been familiar for years, notably in the context of house insurance and motoring. But in the past 20 or so years the insurance industry has started to market policies covering a much wider range of legal problems. Most policies issued in the UK are 'add ons' to existing policies, usually of motor or home insurance policies. It is estimated that about 17 million people have cover under such policies – though often they are unaware of the fact. The 'add-on' policies cost the customer around a mere £15-20. Some of them also provide free, telephone legal advice. (Abbey Legal Protection, for instance, employed eight solicitors and four barristers to provide advice to their legal expenses insurance clients seven days a week and 24 hours a day.[148])

Typically such LEI policies cover lawyers' fees, court costs, costs of witnesses and experts–and costs of the opponent if the insured is ordered to pay them. Normally there is a maximum per claim which may be £25,000 or £50,000. Many of the policies cover all the members of the family.

The policy normally provides that only cases that have a reasonable prospect of success will be supported. But the insured has a right to choose his own lawyer. (This is required by the Insurance Companies (Legal Expenses Insurance) Regulations 1990, SI 1990/1159 implementing EC Directive 87/34 which came into force on 1 July 1990.) Many insurers, however, reserve the right to reject the client's nomination. It is not clear whether this is lawful under the EC Directive.

Most insurers also retain the right to withdraw cover if a reasonable settlement is unlikely to be obtained or if the insured refuses a reasonable offer. (In all these respects insurance is much like having legal aid.)

---

[145]   See especially House of Lords *Hansard*, 21 January 1999, vol 596, cols 782-90.
[146]   House of Commons, Standing Committee 'E', 13 May 1999, cols 376-80.
[147]   The question was raised yet again in the Law Society's Consultation Paper *The Future of Publicly Funded Legal Services*, February 2003, paras.71-77.
[148]   *Law Society's Gazette*, 5 March 1998, p 4.

Most policies exclude matrimonial disputes. Many also exclude building disputes, defamation, tax matters and defence of criminal prosecutions involving violence.

It was said in 1991 that the Association of British Insurers estimated that total premiums were then worth about £40–£50m pa, which represented a significant increase of some 100% on the previous two or three years. This divided between 50% motor related, 20% general family policies and 30% commercial. About 10 million people had some form of cover, though in many cases it amounted only to access to a telephone advisory service.

A survey carried out in 1991 for the Law Society and the Consumers' Association suggested that only 7% of the population had some form of legal expenses insurance proper (compared with around 50% in Germany).[149]

The concept of BTE policies was boosted by the Court of Appeal's decision in *Sarwar v Alam*[150]. S had been injured while a passenger in A's car. S sued A. His solicitor took the case on a CFA. The case was settled save for the costs. In costs-only proceedings the trial judge held that S's solicitors were not entitled to recover the ATE premium on the CFA because he was covered by A's BTE policy which covered both damages and costs. The fact that was not aware that he was covered was irrelevant. On appeal, the Court of Appeal noted that two-fifths of all motor policies carried such cover and that normally it extended to passengers. Allowing the appeal, the court said there were in this case reasons that justified the solicitors advising that a separate ATE policy be taken out so that the ATE premium was recoverable. But it said, obiter, that in motor accident cases it was desirable that solicitors should ask clients to bring to their first interview any relevant motor insurance, household insurance or other stand-alone BTE insurance policy whether belonging to the client or a spouse oo partner living in the same house as the client. If BTE cover was available, the claim was modest and there were no features of the cover that made it inappropriate, the solicitors should refer the case to the BTE insurer without further ado.

Commenting on the decision, Professor John Peysner suggested that it could have profound effects. Over the previous two or three years, as a matter of deliberate policy, liability insurers and legal expenses insurers had created joint ventures to bolt on legal expenses cover at modest or no extra charge, to house and motor insurance policies. The hope was that they could be used to defeat the recoverability of costly ATE insurance premiums and success fees in CFAs. Solicitors on the panels of legal

---

149   See *Legal Expenses Insurance in the UK* (Law Society, January 1991), summarised in *Law Society's Gazette*, 6 February 1991, p 3, and *Solicitors' Journal*, 7 June 1991, p 608. See also the *Which?* survey, April 1991, pp 223–9. For a broad assessment including international comparisons see two papers in Zuckerman and Cranston (ed) *Reforming Civil Procedure–Essays on Access to Justice* (Clarendon, Oxford, 1995): N Rickman and A Gray, 'The Role of Legal Expenses Insurance in Securing Access to the Market for Legal Services' pp 305–25; Vivien Prais, 'Legal Expenses Insurance', pp 431–46.

150   [2001] EWCA Civ 1401, [2001] 4 All ER 541.

expenses insurers charged modest rates without success fees. By replacing the client's own lawyer with the insurer's panel lawyer cheap lawyers would replace expensive ones.

> The implication is that the market for this type of work will alter its profile from provision by a range of independent solicitors buying after-the-event premiums on the open market ... to a relatively small number of panel solicitors (possibly no more than 200 firms in the whole country) who will corner the market for modest claims. Their work will be controlled by legal expenses insurers who are closely linked to the insurers for the defendant .... A scheme where access to legal help is concentrated in a few hands, in the absence of an effective regulator, is a matter of serious concern.[151]

In Germany, premium income from legal expenses insurance in 1997 was almost DM5bn (about £1.7bn). Approximately DM2.4bn (about £800m) was paid out to lawyers. The breakdown of some 3m insurance cases a year included: 80,000 social law cases; 110,000 consultations in family law and inheritance law; 400,000 tenancy and law relating to neighbour problems; 450,000 employment law problems; 570,000 contractual matters; 660,000 tort liability cases; 680,000 criminal law and breaches of regulations.[152]

The Lord Chancellor's March 1998 Consultation Paper (*Access to Justice with Conditional Fees*) said that the Government was keen to encourage the wider use of legal expenses insurance more generally, both before-the-event and after-the-event insurance. It wanted to do what it reasonably could to assist the legal expenses insurance industry and would welcome views on how it could facilitate the development of such insurance whether through changes in the law or otherwise (para 4 13, p 30). But it is easier to pose the question than to find an answer.

8. Pro bono work done by the profession

It has always been the case that lawyers have done work pro bono – ie free of charge. But in recent years both sides of the profession have made significant efforts to institutionalise the concept of pro bono work. At the Bar the way was led by young members of the profession, who in 1972 set up the Free Representation Unit (FRU) to represent clients free of charge in tribunal cases. In 2002, young barristers and Bar students working through FRU were handling some 1,250 cases per year.

In August 1996, on the initiative of Mr Peter Goldsmith QC, former chairman of the Bar (later Lord Goldsmith, Attorney General) the Bar Pro Bono Unit was launched as a charity to provide free legal advice and representation in deserving

---

[151]   J Peysner, 'Turning into trouble', 10(2) *Nottingham Law Journal*, 2001, 64, 66-67. See to similar effect D Lock, 'Funding Faces Tough Future', 16 *Litigation Funding*, 2001, 6.

[152]   A Schiller, 'Legal Expenses Insurance in Germany', in V Pais (ed) *Legal Expenses in Germany, France and the Netherlands* (London School of Economics, December 1998), p 9.

cases where legal aid is not available and the applicant cannot afford legal assistance. Advice and representation are provided by barristers who have volunteered their services. Each agrees to donate a minimum of three days a year. By 2003 it had some 1,350 barrister members.[153]

In 2000 the Bar launched 'Bar in the Community' which provides barristers willing to serve on the Management Committee of voluntary sector organisations. Over 500 barristers have volunteered.

Equivalent activity by the solicitors' branch started in 1992 with the decision by 24 City firms together with some barrister' chambers to provide assistance to Citizens' Advice Bureaux with free advice on debt, housing and employment matters In August 1993, 10 major City firms said they would do pro bono work for Liberty.[154] In March 1995 it was announced that over 40 law firms in different parts of the country had pledged to provide at least £5,000 worth of free advice annually to community projects aimed at job creation, inner city regeneration and environmental improvements.[155]

The Law Society's Pro Bono Working Party which reported in May 1994 was not prepared to recommend that solicitors be obliged to take part in pro bono work.[156] But in November 1996 a meeting organised by solicitor Andrew Phillips (now Lord Phillips) with the backing of the Law Society and the charity Business in the Community established the Solicitors' Pro Bono Group to boost the amount of such work done by the solicitors' branch.[157] The Group started work in September 1997.[158] In March 1998 the group launched a national membership drive with the backing, inter alia, of the Lord Chief Justice. But take-up was not remarkable. A year later the membership drive was relaunched. At that time there were some 160 members ranging from substantial firms to trainee solicitors. Five years later, in Spring 2003 the number of members had crept up to 220, of which 189 were firms. About a dozen of the larger firms had full-time pro bono administrators. It seems therefore as if a more generous and more systematic approach to pro bono work had finally begun to emerge among some leading solicitors' firms.[159]

In 1999 the Law Society gave the Solicitors' Pro Bono Group a two-year grant of £90,000 to enable it to develop its work. In 2002 a National Pro Bono week consisting

---

153   For further details see M Phelan, 'Effective Access to Justice', *Counsel*, March/April 1996, p 16.
154   *Solicitors' Journal*, 27 August 1993.
155   *The Lawyer*, 15 March 1995, p 1.
156   See E Gilvarry, 'The Pro Bono Push', *Law Society's Gazette*, 25 May 1994, p 4.
157   Start up funding for the SPBG was provided by Allen & Overy, Clifford Chance, Clyde & Co, Dibb Luptn Alsop, Freshfields, Hammond Suddards, Herbert Smith, Linklaters, Lovell White Durrant, Norton Rose, Slaughter & May.
158   See *Law Society's Gazette*, 17 September 1997, p 12.
159   The English legal profession came to institutionalised pro bono work at least a quarter of a century after the American: See M Zander, 'Pro Bono Publico', *Law Society Gazette*, 27 September 1972; A Boon and R Alley, 'Moral Agendas? Pro Bono Publico in Large Law Firms in the United Kingdom', 60 *Modern Law Review*, 1997, pp 630-54.

of events in different parts of the country was organised jointly by the Bar, the Law Society and the Institute of Legal Executives to promote the pro bono concept for the profession, advice agencies and the general public. The second National Pro Bono week was held in June 2003.

For the Bar's Pro Bono website see www.barcouncil.org.uk – Links – Other. For the Solicitors' Pro Bono Group website see www.probonogroup.org.uk.

In 2002 the Attorney General, Lord Goldsmith established a new pro bono committee comprising the Law Officers, the main pro bono organisations, the Bar Council and the Law Society. In June 2003 he launched a website – www.probonouk.net – to make the free services of lawyers better known to members of the public. (See J Robins, 'Social conscience', *The Lawyer*, 9 June 2003, p 18.)

Chapter 7

Appeals

An appeal system is necessary to perform a variety of functions. One is to provide an opportunity for the disappointed litigant to test the validity of the decision at first instance. A second is to allow the court 'to correct an error, unfairness or wrong exercise of discretion which has led to an unjust result'.[1] A third purpose of the appeal system is to preserve some measure of uniformity in the decision-making of lower courts. The doctrine of precedent is an important aide in this process. Lower courts are encouraged and in some circumstances are required to follow the indications of the higher courts on matters of law and practice, the assessment of damages and even fact-finding.[2] A fourth function of the appeal court is to keep the law abreast of changing circumstances. A fifth reason is to promote public confidence in the administration of justice. (For exploration of the nature, functions and limitations of appeals in the context of recent reforms see R Nobles and D Schiff, 'The Right to Appeal and Workable Systems of Justice', (2002) 65 *Modern Law Review* 676-701.)

In the earliest days of the system the appeal process was exceedingly limited. In civil cases, procedure was by writ of error and the basis of the appeal was that there was some error appearing on the face of the record. Since only certain things appeared on the record there were many issues on which no appeal was possible. Later the courts allowed each party to move a Bill of Exceptions, in which the trial judge was asked to note that a particular point had been rejected by the judge and this was then treated as part of the record for the purpose of an appeal. This helped somewhat, but it was still limited in scope and required the point to be seen and taken at the trial itself. Moreover, a further problem was that if the appeal was successful the court

---

[1] Bowman *Review of the Court of Appeal (Civil Division)*, September 1997, p 25. The Bowman Review – see below – said that the mere fact that there was an error does not mean that there should be a successful appeal. The important point is to establish 'whether what has happened means that a judgement or order should not be allowed to stand' (ibid).

[2] The operation of the precedent system is considered in the writer's *The Law-Making Process* (5th edn, Butterworths, 1999).

had no power to substitute its own decision for that of the court below. It could only order a fresh trial.

Appeals on questions of fact were even more difficult. Originally, when cases were heard by juries and the jury was supposed to decide cases of its own knowledge a wrong verdict was practically a matter for the disciplining of the jury. A writ of attaint could be brought to try the truth of the jury's verdict and, if the attaint jury thought the first jury was mistaken, the first jury was liable to punishment. It was only in the seventeenth century that juries were no longer liable to be punished for their verdicts and that the common law courts were prepared to order a new trial on the ground that a jury's decision had been against the weight of the evidence.

Juries in civil cases are now virtually unknown so the question normally is whether the appeal court is prepared to interfere with a decision rendered by the trial judge. As will be seen, the appeal court has the power to take a different view of the facts from that of the court below – though it is generally reluctant to do so. But in other respects, the appellate court has extensive powers not only to order a retrial but to substitute its own decision.

In criminal cases the situation was even more remarkable. There was no appeal from conviction at all until well into the nineteenth century. At some point the judges started informally to refer a question of law to other judges before they summed up to the jury or before sentence was executed. In 1848 this informal arrangement was regularised with the establishment of the Court for Crown Cases Reserved. But it was still available only on reference from the judge–though the procedure was extended also to quarter sessions. Parliament considered the question of an appeal in criminal cases no fewer than 28 times in the last seventy years of the nineteenth century. But it was only after an especially serious miscarriage of justice, the Adolf Beck case, that the Court of Criminal Appeal was finally established in 1907. Its powers include quashing a conviction, ordering a retrial and reducing the sentence.

1. The structure of appeal courts

(a) Civil cases

In the nineteenth century the appeal courts in civil cases were in a considerable muddle. Appeals from the old Court of Common Pleas went to the Court of King's Bench. Appeals from the old Court of Exchequer went to the Court of Exchequer Chamber. When the Court of King's Bench began hearing cases at first instance in the sixteenth century, a second Court of Exchequer Chamber was set up to hear appeals from that body. In 1830 the two courts of Exchequer Chamber were replaced by a third. This court was established to hear appeals from all three common law courts– Queen's Bench, Common Pleas and Exchequer. The members of the court were drawn from the two from which the appeal did not come. In addition there was the Court of Appeal in Chancery which heard appeals from the Court of Chancery, not in the traditional way by writ of error but by a rehearing. Appeals from the Court of Admiralty went to the Privy Council and from 1833 to the Judicial Committee of the Privy Council. Appeals from the Divorce Court established in 1857 went at first from the single judge to the full court and from 1868 to the House of Lords.

The Judicature Commissioners reported in 1869 and recommended a new structure. They proposed that there should be one Supreme Court, comprising a High Court and a Court of Appeal. The Court of Appeal should take appeals from all the divisions of the High Court. This reform was achieved in the Judicature Acts 1873–1875. Its constitution and the statutory framework are now to be found in the Supreme Court Act 1981. In 1966 the Court of Criminal Appeal became the Court of Appeal Criminal Division, so that from that date there was a Civil Division and a Criminal Division of that court.

The Civil Division is presided over by the Master of the Rolls and sits in several divisions–almost always in London. Lord Justices of Appeal sit as the judges. The Court of Appeal normally sits with three judges. However the Supreme Court Act 1981provided for two-judge courts to hear appeals on interlocutory matters or any other matter prescribed by order made by the Lord Chancellor and the Access to Justice Act 1999 stated that the Court of Appeal is validly constituted if it consists of one or more judges.[3] For very important cases occasionally the Court of Appeal sits with five judges. Until very recently the Court of Appeal Civil Division heard appeals from both the High Court and the county court, but, as will be seen below, under the post Woolf reforms of the appellate system since May 2000 most appeals from the county court now go to the High Court. The basic concept introduced by these reforms is that an appeal should go to the next level in the hierarchy and that second appeals be severely restricted. (See p 625 below.)

Appeals from the civil jurisdiction of the magistrates' courts go to the Divisional Court of the Family Division, which consists of two or three judges usually of the High Court. Appeals from the Divisional Court in a civil case lie to the Court of Appeal.

Appeals from the Court of Appeal have hitherto gone to the House of Lords. In modern times the House of Lords has consisted of judges specifically appointed for the purpose known as Lords of Appeal in Ordinary, plus the Lord Chancellor and any former Lord Chancellors.

The judicial functions of the House of Lords are as old as Parliament itself. By 1600 it enjoyed an undisputed role as a court of appeal. It heard cases by way of writ of error from the Courts of Exchequer Chamber. But until 1844 lay peers were able to participate in the judicial work, and occasionally they did so. The appellate jurisdiction of the House of Lords was threatened and almost abolished in the court reforms of the 1873–5 era but in the end it was preserved in the Appellate Jurisdiction Act 1876, which provided for salaried law lords. Though nominally the final appeal remained

---

[3]   AJA 1999, s 59 substituting a new s 54(2) into the SCA 1981.

in the hands of the hereditary chamber, in reality it was transferred to a court of law under the control of a professional judiciary.

In 2000 the Report of the Royal Commission on reform of the House of Lords concluded 'There is no reason why the second chamber should not continue to exercise the judicial functions of the present House of Lords'.[4] It recommended that the law lords should continue to be *ex officio* members of the reformed second chamber. If ordinary members of the reformed chamber became subject to a limited term of service this should apply also to the law lords but they should have an automatic right to be reappointed until retirement.

A different view was expressed by Lord Bingham of Cornhill, successively Master of the Rolls, Lord Chief Justice and senior law lord, in a lecture in which he advanced reasons for a supreme court not in the House of Lords – 'A new supreme court for the United Kingdom' www. ucl.ac.uk/constitution-unit/reports/lecture.htm. (The lecture, p 13, contains a rare description of the process of choosing the judges for a particular case.) See also Lord Steyn, 'The Case for a Supreme Court', 118 *Law Quarterly Review*, 2002, p 382. On the problem of selecting the judges see Sir Sydney Kentridge, 'The Highest Court: Selecting the Judges', 62 *Cambridge Law Journal*, 2003, pp 55-71. For consideration of the functions of the House of Lords – and of the Judicial Committee of the Privy – see Andrew Le Sueur and Richard Cornes, *What do the Top Courts Do?*, Constitution Unit, June 2000.

The House of Lords usually sits with five judges but on occasion seven are empanelled. The hearings are conducted in one of the committee rooms of the Palace of Westminster, but judgment is always given in the legislative chamber itself. Nowadays the judgments (called 'speeches') are not read; they are handed to the parties and the procedure consists simply of the presiding judge putting the issue to the vote as if it was an ordinary legislative matter. ('My Lords, I beg to move that the Report of the Appellate Committee be now considered.') When this has been approved ('the Contents have it'), each law lord stands up in order of seniority and says merely that he would allow or dismiss the appeal 'for the reasons given in my printed speech'.

Abolition of the post of Lord Chancellor, of the Lord Chancellor's Department and of the House of Lords in its judicial capacity As previously noted, on 12 June 2003, with no warning and no prior consultation[5], the Prime Minister Mr Tony Blair made the startling announcement that (1) the position of Lord Chancellor was to be abolished; (2) the Lord Chancellor's Department was to be transformed into a new Department

---

4   *A House for the Future*, Cm 4534, 2000, pp 92-93.

5   Apparently, the Cabinet that met that day was not informed of the Prime Minister's impending announcement. Nor was there consultation with the judiciary. The way in which this announcement was made and the lack of proper consultation or planning was the subject of strong criticism from a wide spectrum of opinion.

for Constitutional Affairs; (3) the final court of appeal would be removed from the House of Lords and become a separate Supreme Court; and (4) the appointment of judges would be taken over by an independent Judicial Appointments Commission. No detail was announced – and none seemed to have been worked out – but it soon emerged that, contrary to initial impressions, the project might take some years to complete.

Lord Irvine of Lairg, who had been Lord Chancellor from the start of the Blair Prime Ministership in May 1977, objected to the plans and was retired. Lord Falconer of Thoroton QC was appointed Secretary of State for the new Department which took over the offices of the Lord Chancellor's Department. (It also took over responsibility for the Scottish Office and the Welsh Office.) Pending the establishment of the new system, Lord Falconer also took over the office of Lord Chancellor. So for the transitional period, the appointment of judges, magistrates and the like continued to be conducted as before. However, the Secretary of State announced that he would not sit as a judge. He also announced that he would relinquish the role of Speaker of the House of Lords once a new method for appointing a Speaker had been agreed by the House of Lords.

The necessary legislation would be brought forward in the session 2003/04. (See the national press 13 June 2003 and days following.)

On 14 July, Lord Falconer, the Secretary of State for Constitutional Affairs and Lord Chancellor, issued a Consultation Paper regarding the Supreme Court[6] (*Constitutional Reform: A Supreme Court for the United Kingdom* – www.lcd.gov.uk (Consultation Papers)). The first appointees would be the present 12 Law Lords. While members of the court, they would no longer be able to sit and vote in the House of Lords, though since they would retain their titles, they could do so on retirement.[7]

See further R Cornes, 'The UK Supreme Court', *New Law Journal*, 4 July 2003, p 1019.

---

[6] On the same day he published two further Consultation Papers: Constitutional reform: a new way of appointing judges (CP 10/03); and Constitutional reform: the future of Queen's Counsel (CP 08/03).

[7] Questions on which the Consultation Paper sought views included: should the number of members of the court remain at 12; the method for appointing the members of the new court and for selecting the President of the Court; whether the system of selection should include open applications; whether academics should be considered for appointment; whether the retirement age should be 70 or 75; whether retiring members of the court should be appointed to the House of Lords; whether the court should continue to sit in panels, as opposed to all sitting; whether lower courts should have the power to give leave to appeal; and what the members of the court should be called. The consultation process would close on 7 November 2003.

RADICAL REFORM OF CIVIL APPEALS FOLLOWING BOWMAN

The civil appeal system has recently undergone drastic reform – described by Lord Brooke as 'the most significant changes in the arrangements for appeals in civil proceedings in this country for 125 years'.[8] Under the previous system litigants had extensive rights of appeal. In the case of a final judgment there was generally the right to appeal to the Court of Appeal; in the case of an interlocutory decision by the master or district judge there was generally the possibility of two appeals – first to the judge and then on to the Court of Appeal. Appeals from a district judge or master to a judge were full re-hearings. Appeals to the Court of Appeal were more restricted in their nature.

In his final report *Access to Justice* (1996) Lord Woolf recommended that leave to appeal should be required for all interlocutory appeals; that some appeals should lie to lower courts than the Court of Appeal; that all appeals should be of the 'limited Court of Appeal rehearing type'; and that there should be greater uniformity in the procedure for appeal.

Instead of moving ahead with these recommendations, the Lord Chancellor announced in March 1996 that there would be a full separate review of the civil division of the Court of Appeal. This began a few months later under the chairmanship of Sir Jeffrey Bowman, former senior partner of Price Waterhouse. The terms of reference were to inquire into the Court's rules, procedures and working methods, its jurisdiction and the legal and administrative support system. The five other members of the Review team included Lord Woolf., who at the time was still Master of the Rolls presiding judge in the Court of Appeal. (Lord Woolf became Lord Chief Justice in 2000.)

The 224-page Bowman report was published in September 1997 (www.lcd.gov.uk (Major Reports). For a lengthy review see J Jacob, 'The Bowman Review of the Court of Appeal', *Modern Law Review*, 1998, pp 390-400.) Due to the complex nature of routes of appeal in family matters, Bowman recommended that a specialist committee should examine this area. The Family Appeal Review Group, chaired by Lord Justice Thorpe, published its recommendations in July 1998.

The Bowman Report said that the Court of Appeal was being asked to consider appeals that were not of sufficient weight or complexity to require two or three of the country's most senior judges and which had already been through one or more levels of appeal.[9] The same considerations of justice, expedition and moderation of costs should apply to appeals as to first instance proceedings. An appeal should no longer be seen as an

---

8   *Tanfern Ltd v Cameron MacDonald (Practice Note)* [2000] 2 All ER 801, [2000] 1 WLR 1311, para 50.
9   Thus a decision by a district judge in a non-family case in the county court could be appealed to a circuit judge and then to the Court of Appeal. In High Court cases an appeal lay against an interlocutory decision by a master or district judge to a High Court judge and then to the Court of Appeal.

automatic further stage in a case. A dissatisfied litigant's right should be not to appeal but to have his request to appeal considered. The requirement of permission to appeal should be the norm. Also appeals should be dealt with in ways proportionate to the grounds of complaint and the subject matter of the dispute. More than one level of appeal could normally only be justified if there was an important point of principle or practice at stake.

The Report made 146 recommendations. Many were implemented by the Access to Justice Act 1999 and CPR Part 52 which came into force from 2 May 2000. (The new scheme is described in great detail in the judgment of the Court of Appeal delivered by Lord Justice Brooke in *Tanfern* (above).) The same system was applied to small claims cases as from October 2000.

AJA 1999, s 55 provides that where an appeal is taken to a county court or the High Court, no further appeal can be taken to the Court of Appeal unless the Court of Appeal considers that '(a) the appeal would raise an important point of principle or practice, or (b) there is some other compelling reason for the Court of Appeal to hear it' (s 55(1)).

AJA 1999, s 56 gives the Lord Chancellor the power by statutory instrument to prescribe alternative routes for the destination of appeals. This was done by the Access to Justice Act 1999 (Destination of Appeals) Order 2000, SI 2000 No 1071 – the Destination Order. (For details again see the Court of Appeal's decision in *Tanfern* (above).)

The Destination Order provides that appeals which previously would have gone to the Court of Appeal will now go to a lower court. The general principle is that appeal lies to the next level of judge in the judicial hierarchy. Thus appeals from masters or district judges of the High Court lie to a High Court judge (art 2). Appeals from a district judge of the county court lie to a circuit judge (art 3). Appeals from any other county court judge (ie a circuit judge or recorder) lie to a High Court judge (art 3).

However, art 4 of the Destination Order sets out two exceptions. Article 4(a) provides that the normal route of appeal does not apply where a 'final decision'[10] is given in a multi track case[11]. An appeal lies instead direct to the Court of Appeal.

Article 4(b) provides that where a final decision is made by a specialist jurisdiction, regardless of the level of the judge, appeal lies direct to the Court of Appeal.

Article 5 provides that second appeals go to the Court of Appeal itself.

AJA 1999, s 57 give the Master of the Rolls the power to 'call in' any appeal going to a lower court so that it can be heard instead by the Court of Appeal. This power

---

[10]   As to the meaning of 'final decision' see *Roerig v Valiant Trawlers Ltd* [2002] EWCA Civ 21, [2002] 1 WLR 2304.

[11]   The exception does not apply to cases not on the multi track – *Clark (Inspector of Taxes) v Perks* [2001] 1 WLR 17, paras 7 and 54.

will enable the Court of Appeal to give a ruling on issues that are causing serious difficulties.

Running the office The Supreme Court Act 1981 created the position of Registrar of Civil Appeals who took office in 1982. The Registrar was a judicial officer with limited judicial powers such as granting extensions of time in which to appeal, leave to amend, ordering security for costs and resolving listing disputes. He also had administrative responsibilities, including deciding 'constitutions' (which judges sit in the up-to-11 courts that may be sitting at any time). Constitutions generally stay together for three or so weeks. He did not, however, have line management responsibility for the Civil Appeal Office which was set up in 1982. The Civil Appeal Office processes all appeals and applications for leave to the Court of Appeal. (See *Practice Direction* [1990] 3 All ER 981.)

Bowman recommended that the Head of the Civil Appeals Office should have line management responsibility for the staff and for the running of the Office. His judicial functions should normally be performed by two designated senior legal officers though anyone dissatisfied with their decision should have the right to refer it to a Lord Justice. Accepting this recommendation, the Access to Justice Act 1999, s 70, abolished the office of Registrar of Civil Appeals. His administrative functions were taken over by the Head of Civil Appeals.

Bowman said that the office should undertake much more management of a case from beginning to end. ('Lord Woolf laid great emphasis in his [Access to Justice Report] on case management and the role of the judges in this process. We believe that the principle of case management can be applied in the CA and that the Lords Justices have a very important role to play' (p 75)). But much of the management should be done by staff in the office rather than the judges.

Between 1982 and 2003 the full-time staff increased from 19 to 70, including 10 lawyers. The main duties of the lawyers are to write brief legal abstracts of each case onto the computer. Until recently they prepared summaries of cases of litigants in person. A recent development has been the introduction of some (currently 9) part-time 'judicial assistants' – young, high-calibre pupil barristers or trainee solicitors. Initially they were mainly used to clear up a large number of applications for leave to appeal, especially of litigants in person.[12]

Bowman made various other recommendations for improving the way cases were handled:

- When a judge gave leave to appeal he should give directions on the future handling of the case on such matters as the scope for ADR, security for costs, hearing times, the need for a specialist court and whether the appeal should be limited to certain points. That could normally be done on the papers without an oral hearing.

[12] For a description of the work done by the judicial assistants in the Court of Appeal see *Counsel*, June 1998, p 22; and June 2002, p 18.

- All Lords Justices needed to take responsibility for ensuring that all cases are heard as speedily and efficiently as possible.
- All judgments in county courts should be recorded to permit proper consideration on appeal. (On the proper recording of all decisions see now the Court of Appeal's decision in *Tanfern Ltd* (above) at paras 34-35.)
- There should be a strong presumption that time-limits should not be extended save in exceptional circumstances. If rules were not complied with the applicant/ appellant should be at risk of having the case dismissed or at least of being penalised in costs (p 92).
- The Lord Justice who gave leave should consider whether the case was suitable for mediation or other alternative dispute resolution (p 92).
- The judges should spend more time off the bench reading. ('In our view, time spent considering and preparing cases outside court is likely to save time overall' (p 93).) (In his annual report for 2001-02 the Master of the Rolls stated that members of the court now had five reading and writing days in each three-week period.)
- IT for case management and case tracking should be introduced. Telephone and video conferencing systems should be piloted. Lords Justices should be provided with (the same) appropriate IT. (The annual report for 2001-02 stated: 'The Civil Appeals Office continues with its modernisation programme and use of new IT. The Court has again dealt with applications by video and telephone link'. For further information on IT matters see speeches given by Lord Justice Brooke, the judge in charge of Modernisation, on the LCD website.)
- There should be more help provided for litigants in person. (In 1996, 29% of all applications for leave to appeal and 10% of all appeals were brought by litigants in person (p 16)).

In April 1999 a 54-page Practice Note was published consolidating with some amendments all the principle practice directions relating to proceedings in the Court of Appeal [1999] 2 All ER 490. See now the Practice Direction attached to Part 52. (On practice directions generally see JA Jolowicz, 'Practice Directions and Civil Procedure Rules' [2000] *Cambridge Law Journal* p 53.)

(b)   Criminal cases

Appeals from the old quarter sessions and assize courts went to the Court of Criminal Appeal. When the Court of Appeal, Criminal Division was established in 1966, they went to that court instead. Then in 1972 when the Crown Courts replaced the quarter sessions and assize courts, appeals accordingly went from the Crown Court to the Court of Appeal, Criminal Division. The Court of Appeal, Criminal Division sits normally with three judges. The presiding judge is either the Lord Chief Justice or a Lord Justice of Appeal. The other judges can be Lords Justice, High Court judges or senior circuit judges. Appeals from the Court of Appeal, Criminal Division go, with leave, to the House of Lords.

Appeals from decisions of the magistrates' courts in criminal cases may go in two alternative directions. There can be an appeal to the Crown Court, which sits for this purpose with a judge and two or more magistrates but without a jury. Alternatively appeals lie by way of case stated (see p 643 below) from the magistrates' court to the Divisional Court of the Queen's Bench Division sitting with two or three High Court judges, though the Lord Chief Justice often presides in the Divisional Court. Appeals from the appellate jurisdiction of the Crown Court go to the Divisional Court of the QBD on a point of law by way of case stated. Appeals in criminal cases go direct from the Divisional Court to the House of Lords.

Lord Justice Auld in his Report recommended that both appeals as of right to the Crown Court by way of rehearing and appeals to the Divisional Court by way of case stated or for judicial review should be abolished. Appeals from the magistrates' court, he proposed, should be to a single judge in the Crown Court and such an appeal should require leave. There would be a possibility of a further appeal to the Court of Appeal which would exercise the supervisory jurisdiction now exercised by the Divisional Court.[13] These recommendations were not accepted by the Government. (Its Response to the Report attached to the 2002 White Paper *Justice for All* said, 'We consider that the existing arrangements work satisfactorily'(p 43).)

(c)   The Judicial Committee of the Privy Council

The Judicial Committee of the Privy Council is primarily a Commonwealth court. It is the final court of appeal for over 20 Commonwealth territories and six independent Republics within the Commonwealth.

These include New Zealand, Jamaica and Barbados. It also hears appeals from dependent territories such as Gibraltar and Bermuda. Its jurisdiction, which is based on the Judicial Committee Act 1833, was enlarged to enable it to hear appeals from certain republican countries in the Commonwealth such as Mauritius, and Trinidad and Tobago. (The right of appeal from Australia was abolished in 1986. Singapore abolished the appeal to the Judicial Committee in 1994.) The up-to-date list of countries is on the Judicial Committee's website – www.privycouncil.gov.uk or www.privy-council.org.uk.

The Judicial Committee of the Privy Council was given a potentially major new role under the three devolution Acts passed in 1998 by the Blair Government.

The devolution legislation for Scotland, Wales and Northern Ireland makes the Judicial Committee of the Privy Council the final court of appeal on devolution matters. Normally the decisions of the Judicial Committee, though treated with great respect, are not binding on the UK courts. But decisions on devolution matters are

---

[13]   Chapter 12, pp 620-22.

binding on all courts in the United Kingdom – though not on the Privy Council itself.[14] The Privy Council rather than the House of Lords was made the final court of appeal for devolution issues because it was felt inappropriate that a part of the Westminster Parliament should be the arbiter of devolution matters, including decisions as to the competence of the devolved assemblies.

Under the three devolution Acts the Privy Council may take references on devolution issues arising in the course of litigation, it may hear appeals against determination of a devolution issue from the High Court, the Court of Appeal, the Inner House of the Court of Session in Scotland, or the Court of Appeal in Northern Ireland.[15] The House of Lords may refer devolution issues to the Judicial Committee – though each of the three Act states that it may also decide the matter itself if it 'considers it more appropriate'[16] (For a Practice Note on devolution in Wales see [1999] 3 All ER 466.)

The Judicial Committee includes the present and retired Law Lords, past and present Lord Chancellors, and past and retired Lords Justices of Appeal. If the Lord Chancellor sits, he presides, though the composition of the Judicial Committee is by convention a matter for the senior Law Lord. The devolution Acts, however, contain provisions specifically excluding Commonwealth judges from hearing such cases.[17]

The Judicial Committee, like the House of Lords, normally sits with five judges.

The Government's Consultation Paper published on 14 July 2003 (*Constitutional reform: a Supreme Court for the United Kingdom*, CP11/03) stated that on balance the Government believed that it would be right to transfer the jurisdiction on devolution cases from the Judicial Committee to the new Supreme Court with arrangements which enabled additional Scottish and Northern Ireland judges to sit in such cases where that was appropriate. (para 21)

> The establishment of the new court gives us the opportunity to restore a single apex to the UK's judicial system where all the constitutional issues can be considered. (para 20)

---

[14]   See Scotland Act 1998, s 103; Government of Wales Act 1998, Sch 8, para 32; and the Northern Ireland Act 1998, s 82.
[15]   Scotland Act, ss 32, 33, 98 and Sch 6; Government of Wales Act 1998, s 109 and Sch 8; Northern Ireland Act 1998, ss 11, 79 and 82 and Sch 10.
[16]   Scotland Act 1998, Sch 6, para 32; Government of Wales Act 1998, Sch 8, para 29; Northern Ireland Act 1998, Sch 10, para 32.
[17]   Scotland Act 1998, s 103(2); Government of Wales Act 1998, Sch 8, para 33; Northern Ireland Act 1998, s 82(2).

2. The appeal process

(a) A right to appeal?

(1) CIVIL CASES

As has been seen, the position as regards right to appeal has been transformed by the reforms flowing from the Woolf and Bowman Reports.

The Access to Justice Act 1999, s 54 provides for rights of appeal to be exercised only with permission as prescribed by rules of court. The Explanatory Notes to the Act stated that for the future, with few exceptions, rules would require permission to appeal to be obtained in all appeals to the county courts, High Court or Civil Division of the Court of Appeal. The exceptions were appeals against committal to prison, against a refusal of habeas corpus and against secure accommodation orders under the Childrens Act 1989.[18]

CPR 52.3(6) provides that permission to appeal will only be given where '(a) the court considers that the appeal would have a real prospect of success; or (b) there is some other compelling reason why the appeal should be heard'.

AJA 1999, s 54 (4) provides that there is no appeal against a refusal of permission to appeal (sub-s (4)).[19] However, if the refusal of permission to appeal is made on the papers, the would-be appellant is entitled to have the matter reconsidered by the same court at an oral hearing.

AJA 1999, s 55 provides that where the county court or High Court has decided an appeal, no appeal may be made to the Court of Appeal unless the Court of Appeal considers that the appeal raises an important point of principle or practice or there is some other compelling reason.

A refusal of permission must be reasoned to comply with art 6 of the ECHR – see *Hyams v Plender* [2001] 1 WLR 32 at para 17.

Appeals to the House of Lords require leave–either of the Court of Appeal or of the House of Lords itself. Such appeals are supposed always to be on points of law of general public importance. (For exploration of this issue L Blom-Cooper and G Drewry, *Final Appeal*, Clarendon, 1972, pp 117–51.)

---

18 CPR 52.3 sets out some of the exceptions. Other exceptions are dealt with by Lord Justice Brooke in his judgment in *Tanfern* (above) at paras 24-26.

19 For a disturbing illustration of the effect of this provision see *Gregory v Turner* [2003] EWCA Civ 183, [2003] 2 All ER 1114. The Court of Appeal commiserated with the claimant that it did not have the power to allow an appeal in a case where something had plainly gone wrong below.

(2) CRIMINAL CASES

In criminal cases no leave is required for an appeal from the magistrates' court–whether by way of rehearing to the Crown Court, or by way of case stated on a point of law to the Divisional Court of the Queen's Bench Division. Leave is, however, required for an appeal from the Crown Court to the Court of Appeal, Criminal Division. The exception was for an appeal on a point of law only, where no leave was required until 1995 when the exception was abolished by the Criminal Appeal Act 1995, s 1. Leave is also required for an appeal to the House of Lords, either from the Court of Appeal (or the Divisional Court) or from the House of Lords itself. In addition, in a criminal case, the Court of Appeal (or the Divisional Court) must certify that the case is one raising a point of law of general public importance. To this extent it is harder to appeal in a criminal than in a civil case, since there is no equivalent requirement in civil cases. The Runciman Royal Commission on Criminal Justice recommended that the requirement of this certificate be abolished (p 178, para 79), but this was not implemented.

(b) Appeals by the prosecution

Normally the prosecution has no right of appeal against an acquittal, but there were two exceptions. One was in regard to an appeal on a point of law by way of case stated from the magistrates' court to the Divisional Court. If the prosecution are successful, the result of such an appeal is that the case can be sent back to the magistrates with a direction to convict or to reconsider the matter in the light of the Divisional Court's ruling on the point of law. But where the prosecution applies instead for an order of judicial review to quash an acquittal for some breach of natural justice or lack of jurisdiction, there is no power to do this unless the original trial can be held to have been a total nullity. (See *R v Dorking Justices, ex p Harrington* [1983] 3 All ER 29, applying *R v Middlesex Quarter Sessions Chairman, ex p DPP* [1952] 2 QB 758, in which the court held that nothing could be done when the trial judge quite wrongly told the jury that it 'was a complete waste of their time to listen to the prosecution evidence' and invited them to acquit, which they did. (See WT West, 'Wrongful Acquittals', *Justice of the Peace*, 8 October 1983, p 647.)

Until 1972 there was no right for the prosecution to appeal from acquittals in the Crown Court but the Criminal Justice Act of that year gave the prosecution a limited right of appeal. Section 36 provided for appeals to the Court of Appeal by the Attorney-General in a case tried on indictment where the defendant has been acquitted. The section limits such appeals to points of law. The result of the appeal does not, however, affect the outcome of the trial. For a comment on the section, see DJ Stephens, 'In Jeopardy' (1972) *Criminal Law Review*, p 361, and J Jaconelli, 'Attorney-General's References– a Problematic Device' (1981) *Criminal Law Review*, p 543.

Lord Widgery said, in *A-G's Reference (No 1 of 1975)* [1975] 3 WLR 11 at 13, that the procedure should be used exclusively' for short but important points which require a quick ruling of this court before a potentially false decision of law has too wide a circulation in the courts'. After the Court of Appeal have given their view they can refer the point to the House of Lords if they believe the point ought to be considered by the House. But there is no power to refer theoretical questions of law (*A-G's Reference (No 4 of 1979)* (1980) 71 Cr App Rep 341).

In October 1987, at the Conservative Party Conference, the Home Secretary announced that he had decided to give the Attorney-General a right of appeal against overly lenient sentences which *would* have an effect on the disposition of the actual case. This intention was carried into effect by s 36 of the Criminal Justice Act 1988. See S Shute, 'Prosecution Appeals Against Sentence', 57 *Modern Law Review*, 1994, pp 745–72.

Only the Attorney-General can activate this new power and it also requires the leave of the Court of Appeal. The Solicitor-General told the House of Commons in 2003 that in the previous fourteen years 845 cases had been referred to the Court of Appeal, and 606 had resulted in the sentence being increased. On average the Attorney referred just under half the cases that were sent to him. (House of Commons, *Hansard*, vol 402, 24 March 2003, col 23WA.)

The Royal Commission on Criminal Justice recommended that where a person is convicted of conspiracy to pervert the course of justice by 'jury nobbling' in a case which led to an acquittal, the prosecution should be entitled to restart the case against the acquitted defendant (p 177, para 74). Section 54 of the Criminal Procedure and Investigations Act 1996 gave the High Court the power to quash the conviction if satisfied that the acquittal would not have occurred had it not been for the interference with or intimidation of the jury.

The Royal Commission rejected the suggestion that the prosecution should have a right to appeal against a perverse verdict or where a defendant was acquitted, (or convicted on a less serious charge) as a result of an error by a prosecution witness. ('We have every sympathy for the victims and families of victims in such cases, especially where they have suffered bereavement or injury. We believe, however, that the right answer is for the investigating and prosecuting authorities to prepare their cases thoroughly' (p 177, para 76).)

As was seen above, Lord Justice Auld proposed that there should be legislation to provide that juries may not give perverse acquittals. He did not however go so far as to propose that the prosecution be given a right to appeal against a perverse verdict.

Appeals against terminating rulings The Criminal Justice Bill 2002-2003, Part 9 gave the prosecution the right to appeal against a ruling by a Crown Court judge that there is no case to answer or any other ruling that terminates the trial made at a pre-trial hearing or during the trial at any stage before its end. This includes not only rulings that are terminating in themselves but also those that are so serious a blow to the prosecution that, in the absence of a right of appeal, it would offer no or no further evidence.

The provisions are based on recommendations first proposed by the Law Commission.[20] They also had the support of Lord Justice Auld[21] Leave to appeal must be obtained either from the judge or the Court of Appeal. A ruling effectively acquitting the defendant will not take effect while the prosecution decides whether to appeal, and, if an appeal is pursued, until it is concluded. Both the prosecution and the defence have the right to appeal to the House of Lords on a point of law of general public importance.

But should the prosecution have the right to appeal if solid new evidence comes to light after an acquittal suggesting that the accused was in fact guilty?

ABOLITION OF THE DOUBLE JEOPARDY RULE

It has for centuries been a generally accepted principle that a person should not be put in peril of conviction twice for the same offence. The principle is expressed in the ancient common law doctrine of *autrefois acquit*, better known as the rule against double jeopardy.

Recently, largely stimulated by the Stephen Lawrence case, the question was raised whether the rule against double jeopardy should be curtailed. In 1999 the Macpherson Report on the Stephen Lawrence case recommended that consideration be given to giving the Court of Appeal the power to permit prosecution appeals after acquittal where 'fresh and viable' evidence is presented.[22] In 1999/2000 the Home Affairs Committee of the House of Commons recommended that the double jeopardy rule should be relaxed where there is new evidence that makes an acquittal unsafe and also where the offence carries a life sentence and the Attorney-General considers it to be in the public interest for the conviction to be quashed.[23] In March 2001 the Law Commission in its report *Double Jeopardy and Prosecution Appeals* recommended that in murder cases[24] the Court of Appeal should be given power to set aside an acquittal where there was apparently reliable and compelling new evidence of guilt and it was in the interests of justice to do so.

---

[20] See *Prosecution Appeals Against Judges' Rulings*, Law Comm. Consultation Paper, No.158, 2000; and final report *Double Jeopardy and Prosecution Appeals*, Report No.267, 2001.For critical comment on the Consultation Paper see R Pattenden, 'Prosecution Appeals Against Judges' Rulings' [2000] *Criminal Law Review*, 971-86.

[21] Chapter 12, pp 634-35.

[22] *Report of an Inquiry into the Stephen Lawrence case* by Lord Macpherson of Cluny, Cm 4262, 1999, Recommendation 38.

[23] 3rd Report of the 1999-2000 session, paras 39-41 and 21-24.

[24] In its earlier consultation paper, at para 5.29, it had proposed that the power should apply to all cases in which the sentence would be likely to be at least three years' imprisonment.

Lord Justice Auld in his Report in October 2001 agreed with the Law Commission's recommendation but proposed that it should be extended to 'other grave offences punishable with life and/or long terms of imprisonment as Parliament might specify'. ('Why should an alleged violent rapist or robber, who leaves his victim near dead. . . not be answerable to the law in the same way as an alleged murderer?' (ch 12, para 60, p 633).)

The Law Commission proposed that the personal consent of the DPP should be required for an application to quash an acquittal. Auld agreed but urged that the DPP's consent should also be required for the reopening of an investigation after an acquittal.

The White Paper *Justice for All* (July 2002) signalled that the Government intended to implement these recommendations and outlined the detailed shape of the intended legislation (paras 4-63-66). The proposals were incorporated in Part 10 of the Criminal Justice Bill 2002/03. Part 10 was debated in the Committee stage in the House of Lords for just under three hours on 17 July. But no amendment was tabled and there was no vote, though the principle was strongly opposed, notably by Baroness (Helena) Kennedy QC (see p 636 below). She promised to table an amendment on Report in September when the debate on Part 10 was to be resumed.

The Criminal Justice Bill 2002/03

- The provisions affect a person who has been acquitted of a qualifying offence (or its equivalent) anywhere in the world except Scotland[25]
- The provision is retrospective and therefore applies to acquittals that occurred before the Act (cl 69(6)). This was the subject of considerable criticism in the Committee stage debate in the Lords on 17 July.
- 'Qualifying offences', are listed in Part 1 of Sch 4 (set out over three-and-a-half pages). They are all offences carrying a maximum sentence of life imprisonment and which according to the Explanatory Notes accompanying the Bill (para 279) 'have a particularly serious impact either on the victim or on society more generally'. The length of the list was subjected to fierce criticism in the debate on the Committee stage of the Bill in the Lords on 17 July.
- The prosecutor may apply to the Court of Appeal for an order quashing an acquittal and permitting a retrial for the 'qualifying offence' (cl 70 (1)).
- Such an application requires the personal written consent of the DPP (cl 70 (2)).
- The DPP can only give his consent if satisfied both that the requirements of s 72 as to there being new and compelling evidence (below) are met and that it is in the public interest (cl 70 (4)).
- Such an application can only be made once (cl 70 (5))
- The requirement for making an order is that there is 'new and compelling evidence' that the acquitted person is guilty of the qualifying offence (cl 72 (1)).

[25] Cls 69 (1),(4),(5) and 89. Scotland is excluded because the Scottish devolved executive decided not adopt this modification of the double jeopardy rule.

- The test whether the evidence is 'new' is merely that it was not adduced in the trial leading to the acquittal.[26] It was repeatedly urged in the House of Lords debate on 17 July that this definition of 'new' was unacceptably broad and that it should be narrowed to include only evidence that was genuinely new since the acquittal. The Attorney-General's reply was that in considering whether to give permission for a retrial under cl 73 the Court of Appeal was required to consider to what extent the evidence was new and whether there was any lack of diligence on the part of the police or the prosecution either in the original trial or in the new proceedings – see col 1082.

- Evidence is 'compelling' if it is reliable, substantial and if, 'in the context of the outstanding issues, it appears highly probative of the case against the acquitted person' (cl 72 (3)). The 'outstanding issues' are the issues in dispute in the proceedings' (cl 72 (4)).

- It is irrelevant whether evidence is admissible or inadmissible (cl 72 (5)).

- The interests of justice test must be determined having regard in particular to (a) whether existing circumstances make a fair trial unlikely; (b) the length of time since the offence was committed; (c) whether it is likely that the new evidence would have been available at the time of the original proceedings but for a failure by an officer or prosecutor to act with due diligence; (d) whether an officer or prosecutor has failed to act with due expedition since the new evidence became available (cl 73).

- The person concerned is entitled to be present at the hearing of the application (cl 74 (4)).

- If it thinks it necessary or expedient, the Court of Appeal can order the production of any document or order any witness who would be a compellable witness to attend for examination (cl 74 (6)).

- Reporting restrictions aimed at ensuring that there can be a fair trial can only be sought by the DPP or they can be imposed by the court of its own motion. The court will decide what, if any, restrictions are required and their content and duration. (cl 76).

- An acquitted person may only be retried on an indictment preferred by the direction of the Court of Appeal. Such arraignment must be within two months of the order for a retrial unless the court allows a longer period (cl 77(1), (2)).

- Re-opening an investigation after an acquittal requires the written consent of the DPP. (cl 78(2)(b)) A reinvestigation for these purposes means arrest or questioning the acquitted person, searching him or premises owned or occupied by him, searching a vehicle owned by him, seizing anything in his possession or taking his fingerprints or a bodily sample from him (cl 78(2), (3)). ('This provides a safeguard against any potential harassment of acquitted persons. The requirement for the DPP's consent is not intended to hamper the police making other enquiries which do not directly impact on the life of the individual, for

---

[26] Cl 72(2). When the Bill was first published it was 'new' if it was 'not available or known to an officer or prosecutor at or before the time of the acquittal' (original cl 65(2)).

example by interviewing new or previous witnesses, or comparing fingerprint or DNA samples with records which they already hold' (Explanatory Notes to the Bill, para 299).). The DPP can only give his consent if he is satisfied that there is sufficient new evidence already, or that such new evidence is likely to come to light if the investigation goes ahead (cl 78 (6)).

- If urgent action is needed to prevent an investigation being substantially and irrevocably prejudiced or to prevent death or serious injury it is permitted provided it is authorised by an officer of the rank of superintendent or above (cl 79). ('Urgent action may be needed in cases where new evidence is found during the course other investigations, or where information provided to the police indicates that new evidence is at a particular location' (Explanatory Notes, para 303).).
- A person may be arrested under warrant issued by a magistrate on suspicion of a qualifying offence. A charge for such an offence requires the decision of a superintendent. (cl 80 (1), (3)).
- He must be brought before the Crown Court within 24 hours (excluding Sundays, bank holidays etc) and can then be remanded on bail or in custody for up to 42 days, which can be extended on application (cl 81).
- Prosecutorial decisions in such cases must be taken by the DPP personally, unless he is unavoidably absent in which case he may nominate someone to act in his place.(cl 85)

Needless to say, these proposals were extremely controversial. For two articles written before the Bill was published see Ian Dennis, 'Rethinking Double Jeopardy: Justice and Finality in the Criminal Process' [2000]*Criminal Law Review*, 933-51 and Paul Roberts, 'Justice for All? Two bad arguments [and several good suggestions] for resisting double jeopardy reform' (2002) 6 *International Journal of Evidence and Proof*, 197-217.

In the House of Lords Committee Stage debate on 17 July 2003 a powerful speech against the proposal was made by Baroness (Helena) Kennedy QC:

We are talking about a rule of constitutional importance which is recognised throughout the common law world and even beyond. . . . In denying the principle, we are creating something new. In murder trials and in other serious trials, we are creating the conditional acquittal. I want the Committee to think seriously about that. A person who stands trial will not be able to leave the court building sighing with relief. . . .

[0]ne of the problems is that, in the contemporary world, it is not just the policeman who can put his hand on one's shoulder; the press can do it too. When a man or woman steps out of a courtroom acquitted in a particular kind of case, a campaign will immediately be mounted to have that person brought back before the court. That is a terrible thing to visit on our system. There is a risk that disappointed investigators, particularly in high profile cases, will

wish to recommence investigations immediately after an acquittal, especially if there is pressure from the media, from victims and their families, who will have a higher expectation, and from politicians who want to jump on the bandwagon. Those with previous convictions known to the investigating officer would also be a target. Officers with a personal animus against an accused may wish to pursue him, despite an acquittal. That is a worrying thing to introduce into our system. (cols 1061-62)

Although a variety of amendments were moved in the Lords Committee Stage debate in respect of the proposal, the front benches of the two main Opposition parties having indicated that they would not vote against it, the amendments were all withdrawn and the Committee stood adjourned for two months for the summer recess.

(c) Practice and procedure of appeals

An appeal was formerly said to be by way of rehearing. But with one exception this did not mean what it appeared to mean. The exception was an appeal from the magistrates' court to the Crown Court, where the case started (and still starts) afresh with all the witnesses as if it had never been heard before. (As was seen above, Lord Justice Auld recommended that this form of appeal should be abolished.[27] But the recommendation was rejected by the Government.)

In all other cases the appeal court heard the appeal on the basis of the decision below. In other words, the appellant argued that something went wrong in the court below and for that purpose he would normally have to show what did happen – by producing the judgment which he claimed was wrong in law, or by having a transcript of the whole or part of the proceedings below to show that, for instance, the decision was against the weight of the evidence or that some impropriety had occurred. Occasionally, but very rarely indeed, the Court of Appeal was prepared to listen to witnesses, but only if they were new and then only in exceptional circumstances. Otherwise, testimony was presented to the appeal court via the written word through the transcript of the trial or a note of the proceedings taken by the judge, the lawyers or the court clerk.

Under the former Rules of the Supreme Court, the Court of Appeal had 'all the authority and jurisdiction of the court or tribunal from which the appeal was brought' and the power 'to give any order which ought to have been given or made, and to make such further order as the case may require'.[28] Its powers meant that the Court of Appeal was indeed a court of appeal – as opposed to what in continental systems is called a court of cassation where the court basically has to reach its decision on the basis of the findings of fact of the court below and may not even have the power to

---

[27] Chapter 12, p 622.
[28] Supreme Court Act 1981, s 15(3); RSC Ord 59, rr 10(1), (3).

substitute its own decision so that it can only quash the decision and send the case back for a new start.[29]

Under the new rules for appeals that came into force in May 2000 (Part 52 of the CPR), there is still reference to re-hearing[30] but this form of appeal is now relegated to a secondary position by the new rule that, subject to two exceptions, 'every appeal will be limited to a review of the decision of the lower court'.[31] The exceptions are where a Practice Direction makes different provisions[32] and, secondly, where 'the court considers that in the circumstances of an individual appeal it would be in the interests of justice to hold a re-hearing'.

The intention apparently was that 'review' is to be different from, and probably something more limited than, 'rehearing'. The question is what is that difference and, in particular, does an appeal court, and especially the Court of Appeal, retain the previous power to reach its own decision in regard to all, or any aspect of, the case? An appeal court still has all the powers of the lower court[33] including the power to 'affirm, set aside or vary any judgment or order made or given by the lower court'[34], to receive oral evidence or evidence which was not before the lower court if it so orders[35], and to draw any inference of fact which it considers justified on the evidence.[36]

So in what way does the new power of revision differ from the previous power to rehear? It has been argued that 'rehearing' should now be confined to the rare case of a real rehearing of the entire case whereas 'revision' should be used in relation to all the other powers of the Court.[37] If this is correct not much will have changed. It seems more likely that the intention was to effect a significant change but mainly in regard to interlocutory appeals. In *Tanfern Ltd* (above) Lord Justice Brooke, having set out the new CPR provisions stating that as a general rule every appeal will be limited to a review of the decision below (CPR 52.11(1)), went on:

29   That traditionally was the position in France though in modern times the Cour de Cassation does have the power to substitute its own decision thus blurring the distinction between appeal and cassation.

30   As opposed to 'rehearing' in the former rules – presumably a spelling change that was not intended to have significance.

31   CPR 52.11(1).

32   The most relevant provision of the Practice Direction is para 9.1 which requires a hearing if the appeal is from a minister, person or body who (1) did not hold a hearing to come to that decision or (2) held a hearing but the procedure did not provide for consideration of evidence.

33   CPR 52 10(1).

34   CPR 52.10(2)(a).

35   CPR 52.11(2). The rule now says that the court will *not* receive oral evidence or fresh evidence unless it so orders; the previous rule (RSC Ord 59, r 10(2)) said it should not do so except on special grounds.

36   CPR 52.11(4).

37   J A Jolowicz, 'The New Appeal: re-hearing or revision or what?' 20 *Civil Justice Quarterly* 2001, pp 7-12.

This marks a significant change in practice, in relation to what used to be called 'interlocutory' appeals from district judges or masters. Under the old practice, the appeal to a judge was a rehearing in the fullest sense of the word, and the judge exercised his/her discretion afresh, while giving appropriate weight to the way the lower court had exercised its discretion in the matter. Under the new practice, the decision of the lower court will attract much greater significance, The appeal court's duty is now limited to a review of that decision, and it may only interfere in the quite limited circumstances set out in r 52.11(3). [at para 31]

On the difference between 'review' and 're-hearing' see also *Assicurazioni Generali Spa v Arab Insurance Group (BSC)* [2002] EWCA Civ 1642, [2003] 1 WLR 577, per Clarke LJ para 6 and Ward LJ para 193.

There are several peculiarities of the appeal system which should be noted.

(I) THE PROCEDURE FOR CIVIL APPEALS TO THE COURT OF APPEAL

Applying for leave

Where an application for leave to appeal reaches the Court of Appeal, Civil Division the way it was handled depended on whether it was prepared by a lawyer or by a litigant in person. If the application was prepared by a lawyer, it was normally sent to a single Lord Justice who considered it on the papers, without a hearing. If he refused leave, the applicant had the right to renew the application to the full court where it was argued *ex parte* (in the absence of the other side) before two other Lords Justices. If the application was presented by a litigant in person, it could be dealt with in the same way or, alternatively, since litigants in person are more likely to renew their applications, it could be heard immediately in open court by two Lords Justices as a way of cutting out one stage.

The Bowman Committee proposed some changes. All applications for leave should be considered initially by a single Lord Justice. He could then do one of three things: l) allow the application on the papers; 2) decide to hear the application in open court either alone or with another Lord Justice; or, 3) if minded to refuse leave, to write to the applicant giving reasons but offering to hold an oral hearing. If the offer were not accepted within the time-limit, the application would be dismissed on the papers with no right of renewal. These proposals were adopted.

(2) THE PROCEDURE FOR CRIMINAL APPEALS TO THE COURT OF APPEAL

Applying for leave

All appeals require leave, which is usually sought from the Court of Appeal. Applications for leave are made to a single judge (normally a High Court judge) who deals with the matter by considering the papers only. There is no hearing. If he refuses leave, the applicant has the right to renew the application by asking for leave from the full court of three judges. This is at an actual hearing in open court, though usually neither the prosecution nor the applicant is present. It is very rare for leave to be given by the full court. If leave is given, quite frequently the hearing of the application is combined with the hearing of the appeal, counsel having been warned in advance to prepare themselves for the argument on the merits.

One unsatisfactory feature of the system is that, if the defendant is legally aided (most are),[38] his lawyers' duties cease after they have advised as to whether there are grounds of appeal and if so, have drafted them. The legal aid certificate does not cover advice as to whether to renew an application once it has been turned down by the single judge. Application for legal aid for the renewal hearing can however be made to the Registrar.

The Runciman Royal Commission (p 167, para 25) said this was a gap in the system which should be closed by providing that the original legal aid cover also the question of renewing the application after it has turned down by the single judge. But this recommendation was not implemented.

If leave to appeal is granted, the Registrar of Criminal Appeals prepares a summary of the appellant's case[39] and assigns counsel, usually the same barrister who appeared at the trial. The Registrar therefore has a dual function, as administrative officer of the court and in something like the role of instructing solicitor.

The success rate on a renewal to the full court, not surprisingly, is statistically much affected by whether the appellant is represented. Research for the Runciman Royal Commission showed that in 1989 there were 6,853 applications for leave to appeal considered by the single judge. The Criminal Appeal Office estimated that 95% of these were legally represented. (K Malleson, *Review of the Appeal Process*, Royal Commission on Criminal Justice, Research Study No 17, 1993, p 32.)

However, in a sample of cases between October and December 1990, only 22% of defendants who renewed their application from the single judge to the full court had counsel, but their success rate was 48% compared with only 15% of the much larger number without counsel. (Evidence of Lord Chancellor's Department to Runciman Royal Commission, Chap 4, Table 2.)

---

[38]   Currently around 95% of defendants in the Crown Court have legal aid and an unknown additional proportion are represented privately.

[39]   The summary, which can run to many pages, is prepared by lawyers employed by the Registrar or by barristers employed ad hoc. They do not make recommendations. Formerly these summaries were not seen by the appellant's lawyers, but shortly after he became Lord Chief Justice this was changed by Lord Taylor.

Time loss rules

The court can order that some of the time spent appealing not count toward the sentence, as a penalty for making a frivolous application. This threat acts powerfully on the minds of prisoners. In 1966 the grounds for quashing a conviction were altered and became more favourable to the appellant (see p 660 below). This resulted in a flood of new applications for leave to appeal, which were running at the rate of about 12,000 a year compared with about 2,000 in 1963. This caused an announcement to be made in 1970 by the Lord Chief Justice, Lord Parker that in future the power to order that time not count if the application was thought to be frivolous would be used more often (*Practice Note* [1970] 1 WLR 663). The announcement had an immediate and dramatic effect. The numbers of applications for leave went down by about half and remained at that lower figure of some 6,000 a year for several years.

Would-be appellants were reminded of the existence of the power in a further *Practice Note* in 1980 ([1980] 1 All ER 555). The warning was in fierce and forbidding terms: 'It may be expected that such a direction [ordering loss of time for a hopeless appeal] will normally be made unless the grounds are not only settled and signed by counsel, but also supported by the written opinion of counsel'.

What is not realised by prisoners is how rarely the power to order that time spent appealing should not count is exercised or that the power is limited to adding on 90 days to the sentence. An action against the UK Government under the European Convention on Human Rights challenging the legality of the power was rejected by the European Court in March 1987. The European Court of Human Rights was told that, although there were no statistics, loss of time was ordered in some 60 or so cases per year by the single judge or the full court. The normal order was for 28 days to be added on, though such orders ranged from 7 days to 64 days (*Case of Monnell and Morris*). In the nine month period from October 1990 to July 1991 only five such orders were made, each for 28 days. (Evidence of the Lord Chancellor's Department to the Runciman Royal Commission on Criminal Justice, Chap 6, para 6.1.)

Research conducted for the Runciman Royal Commission on Criminal Justice showed that there is a great deal of misinformation in the prisons about the time loss rules. Many prisoners are under the erroneous impression that *all* the time spent appealing can be added on by the Court of Appeal. (This error is less surprising when seen against the fact that many solicitors appeared to share the same misapprehension and that over half of all solicitors responding to the survey thought that the Court of Appeal still had the power to increase sentences which had been abolished twenty five years earlier in 1966.) A third of the sample of prisoners who did not appeal said the threat of time being added on had been the reason. (J Plotnikoff and R Woolfson, *Information and Advice for Prisoners about Grounds for Appeal and the Appeals Process*, Royal Commission Research Study No 18, 1993, pp 79–82.)

The Runciman Commission recommended that prisoners (and lawyers) be made aware of the true position. ('We think it wrong that appellants who spend several months awaiting appeal should be left with the impression that if they fail, those months will be added to their sentences. Nor should they have reason to fear that the Court of Appeal will increase their sentence' (pp 165-66, para 19).) It recommended that the Court of Appeal issue a new Practice Direction dealing with the issue and that the official guides issued by the Criminal Appeal Office, the Bar Council and the Law Society make matters clear, even though the result would be likely to be an increase in the number of applications for leave to appeal. ('We would regard it as an unavoidable result of correcting an important piece of misinformation common among prisoners' (ibid).) This recommendation has, however, not been acted upon.

The great majority of appeals are against sentence. In the years between 1992 and 2001 the number of applications for leave to appeal against conviction varied very little from a low of 1,943 to a high of 2,393; the number of applications for leave to appeal against sentence fluctuated in the same period between a low of 4,848 and a high of some 7,160. (*Judicial Statistics*, 2001, Table 1.7.) In 2001, of the applications for leave to appeal considered by a single judge, 28% were granted against conviction and 31% against sentence. Of those applications which were refused, 37% were renewed to the full court against conviction and 22% against sentence. Just over a third (35%) of the renewed applications against conviction and just under a third (32%) of those against sentence were successful. (*Judicial Statistics*, 2001, Table 1.7.)

Legal advice for appellants in criminal cases

The Criminal Justice Act 1967 introduced provisions regarding legal advice on the question of an appeal in cases where the accused is represented at the trial on legal aid. Under these provisions a defence barrister in a legally aided case must advise his client at the end of the case whether he has grounds of appeal, and if so, to draft those grounds. The procedure is set out in a pamphlet issued by the Criminal Appeal Office entitled *A Guide to Proceedings in the Court of Appeal, Criminal Division, 1997*– see [1997] 2 Cr App Rep 459 and the current edition of *Archbold Criminal Pleading Evidence & Practice*.(The Guide is also accessible on the web at www.courtservice.gov.uk/fandl/menu.crim.htm.) The procedure requires that counsel fill out a form right away at court which will tell the client whether it is thought that there are grounds of appeal or whether counsel needs time to consider the matter. He is required then to deliver written advice to the solicitor within 14 days, including where appropriate, signed grounds of appeal. The solicitors should send it on to the client so that he receives it within 21 days measured from his conviction or sentence.

Research done for the Runciman Royal Commission by J Plotnikoff and R Woolfson (*Information and Advice for Prisoners about Grounds for Appeal and the Appeals Process*) showed that in various respects this system was not functioning as it should. Thus 9% of prisoners said they had not been visited in the cells at the end of the case and 23% said they had been visited but an appeal had not been discussed. The Royal Commission said it regarded these as serious matters and called on both branches of the profession to 'take all necessary steps to ensure that practitioners not only perform their duty to see the client at the end of the case, as most do, but also give preliminary advice both orally and in writing' (pp 164–65, para 14).

Where it appears that the defendant has submitted his own grounds, the Criminal Appeal Office writes to the solicitors who acted at the trial to ask if advice was given. A survey of 67 'own ground' cases from July to September 1991 indicated that no advice had been given in 8 cases. This represented 12% of the 'own grounds' cases and 0.8% of all the cases received in that period (ibid, Chap 4, para 4.5).

(3) APPEALS BY WAY OF CASE STATED

An appeal may be brought against a decision of the magistrates' court on the ground that it is wrong in law or in excess of jurisdiction, by asking the magistrates to state a case to the Divisional Court (Magistrates' Courts Act 1980, s 111 (1)). This must be done within 21 days. There is no power to give an extension of time. In a criminal case the prosecution may ask for a case to be stated, as can the defence. The magistrates draw up a statement of the facts found, the cases cited, the decision and the issue for the consideration of the Divisional Court. If the appeal is based on the argument that there was no evidence on which the magistrates could have reached their decision, the case stated also includes a resumé of the evidence. The court supplies the parties with a draft of the case to be stated and invites their comments. In the event that a party is dissatisfied with the way in which the case has been put, he can apply to the Divisional Court asking for the case to be remitted to the magistrates for restatement of the facts. The magistrates can refuse to state a case on the grounds that it is a frivolous request. However an unreasonable refusal to state a case can be the subject of an application for judicial review – *Sunworld Ltd v Hammersmith and Fulham London Borough Council* [2000] 2 All ER 837, Div Ct.

(See generally A Murdie, 'Appeals by Case Stated from the Magistrates' Court', *Solicitors' Journal*, 6 October 1995, p 984; J A Backhouse, 'Right of Appeal by way of Case Stated–Should it be Simplified?', *Justice of the Peace*, 16 May, 1992, p 310.)

(4) LEAPFROG APPEALS

In 1969 a new procedure was devised to enable appeals to go direct from the High Court to the House of Lords in certain limited circumstances:

To the House of Lords

Administration of Justice Act 1969

s 12(3)–that a point of law of general public importance is involved in that decision and that that point of law either:

(a)　related wholly or mainly to the construction of an enactment or of a statutory instrument, and has been fully argued in the proceedings and fully considered in the judgment of the judge in the proceedings, or

(b)　is one in respect of which the judge is bound by a decision of the Court of Appeal or of the House of Lords in previous proceedings, and was fully considered in the judgments given by the Court of Appeal or the House of Lords (as the case may be) in those previous proceedings.. . .

The power has been used very little.

To the Court of Appeal, Civil Division

Where an appeal would otherwise be heard on appeal by the county court or the High Court it can be transferred direct to the Court of Appeal if the Master of the Rolls or the court from which the appeal is taken or the court to which the appeal is going considers that it raises an important point of principle or practice or 'there is some other compelling reason for the Court of Appeal to hear the case'.[40]

To the Court of Appeal, Criminal Division

Lord Justice Auld recommended in his Report that the leapfrog appeal be extended to criminal cases for use where there are conflicting decisions of the Court of Appeal that can only be resolved by the House of Lords (ch 12, para 117, p 657). This has not been implemented.

(5)　GENERAL

In the early 1960s a team of eminent English and American judges and lawyers spent a period in each other's countries studying the appeal system. The object was for each to assess the strengths and weaknesses of both systems. A member of the American team reported on the meeting (Delmar Karlen, 'Appeal in England and the United States', 78 *Law Quarterly Review*, 1962, p 371). What follows distils the main points of comparison at that time and (in editorial square brackets or footnotes) what has happened to the English system in the intervening 40 or more years. As will appear, although the English system has moved somewhat in the direction of the American, many of the differences identified then are still valid.

The decision

In the United States, almost all decisions are reserved and rendered in written form. Rarely is one pronounced from the bench. Furthermore, an attempt is always made to have the judges agree upon an opinion for the court as a whole, or, if that cannot be done, to secure as broad a base of agreement as possible.

---

[40]　Access to Justice Act 1999, s 57 and CPR 52.14.

While concurring opinions are not unusual and even multiple separate dissents not unknown, it is not expected that each judge will express his own views. The ideal is a unanimous opinion for the court, or, failing that, one majority opinion and one dissent.

[The English system is moving strongly in that direction. In his annual report for 2001-02, Lord Phillips MR said: 'It is now more common for a constitution of the Court to deliver a single judgment to which all members of the court have contributed. This is a trend which has my support. Profusion of precedent is the bain of judges and practitioners alike. A single judgment reduces the material that has to be read, avoids the opportunity for differences of interpretation and provides greater clarity.' (ed.)]

In England, few decisions are either reserved or written, in the Court of Appeal, the practice is for each judge to express his individual views orally and extemporaneously immediately upon the close of argument. In the Court of Criminal Appeal a single opinion for the court is customarily expressed, but almost always orally and extemporaneously. Only in the House of Lords and the Privy Council are decisions customarily reserved and written.

[This was the position in the Civil Division and remains the position in the Criminal Division. But the proportion of cases in which the decision is reserved in the Civil Division is now very considerable. The Bowman Report in 1997 said (p 90) the Court of Appeal reserved judgment in a quarter to a third of cases. The Master of the Rolls' annual report for 2001/02 showed that the proportion had risen to over half (54%). As the simpler appeals were dealt with by lower courts, the proportion of complex cases heard by the Court of Appeal in which it was necessary to reserve judgment was inevitably rising. (ed)]

The American approach entails different internal operating procedures than are usual in England. Conferences, both formal and informal, are a prominent feature of American practice. So are exchanges of memoranda and draft opinions. On the other hand, since reading and writing are by their nature solitary operations, American judges, who are compelled to do much of both, spend many, if not most, of their working hours alone. They are frequently required to shift their attention from one case to another and then back again, because, with cases being heard in batches, several are awaiting decision at any given time.

To the limited extent that the English practice conforms to the American pattern, the same internal procedures doubtless apply. In the great majority of English appeals, however, the judges follow a vastly different routine. Most of their working time is spent together sitting on the bench, listening and talking rather than reading and writing. The discussions they hold are brief and seemingly casual, although highly economical, by reason of the fact that cases are heard and decided one at a time. The judges' minds are already focused on the problems at hand and not distracted by other cases which have been heard and are awaiting decision. They whisper between themselves on the bench; they converse as they walk to and from the courtroom; and they indirectly make comments to each other as they carry on Socratic dialogues with counsel. But they do not ordinarily exchange memoranda or draft opinions or engage in full scale conferences.[41]

In short, the appellate judge in England spends most of his working time in open court, relatively little in chambers, whereas his counterpart in America spends most of his working time in chambers, and relatively little in open court. This is neatly illustrated by the times of sitting for comparable courts in the two nations. In the United States Court of Appeals for the Second Circuit, each judge hears arguments one week out of four, and uses the other three for studying written briefs and records on appeal, conferring with his brother judges, and writing opinions. By way of contrast, each judge on the English Court of Appeal hears arguments, day after day, five days a week, throughout each term.

[As has been seen, the English Court of Appeal judges now spend five writing days in a three-week period (ed)]

Supporting personnel

In the United States, most appellate judges have law clerks, sometimes more than one. These typically are young men, recently graduated from law school with fine academic records, who serve for a period of a year or two. They are chosen by and answerable to the judges, although paid out of public funds. The services they perform vary greatly from one judge to another, but in general they carry on research, prepare memoranda, discuss the cases to be decided with the judges for whom they work, and sometimes even draft opinions or parts of opinions to be rendered. They participate in the decisional process to the extent that their judges wish them to participate . . .

In England there are no law clerks.[42]

[Professor Karlen went on to make the point that since in the English system written briefs are not used, and most opinions are given extemporaneously at the close of oral argument, it was difficult to see what use law clerks would be in most English appellate courts. As will be seen, skeleton arguments – mini versions of the fully argued American written brief – are now an established part of the English system. But the majority of decisions of the Court of Appeal, Civil Division and the

---

41 See to like effect K Malleson, 'Decision-making in the Court of Appeal: the burden of proof in an inquisitorial process', *International Journal of Evidence and Proof*, vol 1, 1997, 175-86 (ed).

42 But, as has been seen, the Court of Appeal, Civil Division does now employ young judicial assistants. For a fascinating, and possibly disturbing, insider's description and critique of the way the justices of the US Supreme Court operate as seen by a former clerk, see E Lazarus, *Closed Chambers* (1999, Penguin) (ed).

overwhelming majority of the decisions of the Court of Appeal Criminal Division are still rendered extemporaneously at the end of the case. Judicial assistants are not generally used to work on the skeleton arguments (ed)]

Finality

In the United States, appellate decisions possess less finality. New trials can be granted in all types of cases, criminal as well as civil. Rehearings are frequently asked for and occasionally allowed. Existing side by side with appeals are a variety of methods of collateral attack, including habeas corpus, sometimes entailing successive re-examination of a single case by courts of coordinate jurisdiction.

Finally, the American doctrine of precedent is such that a decision is never beyond the reach of challenge in a new lawsuit. If conditions or thinking have changed, sometimes if only the personnel of the court has changed, there is always the possibility that the unwanted decision may be overruled.

[The difference between the two civil systems in this respect is even greater today than it was then, since the Court of Appeal has taken such strong action post-Bowman to reduce second appeals. As will be seen, retrials in criminal cases are not quite so rare today as they were then but they are still very rare. (ed)]

Oral argument

In the United States, oral arguments are secondary in importance to the briefs, and are rigidly limited in duration. In the United States Supreme Court, one hour is allowed to each side, but in many appellate courts, less time than that is permitted, frequently no more than fifteen minutes or a half-hour for each side. Reading by counsel is frowned upon. The judges do not wish to hear what they can read for themselves. They expect to get all the information they need about the judgment below, the evidence, and the authorities relied upon from studying the briefs and record on appeal. They do not even encourage counsel to discuss in detail the precedents claimed to govern the decision, preferring to do that job by themselves in the relative privacy of their chambers, with or without the assistance of law clerks.

In England, where there are no written briefs,[43] oral arguments are all-important. They are never arbitrarily limited in duration. While some last for only a few minutes, others go on for many days, even weeks. The only controls ordinarily exercised over the time of oral arguments are informal, *ad hoc* suggestions from the judges. Thus when counsel wishes to cite a case as authority, the presiding judge may ask him: for what proposition? If the judges indicate that they accept the proposition as stated, there is no need to read the case. Similarly if counsel has persuaded the judges on a certain point, they may

---

43   Written 'skeleton arguments' are, however, now required–see below (ed).

indicate that it is unnecessary for him to pursue it further. If counsel for the appellant, by the time he finishes his argument, has failed to persuade the court that the decision below should be reversed or modified, the court informs counsel for the respondent that it does not wish to hear from him at all, and proceeds forthwith to deliver judgment. Despite such controls as these, the time spent in England in oral arguments tends to be very much greater than that spent in the United States.

[As will be seen below, the English system does now make some attempts to restrict oral argument but so far at least they have not gone far. The basic difference between the system is still very great indeed. (ed)]

Various steps have been taken to improve the efficiency of the Court of Appeal. One is to pay vastly more attention to getting the parties to prepare the bundle of documents for the court in proper form.(See Practice Direction 39PD 3, para 3.2.) Another is to have the judges pre-read so that when the oral argument commences the judges, supposedly, will be able to focus on the important issues.

(6)   SKELETON ARGUMENTS

The beginnings of the skeleton argument were in a Practice Note issued by Lord Donaldson, the then Master of the Rolls in 1983 – [1983] 2 All ER 34. These should consist of numbered points which counsel intended to argue, stated in not more than one or two sentences together with full references to be used in support of each point. It should also contain, he added, anything that would otherwise have to be dictated to the bench such as propositions of law, chronologies of events, lists of *dramatis personae* or, where necessary glossaries of terms. No one would be held to the contents of such a document. The document should, however, be sent to the court (and the other side) well before the hearing or, at the latest, when counsel rose. (See [1983] 2 All ER 34.)

A somewhat similar development had in fact already taken place in the House of Lords. In 1982 in *MV Yorke Motors v Edwards* [1982] 1 All ER 1024, Lord Diplock set out what the House of Lords would in future require by way of written documents in a case. Previously the case presented by the parties would contain a summary of the facts, the proceedings in the courts below, the judgments and the arguments on appeal. But now Lord Diplock said that the case should start 'with a statement of what the party conceives to be the issues that arise on the appeal' (p 1025). Counsel should bear in mind that the members of the appellate committee would have read the judgments below. Each issue should be mentioned in a sentence or two. If there were points that it was not intended to pursue, this should be stated; conversely, if it was intended to take a point that was not argued below, the case should mention the fact. If there was an intention to ask the House of Lords not to follow one of its own previous decisions this should be made clear. Heads of argument should be prepared, setting out the chief authorities to be relied on. Lord Diplock said that it was not intended to move towards the American written brief. Counsel for one side had put in a document of 39 pages, which was far too long. Counsel for the other side had put in one a sixth of that length, which was perfectly adequate.

For a powerful critique of the innovation of skeleton arguments see FA Mann, 'Reflections on English Civil Justice and the Rule of Law', 2 *Civil Justice Quarterly*, 1983, p 320. But Dr Mann notwithstanding, skeleton arguments are here to stay. What started as an experiment with a voluntary system became mandatory in 1989. The rule is now stated in the Practice Direction accompanying CPR r 52.4. The post-CPR White Book states that paragraphs 5.10 and 5.11 of the Practice Direction 'replace voluminous earlier practice directions concerning skeleton arguments'. They should be succinct: 'The practice of drafting diffuse skeleton arguments (which some advocates favoured under the former regime) is not appropriate'.[44]

Since 1999 the rule has been that the skeleton argument must be presented with the application for permission to appeal, failing which within 14 days thereafter. The new approach was criticised by David Pannick QC (*The Times*, 26 January 1999). He argued that it would be wasteful for counsel to prepare a skeleton argument many months before the hearing of the appeal. A skeleton prepared so long in advance would lack quality and focus. Also, the lawyers would have to prepare the case twice – once to draft the skeleton argument and again for the actual appeal hearing. Lord Woolf replying, (*The Times*, 2 February 1999) said early presentation of the skeleton was vital if the court was to be able to take the necessary case management decisions.

(7) RESTRICTIONS ON ORAL ARGUMENT—WILL THE COURT OF APPEAL EVENTUALLY ADOPT AMERICAN PRACTICE?

One of the features of American appellate practice, as has been seen, is drastic restriction of oral argument. This has not yet come to the English system. Despite the requirement of skeleton arguments, counsel are still permitted to argue their case at length–indeed basically at the length that *they* think appropriate.

In 1991 an American scholar, Professor Robert Martineau spent three months in the Court of Appeal, Civil Division to study the English oral tradition. He started with the hypothesis that the American system could probably learn much from the English. He ended with the opposite conclusion. Moreover, he was not overly impressed with the quality of the oral advocacy he observed. ('Most English barristers are not effective appellate advocates.') The situation in England seemed to him to be pretty much the same as in the USA. In both countries, he thought, 15% of appellate advocates were highly competent, 30 to 40% were competent and 50 to 60% were incompetent. (*Appellate Justice in England and the United States*, William Hein, 1991; and see an article based on the book by the present writer–'A Brief Encounter', *New Law Journal*, 12 April 1991, p 491.)

[44] *Civil Procedure*, 2003, 52.4.3.

The chief step taken so far towards limited oral argument in the Court of Appeal has been a rule that counsel is required to give an estimate of time for the case. There are no penalties as yet for overrunning–but maybe this could become the basis of a form of control over the length of oral argument. There is, however, little sign of much appetite for this among English judges. Martineau found that even judges who have pre-read the papers generally leave counsel to develop his oral argument in his own way and at his own length, out of belief in the virtues of the oral tradition. This was confirmed in a paper by Lord Justice Leggatt written for the Anglo-American judicial exchange in 1994, published in *Civil Justice Quarterly*, January 1995 at p 11, under the title 'The Future of the Oral Tradition in the Court of Appeal'. He acknowledged that skeleton arguments help by telling the judges what appeals are about before they start but 'it sometimes effects little perceptible saving of time, because counsel are suffered to repeat orally what they have already rendered in writing' (pp 12–13). That some presiding judges allowed that to happen was 'another example of the oral tradition dying hard'. He suggested that the court was in that respect falling between two stools because skeleton arguments (which were sometimes of inordinate length) were required, yet oral argument essentially was open-ended. The Practice Direction required counsel to open his appeal by going directly to the ground of appeal in the forefront of the appellant's case but this enjoinder was not always obeyed.

Lord Justice Leggatt said that 'immoderate periods of time are spent in informing the courts about the facts and the law, as distinct from presenting the critical reasons why they support the cause of the one side or the other' (p 14). In 1954 there had been eight Lords Justices, in 1974, 16 and in 1994 there were 29. Yet the delays increased. The average time taken from setting down to judgment had lately risen to an average of 8.4 months from an average between 1985 and 1994 of 7.3 months. It was clear, he suggested, that the only alternative to increasing the number of judges was to reduce the time taken to resolve appeals. 'That can only be done by reversing the traditional practice of allowing counsel to state how long they want and substituting a system whereby the court stipulates the length of time for which counsel shall be permitted to address the court' (p 15).

In 1986 the Commercial Court had introduced a table of the periods for which particular kinds of application would be allowed to last, unless counsel had previously obtained permission to take more time.(See now *Admiralty and Commercial Courts Guide* F10.[45]) This worked well and more time was only rarely sought. It was the experience of commercial judges that 'competent counsel can on demand tailor their submissions to take no longer than a stipulated period of time, however short' (ibid).

> Not only can counsel adapt to the time available, but unless the curtailment is too drastic, the quality of the argument will almost always be improved. Increase in the intensity of oral argument may reasonably be expected to increase its quality. The best counsel are invariably concise; lesser counsel

[45]   The White Book, *Civil Procedure*, 2003, vol 2, 2A-93.

would usually be better if they were so. That they are not concise is mainly due to lack of the discipline that limitations of time impose (ibid).

Lord Justice Leggatt said that, although he had no statistics on the matter, it was comparatively uncommon for members of the court to change their minds about whether to allow or to dismiss an appeal once they had read the skeleton arguments. There was no reason to suppose that the judges would change their minds less often if speeches were shorter.

In ordinary cases the appellant's solicitors must lodge an estimate of time needed for the hearing, signed by counsel. A copy must be sent to the respondent who then has the opportunity of disagreeing the time estimate. Failure to do so is taken as acceptance of the proposed time-limit. Any revised time estimate must be lodged with the court, signed by the advocate concerned.

Since 1991 the House of Lords too has required that counsel should notify the Judicial Office how many hours were needed for argument and broadly expects them to keep within that estimate (*Procedure Direction* [1991] 3 All ER 608).

See also the Patent Court *Practice Direction* [1998] 3 All ER 372 which required the parties to give estimates of time needed for the trial and for the judge to read the papers before the hearing. Parties were reminded of 'the court's power to impose guillotines on the duration of submissions and cross-examination'. This power, the Practice Direction warned, 'will be exercised in any case where it is of the view that a case is not being conducted with reasonable expedition' (para 21).

The Bowman Committee said in its 1997 Report that although it did not favour the drastic American approach to time-limits for oral argument it did think that 'there is a greater need to impose appropriate time-limits for individual appeals' (p 88). But it did not wish 'to see counsel being prevented from making relevant submissions because they are abruptly cut off in mid-sentence' (p 89).

The Court of Appeal today The message given in the Master of the Rolls' annual report for the legal year 2001-2002 was distinctly upbeat. The number of appeals outstanding at 703 was approaching half the figure of only four years before and was the lowest figure in the modern history of the Court. CPR Part 52 and the Access to Justice Act 1999 (Destination of Appeals) Order 2000 had resulted in a marked decrease in the number of interlocutory appeals filed from the QBD and the county court. County court interlocutory appeals, for instance, went from 161 in 1998/99 to a mere 39 in 2001/02. On the other hand, commercial final appeals had gone up in the same period from 22 to 70. Almost three in four applications for permission to appeal were dealt with within four months of being filed and 88% were disposed of within six months. Many cases involving children were dealt with within a month. As to the actual appeals, almost 30% were disposed of within four months and nearly two-third (62.5%) within eight months. Only 10% of appeals were not disposed of within a year of being filed.

(d)   The grounds of appeal

An appeal can be brought on a variety of grounds. In a civil case it can be on fact or law, on the amount of damages, on the wrong exercise by the trial court of a discretion, or an allegation that the court exceeded its jurisdiction.

In a criminal case the appeal can be against conviction or sentence. If the appeal is against conviction, it can be either on the facts (that the court or the jury reached the wrong result), on a point of law, on a question of mixed fact and law, or on any other ground which appears sufficient (Criminal Appeal Act 1968, s 1(2)(b)).

Mistakes of counsel Generally the Court of Appeal takes the position that it will not entertain an appeal on the ground that counsel at the trial made a mistake–*Gautam* [1988] Crim LR 109. But if the advocate was flagrantly incompetent that might be a ground of appeal–*Ensor* [1989] 1 WLR 497; *Crabtree, Foley, McCann* [1992] Crim LR 65.

In *Clinton* [1993] 2 All ER 998 the Court of Appeal went further. It quashed a conviction because defence counsel had failed to call the defendant at the trial and as a result the jury had had no evidence about differences between the defendant's appearance and the victim's description of the assailant. Where counsel's conduct rendered the verdict unsafe or unsatisfactory the court would not seek to assess the qualitative value of counsel's alleged incompetence but would seek to assess its effect on the trial and the verdict.

Again, in *Boal* [1992] 3 All ER 177 the Court of Appeal quashed a conviction even though Boal had pleaded guilty and even though his counsel had not been guilty of flagrantly incompetent advocacy. Mr Boal had been deprived of what was in all likelihood a good defence in law–that he was not liable as manager of a body corporate for offences under the Fire Precautions Act. See also *Irwin* [1987] 2 All ER 1085 (conviction quashed where defence counsel decided not to call alibi witnesses without consulting the defendant) and *Ahluwalia* [1992] 4 All ER 889 (conviction of murder quashed and retrial ordered to permit defence of diminished responsibility to be run. It was not clear why this possibility had been overlooked at trial).

The Runciman Royal Commission recommended that the Court of Appeal's attitude to errors by counsel be based (as suggested in *Clinton*) by its effect rather than on the degree of incompetence. ('It cannot possibly be right that there should be defendants serving prison sentences for no other reason than that their lawyers made a decision which later turns out to have been mistaken. What matters is not the degree to which the lawyers were at fault but whether the particular decision, whether reasonable or unreasonable, caused a miscarriage of justice' (p 174, para 59).)

Nevertheless in November 1994 in *Driver* (No 93/1492/W5) the court again emphasised the need to demonstrate that counsel was guilty of 'flagrantly incompetent advocacy' as stated in *Ensor* and ten days earlier in *Ali and Charlton* (No 91/1863/SI) a differently constituted Court of Appeal, Criminal Division said that instances where counsel's conduct could form the basis of an appeal 'must be wholly exceptional'.

In December 1995 the Court of Appeal in *Satpal Ram* (1995) Times, 7 December went further still. The court rejected the defendant's appeal against his conviction for murder. At his trial he had been advised by counsel to base his defence on provocation when self-defence was a conceivable alternative. The court said that there seemed to be an increasing tendency to believe that it was only necessary to assert the fault of trial counsel to sustain an argument that the conviction was unsafe or unsatisfactory. Whether that was due to a mistaken interpretation of the observations on that subject by the Royal Commission on Criminal Justice their Lordships did not know, but they did see far- reaching implications in the Commission's suggestion that even a reasonable decision of counsel could be the cause of a miscarriage of justice. The court could not countenance a case in which the defendant was serving a prison sentence for no other reason than a mistake on counsel's part but equally, where counsel's judgment had been reasonable, there was a strong public interest that the legal process should not be indefinitely prolonged on the ground for example that a defendant's case advanced within a different framework might have stood a greater chance of success. 'It was easy, as Lucretius had observed, to stand on the safety of the shore and pass judgment on the work of those battling against the wind and waves in a high sea.' But see *Scollan and Smith* [1999] Crim LR 566 and *Boodam v The State* [2002] Crim LR 524.

The approach adopted by the European Court of Human Rights is based on the question – was the defendant deprived of his right to a fair trial? See Commentary on *Nangle* [2002] Crim LR 506, 507.

For a review of the English and Scottish cases see Neil Gow, 'Flagrant Incompetency" of Counsel', *New Law Journal*, 29 March 1996, p 453; Robert S Shiels, 'Blaming the Lawyer' [1997] *Criminal Law Review*, 740-44.

Only one appeal

In *Pinfold* [1988] 2 All ER 217 it was held that an appellant only had a right to appeal once. The court had no jurisdiction to hear a second appeal–even on the grounds of fresh evidence. The only recourse for the defendant then was to ask the Home Secretary to refer the case back to the Court of Appeal under his powers under s 17 of the Criminal Appeal Act and is now to try to get the Criminal Cases Review Commission (CCRC, see pp 690-96 below) to do so.

It has been held that when the CCRC refers a case back to the Court of Appeal, the court is not bound by the decision in *Pinfold* and in exceptional circumstances it can therefore reconsider an issue that it has previously determined – *Thomas* [2002] EWCA Crim 941, [2002] Crim LR 912; *Wallace Duncan Smith (No 3)* [2002] EWCA Crim 2907, [2003] 1 Cr App Rep 648; *Mills (No 2), Poole (No 2)* (2003) Times, 26 June.

(e) Powers of the Court of Appeal

(1) COURT OF APPEAL, CIVIL DIVISION

The Court of Appeal can make any order which could have been made in the court below and substitute its own decision as to liability, quantum of damages or costs. It is not limited to points raised in the notice of appeal. It can, though it rarely does, take further points itself, for instance as to the illegality of a contract.

The court can order a retrial. Where the court is considering an award of damages by a jury, however, it had no power to substitute its own award for that of the jury unless the parties consented (which generally they did). Absent such consent, it had to order a retrial. However, the Courts and Legal Services Act 1990, s 8, gave a power for rules to be made to permit the court to change the amount of damages.[46] Usually, the Court of Appeal intervenes to reduce damages but it can equally increase them. (For a rare example see *Clark v Chief Constable of Cleveland Constabulary* [1999] 21 LS Gaz R 38 when the court increased an award of damages for malicious prosecution from £500 to £2,000.)

(2) COURT OF APPEAL, CRIMINAL DIVISION

The Court of Appeal, Criminal Division can quash a conviction or reduce a sentence. Since 1966 it has not had the power to increase sentences–though this power is still exercisable by the Crown Court when it hears appeals from the magistrates' courts. The Court of Appeal also has a right to order a retrial.

(f) The grounds for allowing appeals

(1) CIVIL CASES

Pre-CPR

Under the former system there was no rule in either statute or the rules of court as to the grounds for allowing an appeal. The Rules of the Supreme Court simply said that the Court of Appeal 'shall have power to draw inferences of fact and to give any judgment and make any order which ought to have been given or made, and to make such further or other order as the case may require' (RSC Ord 59, r 10(3).) Case law and commentaries such as the White Book for the High Court and the equivalent Green Book for the county court established the principles on which the courts acted.

Now the rules on the hearing of appeals provide that the appeal court will allow an appeal 'where the decision of the lower court was (a) wrong; or (b) unjust because of

---

[46] See RSC (Amendment No 3) 1990, SI 1990 No 2599, reg 13, amending CPR Sch 1, RSC Ord 59, r 11.

a serious procedural or other irregularity in the proceedings in the lower court' (CPR 52.11(3).) These rules apply not just to the Court of Appeal. They apply to all civil courts exercising appellate functions.

The editors of the White Book suggest that 'wrong' presumably means that the court below (i) erred in law, or (ii) erred in fact or (iii) erred in the exercise of its discretion.

As regards errors of fact, the Court of Appeal has always been chary of taking a different view of the facts from that taken by the trial court, especially where the findings of fact were based on testimony given by witnesses. When the decision was that of a jury the reluctance was even greater. The position was described by the House of Lords in a case in 1927.

SS Hontestroom (Owners) v SS Sagaporack (Owners) [1927] AC 37 (House of Lords)

[In actions arising out of a collision between two ships the trial judge found that the *Sagaporack* was wholly to blame. His decision was reversed by the Court of Appeal which found the other ship was wholly to blame.

On appeal to the House of Lords, Lord Sumner, giving the judgment for the majority, said:]

The learned President, after seeing both pilots, accepted the story of the *Hontestroom*. Though he does not expressly say so, it is evident that he regarded the *Hontestroom's* pilot as an honest and a credible witness and, conversely, that he did not accept the story of the pilot of the *Sagaporack*, not thinking that his memory could be trusted. . . .

What then is the real effect on the hearing in a Court of Appeal of the fact that the trial judge saw and heard the witnesses? I think it has been somewhat lost sight of. Of course, there is jurisdiction to retry the case on the shorthand note, including in such retrial the appreciation of the relative values of the witnesses, for the appeal is made a rehearing by rules which have the force of statute: Order 68, r 1. It is not, however, a mere matter of discretion to remember and take account of this fact; it is a matter of justice and of judicial obligation. None the less, not to have seen the witnesses puts appellate judges in a permanent position of disadvantage as against the trial judge, and, unless it can be shown that he has failed to use or has palpably misused his advantage, the higher court ought not to take the responsibility of reversing conclusions so arrived at, merely on the result of their own comparisons and criticisms of the witnesses and of their own view of the probabilities of the case. The course of the trial and the whole substance of the judgment must be looked at, and the matter does not depend on the question whether a witness has been cross-examined to credit or has been pronounced by the judge in terms to be unworthy of it. If his estimate of the man forms any substantial part of his reasons for his judgment the trial judge's conclusion of fact should, as I understand the decisions, be let alone. In *The Julia* (1860) 14 Moo PC 210, 235 Lord Kingsdown says: 'They, who require this Board, under such circumstances, to reverse a decision of the court below upon a point of this description, undertake a task of great and almost insuperable difficulty . . . We must, in order to reverse, not merely entertain doubts whether the decision below is right, but be convinced that it is wrong'. . . .

My Lords, for these reasons I do not propose to retry this case, nor do I think that the Court of Appeal should have done so.

For rarely expressed scepticism about the value to trial courts of observing the demeanour of the witnesses, see, however, a lecture given by Sir Thomas Bingham given at an early stage of his illustrious judicial career –'The Judge as Juror', *Current Legal Problems*, 1985, p 1 at 6–13.

But sometimes the Court would reverse a judge's finding of fact on the ground that he was plainly wrong. (See, for instance, *The Ikarian Reefer* [1995] Lloyd's Rep 455 reversing the finding that insured shipowners had not intentionally scuttled their vessel.) And very exceptionally, the Court of Appeal was prepared to reverse even a jury's decision if it found it to be perverse. A recent example was *Grobbelaar v News Group Newspapers Ltd*[47] The Court of Appeal set aside a jury's award of £85,000 libel damages awarded to Bruce Grobbelaar the well-known goalkeeper. He had sued the *Sun* newspaper which in a series of sensational articles published over seven days had accused him of taking bribes to fix games. The Court of Appeal said it had a duty to intervene where the verdict was so plainly wrong that no jury acting reasonably could have reached such a decision on a balance of probabilities. Having regard to the evidence, Grobelaar's story was simply incredible and he should not be permitted to retain an unmerited award of damages. (For critical commentary on the decision see P Robertshaw, 'The Review Roles of the Court of Appeal: *Grobelaar v News International*', 64 *Modern Law Review*, 2001, 923-32.) On appeal, the House of Lords reversed the Court of Appeal's decision on the ground that although the Court of Appeal could and should quash a perverse jury decision, in this case it did not agree that the jury's decision was perverse. (Any satisfaction Mr Grobbelaar might have taken in the law lords' decision will have been considerably diminished by their decision to reduce his award of damages to a nominal £1 and to order that he pay two-thirds of the *Sun* newspaper's costs.[48])

The position was somewhat different when the appeal court was asked to review the drawing of inferences from facts by the trial judge. In such cases the appeal court regarded itself as permitted to draw different inferences even though it had not seen

---

47   [2001] EWCA Civ 33, [2001] 2 All ER 437.
48   [2002] UKHL 40, [2002] 4 All ER 732. The law lords said that although the jury must have accepted that G had corruptly accepted bribes, it must also have found that he did not in fact 'throw' matches. To that extent, on the evidence, the jury's decision was not perverse. But the law lords held that it would be an affront to justice if a court of law were to award substantial damages to a man shown to have acted in such flagrant breach of his legal and moral obligations.

the witnesses – see *Benmax v Austin Motor Co Ltd* [1955] AC 370 ; or *Whitehouse v Jordan* [1981] 1 All ER 267.

But in *Biogen Inc v Medeva plc* [1997] RPC 1 at p 45 Lord Hoffmann warned against treating *Benmax* as authorising an appellate court from undertaking a fresh evaluation of the evidence where there was no question of the credibility of witnesses. The need for judicial caution in reversing the judge's evaluation of the fact was based on much more than professional courtesy. 'It is because specific findings of fact, even by the most meticulous judge, are inherently an incomplete statement of the impression which was made upon him by the primary evidence. The expressed findings are always surrounded by a penumbra of imprecision as to emphasis, relative weight, minor qualification and nuance. . . of which time and language do not permit exact expression but which play an important part in the judge's overall evaluation.' An appellate court should be very cautious in differing from the judge's evaluation.

The Court of Appeal's attitude to altering awards of damages was again similar. It was more reluctant to interfere with an award by a jury than a judge but it would alter an award even of a jury if it thought it to be wholly wrong. (For examples see *Lewis v Daily Telegraph Ltd* [1964] AC 234 (damages manifestly too high) or *English and Scottish Co-op Properties Mortgage and Investment Society Ltd v Odhams Press Ltd* [1940] 1 KB 440 (damages manifestly too low).) But the court would uphold an award of damages even if it thought it was considerably more than it would itself have awarded. (In *Blackshaw v Lord* [1983] 2 All ER 311 the Court refused to interfere with libel damages of £45,000 awarded by a jury even though all three judges thought it was far too high.)

In regard to review of discretionary decisions the classic rule has again been that the appeal court would not interfere, even if it disagreed with the decision, unless it could be shown that the judge below had erred in law or had acted on wrong principles – such as taking into account irrelevant matters, acting under a misapprehension of fact or failing to exercise the discretion. (See for instance, *Culver v Beard* [1937] 1 All ER 301 (court refuses to change allocation of case from county court to High Court); *Stevens v Walker* [1936] 2 KB 215 (court interfered because the judge had not considered matters he should have taken into account); *Eagil Trust Co Ltd v Pigott-Brown* [1985] 3 All ER 119 (dismissal for want of prosecution – court's role is to review the exercise of discretion, not to substitute its own decision).)

Post-CPR

It appears that the position under the CPR is much the same. In *Designers Guild Ltd v Russell Williams (Textiles) Ltd* [2001] 1 All ER 700 the House of Lords held that the Court of Appeal had been wrong to substitute its own assessment of the evidence for that made by the trial judge. The question at issue was whether there had been infringement of copyright. Lord Bingham (at 702) said that the Court of Appeal had approached this issue ' more in the manner of a first instance court making original findings of fact than as an appellate court reviewing findings already made ... It was not for the Court of Appeal to embark on the issue of substantiality afresh, unless the judge had misdirected himself, which in my opinion he had not.' Lord Hoffmann said that although the issue had not involved assessment of the credibility of witnesses, nevertheless the trial court had had the benefit of expert testimony. The court's decision involved the application of a not altogether precise legal standard to a combination of features of varying importance. The case fell into a class of case in which an appellate court should not reverse a judge's decision unless he has erred in principle.

In *Assicurazioni Generali SpA v Arab Insurance Group (BSC)* [2002] EWCA Civ 1642, Ward LJ said that two factors led appellate judges to be cautious about interfering.

> First, the appellate court recognises that judging the witness is a more complex task than merely judging the transcript. Each may have its intellectual component but the former can also crucially rely on intuition. That gives the trial judge the advantage over us in assessing the witness's demeanour, so often a vital factor in deciding where the truth lies. Secondly, judging is an art not a science. So the more complex the question, the more likely it is that different judges will come to different conclusions and the harder it is to determine right from wrong. Borrowing language from other jurisprudence, the trial judge is entitled to 'a margin of appreciation'. [at para 196]

This is familiar language which could equally have come from the pre-CPR era.

As to what constitutes sufficient error in the exercise of discretion to justify interference by the appeal court, in *Tanfern Ltd* Brooke LJ referred to Lord Fraser's speech in *G v G (Minors: Custody Appeals)* [1985] 1 WLR 647:

> ... the appellate court should only interfere when they consider that the judge of first instance has not merely preferred an imperfect solution which is different from an alternative imperfect solution which the Court of Appeal might or would have adopted, but has exceeded the generous ambit within which a reasonable disagreement is possible. [at 652]

Again, one would say that that represents business as usual.

(2) CRIMINAL CASES

The conditions for the court to allow an appeal were first laid down in s 4 of the Criminal Appeal Act 1907. (As will be seen, this was replaced in 1966 by s 2 of the Criminal Appeal Act 1966, which became s 2 of the Criminal Appeal Act 1968. Section 2 was in its turn replaced by s 2 of the Criminal Appeal Act 1995.)

Criminal Appeal Act 1907

4.–(1) The Court of Criminal Appeal on any such appeal against conviction shall allow the appeal if they think that the verdict of the jury should be set aside on the ground that it is unreasonable or cannot be supported having regard to the evidence, or that the judgment of the court before whom the appellant was convicted should be set aside on the ground of a wrong decision of any question of law or that on any ground there was a miscarriage of justice, and in any other case shall dismiss the appeal:

Provided that the court may, notwithstanding that they are of opinion that the point raised in the appeal might be decided in favour of the appellant, dismiss the appeal if they consider that no substantial miscarriage of justice has actually occurred.

The Court of Appeal's attitude to jury verdicts in criminal cases was, if anything, even more deferential than that it adopted in civil cases. The case that follows was typical:

R v Hopkins-Husson (1949) 34 Cr App Rep 47 (Court of Criminal Appeal)

[Lord Goddard CJ, giving the judgment of the court, said:]

With regard to the other six cases, the jury found a verdict of Not Guilty in five of them, and in the case of one boy, a boy called Allan Simpson, they found the appellant Guilty. It is fair and right to say that the learned judge said in terms that he was surprised at the verdict, and he himself would obviously have preferred a verdict of acquittal; but it is also right to say that from a very early period in the history of this court it has been laid down, and has been laid down frequently since, that the fact that the trial judge was dissatisfied with the verdict, although it is a matter to be taken into account in this court, must not be taken as a ground by itself for quashing the conviction. If it were, it would mean that we should be substituting the opinion of the judge for the opinion of the jury, and that is one of the things which this court will never do.

In just the same way it has been held from an equally early period in the history of this court that the fact that some members or all the members of the court think that they themselves would have returned a different verdict is again no ground for refusing to accept the verdict of the jury, which is the constitutional method of trial in this country. If there is evidence to go to the jury, and there has been no misdirection, and it cannot be said that the verdict is one which a reasonable jury could not arrive at, this court will not set aside the verdict of Guilty which has been found by the jury.

A commentator in 1966, describing the attitude of the court to its powers, wrote: 'The broad picture that emerged was a court concerned in appeals against conviction, with the judge's direction, evidence and procedure and the occasional point of substantive law rather than the "merits" of the case. An appellant who could point to a clear misdirection, the wrongful admission or exclusion of evidence or some procedural irregularity, had better prospects of success than the appellant who simply

claimed that he was innocent and that the jury had come to the wrong decision.'
(Michael Dean, 'Criminal Appeal Act 1966' [1966] *Criminal Law Review*, pp 535,
539.)

A JUSTICE Committee in 1964 thought 'it seems absurd and unjust that verdicts
which experienced judges would have thought surprising and not supported by really
adequate evidence, should be allowed to stand for no other reason than that they
were arrived at by a jury' (*Criminal Appeals*, 1964, para 59). In 1965 the Donovan
Committee took a similar view. (*Report of the Interdepartmental Committee on the Court
of Criminal Appeal*, 1965, Cmnd 2755):

> Under the terms of s 4(1), if it is strictly construed, there is, in the case of an
> innocent person who has been wrongly identified and in consequence wrongly
> convicted, virtually no protection conferred by his right to appeal . . .provided
> that the evidence of identification was, on the face of it, credible. We think that
> this defect should be remedied [p 33, para 145].

It recommended the adoption of a broader formula, one originally proposed by Mr
FE Smith(the later Lord Chancellor) during the debates on the Criminal Appeal
Bill in 1907, that the court should quash a conviction where the verdict in the opinion
of the court was 'under all the circumstances of the case unsafe or unsatisfactory'.
This was duly achieved in the Criminal Appeal Act 1966, which was then
incorporated into the 1968 Act and became s 2(1)(*a*) of that Act.

Criminal Appeal Act 1968

2.–(1) Except as provided by this Act, the Court of Appeal shall allow an appeal
against conviction if they think:
(*a*)   that the verdict of the jury should be set aside on the ground that under
        all the circumstances of the case it is unsafe or unsatisfactory; or
(*b*)   that the judgment of the court of trial should be set aside on the ground
        of a wrong decision of any question of law; or
(*c*)   that there was a material irregularity in the course of the trial, and in
        any other case shall dismiss the appeal:
Provided that the court may, notwithstanding that they are of opinion that the
point raised in the appeal might be decided in favour of the appellant, dismiss
the appeal if they consider that no miscarriage of justice has actually occurred.

In the case of an appeal against conviction the court shall, if they allow the
appeal, quash the conviction.

Note–'unsafe or unsatisfactory'

In the final appeal of the Birmingham Six the prosecution argued that the two words
had separate meanings and that therefore convictions could be unsatisfactory but
not unsafe. The Court of Appeal rejected this view. The two words, it said, were
indistinguishable.

COOPER AND THE 'LURKING DOUBT' TEST

In 1969 the Court of Appeal, Criminal Division decided the *Cooper* case, in which it pronounced a philosophy in regard to the way in which the court should approach jury verdicts that was very different from the approach shown in the *Hopkins-Husson* decision.

R v Cooper [1969] 1 QB 267 (Court of Appeal, Criminal Division)

[Defendant was convicted of assault occasioning actual bodily harm after an incident in which a 22-year-old girl was attacked by one of a group of three drunken youths. At an identification parade six weeks after the offence she picked out the defendant. In his own words: 'She never looked at anyone else' and according to the court she clearly had no doubt at all. The question for the court was whether the conviction was unsafe by reason of the evidence at the trial that B had told D that he rather than the defendant had committed the attack. There was close physical similarity between the defendant and B. Nevertheless the jury convicted.

Widgery LJ, giving the judgment of the court, said:]

The important thing about this case is that all the material to which I have referred was put before the jury. No one criticises the summing-up, and, indeed, Mr Frisby for the defendant has gone to some lengths to indicate that the summing-up was entirely fair and that everything which could possibly have been said in order to alert the jury to the difficulties of the case was clearly said by the presiding judge. It is, therefore, a case in which every issue was before the jury and in which the jury was properly instructed, and, accordingly, a case in which this court will be very reluctant indeed to intervene. It has been said over and over again throughout the years that this court must recognise the advantage which a jury has in seeing and hearing the witness, and if all the material was before the jury and the summing-up was impeccable, this court should not lightly interfere. Indeed, until the passing of the Criminal Appeal Act 1966, provisions which are now to be found in s 2 of the Criminal Appeal Act 1968, it was almost unheard of for this court to interfere in such a case.

However, now our powers are somewhat different, and we are indeed charged to allow an appeal against conviction if we think that the verdict of the jury should be set aside on the ground that under all the circumstances of the case it is unsafe or unsatisfactory. That means that in cases of this kind the court must in the end ask itself a subjective question, whether we are content to let the matter stand as it is, or whether there is not some lurking doubt in our minds which makes us wonder whether an injustice has been done. This is a reaction which may not be based strictly on the evidence as such; it is a reaction which can be produced by the general feel of the case as the court experiences it.

We have given earnest thought in this case to whether it is one in which we ought to set aside the verdict of the jury, notwithstanding the fact they had every advantage and, indeed, some advantages we do not enjoy. After due consideration, we have decided we do not regard this verdict as safe, and accordingly we shall allow the appeal to quash the conviction. As far as this matter is concerned the appellant is discharged.

If the very broad 'lurking doubt' test as formulated in *Cooper* reflected the Court of Appeal's normal attitude, a high proportion of appellants against conviction might stand a reasonable chance of getting their convictions overturned. In fact, however, the Court of Appeal was not easily persuaded to adopt the 'lurking doubt' test. One expert stated in 1983: 'The lurking doubt' test, enunciated by Lord Widgery when he was first appointed, has been quietly buried' (Tom Sargant, *More Law Reform Now* (Barry Rose, 1983), p 91). Research carried out for JUSTICE almost 20 years after the decision stated that only six reported cases had been found where the court had quashed a conviction on the grounds that there was a lurking doubt about the conviction and there was nothing new to throw doubt on it. (JUSTICE, *Miscarriages of Justice*, 1989, para 4.19, p 49).

An important insight into the Court of Appeal's marked reluctance to use the 'lurking doubt' test was supplied by former Lord Justice Lawton, a vastly experienced criminal appeal judge, in his evidence to the Runciman Royal Commission :

Until the decision of the Court of Appeal in *R v Cooper* it had been assumed that a conviction should not be quashed unless there was some reason in law for doing so. In that case however it was adjudged that the court could apply a subjective test–had it a lurking doubt or reasoned unease which made it wonder whether an injustice had been done. In simpler terms this means that the court can quash a conviction if it has a hunch that there has been an injustice. This cannot be a sound way of administering criminal justice; and since 1969 the judges seem to have appreciated that it was not because only six appeals have been allowed on this ground.

Or, in other words, the judges did not apply the 'lurking doubt' test because they did not like it. They believed that to apply it would be to usurp the function of the jury.

Report of the Runciman Royal Commission

The Runciman Royal Commission said it had received conflicting evidence about the 'lurking doubt' test. On the one hand, there were those who pointed out that the Court of Appeal had only very rarely acknowledged that it was applying this test. On the other hand, it had been suggested to the Royal Commission that the Court of Appeal had not infrequently allowed appeals on what had in truth been the 'lurking doubt' principle, even though there had been no reference to the phrase. These were cases where there was no error at the trial nor any error in law 'but nevertheless the combined experience of the three members of the court leads them to conclude that there may have been an injustice in the trial and in the jury's verdict'. They consequently allowed the appeal on the ground that, at the least, the jury's verdict was unsatisfactory. 'There is no real difference between this approach and an application of the 'lurking doubt principle' (p 171, para 45). The Commission's conclusion on the matter was to encourage the court to use this power when it felt it right to do so:

> We fully appreciate the reluctance felt by judges sitting in the Court of Appeal about quashing a jury's verdict. The jury has seen the witnesses and heard their evidence; the Court of Appeal has not. Where, however, on reading the transcript and hearing argument the Court of Appeal has a serious doubt about the verdict, it should exercise its power to quash. We do not think that quashing the jury's verdict where the court believes it to be unsafe undermines the system of jury trial. We therefore recommend that, as part of the redrafting of s 2, it be made clear that the Court of Appeal should quash a conviction notwithstanding that the jury reached their verdict having heard all the relevant evidence and without any error of law or material irregularity having occurred if after reviewing the case, the court concludes that the verdict is or may be unsafe [Report, pp 171–72, para 46].

For an example of the Court of Appeal adopting this approach see *R v Haughton*, unreported (No 589/SI/91) 21 May 1992. The case was referred back to the Court of Appeal by the Home Secretary on the ground that the ESDA test appeared to show that police officers had fabricated the appellant's confession. The Court of Appeal rejected that argument, but it said that its duty was 'to review the case generally'. Having done that, it found that the verdict was unsafe and unsatisfactory even though there was nothing new that had not been before the jury.

As will be seen below, the Government accepted the Royal Commission's proposal that s 2 be redrafted but it did not adopt the proposal in the form suggested by the Commission. The status of the 'lurking doubt' test was uncertain.

Note – do appeal judges have the time it takes?

A practical point made in a powerful lecture on the problem of miscarriages of justice by the distinguished Australian judge the Hon Justice Michael Kirby, is that appeal judges do not have the time to consider the trial evidence properly. Nor, typically, do they have the time, all of them, to read the entirety of the transcript of what may have been a trial lasting many days or even weeks. 'They visit the evidence, on the invitation of counsel, skipping from one passage to another. Rarely do they capture the subtle atmosphere of the trial, for such things do not readily emerge from cold pages. These are the reasons why so much deference is paid to the advantages of the trial judge or jury, who see the evidence unfold in sequence and observe the witnesses giving their testimony.' ('Miscarriages of Justice', The Child and Co Lecture, London, 1991, p 26.)

The burden of reading papers is already enormous. The Evidence of the Lord Chancellor's Department to the Runciman Royal Commission stated that in a typical week in September 1991, the one Division of the Court of Appeal Criminal Division that was then sitting was provided with 4,800 pages of documentation.

About half the Court of Appeal's time was spent on sentence appeals. Such appeals were declining while the proportion of appeals against conviction was increasing. In a normal sitting day, each Division of the Court could deal with up to ten sentence cases and one or two conviction cases. It seems clear that if the Court were to take on more conviction appeals it would need further resources (ibid).

QUASHING THE JURY'S VERDICT ON ACCOUNT OF ERROR AT TRIAL

Research shows that by far the most frequent reason for the Court of Appeal to quash a conviction is because of some error at trial, usually error by the trial judge in the form of misdirection of the jury on the law or some other defect in the summing up, or a wrong decision to allow or to exclude evidence. The Runciman Royal Commission cited Dr Kate Malleson's research on appeals in 1989, 1990 and 1992. Thus in the 1990 sample, errors of this kind were involved in 82% of successful appeals.

Under the Criminal Appeal Act 1968, errors at trial could be dealt with in three alternative ways. One was to treat the error as inconsequential by applying 'the proviso' (on 'the proviso' see pp 667-68 below). The second was to quash the conviction and order a retrial (on retrials see pp 681-83 below). The third and according to Malleson's research by far the most common was to quash the conviction.

A majority of the Runciman Royal Commission proposed a different scheme:

(1) If the court believes that the conviction is safe despite the error, the appeal should be dismissed.
(2) If the court believes the error has rendered the verdict unsafe, the appeal should be allowed and the conviction quashed.
(3) If it believes the conviction may be unsafe as a result of the error, it should quash the conviction and order a retrial (Report, p 170, para 38).

Three of the Commission's members wished to add a further category for cases where there is an error at trial sufficiently serious to affect the trial materially but not sufficiently serious to make the conviction unsafe. In such a case they thought the court should order a retrial. The majority disagreed–'The majority of us do not believe that a person who is clearly guilty should be accorded a retrial merely because there has been some error at the trial' (p 170, para 38). As will be seen below, when it came to redrafting of s 2, the majority view prevailed.

QUASHING THE JURY'S VERDICT ON ACCOUNT OF PRE-TRIAL MALPRACTICE OR PROCEDURAL IRREGULARITY

Where an appeal is based on some pre-trial matter (which might be anything from fabrication of evidence to some serious irregularity in the implementation of PACE) a majority of nine out of eleven members of the Runciman Royal Commission thought the Court of Appeal should only act if it thought the matter was such as to make or maybe make the conviction unsafe. If there was plenty of other, untainted evidence showing the defendant to be guilty his conviction should not be quashed even if there were some gross impropriety in the pre-trial handling of the case. The minority of two (which included the writer) thought that there could be occasions when the Court should quash a conviction even though there was clear evidence of guilt.

The majority view:

49. In the view of the majority, even if they believed that quashing the convictions of criminals was an appropriate way of punishing police malpractice, it would be naive to suppose that this would have any practical effect on police behaviour. In any case it cannot in their view be morally right that a person who has been convicted on abundant other evidence and may be a danger to the public should walk free because of what may be a criminal offence by someone else. Such an offence should be separately prosecuted within the system. It is also essential, if confidence in the criminal justice system is to be maintained, that police officers involved in malpractice should be disciplined, and in this connection we attach great importance to the recommendations in chapter three, which should lead to more effective police disciplinary procedures. The Court of Appeal must report any cases of malpractice by police officers which come to their attention to chief officers of police. We also envisage that the more serious the malpractice the less likely it is that the court would conclude that the verdict could be safe.

50. In the view of the majority, the minority view is illogical. It would only be effective if the judge at first instance had allowed the tainted evidence to be heard by the jury. If the judge had properly excluded the evidence then the verdict would be unassailable. The minority view must logically involve the trial judge in stopping a case on the basis of tainted evidence which he or she nevertheless proposed to exclude. The majority believe this to be unacceptable precluding as it must the jury from returning a verdict on the basis of evidence which was safe, admissible, and probative. It is only the tainted evidence which is excluded

by section 78 of PACE. That section does not allow the court to stop the case if there remains admissible probative evidence to support it [p 23].

The minority view

[The minority view was expressed in the writer's Dissent:]

68. I cannot agree. The moral foundation of the criminal justice system requires that if the prosecution has employed foul means the defendant must go free even though he is plainly guilty. Where the integrity of the process is fatally flawed, the conviction should be quashed as an expression of the system's repugnance at the methods used by those acting for the prosecution.

69. The majority's position would I believe encourage serious wrongdoing from some police officers who might be tempted to exert force or fabricate or suppress evidence in the hope of establishing the guilt of the suspect, especially in a serious case when they believe him to be guilty. There have unfortunately been some gross examples of such conduct.

70. The position adopted by the majority also seems to me to risk undermining the principle at the heart of section 78 of PACE which explicitly gives the court the power to exclude evidence on the ground that it renders the proceedings 'unfair'. The word 'unfair' expresses the underlying moral principle and the Court of Appeal has repeatedly used this new statutory power very broadly to express its refusal to uphold convictions based on unacceptable police practices even when it could not be said that the misconduct had any impact on the jury's verdict.

71. Section 78 would of course remain – but the majority would in effect be encouraging the Court of Appeal to undercut a part of its moral force by saying that the issue of 'unfairness' can be ignored where there is sufficient evidence to show that the defendant is actually guilty. Any judge concerned to discourage prosecution malpractice would I believe be dismayed by the majority's position. In terms of the message sent to the police service and other prosecution agencies it could undo much of the good effect being achieved by the attitude of the judges to section 78 of PACE.

72. But the matter goes beyond discouraging prosecution malpractice. At the heart of the criminal justice system there is a fundamental principle that the process must itself have integrity. The majority suggest that the answer to prosecution wrongdoing in the investigation of crime is to deal with the wrongdoers through prosecution or disciplinary proceedings. Even were this to happen (and often in practice it would not), the approach is not merely insufficient, it is irrelevant to the point of principle. The more serious the case, the greater the need that the system upholds the values in the name of which it claims to act. If the behaviour of the prosecution agencies has deprived a guilty verdict of its moral legitimacy the Court of Appeal must have a residual power

to quash the verdict no matter how strong the evidence of guilt. The integrity of the criminal justice system is a higher objective than the conviction of any individual [pp 234–5].

NOT QUASHING THE JURY'S VERDICT— APPLICATION OF 'THE PROVISO'

No one suggests that a conviction should be quashed, or even a retrial ordered, where the matter complained of by the appellant is trivial. (In the United States this is known as 'harmless error'.) Here the matter has previously been dealt with by what was called 'the proviso'.

The proviso referred to here is that at the end of CAA 1968, s 2 – p 660 above – 'Provided that the court may, notwithstanding that they are of opinion that the point raised in the appeal might be decided in favour of the appellant, dismiss the appeal if they consider that no miscarriage of justice has actually occurred'.

The application of the proviso was explored by Michael Knight in his book on criminal appeals. In this he showed that, contrary to what was often maintained, the 'great majority of cases where the power [of the proviso] has been exercised are cases of serious error' in the trial (p 15). Before substantiating this controversial assertion, he set out the test which the court had applied for the application of the proviso:

Michael Knight, *Criminal Appeals*, 1970, pp 9–53

The test which the appellate court goes by is not the degree of error but whether there is, despite the fault, sufficient evidence and a sufficient direction for a reasonable jury inevitably to convict for, if so, there is no substantial miscarriage of justice.[49] However, if it is correct to say that the error can have had any crucial influence on a reasonable jury the conviction must be quashed, for to uphold it then would be a miscarriage of justice. The court metaphorically blot out the fault–the error in the direction, the piece of inadmissible evidence, the impact of the wrongly drafted indictment–and ask if, without it, there is a strong enough case for an inevitable conviction. And if they can answer 'yes' to this question, they show the Nelson Touch by turning a blind eye to the fault [p 16].

Knight then gave numerous examples of cases where the proviso was applied in spite of serious errors in the trial, eg:

Haddy (1944) 29 Cr App Rep 182–jury wrongly invited to infer guilt from accused's silence.

Farid (1945) 30 Cr App Rep 168–jury not warned by judge that corroboration desirable for accomplices to other offences.

---

[49]   The test was laid down in *Stirland v DPP* [1944] AC 315 (ed).

Whybrow (1951) 35 Cr App Rep 141–misdirection as to intent in attempted murder.

Slinger (1961) 46 Cr App Rep 244–judge did not tell jury that onus of proof lay on prosecution.

Knight also produced sixteen examples of cases where the proviso was applied although the jury had wrongly been informed of the defendant's previous convictions (pp 19–21). He continued (p 21):

> Certainly in recent years the appellate court in their judgments go extremely carefully through the evidence other than the inadmissible evidence wrongly let in plus the direction, or the direction minus the offending portion plus the evidence, to show that it is fair to say that a reasonable jury would inevitably have convicted. This definite and very often scrupulous care betrays a sense of uneasiness and dislike which can be taken as further recognition of the regularity of use–in serious fault cases [of the proviso].

> The line between some of the cases where the proviso has been exercised and some where it has not is sometimes so narrow as to be almost non-existent, and the answer to this conundrum lies in the amount of evidence and the standard of the direction outside of the fault.

> Occasionally, use of the proviso is declined because a particular fault is of its nature so serious that, even though the appellate court would like to uphold the conviction, and, even though there probably would be sufficient evidence and direction apart from the fault to justify in their opinion an inevitable finding of guilty by a reasonable jury, their desire to have a deserved conviction must be sacrificed to the general principle of fairness in our criminal trial. This is the principle stated in *Maxwell v DPP*:[50] It is often better that one guilty man should escape than that the general rules evolved by the dictates of justice for the conduct of criminal prosecutions should be disregarded or discredited …

THE REDRAFTING OF s 2

The Runciman Royal Commission

The Royal Commission unanimously agreed that CAA 1968, s 2 needed to be redrafted. (For an article detailing the drafting defects of the section see R Buxton, 'Miscarriages of Justice and the Court of Appeal' *Law Quarterly Review*, January 1993, p 66.) But the Commission was not agreed as to how it should be redrafted. The majority of eight recommended that the different grounds of appeal set out in s 2(1)(a), (b) and (c) (p 660 above) should be replaced by a single new ground–that the conviction 'is or may be unsafe'. If the court is satisfied that the conviction *is* unsafe it should

---

50   [1935] AC 309.

quash the conviction; if the court is satisfied that the conviction *may be* unsafe it should quash the conviction and order a retrial unless there are reasons which make a retrial impracticable or undesirable (p 170, para 38). Under that scheme the proviso would be redundant.

The minority of three argued that it would be confusing to wrap up all possible grounds of appeal in the one word 'unsafe'. That word implied that there was something wrong with the jury's verdict whereas the defect might be 'some irregularities or errors of law or procedure which did not necessarily affect the jury's verdict but were so serious that the conviction should not stand' (Report, p 169, para 34). Furthermore, in the view of the minority, an umbrella formula would not give the Court of Appeal sufficient guidance. In the view of the minority the grounds of appeal should distinguish between appeals claiming that the jury reached the wrong result and those alleging material irregularities or errors of law or procedure in or before the trial (ibid).

The Criminal Appeal Act 1995

The Government did not accept the Royal Commission's recommendation that the formula should distinguish between 'is unsafe' and 'maybe unsafe'. The formula in the new Act is simply whether the conviction is unsafe. The Criminal Appeal Act 1995, s 2 replaced CAA 1968, s 2 (including the proviso) with the following new provision:

> Subject to the provisions of this Act, the Court of Appeal (a) shall allow an appeal against conviction if they think that the conviction is unsafe; and (b) shall dismiss such an appeal in any other case.

The Government therefore rejected the view of the minority but it also rejected the majority's view that the formula should include the words 'or may be unsafe'. The Home Office Minister Mr Nicholas Baker, speaking in the Committee stage of the Bill said: 'The difficulty with the phrase "may be unsafe" is that it is inherently uncertain. Almost any conviction may be unsafe. The test might well result in the Court of Appeal having to allow a considerably greater number of appeals than at present, simply because it did not know for certain that the conviction was safe.' (House of Commons, Standing Committee B, 21 March 1995, col 27). Also, 'may be unsafe' had about it a suggestion of subjectivity on the part of someone other than the Court of Appeal. 'That would go far broader than current practice and far broader than the Committee would wish. . . we do not intend it to result in fewer convictions being overturned than at present. We want to consolidate the existing practice of the Court of Appeal' (ibid).

Professor Sir John Smith, addressing this issue, basically agreed with the Government's view that the words 'may be unsafe' added nothing:

> A conviction is unsafe if the court has nothing more than a lurking doubt whether the appellant is guilty—that is the court thinks that he may have been

wrongly convicted. What then is the difference between 'We think that the appellant may have been wrongly convicted?' and 'We think that it may be that he may have been wrongly convicted?' Surely there is no difference. Either the court has a lurking (or greater) doubt, or it does not. It is submitted that the Government was right to insist on the exclusion of the words, 'or may be', which could have led only to confusion, and possibly, to the Court feeling obliged to give a narrow meaning to 'unsafe' [[1995] *Criminal Law Review*, p 922].

The Court of Appeal had previously quite often quashed a conviction on the ground that there was an error of law or a material irregularity even though it probably had no doubt that the defendant was guilty. If the court were to hold that a conviction was only 'unsafe' if the court had a lurking (or greater) doubt about the defendant's conviction, that would be a drastic restriction of the court's power. But the Parliamentary debates make it clear that this was not the Government's intention. In moving the Second Reading of the Bill, the Home Secretary said of this section, 'In substance, it restates the existing practice of the Court of Appeal . . .' (House of Commons, *Hansard*, 6 March 1995, col 24).

The Home Office Minister rejected an amendment to retain the words 'or unsatisfactory'. The Government, he said, agreed with the majority of the Royal Commission that there was no real difference between 'unsafe' and 'unsatisfactory'. It had been argued by some that 'unsafe' referred to evidential flaws whilst 'unsatisfactory' connoted procedural flaws. But in the Government's view 'the word "unsafe" is sufficient to deal with convictions which are unacceptable because of flaws in the manner in which a case is prosecuted or tried, and because of evidence which undermines the prosecution case. If a procedural flaw is sufficiently serious to cast doubt on the safety of a conviction, the court will allow the appeal' (ibid col 27).

Speaking in the Second Reading debate in the House of Lords, the Lord Chief Justice, Lord Taylor said the new formula–whether the conviction is unsafe–'will in my view be concise, just and comprehensible to the ordinary citizen without narrowing the present grounds of appeal' (House of Lords, *Hansard*, 15 May 1995, col 311).

On the redrafting of s 2, see D Schiff and R Nobles, 'Criminal Appeal Act 1995: the Semantics of Jurisdiction', *Modern Law Review*, May 1996, p 299. See also A Clarke, 'Safety or Supervision' [1999] *Criminal Law Review* 108 and V Tunkel, 'When safe convictions are unsafely quashed' (1999) 149 *New Law Journal* 1089.

At first it seemed that, despite what had been said in Parliament, changing 'unsafe or unsatisfactory' to the simple 'unsafe' had resulted in a significant narrowing of the Court of Appeal's power to quash a conviction where something has gone wrong either at the trial or pre-trial but there is enough evidence to show that the defendant was correctly found guilty. In *R v Chalkley and R v Jeffries* (1998) 2 Cr App Rep 79, [1998] 2 All ER 155, the police arrested C in connection with credit card frauds as a pretext in order to be able to place a listening device in his home in connection with conspiracies to commit robberies. The defendants changed their plea to guilty after the judge ruled that the evidence of the tape-recorded conversations was admissible. The Court of Appeal held that the court had no power to allow an appeal 'if it does not think the conviction unsafe but is dissatisfied in some way with what went on at the trial' (p 172).

The decision in *Chalkley* was applied by the Court of Appeal in several later cases – *Kennedy*[51], *Hewitson and Bramwich*[52], *Rajcoomar*[53], *Thomas*[54].

But in *Mullen* [2000] QB 520, [1999] Crim LR 561, the Court of Appeal took a completely different approach. The appellant had been brought unlawfully to this country by collusion between the British and the Zimbabwean authorities. He was deported without regard to normal extradition procedures. He was convicted here of terrorist offences and was sentenced to 30 years' imprisonment. Some years later he was given leave to appeal out of time on the ground that the whole trial was vitiated by the illegality of his deportation. The Court of Appeal held that, despite the gravity of the charges, the conduct of the British authorities was so shameful that it was an affront to the public conscience to allow the conviction to stand. There had been a blatant and extremely serious failure to adhere to the rule of law. All the relevant circumstances had to be weighed. Here they came down decisively against the prosecution. In light of conflicting views expressed in the cases, the meaning of the word 'unsafe' in the Criminal Appeal Act as amended in 1995 was sufficiently ambiguous to permit recourse to *Hansard* from which it was apparent that the new form of s 2 was intended to restate the previous practice of the Court of Appeal which had allowed abuse of process as a ground for quashing a conviction. Furthermore, for a conviction to be safe, it had to be lawful. If it resulted from a trial that should never have taken place, it could hardly be regarded as safe. In his commentary in the *Review*, Professor Sir John Smith wrote: 'we seem now to be close to achieving the result intended by Parliament – ie no change' (at pp 562–63).

Cases following *Mullen* in which convictions were quashed despite there being little doubt as to the factual guilt of the accused include *Togher*[55], *Davis, Johnson and Rowe*[56], and *Sargent*[57] By 2003 it seemed that the Court of Appeal had rejected the approach in *Chalkley*.

In his report in October 2001 Lord Justice Auld (who gave the Court's judgment in *Chalkley*) called for legislative clarification of whether the approach in *Chalkley* or that in *Mullen* was to be preferred. ('In my view, consideration should be given to

---

51   [1999]1 Cr App Rep 54.
52   [1999] Crim LR 307.
53   [1999] Crim LR 728.
54   [2000] 1 Cr App Rep 447.
55   [2001] Cr App Rep 457, [2001] 3 All ER 463. For commentary see especially R Nobles and D Schiff, 'Due Process and Dirty Harry Dilemmas: Criminal Appeals and the Human Rights Act', 64 *Modern Law Review*, 2001, 911-22.
56   [2000] Crim LR 1012. For commentary see Professor Andrew Ashworth at 1017.
57   [2001] UKHL 54, [2003] Crim LR 276.

amendment of the present statutory test to make clear whether and to what extent it is to apply to convictions that would be regarded as safe in the ordinary sense of that word but follow want of due process before or during trial.' (p 614, para 10).) He did not, however, indicate his own preference. Pending any such statutory amendment (of which there has been no sign), it seems that the Court of Appeal has decided that it is *Mullen* rather than *Chalkley* that should prevail.

Has the Human Rights Act changed the position? What is the relationship between the statutory test of 'unsafe' under the 1995 Act and the question whether the defendant has had a fair trial within the meaning of the European Convention on Human Rights. If there have been breaches of the defendant's right to a fair trial under art 6 of the Convention does that mean that the conviction is automatically unsafe? In July 2000 the Court of Appeal dealing with the matter in *Davis, Johnson and* Rowe said the two questions must be kept separate. It was not helpful to think in terms of there being a presumption that a finding of a violation by the European Court meant that the conviction was unsafe. The effect of a breach of the Convention on the safety of the conviction would vary according to the nature and degree of the breach.[58] A few months later in *Togher*, Lord Woolf, giving the judgment of the Court, said that 'the circumstances in which there will be room for a different result before this court and before the European Court because of unfairness based on the respective tests we employ will be rare indeed' and 'if a defendant has been denied a fair trial it will be almost inevitable that the conviction will be regarded as unsafe' [59]

But in *Cranwell* [60] the Court of Appeal said: 'Although in very many cases a trial which is unfair will result in a conviction which is unsafe, this is not necessarily the case. There may be cases, for example, in which, though there has been unfairness, the evidence of the guilt of the defendant is so strong that there can be no doubt that the verdict is safe.'

It seems unlikely that the Strasbourg Court will rule that a breach of the Convention automatically makes a conviction unsafe.[61] In *Condron v United Kingdom* the Strasbourg Court said, 'In the court's opinion, the question whether or not the rights of the defence guaranteed to an accused under art 6 of the convention were secured in any given case cannot be assimilated to a finding that his conviction was safe in the absence of any enquiry into the issue of fairness.' It seems equally unlikely that legislative amendment to the 1995 Act will lay down such a rule[62] In all probability therefore the matter will remain fuzzy. In most cases 'unfair' will equate to 'unsafe' but in some cases it will not. There will be no rule. The real question for the future is whether the number of exceptions is great or small.

---

[58]   [2000] Crim LR 1012 at 1015. See to the same effect the Court's decision in *Francom* [2000] Crim LR 1018, per Lord Woolf.

[59]   [2001] 1 Cr App Rep 457, [2001] 3 All ER 463, at para 33.

[60]   [2001] EWCA Crim 1216.

[61]   (2000) 8 BHRC 290 at para 65.

[62]   K Malleson and S Roberts proposed such an amendment in 'Streamlining and Clarifying the Appellate Process' [2002] *Criminal Law Review* 272, 277.

For a powerful statement that the courts should give particular emphasis to the right to a fair trial see A Jennings, A Ashworth and B Emmerson, 'Silence and Safety: The Impact of Human Rights Law' [2000] *Criminal Law Review*, 879, 893-94 which concluded: 'One effect of bringing Convention rights into English law must be to ensure, at every level of the criminal process, that justice is not only done but is seen to be done.' D Ormerod has argued that breaches of the Convention should at least create a presumption that the evidence be excluded – 'ECHR and the Exclusion of Evidence: Trial Remedies for Article 8 Breaches?' [2003] *Criminal Law Review* 61. For scepticism as to the likelihood of the Court of Appeal changing its traditional approach in light of the Human Rights Act see R Nobles and D Schiff, 'Due Process and Dirty Harry dilemmas', (n 50 above) which concluded:

> The grounds for appeal have undergone a number of changes since the Court of Criminal Appeal was founded in 1907. In each case, the formal grounds for quashing convictions, represented by the statutory wording of the Court's jurisdiction, has mattered less than the Court's sense of what constitutes an appropriate basis for appeal, based on its own professional experience. Those standards have always included a strong deference towards a jury's verdict, and a willingness to regard less serious breaches of due process as insufficient reasons to quash convictions. Changing the Court of Appeal's legal authority by statutory amendment has, in the past, done little to alter its treatment of appeal cases. The Human Rights Act can be viewed as simply another alteration to the formal grounds for appeal. But unless it alters the Court's view of what constitutes a serious irregularity it will make little difference to the outcome of appeals. While the language of rights may be a new addition to Court of Appeal judgements it will not, by itself, alter the Court's view of which irregularities justify freeing those thought to be guilty. . . of serious offences.' (p 922)

Is the test of unsafeness that of then or of now? Since the Court of Appeal normally hears an appeal within a relatively short time after the trial, it is not often that the relevant law or procedure will have changed significantly in the interim. But where the Court of Appeal deals with a case that has been referred to it by the Criminal Cases Review Commission, the trial may have occurred years earlier. (In the case of Derek Bentley it occurred 45 years earlier; in the James Hanratty case it took place 40 years earlier.) When considering whether the original conviction is unsafe should the Court of Appeal apply the standards applicable at the time of the trial or those applicable at the time of the review?

In *Bentley*[63], in a judgment given by Lord Bingham, the Court of Appeal held that the statutory law of homicide had to be taken as it was at the time of the trial but that the common law was that current at the time of the review and that the conduct of the trial and the judge's direction of the jury should likewise be judged by the standards

---

[63]   [2001] 1 Cr App Rep 307, [1999] Crim LR 330.

that would now apply. This has remarkable implications. Commenting on the decision, Professor Sir John Smith wrote, 'How many convictions of, say, more than 20 years ago could be regarded as "safe" in the light of the changed, but relevant, conditions of today?' It was depressing, he said, to think that so many, perhaps a majority of the convictions in our courts were 'unsafe' – ie wrong in law. 'Is there any satisfactory way of preventing this rewriting of legal history? No one really believes that the present common law was the common law in 1189.'[64]

In a helpful commentary on a further case raising the same issue[65] DC Ormerod suggested a differentiation between three types of case: (1) cases where new evidence has come to light which throws doubt on the conviction; (2) cases where there is no new material but there is a new understanding of material in existence at the time of the trial – for instance, new scientific knowledge; (3) cases where there has been a change in the law's attitude prompted solely by legal developments, such as more liberal procedures or changes, perhaps driven by the ECHR, in regard to such matters as the admissibility of evidence, providing access to legal advice, or in regard to disclosure of unused evidence. It was the third category that gave rise to problems. 'If the Court of Appeal is prepared to quash convictions as "unsafe" because the law has changed its perception of what is "fair" to defendants, irrespective of whether that also undermines the reliability of the conviction, this really opens the floodgates.' Even if the third category was restricted to cases of potential unreliability, it would leave an enormous number of cases open to challenge – 'for example, all convictions based on old disclosure rules'.

In *Hanratty (decd)*[66] the Court of Appeal seems to have taken the point. The court said (at para 98):

> In order to achieve justice, non-compliance with rules which were not current at the time of the trial may have to be treated differently from rules which were in force at the time of the trial. If certain of the current requirements of, for example, a summing up are not complied with at a trial which takes place today this can almost automatically result in a conviction being set aside but this approach should not be adopted in relation to trials which took place before the rule was established. The fact that what has happened did not comply with a rule which was in force at the time of the trial makes the non-compliance more serious than it would be if there was no rule in force. Proper standards will not be maintained unless this Court can be expected when appropriate, to enforce the rules by taking a serious view of a breach of the rules at the time

---

64 [1999] Crim LR 330 at 332. See to the same effect a critique of Lord Bingham's judgment by Francis Bennion, 'Rewriting history in the Court of Appeal', *New Law Journal*, 14 August 1998, 1228. ('The past is a foreign country; they do things differently there. Or to put it even more succinctly: you can't change history, and you shouldn't even try' (1243).) But the principle enunciated in *Bentley* was applied in *O'Brien, Hall, Sherwood* [2000] Crim LR 676 CA.

65 *King* [2000] Crim LR 835, 838-41.

66 [2002] EWCA Crim 1141, [2002] Crim LR 650.

they are in force. It is not appropriate to apply this approach to a forty-year old case.

The court upheld the conviction even though it found that much material that today would today be required to be disclosed by the prosecution had not been disclosed.

(g) The power of appeal courts to receive fresh evidence

The Court of Appeal, both civil and criminal, had and still has full power to receive fresh evidence. The issue has rather been how the court chooses to exercise that power.

In civil cases, pre-CPR, the Rules of the Supreme Court (Ord 59, r 10) provided that although the court had the power to receive fresh evidence 'no such evidence ... shall be admitted except on special grounds'. The White Book's gloss pre-CPR stated, 'After there has been a trial or hearing on the merits, fresh evidence will not be admitted in the Court of Appeal unless the conditions in *Ladd v Marshall* are satisfied. A strict approach is adopted.'

The CPR puts the matter even more narrowly: 'Unless it orders otherwise, the appeal court will not receive (a) oral evidence; or (b) evidence which was not before the lower court' (CPR 52.11(2)). But despite the fact that there is no longer reference to 'special grounds', the principles laid down by the Court of Appeal in *Ladd v Marshall* still govern the situation.[67] Lord Phillips has said that the principles of *Ladd v Marshall* are consistent with those of the overriding objective in the CPR[68]

In *Ladd v Marshall* [1954] 1 WLR 1489 CA the plaintiff called the defendant's wife as his witness. She was a reluctant witness and said she did not remember a particular incident. Judgment was given for the defendant. Subsequently, after she had obtained a divorce, she informed the plaintiff's solicitors that she now did remember the incident and that she wished to change her evidence. The plaintiff asked the court either to order a new trial or itself to hear the evidence. The Court of Appeal dismissed the appeal. Lord Denning gave the court's judgment:

> To justify the reception of fresh evidence or a new trial, three conditions must be fulfilled: first, it must be shown that the evidence could not have been obtained with reasonable diligence for use at the trial; secondly, the evidence must be such that, if given, it would probably have an important influence on the result of the case, though it need not be decisive; thirdly, the evidence must be such as is presumably to be believed, or in other words, it must be apparently credible, though it need not be incontrovertible.

We have to apply those principles to the case where a witness comes and says: 'I told a lie but nevertheless I now want to tell the truth'. It seems to me that the fresh evidence

---

[67] See *Hertfordshire Investments Ltd v Bubb* [2000] 1 WLR 2318, per Hale LJ at 2325.
[68] See *Hamilton v Al Fayed* (2001) Times, 16 January, CA.

of such a witness will not as rule satisfy the third condition. A confessed liar cannot usually be accepted as being credible.

In regard to criminal cases, the Criminal Appeal Act 1968, s 23(2) permitted the court to receive fresh evidence if 'it appears to them that the evidence is likely to be credible and would have been admissible' and 'there is a reasonable explanation for the failure to adduce it' in the earlier proceedings. On the recommendation of the Runciman Royal Commission, the definition of admissible fresh evidence was broadened by the Criminal Appeal Act 1995 to evidence 'which appears to the Court to be capable of belief'.[69]

The decision of the Court of Criminal Appeal in *R v Flower* (1965) 50 Cr App Rep 22 showed that the Court's policy regarding the admission of fresh evidence was similar to that expressed in *Ladd v Marshall*. Widgery J, giving the judgment of the court, said:

> When this court gives leave to call fresh evidence which appears at the time of the application for leave to be credible, it is still the duty of the court to consider and assess the reliability of that evidence when the witness appears and is cross-examined, and this is particularly true when evidence is called in rebuttal before this court. Having heard the fresh evidence and considered the reliability of the witness, this court may take one of three views with regard to it. If satisfied that the fresh evidence is true and that it is conclusive of the appeal the court can, and no doubt ordinarily would, quash the conviction. Alternatively, if not satisfied that the evidence is conclusive, the court may order a new trial so that a jury can consider the fresh evidence alongside that given at the original trial. The second possibility is that the court is not satisfied that the fresh evidence is true but nevertheless thinks that it might be acceptable to, and believed by, a jury, in which case as a general proposition the court would no doubt be inclined to order a new trial in order that the evidence could be considered by the jury, assuming the weight of the fresh evidence would justify that course. Then there is a third possibility, namely that this court, having heard the evidence, positively disbelieves it and is satisfied that the witness is not speaking the truth. In that event, and speaking generally again, no new trial is called for because the fresh evidence is treated as worthless and the court will then proceed to deal with the appeal as though the fresh evidence had not been tendered.

A dramatic example of the narrowness of the approach of the Court of Appeal to fresh evidence was the case of Luke Dougherty. Dougherty was charged with shoplifting, having been identified by two witnesses. The offence occurred at a time when Dougherty was in fact on a bus outing with some 20 others, many of whom knew him. In the event only two were produced at the trial. One was his girlfriend and the other was someone with previous convictions. The jury disbelieved the alibi

---

[69] CAA 1968, s 23(2)(a) inserted by CAA 1995, s 4(1) – replacing 'likely to be credible'.

and convicted. He received a sentence of six months' imprisonment, and the judge also activated a nine months' suspended sentence, making 15 months in all.

The case was taken up by JUSTICE. On the application for leave to appeal, the single judge ruled that there was no ground to appoint a solicitor and that the fresh evidence could not be called. In conversation between counsel for Dougherty and the Registrar of the court, the Registrar said that 'this kind of case is unlikely to get off the ground' and that there were various unreported decisions in which the court had refused to allow the calling of fresh evidence where counsel at the trial had not called witnesses in spite of the client's request that they be called. When the case was argued before the full court, the fresh-evidence point was not even argued. Counsel proceeded instead on a different issue (that of the dock identification). Nevertheless the court in dismissing the appeal said that if the point had been argued 'the conditions necessary before such evidence could be received before this court could not be fulfilled'.

JUSTICE pursued its concern over the case and eventually in November 1972, through the good offices of the former Lord Chancellor, Lord Gardiner, it was referred back to the Court of Appeal by the Home Secretary. Dougherty's release was ordered immediately by the court. An examination of the alibi witnesses was then ordered, and on the hearing the prosecution did not contest the contention on behalf of Dougherty that the conviction was unsafe and unsatisfactory.

The whole sorry story was told in the Report of the Devlin Committee, which was set up partly as a result of this case (see *Report of the Departmental Committee on Evidence of Identification in Criminal cases*, 1976, House of Commons Paper 338, ch 2). Commenting on this aspect of the case, the Devlin Committee said that our administration of justice was based on the adversary system and the trial retained many characteristics of a battle. ('In a battle it is the responsibility of each side to get all its troops on the field on time. Napoleon could not appeal against the verdict of Waterloo on the ground that Marshall Grouchy and his army were still on their way when Blucher and the Prussians arrived in the nick of time', para 6.3.) Under the adversary system, relief was granted if the lack of evidence at the time of trial was due to misfortune, but not if it was due to lack of diligence or to a deliberate decision to do without the evidence. The rule was the same for civil as for criminal cases. However, it was no longer acceptable that an innocent person should continue to spend time in prison 'on the principle of "woe to the conquered" '. But the remedy lay chiefly with the executive in exercising the prerogative of mercy by pardon (see p 686 below).

A more relaxed attitude to the problem of fresh evidence was shown by the Court of Appeal, Civil Division in *Dixon v Dixon* (1983) 133 NLJ 305. A husband was ordered to pay maintenance for a child that he claimed was not his. After the magistrates' court hearing, the husband had blood tests done which showed conclusively that the child was not his. He applied to the Divisional Court for leave to appeal out of time against the order for periodic payments and for leave to admit the fresh evidence of the blood test. The Divisional Court refused leave to admit the fresh evidence on the ground that the evidence was available or could have been available if the husband had used reasonable diligence at the time of the hearing before the magistrates.

On appeal, the Court of Appeal remitted the matter to the magistrates to hold a re-hearing with the fresh evidence. The court said it was a very serious matter to exclude evidence which was wholly conclusive in favour of an applicant on the ground that it could have been available with reasonable diligence at the time of the hearing. It would be most undesirable that an order of the court should be allowed to stand which was based on crucial facts that everyone knew were incorrectly stated.

A few months later the House of Lords took a less generous view. In *Linton v Ministry of Defence* (1983) 133 NLJ 1103, it upheld a decision from Northern Ireland denying a fresh trial and permission to introduce fresh evidence to a plaintiff who had been shot by a soldier. He claimed that he was an innocent passer-by caught in a hail of bullets exchanged between soldiers and IRA terrorists. The army claimed that he had been one of the terrorists himself. He sued for damages for his injuries. A crucial piece of evidence concerned an employment card which he said he had had in his jeans' back-pocket, which proved that he was on his way to a job interview at the time of the incident. He was unable, however, to explain on cross-examination why it was neither bloodstained nor crumpled. The barrister for the army suggested to the jury that he had not in fact had it on him and the jury rejected his claim.

On appeal he sought to introduce fresh evidence of two kinds. First, he said he now remembered that he had actually been carrying the card in his jacket, which would explain why it was not bloodstained or crumpled. Second, he wanted to produce the entry in the hospital record where he was taken unconscious after being shot, which showed that his effects included an employment card which Lord Scarman said was almost certainly the card which he had been talking about at the trial.

Giving judgment for a unanimous House of Lords, Lord Scarman said that the appellant had satisfied the second and third of the tests laid down in *Ladd v Marshall*. The evidence was important and it was apparently credible. But he could not satisfy the first test. He (or his lawyers) had lacked reasonable diligence in not producing the new evidence at the trial. 'Ours is an adversarial system and it is the duty of a plaintiff to come to court with the evidence to prove his case.' He cited with approval the dictum of the Lord Chief Justice of Northern Ireland in the court below: 'A new trial cannot be granted or fresh evidence admitted just because the result of the first trial was or may have been occasioned or made more likely by the unsuccessful party's inattention or faulty memory or by an innocent mistake.'

Sometimes, however, the Court of Appeal receives fresh evidence even though there is no reasonable explanation as to why it was not adduced at the trial – simply on the basis that it is expedient to do so in the interests of justice. (See *Cairns* [2000] Crim LR 473.) The trouble is that the attitude of the court is unpredictable.

The Runciman Royal Commission suggested that possibly the court had construed its powers too narrowly. It was understandable that the court should view fresh evidence with suspicion. There was the fear that the allegedly fresh evidence might be manufactured. It agreed that defendants and their lawyers should not be encouraged to think of trials 'as nothing more than a practice run which in the event of a conviction will leave them free to put an alternative defence to the Court of Appeal in whatever manner they please' (ibid, p 173, para 55).

On the other hand, the court should 'be alive to the possibility that the fresh evidence, if true, may exonerate the appellant or at least throw serious doubts on the conviction' (ibid). The court had to consider whether the fresh evidence was available at the trial and if so, whether there was a reasonable explanation for the failure to adduce it. It had been suggested to the Commission that the attitude of the court had on occasion been excessively restrictive. It said: 'We would urge that in general the court should take a broad, rather than a narrow, approach to them' (ibid, para 56).

Thus, where the witness wished to change his evidence, the Court of Appeal was right to look at it very carefully, but if there was some reasonable explanation why the witness gave the previous evidence from which he wants to depart, the court should receive it (p 174, para 57).

Despite the frequently narrow and negative attitude of the Court of Appeal to its powers to receive fresh evidence, there is no doubt that the court has the power to receive any admissible evidence if it so chooses and it can call and hear such evidence on its own initiative. It seems that it can even receive evidence that is inadmissible under the rules of evidence – see *D and J* [1996] 1 All ER 881,886 at d CA. (The Runciman Royal Commission had said that if there were convincing but inadmissible evidence showing that a miscarriage of justice had occurred it should be dealt with through the Royal Prerogative of Mercy rather than by the Court of Appeal. ('If the fresh evidence sought to be admitted is inadmissible under the rules of evidence, in our view the court should not receive it' (p 176, para 67).)

Fresh evidence can be introduced by the prosecution just as much by the defence. That is what happened in the hearing in 2002 of the appeal in the case of James Hanratty who was hanged for murder in 1962. The case, which had been the subject of much controversy over many years, had been referred back to the Court of Appeal by the Criminal Cases Review Commission. The prosecution wished to introduce DNA evidence obtained in 2000 after the body was exhumed at the request of the defence, which, it argued, proved conclusively that Hanratty was guilty. Allowing the application, the Court of Appeal held that the overriding consideration was whether the evidence would assist the court to achieve justice. [70]

The situation is obviously different when the fresh evidence concerns matters that occurred after the trial. But here too the appeal courts have traditionally taken a rather

---

[70]   *R v Hanratty* [2002] EWCA Crim 1141, [2002] 3 All ER 534.

narrow approach, on the basis that there should be an end to litigation and that cases should not be re-opened unless there are very good grounds. Thus in *Mulholland v Mitchell* [1971] AC 666, the plaintiff had suffered very serious injuries, and damages had been assessed by the judge on the basis that he could be looked after either at home or in an ordinary nursing home. The appeal was on the basis that after the trial his condition had deteriorated dramatically. The Court of Appeal allowed fresh evidence to be given to establish the facts. On appeal to the House of Lords, the law lords held that the Court of Appeal had exercised its discretion reasonably but, generally, fresh evidence should not be admitted relating to a matter of uncertainty taken into account by the judge unless the basis on which he had given his decision had been clearly falsified by subsequent events.

When a case is referred back to the Court of Appeal (formerly by the Home Secretary, and now by the Criminal Cases Review Commission, pp 687, 692-94 below) the power to receive fresh evidence is less restrictive than on an ordinary appeal. This emerges from a number of cases: *McGrath* [1949] 2 All ER 495; *Sparkes* [1956] 1 WLR 505; *Swabey* [1972] 2 All ER 1094; *Graves* [1978] Crim LR 216.

NEW POINTS TAKEN ON APPEAL

The Court of Appeal's attitude to new points taken on appeal is rather similar to its attitude to fresh evidence. If they could have been taken at the trial, the Court of Appeal will generally not allow them to be advanced for the first time at the appellate stage. So in *Re Tarling* [1979] 1 All ER 981, Gibson J in a habeas corpus case said: 'It is clear to the court that an applicant for habeas corpus is required to put forward on his initial application the whole of the case which is then fairly available to him–it becomes an abuse of process to raise in subsequent proceedings matters which could, and therefore should, have been litigated in earlier proceedings' (at p 987). In the same year in *Maynard* (1979) 69 Cr App Rep 309, Roskill LJ said: 'We have often said in this court that where a question, and in particular a question of the admissibility of evidence, is deliberately not raised at the trial it is only in very rare cases that we allow the matter to be raised in this court for the first time. To hold otherwise would be to encourage counsel to keep points of this kind up their sleeve and then reserve them for the Court of Appeal and thus have a second bite at the forensic cherry.'

In *Stirland v DPP* [1944] AC 315, the House of Lords rejected any firm rule that the courts could not allow an appeal on admissibility of evidence where counsel had failed to take objection at the trial. But, it said, 'the failure of counsel to object may have some bearing on the question whether the accused was really prejudiced'. It was not 'a proper use of counsel's discretion to raise no objection at the time in order to preserve a ground of objection for a possible appeal' (at p 328).

In 1995 in *R v Cox (Andrew Mark)* [1995] Crim LR 741 the Court of Appeal said it was most unsatisfactory that a matter not relied on at trial could found an appeal against conviction. At the trial prosecution and the trial judge had agreed that it would confuse the jury for the judge to put the issue of provocation as a possible defence to murder in his summing up. Defence counsel had said nothing. The defence at trial was based on diminished responsibility. On appeal it was argued that the judge had misdirected the jury in not dealing with the issue of provocation. The court upheld the defence submission but dismissed the appeal by applying the proviso (see p 667 above). The court said that for the future it must be made clear that both counsel had an obligation to the trial court. If it appears to either counsel that there is evidence supporting a defence of provocation it was their job to invite the judge to deal with the matter and to remind him that he was required by statute to leave the issue to the jury. The Court of Appeal said this was the formulation of a new duty and that no criticism could therefore attach to either counsel.

It remains to be seen whether this duty extends generally to all points that could be taken at trial or only to the special case of provocation where statute requires the judge to leave the issue to the jury if there is any evidence to support such a defence even when the judge takes the view that no reasonable jury could find the defence made out–see *R v Cambridge* [1994] 2 All ER 760.

See further R Munday, 'Trial Tactics and the Appellate Imagination', *Law Society's Gazette*, 27 May 1987, p 1554.

(h)   The power to order retrials in criminal cases

Until 1988 the power to order a retrial in a criminal case existed only in one situation –where the court allowed an appeal on the ground of fresh evidence. The basic statutory provision regulating the right to order retrials was s 7 of the Criminal Appeal Act 1968:

Criminal Appeal Act 1968

Retrial

7–(1) Where the Court of Appeal allow an appeal against conviction [and do so only by reason of evidence received or available to be received by them under section 23 of this Act[71]] and it appears to the court that the interests of justice so require, they may order the appellant to be retried.

The question whether there ought to be a general right to order a retrial was considered in 1954 by the Tucker Committee (*Report of the Departmental Committee on New Trials in Criminal Cases*, 1954, Cmnd 9150) and in 1964 by a committee of JUSTICE. The Tucker Committee was divided on whether there should be a general power to order a retrial (5 to 3 against). The JUSTICE committee was divided 9 to 4 in favour. Both committees were unanimous that there should be a power to order a retrial when there was fresh evidence.

---

[71]   The words in brackets were removed by the Criminal Justice Act 1988, s 43 (ed).

A general power to order retrials became law through s 43 of the Criminal Justice Act 1988. It applies whenever the court thinks it to be in the interests of justice. However, there was not at first any great increase in the tiny number of retrials ordered. In the 19-month period from August 1989 to March 1991 only four retrials were ordered by the Court of Appeal Criminal Division,[72] But in the ten years 1993–2002 the number of retrials was respectively 39, 66, 54, 51, 40, 79, 61, 69, 45, 48 –showing that the court has significantly altered its attitude to the matter.[73]

The Runciman Royal Commission strongly supported the Court of Appeal ordering more retrials:

> We welcome and wish to encourage the increasing exercise of this power. Although... re-trials will not be practicable or desirable in a significant number of cases, they offer the Court of Appeal an attractive solution for its understandable reservations about speculative prediction of a hypothetical jury's decision. Where the court is not in doubt, there is no difficulty in allowing or dismissing the appeal as appropriate. Where, on the other hand, the court is in doubt and would like to see the evidence or arguments more fully tested, then, other things being equal, retrials seem to all of us the better way to proceed, even if some of us would not like them to be as frequently ordered as would others [Report, p 175, para 65].

The Royal Commission was split down the middle as to what should happen if for one or another reason a retrial, though desirable, was felt to be impracticable and fresh evidence was not involved. Six members of the Commission thought that in that situation the Court of Appeal should quash the conviction, on the basis that, by definition, in order to want a retrial it must already have decided that the conviction might be unsafe. Five members of the Commission thought that in that situation the Court of Appeal should still decide the matter for itself (ibid, para 66).

The interests of justice in having or not having a retrial were considered by the House of Lords in *DPP for Northern Ireland v Lynch* (1975) 61 Cr App Rep 6 at pp 16, 22 and 47–8 and by the Privy Council in *Holder* (1978) 68 Cr App Rep 120 and *Au Pui -Kuen* (1979) 69 Cr App Rep 33. Retrials were ordered there after three, four and three years respectively.

The Tucker Committee found that retrials worked satisfactorily in Australia, Canada, New Zealand and Ceylon. Michael Knight in his book *Criminal Appeals* (Stevens, 1970) surveyed the widespread use of retrials in Ireland since 1928 and found (p 151) that they had been ordered in three-quarters of all quashed conviction cases in the period 1954 to 1964.

In *Reid v R* [1980] AC 343, PC, Lord Diplock, giving the judgment of the Judicial Committee of the Privy Committee, said that the factors the court should consider when deciding whether to order a retrial included the seriousness and prevalence of

---

[72]   House of Commons, *Hansard*, 11 March, 1991, vol 187 col 361–2.
[73]   Figures supplied to the author by the Registrar of the Court.

the offence; the probable duration and cost of a new trial; the ordeal to be faced by the defendant in being tried a second time; the lapse of time since the commission of the offence and its effect on the quality of the evidence; and the strength of the prosecution case. A retrial should not be permitted where the prosecution failed for lack of evidence. ('It is not in the interests of justice as administered under the common law system of criminal procedure that the prosecution should be given another chance to cure evidential deficiencies in its case against the defendant.' (at 350).)

The rule regulating retrials does not prevent the court from ordering a new trial where none has taken place initially – for example because the jury failed to agree on a verdict. Sometimes the court holds that an irregularity vitiates the trial and orders a fresh start (*venire de novo*). In order for *venire de novo* to lie, the court must be in a position to rule that the trial was void from the outset – a nullity. For examples see *Crane v DPP* [1921] 2 AC 299 and *Cronin* [1940] 1 All ER 618. For examples of cases where the court did not feel able to order a retrial on this ground, see *Neal* [1949] 2 KB 590; *McKenna* [1960] 1 QB 411; and the House of Lords' decision in *Rose* [1982] 2 All ER 731. In *Rose* the House of Lords quashed a conviction for murder when the judge was shown to have brought pressure on the jury to hasten its decision. But it held that *venire de novo* could not be ordered as the trial had been validly commenced and could not be said to have been void from the outset.

The most authoritative study of the issue is by Sir Robin Cooke (as he then was) in (1955) 71 *Law Quarterly Review*, p 100.

IN FRESH EVIDENCE CASES SHOULD THE COURT OF APPEAL ORDER RETRIALS OR DECIDE FOR ITSELF?

In his book *The Judge* (OUP, 1979, pp 148–76) Lord Devlin argued powerfully that the Court of Appeal had started to usurp the function of the jury in deciding doubtful cases by either quashing the conviction or by applying the proviso. He took as his text *Stafford* v *DPP* [1974] AC 878 and the Luton Murder Case, in which the Court of Appeal repeatedly refused to order a new trial even though crucial new evidence came to light.

In *Stafford* the House of Lords held unanimously that the task of the Court of Appeal in fresh evidence cases was to decide whether *it* thinks the verdict unsafe or unsatisfactory. It should consider the weight of the evidence and not concern itself so much with the question as to what effect it might have had on a jury. Lord Devlin had strongly criticised this approach on the ground that it usurped the function of the jury (see *The Judge*, pp 148–76). Under the rule adopted in *Stafford*, Stafford was not, in his view, convicted by a jury but rather by a mixed trial by judges and jury. It was in effect now the judges who had to evaluate the impact of fresh evidence. ('If the court has no reasonable doubt about the verdict, it follows that the court does not think that the jury could have one; and conversely, if the court says that a jury might in the light of new evidence have a reasonable doubt, that means that the court has a reasonable doubt', *Stafford v DPP* per Lord Dilhorne at p 893.) But the danger of that approach in Lord Devlin's view was that it could lead to an end to the jury ('If judge and jury are bound to give the same answer why bother with a jury?').

For a recent illustration of the principle being applied see *R v Trevor* [1998] Crim LR 652. See further Patrick O'Connor (1990) 'The Court of Appeal:Retrials and Tribulations', *Criminal Law Review*, pp 620–5, and generally Kate Malleson, 'Miscarriages of Justice and the Accessibility of the Court of Appeal' (1991) *Criminal Law Review*, p 323.

The issue came up again in *Pendleton*[74]. In 1985 P was convicted of a murder committed in 1971. In 1999 the case was referred back to the Court of Appeal by the Criminal Cases Review Commission in light of fresh evidence. The Court of Appeal received the fresh evidence but held that it did not affect the safety of the conviction. P appealed to the House of Lords and, surprisingly, persuaded their lordships to overturn the Court of Appeal's decision. (Lord Hobhouse in a concurring opinion expressed his disquiet that the House of Lords should become involved in a question that was properly the province of the Court of Appeal.) On the question of principle the law lords unanimously affirmed *Stafford*. Lord Bingham, with the approval of all the judges, said that the test to be applied was the effect of the fresh evidence on their minds, not the effect it would have had on the mind of the jury (para 19). But in approving *Stafford*, Lord Bingham put a slightly new spin on the issue. Counsel for the appellant, Mr Michael Mansfield, had argued for the view urged by Lord Devlin. This, Lord Bingham said, had the merit of reminding the Court of Appeal that it was not and should never become the primary decision-maker. Secondly, it reminded the Court of Appeal that it had an imperfect and incomplete understanding of the full processes which led the jury to convict.

> For these reasons it will usually be wise for the Court of Appeal, in a case of any difficulty, to test their own provisional view by asking whether the evidence, if given at the trial, might reasonably have affected the decision of the trial jury to convict. If it might, the conviction must be thought to be unsafe. (para 19)

The question for consideration, Lord Bingham said, was 'whether the conviction is safe and not whether the accused is guilty' (para 19). That question had to be separated from the quite different question whether there could or should be a retrial. ('A conviction cannot be thought unsafe if a retrial can be ordered but safe if it cannot.' (para 20).).

In his concurring speech Lord Hobhouse took a more robust approach. He pointed out that if the jury's decision should be paramount – it was Mr Mansfield's argument that was unprincipled – 'since it is he who is seeking to escape from the verdict of a jury merely upon the possibility (which will exist in almost every case) that the jury might have returned a different verdict' (para 36).

Commenting on the decision Professor Sir John Smith suggested that if Lord Devlin

[74] [2001]UKHL 66, [2002]1 All ER 524, [2002] Crim LR 398.

were alive he would not have been satisfied by it but that did not mean that the decision was wrong: 'Giving effect to Lord Devlin's opinion would have meant that in all cases where fresh evidence was admissible there would have to be either a new trial or, if that was impracticable, a final acquittal'.[75]

In *Mills (No 2), Poole (No 2)* [2003] EWCA Crim 1753, (2003) Times, 26 June), the Court of Appeal, quashing two 1990 murder convictions, held that what it called the *Pendleton* impact test as a range of permissible intrusion into the jury's thought processes was equally applicable where the new matter was one of argument, either of law, or interpretation of or inference from the evidence at trial.

The Runciman Royal Commission considered Lord Devlin's criticism that the Court of Appeal usurped the function of the jury if it decided the effect of fresh evidence on the result. It agreed with Lord Devlin save if the fresh evidence was so clear cut as to satisfy the Court of Appeal that it rendered the conviction unsafe–in which case it should quash the conviction. Otherwise, having admitted fresh evidence on the basis that it was relevant and capable of belief which could have affected the outcome of the case, it should order a retrial unless that was not practicable or desirable. ('The Court of Appeal, which has not seen the other witnesses in the case nor heard their evidence, is not in our view the appropriate tribunal to assess the ultimate credibility and effect on a jury of fresh evidence' (p 175, para 62).)

Where a retrial was not practicable or was otherwise undesirable in an appeal based on fresh evidence the Commission unanimously thought that there was no alternative other than the Court of Appeal deciding the matter for itself (p 175, para 63).

It is to be noted that there is in fact no way of taking away from the Court of Appeal the duty of deciding what *it* thinks about fresh evidence since, unavoidably, it always has to decide the initial questions – is the evidence capable of belief and significant. This is not usurping the role of the jury but it does involve consideration of the credibility and importance of the evidence – *pace* Lord Devlin.

3. The machinery for avoiding a miscarriage of justice in criminal cases

The problem of the machinery for dealing with miscarriages of justice has been a contentious issue for years. It came sharply into focus especially in the context of the three IRA cases–the Guildford Four, the Maguire Seven and the Birmingham Six.[76] In all three cases the defendants had their convictions quashed by the Court of Appeal.

---

[75] [2002] Crim LR 400.

[76] Mountains of newsprint, major television programmes and books all played an important part in the saga of these three cases. On the Guildford Four and Maguire cases see in particular Grant McKee and Ros Franey, *Time Bomb*, (Bloomsbury, 1988), Robert Kee, *Trial and Error* (Hamish Hamilton, 1986) and Sir John May, *Interim Report on the Maguire Case*, July 1990, HMSO, HC 556 and *Second Report on the Maguire Case*, 1992, HC 296. On the case of the

In all three the defendants had served long terms of imprisonment. In all three it took years of campaigning to get them set free and in each case it was eventually proved that they had been the victims of a miscarriage of justice. The Government announced the establishment of the Royal Commission on Criminal Justice on the same day that the Birmingham Six were set free, 14 March 1991. One of the topics specifically referred to in the terms of reference of the Commission was 'the arrangements for considering and investigating allegations of miscarriages of justice when appeal rights have been exhausted'. As will be seen below, the Royal Commission recommended that a new system be established for dealing with this problem and the recommendation was implemented in the Criminal Appeal Act 1995 which received the Royal Assent in July 1995.

The problem has been the subject of a number of reports and studies over the past quarter of a century. A distinguished role in this long battle to set things right was played by JUSTICE, the British Section of the International Commission of Jurists. Its report in 1968 (*Home Office Review of Criminal Convictions*) was effectively the first to examine the machinery critically. Since then, as will be noted below, there have been various further reports.

(a) Powers of the Home Secretary

When someone has exhausted his right of appeal to the courts his last recourse is to appeal to the executive. The Minister responsible for such matters is the Home Secretary. There are various powers that may be deployed.

(1) FREE PARDON

The Minister could recommend that the person be given a free pardon. This wipes out the effects of conviction and sentence though, curiously, not the conviction itself. (See *Foster* [1984] Crim LR 423). In *R v Secretary for the Home Department, ex p Bentley* [1993] 4 All ER 442 the Divisional Court held that the courts could review the refusal by the Home Secretary to recommend the grant of a pardon. The court accepted that to get a free pardon it was necessary to establish both moral and technical innocence. See to the same effect the evidence of the Home Office to the Home Affairs Committee of the House of Commons: 'It is a long-established policy that the Free Pardon, as an exceptional act of grace, should be confined as far as possible to those who are morally as well as technically innocent. This "Clean Hands" doctrine means that the Home Secretary must be satisfied before recommending a Free Pardon that in the incident in question the defendant had no intention of committing an offence

---

Birmingham Six see especially Chris Mullin's *Error of Judgment* (Poolbeg, 1990). Apart from the reports and articles referred to in the following pages, see also the special issue of the *New Law Journal* on miscarriages of justice, 17 May 1991.

and did not in fact commit one' (JUSTICE, Miscarriages of Justice, 1982, p 3, para 12).

(2)   CONDITIONAL PARDON

The conditional pardon substitutes one form of punishment for another, again leaving the original conviction standing.

See, on these alternatives, ATH Smith, 'The Prerogative of Mercy, the Power of Pardon and Criminal Justice' (1983) *Public Law*, p 398. See also Alison Wolfgarten, 'Free Pardon', *Solicitors' Journal*, 28 February 1986, p 157.

Most free pardons occur in road-traffic and minor offences, usually for technical reasons. Frequently, for instance, the reason is that a whole batch of speeding convictions is cancelled when it is discovered that the stretch of road in question was not properly marked.

The Home Office's evidence in 1982 to the House of Commons Home Affairs Committee gave statistics about the use of the free pardon. In the eight year period 1972 to 1980 there had been 2,180 instances in which free pardons had been granted in regard to the original conviction. In nine-tenths of the cases the conviction had been for minor motoring offences. There had also been a total of 1,519 cases in which action had been taken on other grounds, such as compassionate remission of imprisonment or early release resulting from assistance given to the prison authorities (*Sixth Report of the House of Commons Home Affairs Committee*, 'Miscarriages of Justice', 1982,Cm 421, Appendix A, p 7).

For a suggestion that failure to exercise the power of mercy might in some circumstances be open to judicial review see BV Harris, 'Judicial Review and the Prerogative of Mercy? *Public Law*, Autumn 1991, p 386.

(3)   REMISSION

Remission, also under prerogative, consists of a reduction in a sentence without a change in the nature of the sentence.

(4)   REFERENCE TO THE COURT OF APPEAL, CRIMINAL DIVISION UNDER THE CRIMINAL APPEAL ACT 1907, s 17 (AS AMENDED)

The Home Secretary could refer a case to the Court of Appeal. In the eight years 1981 to 1989 the Home Secretary referred a total of 39 cases involving 54 defendants. In 18 of these cases the appeals were allowed. (Home Office evidence to the May Inquiry into the Guildford and Woolwich pub-bombings.) The Report of the Runciman Royal Commission, (p 181, fn 5) stated that in the three years from 1989 to 1992 there were a total of 28 cases referred involving 49 defendants. 35 had their convictions quashed. Two were ordered to be retried and in both cases the defendant was acquitted. One appeal was dismissed. The rest were then still pending.

(b) Other powers

In particular cases, the Home Secretary may be in a position to release a prisoner on licence, by virtue of his sentence of life imprisonment. Although these powers are normally exercised on considerations not affecting the original conviction, there is some evidence that they are occasionally used in this way.

(c) Principles upon which the powers of the Home Secretary were exercised

The 1968 JUSTICE Report (above) reported on the criteria for acting adopted by the Home Office:

> The overriding factor governing the exercise of the powers available to the Home Secretary is a proper concern to avoid even the appearance of interfering with the independence of the judiciary. Home Secretaries have accordingly taken a very restricted view of the proper scope for executive intervention—a matter which has been dealt with before a competent court is not normally considered to be reviewable. As a consequence, a Home Secretary will only intervene in cases where evidence is presented by the petitioner which was not available to the courts which dealt with the case. At the level of executive review, the onus of proof is effectively reversed. In cases where the petitioner fails to convince the Home Secretary of his innocence, but establishes that a serious doubt exists as to his guilt, he may be granted some remission of his sentence, or released on licence if the sentence is appropriate. Remission is more commonly granted however in respect of matters arising during the currency of the sentence, such as ill health, or as reward for assistance to the police or prison authorities.

(d) Procedure

The Home Office would rarely move on its own initiative. The Chief Constable of the police force in question was often asked to investigate any fresh evidence. Sometimes a different force would investigate.

Prisoners, inevitably, had great difficulty in putting their points effectively. They usually had no legal or other professional help. Unless there was a public campaign by the media or some individual journalist or an organisation like JUSTICE, the Home Office usually paid little attention to prisoners' petitions. Perhaps understandably, neither the Home Office nor the police showed much enthusiasm for re-examining cases.

In the years from 1968 to the Report of the Runciman Royal Commission in 1993 this topic was considered by JUSTICE (1968)[77]; the Devlin Committee (1970)[78]; the House of Commons Home Affairs Committee (1982)[79]; and JUSTICE again (1989)[80] The main recommendations of these reports, which were covered in the previous edition of this work, are not included here as they are now of purely historical interest.

The case for a new independent system to investigate miscarriages of justice was made by the Home Affairs Committee in 1982 and by JUSTICE in 1989. In October 1989 the Home Secretary and the Attorney-General appointed Lord Justice May to inquire into the circumstances leading to the conviction of the 'Guildford Four' and the Maguire family in respect of the pub bombings in Guildford and Woolwich in 1974.[81] The inquiry was partly about the circumstances of the particular cases but it was also about the general problem of miscarriages of justice. Many of those who gave evidence to the May Inquiry supported the call for some form of independent body to assist the Home Secretary to identify cases. In addition to JUSTICE they included the Criminal Bar Association, the Law Society, the National Association of Probation Officers, the Society of Labour Lawyers and the Legal Action Group.

The most significant (and surprising) piece of evidence to the May Inquiry on this matter was the oral statement of Mr Douglas Hurd, then the Foreign Secretary, who had been the Home Secretary between 1985 and 1989 and in that capacity had been concerned with the Maguire case. In his evidence on 2 October 1991 Mr Hurd said that he was now persuaded that the power to refer possible miscarriages of justice should be removed from Home Secretaries and given to an independent standing body with investigative facilities.

In 1987 he had told the House of Commons that cases should be referred to the Court of Appeal only when new evidence or new considerations of substance cast doubt on a conviction. It was important that Home Secretaries not bow to other pressures. He told the May Inquiry that Home Secretaries came under 'fairly continuous pressure in case after case to use the power to reopen arguments already before the courts'. In the face of that, successive Home Secretaries had 'tried to establish rules and criteria which would enable them to exercise the power without getting into a position where they are in effect substituting themselves for the court'. He explained to the May Inquiry that he had refrained from referring the cases back

77   *Home Office Review of Criminal Convictions*. For the Government's response see House of Commons, *Hansard*, 22 July 1971, col 1652.

78   *Evidence in Identification in Criminal Cases* (1976), House of Commons Paper 338.

79   'Miscarriages of justice', Sixth Report from the Home Affairs Committee, 1982, Cm 421. See also *The Government Reply to the Sixth Report from the Home Affairs Committee*, 1983.

80   *Miscarriages of Justice*.

81   Sir John May was a member of the Runciman Royal Commission. The *general* question of the machinery for handling miscarriage of justice cases was transferred by his Inquiry to the Royal Commission.

to the Court of Appeal for fear of undermining public confidence. It would be better if these pressures could be handled by some new machinery. Possibly it might consist of some form of 'court of last resort' or an independent investigatory bureau. But it should have the power itself to refer cases to the Court of Appeal.

(e)   The Runciman Royal Commission on Criminal Justice

The Runciman Commission reported in July 1993. Its recommendations on the machinery for dealing with miscarriage of justice cases were unanimous. The main recommendation was that the responsibility for dealing with these cases should be taken away from the Home Office and given instead to a new body independent of Government. Most of the witnesses who gave evidence to the Runciman Commission, including the Home Office, the Home Secretary and two former Home Secretaries, had urged this upon the Commission.

The Royal Commission said (Report, p 182, para 9)

> Our recommendation is based on the proposition, adequately established in our view by Sir John May's Inquiry, that the role assigned to the Home Secretary and his Department under the existing legislation is incompatible with the constitutional separation of powers as between the courts and the executive. The scrupulous observance of constitutional principles has meant a reluctance on the part of the Home Office to enquire deeply enough into the cases put to it and, given the constitutional background, we do not think that this is likely to change significantly in the future.

It recommended that a new body be set up 'to consider alleged miscarriages of justice, to supervise their investigation if further inquiries are needed, and to refer appropriate cases to the Court of Appeal' (ibid, para 11). It suggested that the new body might be called the Criminal Cases Review Authority (CCRA). In the event, the Government decided instead that it should be called the Criminal Cases Review Commission (CCRC). (For convenience the new body will be referred to here as the CCRC, whether reference is being made to the recommendations of the Royal Commission or to the provisions of the Criminal Appeal Act 1995.)

The Royal Commission proposed that the applicant could apply to the new body only after his appeal against conviction had been turned down or he had been refused leave to appeal. The CCRC would investigate the case if it thought an investigation was called for. Where it instructed the police to conduct investigations, it would be responsible for supervising the investigation and would have the power to require the police to follow up lines of inquiry it thought necessary. If the investigation suggested that a miscarriage of justice might have occurred, the CCRC would refer the case to the Court of Appeal which would consider it as if it were an appeal referred by the Home Secretary under s 17. The CCRC would provide the court with a statement of reasons and such (admissible) supporting material as it thought desirable (Report, pp 182–83. paras 12, 16).

If it considered there were no grounds for a reference it would explain this decision, with its reasons, to the applicant (Report, pp 183, para 12).

The CCRC would be independent of Government but there would have to be a Minister answerable for it in Parliament. That should be the Home Secretary. The CCRC would report annually to the Minister who would lay the report before Parliament. The chairman should be appointed by the Queen on the advice of the Prime Minister. The other members could be appointed by the Lord Chancellor (p 182, paras 13–14).

The Court of Appeal should have power to refer cases to the CCRC for investigation and the CCRC would report to the Court of Appeal about the outcome of any such investigation. But the CCRC would be wholly separate from the Court of Appeal and would not form a part of the court structure (p 183, para 15).

When the Court of Appeal received a reference from the CCRC it would ensure that the defence and the prosecution had a copy of the statement of reasons and the supporting material together with any additional material that it thought fit, so far as that was not prohibited by public interest immunity (p 183, para 13 and p 187, para 31). The appellant would present his case as he saw fit and he would be able, as before, to raise any matter of fact or law regardless of whether it was included in the papers sent to the CCRC (p 183, para 16).

The Home Secretary could continue, very exceptionally, to exercise the Royal Prerogative of Mercy especially for cases that the Court of Appeal could not consider under the existing rules, for instance because of the rules of evidence (p 184, paras 17-18).

The CCRC should not be subject to judicial review in respect of its decisions. (p 184, para 19).

The CCRC should consist of several members, some lawyers, some lay persons. Not all would need to be full-time. The chairman should not be a serving member of the judiciary (p 184, para 20). It should be supported by a staff of lawyers and administrators and it should have access to specialist advisers such as forensic scientists, as necessary. It might be desirable for it to have on its staff one or two people expert in investigations especially to assist it in supervising police investigations (p 185, para 21).

In its annual report the CCRC should be able to draw attention to general features of the criminal justice system which it found unsatisfactory and to make any recommendations for change it thought fit (p 185, para 22).

The Royal Commission did not attempt to define the test the new body should use in deciding whether to investigate a case. ('In practice, it will need no further justification for investigating a case than a conclusion on the part of its members that there is, or may be on investigation, something to justify referring it to the Court of Appeal' (p 185, para 24).) The CCRC would need to devise its own rules and procedures for selecting cases for investigation.

The CCRC should be resourced sufficiently to enable it when appropriate to discuss cases direct with applicants. ('It is not always possible for people who have suffered a miscarriage of justice and then been sentenced to a long term of imprisonment to set out their case clearly and cogently in writing and an interview may sometimes be the best way of convincing the [Commission] that the case is one worth investigation' (p 185, para 25).)

The Royal Commission considered but rejected the idea that investigations should be carried out by persons other than the police. 'Given the size and scope of the inquiries that sometimes have to be made in these cases, and the resources required, there is in our view no practicable alternative to the police carrying out the investigation' (p 186, para 28).

There would need to be adequate arrangements for granting legal aid to convicted persons after they had lost their appeals to enable them to make representations to the Commission (p 187, para 32).

(f) The Criminal Appeal Act 1995 establishing the Criminal Cases Review Commission

The recommendations of the Royal Commission were broadly implemented in the Criminal Appeal Act 1995. The Act established the Criminal Cases Review Commission (CCRC), consisting of not fewer than 11 persons, all of whom have to be appointed by the Queen on the recommendation of the Prime Minister. At least one-third have to be legally qualified. At least two- thirds must be persons with knowledge or experience of the criminal justice system. There is no prohibition on a serving judge being on or chairman of the Commission. The first chairman, Sir Frederick Crawford, was a lay person, a distinguished scientist. The Commission began work in 1997.

In Scotland, following the recommendations of the Sutherland Committee[82] an equivalent Scottish Criminal Cases Review Commission was set up in 1999.[83]

The CCRC's power to refer a case to the Court of Appeal applies not only to Crown Court conviction issues but also to Crown Court sentencing issues and to conviction and sentence cases dealt with by magistrates. It also applies to Northern Ireland cases.

A reference to the Court of Appeal cannot be made unless the Commission 'considers that there is a real possibility that the conviction, verdict, finding or sentence would not be upheld were the reference to be made ... because of an argument, or evidence, not raised in the proceedings which led to it or on any appeal or application for leave to appeal against it' (s 13(1)(a), (b)). In the case of a sentence, it must be a new point of law or information (s 13(1)(c)).

---

[82] *Criminal Appeals and Alleged Miscarriages of Justice*, 1996, Cmnd 3425, ch 5.
[83] The Crime and Punishment (Scotland) Act 1997, s 24 inserted a new Pt (XA) into the Criminal Procedure (Scotland) Act 1995.

A pre-condition in either case is that an appeal has been determined or leave to appeal has been refused. However, the CCRC retains a discretion to make a reference even if these conditions are not fulfilled 'if it appears to the Commission that there are exceptional circumstances which justify making it' (s 13(2)).

The Minister told the House of Commons during the Committee Stage of the Bill that these criteria were wide enough 'to enable a conviction, verdict or finding to be referred if there was new evidence, or new argument in relation to evidence which has already been raised, which is of sufficient weight in the context of the whole case to give rise to a real possibility of the conviction, verdict or finding not being upheld on appeal' (House of Commons, Standing Committee B, 30 March 1995, col126).

In *R v Criminal Cases Review Commission, ex p Pearson* [1999] 3 All ER 498, in a lengthy judgment delivered by Lord Bingham, Lord Chief Justice, the Divisional Court reviewed the functions and powers of the Commission. Its task, he said, was to predict what view the Court of Appeal would take as to whether a conviction was unsafe. That phrase included cases in which the court, though not persuaded of the appellant's innocence, was 'subject to some lurking doubt or uneasiness whether an injustice has been done'.[84] That was a judgment entrusted to the Commission and to no one else. If a decision not to refer a case was challenged, the courts would not consider whether the CCRC's judgment had been objectively right or wrong. The court would only consider whether it was reasonable and lawful.

The Scottish Commission has broader statutory powers. It may refer a case if it believes '(a) that a miscarriage of justice may have occurred; and (b) that it is in the interests of justice that a reference should be made'.[85] So, at least according to the statutes, unlike the English Commission, the Scottish is not required to 'second-guess' the Court of Appeal's approach to the referral.[86]

In a decision of major importance, the House of Lords in *Kansal (No2)*[87] held that an appellant who had been convicted before the implementation of the Human Rights Act 1998 could not rely on convention rights in an appeal heard after the implementation of the Act.[88] This has obvious implications for the work of the CCRC since it will have to adopt the same approach.

---

[84] P 503, citing *Cooper*, above.

[85] Criminal Procedure (Scotland) Act 1995, s 194C as amended.

[86] See, however, the decision of the High Court of Justiciary in *Crombie v Clark* 2001 SLT 635 which suggests that the Scottish Commission must have some regard to the likely attitude of the High Court. The difference in the statutory provision was based on the Sutherland Committee's apparent view that the English criteria were too stringent – see its report para 5.62. For consideration of the implications of the difference between the English and the Scottish statutes in this regard see P Duff, 'Criminal Cases Review Commissions and "Defence" to the Courts: The Evaluation of Evidence and Evidentiary Rules' [2001] *Criminal Law Review* 341-62 and the follow-up correspondence at 761-63.

[87] [2001] UKHL 62, [2002] 2 AC 69, [2002]1 All ER 257.

[88] Applied in *Rezvi* [2002] UKHL 1, [2003] 1 AC 1099, [2002] 1 All ER 801 and *Benjafield* [2002] UKHL 2, [2003] 1 AC 1099, [2002] 1 All ER 815.

During the Lords Committee stage of the Criminal Appeal Bill, the Minister rejected a Labour attempt to amend the Bill so as to permit a reference where a point was new because it had not been adequately considered at the trial or the appeal. That amendment, Baroness Blatch said, 'would enable the Commission to refer a case on no grounds other than that, in its opinion, the courts had given insufficient consideration to some matter or matters that had come before it' (House of Lords, *Hansard*, 8 June 1995, col 1515). That would not be right 'as it would put the Commission in the invidious position of asserting its opinion or judgment on a matter above that of the courts' (ibid). The Commission was not 'a court of last resort, second guessing, sitting over and above the appellate courts' (ibid).

However, 'Where an argument was so poorly presented that the courts may have been misled, or where the appellant's case was not put to the court, then the Commission could reasonably regard such matters as new and could refer' (ibid).

When making a reference the CCRC gives the court and all the parties a statement of its reasons (s 14(4)). Equally, if the Commission decides not to refer a case, it must give a statement of its reasons to the applicant (s 14(6).) But regardless of the CCRC's reasons for the reference to the Court of Appeal, the convicted person is at liberty to raise any point he wishes – s 14(5).[89]

In *R v Secretary of State for the Home Department, ex p Hickey (No 2)* [1995]1 All ER 490 the Divisional Court held that before the Home Secretary made a decision whether to refer a case under s 17 of the 1968 Act the convicted prisoner was entitled to disclosure of fresh information revealed by inquiries about his case. Lord Justice Simon Brown, giving judgment, said that advance disclosure was required in the interests of both fairness and informed decision-making and the guiding principle on the level of disclosure to be sufficient should be such as to enable the petitioner to present his best case effectively. He could only do that if he adequately appreciated the nature and extent of the evidence that had been produced by the Home Secretary's inquiries. The CCRC is subject to the same duty of disclosure.

The CCRC has the power to obtain documents (ss 17, 18). This includes access 'to all relevant information held by the Secretary of State, whether it is representations by, or on behalf of, any person claiming wrongful conviction, or police reports, forensic science reports, opinions from lawyers, doctors, and other independent experts, transcripts of legal proceedings, correspondence and records of telephone conversations' (House of Lords, *Hansard*, 8 June 1995, col 1529). It does not, however, receive advice to Ministers about cases from their civil servants. That would put the Commission in an invidious position. It would be vulnerable to the charge of having been unduly influenced by the views taken during the earlier consideration of the case by a different authority.

---

[89]   See *Smith (Wallace Duncan)(No 3)* [2000] EWCA Crim 2907, [2003]1 Cr App Rep 648, [2003] Crim LR 398.

The powers of the Scottish Commission are greater since, on application to a court, it may seek documents held by anyone (not only by public bodies) and it can apply for a warrant to compel anyone to give a statement on oath (known as a precognition).

As proposed by the Royal Commission, when investigations are conducted on behalf of the CCRC they are generally conducted by the police. In supervising or directing the police, the CCRC play a role similar to that played by the Police Complaints Authority. The CCRC can require a chief officer of police to appoint a person from his own force or another force to carry out an investigation (s 19). It also has a power of veto over the selection of the officer by the chief constable (ibid). It can direct the actual investigations made and can sack the investigating officer (s 20). In practice, however, the Commission generally carries out its own investigations.

The Home Secretary told the House of Commons on the 2nd Reading debate that the Government expected that, at least initially, the CCRC would have double the caseload of the existing machinery. It would need to employ a staff of about 60– some three times the Home Office staff in C3 division dealing with miscarriages of justice (House of Commons, *Hansard*, 6 March 1995, col 25).

At the outset the Commission took over the existing Home Office caseload (279 files). Understandably, there was a considerable initial surge of fresh applications – some of which related to cases previously rejected by the Home Office. The number of applications in the two first years was 1,103 and 1,037. In the next three years the numbers were somewhat lower – 777, 800 and 834 (*Annual Report*, 2001-02, p 17). But the backlog of cases, though reducing, is still great and the delay in getting a case reviewed is considerable. The number of cases where the review process had not yet begun peaked at 1,208 in May 1999, but had been reduced to 338 by March 2002.

The Commission has a residual power under s 16 of the 1995 Act to refer cases to the Home Secretary for consideration of the Royal prerogative of mercy where a reference to the CCRC is not possible. This might occur where the Commission is convinced that the applicant is innocent but the Court of Appeal would appear not to be able to quash the conviction. By March 2003 no such reference had been made.

All the posts on the board of the Commission including that of chairman were advertised publicly. In addition to the chairman, there were 13 other Commissioners. In March 2002 the CCRC had total staff of 92 including 49 Case Review Managers (CRMs). (By comparison, in 1995, C3 in the Home Office had a staff of 21.) The operating budget in 2001-02 was £6.4m.

The Commission started handling casework as from 31 March 1997. By March 2002, it had received a total of 4,830 cases and had completed 4,128. There had been a total of 161 referrals to the Court of Appeal. (161 referrals in five years is an average of some 30 per year compared with an average of under 10 per year by the Home Secretary pre-CCRC.) Of the 161 referrals, 94 had been determined. Two-thirds (66%) had resulted in the conviction being quashed; one third (34%) in it being upheld. Ten sentences (83%) had been varied, two (17%) had been upheld (*Annual Report*, 2001-02, pp 20-21).

The Commission posts a great deal of information about its work on its website: www.ccrc.gov.uk.

On the pre-CCRC era see for instance, K Malleson, 'The Criminal Cases Review Commission' [1995] *Criminal Law Review*, pp 929–37. See also R Nobles, D Schiff et al, 'The Inevitability of Crisis in Criminal Appeals' [1993] *The International Journal of the Sociology of Law*, 21; DS Greer, 'Miscarriages of Criminal Justice Reconsidered', 57 *Modern Law Review*, 1994, pp 58–74; Nobles and Schiff, 'Miscarriages of Justice: A Systems Approach', 58 *Modern Law Review*, 1995, p 299; Schiff and Nobles, 'Criminal Appeal Act 1995: the Semantics of Jurisdiction', *Modern Law Review*, May 1996, p 299.

For an assessment of the work of the Commission see, for instance, A James, N Taylor, C Walker, 'The Criminal Cases Review Commission: Economy, Effectiveness and Justice' [2000] *Criminal Law Review*, 140-53; R Nobles and D Schiff, 'The Criminal Cases Review Commission: Reporting Success?' 64 *Modern Law Review*, 2001, 280-99; the House of Commons Select on Home Affairs, *The Work of the Criminal Cases Review Commission*, HC 106 (1999);and HC 429 (2000).

See also generally, C Walker and K Starmer (eds), *Miscarriages of Justice: A Review of Justice in Error* (London, Blackstone Press, 1999); R Nobles and D Schiff, *Understanding Miscarriages of Justice: Law, the Media and the Inevitability of Crisis* (Oxford, OUP, 2000).

(g)   Compensation for wrongful conviction

Until 1988, compensation for wrongful conviction was paid by the Home Office on an ex gratia basis. Such payments, it was explained in a Parliamentary statement in 1976, were made 'not as recognition of liability but in recognition of hardship suffered'.[90] Normally it was on the basis that there had been some 'misconduct or negligence on the part of the police or some public authority'[91]. Such payments could be made to persons who had received a free pardon or whose convictions had been quashed after a reference to the Court of Appeal by the Home Secretary.

In 1985 the Home Secretary announced that in future he would pay such compensation where this was required by international obligations:

> The International Covenant on Civil and Political Rights (Art 14.6) provides that, "When a person has by a final decision been convicted of a criminal offence, or he has been pardoned, on the ground that a new or newly discovered

---

[90]   House of Commons, *Hansard*, vol 916, 29 July 1976, cols 328-30.

[91]   Statement of the Home Office Minister, House of Commons, *Hansard*, vol 929, 1977, cols 835-36.

fact shows conclusively that there has been a miscarriage of justice, the person who has suffered punishment as a result of such conviction shall be compensated according to law, unless it is proved that the non-disclosure of the unknown fact in time is wholly or partly attributable to him."

I remain prepared to pay compensation to people who do not fall within the terms of the preceding paragraph but who have spent a period in custody following a wrongful conviction or charge, where I am satisfied that it has resulted from serious default on the part of a member of a police force or some other public authority.

There may be exceptional circumstances that justify compensation in cases outside these categories. In particular, facts may emerge at trial or on appeal within time, that completely exonerate the accused person. I am prepared, in principle, to pay compensation to people who have spent a period in custody or have been imprisoned in cases such as this. I will not, however, be prepared to pay compensation simply because at the trial or an appeal the prosecution was unable to sustain the burden of proof beyond a reasonable doubt in relation to the specific charge that was brought.[92]

The courts held, however, that the matter was entirely one for ministerial discretion[93] and that there was no duty to give reasons.[94]

In November 1987 the Home Office unexpectedly announced during the debate on the Criminal Justice Bill that it intended to move an amendment to give a statutory right of compensation where a court's final decision resulted in a conviction which was later reversed on the ground that new facts showed conclusively that the defendant was the victim of a miscarriage of justice—unless it was shown that the non-disclosure of the facts was due to the defendant's own fault (House of Lords, *Hansard*, 19 November 1987, cols 398–9). This became s 133 and Sch 12 of the Criminal Justice Act 1988.

Section 133(1) of the CJA 1988 states: 'when a person has been convicted of a criminal offence and when subsequently his conviction has been reversed or he has been pardoned on the ground that a new or newly discovered fact shows beyond reasonable doubt that there has been a miscarriage of justice, the Secretary of State shall pay compensation for the miscarriage of justice . . .unless the non-disclosure of the unknown fact was wholly or partly attributable to the person convicted'. It is for the Home Secretary to make the decision whether compensation is payable (s 133(3)). If payable, the amount is determined by an assessor appointed by the Home Secretary (s 133(4)).

---

92   House of Commons, *Hansard*, vol 87, 29 November 1985 WA col 689.
93   *R v Secretary of State for the Home Office, ex p Chubb* [1986] Crim LR 809 (Div Ct).
94   *R v Secretary of State for the Home Department, ex p Harrison* [1988] 3 All ER 86.

In 2002, the Divisional Court ruled that CJA 1988, s 133 only provided compensation for those ultimately proved innocent.[95] But the decision was reversed by the Court of Appeal.[96] As was seen above (p 621) the claimant had served 10 years of a 30-year sentence for IRA terrorism offences when his conviction was quashed by the Court of Appeal on the ground that his deportation to the UK after being arrested in Zimbabwe had been unlawful as an abuse of process. The Divisional Court held that 'miscarriage of justice' in the International Covenant on Civil and Political Rights (above) had a narrow meaning and that CJA 1988, s 133(1) was intended to have the same narrow meaning. Reversing the decision, the Court of Appeal said that the *travaux préparatoires* to the International Covenant showed that the phrase 'miscarriage of justice' was used in its wider rather than its narrower sense. There was no indication that the parties had intended that the claimant had to establish his innocence. Even if that were wrong, the phrase 'miscarriage of justice' was wide enough to embrace such circumstances as had occurred in this case. The presumption of innocence required that Acts of Parliament be interpreted on the basis that that it had not been intended that the state should proceed on the footing that a wrongly convicted man was guilty. If Parliament had intended that the claimant had to be proved innocent it could have said so.[97]

The Criminal Appeal Act 1995 added a new subsection 4A to section 133 that in assessing the amount of compensation in regard to loss of reputation, the assessor should have regard in particular to (a) the seriousness of the offence and the severity of the punishment; (b) the conduct of the investigation and prosecution; and (c) any other convictions of the person and any punishment in respect of those previous convictions. No doubt subsection (c) of this amendment was intended to lower the level of damages paid in such cases.

In June 1997 the Home Secretary issued a document to guide applicants: 'Compensation for Miscarriages of Justice: Note for Successful Applicants'. The note stated, 'In reaching his assessment, the assessor will apply principles analagous to those governing the assessment of damages for civil wrongs' (para 5).

A rare glimpse of the workings of system came in judicial review proceedings brought by cousins Vincent and Michael Hickey, who spent nearly 20 years in prison wrongly convicted of murdering paperboy Carl Bridgewater, and Michael O'Brien who had spent 11 years in prison after being wrongly convicted of the murder of newsagent Philip Saunders. The independent assessor, Lord Brennan QC, former chairman of the Bar, had awarded Vincent Hickey £506,000, Michael Hickey £ 990,000 and O'Brien £650,000. In each case he had reduced the amount attributable to loss of earnings by an amount representing the living expenses they had saved by virtue of being in prison! In his judgment Mr Justice Kay held that the deduction for saved

---

[95]   *R (Mullen) v Secretary of State for the Home Department* [2002] EWHC 230 (Admin), [2002] 1 WLR 1857.
[96]   [2002] EWCA Civ 1882, [2003] QB 993, [2003] 1 All ER 613.
[97]   Leave to appeal to the House of Lords was granted.

living expenses was wrong. But he upheld the assessor's rejection of a claim for the costs of financial advice and for counselling costs for one of the mothers.[98]

For consideration of the assessor's approach to damages see R Kapila, 'Compensation for miscarriages of justice', 153 *New Law Journal*, 16 May 2003, p 742. See generally Stephanie Roberts, '"Unsafe" Convictions: Defining and Compensating Miscarriages of Justice', 66 *Modern Law Review*, 2003, p 441.

---

[98]   *R (on the application of O'Brien) v Independent Assessor* [2003] EWHC 855 (Admin); [2003] NLJR 668.

Chapter 8

The legal profession

1. The component parts of the profession

The legal profession is divided into two main branches–the Bar and the solicitors' branch. The Bar is divided into two main parts–Queen's Counsel and juniors. The solicitors' branch consists of principals or partners, assistant solicitors and legal executives. Trainee barristers are known as pupils; trainee solicitors used to be called articled clerks. The office manager for barristers, who also fixes the fees and manages the allocation of work, is the clerk. Barristers practise in chambers ; they may not form partnerships. They must join an Inn of Court and may join a circuit. The affairs of the Bar are run by the General Council of the Bar and of the Inns of Court (the 'Bar Council') and its committees (The Bar Council's website is www.barcouncil.org.uk) The solicitors' branch is run by the Law Society and local law societies (the Law Society's website is www.lawsociety.org.uk).

A short elaboration of these basic features of the structure of the profession follows.

(a) The Bar

ORIGIN

The Bar dates back to the end of the thirteenth century. Originally and for a very long time, barristers could and did receive instructions direct from the lay client. It was not until the nineteenth century that it was finally settled that a barrister had to have instructions from a solicitor to appear in court.

INNS OF COURT

The profession's connection with what are now the Inns of Court dates back to the early fourteenth century when, on the dissolution of the crusading order of the Knights

Templar, the buildings were occupied by the lawyers who had previously lived in the area around the courts. By the end of the fourteenth century there were four societies in existence–the Inner and Middle Temples, Lincoln's Inn and Gray's Inn. In the seventeenth century the right to practise in the Royal Courts became restricted to members of the Inns of Court, and since that time they have enjoyed a monopoly over the right of admission to the Bar.

There are three categories of members of the Inns–benchers, barristers and students. Control of the Inns is vested in the benchers who are appointed by the existing body of benchers, normally from the ranks of judges and senior practitioners.

The Inns today have five main functions. They own and administer accommodation which is rented to barristers for professional chambers and to other persons for professional, commercial or residential purposes. They provide law libraries and common rooms for barristers and students. They provide lunches and dinners for their members. They award scholarships and bursaries for students and young barristers. They also play some part in the training of students and young barristers by the traditions of keeping term through the eating of dinners, by moots, talks and practical exercises both after dinner and at weekend meetings in places such as Cumberland Lodge in Windsor Great Park.

Most of the income of the Inns (some 90%) comes from rents. In 1974 the Inland Revenue agreed to treat the Inns as charities except to the extent that their income was applied to non-charitable purposes.

In June 2000 a Working Party on the Future of the Inns of Court chaired by Sir Murray Stuart-Smith recommended that membership of the Inns should be offered to solicitors entitled to appear in the higher courts – on payment of an entrance fee of £1,000. [1] The recommendation, however, proved highly controversial and it was not adopted. [2]

ENTRY AND TRAINING

Qualification for the Bar involves three stages: the academic stage; vocational training prior to Call to the Bar; and vocational training after Call to the Bar (pupillage).

---

[1]   Robert Seabrook, 'Read Beyond the Headlines', *Counsel*, August 2000, p 14. See also M.Bowley, 'A missed opportunity', 150 *New Law Journal*, 16 June 2000, p 907.

[2]   On 27 November 2000 the four Inns of Court in a press statement regarding the report said: 'This proposal was canvassed extensively throughout the membership of the four Inns, three of them holding open meetings to encourage the widest possible debate. It became clear that there was insufficient support for the proposal to be accepted at the present time. The fundamental problem lies in the structural and practical distinction between the two professions, which the members of the Inns do not believe should be compromised.' The statement said that 'the Council of the Inns of Court will however keep these developments under review'.

Joining an Inn and 'keeping term' A would-be barrister must become a member of one of the four Inns of Court.[3] One must then 'keep term'- which mainly means eating the required number of dinner in one's Inn.[4]

The academic stage The academic stage is normally fulfilled by taking a law degree but a person with a degree in some other subject is permitted to pass the academic stage by taking a one-year conversion course known as the Common Professional Examination (CPE) or Diploma in Law which for this purpose is deemed to be the equivalent of a law degree. About one quarter of all barristers enter the Bar via this route.

The vocational stage before Call – the BVC Thereafter, one must take the one-year full-time Bar Vocational Course (BVC). (Until recently a person not intending to practise in this country could simply take the Bar Examination and thereby call himself Barrister-at-law. But this has now been stopped. The last date for registering to take the Bar Examination was July 1997.) The Bar Examination course used to be highly academic and theoretical but it was re-vamped in 1989-90, since when it has been essentially designed to train young beginners in the kind of practical skills they will actually need in practice.[5] (For further information see www.bvconline.co.uk.)

The vocational stage after Call – pupillage After the BVC, would-be barristers have to find a set of chambers willing to take them on to do pupillage. The BVC provides only simulations. [6] Pupillage puts flesh on the skeleton by providing real-life experience under tutelage of a pupil master/mistress.[7] One must complete a full year of pupillage, though it is common to do two of six months each. At the end of the first six months the pupil is issued with a provisional practising certificate which allows him/her to accept instructions and to conduct cases. At the end of the satisfactory completion of the full 12 months the provisional practising certificate become a final

---

3   Until recently one had to join an Inn before registering for the vocational training course but this rule was abolished in 1997.

4   The requirement used to be to consume 36 dinners spread over 12 terms, of which there were four per year. The process therefore took at least three years, two of which had to be before Call to the Bar. That rule was changed so that students could 'keep term' by eating only 12 dinners spread over two years, one year of which could be after Call. More recently the dining requirement has been linked (as it was in the sixteenth and seventeenth centuries) to educational activities. After May 1998, 'keeping term' has meant attending 12 'qualifying sessions' spread over two years. A 'qualifying session' is defined as 'an event of an educational and collegiate nature arranged by or on behalf of an Inn'. (See Colleen Graffy, 'Coming to terms with keeping terms', *Counsel*, March/April 1997, p 14.)

5   See M Taylor, 'Pioneering Legal Skills Training', *Legal Action*, April 1995, p 6; J Shapland, 'Training for the Bar', *Counsel*, January / February 1995, p 19.

6   For the proposal that the course should include a period in chambers see N Bastin, 'Survival of the fittest', *Counsel*, October 1999, p 28.

7   For a summary of pupillage past, present and future see N Bastin, 'New pupils for a new century', *Counsel*, April 1998, p 30; J Shapland et al, *Pupillage and the vocational course*, (1995, Sheffield); J Shapland and A Sorsby, *Starting Practice:work and training at the junior Bar*, (1995, Sheffield); J Shapland and A Sorsby, *Good practice in pupillage* (1998, Bar Council).

certificate. There is no formal examination at the end of the pupillage. (The rules were recently amended to permit the first six months of pupillage to be spent in employment rather than with a barrister in private practice and to allow the second six to be spent training with a solicitor or with a lawyer in an EU country.)

Pre-1996, applicants had to apply for pupillages directly to chambers. As a result, chambers were inundated with applications; would-be pupils had to send dozens, or even hundreds, of applications. Inevitably the system favoured those with contacts. As from April 1996, in order to bring order into the system and to create a more level playing field, the Bar established the Pupillage Applications Clearing House (PACH) to operate in a similar way to the UCAS system for entry to university. Students were permitted to make only a limited number of applications. PACH collected the application forms, transmitted them to the participating chambers and communicated chambers' decisions to applicants. About 80% of chambers participated in this system. [8]

In October 2000 the Bar Council decided to move to a new online system of application – the On Line Pupillage Application System (OLPAS). [9] The new system went live in October 2002. As from 1 January 2003, save for recognized exceptions, all pupillage vacancies must be advertised on the OLPAS website (www.pupillageonline.co.uk)[10] One is only permitted applications to 12 sets of chambers. The system has a summer and an autumn season. Chambers are prohibited from making offers in respect of summer applicants before 31 July and in respect of autumn applicants before 31 October.

BVC providers Until 1997 the only way to become a practising barrister was to take the course provided by the Inns of Court School of Law (ICSL) in London. In a report in March 1991, the Taylor Working Party recommended that entry to vocational training for the Bar should be led by the requirement of numbers of practising barristers and that there should be a limit of 700 to 800 on the numbers admitted to the ICSL, the maximum that institution could accommodate. Instead, in June 1994, the Bar Council decided to permit institutions other than the ICSL to teach the BVC. The recommendation that there should be a limit on numbers admitted to the course was abandoned. A number of other institutions were validated to teach the course as from autumn 1997. Currently there are a total of eight: BPP Law School, the College of Law (London), Nottingham Trent University, the University of Northumbria, the University of the West of England (Bristol) and the Cardiff Law School and Manchester Metropolitan University.[11]

---

[8]   For discussion of the failings of PACH see N Shaw, 'The class of 2000', *Counsel*, February 2001, p 18.

[9]   'The way we are to recruit', *Counsel, December 2000*, p 16.

[10]   The exceptions are for pupillages sponsored with recognised training organisations; overseas pupils who intend to return to their own countries; solicitors or other qualified lawyers and academic lawyers.

[11]   For further information see www.legaleducation.org.

Between them the institutions offering the BVC have some 1,500 places. (In 2001–02 there were 2,116 applications for 1,540 places.)

The problem of numbers There has for many years been concern about the 'wastage' involved in the high proportion of students who get as far as taking the vocational course and then cannot find a pupillage, let alone a tenancy. The number of pupillages in 2002 was 766. The number of new tenancies each year is around 500. (In 2001–02 it was 527; in 2001–02 it was 490.) So around a third of those who take the BVC cannot start in practice.

The funding of the BVC The cost of the BVC in 2002–03 ranged between £7,000 and £9,750 (the average was £8,090), plus maintenance, estimated at that date at £6,500–7,500.

As recently as 1990-91, over 60% of students on the BVC received some kind of local education authority grant and nearly 50% received a grant covering their fees in full. This situation has changed dramatically. Six years later, in 1996-97, only 6% of students on the BVC had a grant and less than 3% received an award covering full fees.[12] (Students on the BVC raised the money needed for the vocational course mainly from a combination of loans (26%), Inn scholarships (28%) and parental support (25%) with the balance made up of a variety of sources.[13]) By 2003, local authority funding for the BVC had effectively ceased.

The 2002 *Report of the (Mountfield) Committee to Review Financial Support for Entrants to the Bar*[14] said (paras 5-6) that the effect of the withdrawal of local authority support for the BVC year had been compounded by the imposition of fees of £1,100 for the undergraduate period and the complete replacement of university maintenance grants by student loans. The result was that the average student left university with a debt of £10,000 and, on some estimates, more. If the student had to pay for the BVC and for subsistence he would approach pupillage with a debt of £25,000. For the student who had previously taken the one-year Common Professional Examination (CPE) to transfer from a non-law degree, the debt could be of the order of £36,000.

Referring to the broader social effects of such high debts, the 2002 Mountfield Report said:

> There is a wide consensus that the Bar needs to reflect, and be seen to reflect, the society it serves. Unless it does so, the Bar will increasingly be viewed with hostility and envy by the world at large, as an apparently privileged group drawn from a restricted segment of British society. The social background, gender and ethnic balance had been improving, driven by changes in higher education and by enlightened attitudes by the Bar. There is now a grave and immediate danger that these trends will be reversed because of the changes in public

---

[12]   *Report of the (Goldsmith) Working Party on Financing Entry to the Bar*, 1998, above, p 22.
[13]   Goldsmith Report, p 21.
[14]   Accessible *on* www.barcouncil.org.uk

support for students in higher education and the debt burden of students contemplating a career at the Bar. The social bias in the university system and even further back in the chain, in the school system, has the result that academically high achievers, as conventionally measured, tend to be concentrated in the white middle classes. Fewer than one in five young people from the lower socio-economic groups participate in higher education, well below the 45 percent who participate from the higher ones. [p.3, paras8-9]

The Inns of Court provide significant sums in scholarships. In 1998 the Goldsmith Report said that the Inns of Court provided about £1.75m scholarship and other moneys for students during the BVC year. The Mountfield Report said that by 2002 this had risen to some £2.3m. A general review of funding entry to the profession said that around a quarter of Bar students at that time received financial help from the Inns, with over half obtaining between £3,000 and £6,000.[15]

The 1998 Goldsmith Report recommended that the Bar should provide or procure direct financial assistance to the number of students who were likely to get tenancies, which it took at around 500. In respect of those 500 the Bar should increase its contribution to supporting the cost of the BVC year by £2m per annum. One way to achieve this would be if more chambers provided funding for the BVC year, which it, however, did not think was likely to be achievable. The best way, it thought, would be to raise money through an annual subscription for membership of the Inns of Court or by loans.

Four years later, the Mountfield Report said that chambers provided some £0.33m. in respect of the BVC year [16] In the Committee's view this was insufficient. It recommended that there should be a levy on the senior members of the profession to make it possible to fund some 400 BVC scholarships of about £8,000. Such funding, it said, was necessary to enable the Bar to compete for the ablest entrants with the support provided, for instance, by City solicitors' firms.

According to the Report, the cost would be some £3.5m, which it said was about 0.25% of the Bar's gross income. The levy, it recommended, should be based on barristers' gross income which should be imposed either wholly or mainly on those earning over £100,000. The money could be raised by requiring a charge of 0.25% of gross income for those earning between £100,000 and £250,000 and 0.5% for those earning about £250,000. (That would translate to £250 for the former and £625 for the latter – though the actual cost would be only half after tax and national insurance.)

However, the practising Bar, led by the commercial Bar rejected the Mountfield proposal. [17] The Chairman of the Bar, Mr David Bean QC, who had strongly urged

---

[15]   R.Epstein,'Learning the law-finding the funds' 152 *New Law Journal*, January 25, 2002, pp 91-92.

[16]   Annex D.

[17]   See *Counsel*, October 2002, p.6; December 2002, p.5.

the Bar to accept the proposal, said in the Bar Council's 's Annual Report for 2002 that the Director of Public Prosecutions, Sir David Calvert-Smith, was chairing a new Working Party which would report as to how to address the problem by July 2003. (For the Working Party's Report see the Bar Council's website.)

The funding of pupillage So far as concerns the funding of pupillage, in 1989, a working party under William Blackburne QC recommended that the Bar should finance a scheme by a levy on the profession whereby pupils would receive a minimum income of £6,000 pa during their pupillage year. Their report led to the establishment of a second working party under Sir Nicholas (now Lord) Phillips which took the view that it was neither practical nor lawful to impose on the Bar a scheme such as that proposed by the Blackburne Working Party. Instead it proposed that each set of chambers should be expected to offer a quota of funded pupillage places. The target would be 450 such funded places. This recommendation was adopted by the Bar Council in January 1990 and began in that year. By 1997, chambers were putting £5.3m. into the scheme and five years later in 2002 that figure had risen to £6m. [18]

The Goldsmith Report in 1998 proposed that the minimum of £6,000 pa should be increased to £10,000. [19] This proposal was implemented as from December 31, 2002. [20]

Continuing education From October 1 1997, new practitioners have been required to undertake a total of 42 hours of continuing education over a three-year period which must include further advocacy training and courses in ethics. In addition, attendance at an approved accountancy course is required.

From January 2003, compulsory continuing education (CPD) applied to practitioners called during or after 1990. The requirement is to complete 12 CPD hours per calendar year, of which four hours must be satisfied through 'accredited courses'. [21] (Details of accredited courses are available on the on-line database at www.legaleducation.org.uk.)

From January 2004 this will apply to those called between 1980 and 1989 and from January 2005 it will apply to all practising barristers called before 1980. [22] (On the importance of continuing legal education for barristers whether employed or in

---

[18]   The Mountfield Report, 2002, Annex D.
[19]   In the second six months of the pupillage, £5,000 could be earned by way of guaranteed receipts.
[20]   *Counsel*, April 2002, p.5. See also E Bowles, 'To fund or not to fund?, *Counsel*, February 2001, p 10. There was obviously a possibility that the mandatory payment of £10,000 would result in fewer pupilages – see *New Law Journal*, 22 November 2002, p 1744, reporting that the latest annual survey of the Bar by BDO Stoy Hayward suggested that the number of pupilages could drop by as many as 139.
[21]   J Creaton, 'To be continued', *The Lawyer*, 5 November 2001, p 33.
[22]   *Counsel*, June 2002, p.26. See www.legaleducation.org.uk

independent practice see Report of the Collyear Committee *Education and Training for the Bar, Blueprint for the Future*, June 1999.)

NUMBERS AT THE BAR AND RECRUITMENT

There has been a remarkable growth in the size of the Bar over the past 30 or so years. During the 1950s the number of barristers fluctuated at or somewhat below the figure of 2,000. In 1954, for instance, there were 2,010. Six years later, in 1960, the number had actually declined to 1,919. But in the years since then the number has more than quintupled. In 2002 it was 10,747.

From 1986 to 1998 the number of barristers grew at an average annual rate of 4.9%. In 1999, however, this rate of increase slowed to 2.4% and in 2000 it went to 2%. [23]

A considerable minority of those called to the Bar each year are from overseas. (In 2002, 18%.) It is also still the case that many qualify who never intend to practise.

The Bar estimated in 1991 that in the next decade it would need some 400 to 500 new 'starts in practice' to maintain an adequate flow into the private profession, plus another 150 to 200 or so coming to the Employed Bar to provide manpower for the Government Legal Service, the Crown Prosecution Service, commerce, finance and industry, local government, the armed forces, parliamentary counsel, etc (*Report of the* (Taylor) *Bar Entry and Training Working Party*, 1991).

It is estimated that there are some 3,000 or more 'employed' barristers. (On the position of Employed barristers see p 763 below.) There are also 'non-practising barristers' defined as barristers who are neither in chambers nor employed who may or may not be practising law. (The category includes lecturers, MPs, barristers working in law centres and some who offer specialised services from home or a private office.[24] Their organisation, called the Employed and Non-Practising Barristers' Association (ENPBA) has a website – www.enpba.org.)

CHAMBERS

A barrister does not have an office; he works in 'chambers'. In the past every practising barrister had to be a member of professional chambers. (As will be seen below a barrister who has been in practice for at least three years can now practise from home – but, though growing, this is still highly exceptional.)

Numbers of sets There are currently some 350 sets of chambers – a slight decline in the past few years resulting from mergers.[25] (In 1992-93 there were a total of 373 sets; five years later in 1997 there were 417 sets. [26]

---

[23]   BDO Stoy Hayward, *Report on the 2001 Survey of Barristers' Chambers*, p 8.
[24]   See G Parasie, ' Time, Gentlemen Please', *Counsel*, December 1999, p 26.
[25]   See 'D.Platt, 'The Urge to Merge', *Counsel*, April 2000, p.21.
[26]   Source: the Bar's Annual Report.

Practising outside the Inns of Court Until 1987 there was an unwritten rule that London barristers had to practise in the physical precincts of the Inns of Court. The rule was supported by the long-standing policy that barristers should be charged rents by the Inns that were distinctly lower than the going level of commercial rents. This rule, combined with the explosion of numbers at the Bar, resulted in a very serious accommodation crisis. (A survey in 1986 showed that 10% of London barristers were sharing a desk. Inner Temple had 2.14 barristers per room!)

In summer 1987 the Bar Council issued a statement that the Bar and the Inns had reached agreement on a new policy to ensure the availability of sufficient accommodation for the practising profession, especially in London. The two crucial elements were that the accommodation would, if necessary, be outside the Inns and that the rent would be at a commercial level. The capital for the development would come from moneys raised by mortgage on the properties of the Inns, which were then thought to be worth over £200m. (*New Law Journal*, 26 June 1987, p 580)

At first, the change in policy did not seem to have much effect. But then more and more chambers began to move out of the hallowed precincts of the Inns to more spacious and modern office accommodation in the neighbourhood.

An article in the Bar's journal *Counsel* in July 1991 said that 'Only a few years ago, any suggestion that chambers should move out of the confines of the Inns would have been greeted with horror as a culture shocking break with the past.' But now it was no longer so. 'What has promoted the departure of about a dozen seats from the Temple in the last twelve months has been overcrowding.' In some cases the Inns had assisted the process of moving out by becoming intermediate landlords.

The Benson Royal Commission in 1979 recommended that a barrister should be permitted to practise from home without a clerk but it took until 1989 before this was allowed. The rule is that a barrister who has been in chambers for not less than three years can practise on his own. The first year in which the Bar Council statistics reported the number of sole practitioners was 1993 when there were 68 out of a total of 7,735 barristers in private practice (0.8%). In 2002 it was 208 out of 10,747 (1.9%).

Chambers outside London Traditionally the Bar has been heavily a London-based profession but the proportion of barristers practising in the provinces has increased significantly. In the 1960s it was about one quarter. In the late 1990s it was one third. In 2002 it was 36%. The number of towns and cities outside London where there is a local Bar recently more than doubled. (In 1978 there were 28 cities outside London where barristers practised; 20 years later in 1997/78 there were 58.[27])

The trend is to establish more local Bars. The report 'Strategies for the Future', prepared by the Bar's Strategy Group and issued in October 1990 by the Bar Council, said that, reflecting the Government's policy there was likely to be a long-term trend towards administering justice from a small number of major regional centres. As part of this policy more legal services activity was likely to take place outside London.

[27]   The figure for 2002 was not available.

The county courts were taking on an increasing number of the larger cases. The Bar should 'support and encourage the broad policy of the further development of legal centres outside London' (para 3.16).

For the exploration of these trends by a geographer and a barrister see further M Blacksell and C Fussell, 'Barristers and the growth of local justice in England and Wales', 1994, 19 *Transactions Brit Inst Geogr NS*, pp 482-93. Their conclusion was that 'a more loosely-knit and regionally diverse legal culture was beginning to emerge' at the Bar.

Size of chambers Barristers' chambers have been getting larger and larger. The same 1990 report said: 'The ability of barristers to organise themselves into economic units that offer the best combination of efficiency and accessibility is critical to the future of the Bar' (para 3.24). The size of chambers had doubled in the previous twenty years to an average size of about 15, but the upward trend continued. The report recommended that the optimum size of chambers was at least 25 and that it could in some instances be as high as 50 or even more. ('Only highly specialised sets in high fee-earning areas of the law will be able to practise successfully in smaller units', para 3.28.) One reason for increasing the size of chambers was increased profitability. Barristers in larger chambers had higher gross and net earnings. A study published in July 1999 showed that some 15% of barristers were practising in chambers of over 50 members, 14% were practising in chambers of between 41 and 50 members, 30% were in chambers with 31–40 members, and 24% in chambers with 21–30 members. Only about 17% were in chambers with under 20 members.[28] In 2001, the average size of chambers had risen to 28.[29]

Efficiency The 1990 Bar Council report also dismissed as out-of-date the notion that chambers were still Dickensian in aspect. 'Most sets are now computerised either substantially or to some extent, with applications ranging from word processing, document transmission (fax) and routine accounting such as fee recording and billing, to more complex applications such as legal databases or the production of management information' (para 3.25). (A study had shown that non-computerised sets of chambers had between £0.5m. and £1m. more fees outstanding than computerised sets, resulting in a loss of interest on capital of up to £130,000 pa. This obviously far exceeded the annual cost of leasing basic level computerisation, which was around £7,000 (para 3.85).)

THE CLERK

The rule has been that each set of chambers must have a clerk.[30] Most sets have more than one clerk—one is then the senior clerk and the rest are junior clerks. The junior

---

[28]   BDO Stoy Hayward, *Report on the 1999 Survey of Barristers' Chambers*, p 8.

[29]   BDO Stoy Hayward, *Report on 2001 Survey of Barristers' Chambers*, p.14.

[30]   Technically this rule was changed in 1990 but few barristers choose to practise without a clerk. For description of such a rare case see P Norman, 'Practice without a clerk', *New Law Journal*, 11 July 1997, p 1039.

clerks perform functions that are normally understood by the term, 'clerical', but senior clerks have functions that go well beyond this. The Royal Commission on Legal Services (para 34.3) described the role as having three main components:

(1) *Office administrator and accountant* He maintains the accounts for the chambers as a whole and ensures that each member of chambers has adequate secretarial and other similar services.

(2) *Business manager* He works for each member of chambers individually in maintaining his professional diary; checking court lists for cases in which he is retained; negotiating fees; sending out fee notes and reminders; keeping the individual accounts.

(3) *Agent advising* barristers on the development of their practices; ensuring that beginners receive work according to their abilities and experience; advising solicitors as to which barristers to instruct; and advising on the allocation of work as between members of chambers.

This bald recital does not, however, convey the extent to which the clerk is the lynch-pin of the whole system. A high proportion of work coming into any set of chambers is actually allocated by the clerk. This is for a number of different reasons. Sometimes the solicitor asks on behalf of the lay client for Mr A. The clerk informs him that Mr A is not available to take the case on that date but that he has an excellent Mr B who will be free. The solicitor client will commonly agree to the suggestion that Mr B do the case–especially if he has previously been to those chambers and been broadly satisfied with the quality of the barristers he has instructed. Or the solicitor may be told that Mr A is available, but a day or so before the hearing he is told by the clerk that unfortunately Mr A has not completed his previous case (he is 'part heard' elsewhere) and the clerk suggests Mr B or Miss C both of whom are from the same chambers. The solicitor usually has little choice but to accept the recommendation, especially at the last moment. Another common situation is when the solicitor says from the outset that he has a particular kind of routine case and asks the clerk to find someone of the appropriate level of experience from his chambers to handle it.

The clerk also plays a crucial role in negotiating fees. His own remuneration, until very recently at least, was on a commission basis–in the order of 5 to 7% of gross chambers income without any contribution to chambers' expenses, or 8 to 10% of gross income with the clerk making some contribution towards expenses like a barrister member. It follows that the senior clerk has a direct financial stake in the level of fees earned by his principals. His interest is to set the fees as high as possible consistent with the aim of not losing the work. A solicitor who wishes to discuss the fee with the barrister is permitted to do so, but it is very rarely done. The earning capacity of the clerks is therefore extraordinary. A senior clerk on full commission could be drawing anything from 5% to 10% of the professional earnings of 20-50 or more barristers. He will normally be earning considerably more than most members of the chambers. However, the modern trend is for the senior clerks to be paid on a salary rather than a commission basis or on a combination of salary and commission.[31] *The Lawyer* reported in 2000 that senior clerks were 'facing concerted pressure to reduce their earnings as chambers cut overheads'.[32] Senior clerks at the five leading commercial sets were 'earning between £100,00 and £350,000 a year'.

The Benson Royal Commission said that most clerks go to great trouble to help newly qualified barristers to establish themselves. Nevertheless sometimes the power of allocation of work was not exercised fairly. This was to be deplored and must be avoided (para 34.37).

The only extended treatment of the arcane subject of the clerking system is John Flood's book *Barristers' Clerks* (Manchester University Press, 1983). For a short and racy piece see Ravinder Singh Chahal, 'Clerks no more on borrowed time', *The Lawyer*, 29 October 1996 and by the same author, 'A tough niche to carve', *The Lawyer*, 4 February 1997.

But the system is gradually changing with the growth in the size, complexity and modernisation of chambers and the increasing concern at the Bar for a more acceptable image. A woman clerk, for instance, is no longer a rarity. Clerks are increasingly likely to have considerable educational and other qualifications. Traditionally clerks came straight from school with few, if any, qualifications. Today they need considerable skills including the capacity to mastermind a multi-million-pound business. Sets of chambers looking for a new chief clerk are these days increasingly likely to advertise for an 'Administrator', 'Practice Manager' or 'Chief Executive'. (In 2001 some 22% of chambers had a Practice Manager or Chief Executive.[33])

The Bar's 1990 report, 'Strategies for the Future', said (para 3.46) that the present clerking arrangements suffered from a number of weaknesses including:
(1) the wide range of functions and skills required of clerks;
(2) inadequate specialist skills in marketing, performance management, information technology and accountancy;
(3) high costs associated with the commission-based remuneration of the clerk ('with some clerks earning significantly more than experienced barristers within their employing chambers');
(4) the potential for patronage or influence over the careers of barristers and undue lack of accountability to members of the set;
(5) unclear contractual relationships.

The report recommended that chambers should aim to have a staff (on normal pensionable employment contracts) consisting of two main figures. One would be

---

[31] The 2001 BDO Stoy Hayward Survey of Barristers Chambers showed (p.25) that 35% of chief clerks were on salary only (compared with 23% in 1999), while 29% were on commission only (compared with 35% in 1999 and 43% in 1997).

[32] 16 October 2000, p 1.

[33] BDO Stoy Hayward *Survey of Barristers Chambers*, 2001, p.20.

the Practice Manager, dealing with such matters as marketing and promotion, pricing, fee negotiation, practice development and accommodation strategy. The second would be the Administrator, dealing with accounting, billing, secretarial services, information technology, library facilities, etc.

They should be remunerated by a basic salary plus an annual performance-related bonus awarded by a management committee. 'There should be no commission or percentage element' (para 3.53). (The Practice Manager, it suggested, might in 1990 earn a maximum of, say, £48,000; the Administrator, say, £29,000 (para 3.55).)

Such new arrangements would need to be phased in. To convert the clerking system into an effective management capability would 'require determined action from the profession'. 'It will not be adequate to introduce change simply by waiting for retirements' (para 3.49).

QUEEN'S (OR KING'S) COUNSEL

On 29 April 2003 at the annual ceremony in the House of Lords when the new QCs are sworn in, Lord Irvine, the Lord Chancellor, announced, with no prior warning, that the competition for appointment as Queen's Counsel for 2004 was being suspended. 'The question I must resolve', he told the no doubt astonished and probably dismayed silks and their families, 'is whether the award of a quality mark is of such central importance to the effective operation of our legal system that it should continue to be made by the state. If the view prevails that a quality mark should still be awarded, but independently of government, then the state should stand aside and the grant of a quality mark would become an issue for the professions alone: the rank of Queen's Counsel would therefore go.' [34] He had already, four weeks earlier, on 2 April, told the new Lord Chancellor's Department Select Committee that a consultation paper would be issued 'before the summer in which the principal issue will be whether the status of Queen's Counsel should continue to exist'. (It was published on 14 July – see below.) It was clear from Lord Irvine's announcement on 29 April that the 2003 batch of new QCs could be the last to be appointed by the Queen. This impression was strengthened when six weeks later, on 12 June, the Prime Minister, Tony Blair, announced that the office of Lord Chancellor itself was to be abolished. (When Lord Irvine demurred he was told by Mr Blair that he was being replaced.). What follows was written before these extraordinary developments. It could now be of mainly historical interest.

Originally the division in the profession was between 'sergeants-at-law' and barristers. The first King's Counsel were appointed in the 17th century but at that time the title did not signify seniority in the profession but rather the function of assisting the law officers of the Crown in cases in which the Crown had an interest. In the course of

[34]   See S Hawthorne, 'Last of the line?',*Counsel*, June 2003, p 46.

the 18th and 19th centuries, appointments to the rank of King's Counsel came to be regarded as a mark of pre-eminence in the profession. By the end of the nineteenth century, no more appointments of sergeants-at-law were made and the senior rank amongst barristers was limited to King's (Queen's) Counsel– otherwise known as KC or QC or 'leaders' or 'silks'.

QCs have been appointed by the Queen on the advice of the Lord Chancellor. Toward the end of each year a notice was published in the legal journals informing practitioners who wished to be considered to submit their names to the Lord Chancellor. Only those who applied were considered. The process of selection has been described by the Lord Chancellor.[35] Applicants put in their curriculum vitae and the Lord Chancellor had inquiries made about each applicant by senior members of his staff. The list of applicants was sent to the law lords, the judges in the Court of Appeal and to all High Court judges as well as to certain senior circuit judges. The list also went to the Chairman of the Bar and to the leaders of the circuits and specialist Bars. Those consulted were encouraged to express their views about those on the list – after having taken discreet soundings among other leading silks. The Lord Chancellor's staff met the Bar Leaders and the Presiding Judges from each circuit. The staff had some 35 meetings on the subject. A provisional list of appointments was discussed with the Heads of Divisions (Lord Chief Justice, Master of the Rolls, President of the Family Division and Vice Chancellor, head of the Chancery Division).

A Bar Council Working Party (the Kalisher Committee) set up 'to investigate the methods, procedures and criteria for the appointment of Queen's Counsel', which reported in 1994, recommended that the pool of those consulted should be wider still – for instance by including Masters and Resident Circuit judges in main court centres.[36]

The Lord Chancellor takes into account not only the personal qualities of the applicant but also the total number of silks generally and the total number in the field in which the applicant practises. (The form filled out by those consulted has a space 'Ready for silk now, but not recommended for appointment this year because other, named, candidates are preferred in this field'.)

A person who is not appointed one year may apply again and it is very common to apply several times before being appointed.

The proportion of QCs to junior barristers has been kept at about 10% for many years. The percentage of successful applicants in the past 8 years has been between 12 and 17%, except for 2002 when it jumped to 26% and 2003 when it was 31%.[37] The number of appointments in 2002 was dramatically higher than in any previous year. Between 1994 and 2001 the annual number was around 70 with a high of 78.

[35]   See Lord Mackay, 'The Myths and Facts about Silk', *Counsel*, October 1993, p 11.
[36]   See C Frazer, 'The Silk Round', *Counsel*, July/August 1994, p 22.
[37]   *Counsel*, June 2002, Table 1, p.42; June 2000, Table 1, p 47.

For whatever reason,[38] it jumped in one year from 77 in 2001 to 113 in 2002 and to 121 in 2003.[39] The total number of QCs in December 2002 was 1,145–10.6% of the practicing Bar.

A person applied to become a QC for a number of reasons. One is the desire for advancement in the profession. QCs generally enjoy higher incomes and have a higher status. (They even have a separate bench to sit on in court.) The second reason is to lighten the load of work. The work of barristers is divided between advocacy, opinion and 'paper work', meaning in the main drafting of pleadings and similar documents. By tradition, paper work is reserved for junior barristers. It is not very well remunerated and is burdensome. Practitioners are usually happy to escape this work and to concentrate their efforts on advocacy in heavy cases and opinion work.

Applying for silk, however, is a gamble, mainly because of the old 'Two Counsel' rule. This was the rule that, normally, a Queen's Counsel should appear in court only with a junior as well. (There used to be a further rule that the junior was paid a fee equivalent to two-thirds of that paid to the QC. This was abolished by the Bar in 1971, but the junior is still normally paid the equivalent of either two-thirds or half the leader's fee.)

In 1976 the Monopolies and Mergers Commission in a special report (*Two-Counsel Rule*) stated that this restrictive rule was contrary to the public interest, though it accepted that paper work (eg drafting) should normally be done by juniors. This report was accepted by the Bar, which abolished the Two Counsel rule at the next AGM in 1977. Since then a QC has had the right to appear in court without a junior. But he is entitled to expect that a junior will be instructed unless the contrary is stated, and he may decline to accept instructions to appear without a junior if he thinks this would prejudice his ability to conduct the case or any other case or to fulfil his other professional obligations. In general, QCs tend to be employed in heavy matters where two counsel are appropriate.

It follows that when applying for silk the applicant must consider that clients are willing to pay not only the higher fees normally paid to leaders but also the fee of the junior who would normally appear with him. Some of those appointed as QCs do not become successful as leaders even though they had been highly successful as juniors.

The question whether the institution of silk should be scrapped came up periodically. In 1999, an early day motion proposing the abolition of QCs tabled by Mr Andrew Dismore, a backbench Labour MP, won the support of over 100 MPs. He also put down a series of parliamentary questions which elicited, inter alia, that the LCD's selection process cost the taxpayer a fair amount of money. Mr Geoff Hoon, at that

---

[38]   There was speculation that it was a defensive response to the threatening sounds about the institution emanating from the Office of Fair Trading – on which see pp 717, 765 below.)
[39]   *Counsel*, June 2001, p.42, *Counsel*, June 2003, p 47.

time Minister of State in the LCD[40], told the House of Commons during the Committee stage of the Access to Justice Bill that the total cost was of the order of £130,000, of which £120,000 was attributable to the elaborate consultation process.[41] (In 2002 there were 429 applications; in 2003 there were 394.) The Bar Council accepted that this cost should instead be borne by applicants and the Government introduced an amendment to the Access to Justice Bill to permit this.[42] In 1999 the fee was fixed at £335. By 2002 it had been raised to £720.

Mr Dismore's efforts to persuade the Government to abolish QCs initially met with less success. His proposed amendment was very simple, 'The office of Queen's Counsel is abolished'. Of the various argument he deployed the most weighty was the inflationary effect on fees. ('It simply enables QCs to charge more money for doing exactly the same work.[43]) Speaking to the amendment, the Minister, Mr Hoon, said that the rank of Queen's Counsel had existed since the end of the 16th century when it was first bestowed on Francis Bacon. Not that the Government would regard that as conclusive. ('We are a reforming Government and we would not be afraid to abolish an institution whose only value is as a relic of the past.'[44]) But, he said, the Lord Chancellor (who until the election in May 1997 was himself a practising QC) took 'a positive view' of the value of Queen's Counsel. 'By identifying the best advocates through a tough system of peer and judicial assessment, the award of silk is a kite mark of quality'. It enabled lawyers and clients to identify the leading members of the profession and to make more informed choices. It also provided an incentive to attain the highest standards of advocacy and integrity. It was right that the system should be conducted under the Government's auspices. The process of selection was open and was explained in a guide that was available on the LCD's website.[45]

In July 1999, however, the Lord Chancellor announced that he had asked Sir Leonard Peach, former Commissioner for Public Appointments, to examine the selection procedures for appointing both QCs and judges. (*The Times*, 28 July 1999.) The Peach Report (*An Independent Scrutiny of the Appointment Processes of Judges and Queen's Counsel in England and Wales* – www.lcd.gov.uk/majrepfr.htm) was published in December 1999. It stated that:

- the judges and the Bar's representatives seen were 'largely content' with the system;
- the officers of the Law Society were opposed to the concept of Silk and were 'firmly opposed to the consultation system';[46]

---

[40]   Before he became Secretary of State for Defence.

[41]   House of Commons, Standing Committee 'E', May 11, 1999, col 358.

[42]   House of Commons, Standing Committee 'E', May 11, 1999, col 357. See Access to Justice Act 1999, s 45.

[43]   House of Commons, Standing Committee 'E', May 11, 1999, col 363.

[44]   House of Commons, Standing Committee 'E', May 11, 1999, cols 372-73.

[45]   House of Commons, Standing Committee 'E', May 11, 1999, cols 373-74.

[46]   The Law Society had announced in October 1999 that it would no longer take part in the consultation processes of appointing judges and QCs. ('Law Society turns its back on "secret soundings"', *Solicitors' Journal*, 1 October 1999, p.895.)

- some specialist groups of barristers and solicitors, notably employed lawyers, felt they were unfairly excluded from consideration;
- equal opportunity and ethnic minority representatives agreed that the system needed revision to give them a better chance of appointment.[47]

Sir Leonard made proposals for minor changes:

- the assessment form should be slightly restructured;
- the number of consultees nominated by the applicant should be restricted to 3-6 – 'an unlimited number simply aids the well known candidate';
- all applicants should be required to give reasons for their own suitability for Silk in relation to the criteria;
- a table should be published showing the fee earnings of candidates in quartiles. (This is now done. [48] The range was from £705,000 at the top to £63,000 at the bottom for successful candidates and from £684,000 to £46,000 for unsuccessful candidates.);
- there should be power in exceptional circumstances to interview someone regarded as a good candidate about whom there is insufficient information.

By recommending only minor changes in the system, the Peach Report in effect validated it. But in March 2001 the Office of Fair Trading (OFT) in a fierce and wide-ranging report on restrictions on competition in professions (*Competition in professions*, OFT328) raised the fundamental question whether the award of the title Queen's Counsel was on balance of value to consumers. The OFT has real powers and this report represented a serious threat to the continued existence of the rank of Queen's Counsel. (On the OFT's report see pp 764-68 below. On the arguments pro and con see pp 743-44 below.)

Speaking at the Bar's annual conference in 2002, Lady Justice Hale questioned whether the Bar was sensible to rely on a Government minister to bestow this mark of superior quality. She asked, 'what is a profession, a large part of whose function is to stand up for the citizen against the state, doing when it looks to Government for preferment?' [49] In March 2003, the Bar Council's Working Party on Judicial Appointments and Silk, chaired by Sir Iain Glidewell, a former Court of Appeal judge, recommended that Silks should no longer be appointed by the Lord Chancellor. Instead, appointment should be on the recommendation of a panel chaired by a retired senior judge and a broad membership. (See *Counsel*, April 2003, p 8.)

A month later, as has been seen, the Lord Chancellor, giving evidence to the new House of Commons Select Committee on his Department stated that he would

---

[47] For research on this see K.Malleson and F.Banda, *Factors Affecting the Decision to Apply for Silk and Judicial Office*, LCD Research Series, June 2000 – www.lcd.gov.uk/research/2000/res00fr.htm.

[48] See *Counsel*, June 2002, p 42. The table showed that the average earnings of all applicants was £206,000 (£269,000 for successful and £184,000 for unsuccessful candidates).

[49] *Counsel*, December 2002, p.32.

shortly be issuing a consultation paper which would invite views both on the method of appointing Silks and on 'whether the status of Queen's Counsel should continue to exist or not' [50] (On the Consultation Paper, see p 767.)

PARTNERSHIPS AMONG BARRISTERS

It is a rule of Bar conduct and etiquette that barristers may not form partnerships. The members of chambers share the services of the clerk and share office expenses such as secretarial facilities, library and other costs. But they may not agree to share fees. The traditional basis of the rule is that the barrister is an individual and should take responsibility for his work as an individual. The reason for the rule has somewhat altered nowadays when so much of the work is either not earmarked for any individual or gets reallocated because of the eventual non-availability of the selected individual.

From time to time the issue has been considered by the Bar. In 1961 a Committee recommended that the rule be adhered to, and this view was taken again by a different committee in 1969 and again by the Senate when it came to give evidence to the Benson Royal Commission on Legal Services.

The Royal Commission did not go into the issue very deeply. But it unanimously adopted the prevailing view that partnerships should not be allowed. Partnerships, it thought, would erode the right of the client to select a particular individual by reason of his capabilities. ('Both by law and in practice, a partnership involves the sharing of work and responsibility and a common interest in earning profits so that if one member of a partnership cannot, or does not wish to, deal with a particular matter another partner, who may not either be known, or acceptable, to the client does so' (para (33.65).) The Commission said it was particularly influenced by the fact that partnerships would restrict the client's choice–especially in some of the small specialised Bars and in provincial centres, some of which only had one set of chambers.

Another problem with partnerships, which the Commission did not mention, is that many members of the Bar perform part-time judicial functions. It would presumably be impossible for one member of a partnership to appear as an advocate in a case in which a partner of his was the judge. This would mean that if the barrister came to court and found that his partner was to be the judge he would have to withdraw at the last moment. Even if the problem were appreciated earlier, it would still create considerable administrative difficulties which would add yet a further dimension to the already complex matter of listing cases.

The Royal Commission concluded: 'Partnerships would often we think be convenient or advantageous to barristers but the point of overriding importance is the public interest. We therefore consider that partnerships between barristers should not be permitted' (para 33.66).

---

[50] Oral evidence of April 2, 2003, Q.73. The evidence is accessible on www.parliament.uk.

A later inquiry into the issue resulted in a statement by the Bar in May 1987 that it adhered to the rule that barristers could not form partnerships, but that it would for the first time permit 'purse sharing' arrangements in the form of the pooling of fees and their distribution according to some agreed formula. Solicitors would have to be informed that such arrangements operated in the chambers, and barristers in such chambers would not be allowed to appear against each other or in a case in which a member of the chambers was acting as judge. (See *Law Society's Gazette*, 27 May 1987, p 1566.) So far as the writer is aware this system for distribution of fees is exceedingly rare.

One of the many proposals canvassed in Lord Mackay's 1989 Green Papers (p 742 below) was that barristers should be able to form partnerships with one another. The Bar's response on this (as on virtually all the proposals in the Green Papers) was negative.

The matter was considered again by the 1990 Bar Council's report entitled 'Strategies for the Future'. This said that the supposed advantages of partnership were greatly exaggerated. In particular, a partnership no longer had any distinct tax benefits. Moreover the advantages were greatly outweighed by the disadvantages. It had therefore approached its work on the basis that partnerships would continue to be prohibited.

In its view most of the main advantages of a partnership in terms of a cohesive group structure could be achieved without a formal partnership. A set of chambers, it suggested, needed a clear and efficient decision-making structure to permit it to assess options and determine courses of action on the basis of full discussion–but without the need for unanimous decisions. The present informal consensus process needed to be replaced by machinery that allowed for rapid and effective decisions to be taken for all. The larger the set, the greater the need for such machinery.

The question of partnerships at the Bar was raised most recently by the OFT's 2001 report *Competition in professions*. (For details and further developments see pp 769-70 below.)

WOMEN AT THE BAR

In 1955 women made up only 3.2% of the practising Bar. The proportion has risen very considerably: by 1965, 4.6%; 1975, 7.1%; 1985, 13%; 1995, 22%. In 2002, it was 28%. [51] In 2002, exactly 50% of those Called to the Bar were women. Of barristers of up to five years Call, women are now some 38% of the cohort.[52] Of the cohort of over 10, 15 and 20 years call the proportions are 20%, 16%, 13%.[53] Because women have only quite recently begun to come into the profession in large numbers there

---

[51]   Bar Council's *Annual Report* 2002, p 31.
[52]   BDO Stoy Hayward Report, op cit, n 33 above para 3.2.
[53]   LCD, *Judicial Appointments, 4th Annual Report, 2001-2002*,p 9.

are very few in the ranks of senior practitioners, let alone on the bench as judges. In 2002, the number of women appointed QC was 11% of all such appointments – but projections suggested that by 2005 the proportion of appointments could be 17% and by 2010, could be 20%.[54] In 2002, the total number of women QCs was 95 out of 1,145 (8%) One aspect of the problem is that so few women put themselves forward for consideration. In both 2002 and 2003, only 10% of applicants for Silk were women.

On 1 March 2003, the number of High Court judges was 105 – of whom only 6 were women. There were three women out of 36 Lords Justices of Appeal and no woman among the 12 law lords. Of the 533 circuit judges, 50 (9.4%) were women. Of the 1,217 recorders, 143 (11.7%) were women. Of the 35 District Judges (Magistrates' Courts, 11 (31%) were women. (The current figures are to be found on the LCD website – www.lcd.gov.uk)

In 1992 research published by the Bar Council concluded 'It is unlikely that the judicial appointment system offers equal access to women or fair access to promotion to women judges... The system depends on patronage, being noticed and being known.'[55]

For details of a survey of women barristers regarding their experience of sex discrimination see B Hewson, 'Sex and the Bar', *Counsel*, February 1993, p 12. See also C McGlynn, 'Appointing women judges', *New Law Journal*, 24 April 1998, p 59.C Barton and C Farrelly, `Women in the legal profession', *New Law Journal*, 24 April 1998, p 599. K Malleson and F Banda, *Factors Affecting the Decision to Apply for Silk and Judicial Office*, LCD Research Series, June 2000 – www.lcd.gov.uk/research/2000/res00fr.htm.

For details of the continuing efforts made by the LCD to increase diversity in judicial appointments see the LCD's annual reports on *Judicial Appointments* and speeches made from time to time by the Lord Chancellor accessible on the LCD's website.

ETHNIC MINORITIES AT THE BAR

In 2002 ethnic minority barristers made up just under 10% of the practicing Bar – though as many as 20% of pupils were from the ethnic minorities. [56]

There has been concern for many years about the problems of members of ethnic minorities in getting entry to the Bar, and even more about the fact that most practise in 'ghetto chambers' consisting largely of members of the minority in question.

Research in 1989 showed that more than half of chambers had no ethnic minority tenants and slightly more than half of the practising black barristers were concentrated in 16 sets. There were only six non-white QCs.

---

54 LCD, *Judicial Appointments, 3rd Annual Report, 2000-2001*, p 8.
55 'Without Prejudice? Sex Equality at the Bar and in the Judiciary', 1992, para 48(1).
56 Bar Council's Annual Report, 2002, p 31.

In 2002 the number of ethnic minority barristers applying for Silk was 19 out of 429 (4%) Seven were appointed – 6% of the 113 appointments made but 37% of those from ethnic minorities applying. In 2003, the number applying was 23 out of 394 (6%). The same number, seven, were appointed – again 6% of the total applying, but 30% of those applying from ethnic minorities.

In October 1991 the Bar Council adopted a race-equality policy which included a recommendation to all chambers that they should aim to have 5% of their members drawn from ethnic minorities. This recommendation does not seem to have had much, if any, impact. The policy also envisaged a Code of Practice on the non-discriminatory selection and treatment of pupils and tenants and for the distribution of work in chambers. The Bar's new selection procedures for entry to the Inns of Court School of Law would be monitored to ensure that they were not discriminatory. For comment see Jake Gordon Clark, 'Race discrimination at the Bar', *New Law Journal*, 26 September 1997, p 1400.

CIRCUITS

The country is divided into six circuits, each with its own rules and customs, officers and controlling committee. A barrister can only be a member of one circuit but he can appear in a court on another circuit. The circuit is concerned with the administration of criminal justice in its area together with the Circuit Administrator who is a senior official of the Lord Chancellor's Department. The circuits are also concerned with the establishment of new chambers in their area. The circuit leader will take an interest in the conduct of members of the circuit and will give advice and guidance to any barrister who seems to require it. The circuits have no formal function in respect of disciplinary proceedings.

ADVERTISING BY BARRISTERS

In 1989 the Bar Council changed its rules to permit a barrister to engage in any advertising or promotion in connection with his practice which conforms to the British Code of Advertising Practice, including the use of photographs, statements of rates and methods of charging, statements about the nature and extent of his services and, with the client's written consent, the name of any professional or lay client. Such advertising must not be inaccurate or likely to mislead, or be likely to diminish public confidence in the legal profession. It must not make comparisons with other barristers ('knocking copy' or fee comparisons) or include statements about the quality of the barrister's work, the size or success of his practice or his success rate. (See Bar Code of Conduct, 2000, 7th edn, para 710 – the Code can be accessed on the Bar Council's website – wwwbarcouncil.org.uk.) Most chambers have so far confined their advertising to chambers' brochures.

The Office of Fair Trading (OFT)'s report *Competition in professions*, March 2001, said that the restriction on direct comparison with other barristers and on referring to success rates 'may restrict competition, perhaps especially for individuals and smaller clients, and they may limit the ability of prospective clients to compare relative value for money' (p 15).

In its response, the Bar Council said that the Bar's attitude to advertising had undergone a sea-change in recent years – moving from one in which all advertising was prohibited with a few exceptions, to one, in which all advertising was permitted with a few exceptions.

In regard to advertising success rates it argued that such advertising would be inherently misleading, partly because often there is no clear definition of success or failure and also for the fundamental reason that the outcome of a case depends on many factors other than the skill of the advocate. The more skilful a barrister the more likely that he will be instructed in the most difficult cases. No member of the profession would regard success rates as an indication of quality of the barrister but there was a danger that uninformed persons might do so. Also if success rates could be advertised barristers might tend to avoid the more difficult cases in order not to compromise their position in some league table. Those consulted unanimously took the view that the prohibition on such advertising should remain. These arguments were apparently persuasive as the OFT said in its *Progress Statement* of April 2002, 'We do not at present intend to pursue this issue further' (para 3.24, p 14).

Different considerations, the Bar's response stated, applied to comparative advertising. No one favoured comparisons in terms of quality with, or criticisms of individuals or other sets of chambers. Such comparisons were calculated only to disparage while being unverifiable. But comparing fees would not be open to that objection providing it was accurate and not likely to mislead. The Bar Council changed the rule to make that possible on 23 March 2002 with effect from that date. (One consequence is that the world now knows what top QCs charge. On 28 April 2003, under the heading 'Fees squeezed at commercial bar' ,*The Lawyer* reported that although three QCs (Lord Grabiner[57], Jonathan Sumption and Gordon Pollock) now charged £1,000 per hour, the 'headline rate' across the rest of the commercial bar had been 'hit hard'. Due to competitive pressures and the relatively slow rate of incoming work, a range as 'low' as £500-£600 per hour was prevalent among the 40 top commercial silks.)

BARRISTERS' INCOME FROM PUBLIC FUNDS

A substantial part of barristers' income is derived from public funds.

In 1971, the Benson Royal Commission on Legal Services estimated that public funds accounted for as much as 48% of the Bar's gross fees.[58] In 2002, the annual survey of the Bar by BDO Stoy Hayward showed that the proportion at 46% was much the

---

[57]   Lord Grabiner had previously made headlines as the first barrister to earn over £1m per year.
[58]   Cmnd 7648, 1979, p 520.

same – 27% coming from prosecution and defence criminal work, 13% from family work and 6% from other publicly funded work (Table 7, p 30). The survey also reported (p 29) that income for chancery, commercial and other specialist practitioners was roughly twice as high as for practitioners undertaking criminal and family work – and whereas receipts for publicly funded work had been fairly static, in chancery and commercial work there had been a 33% increase in gross receipts since the previous year.

It is too early to predict the likely impact on the Bar's earnings of changes in funding of legal aid, of the development of conditional fee agreements, or of changes in the rights of audience for solicitors or 'employed lawyers' and, in particular, those employed by the CPS. For members of the Bar who derive a large part of their income from public funds the impact of these changes could in the medium to long term be considerable.

MANAGEMENT OF THE BAR

For most of the past century the affairs of practitioners have been run by the Bar Council. Its origins were the Bar Committee, which was created in 1883 and which in 1895 became the General Council of the Bar, known as the Bar Council. It was expressly barred from interfering with 'the property, jurisdiction, powers or privileges of the Inns'. Disciplinary matters at that time remained in the hands of the Inns but the rulings of the Bar Council on matters of etiquette became recognised as binding on barristers as a whole.

During the 1950s and 1960s the relationship between the Bar Council and the Inns became increasingly strained and in 1966 a new body, the Senate of the Four Inns of Court, was established by resolution of the Inns and the Bar Council. Its purpose was to provide one body that could act collectively in matters of common interest. It had seven representatives from each Inn and six representatives of the Bar Council. But it could take no decisions that involved expense to the Inns without getting their agreement.

This proved unsatisfactory and in 1971 at the instance of Lord Hailsham, then Lord Chancellor, a committee under Lord Pearce was set up to consider the problem. The 1972 interim report of the Pearce Committee identified the faults of the system. It pointed to the fact that there were no fewer than six autonomous bodies to run a profession of fewer than 3,000 practitioners–the four Inns, the Senate and the Bar Council. There was a multiplicity of overlapping committees–in 1971 some 61 standing bodies. The whole system was wasteful of manpower, accommodation, money and time. Also, junior members were virtually excluded from all decision-making.

There was a critical shortage of accommodation for practitioners in London. The Inns had no common rent policy, no common policy on libraries and lacked control over pupils. The Pearce Committee concluded that there should be one effective central governing body with sufficient financial resources to carry out its policies.

On the basis of these recommendations, a new body, the Senate of the Four Inns of Court and the Bar, was set up and came into existence in 1974. It had six representatives of each Inn, appointed by the benchers; three barrister representatives of each Inn, elected by the members of the Inns other than the benchers; and 39 barristers elected by the Bar, of whom 18 had to be practising juniors and under seven years since Call. There were 10 ex-officio members, such as the Law Officers and the leaders of the six circuits, and up to 16 additional members appointed by the Senate. The practising Bar, therefore, had a slight majority on the Senate.

The functions of the Senate were to lay down general policy for the profession and to decide on the contents of the Consolidated Regulations of the Inns. The Inns undertook to abide by the general policy laid down from time to time by the Senate subject to certain understandings, the gist of which is that they must not be expected to bear an unfair burden of cost. The trade-union affairs of the profession were handled by the Bar Council, which was a sub-committee of the Senate and which consisted of the 39 Bar representatives of the Senate, the leaders of the circuits and up to 12 co-opted members.

The Benson Royal Commission on Legal Services in 1979 made several recommendations regarding the organisation of the Bar. It thought that the existing arrangements were 'neither sufficiently co-ordinated nor adequately representative of the profession as a whole to provide the necessary direction' (para 32.67) and it proposed that the Senate should be given power to take decisions binding on the Inns. Some 60 members of the Senate should be elected by the Bar in such a way as to ensure adequate representation for different levels of seniority, specialists, barristers practising in different parts of the country, and those employed in commerce and industry. There was no need to have barristers appointed by the Inns on the Senate. It would be right to continue to have some representation of the judges in the Senate and some method should be found to have between 10 and 20 whether by appointment, election by the judges or co-option. The Inns should have representatives in the form of the Treasurer and Chairman of its Finance Committee.

In 1985 the Bar set up a new committee under the chairmanship of Lord Rawlinson to 'consider the constitution and composition of the governing body of the profession and to make recommendations'. The committee reported in the spring of 1986. Its main conclusion was that the management of the Bar should be in the hands solely of practitioners. The government of a profession, particularly one like the Bar which engaged in a great deal of publicly funded work, should not be in the hands even partially of judges.

Accordingly it recommended that there should be a new General Council of the Bar and of the Inns of Court consisting of barristers alone. Decisions which might affect the Inns should be taken by a Treasurers' Council of the Inns. It should consist of the treasurers, certain other benchers, the chairman of the Council of Legal Education and the officers of the new Bar Council.

The Treasurers' Council would have power to refer back to the Bar Council any policies and the Bar Council would then consider its views. But if the Bar Council affirmed the policy, the Treasurers' Council would have the duty to secure its implementation. (The relationship would in a sense be like that between the House of Commons and the House of Lords, with the Commons having the ultimate power to insist on a policy.)

The Bar Council would include a system of constituencies. It should consist of two representatives of each circuit (of whom one would be a junior barrister), one from each Bar Association, 3 representatives of each Inn and 51 elected members, of whom 9 would be Queen's Counsel and 12 would be under seven years' call.

These proposals were adopted by the Bar in June 1986 and came into effect on 1 January 1987. [59]

In 1991, Lord Benson, the former Chairman of the Royal Commission on Legal Services, urged that the time had come to place management of all the Inns' properties under the authority of the Bar Council. Writing in the Bar's house journal *Counsel* (July 1991, pp 14–15), he said that very large sums of money would shortly be needed to modernise the properties held by the Inns, to bear the cost of improving recruitment, the vocational training of students, remuneration in pupillage and continuing professional education. The Bar, though tiny, still had six governing bodies–the Bar Council, the four Inns of Court and the Inns' Council. The division of responsibility was wasteful in time and money.

The Inns owned extremely valuable properties in London and were therefore one of the best-endowed professions in the country. Each of the Inns managed its properties in its own way. For years they had charged low rents and had therefore failed to build up reserves. Now they would have to borrow large sums at high interest.

The Bar had the duty under the Courts and Legal Services Act 1990 for education and training of barristers. It was vital to give the Bar Council the authority to discharge its responsibilities. The Inns were reluctant to allow the Bar Council to decide how to administer their valuable assets. Under the 1987 agreement the Bar could in theory impose its will on the Inns but the procedure was complex. Lord Benson thought, moreover, that it was incompatible with the Bar Council's new statutory obligations and in his view was unworkable.

In 1994 the Chairman of the Bar Council said that its budget was £2.7m of which £2m was raised by subscription. (For description of its functions see *Counsel*, March/April 1994, pp 10–12.) In 1999, the Bar Council moved to make subscription to the Bar Council compulsory.[60] It persuaded the Government to introduce an amendment

---

[59]   See *Law Society's Gazette*, 28 May 1986, p 1628, and 23 July 1986, p 2321 and also *Counsel*, September/October 1994, pp 10–14.

[60]   *The Lawyer*, 18 January 1999, p.7.

to the Access to Justice Bill which gave the Bar Council the right to make subscriptions mandatory.[61]

The problem of the management of the Bar continues to be an issue. Martin Bowley QC, writing in the Bar's house journal in 1996 said: 'The central issue which apparently no one is prepared to face – is that we just cannot afford the waste of resources, both human and financial, involved in our current system of government which involves a Bar Council, four Inns of Court, six Circuits and something like 20 specialist associations, all with differing agendas and differing priorities.' (*Counsel*, May/June 1996, p 16)

EMPLOYED AND 'NON PRACTISING' BARRISTERS

There are many barristers who, having been called to the Bar, do not become self-employed barristers in chambers but who do provide legal services. They used to be called 'non-practising barristers', despite the fact that they worked as lawyers. But in the 1980s those who offered legal services to their own employer came to be called 'employed barristers'. Until the end of the 1980s, employed barristers had no right to appear as advocates in the courts. But in 1989 the Bar Council agreed that employed barristers should be treated in the same way as solicitors. Providing they had completed pupillage or had been in employment for five years they were given the same rights of audience as solicitors in the lower courts. They were also permitted to instruct barristers in private practice. But they were not allowed to conduct litigation. In 1997, as will be seen below, employed solicitors were granted full rights of audience and the Bar Council moved to grant similar rights to employed barristers but these moves were overtaken by the Access to Justice Act 1999 which required the Bar Council to grant full rights of audience to employed barristers who satisfied equivalent training requirements to those for self-employed barristers. In order to obtain rights of audience in the higher courts a barrister must not only have completed pupillage but must for three years following pupillage work from the office of a 'qualified person'. The majority of employed barristers and most solicitors do not at present meet the criteria for being 'qualified persons'[62] This creates a barrier for newly qualified barristers.

There are now three categories of employed barristers. There are employed barristers who offer legal services only to their own employer. This is the position of barristers who are employed in the government legal service or in local government and in-house lawyers in commerce, finance and industry. [63]

---

61   See Access to Justice Act 1999, s 46.
62   Defined as someone who for six years has practiced as a barrister or a member of an authorised body and for the previous two years has made such practice his primary occupation and who has been entitled to exercise a right of audience in all the courts.(Code of Conduct rule 203.3)
63   Those who were Called before January 2002, need only to have completed their Bar Vocational Course (or the previous Bar Finals) to be eligible for this status. Those called after January 2002 need also to have completed a pupillage.

Secondly, there are barristers who offer legal services to the general public through their employers. They can only hold themselves out as practising barristers if they have higher rights of audience and work for an organisation approved under the Code of Conduct. The organisations that are approved include solicitors' firms and law centres.

Thirdly, there are employed barristers who may not hold themselves out as barristers – for instance because although they work for an approved organisation such as a firm of solicitors, they have not done pupillage. (An example is Allen & Overy which employs some 150 barristers most of whom are not practicing.) Another group are those who may have higher rights of audience but who offer legal services to the public at large working for non-authorised organisations such as accountants' firms, or as claims advisers for insurance companies.

(b) The solicitor's branch

ORIGIN AND HISTORY

The solicitors' branch grew out of the variety of different practitioners who operated in different capacities in the legal system other than the barrister and the sergeant-at-law. By the late thirteenth century, attorneys existed to handle the technicalities of law suits. Solicitors seem first to have emerged in the sixteenth century. By the end of the seventeenth century the different categories included sergeants, two ranks of barristers, solicitors, attorneys, conveyancers or scriveners, pleaders, and proctors. Pleaders were absorbed by the Bar, scriveners' work was taken over by solicitors and attorneys, and the differences between attorney and solicitors were gradually eliminated. Attorneys were advisers to the parties, solicitors were especially associated with matters concerned with land, and proctors were concerned with ecclesiastical law and matrimonial affairs.

The 1873 Judicature Act merged the functions of solicitors, attorneys and proctors, and the title 'solicitor' was adopted as a generic title for them all. Statute now reserves that title to those qualified as solicitors. (There is no equivalent statute in relation to barristers.)

For information about the profession at present, including much statistical information covering recent years see www.research.lawsociety.org.uk. Note especially very helpful fact sheets. On the history of the profession see, for instance, M Birks, *Gentlemen of the Law* (Stevens, 1960).

ENTRY AND TRAINING

As for the barrister the process of qualifying to be a solicitor consists of an academic stage, a stage of vocational training and a period under training 'on the job', formerly known as articles and today called traineeship.

The academic stage A person wishing to be a solicitor can pass the academic requirement by taking a law degree but, as with barristers, a non-law degree plus the one-year law conversion course (the Common Professional Examination or CPE) is deemed to be the equivalent. In 2000-2001 there were 6,218 persons admitted as solicitors. Of these three-quarters (74%) came by way of direct entry, 20% were by transfer. [64] Of those who came by direct entry, 73% had law degrees and 27% had non-law degrees. Of the transfers, 13% were former barristers, 9% were legal executives, 3% were justices' clerks and 75% were foreign lawyers – (in order) from Australia, New Zealand, Hong Kong, North America, Singapore, EU countries, Scotland, the Indian sub-continent. [65]

Vocational training for solicitors–the Legal Practice Course The Law Society's vocational Legal Practice Course(LPC) was drastically reformed as from 1993. The aim was to make the course more genuinely vocational, based as much as possible on skills training. The course is taught at the five branches of the College of Law and at over 20 universities. Whereas previously the course was virtually identical wherever it was taught, there is now a measure of freedom for teaching institutions subject to accreditation by the Law Society's Legal Practice Course Board. The content has a practical basis with an emphasis on the use of 'black letter law' and practical know-how. The course consists of both compulsory subjects (conveyancing, wills, probate, administration, business law and practice, and litigation and advocacy) and optional subjects. Matters of professional conduct and the influence of European law, revenue law and financial services law are supposed to be taught throughout the course. Skills training is supposed to focus on interviewing and advising, legal research, writing and drafting, negotiating and advocacy. The course can be either full-time over one year or part-time over two academic years. (See further *Law Society's Gazette*, 23 May 1990, p 4; 20 June 1990, p 2; 6 February 1991, p 6; 2 October 1991, p 4. For critical assessment and a reply see *Legal Action*, July 1994, p 8 and September 1994, p 9. See also the study by the Policy Studies Institute–M Shiner and T Newburn, *Entry into the Legal Professions: The Law Student Cohort Study Year 3*, The Law Society, 1995.) The course was revised in 1997 to place greater emphasis on law in general and business law in particular, to give more opportunity for options. (For a description see Nigel Savage, `Reshaping the legal practice course', *New Law Journal*, 19 September 1997, p 1358.)

The number of places for full-time students on the LPC in the three years from 1999-2001 was 7,088, 7,376 and 7,486. (That is the number of places not the number of students.) The number of part-time places in those years was 1,526, 1,500 and 1,632.[66]

---

64   No information was available as to the route of entry of 5% persons.

65   Law Society, *Trends in the Solicitors' Profession, Annual Statistical Report 2001* ('*Annual Statistics 2001*'), pp 67-69. The annual statistical report is accessible on the Law Society's website – www.lawsociety.org.uk.

66   *Annual Statistics 2001*, Table 9.3, p 58.

Funding the LPC For those who obtain traineeship contracts with large firms, the costs of the LPC course are normally paid by the firm. (According to the 2002 Mountfield Report[67] the typical financial package offered by the large firms, covers: costs of the course, CPE as well as LPC, plus maintenance of £5,000 pa; a salary of £28,000 for the first year of the traineeship, £32,000 for the second year and £50,000 on qualification.) Obviously, few small firms can offer such inducements.

However, in a major new initiative, the Legal Services Commission, in order to encourage young lawyers into publicly funded work, has started to pay LPC fees. As from October 2002, it is making 100 grants a year. The grants will continue to cover a part of the Law Society's minimum salary for the traineeship stage. In the first year grants were being targeted at firms in smaller urban and rural areas. Firms must derive over 50% of their income from legal aid. The grants are premised on an expectation that the solicitor will stay with the firm for at least two years after qualification.[68]

Traineeship Most entrants undergo a two-year period as trainees. In 2000-2001 there were 5,162 new traineeships registered (compared with 3,841 10 years earlier, an increase of a third).[69] Well over half (59%) were women (compared with 54% in 1990-1991).[70] Of those with known ethnicity, ethnic minority trainees were 17%. (In regard to 11% of trainees there was no information as to ethnicity.)[71] Since 1987, the Law Society has recommended national minimum starting salaries for trainee solicitors. (In June 2003 the Law Society fixed its recommended minimum salary for trainee solicitors at £16,200 in London and £14,450 elsewhere.) Most trainees are paid over the minimum rate. The average starting salary in 2000-2001 was £18,300 – though in Central London it was £24,000. [72] Male trainees were offered starting salaries that were 5% above the average for females.[73]

The small number of large firms took a completely disproportionate number of the trainees. Just under a half (49%) of all traineeships registered in 2000-2001 were with the 1% of firms with 26 or more partners, 15% were with the 4% of firms with 11-25 partners, 13% were with the 11% of firms with 5 to 10 partners, and 23% were with the 82% of 1-4 partner firms.[74]

Continuing education The Law Society introduced compulsory continuing education for new entrants as from 1984. In 1990 it was extended to all members of the profession qualifying after 1987, who have to undertake 16 hours per annum at

---

[67]   *Report of the Committee on Financial Support for Entrants to the Bar*, July 2002, Annex B.
[68]   See Legal Services Commission's Consultation Paper *Developing Legal Aid Solicitors*; Press Release of 12 June 2002 ('Over £1.5m to help fund the next generation of legal aid solicitors'); www.legalservices.gov.uk.
[69]   *Annual Statistics 2001*, paras.9.6-9.7, p 59.
[70]   *Annual Statistics 2001*, Table 9.7, p 60.
[71]   *Annual Statistics 2001*, para 9.8.
[72]   *Annual Statistics 2001*, Table 9.13, p.64.
[73]   *Annual Statistics 2001*, para 9.14, p 64.
[74]   *Annual Statistics 2001*, Table 9.11, p 63.

continuing education courses or activities of one sort or another for the rest of their careers. As from November 1998 the same obligation to undertake continuing education was extended to all solicitors of whatever seniority. The obligation can be met by engaging in a variety of educational activities.

NUMBER OF SOLICITORS

A solicitor who acts as a solicitor within the meaning of the Solicitors Act 1974 must hold an annual practising certificate. In 2001, there were 109,553 solicitors on the Roll of whom 86,603 (79%) held practising certificates. Of these, 68,466 (79%) were in private practice.[75]

There has been a dramatic increase in the number of solicitors with practising certificates. For the first half of this century it was under 20,000. In 1950 it was 17,000. In 1968 the number was just under 23,000; in 1978, almost 34,000;in 1988, just over 51,500 and in 1998, just over 75,000.[76] (A feature of the growth of the number of solicitors with practising certificates is the growth in the number and proportion not in private practice, who mainly work in commerce, industry and the public sector.' Between 1991 and 2001 this proportion rose from 16% to 21%.[77]

The large growth in the size of the Bar in the 1960s and 1970s was fuelled to a considerable extent by the exponential increase in grants of representation under legal aid. This was not the case for the solicitors' branch since legal aid forms only a small proportion of their income. (In 1999-2000 it was 13% of gross fees, compared with 9% in 1989-1990 and 15% in 1995-1996.[78]) It was attributable rather to the spread of home ownership in the population. As will be seen below, until 1986 solicitors had a monopoly of the handling of conveyancing which accounted for a very large part of their income. (In 1901 about 10% of dwellings were owner-occupied; the figure in 1971 was 50% and in 1990 was 67%.)

Controlling numbers From time to time the question of regulating numbers coming into the profession surfaces as an issue. In 1995, Mr Martin Mears made this one of the topics on which he campaigned for the Presidency of the Law Society. His proposal was that places on the compulsory Legal Practice Course should be restricted to persons who had training contracts with firms. In 1995/96 there were 7,924 places for the Legal Practice course but the profession only offered some 3,700 training placements. Mr Mears' plan would therefore have resulted in a drastic reduction in the numbers being allowed onto the course. His Vice President, elected at the same time (also after a contested election) went even further. He wanted to reduce places on the LPC to 1,000. (See *Law Society's Gazette*, 26 July 1995, p 8.) This plan ran into

---

75   *Annual Statistics 2001*, para 1.3, p 13.Those without a practising certificate include retired solicitors and others not pursuing a career in the legal profession.
76   *Annual Statistics 2001*, p.11.
77   Law Society, *Quality, Choice and the Public Interest*, November 2002, Annex 2, p 76.
78   *Annual Statistics 2001*, Table 5.8, p 40.

opposition from members of the Council of the Law Society. It was also declared to be unlawful in a formal legal opinion by Richard Drabble QC whose advice had been sought by the Law Society. In his view the Law Society had no power to restrict the numbers entering professional training for reasons unconnected with educational standards. (See *The Lawyer*, 9 January 1996, p 1.)

When this proved to be a blind alley, the working party set up by the President to consider whether, and if so, how to reduce entry to the profession directed its attention to reducing numbers by introducing an aptitude test (*The Lawyer*, 5 March 1996, p 13; *Law Society's Gazette*, 17 January 1996, p 10).

But a report from the Law Society's training committee suggested that the number of students applying for the 1996 Legal Practice Course had dropped by 1,364 by comparison with 1995 and, at the same time, there was a small increase in the number of training contracts. The chairman of the training committee was quoted as saying that 'the serious oversupply of applicants seems to be correcting itself without the need for direct intervention'. (*The Lawyer*, 27 February 1996, p 1; J Ames, 'Student Numbers in Decline', *Law Society's Gazette*, 28 February 1996, p 6.)

This was confirmed by the Lord Chancellor's Advisory Committee on Legal Education and Conduct (ACLEC) in its report on *Legal Education and Training* in April 1996. The report (p 45) opposed the idea of a restriction on the numbers seeking entry to the profession either by arbitrary restrictions on the numbers of places on vocational courses or by externally imposed limitations on the number of training contracts for solicitors (or pupillages for barristers).

THE STRUCTURE OF THE SOLICITORS' PROFESSION

Solicitors practise in firms. A firm may have more than one office. The annual statistics published by the Law Society show the number of firms broken down by numbers of partners. In the five years from 1992/93 to 1997/98 the number of firms increased slightly from 9,754 to 10,120 whilst the overall number of offices remained about the same at just under 14,000.[79] In 2001 there were 9,251 private practice firms, located in 12,966 offices. (The decrease in the number of firms and offices was at least partly due to 'the data cleaning exercise' which had recently taken place on the Law Society's systems.)[80]

Taking just the 8,306 firms with a turnover of at least £15,000, the breakdown of firms by numbers of partners in 2001 was: sole practitioners 42%; 2-4 partner firms 40%; 5-10 partner firms 11%; 11-25 partner firms 4%; 26 or more partner firms 1.5%.[81] So more than four-fifths of these firms have one to four partners.

---

[79]   *Annual Statistics 2001*, Table 3.6, p.24.
[80]   *Annual Statistics 2001*, para 3.4, p 25.
[81]   *Annual Statistics 2001*, Table 3.11, p 29.

But it is the largest firms of which one hears most often. According to the latest annual profile of the 'Top 100' firms by *The Lawyer*[82], in 1998 there were five firms with over 1,000 fee earners : Clifford Chance (with 1,795 fee earners including 178 partners and 1,144 assistant solicitors); Eversheds (1,289 fee earners, 296 partners and 427 assistant solicitors); Freshfields (1,097 fee earners, 122 partners, 631 assistant solicitors); Allen & Overy (1,092 fee earners, 123 partners, 665 assistant solicitors); Linklaters (1,054 fee earners, 146 partners and 594 assistant solicitors). After that it was a steep downward curve. Only 13 of the 100 firms had over 500 fee earners and under half had more than 200. So the very large firms are highly exceptional.

Their importance, however, is enormous. In 2001, firms with 81 or more partners, around 0.4% of the total, employed just over one-fifth (20.9%) of all solicitors. Firms with 26 or more partners, 1.5% of the total, employed over a third (36%) of all solicitors. (At the other end of the spectrum, sole practices, 42% of all firms employed 12% of all principals and 9% of all solicitors.)[83]

The firms with 26 or more partners, a little over 1% of all firms, in 1999-2000 generated no less than 50% of the profession's gross fees. As has been seen, they also train half of all the entrants to the profession.

'Assistant solicitors' are qualified solicitors who are not partners. In recent years a new category has emerged of 'associate solicitors' whose status is between that of assistant solicitor and partner. In 2001, solicitors in firms were partners (42%), assistant solicitors (39%), associate solicitors (7%), consultants (4%), sole practitioners (6%), other (2%).[84]

A solicitor normally cannot establish his own practice within three years of admission to the Roll. He needs the permission of the Law Society to do so.

The fee earners in solicitors' firms also include 'legal executives'.

LEGAL EXECUTIVES

It has been a familiar feature of solicitors' offices for well over a hundred years that they employ unadmitted staff on professional work. Formerly they were known as 'managing clerks', but since the founding of the Institute of Legal Executives in 1963 they have generally been known as legal executives, regardless of whether they were actually members of the Institute. In 2003, there were some 22,500 members of the Institute (including students). There are reckoned to be approximately another 10,000 unadmitted staff in solicitors' offices who are not members of the Institute.

The Institute has three grades of membership–students, Associates (who have passed four papers in law and have served in solicitors' office for at least three consecutive

---

[82]   5 May 1998, p.16
[83]   *Annual Statistics 2001*, Table 4.1, p 33.
[84]   *Annual Statistics 2001*, Table 4.1, p 33.

years); and Fellows (who must be 25 or over, have served eight years in a solicitors' office and who must have passed an examination comprising three papers out of a choice of thirteen).

For further information see the Institute's website www.ilex.org. See also AM Francis, 'Legal executives and the phantom of legal professionalism: the rise and rise of the third branch of the legal profession', 9 *International Journal of the Legal Profession*, 2002, 5-25.

THE DISTRIBUTION OF PERSONNEL IN SOLICITORS' FIRMS

In 2000 there were some 194,000 persons working in solicitors' firms (excluding firms earning less than £15,000 pa). They were divided into principals (17%), assistant solicitors(16%), other fee earners such as legal executives and trainee solicitors(15%), and administrative and support staff such as secretaries, clerks, receptionists etc(52%). Of the 93,839 fee-earners, 34% were principals, 33% were assistant solicitors and 32% were 'other fee –earners'. [85]

As has been seen, the large firms have a disproportionate share of the manpower. Thus in 2000, firms with up to four partners were 83% of all firms but they employed only 24% of assistant solicitors and 32% of all non-solicitor fee earners. The firms with 11 or more partners were 5% of all firms but they employed 60% of all assistant solicitors and 49% of non-solicitor fee earners. [86]

[Note: this information is not available after 2000. Until then it was provided by the Solicitors Indemnity Fund. On the demise of the Indemnity Fund (see p 736 below) the annual statistical report draws its information on private practice staffing from the Society's REGIS system which does not contain information on non-admitted fee-earners or support staff.]

THE DISTRIBUTION OF SOLICITORS' OFFICES IN THE COMMUNITY

The first systematic national study of the location of solicitors' offices was carried out by Ken Foster on the basis of the Law List in 1971 ('The Location of Solicitors', 1973, *Modern Law Review*, p 153). Wide differences emerged in the distribution of solicitors' offices. Various socio-economic factors were then tested to attempt to explain this unequal distribution of solicitors. The strongest correlation was between the distribution of solicitors and the amount per head of retail sales. These high correlations, Foster suggested, indicated that 'the location of solicitors and their offices is governed principally by economic considerations very similar to those that govern the location of retail distribution outlets' (pp 161–2).

[85]   *Annual Statistics 2000*, Table 4.1, p 33.
[86]   *Annual Statistics 2001.*, Table 4.1, p 33.

A second study of the distribution of solicitors was carried out some years later on the data for 1985. (Kim Economides and Mark Blacksell 'Access to Justice in Rural Britain: Final Report', 16 *Anglo-American Law Review*, 1985, pp 353-75) Like Foster, they plotted the distribution of solicitors in the Solicitors' and Barristers Directory. The results showed a very uneven distribution. 'At a regional level, the southeast dominates, with almost half the total and the lowest regional value for the number of persons per solicitor. There is a broad band of relatively well-provided counties stretching from the southwest to East Anglia, while poorly-provided counties covers the north and east Midlands' (ibid, pp 357-58). However, more detailed scrutiny of the data, at district rather than county level, revealed a more complex and more interesting pattern which ran somewhat counter to the general distribution picture. Solicitors were disproportionately well represented in rural areas and poorly represented in rapidly expanding suburban populations on the fringes of the major centres of population.

WOMEN IN THE SOLICITORS' PROFESSION

The remarkable rise in the number of women in the profession is similar to that at the Bar. As recently as 1960 there were virtually no women solicitors. In 1970, they were a mere 3% of those with practising certificates. In 1980, the proportion was 10%, in 1990 25% and in 2001, 37%. Of those admitted as solicitors in 2000-2001, 55% were women.[87]

It seems, however, that women still do not enjoy parity in promotion prospects. The distribution of solicitors in private practice in 2001 was:

	All solicitors	Women	Men
	%	%	%
Partners	42	24	52
Sole practitioners	6	3.5	7
Associate solicitors	7	10	6
Assistant solicitors	39	59	28
Consultant/Other	4	2	6
Other	1	2	1
Total	100	100	100

(Source: *Annual Statistical Report*, 2001, Table 2.9, p 19)

[87]   *Annual Statistics 2001*, Table 10.3, p 66.

The table shows that 52% of men compared with 24% of women were partners. In part this might be because women have only relatively recently begun to enter the profession in significant numbers. But the Statistical Report (para 2.10, p 20) goes on to show that with equivalent levels of experience a higher proportion of men achieve partnership. Of solicitors with 10-19 years of experience, 83% of men were partners compared with 57% of women. This could be partly because, compared with men, women take greater number of career breaks and accumulate fewer years of post-qualifying experience. No doubt it is also due to some extent to gender discrimination.

See further CMS McGlynn, 'The Business of Equality in the Solicitors' Profession', 63 *Modern Law Review*, 2000, 442-56; H Sommerlad, 'Women solicitors in a fractured profession: intersections of gender and professionalism in England and Wales', 9 *International Journal of the Legal Profession*, 2002, pp.213-34. See also Law Society, *Women Solicitors*, Fact Sheet, 2001 – www.research.lawsociety.org.uk.

ETHNIC MINORITIES IN THE SOLICITORS' PROFESSION

The proportion of solicitors from the ethnic minorities has risen considerably in recent years. In 1995 they were 3.8% of solicitors with practising certificates. By 2001 this had risen to 6.6%.[88] Of the students enrolling with the Law Society in 1998, 21% were from ethnic minority groups – compared with 14% in 1991-92.[89] In 2001, 17% of trainee solicitors and 13% of new admissions to the Roll were from ethnic groups.[90]

By far the largest single category of ethnic minority admissions was Asian (54%). Others were Chinese (13%), African (10%) and Afro-Carribbean (6%).[91] The figures for ethnic origin of those admitted as solicitors is not complete since the information about ethnic origin was only available in 2000-2001 for 86% of those admitted. A fuller breakdown of the ethnic minority admissions showed that 59% were women – a higher proportion than for admissions generally. Within the ethnic minorities, the proportion of female admissions was highest amongst Afro-Carribbeans (67%) and lowest amongst Asians (58%).[92]

MANAGEMENT OF THE SOLICITORS' BRANCH

The profession is run by the Law Society (which was established by Royal Charter in 1831) and the 121 autonomous local law societies. The Law Society is both the professional association concerned with the advancement of the interests of solicitors

---

88   *Annual Statistics 2001*, para.2.12, p 21.
89   *Annual Statistics 2001*, para.8.5, p 55.
90   *Annual Statistics 2001*,pp 60,73.
91   *Annual Statistics 2001*, Table 10.11, p 73.
92   *Annual Statistics 2001*, para.10.11, p 73.

and the governing body concerned with dealing with complaints against solicitors and disciplinary matters. It is therefore both the trade union and the regulator. It issues practising certificates to those in private practice. It administers the Compensation Fund against which clients defrauded by solicitors can complain and recoup their losses.[93] It also manages the system of training for those wishing to qualify as solicitors, through its College of Law. Practice Rules regulating the practice, conduct and discipline of solicitors are promulgated by the Law Society with the approval of the Master of the Rolls, under the authority of the Solicitors Act 1933, s 31.

The 121 local law societies perform less important functions. They deal with complaints from the public, help solicitors in difficulties and assist would-be entrants to secure positions in firms. They may arrange lectures and social events. They also play a role in shaping Law Society policy by reacting to proposals emanating from Chancery Lane which are for consideration by the profession as a whole.

The Law Society is run by its Council, which until 2000 consisted of 75 members elected by solicitors throughout the country. The country was divided into constituencies, each of which had a proportionate number of Council members depending on the number of solicitors who practised in that area.

As is normal for a professional body, the Law Society has always been the butt of criticism from its members. But in the past few years the level of criticism has reached new heights (or depths). Dissatisfaction seems to centre partly on the way the Society deals with substantive issues – such as the catastrophe of the shortfall of several hundred million pounds on the Solicitors' Indemnity Fund (SIF) and the resulting gigantic increases in insurance premiums, partly on what is felt to be general inefficiency and partly on lack of rapport with the concerns of the ordinary practitioner.

The crisis over the SIF, after a long and agonising saga, eventually led in June 1999 to a decision by a reluctant Council of the Law Society to allow solicitors to opt between the previously compulsory mutual Fund and making equivalent alternative insurance arrangements in the open market.[94]

The perceived problem of inefficiency and general malaise led to the Council asking for advice from Pearson Group chairman, Sir Dennis (now Lord) Stevenson, a businessman experienced in helping ailing companies. His verdict: 'The Law Society

---

93   In 2001, payments from the Fund amounted to £17m. (Law Society's *Annual Report*, 2001, p 14.)

94   *Law Society's Gazette* 30 June 1999, p 3. The story can be traced over months through the columns of the *Gazette*. For a potted history of professional indemnity insurance for solicitors see *Law Society's Gazette*, 17 February 1999, p 22. For a full account see M Davies, 'Wither mutuality? A recent history of solicitors' professional indemnity insurance', 5 *International Journal of the Legal Profession*, 1998, 29-61 For the new scheme, see *Law Society's Gazette*, 11 August 1999, p 46, 20 April 2001, p 24; *New Law Journal*, 15 June 2001, p 881; *The Lawyer*, 25 June 2001, p 33.

does not work. Its very structure prevents effective decision-making, and when decisions are made, there is no means of ensuring that they are implemented'. He recommended that the Society's 141 committees, and working parties should be reduced to a core; that greater use be made of ad hoc task forces; that an executive committee should oversee implementation of the Council's policy decisions; and that elections should be restricted to the Deputy Vice President level to avoid damaging contests.[95] The Council took his advice. In January 1999 some 50 committees were abolished. A new organisational system was established to come into force in January 2000. In the meanwhile a small Interim Executive Committee and 12 working parties on major policy areas were established.[96]

Regarding the standing of the profession, Sir Dennis (now Lord) Stevenson advised that the Society should vigorously promote the contribution made by solicitors to society, the economy and to protecting human rights.

In 1999-2000 the Law Society engaged in a further bout of major reform. In December 1999 the Interim Executive Committee approved the appointment of consultants Corporate Edge to advise on a redefinition of the Society's activities. In April 2000, the Council received reports from three working parties on Future of Regulation, Regulation Review, and Sections and Specialisation. It agreed that reform should be taken forward by a specially convened Reform Co-ordination Group (RCG). This eventually resulted in a Consultation Paper which was sent to the profession in October 2000.The Consultation Paper made a number of central proposals:

- *An enlarged and more representative Council* – size to be increased from 75 to a 100 – representation not only for geographical constituencies but also for sectional and specialist interests possibly to be elected by national ballot or nominated by the interest groups – primary role of Council to approve strategic priorities, determine policy and set budget – it would elect and delegate authority to a Main Board – the Council would only meet four to six times a year.
- *Redesignation of the Society's functions* – proposed they be Standards; Adjudication & Compliance[97]; Law reform; Representation; Services; and Finance and Administration.
- *A Board per function, chaired by a Council member* – each Board to consist of a mixture of Council, non-Council and lay members – the first two named Boards to have 50% lay membership.
- *The Main Board to operate as 'cabinet' government* – consisting of three office holders, Council member chairs of the individual boards, the Chief Executive and the staff director of each function – its role overseeing the strategic plan and budget.

---

[95] *The Lawyer*, 22 September 1998, p 1.
[96] For the developing story see *Law Society's Gazette*, 20 September 1998, p 4; 18 November 1998, p 22; November 25,1998, p 22; 2 December 1998, p 15; 20 January 1999,p 16; 26 May 1999, p 18.
[97] See further p 762 below.

The reform package met opposition. [98] But it was approved by the profession – first in responses to the consultation exercise and then at a Special General Meeting in May 2001. The postal ballot, in which over 17,000 voted, approved a series of resolutions by more than the required two-thirds majority. [99]

The Society's annual report for the year ending December 2001 gave details of the initial phase under the new system. The new Council had 61 seats for geographical constituencies plus up to 39 specialist seats and five lay members. So far, 36 of the 39 seats had been designated. The first lay members had been appointed by the Master of the Rolls in July 2001. The Standards Board had eight Council members and three lay members. Half the members of the Compliance Board which dealt with enforcement of rules, regulations and standards were lay persons.

NB It is not required that qualified solicitors be members of the Law Society, but over 80% are.

2. The divided profession

Many assume that the division of the legal profession goes back into the mists of antiquity, but this is not so. As Australian scholar John Forbes pointed out, division presupposes two or more parts of a whole, but it was not until the seventeenth or even eighteenth century that solicitors could be said to have emerged as a distinct or identifiable professional group. The Bar had by then had centuries of development. The distinction in those days was therefore not between two parts of the same profession, but between lawyers and sub-lawyers. In 1765 Blackstone set out the hierarchy of the legal profession without even mentioning solicitors. Even a hundred years later Dicey lectured on legal education without referring to solicitors. Until the late eighteenth and into the early nineteenth century, solicitors could be described as 'an unorganised, ill-disciplined, ill-educated category of sub-professional agents, living wholly or partly on the sub-professional trivia of litigation and conveyancing and sharing even this subject matter with court clerks, law students and laymen' (Michael Birks, *Gentlemen of the Law*, Stevens, 1960, p 105).

But in the nineteenth century the solicitors' branch gradually established itself and carved out areas of work in which it specialised. The Bar was persuaded first to give up seeing clients direct and then to cease to do conveyancing. In return the Bar had a monopoly over the right to appear as an advocate (the 'right of audience') in the higher courts and a virtual monopoly over appointments to the bench.

---

[98]   See for instance, D Keating, 'Reform at the Law Society', *New Law Journal*, September 29, 2000, p 1396; M Mears, 'Keep the status quo', *Law Society's Gazette*, 16 November 2000, p 26.

[99]   See M Napier, 'End of the beginning', *Law Society's Gazette*, 3 May 2001, p 20; and for the resolutions passed see 'The Law Society's special general meeting', *Law Society's Gazette*, 11 May 2001, p 14.

Today the division is still maintained. One cannot practise both as a barrister and a solicitor at the same time. Barristers and solicitors are not permitted to form partnerships nor can they work in each other's offices. The Bar is still the senior branch. The solicitor attends on the barrister in his chambers rather than the reverse. The barrister is in charge of the running of the case and will tell the solicitor how he intends to conduct it. The barrister team and the solicitor team in a case still tend to work separately in doing their respective parts of the work. Barristers no longer have their former monopoly in regard to rights of audience in the higher courts, but they still do by far the bulk of that work. (The Law Society has conceded that in some cases it is not necessary for a solicitor to attend counsel at court.[100]) Similarly, although barristers no longer have their former monopoly over all higher judicial appointments[101] the great majority of such appointments in fact are still from the ranks of barristers. (Thus in 2002, of 1,356 recorders only 139 (10%) were former solicitors. The number of solicitor circuit judges was 88 out of 621 (14%).) In 2001-2002, of 19 High Court judges appointed, none was a solicitor; of 72 circuit judges appointed, 13 were solicitors; of 90 recorders appointed, 8 were solicitors. [102])

As will be seen, there are more and more signs of overlap in the work done by barristers and solicitors and of direct competition between the two branches. (The Bar's Response to the OFT Report said, 'All the services that barristers provide can now be and are increasingly provided by solicitors.' (para 2.19)) As from 2003 it will even be possible for lay clients to seek advice from a barrister without the intervention of a solicitor (see p 763 below). This is the most radical step yet in the changing relationship between the two branches of the profession. But although the Labour Government which took office in May 1997 has espoused radical reforms of some aspects of the legal profession, there has been no indication, so far at least, that it intends to move to abolish the distinction between barristers and solicitors or to undertake any form of 'fusion' of the two branches.[103]

Transfer between the two branches

It has become very much easier than it previously was to transfer from one branch to the other. Under the Qualified Lawyer Transfer Regulations 1990 a barrister wishing

[100] See *Guide to the Professional Conduct of Solicitors*, 20.04 – www.lawsociety.org.uk which replaces the version of 20.04 in the printed Guide. It applies in magistrates' courts, in small claims track, in fast track cases and in some Crown Court cases - where the solicitor considers it reasonable in that neither the client's interests nor the interests of justice will be prejudiced.

[101] Solicitors gained the right to be appointed recorders and circuit judges by the Courts Act 1971. (See also Administration of Justice Act 1977, s 12.) They won the right to be appointed judges in the High Court and above by the Courts and Legal Services Act 1990, s 71.

[102] *Judicial Appointments Annual Report*, Annex H.

[103] It was reported however in October 2001 that a set of chambers at 2 Hare Court was putting in place restructuring to enable it in due course to establish formal ties with a firm of solicitors. A member of chambers was quoted, 'The chambers is particularly conscious of the OFT report and we're preparing, so that in five years we will be ready to form a partnership' (*The Lawyer*, 29 October 2001, p 2).

to practise as a solicitor must pass a test in Professional Conduct and Accounts (a combined paper). In addition, they must either have completed 12 months' pupillage and 12 months' legal practice after pupillage, or complete two years' legal practice. Providing they have had recent advocacy experience, they do not have to requalify for rights of audience in the higher courts. [104] Barristers who switch to practise as solicitors do not have disbar themselves. They remain subject to the Bar Council Code as 'non-practising barristers'. Solicitors who switch to become barristers, do not have to come off the Roll but they cannot have a practising certificate. Unless they have higher rights of audience, solicitors transferring to the Bar must undertake pupillage.

About 70 solicitors apply each year to become barristers; some 150-200 barristers apply each year to become solicitors.

3. Law centres

Law centres are offices providing legal services in poverty areas staffed by lawyers whose salaries are paid out of public funds. The funding is a mixture of central and local government money and ordinary payments out of the legal aid fund. For the clients the services are entirely free of charge.

Law centres were first proposed in 1968 in the Society of Labour Lawyers' pamphlet *Justice for All*. At the time the concept was opposed by the Law Society, which saw law centres as a threat to the private practitioner. The first centre was set up in 1970 in North Kensington. By the end of that decade there were some 30. During most of the 1980s there were some 50 law centres and that remains the approximate number.

The original opposition of the Law Society soon melted away as it began to be appreciated that law centres could feed paying work to the local profession whilst handling unremunerative work that the profession was not keen to undertake. Law centres are generally regarded as an important resource filling gaps in the legal aid system, often specialising in areas of work that private practitioners do not handle.

Law centre lawyers have developed skills and specialisms which have been copied by private practitioners. They have pioneered means of delivering legal services, such as, 24-hour services (a precursor of the police station Duty Solicitor scheme); multi-plaintiff work in areas other than personal injuries; peripatetic advice sessions; advice over the telephone for those who find it difficult to get to the office; or pro-active lawyering, for instance through advice and training to groups. Law centres have also played a major role in providing representation in tribunals and thereby opening up an area of need not covered by the traditional legal aid system.

The former Legal Aid Board's annual reports showed payments to law centres by way both of grant and of ordinary payments under the legal aid scheme. (Thus, in

---

[104] Courts Qualifications Regulations 2000 made under the Access to Justice Act 1999.

1997-98 law centres received grant income of £899,000 and payments under the legal aid scheme of £3.5m.(p.115).) As was seen earlier, by 2003 the Legal Services Commission was supporting 53 law centres with payments of some £7m a year .

4. The use of solicitors and clients' perceptions

There have been various surveys about use of lawyers. The largest study was that conducted in the late 1970s for the Benson Royal Commission on Legal Services based on interviews with a random sample of 7,941 households (Cmnd 7648, 1979, vol 2, pp 173–298 -'Royal Commision survey'). A study by the Law Society's Research and Planning Unit was based on interviews with a representative sample of 1,630 people aged over 18 (J.Jenkins and V.Lewis, 'Client Perceptions', Research Study No 17, 1995 – '1995 Law Society Survey'). See also J Jenkins, E Skordaki and C Willis, 'Public Use and Perception of Solicitors' Services', Law Society Research Study No 1, 1989 and R Craig, M Rigg, R Briscoe, and P Smith, *Client Views*, Law Society, Research Study No 40, 2001.

The main findings of these surveys are:

(1) Use of lawyers is quite common. Nearly three-fifths of people over 18 had seen a solicitor in regard to a personal problem at some point. 14% had done so in the previous twelve months (Royal Commission, Table 8.3, p 185). 34% had used a solicitor in the past five years for a personal problem. (Law Society, 1995 p 5)

(2) The age-group that uses lawyers most are those between 25 and 34 (Royal Commission, para 8.27, p 184; Law Society, 1995, pp 5-6). Given that buying a home is the most common reason for using a solicitor, this is not surprising.

(3) The main services are buying and selling a home, making a will, divorce and matrimonial problems, dealing with someone's estate and compensation for injury. (All three surveys)

(4) Use of lawyers varies by socio-economic group. A solicitor in 1977 was used by: 25% of the professional class; 21% of employers and managers; 19% of intermediate and junior non-manual workers; 13% of skilled manual workers and workers who worked on their own account; 11% of semi-skilled workers; and 10% of unskilled manual workers (Royal Commission, Table 8.8, p 190).

(5) Those in non-manual households (one-third of the population) accounted for over a half of all use of lawyers for the buying and selling of property, dealing with the estates of deceased persons and making or altering wills (Royal Commission, para 8.110). In divorce, motoring offences and personal injury claims arising out of road traffic accidents those who used lawyers were roughly in proportion to their size in the general population (para 8.111). Manual households used lawyers considerably more (proportionately) than non-manual in claims for industrial injury compensation, and marginally more in offences other than motoring (para 8.112). But in matters which were not connected with property, 'the profile of users of lawyers'

services by socio-economic group is not greatly different from that of the adult population in general (Royal Commission, para 8.115).

These results demonstrate that use of lawyers is problem-connected even more than it is type-of-person connected. In other words, socio-economic background is not the best explanation of the fact that different categories in the socio-economic scale use lawyers to a different extent. In fields where property is involved (conveyancing, probate, wills, etc), naturally those with property see lawyers much more than those who do not. Since this is the largest single source of work for the solicitors' profession it explains why lawyer-use seems to reflect the differences between classes. But the impression is misleading. If one looks at non-property types of work, the use of lawyers is relatively even as between members of different socio-economic backgrounds.

(6) The image of solicitors is generally good. Of the professions evaluated (the others were bank managers, estate agents, dentists, NHS doctors, social workers), solicitors came in the middle range, with doctors rated most highly on all criteria. (Law Society, 1995, ch.3) The vast majority of clients were extremely satisfied with their own solicitor. (Ibid, para3.9)

People distinguished between their own solicitor and the profession as a whole. Thus 31% thought solicitors were approachable and easy to talk to. When asked about their own solicitor, the percentage was 74%. (Ibid, para 3.10)

The ratings for all the professions were generally down from the previous survey in 1989. ('The evidence supports the opinion that the public are now more questioning and demand higher level of service from all professions'. (Ibid, para 3.12).)

For a study by the Consumers' Association conducted since the establishment of the Community Legal Service see *The Community Legal Service: access for all?*, 2000, summarised in *Legal Action*, July 2000 pp 8-9.

5.   Reform of the profession and current topics

Reform of the legal profession has been a live topic for most of the period since the 1960s. The affairs of the profession were examined in the 1960s by three reports from the now defunct National Board for Prices and Incomes (1968, 1969,1971) and in the 1970s by three reports from the Monopolies Commission (on restrictive practices generally, 1970, on The Two Counsel Rule, 1976, and on restrictions on advertising 1976). In 1979 the Benson Royal Commission on Legal Services published its report (Cmnd 7648). In 1988 there was *A Time for Change*, the report of the Marre Committee set up jointly by the Bar Council and the Law Society. (For reasons of space, these reports are dealt with here only to the extent necessary to understand current issues.)

The aggregate effect of all these inquiries was not great. Then, in January 1989, the then Lord Chancellor, Lord Mackay launched his famous three Green Papers making a whole raft of radical proposals for reform of the profession. The Green Papers provoked uproar.[105] The legal profession and the judges reacted fiercely, forcing Mrs Thatcher's Government to retreat. The White Paper published in July 1989 was significantly less radical than the Green Papers of January. (For a detailed account of the battle over the Green Papers see M Zander, 'The Thatcher Government's Onslaught on the Lawyers: Who Won?', *International Lawyer*, vol 24, 1990, pp 753–85.)

The White Paper was broadly implemented in the Courts and Legal Services Act 1990. That Act created a new structure for dealing in particular with the endlessly vexing battles over rights of audience (on which see below). But in December 1997, Lord Irvine, the new Labour Lord Chancellor, indicated that he was dissatisfied with the new system for dealing with rights of audience created by the CLSA 1990 and that legislation would be introduced to reform it. A Consultation Paper ('Rights of Audience and Rights to Conduct Litigation: The Way Ahead') was issued in June 1998 followed in December 1998 by a wide-ranging White Paper (*Modernising Justice*, Cm 4155) dealing with legal services, civil legal aid, the civil courts, criminal justice and criminal defence. At the same time Lord Irvine published his Access to Justice Bill.

The 2001 Report of the Office of Fair Trading (OFT) The latest developments flowed from the publication in March 2001 of the Office of Fair Trading's Report *Competition in professions* (OFT328 – accessible on www.oft.gov.uk[106]).

The OFT's report was commissioned under s 2 of the Fair Trading Act 1973. The terms of reference were to identify restrictions which have the effect of 'preventing, restricting or distorting competition in professional services to a significant extent'. Although any consumer benefits claimed for the restrictions were also to be identified,

---

105   There were three Green Papers: *The Work and Organisation of the Legal Profession* (Cm 570, 1989); *Conveyancing by Authorised Practitioners* (Cm 572, 1989); and *Contingency Fees* (Cm 571, 1989). They were followed in swift succession by the Government's *White Paper on Legal Services* in July 1989 (Cm 740, 1989) and in the autumn the Courts and Legal Services Bill, which became the CLSA 1990 of that name. For an extended review of the proposals in the Green Papers see 'The Green paper on Contingency Fees', *Civil Justice Quarterly*, April 1989, pp 97–103; and 'The Realignment of the English Legal Profession', *Civil Justice Quarterly*, July 1989, pp 202–14. For a review of the White Paper see 'The White Paper on Legal Services', *Civil Justice Quarterly*, January 1990, pp 6–12. For an account of the CLSA 1990 see 'Courts and Legal Services Act 1990', *Civil Justice Quarterly*, April 1991, p 97.

106   For a summary see *New Law Journal*, 23 February 2001, p 370. The report was on restrictions on competition in three professions – lawyers, accountants and architects - but the lawyers were the main focus. The recommendations in the report were wide-ranging and, if implemented, potentially extremely serious for both branches of the profession: the professions to lose their partial exemption from competition law; banks, insurance companies and building societies to be allowed to compete for conveyancing and probate work; solicitors and barristers employed by non-lawyers to be permitted to offer legal services to the public; scrapping of the rank of QC; abolition of the restrictions on lay clients having direct access to barristers, on barristers forming partnerships and on barristers and solicitors forming multi-disciplinary partnerships etc. This was, in effect, a reprise of Lord Mackay's 1989 Green Papers.

the terms of reference expressly stated that the question whether such benefits justified the restrictions was to be left 'for further consideration'.

Section 9 of the Competition Act 1998 sets out the criteria that must be met if a restrictive agreement is to be given an exemption. The test is a narrow economic one – namely, whether (a) the restriction on competition in question is justified on the ground that it improves production, distribution or economic progress, while allowing consumers a fair share of the resulting benefit and (b) does not impose restrictions that are not indispensable to the attainment of those objectives or give the profession concerned the possibility of eliminating competition in respect of a substantial part of the work in question.

The OFT's document consisted of two parts – the 137-page report of its consultants, Law and Economics Consulting Group Ltd (LECG), and its own 19-page conclusions based on that report. LECG's report was prepared under severe time constraints and was based on skimpy field research. (For instance, it did not include a visit to a single set of chambers!) They also drew up their extensive reform agenda despite admitting that their inquiries 'did not uncover significant concerns among users of professional services, whether about quality, price or innovation' (para 20). (The Report said that there were two possible explanations. 'One is that the professions are providing a high standard of service at a reasonable price. The other is that they may not be, but that clients have difficulty in judging whether they have received good service and what would constitute a reasonable price.' (para 20).)

Despite these serious shortcomings, the OFT adopted LECG's report. It called for consideration of legislative action by government. It urged the professions to take prompt action to remove those restrictions that did not have a proper justification and warned that, failing readiness to take such action within 12 months, it would 'use its available powers with a view to removal of those restrictions'. (para 49)

The then Secretary of State at the Department of Trade and Industry, Mr Stephen Byers, said in the Commons on 8 March 2001 that the Government accepted and would implement the recommendation to make the professions fully subject to competition law [107], but that for the rest it seemed appropriate to consider comments on the report and that the Government would be issuing a formal consultation paper.

The Bar's Response The Bar published a 41-page response to the OFT in February 2002 (accessible on www.barcouncil.org). The Response was prepared by a committee chaired by Sir Sydney Kentridge QC. It started with arguments as to why the divided profession was in the public interest. LECG's report had not addressed this question[108]

---

[107] This was done by repeal of Sch 4 of the Competition Act 1998 by the Enterprise Act 2002 which took effect on 1 April 2003.

[108] Except that it stated that it had no objection to the title 'barrister' and 'solicitor' continuing provided that restrictions on direct access of clients to barristers and on conducting litigation

The Bar's Response said that the divided profession not only had the advantages of enabling barristers to hone specialist skills as advocates and of providing objective advice to solicitors and their clients, it also enabled them to do their work 'more efficiently and cheaply than solicitors' (para 2.10). This was because barristers' overheads were so much lower – typically 28% of gross income compared with 70% for solicitors.[109] The market for their services, the Bar said, would work less efficiently if the client did not have the solicitor to match the barrister to the client's needs and to monitor the quality of the barrister's work. The divided profession also promoted competition between solicitors by giving even small firms access to the full range of expertise at the Bar which enabled them better to compete with larger firms. 80% of solicitors' firms had five or fewer partners. The availability of the Bar enabled them 'to provide a much higher quality and range of services than would otherwise be possible' (para 2.17). The divided profession also permitted barristers to operate the cab-rank rule which prohibited picking and choosing clients. (The rule requires a barrister to accept instructions in regard to work within his competence on being offered a proper fee.[110]) Because, as a result, barristers were not identified with their clients, even the most unpopular could secure proper representation. The cab-rank rule did not apply to solicitors. The Bar ended the general introductory section of its Response by quoting the writer, commenting on the OFT report, that it was an over-simplification to believe

> ... that equating the work done by professional people to business will necessarily improve the position of the consumer when the reality is that sometimes it may rather worsen it. Certainly one wants competition to ensure that professional fees are no higher than they need to be and that professional rules do not unnecessarily inhibit efficiency. But what one looks for from the professions even more is standards, integrity and concern for the client of a higher order than that offered in the business world.[111]

The Response then addressed the specific restrictive rules at issue: partnerships, including multi-disciplinary partnerships; direct access to barristers by lay clients; advertising; the right to conduct litigation; Queen's Counsel; and legal professional privilege. The arguments are noted in the relevant sections below.

---

were removed. (para 252, p 74). but the OFT report (para.49) had said, 'The dual structure of the legal profession, with its separate roles for solicitors and barristers, may add unnecessarily to costs'. In the Director General's view, rather than pressing now for restructuring to end the dual structure of the legal profession, 'the best approach is to address its remaining adverse effects through further liberalisation of professional rules'.

[109] It quoted the current average hourly rates for barristers: 0-5 years call, £78; 5-10 years call, £113; over 10 years call, £166; QCs, £293 by comparison with the rates for solicitors: 0-5 years post-qualification, £181; over five years' post-qualification £245; equity partner £323. BDO Stoy Hayward *Survey of Barristers' Chambers*, 2001, para.6.5.

[110] See A Watson, 'Advocacy for the Unpopular: The Barrister's Cab-rank Rule in England and Wales – Past, Present and Future?' 162 *Justice of the Peace*, 20 June 1998, p 476, 499, 576.

[111] M Zander, 'Should the legal profession be shaking in its boots?' *New Law Journal*, 23 February 2001, p 369.

The Law Society's Response The Law Society's Response to the OFT's report in December 2000 (www.lawsociety.org.uk) was quite brief. It stated that the Law Society had a Working Party on Multi-disciplinary Partnerships (see p 733 below) and a Regulation Review Working Party reviewing all the current restrictions on competition. It explained the rules regarding entry to the profession, fee sharing with non-solicitors and advertising and argued that they were in the public interest.

In July 2002 the LCD issued a Consultation Paper regarding those matters in the OFT's report (*In the public interest?* CP 07/02 – www.lcd.gov.uk.) which fell to the Department.[112] It stated, 'On all the issues raised in this consultation, the Government's position is that the market should be opened up to competition unless there are strong reasons why that should not be the case, such as evidence that real consumer detriment might result from such a change' (p.5). The Government had decided to review the whole regulatory framework for legal services, the first step of which would be to settle the scope of such an exercise and how to complete it. It posed a series of questions.

In November 2002 both the Bar and the Law Society published their responses to the LCD's consultation paper *In the public interest?* (For the Bar's response see www.barcouncil.org.uk); for the Law Society's response (*Quality, Choice and the Consumer Interest*) see www.lawsociety.org.uk.)

In April 2002 the OFT issued a 21-page progress statement. [113] The accompanying press release was headed 'Competition in professions – improvement but more action needed'. In November 2002, the OFT issued a brief response to the LCD's Consultation Paper *In the public interest?* (Press Release, 21 November 2002.)

What follows is a treatment of a variety of current topics including in particular issues raised by the OFT. A topic that is no longer treated is that of fusion of the two branches. At one time this issue excited a great deal of interest. The writer wrote extensively on the subject.[114] In the first five editions of this work a good deal of space was given to

---

112   Five topics were addressed: legislation on conveyancing and probate; multi-disciplinary partnerships for solicitors; legal professional privilege; and the QC system.

113   OFT385, www.oft.gov.uk.

114   The argument for unification of the legal profession was perhaps most fully developed in M Zander, *Lawyers and the Public Interest* (Weidenfeld and Nicolson, 1968, now out of print), pp 270–332. See also M Zander, *Cases and Materials on the English System*, (5th edn, Weidenfeld and Nicolson, 1988), pp 592–603; P Reeves, *Are Two Legal Professions Necessary?* (Waterlows, 1986).

   For a direct response to the arguments in *Lawyers and the Public Interest*, see Gerald Gardiner, 'Two Lawyers or One?', 23 *Current Legal Problems*, 1970, p 1. See also: R E Megarry, *Lawyer and Litigant in England*, (Stevens, 1962); C P Harvey, *The Advocate's Devil* (Stevens, 1958); EJ Cohn, 'The German Attorney–Experiences with a United Profession', 9 *International and Comparative Law Quarterly*, 1960, pp 580–99, and 10 *International and Comparative Law Quarterly*, 1961, pp 103–22; and FA Mann, 'Fusion of the Legal Profession', *Law Quarterly Review*, July 1977, p 367.

   For the history see J Forbes, 'Division of the Profession: Ancient or Scientific', *Law Society's Gazette*, 26 January 1977, p 67.

the subject. But in 1992 in the sixth edition this material was dropped – not because the topic lacked interest, but because it no longer seemed to be of practical importance. The Benson Royal Commission on the Legal Profession in its 1979 Report had concluded unanimously (15-0) that the divided profession was in the public interest.[115] It seemed improbable that this verdict would be overturned. It is true that the relevant Green Paper in 1989 proposed that barristers and solicitors should be permitted to form partnerships with eachother and that the Courts and Legal Services Act 1990, s.66 permitted both barristers and solicitors to enter into partnerships with, respectively, non-barristers and non-solicitors. But it also specifically permitted the Law Society and the Bar Council to make rules prohibiting their members from entering into such partnerships and both branches have, and apparently intend to maintain, such rules. In other words, the legislation left it to the profession to regulate the matter and with both branches of the profession strongly opposed to 'fusion', the issue did not seem to be a live one. The fact that the OFT did not deal with the question in its 2001 report on restrictions on competition in the professions confirmed this view.

[Abbreviations: In the text that follows MGP is the main Green Paper *The Work and Organisation of the Legal Profession*, (1989, Cm570), WP is the White Paper (*Legal Services: A Framework for the Future*, 1989, Cm 740).]

(a)   Rights of audience for lawyers

The battle between barristers and solicitors over rights of audience in the higher courts has, over the years been the issue between the two branches of the legal profession that has provoked sharper differences than any other. The right of audience is a technical term meaning the right to appear for a client as an advocate in a court or tribunal. Traditionally the question of who can appear as an advocate in an English court was decided by the judges.[116] From the nineteenth century, Parliament also became involved through legislation. (Thus, for instance, since their establishment in 1846, legislation provided that both barristers and solicitors have the right to appear as advocates in the county courts.) In recent years the battle expanded beyond the respective interests of barristers and solicitors in private practice to the question whether rights of audience in the higher courts should be given to employed lawyers and especially those employed by the Crown Prosecution Service. As will be seen, it now also embraces rights of audience for non-lawyers.

In 1979, the Benson Royal Commission, by a bare majority of 8 to 7, recommended that the Bar should retain its ancient monopoly over the right of audience in the higher courts. The 1989 Green Paper proposed instead that the right to appear as an advocate should be based not on status as a barrister or a solicitor but on individual

---

[115]   Chapter 17, pp.187-202.
[116]   For a helpful modern review of the history and the cases see *Abse v Smith* [1986] QB 536, [1986]] 1 All ER 350.

qualification for the particular court. The test should be whether the relevant professional body had been authorised to certify advocates and whether the individual had the prescribed qualifications. Lay advocates could also be given rights of audience.

However, after furious debate, the 1989 White Paper more or less abandoned the 1989 Green Paper approach. The White Paper (paras 3.4–3.17) proposed first, that the existing complex arrangements for rights of audience under statute and common law should be replaced by statutory rights of audience in all courts and appropriate tribunals. The Bar Council and the Law Society would both be authorised bodies able to grant rights of audience and the members of both professional bodies would be deemed to enjoy their existing rights of audience. Thus, on qualification, barristers in private practice would have full rights of audience in all the courts; solicitors in private practice would have their existing rights of audience in the lower courts and such other rights of audience in the higher courts as they already enjoyed; lawyers employed other than in private practice would only have rights of audience in the lower courts.

But additional rights of audience could be sought by the Law Society and by bodies representing employed lawyers, or by bodies representing non-lawyers. The White Paper laid out a complex process by which such claims would be handled. The claim would be put to the Lord Chancellor who would refer it to his Advisory Committee on Legal Education and Conduct (ACLEC). If ACLEC approved, it would then have to be approved by the Lord Chancellor with the concurrence of four senior judges: the Lord Chief Justice, the Master of the Rolls, the President of the Family Division, and the Vice-Chancellor of the Chancery Division.

The Lord Chancellor and the four judges would have to consider the matter 'having regard' to the views of the Advisory Committee. Each judge would have to agree; each would therefore have a veto. Failure to agree would have to be explained in written reasons (which would be subject to judicial review for unreasonableness). In addition, the question would be referred to the Director-General of the Office of Fair Trading for his assessment from the point of view of competition policy.

This scheme was translated into law in Part II of the CLSA 1990 subject to the requirement that decisions fulfill the 'statutory objective' [117] and the 'general principle'[118]

---

[117]   Section 17(1) stated, 'The general objective of this Part is the development of legal services . . . by making provision for new or better ways of providing such services and a wider choice of persons providing them, while maintaining the proper and efficient administration of justice.

[118]   Section 17 (3) stated, 'As a general principle' the question whether a person should be granted a right of audience or be granted a right to conduct litigation had to be determined by reference '*only*' (emphasis supplied) to four considerations: qualifications; being a member of a professional body capable of enforcing rules of conduct; whether it had an equivalent to the Bar's cab-rank rule; and whether the rules of conduct were 'appropriate in the interests of the proper and efficient administration of justice'

Almost as soon as the CLSA 1990 received the Royal Assent, the Law Society put in its application for additional rights of audience and, shortly after, a second application was put in by the Head of the Government Legal Service and the Director of Public Prosecutions on behalf of Government lawyers and the CPS respectively.

There then ensued a tortuous process lasting several years. (The story was told by the writer in some six pages in the 8th edition of this work and at much greater length elsewhere[119].) In brief, in 1993 solicitors won the right to qualify as advocates in the higher courts under the CLSA 1990. [120] The Lord Chancellor and the Lord Chief Justice greatly irritated the solicitors' branch when they decided in 1994 that solicitor advocates in the higher courts could not wear wigs. [121]

Eventually, in February 1997, the Lord Chancellor announced acceptance of the Law Society's request for extended rights of audience for employed lawyers subject to certain conditions. The Bar, in July 1997, requested the same extension for employed barristers but, whilst this was under consideration, Lord Irvine, the Lord Chancellor announced that he would be introducing major changes in the system for granting rights of audience. He was clearly frustrated both at the cumbersome nature of the vetting system under the CLSA 1990, at the low take-up of their new rights of audience by solicitors[122] and at the barriers put in the way of employed lawyers. The qualification rules for solicitors would be eased. Employed lawyers would basically be given the same rights of audience as lawyers in private practice. ACLEC would be abolished. The proposal to give employed lawyers (ie CPS employees) the right to have full rights of audience provoked huge controversy focussed especially on whether CPS advocates could be sufficiently independent. [123]

The Lord Chancellor's promise (or threat) was implemented by the Access to Justice Act 1999. Section 36 provided that every barrister and every solicitor has rights of

[119]   M Zander, 'Rights of audience in the higher courts in England and Wales since the 1990 Act: what happened?' 4 *International Journal of the Legal Profession*, 1997, pp 167-196.

[120]   For the original regulations laying down the mode of qualification for extended rights of audience for solicitors in private practice see *Law Society's* Gazette, 17 December 1993, pp 29-30.

[121]   See Practice Direction (Court Dress) – *The Times*, 20 July 1994. On the history of the wigs see JF McLaren, 'A brief history of wigs in the legal profession', 6 *International Journal of the Legal Profession*, 1999, 241-50. (At the time of writing, summer 2003, the LCD was in the process of a consultation exercise on court attire including wigs – see *Counsel*, June 2003, p 5. For the results of the Bar's own survey, in which 3,751 barristers took part, see *Counsel*, July 2003, pp 21-22.

[122]   He was quoted as saying of the low take-up, 'There must therefore be a question whether solicitors have a significant appetite to become advocates'. (*Law Society's Gazette*, 17 February 2000, p 4.)

[123]   Unsurprisingly, the Bar and the great majority of judges strongly opposed the change. For a sceptical view see also M Zander, 'Will the reforms serve the public interest?, *New Law Journal*, 3 July 1998, p 969 . For the contrary view see, for instance, A Darlington, 'The CPS and rights of audience', September 1997, p.1395. Both Lord Bingham, then Lord Chief Justice, and Lord Woolf, then Master of the Rolls, supported the change – see House of Lords, *Hansard*, vol.595, 14 December 1998, cols 1125-26, and 1153.

audience in all the courts 'exercisable in accordance with the qualification regulations and rules of conduct' of the Bar Council and the Law Society. These regulations were promulgated in March 2000 (see below).

AJA 1999, s 37 added that qualification regulations were invalid insofar as they imposed special restrictions on employed lawyers as to the courts or the cases in which the right of audience could be exercised. The Lord Chancellor attempted to meet concerns about the independence of employed lawyers by s 42 which stated that everyone exercising rights of audience 'has (a) a duty to the court to act in the interests of justice; and (b) a duty to comply with rules of conduct of the body relating to the right and approved for the purposes of this section; and those duties shall override any obligation which the person may have (otherwise than under the criminal law) if it is inconsistent with them'.(The Explanatory Notes said this meant that an advocate must refuse to do anything that is not in the interests of justice.)

The effect of the changes As just noted, take-up by solicitors of the new right to seek rights of audience in the higher courts was slow. The first solicitor to appear in the higher courts did so in February 1994. By 2000, when the regulations under the AJA 1999, were being worked out, the number of solicitors who had qualified for rights of audience in the higher civil or higher criminal courts or both was only some 1,000. (Over two-thirds (69%) had qualified for criminal proceedings, 15% had qualified for civil proceedings, and 16% had qualified for both civil and criminal cases.)

Research conducted for ACLEC before the AJA 1999 suggested that this somewhat sluggish start to the new era of rights of audience in the higher courts for solicitors was unlikely to alter swiftly. There were many reasons. One was the cost of qualification which had risen from £2,000 in 1994 to some £4,000. Another was the difficulty of the exam. (In September 1995 only 29% of the 53 candidates passed the evidence and procedure test.)[124] For City firms, one reason was the problem of enabling their members to get the required 'flying hours' of advocacy in the lower courts when such firms rarely had cases in those courts. City firms argued that they should be allowed to train their members themselves.[125] But the main reasons were that solicitors did not yet see higher court advocacy fitting in with their way of practising and that they preferred to continue to use the Bar.[126]

---

[124]   *Law Society's Gazette* 14 February 1996, p.1.

[125]   *The Lawyer*, 6 February 1996. In 1998 the Law Society eased the problem by agreeing a third training route to qualification by use of a discretion in regard to advocacy experience in the lower courts. See *The Lawyer*, 28 April 1998, p.3

[126]   See 'Solicitor advocates no threat to Bar', *Solicitors' Journal* 15 November 1996, p 1092; G Davis et al, 'Solicitor advocacy and higher court rights', *New Law Journal*, 14 February 1997, p 212; M Zander, 'The long shadow of the Bar', *New Law Journal*, 2 October 1998, p 1422; L Hickman, 'A higher calling', *Law Society's Gazette*, 5 May 2001, p 38. See also R Kerridge and G Davis, ' Reform of the Legal Profession: An Alternative Way Ahead', 62 *Modern Law Review*, 1999, pp 807-23.

Implementation of the rights of audience provisions in the AJA 1999 resulted in a simpler, cheaper system of qualification for solicitors. The Higher Rights Qualification Regulations 2000 provided for three routes to qualification:

- *exemption* – for solicitors who have practised as barrister or solicitor for at least three years and who can demonstrate experience of advocacy in the higher courts;
- *accreditation* – for solicitors who have practised for three or more years as a barrister or solicitor who by reason of their experience of litigation in the higher courts have a sound understanding of the applicable procedure, evidence and ethics – can apply for a Certificate of Eligibility to attempt an Advocacy Assessment; and
- *development* – training and assessment in higher court procedure, evidence, ethics and advocacy skills plus one year's litigation and advocacy experience working with a mentor. Six months of the one year can be during the solicitor's training contract period.

From 2005 only the third of these routes will be available. For further details see the Law Society's website.[127]

The signs were that many of the large and even medium-size solicitors' firms were starting to develop advocacy training on a significant scale. [128]

By April 2003, a total of 1,768 solicitors had qualified for rights of audience in the higher courts. (Of these, 955 had criminal certificates, 421 civil and 392 had both.) But no information was available regarding the crucial question as to how often such rights of audience were actually being used.

For views based on comparable reforms in Scotland see G Hanlon and JD Jackson, 'Last Orders at the Bar? Competition, Choice and Justice for All – the Impact of Solicitor-Advocacy', 19 *Oxford Journal of Legal Studies*, 1999, 555-82.

In regard to the CPS, by April 2003 a total of 421 CPS lawyers (out of 1,963) had taken the Higher Courts Advocacy training.[129] In the year to April 2003, they had taken a total of 4,984 half day Crown Court sessions – mainly pre-trial Plea and Directions Hearings and guilty pleas. The HM Chief Inspector's Annual Report on the CPS for 2001-2002 stated that inspectors saw 187 advocates perform. The general level of performance was good. About half were rated 'competent in all respects'.

---

127   www.lawsociety.org.uk – Contents – Law Society Members – Our services (Specialist Panels) – Rights of Audience in the Higher Courts.

128   'Top City firms take advocacy in-house', *Law Society's Gazette*, 30 March 2000, p 1; 'City firm joins advocacy trend', *Law Society's Gazette*, 6 April 2000, p 1; 'Advocacy training courses attract the interest of mid-sized commercial firms', *Law Society's Gazette*, 22 June 2000, p 9; 'Linklaters to introduce its own advocacy qualification', *Law Society's Gazette*, 17 August 2000, p 8; 'The best of both worlds', *The Lawyer*, 11 March 2002, p 27; and, more generally, N Armstrong and D Urpeth, ' Solicitor advocacy', *New Law Journal*, June 2, 2000, p 835.

129   Stage 1 is a one-day course to test legal knowledge and advocacy skills. Stage 2 is a three-and-a-half day course working with different case scenarios and mock trials, assessed by an external examiner.

About 25% were rated 'above average in some respects'. About 10% were 'very good'. Under 10% were 'less than competent' or 'very poor' (pp 14-15).

(b)   Rights of audience for non-lawyers

The 1989 Green Paper had suggested that bodies other than lawyers could be authorised to licence advocates in the courts. This was confirmed in the 1989 White Paper and was reflected in the machinery of the CLSA 1990 described above. A body representing, say, accountants, surveyors or patent agents could apply to be approved by the Advisory Committee, the designated judges and the Lord Chancellor in precisely the same way as the Bar Council and the Law Society which were approved as authorised bodies by the Act.

In 1993 the Institute of Legal Executives (ILEX) applied to become an authorised body to grant rights of audience for certain proceedings in county courts, magistrates' courts and coroners courts. (In open court in the county court for matters within the jurisdiction of district judges and in magistrates' courts in specified matrimonial proceedings.) ACLEC approved the application in December 1995. ILEX applied to the Lord Chancellor in March 1996 and the application was approved in November 1997. The new rights of audience became effective as from April 1998. They apply to Fellows of ILEX with at least five-years' post qualification experience.

The second such application to be approved had been made in 1991 by the Chartered Institute of Patent Agents. It applied for its members to conduct litigation and to have rights of audience in patent and related intellectual property proceedings in the High Court. At first the application foundered on various objections raised by ACLEC. But it was reactivated and eventually a fresh application was made. This was formally approved by ACLEC in November 1998 and by the designated judges and the Lord Chancellor in May 1999.

Rights of audience and other extended powers for non-lawyers in the CPS The Narey Report on Delay in the Criminal Justice System (February 1997) proposed that non-lawyers in the CPS should be able to review files and to present uncontested cases in the magistrates' courts.: 'One of the things which most struck me on visiting CPS offices was the amount of entirely straightforward work being handled in the office and at court by lawyers. Much of this work must be dispiriting. I am convinced that administrative staff, managed by lawyers and dealing exclusively with uncontested cases, could successfully and efficiently present cases at court, freeing lawyers to concentrate on contested cases.' (p 15).

The Labour Government acted on the Narey recommendation in the Crime and Disorder Act 1998 but took it further than Narey proposed. Section 53 gave the DPP the power to designate non-lawyers in the CPS to conduct bail applications, and all proceedings in the magistrates' courts other than (1) contested cases (from the opening until conviction), (2) cases which can only be tried on indictment or where the defendant has opted for Crown Court trial or (3) a notice of transfer (p 328) has been served. An experienced solicitor, Mr Anthony Edwards[130] expressed his concern, 'the review function of the Crown Prosecution Service will be significantly diminished if less qualified staff are not able to identify where there is insufficient evidence to justify a prosecution or allow charges to proceed at the wrong level' ([1999]*Criminal Law Review*, p 32). The same view had been expressed in 1997 by Lord Bingham, the Lord Chief Justice, who said that the proposal for lay CPS staff to review files and to prosecute undefended cases 'appears to reflect a belief that such matters are relatively straightforward and call for little technical understanding'. 'In many cases this is no doubt true. In other cases it is not.' (J.Malpas, 'Lay prosecutors: revolution by the back door', *The Lawyer*, August 12 1997, p 2.) The journal *Justice of the Peace* commenting editorially said: 'We see this as yet another disappointing development in the still young life of the CPS. Low morale, overstretched resources and the recent loss of many experienced lawyers have all hit the service very hard indeed. Despite the Government's denials we are in no doubt that the true reason behind this initiative is to cut costs. . . . Administrative staff in the CPS do fine work day in day out, but they are not lawyers and appropriate qualifications and experience are necessary to carry out proper case reviews and to prosecute even simple guilty pleas. Assurances about 'appropriate training' for the new 'lay reviewers and presenters' do not allay our concerns, and they will not allay the concerns of others.' (vol 162, 14 March 1998, p 194) The Government was mistaken, the journal said, in suggesting that CPS non-lawyers could do the job because it was done for instance by Customs and Excise. The CPS had much broader responsibilities than Customs and Excise. Moreover the quality of lay presenters varied greatly. The journal said it was especially noteworthy that the Government replaced the Narey recommendation that lay prosecutors should be subject at all times to direction by legally qualified staff with the very different requirement of 'subject to such instructions as are given to him by the director'. (('The danger we foresee is that lay prosecutors, after passing their initial and as yet unspecified training, will be issued with numerous circulars on how to do this or that and then be left to get on with it with little, if any, *de facto* supervision by lawyers. (ibid))

The Glidewell Report (*Review of the Crown Prosecution Service*, Cm 3960, June 1998), which was published after the provisions dealing with this issue had already been adopted in the Crime and Disorder Bill, said that many CPS lawyers were opposed to the Narey proposals for an expanded role for non-lawyers in the CPS seeing them as 'an attack on their proper area of work'. The point was also made that even in the simplest of cases there can be difficulties with which a non-lawyer could not be expected to deal competently. Non-lawyers expressed the fear that they might be obliged to do work for which they had neither aptitude nor training. (p 130, para 16). Glidewell rejected these worries. But it drew a distinction between lay review and lay representation. In regard to lay representation, if the list included only guilty plea cases within the Narey criteria it saw no disadvantage and considerable advantage

---

130   As noted above, Mr Edwards subsequently became Professional Head of Service for the Public Defence Service run by the Legal Services Commission.

in the prosecution being presented by an experienced but not legally qualified caseworker. But if the list included a mixture of cases it would be 'positively wasteful' to have both the lawyer and a non-lawyer to present the cases. Also non-lawyer caseworkers would have to be trained to do the work. And only those who wanted to do such work should be used. There should be no element of compulsion.

As to review of case files by non-lawyers, Glidewell said it had 'more reservations' (para 19). The Narey recommendation related to a substantial proportion of cases prosecuted by the CPS. 'If it means no more than ensuring that the statement of evidence apparently justifies the charge, that the charge is within the agreed criteria and that the defendant, usually after having legal advice (which will often be from a duty lawyer) intends to plead guilty, then we think that an experienced caseworker could properly so decide. . . But if more than that is to be involved in the process of reviewing expedited cases, the skills necessary for such review will be those of a lawyer. If a lawyer is to acquire them, he will require both instruction in the law and practice and some experience. Whether the overall benefit in those circumstances will be worthwhile, we doubt.' (ibid)

It is to be noted that both Narey and Glidewell's stated pre-condition for non-lawyers to undertake either the review or the presentation function is that they be properly trained for the task. One has to be sceptical whether adequate training will be given.

Lay representation in small claims cases The 1989 Green Paper supported the recommendation of the Civil Justice Review that litigants should have the right to select a lay representative in small claims cases and debt and housing cases in the county court. This was implemented in s 11 of the Courts and Legal Services Act 1990, which gave the Lord Chancellor the power to make such provision by order. In 1992 the Lord Chancellor issued a Practice Direction giving effect to s 11 (SI 1992/1966) in respect only of small claims cases. The order entitled anyone to speak at a small claims hearing on behalf of a party. The party being represented must be present. The court retained the power to bar a lay representative who behaves in an unruly fashion.

The 1999 Civil Procedure Rules preserved that position in small claims cases. ('A party may present his own case at a hearing or a lawyer or lay representative may present it for him'. But, unless the court agrees, the lay representative can only present the case if the lay client is present. (CPR PD. 27.3)) See also pp 393-95 above for the position of the 'McKenzie man'.

(c)   Conducting litigation

Prior to the CLSA 1990 it was an offence under the Solicitors Act 1974, s 20, for anyone other than a solicitor to start or conduct litigation in any civil or criminal court, except as a litigant in person. The 1989 Green Paper proposed that this monopoly should be ended and that anyone should be capable of becoming a litigator. The 1989 White Paper (ch 4) confirmed this proposal. It stated that the right to conduct litigation, like the right to appear as an advocate, should be granted to practitioners by the professional bodies or institutions to which they belonged, if the bodies could demonstrate that they could set and maintain appropriate standards of competence and conduct. All litigators would also be subject to the existing powers of the High Court over solicitors as officers of the court. The Law Society would become an authorised body under the Act. Other bodies could become authorised bodies by an Order in Council made, following advice from ACLEC, on the recommendation of the Lord Chancellor and subject to the concurrence of the four designated judges. This scheme was implemented by ss 28–9 of the CLSA 1990. By 1999 no new body had been granted the right to initiate or to conduct litigation. The application by a newly formed Institute of Commercial Litigators was rejected by the ACLEC in February 1996. The Institute was informed by the Committee that the application fell 'far short of what is required by the statutory objective and the general principle'.

But in the LCD's June 1998 Consultation Paper *Rights of Audience and Rights to Conduct Litigation* the question was posed whether legislation should authorise bodies other than the Law Society to conduct litigation. The two bodies which would be obvious candidates, it suggested, were the Bar Council and the Institute of Legal Executives both of which were authorised bodies in regard to rights of audience. There would be no compulsion to take up rights to conduct litigation and most barristers would probably prefer not to do so. But some, such as those employed as lawyers in commerce and industry, might find it useful to be able to become authorised litigators. (para 5.5) Most legal executives worked in solicitors' offices but some might benefit from being able to set up in their own independent practices.

This suggestion was implemented in the Access to Justice Act, s 40 which made both the Bar Council and the Institute of Legal Executives authorised bodies for this purpose. The Bar has exercised this power – but only in respect of employed lawyers providing such services for their own employers. [131]

The 2001 OFT Report, *Competition in Professions* (see p 743 above) said the restriction on private practitioners conducting litigation 'prevents potential efficiencies and limits the numbers of lawyers who are able to conduct litigation on behalf of clients'.[132] In its Response the Bar argued that adding a few barristers to the number of lawyers eligible to conduct litigation would produce negligible benefits for consumers. They already had 85,000 lawyers in some 8,000 firms available for the purpose. On the other hand, to permit barristers to perform the function would undermine the distinction between barristers and solicitors. By absorbing time in collecting evidence, correspondence, handling disclosure, it would dilute the barristers' specialist skills and would thereby seriously diminish the quality of their advocacy and advice. Also

---

[131]   See Employed Barristers (Conduct of Litigation) Rules – www.barcouncil.org.uk - (Rules and Guidance). Exceptionally, however, an employed barrister may offer the service to the public – ie when employed in a solicitor's office or in a law centre.

[132]   At p 15. Based on the view expressed in the LECG Report at paras 258-61.

barristers' overheads would increase if they had to maintain the systems and staff necessary to conduct litigation. If barristers were to handle client moneys they would need to be regulated as solicitors are regulated. Such a regulatory system could cost as much as £1m per year to run.

In a statement issued on 25 April 2002 regarding progress the OFT said it remained concerned that the Bar did not intend to lift the blanket prohibition on the conduct of litigation by barristers in independent practice and that it would be investigating the matter further. It did not object to the divided profession but to a rule that imposed specialisation and which restricted what barristers were free to do. Permitting barristers who wished to conduct litigation to do so would not prevent other barristers from continuing to be specialists who did not offer that service. The OFT said it was not persuaded by the argument about the cost of regulating the holding of client moneys. One solution would be to prohibit it. Another would be to find cost effective ways of solving the problem.

Neither the LCD's Consultation Paper *In the public interest?* nor the OFT's Response to the Consultation Paper referred to the topic.

If barristers were permitted to conduct litigation it seems unlikely that any significant number would avail themselves of the possibility.

CLAIMS ASSESSORS

The Lord Chancellor announced in June 1999 that he was setting up a committee to examine the activities of claims assessors who assisted claimants with their claims in return for a commission on damages recovered. There had been some complaints. The *Solicitors' Journal* reported that lawyers groups had long been warning 'that consumers [were] being ripped off by unscrupulous and incompetent assessors'. They were wholly unregulated. Anyone could set himself up to bring compensation claims for a share of the damages. Because they were not permitted to issue legal proceedings they were tempted to settle for too low a figure rather than hand the case to a solicitor. Also their fees were unregulated. A Law Society spokesman was quoted as saying, 'At worst, these unqualified legal advisers are just cowboys or crooks. At best, they can only provide a second-rate service.(*Solicitors' Journal*, 18 June, 1999, p 575.) The Committee reported in April 2000 that it did not think that there was a present need for legislation. (See *Report on the Activities of non-legally qualified Claims Assessors and Employment Advisers* – accessible on www.lcd.gov.uk (Major Reports/Reviews).)

(d)   The Lord Chancellor's Advisory Committee (ACLEC) replaced

The 1989 Green Paper proposed that the Lord Chancellor should have an advisory committee with a lay majority. The functions of the advisory committee, it suggested, should include advice on the arrangements for legal education and training, on the need for recognising areas of specialisation and how specialists should be trained, and on codes of conduct.

The WP (ch 12) confirmed that there would be an advisory committee with a lay majority. The Committee was established by s 20 of the Act. Its general duty was to assist 'in the maintenance and development of standards in the education, training and conduct of those offering legal services' (s 21(1)). Its functions, set out in Schedule 2 of the Act, included advising the Lord Chancellor on all stages of education and training of lawyers; qualification regulations and rules of conduct (whether related to advocacy or the conduct of litigation or not); and specialisation schemes.

The Advisory Committee on Legal Education and Conduct (known as ACLEC) was clearly intended to be the lead policy-making body under the CLSA 1990–with the designated judges playing a subsidiary monitoring role.

Replacement of ACLEC In its June 1998 Consultation Paper (above) the Lord Chancellor's Department said that the Government intended to abolish ACLEC. The Committee, it said, had attracted distinguished membership but it had not succeeded in 'significantly furthering the statutory objective of developing new or better ways of providing legal services and a wider choice of persons providing them' (para 4.6) Partly this might have been due to the carefully balanced membership representative of various legal interest groups.

The Consultation Paper did not comment on the role played by the designated judges. But its overall summary was that 'the approval mechanism which was put in place to consider changes to rights of audience and rights to conduct litigation is much too complicated, cumbersome and slow, and is a major factor which has led to the frustration of the intention of the CLSA 1990 to extend the provision of legal services'. Instead the Government proposed 'a streamlined approval procedure, and that ACLEC should be replaced by a small, more focused body, which will concentrate on providing specialist advice about how, or whether, proposed changes would work, rather than on broad issues of policy' (para 4.15).

There should be a new body to be called the Legal Services Consultative Panel with a Chairman and perhaps ten members appointed for their individual expertise rather than as representatives of interest groups. (para 4.16) The Panel would be asked to consider all applications from new bodies for authorisation under the CLSA 1990, any applications for the approval of rule changes on which the Lord Chancellor required advice 'and any other matters concerning the provision of legal services on which the Lord Chancellor required advice' (para 4.17).

Under the new approval procedure applications for approval as an authorised body would be made direct to the Lord Chancellor. He would refer the application to the new Consultative Panel and to the Director General of Fair Trading for their advice – and would have the power to impose a timetable. The applicant would be able to comment and to modify the application. The Lord Chancellor would then consult the designated judges. Instead of a requirement that they must each agree as under the CLSA 1990, the Lord Chancellor would merely have to have regard to their advice 'but would not be bound to follow it' (para 4.18). He would however remain subject to the obligation to comply with the general principle and to further the statutory objective (see nn 117 and 118, p 748 above). If the Lord Chancellor decided that the applicant should be authorised, a draft Order in Council would be laid before Parliament for approval as at present.

Under the CLSA 1990, changes in the rules of conduct of authorised bodies so far as they affected rights of audience or the conduct of litigation had to be referred to ACLEC and required the consent of the designated judges. The Consultation Paper proposed a radical change. The Lord Chancellor would have a choice. Either he might write to the designated judges informing them of his intended decision and asking for their views. The Consultation Paper said that this should mean that most rule changes, 'which are straightforward', could be brought into effect much more quickly than at present. But if the Lord Chancellor thought the matter deserved wider consideration, he could refer it to the new Consultation Panel or to the Director of Fair Trading or both for their advice. The final decision, however, would be for the Lord Chancellor and he would not need anyone's consent. The only concession suggested was that the Lord Chancellor might be made subject to statutory criteria, along the lines of those in the CLSA 1990, to ensure 'that the Lord Chancellor's powers were limited to what was necessary to achieve the aim of extending rights of audience. Thus the Lord Chancellor might be required to have regard, *inter alia*, to 'promoting the proper and efficient administration of justice' (para 3.8).

Reacting to these proposals, Sir Sydney Kentridge QC, one of the most distinguished members of the South African as well as of the English Bars, wrote that implementation of these proposals to transfer the power over rights of audience from the judges to a Cabinet Minister 'would constitute a quiet constitutional revolution'. The Lord Chancellor would be able to change the rules without the consent either of the Bar or of the judges – ' a decision which could seriously undermine the independence of the Bar, and in the hands of another Lord Chancellor less committed to the independence of the Bar, destroy it.' During apartheid in South Africa there were frequent threats from the government to place the Bar under the control of a central council with government nominated members. 'This proposal was consistently and successfully resisted by the whole of the Bar. . . It was well understood that to remove the control of the profession from the provincial Bar Councils and General Council of the Bar would have meant the end of the independence of the profession.' (S Kentridge, 'A Quiet Revolution?', *Counsel*, December 1998, p 24.) See also Robin de Wilde, 'A constitutional issue-the judges and the Bar', *New Law Journal*, 2 October 1998, p 1424 and Lord Ackner powerfully supporting the same view 'More power to the Executive?', *New Law Journal* 16 October 1998, p 1512.

The writer was another of those critical of the proposals in the Consultation Paper on the abolition of ACLEC and greater powers for the Lord Chancellor:

The most far-reaching proposed change is to abolish the judge's veto. . . The 1990 Courts and Legal Services Act established a system of checks and balances. Extensions of rights of audience involves a process of decision making involving ACLEC, the Director General of Fair Trading, the four 'designated judges' and the Lord Chancellor. All have to agree to changes. The need to secure the agreement of the Lord Chief Justice, the Master of the Rolls, the President of the Family Division and the Vice Chancellor recognises both the historic role of the judges in regulating rights of audience and that changes in a matter so intimately affecting the work of the courts as rights of audience should have the approval of the judiciary. . . The system under the CLSA 1990 has proved to be slow, but legitimacy of decisions is even more important than speed. Changes in rights of audience take years to have an impact in any event. It is hard to see the need for urgency. . . .

The Consultation Paper, however, is not confined to rights of audience. It also proposes that the Lord Chancellor should be able to 'call in' any of the rules of the Bar and the Law Society. . . . The pretext for all these drastic proposals is to speed up the process. . . The real agenda is for the Lord Chancellor to take control. When Lord Mackay in his 1989 Green Papers proposed to transfer vast new powers over the profession to the Lord Chancellor, the resulting uproar forced him to back off. Lord Irvine is apparently bent on completing the job. (M Zander, 'More Louis XIV than Cardinal Wolsey', *New Law Journal*, 24 July 1998, p 1084.)

ACLEC, in its response to the Consultation Paper, stoutly defended its record. [133] It also argued that the Lord Chancellor's proposals did not provide adequately for performance of the function of assisting applicants develop their applications nor the provision of independent, expert advice on appropriate standards of legal education, training and conduct. These functions should not be performed by the executive. The independence of a suitable body was best secured if its work was not limited to ad hoc references made by the Lord Chancellor, and if it was free to set its own agenda. It should have a permanent secretariat and the ability to represent the consumer perspective.

The Access to Justice Act, s 35(1) starts, 'The Lord Chancellor's Advisory Committee on Legal Education and Conduct is abolished.' Subsection (2) sets up the Legal Services Consultative Panel with the function, first, of 'assisting in the maintenance and development of standards in the education, training and conduct of persons offering legal services by considering relevant issues in accordance with a programme of work approved by the Lord Chancellor' and making recommendations ; and, secondly, giving the Lord Chancellor advice at his request on any aspect of the provision of legal services. The Explanatory Notes said, 'The Panel will be required

---

[133]   See also 'Farewell to ACLEC' by Lord Justice Potter its last chairman in *Counsel*, April 1999, p 26.

to draw up its own programme of work on these topics, to be agreed with the Lord Chancellor'. The Panel would also have a significant role in working the new approval system set out in Schedule 5.

When first published the Bill contained no guiding criteria equivalent to the 'statutory objective' or 'the general principle' in s 17 of the CLSA 1990. This was the subject of criticism by the Select Committee on Delegated Powers and Deregulation in its report on the Bill. ('The Committee's concern is that the Bill does not provide any indication as to the basis on which the Lord Chancellor is to form his opinion. . .

Serious criticism of the extent and untrammelled nature of the Lord Chancellor's proposed powers under the Bill was made in January 1999 by the House of Lords Select Committee on Delegated Powers and Deregulation.(HL Paper 17). It urged that the bill should include statements of principle and criteria to be taken into account by the Lord Chancellor when giving directions. It also wished to see more use made of parliamentary accountability. The Funding Code, for instance, should be laid before Parliament in draft and be subject to affirmative resolution; the power to 'call in' and alter professional qualification regulations or rules of conduct should be circumscribed – to be used 'if, and only if,' the Lord Chancellor thought the regulations unreasonably restricted rights of audience. The Lord Chancellor stated that he accepted these various suggestions and amended the Bill accordingly. [134]

For details of the Panel's work see www.lcd.gov.uk – Access to Justice.

(e)   *Right of direct access to the Bar for professional and lay clients*

In earlier times there was no rule preventing barristers from dealing directly with clients. But by the mid-nineteenth century it had become an understanding. In 1888 the Attorney-General gave an opinion that in contentious matters a barrister should not act or advise without the intervention of a solicitor – chiefly because the barrister was not in a position to ascertain the facts of the case.[135] It remained permissible, though uncommon for barristers to accept instructions directly from clients in non-contentious matters. But in 1955 the then Attorney-General declared the practice to be wrong and this opinion was adopted by the Bar Council at its 1956 Annual General Meeting. It remained a firm rule until 1989.

The 1989 Green Paper recommended that lay clients should have a right of direct access to barristers. Many commentators, including the writer, argued that this would lead to the destruction of the Bar as a second-tier consultancy service and the Government conceded the point. The 1989 White Paper (para 11.7) said that this matter would be left to the Bar to determine.

---

[134]   For the Lord Chancellor's speech see House of Lords, *Hansard*, 19 January 1999, vol 596, cols 483-87. See Access to Justice Act 1999, ss 4(4), 9(4), 25(9), 42(1) and Sch 5, para 17.
[135]   (1888) 85 LT Jo 176.

In 1989, in the context of the furious debate over the Green Papers, the Bar altered its rules to permit Direct Professional Access (DPA) to some professional clients to instruct barristers direct, without having to go via a solicitor. By 1999 there were nearly 40 professional bodies with this right. They included: architects, accountants, loss adjusters, ombudsmen, actuaries, valuers and auctioneers, Royal Town Planning Institute, Royal Institution of Chartered Surveyors, Association of Average Adjusters, Chartered Association of Certified Accountants, Institution of Mechanical Engineers, Institution of Chemical Engineers, Institute of Taxation, Institute of Chartered Secretaries and Administrators.

In May 1996 the Bar Council agreed in principle that bureau workers in designated Citizens' Advice Bureaux should be able to refer work direct to a barrister. [136] After completion of a pilot, this scheme became effective for advice agencies with franchises from the Legal Aid Board as from January 1999. [137]

A Bar Council Policy Unit (think-tank) appointed in 1994 'to think the unthinkable' produced a Consultation Paper in February 1994 which, amongst other things, proposed that direct access for *lay clients* to a barrister should be permitted in non-contentious work–ie for legal advice. For contentious matters (litigation) the lay client should also be allowed direct access to a barrister but the barrister should then be under a duty to refer the client to an appropriate professional intermediary who would usually be a solicitor. This proposal was considered but rejected at the Bar's Annual Meeting in July 1994.

Spokesmen for the Labour Party (notably Mr Paul Boateng MP) said before the 1997 General Election that a Labour Government would abolish the rule prohibiting direct access for lay clients to a barrister but, in the event, after Labour was returned to power in the General Election this threat was quietly dropped.

Neither the LCD's 1998 Consultation Paper nor the Access to Justice Act 1999 contained any provision on the subject.

However, in October 1998 the Bar Council issued a short but potentially important Consultation Paper addressing the issue of direct access. ('Contracts and Access to the Bar' prepared by a sub-committee, known as the Contracts Working Party, under the Chairmanship of James Munby QC who had also chaired the Bar Council Policy Unit which produced the 1994 consultation paper). The Munby Committee said that barristers were restricted not only by rules about the source of their work (ie from whom they were permitted to receive instructions), but also regarding the nature of the work they could do. They were not permitted to do certain categories of work done by solicitors – defined in the Bar's Code of Conduct para 901. (This 'excepted work' includes the management, administration or general conduct of a lay client's

---

[136] See H Heilbron, 'Moving with the times – an opportunity for the Bar', *Counsel*, July/August 1996, p.18.
[137] See D Payne, 'Welcome advice', *Counsel*, April 1999, p 24.

affairs, the management, administration or general conduct of litigation and the receipt and handling of clients' money.)

The Munby committee suggested that the Bar had various options. One was to maintain the status quo. The second was to expand the categories eligible to refer Direct Professional Access (DPA) work. The third was to permit direct access by lay clients. The fourth was both to permit direct access to lay clients and to scrap the restrictions on the work that barristers could do. The fifth, was also to permit barristers to conduct litigation. The last two would lead to an assimilation of the functions and roles of barristers and solicitors.

Direct licensed access (DLA) Expansion of the categories of those able to refer clients to the barrister could include people not members of a professional body provided they were recognised by the Bar Council as (1) competent in some identifiable area of expertise or experience, (2) having the necessary skills to organise papers and information and (perhaps) (3) subject to some suitable disciplinary or regulatory tribunal or at least some rules. There were many potential candidates including banks, building societies, insurance companies, trade unions, trade associations, employers' associations, consumer bodies, housing associations, charities.

If the Bar Council had the responsibility for deciding who had the right to refer to barristers, this would free 'individual barristers and chambers from the administrative and other burdens of dealing with any and every layman who simply walks in off the street'. Also unrestricted direct access by lay clients would raise overheads and would have significant client care implications. (para 5.5)

The Munby Committee said it saw no reason to distinguish between contentious and non-contentious work for the purpose of the Direct Access rules. It did not think that holding to the status quo was right. It was strongly opposed to permitting unrestricted direct access. If the Bar was going to survive it would do so 'only because there is a real and perceived difference between what barristers do and what solicitors (and others) do. . . Barristers should do barristers' work; they should not do solicitors' work' (para 5.9(4)).

So the choice effectively lay between an extension of DPA, the introduction of DLA or the extension of direct access to all lay clients. There was little scope for extension of DPA. There were few professional bodies not already on the list that would satisfy the criteria. The Munby Committee favoured DLA over direct access to all lay clients.

This view prevailed. In 1999 the Bar Council approved a scheme for Direct Licensed Access, Bar DIRECT. (See J Munby, 'Extending a Helping Hand', *Counsel*, October 1999, p 26.) The scheme was extended to include police forces, probation, services, trading standards offices, clinical negligence and other insurers, trading companies, banks, insolvency practitioners and trades unions. By 2003 over 100 licences had been approved. Details are on the Bar Council's website – www.barcouncil.org.uk. (The list was published in *Counsel*, March 2003, p vi.)

In March 2001 the Office of Fair Trading's report *Competition in professions* said (p 15) that while there was no objection to a barrister choosing not to deal with clients without the intermediary of a solicitor there was objection to the professional rule denying freedom of choice. In response to the criticism, the Bar Council, acting on the recommendation of a committee chaired by Sir Sydney Kentridge, unanimously approved changes to its professional rules to broaden the scope for lay clients to have direct access to barristers.

The Kentridge Committee's recommendation was that the new regime should be implemented cautiously, with restricted direct access in criminal and family cases, notably for advice and in a very few court matters where it is clear that the additional role of the solicitor is not necessary. A consultation paper on the response to the OFT's report was issued by the Bar in April 2002. This proved to be the most controversial issue in the consultation paper. A working group then put forward detailed rules which were approved by the Bar Council at its meeting on 16 November 2002. The final version was approved by the Bar Council on 29 March 2003 and was then sent to the Lord Chancellor for his approval

Under the new rules, direct access would be permitted in civil work other than family and immigration matters providing it can be done without a solicitor. So a barrister could not take on work on the instructions of a lay client which involved investigation of facts or the taking of statements from witnesses. It could be undertaken in limited categories of family and criminal work such as advice (but not advice in police stations) and appeals but not for trials. Special Bar Council approved training would be a requirement. Barristers with under three years' experience could not undertake direct access work. Existing prohibitions on conducting litigation and handling client moneys would remain. The barrister would be required to send a client care letter setting out what he or she was and was not able to do, the likely fees to be charged and any other information the client needed. The subject would be reviewed after two years.[138]

Writing about the potential impact of the new direct access rules, the marketing director of a major set of chambers suggested, 'The strongest example of how the model can work is at the tax bar, where members receive up to 60% of their work on a direct access basis, compared with under 5% for the Bar as a whole'. It could offer new streams of work which would be welcome news 'at a time when a general downturn in civil litigation is reported, with a shift to solicitors doing more preparatory work themselves, with a reduction in the levels of public funding, and a more costs conscious and risk averse economy'. It also offered the Bar an opportunity to 'enhance its image by ridding itself of the mantle of exclusivity and inaccessibility, and to market itself effectively in the business community'. The downside lay in the fundamental changes in working practices that had to be adopted. 'Satisfactory conduct of direct access work will mean a commitment to administrative and support

[138]   See *Counsel*, February 2003, p iv.

functions in chambers and to the cost of adopting these. [139] The chief executive of another set of chambers writing in the same issue of *Counsel* expressed similarly bullish thoughts. In his view the new system would have an especial impact in six different types of work: early advice as to whether it was worth instructing solicitors; in-house lawyers keeping work longer with the Bar's advice; professional firms that already use DPA would use it more; business organisations with significant legal costs incurred in many disputes; new litigation organisations were likely to come into the market.[140]

NOTE

In 1990 the Bar authorised a new type of practice – that of 'non-practising employed barristers' working, say, for a firm of accountants or foreign lawyers. Such a barrister was allowed to advise his firm's clients but not to hold himself out to be a practising barrister nor to appear as counsel in court. But the rules only allow a non practising barrister to call himself such if he has completed a pupillage. The consultants LECG in their report attached to the OFT's report *Competition in professions* said that only about 100 individuals had registered with the Bar Council to continue using the title (para 269, p 77). It doubted whether the requirement of a pupillage as the basis for using the title was necessary. It called this a backward step to inhibit a source of competition for non-advocacy services (ibid).

(f)   Queen's Counsel

Eligibility of solicitors The 1989 Green Paper did not question the value of the status of QC but it proposed that all those who held full advocacy certificates should be eligible to become QCs. The White Paper slightly amended this by stating (para 3.21) that the Lord Chancellor would in future regard as eligible those who held rights of audience *either* in the High Court *or* the Crown Court. This did not need legislation and was therefore not included in the CLSA 1990.

In July 1995 it was announced that solicitor advocates were eligible to apply to become QCs. By 2003 only eight had been appointed. [141] In the eight years 1996 to 2003 there were a total of 3,837 applications for silk, an average of 480 per year. Of these, 73 were made by solicitors. The highest number of solicitor applications in any year was 2001, when 12 applied.[142] In 2003 there were only 10 of whom one was appointed.[143]

---

[139]   Liz Heathfield, 'Handle with care', *Counsel*, May 2003, p 15.
[140]   P Bennett, 'Moving the goalposts', *Counsel*, May 2003, pp 18-19.
[141]   One, Laurence Collins, a partner in Messrs. Herbert Smith, appeared for the Chilean Government in the second Pinochet case in the House of Lords and was subsequently the first solicitor to be appointed to the High Court bench.
[142]   *Counsel*, June 2003, p 47.
[143]   *Counsel*, June 2003, p 47.

Should QCs continue to exist? As was seen above (p 717) the question whether the status of QC benefited consumers was raised by the Office of Fair Trading in its 2001 report *Competition in professions.*

The Bar's Response to the OFT report argued that the QC system had real value both for the purchasers of advocacy services and to the administration of justice. Appointment as QC was public recognition of outstanding ability. It was of value to purchasers of advocacy services such as solicitors and especially to those who did not regularly instruct counsel in the particular field of work. Internationally it helped to make English advocates competitive in litigation and arbitrations outside the UK. It also helped to maintain standards since QCs were selected not only for their legal skills. Integrity, and independence were also assessed. The question whether it should be the Lord Chancellor who made the selection was, it suggested, a constitutional rather than a competition question. At least no one suggested that political considerations played any part in the process. The level of consultation and the work involved would make it difficult for a professional body to undertake.

The OFT suggested that there was inadequate peer review. The Bar said, on the contrary, the selection process involved an intense and wide-ranging process of peer review. The OFT pointed out that there were no professional examinations that had to be taken to become a QC. The Bar's reply was that what was being assessed – experience, advocacy skills and professional qualities demonstrated in practice – were not measurable by formal examinations. The OFT argued that there was no continuous quality appraisal of QCs. The Bar said it was not aware that this caused any problem. Market forces were the main safeguard. But there might be a case for a procedure whereby the rank of QC could be removed if the Lord Chancellor was satisfied that there had been a serious or sustained failure by the QC to meet the standards reasonably to be expected of a QC. [144]

In its report on progress in April 2002, the OFT (para 3.39) said a quality mark was only of value to consumers if it was awarded according to clear criteria and in a transparent way. Whether the QC system met this condition was open to debate. Another condition was that the mark should be capable of being lost as well as won. The QC system did not qualify in that regard. Also, it said, 'we remain concerned that the QC system may operate to distort competition'. One sign of this was 'the step-change in fees that QCs are said to command upon taking silk'; another was that 'custom and practice had given rise to some de facto demarcations as to what work is and is not suitable for QCs'. It had also been suggested that the system displayed elements of a quota system and that some quantitative as distinct from purely qualitative criteria might apply. (It added, pointedly, 'we note with interest that the number of QCs appointed in 2002 is markedly higher than in any other recent year'.[145])

[144]   See paras 7.1-7.15.
[145]   As noted above, in previous years the number appointed was 60-70 and the success rate of applications was as low as an average of 14%. In 2002 the number was 113 from 429

The LCD's Consultation Paper *In the Public Interest?*, issued in July 2002, devoted 11 pages to the issue It seemed to lean toward affirmation of the utility of the status of QCs: 'In so far as users of a service are insufficiently informed about the full range of quality on offer, an effective and accurate mark of quality which differentiates the leading players will improve the amount of information available to users of the service'. (para 127) Not all users of the service would have the information to identify the top specialists. Since barristers were self-employed, many of the usual mechanisms to signal information on quality – such as becoming a partner – were not available to barristers. In the absence of reliable information on the quality of providers, users would tend to stick with the barristers they had tried previously. A mark of quality 'therefore facilitates competition by enabling the user to "switch" to new providers, ie to instruct with confidence a barrister of whom they have little or no experience'. (para 131) The QC system also provided a career structure within the legal system 'marking the achievement of a level of status, excellence and seniority which is broadly analogous to that found within other professions (senior partners in solicitors' firms, hospital consultants, professors in the academic world, etc)'. (para 134)

The Lord Chancellor, it suggested was well-positioned to be custodian of the process. There was no quota on appointments. The appointment process was described. (For a fuller statement see www.lcd.gov.uk/judicial.

On the question of increased fees the paper said that there was considerable overlap between what could be earned by a successful junior and a QC. The junior could be earning more than the QC even in the same area of practice.

The Law Society in its response to the Consultation Paper criticised the system. It referred to the evidence it gave in 1999 to the enquiry by Sir Leonard Peach on the operation of the Judicial and QC appointments procedures when it said: 'The designation is a mark of patronage that is inappropriate in the modern age'. (para 5.3) The Council of the Law Society had confirmed that opinion in September 2000 in deciding to continue to remain outside the automatic consultation process for judicial appointments and silk.

The Law Society in its Response to the July 2002 consultation paper (para 5.5) said it had three main concerns. One was about the consultation process which at least until recently gave excessive weight to the views of the judges and not enough to key consumers such as solicitors. Secondly, it was undesirable for leaders of an independent profession to be selected by a Government Minister – though there was no evidence that the appointment function had been abused in the recent past. Thirdly, there was concern that, 'at least until very recently', a quota system had operated. The QC system was helpful in identifying specialists for non-specialists.

---

applications, a success rate of 26%.In 2003 it was even higher – 121 from 394 applications, a success rate of 31%. This apparent 'watering of the brandy' led to criticism – see B Malkin, 'Irvine under fire for silk appointment hike', *The Lawyer*, 21 April 2003, p 2.

But it said that solicitors reported 'a substantial increase in fees when barristers are appointed QC – indeed, solicitors thought that this was the whole point, from the applicants' perspective' (Q.57, p 60). It agreed with the OFT that 'reports from solicitors suggest a step-change [in higher fees] that is not always justified by the superior skills claimed' (Q 59, p 60). Sometimes a QC was instructed solely because the client was anxious to have apparent equality of arms with the opponent. Another point of criticism was that the courts too often placed greater weight on an argument put by a QC than on the same argument put by a junior.

If the system continued, the Law Society thought it should be replaced by an accreditation system for experienced members of the Bar. ('Ideally, accreditation would be achieved by candidates being able to demonstrate by objective methods that they had achieved the required level of work experience and specialised knowledge.' (para 5.8)) Such a scheme would also require members to seek re-accreditation, say, every five years. No indication was given as to what 'objective methods' could be used for such accreditation.

For other responses to this part of the Consultation Paper *In the public interest?* see www.dca.gov.uk/consult/general/oftreptresp.htm#ch5.

Given the markedly approving tenor of the LCD's presentation of the issues in July 2002, it was surprising that, as has been seen, on 2 April 2003 the Lord Chancellor told the new House of Commons Select Committee on his Department that he would be issuing a consultation paper to canvass, inter alia, the question whether the QC system should continue to exist and even more surprising that on 29 April 2003 he announced that he was suspending the entire process of selection.

The Government's further Consultation Paper (*Constitutional reform: the future of Queen's Counsel*, CP 08/03, accessible on www.dca.gov.uk/consult/qcfuture) was issued on 14 July 2003. Its substantive part was 31 pages long. In the Foreword the new Lord Chancellor, Lord Falconer, said 'I have no predetermined answers to the questions raised in this paper', but the paper gave rather more emphasis to the negative aspects of the system than had its July 2002 paper.

It first addressed whether it was appropriate for the appointment to be made by the Queen on the advice of ministers. There was need for a strong case to justify it. ('The indications from customers certainly suggest that the rank of QC in the legal services market does not provide a useful kitemark in practice, and that the market might work more effectively if the QC mark were to be removed' (para 22)) The Government's provisional view was that retention of the rank in its present form could only be justified if–
- it serves a helpful purpose for users of legal services
- any benefits clearly outweigh any problems and in particular the extent to which it may distort competition in the market for legal services and its possible effect on fees; and
- its possible benefits cannot be provided in other ways free of such disadvantages (p 22)

The responses to *In the Public Interest?* had not produced many concrete examples of the QC rank being used as an effective guide when selecting an advocate.

> A number of respondents said that it had a general usefulness, but more detailed responses tended to argue that what was relevant to an instructing solicitor was the individual advocate's experience and skills. They had frequently found the right junior counsel to be of better value than a QC. It was also said that the rank of QC drove up legal costs unjustifiably. There was a perception that QCs were now instructed in circumstances where their particular skills were not really needed: for example because it mighty be thought that judges would pay more attention to a QC's argument, or because a simple equality of arms was needed – just because the other side had already instructed a QC. Such perceptions could have the effect of tilting the market in favour of QCs and against experienced juniors. (para 49)

Abolition of the rank could therefore have two beneficial effects. First, it could lead to a more effective reliance on information about individual advocates and their skills 'so that consumers would pay only the price reflecting the real value of the service they are buying rather than paying for a badge or QC "brand".' (para 50) Providing information flowed freely, the market would determine which barristers could command higher prices on the basis of the quality of their work. (para 50) Secondly, if QCs lowered their fees to be competitive with experienced juniors. costs would come down. (On the other hand, if individuals were already paid according to their skills, there would be little or no change. A different possibility was that experienced juniors might put their fees up.)

The paper considered the implications for existing QCs if the rank were removed and the ways in which it might be done. The final section discussed what sort of award system might replace the present system. Annexes dealt with the current criteria for the award, the current selection procedures, the position in other jurisdictions and quality marks in other UK professions and trades. The consultation period closed on 7 November and the Government intended to announce its decision early in 2004.

(g) BarMark

In 1999 the Bar Council decided to introduce the BarMark scheme whereby chambers can be accredited as efficient. [146] The Quality Mark can be obtained either through the British Standards Institution or through the Legal Services Commission. The latter is free whereas the BSI has a cost. To qualify the chambers has to be able to show that its systems and documentation are consistent with the required quality standards. The tests are quite demanding but by February 2003 some 60 sets of chambers had obtained the qualification[147] and a large number of chambers stated

---

[146] See *Counsel*, June 2000, pp 3, 28.
[147] *Counsel*, February 2003, p vi.

that they intended to apply for it. The BDO Stoy Hayward survey of the Bar for 2002 stated (p 5) that 71% of the chambers that responded to the survey intended to apply for BarMark accreditation within the next 12 months. [148] (See J Chase, 'Nine easy steps to BarMark status', *Counsel*, June 2000, p 28 and the Bar Council's website – www.barcouncil.org.uk.)

(h) Partnerships between lawyers and between lawyers and non-lawyers

As was seen above (p 718), in 1979 the Report of the Benson Royal Commission supported the Bar's traditional rule forbidding partnerships. (The sole exception is that, curiously, a barrister has for many years been allowed to form a partnership with an overseas lawyer.) Ten years later, the February 1989 Green Paper proposed (1) that barristers and solicitors should be able to form partnerships with each other; (2) that each should be able to join in partnerships with members of other professions ('multi-disciplinary partnerships' or 'MDPs'); (3) that each should be able to join in partnership with foreign lawyers ('multi-national partnerships' or 'MNPs'); and (4) that barristers should be able to form partnerships with other barristers.

But the July 1989 White Paper (ch 12) played a very different tune. ('The Government ... believes that the regulation of how the members of professional bodies organise themselves to meet their clients' needs is best left to the professions themselves, subject to a proper scrutiny to avoid unnecessary or undesirable anti-competitive effects' (para 12.2).

The 1990 Courts and Legal Services Act s 66 abolished the statutory prohibition on solicitors forming partnerships with non-solicitors and stated that there is no common law rule that prevents barristers from forming such relationships. But s 66 also specifically permits the Bar to make rules preventing barristers from entering such partnerships. The Bar has so far maintained its prohibition on partnerships.

PARTNERSHIPS BETWEEN BARRISTERS

The publication in February 2001 of the report of the Office of Fair Trading *Competition in professions.* (p 743 above) suddenly made the issue – at least of partnerships between barristers – a live one. The report said:

> The requirement that only sole practitioners can supply barristers' services is anomalous in the context of professional services and beyond. A similar requirement for, say, booksellers would have clear disadvantages in terms of, inter alia, costs, price, efficiency, innovation and choice. While bookselling and the supply of legal services by barristers have rather different economic characteristics, the same general economic principles should apply. Moreover, the sole practitioner requirement might also have the effect of deterring some

[148] Just under a third of chambers responded – Appendix B.

people from a career as a barrister who would be at least as able professionally as those who become barristers, but who do not have the financial resources to fall back on if their flow of business were to fall off, or who are quite reasonably averse to such financial risk. Lifting of the restriction could therefore help to broaden access to and diversity in the profession.' [149]

The Bar's Response to the OFT's report devoted six pages to the topic. (pp 13-20) It argued that the rule ensured the widest availability of barristers' services to the public in three ways:

• Competition was promoted by maximising the number of competing undertakings – barristers in the same chambers often appeared against each other which would be impossible if they were partners – this was especially important in specialised fields with small numbers of practitioners.

• Minimising costs – individuals working for themselves had lower overheads.

• The cab-rank principle (p 745 above) would be undermined with partnerships – conflict of interest problems would be greatly increased as the barrister would have to consider not only the interests of his own clients but those of all the clients of the partnerships – even if there were no technical conflict of interest, partners would sometimes pressurise each other not to take a client – representation would be subject to the will of the majority. The LECG report suggested that the freedom to form partnerships was more important than the cab-rank rule. This showed 'little understanding of the importance of the rule to British justice'. To reduce this valuable public benefit in the name of personal financial advantage and greater security for barristers was contrary to the public interest.

Features that made the OFT's comparison with bookselling inappropriate included:
• the adversarial nature of litigation with the potential for conflicts of interest;
• the small number of barristers with relevant specialist skills;
• the public interest in ensuring that such expertise was as widely available as possible;
• the public duties to which barristers were subject.

There was no evidence that the rule deterred would-be entrants. There was a heavy demand for pupillages and tenancies. Most entrants did not have private means and were dependent on funding provided by chambers.

In its April 2002 progress statement regarding *Competition in professions* the OFT responded to the Bar's three main arguments. It questioned whether it was true that abolishing the rule would diminish competition. Not all specialist areas were small and moreover competition rules existed to prevent concentration of work in few hands. As to the relative overhead costs of barristers and solicitors it was premature to draw the conclusion that this was due to a difference in their respective business structures. As to the cab-rank rule, it would still apply to barristers not in partnerships and might apply also to those in partnerships. The OFT said that it intended to give further detailed consideration to the issue.

---

[149]   At p 15 and see also the accompanying report of the consultants LECG pp 80-82.

PARTNERSHIPS BETWEEN BARRISTERS AND MEMBERS OF OTHER PROFESSIONS

The OFT report did not address additional words to the prohibition on barristers forming multi-disciplinary partnerships (MDPs). The consultants LECG's report said the arguments were similar to those that applied to partnerships between barristers. It concluded that the current restrictions on barristers forming MDPs were 'inhibiting competition, potential cost efficiencies and customer choice and convenience' (para 291 p 82).

The Bar's Response said that all the reasons for prohibiting barristers from forming partnerships with one another applied equally to MDPs. In addition, MDPs would give rise to difficulties of differing professional standards, differing approaches to conflicts of interest and differing rules concerning client confidentiality and the operation of legal professional privilege. (p 19, para 3.27) The LECG report recognised these difficulties but did not propose any solution to them. There had been no support in the consultation conducted by the Kentridge Committee for barristers to enter MDPs. In conclusion on this topic it quoted a recent speech by Lord Woolf, Lord Chief Justice, in which, referring to the OFT report he had said, 'I want to say that I believe that partnership is inconsistent with the independence of the Bar and with the public interest'.

MNPS AND MDPS FOR SOLICITORS

Section 66(1) of the Courts and Legal Services Act 1990 provided, 'Section 39 of the Solicitors Act 1974 (which, in effect, prevents solicitors entering into partnership with persons who are not solicitors) shall cease to have effect'. However, subsection (2) went on to permit the Law Society to continue to prohibit or restrict such partnerships.

One of the few policies proposed in the 1989 Green Papers to be implemented was the recommendation that solicitors should be permitted to form partnerships with foreign lawyers (MNPs). Under the Multinational Practice Rules 1991 a MNP operating in England and Wales has to comply with all the rules that apply to solicitors. All the partners must be either solicitors or Registered Foreign Lawyers (RFLs). One becomes an RFL by going through a process of registration with the Law Society, set out in s 89 and Sch 14 of the CLSA 1990. [150] In April 2003 there were just over 200 such MNPs registered with the Law Society.

However, partnerships between solicitors and members of other professions (MDPs) are still prohibited by reasons of Solicitors' Practice Rules 4 and 7. Rule 4 prohibits solicitors employed by non-solicitors acting for third parties; Rule 7 prohibits solicitors sharing fees with non-solicitors. Whether MDPs should be permitted has been the subject of deep divisions in the profession since the 1980s. (The previous edition of this work gave details of the progress of this debate from 1987 to 1998.) In

---

[150] For a review of the various forms of alliances being formed with European lawyers see 'Rocky road to union', *Law Society's Gazette*, 26 June 2001, p 26.

1987, in response to a consultation document issued by the Law Society, 54% of respondents favoured a relaxation of the ban on mixed partnerships. In January 1993 the Law Society issued a fresh consultation document ('Multi-Disciplinary Practice') inviting the profession's views. The response rate to the survey conducted by the Law Society was very low, but of those who replied, 49% of solicitors and 56% of Local Law Societies were opposed, 33% were in favour. The Council of the Law Society decided in March 1994 to take no further action on the matter for the time being.

In June 1996 the Council of the Law Society decided to reopen the topic which led in October 1998 to the Law Society issuing yet another consultation paper on the question. ('MDPs: Why?...Why Not?') It stated that solicitors could currently work with non-lawyers in four different ways short of partnership: 1) A firm of solicitors could have a close association with a firm of non-lawyers with a referral arrangement. Most of the major accountancy firms had such arrangements with firms of solicitors. They were permitted – provided the firm had only lawyer owners and fees were not shared with non-lawyers. 2) A solicitor could have a business that was not a solicitors' business with a non-lawyer. Such a firm could provide business adviser services but not legal services. 3) A solicitor employed by non-lawyers could do legal work for customers but not as a practising solicitor. 4) A solicitor who is not practising could own a non-lawyer business jointly with a non-lawyer. Such a business was not a practice.

The consultation paper set out pros and cons of MDPs in general and proposed six alternative models. This time a large majority of those who responded favoured relaxation of the rules and in October 1999 the Council resolved that solicitors who wished to do so should be allowed to provide any legal service through any medium to anyone whilst still providing safeguards to protect the public interest. It was accepted that this would require legislation.[151] It authorised its working party to develop two interim models of MDPs: Model A, a solicitors' firm with a minority of non-solicitor partners; and Model B, 'linked' partnerships of lawyers and non-lawyers to share fees.

The main interim model proposed by the Working Party was Model A – 'Legal Practice Plus' – which would allow solicitors to take non-solicitors into partnership (NSPs) provided the practice remained in the control of the solicitor partners and the services provided were of the kind normally provided by a solicitor's practice. The proposal was that the NSPs would be regulated by the Society under a contractual scheme established under its Charter (as opposed to its statutory) powers. In return for being entered on a register, NSPs would agree to be subject to Law Society regulation. However, leading counsel advised in 2001 that this model could not be achieved without legislation.

---

[151] See 'Multi-disciplinary partnerships on horizon after "seismic" vote', *Law Society's Gazette*, 20 October 1999, p 3.

A second interim solution proposed by the MDP Working Party was Model B under which solicitors could fee-share but not enter into partnerships with a non-solicitor business. Examples might include franchising and licensing arrangements.

A third model being canvassed, dubbed 'TescoLaw', would allow any organisation, including supermarkets, to deliver legal services provided it was properly regulated.[152] Regulation might be achieved by 'ring fencing' the solicitors' practice part of the operation as an incorporated practice. Again this would require legislation to allow non-solicitors to participate in the ownership and control of an incorporated practice. The Law Society would also need new powers to disqualify individuals from owning a practice so as to protect the public.

The Law Society said that consideration was also being given to relaxation of the restrictions on employed solicitor acting for third parties. Solicitors employed by non-solicitors could act as solicitors only for their employers, though there was an exception, for instance, for trades unions and for lawyers employed by law centres. If this rule were removed, the regulation of solicitors employed by non-solicitors could be achieved by a system where individual practitioners rather than business structures were regulated.

The consultants LECG for the OFT report *Competition in professions* said that there was some demand for MDPs among solicitors – notably in the fields of property (solicitors with surveyors and estate agents), financial services (solicitors with accountants and financial advisers), and family law (solicitors and mediators). In its view, the current restrictions on the formation of MDPs were 'inhibiting competition, potential cost efficiencies, and customer choice and convenience' (para 204, p 62). However, it admitted that 'there could be a risk that a small number of accountancy firms could come to dominate the market for legal services' though this, it said, should be addressed by competition law against abuse of a dominant position.

In its April 2002 statement on progress the OFT said the Law Society had been active in addressing the issues raised in its 2001 report. The Law Society Council had adopted a recommendation from its Regulatory Review Working Party to amend Practice Rule 4, subject to the implementation of measures necessary for consumer protection. This amendment would allow solicitors employed by non-solicitors to provide services to members of the public. The Council was to be asked by the Working Party to reconsider a proposal, which it had previously rejected, to remove the ban in Practice Rule 7 on sharing fees with non-solicitor professionals. Legislation might be needed to enable the Law Society to regulate non-solicitor partners of MDPs. These were concerns for the Lord Chancellor's Department to address.

In its consultation paper *In the interests of justice?* issued in July 2002 (www.lcd.gov.uk), the LCD devoted 16 pages to MDPs and the provision of legal services by lawyers employed by non-lawyers. It said that the Government's position was that unjustified

---

152 See J Robins, 'Basket cases', *The Lawyer*, 18 February 2002, p 22; M Patterson, 'De-regulation cannot be avoided', *Solicitors' Journal*, 5 April 2002, p 300.

restrictions on competition should be removed subject to the need for adequate protection of the consumers. It asked for answers to 30 relevant questions. In its Response, the Law Society had 15 pages on the topic (*Quality, Choice and the Public Interest* – www.lawsociety.org.uk, pp 37-52) It anticipated that liberalisation of the rules would bring potential benefits both to consumers and to the public. Capital injections whether through MDPs or commercial organisations offering legal services direct to the public 'could increase competition' (para 3.19, p 42). Significant capital investment could help solicitors to 'market a range of methods of delivery of services to consumers. Increasingly organisations would want to meet the diverse expectations of clients which might lead to changes in traditional office hours, remote access, access to services through the internet and the like (para 3.20, p.42) Many firms were concerned that they could not compete effectively with well resourced non-qualified providers of legal services. Liberalisation of rules, allowing input of venture capital would help firms to compete on a more level playing field. Some firms already employed other professionals such as accountants. With MDPs they could offer such persons partnerships – 'giving them a real stake in the future prosperity of their business' (para 3.21, p 42). If solicitors employed in commerce and industry could offer legal services to the public new career options would open for members of the profession which might for instance be attractive to those wishing to work part-time or to take career breaks.

Addressing 'Perceived risks', the Law Society said MDPs could result in a reduction of choice for consumers – if monster accountant firms swallowed solicitors' firms. It was even more concerned that the result could be a shrinking of consumer access to legal services. Larger organisations would be likely to be attracted to the profitable areas of work such as probate, personal injury and professional negligence and to neglect less profitable ones affecting people facing social exclusion, the poor, the homeless and those with mental health problems. Solicitors practising in the field of social welfare law might become increasingly thin on the ground. To minimise that risk the Government should provide proper level of funding for those services. A related issue was that larger commercial organisations were likely to take tough commercial decisions as to the closing of satellite offices in smaller communities. In the same way that banks, building societies and supermarkets had moved away from small market towns towards more central locations, so too might large organisations offering legal services. Technology would help to bridge the gap through video-conferencing and internet access. But a significant proportion of clients were not ready for such developments, preferring face-to-face contact with an adviser. Research suggested that under half the population was willing to consider video-conferencing or the internet to obtain legal advice. (para 3.27, p 44)

The risks to the profession mirrored the risks to the public. 'The liberalisation of practice, opening up competition, could lead to the gradual disintegration of the current high street network of firms ... this could have a significant impact for consumers on choice of and access to legal advice' (para 3.30, p 45). A major concern was whether MDPs and incorporated practices would provide the necessary commitment to train young solicitors.

The Law Society's conclusion was that while it was likely to be possible to provide a satisfactory *regulatory* framework for solicitors employed by commercial organisations to provide services to the public by adopting the incorporated practice regime there was a 'strong possibility that such a development could seriously damage access to justice, especially in rural areas' (para 3.32, p 45). It urged the Government to undertake further research and to carry out detailed economic analysis before taking firm decisions.

In February 2002 the European Court of Justice ruled that the Netherlands (and therefore the other member states) had the right to prevent lawyers from entering into MDPs with accountants even though it accepted that this might restrict competition in legal services. The Netherlands Bar refused to allow two Dutch lawyers to enter into partnership respectively with Arthur Andersen and PriceWaterhouse-Coopers on the ground that it threatened the lawyer's duty to act for clients in complete independence, to avoid all risk of a conflict of interest and to observe strict professional secrecy. The judges found there was incompatibility between the advisory activities of the lawyers and the supervisory activities of accountants who are not subject to the same duty of secrecy as legal practitioners. (Case C-309/99 *Wouters*, Judgment of 19 February 2002 – http://europa.eu.int/jurisp/cgi-bin/form.pl?lang=en.)

For a helpful succinct general overview of these issues see A Bogan, 'Multi-disciplinary partnerships – Is it a brave new world or a glimpse into chaos', *New Law Journal*, 9 March 2001, p 354; S Young, 'Multi-disciplinary partnerships', *New Law Journal*, 29 November 2002, p 1810. See also 8 *International Journal of the Legal Profession*, 2001 a special issue with four articles on MDPs : J Fish, 'Ethics, MDPs and the European Dimension', 103-108; E Deards, 'MDPs: a cause for concern or celebration?', 125-50; LS Terry, 'MDPs: reflections from the US perspective', 151-60; and AA Paterson, 'Multi-disciplinary partnerships – a critique', 161-68.

The accountants and legal services It is clear that the gigantic firms of accountants will play an increasing part in the provision of legal services to multinational corporations. In the past few years they have been moving seriously into this field both by employing large numbers of lawyers on their staff and, more recently, by establishing their own law firms as subsidiaries on a world-wide basis. (For the role in the story of the big accountancy firms see H McVea, 'Predators and the Public Interest – the "Big Four" and Multi-Disciplinary Practices', 65 *Modern Law Review*, 2002, 811-33. See also A Mizzi, 'Counter culture', *Law Society's Gazette*, 14 June 2001, p 34; H Power, 'Survival techniques', *The Lawyer*, 28 April 2003, p 18.)

(i)   Incorporation and limited liability

Solicitors were permitted to incorporate by the Solicitors Incorporated Practice Rules 1988. By 2003 there were some 600 firms that had done so. The chief advantage of incorporation is the protection it gives to the personal assets of partners not involved in the actionable advice. But, unlike accountants or surveyors, solicitors are not allowed to issue shares or to offer directorships to non-solicitors. One therefore cannot obtain external financing.

Another important consideration is financial disclosure. Annual accounts must be filed at Companies House. (See C.Davis,'Coming aboard', *Law Society's Gazette*, 15 May 1996, p 26.) Under the existing rules liability cannot be limited but the question of limited liability has been under consideration for some years especially as a result of the fear of massive claims against lawyers' and accountants' firms.[153]

In February 1997 the Conservative Government published a consultation paper on limited liability partnerships but in May of that year Labour was returned at the General Election. The Labour Government took over the project. The Limited Liability Partnerships Act 2000 became effective as from April 2001. The LLP is a new form of body corporate with members not partners. The members act as agents of the LLP not of eachother. In the event of a claim, only members who assume a personal duty of care to a client would be liable for the losses arising from the LLP's work. So innocent members would no longer be liable. Moreover the member's liability is limited to the capital they have in the firm. So private wealth is not at risk. It does not have share capital and the tension between directors and shareholders therefore does not arise. The LLP can sue and be sued. In some ways it is like a partnership. It is taxed like a partnership in the hands of its members. The main disadvantage is the requirement of financial transparency. An LLP must file 'true and fair' accounts audited to generally accepted accounting standards – including a requirement, if the total divisible profit exceeds £200,000, to show the income of the highest paid member. (The requirements as to financial disclosure in the United States are less demanding. Clifford Chance became an LLP under New York law, it is said, in order to gain the benefits without the disadvantage of financial disclosure.) By April 2003 there were some 60 LLPs.

(For a review of the first year of LLPs see R Foster, 'Limited liability partnerships-could they save your home?', *New Law Journal*, 14 June 2002, p 919.)

(j)   Specialisation

Specialistion has been promoted actively by the Law Society principally through a policy of developing panels of experts who can hold themselves out as such. There are now eleven such panels on: Family Law, Immigration Law, Personal Injury, Clinical Negligence, Children, Mental Health, Family Mediation, Criminal Litigation, Planning Law, Insolvency and Higher Courts.

---

[153]   In December 1995, for instance, the 150 partners of accountants Binder Hamlyn were ordered to pay damages of £34m for failing in their duty of auditing. (*The Times*, 1 December 1995; 8 December 1995)

To get on to a specialist panel, practitioners need to establish that they have the necessary knowledge and experience. Typically applicants have to submit a detailed application about their experience which is then judged by expert assessors. In the case of some panels, such as that for Mental Health and Children, an interview is a part of the process. Membership of the Family Mediation panel requires completion of approved family mediation training.

Barristers are even more specialised than solicitors and it is not only the individual barristers but their chambers that specialise. A 1999 survey showed that 60% of London chambers and 53% of chambers outside London did only one category of work. The largest category was Criminal, followed by General Civil and Family.[154]

(k)   Conveyancing

Until the 1970s conveyancing accounted for half the solicitors' profession's income. Solicitors enjoyed a statutory monopoly. The continuation of the monopoly was therefore felt to be of critical importance to solicitors. In 1979 the Benson Royal Commission recommended by 10 to 5 that, on balance, it was in the public interest that the monopoly continue – mainly so as to give the consumer the protection of work done by a person with the necessary skills. The Government at first accepted this recommendation but subsequently it changed its mind. In 1985 Parliament enacted the Administration of Justice Act which permitted competition for solicitors from licensed conveyancers. The solicitors' profession was deeply apprehensive about competititon from licensed conveyancers but this proved an unreal fear. The competition turned out to be insignificant. In 1999 the Law Society stated that solicitors accounted for 95% of the market share in the provision of conveyancing services.[155] Licensed conveyancers accounted for the rest apart from 1% attributable to DIY. In April 2003 there were 805 licensed conveyancers of whom 285 had full licences allowing them to practise on their own, or in a partnership or in a recognised body. The rest were employed mainly by small firms of solicitors or other licensed conveyancers.[156] (At the same date there were an estimated 15,000 solicitors working in the field of conveyancing.)

In 1989 a much greater threat emerged when the Government's Green Paper (*Conveyancing by Authorised Practitioners*, 1989, Cm 572) proposed that banks, building societies and other financial institutions should be permitted to compete for conveyancing work with solicitors in private practice – though the financial institutions would be required to use either solicitors or licensed conveyancers. The proposal caused consternation among solicitors.

---

[154]   BDO Stoy Hayward, *1999 Survey of Barristers' Chambers*.4.4.
[155]   Law Society, *The Changing Legal Market Place*, September 1999, p 31, para 7.4.
[156]   The Council of Licensed Conveyancers' website is at www.theclc.gov.uk.

In the 1989 White Paper the proposal survived– subject to several qualifications, all designed to promote a 'level playing field' (paras 5. 13–5. 16):(1) There would have to be an identified solicitor or licensed conveyancer responsible for the conveyancing part of the transaction.(2)The client would have to be offered at least one personal interview with the solicitor or licensed conveyancer to review any possible conflict of interest between the client and the provider of the service.(3)In order to restrict conflicts of interest, the code of practice would prevent financial institutions ('authorised practitioners') from providing services both to buyer and seller. They would also be prohibited from offering conveyancing services if they (or a subsidiary or associated company) was also providing estate agency services to another party. These restrictions could not be overridden even by written consent.(4) The code would prohibit 'tying-in' by a rule that conveyancing services should not be made conditional on other services being undertaken, or other services be made conditional on conveyancing services being undertaken.

The early signals were that the financial institutions would not want to compete by using in-house solicitors or licensed conveyancers. They appeared likely to compete instead by using existing local practitioners on non-exclusive panels. The threat to the profession was (1) that profit margins would be cut even further and (2) that solicitors' firms that were not on the panels would lose much of their conveyancing work.

The Courts and Legal Services Act 1999, ss 34-52 enacted provisions which would permit non-lawyers to become 'authorised practitioners' to undertake conveyancing work in competition with solicitors in private practice. The process would be supervised by an independent regulatory authority (the Authorised Conveyancing Practitioners Board) and be subject to regulations. The Board was set up in 1991 and draft regulations were circulated for comment. But in March 1992 the Lord Chancellor announced unexpectedly that he had decided to postpone the implementation of the scheme because of a lack of demand from potential providers.[157]

Nearly 10 years later the topic was reactivated when the Office of Fair Trading in its report *Competition in professions* (2001) recommended that 'fresh consideration should be given to implementing the parts of CLSA 1990, ss 34-52 not so far implemented, with a view to increase competition in the provision of conveyancing services' (p 17). At present, it said, solicitors faced little competition. (The report of its consultants LECG said that the wide variation in solicitors'charges for conveyancing work indicated a lack of competition.) Implementation of the rest of ss 34-52 ' would allow, for example, banks and building societies to provide conveyancing services' (p 17).

In its Consultation Paper, *In the Interests of Justice*, in July 2002, the LCD said, 'The Government favours opening up the conveyancing market further and in principle is willing to incur the cost of establishing an independent regulator, if that represents

---

[157]   House of Lords, *Hansard*, 11 March 1992, WA col 71.

good use of public funds' [158] The conveyancing market was in the process of considerable developments. The Land Registry already delivered many of its services on-line and was moving toward a system of electronic conveyancing. This 'could ignite the interest of potential new providers of conveyancing services' (para 8, p 13). The current proposals for a seller's pack of documents required by a purchaser could have the same effect. There was evidence of an increasingly specialist approach in some firms which had developed 'conveyancing factories' providing clients access seven days a week. They often had a small number of solicitors or licensed conveyancers supervising much larger numbers of non-legally qualified staff. The introduction of a compulsory seller's pack might result in specialist providers of such packs. There might also be 'guaranteed seller's packs' backed by insurance.

On the other hand, the Consultation Paper suggested, the introduction of new providers threatened the existence of small firms. For firms with fewer than five partners, residential conveyancing represented nearly a quarter (23%) of gross fee income. Loss of that income could lead to firms closing or amalgamating which would be of especial concern in rural areas where there were fewest firms. The Government had made 'rural proofing' a part of its formal policy-making process.

The Law Society, in its response (*Quality, Choice and the Public Interest*, November 2002) drew attention to the range of protections enjoyed by solicitors' clients including in particular compulsory insurance up to £1m. on each claim and the Compensation Fund which was good for £1m. per claim. If banks and building societies could offer conveyancing there was the prospect of buyers and borrowers being required to use the in-house service with the consequential loss of independent advice. The 1991 draft regulations had dealt with this by requiring that the client must have a personal interview with a solicitor. The financial institutions disliked this as it would have reduced their profits.

The Law Society agreed with the LCD that the effect of competition with banks and building societies might be the disappearance of large parts of the network of solicitors' firms. It recommended that the only satisfactory vehicle in regulatory terms to enable new providers to enter this market would be through enabling employed solicitors to provide services to the employers' customers through ring-fenced incorporated solicitors' practices – provided that a proper scheme of regulation for such bodies could be developed.

(l)   Probate

Prior to the CLSA 1990, it was an offence for anyone other than a solicitor, barrister or notary to draft for a fee the papers on which a grant of probate or letters of

---

[158]   Paragraph 6, p 12. The cost of running the Board it thought would be some £1.3m some of which would be recovered through a levy on fees charged by the Board to authorised practitioners - para 15, p 16.

administration depend. (Probate is granted where the deceased left a will to enable his affairs to be dealt with; if there is no will, the equivalent authorisation is called letters of administration.) The 1989 Green Paper proposed that this monopoly should be abolished. It offered two possible ways of achieving more competition. One was to widen the class of persons who could apply for probate for reward; the second was to abolish the restriction altogether.

The response to the Green Paper strongly supported the former rather than the latter alternative and this was stated to be the Government's decision. The CLSA 1990, s 54, stated that banks, building societies and insurance companies could also do such work provided that they were parties to a scheme for complaints and complied with any regulations made by the Lord Chancellor for such a scheme.[159] Section 55 would enable the Lord Chancellor – subject to the approval procedure set out in Sched.9 of the Act which requires him to consult with the Legal Services Consultative Panel and the President of the Family Division – to add to the list of approved bodies whose members could provide probate services. But this scheme was not implemented.

The Office of Fair Trading's report *Competition in professions* recommended that fresh consideration should be given to activating sections 54 and 55 so as to promote competition in this field. The LCD's Consultation Paper *In the public interest?*, said again, as it had for conveyancing, that the Government favoured the opening up of the market and was in principle willing to incur the cost providing that represented a good use of public money. It invited views whether the method of regulation proposed in s 54 and the approval procedure in s 55 were sufficient protection for consumers.

The Law Society in its response (*Quality, Choice and the Public Interest*, November 2002) urged that implementing ss 54 and 55 would provide significantly weaker protections for the users of new providers than was available for solicitors' clients (para 2.17, p 30). It would confuse members of the public about regulators. The Law Society was considering whether solicitors employed by bodies such as banks and lending organisations should be allowed to offer probate service to their customers through an incorporated solicitors' practice. But basically the existing arrangements worked well. The main problem, it suggested, was the absence of safeguards against excessive fees charged by banks and trust corporations.

(m)   Client care and handling complaints

In the interests of reducing the number of complaints against solicitors, the Law Society has strengthened the Solicitors' Costs Information and Client Care Code.

---

[159] The Financial Services and Markets Act 2000 (FSMA) altered the reference to banks, building societies and insurance companies in s 54 to persons with permission under Pt IV of FSMA to accept deposits or effect contracts of insurance. This would bring in credit unions.

The Code requires that clients 'are given the information they need to understand what is happening generally, and in particular on (i) the cost of legal service both at the outset and as the matter progresses; and (ii) responsibility for client matters. Clients should be given the best information possible about the likely costs, including a breakdown between fees, disbursements and VAT. The Code states that giving the best information includes agreeing a fixed fee or giving a realistic estimate or giving a forecast within a range of possible costs or explaining why none of those are possible. The solicitor is supposed to explain on what basis charges are calculated.

If charging is on an hourly basis, that should be made clear. All solicitors' firms are under an obligation to have a written complaints procedure. Clients must be told the name *and status* of the person who is handling the matter and who to contact in case they have a complaint. Failing to comply with these rules has serious consequences – see *Pilbrow v Pearless De Rougemont & Co* [1999] 3 All ER 355, CA. The client paid £800 on account of the bill but then refused to pay the balance of £1,800 on the ground that he had asked to see a solicitor but the matter had been handled by someone who was not a solicitor nor a qualified legal executive. Despite the fact that the work had been done competently, the court upheld the client's refusal to pay the solicitors' bill.

For the full text of the 18-page Solicitors' Costs Information and Client Care Code, as amended in March 1999, see *Law Society's Gazette*, 21 April 1999 or the full text of the Code at www.lawsociety.org.uk. For a study of the previous system see C Christensen, S Day and J Worthington, 'Learned Profession? – the stuff of sherry talk': the response to Practice Rule 15?', 6 *International Journal of the Legal Profession*, 1999, 27-69.

(n) Regulation and complaints

One of the attributes of the professions is the concept of self-regulation. Yet over the past years this concept has increasingly been modified as more and more systems of regulation have been put in place. The Legal Services Ombudsman (www.olso.org) entitled her report for 2001-2002 *The Regulatory Maze*. ('There are too many different agencies with their own approaches and priorities, and too few co-ordinating influences, for the regulation of legal services to be seen to be operating in the public interest.' (p 11).) A report in 1997 said that the areas regulated included entry, training, planning, competition, cost and quality of, and access to services and complaints. [160] The bodies and agencies involved include the Lord Chancellor's Department, Parliament, the Master of the Rolls, the Attorney-General, the National Audit Office, the Office of Fair Trading, the courts, the Legal Aid Board (now the Legal Services Commission) and the Legal Services Ombudsman. The advent of MDPs and direct access to barristers would create the need for more regulation. In the Ombudsman's view:

[160] R Baldwin, *Regulating Legal Services*, LCD Research Programme No 5/97.

At the most general level, the existence of numerous responsible bodies acts as an obstacle to the identification of clear, authoritative objectives, driven by an overriding sense of purpose and underpinned with a unified set of principles. At the same time, efficient delivery is compromised. The result is likely to be reforms which are piecemeal at best, with the ever-present prospect of inefficiency, duplication, oversight and incompatibility. Without an overarching regulatory strategy, it is difficult to see how the provision of legal services can be effectively modernised.' (p 13)

In the field of financial services, the Financial Services and Markets Act 2000 had created a unified system. This might prove a model for legal services.

The Legal Services Ombudsman (LSO) was established as a result of the 1989 Green Papers. Prior to that there had been the statutory Lay Observer whose remit was limited to supervising complaints against solicitors. The proposals in the Green Paper were implemented by ss 21-6 of the Courts and Legal Services Act 1990. When a complaint was upheld, the LSO could recommend that the professional body pay compensation. The Access to Justice Act 1999, s 49 changed this to a power to *order* compensation.

The LSO supervises complaints against solicitors, barristers, legal executives, licensed conveyancers and patent agents. Since the solicitors' profession is by far the largest of these professions it is not surprising that the bulk of the LSO's work concerns solicitors. For many years the LSO's annual report has been extremely critical in particular of the Law Society's systems for handling complaints. The systems have changed over the years but the criticisms, if anything, have become even sharper. (For a brief bullet-points account of the main events from 1990 to 2000 see the LSO's annual report for 2000-01, pp 9-12.)

The Legal Services Ombudsman from 1997 to 2002 was Ms Ann Abraham. In her report for 1999-00 she said that in her previous report she had described the Law Society's Office for the Supervision of Solicitors (OSS) as 'spiralling out of control' and that the Law Society was considering an alternative strategy for dealing with an ever increasing volume of cases. At the core of that alternative strategy was the devolution of complaints handling from the OSS to the practising profession. 'If the burden of casework at the OSS was to be eased, solicitors themselves would have to accept greater responsibility for tackling the discontent which they had caused.' Following on a report commissioned by Ernst & Young, in June 1999 the Law Society made a series of changes and added 23 permanent and 83 temporary case workers in order to clear the backlog of complaints by the end of 2000. The Law Society agreed to develop a client care programme that would help solicitors set up in-house complaints handling. Local law societies would become involved in settling complaints. There would be a new and tougher Practice Rule 15 on client care and complaints handling. The Government had made it clear that it would act, if the Society failed to put its house in order. The Access to Justice Act 1999 included a provision (s 51) for the establishment of a new office of Legal Services Complaints

Commissioner with powers to set standards for complaints handling and the power to fine professional bodies if they were not met.

In the result, the LSO said she had been satisfied with the way the OSS had dealt with complaints in only 59% of cases and although progress had been made to clear the backlog, the Law Society had failed to meet most of the casework targets set by the Lord Chancellor. Progress against broader strategy initiatives, such as client care, regulatory review and more comprehensive and regular research, had also been slow and unco-ordinated. (p 6)

The following year's annual report (for 2000-2001) said the LSO had been satisfied with the way the OSS handled complaints in only 57% of cases (an all-time low). The Law Society had met the target to reduce the outstanding caseload to no more than 6,000 cases by the end of December 2000 but other targets for turn round time, quality of casework and the level of cases referred to the Ombudsman had not been met. The Law Society had introduced a radical package of reform of their governance and management structure (on which see pp 736-38 above) but there had been 'disappointingly slow progress' in the development of their proposed new complaints redress system which had been billed as 'a cornerstone of the Society's plans to become a model regulator' (p 6).

The report for 2001-2002 reported satisfaction with the way the Law Society handled complaints had gone up from 57% of cases – to 58%! Problems with its statistical systems made it impossible to say with accuracy whether the specific performance targets agreed with the LCD had been met. However, the report said, 'it is apparent that sustained and continuing improvement in the Law Society's complaint handling activities has not been achieved.' (p 7)

The Law Society had added a new Consumer Redress Scheme which it said was the 'centrepiece' of its new approach to regulation. The Ombudsman said she was concerned that the new Scheme was 'disappointingly unambitious and unlikely to deliver the necessary improvements in public confidence' (p 7). She doubted whether the Law Society's decision to appoint an Independent Commissioner[161] as part of the Scheme would 'add anything other than symbolic value to the Law Society's complaint-handling arrangements' (p 7). The Law Society had issued a Consultation Paper on the subject in August 2001. This had resulted in comments from the LSO and others. But in the LSO's view, the Law Society had been determined to press ahead with the Scheme as originally envisaged 'taking little note of my views, or indeed those of other stakeholders' (p 26). In January 2002, the LSO had therefore used her powers under s 24(1) of the Courts and Legal Services Act 1990 to make recommendations to which the professional body was obliged to have regard. [162] The Law Society had indicated that it would respond positively to the recommendations

---

[161]   In July 2002 the Law Society appointed Sir Stephen Lander, Director-General of MI5, as its first Independent Commissioner to oversee the solicitors' complaints system and to help restore public confidence in the system.

[162]   They are set out on p 27 of the report.

but the LSO said she was concerned about the lack of consultation by the Law Society with her office and other stakeholders in relation to the introduction of such an important new scheme. (p 28)

In 2001-2002, the LSO investigated 1,629 allegations about the handling of complaints by the OSS. (This was just over 91% of her total caseload.) She formally criticised the OSS in 11% of cases and made a total of 554 recommendations. (In 270 the recommendation was that the OSS should reconsider the complaint; in 284 it was that the OSS should pay compensation for administrative failings such as delay.) Because of the defects in the statistical systems the Lord Chancellor had decided that it 'would not be productive' to set new performance targets for the coming year. Instead he had asked the LSO 'to maintain an increased oversight of the work of the OSS'.

The report said that the debate about targets and whether or not they had been met, had created a smokescreen that had obscured the bigger picture.' Undoubtedly there has been target-driven behaviour at the OSS, such as premature and inappropriate closure of files ... but even more worryingly, it seems that in chasing artificial targets at the expense of real progress, the OSS have lost sight of the main objective – that is, sustained and continuing improvement in their complaint-handling activities' (p 26). And as the smokescreen started to clear it was 'now apparent that sustained and continuing improvement has not taken place: the volume of incoming cases to the OSS is not reducing, despite initial indications to the contrary; the OSS are now closing considerably fewer cases than they are receiving; and there is a danger of a new backlog of 'older cases' building up; the quality of the OSS' decision-making remains disappointingly low; the performance of the new Customer Assistance Unit has been mixed; and the Society's core strategy of ensuring that solicitors deal promptly with complaints at a local level is not being effectively monitored'. (p 26)

Ms Ann Abraham was succeeded as Ombudsman by Ms Zaheeda Manzoor CBE. Her first annual report, published in July 2003, made it clear that things continued to go from bad to worse. The number of complaints received by the OSS had jumped in 2002-03 from 10,585 to 14,880. Since the Law Society's declared strategy had been to have more complaints handled locally through solicitors' own internal complaints-handling procedures, 'any outcome other than the intended reduction to their caseload must be seen as a failure in their complaints management strategy' (p 5). It was disappointing, she said, that there was nothing new about these increases in complaints 'nor the questions they raise regarding public confidence in lawyers, their professional bodies or the validity of self-regulation' (p 5).

Her report said that the complaints-handling procedures must deliver a more effective service, hitting more satisfactory levels for turnaround times, responsiveness of communications and quality of decisions. Redress mechanisms should be designed from the perspective and needs of the complainants.

The LSO's comments on complaint-handling by the Bar have been less critical. The proportion of complaints that are upheld is very low. In 2001-2002 the Ombudsman's report said, 'Generally the Bar Council maintained their high standard of complaint handling and in 93% of cases I found no cause for recommendation against, or criticism of, either the Bar Council, or the barrister complained about' (p 38). In the most serious case of poor service dealt with by the professional body, a barrister was directed to pay compensation of £2,000 and to forego fees of £1,888. The Ombudsman said that this demonstrated that the Bar Council was making full use of its powers.

However, Ms Abraham warned that although the Bar Council was then coping quite comfortably, if the number of complaints increased significantly the problems that had engulfed the solicitors' branch of the profession 'might be just around the corner' (p 29). Adoption by the Bar of increased direct access was likely to generate an increasing volume of complaints. From February 2002 barristers in private practice had to comply with an appropriate written complaints procedure and on request to make a copy available to clients. The Bar Council had produced a model chambers complaints procedure and guidance on its operation. 'These', Ms Abraham said in her report for 2002-2002, 'are significant and important developments – particularly for a profession of which it has been said that "allowing others within chambers to adjudicate a complaint against an individual member, was viewed as subjugation of ... independence and autonomy".' But requiring barristers to operate a complaints procedure for both lay and professional clients was just the beginning. 'The Bar Council must now ensure that there is effective monitoring of complaint handling by barristers and that chambers operate their complaints procedures in practice and not just on paper.' (p 40) The Bar's system has from the outset been run by a lay complaints commissioner.

In her first report Ms Manzoor referred to the MORI survey of the Bar Council's complaint-handling system which found that complainants tended to be people who were already dissatisfied with the outcome of a legal process. Their perceptions of 'the system' were already likely to be negative. Given that, it was especially important that ways be found to develop and maintain confidence-building measures in order to mitigate those early negative perceptions. She welcomed the 'enthusiasm' the Bar Council had shown in addressing these issues promptly. It was undertaking a review with strong lay involvement of its processes to address perceptions of bias, was looking at written guidance supplied to complainants and at communications generally' (p 43)

On the Bar's system see M Ross and Y Enoch, ' Procedures for Complaint against Counsel in the United Kingdom: Internal Purification versus External Vindication?', 19 *Civil Justice Quarterly*, 2000, pp 405-31.

For a comparative study, see M Ross and Y Enoch, 'Complaints against Solicitors: A Comparative Study of the Solicitors' Complaints Procedures in Scotland, England and Wales, and Northern Ireland', *Scottish Law and Practice Quarterly*, 1996, pp 145-58, 216-23 and 331-39.

For an evaluation of the role of the Ombudsman see R James and M Seneviratne, 'The Legal Services Ombudsman: Form versus Function?', 58 *Modern Law Review*, 1995, pp 187-209.

See also M Seneviratne, ' Consumer complaints and the legal profession: making self-regulation work', 7 *International Journal of the Legal Profession*, 2000, pp 39-58.

Legal Services Complaints Commissioner Section 51 of the Access to Justice Act 1999 gave the Lord Chancellor the power to appoint a Legal Services Complaints Commissioner. Section 52 sets out the powers of the Commissioner. The Commissioner would have the power to intervene to improve standards of complaints handling by the legal professional bodies. He would have the right to investigate and to make recommendations about the arrangements for the handling of complaints and any aspect of complaints handling. He would have power to impose targets for the handling of complaints, to ask for a plan for meeting such targets and to levy fines for failure to meet targets. The post would be financed by a levy on the professional bodies. But the provisions would only come into force 'if it appears to the Lord Chancellor that complaints about members of any professional body are not being handled effectively and efficiently'. The Lord Chancellor would use the power 'only after a great deal of thought and with a great deal of reluctance'. [163] The Minister said that, in all probability, if the Commissioner were appointed, it would be the Legal Services Ombudsman.[164] To date the threat to appoint the Commissioner has not been carried out – though there were indications in mid-2003 that it might indeed happen.

(o)   EU lawyers – reciprocal rights

There are three EU Directives that apply to European lawyers working in Great Britain. The first was the 1977 Services Directive (77/249/EEC). This allowed lawyers to cross borders within the European Union, and provide temporary services, including advocacy services in local courts. It allowed lawyers to follow their clients across borders in individual cases.

The second was the 1989 Mutual Recognition of Diplomas Directive (89/48/EEC) under which each state requires lawyers applying for recognition to undergo certain tests. In the case of the Law Society these are prescribed by the Qualified Lawyers Transfer Regulations 1990.

The third is the European Rights of Establishment Directive (98/5/EC) which came into force in March 2000 after being in gestation for more than 20 years. [165] (At the

---

[163]   House of Commons, *Hansard*, vol 333, 22 June 1999, col 1032.

[164]   House of Commons, *Hansard*, vol 333, 22 June 1999, col 1033. The advertisement for the replacement of Ms Ann Abraham as Legal Services Ombudsman made it clear that the appointee would also become Legal Services Complaints Commissioner should that post be established.

[165]   See European Communities (Lawyer's Practice) Regulations 2000, SI 2000 No 1119.

time of writing the Establishment Directive had not been brought into force in France, Ireland or the Netherlands.)

This third Directive has dramatic implications. The three main consequences are:

- European Union lawyers have the right to practise law – including the law of another EU member state in which they are established – under their own professional title (Art 3). So a German lawyer working in London can hold himself out to advise clients on English law. Equally, English lawyers can practise under their title of barrister or solicitor, in other EU countries. The lawyer wishing to avail himself of this must be registered with a competent authority in the host state. The relevant competent authority in England would be the Law Society or the Bar Council.
- Once registered, EU lawyers have the right to representation in the professional association and have a full right to vote in elections.
- After three years of 'practice of host state law', under Art 10 of the Directive EU lawyers have the right to be admitted to the local profession without examination. However in summer 2003 the Law Society was considering the form of any additional requirement. Certainly they have to make clear the nature of their qualifications on their notepaper so that the public are not misled but the Law Society may require some evidence that the lawyer has indeed been practising English law during the previous three years. The foreign lawyer can choose whether he wants to become barrister or solicitor.[166] By June 2003 none had chosen to be barristers.

In 1999 it was estimated that there were some 600 EU lawyers working in England Wales. The Establishment Directive makes registration mandatory for EU nationals working as lawyers in England on a permanent basis. But by June 2003 only just over 200 EU lawyers had registered with the Law Society under the Directive. Whether the relatively small number who have registered is because they did not know about the requirement, or because of the cost (£820 in 2003), or for other reasons was not known.

The Law Society has a helpful pack of relevant materials entitled Registered European Lawyers.

(p)   New government review of the regulation of the legal services market

On 24 July 2003 (only days before this book was sent for printing), Lord Falconer, Lord Chancellor and Secretary of State for Constitutional Affairs, announced that there was to be a wide-ranging review of the regulation of the legal services market aimed at promoting competition and innovation and improving services for the customer. It would be led by Mr David Clementi, chairman of Prudential plc and

[166]   *The Lawyer*, 31 May 1999, p 7.

former Deputy Governor of the Bank of England. He was asked to complete his review by the end of 2004.

Lord Falconer said: 'The legal services regulatory system is complex and fragmented. There is a wide range of regulators with overlapping powers and responsibilities. This lacks transparency and is confusing to the public and therefore seems not to be very accountable. We need to establish whether or not the system meets the demands of a modern, changing legal services market.' (Press Release 310/03)

The review was announced in the Department for Constitutional Affairs' report, *Competition and Regulation in the Legal Services Market* giving the Government's conclusions on the matters raised by the Consultation Paper, *In the Public Interest?* of July 2002. (For the full report see www.dca.gov.uk. Appendix A considered the impact of opening up probate services. The 133-page Scoping Study in Appendix B found that there were no fewer than 22 regulators involved in legal services.)

The report announced that:
- In advance of the review, the probate market would be opened up to banks, building societies and insurance companies, subject to the controls in ss 54 and 55 of the Courts and Legal Services Act 1990 which would be brought into effect, as recommended by the Office of Fair Trading. The Government's calculation was that, over a decade, solicitors were unlikely to lose more than 7-8% of their market share in this area, which represented only one per cent of solicitors' overall gross income. (See Annex A)
- The Government favoured allowing new types of businesses such as MDPs giving 'one-stop' services and corporations wider access to the market but would leave it to the Clementi review to recommend how best to regulate them to safeguard the independence of the professions and consumers' interests. ('Appropriate regulation, adequate and stringent enough to protect both the interests of the public and the core values of the professions, is the key to the successful development of these new style businesses.')[167]
- Legal professional privilege would not be extended to clients of non-lawyers. (There was no evidence that the existing privilege was significantly distorting the market in favour of lawyers and it was contrary to the public interest to increase the right of non-disclosure, both from the courts and from the Revenue and Customs and Excise.)
- Pending the review, the conveyancing market would not be opened up to banks or building societies. (The set-up costs for government in respect of regulation would be high. In the early 1990s, take-up by such competitors was low. The conveyancing market was no longer a monopoly and was already competitive - providers now gave quotes to consumers who could shop around.)

---

[167] For sharp critical reaction from a sole practitioner to the prospect of what has been dubbed 'Tesco law' see C Sutton, 'A "Special offer" the public must refuse', *New Law Journal*, 1 August 2003, p 1185.

Index